Summary of Selected Financial Ratios

RATIO NAME	FORMULA	PAGE REFERENCE
Liquidity Analysis		
Working capital	Current Assets − Current Liabilities	63, 635
Current ratio	$\dfrac{\text{Current Assets}}{\text{Current Liabilities}}$	63, 403, 636
Acid-test ratio (quick ratio)	$\dfrac{\text{Cash} + \text{Marketable Securi\ldots}}{\text{Current \ldots}}$	403, 637
Cash flow from operations to current liabilities ratio	$\dfrac{\text{Net Cash Provided by Oper\ldots}}{\text{Average Current Liabilities}}$	637
Accounts receivable turnover ratio	$\dfrac{\text{Net Credit Sales}}{\text{Average Accounts Receivable}}$	638
Number of days' sales in receivables	$\dfrac{\text{Number of Days in the Period}}{\text{Accounts Receivable Turnover}}$	639
Inventory turnover ratio	$\dfrac{\text{Cost of Goods Sold}}{\text{Average Inventory}}$	265, 639
Number of days' sales in inventory	$\dfrac{\text{Number of Days in the Period}}{\text{Inventory Turnover}}$	267, 640
Accounts payable turnover ratio	$\dfrac{\text{Purchases}}{\text{Average Accounts Receivable}}$	640
Number of days' purchases in payables	$\dfrac{\text{Number of Days in the Period}}{\text{Accounts Payable Turnover}}$	640
Cash to cash operating cycle	Number of Days' Sales in Inventory + Number of Days' Sales in Receivables − Number of Days' Purchases in Payables	641
Solvency Analysis		
Debt-to-equity ratio	$\dfrac{\text{Total Liabilities}}{\text{Total Stockholders' Equity}}$	483, 642
Times interest earned ratio	$\dfrac{\text{Net Income} + \text{Interest Expense} + \text{Income Tax Expense}}{\text{Interest Expense}}$	483, 643
Debt service coverage ratio	$\dfrac{\text{Cash Flow from Operations Before Interest and Tax Payments}}{\text{Interest and Principal Payments}}$	483, 643
Cash flow from operations to capital expenditures ratio	$\dfrac{\text{Cash Flow from Operations} - \text{Total Dividends Paid}}{\text{Cash Paid for Acquisitions}}$	637
Book value per share	$\dfrac{\text{Total Shareholders' Equity}}{\text{Number of Common Shares Outstanding}}$	533
Profitability Analysis		
Gross profit ratio	$\dfrac{\text{Gross Profit}}{\text{Net Sales}}$	216, 633
Profit margin	$\dfrac{\text{Net Income}}{\text{Net Sales}}$	64, 218, 633
Return on assets ratio	$\dfrac{\text{Net Income} + \text{Interest Expense, Net of Tax}}{\text{Average Total Assets}}$	645
Return on sales ratio	$\dfrac{\text{Net Income} + \text{Interest Expense, Net of Tax}}{\text{Net Sales}}$	646
Asset turnover ratio	$\dfrac{\text{Net Sales}}{\text{Average Total Assets}}$	375, 646
Return on assets	Return on Sales × Asset Turnover	645
Return on common stockholders' equity ratio	$\dfrac{\text{Net Income} - \text{Preferred Dividends}}{\text{Average Common Stockholders' Equity}}$	647
Earnings per share	$\dfrac{\text{Net Income} - \text{Preferred Dividends}}{\text{Weighted Average Number of Common Shares Outstanding}}$	648
Price/earnings ratio	$\dfrac{\text{Current Market Price}}{\text{Earnings per Share}}$	649

Nelson Education
FINANCIAL STATEMENT TUTORIALS

Nelson Education Financial Statement Tutorials prepared by Irene Herremans (University of Calgary) are designed to help you learn the basic preparation of and the concepts behind financial statements and how they are used to understand a company's performance. These visually impressive modules also include quizzes and many practical examples from well-known companies to provide relevance to the discussion on financial statements.

A unique one-time password is required to access the tutorials and can be ordered as part of your book package by your instructor or by contacting Nelson Education Customer Support at www.nelson.com.

The tutorials cover:

the Balance Sheet • the Income Statement • the Cash Flow Statement • Recording Transactions

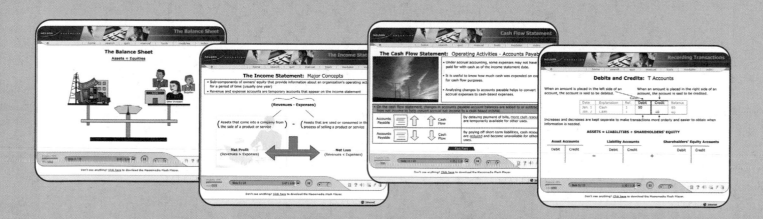

• Coming Soon: IFRS Module

www.porter2ce.nelson.com/tutorials

NELSON / EDUCATION

NAVIGATING THE TUTORIALS

The *navigation menu* items open various resources.

Home – takes you to the first screen

Search – allows you to look up or search for specific terms or concepts

Quiz – test your knowledge of the tutorial

Manual – download a PDF version of the tutorials for easy printing

Tools – opens a glossary of terms

Modules – opens the tutorial menu

Index – opens a list of all slides and their descriptions

Use the *navigation icons* at the bottom of the screen to go to the next slide, return to a previous slide, or pause a slide.

Directional icons at the bottom-right of the screen allow you to navigate through the module

Notepad – allows you to type, save, and print notes

? – provides help and FAQs

Audio – toggles audio on and off

Print – prints the current screen

Hi-liter – allows you to hi-lite on the screen

History – allows you to view a history of your work

Map – (bottom-left of the screen) allows you to skip to any slide

Progress – shows where you are in the tutorial

Application functions may appear within the tutorials.

Quick Click – short quiz with instant feedback to test your learning thus far

Fast Facts – interesting or unique facts

Case Study – mini case study of an actual organization

Application – real-world example or illustration of an applied concept

More Information – fuller explanation of the subject matter

Guess the Best – additional industry-related questions

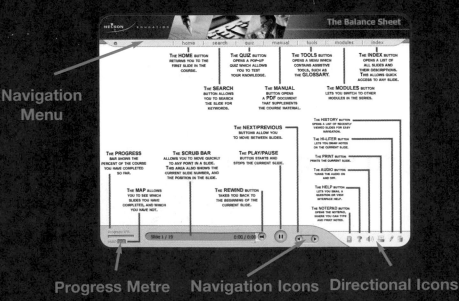

Enjoy your study of the financial accounting process!

FINANCIAL ACCOUNTING:
The Impact on Decision Makers

Second Canadian Edition

FINANCIAL ACCOUNTING:
The Impact on Decision Makers

Second Canadian Edition

Gary A. Porter
University of St. Thomas—Minnesota

Curtis L. Norton
Northern Illinois University

G. Richard Chesley
Saint Mary's University

Xiaofei Song-Bauld
Saint Mary's University

NELSON / EDUCATION

NELSON / EDUCATION

Financial Accounting: The Impact on Decision Makers, Second Canadian Edition
by Gary A. Porter, Curtis L. Norton, G. Richard Chesley, and Xiaofei Song-Bauld

Associate Vice President, Editorial Director:
Evelyn Veitch

Editor-in-Chief, Higher Education:
Anne Williams

Senior Acquisitions Editor:
Craig Dyer

Marketing Manager:
Kathaleen McCormick

Developmental Editor:
James Polley and Toula Kanellopoulos

Photo Researcher and Permissions Coordinator:
Melody Tolson

Content Production Manager:
Susan Wong

Production Service:
GEX Publishing Services

Copy Editor:
Karen Rolfe

Proofreader:
GEX Publishing Services

Supplements Developmental Editor:
Rod Banister

Indexer:
GEX Publishing Services

Manufacturing Coordinator:
Joanne McNeil

Design Director:
Ken Phipps

Interior Design:
Peter Papayanakis

Cover Design:
Johanna Liburd

Cover Image:
© Ken Taylor / Alamy

Compositor:
GEX Publishing Services

Printer:
Transcontinental Printing

Library and Archives Canada Cataloguing in Publication Data

Financial accounting: the impact on decision makers / Gary A. Porter ... [et al.]. -- 2nd Canadian ed.

Includes bibliographical references and index.

1. Accounting--Textbooks.

2. Accounting--Decision making--Textbooks. I. Porter, Gary A., 1950-
HF5636.F55 2008a   657
C2008-907354-1

ISBN-13: 978-0-17-610445-0
ISBN-10: 0-17-610445-3

To those who really "count":
Dianna
Don, Noah, Kyle

Balance of *Preparer Perspective* and *User Focus*. Discover the Best of Both with Porter/Norton/Chesley/ Song-Bauld!

Anyone who works out regularly appreciates the need to maintain a healthy balance between cardiovascular/aerobic training and muscular/strength training. Likewise, the study of accounting requires a balance between an understanding of the preparation of financial statements and the use of those statements in decision making.

A STUDENT finishing a financial accounting course needs to be able to *read and understand* an annual report. At the same time, he or she needs a solid understanding of the preparation of financial statements from transactions. This is why, from the very first edition, we have pursued "a balance between a **Preparer Perspective** and a **User Focus**. From our experience, students need to understand both how transactions are recorded and statements are prepared and also how accounting information is used and why it is important for financial decision making.

WE INVITE you to discover the best of both with *Financial Accounting: The Impact on Decision Makers*, Second Canadian Edition.

Brief Contents

Contents

Preface

◼ ALL ABOARD!

No one can doubt the important role that railways played in the development of Canada. As the pioneers pushed from east to west, the railways opened up prosperity and new opportunities. In a similar fashion, your first course in financial accounting will introduce you to a new world: a world full of challenges and opportunities. As you take the "trip" through our text, you will encounter the key information you need in order to understand the business environment; you will also learn about the important role of financial accounting in that environment. You will learn the process of transforming information from business transactions into financial reports, how to decipher the important information contained in those reports, and how to analyze reports in order to make financial decisions. Welcome to your Journey to Success!

A Balanced View

While developing this book, we found that most instructors want the best of two worlds: a *decision-making focus* featuring elements that capture student interest, and solid coverage of the *preparation of financial statements from transactions*. By striking *the correct balance* and by combining topical coverage with pedagogical features that are useful to both these valid approaches, we lead the way in successfully presenting financial accounting. This Second Canadian Edition builds on the success of the First Canadian Edition and of six previous U.S. editions in providing a truly balanced approach.

In order to meet a variety of needs for courses and students, we provide *many choices* for coverage. As reflected on the contents pages, several chapters have appendixes that provide additional procedural and decision-focused coverage. These appendixes can be included or excluded as desired. In addition, we provide a large selection of pedagogical elements and assignments to allow *flexibility* and *variety*.

As suggested by the Journey to Success map presented on the inside front cover, the text directs a journey across Canada, with side trips as necessary to customize your journey.

◼ TRAVEL ON A FIRM FOUNDATION

We are committed to four principles that have been instrumental to student success:

- ◼ An emphasis on *pedagogy* and *student appeal* to accommodate most learning styles.
- ◼ A focus on *financial statements*.
- ◼ A focus on *actual public companies*.
- ◼ A *decision-making* emphasis.

Our adherence to these principles means that business majors and accounting majors alike will be prepared for future success when using accounting information in the business environment.

Rely on the Text's Solid Infrastructure

To support the principles set for the text, we have developed the presentation around transaction processing, the income statement, the balance sheet, and the statement of cash flows. Tying that structure together is a flagship company, **Canadian National Railway Company (CN),** which students will return to many times as they develop their understanding of financial information.

Information about CN is woven throughout the text. Readers are introduced to the company in Chapter 1. In later chapters, CN's financial statements are revisited many times. Also, the company's 2007 financial statements from its annual report are reproduced in Appendix A to provide an integrated view of the particulars presented in each chapter.

Browse Our Itinerary

Our **Journey to Success** guides you through the text. This master map, which appears at the beginning of the text, provides an overview of the textbook. Each Part Opener introduces you to an important new area of financial accounting and includes a statement about the core focus of that part. This will serve as an ongoing reminder of the text's direction and coverage.

We start our trip on the East Coast with Part I: "Planning for the Trip." Part I is designed to orient readers to the business world so that all will have basic information about the structure of businesses, the importance of financial accounting, and the decision makers in the business environment. The story of CN begins its path through the text in Chapters 1 and 2. We'll answer questions such as "Why Study Accounting?" and "What Is Accounting?" and we'll look at the needs of accounting's users. These chapters introduce and describe the four main financial statements and supporting information found in annual reports. This brief overview of the four financial statements will help plan the journey's itinerary.

Heading inland, Part II: "Getting Basic Training," focuses on the accounting process from transaction analysis and recording through to financial statement preparation. Chapter 3 discusses the effects of transactions on accounting equations and how transactions are recorded and processed systematically using double-entry accounting. Chapter 4 introduces recognition and measurement issues and completes our discussion of the accounting cycle.

As our journey enters Part III: "Touring the Income Statement," we look at the elements of that statement that are key for assessing the performance of a company and for valuing investment in a company. Revenues, expenses, and classification issues are described so that an assessment can be made of a company's operations. Chapter 5 presents the income statement, while Chapter 6 focuses on inventories and cost of goods sold.

We continue the journey in Part IV: "Touring the Balance Sheet," where we describe the nature and classification of a company's investment and financing activities. In this way we show the relationship between operating results and the investment required to achieve those results. In this part we discuss each major area of the balance sheet. In Chapter 7 we talk about cash and other investments used to operate the business. In Chapter 8 we describe the long-term investments used in business operations. Chapters 9 and 10 discuss the short- and long-term financing of businesses. Chapter 11 completes Part IV by presenting the financing provided by business owners.

As the journey nears its destination, Part V: "Touring the Cash Flow Statement," links together the basic descriptions of the cash flows presented as part of earlier discussions. Chapter 12 also illustrates the cash linkages in the financial statements.

Part VI: "Final Destination," discusses the decision analysis that investors and managers require in order to assess financial reports. Earlier discussions introduced the ideas behind this assessment; this part presents an integrated view of the interpretation process. Chapter 13 ends the journey with a comparison of CN and CP, using all the concepts you've learned on your journey to success!

Revisions in the Second Canadian Edition

The Second Canadian Edition provides the opportunity to incorporate the lessons learned from a number of classroom tests of the preliminary first edition and a second round of reviews. As a result, we made changes that we believe improve an already excellent text.

Specific changes include the following topics:

- IFRS regulations or proposals have been incorporated wherever possible to reflect developments in the international harmonization of accounting. We encourage investigation of two recent books[1] focused directly on the specifics of the IFRS requirements and the impact on Canadian accounting.

- A revised presentation of the ethics material.

- Incorporation of internal control discussions in the main chapter.

- A discussion of the revised nature of Canadian GAAP that broadens its scope to reflect practices permitted by a company such such companies as Canadian National Railway.

- Increased discussion of comprehensive income as stated by Canadian GAAP along with a reduced presentation of LIFO inventory cost allocation as implied by Canadian developments.

- Movement of short-term investments to an appendix that permits a discussion appropriate for its new complexity.

- An expansion of the discussion of depreciation to reflect the impact of international changes on Canadian practice.

- A revised description of income trusts that accommodates the changes in Canadian law.

Besides the specific changes listed above, numerous changes are incorporated in most of the chapters. The following summarizes these revisions.

- All chapters present revised chapter openers and illustrations.

- Study links were placed at the beginning of each chapter to assist the reader to integrate the material contained therein.

- Chapter highlights were written to conform to the learning objectives of each chapter to assist reviews.

- Account highlights and ratios are redesigned to improve readability and to summarize the contents of each chapter and improve decision relevance of accounting presentations.

- Nearly all exercises, problems, and cases are revised.

- New comprehensive problems were added.

- Significant edits were made to improve clarity where needed.

- A complete supplements package was developed to provide support and assistance to students and faculty using this text.

We believe the changes we made provide a text discussion appropriate to our readers in both universities and colleges and incorporate the suggestions of our reviewers as best we can. New improvements can be requested by both students and faculty and we encourage feedback by contacting our publisher at www.nelson.com. Such feedback will enable us to improve the next edition of this wonderful text.

---

[1] I.M. Wiecek and N. M. Young , IFRS Primer: International GAAP Basics (Mississauga, Ont.: John Wiley and Sons Canada Ltd., 2009. A. Melville, International Financial Reporting: A Practice Guide (Toronto, Ont.: Prentice-Hall, 2008.

PEDAGOGICAL FEATURES

Each chapter begins with an opener that focuses on financial reports. CN is used to illustrate many of the topics and end-of-chapter materials. However, CN's competitor, Canadian Pacific (CP), and other prominent Canadian companies such as HBC, Alimentations Couche-Tard, and Loblaw provide specifics and will help you compare and understand the financial reports of CN.

Each chapter contains a number of pedagogical features to help you understand financial accounting:

- **Learning Objectives** allow you to focus on the key information in each chapter. Each learning objective is keyed to relevant chapter content and is tied to the Chapter Highlights summary and to related problems and exercises.

- **Study links** provide connections with the previous chapter and links to upcoming chapters.

- **Focus on Financial Results** opens each chapter with a case study to develop a real-world setting for each chapter's topic coverage.

- **Margin glossaries** provide definitions for new terms the first time they appear; a full glossary appears at the end of the book.

- **Study Tips** appear in the margins to further focus your reading on important concepts. These are also useful study tools.

- **Two-Minute Reviews** are quick reviews of the section you just read. Answers to the Two-Minute Reviews are at the end of the chapter.

- **Accounting for Your Decisions** illustrates applications of the concepts developed by allowing you to assume the role of a user of financial information, a decision maker, or business person and to respond to a realistic situation you may encounter on the job.

- **Ratio Review sections** appear in chapters where ratios and other key calculations are introduced.

- **Impact on the Financial Reports** shows, in one place, the impact of the chapter's topical coverage on one or more of the four financial statements.

- **End-of-chapter materials** include chapter highlights tied to learning objectives, warmup exercises (with solutions), review problems (with solutions), key terms quizzes, questions, exercises, problems, alternative problems, and cases. Most cases involve reading and interpreting financial statements, comparing two companies in the same industry, ethics-in-accounting cases, and Internet research. Relevant learning objectives are keyed to the exercises, problems, and cases to provide students with easy access to related text information when working through end-of-chapter materials.

Supporting several chapters are appendixes that contain special "topics." These include coverage of a work sheet (Chapter 4), sales tax (Chapter 5), the perpetual inventory method (Chapter 6), short-term investments (Chapter 7), interest calculations (Chapter 9), taxes and pensions (Chapter 10), and unincorporated business (Chapter 11). These appendixes represent important side trips for various stages of the journey.

Five integrative problems have been incorporated at the end of Part I, Part II, Chapter 8, Chapter 11, and Part VI. Each assignment challenges the student to think through a multi-faceted problem that requires knowledge learned throughout that section of the text.

For quick reference, a comprehensive **glossary of key terms** is located at the end of the text, along with a subject index to help in locating specifics within the text.

HELPING STUDENTS SUCCEED

CengageNOW CENGAGENOW™

Prepared by Helen Vallee (Kwantlen Polytechnic University) this powerful and fully integrated on-line teaching and learning system provides you with flexibility and control, saves valuable classroom time, and improves outcomes. Your students benefit by having a learning pathway customized and tailored to their unique needs.

- This unique learning path is organized by topic so that each student is directed to complete a **diagnostic pre-assessment**.
- The results of the pre-assessment generate an **individualized learning pathway** that connects the student to additional resources that they can access to help them master the course content.
- A **post-assessment** is also available, so that students may gauge their progress and comprehension of the concepts and skills necessary to succeed in introductory accounting.

Using **CengageNOW**, you and your students may:

- Complete, self-grade, and track student homework.
- Access an integrated e-book.
- Take advantage of a personalized learning path.
- Teach and learn using interactive course assignments.
- Test and teach using a flexible set of assessment options.
- Make use of test delivery options.
- Use a full range of course management tools.
- Have full confidence of WebCT™ and Blackboard® integration.

Contact your Nelson Education sales representative for more information about CengageNOW.

Nelson Education Financial Statement Tutorials The Nelson Education Financial Statement Tutorials prepared by Irene Herremans (University of Calgary) are designed to help you learn the basic preparation of and the concepts behind financial statements and how they are used to understand a company's performance. A unique one-time-use password is required to access the tutorials and can be ordered as part of your book package by your instructor or by contacting Nelson Education Customer Support at www.nelson.com.

Student Solutions Manual (ISBN 0-17-610450-X) Written by the text authors, the Student Solutions Manual contains solutions to the odd-numbered exercises, problems, and cases in the text.

Excel® Templates Prepared by Heather Sceles, (Saint Mary's University), many problems in each chapter may be solved on a Microsoft Excel spreadsheet to increase student awareness of basic software applications. Those selected assignments that may be solved using the Excel spreadsheets are available from the student resource section of the text's Web site.

Web Resources This text's supporting Web site at www.porter2ce.nelson.com provides web quizzes to test your learning, crossword puzzlcs, flashcards, on-line glossary and downloadable Excel spreadsheets for selected problems in the text. The web quizzes were prepared by Prem Lobo (York University).

HELPING INSTRUCTORS SHINE

An unsurpassed package of supplementary resources helps you **plan**, **manage**, and **teach** your course. Additionally, special resources are available to help **assess** the progress of your students.

Instructor's Resource CD-ROM This all-in-one resource contains all of the key instructor ancillaries (solutions manual, instructor's manual, electronic test bank files, ExamView® computerized test bank, PowerPoint® presentation slides, Turning Point Slides, Excel templates, and Day One Slides), giving instructors the ultimate tool for customizing lectures and presentations.

Instructor's Resource Manual Prepared by Fayez Elayan (Brock University) and available on the Instructor's Resource CD-ROM and from the text's Web site, this resource helps you plan for your course by providing detailed chapter outlines, lecture topics, and suggestions for classroom activities.

Solutions Manual (ISBN 0176104593) Prepared by the text authors, this material is also available in electronic form on the Instructor's Resource CD-ROM.

Instructor's PowerPoint® Slides Prepared by Xiaofei Song-Bauld (Saint Mary's University) and located on the Instructor's Resource CD-ROM and on the text's Web site, these colourful slides reinforce chapter content and provide a rich tool for in-class lectures and out-of-class reviewing.

Turning Point: JoinIn™ on Turning Point® Prepared by Xiaofei Song-Bauld, this powerful lecture tool transforms PowerPoint® into a two-way learning experience. Enliven your classroom by integrating interactive quizzes and activities directly into your PowerPoint® lectures, and provide immediate feedback on student comprehension. If you can use PowerPoint, you can use JoinIn on Turning Point!

Computerized Test Bank The Test Bank, by Gordon Holyer (Vancouver Island University) is a complete and plentiful set of revised test items that is also available in electronic form (using ExamView® software), provided on the Instructor's Resource CD-ROM. The Test Banks files are also available in electronic format as Word files on the Instructor's Resource CD-ROM.

■ ACKNOWLEDGMENTS

We have had the benefit of adapting the successful work of Gary Porter and Curtis Norton, currently in its sixth edition; we thank Professors Porter and Norton for their confidence and for their initial work on this text.

In preparing this Second Canadian Edition, we have benefited from extensive feedback from the following people who were either reviewers or user diarists:

Ronald Baker, University of Regina

Margaret Beresford, Kwantlen Polytechnic University

Kristie Dewald, University of Alberta

Robert Ducharme, University of Waterloo

Leo Gallant, St. Francis Xavier University

George Andrew Gekas, Ryerson University

Jingyu Li, Brock University

David J. McConomy, Queen's University

Patti Proulx, Carleton University

Helen Vallee, Kwantlen Polytechnic University

Elisa Zuliani, University of Toronto, Rotman

A large number of reviewers provided feedback that contributed to the success of the Preliminary Canadian Edition:

Hilary Becker, Carleton University

H. Donald Brown, Brock University

Elizabeth Farrell, York University

Larry Goldsman, British Columbia Institute of Technology

Michael Konopaski, Trent University

Ken MacAuley, St. Francis Xavier University

Mark Mellon, University of New Brunswick, Saint John

Anthony Moung Yin Chan, Ryerson University

Jeanbih Pai, University of Manitoba

Akash S. Rattan, British Columbia Institute of Technology

Bob Sproule, University of Waterloo

In addition, we are grateful for the administrative support of the staff of the editorial department of Nelson, as well as to Ross Meacher for completing an accuracy check of the solutions. Ross Meacher is a chartered accountant with a Master's degree in mathematics.

We would appreciate any questions and feedback from readers of the text. Contact can be made through your Nelson sales representative.

Meet the Authors

Gary A. Porter is Professor of Accounting at the University of St. Thomas—Minnesota. He earned Ph.D. and M.B.A. degrees from the University of Colorado and his B.S.B.A. from Drake University. He has published in *Journal of Accounting Education*, *Journal of Accounting, Auditing & Finance*, and *Journal of Accountancy*, among others, and has conducted numerous workshops on introductory accounting education and corporate financial reporting. Dr. Porter's professional activities include experience as a staff accountant with Deloitte & Touche in Denver, participation in KPMG Peat Marwick Foundation's Faculty Development program, and a leading role in numerous bank training programs.

He has won an Excellence in Teaching Award from the University of Colorado and Outstanding Professor Awards from both San Diego State University and the University of Montana. He has served on the Illinois CPA Society's Innovations in Accounting Education Grants Committee, the steering committee of the Midwest region of the American Accounting Association, and the board of directors of the Chicago chapter of Financial Executives International.

Curtis L. Norton has been a professor at Northern Illinois University in Dekalb, Illinois, since 1976. He earned his B.S. from Jamestown College, North Dakota, his M.B.A. from the University of South Dakota, and his Ph.D. from Arizona State University. His extensive publications include articles in *Accounting Horizons*, *Journal of Accounting Education*, *Journal of Accountancy*, *Journal of Corporate Accounting*, *Journal of the American Taxation Association*, *Real Estate Review*, *Accounting Review*, and *CPA Journal*. In 1988–89 he received the University Excellence in Teaching Award—the highest university-wide teaching recognition at NIU. He is also a consultant and has conducted training programs for government departments, banks, utilities, and other entities. Dr. Norton is a member of the American Accounting Association and a member and officer of Financial Executives International.

G. Richard Chesley is Professor Emeritus of Accounting at the Sobey School of Business, Saint Mary's University, Halifax, Nova Scotia. He graduated from Mount Allison University and Ohio State University holding B.Comm., M.A., and Ph.D. degrees. He has been involved in eleven previous books as well as numerous articles and presentations on a wide variety of subjects, including ethics, corporate governance, derivatives, environmental reporting, accounting regulation, and forecast bias. He has published in *Accounting Review*, *Journal of Accounting Research*, *CA Magazine*, and *CMA Management Magazine*, and has been involved in designing many courses and programs. In recognition of his extensive efforts, he was awarded the L.S. Rosen Outstanding Educator Award by the Canadian Academic Accounting Association, as well as the Saint Mary's University President's Exemplary Service Award. He has held appointments at the University of Pennsylvania, Dalhousie University, Lingnan University, and the University of Iowa. In 2007, Saint Mary's University appointed him to the position of Professor Emeritus.

Xiaofei Song-Bauld is an Associate Professor of Accounting at the Sobey School of Business, Saint Mary's University, Halifax, Nova Scotia. She holds a B.Sc. from Fudan University, an M.Sc. from Shanghai Jiao Tong University, an M.B.A. from Saint Mary's University, and a Ph.D. from Baruch College, City University of New York. She is also a certified general accountant. Her research in financial reporting has been published in *Journal of Accounting, Auditing, and Finance* and *Journal of Accounting and Public Policy* and has been presented at numerous conferences. She has held academic positions at Fudan University, Baruch College, and Pace University.

COURTESY CN RAIL

Planning for the Trip

A Word to Readers About This Book

Knowing accounting is just plain smart for everyone in today's job market. This book is therefore not just for accounting majors—it's for anyone who wants to learn how to read and understand financial information. You'll work with numbers in this book. But at every turn, this book and its study aids—not to mention your instructor—will walk you through the details. You'll write some memorandums backing up your calculations, pitting your analytical skills against real financial statements and problems. And you'll have the chance to place yourself in different business roles.

In fact, this book will help you think, talk, and write skillfully about accounting information.

LEARNING OBJECTIVES

After studying this chapter, you should be able to:

LO 1 Distinguish among the forms of organizations.

LO 2 Describe the various types of business activities.

LO 3 Identify the primary users of accounting information and their needs.

LO 4 Explain the purpose of each of the financial statements and the relationships among them, and prepare a set of simple statements.

LO 5 Identify and explain the primary assumptions made in preparing financial statements.

LO 6 Describe the various roles of accountants in organizations.

Accounting Communication— An Introduction

CP PHOTO/ JEFF MCINTOSH

STUDY LINKS

A Look at This Chapter

Business is the foundation upon which accounting rests. This introduction explains the nature of business, the different forms of organizations, and the types of activities in which businesses engage. We begin the study of accounting by considering what accounting is and who uses the information it provides. We will see that accounting is an important form of communication and that financial statements are the medium that accountants use to communicate with those who have some interest in the financial affairs of a company.

Chapter 1 introduces you to accounting and the output of an accounting system, the financial statements. As a form of communication, we will explore how accounting provides useful information to a variety of users and the various roles that accountants play in organizations.

A Look at an Upcoming Chapter

In Chapter 2 we look in more detail at the composition of the statements and the conceptual framework that supports the work of an accountant.

Focus on Financial Results

Canadian National Railway Company (CN for short) is a major component of Canada's transportation industry and a Canadian institution. A recent study by Statistics Canada estimates that transportation in the year 2000 represents $64 billion of the total Canadian economy, ranking behind only four other sectors and ahead of such sectors as oil and gas and mining.[1]

CN is a major component of Canada's transportation sector. Many groups, from investors to employees, are interested in the financial affairs of CN. As presented in the financial summary (see below), CN's operations generated $7.9 billion in revenues and $2.2 billion in income after expenses and income taxes. It owed $5.6 billion to creditors on its assets of $23.5 billion. These key facts are only a few of the financial items concerning the health of CN that are available to readers of its annual report. More details will become evident in Chapter 1 and in each of the subsequent chapters explored as part of your journey through this book.

[1]"Economic Importance of Transportation," *The Daily*, May 19, 2006, www.statcan.ca.

CN 2007 ANNUAL REPORT   http://www.cn.ca

$ in millions, except per share data, or unless otherwise indicated	2007[1]	2006[1][2]	2005[2]
Financial results			
Revenues	$7,897	$7,929	$7,446
Operating income	2,876	3,030	2,624
Net income	2,158	2,087	1,556
Diluted earnings per share	4.25	3.91	2.77
Dividend per share	0.84	0.65	0.50
Net capital expenditures	1,387	1,298	1,180
Financial position			
Total assets	23,460	24,004	22,188
Long-term debt, including current portion	5,617	5,604	5,085
Shareholders' equity	10,177	9,824	9,249
Financial ratios *(%)*			
Operating ratio	63.6	61.8	64.8
Debt to total capitalization	35.6	36.3	35.5

(1)   The Company's financial results for 2007 and 2006 include items affecting the comparability of the results of operations as discussed on page 33 of this report.

(2)   The 2006 and 2005 comparative figures have been reclassified in order to be consistent with the 2007 presentation as discussed on page 42 of this report.

This excerpt from CN's 2007 Annual Report appears courtesy of CN. This section of the CN Annual Report appears in the Appendix of this textbook.

Why study accounting? There are many reasons to do so. This book will show you the benefits of such study by describing the details of a subset of accounting known as "financial accounting." In this book we focus on financial accounting because of its pervasive nature and long history. To discuss all of accounting would not be useful because the field is too broad.

Organization A collection of individuals pursuing the same goal or objective.

Individuals come together to pursue goals. The result of this gathering is an **organization**, defined as a collection of individuals pursuing the same goal or objective. Many organizations will already be familiar to you—for example, a student group, a government, a business, a club, or a charity.

All organizations, whatever their size, require finances and must make financial decisions. Thus organizations need financial information in order to describe the resources they hold and to support the various financial decisions they make.

▪ FORMS OF ORGANIZATIONS

LO 1 Distinguish among the forms of organizations.

There are many different types of organizations in our society. One convenient way to categorize the myriad types is to distinguish between those that are organized to earn income and those that exist for some other purpose. Although the lines can become blurred, *business entities* generally are organized to earn an income, whereas *non-business entities* generally exist to serve various segments of society. Both types are summarized in Exhibit 1-1.

Exhibit 1-1 Forms of Organization

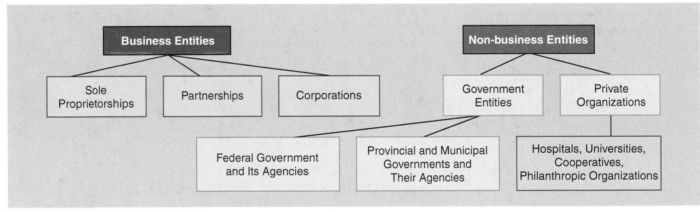

SOUTH-WESTERN PUBLISHING

Business Entities

Business entities are organized to earn an income (commonly termed a profit). Legally, a profit-oriented company is one of three types: a sole proprietorship, a partnership, or a corporation.

Sole proprietorship A business with a single owner.

Economic entity concept The assumption that a single, identifiable unit must be accounted for in all situations.

Sole Proprietorships   This form of organization is characterized by a single owner. Many small businesses are organized as **sole proprietorships.** Very often the business is owned and operated by the same person. Despite the close relationship between the owner and the business, the affairs of the two must be kept separate. This is one example in accounting of the **economic entity concept,** which requires that a single, identifiable unit of an organization be accounted for in all situations. For example, assume that Bernie Berg owns a neighbourhood grocery store. In paying the monthly bills, such as utilities and supplies, Bernie must separate his personal costs from the costs associated with the grocery business. In turn, financial statements prepared for the business must not intermingle Bernie's personal affairs with the affairs of the entity.

Unlike the distinction made for accounting purposes between an individual's personal and business affairs, the **Canada Revenue Agency** does not recognize the separate existence of a proprietorship from its owner. That is, a sole proprietorship is not a taxable entity; any income earned by the business is taxed on the tax return of the individual.

http://www.cra-arc.gc.ca

Partnerships   A **partnership** is a business owned by two or more individuals. Many small businesses begin as partnerships. When two or more partners start out, they need an agreement as to how much each will contribute to the business and how they will divide the income. In large businesses, like the accounting firm of **PricewaterhouseCoopers**, the partnership agreement is formalized in a written document.

Although a partnership may involve just two owners, some have thousands of partners. Public accounting firms, law firms, and other types of service companies are often organized as partnerships. Like a sole proprietorship, a partnership is not a taxable entity. The individual partners pay taxes on their proportionate shares of the income of the business.

Partnership A business owned by two or more individuals and with the characteristic of unlimited liability.

http://www.pwc.com/ca

Corporations   Although sole proprietorships and partnerships dominate in sheer number, corporations control an overwhelming majority of the private resources in this country. A **corporation** is an entity organized under the laws of a particular province or the federal government. Each of the provinces is empowered to regulate the creation and operation of businesses organized as corporations in it.

To start a corporation, one must file articles of incorporation with the government. If the articles are approved by the government, a corporate charter is issued, and the corporation can begin to issue shares. A **share** is a certificate that acts as evidence of ownership in a corporation. Although not always the case, shares of many corporations are traded on organized stock exchanges, such as the **Toronto** and **Toronto Venture Stock Exchanges**.

What are the advantages of running a business as a corporation rather than a partnership? One key advantage of the corporate form of organization is that it makes it possible to raise large amounts of money in a relatively brief period of time. To raise money, the company can sell a specific type of security: shares. As stated earlier, a share is simply a certificate that evidences ownership in a corporation. Sometimes corporations issue another type of security called a bond or debenture. A **bond** is similar to a share in that it is a certificate or piece of paper issued to someone. However, it is different from a share in that a bond represents a promise by the company to repay a certain amount of money at a future date. In other words, if you were to buy a bond from a company, you would be lending it money. Interest on the bond is usually paid semiannually. We will have more to say about shares and bonds later, when we discuss financing activities.

The ease of transfer of ownership in a corporation is another advantage of this form of organization. If you hold shares in a corporation whose shares are actively traded and you decide to sell, you simply call your broker and put in an order to sell. Another distinct advantage is the limited liability of the shareholder. Generally speaking, a shareholder is liable only for the amount contributed to the business. That is, if a company goes out of business, the most the shareholder stands to lose is the amount invested. On the other hand, both proprietors and general partners usually can be held personally liable for the debts of the business.

Corporation A form of entity organized under the laws of a particular province or the federal government; ownership evidenced by shares.

Share A certificate that acts as ownership in a corporation.

http://www.tsx.com

Bond A certificate that represents a corporation's promise to repay a certain amount of money and interest in the future.

Non-Business Entities

Most **non-business entities** are organized for a purpose other than to earn an income. They exist to serve the needs of various segments of society. For example, a hospital is organized to provide health care to its patients. A municipal government is operated for the benefit of its citizens. A local school district exists to meet the educational needs of the youth in the community.

Non-business entity Organization operated for some purpose other than to earn a profit.

All these entities are distinguished by the lack of an identifiable owner. The lack of an identifiable owner and of the profit motive changes to some extent the type of accounting used by non-business entities. This type, called *fund accounting,* is discussed in advanced accounting courses. Regardless of the lack of a profit motive in non-business entities, there is still a demand for the information provided by an accounting system. For example, a local government needs detailed cost breakdowns in order to manage its tax collections. A hospital may want to raise money and will need financial statements to present to the prospective contributor or the government.

Organizations and Social Responsibility

Although non-business entities are organized specifically to serve members of society, business entities also have become more sensitive to their broader social responsibilities. Because they touch the lives of so many members of society, most large corporations recognize the societal aspects of their overall mission and have established programs to meet their social responsibilities. Some companies focus their efforts on local charities, while others donate to national or international causes.

■ THE NATURE OF BUSINESS ACTIVITY

LO 2 Describe the various types of business activities.

Because corporations dominate business activity in Canada, in this book we will focus on this form of organization. Corporations engage in a multitude of different types of activities. It is possible to categorize all of them into one of three types, however: financing, investing, and operating. Exhibit 1-2 displays a statement of cash flows, which captures the financing, investing, and operating cash activities of businesses. This required accounting disclosure contains a summary of these three activities for the Canadian National Railway Company. Some of the specific disclosures will be described in the next few pages. More specifics will become evident as later chapters are studied.

Financing Activities

CN
http://www.cn.ca

All businesses must start with financing. Simply put, money is needed to start a business. CN began operations in 1830. During part of its expansion and growth it was an agency of the federal government, termed a Crown corporation, but in 1995 it became a corporation under the Canada Business Corporations Act, selling 100 percent of its ownership on various stock exchanges. To implement the transfer of ownership, the company issued 83,800,000 shares for an offering price of $27 per share.

As you will see throughout this book, accounting has its own unique terminology. In fact, accounting is often referred to as *the language of business.* The discussion of financing activities brings up two important accounting terms: liabilities and capital stock. A **liability** is an obligation of a business; it can take many different forms. When a company borrows money at a bank, the liability is called a *note payable.* When a company sells bonds, the obligation is termed *bonds payable.* Amounts owed to the government for taxes are called *taxes payable.* Assume that CN buys diesel oil from Petro-Canada and that Petro-Canada gives CN 30 days to pay for purchases. During this 30-day period, CN has an obligation called *accounts payable.*

Liability An obligation of a business.

http://www.petro-canada.ca

Capital stock is the term used by accountants to indicate the dollar amount of shares sold to the public. Capital stock differs from liabilities in one very important respect. Those who buy shares in a corporation are not lending money to the business, as are those who buy bonds in the company or who make a loan in some other form to the company. Someone who buys shares in a company is called a **shareholder,** and that person is providing a permanent form of financing to the business. In other words, there is not a due date at which time the shareholder will be repaid. Normally, the only way for a shareholder to get back his or her original investment from buying shares is to sell them to someone else. Someone who buys bonds in a company or in some other way

Capital stock Indicates the owners' contributions to a corporation.

Shareholder Someone who buys shares in a company.

Exhibit 1-2 Canadian National Railway Company Consolidated Statement of Cash Flows

In millions — Year ended December 31,	2007	2006	2005
Operating activities			
Net income	$ 2,158	$ 2,087	$ 1,556
Adjustments to reconcile net income to net cash provided from operating activities:			
Depreciation and amortization	678	653	630
Deferred income taxes (Note 15)	(82)	3	547
Gain on sale of Central Station Complex (Note 5)	(92)	–	–
Gain on sale of Investment in English Welsh and Scottish Railway (Note 6)	(61)	–	–
Other changes in:			
Accounts receivable (Note 4)	229	(17)	142
Material and supplies	18	(36)	(25)
Accounts payable and accrued charges	(351)	197	(156)
Other net current assets and liabilities	39	58	8
Other	(119)	6	6
Cash provided from operating activities	2,417	2,951	2,708
Investing activities			
Property additions	(1,387)	(1,298)	(1,180)
Acquisitions, net of cash acquired (Note 3)	(25)	(84)	–
Sale of Central Station Complex (Note 5)	351	–	–
Sale of Investment in English Welsh and Scottish Railway (Note 6)	114	–	–
Other, net	52	33	105
Cash used by investing activities	(895)	(1,349)	(1,075)
Financing activities			
Issuance of long-term debt	4,171	3,308	2,728
Reduction of long-term debt	(3,589)	(3,089)	(2,865)
Issuance of common shares due to exercise of stock options and related excess tax benefits realized (Note 12)	77	120	115
Repurchase of common shares (Note 11)	(1,584)	(1,483)	(1,418)
Dividends paid	(418)	(340)	(275)
Cash used by financing activities	(1,343)	(1,484)	(1,715)
Effect of foreign exchange fluctuations on U.S. dollar-denominated cash and cash equivalents	(48)	(1)	(3)
Net increase (decrease) in cash and cash equivalents	131	117	(85)
Cash and cash equivalents, beginning of year	179	62	147
Cash and cash equivalents, end of year	$ 310	$ 179	$ 62
Supplemental cash flow information			
Net cash receipts from customers and other	$ 8,139	$ 7,946	$ 7,581
Net cash payments for:			
Employee services, suppliers and other expenses	(4,323)	(4,130)	(4,075)
Interest	(340)	(294)	(306)
Workforce reductions (Note 9)	(31)	(45)	(87)
Personal injury and other claims (Note 18)	(86)	(107)	(92)
Pensions (Note 13)	(75)	(112)	(127)
Income taxes (Note 15)	(867)	(307)	(186)
Cash provided from operating activities	$ 2,417	$ 2,951	$ 2,708

See accompanying notes to consolidated financial statements.

This excerpt from CN's 2007 Annual Report appears courtesy of CN. This section of the CN Annual Report appears in the Appendix of this textbook.

Creditor Someone to whom a company or person has a debt.

makes a loan to it is called a **creditor.** A creditor does *not* provide a permanent form of financing to the business. That is, the creditor expects repayment of the amount loaned and, in many instances, payment of interest for the use of the money as well.

Exhibit 1-2 shows CN's financing activities. The issue and repurchase of common shares are classified as financing activities. Long-term debt (long-term liabilities) is also shown as a financing activity. However, other liabilities such as accounts payable and accrued charges are shown as operating activities. For now, we must ask that you accept this confusion; later, we will explain it.

Investing Activities

There is a natural progression in a business or other type of organization from financing activities to investing activities. That is, if operating activities are insufficient to permit all desired investing, then funds must be obtained from creditors and shareholders.

Asset A future economic benefit to an organization.

http://www.bcrco.com/
http://gltvtc.proboards57.com/

An **asset** is a future economic benefit to an organization. Money spent on certain assets is classified as investing. For example, purchases of land, buildings, and equipment would appear in financial statements as investments in properties. Purchases of other companies such as **BC Rail** and **Great Lakes Transport** (GLT) are also considered investments in assets because of the benefits expected.

Yet in Exhibit 1-2 you will notice that changes in other assets (such as accounts receivable from customers, and material and supplies on hand) are shown under operating activities. This dual treatment of assets is similar in nature to the treatment of financing activities. Later chapters will explain why such treatment is required.

Operating Activities

Once funds are obtained from financing activities and investments are made in productive assets, a business is ready to begin operations. Every business is organized with a purpose in mind. The purpose of some businesses is to sell a *product.* Other companies provide *services.* Service-oriented businesses are becoming an increasingly important sector of the Canadian economy. Some of the largest corporations in this country, such as transportation companies and banks, sell services rather than products. Some companies sell both products and services.

Revenue Inflows of assets resulting from the sale of products and services.

Accountants have a name for the sale of products and services. **Revenue** is the inflow of assets resulting from the sale of products and services. When a company makes a cash sale, the asset it receives is cash. When a sale is made on credit, the asset received is an account receivable. For now, you should understand that revenue represents the dollar amount of sales of products and services for a specific period of time.

We have thus far identified one important operating activity: the sale of products and services. However, costs must be incurred to operate a business. Employees must be paid salaries and wages. Suppliers must be paid for purchases of inventory, and the utility companies have to be paid for heat and electricity. The government must be paid the taxes owed it. All of these are examples of important operating activities of a business. As you might expect by now, accountants use a specific name for the costs incurred in operating a business. An **expense** is the outflow of assets resulting from the sale of goods and services.

Expense Outflows of assets resulting from the sale of goods and services.

Exhibit 1-3 summarizes the three types of activities conducted by a business. Our discussion and the exhibit present a simplification of business activity, because actual businesses are in a constant state of motion with many different financing, investing, and operating activities going on at any one time. The model as portrayed in Exhibit 1-3 should be helpful as you begin the study of accounting, however. To summarize, a company obtains money from various types of financing activities, uses the money raised to invest in productive assets, and then provides goods and services to its customers.

Going back to Exhibit 1-2 note the $2,417 figure appears twice on the statement of cash flows. The first is as a subtotal at the top of the statement under cash provided from operating activities. The second is at the bottom under supplemental cash flow information. A quick review of both sections of the statement will reveal that the section totals are the same but the internal makeup of each is different. Such alternative disclosures are

Exhibit 1-3 A Model of Business Activities

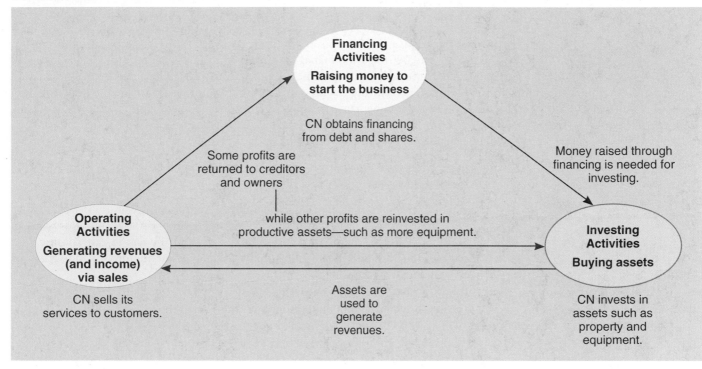

possible in accounting reports, but careful study of later chapters will help to avoid potential confusion. At present, we will describe a few of the supplemental cash flows in the bottom disclosure.

CN derived cash from operating activities in 2007 in the amount of $2,417 million. While the upper presentation is perhaps a challenge to the reader, the supplemental description at the bottom of Exhibit 1-2 shows receipts from customers of $8,139 million and payments for expenses and other services of $4,323 million, $340 million for interest, and $867 million for taxes—descriptions that are usually easier to interpret.

▌ WHAT IS ACCOUNTING?

Many people have preconceived notions about what accounting is. They think of it as a highly procedural activity practised by people who are "good in math." This notion of accounting is very narrow and focuses only on the record-keeping or bookkeeping aspects of the discipline. Accounting is in fact much broader than this in its scope. Specifically, **accounting** is "the process of identifying, measuring, and communicating economic information to permit informed judgments and decisions by users of the information."[2]

Each of the three activities in this definition—*identifying, measuring,* and *communicating*—requires the judgment of a trained professional. We will return later in this chapter to accounting as a profession and the various roles of accountants in our society. Note that the definition refers to the users of economic information and the decisions they make. Who *are* the users of accounting information? We turn now to this important question.

> **Accounting** The process of identifying, measuring, and communicating economic information to various users.

▌ USERS OF ACCOUNTING INFORMATION AND THEIR NEEDS

It is helpful to categorize users of accounting information on the basis of their relationship to the organization. Internal users, primarily the managers of a company, are involved in the daily affairs of the business. All other groups are external users.

> **LO 3** Identify the primary users of accounting information and their needs.

[2]American Accounting Association, *A Statement of Basic Accounting Theory* (Evanston, Ill.: American Accounting Association, 1966), p. 1.

Internal Users

Management accounting The branch of accounting concerned with providing management with information to facilitate planning and control.

The management of a company is in a position to obtain financial information in a way that best suits its needs. For example, if a CN manager needs to know the cost of shipping a carload of coal to Vancouver, this information exists in the accounting system and can be reported. If the same manager wants to find out if the monthly payroll is more or less than the budgeted amount, a report can be generated to provide the answer. **Management accounting** is the branch of accounting concerned with providing internal users (management) with information to facilitate planning and control. The ability to produce management accounting reports is limited only by the extent of the data available and the cost involved in generating the relevant information.

External Users

External users, those not involved directly in the operations of a business, need information that differs from that needed by internal users. In addition, the ability of external users to obtain the information is more limited. Without the day-to-day contact with the affairs of the business, outsiders must rely on the information presented to them by the management of the company.

Certain external users, such as the Canada Revenue Agency, the Canadian federal income tax administrator, require that information be presented in a very specific manner, and they have the authority of the law to ensure that they get the required information. Shareholders, bondholders, and other creditors must rely on *financial statements* for their information.[3] **Financial accounting** is the branch of accounting concerned with communication with outsiders through financial statements.

Financial accounting The branch of accounting concerned with the preparation of financial statements for outsider use.

Shareholders and Potential Shareholders Both existing and potential shareholders need financial information about a business. If you currently own shares in a company, you need information that will aid in your decision either to continue to hold the shares or to sell them. If you are considering buying shares in a company, you need financial information that will help in choosing among competing alternative investments. What has been the recent performance of the company in the stock market? What were its profits for the most recent year? How do these profits compare with those of the prior year? How much did the company pay in dividends? One source for much of this information is the company's financial statements.

Bondholders, Bankers, and Other Creditors Before buying a bond in a company (remember that you are lending money to the company), you need to feel comfortable that the company will be able to pay you the amount owed at maturity and the periodic interest payments. Financial statements can help you decide whether to purchase a bond. Similarly, before lending money, a bank needs information that will help it to determine the company's ability to repay both the amount of the loan and interest. Therefore, a set of financial statements is a key ingredient in a loan proposal.

Government Agencies Numerous government agencies have information needs specified by law. For example, the Canada Revenue Agency is empowered to collect a tax on income from both individuals and corporations. Every year a company prepares a tax return to report the amount of taxable income it earned. Another government agency, the **Ontario Securities Commission** (OSC), sets the rules under which financial statements must be presented for corporations that sell their shares to the public.

http://www.osc.gov.on.ca

Other External Users Many other individuals and groups rely on financial information given to them by businesses. A supplier of raw material needs to know the creditworthiness of a company before selling it a product on credit. To promote its industry, a trade association must gather financial information on the various companies in the

---

[3]Technically, shareholders are insiders because they own shares in the business. In most large corporations, however, it is not practical for shareholders to be involved in the daily affairs of the business. Thus, they are better categorized here as external users because they normally rely on general-purpose financial statements, as do creditors.

industry. Other important users are financial analysts. They use financial reports in advising their clients on investment decisions. In reaching their decisions, all of these users rely to a large extent on accounting information provided by management. Exhibit 1-4 summarizes the various users of financial information and the types of decisions they must make.

Exhibit 1-4 Users of Accounting Information

CATEGORIES OF USERS	EXAMPLES OF USERS	COMMON DECISION	RELEVANT QUESTION
Internal	Management	Should we build another facility?	What will be the cost to construct the plant?
External	Shareholder	Should I buy shares of CN?	How much did the company earn last year?
	Banker	Should I lend money to CN?	What existing debts or liabilities does the company have?
	Employee	Should I ask for a raise?	How much is the company's revenue, and how much is it paying out in salaries and wages? Is it paying out too much in compensation compared to its sales?
	Supplier	Should I allow CN to buy diesel fuel from me and pay me later?	What is the current amount of the company's accounts payable?

▪ FINANCIAL STATEMENTS: HOW ACCOUNTANTS COMMUNICATE

The primary focus of this book is financial accounting. This branch of accounting is concerned with informing management and outsiders about a company through financial statements. We turn our attention now to the composition of three of the major statements: the balance sheet, the income statement, and the statement of retained earnings.[4]

The Accounting Equation and the Balance Sheet

The accounting equation is the foundation for the entire accounting system:

Assets = Liabilities + Owners' Equity

The left side of the accounting equation refers to the *assets* of the company. Those items that are valuable economic resources and that will provide future benefit to the company should appear on the left side of the equation. The right side of the equation indicates who provided, or has a claim to, those assets. Some of the assets were provided by creditors, and they have a claim to them. For example, if a company has a delivery truck, the dealer that provided the truck to the company has a claim to the truck until the dealer is paid. The delivery truck would appear on the left side of the equation as an asset to the company; the company's *liability* to the dealer would appear on the right side of the equation. Other assets are provided by the owners of the business. Their claims to these assets are represented by the portion of the right side of the equation called **owners' equity.**

The term *shareholders' equity* is used to refer to the owners' equity of a corporation. **Shareholders' equity** is the mathematical difference between a corporation's assets and its obligations or liabilities. That is, after the amounts owed to bondholders, banks, suppliers, and other creditors are subtracted from the assets, the amount remaining is the shareholders' equity, the amount of interest or claim that the owners have on the assets of the business.

LO 4 Explain the purpose of each of the financial statements and the relationships among them, and prepare a set of simple statements.

Study Tip

The accounting equation and the financial statements are at the heart of this course. Memorize the accounting equation, and make sure you study this introduction to how the financial statements should look, how to read them, and what they say about a company.

Owners' equity The owners' claims on the assets of an entity.

Shareholders' equity The owners' equity in a corporation.

---

[4]The fourth major financial statement is the statement of cash flows. This important statement was shown earlier, in Exhibit 1-2.

Shareholders' equity arises in two distinct ways. First, it is created when a company issues shares to an investor. As we noted earlier, capital stock reflects ownership in a corporation in the form of a certificate. It represents the amounts contributed by the owners to the company. Second, as owners of shares in a corporation, shareholders have a claim on the assets of a business when it is profitable. **Retained earnings** represents the owners' claims to the company's assets that result from its earnings that have not been paid out in dividends. It is the earnings accumulated or retained by the company.

The **balance sheet** (sometimes called the *statement of financial position*) is the financial statement that summarizes the assets, liabilities, and owners' equity of a company. It is a "snapshot" of the business at a certain date. A balance sheet can be prepared on any day of the year, although it is most commonly prepared on the last day of a month, quarter, or year. At any point in time, the balance sheet must be "in balance." That is, assets must equal liabilities plus owners' equity.

Balance sheets for CN at the ends of two recent years are shown in Exhibit 1-5. Note the headings on the two columns of the balance sheet: December 31, 2007, and December 31, 2006. Although December 31 is the most common year-end, some companies use a date other than December 31 to end their year. Often this choice is based on when a company's peak selling season ends.

As the exhibit makes clear, there are three main sections of the balance sheet corresponding to the three elements of the accounting equation: Assets, Liabilities, and Shareholders' Equity.

In the following list, note some of the main types of items that appear on the balance sheet:

1. Cash and cash equivalents: Includes cash on hand as well as cash in various bank accounts
2. Accounts receivable: Arises from selling services to customers and allowing them to pay later
3. Material and supplies: Refers to products that the company uses in its operations
4. Properties: Includes land, buildings, machinery, and transportation equipment that are all needed to conduct rail services
5. Accounts payable and accrued charges: Arise from buying supplies and other materials and being allowed to pay later
6. Retained earnings: Amount of income earned less dividends accumulated over life of the company

Exhibit 1-6 summarizes the relationship between the accounting equation and the items that appear on a balance sheet.

The Income Statement

An **income statement,** or statement of earnings, as it is sometimes called, summarizes the revenues and expenses of a company for a period of time. Comparative income statements for CN for three recent years are shown in Exhibit 1-7. Unlike the balance sheet, an income statement is a *flow* statement. That is, it summarizes the flow of revenues and expenses for the year. As was the case for the balance sheet, you are not expected at this point to understand fully all of the complexities involved in preparing an income statement. However, note the three largest items on the income statement—revenues, operating expenses, and income tax expense.

The Statement of Retained Earnings

As discussed earlier, retained earnings represents the accumulated earnings of a corporation less the amount paid in dividends to shareholders. **Dividends** are distributions of the net income or profits of a business to its shareholders. Not all businesses pay cash dividends. Among those companies that do pay dividends, the frequency with which they pay differs. For example, CN paid a cash dividend of $0.84 per share for 2007. (See page 5 and Exhibit 1-8).

Retained earnings The part of owners' equity that represents the income earned less dividends paid over the life of an entity.

Balance sheet The financial statement that summarizes the assets, liabilities, and owners' equity at a specific point in time.

Income statement A statement that summarizes revenues and expenses.

Dividends A distribution of the net income of a business to its owners.

In millions December 31,	2007	2006
Assets		
Current assets:		
Cash and cash equivalents	$ 310	$ 179
Accounts receivable *(Note 4)*	370	692
Material and supplies	162	189
Deferred income taxes *(Note 15)*	68	84
Other	138	192
	1,048	1,336
Properties *(Note 5)*	20,413	21,053
Intangible and other assets *(Note 6)*	1,999	1,615
Total assets	$23,460	$24,004
Liabilities and shareholder's equity		
Current liabilities:		
Accounts payable and accrued charges *(Note 8)*	$ 1,282	$ 1,823
Current portion of long-term debt *(Note 10)*	254	218
Other	54	73
	1,590	2,114
Deferred income taxes *(Note 15)*	4,908	5,215
Other liabilities and deferred credits *(Note 9)*	1,422	1,465
Long-term debt *(Note 10)*	5,363	5,386
Shareholders' equity:		
Common shares *(Note 11)*	4,283	4,459
Accumulated other comprehensive loss *(Note 20)*	(31)	(44)
Retained earnings	5,925	5,409
	10,177	9,824
Total liabilities and shareholders' equity	$23,460	$24,004

See accompanying notes to consolidated financial statements.

This excerpt from CN's 2007 Annual Report appears courtesy of CN. This section of the CN Annual Report appears in the Appendix of this textbook.

Assets = Liabilities + Shareholders' Equity

Economic resources	**Creditors' claims to the assets**	**Owners' claims to the assets**
Examples:	Examples:	Examples:
• Cash	• Accounts payable	• Capital stock
• Accounts receivable	• Long-term debt	• Retained earnings
• Inventory		

Exhibit 1-6

The Relationship between the Accounting Equation and the Balance Sheet

Exhibit 1-6 refers to Owners' Equity, while Exhibit 1-5 refers to Shareholders' Equity. Remember, both are correct! "Owners' equity" is the general term by which we refer to ownership. "Shareholders' equity" refers only to ownership of a corporation by shareholders.

Exhibit 1-7 Canadian National Railway Company Consolidated Statement of Income

In millions, except per share data Year ended December 31,	2007	2006	2005
Revenues[1]	**$7,897**	$7,929	$7,446
Operating expenses[1]			
Labor and fringe benefits	**1,701**	1,823	1,856
Purchased services and material	**1,045**	1,027	993
Fuel	**1,026**	892	730
Depreciation and amortization	**677**	650	627
Equipment costs	**247**	198	192
Casualty and other	**325**	309	424
Total operating expenses	**5,021**	4,899	4,822
Operating income	**2,876**	3,030	2,624
Interest expense	**(336)**	(312)	(299)
Other income *(Note 14)*	**166**	11	12
Income before income taxes	**2,706**	2,729	2,337
Income tax expense *(Note 15)*	**(548)**	(642)	(781)
Net income	**$2,158**	$2,087	$1,556
Earnings per share (Note 17)			
Basic	**$ 4.31**	$ 3.97	$ 2.82
Diluted	**$ 4.25**	$ 3.91	$ 2.77

(1)   *Certain of the 2006 and 2005 comparative figures have been reclassified in order to be consistent with the 2007 presentation (see Note 21).*

This excerpt from CN's 2007 Annual Report appears courtesy of CN. This section of the CN Annual Report appears in the Appendix of this textbook.

Statement of retained earnings
The statement that summarizes the income earned and dividends paid over the life of a business.

A **statement of retained earnings** (see Exhibit 1-8) explains the change in retained earnings during the period. The basic format for the statement is as follows:

Beginning balance	$xxx,xxx
Add: Net income for the period	xxx,xxx
Deduct: Dividends for the period	xxx,xxx
Ending balance	$xxx,xxx

Revenues minus expenses, or net income, is an increase in retained earnings, and dividends are a decrease in the balance. Why are dividends shown on a statement of retained earnings instead of on an income statement? Dividends are not an expense and thus are not a component of net income, as are expenses. Instead, they are a *distribution* of the income of the business to its shareholders.

In millions	Retained earnings
Balance December 31, 2005	$4,891
Net income	2,087
Share repurchase programs *(Note 11)*	(1,229)
Dividends ($0.65 per share)	(340)
Balance December 31, 2006	5,409
Adoption of accounting pronouncements *(Note 2)*	95
Restated balance, beginning of year	5,504
Net income	2,158
Share repurchase programs *(Note 11)*	(1,319)
Dividends ($0.84 per share)	(418)
Balance December 31, 2007	**$5,925**

This excerpt from CN's 2007 Annual Report appears courtesy of CN. This section of the CN Annual Report appears in the Appendix of this textbook.

Recall that shareholders' equity consists of two parts: capital stock and retained earnings. In lieu of a separate statement of retained earnings, many corporations prepare a comprehensive statement to explain the changes both in the various capital stock accounts and in retained earnings during the period. CN, for example, presents the more comprehensive statement of changes in shareholders' equity. (It is not shown here, but you will find it in the printed annual report.)

Accounting for Your Decisions

You Are a Potential Shareholder

You are deciding whether to invest in a company's shares. Which financial statement would you want to see, and which areas would you be most interested in?

ANSWER: All of them. The balance sheet will show the relative size of the assets and liabilities, and the shareholders' equity section should state how many shares have been sold (outstanding shares) and how many more are available (authorized but not yet issued). The income statement's revenues, operating income, and net income are important, not only for the most current year but also for previous years to determine trends. The statement of retained earnings will report whether dividends were paid and, if so, the amount.

Relationships between CN's Income Statement and Balance Sheet

Because the statements of a company such as CN are complex, it may not be easy at this point to see the important links among them. The relationships among the statements are summarized in Exhibit 1-9. Recall that in its annual report, CN does not present a separate statement of retained earnings. The information for the statement of retained earnings in Exhibit 1-9 appears as one of the columns in CN's statement of changes in shareholders' equity. Three important relationships are seen by examining the exhibit (NOTE: Here and throughout the book, the numbers that follow correspond to the highlighted numbers in the exhibit; numbers in this exhibit are stated in millions of dollars):

1 The 2007 income statement reports net income of $2,158. Net income increases retained earnings, as reported on the statement of retained earnings.

2 Cash dividends in the amount of $418 decrease retained earnings and, therefore, are shown as a deduction on the statement of retained earnings.

3 Share repurchase program represents $1,319 paid to common shareholders in excess of what common shareholders paid for the shares when CN originally issued them to shareholders.

4 The ending balance of $5,925 in retained earnings, as reported on the statement of retained earnings for 2007, is transferred to the balance sheet at the end of 2007.

Exhibit 1-9
Relationships among Financial Statements: CN Example

INCOME STATEMENT FOR 2007

Revenues	$ xxx
Less: Expenses	xxx
Net income	$2,158

STATEMENT OF RETAINED EARNINGS FOR 2007

Beginning balance, retained earnings	$5,409
Adoption of accounting pronouncements	95
Restated balance, beginning of year	5,504
Add: Net income	2,158
Deduct: Cash dividends	(418)
Share repurchase program	(1,319)
Ending balance, retained earnings	$5,925

BALANCE SHEETS

	END OF 2007	2006
Total assets	$ xxx	$ xxx
Liabilities	$ xxx	$ xxx
Capital stock	xxx	xxx
Retained earnings	5,925	5,409
Total liabilities and shareholders' equity	$ xxx	$ xxx

This excerpt from CN's 2007 Annual Report appears courtesy of CN. This section of the CN Annual Report appears in the Appendix of this textbook.

Two-Minute Review

1. State the accounting equation, and indicate what each term means.
2. What are the four financial statements presented in this chapter?
3. How do amounts in the three of the four statements interrelate?

Answers on p. 26

THE CONCEPTUAL FRAMEWORK: FOUNDATION FOR FINANCIAL STATEMENTS

LO 5 Identify and explain the primary assumptions made in preparing financial statements.

Many people perceive the work of an accountant as being routine. In reality, accounting is anything but routine and requires a great deal of judgment on the part of the accountant. The record-keeping aspect of accounting—what we normally think of as bookkeeping—is the routine part of the accountant's work and only a small part of it. Most of the job deals with communicating relevant information to financial statement users.

The accounting profession has developed a *conceptual framework for accounting* that aids accountants in their role as interpreters and communicators of relevant information. The purpose of the framework is to act as a foundation for the specific principles and standards needed by the profession. An important part of the conceptual framework is a set of assumptions accountants make in preparing financial statements. We will briefly consider these assumptions, returning to a more detailed discussion of them in later chapters.

> **Study Tip**
>
> The concepts in this section underlie everything you will learn throughout the course. You'll encounter them later in the context of specific topics.

The *economic entity concept* (page 6) was introduced when we first discussed different types of business entities. This assumption requires that an identifiable, specific entity be the subject of a set of financial statements. For example, even though some of CN's employees are shareholders and therefore own part of CN, their personal affairs must be kept separate from the business affairs. When we look at a balance sheet, we need assurance that it shows the financial position of that entity only and does not intermingle the personal assets and liabilities of the employees or any of the other shareholders.

The **cost principle** requires that accountants record assets at the cost paid to acquire them and continue to show this amount on all balance sheets until the company disposes of them. With a few exceptions, companies do not carry assets at their market value (how much they could sell the asset for today) but at original cost. Accountants use the term *historical cost* to refer to the original cost of an asset. Why not show an asset such as land at market value? The *subjectivity* inherent in determining market values supports the practice of carrying assets at their historical cost. The cost of an asset is verifiable by an independent observer and is much more *objective* than market value.

Cost principle Assets are recorded at the cost to acquire them.

Accountants assume that the entity being accounted for is a **going concern.** That is, they assume that CN is not in the process of liquidation and that it will continue indefinitely into the future. Another important reason for using historical cost rather than market value to report assets is the going concern assumption. If we assume that a business is *not* a going concern, then we assume that it is in the process of liquidation. If this is the case, market value might be more relevant than cost as a basis for recognizing the assets. But if we are able to assume that a business will continue indefinitely, cost can be more easily justified as a basis for valuation. The **monetary unit** used in preparing the statements of CN was the dollar. The reason for using the dollar as the monetary unit is that it is the recognized medium of exchange. It provides a convenient measure for the position and earnings of the business. As a measure, however, the dollar, like the currencies of all other countries, is subject to instability. We are all well aware that a dollar will not buy as much today as it did 10 years ago.

Going concern The assumption that an entity is not in the process of liquidation and that it will continue indefinitely.

Monetary unit The yardstick used to measure amounts in financial statements, the dollar.

Interestingly, CN issues its financial statements using Canadian dollars and United States generally accepted accounting principles (U.S. GAAP) to accommodate both Canadian and American shareholders and creditors. CN started this practice during the 2005 fiscal year and prepared at that time an analysis of the differences between Canadian GAAP results and U.S. GAAP results. While some differences in results do appear, CN obviously believes the differences are not significant to its statement users. The harmonization of Canadian and U.S. GAAP is ongoing at present, and CN provides evidence of the results of this harmonization and the need to recognize the dependence of CN on U.S. investors. Where it is needed in discussions in later chapters, explanation of the differences will be provided.

Inflation is evidenced by a general rise in the level of prices in an economy. Its effect on the measuring unit used in preparing financial statements is an important concern to the accounting profession. Although accountants have experimented with financial statements adjusted for the changing value of the measuring unit, the financial statements now prepared by corporations are prepared under the assumption that the monetary unit

Time period Artificial segment on the calendar, used as the basis for preparing financial statements.

is relatively stable. At various times in the past, this has been a reasonable assumption and at other times not so reasonable.

Under the **time period** assumption, accountants assume that it is possible to prepare an income statement that accurately reflects net income or earnings for a specific time period. In the case of CN, this time period was one year. It is somewhat artificial to measure the earnings of a business for a period of time indicated on a calendar, whether it be a month, a quarter, or a year. Of course, the most accurate point in time to measure the earnings of a business would be at the end of its life. Accountants prepare periodic statements, however, because the users of the statements demand information about the entity on a regular basis.

Generally accepted accounting principles (GAAP) The various methods, rules, practices, and other procedures that have evolved over time in response to the need to regulate the preparation of financial statements.

Financial statements prepared by accountants must conform to **generally accepted accounting principles (GAAP)**. This term refers to the various methods, rules, practices, and other procedures that have evolved over time in response to the need for some form of regulation over the preparation of financial statements. As changes have taken place in the business environment over time, GAAP have developed in response to these changes.

Accounting as a Social Science

Accounting is a service activity. As we have seen, its purpose is to provide financial information to decision makers. Thus, accounting is a *social* science. Accounting principles are much different from the rules that govern the *physical* sciences. For example, it is a rule of nature that an object dropped from your hand will eventually hit the ground rather than be suspended in air. There are no rules comparable to this in accounting. The principles that govern financial reporting are not governed by nature but instead develop in response to changing business conditions. For example, consider the lease of an office building. Leasing has developed in response to the need to have access to valuable assets, such as office space, without spending the large sum necessary to buy the asset. As leasing has increased in popularity, it has been left to the accounting profession to develop guidelines, some of which are quite complex, to be followed in accounting for leases. Those guidelines are now part of GAAP.

Two-Minute Review

1. Name the four concepts (other than the economic entity concept) in the conceptual framework presented in this section.

2. Give a brief example of each concept.

3. What are "GAAP"?

Answers on p. 26

Who Determines the Rules of the Game?

Who determines the rules to be followed in preparing an income statement or a balance sheet? No one group is totally responsible for setting the standards or principles to be followed in preparing financial statements. The process is a joint effort among various groups.

In Canada, the primary body that sets accounting standards is the Accounting Standards Board (AcSB). Its membership and specific terms of reference are approved by an oversight body called the Accounting Standards Oversight Council. The three primary accounting professional groups—CAs (Chartered Accountants), CGAs (Certified General Accountants), and CMAs (Certified Management Accountants)—sit as members of the AcSB, with the dominant role taken by the **Canadian Institute of Chartered Accountants** (CICA). Authority for this body to pronounce accounting standards in Canada can be found in the Companies Acts issued federally and provincially as well as in securities acts regulating companies issuing bonds and shares to the public.

http://www.cica.ca

Securities and Exchange Commission (SEC) The U.S. federal agency with ultimate authority to determine the rules in preparing statements for companies whose shares are sold to the public.

In the United States, Canada's major trading partner, the federal government, through the **Securities and Exchange Commission (SEC),** has the ultimate authority to determine the rules for preparing financial statements by companies whose securities are sold to the general public. However, for the most part, the SEC has allowed the accounting profession to establish its own rules.

The **Financial Accounting Standards Board** (**FASB**) sets these accounting standards in the United States. This small independent group with a large staff has issued more than 140 financial accounting standards, and seven statements of financial accounting concepts, since its creation in the early 1970s. These standards deal with a variety of financial reporting issues, such as the proper accounting for lease arrangements and pension plans, and the concepts are used to guide the board in setting accounting standards.

Finally, if you are considering buying shares in **Porsche**, the German-based car manufacturer, you'll want to be sure that the rules Porsche followed in preparing the statements are similar to those the FASB requires for American companies or AcSB for Canadian companies. Unfortunately, accounting standards can differ considerably from one country to another. The **International Accounting Standards Board** (**IASB**) was created in 2001. Prior to that time, the organization was known as the International Accounting Standards Committee (IASC), which was formed in 1973 to develop worldwide accounting standards. Organizations from many different countries, including the AcSB in this country, participate in the IASB's efforts to develop international reporting standards. Currently, Canada through the AcSB and the United States through FASB are attempting to make their GAAPs consistent with the pronouncements of the IASB. Although the IASB has made considerable progress, compliance with its standards is voluntary, and much work remains to be done in developing international accounting standards.

Financial Accounting Standards Board (FASB) The group in the American private sector with authority to set accounting standards.

http://www.porsche.com

International Accounting Standards Board (IASB) The organization formed to develop worldwide accounting standards.

◤ THE ACCOUNTING PROFESSION

Accountants play many different roles in society. Understanding the various roles will help you to appreciate more fully the importance of accounting in organizations.

LO 6 Describe the various roles of accountants in organizations.

Employment by Private Business

Many accountants work for business entities. Regardless of the types of activities companies engage in, accountants perform a number of important functions for them. A partial organization chart for a corporation is shown in Exhibit 1-10. The chart indicates that three individuals report directly to the chief financial officer: the controller, the treasurer, and the director of internal auditing.

The **controller** is the chief accounting officer for a company and typically has responsibility for the overall operation of the accounting system. Accountants working for the controller record the company's activities and prepare periodic financial statements. In this organization, the payroll function is assigned to the controller's office, as well as responsibility for the preparation of budgets.

The **treasurer** of an organization is typically responsible for both the safeguarding and the efficient use of the company's liquid resources, such as cash. Note that the director of the tax department in this corporation reports to the treasurer. Accountants in the tax department are responsible for both preparing the company's tax returns and planning transactions in such a way that the company pays the least amount of taxes possible within the boundaries of the Income Tax Act.

Internal auditing is the department responsible in a company for the review and appraisal of accounting and administrative controls. The department must determine whether the company's assets are properly accounted for and protected from losses. Recommendations are made periodically to management for improvements in the various controls.

Controller The chief accounting officer for a company.

Treasurer The officer responsible in an organization for the safeguarding and efficient use of a company's liquid assets.

Internal auditing The department responsible in a company for the review and appraisal of its accounting and administrative controls.

Employment by Non-Business Entities

Non-business organizations, such as hospitals, universities, and various branches of the government, have as much need for accountants as do companies organized to earn a profit. Although the profit motive is not paramount to non-business entities, all organizations

Exhibit 1-10 Partial Organization Chart

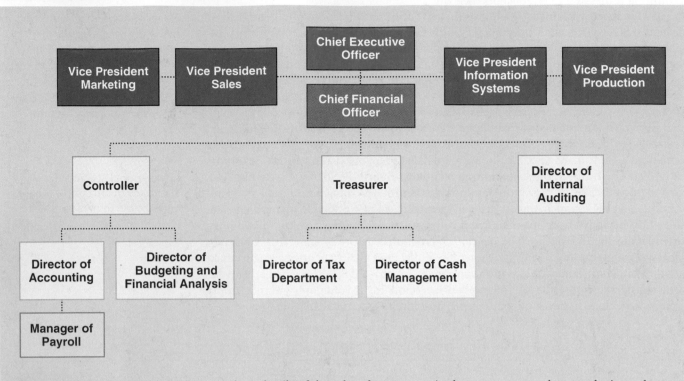

This partial organization chart does not show details of the other departments in the company—such as marketing, sales, production, and so on. That does not mean they are unimportant to the flow of accounting information. In fact, accounting information for internal decision making forms a complex system of reporting, responsibility, and control collectively known as management accounting.

must have financial information to operate efficiently. A municipal government needs detailed cost information in determining the taxes to levy on its constituents. A university must pay close attention to its various operating costs in setting the annual tuition rates. Accountants working for non-business entities perform most of the same tasks as their counterparts in the business sector. In fact, many of the job titles in business entities, such as controller and treasurer, are also used by non-business entities.

Employment in Public Accounting

Public accounting firms provide valuable services in much the same way as do law firms or architectural firms. They provide a professional service for their clients in return for a fee. The usual services provided by public accounting firms include auditing, tax, and management consulting services.

Auditing Services   The auditing services rendered by public accountants are similar in certain respects to the work performed by internal auditors. However, there are key differences between the two types of auditing. Internal auditors are more concerned with the efficient operation of the various segments of the business, and therefore, the work they do is often called *operational auditing*. On the other hand, the primary objective of the external auditor, or public accountant, is to assure shareholders and other users that the statements are fairly presented. In this respect, **auditing** is the process of examining the financial statements and the underlying records of a company in order to render an opinion as to whether the statements are fairly presented.

As we discussed earlier, the financial statements are prepared by the company's accountants. The external auditor performs various tests and procedures to be able to render his or

Auditing The process of examining the financial statements and the underlying records of a company in order to render an opinion as to whether the statements are fairly presented.

her opinion. The public accountant has a responsibility to the company's shareholders and any other users of the statements. Because most shareholders of public companies like CN are not actively involved in the daily affairs of the business, they must rely on the auditors to ensure that management is fairly presenting the financial statements of the business.

Note that the **auditors' report** is an *opinion,* not a statement of fact. For example, one important procedure performed by the auditor to obtain assurance as to the validity of a company's inventory is to observe the year-end physical count of inventory by the company's employees. However, this is done on a sample basis. It would be too costly for the auditors to make an independent count of every single item of inventory.

The auditors' report on the financial statements for CN is shown in Exhibit 1-11. Note first that the report is directed to the company's shareholders. The company is audited by **KPMG**, a large international accounting firm. Public accounting firms range in size from those with a single owner to others, such as KPMG, that have thousands of partners. The opinion given by KPMG on the company's financial statements is the *standard auditors' report.* The first paragraph indicates that the firm has examined the company's balance sheet and the related statements of income, changes in shareholders' equity, and cash flows. Note that the second paragraph of the report indicates that evidence supporting the amounts and disclosures in the statements was examined on a *test* basis. The third paragraph states the firm's *opinion* that the financial statements are fairly presented in conformity with GAAP. Paragraph four contains comments on a special audit area dealing with the effectiveness of the company's system for controlling its information, termed internal control. Later chapters will explain more about internal control.

Public companies like CN require an audit. Proprietorships, partnerships, and private companies can have an audit if desired for various reasons such as the satisfaction of a creditor, but they can vote not to have one because of the proximity of the owners to an organization. For most of our discussions in the following chapters we shall describe the audit situation.

Tax Services   In addition to auditing, public accounting firms provide a variety of tax services. Firms often prepare the tax returns for the companies they audit. They also usually work throughout the year with management to plan acquisitions and other transactions to take full advantage of the tax laws. For example, if tax rates are scheduled to decline next year, a public accounting firm would advise its client to accelerate certain expenditures this year as much as possible to receive a higher tax deduction than would be possible if waiting until next year.

Management Consulting Services   By working closely with management to provide auditing and tax services, a public accounting firm becomes very familiar with various aspects of a company's business. This vantage point allows the firm to provide expert advice to the company to improve its operations. The management consulting services rendered by public accounting firms to their clients take a variety of forms. For example, the firm might advise the company on the design and installation of a computer system to meet its needs. The services provided in this area have grown dramatically to include such diverse activities as advice on selection of a new plant site or an investment opportunity.

Accountants in Education

Some accountants choose a career in education. As the demand for accountants in business entities, non-business organizations, and public accounting has increased, so has the need for qualified professors to teach this discipline. Accounting programs range from two years of study at community colleges to doctoral programs at some universities. All of these programs require the services of knowledgeable instructors. In addition to their teaching duties, many accounting educators are actively involved in research. The **Canadian Academic Accounting Association** is a professional organization of accounting educators and others interested in the future of the profession. The group advances its ideas through its many committees and the publication of a number of journals.

Auditors' report The opinion rendered by a public accounting firm concerning the fairness of the presentation of the financial statements.

http://www.kpmg.com

Canadian Academic Accounting Association The professional organization for accounting educators.

Exhibit 1-11 Auditors' Report

Report of Independent Registered Public Accounting Firm

To the Board of Directors and Shareholders of Canadian National Railway Company

We have audited the accompanying consolidated balance sheets of Canadian National Railway Company (the "Company") as of December 31, 2007 and 2006, and the related consolidated statements of income, comprehensive income, changes in shareholders' equity and cash flows for each of the years in the three-year period ended December 31, 2007. These consolidated financial statements are the responsibility of the Company's management. Our responsibility is to express an opinion on these consolidated financial statements based on our audits.

We conducted our audits in accordance with Canadian generally accepted auditing standards and with the standards of the Public Company Accounting Oversight Board (United States). Those standards require that we plan and perform the audit to obtain reasonable assurance about whether the financial statements are free of material misstatement. An audit includes examining, on a test basis, evidence supporting the amounts and disclosures in the financial statements. An audit also includes assessing the accounting principles used and significant estimates made by management, as well as evaluating the overall financial statement presentation. We believe that our audits provide a reasonable basis for our opinion.

In our opinion, the consolidated financial statements referred to above present fairly, in all material respects, the financial position of the Company as of December 31, 2007 and 2006, and the results of its operations and its cash flows for each of the years in the three-year period ended December 31, 2007, in conformity with generally accepted accounting principles in the United States.

We also have audited, in accordance with the standards of the Public Company Accounting Oversight Board (United States), the Company's internal control over financial reporting as of December 31, 2007, based on criteria established in Internal Control – Integrated Framework issued by the Committee of Sponsoring Organizations of the Treadway Commission (COSO), and our report dated February 11, 2008 expressed an unqualified opinion on the effectiveness of the Company's internal control over financial reporting.

(signed)
KPMG LLP
Chartered Accountants

Montreal, Canada
February 11, 2008

This excerpt from CN's 2007 Annual Report appears courtesy of CN. This section of the CN Annual Report appears in the Appendix of this textbook.

Accounting as a Career

As you can see, a number of different career paths in accounting are possible. The stereotypical view of the accountant as a "numbers person and not a people person" is a seriously outdated notion. Various specialties are now emerging, including tax accounting, environmental accounting, forensic accounting, software development, and accounting in the entertainment and telecommunications industries. Some of these opportunities exist in both the business and the non-business sectors. For example, forensic accounting has become an exciting career field as both corporations and various agencies of the federal government, such as the RCMP, concern themselves with fraud and white-collar crime.

As in any profession, salaries in accounting vary considerably depending on numerous factors, including educational background and other credentials, number of years of experience, and size of the employer.

Accountants and Ethical Judgments

Remember the primary goal of accounting: to provide useful information to aid in the decision-making process. As discussed, the work of the accountant in providing useful information is anything but routine and requires the accountant to make subjective judgments about what information to present and how to present it. The latitude given accountants in this respect is one of the major reasons accounting is a profession and its members are considered professionals. Along with this designation as a professional, however, comes a serious responsibility. As we noted, financial statements are prepared for external parties who must rely on these statements to provide information on which to base important decisions. Exhibit 1-12 provides a summary of the ethical decision process.

Exhibit 1-12 Ethics and Accounting: A Decision Making Model

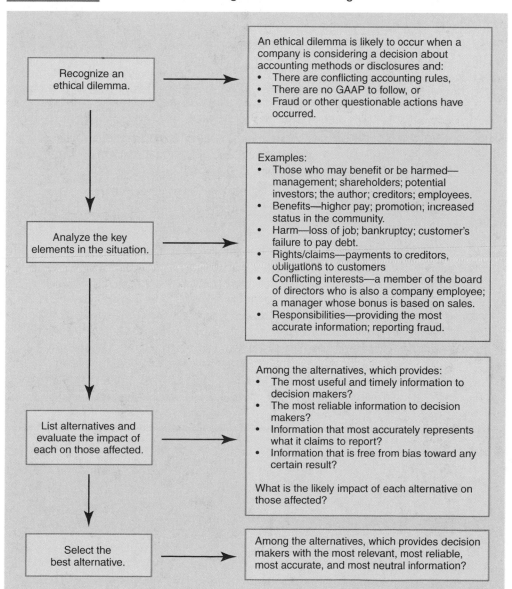

Each chapter has cases titled "Accounting and Ethics: What Would You Do?" The cases require you to evaluate difficult issues and make a decision. Judgment is needed in deciding which accounting method to select or how to report a certain item in the statements. As you are faced with these decisions, keep in mind the trust placed in the accountant by various financial statement users. This is central to reaching an ethical decision.

▪ A FINAL NOTE ABOUT CANADIAN NATIONAL RAILWAY COMPANY

As you have seen in this chapter, accounting is a practical discipline. Financial statements of real companies, including CN, are used throughout the remainder of the book to help you learn more about this practical discipline. For example, some of the sidebars in future chapters will require you to return to the financial statements of CN, as will some of the cases at the ends of the chapters. Because no two sets of financial statements look the same, however, you will be introduced to the financial statements of many other real companies as well. Use this opportunity to learn more not only about accounting but also about each of these companies.

Answers to the Two-Minute Reviews

Two-Minute Review on Page 18

1. Assets = Liabilities + Owners' Equity

   Assets are economic resources. Liabilities are creditors' claims against assets. Owners' Equity is owners' claims against assets. See Exhibit 1-6.

2. The four financial statements are the balance sheet, the income statement, the statement of retained earnings, and the cash flow statement.

3. Net income on the income statement increases retained earnings on the statement of retained earnings. The ending balance in retained earnings is transferred to the balance sheet. See Exhibit 1-9.

Two-Minute Review on Page 20

1. Cost principle, going concern, monetary unit, and time period assumption.

2. Under the cost principle, we record assets at their cost rather than at market value. *Example:* CN would record a new machine at its purchase price. Under going concern, we assume that the company will continue existing indefinitely. *Example:* CN will continue to operate rather than begin liquidating its assets. The monetary unit, such as the dollar, is the company's recognized medium of exchange. *Example:* CN uses the dollar as the monetary unit. The time period assumption imposes, for reporting purposes, an arbitrary time period (such as a year) that is shorter than the company's life span. *Example:* CN's income statement is for the fiscal year ended December 31, 2007.

3. GAAP are the methods, rules, practices, and other procedures that have evolved to govern the preparation of financial statements.

Chapter Highlights

1. **LO 1** **Distinguish among the forms of organizations (page 6).**
   - Corporations, proprietorships, partnerships, and non-business

2. **LO 2** **Describe the various types of business activities (page 8).**
   - Financing—Sources of cash
   - Investing—Uses of cash to procure future benefits (assets)
   - Operating—Cash flows from operating activities

3. **LO 3** **Identify the primary users of accounting information and their needs (p. 11).**
   - The primary users of financial statements are those who depend upon the economic information conveyed in those statements to make decisions. Primary users may be broadly classified as internal users and those external to the company.
     - Internal users are usually managers of a company.
     - External users include shareholders, investors, creditors, and government agencies.

4. **LO 4** **Explain the purpose of each of the financial statements and relationships among them, and prepare a set of simple statements (p. 13).**
   - There are three major financial statements covered in this chapter: balance sheet, income statement, and statement of retained earnings.
     - The balance sheet is a snapshot of a company's financial position at the end of the period. It reflects the assets, liabilities, and shareholders' equity accounts.
     - The income statement summarizes the financial activity for a period of time. Items of revenues, expenses, gains, and losses are reflected in the income statement.

   - Ultimately, all net income (loss) and dividends are reflected in retained earnings on the balance sheet. The statement of retained earnings links the income statement to the balance sheet by showing how net income (loss) and dividends affect the retained earnings account.

5. **LO 5** **Identify and explain the primary assumptions made in preparing financial statements (p. 19).**
   - The usefulness of accounting information is enhanced through the various assumptions set forth in the conceptual framework for the methods, rules, and practices that comprise generally accepted accounting principles (GAAP).
   - Important assumptions in the conceptual framework are:
     - Economic entity concept
     - Cost principle
     - Going concern
     - Monetary unit
     - Time period

6. **LO 6** **Describe the various roles of accountants in organizations (p. 21).**
   - Accountants play an important role in the measurement, analysis, and communication of financial information and are employed by business, non-business, and governmental entities.
   - Public accounting also employs many accountants that provide auditing, tax, and management consulting services.

Key Terms Quiz (1)

Read each of the following definitions and then write the number of that definition in the blank beside the appropriate term it defines. The first one has been done for you. The solution appears at the end of this chapter. When reviewing terminology, come back to your completed key terms quiz. Study tip: also check the glossary in the margin or at the end of the book.

_____	Business	_____	Non-business entity
_____	Business entity	_____	Liability
_____	Economic entity concept	_____	Capital stock
_____	Sole proprietorship	_____	Shareholder
_____	Partnership	_____	Creditor
_____	Corporation	1	Asset
_____	A share	_____	Revenue
_____	Bond	_____	Expense

1. A future economic benefit.
2. A business owned by two or more individuals; organization form often used by accounting firms and law firms.
3. An inflow of assets resulting from the sale of goods and services.
4. A form of entity organized under the laws of a particular jurisdiction; ownership evidenced by shares.
5. Organization operated for some purpose other than to earn a profit.
6. An outflow of assets resulting from the sale of goods and services.
7. An obligation of a business.
8. A certificate that acts as ownership in a corporation.

(continued)

9. A certificate that represents a corporation's promise to repay a certain amount of money and interest in the future.

10. One of the owners of a corporation.

11. Someone to whom a company or person has a debt.

12. The assumption that a single, identifiable unit must be accounted for in all situations.

13. Form of organization with a single owner.

14. Indicates the owners' contributions to a corporation.

15. All the activities necessary to provide the members of an economic system with goods and services.

16. Organization operated to earn a profit.

Answers on p. 48.

Key Terms Quiz (2)

Read each definition below and then write the number of that definition in the blank beside the appropriate term it defines. The quiz solutions appear at the end of the chapter.

_____ Accounting
_____ Management accounting
_____ Financial accounting
_____ Owners' equity
_____ Shareholders' equity
_____ Retained earnings
_____ Balance sheet
_____ Income statement
_____ Dividends
_____ Statement of retained earnings
_____ Cost principle
_____ Going concern
_____ Monetary unit
_____ Time period

_____ Generally accepted accounting principles (GAAP)
_____ Securities commissions
_____ Accounting Standards Board
_____ Certified General Accountants
_____ International Accounting Standards Board (IASB)
_____ Controller
_____ Treasurer
_____ Internal auditing
_____ Auditing
_____ Auditors' report
_____ Canadian Academic Accounting Association

1. A statement that summarizes revenues and expenses for a period of time.

2. The statement that summarizes the income earned and dividends paid over the life of a business.

3. The owners' equity of a corporation.

4. The process of identifying, measuring, and communicating economic information to various users.

5. The branch of accounting concerned with communication with outsiders through financial statements.

6. The owners' claims to the assets of an entity.

7. The financial statement that summarizes the assets, liabilities, and owners' equity at a specific point in time.

8. The part of owners' equity that represents the income earned less dividends paid over the life of an entity.

9. The branch of accounting concerned with providing management with information to facilitate the planning and control functions.

10. A distribution of the net income of a business to its shareholders.

11. The various methods, rules, practices, and other procedures that have evolved over time in response to the need to regulate the preparation of financial statements.

12. Assets are recorded and reported at the cost paid to acquire them.

13. Agencies with ultimate authority to determine the rules in preparing statements for companies whose shares are sold to the public.

14. The professional organization for accounting educators.

15. The officer of an organization who is responsible for the safeguarding and efficient use of the company's liquid assets.

16. The assumption that an entity is not in the process of liquidation and that it will continue indefinitely.

17. The group in the private sector with authority to set accounting standards.

18. The currency used to measure amounts in financial statements; the dollar.

19. The professional organization for certified general accountants.

20. The department in a company responsible for the review and appraisal of a company's accounting and administrative controls.

21. A length of time on the calendar used as the basis for preparing financial statements.

22. The chief accounting officer for a company.

23. The process of examining the financial statements and the underlying records of a company in order to render an opinion as to whether the statements are fairly presented.

24. The organization formed to develop worldwide accounting standards.

25. The opinion rendered by a public accounting firm concerning the fairness of the presentation of the financial statements.

Answers on p. 49.

Alternate Terms

Auditors' report Report of independent accountants

Balance sheet Statement of financial position

Cost principle Original cost; historical cost

Creditor Lender

Income statement Statement of income

Net income Profits or earnings

Shareholder Stockholder

Warmup Exercises and Solutions

Warmup Exercise 1-1 *Your Assets and Liabilities* **LO 2**
Consider your own situation in terms of assets and liabilities.

Required

1. Name three of your financial assets.
2. Name three of your financial liabilities.

Key to the Solution Refer to Exhibit 1-6 for definitions of assets and liabilities.

Warmup Exercise 1-2 *CN's Assets and Liabilities* **LO 2**
Think about CN's business in balance sheet terms.

Required

1. Name three of CN's assets.
2. Name three of CN's liabilities.

Key to the Solution Refer to Exhibit 1-5 if you need to see CN's balance sheet. Also consult the list on page 15.

Warmup Exercise 1-3 *CN and the Accounting Equation* **LO 2**
Place CN's total assets, total liabilities, and total shareholders' equity in the form of the accounting equation.

Key to the Solution Refer to Exhibit 1-5. You will have to add up the liabilities since they are not totaled for you.

> **Study Tip**
>
> Use these exercises to get accustomed to the assignments that follow.

CN
http://www.cn.ca

Solutions to Warmup Exercises

Warmup Exercise 1-1

1. Possible personal financial assets might include chequing accounts, savings accounts, shares, bonds, and mutual funds.
2. Possible personal financial liabilities might include student loans, car loans, home mortgages, and amounts borrowed from relatives.

Warmup Exercise 1-2

1. CN's assets are cash and cash equivalents, accounts receivable, materials and supplies, prepaid expenses, deferred income taxes, properties, and intangible and other assets.
2. CN's liabilities are accounts payable and accrued charges, deferred income taxes, and long-term debt and other liabilities.

Warmup Exercise 1-3

$$\text{Assets} = \text{Liabilities} + \text{Shareholders' Equity}$$
$$\$23,460 = \$13,283^* + \$10,177$$

$$^* \$1,590 + \$4,908 + \$1,422 + \$5,363 = \$13,283$$

Review Problem and Solution

Study Tip

Note to the student: At the end of each chapter is a problem to test your understanding of some of the major ideas presented in the chapter. Try to solve the problem before turning to the solution that follows it.

Greenway Corporation is organized on June 1, 2008. The company will provide lawn-care and tree-trimming services on a contract basis. Following is an alphabetical list of the items that should appear on its income statement for the first month and on its balance sheet at the end of the first month (you will need to determine on which statement each should appear).

Accounts payable	$ 800	Lawn-care revenue	1,500
Accounts receivable	500	Notes payable	6,000
Building	2,000	Retained earnings (beginning balance)	–0–
Capital stock	5,000	Salaries and wages expense	900
Cash	3,300	Tools	800
Gas, utilities, and other expenses	300	Tree-trimming revenue	500
Land	4,000	Truck	2,000

Required

1. Prepare an income statement for the month of June.

2. Prepare a balance sheet at June 30, 2008. *Note:* You will need to determine the balance in retained earnings at the end of the month.

3. The financial statements you have just prepared are helpful, but in many ways they are only a starting point. Assuming this is your business, what additional questions do they raise that you need to consider?

Solution to Review Problem

1.

GREENWAY CORPORATION
INCOME STATEMENT
FOR THE MONTH ENDED JUNE 30, 2008

Revenues:		
Lawn care	$1,500	
Tree trimming	500	$2,000
Expenses:		
Salaries and wages	900	
Gas, utilities, and other expenses	300	1,200
Net income		$ 800

2.

GREENWAY CORPORATION
BALANCE SHEET
JUNE 30, 2008

Assets		Liabilities and Shareholders' Equity	
Cash	$ 3,300	Accounts payable	$ 800
Accounts receivable	500	Notes payable	6,000
Truck	2,000	Capital stock	5,000
Tools	800	Retained earnings	800
Building	2,000		
Land	4,000		
		Total liabilities and	
Total assets	$12,600	shareholders' equity	$12,600

3. Some additional questions would be: future cash flows, collection of accounts, payments on loan, desired earnings, growth expectations.

Questions

1. What is business about? What do all businesses have in common?
2. What is an asset? Give three examples.
3. What is a liability? How does the definition of *liability* relate to the definition of *asset*?
4. Business entities are organized as one of three distinct forms. What are these three forms?
5. What are the three distinct types of business activities in which companies engage? Assume you start your own company to rent bicycles in the summer and skis in the winter. Give an example of at least one of each of the three types of business activities in which you would engage.
6. What is accounting? Define it in terms understandable to someone without a business background.
7. How do financial accounting and management accounting differ?
8. What are five different groups of users of accounting information? Briefly describe the types of decisions each group must make.
9. How does owners' equity fit into the accounting equation?
10. What are the two distinct elements of owners' equity in a corporation? Define each element.
11. What is the purpose of a balance sheet?
12. How should a balance sheet be dated: as of a particular day or for a particular period of time? Explain your answer.
13. What does the term *cost principle* mean?
14. What is the purpose of an income statement?
15. How should an income statement be dated: as of a particular day or for a particular period of time? Explain your answer.
16. Rogers Corporation starts the year with a Retained Earnings balance of $55,000. Net income for the year is $27,000. The ending balance in Retained Earnings is $70,000. What was the amount of dividends for the year?
17. How do the duties of the controller of a corporation typically differ from those of the treasurer?
18. What are the three basic types of services performed by public accounting firms?
19. How would you evaluate the following statement: "The auditors are in the best position to evaluate a company because they have prepared the financial statements"?
20. What is the relationship between the cost principle and the going concern assumption?
21. Why does inflation present a challenge to the accountant? Relate your answer to the monetary unit assumption.
22. What is meant by the phrase *generally accepted accounting principles*?
23. What role have the securities commissions played in setting accounting standards? Contrast their role with that played by the Accounting Standards Board.

Exercises

Exercise 1-1 *Users of Accounting Information and Their Needs* **LO 3**

Listed below are a number of the important users of accounting information. Below the list are descriptions of a major need of each of these various users. Fill in the blank with the one user group that is most likely to have the need described to the right of the blank.

Company management   Banker

Shareholder   Supplier

Securities commissions   Labour union

Canada Revenue Agency

User Group   **Needs Information About**

_____   1. The profitability of each division in the company

_____   2. The prospects for future dividend payments

_____   3. The profitability of the company since the last contract with the work force was signed

_____   4. The financial status of a company issuing securities to the public for the first time

_____   5. The prospects that a company will be able to meet its interest payments on time

_____   6. The prospects that a company will be able to pay for its purchases on time

_____   7. The profitability of the company based on the tax law

Exercise 1-2 *The Accounting Equation* **LO 4**

For each of the following independent cases, fill in the blank with the appropriate dollar amount.

	Assets	=	Liabilities	+	Owners' Equity
Case 1	$100,000		$ 75,000		$_____
Case 2	200,000		_____		75,000
Case 3	_____		220,000		85,000

Exercise 1-3 *The Accounting Equation* **LO 4**

Able Enterprises began the year with total assets of $250,000 and total liabilities of $125,000. Using this information and the accounting equation, answer each of the following independent questions.

1. What was the amount of Able's owners' equity at the beginning of the year?

2. If Able's total assets increased by $50,000 and its total liabilities increased by $38,500 during the year, what was the amount of Able's owners' equity at the end of the year?

3. If Able's total liabilities increased by $66,000 and its owners' equity decreased by $116,000 during the year, what was the amount of its total assets at the end of the year?

4. If Able's total assets doubled to $500,000 and its owners' equity remained the same during the year, what was the amount of its total liabilities at the end of the year?

Exercise 1-4 *The Accounting Equation* **LO 4**

Using the accounting equation, answer each of the following independent questions.

1. Berwick Company starts the year with $50,000 in assets and $40,000 in liabilities. Net income for the year is $12,500, and no dividends are paid. How much is owners' equity at the end of the year?

2. Bedford Ltd. doubles the amount of its assets from the beginning to the end of the year. Liabilities at the end of the year amount to $20,000, and owners' equity is $10,000. What is the amount of Bedford's assets at the beginning of the year?

3. During the year, the liabilities of David Inc. triple in amount. Assets at the beginning of the year amount to $40,000, and owners' equity is $15,000. What is the amount of liabilities at the end of the year?

Exercise 1-5 *Changes in Owners' Equity* **LO 4**

The following amounts are available from the records of B & B Inc. at the end of the years indicated:

December 31	Total Assets	Total Liabilities
2006	$ 50,000	$ 24,000
2007	39,500	34,500
2008	92,000	68,500

Required

1. Compute the changes in B & B's owners' equity during 2007 and 2008.

2. Compute the amount of B & B's net income (or loss) for 2007, assuming that no dividends were paid during the year.

3. Compute the amount of B & B's net income (or loss) for 2008, assuming that dividends paid during the year amounted to $15,000.

Exercise 1-6 *The Accounting Equation* **LO 4**

For each of the following independent cases, fill in the blank with the appropriate dollar amount.

	Case 1	Case 2	Case 3	Case 4
Total assets, end of period	$50,000	$75,000	$_____	$40,000
Total liabilities, end of period	10,000	25,000	15,000	_____
Capital stock, end of period	15,000	20,000	5,000	10,000
Retained earnings, beginning of period	20,000	10,000	8,000	15,000
Net income for the period	9,000	_____	7,000	8,000
Dividends for the period	_____	3,000	1,000	2,000

Exercise 1-7 *Classification of Financial Statement Items* **LO 4**

Classify each of the following items according to (1) whether it belongs on the income statement (IS) or balance sheet (BS) and (2) whether it is a revenue (R), expense (E), asset (A), liability (L), or owners' equity (OE) item.

Item	Appears on the	Classified as
Example: Cash	BS	A
1. Salaries expense		
2. Equipment		
3. Accounts receivable		
4. Membership fees earned		
5. Advertising expense		
6. Accounts payable		
7. Buildings		
8. Capital stock		
9. Retained earnings		

Exercise 1-8 *Net Income (or Loss) and Retained Earnings* **LO 4**

The following information is available from the records of Lonas Landscape Design Inc. at the end of the 2008 calendar year:

Accounts payable	$ 10,000	Office equipment	$ 15,000
Accounts receivable	8,000	Rent expense	13,000
Capital stock	16,000	Retained earnings,	
Cash	26,000	beginning of year	17,000
Dividends paid		Salary and wage expense	24,000
during the year	6,000	Supplies on hand	1,000
Landscaping revenues	50,000		

Required

Use the information above to answer the following questions:

1. What is Lonas's net income for the year ended December 31, 2008?
2. What is Lonas's retained earnings balance at the end of the year?
3. What is the total amount of Lonas's assets at the end of the year?
4. What is the total amount of Lonas's liabilities at the end of the year?
5. How much owners' equity does Lonas have at the end of the year?
6. What is Lonas's accounting equation at December 31, 2008?

Exercise 1-9 *Statement of Retained Earnings* **LO 4**

Zee Corporation has been in business for many years. Retained earnings on January 1, 2008, is $117,900. The following information is available for the first two months of 2008:

	January	February
Revenues	$41,500	$48,000
Expenses	44,500	41,000
Dividends paid	0	2,500

Required

Prepare a statement of retained earnings for the month ended February 29, 2008.

Exercise 1-10 *Accounting Principles and Assumptions* **LO 5**

The following basic accounting principles and assumptions were discussed in the chapter:

Economic entity

Monetary unit

Cost principle

Going concern

Time period

(continued)

Fill in each of the blanks with the accounting principle or assumption that is relevant to the situation described.

_____ 1. SMU Ltd. is now in its 30th year of business. The founder of the company is planning to retire at the end of the year and turn the business over to his daughter.

_____ 2. North Company purchased a 10-hectare parcel of property on which to build a new factory. The company recorded the property on the records at the amount of cash given to acquire it.

_____ 3. Jim Cann enters into an agreement to operate a new law firm in partnership with a friend. Each partner will make an initial cash investment of $20,000. Jim opens a chequing account in the name of the partnership and transfers $20,000 from his personal account into the new account.

_____ 4. Far East Ltd. has a division in Hong Kong. Prior to preparing the financial statements for the company and all its foreign divisions, Far East translates the financial statements of its Hong Kong division from yuan to Canadian dollars.

_____ 5. Canning Company has always prepared financial statements annually, with a year-end of June 30. Because the company is going to sell its shares to the public for the first time, quarterly financial reports will also be required by the Ontario Securities Commission.

Exercise 1-11 *Organizations and Accounting* **LO 6**
Match each of the organizations listed below with the statement that most adequately describes the role of the group.

Ontario Securities Commission

International Accounting Standards Board

Accounting Standards Board

Certified General Accountants

Canadian Academic Accounting Association

_____ 1. Provincial agency with ultimate authority to determine rules used in preparing financial statements for companies whose shares are sold to the public

_____ 2. Professional organization for accounting educators

_____ 3. Group in the private sector with authority to set accounting standards

_____ 4. Professional organization for accountants

_____ 5. Organization formed to develop worldwide accounting standards

Multi-Concept Exercises

Exercise 1-12 *Users of Accounting Information and the Financial Statements* **LO 3, 4**
Listed below are a number of users of accounting information and examples of questions they need answered before making decisions. Fill in each blank to indicate whether the user is most likely to find the answer by looking at the income statement (IS), the balance sheet (BS), or the statement of retained earnings (RE).

User	Question	Financial Statement
Shareholder	How did this year's sales compare to last year's?	_____
Banker	How much debt does the company already have on its books?	_____
Supplier	How much does the company currently owe to its suppliers?	_____
Shareholder	How much did the company pay in dividends this past year?	_____
Advertising account manager	How much did the company spend this past year to generate sales?	_____
Banker	What collateral or security can the company provide to ensure that any loan I make will be repaid?	_____

Exercise 1-13 *CN's Inventories* **LO 4, 5**

Refer to Canadian National Railway's balance sheet reproduced in the chapter.

Required

What was the amount of Inventories at December 31, 2007? What does this amount represent (i.e., cost, market value)? Why does CN carry its inventories at one or the other?

Exercise 1-14 *Roles of Accountants* **LO 3, 6**

One day on campus, you overhear two non-business majors discussing the reasons each did not major in accounting. "Accountants are bean counters. They just sit in a room and play with the books all day. They do not have people skills, but I suppose it really doesn't matter because no one ever looks at the statements they prepare," says the first student. The second student replies, "Oh, they are very intelligent, though, because they must know all about the tax laws, and that's too complicated for me."

Required

Comment on the students' perceptions of the roles of accountants in society. Do you agree that no one ever looks at the statements they prepare? If not, identify who the primary users are.

Problems

Problem 1-1 *You Won the Lottery* **LO 3**

You have won a lottery! You will receive $200,000 each year for the next five years.

Required

Describe the process you will go through in determining how to invest your winnings. Consider at least two options and make a choice. You may consider the shares of a certain company, bonds, real estate investments, bank deposits, and so on. Be specific. What information did you need to make a final decision? How was your decision affected by the fact that you will receive the winnings over a five-year period rather than in one lump sum? Would you prefer one payment? Explain.

Problem 1-2 *Users of Accounting Information and Their Needs* **LO 3**

LaHave Company would like to buy a building and equipment to produce a new product line. Some information about LaHave is more useful to some people involved in the project than to others.

Required

Complete the following chart by identifying the information listed on the right with the user's need to know the information. Identify the information as
a. *need* to know;
b. *helpful* to know; or
c. *not necessary* to know.

Information	User of the Information		
	Management	Shareholders	Banker
1. Amount of current debt, repayment schedule, and interest rate			
2. Fair market value of the building	____	____	____
3. Condition of the roof and heating and cooling, electrical, and plumbing systems	____	____	____
4. Total cost of the building, improvements, and equipment to set up production	____	____	____
5. Expected sales from the new product, variable production costs, related selling costs	____	____	____
	____	____	____

Problem 1-3 *Balance Sheet* **LO 4**

The following items are available from records of Fredricton Ltd. at the end of the 2008 calendar year:

Accounts payable	$25,100
Accounts receivable	47,840

(continued)

Advertising expense	4,200
Buildings	170,000
Capital stock	50,000
Cash	8,440
Notes payable	100,000
Office equipment	24,000
Retained earnings, end of year	75,180
Salary and wage expense	16,460
Sales revenue	28,440

Required

Prepare a balance sheet. *Hint:* Not all the items listed should appear on a balance sheet. For each of these items, indicate where it should appear.

Problem 1-4 *Corrected Balance Sheet* LO 4

Jane is the president of JJ Consulting Inc. JJ began business on January 1, 2008. The company's controller is out of the country on business. Jane needs a copy of the company's balance sheet for a meeting tomorrow and asked her assistant to obtain the required information from the company's records. He presented Jane with the following balance sheet. She asks you to review it for accuracy.

JJ CONSULTING INC.
BALANCE SHEET
FOR THE YEAR ENDED DECEMBER 31, 2008

Assets		Liabilities and Shareholders' Equity	
Accounts payable	$39,000	Accounts receivable	$48,000
Cash	63,000	Capital stock	60,000
Cash dividends paid	48,000	Net income for 2008	216,000
Furniture and equipment	129,000	Supplies	27,000

Required

1. Prepare a corrected balance sheet.

2. Draft a memo explaining the major differences between the balance sheet Jane's assistant prepared and the one you prepared.

Problem 1-5 *Income Statement, Statement of Retained Earnings, and Balance Sheet* LO 4

Shown below is a list of the various items that regularly appear on the financial statements of Neptune Theatres Corp. The amounts shown for balance sheet items are balances as of September 30, 2008 (with the exception of retained earnings, which is the balance on September 1, 2008), and the amounts shown for income statement items are balances for the month ended September 30, 2008:

Accounts receivable	$ 6,410
Advertising expense	14,500
Buildings	60,000
Capital stock	46,160
Cash	15,230
Concessions revenue	60,300
Cost of concessions sold	23,450
Dividends paid during the month	8,400
Furniture and fixtures	34,000
Accounts payable	17,600
Land	26,000
Notes payable	20,000
Projection equipment	25,000
Rent expense—movies	25,300
Retained earnings, beginning of month	73,780
Salaries and wages expense	23,250
Ticket sales	47,550
Water, gas, and electricity	3,850

Required

1. Prepare an income statement for the month ended September 30, 2008.

2. Prepare a statement of retained earnings for the month ended September 30, 2008.

3. Prepare a balance sheet at September 30, 2008.

4. You have $1,000 to invest. On the basis of the statements you prepared, would you use it to buy shares in Neptune? What other information would you want before making a final decision?

Problem 1-6 *Income Statement and Balance Sheet* LO 4

Canso Ltd. began business in July 2008 as a commercial fishing operation and passenger service between islands. Shares were issued to the owners in exchange for cash. Boats were purchased by making a down payment in cash and signing a note payable for the balance. Fish catches are sold to local restaurants on open account, and customers are given 15 days to pay their account. Cash fares are collected for all passenger traffic. Rent for the dock facilities is paid at the beginning of each month. Salaries and wages are paid at the end of the month. The following amounts are from the records of Canso Ltd. at the end of its first month of operations:

Accounts receivable	$37,000
Boats	160,000
Capital stock	80,000
Cash	15,460
Dividends	10,800
Fishing revenue	42,600
Notes payable	120,000
Passenger service revenue	25,120
Rent expense	8,000
Retained earnings	???
Salary and wage expense	36,460

Required

1. Prepare an income statement for the month ended July 31, 2008.

2. Prepare a balance sheet at July 31, 2008.

3. What information would you need about Notes Payable to assess Canso's long-term viability fully? Explain your answer.

Problem 1-7 *Corrected Financial Statements* LO 4

Home Cleaners Ltd. operates a small cleaning business. The company has always maintained a complete and accurate set of records. Unfortunately, the company's accountant left after a dispute with the president and took the 2008 financial statements with him. The balance sheet below and the income statement shown on the next page were prepared by the company's president.

HOME CLEANERS LTD.
INCOME STATEMENT
FOR THE YEAR ENDED DECEMBER 31, 2008

Revenues:		
Accounts receivable	$30,400	
Cleaning revenue—cash sales	65,000	$95,400
Expenses:		
Dividends	8,000	
Accounts payable	9,000	
Utilities	24,400	
Salaries and wages	34,200	75,600
Net income		$19,800

(continued)

HOME CLEANERS LTD.
BALANCE SHEET
DECEMBER 31, 2008

Assets		Liabilities and Shareholders' Equity	
Cash	$ 14,800	Cleaning revenue—	
Building and equipment	160,000	credit sales	$ 52,400
Less: Notes payable	(100,000)	Capital stock	40,000
Land	80,000	Net income	19,800
		Retained earnings	42,600
		Total liabilities and	
Total assets	$154,800	shareholders' equity	$154,800

The president is very disappointed with the net income for the year because it has averaged $50,000 over the last 10 years. She has asked for your help in determining whether the reported net income accurately reflects the profitability of the company and whether the balance sheet is prepared correctly.

Required

1. Prepare a corrected income statement for the year ended December 31, 2008.

2. Prepare a statement of retained earnings for the year ended December 31, 2008. (The actual balance of retained earnings on January 1, 2008, was $85,400. Note that the December 31, 2008, retained earnings balance shown above is incorrect. The president simply "plugged" this amount in to make the balance sheet balance.)

3. Prepare a corrected balance sheet at December 31, 2008.

4. Draft a memo to the president explaining the major differences between the income statement she prepared and the one you prepared.

Problem 1-8 *Statement of Retained Earnings for the Oxner Company* LO 4

The Oxner Company reported the following amounts (in thousands) in various statements included in its 2008 annual report:

Net loss for 2008	$ (36)
Dividends declared and paid in 2008	98
Retained earnings, September 30, 2007	2,838
Retained earnings, September 30, 2008	2,704

Required

1. Prepare a statement of retained earnings for the Oxner Company for the year ended September 30, 2008.

2. The Oxner Company does not actually present a statement of retained earnings in its annual report. Instead, it presents a broader statement of shareholders' equity. Describe the information that would be included on this statement and that is not included on a statement of retained earnings.

Problem 1-9 *Role of the Accountant in Various Organizations* LO 6

The following positions in various entities require a knowledge of accounting practices:

1. Chief financial officer for the subsidiary of a large company

2. Tax adviser to a consolidated group of entities

3. Independent computer consultant

4. Financial planner in a bank

5. Real estate broker in an independent office

6. Production planner in a manufacturing facility

7. Quality control adviser

8. Superintendent of a school district

9. Manager of one store in a retail clothing chain

10. Salesperson for a company that offers subcontract services, such as food service and maintenance to hospitals

Required

For each position listed previously, identify the entity in which it occurs as business or non-business and describe the kind of accounting knowledge (such as financial, managerial, taxes, non-business) required by each position.

Problem 1-10 *Information Needs and Setting Accounting Standards* LO 3

The Accounting Standards Board requires companies to supplement their consolidated financial statements with disclosures about segments of their businesses. To comply with this standard, CN's annual report (see note 16) provides various disclosures for the two geographic segments in which it operates: Canada and the United States.

Required

Which users of accounting information do you think the Accounting Standards Board had in mind when it set this standard? What types of disclosures do you think these users would find helpful?

Multi-Concept Problem

Problem 1-11 *Primary Assumptions Made in Preparing Financial Statements* LO 4, 5

John Hale opened a machine repair business in leased retail space, paying the first month's rent of $600 and a $2,000 security deposit with a cheque on his personal account. He took tools worth about $15,000 from his garage to the shop. He also bought some equipment to get started. The new equipment had a list price of $10,000, but John was able to purchase it on sale at **Home Depot** for only $8,400. He charged the new equipment on his personal Home Depot credit card. John's first customer paid $800 for services rendered, so John opened a chequing account for the company. He completed a second job, but the customer has not paid John the $5,000 for his work. At the end of the first month, John prepared the following balance sheet and income statement.

http://www.homedepot.ca

HALE'S MACHINE REPAIR
BALANCE SHEET
JULY 31, 2008

Cash	$ 800		
Equipment	10,000	Equity	$10,800
Total	$10,800	Total	$10,800

HALE'S MACHINE REPAIR
INCOME STATEMENT
FOR MONTH ENDED JULY 31, 2008

Sales		$ 5,800
Rent	$ 600	
Tools	8,400	9,000
Net loss		$(3,200)

John believes that he should show a greater profit next month because he won't have large expenses for items such as tools.

Required

Identify the assumptions that John has violated and explain how each event should have been handled. Prepare a corrected balance sheet and income statement.

Problem 1-1A *What to Do with a Million Dollars* LO 3

You have inherited $1 million!

Required

Describe the process you will go through in determining how to invest your inheritance. Consider at least two options and choose one. You may consider the shares of a certain company, bonds, real estate investments, bank deposits, and so on. Be specific. What information did you need to make a final decision? Where did you find the information you needed? What additional information will you need to consider if you want to make a change in your investment?

Problem 1-2A *Users of Accounting Information and Their Needs* LO 3

Bedford Ltd. would like to buy a franchise to provide a specialized service. Some information about Bedford is more useful to some people involved in the project than to others.

Required

Complete the following chart by identifying the information listed on the left with the user's need to know the information. Identify the information as

a. *need* to know;

b. *helpful* to know; or

c. *not necessary* to know.

User of the Information			
Manager	Shareholders	Franchisor	Information
_____	_____	_____	1. Expected revenue from the new service.
_____	_____	_____	2. Cost of the franchise fee and recurring fees to be paid to the franchisor.
_____	_____	_____	3. Cash available to Bedford, the franchisee, to operate the business after the franchise is purchased.
_____	_____	_____	4. Expected overhead costs of the service outlet.
_____	_____	_____	5. Bedford's required return on its investment.

Problem 1-3A *Balance Sheet* LO 4

The following items are available from the records of Hubbards Ltd. at the end of its fiscal year, July 31, 2008:

Accounts receivable	$ 5,700
Sales revenue	14,220
Buildings	70,000
Butter and cheese inventory	12,100
Capital stock	47,000
Cash	21,800
Computerized mixers	25,800
Accounts payable	16,900
Delivery expense	4,600
Notes payable	75,000
Office equipment	24,000
Retained earnings, end of year	26,300
Salary and wage expense	8,230
Tools	5,800

Required

Prepare a balance sheet. *Hint:* Not all the items listed should appear on a balance sheet. For each of these items, indicate where it should appear.

Problem 1-4A *Corrected Balance Sheet* **LO 4**

Oscar is the president of PEI Enterprises. PEI Enterprises began business on January 1, 2008. The company's controller is out of the country on business. Oscar needs a copy of the company's balance sheet for a meeting tomorrow and asked his assistant to obtain the required information from the company's records. She presented Oscar with the following balance sheet. He asks you to review it for accuracy.

PEI ENTERPRISES
BALANCE SHEET
FOR THE YEAR ENDED DECEMBER 31, 2008

Assets		Liabilities and Shareholders' Equity	
Accounts payable	$ 14,800	Accounts receivable	$ 11,600
Cash	7,375	Capital stock	50,000
Cash dividends paid	8,000	Net income for 2008	56,925
Building and equipment	88,650	Supplies	6,100

Required

1. Prepare a corrected balance sheet.

2. Draft a memo explaining the major differences between the balance sheet Oscar's assistant prepared and the one you prepared.

Problem 1-5A *Income Statement, Statement of Retained Earnings, and Balance Sheet* **LO 4**

Shown below, in alphabetical order, is a list of the various items that regularly appear on the financial statements of Susan's Rental Ltd. The amounts shown for balance sheet items are balances as of December 31, 2008 (with the exception of retained earnings, which is the balance on January 1, 2008), and the amounts shown for income statement items are balances for the year ended December 31, 2008:

Accounts payable	$ 9,000
Accounts receivable	600
Advertising expense	29,000
Audio tape inventory	140,000
Capital stock	100,000
Cash	4,980
Display fixtures	90,000
Dividends paid during the year	24,000
Notes payable	20,000
Rental revenue	251,800
Rent paid on building	120,000
Retained earnings, beginning of year	70,780
Salaries and wages expense	35,800
Water, gas, and electricity	7,200

Required

1. Prepare an income statement for the year ended December 31, 2008.

2. Prepare a statement of retained earnings for the year ended December 31, 2008.

3. Prepare a balance sheet at December 31, 2008.

4. You have $1,000 to invest. On the basis of the statements you prepared, would you use it to buy shares in this company? What other information would you want before deciding?

Problem 1-6A *Income Statement and Balance Sheet* **LO 4**

Calgary Ltd. began business in January 2008 as a commercial carpet cleaning and drying service. Shares were issued to the owners in exchange for cash. Equipment was purchased by making a down payment in cash and signing a note payable for the balance. Services are performed for local restaurants and office buildings on open account, and customers are given 15 days to pay their

(continued)

account. Rent for office and storage facilities is paid at the beginning of each month. Salaries and wages are paid at the end of the month. The following amounts are from the records of Calgary at the end of its first month of operations:

Accounts receivable	$49,500
Capital stock	160,000
Cash	103,300
Cleaning revenue	91,800
Dividends	11,000
Equipment	124,000
Note payable	60,000
Rent expense	7,200
Retained earnings	???
Salary and wage expense	16,800

Required

1. Prepare an income statement for the month ended January 31, 2008.

2. Prepare a balance sheet at January 31, 2008.

3. What information would you need about Note Payable to assess Calgary's long-term viability fully? Explain your answer.

Problem 1-7A *Corrected Financial Statements* LO 4

Mahone Bakery Ltd. operates a small pastry business. The company has always maintained a complete and accurate set of records. Unfortunately, the company's accountant left in a dispute with the president and took the 2008 financial statements with her. The balance sheet and the income statement shown below were prepared by the company's president.

MAHONE BAKERY LTD.
INCOME STATEMENT
FOR THE YEAR ENDED DECEMBER 31, 2008

Revenues:		
Accounts receivable	$ 46,500	
Pastry revenue—cash sales	71,100	$117,600
Expenses:		
Dividends	16,800	
Accounts payable	20,400	
Utilities	28,500	
Salaries and wages	54,600	120,300
Net loss		$ (2,700)

MAHONE BAKERY LTD.
BALANCE SHEET
DECEMBER 31, 2008

Assets		Liabilities and Shareholders' Equity	
Cash	$ 11,100	Pastry revenue—	
Building and equipment	180,000	credit sales	$ 66,300
Less: Notes payable	(120,000)	Capital stock	90,000
Land	150,000	Net loss	(2,700)
		Retained earnings	67,500
		Total liabilities and	
Total assets	$221,100	shareholders' equity	$221,100

The president is very disappointed with the net loss for the year because net income has averaged $63,000 over the past 10 years. He has asked for your help in determining whether the reported net loss accurately reflects the profitability of the company and whether the balance sheet is prepared correctly.

Required

1. Prepare a corrected income statement for the year ended December 31, 2008.

2. Prepare a statement of retained earnings for the year ended December 31, 2008. (The actual amount of retained earnings on January 1, 2008, was $119,700. The December 31, 2008, retained earnings balance shown previously is incorrect. The president simply "plugged" this amount in to make the balance sheet balance.)

3. Prepare a corrected balance sheet at December 31, 2008.

4. Draft a memo to the president explaining the major differences between the income statement he prepared and the one you prepared.

Problem 1-8A *Statement of Retained Earnings* LO 4

Bennett Corporation reported the following amounts in various statements included in its 2008 annual report (all amounts are stated in millions of dollars):

Net earnings for 2008	$ 27
Cash dividends declared and paid in 2008	15
Retained earnings, December 31, 2007	348
Retained earnings, December 31, 2008	360

Required

1. Prepare a statement of retained earnings for Bennett Corporation for the year ended December 31, 2008.

2. Bennett does not actually present a statement of retained earnings in its annual report. Instead, it presents a broader statement of shareholders' equity. Describe the information that would be included on this statement and that is not included on a statement of retained earnings.

Problem 1-9A *Role of the Accountant in Various Organizations* LO 6

The following positions in various entities require a knowledge of accounting practices:

_____	1. Chief financial officer for the subsidiary of a large company
_____	2. Tax adviser to a consolidated group of entities
_____	3. Accounts receivable computer analyst
_____	4. Financial planner in a bank
_____	5. Budget analyst in a real estate office
_____	6. Production planner in a manufacturing facility
_____	7. Quality control adviser
_____	8. Manager of the team conducting an audit on a provincial lottery
_____	9. Assistant superintendent of a school district
_____	10. Manager of one store in a retail clothing chain
_____	11. Controller in a company that offers subcontract services, such as food service and maintenance to hospitals
_____	12. Staff accountant in a large audit firm

Required

For each position listed above, fill in the blank to classify the position as one of the general categories of accountants listed below.

Financial accountant	**Accountant for non-business organization**
Managerial accountant	**Auditor**
Tax accountant	**Not an accounting position**

Problem 1-10A *Information Needs and Setting Accounting Standards* LO 3

The Accounting Standards Board requires companies to supplement their consolidated financial statements with disclosures about segments of their businesses. To comply with this standard, **Canadian Pacific Railway**'s annual report provides various disclosures for the three geographic segments in which it operates: Canada, the United States, and other in footnote 23.

http://www.cpr.ca

Required

Which users of accounting information do you think the Accounting Standards Board had in mind when it set this standard? What types of disclosures do you think these users would find helpful?

Alternate Multi-Concept Problem

Problem 1-11A *Primary Assumptions Made in Preparing Financial Statements* LO 4, 5

Michael Peek opened a ceramic studio in leased retail space, paying the first month's rent of $900 and a $3,000 security deposit with a cheque on his personal account. He took moulds and paint, worth about $22,500, from his home to the studio. He also bought a new firing kiln to start the business. The new kiln had a list price of $15,000, but Michael was able to trade in his old kiln, worth $1,500 at the time of trade, on the new kiln, and therefore he paid only $13,500 cash. He wrote a cheque on his personal chequing account. Michael's first customers paid a total of $4,200 to attend classes for the next two months. He opened a chequing account in the company's name with the $4,200. He has conducted classes for one month and has sold for $9,000 unfinished ceramic pieces called *greenware.* Greenware sales are all cash. Michael incurred $3,000 of personal cost in making the greenware. At the end of the first month, Michael prepared the following balance sheet and income statement.

MICHAEL'S CERAMIC STUDIO
BALANCE SHEET
JULY 31, 2008

Cash	$ 4,200		
Kiln	15,000	Equity	$19,200
Total	$19,200	Total	$19,200

MICHAEL'S CERAMIC STUDIO
INCOME STATEMENT
FOR THE MONTH ENDED JULY 31, 2008

Sales		$13,200
Rent	$ 900	
Supplies	1,800	2,700
Net income		$10,500

Michael needs to earn at least $9,000 each month for the business to be worth his time. He is pleased with the results.

Required

Identify the assumptions that Michael has violated and explain how each event should have been handled. Prepare a corrected balance sheet and income statement.

Cases

Reading and Interpreting Financial Statements

Case 1-1 *An Annual Report As Ready Reference* LO 3, 4

Refer to the CN annual report, and identify where each of the following users of accounting information would first look to answer their respective questions about CN:

1. Investors: How much did the company earn for each share I own? How much of those earnings did I receive, and how much was reinvested in the company?

2. Potential investors: What amount of earnings can I expect to see from CN in the near future?

44   **CHAPTER 1**   Accounting Communication—An Introduction   NEL

3. Bankers and creditors: Should I extend the short-term borrowing limit for CN? Does it have sufficient cash or cash-like assets to repay short-term loans?

4. Canada Revenue Agency: How much does CN owe for taxes?

5. Employees: How much money did the president and vice presidents earn? Should I ask for a raise?

Case 1-2 *Reading and Interpreting CN's Financial Statements* **LO 4**

Refer to the financial statements for CN reproduced in the appendix and answer the following questions:

1. What was the company's net income for 2007?

2. State CN's financial position on December 31, 2007, in terms of the accounting equation.

3. Explain the reasons for the change in retained (or reinvested) earnings from a balance of $5,409 on December 31, 2006, to a balance of $5,925 on December 31, 2007. Also, what amount of dividends did the company pay in 2007?

Case 1-3 *Comparing Two Companies in the Same Industry: CN and CP* **LO 4, 6**

Refer to the financial information for CN and CP reproduced in Appendices A and B at the end of the book and answer the following questions:

1. What was the total revenue amount for each company for 2007? Did each company's revenues increase or decrease from its total amount in 2006?

2. What was each company's net income for 2007? Did each company's net income increase or decrease from its net income for 2006?

3. What was the total asset balance for each company at the end of its 2007 fiscal year? Among its assets, what was the largest asset each reported on its 2007 fiscal year-end balance sheet?

4. Did either company pay its shareholders any dividends during 2007? Explain how you can tell whether they did or did not pay any dividends.

5. Compare the auditors' reports for the two companies. Are the formats of the reports the same? If not, how do they differ? Do they contain the same basic information?

Case 1-4 *Canadian National Railways* **LO 1, 2**

Refer to the financial statements of CN presented in Appendix A and examine the statement of cash flows.

Required

1. What form of organization is CN?

2. What cash flow activities did CN have for 2007?

3. How much did CN spend or receive for its activities in 2007? List the amount for each class of activity.

4. How did CN finance its investing cash requirements for 2007?

Making Financial Decisions

Case 1-5 *An Investment Opportunity* **LO 3**

You have saved enough money to pay for your university tuition for the next three years when a high school friend comes to you with a deal. He is an artist who has spent most of the past two years drawing on the walls of old buildings. The buildings are about to be demolished and your friend thinks you should buy the walls before the buildings are demolished and open a gallery featuring his work. Of course, you are levelheaded and would normally say "No!" Recently, however, your friend has been featured on several local radio and television shows and is talking to some national networks about doing a feature on a well-known news show. To set up the gallery would take all your savings, but your friend feels that you will be able to sell his artwork for 10 times the cost of your investment. What kinds of information about the business do you need before deciding to invest all your savings? What kind of profit split would you suggest to your friend if you decide to open the gallery?

Case 1-6 *Preparation of Projected Statements for a New Business* **LO 4**

Upon graduation from the University of Sherbrooke, you and your roommate decide to start your respective careers in accounting and salmon fishing in Shag Harbour. Your career as a public accountant in Shag Harbour is going well, as is your roommate's job as a commercial fisherman. After one year in Shag Harbour, he approaches you with a business opportunity.

> As we are well aware, the video rental business has yet to reach Shag Harbour, and the nearest rental facility is 250 kilometres away. We each put up our first year's savings of $5,000 and file for incorporation with Ontario to do business as Shag Video World. In return for our investment of $5,000, we each receive equal shares of capital stock in the corporation. Then we go to Corner Bank and apply for a $12,000 loan. We take the total cash of $22,000 we have now raised and buy 2,000 videos at $10 each from a mail-order supplier. We rent the movies for $3 per title and sell monthly memberships for $25, allowing a member to check out an unlimited number of movies during the month. Individual rentals would be a cash-and-carry business, but we would give customers until the 10th of the following month to pay for a monthly membership. My most conservative estimate is that during the first month alone, we will rent 800 movies and sell 250 memberships. As I see it, we will have only two expenses. First, we will hire four high school students to run the store for 15 hours each per week and pay them $7 per hour. Second, the landlord of a vacant store in town will rent us space in the building for $1,000 per month.

Required

1. Prepare a projected income statement for the first month of operations.

2. Prepare a balance sheet as it would appear at the end of the first month of operations.

3. Assume that the bank is willing to make the $12,000 loan. Would you be willing to join your roommate in this business? Explain your response. Also, indicate any information other than what he has provided that you would like to have before making a final decision.

Accounting and Ethics: What Would You Do?

Case 1-7 *Identification of Errors in Financial Statements and Preparation of Revised Statements* **LO 3, 4**

Burnside Inc. is a minor-league baseball organization that has just completed its first season. You and three other investors organized the corporation; each put up $20,000 in cash for shares of capital stock. Because you live out of the province, you have not been actively involved in the daily affairs of the club. However, you are thrilled to receive a dividend cheque for $20,000 at the end of the season—an amount equal to your original investment! Included with the cheque are the following financial statements, along with supporting explanations.

BURNSIDE INC.
INCOME STATEMENT
FOR THE YEAR ENDED DECEMBER 31, 2008

Revenues:		
Single-game ticket revenue	$840,000	
Season-ticket revenue	280,000	
Concessions revenue	560,000	
Advertising revenue	200,000	$1,880,000
Expenses:		
Cost of concessions sold	220,000	
Salary expense—players	450,000	
Salary and wage expense—staff	300,000	
Rent expense	420,000	1,390,000
Net income		$ 490,000

BURNSIDE INC.
STATEMENT OF RETAINED EARNINGS
FOR THE YEAR ENDED DECEMBER 31, 2008

Beginning balance, January 1, 2008	$ 0
Add: Net income for 2008	490,000
Deduct: Cash dividends paid in 2008	(80,000)
Ending balance, December 31, 2008	$410,000

BURNSIDE INC.
BALANCE SHEET
DECEMBER 31, 2008

Assets		Liabilities and Shareholders' Equity	
Cash	$ 10,000	Notes payable	$ 100,000
Accounts receivable:		Capital stock	240,000
Season tickets	280,000	Parent club's equity	250,000
Advertisers	200,000	Retained earnings	410,000
Auxiliary assets	160,000		
Equipment	100,000		
Player contracts	250,000	Total liabilities and	
Total assets	$1,000,000	shareholders' equity	$1,000,000

Additional information:

a. Single-game tickets sold for $8 per game. The team averaged 1,500 fans per game. With 70 home games × $8 per game × 1,500 fans, single-game ticket revenue amounted to $840,000.

b. No season tickets were sold during the first season. During the last three months of 2008, however, an aggressive sales campaign resulted in the sale of 500 season tickets for the 2009 season. Therefore, the controller (who is also one of the owners) chose to record an Account Receivable— Season Tickets and corresponding revenue for 500 tickets × $8 per game × 70 games, or $280,000.

c. Advertising revenue of $200,000 resulted from the sale of the 40 signs on the outfield wall at $5,000 each for the season. However, none of the advertisers have paid their bills yet (thus, an account receivable of $200,000 on the balance sheet) because the contract with Burnside required them to pay only if the team averaged 2,000 fans per game during the 2008 season. The controller believes that the advertisers will be sympathetic to the difficulties of starting a new franchise and be willing to overlook the slight deficiency in the attendance requirement.

d. Burnside has a working agreement with one of the major-league franchises. The minor-league team is required to pay $10,000 *every* year to the major-league team for each of the 25 players on its roster. The controller believes that each of the players is certainly an asset to the organization and has therefore recorded $10,000 × 25, or $250,000, as an asset called Player Contracts. The item on the right side of the balance sheet entitled Parent Club's Equity is the amount owed to the major league team by February 1, 2009, as payment for the players for the 2008 season.

e. In addition to the cost described in **d**, Burnside directly pays each of its 25 players a $18,000 salary for the season. This amount—$450,000—has already been paid for the 2008 season and is reported on the income statement.

f. The items on the balance sheet entitled auxiliary assets on the left side and capital stock on the right side represent the value of the controller's personal residence. She has a mortgage with the bank for the full value of the house.

g. The $100,000 note payable resulted from a loan that was taken out at the beginning of the year to finance the purchase of bats, balls, uniforms, lawn mowers, and other miscellaneous supplies needed to operate the team (equipment is reported as an asset for the same amount). The loan, with interest, is due on April 15, 2009. Even though the team had a very successful first year, Burnside is a little short of cash at the end of 2008 and has therefore asked the bank for a three-month extension of the loan. The controller reasons, "By the due date of April 15, 2009, the cash due from the new season ticket holders will be available, things will be cleared up with the advertisers, and the loan can easily be repaid."

(continued)

Required

1. Identify any errors that you think the controller has made in preparing the financial statements.

2. On the basis of your answer in **1**, prepare a revised income statement, statement of retained earnings, and balance sheet.

3. On the basis of your revised financial statements, identify any ethical dilemma you now face. Do you have a responsibility to share these revisions with the other three owners? What is your responsibility to the bank?

Internet Research Case

INTERNET

CN

http://www.cn.ca

Case 1-8 Canadian National Railway

CN is a name synonymous with railways; the company has been a leader in the rail transport industry for many years. Its fiscal year 2006 saw an increase in revenue and an increase in net income.

1. What was the amount of CN's revenues and operating expenses for the 2006 fiscal year as reported on its income statement? Was there an increase or a decrease in each of these amounts in 2006? What was the percentage increase or decrease in each amount from the prior year?

2. What was the amount of cash dividends paid, both in total and per share, for the 2006 fiscal year as reported on CN's statement of changes in shareholders' equity? Was there any change in the dividends paid per share from the prior year?

3. What was the amount of total assets as reported on CN's balance sheet at the end of the 2007 fiscal year? Did total assets increase or decrease during the year? What was the percentage increase or decrease?

Solutions to Key Terms Quiz (1)

_15_	Business		_5_	Non-business entity
_16_	Business entity		_7_	Liability
_12_	Economic entity concept		_14_	Capital stock
_13_	Sole proprietorship		_10_	Shareholder
_2_	Partnership		_11_	Creditor
_4_	Corporation		_1_	Asset
_8_	A share		_3_	Revenue
_9_	Bond/debenture		_6_	Expense

4	Accounting	21	Time period
9	Management accounting	11	Generally accepted accounting principles (GAAP)
5	Financial accounting		
6	Owners' equity	13	Securities commissions
3	Shareholders' equity	17	Accounting Standards Board
8	Retained earnings	19	Certified General Accountants
7	Balance sheet	24	International Accounting Standards Board (IASB)
1	Income statement		
10	Dividends	22	Controller
2	Statement of retained earnings	15	Treasurer
12	Cost principle	20	Internal auditing
16	Going concern	23	Auditing
18	Monetary unit	25	Auditors' report
		14	Canadian Academic Accounting Association

CHAPTER 2

Financial Statements and the Annual Report

PHOTOS.COM

STUDY LINKS

A Look at the Previous Chapter

Chapter 1 introduced how investors, creditors, and others use accounting and the outputs of the accounting system—financial statements—in making business decisions. Chapter 1 introduced the Ethical Decision Framework—a key decision tool needed for informed and ethical decision making.

A Look at This Chapter

Chapter 2 takes a closer look at the financial statements as well as other elements that make up an annual report.

A Look at the Upcoming Chapter

Chapter 3 steps back from a firms's financial statement to show how business transactions and the resulting accounting information are handled. We begin by looking at transactions—what they are, how they are analyzed, and how accounting procedures facilitate turning them into journal entries, ledger accounts, and trial balances on which financial statements are based.

Focus on Financial Results

The annual report of a company like CN represents a communication by the management of CN to various interested groups and individuals (termed stakeholders). Besides the financial statements and footnotes to those statements mentioned in Chapter 1, the annual report contains a long section referred to as management discussion and analysis (MD&A for short). MD&A contains a wealth of financial and other information of interest to readers that typically does not lend itself to recognition in the financial statements. The full MD&A for CN for 2007 is provided in Appendix A of this book. Various activities and important facts are conveyed in an MD&A; a sample is provided below.

CN 2007 ANNUAL REPORT (EXCERPT)   http://www.cn.ca

Management's discussion and analysis (MD&A) relates to the financial condition and results of operations of Canadian National Railway Company, together with its wholly-owned subsidiaries, collectively "CN" or "the Company". Canadian National Railway Company's common shares are listed in the Toronto and New York stock exchanges. Except where otherwise indicated, all financial information reflected herein is expressed in Canadian dollars and determined on the basis of United States generally accepted accounting principles (U.S. GAAP). The Company's objective is to provide meaningful and relevant information reflecting the Company's financial condition and results of operations. In certain instances, the Company may make reference to certain non-GAAP measures that, from management's perspective, are useful measures of performance. The reader is advised to read all information provided in the MD&A in conjunction with the Company's 2007 Annual Consolidated Financial Statements and Notes thereto.

Business profile

CN is engaged in the rail and related transportation business. CN's network of approximately 20,400 route miles of track spans Canada and mid-America, connecting three coasts: the Atlantic, the Pacific and the Gulf of Mexico. CN's extensive network, in addition to co-production arrangements, routing protocols, marketing alliances, and interline agreements, provide CN customers access to all three North American Free Trade Agreement (NAFTA) nations.

CN's freight revenues are derived from seven commodity groups representing a diversified and balanced portfolio of goods transported between a wide range of origins and destinations. This product and geographic diversity better positions the Company to face economic fluctuations and enhances its potential for growth opportunities. In 2007, no individual commodity group accounted for more than 20% of revenues. From a geographic standpoint, 19% of revenues came from United States (U.S.) domestic traffic, 32% from transborder traffic, 23% from Canadian domestic traffic and 26% from overseas traffic. The Company originates approximately 87% of traffic moving along its network, which allows it both to capitalize on service advantages and build on opportunities to efficiently use assets.

This excerpt from CN's 2007 Annual Report appears courtesy of CN. This section of the CN Annual Report appears in the Appendix of this textbook.

WHAT FINANCIAL STATEMENTS TELL ABOUT A BUSINESS

As we saw in Chapter 1, a variety of external users need information to make sound business decisions. These users include shareholders, bondholders, bankers, and other types of creditors, such as suppliers. All of these users must make an initial decision about investing in a company, regardless of whether it is in the form of a share, a bond, or a note. The balance sheet, the income statements, the statement of cash flow, along with the supporting notes and other information found in an annual report, are the key sources of information needed to make sound decisions.

- The balance sheet tells what obligations will be due in the near future and what assets will be available to satisfy them.
- The income statement tells the revenues and expenses for a period of time.
- The statement of cash flow tells where cash came from and how it was used during the period.
- The notes provide essential details about company's accounting policies and other key factors that affect its financial condition and performance.

To use the basic information that is found, decision makers must understand the underlying accounting principles that have been applied to create the reported information in the statements. In preparing financial statements, accountants consider:

- The objectives of financial reporting.
- The characteristics that make accounting information useful.
- The most useful way to display the information found in the balance sheet, the income statement, and the statements of cash flows.

OBJECTIVES OF FINANCIAL REPORTING

LO 1 Describe the objectives of financial reporting.

CN
http://www.cn.ca

The users of financial information are the main reason that financial statements are prepared. After all, it is the investors, creditors, and other groups and individuals outside and inside the company who must make economic decisions based on these statements. Therefore, as we learned in Chapter 1, financial statements must be based on agreed upon assumptions like time-period, going concern, and other generally accepted accounting principles.

When the accountants for companies like **CN** prepare their financial statements, they must keep in mind financial reporting objectives, which are focused on providing the most understandable and useful information possible. Financial reporting has one overall objective and a set of related objectives, all of them concerned with how the information may be useful to the readers.

The Primary Objective: Provide Information for Decision Making

The primary objective of financial reporting is *to communicate information to permit users of the information to make informed decisions.* Users include both the management of a company (internal users) and others not involved in the daily operations of the business (external users). Without access to the detailed records of the business and without the benefit of daily involvement in the affairs of the company, external users make their decisions based on *financial statements* prepared by management. According to the Accounting Standards Board (AcSB), financial reporting should provide information that is useful to investors, members, contributors, creditors, and other users in making their resource allocation decisions and/or assessing management stewardship.[1]

We see from this statement how closely the objective of financial reporting is tied to decision making. *The purpose of financial reporting is to help the users reach their decisions in an informed manner.*

---

[1]AcSB, General Accounting Section 1000, Financial Statement Concepts, para. 15, The CICA Virtual Professional Library, 2005. Hereafter, reference will be shortened to AcSB Section 1000, para. 15.

Supporting Objective: Reflect Prospective Cash Receipts to Investors and Creditors

Present shareholders must decide whether to hold their shares in a company or sell them. For potential shareholders, the decision is whether to buy the shares in the first place. Bankers, suppliers, and other types of creditors must decide whether to lend money to a company. In making their decisions, all these groups rely partly on the information provided in financial statements. (Other sources of information are sometimes as important, or more important, in reaching a decision. For example, the most recent income statement may report the highest profits in the history of a company. However, a potential investor may choose not to buy shares in a company if news reports such as *Report on Business* or *The Financial Post* report that a strike is likely to shut down operations for an indeterminable period of time.)

If you buy shares in a company, your primary concern is the *future cash to be received from the investment.* First, how much, if anything, will you periodically receive in *cash dividends?* Second, how much cash will you receive from the *sale of the shares?* The interests of a creditor, such as a banker, are similar. The banker is concerned with receiving the original amount of money lent and the interest on the loan. In summary, another objective of financial reporting is to provide information to help present and potential investors and creditors "in predicting the ability of the entity to earn income and generate cash flows in the future to meet its obligations and to generate a return on investment."[2]

As an investor your ultimate concern is not the company's cash flows—how much comes in and goes out in the course of doing business—but the cash you receive from your investment. But since your investment depends to some extent on the company's business skills in managing its cash flows, another objective of accounting is to provide information that will allow users to make decisions about the future cash flows of a company.

Supporting Objective: Reflect the Enterprise's Resources and Claims to Its Resources

The AcSB emphasizes the roles of the balance sheet and the income statement in providing useful information. These financial statements should reflect what *resources* (or assets) the company or enterprise has, what *claims to these resources* (liabilities and shareholders' equity) there are, and the effects of transactions and events that change these resources and claims. Thus, another objective of financial reporting is to show "how the management of an entity has discharged its stewardship responsibility to those that have provided resources to the entity."[3]

Exhibit 2-1 summarizes the objectives of financial reporting as they pertain to someone considering whether to buy shares in CN. The exhibit should help you understand how something as abstract as a set of financial reporting objectives can be applied to a decision-making situation.

Exhibit 2-1 The Application of Financial Reporting Objectives

FINANCIAL REPORTING OBJECTIVE	POTENTIAL INVESTOR'S QUESTIONS
1. The primary objective: Provide information for decision making.	"Based on the financial information, should I buy shares in CN?"
2. Supporting objective: Assist with the prediction of cash receipts to investors and creditors.	"How much cash will I receive in dividends each year and from the sale of the shares of CN in the future?"
	"After paying its suppliers and employees, and meeting all of its obligations, how much cash will CN take in during the time I own the shares?"
3. Supporting objective: Reflect the management's stewardship of resources and claims to resources.	"How much has CN invested in new property and equipment?"

---

[2] AcSB, Section 1000, para. 12.
[3] AcSB, Section 1000, para. 14.

What Makes Accounting Information Useful? Qualitative Characteristics

Since accounting information must be useful for decision making, what makes this information useful? This section focuses on the qualities that accountants strive for in their financial reporting and on some of the challenges they face in making reporting judgments. It also reveals what users of financial information expect from financial statements.

Quantitative considerations, such as tuition costs, certainly were a concern when you chose your current school. In addition, your decision required you to make subjective judgments about the *qualitative* characteristics you were looking for in a university or college. Similarly, there are certain qualities that make accounting information useful.

Understandability The quality of accounting information that makes it comprehensible to those willing to spend the necessary time.

Understandability   For anything to be useful, it must be understandable. Usefulness and understandability go hand in hand. However, **understandability** of financial information varies considerably, depending on the background of the user. For example, should financial statements be prepared so that they are understandable by anyone with a university education? Or should it be assumed that all readers of financial statements have completed at least one accounting course? Is a background in business necessary for a good understanding of financial reports, regardless of one's formal accounting training? As you might expect, there are no simple answers to these questions. However, the AcSB believes that financial information should be comprehensible to those who possess a reasonable understanding of business and economic activities and accounting, and have a willingness to study the information with reasonable diligence.[4]

Relevance The capacity of information to make a difference in a decision.

Relevance   Understandability alone is certainly not enough to render information useful. To be useful, information must be relevant. **Relevance** is the capacity of information to make a difference in a decision.[5] For example, assume that you are a banker evaluating the financial statements of a company that has come to you for a loan. All of the financial statements point to a strong and profitable company. However, today's newspaper revealed that the company has been named in a multimillion-dollar lawsuit. Undoubtedly, this information would be relevant to your talks with the company, and disclosure of the lawsuit in the financial statements would make them even more relevant to your lending decision.

Two types of value reflect two approaches to prediction. Predictive value helps users predict future results. Feedback value reflects the use of financial statements in confirming or correcting previous decisions. In both cases, financial statements must be timely in order to influence decisions.

 ## Accounting for Your Decisions

You Are the Shareholder

ABC Technology produces a highly technical product used in the computer industry. You are a shareholder and are currently in the process of reading this year's annual report. You find that you can't understand the report because it contains so much accounting jargon. But the annual report contains a 1-800 number for shareholder inquiries. You call the number and complain about the annual report, but the corporate spokesman politely tells you that "that's the way people talk in accounting." Is your complaint valid?

> **ANSWER:** One of the purposes of an annual report is to interest potential shareholders in the company. A small percentage of those potential investors are professional money managers who are familiar with the accounting terminology. However, most readers are individual investors who probably don't have a sophisticated accounting background. It is true that the report must assume a minimum level of formal education; accountants expect those who read the report to take the time to understand it. Technicalities aside, however, it is important to write an annual report for as broad an audience as possible.

---

[4]AcSB, Section 1000, para. 19.
[5]AcSB, Section 1000, para. 20.

Reliability   What makes accounting information reliable? According to the AcSB, information is reliable "when it is in agreement with the actual underlying transactions and events, the agreement is capable of independent verification and the information is reasonably free from error and bias."[6]

Reliability has four basic characteristics:

- *Verifiability*   Information is verifiable when we can make sure that it is free from error—for example, by looking up the cost paid for an asset in a contract or an invoice.

- *Representational faithfulness*   Information is representationally faithful when it corresponds to an actual event—such as when the purchase of land corresponds to a transaction in the company's records.

- *Neutrality*   Information is neutral when it is not slanted to portray a company's position in a better or worse light than the actual circumstances would dictate—such as when the probable losses from a major lawsuit are disclosed accurately in the notes to the financial statements, with all their potential effects on the company, rather than minimized as very remote possible losses.

- *Conservatism*   Information that is uncertain should be presented so that assets and revenues are not overstated while liabilities and expenses are not understated. Care is needed here to avoid the creation of bias as a result of being conservative. Various accounting rules are based on the concept of conservatism. For example, inventory held for resale is reported on the balance sheet at the *lower of cost and market* value. This rule requires a company to compare the cost of its inventory with the market price, or current cost to replace that inventory, and report the lower of the two amounts on the balance sheet at the end of the year. In Chapter 6 we shall more fully explore the lower of cost and market rule as it pertains to inventory.

Reliability The quality that makes accounting information dependable in representing the events that it purports to represent.

Comparability and Consistency

Comparability allows comparisons to be made *between or among companies*. Generally accepted accounting principles (GAAP) allow a certain amount of freedom in choosing among competing alternative treatments for certain transactions.

For example, under GAAP, companies may choose from a number of methods of accounting for the depreciation of certain long-term assets. **Depreciation** (amortization) is the process of allocating the cost of a long-term tangible asset, such as a building or equipment, over its useful life. Each method may affect the value of the assets differently. (We discuss depreciation in Chapter 8.) How does this freedom of choice affect the ability of investors to make comparisons between companies?

Assume you were considering buying shares in one of three companies. As their annual reports indicate, two of the companies use what is called the "accelerated" depreciation method, and the other company uses what is called the "straight-line" depreciation method. (We'll learn about these methods in a later chapter.) Does this lack of a common depreciation method make it impossible for you to compare the performance of the three companies?

Obviously, comparisons among the companies would be easier and more meaningful if all three used the same depreciation method. However, comparisons are not impossible just because companies use different methods. Certainly, the more alike—that is, uniform—statements are in terms of the principles used to prepare them, the more comparable they will be. However, the profession allows a certain freedom of choice in selecting from among alternative generally accepted accounting principles.

To render statements of companies using different methods more meaningful, *disclosure* assumes a very important role. For example, as we will see later in this chapter, the first note in the annual report of a publicly traded company is the disclosure of its accounting policies. The reader of this note for each of the three companies is made aware that the companies do not use the same depreciation method. Disclosure of accounting policies allows the reader to make some sort of subjective adjustment to the statements of one or more of the companies and thus to compensate for the different depreciation method being used.

Comparability For accounting information, the quality that allows a user to analyze two or more companies and look for similarities and differences.

Depreciation The process of allocating the cost of a long-term tangible asset over its useful life. Also termed amortization.

---

[6]AcSB, Section 1000, para. 21.

Consistency For accounting information, the quality that allows a user to compare two or more accounting periods for a single company.

Consistency is closely related to the concept of comparability. Both involve the relationship between two numbers. However, whereas financial statements are comparable when they can be compared between one company and another, statements are consistent when they can be compared within a single company from one accounting period to the next.

Occasionally, companies decide to change methods from one accounting method to another. Will it be possible to compare a company's earnings in a period in which it switches methods with its earnings in prior years if the methods differ? Like the different methods used by different companies, changes in accounting methods from one period to the next do not make comparisons impossible, only more difficult. When a company makes an accounting change, accounting standards require various disclosures to help the reader evaluate the impact of the change.

Canadian National Railway Company
Notes to Consolidated Financial Statements

H. Depreciation

The cost of properties, including those under capital leases, net of asset impairment write-downs, is depreciated on a straight-line basis over their estimated useful lives as follows:

Asset class	Annual rate
Track and roadway	2%
Rolling stock	3%
Information technology	11%
Other	8%

The Company follows the group method of depreciation for railroad properties and, as such, conducts comprehensive depreciation studies on a periodic basis to assess the reasonableness of the lives of properties based upon current information and historical activities. Changes in estimated useful lives are accounted for prospectively. In 2007, the Company completed a depreciation study for all it U.S. assets, for which there was no significant impact on depreciation expense. The Company is also conducting a depreciation study of its Canadian properties, plant and equipment, and expects to finalize this study by the first quater of 2008.

I. Intangible assets

Intangible assets relate to customer contracts and relationships assumed through past acquisitions and are being amortized on a straight-line basis over 40 to 50 years.

This excerpt from CN's 2007 Annual Report appears courtesy of CN. This section of the CN Annual Report appears in the Appendix of this textbook.

Materiality The magnitude of an accounting information omission or misstatement that will affect the judgment of someone relying on the information.

Materiality For accounting information to be useful, it must be relevant to a decision. The concept of **materiality** is closely related to relevance and deals with the size of an error in accounting information. The issue is whether the error is large enough to affect the judgment of someone relying on the information. Consider the following example. A company pays cash for two separate purchases: one for a $5 pencil sharpener and the other for a $50,000 computer. Theoretically, each expenditure results in the acquisition of an asset that should be depreciated over its useful life. However, what if the company decides to account for the $5 as an expense of the period rather than treating it in the theoretically correct manner by depreciating it over the life of the pencil sharpener? *Will this error in any way affect the judgment of someone relying on the financial statements?* Because such a slight error will *not* affect any decisions, minor expenditures of this nature are considered *immaterial* and are accounted for as an expense of the period.

The *threshold* for determining materiality will vary from one company to the next, depending to a large extent on the size of the company. Many companies establish policies that *any* expenditure under a certain dollar amount should be accounted for as an expense of the period. The threshold might be $50 for the corner grocery store but $1,000 for a large corporation. Finally, in some instances the amount of a transaction may be immaterial by company standards but may still be considered significant by financial statement users. For example, a transaction involving either illegal or unethical behaviour by a company officer would be of concern, regardless of the dollar amounts involved.

Benefit versus Cost Constraint The benefits of accounting information should exceed the costs of providing the information. Such a judgment is a challenge for standard setters and accountants because of the wide variety of users. A recent section of the standards, "Differential Reporting," provides some options for certain qualified firms so that they can avoid the costs of the more complex standards, particularly when the firm's owners consent to such adjustments on the grounds of their involvement with the management of the organization. If this close contact is combined with the need to be accountable to a limited number of stakeholders, the organization can select the provisions of the section on differential reporting to use certain prescribed accounting procedures.[7]

Exhibit 2-2 below provides a convenient review of various qualitative characteristics of accounting information.

Exhibit 2-2 Qualitative Characteristics of Accounting Information

SITUATION A bank is trying to decide whether to extend a $1 million loan to Russell Corporation. Russell presents the bank with its most recent balance sheet, showing its financial position on a historical cost basis. Each quality of the information is summarized in the form of a question.

QUALITY	QUESTION
Understandability	Can the information be used by those willing to learn to use it properly?
Relevance	Would the information be useful in deciding whether or not to lend money to Russell?
Reliability	
Verifiability	Can the information be verified? Is the information free from error?
Representational faithfulness	Is there agreement between the information and the events represented?
Neutrality	Is the information slanted in any way to present the company more favourably than is warranted?
Conservatism	If there is any uncertainty about any of the amounts assigned to items on the balance sheet, are they recognized using the least optimistic estimate?
Comparability	Are the methods used in assigning amounts to assets the same as those used by other companies?
Consistency	Are the methods used in assigning amounts to assets the same as those used in prior years?
Materiality	Will a specific error in any way affect the judgment of someone relying on the financial statements?
Benefits exceed costs	Is the company using the differential reporting provisions in its accounting reports?

Financial Reporting: An International Perspective

In Chapter 1 we introduced the International Accounting Standards Board (IASB) and its efforts to improve the development of accounting standards around the world. Interestingly, four of the most influential members of this group, representing the standard-setting bodies in the United States, the United Kingdom, Canada, and Australia, agree on the primary objective of financial reporting. All recognize that the primary objective is to provide information useful in making economic decisions.

The standard-setting body in the United Kingdom distinguishes between qualitative characteristics that relate to *content* of the information presented and those that relate to *presentation*. Similar to the FASB in the United States, this group recognizes relevance and reliability as the primary characteristics related to content. Comparability and understandability are the primary qualities related to the presentation of the information.

---

[7]AcSB, Section 1300.

Objectives of Financial Reporting   **57**

The concept of conservatism is also recognized in other countries. For example, both the IASB and the standard-setting body in the United Kingdom list "prudence" among their qualitative characteristics. Prudence requires the use of caution in making the various estimates required in accounting. Like the Canadian standard-setting body, these groups recognize that prudence does not justify the deliberate understatement of assets or revenues or the deliberate overstatement of liabilities or expenses.

The apparent consensus of these standard setting bodies about the concepts of accounting should help with harmonization of GAAP around the world.

■ THE CLASSIFIED BALANCE SHEET

LO 2 Explain the concept and purpose of a classified balance sheet and prepare the statement.

Chapter 1 provided a description of some of the key elements of accounting reports such as assets, liabilities, revenues, and cash flows from investing. Underlying these disclosures are concepts such as usefulness. We now turn to the outputs of the system: the financial statements. First, we will consider the significance of a *classified balance sheet*. We will then examine the *income statement*, the *statement of retained earnings*, and the *statement of cash flows*. The chapter concludes with a brief look at the financial statements of a real company, CN, and at the other elements in an annual report.

What Are the Parts of the Balance Sheet? Understanding the Operating Cycle

Operating cycle The period of time between the purchase of inventory and the collection of any receivable from the sale of the inventory.

In the first part of this chapter, we stressed the importance of *cash flow*. For a company that sells a product, the **operating cycle** begins when cash is invested in inventory and ends when cash is collected by the enterprise from its customers.

Assume that on August 1 a retailer, Laptop Computer Sales, buys a computer for $5,000 from the manufacturer, BIM Corp. At this point, Laptop has merely substituted one asset, cash, for another, inventory. On August 20, twenty days after buying the computer, Laptop sells it to an accounting firm, Price & Company, for $6,000. Under the purchase agreement, Price will pay for the computer within the next 30 days. At this point, both the form of the asset and the amount have changed. The form of the asset held by Laptop has changed from inventory to account receivable. Also, because the inventory has been sold for $1,000 more than its cost of $5,000, the size of the asset held, the account receivable, is now $6,000. Finally, on September 20, Price pays $6,000 to Laptop, and the operating cycle is complete. As we will explore more fully in later chapters, Laptop has earned $1,000, the difference between what it sold the computer for and what it initially paid for the computer. The cycle starts again when Laptop buys another computer for resale.

Laptop's operating cycle is summarized in Exhibit 2-3. The length of the company's operating cycle was 50 days. The operating cycle consisted of two distinct parts. From the time Laptop purchased the inventory, 20 days elapsed before it sold the computer. Another 30 days passed before the account receivable was collected. The length of the operating cycle depends to a large extent on the nature of a company's business. For example, in our illustration, the manufacturer of the computer, BIM Corp., received cash immediately from Laptop and did not have to wait to collect a receivable. However, additional time is added to the operating cycle of BIM Corp. to *manufacture* the computer.

The operating cycle of the accounting firm in our example, Price & Company, differs from that of either the manufacturer or the retailer. Price sells a service rather than a product. Its operating cycle is determined by two factors: the length of time involved in providing a service to the client and the amount of time required to collect any account receivable.

A classified balance sheet for a hypothetical company, Dixon Sporting Goods Inc., is shown in Exhibit 2-4. You will want to refer to it as you learn about the different categories on a classified balance sheet. (The bulleted numbers to follow refer to Exhibit 2-4.)

Study Tip

The operating cycle of a business is the basis for deciding which assets are current and which are non-current. When you look at a company's balance sheet, be sure you understand the length of its operating cycle so that you are clear about how it classifies its assets.

Exhibit 2-3 The Operating Cycle for a Retailer

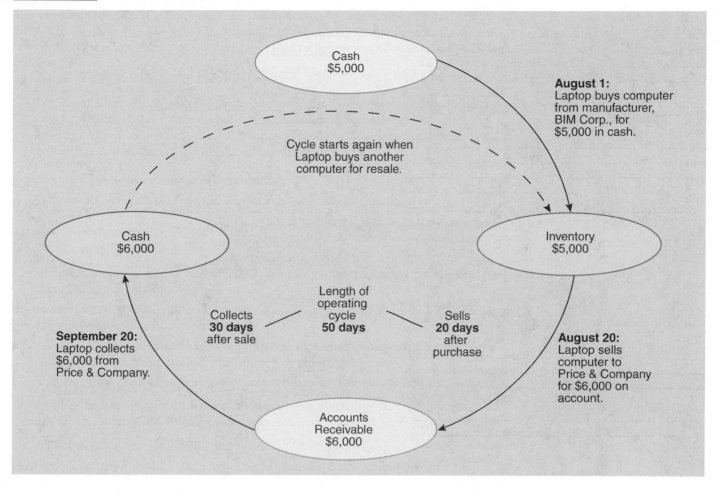

Current Assets 1

The basic distinction on a classified balance sheet is between current and non-current items. **Current assets** are cash and other assets that are reasonably expected to be realized in cash or sold or consumed during the normal operating cycle of a business or within one year if the operating cycle is shorter than one year.[8]

Most businesses have an operating cycle shorter than one year. The operating cycle for Laptop Computer Sales in our illustration was 50 days. Therefore cash, accounts receivable, and inventory are classified as current assets because they *are* cash, will be *realized* in (converted to) cash (accounts receivable), or will be *sold* (inventory) within one year.

Can you think of a situation in which a company's operating cycle is longer than one year? A construction company is a good example. A construction company essentially builds an item of inventory, such as an office building, to a customer's specifications. The entire process, including constructing the building and collecting the sales amount from the customer, may take three years to complete. According to our earlier definition, because the inventory will be sold and the account receivable will be collected within the operating cycle, they will still qualify as current assets.

In addition to cash, accounts receivable, and inventory, the two other most common types of current assets are temporary investments and prepaid expenses. Excess cash is often invested in the shares and bonds of other companies, as well as in various government instruments. If the investments are made for the short term, they are classified as current and are typically called either *temporary investments* or *marketable securities*.

> **Current asset** An asset that is expected to be realized in cash or sold or consumed during the operating cycle or within one year if the cycle is shorter than one year.

[8]AcSB, Section 1510, para. 1.

Exhibit 2-4 Balance Sheet for Dixon Sporting Goods

DIXON SPORTING GOODS INC.
BALANCE SHEET
AT DECEMBER 31, 2008

ASSETS

1 These assets are realizable, sold, or consumed in one year or operating cycle.

Current assets

► Cash		$ 5,000
► Temporary investments		11,000
► Accounts receivable		23,000
► Merchandise inventory		73,500
► Prepaid insurance		4,800
► Store supplies		700
Total current assets		$118,000

2 These assets will not be realizable, sold, or consumed within one year or operating cycle.

Investments

► Land held for future office site			150,000
Property, plant, and equipment			
► Land		100,000	
► Buildings	$150,000		
Less: Accumulated depreciation	60,000	90,000	
► Store furniture and fixtures	42,000		
Less: Accumulated depreciation	12,600	29,400	
Total property, plant, and equipment			219,400
Intangible assets			
► Franchise agreement			55,000
Total assets			$542,400

LIABILITIES

3 These are liabilities that will be satisfied within one year or operating cycle.

Current liabilities

► Accounts payable		$ 15,700
► Salaries and wages payable		9,500
► Income taxes payable		7,200
► Interest payable		2,500
► Bank loan payable		25,000
Total current liabilities		$ 59,900

4 These are liabilities that will not be satisfied within one year or operating cycle.

Long-term liabilities

► Notes payable, due December 31, 2016		120,000
Total liabilities		179,900

SHAREHOLDERS' EQUITY

5 These are owners' claims on assets.

Contributed capital

Capital stock, 5,000 no par shares		
issued and outstanding	75,000	
Retained earnings	287,500	
Total shareholders' equity		362,500
Total liabilities and shareholders' equity		$542,400

(Alternatively, some investments are made for the purpose of exercising influence over another company and thus are made for the long term. These investments are classified as non-current assets.) Various prepayments, such as office supplies, rent, and insurance, are classified as *prepaid expenses* and thus are current assets. These assets qualify as current because they will usually be *consumed* within one year.

Non-current Assets **2**

Any assets that do not meet the definition of a current asset are classified as *long-term* or *non-current assets*. Three common categories of long-term assets are: investments; property, plant, and equipment; and intangibles.

Investments   Recall, from the discussion of current assets, that shares and bonds expected to be sold within the next year are classified as current assets. Securities that are not expected to be sold within the next year are classified as *investments*. In many cases, the investment is in the common stock of another company. Sometimes companies invest in another company either to exercise some influence or actually to control the operation of the other company. Other types of assets classified as investments are land held for future use and buildings and equipment not currently used in operations.

CN has two types of investments. Through *subsidiary investments*, it has voting control of other companies. Such investments are treated by consolidation, which means that CN includes the assets, liabilities, revenues, and expenses of these subsidiaries in its consolidated statements. For example, CN consolidates (includes) the financial results of its subsidiaries Great Lakes Transportation and BC Rail, both of which it acquired in 2004 through the purchase of their common shares. With other companies, CN owns shares but does not have voting control. These companies are accounted for as long-term investments. For example, in November 2007, CN sold its 32% ownership interest in the **English Welsh and Scottish Railway Company**, a major freight service in Great Britain and the Channel Tunnel. This investment was held in its long-term investments in 2006. Only controlled companies (i.e., those with more than 50% of voting shares owned by CN) are consolidated.

http://www.ews-railway.co.uk

Property, Plant, and Equipment   This category consists of the various *tangible, productive assets* used in the operation of a business. Land, buildings, equipment, machinery, furniture and fixtures, trucks, and tools are all examples of assets held for use in the *operation* of a business rather than for *resale*. The distinction between inventory and equipment, for example, depends on the company's *intent* in acquiring the asset. For example, **IBM** classifies a computer system as inventory because its intent in manufacturing the asset is to offer it for resale. However, this same computer in the hands of a law firm would be classified as equipment because its intent in buying the asset from IBM is to use it in the long-term operation of the business.

http://www.ibm.com/us/

The relative size of property, plant, and equipment depends largely on a company's business. Consider that CN had over $23.4 billion in total assets at the end of 2007. Over 87% of the total assets were invested in property, plant, and equipment. On the other hand, property and equipment represented less than 3% of the total assets of **Microsoft**, the highly successful software company. Regardless of the relative size of property, plant, and equipment, all assets in this category are subject to depreciation, with the exception of land. A separate accumulated depreciation account is used to account for the depreciation recorded on each of these assets over its life.

http://www.microsoft.com/

Intangibles   Intangible assets are similar to property, plant, and equipment in that they provide benefits to the firm over the long term. The distinction is in the *form* of the asset. *Intangible assets lack physical substance.* Trademarks, copyrights, franchise rights, patents, and goodwill are examples of intangible assets. The cost principle governs the accounting for intangibles, just as it does for tangible assets. For example, the amount paid to an inventor for the patent rights to a new project is recorded as an intangible asset. Similarly, the amount paid to purchase a franchise for a fast-food restaurant for the exclusive right to operate in a certain geographic area is recorded as an intangible asset. Like tangible assets, intangibles may be written off to expense over their useful lives. *Depreciation* is the name given to the process of writing off tangible assets; the same process for intangible assets is called *amortization*. One should note that the term amortization is often used in Canada for writing off both tangible and intangible assets. Depreciation and amortization are both explained more fully in Chapter 8.

Two-Minute Review

1. Give at least three examples of current assets.

2. Give the three common categories of non-current assets.

Answers on page 70.

The Classified Balance Sheet

Current Liabilities ③

Current liability An obligation that will be satisfied within the next operating cycle or within one year if the cycle is shorter than one year.

The definition of a current liability is closely tied to that of a current asset. A **current liability** is an obligation that will be satisfied within the next operating cycle or within one year, if the cycle is shorter than one year. For example, the classification of a note payable on the balance sheet depends on its maturity date. If the note will be paid within the next year, it is classified as current; otherwise, it is classified as a long-term liability. On the other hand, accounts payable, wages payable, and income taxes payable are all short-term or current liabilities.

Most liabilities, such as those for purchases of merchandise on credit, are satisfied by the payment of cash. However, certain liabilities are eliminated from the balance sheet when the company performs services. For example, the liability Subscriptions Received in Advance, which would appear on the balance sheet of a magazine publisher, is satisfied not by the payment of any cash but by the delivery of the magazine to the customers. Finally, it is possible to satisfy one liability by substituting another in its place. For example, a supplier might ask a customer to sign a written note to replace an existing account payable if the customer is unable to pay at the present time.

Long-Term Liabilities ④

Any obligation that will not be paid or otherwise satisfied within the next year or the operating cycle, whichever is longer, is classified as a long-term liability, or long-term debt. Notes payable and bonds payable, both promises to pay money in the future, are two common forms of long-term debt. Some bonds have a life as long as 25 or 30 years.

Shareholders' Equity ⑤

Recall that shareholders' equity represents the owners' claims on the assets of the business. These claims arise from two sources: *contributed capital* and *earned capital.* Contributed capital appears on the balance sheet in the form of capital stock, and earned capital takes the form of retained earnings. *Capital stock* indicates the owners' investment in the business. *Retained earnings* represents the accumulated earnings, or net income, of the business since its inception less all dividends paid during that time.

Most companies have a single class of capital stock called *common stock.* This is the most basic form of ownership in a business. All other claims against the company, such as those of *creditors* and *preferred shareholders,* take priority. *Preferred shares* are a form of capital stock that, as the name implies, carries with it certain preferences. For example, the company must pay dividends on preferred shares before it makes any distribution of dividends on common shares. In the event of liquidation, preferred shareholders have priority over common shareholders in the distribution of the entity's assets.

Capital stock may appear as two separate items on the balance sheet: *par value* (a legal term for shares used in some jurisdictions outside Canada) and *paid-in capital in excess of par value.* The total of these two items tells us the amount that has been paid by the owners for the shares. We will take a closer look at these items in Chapter 11.

Study Tip

Do not try to memorize each of the items on the balance sheet in Exhibit 2-4. Instead, read each account title and try to understand what would be included in each of the accounts. Account titles vary from one company to the next, but the names used by a company should give you an indication of what is included in the account.

Using a Classified Balance Sheet

As we have now seen, a classified balance sheet separates both assets and liabilities into those that are current and those that are non-current. This distinction is very useful in any analysis of a company's financial position.

Working Capital   Investors, bankers, and other interested readers use the balance sheet to evaluate the liquidity of a business. **Liquidity** is a relative term and deals with the ability of a company to pay its debts as they come due. As you might expect, bankers and other creditors are particularly interested in the liquidity of businesses to which they have lent money. A comparison of current assets and current liabilities is a starting point

Liquidity The ability of a company to pay its debts as they come due.

in evaluating the ability of a company to meet its obligations. **Working capital** is the difference between current assets and current liabilities at a point in time. Referring back to Exhibit 2-4, we see that the working capital for Dixon Sporting Goods on December 31, 2008, is as follows:

Working capital Current assets minus current liabilities.

WORKING CAPITAL

FORMULA	FOR DIXON SPORTING GOODS
Current Assets − Current Liabilities	$118,000 − $59,900 = $58,100

The management of working capital is an important task for any business. A company must constantly strive for a *balance* in managing its working capital. For example, too little working capital—or in the extreme, negative working capital—may signal the inability to pay creditors on a timely basis. However, an overabundance of working capital could indicate that the company is not investing enough of its available funds in productive resources, such as new machinery and equipment.

Current Ratio   Because it is an absolute dollar amount, working capital is limited in its informational value. For example, $1 million may be an inadequate amount of working capital for a large corporation but far too much for a smaller company. In addition, a certain dollar amount of working capital may have been adequate for a company earlier in its life but be inadequate now. However, a related measure of liquidity, the **current ratio,** allows us to *compare* the liquidity of companies of different sizes and of a single company over time. The ratio is computed by dividing current assets by current liabilities. Dixon Sporting Goods has a current ratio of just under 2 to 1:

Current ratio Current assets divided by current liabilities.

CURRENT RATIO

FORMULA	FOR DIXON SPORTING GOODS
$\dfrac{\text{Current Assets}}{\text{Current Liabilities}}$	$\dfrac{\$118,000}{\$59,900} = 1.97 \text{ to } 1$

Some analysts use a rule of thumb of 2 to 1 for the current ratio as a sign of short-term financial health. However, as is always the case, rules of thumb can be dangerous. Historically, companies in certain industries have operated quite efficiently with a current ratio of less than 2 to 1, whereas a ratio much higher than this is necessary to survive in other industries. Consider **Canadian Pacific Railway (CP)**. At the end of fiscal 2007, it had a current ratio of 0.87 to 1. On the other hand, manufacturing companies routinely have current ratios well over 1 to 1. **Maax Inc.,** a leading manufacturer of bathroom and kitchen products, had a current ratio at the end of 2007 of 1.68 to 1.

http://www.cpr.ca

http://www.maax.com

Unfortunately neither the amount of working capital nor the current ratio tells us anything about the *composition* of current assets and current liabilities. For example, assume two companies both have total current assets equal to $100,000. Company A has cash of $10,000, accounts receivable of $50,000, and inventory of $40,000. Company B also has cash of $10,000 but accounts receivable of $20,000 and inventory of $70,000. All other things being equal, Company A is more liquid than Company B because more of its total current assets are in receivables than inventory. Receivables are only one step away from being cash, whereas inventory must be sold and then the receivable collected. Note that Dixon's inventory of $73,500 makes up a large portion of its total current assets of $118,000. An examination of the *relative* size of the various current assets for a company may reveal certain strengths and weaknesses not evident in the current ratio.

In addition to the composition of the current assets, the *frequency* with which they are "turned over" is important. For instance, how long does it take to sell an item of inventory? How much time is required to collect an account receivable? Many companies could not exist with the current ratio of 0.87 reported by the CP at the end of 2007.

The frequency of its sales and thus the numerous operating cycles within a single year mean that it can operate with a much lower current ratio than a manufacturing company, for example.

THE INCOME STATEMENT

LO 3 Explain the components of an income statement.

The income statement is used to summarize the results of operations of an entity for a *period of time*. At a minimum, all companies prepare income statements at least once a year. Companies that must report to securities commissions prepare financial statements, including an income statement, every three months. Monthly income statements are usually prepared for internal use by management.

What Appears on the Income Statement?

From an accounting perspective, it is important to understand which transactions of an entity should appear on the income statement. In general, the income statement reports the excess of *revenues over expenses,* that is, the *net income,* or in the event of an excess of *expenses over revenues,* the *net loss* of the period. As a reference to the "bottom line" on an income statement, it is common to use the terms *profits* or *earnings* as synonyms for *net income.*

As discussed in Chapter 1, *revenue* is the inflow of assets resulting from the sale of products and services. It represents the dollar amount of sales of products and services for a period of time. An *expense* is the outflow of assets resulting from the sale of goods and services for a period of time. The cost of products sold, wages and salaries, and taxes are all examples of expenses.

Certain special types of revenues, called *gains,* are sometimes reported on the income statement, as are certain special types of expenses, called *losses.* For example, assume that Sanders Company holds a parcel of land for a future building site. The company paid $50,000 for the land 10 years ago. The province pays Sanders $60,000 for the property to use in a new highway project. Sanders has a special type of revenue from the sale of its property. It will recognize a *gain* of $10,000: the excess of the cash received from the province, $60,000, over the cost of the land, $50,000.

Format of the Income Statement

One form used by companies is termed a single-step format, implying that revenues are totalled, expenses are totalled, and the difference is net income (loss).

Single-step income statement An income statement in which all expenses are added together and subtracted from all revenues.

Exhibit 2-5 presents a **single-step income statement** for Dixon Sporting Goods Inc. The format here is similar to the one used by CN, except that CN's contains some elaborations that will be discussed in Chapter 5. The primary advantage of the single-step format is its simplicity. No attempt is made to classify either revenues or expenses or to associate any of the expenses with any of the revenues.

Using a Single-Step Income Statement

Profit margin Net income divided by sales.

An important use of the income statement is to evaluate the *profitability* of a business. For example, a company's **profit margin** is the ratio of its net income to its sales. Some analysts refer to a company's profit margin as its *return on sales.* Dixon's profit margin is as follows:

PROFIT MARGIN

FORMULA	FOR DIXON SPORTING GOODS
$\dfrac{\text{Net Income}}{\text{Sales}}$	$\dfrac{\$41,000}{\$357,500} = 11\%$

For every dollar of sales, Dixon has $0.11 in net income.

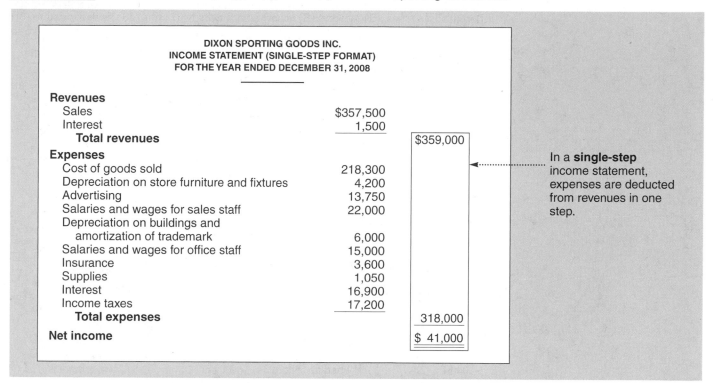

DIXON SPORTING GOODS INC.
INCOME STATEMENT (SINGLE-STEP FORMAT)
FOR THE YEAR ENDED DECEMBER 31, 2008

Revenues		
Sales	$357,500	
Interest	1,500	
Total revenues		$359,000
Expenses		
Cost of goods sold	218,300	
Depreciation on store furniture and fixtures	4,200	
Advertising	13,750	
Salaries and wages for sales staff	22,000	
Depreciation on buildings and amortization of trademark	6,000	
Salaries and wages for office staff	15,000	
Insurance	3,600	
Supplies	1,050	
Interest	16,900	
Income taxes	17,200	
Total expenses		318,000
Net income		$ 41,000

In a **single-step** income statement, expenses are deducted from revenues in one step.

Two important factors should be kept in mind in evaluating any financial statement ratio. First, how does this year's ratio differ from ratios of prior years? For example, a decrease in the profit margin may indicate that the company is having trouble this year controlling certain costs. Second, how does the ratio compare with industry norms? For example, in some industries the profit margin is considerably lower than in many others, such as in mass merchandising. (**Loblaw Companies Limited**'s profit margin for 2006 was reported as –0.76%.) It is always helpful to compare key ratios, such as the profit margin, with an industry average or with the same ratio for a close competitor of the company. (For example, the **Sobeys Inc.** profit margin for the same time period was reported as 1.47%.)

http://www.loblaw.ca

http://www.sobeys.com/corporate

THE STATEMENT OF RETAINED EARNINGS

The purpose of a statement of shareholders' equity is to explain the changes in the components of owners' equity during the period. Retained earnings and capital stock are the two primary components of shareholders' equity. If there are no changes during the period in a company's capital stock, it may choose to present a statement of retained earnings instead of a statement of shareholders' equity. A statement of retained earnings for Dixon Sporting Goods is shown in Exhibit 2-6.

LO 4 Identify the components of the statement of retained earnings and prepare the statement.

DIXON SPORTING GOODS INC.
STATEMENT OF RETAINED EARNINGS
FOR THE YEAR ENDED DECEMBER 31, 2008

Retained earnings, January 1, 2008	$271,500
Add: Net income for 2008	41,000
	312,500
Less: Dividends declared and paid in 2008	(25,000)
Retained earnings, December 31, 2008	$287,500

Exhibit 2-6

Statement of Retained Earnings for Dixon Sporting Goods Inc.

The statement of retained earnings provides an important link between the income statement and the balance sheet. Dixon's net income of $41,000, as detailed on the income statement, is an *addition* to retained earnings. Note that the dividends declared and paid of $25,000 do not appear on the income statement because they are a payout, or *distribution,* of net income to shareholders rather than one of the expenses deducted to arrive at net income. Accordingly, they appear as a direct deduction on the statement of retained earnings. The beginning balance in retained earnings is carried forward from last year's statement of retained earnings.

THE STATEMENT OF CASH FLOWS

LO 5 Identify the components of the statement of cash flows and prepare the statement.

All publicly held corporations are required to present a statement of cash flows in their annual reports. The purpose of the statement is to summarize the cash flow effects of a company's operating, investing, and financing activities for the period.

The Cash Flow Statement for Dixon Sporting Goods

The statement for Dixon Sporting Goods is shown in Exhibit 2-7. The statement consists of three categories: operating activities, investing activities, and financing activities. Each of these three categories can result in a net inflow of cash or a net outflow of cash.

Dixon's *operating activities* generated $56,100 of cash during the period. Operating activities **1** concern the purchase and sale of a product, in this case the acquisition of sporting goods from distributors and the subsequent sale of those goods. As we can readily see, Dixon had one major source of cash, the collection from its customers of $362,500. Similarly, Dixon's largest use of cash was the $217,200 it paid for inventory. In Chapter 12, we will discuss the statement of cash flows in detail and the preparation of this section of the statement.

Financing and investing activities were described in Chapter 1. *Investing activities* **2** involve the acquisition and sale of long-term or non-current assets, such as long-term investments, property, plant, and equipment, and intangible assets. *Financing activities* **3** result from the issuance and repayment, or retirement, of long-term liabilities and capital stock. The one investing activity on Dixon's statement of cash flows, the purchase of land for a future office site, required the use of cash and thus is shown as a net outflow of $150,000. Dixon had two financing activities: dividends of $25,000 required the use of cash, and the issuance of a long-term note generated cash of $120,000. The balance in cash on the bottom of the statement of $5,000 must agree with the balance for this item as shown on the balance sheet in Exhibit 2-4.

The Financial Statements for CN

The previous financial statements for Dixon Sporting Goods Inc. are hypothetical results the purpose of which is to introduce the major categories used by financial statements. CN's financial statements, presented in Appendix A and described in more detail in later chapters, involve more items and categories, which are intended to provide more detailed information to the user. However, as you journey through the remaining chapters of this book, you will better understand details such as those for CN by keeping in mind the major categories of Dixon's financial statements, since their structure is similar to that of CN.

One term used for CN's statements that cannot be used for those of Dixon is "consolidated," as in consolidated balance sheet, consolidated income statement, and so on. The word "consolidated" is used in the case of CN because it implies that the statements reflect all of the operations of other companies controlled (usually by owning more than 50% of the voting shares of a company) by CN. By contrast, Dixon does not control another company, so the term cannot apply.

Exhibit 2-7 Statement of Cash Flows for Dixon Sporting Goods Inc.

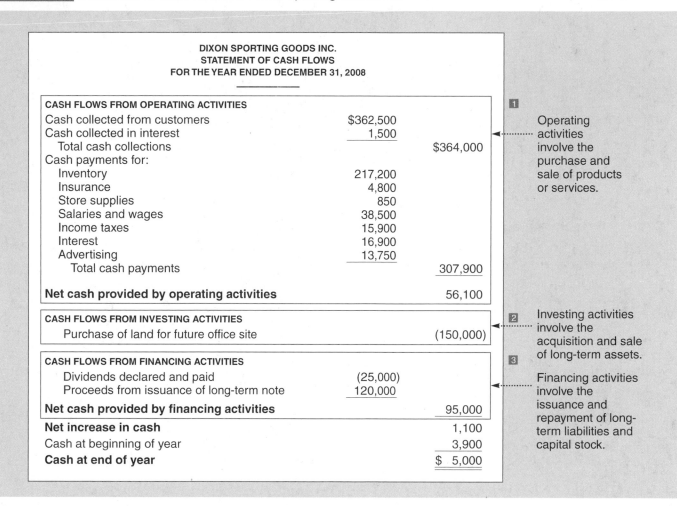

DIXON SPORTING GOODS INC.
STATEMENT OF CASH FLOWS
FOR THE YEAR ENDED DECEMBER 31, 2008

CASH FLOWS FROM OPERATING ACTIVITIES		
Cash collected from customers	$362,500	
Cash collected in interest	1,500	
Total cash collections		$364,000
Cash payments for:		
Inventory	217,200	
Insurance	4,800	
Store supplies	850	
Salaries and wages	38,500	
Income taxes	15,900	
Interest	16,900	
Advertising	13,750	
Total cash payments		307,900
Net cash provided by operating activities		56,100
CASH FLOWS FROM INVESTING ACTIVITIES		
Purchase of land for future office site		(150,000)
CASH FLOWS FROM FINANCING ACTIVITIES		
Dividends declared and paid	(25,000)	
Proceeds from issuance of long-term note	120,000	
Net cash provided by financing activities		95,000
Net increase in cash		1,100
Cash at beginning of year		3,900
Cash at end of year		$ 5,000

1 Operating activities involve the purchase and sale of products or services.

2 Investing activities involve the acquisition and sale of long-term assets.

3 Financing activities involve the issuance and repayment of long-term liabilities and capital stock.

OTHER ELEMENTS OF AN ANNUAL REPORT

No two annual reports look the same. The appearance of an annual report depends not only on the size of a company but also on the budget devoted to the preparation of the report. Some companies publish "bare-bones" annual reports, whereas others issue a glossy report complete with pictures of company products and employees. In recent years, many companies, as a cost-cutting measure, have scaled back the amount spent on the annual report. The creativity in annual reports varies as well. For example, a recent annual report for *Reader's Digest* gave the appearance in size of the well-recognized publication itself.

Privately held companies tend to distribute only financial statements, without the additional information normally included in the annual reports of public companies. For the annual reports of public companies, however, certain basic elements are considered standard. A letter to the shareholders from either the president or the chairman of the board of directors appears in the first few pages of most annual reports. A section describing the company's products and markets is usually included. At the heart of any annual report is the financial report or review, which consists of the financial statements accompanied by notes to explain various items on the statements.

On the next page, Exhibit 2-8 presents a statement by the financial executives of CN in which they accept responsibility for the internal controls over financial reporting and the approval they received from the auditors for these controls.

LO 6 Identify other components of an annual report and their usefulness.

http://www.rd.com

Exhibit 2-8 Management Report

Management is responsible for establishing and maintaining adequate internal control over financial reporting. Internal control over financial reporting is a process designed to provide reasonable assurance regarding the reliability of financial reporting and the preparation of financial statements for external purposes in accordance with generally accepted accounting principles. Because of its inherent limitations, internal control over financial reporting may not prevent or detect misstatements.

Management has assessed the effectiveness of the Company's internal control over financial reporting as of December 31, 2007 using the criteria set forth by the Committee of Sponsoring Organizations of the Treadway Commission (COSO) in Internal Control – Integrated Framework. Based on this assessment, management has determined that the Company's internal control over financial reporting was effective as of December 31, 2007.

KPMG LLP, an independent registered public accounting firm, has issued an unqualified audit report on the effectiveness of the Company's internal control over financial reporting as of December 31, 2007 and has also expressed an unqualified opinion on the Company's 2007 consolidated financial statements as stated in their Reports of Independent Registered Public Accounting Firm dated February 11, 2008.

(signed)
E. Hunter Harrison
President and Chief Executive Officer

February 11, 2008

(signed)
Claude Mongeau
Executive Vice-President and Chief Financial Officer

February 11, 2008

This excerpt from CN'S 2007 Annual Report appears courtesy of CN. This section of the CN Annual Report appears in the Appendix of this textbook.

Exhibit 2-9 presents the auditors' statement of their responsibility for the financial statements based on the audit review they have conducted.

Besides these two important testimonials as to the reliability of the financial statements, the MD&A section of the annual report—a portion of which was illustrated at the beginning of this chapter (and which is presented in detail in Appendix A)—provides a variety of financial highlights and management decisions (termed strategies). Also described are financial risks, financing activities, labour negotiations, and regulation, as well as operating risks such as injury claims and environmental claims.

Careful reading of MD&A and other disclosures can provide information that is not offered in the financial statements because it does not satisfy the recognition rules of accounting. The same sections can also suggest the underlying views and attitudes of management toward the financial statements.

Notes to Consolidated Financial Statements   The sentence "See accompanying notes to the consolidated financial statements" appears at the bottom of each of CN's four financial statements. These comments, or *notes,* as they are commonly called, are necessary to satisfy the need for *full disclosure* of all the facts relevant to a company's results and financial position. The first note in all annual reports is a summary of

Exhibit 2-9 Report of Independent Registered Public Accounting Firm

To the Board of Directors and Shareholders of Canadian National Railway Company

We have audited the accompanying consolidated balance sheets of Canadian National Railway Company (the "Company") as of December 31, 2007 and 2006, and the related consolidated statements of income, comprehensive income, changes in shareholders' equity and cash flows for each of the years in the three-year period ended December 31, 2007. These consolidated financial statements are the responsibility of the Company's management. Our responsibility is to express an opinion on these consolidated financial statements based on our audits.

We conducted our audits in accordance with Canadian generally accepted auditing standards and with the standards of the Public Company Accounting Oversight Board (United States). Those standards require that we plan and perform the audit to obtain reasonable assurance about whether the financial statements are free of material misstatement. An audit includes examining, on a test basis, evidence supporting the amounts and disclosures in the financial statements. An audit also includes assessing the accounting principles used and significant estimates made by management, as well as evaluating the overall financial statement presentation. We believe that our audits provide a reasonable basis for our opinion.

In our opinion, the consolidated financial statements referred to above present fairly, in all material respects, the financial position of the Company as of December 31, 2007 and 2006, and the results of its operations and its cash flows for each of the years in the three-year period ended December 31, 2007, in conformity with generally accepted accounting principles in the United States.

We also have audited, in accordance with the standards of the Public Company Accounting Oversight Board (United States), the Company's internal control over financial reporting as of December 31, 2007, based on criteria established in Internal Control – Integrated Framework issued by the Committee of Sponsoring Organizations of the Treadway Commission (COSO), and our report dated February 11, 2008 expressed an unqualified opinion on the effectiveness of the Company's internal control over financial reporting.

(signed)
KPMG LLP
Chartered Accountants

Montreal, Canada
February 11, 2008

This excerpt from CN'S 2007 Annual Report appears courtesy of CN. This section of the CN Annual Report appears in the Appendix of this textbook.

significant accounting policies. A company's policies for consolidating other companies, recognizing revenues, dealing with foreign currency (particularly U.S. dollars), and treating receivables, materials, properties, and other financial statement items are described.

This completes our discussion of the makeup of the annual report. By now you should appreciate the flexibility that companies have in assembling the report, aside from the need to follow generally accepted accounting principles in preparing the statements. The accounting standards followed in preparing the statements, as well as the appearance of the annual report itself, differ in other countries. As has been noted elsewhere, although many corporations operate internationally, accounting principles are far from being standardized.

The Ethical Responsibility of Management and the Auditors The management of a company and its auditors share a common purpose: to protect the interests of shareholders. In large corporations, the shareholders are normally removed from the daily affairs of the business. The need for a professional management team to run the business is a practical necessity, as is the need for a periodic audit of the company's records.

Because shareholders cannot run the business themselves, they need assurances that the business is being operated effectively and efficiently and that the financial statements presented by management are a fair representation of the company's operations and financial position. The management and the auditors have a very important ethical responsibility to their constituents, the shareholders of the company.

Chapter Highlights

1. **LO 1** **Describe the objectives of financial reporting (p. 52)**

The primary objective of financial reporting is to provide information that is useful in making investment, credit, and similar decisions.

- Investors and creditors are ultimately interested in their own prospective cash receipts from dividends or interest and the proceeds from the sale, redemption, or maturity of securities or loans. Because these expected cash flows are related to the expected cash flows of the company, its cash flows are of interest to investors and creditors. The entity's economic resources, claims to them, and the effects of transactions that change resources and claims to those resources are also of interest.

- Financial information should be *understandable* to those who are willing to spend the time to understand it. To be useful, the information should be *relevant* and *reliable*. *Relevant* information has the capacity to make a difference in a decision. *Reliable* information can be depended on to represent the economic events that it purports to represent.

- *Comparability* is the quality that allows for comparisons to be made between two or more companies, whereas *consistency* is the quality that allows for comparisons to be made within a single company from one period to the next. These two qualities of useful accounting information are aided by full disclosure—in the notes to the financial statements—of all relevant information.

2. **LO 2** **Explain the concept and purpose of a classified balance sheet and prepare the statement (p. 58)**

- The operating cycle depends to a large extent on the nature of a company's business. For a retailer, it encompasses the period of time from the investment of cash in inventory to the collection of any account receivable from sale of the product. The operating cycle for a manufacturer is expanded to include the period of time required to convert raw materials into finished products.

- *Current assets* will be realized in cash or sold or consumed during the operating cycle or within one year if the cycle is shorter than one year. Because most businesses have numerous operating cycles within a year, the cutoff for classification as a *current asset* is usually one year. Cash, accounts receivable, inventory, and prepaid expenses are all examples of *current assets*.

- The definition of *current liability* is related to that of *current asset*. A current liability is an obligation that will be satisfied within the operating cycle or within one year if the cycle is shorter than one year. Many liabilities are satisfied by making a cash payment. However, some obligations are settled by rendering a service.

- A classified balance sheet is helpful in evaluating the liquidity of a business. Working capital, the difference between current assets and current liabilities, indicates the buffer of protection for creditors. The current ratio, current assets divided by current liabilities, provides the reader with a relative measure of liquidity.

3. **LO 3** **Explain the components of an income statement (p. 64)**

- All expenses are added together and subtracted from all revenues in a single-step income statement. Profitability analysis includes such measures as the profit margin (the ratio of net income to sales).

4. **LO 4** **Identify the components of the statement of retained earnings and prepare the statement (p. 65).**

- The statement of retained earnings provides a link between the income statement and balance sheet.

   - It explains the changes in retained earnings during the period, of which net income (loss) is an important component.

5. **LO 5** **Identify the components of the statement of cash flows and prepare the statement (p. 66).**

- The statement of cash flows classifies cash inflows and outflows as originating from three activities: operating, investing, and financing.

   - Operating activities are related to the primary purpose of a business.

   - Investing activities are those generally involved with the acquisition and sale of non-current assets.

   - Financing activities are related to the acquisition and repayment of capital that ultimately funds the operations of a business; for example, borrowing or the issuance of shares.

6. **LO 6** **Identify other components of an annual report and their usefulness (p. 67).**

- Annual reports contain more information than just the financial statements. This information can be used alone or in conjunction with the financial statements to gain a more complete financial picture of a company.

  ○ Management's discussion and Analysis provides explanatory comments about certain results reflected in the financial statements and sometimes forward-looking commentary.

  ○ The Report of Independent Accountants is provided by the company's auditor, whose job it is to express an opinion on whether the financial statements fairly represent the accounting treatment of a company's economic activity for the year.

  ○ Notes to the Consolidated Financial Statements are generally supplementary disclosures required by GAAP that help to explain detail behind the accounting treatment of certain items in the financial statements.

Ratio Review

Working Capital = Current Assets (balance sheet) – Current Liabilities (balance sheet)

$$\text{Current Ratio} = \frac{\text{Current Assets (balance sheet)}}{\text{Current Liabilities (balance sheet)}}$$

$$\text{Profit Margin} = \frac{\text{Net Income (income statement)}}{\text{Sales or Revenues (income statement)}}$$

Key Terms Quiz

Read each definition below and then write the number of that definition in the blank beside the appropriate term it defines. The quiz solutions appear at the end of the chapter.

_____ Understandability   _____ Operating cycle

_____ Relevance   _____ Current asset

_____ Reliability   _____ Current liability

_____ Comparability   _____ Liquidity

_____ Depreciation   _____ Working capital

_____ Consistency   _____ Current ratio

_____ Materiality   _____ Single-step income statement

_____ Conservatism   _____ Profit margin

1. An income statement in which all expenses are added together and subtracted from all revenues.

2. The magnitude of an omission or misstatement in accounting information that will affect the judgment of someone relying on the information.

3. The capacity of information to make a difference in a decision.

4. The practice of using the least optimistic estimate when two estimates of amounts are about equally likely.

5. The quality of accounting information that makes it comprehensible to those willing to spend the necessary time.

6. Current assets divided by current liabilities.

7. The quality of accounting information that makes it dependable in representing the events that it purports to represent.

8. An obligation that will be satisfied within the next operating cycle or within one year if the cycle is shorter than one year.

9. The period of time between the purchase of inventory and the collection of any receivable from the sale of the inventory.

10. Current assets minus current liabilities.

11. Net income divided by sales.

12. The quality of accounting information that allows a user to analyze two or more companies and look for similarities and differences.

13. An asset that is expected to be realized in cash or sold or consumed during the operating cycle or within one year if the cycle is shorter than one year.

14. The ability of a company to pay its debts as they come due.

15. The quality of accounting information that allows a user to compare two or more accounting periods for a single company.

16. The allocation of the cost of a tangible, long-term asset over its useful life.

Answers on p. 89.

Alternate Terms

Balance sheet Statement of financial position or condition

Capital stock Contributed capital

Income statement Statement of income

Income tax expense Provision for income taxes

Long-term assets Non-current assets

Long-term liability Long-term debt

Net income Profits or earnings

Report of independent accountants Auditors' report

Retained earnings Earned capital

Shareholders' equity Stockholders' equity

Warmup Exercises and Solutions

Warmup Exercise 2-1 *Identifying Ratios* **LO 2, 3**

State the equation for each of the following ratios:

1. Current ratio

2. Profit margin

Key to the Solution Review the various ratios as discussed in the chapter.

Warmup Exercise 2-2 *Calculating Ratios* **LO 3**

Bridger reported net income of $150,000, sales of $1,000,000, and cost of goods sold of $800,000.

Required

Compute the profit margin for Bridger.

Key to the Solution Recall the equation for the ratio as presented in the chapter.

Warmup Exercise 2-3 *Determining Liquidity* **LO 2**

Big has current assets of $500,000 and current liabilities of $400,000. Small reports current assets of $80,000 and current liabilities of $20,000.

Required

Which company is more liquid? Why?

Key to the Solution Calculate the current ratio for each company and compare the two figures.

Solutions to Warmup Exercises

Warmup Exercise 2-1

1. $$\text{Current ratio} = \frac{\text{Current Assets}}{\text{Current Liabilities}}$$

2. $$\text{Profit margin} = \frac{\text{Net Income}}{\text{Sales}}$$

Warmup Exercise 2-2

$$\frac{\$150,000}{\$1,000,000} = 15\%$$

Warmup Exercise 2-3

Small appears on the surface to be more liquid. Its current ratio of $80,000/$20,000, or 4 to 1, is significantly higher than Big's current ratio of $500,000/$400,000, or 1.25 to 1.

Review Problem and Solution

Shown below are items taken from the records of Grizzly Inc., a chain of outdoor recreational stores in Alberta. Use the items to prepare two statements. First, prepare an income statement for the year ended December 31, 2008. The income statement should be in single-step form. Second, prepare a classified balance sheet at December 31, 2008. All amounts are in thousands of dollars.

Accounts payable	$ 6,500
Accounts receivable	8,200
Accumulated depreciation—buildings	25,000
Accumulated depreciation—furniture and fixtures	15,000
Advertising expense	3,100
Buildings	80,000
Capital stock, 10,000 no par shares issued and outstanding	50,000
Cash	2,400
Commissions expense	8,600
Cost of goods sold	110,000
Depreciation on buildings	2,500
Depreciation on furniture and fixtures	1,200
Furniture and fixtures	68,000
Income taxes payable	2,200
Income tax expense	13,000
Insurance expense	2,000
Interest expense	12,000
Interest payable	1,000
Interest revenue	2,000
Land	100,000
Long-term notes payable, due December 31, 2016	120,000
Merchandise inventories	6,000
Office supplies	900
Prepaid rent	3,000
Rent expense for salespersons' autos	9,000
Retained earnings	48,800
Salaries and wages for office staff	11,000
Sales revenue	190,000

Solution to Review Problem

1. Single-step income statement:

GRIZZLY INC.
INCOME STATEMENT
FOR THE YEAR ENDED DECEMBER 31, 2008
(IN THOUSANDS OF DOLLARS)

Sales revenue	$190,000	
Interest revenue	2,000	
Total revenues		$19,200
Expenses		
Cost of goods sold	110,000	
Advertising expense	3,100	
Depreciation on furniture and fixtures	1,200	
Rent expense for salespersons' autos	9,000	
Commissions expense	8,600	
Depreciation on buildings	2,500	
Insurance expense	2,000	
Salaries and wages for office staff	11,000	
Interest expense	12,000	
Income tax expense	13,000	
Total expenses		172,400
Net income		$ 19,600

(continued)

2. Classified balance sheet:

GRIZZLY INC.
BALANCE SHEET
AT DECEMBER 31, 2008
(IN THOUSANDS OF DOLLARS)

Assets

Current assets:			
Cash		$ 2,400	
Accounts receivable		8,200	
Merchandise inventories		6,000	
Office supplies		900	
Prepaid rent		3,000	
Total current assets			$ 20,500
Property, plant, and equipment:			
Land		100,000	
Buildings	$ 80,000		
Less: Accumulated depreciation	25,000	55,000	
Furniture and fixtures	68,000		
Less: Accumulated depreciation	15,000	53,000	
Total property, plant, and equipment			208,000
Total assets			$228,500

Liabilities

Current liabilities:			
Accounts payable		$ 6,500	
Income taxes payable		2,200	
Interest payable		1,000	
Total current liabilities			$ 9,700
Long-term notes payable, due December 31, 2016			120,000
Total liabilities			129,700

Shareholders' Equity

Contributed capital:			
Capital stock, 10,000 no par shares issued and outstanding		50,000	
Retained earnings		48,800	
Total shareholders' equity			98,800
Total liabilities and shareholders' equity			$228,500

Questions

1. How would you evaluate the following statement: "The cash flows to a company are irrelevant to an investor; all the investor cares about is the potential for receiving dividends on the investment"?

2. A key characteristic of useful financial information is understandability. How does this qualitative characteristic relate to the background of the user of the information?

3. What does *relevance* mean with regard to the use of accounting information?

4. What is the qualitative characteristic of comparability, and why is it important in preparing financial statements?

5. What is the difference between comparability and consistency as they relate to the use of accounting information?

6. How does the concept of materiality relate to the size of a company?

7. How does the operating cycle of a retailer differ from that of a service company?

8. How does the concept of the operating cycle relate to the definition of a current asset?

9. What are two examples of how the way a company's intent in using an asset affects the classification of an asset on the balance sheet?

10. How would you evaluate the following statement: "A note payable with an original maturity of five years will be classified on the balance sheet as a long-term liability until it matures"?

11. How do the two basic forms of owners' equity items for a corporation—capital stock and retained earnings—differ?

12. What are the limitations of working capital as a measure of the liquidity of a business as opposed to the current ratio?

13. What is meant by a company's capital structure?

14. What is the major weakness of the single-step form for the income statement?

15. Why might a company's sales increase from one year to the next but its profit margin ratio decrease?

16. How does a statement of retained earnings act as a link between an income statement and a balance sheet?

17. In auditing the financial statements of a company, does the auditor *certify* that the statements are totally accurate and without errors of any size or variety?

18. What is the first note in the annual report of all publicly held companies, and what is its purpose?

---------- *Exercises* ----------

Exercise 2-1 *Characteristics of Useful Accounting Information* LO 1

Fill in the blank with the qualitative characteristic for each of the following descriptions:

_____ 1. Information that users can depend on to represent the events that it purports to represent

_____ 2. Information that has the capacity to make a difference in a decision

_____ 3. Information that is valid, that indicates an agreement between the underlying data and the events represented

_____ 4. Information that allows for comparisons to be made from one accounting period to the next

_____ 5. Information that is free from error

_____ 6. Information that is meaningful to those who are willing to learn to use it properly

_____ 7. Information that is not slanted to portray a company's position any better or worse than the circumstances warrant

_____ 8. Information that allows for comparisons to be made between or among companies

Exercise 2-2 *Classification of Assets and Liabilities* LO 2

Indicate the appropriate classification of each of the following as a current asset (CA), non-current asset (NCA), current liability (CL), or long-term liability (LTL):

_____ 1. Inventory

_____ 2. Accounts payable

_____ 3. Cash

_____ 4. Patents

_____ 5. Notes payable, due in six months

_____ 6. Taxes payable

_____ 7. Prepaid rent (for the next nine months)

_____ 8. Bonds payable, due in 10 years

_____ 9. Machinery

Exercise 2-3 *Income Statement Ratios* LO 3

The 2008 income statement of Amina Enterprises shows net income of $90,000, comprising net sales of $296,600, cost of goods sold of $107,840, selling expenses of $36,620, and general and administrative expenses of $33,980, and interest expense of $1,160. Amina's shareholders' equity was $560,000 at the beginning of the year and $640,000 at the end of the year. The company has 40,000 shares outstanding at December 31, 2008.

Required

Compute Amina's profit margin. What other information would you need to be able to comment on whether this ratio is favourable?

Exercise 2-4 *Statement of Retained Earnings* **LO 4, 6**

Ottawa Corporation was organized on January 2, 2006, with the investment of $50,000 by each of its two shareholders. Net income for its first year of business was $42,600. Net income increased during 2007 to $62,660 and to $72,740 during 2008. Ottawa paid $10,000 in dividends to each of the two shareholders in each of the three years.

Required

Prepare a statement of retained earnings for the year ended December 31, 2008.

Exercise 2-5 *Components of the Statement of Cash Flows* **LO 5**

From the following list, identify each item as operating (O), investing (I), financing (F), or not on the statement of cash flows (N):

_____ 1. Paid for supplies

_____ 2. Collected cash from customers

_____ 3. Purchased land (held for resale)

_____ 4. Purchased land (for construction of new building)

_____ 5. Paid dividend

_____ 6. Issued shares

_____ 7. Purchased computers (for use in the business)

_____ 8. Sold old equipment

Exercise 2-6 *Basic Elements of Financial Statements* **LO 6**

Most annual reports contain the following list of basic elements. For each element, identify the person(s) who prepared the element and describe the information a user would expect to find in each element. Some information is verifiable; other information is subjectively chosen by management. Comment on the verifiability of information in each element.

1. Management's report
2. Product/markets of company
3. Financial statements
4. Notes to financial statements
5. Independent accountants' report

Multi-Concept Exercises

Exercise 2-7 *Financial Statement Classification* **LO 2, 3, 4**

Potential shareholders and lenders are interested in a company's financial statements. For the list below, identify the statement—balance sheet (BS), income statement (IS), retained earnings statement (RE)—on which each item would appear.

_____ 1. Accounts payable

_____ 2. Accounts receivable

_____ 3. Advertising expense

_____ 4. Bad debt expense

_____ 5. Bonds payable

_____ 6. Buildings

_____ 7. Cash

_____ 8. Common stock

_____ 9. Deferred income taxes

_____ 10. Depreciation expense

_____ 11. Dividends

_____ 12. Land held for future expansion

_____ 13. Loss on the sale of equipment

_____ 14. Office supplies

_____ 15. Organizational costs

_____ 16. Patent amortization expense

_____ 17. Retained earnings

_____ 18. Sales

_____ 19. Unearned revenue

_____ 20. Utilities expense

Problem 2-1 *Materiality* LO 1

Joe Howe, a new accountant, wanted to impress his boss, so he stayed late one night to analyze the office supplies expense. He determined the cost by month, for the past 12 months, of each of the following: computer paper, copy paper, fax paper, pencils and pens, note pads, postage, stationery, and miscellaneous items.

1. What did Joe think his boss would learn from this information? What action might be taken as a result of knowing it?
2. Would this information be more relevant if Joe worked for an electronics store or for a real estate sales company? Discuss.

Problem 2-2 *Costs and Expenses* LO 1

The following costs are incurred by a retailer:

1. Display fixtures in a retail store
2. Advertising
3. Merchandise for sale
4. Incorporation (i.e., legal costs, share issue costs)
5. Cost of a franchise
6. Office supplies
7. Wages in a restaurant
8. Computer software
9. Computer hardware

Required

For each of these costs, explain whether all of the cost or only a portion of the cost would appear as an expense on the income statement for the period in which the cost was incurred. If not all of the cost would appear on the income statement for that period, explain why not.

Problem 2-3 *Classified Balance Sheet* LO 2

The following balance sheet items, listed in alphabetical order, are available from the records of Rod Ltd. Corporation at December 31, 2008:

Accounts payable	$ 54,765
Accounts receivable	70,350
Accumulated depreciation—automobiles	67,500
Accumulated depreciation— buildings	120,000
Automobiles	337,500
Bonds payable, due December 31, 2012	480,000
Buildings	600,000
Capital stock, 30,000 no par shares	600,000
Cash	39,690
Income taxes payable	18,600
Interest payable	4,500
Inventory	137,190
Land	750,000
Long-term investments	255,000
Notes payable, due June 30, 2009	30,000
Office supplies	7,020
Patents	120,000
Prepaid rent	4,500
Retained earnings	933,285
Salaries and wages payable	12,600

(continued)

Required

1. Prepare in good form a classified balance sheet as of December 31, 2008.

2. Compute Rod's current ratio.

3. On the basis of your answer to requirement 2, does Rod appear to be *liquid?* What other information do you need to fully answer this question?

Problem 2-4 *Financial Statement Ratios* LO 2

The following items are available from the records of Quick Ltd. as of December 31, 2008 and 2007:

	December 31, 2008	December 31, 2007
Accounts payable	$ 4,200	$ 2,600
Accounts receivable	6,615	9,785
Cash	5,100	4,725
Cleaning supplies	225	350
Interest payable	0	600
Inventory	12,300	13,100
Temporary investments	3,125	2,510
Note payable, due in six months	0	6,000
Prepaid rent	1,800	2,400
Taxes payable	725	615
Wages payable	600	800

Required

1. Calculate the following, as of December 31, 2008, and December 31, 2007:

   a. Working capital

   b. Current ratio

2. On the basis of your answers to requirement **1**, comment on the relative liquidity of the company at the beginning and the end of the year. As part of your answer, explain the change in the company's liquidity from the beginning to the end of 2008.

Problem 2-5 *Working Capital and Current Ratio* LO 2

The balance sheet of Marlene Ltd. includes the following items:

Cash	$ 46,000
Accounts receivable	26,000
Inventory	90,000
Prepaid insurance	1,600
Land	160,000
Accounts payable	109,800
Salaries payable	2,400
Capital stock	200,000
Retained earnings	11,400

Required

1. Determine the current ratio and working capital.

2. Beyond the information provided in your answers to requirement **1**, what does the composition of the current assets tell you about Marlene's liquidity?

3. What other information do you need to fully assess Marlene's liquidity?

Problem 2-6 *Single-Step Income Statement* LO 3

The following income statement items, arranged in alphabetical order, are taken from the records of Simcoe Company for the year ended December 31, 2008:

Advertising expense	$ 4,500
Commissions expense	7,245
Cost of goods sold	87,600
Depreciation expense—office building	8,700
Income tax expense	4,620

Insurance expense—salesperson's auto	6,750
Interest expense	4,200
Interest revenue	4,020
Rent revenue	20,100
Salaries and wages expense—office	37,680
Sales revenue	144,900
Supplies expense—office	2,670

Required

1. Prepare a single-step income statement for the year ended December 31, 2008.

2. What weaknesses do you see in this form for the income statement?

Problem 2-7 *Statement of Cash Flows* LO 5

Winnipeg Corporation was organized on January 1, 2008, with the investment of $125,000 in cash by its shareholders. The company immediately purchased an office building for $150,000, paying $105,000 in cash and signing a three-year note for the balance. Winnipeg signed a five-year, $30,000 promissory note at a local bank during 2008 and received cash in the same amount. During its first year, Winnipeg collected $46,985 from its customers. It paid $32,800 for inventory, $10,200 in salaries and wages, and another $1,550 in taxes. Winnipeg paid $2,800 in cash dividends.

Required

1. Prepare a statement of cash flows for the year ended December 31, 2008.

2. What does this statement tell you that an income statement does not?

Problem 2-8 *Basic Elements of Financial Reports* LO 6

Comparative income statements for Edmonton Inc. are presented below.

	2008	2007
Sales	$ 500,000	$250,000
Cost of sales	(250,000)	(150,000)
Operating expenses	(60,000)	(50,000)
Loss on sale of subsidiary	(200,000)	0
Net income (Loss)	$ (10,000)	$ 50,000

Required

The president and management believe that the company performed better in 2008 than it did in 2007. Write the president's letter to be included in the 2008 annual report. Explain why the company is financially sound and why shareholders should not be alarmed by the $10,000 loss in a year when sales have doubled.

Multi-Concept Problems

Problem 2-9 *Comparing Loblaw and Sobeys* LO 1, 2

The following current items, listed in alphabetical order, are taken from the consolidated balance sheet of **Loblaw** and **Sobeys**:

http://www.loblaw.ca
http://www.sobeys.com/corporate

Loblaw

Accounts payable and accrued liabilities	$2,598
Accounts receivable	728
Bank indebtedness	1
Cash and cash equivalents	669
Commercial paper (current liability)	647
Inventories	2,037
Long-term debt due within one year	27
Prepaid expenses and other assets	187
Short-term investments	327

(continued)

Sobeys

Accounts payable and accrued liabilities	$1,158.8
Cash and cash equivalents	332.1
Future tax liabilities (current liability)	46.1
Inventories	626.8
Other current assets	21.7
Prepaid expenses	45.9
Receivables	208.2
Long-term debt due within one year	25.0

Required

1. Compute working capital and the current ratio for both companies.

2. On the basis of your answers to requirement **1** above, which company appears to be more liquid?

3. As you know, other factors affect a company's liquidity in addition to its working capital and current ratio. Comment on the *composition* of each company's current assets and how this composition affects its liquidity.

Problem 2-10 *Classified Balance Sheet, Single-Step Income Statement, and Statement of Retained Earnings* **LO 2, 3, 4**

In alphabetical order, the following items are taken from Cable's 2008 consolidated financial statements:

(thousands)	2008
Accounts payable	$ 1,164.6
Accounts receivable, net	2,055.9
Cash and cash equivalents	613.2
Cash dividends	1,211.7
Common stock	617.4
Cost of goods sold	9,981.0
Current maturities of long-term debt	2,703.3
Income taxes (expense)	840.0
Interest expense	412.5
Inventories	1,331.4
Long-term debt	2,127.6
Net sales	20,864.1
Notes payable (current liability)	1,455.6
Other assets (long-term assets)	2,287.8
Other current assets	819.9
Other current liabilities	2,154.3
Other income, net	46.2
Other liabilities (long-term liabilities)	2,391.0
Property, net	7,580.7
Restructuring charges (operating expense)	259.5
Retained earnings, beginning of year	1,523.7
Selling, general, and administrative expense	7,654.2

(NOTE: The descriptions in parentheses are not part of the items but have been added to provide you with hints as you complete this problem.)

Required

1. Prepare an income statement for Cable for the year ended December 31, 2008.

2. Prepare a statement of retained earnings for Cable for the year ended December 31, 2008.

3. Prepare a classified balance sheet for Cable at December 31, 2008.

Problem 2-11 *Using Cable's Classified Balance Sheet and Single-Step Income Statement* **LO 2, 3**

(Note: Consider completing this problem after Problem 2-10 to ensure that you have the various items on the financial statements properly classified.)

Refer to the information set forth in Problem 2-10.

Required

1. Compute Cable's working capital and its current ratio at December 31, 2008.

2. Does Cable appear to be liquid? What other factors need to be considered in answering this question?

3. Compute Cable's profit margin for 2008.

4. As a Cable shareholder, would you be satisfied with the company's profit margin? What other factors need to be considered in answering this question?

Problem 2-12 *Cash Flow* LO 1, 2, 5

Victoria Co., a specialty retailer, has a history of paying quarterly dividends of $0.50 per share. Management is trying to determine whether the company will have adequate cash on December 31, 2008, to pay a dividend if one is declared by the board of directors. The following additional information is available:

- All sales are on account, and accounts receivable are collected one month after the sale. Sales volume has been increasing 5% each month.

- All purchases of merchandise are on account, and accounts payable are paid one month after the purchase. Cost of sales is 40% of the sales price. Inventory levels are maintained at $37,500.

- Operating expenses in addition to the mortgage are paid in cash. They amount to $1,500 per month and are paid as they are incurred.

VICTORIA CO.
BALANCE SHEET
SEPTEMBER 30, 2008

Cash	$ 2,500	Accounts payable	$ 2,500
Accounts receivable	6,250	Mortgage note†	75,000
Inventory	37,500	Common stock—25,000 no par	25,000
Note receivable*	5,000	Retained earnings	33,250
Building/land	84,500	Total liabilities	
Total assets	$135,750	and shareholders' equity	$135,750

*Note receivable represents a one-year, 5% interest-bearing note, due November 1, 2008.
†Mortgage note is a 30-year, 7% note due in monthly installments of $600.

Required

Determine the cash that Victoria will have available to pay a dividend on December 31, 2008. Round all amounts to the nearest dollar. What can Victoria's management do to increase the cash available? Should management recommend that the board of directors declare a dividend?

Problem 2-13 *Components of an Annual Report* LO 6

Refer to Exhibits 2-8 and 2-9 contained in this chapter.

Required:

1. On what basis did the financial officers of **CN** assert that the annual report information was reliable?

2. What did the auditors, KPMG LLP, certify and how did they gain their assurance?

CN
http://www.cn.ca

—— Alternate Problems ——

Problem 2-1A *Materiality* LO 1

Dale Coates, a new accountant, wanted to impress his boss, so he stayed late one night to analyze the long-distance calls by area code and time of day placed. He determined the monthly cost, for the past 12 months, by hour and area code called.

Required

1. What did Dale think his boss would learn from this information? What action might be taken as a result of knowing it?

2. Would this information be more relevant if Dale worked for a hardware store or for a real estate company? Discuss.

Problem 2-2A *Costs and Expenses* **LO 1**

The following costs are incurred by a retailer:

1. Scanner systems in a retail store
2. An ad in the yellow pages
3. An inventory-control computer software system
4. Shipping merchandise for resale to chain outlets

For each of these costs, explain whether all of the cost or only a portion of the cost would appear as an expense on the income statement for the period in which the cost is incurred. If not all of the cost would appear on the income statement for that period, explain why not.

Problem 2-3A *Classified Balance Sheet* **LO 2**

The following balance sheet items, listed in alphabetical order, are available from the records of Saskatoon Company at December 31, 2008.

Accounts payable	$ 25,710
Accounts receivable	20,025
Accumulated depreciation—buildings	30,000
Accumulated depreciation—equipment	9,375
Bonds payable, due December 31, 2014	187,500
Buildings	112,500
Capital stock, 200,000 no par	206,250
Cash	45,592
Equipment	63,375
Income taxes payable	5,625
Interest payable	1,650
Land	187,500
Merchandise inventory	84,675
Notes payable, due April 15, 2009	4,875
Office supplies	300
Patents	33,750
Prepaid rent	2,700
Retained earnings	85,132
Salaries payable	5,550
Temporary investments	11,250

Required

1. Prepare a classified balance sheet as of December 31, 2008.
2. Compute Saskatoon's current ratio.
3. On the basis of your answer to requirement **2**, does Saskatoon appear to be *liquid?* What other information do you need to fully answer this question?

Problem 2-4A *Financial Statement Ratios* **LO 2**

The following items, in alphabetical order, are available from the records of Quaker Corporation as of December 31, 2008 and 2007.

	December 31, 2008	December 31, 2007
Accounts payable	$5,250	$ 3,250
Accounts receivable	8,250	13,000
Cash	6,375	5,900
Interest receivable	100	0
Note receivable, due 12/31/2010	6,000	6,000
Office supplies	450	550
Prepaid insurance	200	125
Salaries payable	900	400
Taxes payable	5,000	2,900

Required

1. Calculate the following, as of December 31, 2008, and December 31, 2007:
   a. Working capital
   b. Current ratio

2. On the basis of your answers to requirement **1**, comment on the relative liquidity of the company at the beginning and the end of the year. As part of your answer, explain the change in the company's liquidity from the beginning to the end of 2008.

Problem 2-5A *Working Capital and Current Ratio* LO 2

The balance sheet of Moncton Ltd. includes the following items:

Cash	$ 46,000
Accounts receivable	86,000
Inventory	150,000
Prepaid insurance	5,600
Land	160,000
Accounts payable	169,800
Salaries payable	6,400
Capital stock	200,000
Retained earnings	71,400

Required

1. Determine the current ratio and working capital.

2. Moncton appears to have a positive current ratio and a large net working capital. Why would it have trouble paying bills as they come due?

3. Suggest three things that Moncton can do to help pay its bills on time.

Problem 2-6A *Single-Step Income Statement* LO 3

The following income statement items, arranged in alphabetical order, are taken from the records of Cold Lake Co., a software sales firm, for the year ended December 31, 2008:

Advertising expense	$ 18,000
Cost of goods sold	300,000
Depreciation expense—computer	9,000
Dividend revenue	5,400
Income tax expense	61,400
Interest expense	3,800
Rent expense—office	52,800
Rent expense—salespersons' autos	36,000
Sales revenue	700,000
Supplies expense—office	2,600
Utilities expense	13,500
Wages expense—office	91,200

Required

1. Prepare a single-step income statement for the year ended December 31, 2008.

2. What weaknesses do you see in this form for the income statement?

Problem 2-7A *Statement of Cash Flows* LO 5

Regina Ltd. was organized on January 1, 2008, with the investment of $200,000 in cash by its shareholders. The company immediately purchased a manufacturing facility for $150,000, paying $75,000 in cash and signing a five-year note for the balance. Regina signed another five-year note for $25,000 during 2008 and received cash for the same amount. During its first year, Regina collected $155,000 from its customers. It paid $92,500 for inventory, $15,050 in salaries and wages, and another $20,000 in taxes. Regina paid $2,000 in cash dividends.

Required

1. Prepare a statement of cash flows for the year ended December 31, 2008.

2. What does this statement tell you that an income statement does not?

Problem 2-8A *Basic Elements of Financial Reports* LO 6

Comparative income statements for Theodore Inc. are presented below:

	2008	2007
Sales	$ 500,000	$250,000
Cost of sales	(250,000)	(150,000)
Operating expenses	(60,000)	(50,000)
Gain on the sale of subsidiary	0	200,000
Net income	$ 190,000	$250,000

Required

The president and management believe that the company performed better in 2008 than it did in 2007. Write the president's letter to be included in the 2008 annual report. Explain why the company is financially sound and why shareholders should not be alarmed by the reduction in income in a year when sales have doubled.

Alternate Multi-Concept Problems

Problem 2-9A *Comparing Nortel and RIM* LO 1, 2

http://www.nortel.com
http://www.rim.com

The following current items are taken from the consolidated balance sheets of **Nortel** and **RIM**

Nortel

Trade and other accounts payable	$1,077
Cash and cash equivalents	3,128
Inventories	2,094
Other assets (current)	1,134
Other liabilities (current)	4,707
Accounts receivable, net	2,538
Long-term debt due within one year	697

RIM

Accounts payable	$ 230
Trade receivables	1,037
Accrued and other (current liabilities)	905
Cash and cash equivalents	1,190
Inventories	340
Other (current assets)	273
Short-term investments	407
Current portion of long-term debt	0

(NOTE: the descriptions in parentheses are not part of the items but have been added to provide you with assistance as you complete this problem.)

Required

1. Compute working capital and the current ratio for both companies.

2. On the basis of your answers to requirement 1 above, which company appears to be more liquid?

3. As you know, other factors affect a company's liquidity in addition to its working capital and current ratio. Comment on the *composition* of each company's current assets and how this composition affects its liquidity.

Problem 2-10A *Comparability and Consistency in Income Statements* LO 1, 3

The following income statements were provided by Camphill Company, a wholesale food distributor:

	2008	2007
Sales	$850,000	$750,000
Cost of sales	306,000	225,000
Sales salaries	213,500	199,000

Delivery expense	90,000	87,500
Office supplies	27,500	27,000
Depreciation—truck	20,000	20,000
Computer line expense	11,500	10,000
Total expenses	668,500	568,500
Net income	$181,500	$181,500

Required

Restate each item in the income statements as a percentage of sales. Why did net income remain unchanged when sales increased in 2008?

Problem 2-11A *Classified Balance Sheet, Single-Step Income Statement, and Statement of Retained Earnings for Westminister* **LO 2, 3, 4**

Shown below, in alphabetical order, are items taken from Westminister's 2008 consolidated financial statements. Westminister Co. has a fiscal year ending September 30.

Accounts receivable, net	$ 1,596.6
Accrued expenses and other liabilities	1,875.0
Cash and cash equivalents	33.8
Cash dividends declared	285.0
Common stock	1,352.6
Cost of sales	36,097.8
Deferred income taxes (noncurrent liability)	274.0
Income taxes (current liability)	173.2
Income tax provision (expense)	1,074.2
Interest expense	6.2
Interest income	10.8
Inventories	6,964.8
Net sales	49,246.0
Other current assets	192.6
Other income	44.2
Other noncurrent assets	189.2
Other noncurrent liabilities	956.0
Property and equipment, at cost, less accumulated depreciation and amortization	8,690.6
Retained earnings, beginning of year	7,575.6
Selling, occupancy, and administration (expense)	10,351.6
Short-term borrowings	881.4
Trade accounts payable	3,093.6

(NOTE: The descriptions in parentheses are not part of the items but have been added to provide you with hints as you complete this problem.)

Required

1. Prepare an income statement for Westminister for the year ended September 30, 2008.
2. Prepare a statement of retained earnings for Westminister for the year ended September 30, 2008.
3. Prepare a classified balance sheet for Westminister at September 30, 2008.

Problem 2-12A *Using Westminister's Classified Balance Sheet and Income Statement* **LO 2, 3**
(**Note:** Consider completing this problem after Problem 2-11A to ensure that you have the various items on the financial statements properly classified.)

Refer to the information set forth in Problem 2-11A.

(continued)

Required

1. Compute Westminister's working capital and its current ratio at September 30, 2008.
2. Does Westminister appear to be liquid? What other factors need to be considered in answering this question?
3. Compute Westminister's profit margin for the year ended September 30, 2008.
4. As a Westminister shareholder, would you be satisfied with the company's profit margin? What other factors need to be considered in answering this question?

Problem 2-13A *Cash Flow* LO 1, 2, 5

Corner Brook Ltd., a consulting service, has a history of paying annual dividends of $1 per share. Management is trying to determine whether the company will have adequate cash on December 31, 2008, to pay a dividend if one is declared by the board of directors. The following additional information is available:

■ All sales are on account, and accounts receivable are collected one month after the sale. Sales volume has been decreasing 5% each month.

■ Operating expenses are paid in cash in the month incurred. Average monthly expenses are $20,000 (excluding the biweekly payroll).

■ Biweekly payroll is $9,000, and it will be paid December 15 and December 31.

■ Unearned revenue is expected to be earned in December. This amount was taken into consideration in the expected sales volume.

CORNER BROOK LTD.
BALANCE SHEET
DECEMBER 1, 2008

Cash	$ 30,000	Unearned revenue	$ 4,000
Accounts receivable	80,000	Note payable*	60,000
Computer equipment	240,000	Common stock—50,000 no par	100,000
		Retained earnings	186,000
		Total liabilities and	
Total assets	$350,000	shareholders' equity	$350,000

The note payable plus 3% interest for six months is due January 15, 2009.

Required

Determine the cash that Corner Brook will have available to pay a dividend on December 31, 2008. Round all amounts to the nearest dollar. Should management recommend that the board of directors declare a dividend?

Problem 2-14A *Management Discussion and Analysis* LO 6

Refer to the MD&A exhibit in the Focus on Financial Results opener to this chapter.

Required

Describe what should appear in the MD&A as presented by CN.

Cases

Reading and Interpreting Financial Statements

Case 2-1 *Bombardier Inc.'s Operating Cycle* LO 2

http://www.bombardier.com

In **Bombardier's** annual report, note 1, "Summary of Significant Accounting Policies," includes the following explanation of Bombardier's inventories:

Inventory valuation

a) Aerospace programs
Inventory, determined under the average cost accounting method..., is recorded at the lower of cost or net recoverable value. It includes raw materials, direct labour and manufacturing overhead.

To the extent that inventory costs are expected to exceed their recoverable amount, charges are recorded in cost of sales to reduce inventoried costs to their estimated recoverable value.

b) Long-term contracts
Long-term contract inventory... includes material, direct labour, manufacturing overhead as well as estimated contract margins.

c) Finished products
Finished product inventories, ... are valued at the lower of cost or net realizable value. The cost of finished products includes the cost of materials, direct labour and related manufacturing overhead...

New and pre-owned aircraft available for sale are valued at the lower of cost or net realizable valuations. The Corporation estimates the net realizable value by using both external and internal aircraft valuations including the sales of similiar aircraft in the secondary market. *

*Extracted from Bombardier Inc. annual report for 2007.

Required

1. Based on the previous notes, describe Bombardier's inventory. That is, what types of items would you expect to find in the inventory of this type of company?

2. Why would Bombardier expect that a portion of its inventoried costs would *not* be realized within one year?

3. Based on your answer to requirement **2** above, should Bombardier classify its inventories as current or as non-current assets? Explain your answer.

Case 2-2 *Comparing Two Companies in the Same Industry: CN and CP* LO 2

Refer to the financial information for CN and **CP** reproduced in Appendixes A and B at the end of the book for the information needed to answer the following questions.

http://www.cpr.ca

Required

1. Compute each company's working capital at the end of 2007 and 2006. Also, for each company, compute the change in working capital from the end of 2006 to the end of 2007.

2. Compute each company's current ratio at the end of 2007 and 2006. Compute the percentage change in the ratio from the end of 2006 to the end of 2007.

3. How do CN and CP differ in terms of the accounts that made up their current assets at the end of 2007? What is the largest current asset each reports on the balance sheet at the end of 2007?

4. On the basis of your answers to requirements 2 and 3 above, which company appears to be the most liquid at the end of 2007? Explain your answer.

Making Financial Decisions

Case 2-3 *Analysis of Cash Flow for a Small Business* LO 5

Kathy, a financial consultant, has been self-employed for two years. Her list of clients has grown, and she is earning a reputation as a shrewd investor. Kathy rents a small office, uses the pool secretarial services, and has purchased a car that she is depreciating over three years. The following income statements cover Kathy's first two years of business:

	Year 1	Year 2
Commissions revenue	$ 50,000	$130,000
Rent	24,000	24,000
Secretarial services	6,000	18,000
Car expenses, gas, insurance	12,000	13,000
Depreciation	30,000	30,000
Net income (Loss)	$(22,000)	$ 45,000

Kathy believes that she should earn more than $23,000 for working very hard for two years. She is thinking about going to work for an investment firm where she can earn $80,000 per year. What would you advise Kathy to do?

Case 2-4 *Factors Involved in an Investment Decision* LO 5

As an investor, you are considering purchasing shares in a fast-food restaurant chain. The annual reports of several companies are available for comparison.

Required

Prepare an outline of the steps you would follow to make your comparison. Start by listing the first section that you would read in the financial reports. What would you expect to find there, and why did you choose that section to read first? Continue with the other sections of the financial report.

Many fast-food chains are owned by large conglomerates. What limitation does this create in your comparison? How would you solve it?

Accounting and Ethics: What Would You Do?

Case 2-5 *The Expenditure Approval Process* LO 1

Robert is the plant superintendent of a small manufacturing company that is owned by a large corporation. The corporation has a policy that any expenditure over $2,000 must be approved by the chief financial officer in the corporate headquarters. The approval process takes a minimum of three weeks. Robert would like to order a new labelling machine that is expected to reduce costs and pay for itself in six months. The machine costs $4,400, but Robert can buy the sales rep's demo unit for $3,600. Robert has asked the sales rep to send two separate bills for $1,800 each.

What would you do if you were the sales rep? Do you agree or disagree with Robert's actions? What do you think about the corporate policy?

Case 2-6 *Apply for a Loan* LO 2, 3

Bill, owner of Bill's Bagels, a drive-through bagel shop, would like to expand his business from its current single location to a chain of bagel shops. Sales in the bagel shop have been increasing an average of 8% each quarter. Profits have been increasing accordingly. Bill is conservative in spending and a very hard worker. He has an appointment with a banker to apply for a loan to expand the business. To prepare for the appointment, he instructs you, as the chief financial officer and payroll clerk, to copy the quarterly income statements for the past two years but not to include a balance sheet. Bill already has a substantial loan from another bank. In fact, he has very little of his own money invested in the business.

What should you do? Do you think the banker will lend Bill more money?

Internet Research Cases

INTERNET

http://www.loblaw.ca

Case 2-7 *Interpreting Loblaw's Inventory* LO 2

Refer to the **Loblaw Companies Limited** balance sheet as of December 30, 2006.

Required

1. What is the amount of Loblaw's inventory at December 30, 2006? Did this amount increase or decrease during 2006?
2. Give some examples of the types of costs you would expect to be included in Loblaw's inventory account.

Case 2-8 *Loblaw* LO 2, 3

You can probably do this from your everyday knowledge, but this is good practice in researching a company using the Internet. Find a website or a source of information that will list the competitors to Loblaw. Choose the top two competitors and answer the following questions.

1. Looking at their balance sheets, what are their total current assets and their total current liabilities? From these numbers, calculate each company's working capital and current ratio. How do they compare to these ratios for Loblaw?
2. From their income statements, calculate their profit margins for the latest year available. How do they compare?

Optional Research: From the financial information available on their websites, what other comparisons can you make about these companies? Based on your research, are the companies themselves comparable, in such areas as size, products, assets, liabilities, and net income? If not, explain five ways in which they differ. Is the financial information itself comparable for the three companies? Explain.

Solutions to Key Terms Quiz

5	Understandability	9	Operating cycle
3	Relevance	13	Current asset
7	Reliability	8	Current liability
12	Comparability	14	Liquidity
16	Depreciation	10	Working capital
15	Consistency	6	Current ratio
2	Materiality	1	Single-step income statement
4	Conservatism	11	Profit margin

Part I Integrative Problem

The following problem will give you the opportunity to apply what you have learned by preparing both an income statement and balance sheet.

Shown below are items taken from the records of Larry's Landscaping. Use the items to prepare two statements. First, prepare an income statement for the year ended December 31, 2008. The income statement should be in single-step form. Second, prepare a classified balance sheet at December 31, 2008. All amounts are in thousands of dollars.

Accounts payable	$ 6,500
Accounts receivable	8,200
Accumulated depreciation—buildings	25,000
Accumulated depreciation—equipment	15,000
Advertising expense	3,100
Buildings	80,000
Capital stock, 10,000 no par shares issued and outstanding	50,000
Cash	2,400
Commisions expense	8,600
Depreciation on buildings	2,500
Depreciation on equipment	1,200
Design revenues	50,000
Equipment	68,000
Income tax expense	13,000
Income taxes payable	2,200
Installation revenue	140,000
Insurance expense	2,000
Interest expense	12,000
Interest payable	1,000
Interest revenue	2,000
Land	100,000
Long-term notes payable, due December 21, 2013	120,000
Office supplies	900
Prepaid rent	3,000
Rent expense for salespersons' autos	9,000
Retained earnings	42,800
Salaries and wages for installation staff	110,000
Salaries and wages for office staff	11,000

COURTESY CN RAIL

Getting Basic Training

A Word to Readers About This Part

The final products of an accounting process are financial statements. The inputs of this process are the events that happen in an organization on a day-to-day basis. This part of the book explains the process from analyzing and recording transactions of a business to the production of financial statements. The knowledge of this process will serve as the foundation for understanding the relevance of the accounting issues discussed in the remainder of the book.

CHAPTER 3

Processing Accounting Information

LEARNING OBJECTIVES

After studying this chapter,
you should be able to:

LO 1   Identify transactions for recording.

LO 2   Analyze the effects of transactions on
the accounting equation.

LO 3   Use double-entry accounting and debits
and credits.

LO 4   Journalize transactions.

LO 5   Post to the ledger and prepare a trial
balance.

COURTESY CN RAIL

STUDY LINKS

A Look at Previous Chapters

Up to this point, we have focused on the
role of accounting in decision making and
the way accountants use financial statements to communicate useful information
to the various users of the statements.

A Look at This Chapter

In this chapter, we consider how
accounting information is processed. We
begin by considering the *inputs* to an
accounting system, that is, the transactions entered into by a business. We look
at how transactions are analyzed, and then
we turn to a number of accounting tools

and procedures designed to facilitate the
preparation of the *outputs* of the system,
the financial statements. Ledger accounts,
journal entries, and trial balances are tools
that allow a company to process vast
amounts of data efficiently.

A Look at the Upcoming Chapter

Chapter 4 concludes our overview of the
accounting model. We will examine the
accrual basis of accounting and its effect
on the measurements of income. Adjusting
entries, which are the focus of the accrual
basis, will be discussed in detail in
Chapter 4 along with the other steps in
the accounting cycle.

Focus on Financial Results

CN, directly or through its subsidiaries, is engaged in railway and related transportation businesses. Its network of approximately 20,400 route miles of track spans Canada and mid-America, connecting three coasts: the Atlantic, the Pacific, and the Gulf of Mexico. CN derives its revenues from seven commodity groups and other miscellaneous items as well as a large number of destinations. In its 2007 income statement, CN reported $7,897 million in revenue arising from thousands—perhaps even millions—of freight contracts and other arrangements. To determine this revenue figure, CN had to carefully analyze and systematically record every freight contract and arrangement that took place during the period. In this chapter we discuss the accounting procedures for recording transactions and processing accounting information for financial statements.

In millions, except per share data	Year ended December 31,	2007	2006	2005
Revenues		**$7,897**	$7,929	$7,446
Operating expenses				
Labor and fringe benefits		1,701	1,823	1,856
Purchased services and material		1,045	1,027	993
Depreciation and amortization		1,026	892	730
Fuel		677	650	627
Equipment rents		247	198	192
Casualty and other		325	309	424
Total operating expenses		5,021	4,899	4,822
Operating income		2,876	3,030	2,624
Interest expense		(336)	(312)	(299)
Other income (Note 14)		166	11	12
Income before income taxes		2,706	2,729	2,337
Income tax expense (Note 15)		(548)	(642)	(781)
Net income		$2,158	$2,087	$1,556
Earnings per share (Note 17)				
Basic		$ 4.31	$ 3.97	$ 2.82
Diluted		$ 4.25	$ 3.91	$ 2.77

(1) Certain of the 2006 and 2005 comparative figures have been reclassified in order to be consistent with 2007 presentation (see Note 21).

This excerpt from CN's 2007 Annual Report appears courtesy of CN. This section of the CN Annual Report appears in the Appendix of this textbook.

ECONOMIC EVENTS: THE BASIS FOR RECORDING TRANSACTIONS

LO 1 Identify transactions for recording.

Event A happening of consequence to an entity.

Many different types of economic events affect an entity during the year. A sale is made to a customer. Inventory is purchased from a supplier. A loan is taken out at the bank. A fire destroys a warehouse. A new contract is signed with the union. In short, an **event** is a happening of consequence to an entity.

External and Internal Events

Two types of events affect an entity: internal and external.

External event An event involving interaction between an entity and its environment.

Internal event An event occurring entirely within an entity.

Transaction Any event that is recognized in a set of financial statements.

- An **external event** involves interaction between the entity and its environment. For example, the *payment* of wages to an employee is an external event, as is the hiring of a new sales manager.
- An **internal event** occurs entirely within the entity. The use of a piece of equipment is an internal event.

We will use the term **transaction** to refer to any event, external or internal, that is recognized in a set of financial statements.

What is necessary to recognize an event in the records? Are all economic events recognized as transactions by the accountant? The answers to these questions involve the concept of *measurement*. An event must be measured to be recognized.

Transactions typically include the following two types of events:

1. An external event that involves exchange of assets and liabilities between the entity and external parties. Examples of such external events include paying a monthly utility bill, selling merchandise to a customer, or issuing shares to new shareholders.
2. An internal event, where the effects on the entity can be reliably measured. Examples of such events include using materials and equipment to manufacture a product, incurring losses due to natural disaster, or accruing interest on a bank loan.

There is no definitive answer to the measurement problem in accounting. It is a continuing challenge to the accounting profession and something we will return to throughout the text.

The Role of Source Documents in Recording Transactions

Source document A piece of paper that is used as evidence to record a transaction.

The first step in the recording process is *identification*. A business needs a systematic method for recognizing events as transactions. A **source document** provides the evidence needed in an accounting system to record a transaction. Source documents take many different forms. An invoice received from a supplier is the source document for a purchase of inventory on credit. A cash register tape is the source document used by a retailer to recognize a cash sale. The payroll department sends the accountant the time cards for the week as the necessary documentation to record wages.

Not all recognizable events are supported by a standard source document. For certain events, some form of documentation must be generated. For example, no standard source document exists to recognize the financial consequences from a fire or the settlement of a lawsuit. Documentation is just as important for these types of events as it is for standard, recurring transactions.

Source documents like these receipts are records that document transactions that the business engages in. Shown here are an employee's travel expense receipts, which will be turned in to the company for reimbursement. Other source documents may be contracts, lease agreements, invoices, delivery vouchers, cheque stubs, and deposit slips.

■ ANALYZING THE EFFECTS OF TRANSACTIONS ON THE ACCOUNTING EQUATION

Economic events are the basis for recording transactions in an accounting system. For every transaction, it is essential to analyze its effect on the accounting equation:

LO 2 Analyze the effects of transactions on the accounting equation.

Assets = Liabilities + Shareholders' Equity

We will now consider a series of events and their recognition as transactions for a hypothetical corporation, Glengarry Health Club. The transactions are for the month of January 2008, the first month of operations for the new business.

Transactions of Glengarry Health Club

(1) *Issuance of capital stock.* The company is started when Mary Jo Kovach and Irene McGuinness file articles of incorporation with the government to obtain a certificate of incorporation. Each invests $50,000 in the business. In return, each receives 5,000 shares. Thus, at this point, each of them owns 50% of the outstanding shares of the company and has a claim to 50% of its assets. The effect of this transaction on the accounting equation is to increase both assets and shareholders' equity:

TRANS. NO.	Assets CASH	=	Liabilities	+	Shareholders' Equity CAPITAL STOCK
1	$100,000				$100,000
Total	$100,000				$100,000

As you can see, each side of the accounting equation has increased by $100,000. Cash is increased, and because the owners contributed this amount, their claims to the assets are increased in the form of Capital Stock.

(2) *Acquisition of equipment.* Mary Jo and Irene contact an equipment supplier and buy $150,000 of exercise equipment: treadmills, barbells, stationary bicycles, and so forth. The supplier agrees to accept a $50,000 cash payment and a five-year note for the $100,000 balance. This note, which the health club gives to the seller, is a written promise to repay the principal amount of the loan at the end of five years. To the club, the note is a liability. The effect of this transaction on the accounting equation is to increase net assets by $100,000 (a decrease in cash of $50,000 and an increase in equipment of $150,000) and to increase liabilities by $100,000:

| TRANS. NO. | Assets | | = | Liabilities | + | Shareholders' Equity |
	CASH	EQUIPMENT		NOTES PAYABLE		CAPITAL STOCK
Bal.	$100,000					$100,000
2	-$ 50,000	$150,000		$100,000		
Bal.	$ 50,000	$150,000		$100,000		$100,000
Total		$200,000			$200,000	

(3) *Purchase of supplies on credit.* The owners purchase supplies—towels, shampoos, cleaning supplies, and so on—for $3,000 and agree to pay the supplier for the purchase early next month. These supplies are to be used in running the club and serving its customers and are considered assets. Conversely, the promise to pay the supplier for the supplies purchased is a liability. The effect of this transaction is to increase both assets and liabilities:

| TRANS. NO. | Assets | | | = | Liabilities | | + | Shareholders' Equity |
	CASH	SUPPLY INVENTORY	EQUIPMENT		ACCOUNTS PAYABLE	NOTES PAYABLE		CAPITAL STOCK
Bal.	$50,000		$150,000			$100,000		$100,000
3		$3,000			$3,000			
Bal.	$50,000	$3,000	$150,000		$3,000	$100,000		$100,000
Total		$203,000				$203,000		

(4) *Prepayment of first six months' rent.* The owners find a building that is suitable for the business. They sign a lease and pay $18,000 for the first six months' rent. The payment results in something that will provide a benefit to the company—that is, the use of the building to operate the health club for six months. Thus, this prepayment is an asset. It is similar to the supplies in (3) that are to be used in running the business. The difference between this transaction and (3) is that cash is *paid* instead of promised at a later date. The effect of this transaction is to decrease one type of asset (cash) and increase another (prepaid rent) by the same amount:

| TRANS. NO. | Assets | | | | = | Liabilities | | + | Shareholders' Equity |
	CASH	SUPPLY INVENTORY	PREPAID RENT	EQUIPMENT		ACCOUNTS PAYABLE	NOTES PAYABLE		CAPITAL STOCK
Bal.	$50,000	$3,000		$150,000		$3,000	$100,000		$100,000
4	-$18,000		$18,000						
Bal.	$32,000	$3,000	$18,000	$150,000		$3,000	$100,000		$100,000
Total		$203,000					$203,000		

(5) *Sale of day passes for cash.* Glengarry is a health club, and it generates revenue by providing its customers with the use of its facilities. During January it sells 3,000 day passes—each of which allows a customer one day's access to the club facilities—at $5 each, for a total of $15,000 cash. This increases the company's asset by $15,000. The other side of this transaction is an increase in owners' equity—specifically, Retained Earnings. Recall that an inflow of assets resulting from the sale of goods and services by a business is called *Revenue*. An increase in revenue will cause an increase in the income of the period, which in turn results in an increase in the retained earnings. Remember, retained earnings is the income earned and accumulated or retained in the company. The increase in shareholders' equity indicates that the shareholders' residual interest in the assets of the business has increased by this amount. The change in the accounting equation follows:

	Assets				=	Liabilities		+	Shareholders' Equity		
TRANS. NO.	CASH	SUPPLY INVENTORY	PREPAID RENT	EQUIPMENT		ACCOUNTS PAYABLE	NOTES PAYABLE		CAPITAL STOCK	RETAINED EARNINGS	TYPE OF CHANGE IN RETAINED EARNINGS
Bal.	$32,000	$3,000	$18,000	$150,000		$3,000	$100,000		$100,000		
5	$15,000									$15,000	Day Pass Revenue
Bal.	$47,000	$3,000	$18,000	$150,000		$3,000	$100,000		$100,000	$100,000 $15,000	
Total		$218,000					$218,000				

(6) *Rental of studio space and court time to customers on credit.* In addition to selling day passes, Glengarry also rents out its studio space and court time for classes, games, and other events. The rental fees for January amount to $5,000; however, the customers don't have to pay until February 10. All events take place in January. Glengarry does not have cash from the rental customers; instead, it has a promise from each customer to pay cash in the future. A promise from a customer to pay an amount owed is an asset referred to as an *account receivable*. The other side of this transaction is an increase in owners' equity—specifically, in Retained Earnings:

	Assets					=	Liabilities		+	Shareholders' Equity		
TRANS. NO.	CASH	ACCOUNTS RECEIVABLE	SUPPLY INVENTORY	PREPAID RENT	EQUIPMENT		ACCOUNTS PAYABLE	NOTES PAYABLE		CAPITAL STOCK	CAPITAL EARNINGS	TYPE OF CHANGE IN RETAINED EARNINGS
Bal.	$47,000		$3,000	$18,000	$150,000		$3,000	$100,000		$100,000	$100,000 $15,000	
6		$5,000									$ 5,000	Rental Revenue
Bal.	$47,000	$5,000	$3,000	$18,000	$150,000		$3,000	$100,000		$100,000	$100,000 $20,000	
Total			$223,000					$223,000				

The only difference between this transaction and **(5)** is that a promise to pay at a later date is received, rather than cash. Both transactions result in an increase in an asset by providing the use of the club facilities. Thus, in both cases the company has earned revenue.

(7) *Sale of annual memberships for cash.* Glengarry also offers annual memberships. These allow unlimited access to the club facilities for one year. During January, 100 annual memberships are sold for $480 each—a total of $48,000. The cash received by Glengarry obligates the club to provide the use of its facilities to the members in the future. Thus, the transaction creates a liability called *Unearned Revenue*. The effect on the accounting equation is as follows:

	Assets					=	Liabilities			+	Shareholders' Equity	
TRANS. NO.	CASH	ACCOUNTS RECEIVABLE	SUPPLY INVENTORY	PREPAID RENT	EQUIPMENT		ACCOUNTS PAYABLE	UNEARNED ANNUAL MEMBERSHIP FEES	NOTES PAYABLE		CAPITAL STOCK	RETAINED EARNINGS
Bal.	$47,000	$5,000	$3,000	$18,000	$150,000		$3,000		$100,000		$100,000	$20,000
7	$48,000							$48,000				
Bal.	$95,000	$5,000	$3,000	$18,000	$150,000		$3,000	$48,000	$100,000		$100,000	$20,000
Total			$271,000							$271,000		

The difference between this transaction and (5) and (6) is that the supposed uses of the facilities in this transaction have not yet all been provided. The revenue resulting from providing such services has not yet been earned. Thus, instead of revenue, a liability is increased.

(8) *Payment of wages and salaries.* The wages and salaries for the first month amount to $10,000. The payment of this amount results in a decrease in Cash as well as a decrease in the shareholders' claim on the assets—that is, a decrease in Retained Earnings. More specifically, an outflow of assets from the sale of goods or services is called an *expense*. Expenses of a period reduce the income of the period, which in turn reduces retained earnings. The effect of this transaction is to decrease both sides of the accounting equation:

	Assets					=	Liabilities			+	Shareholders' Equity		
TRANS. NO.	CASH	ACCOUNTS RECEIVABLE	SUPPLY INVENTORY	PREPAID RENT	EQUIPMENT		ACCOUNTS PAYABLE	UNEARNED ANNUAL MEMBERSHIP FEES	NOTES PAYABLE		CAPITAL STOCK	RETAINED EARNINGS	TYPE OF CHANGE IN RETAINED EARNINGS
Bal.	$95,000	$5,000	$3,000	$18,000	$150,000		$3,000	$48,000	$100,000		$100,000	$20,000	
8	-$10,000											-$10,000	Wage and Salary Expense
Bal.	$85,000	$5,000	$3,000	$18,000	$150,000		$3,000	$48,000	$100,000		$100,000	$10,000	
Total			$261,000							$261,000			

(9) *Payment of utilities.* The cost of utilities for the first month is $1,000. Glengarry pays the utility bill with cash, as with (8), the decrease in assets resulting from delivering goods or rendering services is called an *expense*. The effect on the accounting equation follows:

	Assets					=	Liabilities			+	Shareholders' Equity		
TRANS. NO.	CASH	ACCOUNTS RECEIVABLE	SUPPLY INVENTORY	PREPAID RENT	EQUIPMENT		ACCOUNTS PAYABLE	UNEARNED ANNUAL MEMBERSHIP FEES	NOTES PAYABLE		CAPITAL STOCK	RETAINED EARNINGS	TYPE OF CHANGE IN RETAINED EARNINGS
Bal.	$85,000	$5,000	$3,000	$18,000	$150,000		$3,000	$48,000	$100,000		$100,000	$10,000	
9	-$ 1,000											-$ 1,000	Utility Expense
Bal.	$84,000	$5,000	$3,000	$18,000	$150,000		$3,000	$48,000	$100,000		$100,000	$ 9,000	
Total			$260,000							$260,000			

(10) *Collection of accounts receivable.* Even though the January rental fees are not due until the 10th of the following month, some of the customers pay their bills by the end of January. The amount received from customers in payment of their accounts is $4,000. The effect of the collection of an open account is to increase Cash and decrease Accounts Receivable:

		Assets				=	Liabilities			+	Shareholders' Equity	
TRANS. NO.	CASH	ACCOUNTS RECEIVABLE	SUPPLY INVENTORY	PREPAID RENT	EQUIPMENT		ACCOUNTS PAYABLE	UNEARNED ANNUAL MEMBERSHIP FEES	NOTES PAYABLE		CAPITAL STOCK	RETAINED EARNINGS
Bal.	$84,000	$5,000	$3,000	$18,000	$150,000		$3,000	$48,000	$100,000		$100,000	$9,000
10	$ 4,000	–$4,000										
Bal.	$88,000	$1,000	$3,000	$18,000	$150,000		$3,000	$48,000	$100,000		$100,000	$9,000
Total			$260,000						$260,000			

Note that the company simply traded assets: Accounts Receivable for Cash. Thus, the totals for the accounting equation remain at $260,000. Also note that Retained Earnings is not affected by this transaction because revenue was recognized earlier, in **(6)**, when Accounts Receivable was increased.

(11) *Payment of dividends.* At the end of the month, Mary Jo and Irene, acting on behalf of Glengarry Health Club, decide to pay a dividend of $1,000 on the shares owned by each of them, or $2,000 in total. The effect of this dividend is to decrease both Cash and Retained Earnings. That is, the company is returning cash to the owners, based on the profitable operations of the business for the first month. The transaction not only reduces Cash but also decreases the owners' claims on the assets of the company. Dividends are not an expense but rather a direct reduction of Retained Earnings. The effect on the accounting equation follows:

		Assets				=	Liabilities			+	Shareholders' Equity		
TRANS. NO.	CASH	ACCOUNTS RECEIVABLE	SUPPLY INVENTORY	PREPAID RENT	EQUIPMENT		ACCOUNTS PAYABLE	UNEARNED ANNUAL MEMBERSHIP FEES	NOTES PAYABLE		CAPITAL STOCK	RETAINED EARNINGS	TYPE OF CHANGE IN RETAINED EARNINGS
Bal.	$88,000	$1,000	$3,000	$18,000	$150,000		$3,000	$48,000	$100,000		$100,000	$9,000	
11	–$ 2,000											–$2,000	Dividends
Bal.	$86,000	$1,000	$3,000	$18,000	$150,000		$3,000	$48,000	$100,000		$100,000	$7,000	
Total			$258,000						$258,000				

The Cost Principle An important principle governs the accounting for the exercise equipment in **(2)**. The *cost principle* requires that we record an asset at the cost to acquire it and continue to show this amount on all balance sheets until we dispose of the asset. With a few exceptions, an asset is not carried at its market value but at its original cost. Why not show the equipment on future balance sheets at its market value? Although this might seem more appropriate in certain instances, the subjectivity inherent in determining market values is a major reason behind the practice of carrying assets at their historical cost. The cost of an asset can be verified by an independent observer and is much more *objective* than market value.

Companies engage in transactions in many ways. The company from whom this woman is ordering supports sales transactions over the phone using a credit card number. A sales representative may be inputting the card number and the order information into an order database. The company links its order-processing system and other business systems to this customer input.

Two-Minute Review

Assume that on February 1 Glengarry buys additional exercise equipment for $10,000 in cash.

1. Indicate which two accounts are affected and the increase or decrease in each.

2. What will be the total dollar amount of each of the two sides of the accounting equation after this transaction is recorded? (See page 99 for January 31 balance.)

Answers on page 115.

Balance Sheet and Income Statement for the Health Club

To summarize, Exhibit 3-1 indicates the effect of each transaction on the accounting equation, specifically the individual items increased or decreased by each transaction. Note the *dual* effect of each transaction. At least two items were involved in each transaction. For example, the initial investment by the owners resulted in an increase in an asset and an increase in Capital Stock. The payment of the utility bill caused a decrease in an asset and a decrease in Retained Earnings.

You can now see the central idea behind the accounting equation: Even though individual transactions may change the amount and composition of the assets and liabilities, the *equation* must always balance *for* each transaction, and the *balance sheet* must balance *after* each transaction.

A balance sheet for Glengarry Health Club appears in Exhibit 3-2. All of the information needed to prepare this statement is available in Exhibit 3-1. The balances at the bottom of this exhibit are entered on the balance sheet, with assets on the left side and liabilities and shareholders' equity on the right side.

An income statement for Glengarry is shown in Exhibit 3-3. An income statement summarizes the revenues and expenses of a company for a period of time. In our example, the statement is for the month of January, as indicated on the third line of the heading of the statement. Glengarry earned revenues from two sources: (1) day passes and (2) rental fees. Two types of expenses were incurred: (1) salaries and wages and (2) utilities. The difference between the total revenues of $20,000 and the total expenses of $11,000 is the net income for the month of $9,000. Finally, remember that dividends appear on a statement of retained earnings rather than on the income statement. They are a *distribution* of net income of the period, not a *determinant* of net income as are expenses.

We have seen how transactions are analyzed and how they affect the accounting equation and ultimately the financial statements. While the approach we took in analyzing the eleven transactions of the Glengarry Health Club was manageable, can you imagine using this type of analysis for a company with *thousands* of transactions in any one month? We now turn our attention to various *tools* used by the accountant to process a large volume of transactions effectively and efficiently.

		Assets				=	Liabilities			+	Shareholders' Equity		
TRANS. NO.	Cash	Accounts Receivable	Supply Inventory	Prepaid Rent	Equipment		Accounts Payable	Unearned Annual Membership Fees	Notes Payable		Capital Stock	Retained Earnings	Type of change in Retained Earnings
1	$100,000										$100,000		
2	-$50,000				$150,000				$100,000				
Bal.	$50,000				$150,000				$100,000		$100,000		
3			$3,000				$3,000						
Bal.	$50,000		$3,000		$150,000		$3,000		$100,000		$100,000		
4	-$18,000			$18,000									
Bal.	$32,000		$3,000	$18,000	$150,000		$3,000		$100,000		$100,000		
5	$15,000											$15,000	Day Pass Revenue
Bal.	$47,000		$3,000	$18,000	$150,000		$3,000		$100,000		$100,000	$15,000	
6		$5,000										$5,000	Rental Revenue
Bal.	$47,000	$5,000	$3,000	$18,000	$150,000		$3,000		$100,000		$100,000	$20,000	
7	$48,000							$48,000					
Bal.	$95,000	$5,000	$3,000	$18,000	$150,000		$3,000	$48,000	$100,000		$100,000	$20,000	
8	-$10,000											-$10,000	Wage and Salary Expense
Bal.	$85,000	$5,000	$3,000	$18,000	$150,000		$3,000	$48,000	$100,000		$100,000	$10,000	
9	-$1,000											-$1,000	Utility Expense
Bal.	$84,000	$5,000	$3,000	$18,000	$150,000		$3,000	$48,000	$100,000		$100,000	$9,000	
10	$4,000	-$4,000											
Bal.	$88,000	$1,000	$3,000	$18,000	$150,000		$3,000	$48,000	$100,000		$100,000	$9,000	
11	-$2,000											-$2,000	Dividends
Bal.	$86,000	$1,000	$3,000	$18,000	$150,000		$3,000	$48,000	$100,000		$100,000	$7,000	

Total assets $258,000   Total liabilities and shareholders' equity $258,000

GLENGARRY HEALTH CLUB
BALANCE SHEET
JANUARY 31, 2008

Assets		Liabilities and Shareholders' Equity	
Cash	$ 86,000	Accounts payable	$ 3,000
Accounts receivable	1,000	Unearned annual	
Supply inventory	3,000	membership revenue	48,000
Prepaid rent	18,000	Notes payable	100,000
Equipment	150,000	Capital stock	100,000
		Retained earnings	7,000
		Total liabilities	
Total assets	$258,000	and shareholders' equity	$258,000

Exhibit 3-2

Balance Sheet for Glengarry Health Club

Exhibit 3-3

Income Statement for
Glengarry Health Club

GLENGARRY HEALTH CLUB
INCOME STATEMENT
FOR THE MONTH ENDED JANUARY 31, 2008

Revenues:		
Day passes	$15,000	
Court rental	5,000	$20,000
Expenses:		
Wage and salary	10,000	
Utility	1,000	11,000
Net income		$ 9,000

THE DOUBLE-ENTRY SYSTEM

LO 3 Use double-entry accounting and debits and credits.

The origin of the double-entry system of accounting can be traced to Venice, Italy, in 1494. In that year, Fra Luca Pacioli, a Franciscan monk, wrote a mathematical treatise. Included in his book was the concept of debits and credits that is still used almost universally today.

A few basic concepts are introduced in the following sections before we describe the double-entry system.

The Account

Account Record used to accumulate amounts for each individual asset, liability, revenue, expense, and component of shareholders' equity.

An **account** is the record used to accumulate monetary amounts for each asset, liability, and component of shareholders' equity, such as Capital Stock, Retained Earnings, and Dividends. It is the basic recording unit for each element in the financial statements. Each revenue and expense has its own account. In the Glengarry Health Club example, ten accounts were used: Cash, Accounts Receivable, Supply Inventory, Prepaid Rent, Equipment, Accounts Payable, Unearned Annual Membership Fees, Notes Payable, Capital Stock, and Retained Earnings. Later in the chapter we will see that normally each revenue and expense is recorded in a separate account. In the real world, a company might have hundreds, or even thousands, of individual accounts.

No two entities have exactly the same set of accounts. To a certain extent, the accounts used by a company depend on its business. For example, a manufacturer normally has three inventory accounts: Raw Materials, Work in Process, and Finished Goods. A retailer uses just one account for inventory, a Merchandise Inventory account. A service business has no need for an inventory account.

Chart of Accounts

Chart of accounts A numerical list of all the accounts used by a company.

Companies need a way to organize the large number of accounts they use to record transactions. A **chart of accounts** is a numerical list of all of the accounts an entity uses. The numbering system is a convenient way to identify accounts. For example, all asset accounts might be numbered from 100 to 199, liability accounts from 200 to 299, equity accounts from 300 to 399, revenues from 400 to 499, and expenses from 500 to 599. A chart of accounts for a hypothetical retail store is shown in Exhibit 3-4. Note the division of account numbers within each of the financial statement categories. Within the asset category, current assets are numbered from 100 to 149, non-current assets from 150 to 199. Not all of the numbers are currently assigned. For example, only four of the available 50 numbers are currently utilized for current asset accounts. This allows the company to add accounts as needed.

In today's business world, most companies have an automated accounting system. The computer is ideally suited for the job of processing vast amounts of data rapidly. *All of the tools discussed in this chapter are as applicable to computerized systems as they are to manual systems. It is merely the appearance of the tools that differs between manual and computerized systems.* For example, the ledger in an automated system might be contained on a computer file server rather than stored in a file cabinet. Throughout the book, we will use a manual system to explain the various tools, such as ledger accounts. The reason is that it is easier to illustrate and visualize the tools in a manual system. However, all of the ideas apply just as well to a computerized system of accounting.

Exhibit 3-4

Chart of Accounts for a Retail Store

100–199:	ASSETS	
100–149:	Current Assets	
110:	Cash	
120:	Accounts Receivable	
130:	Inventory	
140:	Prepaid Expense	
150–199:	Non-current Assets	
150:	Land	
160:	Building	
165:	Accumulated Depreciation—Building	
170:	Furniture and Fixtures	
175:	Accumulated Depreciation—Furniture and Fixtures	
200–299:	LIABILITIES	
200–249:	Current Liabilities	
210:	Accounts Payable	
220:	Wages and Salaries Payable	
250–299:	Long-Term Liabilities	
250:	Notes Payable	
300–399:	SHAREHOLDERS' EQUITY	
310:	Preferred Shares	
320:	Common Shares	
330:	Retained Earnings	
340:	Dividends	
400–499:	REVENUES	
410:	Sales Revenue	
420:	Other Revenue	
500–599	EXPENSES	
510:	Cost of Goods Sold	
520:	Wages and Salaries	
530:	Insurance	
540:	Utilities	
550:	Depreciation	
551:	Depreciation Expense—Building	
552:	Depreciation Expense—Furniture and Fixtures	
560:	Advertising Expense	
570:	Income Taxes	

The T Account

The form of account often used to analyze transactions is called the *T account*, so named because it resembles the capital letter T. The name of the account appears across the horizontal line. One side is used to record increases and the other side decreases, but as you will see, the same side is not used for increases for every account. As a matter of convention, the *left* side of an *asset* account is used to record *increases* and the *right* side to record *decreases*.

The conventions for using a *T account* can be related to the accounting equation as follows: assets are on the left side of the accounting equation, and increases in an asset are recorded on the *left* side of the *T account*. Liabilities and Shareholders' Equity are on the right side of the accounting equation, and *increases* in a liability or shareholders' equity are recorded in the *right* side of the *T account*. We can summarize the conventions for a T account, the increases and decreases, and the accounting equation as follows:

ASSETS		=	LIABILITIES		+	SHAREHOLDERS' EQUITY	
Increases	Decreases		Decreases	Increases		Decreases	Increases
+	–		–	+		–	+

To illustrate a specific T account, let us examine the Cash account for Glengarry Health Club. The transactions recorded in the account can be traced to Exhibit 3-1.

CASH

INCREASES		DECREASES	
Investment by owners	100,000	Equipment	50,000
Day passes sold	15,000	Prepayment of rent	18,000
Annual memberships sold	48,000	Wage and salary	10,000
Accounts collected	4,000	Utility	1,000
		Dividends	2,000
	167,000		81,000
Bal.	86,000		

The amounts $167,000 and $81,000 are called *footings*. They represent the totals of the amounts on each side of the account. Neither these amounts nor the balance of $86,000 represents transactions. They are simply shown to indicate the totals and the balance in the account.

Debits and Credits

Rather than refer to the left or right side of an account, accountants use specific labels for each side. The *left* side of any account is the **debit** side, and the *right* side of any account is the **credit** side. We will also use the terms *debit* and *credit* as verbs. If we *debit* the Cash account, we enter an amount on the left side. Similarly, if we want to enter an amount on the right side of an account, we *credit* the account. To *charge* an account has the same meaning as to *debit* it. No such synonym exists for the act of crediting an account.

Note that *debit* and *credit* are *locational* terms. They simply refer to the left or right side of a T account. They do *not* represent increases or decreases. As we will see, when one type of account is increased (for example, the Cash account), the increase is on the left or *debit* side. When certain other types of accounts are increased, however, the entry will be on the right or *credit* side.

We can summarize the logic of debits and credits, increases and decreases, and the accounting equation in the following way:

ASSETS		=	LIABILITIES		+	SHAREHOLDERS' EQUITY	
Debits	Credits		Debits	Credits		Debits	Credits
Increases	Decreases		Decreases	Increases		Decreases	Increases
+	–		–	+		–	+

Note again that debits and credits are location-oriented. Debits are always on the left side of an account and credits on the right side.

Debit An entry on the left side of an account.

Credit An entry on the right side of an account.

Accounting for Your Decisions

You Are a Student

A classmate comes to you with a question about the bank statement she has received. Why does the bank credit her account when she makes a deposit to her account, but accounting rules state that cash is increased with a debit?

ANSWER: The bank is looking at customer deposits from its perspective and not the customers'. Chequing account deposits represent liabilities to the bank, such as "Deposits Payable." Thus, when customers make deposits, the bank has increased its liability to those customers, with a credit to its "Deposits Payable."

Debits and Credits for Revenues, Expenses, and Dividends

In our Glengarry Health Club example, revenues were an increase in Retained Earnings. The sale of day passes was not only an increase in the asset Cash but also an increase in the owners' equity account Retained Earnings. The transaction resulted in an increase in the owners' claim on the assets of the business. Rather than being recorded directly in Retained Earnings, however, each revenue item is maintained in a separate account. The following logic is used to arrive at the rules for increasing and decreasing revenues:[1]

1. Retained Earnings is increased with a credit.
2. Revenue is an increase in Retained Earnings.
3. Revenue is increased with a credit.
4. Because revenue is increased with a credit, it is decreased with a debit.

The same logic is applied to the rules for increasing and decreasing expense accounts:

1. Retained Earnings is decreased with a debit.
2. Expense is a decrease in Retained Earnings.
3. Expense is increased with a debit.
4. Because expense is increased with a debit, it is decreased with a credit.

Recall that dividends reduce cash. But they also reduce the owners' claim on the assets of the business. Earlier we recognized this decrease in the owners' claim as a reduction of Retained Earnings. As we do for revenue and expense accounts, we will use a separate Dividends account:

1. Retained Earnings is decreased with a debit.
2. Dividends are a decrease in Retained Earnings.
3. Dividends are increased with a debit.
4. Because dividends are increased with a debit, they are decreased with a credit.

---

[1] We normally think of both revenues and expenses as being only increased, not decreased. Because we will need to decrease them as part of the closing procedure, it is important to know how to reduce these accounts as well as increase them.

Summary of the Rules for Increasing and Decreasing Accounts

The rules for increasing and decreasing the various types of accounts are summarized as follows:

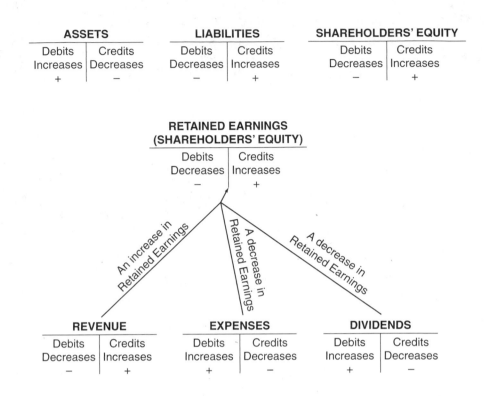

ASSETS	
Debits	Credits
Increases	Decreases
+	−

LIABILITIES	
Debits	Credits
Decreases	Increases
−	+

SHAREHOLDERS' EQUITY	
Debits	Credits
Decreases	Increases
−	+

RETAINED EARNINGS (SHAREHOLDERS' EQUITY)

Debits	Credits
Decreases	Increases
−	+

An increase in Retained Earnings

A decrease in Retained Earnings

A decrease in Retained Earnings

REVENUE	
Debits	Credits
Decreases	Increases
−	+

EXPENSES	
Debits	Credits
Increases	Decreases
+	−

DIVIDENDS	
Debits	Credits
Increases	Decreases
+	−

Normal Account Balances

Each account has a "normal" balance. For example, assets normally have debit balances. Would it be possible for an asset such as Cash to have a credit balance? Assume that a company has a chequing account with a bank. A credit balance in the account would indicate that the decreases in the account, from cheques written and other bank charges, were more than the deposits into the account. If this were the case, however, the company would no longer have an asset, Cash, but instead would have a liability to the bank. The normal balances for the accounts we have looked at are as follows:

Type of Account	Normal Balance
Asset	Debit
Liability	Credit
Shareholders' Equity	Credit
Revenue	Credit
Expense	Debit
Dividends	Debit

Debits Aren't Bad, and Credits Aren't Good

Students often approach their first encounter with debits and credits with preconceived notions. The use of the terms *debit* and *credit* in everyday language leads to many of these notions. "Joe is a real credit to his team." "Nancy should be credited with saving Mary's career." These both appear to be very positive statements. You must resist the temptation to associate the term *credit* with something good or positive and the term *debit* with something bad or negative. *In accounting, debit means one thing: an entry made on the left side of an account. A credit means an entry made on the right side of an account.*

Debits and Credits Applied to Transactions

Recall the first transaction recorded by Glengarry Health Club earlier in the chapter: the owners invested $100,000 cash in the business. The transaction resulted in an increase in the Cash account and an increase in the Capital Stock account. Applying the rules of debits and credits, we would *debit* the Cash account for $100,000 and *credit* the Capital Stock account for the same amount:[2]

CASH		CAPITAL STOCK	
(1) 100,000			100,000 (1)

You now can see why we refer to the **double-entry system** of accounting. Every transaction is recorded so that the equality of debits and credits is maintained, and in the process, the accounting equation is kept in balance. *Every transaction is entered in at least two accounts on opposite sides of T accounts. Our first transaction resulted in an increase in an asset account and an increase in a shareholders' equity account. For every transaction, the debit side must equal the credit side. The debit of $100,000 to the Cash account equals the credit of $100,000 to the Capital Stock account.* It naturally follows that if the debit side must equal the credit side for every transaction, at any point in time the total of all debits recorded must equal the total of all credits recorded. Thus, the fundamental accounting equation remains in balance.

Double-entry system A system of accounting in which every transaction is recorded with equal debits and credits and the accounting equation is kept in balance.

THE JOURNAL

All transactions are first recorded into a file called a **journal**. A journal is a chronological record of transactions. Because a journal lists transactions in the order in which they took place, it is called the *book of original entry*. The process of recording entries in a journal is called *journalizing*. A standard format is normally used for recording journal entries. Consider the original investment by the owners of Glengarry Health Club. The format of the journal entry is as follows:

LO 4 Journalize transactions.

Journal A chronological record of transactions, also known as the book of original entry.

		DEBIT	CREDIT
1	Cash	100,000	
	Capital Stock		100,000
	To record the issuance of 10,000 shares for cash		

Each journal entry contains columns for the date (here replaced by the transaction number), for the accounts used, and for the amounts debited and credited. Accounts credited are indented to distinguish them from accounts debited. A brief explanation normally appears just under the entry.

Transactions are normally recorded in a **general journal**. Specialized journals may be used to record repetitive transactions. For example, a cash receipts journal may be used to record all transactions in which cash is received. Special journals accomplish the same purpose as a general journal, but they save time in recording similar transactions. In this chapter, we will use a general journal to record all transactions.

General journal The journal used in place of a specialized journal.

Recording Transactions for Glengarry Health Club

Now we return to the transactions of the health club. We follow three distinct steps in recording a transaction:

1. First, we *analyze* the transaction. That is, we decide which accounts are increased or decreased and by how much.

---

[2]We will use the numbers of each transaction, as they were labelled earlier in the chapter, to identify the transactions. In practice, a formal ledger account is used, and transactions are entered according to their date.

2. Second, we *recall* the rules of debits and credits as they apply to the transaction we are analyzing.

3. Finally, we *record* the transaction using the rules of debits and credits.

We have already explained the logic for the debit to the Cash account and the credit to the Capital Stock account for the initial investment by the owners. We have also shown the journal entry for the transaction. We now prepare journal entries to record the rest of Glengarry Health Club's transactions in January 2008. Refer to Exhibit 3-1 for a summary of the transaction.

(2) Acquisition of exercise equipment with a $50,000 cash payment and $100,000 note.

Analyze: An asset account, Equipment, is increased by $150,000. Another asset account, Cash, is decreased by $50,000. A liability account, Notes Payable, is increased by $100,000.

Recall: An asset is increased with a debit and decreased with a credit, and a liability is increased with a credit.

Record:

		DEBIT	CREDIT
2	Equipment	150,000	
	Cash		50,000
	Notes Payable		100,000
	To record the purchase of exercise equipment		

(3) Purchase of $3,000 of supplies on credit.

Analyze: An asset account, Supply Inventory, is increased by $3,000. A liability account, Accounts Payable, is increased by the same amount.

Recall: An asset is increased with a debit, and a liability is increased with a credit.

Record:

		DEBIT	CREDIT
3	Supply Inventory	3,000	
	Accounts Payable		3,000
	To record the purchase of supplies		

(4) Prepayment of $18,000 of first six months' rent.

Analyze: An asset account, Prepaid Rent, is increased by $18,000, and another asset account, Cash, is decreased by the same amount.

Recall: An asset is increased with a debit and decreased with a credit.

Record:

		DEBIT	CREDIT
4	Prepaid Rent	18,000	
	Cash		18,000
	To record the prepayment of rent		

(5) Sales of 3,000 day passes for $15,000 of cash.

Analyze: An asset account, Cash, is increased by $15,000. The shareholders' equity, the owners' claim to the assets, is increased by the same amount. Recall, however, that we do not record revenues directly in a shareholders' equity account but instead use a separate revenue account. We will call the account Day Pass Revenue.

Recall: An asset is increased with a debit. Shareholders' equity is increased with a credit. Because revenue is an increase in shareholders' equity, it is increased with a credit.

Record:

		DEBIT	CREDIT
5	Cash	15,000	
	Day Pass Revenue		15,000
	To record the sales of day passes		

(6) Rental Revenue of $5,000 on credit.

Analyze: An asset account, Accounts Receivable, is increased by $5,000. The amount is an asset because the company has the right to collect it in the future. The shareholders' equity is increased by the same amount. This increase in shareholders' equity is recorded as an increase in Rental Revenue.

Recall: An asset is increased with a debit. Shareholders' equity is increased with a credit. Because revenue is an increase in shareholders' equity, it is increased with a credit.

Record:

		DEBIT	CREDIT
6	Accounts Receivable	5,000	
	Rental Revenue		5,000
	To record the rental of court space		

(7) Sales of annual memberships for $48,000 of cash.

Analyze: An asset account, Cash, is increased by $48,000. A liability account, Unearned Revenue, is increased by the same amount. By receiving the amount, the club is now obligated to provide the use of the club facilities to the members in the future.

Recall: An asset is increased with a debit, and a liability is increased with a credit.

Record:

		DEBIT	CREDIT
7	Cash	48,000	
	Unearned Revenue		48,000
	To record the sales of annual memberships		

(8) Payment of $10,000 monthly wages and salaries.

Analyze: The asset account, Cash, is decreased by $10,000. At the same time, the shareholders' equity is decreased by this amount. However, rather than record a decrease directly to Retained Earnings, we set up an expense account, Wage and Salary Expense.

Recall: An asset is decreased with a credit. Shareholders' equity is decreased with a debit. Because expense is a decrease in shareholders' equity, it is increased with a debit.

Record:

		DEBIT	CREDIT
8	Wage and Salary Expense	10,000	
	Cash		10,000
	To record the payment of monthly wages and salaries		

(9) Payment of January utilities of $1,000.

Analyze: An asset account, Cash, is decreased by $1,000. At the same time, the shareholders' equity is decreased by this amount. However, rather than record a decrease directly to Retained Earnings, we set up an expense account, Utilities Expense.

Recall: An asset is decreased with a credit. Shareholders' equity is decreased with a debit. Because expense is a decrease in shareholders' equity, it is increased with a debit.

Record:

		DEBIT	CREDIT
9	Utility Expense	1,000	
	Cash		1,000
	To record the payment of January utilities		

(10) Collection of $4,000 of accounts receivable.

Analyze: Cash is increased by the amount collected from the members, $4,000. Another asset account, Accounts Receivable, is decreased by the same amount. Glengarry has simply traded one asset for another.

Recall: An asset is increased with a debit and decreased with a credit. Thus, one asset is debited and another is credited.

Record:

		DEBIT	CREDIT
10	Cash	4,000	
	Accounts Receivable		4,000
	To record the collection of accounts receivable		

(11) Dividends of $2,000 are distributed to the owners.

Analyze: The asset account, Cash, is decreased by $2,000. At the same time, Shareholders' Equity is decreased by this amount. Earlier in the chapter, we decreased Retained Earnings for dividends paid to the owners. Now we will use a separate account, Dividends, to record these distributions.

Recall: An asset is decreased with a credit. Retained earnings are decreased with a debit. Because dividends are a decrease in retained earnings, they are increased with a debit.

Record:

		DEBIT	CREDIT
11	Dividends	2,000	
	Cash		2,000
	To record the payment of dividends		

Two-Minute Review

1. Assume that Glengarry pays the supplier the amount owed on open account. Record this transaction in the journal.

2. Assume that Glengarry collects the remaining amount owed by customers for rental fees. Record this transaction in the journal.

Answers on page 116.

THE LEDGER AND TRIAL BALANCE

LO 5 Post to the ledger and prepare a trial balance.

Journal entries are used by accountants for the initial recording of transactions. The end result of the accounting process is a set of financial statements. Journalizing provides us with a chronological record of all transactions. However, it is not efficient to prepare financial statements directly from the journal entries. For instance, for the balance sheet we will need the amount of cash on hand at the end of January. In our simple example of Glengarry Health Club, it would be possible to get this information by examining the journal entry by entry and tallying up the changes in the amount of cash on hand. In real-world situations, however, the number of transactions for a given period can be so large that it would be terribly inefficient, if not virtually impossible, to do so.

For the purpose of preparing financial statements, information recorded in the journal is transferred into a second book called a **ledger.** A ledger is an accounting record organized by the accounts, or a file or book that contains the accounts. In a manual system, a separate sheet is used to record the activity in each account. The process of transferring amounts from a journal to the ledger accounts is called **posting:**

Ledger A book, file, hard drive, or other device containing all the accounts.

Posting The process of transferring amounts from a journal to the ledger accounts.

Note that posting does not result in any change in the amounts recorded. It is simply a process of re-sorting the transactions from a chronological order to a topical arrangement.

The posting process for Glengarry Health Club's first two transactions is illustrated in Exhibit 3-5:

Exhibit 3-5 Posting from Journal to Ledger

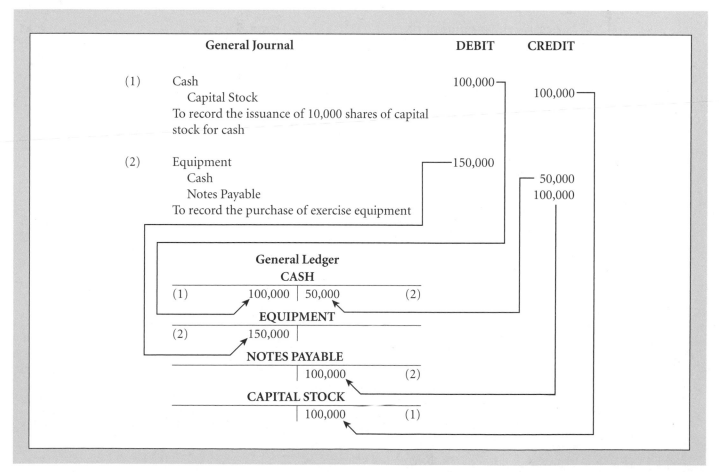

Note the cross-referencing between the journal and the ledger. As amounts are entered in the ledger accounts, the transaction numbers are used as posting references.

The frequency of posting varies among companies, partly based on the degree to which the accounting system is automated. For example, in some computerized systems, amounts are posted to the ledger accounts at the time an entry is recorded in the journal. In a manual system, posting is normally done periodically—perhaps daily, weekly, or monthly. Regardless of when it is performed, the posting process changes nothing. It simply reorganizes the transactions by account.

Exhibit 3-6 shows the ledger of Glengarry Health Club after the January transactions are posted. In addition to the account titles, the entries of each transaction, and the transaction numbers, the footings and balance are also presented for Cash and Accounts Receivable accounts. For the rest of the accounts, the entry in each account is also the balance of the account at the end of January.

Exhibit 3-6 Ledger of Glengarry Health Club

	CASH				ACCOUNTS PAYABLE		
(1)	100,000	50,000	(2)			3,000	(3)
(5)	15,000	18,000	(4)				
(7)	48,000	10,000	(8)		UNEARNED REVENUE		
(10)	4,000	1,000	(9)			48,000	(7)
		2,000	(11)				
	167,000	81,000			NOTES PAYABLE		
Bal.	86,000					100,000	(2)
	ACCOUNTS RECEIVABLE				CAPITAL STOCK		
(6)	5,000	4,000	(10)			100,000	(1)
Bal.	1,000				DAY PASS REVENUE		
	SUPPLY INVENTORY					15,000	(5)
(3)	3,000				RENTAL REVENUE		
	PREPAID RENT					5,000	(6)
(4)	18,000				WAGE AND SALARY EXPENSE		
	EQUIPMENT						
(2)	150,000			(8)	10,000		
	DIVIDENDS				UTILITY EXPENSE		
(11)	2,000			(9)	1,000		

The journal and ledger accounts illustrated in Exhibit 3-6 are in T-account format. This format has the advantage of being intuitively simple and visually appealing; in the real world, however, it is not usually encountered. An example of a real-life general journal and general ledger for a manual system is provided in Exhibit 3-7.

Exhibit 3-7 Example of Journal and Ledger

General Journal   Page No. 1

Date		Account Titles and Explanation	Post. Ref.	Debit	Credit
2008 Jan.	XX	Cash	101	100,000	
		Capital Stock	301		100,000
		Issued 10,000 shares for cash			
	XX	Equipment	151	150,000	
		Cash	101		50,000
		Notes Payable	255		100,000
		Purchased exercise equipment			

General Ledger
Cash   Acct. No. 101

Date		Explanation	Post. Ref.	Debit	Credit	Balance
2008 Jan.	XX	Issued 10,000 shares for cash	GJ1	100,000		100,000
	XX	Purchased exercise equipment	GJ1		50,000	50,000

Capital Stock   Acct. No. 301

Date		Explanation	Post. Ref.	Debit	Credit	Balance
2008 Jan.	XX	Issued 10,000 shares for cash	GJ1		100,000	100,000

Equipment   Acct. No. 151

Date		Explanation	Post. Ref.	Debit	Credit	Balance
2008 Jan.	XX	Purchased exercise equipment	GJ1	150,000		150,000

Notes Payable   Acct. No. 255

Date		Explanation	Post. Ref.	Debit	Credit	Balance
2008 Jan.	XX	Purchased exercise equipment	GJ1		100,000	100,000

In Exhibit 3-7, the *running balance* form is used rather than T-account format for the ledger accounts. A separate column indicates the balance in the ledger account after each transaction. The use of an explanation column in a ledger account is optional. Because an explanation of the entry in the account can be found by referring to the journal, this column is often left blank.

The Posting Reference column in the ledger provides the page number of the journal. For example, GJ1 is used to indicate page 1 from the general journal. (Note that the illustration on the previous page shows a manual accounting record. In computerized accounting systems, transaction numbers or batch numbers, rather than journal page numbers, are more commonly used as posting reference numbers.) The Posting Reference column of the journal is the appropriate account number.

Accounting for Your Decisions

You Are the Manager

You are the community relations manager for a company. You need to determine whether the company is spending its money wisely in promoting its image in the local community.

1. What types of accounts would you examine? Give examples of the possible names for some of these accounts.

2. Would a general journal or a general ledger be more useful to you in making your determination? Explain your answer.

ANSWER: 1. Among the possible accounts that you want to examine are Entertainment, Travel, Promotions, Advertising, and Miscellaneous, in addition to any accounts that might contain expenditures related to community relations.

2. You may want to examine the general ledger for each of the accounts listed in part 1. The ledger contains a record for each of the accounts and the activity in them during the period.

The Trial Balance

Recording transactions in a journal and posting them to ledger accounts are only the first two steps that accountants take when preparing financial statements. The complete accounting procedure, also called the accounting cycle, will be discussed in detail in Chapter 4. Yet another tool that accountants often use when preparing financial statements is the trial balance. A **trial balance** is a list of each account and its balance at a specific point in time. The trial balance is *not* a financial statement but merely a convenient device to prove the equality of the debit and credit balances in the accounts. It can be as informal as an adding-machine tape with the account titles pencilled in next to the debit and credit amounts. A trial balance for Glengarry Health Club as of January 31, 2008, is shown in Exhibit 3-8. The balances of the accounts are taken from Glengarry's ledger accounts in Exhibit 3-6.

Certain types of errors are detectable from a trial balance. For example, if the balance of an account is incorrectly computed, the totals of the debits and credits in the trial balance will not be equal. If a debit is posted to an account as a credit, or vice versa, the trial balance will be out of balance. The omission of part of a journal entry in the posting process will also be detected by the preparation of a trial balance.

Do not attribute more significance to a trial balance, however, than is warranted. It does provide a convenient summary of account balances for preparing financial statements. It also assures us that the balances of all the debit accounts equal the balances of all the credit accounts. But an equality of debits and credits does not necessarily mean that the *correct* accounts were debited and credited in an entry. For example, the entry

Trial balance A list of each account and its balance; used to prove equality of debits and credits.

Exhibit 3-8

Trial Balance for Glengarry
Health Club

GLENGARRY HEALTH CLUB
UNADJUSTED TRIAL BALANCE
JANUARY 31, 2008

	Debit	Credit
Cash	$ 86,000	
Accounts Receivable	1,000	
Supply Inventory	3,000	
Prepaid Rent	18,000	
Equipment	150,000	
Accounts Payable		$ 3,000
Unearned Annual Membership Revenue		48,000
Notes Payable		100,000
Capital Stock		100,000
Dividends	2,000	
Day Pass Revenue		15,000
Rental Revenue		5,000
Wage and Salary Expense	10,000	
Utility Expense	1,000	
Totals	$271,000	$271,000

Study Tip

Remember from p. 106 that every account has a normal balance, either debit or credit. Note the normal balances for each account on this trial balance.

to record the purchase of equipment by signing a promissory note *should* result in a debit to Equipment and a credit to Notes Payable. If the accountant incorrectly debited Cash instead of Equipment, the trial balance would still show an equality of debits and credits. A trial balance can be prepared at any time; it is usually prepared before the release of a set of financial statements.

The series of steps performed by every company in every period that culminate in the preparation of a set of financial statements is called the accounting cycle. In this chapter we cover only the front half of this cycle. The second half of the accounting cycle is discussed in Chapter 4.

Accounting for Your Decisions

You Are the Shareholder

You own 100 shares of CN. Every year you receive CN's annual report, which includes a chairman's letter, a management discussion and analysis (MD&A), a financial section, and notes to the financial statements. Nowhere in the report do you see a general ledger or a trial balance. Is CN hiding something?

CN
http://www.cn.ca

ANSWER: CN's balance sheet, income statement, and statement of cash flows are derived from the company's journal entries, general ledgers, trial balances, and so on. These documents are the building blocks of the final statements. There could literally be millions of transactions during the year—which even the most diehard accounting fan would tire of reading.

Answers to the Two-Minute Reviews

Two-Minute Review on page 100
1. Equipment will increase by $10,000, and Cash will decrease by $10,000.
2. $258,000 (the effect of the transaction is to increase and decrease assets by the same amount).

(continued)

Two-Minute Review on page 110

		Debit	Credit
1.	Accounts Payable	3,000	
	Cash		3,000
	To record the payment of accounts payable		

		Debit	Credit
2.	Cash	1,000	
	Accounts Receivable		1,000
	To record the collection of accounts receivable		

Chapter Highlights

1. **LO 1   Identify transactions for recording (p. 94).**

   - Events that affect an entity are usually recorded in the accouting system as a transaction. Transactions can be:

     ○ External events that involve exchange of assets and liabilities with external parties.

     ○ Internal events whose effects on the entity can be reliably measured.

   - Source documents provide the evidence needed to begin the procedures for recording and processing a transaction. These documents need not be in hard copy form and can come from parties both internal and external to the company.

2. **LO 2   Analyze the effects of transactions on the accounting equation (p. 95).**

   - The accounting equation illustrates the relationship between assets, liabilities, and shareholders' equity accounts. Understanding these relationships helps to see the logic behind the double-entry system in recording transactions.

     ○ The accounting equation:
       Assets = Liabilities + Shareholders' Equity

     ○ This equality must always be maintained. The equation can be expanded to show the linkage between the balance sheet and the income statement through the Retained Earnings account:

       Assets = Liabilities + Capital Stock + Retained Earnings

3. **LO 3   Use double-entry accounting and debits and credits (p. 102).**

   - T-accounts are a convenient way to analyze the activity in any particular account. The left side of a T-account represents debits made to an account, and the right represents credits made to an account.

   - Debits and credits take on meaning only when associated with the recording of transactions involving asset, liability, and equity accounts.

     ○ In general, debits increase asset accounts, and credits increase liability and equity accounts.

     ○ The double-entry system requires that total debits equal total credits for any transaction recorded in the accounting system.

4. **LO 4   Journalizing Transactions (p. 107).**

   - A journal documents the details of transactions by date. Entries are made to a journal every time a transaction occurs.

     ○ Similar transactions that occur regularly may be recorded in special journals.

5. **LO 5   Post to the ledger and prepare a trial balance (p. 110).**

   - Ultimately, information is posted from the journal to the ledgers for each individual account.

   - A ledger is a crucial part of the accounting system that contains all accounts and their balances. The preparation of financial statements requires the current account balances in the ledger.

   - At the end of the period, a trial balance may be prepared that lists all the accounts in the general ledger along with their debit or credit balances.

   - The purpose of the trial balance is to see whether total debits equals total credits. This provides some assurance that the accounting equation was adhered to in the processing of transactions but is no guarantee that transactions have been recorded properly.

Accounts Highlighted

Account Titles	Where it Appears	In What Section	Page Number
Cash	Balance Sheet	Current Assets	95
Capital stock	Balance Sheet	Shareholders' Equity	95
Equipment	Balance Sheet	Noncurrent Assets	96
Notes payable	Balance Sheet	Noncurrent Liability	96
Supply Inventory	Balance Sheet	Current Assets	96
Accounts payable	Balance Sheet	Current Liabilities	96
Prepaid rent	Balance Sheet	Current Assets	96
Retained earnings	Balance Sheet	Shareholders' Equity	97
Accounts receivable	Balance Sheet	Current Assets	97
Day pass revenue	Income Statement	Revenue	97
Rental revenue	Income Statement	Revenue	97
Unearned annual membership fees	Balance Sheet	Current Liabilities	98
Wage and salary expense	Income Statement	Expense	98
Utility expense	Income Statement	Expense	98
Dividends	Statement of Retained Earnings	Shareholders' Equity	99

Key Terms Quiz

Read each definition below, and then write the number of the definition in the blank beside the appropriate term it defines. The quiz solutions appear at the end of the chapter.

_____ Account

_____ Chart of accounts

_____ Event

_____ External event

_____ Internal event

_____ Transaction

_____ Source document

_____ Ledger

_____ Debit

_____ Credit

_____ Double-entry system

_____ Journal

_____ Posting

_____ Journalizing

_____ Trial balance

1. A numerical list of all the accounts used by a company.

2. A list of each account and its balance at a specific point in time; used to prove the equality of debits and credits.

3. A happening of consequence to an entity.

4. An entry on the right side of an account.

5. An event occurring entirely within an entity.

6. A piece of paper, such as a sales invoice, that is used as the evidence to record a transaction.

7. The act of recording journal entries.

8. An entry on the left side of an account.

9. The process of transferring amounts from a journal to the appropriate ledger accounts.

10. An event involving interaction between an entity and its environment.

11. The record used to accumulate monetary amounts for each individual asset, liability, revenue, expense, and component of shareholders' equity.

12. A book, file, hard drive, or other device containing all of a company's accounts.

13. A chronological record of transactions, also known as the *book of original entry*.

14. Any event, external or internal, that is recognized in a set of financial statements.

15. A system of accounting in which every transaction is recorded with equal debits and credits and the accounting equation is kept in balance.

Answers on p. 141.

Alternate Terms

Credit side of an account Right side of an account

Debit an account Charge an account

Debit side of an account Left side of an account

General ledger Set of accounts

Journal Book of original entry

Journalize an entry Record an entry

Posting an account Transferring an amount from the journal to the ledger

Warmup Exercises and Solutions

Warmup Exercise 3-1 *Your Debits and Credits* LO 3

Assume that you borrow $1,000 from your roommate by signing an agreement to repay the amount borrowed in six months.

Required

1. What is the effect of this transaction on your own accounting equation?
2. Prepare the journal entry to record this transaction in your own records.

Key to the Solution Recall Exhibit 3-1 for the effects of transactions on the accounting equation, and refer to the summary of the rules for increasing and decreasing accounts on p. 104.

Warmup Exercise 3-2 *A Bank's Debits and Credits* LO 3

The National Bank loans a customer $5,000 in exchange for a promissory note.

Required

1. What is the effect of this transaction on the bank's accounting equation?
2. Prepare the journal entry to record this transaction in the bank's records.

Key to the Solution Recall Exhibit 3-1 for the effects of transactions on the accounting equation, and refer to the summary of the rules for increasing and decreasing accounts on p. 104.

CN
http://www.cn.ca

Warmup Exercise 3-3 *Debits and Credits for CN* LO 3

Assume **CN** goes to its bank and borrows $50,000,000 by signing a promissory note. The next day the company uses the money to buy a rail car.

Required

1. What is the effect of each of these two transactions on CN's accounting equation?
2. Prepare the journal entries to record both transactions in CN's records.

Key to the Solution Recall Exhibit 3-1 for the effects of transactions on the accounting equation, and refer to the summary of the rules for increasing and decreasing accounts on p. 104.

Solutions to Warmup Exercises

Warmup Exercise 3-1

1. If you borrow $1,000 from your roommate, assets in the form of cash increase $1,000, and liabilities in the form of a note payable increase $1,000.

2. Cash   1,000
     Notes Payable   1,000

Warmup Exercise 3-2

1. If a bank loans a customer $5,000, the bank's assets, in the form of a note receivable, increase $5,000, and its assets, in the form of cash, decrease $5,000.

2. Notes Receivable   5,000
     Cash   5,000

Warmup Exercise 3-3

1. If CN borrows $50,000,000 from its bank, assets, in the form of cash, increase $50,000,000, and liabilities, in the form of a note payable, increase $50,000,000. If the company uses the money to buy a rail car, assets, in the form of equipment, increase $50,000,000, and assets, in the form of cash, decrease $50,000,000.

2. Cash   50,000,000
     Notes Payable   50,000,000

   Equipment   50,000,000
     Cash   50,000,000

———— Review Problem and Solution ————

The following transactions are entered into by Sparkle Car Wash during its first month of operations:

a. Articles of incorporation are filed with the government, and 20,000 shares of capital stock are issued. Cash of $40,000 is received from the new owners for the shares.

b. A five-year promissory note is signed at the local bank. The cash received from the loan is $120,000.

c. An existing car wash is purchased for $150,000 in cash. The values assigned to the land, building, and equipment are $25,000, $75,000, and $50,000, respectively.

d. Cleaning supplies are purchased on account for $2,500 from a distributor. All of the supplies are used in the first month.

e. During the first month, $1,500 is paid to the distributor for the cleaning supplies. The remaining $1,000 will be paid next month.

f. Gross receipts from car washes during the first month of operations amount to $7,000.

g. Wages and salaries paid in the first month amount to $2,000.

h. The utility bill of $800 for the month is paid.

i. A total of $1,000 in dividends is paid to the owners.

Required

1. Prepare a table to summarize the preceding transactions as they affect the accounting equation. Use the format in Exhibit 3-1. Identify each transaction by letter.

2. Prepare an income statement for the month.

3. Prepare a balance sheet at the end of the month.

Solution to Review Problem

1.

SPARKLE CAR WASH
TRANSACTIONS FOR THE MONTH

	Assets				=	Liabilities		+	Shareholders' Equity		
TRANS.	CASH	LAND	BUILDING	EQUIPMENT		ACCOUNTS PAYABLE	NOTES PAYABLE		CAPITAL STOCK	RETAINED EARNINGS	TYPE OF CHANGE IN RETAINED EARNINGS
a.	$ 40,000								$40,000		
b.	120,000						$120,000				
Bal.	160,000						120,000		40,000		
c.	–150,000	$25,000	$75,000	$50,000							
Bal.	10,000	25,000	75,000	50,000			120,000		40,000		
d.											Supplies Expense
						$2,500				$–2,500	
Bal.	10,000	25,000	75,000	50,000		2,500	120,000		40,000	–2,500	
e.	–1,500					–1,500					
Bal.	8,500	25,000	75,000	50,000		1,000	120,000		40,000	–2,500	
f.											Service Revenue
	7,000									7,000	
Bal.	15,500	25,000	75,000	50,000		1,000	120,000		40,000	4,500	
g.											Wage and Salary Expense
	–2,000									–2,000	
Bal.	13,500	25,000	75,000	50,000		1,000	120,000		40,000	2,500	
h.											Utility Expense
	–800									– 800	
Bal.	12,700	25,000	75,000	50,000		1,000	120,000		40,000	1,700	
i.	–1,000									– 1,000	Dividends
Bal.	$ 11,700	$25,000	$75,000	$50,000		$1,000	$120,000		$40,000	$ 700	

Total assets: $161,700

Total liabilities and shareholders' equity: $161,700

2.

SPARKLE CAR WASH
INCOME STATEMENT
FOR THE MONTH ENDED XX/XX/XX

Car wash revenue		$7,000
Expenses:		
Supplies	$2,500	
Wages and salaries	2,000	
Utilities	800	5,300
Net income		$1,700

3.

SPARKLE CAR WASH
BALANCE SHEET
AT XX/XX/XX

Assets		Liabilities and Shareholders' Equity	
Cash	$ 11,700	Accounts payable	$ 1,000
Land	25,000	Notes payable	120,000
Building	75,000	Capital stock	40,000
Equipment	50,000	Retained earnings	700
		Total liabilities	
Total assets	$161,700	and shareholders' equity	$161,700

Questions

1. What are the two types of events that affect an entity? Describe each.

2. What is the significance of source documents to the recording process? Give two examples of source documents.

3. How does an account payable differ from a note payable?

4. What is meant by the statement "One company's account receivable is another company's account payable"?

5. What do accountants mean when they refer to the "double-entry system" of accounting?

6. Shareholders' equity represents the claim of the owners on the assets of the business. What is the distinction relative to the owners' claim between the Capital Stock account and the Retained Earnings account?

7. If an asset account is increased with a debit, what is the logic for increasing a liability account with a credit?

8. A friend comes to you with the following plight: "I'm confused. An asset is something positive, and it is increased with a debit. However, an expense is something negative, and it is also increased with a debit. I don't get it." How can you straighten your friend out?

9. The payment of dividends reduces cash. If the Cash account is reduced with a credit, why is the Dividends account debited when dividends are paid?

10. If Cash is increased with a debit, why does the bank credit your account when you make a deposit?

11. Your friend presents the following criticism of the accounting system: "Accounting involves so much duplication of effort. First, entries are recorded in a journal, and then the same information is recorded in a ledger. No wonder accountants work such long hours!" Do you agree with this criticism?

12. How does the T account differ from the running balance form for an account? How are they similar?

13. What is the benefit of using a cross-referencing system between a ledger and a journal?

14. How often should a company post entries from the journal to the ledger?

15. What is the purpose of a trial balance?

Exercises

Exercise 3-1 *Types of Events* LO 1

For each of the following events, identify whether it is an external event that would be recorded as a transaction (E), an internal event that would be recorded as a transaction (I), or not recorded (NR):

1. A supplier of a company delivers raw material the company ordered.
2. A bank loan is obtained by signing a note.
3. A new chief executive officer is hired.
4. The biweekly payroll is paid.
5. Raw materials are entered into production.
6. A new advertising agency is hired to develop a series of newspaper ads for the company.
7. The advertising bill for the first month is paid.
8. The accountant determines the interest owed based on the notes payable amount and the interest rate.

Exercise 3-2 *Source Documents Matched with Transactions* **LO 1**

Following are a list of source documents and a list of transactions. Indicate by letter, next to each transaction, the source document that would serve as evidence for the recording of the transaction.

Source Documents

a. Purchase invoice

b. Sales invoice

c. Cash register tape

d. Time cards

e. Note

f. Share certificates

g. Monthly statement from utility company

h. No standard source document would normally be available

Transactions

_____ 1. A building is acquired by signing an agreement to repay a stated amount plus interest in six months.

_____ 2. A cash settlement is received from a pending lawsuit.

_____ 3. A sale is made on open account.

_____ 4. Cash sales for the day are recorded.

_____ 5. Equipment is acquired on a 30-day open account.

_____ 6. Shareholders contribute cash to start a new corporation.

_____ 7. The biweekly payroll is paid.

_____ 8. Utilities expense for the month is recorded.

Exercise 3-3 *The Effect of Transactions on the Accounting Equation* **LO 2**

For each of the following transactions, indicate whether it increases (I), decreases (D), or has no effect (NE) on the total dollar amount of each of the elements of the accounting equation.

Transactions	Assets	= Liabilities	+ Shareholders' Equity
Example: Common stock is issued in exchange for cash.	I	NE	I
1. Cash sales are made.			
2. Cash is collected on an account receivable.			
3. Equipment is purchased for cash.			
4. An account payable is paid off.			
5. Sales are made on account.			
6. Advertising bill for the month is paid.			
7. Dividends are paid to shareholders.			
8. Land is acquired by issuing shares of capital stock to the owner of the land.			
9. Buildings are purchased in exchange for a three-year note payable.			

Exercise 3-4 *Types of Transactions* **LO 2**

As you found out in reading the chapter, there are three elements to the accounting equation: assets, liabilities, and shareholders' equity. You also learned that every transaction affects at least two of these elements. Although other possibilities exist, five types of transactions are described on page 123. For *each* of these five types, write out descriptions of at least *two* transactions that illustrate these types of transactions.

Type of Transaction	Assets	= Liabilities +	Shareholders' Equity
1.	Increase	Increase	
2.	Increase		Increase
3.	Decrease	Decrease	
4.	Decrease		Decrease
5.	Increase		
	Decrease		

Exercise 3-5 *Balance Sheet Accounts and Their Use* **LO 2**

Choose from the following list of account titles the one that most accurately fits the description of that account or is an example of that account. An account title may be used more than once or not at all.

Cash	Capital Stock	Retained Earnings
Prepaid Asset	Accounts Receivable	Buildings
Investments	Land	Notes Payable
Taxes Payable	Accounts Payable	Inventory

_____ **1.** A chequing account at the bank

_____ **2.** A warehouse used to store merchandise

_____ **3.** A written obligation to repay a fixed amount, with interest, at some time in the future

_____ **4.** Amounts owed on an open account to a supplier of raw materials, due in 90 days

_____ **5.** An amount owed by a customer

_____ **6.** Claims by the shareholders on the undistributed net income of a business

_____ **7.** Corporate income taxes owed to the federal government

_____ **8.** Five hectares of land used as the site for a factory

_____ **9.** Ownership in a company

_____ **10.** Rent paid on an office building in advance of use of the facility

_____ **11.** Twenty hectares of land held for speculation

Exercise 3-6 *Normal Account Balances* **LO 3**

Each account has a normal balance. For the following list of accounts, indicate whether the normal balance of each is a debit or a credit.

Account	Normal Balance
1. Cash	_____
2. Accounts Payable	_____
3. Retained Earnings	_____
4. Equipment	_____
5. Notes Payable	_____
6. Capital Stock	_____
7. Advertising Fees Earned	_____
8. Wages and Salaries Expense	_____
9. Wages and Salaries Payable	_____
10. Office Supplies	_____
11. Dividends	_____

Exercise 3-7 *Debits and Credits* **LO 3**

The new bookkeeper for Dalhousie Corporation is getting ready to mail the daily cash receipts to the bank for deposit. Because his previous job was at a bank, he is aware that the bank "credits" your account for all deposits and "debits" your account for all cheques written. Therefore, he makes the following entry before sending the daily receipts to the bank:

June 5	Accounts Receivable	10,000	
	Sales Revenue	2,450	
	Cash		12,450
	To record cash received on June 5: $10,000 collections on account and $2,450 in cash sales.		

Required

Explain why this entry is wrong, and prepare the correct journal entry. Why does the bank refer to cash received from a customer as a *credit* to that customer's account?

Exercise 3-8 *Trial Balance* **LO 5**

The following list of accounts was taken from the general ledger of Sackville Corporation on December 31, 2008. The bookkeeper thought it would be helpful if the accounts were arranged in alphabetical order. Each account contains the balance normal for that type of account (for example, Cash normally has a debit balance). Prepare a trial balance as of this date, with the accounts arranged in the following order: (1) assets, (2) liabilities, (3) shareholders' equity, (4) revenues, (5) expenses, and (6) dividends.

Account	Balance
Accounts Payable	$ 7,600
Accounts Receivable	5,300
Advertising Expense	2,000
Buildings	150,000
Capital Stock	100,000
Cash	10,500
Commissions Revenue	12,800
Dividends	2,000
Equipment	85,000
Furniture	9,000
Heat, Light, and Water Expense	1,400
Income Tax Expense	1,700
Income Taxes Payable	2,500
Interest Revenue	1,300
Land	50,000
Notes Payable	90,000
Office Salaries Expense	6,800
Office Supplies	500
Retained Earnings	110,000

Multi-Concept Exercises

Exercise 3-9 *Journal Entries* **LO 2, 3, 4**

Prepare journal entries to record each of the following transactions, using the numbers preceding the transactions to identify them in the journal.

1. Received contribution of $5,000 from each of the three principal owners of the Go-Go Delivery Service in exchange for shares of capital stock.

2. Borrowed $10,000 from the bank by signing a note.

3. Purchased office supplies for cash of $130.

4. Purchased a van for $15,000 on an open account. The company has 25 days to pay for the van.

5. Provided delivery services to residential customers for cash of $125.

6. Billed a local business $200 for delivery services. The customer is to pay the bill within 15 days.

7. Paid the amount due on the van.

8. Received the amount due from the local business billed in transaction (**6**) on previous page.

Exercise 3-10 *Posting Journal Entries to a Ledger* **LO 3, 5**

Refer to the journal entries for Go-Go Delivery Services in Exercise 3-9. Post them to a ledger. Use the transaction numbers to identify them in the accounts.

Exercise 3-11 *Trial Balance* **LO 3, 5**

Refer to the T accounts for the Go-Go Delivery Service in Exercise 3-10. Assume that the transactions all took place during December 2008. Prepare a trial balance at December 31, 2008.

Exercise 3-12 *Determining an Ending Account Balance* **LO 2, 3, 4, 5**

Pam's Pet Shop was established on June 1, 2008. The company received a contribution of $2,000 from Pam. During the month, Pam's Pet Shop had cash sales of $1,400, had sales on account of $450, received $250 from customers in payment of their accounts, purchased supplies on account for $600 and equipment on account for $1,350, received a utility bill for $250 that will not be paid until July, and paid the full amount due on the equipment. Use a T account to determine the company's Cash balance on June 30, 2008.

Exercise 3-13 *Reconstructing a Beginning Account Balance* **LO 2, 3, 4, 5**

During the month, services performed for customers on account amounted to $7,500, and collections from customers in payment of their accounts totalled $6,000. At the end of the month, the Accounts Receivable account had a balance of $2,500. What was the Accounts Receivable balance at the beginning of the month?

Exercise 3-14 *Journal Entries* **LO 2, 3, 4**

Prepare the journal entry to record each of the following independent transactions (use the number of the transaction in lieu of a date for identification purposes):

1. Sales on account of $1,530

2. Purchases of supplies on account for $1,365

3. Cash sales of $750

4. Purchase of equipment for cash of $4,240

5. Issuance of a promissory note for $2,500

6. Collections on account for $890

7. Sale of shares in exchange for a parcel of land; the land is appraised at $50,000

8. Payment of $4,000 in salaries and wages

9. Payment of open account in the amount of $500

Exercise 3-15 *Journal Entries* **LO 2, 3, 4**

Following is a list of transactions entered into during the first month of operations of Yard Corp., a new landscape service company. Prepare in journal form the entry to record each transaction.

April 1: 100,000 shares are issued for $200,000 in cash.

April 4: A six-month note is signed at the bank. Interest at 9% per annum will be repaid in six months with the principal amount of the loan of $100,000.

April 8: Land and a storage shed are acquired for a lump sum of $120,000 cash. On the basis of an appraisal, 25% of the value is assigned to the land and the remainder to the building.

April 10: Mowing equipment is purchased from a supplier at a total cost of $50,000. A down payment of $10,000 is made, with the remainder due by the end of the month.

April 18: Customers are billed for services provided during the first half of the month. The total amount billed of $8,800 is due within 10 days.

April 27: The remaining balance due on the mowing equipment is paid to the supplier.

April 28: The total amount of $8,800 due from customers is received.

April 30: Customers are billed for services provided during the second half of the month. The total amount billed is $13,000.

April 30: Salaries and wages of $4,800 for the month are paid.

Problem 3-1 *Events to Be Recorded in Accounts* LO 1

The following events take place at Ben's Lunch:

1. Food is ordered from vendors, who will deliver the food within the week.
2. Vendors deliver food on account, payment due in 30 days.
3. Employees take frozen food from the freezers and prepare it for customers.
4. Food is served to customers, and sales are rung up on the cash register; sales will be totalled at the end of the day.
5. Trash is taken to dumpsters, and the floors are cleaned.
6. Cash registers are cleared at the end of the day.
7. Cash is deposited in the bank night depository.
8. Employees are paid weekly paycheques.
9. Vendors noted in item 2 are paid for the food delivered.

Required

Identify each event as internal (I) or external (E), and indicate whether each event would be recorded in the *accounts* of the company. For each event that is to be recorded, identify the names of at least two accounts that would be affected.

Problem 3-2 *Transaction Analysis and Financial Statements* LO 2

Fun-on-Wheels Inc. was organized on May 1, 2008, by two college students who recognized an opportunity to make money while spending their days at a beach on Prince Edward Island. The two entrepreneurs plan to rent bicycles and in-line skates to weekend visitors to the beach. The following transactions occurred during the first month of operations:

May 1:	Received contribution of $5,000 from each of the two principal owners of the new business in exchange for shares.
May 1:	Purchased 10 bicycles for $300 each on an open account. The company has 30 days to pay for the bicycles.
May 5:	Registered as a vendor with the city and paid the $15 monthly fee.
May 9:	Purchased 20 pairs of in-line skates at $125 per pair, 20 helmets at $50 each, and 20 sets of protective gear (knee and elbow pads and wrist guards) at $45 per set for cash.
May 10:	Purchased $100 in miscellaneous supplies on account. The company has 30 days to pay for the supplies.
May 15:	Paid $125 bill from local radio station for advertising for the last two weeks of May.
May 17:	Customers rented in-line skates and bicycles for cash of $1,800.
May 24:	Billed the local park district $1,200 for in-line skating lessons provided to neighbourhood kids. The park district is to pay one-half of the bill within five working days and the rest within 30 days.
May 29:	Received 50% of the amount billed to the park district.
May 30:	Customers rented in-line skates and bicycles for cash of $3,000.
May 30:	Paid wages of $160 to a friend who helped out over the weekend.
May 31:	Paid the balance due on the bicycles.

Required

1. Prepare a table to summarize the preceding transactions as they affect the accounting equation. Use the format in Exhibit 3-1. Identify each transaction with the date.
2. Prepare an income statement for the month ended May 31, 2008.
3. Prepare a classified balance sheet at May 31, 2008.
4. Why do you think the two college students decided to incorporate their business rather than operate it as a partnership?

Problem 3-3 *Transaction Analysis and Financial Statements* LO 2

GB Services Inc. was established on March 1, 2008, by two former university roommates. The corporation will provide computer consulting services to small businesses. The following transactions occurred during the first month of operations:

March 2: Received contributions of $5,000 from each of the two principal owners of the new business in exchange for shares.

March 7: Signed a two-year note at the bank and received cash of $15,000. Interest, along with the $15,000, will be repaid at the end of the two years.

March 12: Purchased $700 in miscellaneous supplies on account. The company has 30 days to pay for the supplies.

March 19: Billed a client $6,000 for services rendered by GB in helping to install a new computer system. The client is to pay $1,000 of the bill upon its receipt and the remaining balance within 30 days.

March 20: Paid a $1,300 bill from the local newspaper for advertising for the month of March.

March 22: Received $1,000 of the amount billed the client on March 19.

March 26: Received cash of $2,800 for services provided in assisting a client in selecting software for its computer.

March 29: Purchased a computer system for $8,000 in cash.

March 30: Paid $3,300 of salaries and wages for March.

March 31: Received and paid $1,400 in gas, electric, and water bills.

Required

1. Prepare a table to summarize the preceding transactions as they affect the accounting equation. Use the format in Exhibit 3-1. Identify each transaction with the date.

2. Prepare an income statement for the month ended March 31, 2008.

3. Prepare a classified balance sheet at March 31, 2008.

4. From reading the balance sheet you prepared in requirement 3, what events would you expect to take place in April? Explain your answer.

Problem 3-4 *Transactions Reconstructed from Financial Statements* LO 2

The following financial statements are available for Tower Corporation for its first month of operations:

TOWER CORPORATION
INCOME STATEMENT
FOR THE MONTH ENDED JUNE 30, 2008

Service revenue		$93,600
Expenses:		
Rent	$ 9,000	
Salaries and wages	27,900	
Utilities	13,800	50,700
Net income		$42,900

TOWER CORPORATION
BALANCE SHEET
JUNE 30, 2008

Assets		Liabilities and Shareholders' Equity	
Cash	$ 22,800	Accounts payable	$ 18,000
Accounts receivable	21,600	Notes payable	90,000
Equipment	18,000	Capital stock	30,000
Building	90,000	Retained earnings	38,400
Land	24,000	Total liabilities and	
Total assets	$176,400	shareholders' equity	$176,400

(continued)

Required

Using the format illustrated in Exhibit 3-1, prepare a table to summarize the transactions entered into by Tower Corporation during its first month of business. State any assumptions you believe are necessary in reconstructing the transactions.

Problem 3-5 *Identification of Events with Source Documents* **LO 1**

Many events are linked to a source document. The following is a list of events that occurred in an entity:

a. Sold merchandise to a customer on account.

b. Paid a one-year insurance premium.

c. Paid employee payroll.

d. Identified materials in the warehouse destroyed by flood.

e. Received payment of bills from customers.

f. Purchased land for future expansion.

g. Calculated taxes due.

h. Entered into a car lease agreement and paid the tax, title, and licence.

Required

For each item **a** through **h,** indicate whether the event should or should not be recorded in the entity's accounts. For each item that should be recorded in the entity's books:

1. Identify one or more source documents that are generated from the event.

2. Identify which source document would be used to record an event when it produces more than one source document.

3. For each document, identify the information that is most useful in recording the event in the accounts.

Multi-Concept Problems

Problem 3-6 *Accounts Used to Record Transactions* **LO 2, 3**

A list of accounts, with an identifying number for each, is shown below. Following the list of accounts is a series of transactions entered into by a company during its first year of operations.

Required

For each transaction, indicate the account or accounts that should be debited and credited.

1. Cash	9. Notes Payable
2. Accounts Receivable	10. Capital Stock
3. Office Supplies	11. Retained Earnings
4. Buildings	12. Service Revenue
5. Automobiles	13. Wage and Salary Expense
6. Land	14. Selling Expense
7. Accounts Payable	15. Utilities Expense
8. Income Tax Payable	16. Income Tax Expense

	Accounts	
Transactions	**Debited**	**Credited**
Example: Purchased land and building in exchange for a three-year promissory note.	4, 6	9
a. Issued capital shares for cash.		
b. Purchased land in exchange for a note due in six months.		
c. Purchased 10 automobiles; paid part in cash and signed a 60-day note for the balance.		

d. Paid newspaper for company ads appearing during the month. _____ _____

e. Purchased office supplies; agreed to pay total bill by the 10th of the following month. _____ _____

f. Billed clients for services performed during the month, and gave them until the 15th of the following month to pay. _____ _____

g. Received cash on account from clients for services rendered to them in past months. _____ _____

h. Paid employees salaries and wages earned during the month. _____ _____

i. Received monthly gas and electric bill from the utility company; payment is due anytime within the first 10 days of the following month. _____ _____

j. Computed amount of taxes due based on the income of the period; amount will be paid in the following month. _____ _____

Problem 3-7 *Transaction Analysis Trial Balance, and Financial Statements* LO 2, 5

Four brothers organized Entertainment Enterprises on October 1, 2008. The following transactions occurred during the first month of operations:

October 1: Received contribution of $10,000 from each of the four principal owners of the new business in exchange for shares.

October 2: Purchased the Acadia Theatre for $125,000. The seller agreed to accept a down payment of $25,000 and a seven-year note for the balance. The Acadia property consists of land valued at $35,000 and a building valued at $90,000.

October 3: Purchased new seats for the theatre at a cost of $5,000, paying $2,500 down and agreeing to pay the remainder in 60 days.

October 12: Purchased candy, popcorn, cups, and napkins for $3,700 on an open account. The company has 30 days to pay for the concession supplies.

October 13: Sold tickets for the opening-night movie for cash of $1,800, and took in $2,400 at the concession stand.

October 17: Rented out the theatre to a local community group for $1,500. The community group is to pay one-half of the bill within five working days and has 30 days to pay the remainder.

October 23: Received 50% of the amount billed to the community group.

October 24: Sold movie tickets for cash of $2,000, and took in $2,800 at the concession stand.

October 26: The four brothers, acting on behalf of Entertainment Enterprises, paid a dividend of $750 on the shares owned by each of them, or $3,000 in total.

October 27: Paid $500 for utilities.

October 30: Paid wages and salaries of $2,400 total to the ushers, the projectionist, the concession stand workers, and the maintenance crew.

October 31: Sold movie tickets for cash of $1,800, and took in $2,500 at the concession stand.

Required

1. Prepare a table to summarize the preceding transactions as they affect the accounting equation. Use the format in Exhibit 3-1. Identify each transaction with a date.
2. Prepare a trial balance at October 31, 2008.
3. Prepare an income statement for the month ended October 31, 2008.
4. Prepare a statement of retained earnings for the month ended October 31, 2008.
5. Prepare a classified balance sheet at October 31, 2008.

Problem 3-8 *Journal Entries and Ledger Posting* LO 4, 5

Zunich Advertising Agency began business on January 2, 2008. The following listings are the transactions entered into by Zunich during its first month of operations.

a. Issued 100,000 shares in exchange for $200,000 in cash.

b. Purchased an office building for $150,000 in cash. The building is valued at $100,000, and the remainder of the value is assigned to the land.

(continued)

c. Signed a three-year note at the bank for $120,000.

d. Purchased office equipment at a cost of $50,000, paying $10,000 down and agreeing to pay the remainder in 10 days.

e. Paid wages and salaries of $12,000 for the first half of the month. Office employees are paid twice a month.

f. Paid the balance due on the office equipment.

g. Sold $24,000 of advertising during the first month. Customers have until the 15th of the following month to pay their bills.

h. Paid wages and salaries of $15,000 for the second half of the month.

i. Recorded $3,500 in commissions earned by the salespeople during the month. They will be paid on the fifth of the following month.

Required

1. Prepare in journal form the entry to record each transaction.

2. Post the journal to ledger accounts, using the letters preceding the transactions to identify them in the accounts. Each account involved in the problem needs a separate T account.

3. Prepare a trial balance at January 31, 2008.

Problem 3-9 *The Detection of Errors in a Trial Balance and Preparation of a Corrected Trial Balance* **LO 2, 3**

Hart Inc. was incorporated on January 1, 2008, with the issuance of shares in return for $90,000 of cash contributed by the owners. The only other transaction entered into prior to beginning operations was the issuance of a $75,300 note payable in exchange for building and equipment. The following trial balance was prepared at the end of the first month by the bookkeeper for Hart Inc.

HART INC.
TRIAL BALANCE
JANUARY 31, 2008

Account Titles	Debits	Credits
Cash	$ 19,980	
Accounts Receivable	8,640	
Land	70,000	
Building	50,000	
Equipment	23,500	
Notes Payable		$ 75,300
Capital Stock		90,000
Service Revenue		50,340
Wage and Salary Expense	23,700	
Advertising Expense	4,600	
Utilities Expense	8,420	
Dividends		5,000
Totals	$208,840	$220,640

Required

1. Identify the *two* errors in the trial balance. Ignore depreciation expense and interest expense.

2. Prepare a corrected trial balance.

Problem 3-10 *Journal Entries, Ledger, Trial Balance, and Financial Statements* **LO 3, 4, 5**

Eagle Delivery Service is incorporated on January 2, 2008, and enters into the following transactions during its first month of operations:

January 2: Filed articles of incorporation with the government, and issued 100,000 shares. Cash of $50,000 is received from the new owners for the shares.

January 3: Purchased a warehouse and land for $40,000 in cash. An appraiser values the land at $10,000 and the warehouse at $30,000.

January 4: Signed a three-year note at the National Bank in the amount of $30,000.

January 6: Purchased five new delivery trucks for a total of $25,000 in cash.

January 31: Performed services on account that amounted to $8,500 during the month. Cash amounting to $7,200 was received from customers on account during the month.

January 31: Established an open account at a local service station at the beginning of the month. Purchases of gas and oil during January amounted to $3,600. Eagle has until the 10th of the following month to pay its bill.

Required

1. Prepare journal entries to record the transactions entered into during the month.

2. Post the journal entries to ledger accounts.

3. Prepare a trial balance at January 31, 2008.

4. Prepare an income statement for the month ended January 31, 2008.

5. Prepare a classified balance sheet at January 31, 2008.

6. Assume that you are considering buying shares in this company. Beginning with the transaction to record the purchase of the property on January 3, list any additional information you would like to have about each of the transactions during the remainder of the month.

Problem 3-11 *Journal Entries, Ledger, Trial Balance, and Financial Statements* LO 3, 4, 5

Lacewood Inc. was organized on June 2, 2008, by a group of accountants to provide accounting and tax services to small businesses. The following transactions occurred during the first month of business:

June 2: Received contributions of $20,000 from each of the three owners of the business in exchange for shares.

June 5: Purchased a computer system for $24,000. The agreement with the vendor requires a down payment of $5,000 with the balance due in 60 days.

June 8: Signed a two-year note at the bank and received cash of $40,000.

June 15: Billed $24,700 to clients for the first half of June. Clients are billed twice a month for services performed during the month, and the bills are payable within 10 days.

June 17: Paid a $1,800 bill from the local newspaper for advertising for the month of June.

June 23: Received the amounts billed to clients for services performed during the first half of the month.

June 28: Received and paid gas, electric, and water bills. The total amount is $5,400.

June 29: Received the landlord's bill for $4,400 for rent on the office space that Lacewood leases. The bill is payable by the 10th of the following month.

June 30: Paid salaries and wages for June. The total amount is $11,300.

June 30: Billed $36,800 to clients for the second half of June.

June 30: Declared and paid dividends in the amount of $12,000.

Required

1. Prepare journal entries to record the transactions entered into during the month. Ignore depreciation expense and interest expense.

2. Post the journal entries to the ledger.

3. Prepare a trial balance at June 30, 2008.

4. Prepare the following financial statements:
   a. Income statement for the month ended June 30, 2008.
   b. Statement of retained earnings for the month ended June 30, 2008.
   c. Classified balance sheet at June 30, 2008.

5. Assume that you have just graduated from university and have been approached to join this company as an accountant. From your reading of the financial statements for the first month, would you consider joining the company? Explain your answer. Limit your answer to financial considerations only.

Problem 3-1A *Events to Be Recorded in Accounts* LO 1

The following events take place at Peat Accountants Inc.:

1. Supplies are ordered from vendors, who will deliver the supplies within the week.
2. Vendors deliver supplies on account, payment due in 30 days.
3. New computer system is ordered.
4. Old computer system is sold for cash.
5. Services are rendered to customers on account. The invoices are mailed and due in 30 days.
6. Cash is received from customer and is deposited in the bank night depository.
7. Employees are paid weekly paycheques.
8. Vendors noted in item **2** are paid for the supplies delivered.

Required

Identify each event as internal (I) or external (E), and indicate whether each event would be recorded in the *accounts* of the company. For each event that is to be recorded, identify the names of at least two accounts that would be affected.

Problem 3-2A *Transaction Analysis and Financial Statements* LO 2

Shades Enterprises was organized on June 1, 2008, by two university students who recognized an opportunity to make money while spending their days at a beach along Lake Ontario. The two entrepreneurs plan to rent beach umbrellas. The following transactions occurred during the first month of operations:

June 1: Received contribution of $4,000 from each of the two principal owners of the new business in exchange for shares.

June 1: Purchased 50 beach umbrellas for $250 each on account. The company has 30 days to pay for the beach umbrellas.

June 5: Registered as a vendor with the municipality and paid the $70 monthly fee.

June 10: Purchased $100 in miscellaneous supplies on an open account. The company has 30 days to pay for the supplies.

June 15: Paid a $140 bill from a local radio station for advertising for the last two weeks of June.

June 17: Customers rented beach umbrellas for cash of $2,000.

June 24: Billed a local hotel $4,000 for beach umbrellas provided for use during a convention being held at the hotel. The hotel is to pay one-half of the bill in five days and the rest within 30 days.

June 29: Received 50% of the amount billed to the hotel.

June 30: Customers rented beach umbrellas for cash of $3,000.

June 30: Paid wages of $180 to a friend who helped out over the weekend.

June 30: Paid the balance due on the beach umbrellas.

Required

1. Prepare a table to summarize the preceding transactions as they affect the accounting equation. Use the format in Exhibit 3-1. Identify each transaction with a date.
2. Prepare an income statement for the month ended June 30, 2008.
3. Prepare a classified balance sheet at June 30, 2008.

Problem 3-3A *Transaction Analysis and Financial Statements* LO 2

Four Services Inc. was organized on March 1, 2008, by four former university roommates. The corporation will provide computer tax services to small businesses. The following transactions occurred during the first month of operations:

March 2: Received contributions of $10,000 from each of the four principal owners in exchange for shares.

March 7: Signed a two-year note at the bank and received cash of $15,000. Interest, along with the $15,000, will be repaid at the end of the two years.

March 12: Purchased miscellaneous supplies on account for $700, with payment due in 30 days.

March 19: Billed a client $4,000 for tax preparation services. According to an agreement between the two companies, the client is to pay 25% of the bill upon its receipt and the remaining balance within 30 days.

March 20: Paid a $1,300 bill from the local newspaper for advertising for the month of March.

March 22: Received 25% of the amount billed the client on March 19.

March 26: Received cash of $2,800 for services provided in assisting a client in preparing its tax return.

March 29: Purchased a computer system for $8,000 in cash.

March 30: Paid $3,300 in salaries and wages for March.

March 31: Received and paid $1,400 of gas, electric, and water bills.

Required

1. Prepare a table to summarize the preceding transactions as they affect the accounting equation. Use the format in Exhibit 3-1. Identify each transaction with the date.

2. Prepare an income statement for the month ended March 31, 2008.

3. Prepare a classified balance sheet at March 31, 2008.

4. From reading the balance sheet you prepared in requirement **3**, what events would you expect to take place in April? Explain your answer.

Problem 3-4A *Transactions Reconstructed from Financial Statements* LO 2

The following financial statements are available for Gottington Corporation for its first month of operations:

GOTTINGTON CORPORATION
INCOME STATEMENT
FOR THE MONTH ENDED MAY 31, 2008

Service revenue		$37,700
Expenses:		
Rent	$ 3,000	
Salaries and wages	12,300	
Utilities	6,400	21,700
Net income		$16,000

GOTTINGTON CORPORATION
BALANCE SHEET
MAY 31, 2008

Assets		Liabilities and Shareholders' Equity	
Cash	$ 6,800	Wages payable	$ 3,000
Accounts receivable	12,900	Notes payable	25,000
Equipment	16,000	Unearned service revenue	2,000
Furniture	7,300	Capital stock	15,000
Land	12,000	Retained earnings	10,000
		Total liabilities and	
Total assets	$ 55,000	shareholders' equity	$ 55,000

Required

Describe as many transactions as you can that were entered into by Gottington Corporation during the first month of business.

Problem 3-5A *Identification of Events with Source Documents* LO 1

Many events are linked to a source document. The following is a list of events that occurred in an entity:

a. Signed a note at the bank and received cash.

b. Hired three employees and agreed to pay them $750 per week.

c. Sold merchandise to a customer for cash.

(continued)

d. Reported a fire that destroyed a billboard that is on the entity's property and is owned and maintained by another entity.

e. Received payment of bills from customers.

f. Purchased shares in another entity to gain some control over it.

g. Paid a security deposit and six months' rent on a building.

h. Contracted with a cleaning service to maintain the interior of the building in good repair. No money is paid at this time.

Required

For each item **a** through **h,** indicate whether the event should or should not be recorded in the entity's accounts. For each item that should be recorded in the entity's books:

1. Identify one or more source documents that are generated from the event.

2. Identify which source document would be used to record an event when it produces more than one source document.

3. For each document, identify the information that is most useful in recording the event in the accounts.

Alternate Multi-Concept Problems

Problem 3-6A *Accounts Used to Record Transactions* LO 2, 3

A list of accounts, with an identifying number for each, is shown below. Following the list of accounts is a series of transactions entered into by a company during its first year of operations.

Required

For each transaction, indicate the account or accounts that should be debited and credited.

1. Cash	9. Notes Payable
2. Accounts Receivable	10. Capital Stock
3. Prepaid Insurance	11. Retained Earnings
4. Office Supplies	12. Service Revenue
5. Automobiles	13. Wage and Salary Expense
6. Land	14. Utilities Expense
7. Accounts Payable	15. Income Tax Expense
8. Income Tax Payable	

	Accounts	
Transactions	**Debited**	**Credited**
Example: Purchased office supplies for cash.	4	1
a. Issued shares for cash.	_____	_____
b. Acquired land in exchange for shares.	_____	_____
c. Purchased an automobile and signed a 60-day note for the total amount.	_____	_____
d. Paid employees salaries and wages earned during the month.	_____	_____
e. Received cash from clients for services performed during the month.	_____	_____
f. Purchased flyers and signs from a printer, payment due in 10 days.	_____	_____
g. Paid for the flyers and signs purchased in item **f.**	_____	_____
h. Received monthly telephone bill; payment is due within 10 days of receipt.	_____	_____

i. Paid monthly telephone bill. _____ _____

j. Paid for a six-month liability insurance policy. _____ _____

k. Computed amount of taxes due based on the income of the period and paid the amount. _____ _____

Problem 3-7A *Transaction Analysis, Trial Balance, and Financial Statements* LO 2, 5

Three friends set up Putting Range on October 1, 2008. The following transactions occurred during the first month of operations:

October 1: Received contribution of $10,000 from each of the three principal owners of the new business in exchange for shares.

October 2: Purchased land valued at $15,000 and a building valued at $75,000. The seller agreed to accept a down payment of $9,000 and a five-year note for the balance.

October 3: Purchased new tables and chairs for the lounge at a cost of $25,000, paying $5,000 down and agreeing to pay for the remainder in 60 days.

October 9: Purchased soft balls for $3,500 cash.

October 12: Purchased food and drinks for $2,500 on an open account. The company has 30 days to pay for the concession supplies.

October 13: Sold tickets for cash of $400 and took in $750 at the concession stand.

October 17: Rented out the range to a local community group for $750. The community group is to pay one-half of the bill within five working days and has 30 days to pay the remainder.

October 23: Received 50% of the amount billed to the community group.

October 24: Sold tickets for cash of $500, and took in $1,200 at the concession stand.

October 26: The three friends, acting on behalf of Putting Range, paid a dividend of $250 on the shares of stock owned by each of them, or $750 in total.

October 27: Paid $1,275 for utilities.

October 30: Paid wages and salaries of $2,250.

October 31: Sold tickets for cash of $700, and took in $1,300 at the concession stand.

Required

1. Prepare a table to summarize the preceding transactions as they affect the accounting equation. Use the format in Exhibit 3-1. Identify each transaction with a date.
2. Prepare a trial balance at October 31, 2008.
3. Prepare an income statement for the month ended October 31, 2008.
4. Prepare a statement of retained earnings for the month ended October 31, 2008.
5. Prepare a classified balance sheet at October 31, 2008.

Problem 3-8A *Journal Entries, Ledger Posting, and Trial Balance* LO 3, 4, 5

Centry 21 Consulting began business in February 2008. Listed below are the transactions entered into by Centry 21 during its first month of operations.

a. Issued 10,000 shares in exchange for $50,000 in cash.

b. Paid monthly rent of $400.

c. Signed a five-year note for $50,000 at the bank.

d. Received $5,000 cash from a customer for services to be performed over the next two months.

e. Purchased software to be used on future jobs. The software costs $10,950 and is expected to be used on five to eight jobs over the next two years.

f. Billed customers $12,500 for work performed during the month.

g. Paid office personnel $3,000 for the month of February.

h. Received a utility bill of $100. The total amount is due in 30 days.

(continued)

Required

1. Prepare in journal form the entry to record each transaction.

2. Post journal to ledger accounts, using the letters preceding the transactions to identify them in the accounts. Each account involved in the problem needs a separate T account.

3. Prepare a trial balance at February 29, 2008.

Problem 3-9A *Entries Prepared from a Trial Balance and Proof of the Cash Balance* LO 2, 3

Highland Company was incorporated on January 1, 2008, with the issuance of shares in return for $40,000 of cash contributed by the owners. The only other transaction entered into prior to beginning operations was the issuance of a $50,000 note payable in exchange for equipment and fixtures. The following trial balance was prepared at the end of the first month by the bookkeeper for Highland Company.

HIGHLAND COMPANY
TRIAL BALANCE
JANUARY 31, 2008

Account Titles	Debits	Credits
Cash	$?	
Accounts Receivable	30,500	
Equipment and Fixtures	50,000	
Wages Payable		$ 10,000
Notes Payable		50,000
Capital Stock		40,000
Service Revenue		60,500
Wage and Salary Expense	24,600	
Advertising Expense	12,500	
Rent Expense	5,200	

Required

1. Determine the balance in the Cash account.

2. Identify all of the transactions that affected the Cash account during the month. Use a T account to prove what the balance in Cash would be after all transactions are recorded.

Problem 3-10A *Journal Entries* LO 3, 4

Right-Away Delivery Inc. is incorporated on January 2, 2008, and enters into the following transactions during its second month of operations:

February 2: Paid $800 for wages earned by employees for the week ending January 31.

February 3: Paid $6,460 for gas and oil billed on an open account in January.

February 4: Declared and paid $4,000 cash dividends to shareholders.

February 15: Received $16,000 cash from customer accounts.

February 26: Provided $33,600 of services on account during the month.

February 27: Received a $6,800 bill from the local service station for gas and oil used during February.

Required

1. Prepare journal entries on the books of Right-Away to record the transactions entered into during February.

2. For the transactions on February 2, 3, 4, and 27, indicate whether the amount is an expense of operating in the month of January or February or is not an expense in either month.

Problem 3-11A *Journal Entries, Ledger Posting, Trial Balance, and Financial Statments* LO 3, 4, 5

Bugscontrol Inc. was organized on July 1, 2008, by a group of technicians to provide termite inspections and treatment to homeowners and small businesses. On the next page, the following transactions occurred during the first month of business:

July 2: Received contributions of $6,000 from each of the six owners in exchange for shares.

July 3: Paid $2,000 rent for the month of July.

July 5: Purchased flashlights, tools, spray equipment, and ladders for $36,000, with a down payment of $10,000 and the balance due in 30 days.

July 17: Paid a $400 bill for the distribution of door-to-door advertising.

July 28: Paid August rent and July utilities to the landlord in the amounts of $2,000 and $900, respectively.

July 30: Received $16,000 in cash from homeowners for services performed during the month. In addition, billed $15,000 to other customers for services performed during the month. Billings are due in 30 days.

July 30: Paid commissions of $19,000 to the technicians for July.

July 31: Received $1,200 from a business client to perform services over the next two months.

Required

1. Prepare journal entries on the books of Bugscontrol to record the transactions entered into during the month. Ignore depreciation expense.

2. Post the journal entries to a ledger.

3. Prepare a trial balance at July 31, 2008.

4. Prepare the following financial statments:

   a. The income statement for the month ended July 31, 2008.

   b. The statement of retained earnings for the month ended July 31, 2008.

   c. The classified balance sheet at July 31, 2008.

5. From the balance sheet, what cash inflow and what cash outflow can you predict in the month of August? Who would be interested in the cash flow information and why?

Cases

Reading and Interpreting Financial Statements

Case 3-1 *Reading CN's income statement* LO 5
Refer to the income statements for CN in Appendix A at the end of the book.

Required

1. What is the change in CN's Revenues account from 2006 to 2007?

2. What is the change in CN's Net Income account from 2006 to 2007? How many operating expense accounts does CN report on its income statement? Which of these is the largest amount in 2007? Give an example of a transaction that would affect this account.

3. CN reports taxes on its income statement on the line "Income tax expense." What is the dollar amount of taxes CN reports on its 2007 income statement? Compute the ratio of taxes to income before income taxes for 2006 and 2007. Is CN's ratio the same for both years? What does this ratio tell you?

Case 3-2 *Reading and Interpreting CN's Statement of Cash Flows* LO 2, 3, 4
Refer to CN's statement of cash flows for the year ended December 31, 2007.

Required

1. What amount did the company spend on purchases of properties during 2007? Prepare the journal entry to record these purchases, assuming cash was paid.

2. What amount did the company pay shareholders in cash dividends during 2007? Prepare the journal entry to record the payment.

Case 3-3 *Reading and Interpreting ACE Aviation's Balance Sheet* **LO 1, 2, 5**

The following item appears in the current liabilities section of the balance sheet of **ACE Aviation Holdings Inc.**, formerly **Air Canada**, at December 31, 2007.

Advance ticket sales and loyalty program deferred revenues $1,245 million

In addition, one of the notes states: "Airline passenger and cargo advance sales are deferred and included in current liabilities. Passenger and cargo revenues are recognized when the transportation is provided."

Required

1. What economic event caused ACE Aviation to incur this liability? Was it an external or an internal event?

2. Describe the effect on the accounting equation from the transaction to record the advance ticket sales.

3. Assume that one customer purchases a $500 ticket in advance. Prepare the journal entry on ACE Aviation's books to record this transaction.

4. What economic event will cause ACE Aviation to reduce its advance ticket sales? Is this an external or an internal event?

Making Financial Decisions

Case 3-4 *Cash Flow versus Net Income* **LO 1, 3**

Kim Lee started a real estate business at the beginning of January. After obtaining the certificate of incorporation, she issued 1,000 shares to herself and deposited $20,000 in a bank account under the name Lee Properties. Because business was "booming," she spent all of her time during the first month selling properties rather than keeping financial records.

At the end of January, Kim comes to you with the following plight:

> I put $20,000 in to start this business at the beginning of the month. My January 31 bank statement shows a balance of $17,000. After all of my efforts, it appears as if I'm "in the hole" already! On the other hand, that seems impossible—we sold five properties for clients during the month. The total sales value of these properties was $600,000, and I receive a commission of 5% on each sale. Granted, one of the five sellers still owes me an $8,000 commission on the sale, but the other four have been collected in full. Three of the sales, totaling $400,000, were actually made by my assistants. I pay them 4% of the sales value of a property. Sure, I have a few office expenses for my car, utilities, and a secretary, but that's about it. How can I have possibly lost $3,000 this month?

You agree to help Kim figure out how she really did this month. The bank statement is helpful. The total deposits during the month amount to $22,000. Kim explains that this amount represents the commissions on the four sales collected so far. The cancelled cheques reveal the following expenditures:

Cheque No.	Payee—Memo at Bottom of Cheque	Amount
101	Stevens Office Supply	$ 2,000
102	Why Walk, Let's Talk Motor Co.—new car	3,000
103	City of Westbrook—heat and lights	500
104	Alice Hill—secretary	2,200
105	Ace Property Management—office rent for month	1,200
106	Jerry Hayes (sales assistant)	10,000
107	Joan Harper (sales assistant)	6,000
108	Don's Fillitup—gas and oil for car	100

According to Kim, the $2,000 cheque to Stevens Office Supply represents the down payment on a word processor and a copier for the office. The remaining balance is $3,000 and it must be paid to Stevens by February 15. Similarly, the $3,000 cheque is the down payment on a car for the business. A $12,000 note was given to the car dealer and is due along with interest in one year.

1. Prepare an income statement for the month of January for Lee Properties.

2. Prepare a statement of cash flows for the month of January for Lee Properties.

3. Draft a memorandum to Kim Lee explaining as simply and as clearly as possible why she *did* in fact have a profitable first month in business but experienced a decrease in her Cash account. Support your explanation with any necessary figures.

4. The down payments on the car and the office equipment are reflected on the statement of cash flows. They are assets that will benefit the business for a number of years. Do you think that *any* of the cost associated with the acquisition of these assets should be recognized in some way on the income statement? Explain your answer.

Case 3-5 *Loan Request* LO 2, 3, 4, 5

Scott McKay started a landscaping and lawn care business in April 2008 by investing $20,000 cash in the business in exchange for shares. Because his business is in eastern Canada, the season begins in April and concludes in September. He prepared the following trial balance (with accounts in alphabetical order) at the end of the first season in business.

MCKAY LANDSCAPING
TRIAL BALANCE
SEPTEMBER 30, 2008

	Debits	Credits
Accounts Payable		$16,000
Accounts Receivable	$26,000	
Capital Stock		20,000
Cash	1,200	
Gas and Oil Expense	15,700	
Insurance Expense	2,500	
Landscaping Revenue		33,400
Lawn Care Revenue		24,000
Mowing Equipment	5,000	
Rent Expense	6,000	
Salaries Expense	22,000	
Truck	15,000	
Totals	$93,400	$93,400

Scott is pleased with his first year in business. "I paid myself a salary of $22,000 during the year and still have $1,200 in the bank. Sure, I have a few bills outstanding, but my accounts receivable will more than cover those." In fact, Scott is so happy with the first year that he has come to you in your role as a lending officer at the local bank to ask for a $20,000 loan to allow him to add another truck and mowing equipment for the second season.

Required

1. From your reading of the trial balance, what does it appear to you that Scott did with the $20,000 in cash he originally contributed to the business? Reconstruct the journal entry to record the transaction you think took place.

2. Prepare an income statement for the six months ended September 30, 2008.

3. The mowing equipment and truck are assets that will benefit the business for a number of years. Do you think that any of the costs associated with the purchase of these assets should have been recognized as expenses in the first year? How would this have affected the income statement?

4. Prepare a classified balance sheet as of September 30, 2008. As a banker, what two items on the balance sheet concern you the most? Explain your answer.

5. As a banker, would you loan Scott $20,000 to expand his business during the second year? Draft a memo to respond to Scott's request for the loan, indicating whether you will make the loan.

Accounting and Ethics: What Would You Do?

Case 3-6 *Delay in the Posting of a Journal Entry* LO 2, 3, 4, 5

As assistant controller for a small consulting firm, you are responsible for recording and posting the daily cash receipts and disbursements to the ledger accounts. After you have posted the entries, your boss, the controller, prepares a trial balance and the financial statements. You make the following entries on June 30, 2008:

2008			
June 30	Cash	1,430	
	Accounts Receivable	1,950	
	Service Revenue		3,380
	To record daily cash receipts		
June 30	Advertising Expense	12,500	
	Utilities Expense	22,600	
	Rent Expense	24,000	
	Salary and Wage Expense	17,400	
	Cash		76,500
	To record daily cash disbursements		

The daily cash disbursements are much larger on June 30 than any other day because many of the company's major bills are paid on the last day of the month. After you have recorded these two transactions and *before* you have posted them to the ledger accounts, your boss comes to you with the following request:

> As you are aware, the first half of the year has been a tough one for the consulting industry and for our business in particular. With first-half bonuses based on net income, I am concerned whether you or I will get any bonus this time around. However, I have a suggestion that should allow us to receive something for our hard work and at the same time will not hurt anyone. Go ahead and post the June 30 cash receipts to the ledger but don't bother to post that day's cash disbursements. Even though the treasurer writes the cheques on the last day of the month and you normally journalize the transaction on the same day, it is pretty silly to bother posting the entry to the ledger, since it takes at least a week for the cheques to clear the bank.

Required

1. Explain *why* the controller's request will result in an increase in net income.
2. Do you agree with the controller that the omission of the entry on June 30 "will not hurt anyone"? If not, be explicit as to why you don't agree. Whom could it hurt?
3. What would you do? Whom should you talk to about this issue?

Case 3-7 *Debits and Credits* LO 2, 4

You are controller for an architectural firm whose accounting year ends on December 31. As part of the management team, you receive a year-end bonus directly related to the firm's earnings for the year. One of your duties is to review the journal entries recorded by the bookkeepers. A new bookkeeper prepared the following journal entry:

Dec. 3	Cash	10,000	
	Service Revenue		10,000
	To record deposit from client		

You notice that the explanation for the journal entry refers to the amount as a deposit, and the bookkeeper explains to you that the firm plans to provide the services to the client in March of the following year.

1. Did the bookkeeper prepare the correct journal entry to account for the client's deposit? Explain your answer.

2. What would you do as controller for the firm? Do you have a responsibility to do anything to correct the books?

Solutions to Key Terms Quiz

11	Account	8	Debit
1	Chart of accounts	4	Credit
3	Event	15	Double-entry system
10	External event	13	Journal
5	Internal event	9	Posting
14	Transaction	7	Journalizing
6	Source document	2	Trial balance
12	Ledger		

CHAPTER 4

Accrual Accounting, Adjusting Entries, and Accounting Cycle

PHOTOS.COM

Focus on Financial Results

CN's 2007 income statement reports $2,158 million of net income. However, its statement of cash flows for the same period shows that cash provided from operating activities is $2,417 million. Why does CN have two different operating results? One of the objectives of this chapter is to explain the difference between the accrual basis of accounting and the cash basis of accounting.

CN 2007 ANNUAL REPORT   http://www.cn.ca

Consolidated Statement of Income (excerpt)

In millions	Year ended December 31,	2007	2006	2005
Revenues		$7,897	$7,929	$7,446
Total operating expenses		5,021	4,899	4,822
Operating income		2,876	3,030	2,624
Interest expense		(336)	(312)	(299)
Other income (Note 14)		(166)	11	12
Income before income taxes		2,706	2,729	2,337
Income tax expense (Note 15)		(548)	(642)	(781)
Net income		$2,158	$2,087	$1,556

Consolidated Statement of Cash Flows (excerpt)

In millions	2007	2006	2005
Net cash receipts from customers and other	$8,139	$7,946	$7,581
Net cash payments for:			
Employee services, suppliers and other expenses	(4,323)	(4,130)	(4,075)
Interest	(340)	(294)	(306)
Workforce reductions (Note 9)	(31)	(45)	(87)
Personal injury and other claims (Note 18)	(86)	(107)	(92)
Pension (Note 13)	(75)	(112)	(127)
Income taxes (Note 15)	(867)	(307)	(186)
Cash provided from operating activities	$2,417	$2,951	$2,708

This excerpt from CN's 2007 Annual Report appears courtesy of CN. This section of the CN Annual Report appears in the Appendix of this textbook.

RECOGNITION AND MEASUREMENT IN FINANCIAL STATEMENTS

Accounting is a communication process. To successfully communicate information to the users of financial statements, accountants and managers must answer two questions:

1. What economic events should be communicated, or *recognized*, in the statements?
2. How should the effects of these events be *measured* in the statements?

The dual concepts of recognition and measurement are crucial to the success of accounting as a form of communication.

Recognition

Recognition The process of including an item in the financial statements of an entity.

"**Recognition** is the process of including an item in the financial statements of an entity. Recognition consists of the addition of the amount involved into statement totals together with a narrative description of the item (e.g., "inventory," "sales," or "donations") in a statement."[1] We see in this definition the central idea behind general purpose financial statements. It is a form of communication between the entity and external users. Shareholders, bankers, and other creditors have limited access to relevant information about a company. They depend on the periodic financial statements issued by management to provide the necessary information to make their decisions. Acting on behalf of management, accountants have a moral and ethical responsibility to provide users with financial information that will be useful in making their decisions. The process by which the accountant depicts, or describes, the effects of economic events on the entity is called recognition.

The items, such as assets, liabilities, revenues, and expenses, depicted in financial statements are *representations*. Simply stated, the accountant cannot show a shareholder or other user the company's assets, such as cash and buildings. What the user sees in a set of financial statements is a depiction of the real thing. That is, the accountant describes, with words and numbers, the various items in a set of financial statements. The system is imperfect at best and, for that reason, is always in the process of change. As society and the business environment have become more complex, the accounting profession has striven for ways to improve financial statements as a means of communicating with statement users.

Measurement

Accountants depict a financial statement item in both words and *numbers*. The accountant must *quantify* the effects of economic events on the entity. It is not enough to include an event in the financial statements just because it is important. To be able to recognize it, the statement preparer must measure the financial effects of the event on the company.

Measurement of an item in financial statements requires that two choices be made. First, the accountant must decide on the *attribute* to be measured. Second, a scale of measurement, or *unit of measure,* must be chosen.

The Attribute to Be Measured   Assume that a company holds a parcel of real estate as an investment. What attribute—that is, *characteristic*—of the property should be used to measure and thus recognize it as an asset on the balance sheet? The cost of the asset at the time it is acquired is the most logical choice. *Cost* is the amount of cash, or its equivalent, paid to acquire the asset. But how do we report the property on a balance sheet a year from now?

Historical cost The amount paid for an asset and used as a basis for recognizing it on the balance sheet and carrying it on later balance sheets.

■   The simplest approach is to show the property on the balance sheet at its original cost, thus the designation **historical cost**. The use of historical cost is not only

---

[1] AcSB Section 1000.40.

simple but also *verifiable.* Assume that two accountants are asked to independently measure the cost of the asset. After examining the sales contract for the land, they should arrive at the same amount.

■ An alternative to historical cost as the attribute to be measured is **realizable value.**[2] Realizable value is the amount of cash, or its equivalent, that could be received currently from the sale of the asset. For the company's piece of property, realizable value is the *estimated* selling price of the land, reduced by any commissions or other fees involved in making the sale. But the amount is only an estimate, not an actual amount. If the company has not yet sold the property, how can we know for certain its selling price? We have to compare it to similar properties that *have* been sold recently.

Realizable value The amount of cash, or its equivalent, that could be received by selling an asset currently.

The choice between realizable value and historical cost as the attribute to be measured is a good example of the tradeoff between *relevance* and *reliability.* As indicated earlier, historical cost is verifiable and is thus to a large extent a reliable measure. But is it as relevant to the needs of the decision makers as realizable value? Put yourself in the position of a banker trying to decide whether to lend money to the company. In evaluating the company's assets as collateral for the loan, is it more relevant to your decision to know what the firm paid for a piece of land 20 years ago or what it could be sold for today? But what *could* the property be sold for today? Two accountants might not necessarily arrive at the same realizable value for the land. Whereas value or selling price may be more relevant to your decision on the loan, the reliability of this amount is often questionable.

Because of its objective nature, historical cost is the attribute used to measure many of the assets recognized on the balance sheet. However, certain other attributes, such as realizable value, have increased in popularity in recent years. In other chapters of the book, we will discuss some of the alternatives to historical cost.

The Unit of Measure   Regardless of the attribute of an item to be measured, it is still necessary to choose a yardstick or unit of measure. The yardstick we currently use is units of money. *Money* is something accepted as a medium of exchange or as a means of payment. The unit of money in Canada is the dollar. In Japan the medium of exchange is the yen, and in Great Britain it is the pound.

The use of the dollar as a unit of measure for financial transactions is widely accepted. The *stability* of the dollar as a yardstick is subject to considerable debate, however. Consider an example. You are thinking about buying a certain parcel of land. As part of your decision process, you measure the dimensions of the property and determine that the lot is 80 metres wide and 120 metres deep. Thus, the unit of measure used to determine the lot's size is the square metre. The company that owns the land offers to sell it for $10,000. Although the offer sounds attractive, you decide against the purchase today.

You return in one year to take a second look at the lot. You measure the lot again and, not surprisingly, find the width to still be 80 metres and the depth 120 metres. The owner is still willing to sell the lot for $10,000. This may appear to be the same price as last year. But the *purchasing power* of the unit of measure, the dollar, may very possibly have changed since last year. Even though the metre is a stable measuring unit, the dollar often is not. A *decline* in the purchasing power of the dollar is evidenced by a continuing *rise* in the general level of prices in an economy. For example, rather than paying $10,000 last year to buy the lot, you could have spent the $10,000 on other goods or services. However, a year later, the same $10,000 may very well not buy the same amount of goods and services.

Inflation, or a rise in the general level of prices in the economy, results in a decrease in purchasing power. In the past, the accounting profession has experimented with

What events have economic consequences to a business? The destructive effects of a warehouse fire, for example, will result in losses to buildings and other business assets. These losses will surely be reflected in the next year's financial statements of the affected companies—possibly in the income statement, as a downturn in revenues due to lost sales. What other financial statements would be affected by a big fire?

---

[2]Realizable value is discussed here as an example of alternatives to historical cost. *AcSB* Section 1000.54 lists three alternatives: replacement cost, realizable value, and present value. The other two alternatives are also used, but only in limited circumstances.

financial statements adjusted for the changing value of the dollar. As inflation has declined in recent years in North America, the debate over the use of the dollar as a stable measuring unit has somewhat subsided.[3] It is still important to recognize the inherent weakness in the use of a measuring unit that is subject to change, however.

Summary of Recognition and Measurement in Financial Statements

The purpose of financial statements is to communicate various types of economic information about a company. The job of the accountant is to decide which information should be recognized in the financial statements and how the effects of that information on the entity should be measured. Exhibit 4-1 summarizes the role of recognition and measurement in the preparation of financial statements.

Exhibit 4-1

Recognition and Measurement in Financial Statements

ECONOMIC EVENTS	are	RECOGNIZED with	MEASURED with
Such as: **Purchase of supplies** **Sale of products** **Payment of wages** **Warehouse fire** **Many other events**		*Words:* Cash Land *Numbers:* $3 million $13,927	*Attribute:* Historical cost *Unit of Measure:* The dollar

THE ACCRUAL BASIS OF ACCOUNTING

LO 2 Describe the differences between the accrual and cash bases of accounting.

The accrual basis of accounting is the foundation for the measurement of income in our modern system of accounting. The best way to understand the accrual basis is to compare it with the simpler cash approach.

Comparing the Cash and Accrual Bases of Accounting

The cash and accrual bases of accounting differ with respect to the *timing* of the recognition of revenues and expenses. For example, assume that on July 24, Barbara White, a salesperson for Spiffy House Painters, contracts with a homeowner to repaint a house for $1,000. A large crew comes in and paints the house the next day, July 25. The customer has 30 days from the day of completion of the job to pay and does, in fact, pay Spiffy on August 25. *When* should Spiffy recognize the $1,000 as revenue? As soon as the contract is signed on July 24? Or on July 25, when the work is done? Or on August 25, when the customer pays the bill?

Exhibit 4-2

When is Revenue Recognized?

July 24 Contract is signed	**July 25** House is painted	**August 25** Customer pays for job
No Revenue Yet!	**Accrual Basis:** When house is painted	**Cash Basis:** When cash is received

---

[3]The rate of inflation in some countries, most noticeably those in South America or Africa, has far exceeded the rate in Canada. Companies operating in some of these countries with hyperinflationary economies are required to make adjustments to their statements.

In an income statement prepared on the **cash basis,** revenues are recognized when cash is *received.* Thus, on a cash basis, the $1,000 would not be recognized as revenue until the cash is collected, on August 25. On an **accrual basis,** revenue is recognized when it is *earned.* On this basis, the $1,000 would be recognized as revenue on July 25, when the house is painted. This is the point at which the revenue is earned.

Recall from Chapter 3 the journal entry to recognize revenue before cash is received. Although cash has not yet been received, another account, Accounts Receivable, is recognized as an asset. This asset represents the right to receive cash in the future. The entry on completion of the job is as follows:

July 25	Accounts Receivable	1,000	
	Service Revenue		1,000
	To recognize revenue from house painting		

Recall from Chapter 3 that the accounting equation must balance after each transaction is recorded. Throughout the remainder of the book, each time we record a journal entry, we illustrate the effect of the entry on the equation. The effect of the preceding entry on the equation is as follows:

$$\textbf{Assets} \;=\; \textbf{Liabilities} \;+\; \textbf{Shareholders' Equity}$$
$$\textbf{+1,000} \qquad\qquad\qquad\quad \textbf{+1,000}$$

At the time cash is collected, Accounts Receivable is reduced and Cash is increased:

Aug. 25	Cash	1,000	
	Accounts Receivable		1,000
	To record cash received from house painting		

$$\textbf{Assets} \;=\; \textbf{Liabilities} \;+\; \textbf{Shareholders' Equity}$$
$$\textbf{+1,000}$$
$$\textbf{−1,000}$$

Assume that Barbara White is paid a 10% commission for all contracts and is paid on the 15th of the month following the month a house is painted. Thus, for this job, she will receive a $100 commission cheque on August 15. When should Spiffy recognize her commission of $100 as an expense? On July 24, when White gets the homeowner to sign a contract? When the work is completed, on July 25? Or on August 15, when she receives the commission cheque? Again, on a cash basis, commission expense would be recognized on August 15, when cash is *paid* to the salesperson. But on an accrual basis, expenses are recognized when they are *incurred.* In our example, the commission expense is incurred when the house is painted, on July 25.

Exhibit 4-3 summarizes the essential differences between recognition of revenues and expenses on a cash basis and recognition on an accrual basis.

Cash basis A system of accounting in which revenues are recognized when cash is received and expenses when cash is paid.

Accrual basis A system of accounting in which revenues are recognized when earned and expenses when incurred.

	Cash Basis	Accrual Basis
Revenue is recognized	**When Received**	**When Earned**
Expense is recognized	**When Paid**	**When Incurred**

Exhibit 4-3
Comparing the Cash and Accrual Bases of Accounting

What the Income Statement and the Statement of Cash Flows Reveal

Most business entities, other than the very smallest, use the accrual basis of accounting. Thus, the income statement reflects the accrual basis. Revenues are recognized when they are earned and expenses when they are incurred. At the same time, however, shareholders and creditors are also interested in information concerning the cash flows of an entity. The purpose of a statement of cash flows is to provide this information. Keep in mind that even though we present a statement of cash flows in a complete set of financial statements, the accrual basis is used for recording transactions and for preparing a balance sheet and an income statement.

Recall the example of Glengarry Health Club in Chapter 3. The club earned revenue from two sources, day passes and court rental. Both of these forms of revenue were recognized on the income statement presented in that chapter and are reproduced in the top portion of Exhibit 4-4. Recall, however, that customers have 30 days to pay and that, at the end of the first month of operation, $4,000 of the court rental of $5,000 had been collected.

Now consider the statement of cash flows for the first month of operation, partially presented in the bottom portion of Exhibit 4-4. Because we want to compare the income statement to the statement of cash flows, only the Operating Activities section of the statement is shown. (The Investing and Financing Activities sections have been omitted from the statement.) Why is net income for the month $9,000 but cash from operating activities only $8,000? Of the $5,000 rental revenue reflected on the income statement, only $4,000 was collected in cash. Glengarry has accounts receivable for the other $1,000. Thus, cash from operating activities, as reflected on a statement of cash flows, is $1,000 *less* than net income of $9,000, or $8,000.

Exhibit 4-4 Comparing the Income Statement and the Statement of Cash Flows

Rental revenue is $5,000 but only $4,000 was collected in cash. This $1,000 difference explains why net income is different from cash generated from these operating activities.

Net income and cash generated from operating activities differ by $1,000

The **income statement** for Glengarry Health Club shows the following:

Revenues:		
Day passes	$15,000	
Court rental	5,000	$ 20,000
Expenses:		
Salaries and wages	10,000	
Utilities	1,000	11,000
Net income		$ 9,000

A **partial statement of cash flows** for Glengarry Health Club shows the following:

Cash received from:		
Day passes	$15,000	
Court rental	4,000	$ 19,000
Cash paid for:		
Salaries and wages	10,000	
Utilities	1,000	11,000
Cash generated from operating activities		$ 8,000

Each of these two financial statements serves a useful purpose. The income statement reflects the revenues actually earned by the business, regardless of whether cash has been collected. The statement of cash flows tells the reader about the actual cash inflows during a period of time. The need for the information provided by both statements is summarized by the United States Financial Accounting Standards Board as follows:

> Statements of cash flows commonly show a great deal about an entity's current cash receipts and payments, but a cash flow statement provides an incomplete basis for assessing prospects for future cash flows because it cannot show interperiod relationships. Many current cash receipts, especially from operations, stem from activities of earlier periods, and many current cash payments are intended or expected to result in future, not current, cash receipts. Statements of earnings and comprehensive income, especially if used in conjunction with statements of financial position, usually provide a better basis for assessing future cash flow prospects of an entity than do cash flow statements alone.[4]

---
[4]*SFAC No. 5*, par. 24c.

Accrual Accounting and Time Periods

The *time period* assumption was introduced in Chapter 1. We assume that it is possible to prepare an income statement that fairly reflects the earnings of a business for a specific period of time, such as a month or a year. It is somewhat artificial to divide the operations of a business into periods of time as indicated on a calendar. The conflict arises because earning income is a *process* that takes place *over a period of time* rather than *at any one point in time.*

Consider an alternative to our present system of reporting on the operations of a business on a periodic basis. A new business begins operations with an investment of $50,000. The business operates for 10 years, during which time no records are kept other than a chequebook for the cash on deposit at the bank. At the end of the 10 years, the owners decide to go their separate ways and convert all of their assets to cash. They split among them the balance of $80,000 in the bank account. What is the profit of the business for the 10-year period? The answer is $30,000, the difference between the original cash of $50,000 contributed and the cash of $80,000 available at liquidation.

The point of this simple example is that we could be very precise and accurate in our measurement of the income of a business if it were not necessary to artificially divide operations according to a calendar. Shareholders, creditors, and other interested parties cannot wait until a business liquidates to make decisions, however. They need information on a periodic basis. Thus, the justification for the accrual basis of accounting lies in the needs of financial statement users for periodic information on the financial position as well as the profitability of the entity.

Two-Minute Review

1. Explain the difference between the attribute to be measured and the unit of measure.
2. Explain the difference between what the income statement reveals and what the cash flow statement reveals.

Answers on pages 164.

ACCRUAL ACCOUNTING AND ADJUSTING ENTRIES

The accrual basis of accounting requires that revenues be recognized when earned and that expenses be recognized when incurred.[5] The accrual basis of accounting necessitates a number of adjusting entries at the end of a period. **Adjusting entries** are the journal entries the accountant makes at the end of a period for a company on the accrual basis of accounting. *Adjusting entries are not needed if a cash basis is used. It is the very nature of the accrual basis that results in the need for adjusting entries.* The frequency of the adjustment process depends on how often financial statements are prepared. Most businesses make adjustments at the end of each month.

> **LO 3** Identify and prepare the four major types of adjusting entries.
>
> **Adjusting entries** Journal entries made at the end of a period by a company using the accrual basis of accounting.

Types of Adjusting Entries

Why are there four basic types, or categories, of adjusting entries? The answer lies in the distinction between the cash and the accrual bases of accounting. On an accrual basis, *revenue* can be earned either *before* or *after* cash is received. *Expenses* can be incurred either *before* or *after* cash is paid. Each of these four distinct situations requires a different type of adjustment at the end of the period. We will consider each of the four categories and look at some examples of each.

---

[5]A more detailed discussion of the revenue and expense recognition principles is provided in Chapter 5.

(1) Cash Paid before Expense Is Incurred (Prepaid Expense) Assets are often acquired before their actual use in the business. Insurance policies typically are prepaid, as often is rent. Office supplies are purchased in advance of their use, as are all types of property and equipment. These unexpired costs are assets. As the costs expire and the benefits are used up, the asset must be written off and replaced with an expense.

Assume that on September 1, a company prepays $2,400 in rent on its office space for the next 12 months. The entry to record the prepayment follows:

Sept. 1	Prepaid Rent	2,400	
	Cash		2,400
	To prepay the rent on office space for 12 months		

Assets	**=**	**Liabilities**	**+**	**Shareholders' Equity**
+2,400				
−2,400				

An asset account, Prepaid Rent, is recorded because the company will receive benefits over the next 12 months. Because the rent is for a 12-month period, $200 of benefits from the asset expires at the end of each month. The adjusting entry at the end of September to record this expiration accomplishes two purposes: (1) it recognizes the reduction in the asset Prepaid Rent, and (2) it recognizes the expense associated with using up the benefits for one month. From the last chapter you should recall that an asset is decreased with a credit and that an expense is increased with a debit, as follows:

Sept. 30	Rent Expense	200	
	Prepaid Rent		200
	To recognize $200 of rent expense for the month		

Assets	**=**	**Liabilities**	**+**	**Shareholders' Equity**
−200				−200

T accounts are an invaluable aid in understanding adjusting entries. They allow us to focus on the transactions and balances that will be included in the more formal general ledger accounts. The T accounts for Prepaid Rent and Rent Expense appear as follows after posting the original entry on September 1 and the adjusting entry on September 30:

PREPAID RENT					RENT EXPENSE		
9/1	2,400				9/30	200	
		200	9/30				
Bal.	2,200						

The balance in Prepaid Rent represents the unexpired benefits from the prepayment of rent for the remaining 11 months: $200 × 11 = $2,200. The Rent Expense account reflects the expiration of benefits during the month of September.

☒ Accounting for Your Decisions

You Are the Store Manager

You are responsible for managing a new running shoe store. The landlord requires a security deposit as well as prepayment of the first year's rent. The security deposit is refundable at the end of the first year. After the first year, rent is payable on a monthly basis. After three months in business, the owner asks you for an income statement. How should the security deposit and the prepayment of the first year's rent be recognized on this income statement?

ANSWER: The security deposit will not affect the income statement. It is an asset that will be converted to cash at the end of the first year, assuming that you are entitled to a full refund. One-fourth of the prepayment of the first year's rent should be recognized as an expense on the income statement for the first three months.

Depreciation is the process of allocating the cost of a long-term tangible asset over its estimated useful life. The accountant does not attempt to measure the decline in value of the asset but simply tries to allocate its cost over its useful life. Thus, the adjustment for depreciation is similar to the one we made for rent expense. Assume that on January 1, a company buys a delivery truck, for which it pays $21,000. The entry to record the purchase is as follows:

Jan. 1   Delivery Truck   21,000
              Cash   21,000
              To record purchase of delivery truck for cash

> **Depreciation** The process of allocating the cost of a long-term tangible asset over its useful life.

Assets	=	Liabilities	+	Shareholders' Equity
+21,000				
−21,000				

Two estimates must be made in depreciating the delivery truck: (1) the useful life of the asset, and (2) the residual value of the truck at the end of its useful life. Estimated residual value is the amount a company expects to be able to receive when it sells an asset at the end of its estimated useful life. Assume a five-year estimated life for the truck and an estimated residual value of $3,000 at the end of that time. Thus, the *depreciable cost* of the truck is $21,000 − $3,000, or $18,000. In a later chapter, we will consider alternative methods for allocating the depreciable cost over the useful life of an asset. For now, we will use the simplest approach, called the **straight-line method,** which assigns an equal amount of depreciation to each period. The monthly depreciation is found by dividing the depreciable cost of $18,000 over the estimated useful life of 60 months, which equals $300 per month.

> **Straight-line method** The assignment of an equal amount of depreciation to each period.

The adjustment to recognize depreciation is conceptually the same as the adjustment to write off Prepaid Rent. That is, the asset account is reduced, and an expense is recognized. However, accountants normally use a contra account to reduce the total amount of long-term tangible assets by the amount of depreciation. A **contra account** has a balance that is the opposite of the balance in its related account. For example, Accumulated Depreciation is used to record the decrease in a long-term asset for depreciation, and thus it carries a credit balance. An *increase* in Accumulated Depreciation is recorded with a *credit* because we want to *decrease* the amount of assets and assets are *decreased* by a *credit*. The entry to record depreciation at the end of January is as follows:

> **Contra account** An account with a balance that is opposite that of a related account.

Jan. 31   Depreciation Expense   300
                 Accumulated Depreciation   300
                 To record depreciation on delivery truck

Assets	=	Liabilities	+	Shareholders' Equity
−300				−300

Why do companies use a contra account for depreciation rather than simply reducing the long-term asset directly? If the asset account were reduced each time depreciation is recorded, its original cost would not be readily determinable from the accounting records. Businesses need to know the original cost of each asset, for various reasons. One of the most important of these reasons is the need to know historical cost for computation of depreciation for tax purposes.

The T accounts for Delivery Truck, Accumulated Depreciation, and Depreciation Expense show the following balances at the end of the first month:

DELIVERY TRUCK		DEPRECIATION EXPENSE	
1/1 21,000		1/31 300	

ACCUMULATED DEPRECIATION	
	300 1/31

> **Study Tip**
>
> Think of the Accumulated Depreciation account as simply an extension of the related asset account, in this case the truck. Therefore, although the Delivery Truck account is not directly reduced for depreciation, a credit to its companion account, Accumulated Depreciation, has the effect of reducing the asset.

On a balance sheet prepared on January 31, the contra account is shown as a reduction in the carrying value of the truck:

Delivery Truck	$21,000	
Less: Accumulated Depreciation	300	$20,700

(2) Cash Received before Revenue Is Earned (Unearned Revenue)

You can benefit greatly in your study of accounting by recognizing its *symmetry*. By this we mean that one company's asset is another company's liability. In the earlier example involving the rental of office space, a second company, the landlord, received the cash paid by the first company, the tenant. At the time cash is received, the landlord has a liability because it has taken cash from the tenant but has not yet performed the service to earn the revenue. The revenue will be earned with the passage of time but is unearned at the moment. This is the entry on the books of the landlord on September 1:

Sept. 1	Cash	2,400	
	Unearned Rent Revenue		2,400
	To record receipt of rent on office space for 12 months		

Assets	=	Liabilities	+	Shareholders' Equity
+2,400		+2,400		

The account Unearned Rent Revenue is a liability. The landlord is obligated to provide the tenant uninterrupted use of the office facilities for the next 12 months. With the passage of time, the liability, is satisfied as the tenant is provided the use of the space. The adjusting entry at the end of each month accomplishes two purposes: it recognizes (1) the reduction in the liability, and (2) the revenue earned each month as the tenant occupies the space. Recall that we decrease a liability with a debit and increase revenue with a credit:

Sept. 30	Unearned Rent Revenue	200	
	Rent Revenue		200
	To recognize rent earned for the month		

Assets	=	Liabilities	+	Shareholders' Equity
		−200		+200

The balance in Unearned Rent Revenue reflects the remaining liability, and the balance in Rent Revenue indicates the amount earned for the month:

UNEARNED RENT REVENUE					RENT REVENUE		
		2,400	9/1			200	9/30
9/30	200						
		2,200	Bal.				

Exhibit 4-5 Gift Card

A gift card like this is a good example of an unearned revenue. **Hudson Bay Company** *has received the $100 in payment for the certificate, but because it must wait for the recipient of the gift to pick out some merchandise, it considers the obligation to deliver the merchandise in the future a liability.*

http://www.hbc.com

COPYRIGHT HUDSON'S BAY COMPANY, USED WITH THEIR PERMISSION.

In another example, many professional sports teams sell season tickets, which require payment in advance. Say, for example, that you subscribe to the 2006 **Toronto Blue Jays**, purchasing a season ticket for $2,025. At the time you pay for the subscription, **Rogers Communications Inc.** (which owns the Blue Jays) incurs a liability. It has taken your money but has not yet done anything to earn it. The company is obligated, through the Blue Jays, either to play the games during the season or to refund your $2,025.

http://toronto.bluejays.mlb.com

http://www.rogers.com

Assume that on March 1, the Blue Jays sold 10 season tickets at $2,025 each. The entry to record the receipt of the cash from the 10 season ticket holders is as follows:

Mar. 1	Cash	20,250
	Unearned Season Ticket Revenue	20,250
	To record receipt of cash from sales of 10 season	
	tickets at $2,025 each	

Assets = Liabilities + Shareholders' Equity
+20,250   +20,250

At what point should Rogers recognize the revenue from ticket sales? The team receives cash at the time a ticket is sold. The revenue has not been earned until the team plays the game, however. Thus a team usually recognizes the revenue after the game is played. An excerpt from the 2004 annual report of Rogers Communications Inc. reflects this policy:

> The Blue Jays' revenue, which is composed primarily of home game admission and concession revenue, is recognized as the related games are played during the baseball season.

Regarding season tickets, assume that there are 81 Blue Jays home games scheduled for the season and that 14 are played in April. Here, the season ticket revenue earned in April should be $20,250 × 14/81, or $3,500. Rogers accountants would make the following entry at the end of April:

Apr. 30	Unearned Season Ticket Revenue	3,500
	Ticket Revenue	3,500
	To record ticket revenue earnings in April	

Assets = Liabilities + Shareholders' Equity
−3,500   +3,500

The accounts Unearned Season Ticket Revenue and Ticket Revenue appear as follows after the two entries are posted:

UNEARNED SEASON TICKET REVENUE

		20,250	4/1
4/30	3,500		
		16,750	Bal.

TICKET REVENUE

3,500	4/30

Accounting for Your Decisions

You Are the Banker

A new Maritime publisher comes to you for a loan. Through an aggressive ad campaign, the company sold a phenomenal number of subscriptions to a new sports magazine in its first six months and needs additional money to go national. The first issue of the magazine is due out next month. The publisher presents you an income statement for its first six months and you notice that it includes all of the revenue from the initial subscriptions sold in the Maritimes. What concerns do you have?

ANSWER: First, the accounting treatment for the magazine revenue is improper. Because the magazine has not yet been delivered to the customers, the subscriptions have not yet been earned, and therefore no revenue should be recognized. As a banker, you should be sufficiently concerned that a potential customer would present improper financial statements, and you should deny the loan on that basis alone. That does not even take into account the fact that the company has yet to establish a sufficient track record to warrant the credit risk.

As you know by now, accounting terminology differs among companies. An account title such as Unearned Season Ticket Revenue is only one of any number of possible titles for a liability related to season ticket subscriptions. Another possible account title for such as liability is Season Ticket Subscriptions Collected in Advance.

(3) Expense Incurred before Cash Is Paid (Accrued Liability)

This situation is just the opposite of (1). That is, cash is paid *after* an expense is actually incurred rather than *before* its incurrence, as was the case in (1). Many normal operating costs, such as payroll and utilities, fit this situation. A utility bill is received at the end of the month, but the company has 10 days to pay it. Or consider the biweekly payroll for Jones Corporation. The company pays a total of $28,000 in wages on every other Friday. Assume that the last payday was Friday, May 31. The next two paydays will be Friday, June 14, and Friday, June 28. The journal entry will be the same on each of these paydays:

June 14	Wages Expense	28,000	
(and	Cash		28,000
June 28)	To pay the biweekly payroll		

Assets	=	Liabilities	+	Shareholders' Equity
−28,000				−28,000

On a balance sheet prepared as of June 30, a liability must be recognized. Even though the next payment is not until July 12, Jones *owes* employees wages for the last two days of June and must recognize an expense for the wages earned by employees for these two days. We will assume that the company operates seven days a week and that the daily cost is 1/14th of the biweekly amount of $28,000, or $2,000. In addition to recognizing a liability on June 30, Jones must adjust the records to reflect an expense associated with the cost of wages for the last two days of the month:

June 30	Wages Expense	4,000	
	Wages Payable		4,000
	To record wages for last two days of the month		

Assets	=	Liabilities	+	Shareholders' Equity
		+4,000		−4,000

What entry will be made on the next payday, July 12? Jones will need to eliminate the liability of $4,000 for the last two days of wages recorded on June 30 because the amount has now been paid. An additional $24,000 of expense has been incurred for the $2,000 cost per day associated with the first 12 days in July. Finally, cash is reduced for $28,000, which represents the biweekly payroll. The entry recorded is:

July 12	Wages Payable	4,000	
	Wages Expense	24,000	
	Cash		28,000
	To pay the biweekly payroll		

Assets	=	Liabilities	+	Shareholders' Equity
−28,000		−4,000		−24,000

The following time line illustrates the amount of expense incurred in each of the two months, June and July, for the biweekly payroll:

2 days' expense in June: $4,000	12 days' expense in July: $24,000

Friday, June 28: Last payday	Friday, June 30: End of accounting period	Friday, July 12: Next payday

Another typical expense incurred before the payment of cash is interest. In many cases, the interest on a short-term loan is repaid with the amount of the loan, called the *principal,* on the maturity date. For example, Granger Company takes out a 9%, 90-day,

$20,000 loan with its bank on March 1. The principal and interest will be repaid on May 30. The entry on Granger's books on March 1 follows:

Mar. 1	Cash	20,000	
	Notes Payable		20,000
	To record issuance of 9%, 90-day, $20,000 note		

$$\text{Assets} \;=\; \text{Liabilities} \;+\; \text{Shareholders' Equity}$$
$$+20{,}000 \qquad\quad +20{,}000$$

The basic formula for computing interest follows:

$$I = P \times R \times T$$

where
I = the dollar amount of interest
P = the principal amount of the loan
R = the annual rate of interest as a percentage
T = time in years (often stated as a fraction of a year).

The total interest on Granger's loan is as follows:

$$\$20{,}000 \times 0.09 \times 3/12 = \underline{\$450}$$

Therefore, the amount of interest that must be recognized as expense at the end of March is one-third of $450 because one month of a total of three has passed. Alternatively, the formula for finding the total interest on the loan can be modified to compute the interest for one month:[6]

$$\$20{,}000 \times 0.09 \times 1/12 = \underline{\$150}$$

The adjusting entry for the month of March is as follows:

Mar. 31	Interest Expense	150	
	Interest Payable		150
	To record interest for one month on a 9%, $20,000 loan		

$$\text{Assets} \;=\; \text{Liabilities} \;+\; \text{Shareholders' Equity}$$
$$+150 \qquad\qquad -150$$

The same adjusting entry is also made at the end of April:

Apr. 30	Interest Expense	150	
	Interest Payable		150
	To record interest for one month on a 9%, $20,000 loan		

$$\text{Assets} \;=\; \text{Liabilities} \;+\; \text{Shareholders' Equity}$$
$$+150 \qquad\qquad -150$$

The entry on Granger's books on May 30 when it repays the principal and interest is as follows:

May 30	Interest Payable	300	
	Interest Expense	150	
	Notes Payable	20,000	
	Cash		20,450
	To record payment of a 9%, 90-day, $20,000 loan with interest		

$$\text{Assets} \;=\; \text{Liabilities} \;+\; \text{Shareholders' Equity}$$
$$-20{,}450 \qquad -20{,}300 \qquad\qquad -150$$

---

[6]In practice, interest is calculated on the basis of days rather than months. For example, the interest for March would be $20,000 × 0.09 × 30/365, or $147.95, to reflect 30 days in the month out of a total of 365 days in the year. The reason the number of days in March is 30 rather than 31 is because in computing interest, businesses normally count the day a note matures but not the day it is signed. To simplify the calculations, we will use months, even though the result is slightly inaccurate.

The reduction in Interest Payable eliminates the liability recorded at the end of March and April. The recognition of $150 in Interest Expense is the cost associated with the month of May.[7] The reduction in Cash represents the $20,000 of principal and the total interest of $450 for three months.

(4) Revenue Earned before Cash Is Received (Accrued Asset)

Revenue is sometimes earned before the receipt of cash. Rent and interest are both earned with the passage of time and require an adjustment if cash has not yet been received. For example, assume that Grand Management Company rents warehouse space to a number of tenants. Most of its contracts call for prepayment of rent for six months at a time. Its agreement with one tenant, however, allows the tenant to pay Grand $2,500 in monthly rent any time within the first 10 days of the following month. The adjusting entry on Grand's books at the end of April, the first month of the agreement, is as follows:

Apr. 30	Rent Receivable	2,500	
	Rent Revenue		2,500
	To record rent earned for the month of April		

Assets	=	**Liabilities**	+	**Shareholders' Equity**
+2,500				+2,500

When the tenant pays its rent on May 7, the effect on Grand's books is as follows:

May 7	Cash	2,500	
	Rent Receivable		2,500
	To record rent collected for the month of April		

Assets	=	**Liabilities**	+	**Shareholders' Equity**
+2,500				
−2,500				

Terminology

One of the challenges in learning accounting concepts is to gain an understanding of the terminology. Part of the difficulty stems from the alternative terms used by different accountants to mean the same thing. For example, the asset created when insurance is paid for in advance is termed a *prepaid expense* by some and a *prepaid asset* by others. Someone else might refer to it as a *deferred expense*.

We will use the term **prepaid expense** to refer to a situation in which cash has been paid but the recognition of expense has been deferred to a later date. Because a prepaid expense represents a *future* benefit to a company, it is an *asset*. An alternative name for prepaid expense is *deferred expense*. Prepaid insurance and office supplies are prepaid expenses. An adjusting entry is made periodically to record the portion of the prepaid expense that has expired.

Unearned revenue means that cash has been received but the recognition of any revenue has been deferred until a later time. Because unearned revenue represents an *obligation* of a company, it is a *liability*. An alternative name for unearned revenue is *deferred revenue*. Rent collected in advance is unearned revenue. The period adjusting entry recognizes the portion of the unearned revenue that is earned in that period.

In this chapter, we have discussed in detail the accrual basis of accounting, which involves recognizing changes in resources and obligations as they occur, not simply when cash changes hands. More specifically, we will use the term *accrual* to refer to a situation in which no cash has been paid or received yet but it is necessary to recognize, or accrue, an expense or a revenue. An **accrued liability** is recognized at the end of the period in cases in which an expense has been incurred but cash has not yet been paid. Wages payable and interest payable are examples of accrued liabilities. An **accrued asset** is recorded when revenue has been earned but cash has not yet been collected. Rent receivable is an accrued asset.

Prepaid expense An asset resulting from the payment of cash before the incurrence of expense.

Unearned revenue A liability resulting from the receipt of cash before the recognition of revenue.

Accrued liability A liability resulting from the recognition of an expense before the payment of cash.

Accrued asset An asset resulting from the recognition of a revenue before the receipt of cash.

---

[7]This assumes that Granger did not make a separate entry prior to this to recognize interest expense for the month of May. If a separate entry had been made, a debit of $450 would be made to Interest Payable.

Exhibit 4-6 Terminology

TYPE	SITUATION	EXAMPLES	ENTRY DURING PERIOD	ENTRY AT END OF PERIOD
Prepaid expense	Cash paid before expense is incurred	Insurance policy Supplies Rent Buildings Equipment	Asset Cash	Expense Asset
Unearned revenue	Cash received before revenue is earned	Deposits Rent Subscriptions Gift certificates	Cash Liability	Liability Revenue
Accrued liability	Expense incurred before cash is paid	Salaries and wages Interest Taxes Rent	No Entry	Expense Liability
Accrued asset	Revenue earned before cash is received	Interest Rent	No Entry	Asset Revenue

Summary of Adjusting Entries

The four types of adjusting entries are summarized in Exhibit 4-6. Common examples of each are shown, along with the structure of the entries associated with the four categories. Finally, the following generalizations should help you in gaining a better understanding of adjusting entries and how they are used:

1. An adjusting entry is an internal transaction. It does not involve another entity.

2. Because it is an internal transaction, an adjusting entry *never* involves an increase or decrease in Cash.

3. At least one balance sheet account and one income statement account are involved in an adjusting entry. It is the nature of the adjustment process that an asset or liability account is adjusted with a corresponding change in either a revenue or an expense account.

Two-Minute Review

Assume that a company wants to prepare financial statements at the end of its first month of operations. Each of the following transactions were recorded on the company's books on the first day of the month.

1. Purchased a 24-month insurance policy for $3,600.

2. Collected $4,800 from a tenant for office space that the tenant has rented for the next 12 months.

3. Took out a 6%, 180-day, $10,000 loan at the bank.

Prepare the necessary adjusting journal entries at the end of the month.

Answers on page 164.

Adjusting Entries for Glengarry Health Club

We will now consider the transactions for the first month of operations and the end-of-period adjusting entries for Glengarry Health Club in Chapter 3 as a comprehensive example. The trial balance after posting to the accounts the transactions entered into during the first month of business is reproduced in Exhibit 4-7. As discussed in Chapter 3, a trial balance can be prepared at any point in time. Because the trial balance is prepared *before* taking into account adjusting entries, it is called an *unadjusted*

Exhibit 4-7
Unadjusted Trial Balance

GLENGARRY HEALTH CLUB UNADJUSTED TRIAL BALANCE JANUARY 31, 2008		
	Debit	**Credit**
Cash	$ 86,000	
Accounts Receivable	1,000	
Supply Inventory	3,000	
Prepaid Rent	18,000	
Equipment	150,000	
Accounts Payable		$ 3,000
Unearned Annual Membership Revenue		48,000
Notes Payable		100,000
Capital Stock		100,000
Day Pass Revenue		15,000
Rental Revenue		5,000
Wage and Salary Expense	10,000	
Utility Expense	1,000	
Dividends	2,000	
Totals	$271,000	$271,000

trial balance. This is the first month of operations for Glengarry. Thus, the Retained Earnings account does not yet appear on the trial balance. After the first month, this account will have a balance and will appear on subsequent trial balances.

Glengarry wants to prepare a balance sheet at the end of January and an income statement for its first month of operations. Use of the accrual basis necessitates a number of adjusting entries to update certain asset and liability accounts and to recognize the correct amounts for the various revenues and expenses.

A trial balance is an important tool to use in preparing adjusting entries. The prepaid expenses on Glengarry's trial balance, such as Prepaid Rent, must be reduced, with a corresponding increase in expenses. Similarly, any unearned revenues, such as Unearned Annual Membership Revenue, must be adjusted and a corresponding amount of revenue recognized. In addition, any accrued assets and accrued liabilities, such as Interest Payable, that do not currently appear on the trial balance must be recognized.

At the beginning of January, Glengarry acquired exercise equipment and issued a $100,000 note as part of the payment. The note has an 18-month term and a 9% interest rate. Although interest will not be repaid until the loan's maturity date, Glengarry must accrue interest for the first month. The calculation of interest for one month is $100,000 $\times$ 0.09 $\times$ 1/12 = $750.

The adjusting entry is as follows:

(a) Interest Expense   750
        Interest Payable   750
        To record interest for one month on 9%, $100,000 note

Assets	**=**	**Liabilities**	**+**	**Shareholders' Equity**
+750				−750

At the beginning of January, Glengarry acquired exercise equipment at a cost of $150,000. The exercise equipment has an estimated useful life of 9 years and an estimated residual value of $15,000 at the end of its life. The monthly depreciation is computed by dividing the depreciable cost of $135,000 by the useful life of 120 months:

$$\frac{\$150,000 - \$15,000}{9 \text{ years} \times 12 \text{ months}} = \frac{\$135,000}{108 \text{ months}} = \$1,250 \text{ per month}$$

The entry to record the depreciation on the equipment for January for a full month is as follows:

(b) Depreciation Expense   1,250
          Accumulated Depreciation   1,250
     To record depreciation for the month

Assets = Liabilities + Shareholders' Equity
−1,250   −1,250

Glengarry purchased $3,000 worth of supplies at the beginning of January. This amount is debited to an asset account, Supply Inventory. At the end of January, however, Glengarry finds that the supplies left on hand have a value of $2,500. The $500 of the supplies that are no longer there are the supplies used during January. This is the amount by which the company reduces its asset and recognizes an expense for the month.

(c) Supply Expense   500
          Supply Inventory   500
     To record use of supplies during January

Assets = Liabilities + Shareholders' Equity
−500   −500

Prepaid Rent on the trial balance represents the rent paid at the beginning of January and covers the six-month period from January to June. The portion of the prepaid rent that has expired after the first month should be allocated to January as rent expense:

$$\frac{\$18,000}{6 \text{ months}} = \$3,000 \text{ per month}$$

The adjusting entry to recognize January rent expense is as follows:

(d) Rent Expense   3,000
          Prepaid Rent   3,000
     To record expiration of prepaid rent

Assets = Liabilities + Shareholders' Equity
−3,000   −3,000

In addition to day passes and rental revenues, Glengarry sells annual memberships. The annual memberships allow the members to use the club facilities at any time within the period of 12 months, including the month of the sale. Thus, as the memberships are sold, Glengarry debits Cash and credits a liability account, Unearned Annual Membership Revenue. The sale of $48,000 worth of memberships was recorded during January and is thus reflected on the trial balance. At the end of the first month, Glengarry's remaining obligations to these members become 11 months' use of the facilities. Because one month of memberships has expired, this is the amount by which the company reduces its liability and recognizes revenue for the month:

$$\frac{\$48,000}{12 \text{ months}} = \$4,000 \text{ per month}$$

(e) Unearned Annual Membership Revenue   4,000
          Annual Membership Revenue   4,000
     To record expiration of annual memberships sold

Assets = Liabilities + Shareholders' Equity
                 −4,000   +4,000

Corporations must pay taxes based on their earnings. In preparing its income statement for the month of January, Glengarry must estimate its taxes for the month, even though it may not have to pay them until some time later. We will assume a corporate tax rate of 34% on income before tax. The computation of Income Tax Expense is as follows (the amounts shown for the revenues and expenses reflect the effect of the adjusting entries):

Revenues		
Day Pass Revenue	$15,000	
Rental Revenue	5,000	
Annual Membership Revenue	4,000	$24,000
Expenses:		
Wage and Salary Expense	10,000	
Rent Expense	3,000	
Depreciation Expense	1,250	
Utilities Expense	1,000	
Supply Expense	500	
Interest Expense	750	16,500
Net Income before Tax		7,500
Times the Corporate Tax Rate		× 34%
Income Tax Expense		$ 2,550

Based on this estimate of taxes, the final adjusting entry recorded on Glengarry's books for the month is:

(f)	Income Tax Expense	2,550	
	Income Tax Payable		2,550
	To record estimated income taxes for the month		

$$\textbf{Assets} \quad = \quad \textbf{Liabilities} \quad + \quad \textbf{Shareholders' Equity}$$
$$\textbf{+2,550} \qquad\qquad\qquad \textbf{-2,550}$$

An *adjusted* trial balance, shown in Exhibit 4-8, indicates the equality of debits and credits after the adjusting entries have been recorded. Note the addition of a number of new accounts that did not appear on the unadjusted trial balance in Exhibit 4-6. The new trial balance includes the accounts that were added when adjusting entries were recorded.

Exhibit 4-8

Adjusted Trial Balance

GLENGARRY HEALTH CLUB ADJUSTED TRIAL BALANCE JANUARY 31, 2008		
	Debit	**Credit**
Cash	$ 86,000	
Accounts Receivable	1,000	
Supply Inventory	2,500	
Prepaid Rent	15,000	
Equipment	150,000	
Accumulated Depreciation		$ 1,250
Accounts Payable		3,000
Unearned Annual Membership Revenue		44,000
Income Tax Payable		2,550
Interest Payable		750
Notes Payable		100,000
Capital Stock		100,000
Dividends	2,000	
Day Pass Revenue		15,000
Rental Revenue		5,000
Annual Membership Revenue		4,000
Wage and Salary Expense	10,000	
Rent Expense	3,000	
Depreciation Expense	1,250	
Utility Expense	1,000	
Supply Expense	500	
Interest Expense	750	
Tax Expense	2,550	
Totals	$275,550	$275,550

THE ACCOUNTING CYCLE

We have focused our attention in this chapter on accrual accounting and the adjusting entries it necessitates. Adjusting entries are one key component in the **accounting cycle.** The accountant for a business follows a series of steps each period. The objective is always the same: *collect the necessary information to prepare a set of financial statements.* Together, these steps make up the accounting cycle. The name comes from the fact that the steps are repeated each period.

The steps in the accounting cycle are shown in Exhibit 4-9. Note that step 1 involves not only *collecting* information but also *analyzing* it. Transaction analysis is probably the most challenging of all the steps in the accounting cycle. It requires the ability to think logically about an event and its effect on the financial position of the entity. Once the transaction is analyzed, it is recorded in the journal, as indicated by the second step in the exhibit. The first two steps in the cycle take place continuously.

Journal entries are posted to the accounts on a periodic basis. The frequency of posting to the accounts depends on two factors: the type of accounting system used by a company and the volume of transactions. In a manual system, entries might be posted daily, weekly, or even monthly, depending on the amount of activity. The larger the number of transactions a company records, the more often it posts. In an automated accounting system, posting is likely done automatically by the computer each time a transaction is recorded.

The accrual basis of accounting requires that adjustments be prepared at the end of a period to recognize both accrued and deferred revenues and expenses. The four types of adjusting entries were discussed in detail earlier in this chapter. Just like the transactions

LO 4 Complete the steps in the accounting cycle.

Accounting cycle A series of steps performed each period and culminating with the preparation of a set of financial statements.

Exhibit 4-9 Steps in the Accounting Cycle

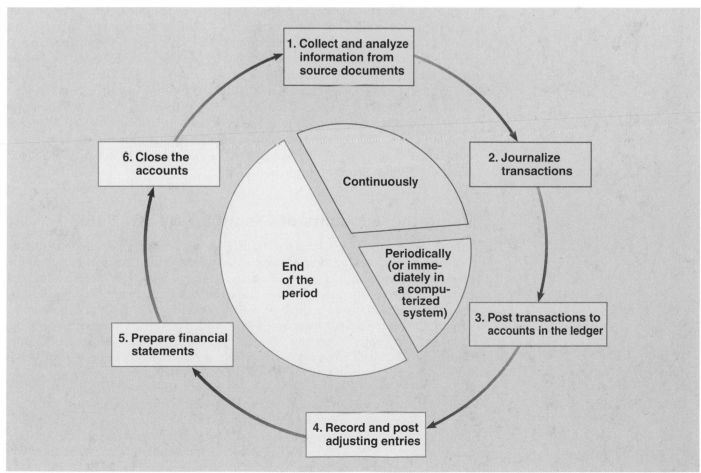

recorded during an accounting period, the adjusting entries need to be journalized first and then posted to ledger accounts. An unadjusted trial balance is often prepared to facilitate the identification and preparation of adjusting entries. An adjusted trial balance is often prepared afterwards to help in the preparation of financial statements. The information needed for the income statement, the statement of retained earnings, and the balance sheet is readily available in an adjusted trial balance. However, additional information and further analysis are needed for the statement of cash flows. The statement of cash flows will be discussed in detail in Chapter 12.

The last step in completing an accounting cycle is to close the accounts. Two types of accounts appear on an adjusted trial balance. Balance sheet accounts are called **permanent accounts** because they are permanent in nature. For this reason, they are never closed. The balance in each of these accounts is carried over from one period to the next. In contrast, revenue, expense, and dividend accounts are **temporary accounts.** The balances in the income statement accounts and the Dividends account are *not* carried forward from one accounting period to the next. For this reason, these accounts are closed at the end of the period.

Closing entries serve two important purposes: (1) to return the balances in all temporary accounts to zero to start the next accounting period, and (2) to transfer the net income (or net loss) and the dividends of the period to the Retained Earnings account.

An account with a debit balance is closed by crediting the account for the amount of the balance. An account with a credit balance is closed by debiting the account for the amount of the balance. Thus, revenue accounts are debited in the closing process. Expense accounts are credited to close them. In this way, the balance of each income statement account is restored to zero to start the next accounting period.

Various approaches are used to accomplish the same two purposes: restore the temporary accounts to zero and update the Retained Earnings account. We will use a holding account called Income Summary to facilitate the closing process. A single entry is made to close all of the revenue accounts. The total amount debited to the revenue accounts is credited to Income Summary. Similarly, a single entry is made to close all of the expense accounts, and the offsetting debit is made to Income Summary. This account acts as a temporary storage account. After closing the revenue and expense accounts, Income Summary has a *credit* balance *if revenues exceed expenses.* Finally, the credit balance in Income Summary is itself closed by debiting the account and crediting Retained Earnings for the same amount. The net result of the process is that all of the revenues less expenses, that is, net income, have been transferred to Retained Earnings.

The Dividends account is closed directly to Retained Earnings. Because dividends are *not* an expense, the Dividends account is not closed first to the Income Summary account, as are expense accounts. A credit is made to close the Dividends account with an offsetting debit to Retained Earnings.

Closing the Accounts of Glengarry Health Club

The four closing entries for Glengarry Health Club are illustrated in Exhibit 4-10. The first closing entry closes the three revenue accounts and credits the total of the month, $24,000, which represents all of the revenue of the period to the Income Summary account. The second entry closes each of the seven expense accounts and transfers the total expenses of $19,050 as a debit to the Income Summary account. The Income Summary account has a credit balance of $4,950, which represents the net income of the period. The third entry closes this temporary holding account and credits the net income to the Retained Earnings account. Finally, the fourth entry closes the Dividends account and debits the $2,000 to the Retained Earnings account.

The posting of closing entries to the ledger accounts is illustrated in Exhibit 4-11. The first closing entry results in a zero balance in each of the three revenue accounts. The second closing entry results in a zero balance in each of the seven expense accounts. The third closing entry transfers the balance of Income Summary account to the Retained Earnings account and leaves the Income Summary account with a zero balance. The Retained Earnings account is now updated to its correct ending balance of $2,950.

Permanent accounts The name given to balance sheet accounts because they are permanent and are not closed at the end of the period.

Temporary accounts The name given to revenue, expense, and dividend accounts because they are temporary and are closed at the end of the period.

Closing entries Journal entries made at the end of the period to return the balance in all temporary accounts to zero and transfer the net income or loss and the dividends to Retained Earnings.

Exhibit 4-10

Recording Closing Entries in the Journal

DATE		ACCOUNT TITLES AND EXPLANATION	POST. REF.	DEBIT	CREDIT
Jan.	31	Day Pass Revenue		15,000	
		Income Summary			15,000
		Rental Revenue		5,000	
		Income Summary			5,000
		Annual Membership Revenue		4,000	
		Income Summary			4,000
		To close revenue accounts to Income Summary			
	31	Income Summary		10,000	
		Wage and Salary Expense			10,000
		Income Summary		3,000	
		Rent Expense			3,000
		Income Summary		1,250	
		Depreciation Expense			1,250
		Income Summary		1,000	
		Utilities Expense			1,000
		Income Summary		500	
		Supplies Expense			500
		Income Summary		750	
		Interest Expense			750
		Income Summary		2,550	
		Income Tax Expense			2,550
		To close expense accounts to Income Summary			

Exhibit 4-11 The Posting of Closing Entries to Ledger Accounts

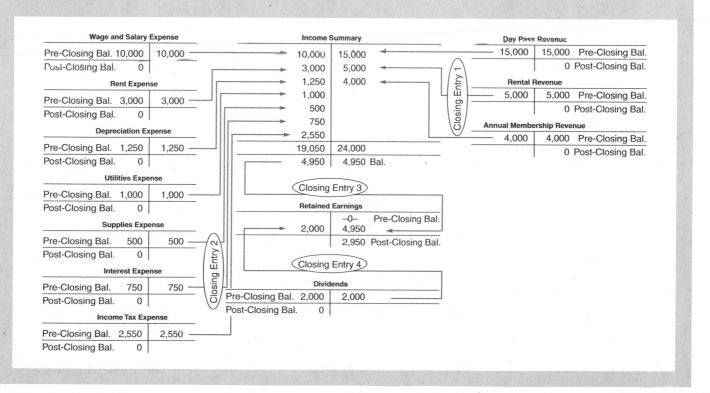

Interim Financial Statements

Interim statements Financial statements prepared monthly, quarterly, or at other intervals less than a year in duration.

We mentioned earlier in this chapter that certain steps in the accounting cycle are sometimes carried out only once a year rather than each month as in our example. For ease of illustration, we have been assuming a monthly accounting cycle. Many companies adjust and close the accounts only once a year, however. Statements prepared monthly, quarterly, or at other intervals less than a year in duration are called **interim statements.** Many companies prepare monthly financial statements for their own internal use. Similarly, corporations whose shares are publicly traded on one of the stock exchanges are required to file quarterly financial statements with the securities commissions.

Suppose that a company prepares monthly financial statements for internal use and completes the accounting cycle in its entirety only once a year. In this case, a work sheet, which is discussed in the Appendix of the chapter, is prepared each month as the basis for interim financial statements. The adjusting entries that appear on the monthly work sheet are not posted to the accounts. They are entered on the work sheet simply as a basis for preparing the monthly financial statements. Formal adjusting and closing entries are prepared only at the end of each year.

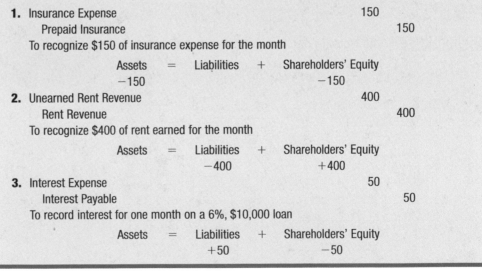

Answers to the Two-Minute Reviews

Two-Minute Review on page 149

1. Accountants must decide whether to use historical cost or another attribute or characteristic of an asset, such as its current value, to measure it. Regardless of the attribute measured, it is necessary to choose a unit of measure. In this country, accountants use the dollar to measure assets and other financial statement items.

2. The income statement reveals the revenues actually earned and the expenses actually incurred by a business, regardless of whether the cash has been collected and paid. The statement of cash flows reveals the actual cash inflows and outflows over a period of time.

Two-Minute Review on page 157

1. Insurance Expense   150
       Prepaid Insurance   150
   To recognize $150 of insurance expense for the month

Assets	=	Liabilities	+	Shareholders' Equity
−150				−150

2. Unearned Rent Revenue   400
       Rent Revenue   400
   To recognize $400 of rent earned for the month

Assets	=	Liabilities	+	Shareholders' Equity
		−400		+400

3. Interest Expense   50
       Interest Payable   50
   To record interest for one month on a 6%, $10,000 loan

Assets	=	Liabilities	+	Shareholders' Equity
		+50		−50

Work sheet A device used at the end of the period to gather the information needed to prepare financial statements without actually recording and posting adjusting entries.

Appendix: Work Sheets

LO 5 Use a work sheet as the basis for preparing financial statements (Appendix).

A **work sheet** is used to organize the information needed to prepare financial statements without recording and posting formal adjusting entries. There is no one single format for a work sheet. We will illustrate a 10-column work sheet by using the information in Chapter 3 and Chapter 4 for the Glengarry Health Club example. The format for a 10-column work sheet appears in Exhibit 4-12. We will concentrate on the *steps* to complete the work sheet, which has already been completed.

Step 1: The Unadjusted Trial Balance Columns

The starting point for the work sheet is the first two columns, which must be filled in with the appropriate amounts from the unadjusted trial balance of Glengarry Health Club as shown in Exhibit 4-7. The trial balance is labelled *unadjusted* because it does not reflect the adjusting entries at the end of the period.

At this point, only the accounts used during the period are entered on the work sheet. Any accounts that are used for the first time during the period because of the adjusting entries will be added in the next step. All but the first two columns of the work sheet should be ignored at this time. Two accounts are included on the work sheet even though they do not have a balance: (1) Accumulated Depreciation, and (2) Retained Earnings. After this first month of operations, these accounts will always have a balance and will appear on an unadjusted trial balance.

Step 2: The Adjusting Entries Columns

The third and fourth columns of the work sheet have been completed in Exhibit 4-12. Rather than take the time now to prepare adjusting entries and post them to their respective accounts, the accountant makes the entries in these two columns of the work sheet. Formal entries can be made after the financial statements have been prepared. The addition of these two columns to the work sheet requires that we add the accounts used for the first time in the period because of the adjustment process. Letters are typically used on a work sheet to identify the adjusting entries and are therefore used here. In practice, the work sheet can be many pages long, and the use of identifying letters makes it easier to locate and match the debit and credit sides of each adjusting entry.

The two columns are totalled to ensure the equality of debits and credits for the adjusting entries. Keep in mind that the entries made in these two columns of the work sheet are *not* the actual adjusting entries; those will be recorded in the journal at a later time, after the financial statements have been prepared.

Step 3: The Adjusted Trial Balance Columns

Columns 5 and 6 of the work sheet represent an adjusted trial balance. The amounts entered in these two columns are found by adding or subtracting any debits or credits in the adjusting entries columns to or from the unadjusted balances. For example, Cash is not adjusted, and thus the $86,000 unadjusted amount is carried over to the Debit column of the adjusted trial balance. The $3,000 credit adjustment to Prepaid Rent is subtracted from the unadjusted debit balance of $18,000, resulting in a debit balance of $15,000 on the adjusted trial balance. Finally, note the equality of the debits and credits on the new trial balance, $275,550.

Step 4: The Income Statement Columns

An adjusted trial balance is the basis for preparing the financial statements. The purpose of the last four columns of the work sheet is to separate the accounts into those that will appear on the income statement and those that will appear on the balance sheet. The income statement columns will be completed next.

The three revenue accounts appear in the credit column, and the seven expense accounts appear in the debit column. These amounts are simply carried over, or extended, from the adjusted trial balance. Glengarry's revenues exceed its expenses. The total of the credit column, $24,000, exceeds the total of the debit column, $19,050. The difference between the two columns, the net income of the period of $4,950, is entered in the debit column. One purpose for showing the net income in this column is to balance the two columns. In addition, the entry in the debit column will be matched with an entry in the balance sheet credit column to represent the transfer of net income to retained earnings. If revenues were *less* than expenses, the *net loss* would be entered in the income statement *credit* column.

Step 5: The Balance Sheet Columns

Why do the income statement columns appear *before* the balance sheet columns on the work sheet? The income statement is in fact a *subset* of the balance sheet, and information from the income statement columns flows into the balance sheet columns. Recall that net income causes an increase in the owners' claim to the assets, that is, an increase in owners' equity, through the Retained Earnings account and, thus, is entered in the balance sheet credit column of the work sheet. In Exhibit 4-12, the amount of *net income,* $4,950, is carried over from the debit column of the income statement to the credit column of the balance sheet. If a company experiences a *net loss* for the period, the amount of the loss is entered in the credit column of the income statement and in the debit column of the balance sheet.

You will note that the Retained Earnings account has a zero balance in the last column of the work sheet, because this is the first month of operations for Glengarry Health Club. On future work sheets, the account will reflect the balance from the *end* of the *previous* month. Dividends appear in the debit column, and net income appears in the credit column. Thus, the ending balance of Retained Earnings can be found by taking its beginning balance, adding the net income of the period, and deducting the dividends. The completed work sheet provides all the necessary information to prepare an income statement, a statement of retained earnings, and a balance sheet.

Exhibit 4-12 The Work Sheet

GLENGARRY HEALTH CLUB
WORK SHEET
FOR THE MONTH ENDED JANUARY 31, 2008

Account Titles	Unadjusted Trial Balance Debit	Unadjusted Trial Balance Credit	Adjusting Entries Debit	Adjusting Entries Credit	Adjusted Trial Balance Debit	Adjusted Trial Balance Credit	Income Statement Debit	Income Statement Credit	Balance Sheet Debit	Balance Sheet Credit
Cash	86,000				86,000				86,000	
Accounts Receivable	1,000				1,000				1,000	
Supply Inventory	3,000			(c) 500	2,500				2,500	
Prepaid Rent	18,000			(d) 3,000	15,000				15,000	
Equipment	150,000				150,000				150,000	
Accumulated Depreciation		0		(b) 1,250		1,250				1,250
Accounts Payable		3,000				3,000				3,000
Unearned Annual Membership Revenue		48,000	(e) 4,000			44,000				44,000
Notes Payable		100,000				100,000				100,000
Retained Earnings		0				—				—
Capital Stock		100,000				100,000				100,000
Dividends	2,000				2,000				2,000	
Day Pass Revenue		15,000				15,000		15,000		
Rental Revenue		5,000				5,000		5,000		
Wage and Salary Expense	10,000				10,000		10,000			
Utility Expense	1,000				1,000		1,000			
	271,000	271,000								
Interest Expense			(a) 750		750		750			
Depreciation Expense			(b) 1,250		1,250		1,250			
Supply Expense			(c) 500		500		500			
Rent Expense			(d) 3,000		3,000		3,000			
Annual Membership Revenue				(e) 4,000		4,000		4,000		
Interest Payable				(a) 750		750				750
Income Tax Expense			(f) 2,550		2,550		2,550			
Income Tax Payable				(f) 2,550		2,550				2,550
			12,050	12,050	275,550	275,550	19,050	24,000	256,500	251,550
							4,950			4,950
							24,000	24,000	256,500	256,500

Chapter Highlights

1. **LO 1** **Explain recognition and measurement issues in financial reporting (p. 144).**

   - Determining which economic events should be recognized and how they should be measured is critical for accounting information to be useful.
     - Recognition drives how and when the effects of economic events are described in the financial statements.
     - Measurement involves deciding on which attribute of an economic event must be measured and the appropriate unit of measure.

2. **LO 2** **Describe the differences between the accrual and cash bases of accounting (p. 146).**

   - Cash and accrual bases are two alternatives to account for transactions or economic events. They differ in the timing of when revenues and expenses are recognized.
     - Under the accrual method, which is the focus of this text, revenues are recognized when earned, and expenses are recognized when incurred.
     - By contrast, under the cash method, revenues are recognized when cash is received, and expenses are recognized when cash is paid.

3. **LO 3** **Identify and prepare the four major types of adjusting entries (p. 149).**

   - Adjusting entries are made at the end of an accounting period to update revenue or expense accounts in accordance with the accrual basis of accounting.
   - There are four basic categories of adjusting entries:
     - Adjustments where cash is paid before expenses are incurred—prepaid expenses.
     - Adjustments where cash is received before revenues are earned—unearned revenue.
     - Adjustments where expenses are incurred before cash is paid—accrued liabilities.
     - Adjustments where revenues are recognized before cash is received—accrued assets.

4. **LO 4** **Complete the steps in the accounting cycle (p. 161).**

   - The accounting cycle involves six steps that are repeated each period (see Exhibit 4-9).
     - Collecting and analyzing data, and journalizing transactions occur on a continuous basis.
     - Periodically, transactions are posted to accounts in the ledger.
     - At the end of the period, adjusting entries are recorded and posted, financial statements are prepared, and accounts are closed.

5. **LO 5** **Use a work sheet as the basis for preparing financial statements. (Appendix—p. 165)**

   - A work sheet is a useful device for organizing the necessary information to prepare financial statements without going through the formal process of recording and posting adjusting entries. A work sheet itself is not a financial statement.
     - The format for a work sheet includes two columns each (debits and credits) for the unadjusted trial balance, the adjustments, the adjusted trial balance, the income statement, and the balance sheet.

Accounts Highlighted

Account Titles	Where it Appears	In What Section	Page Number
Rent expenses	Income statement	Expense	150
Delivery truck	Balance Sheet	Noncurrent Assets	151
Depreciation expense	Income statement	Expense	151
Accumulated depreciation	Balance Sheet	Noncurrent Assets (contra)	151
Interest expense	Income statement	Expense	155
Interest payable	Balance Sheet	Current Liabilities	155
Rent receivable	Balance Sheet	Current Assets	156
Rent revenue	Income statement	Revenue	156
Income tax expense	Income statement	Expense	160
Income tax payable	Balance Sheet	Current Liabilities	161

Read each definition below and then write the number of that definition in the blank beside the appropriate term it defines. The quiz solutions appear at the end of the chapter.

_____ Recognition	_____ Unearned revenue
_____ Historical cost	_____ Accrual
_____ Realizable value	_____ Accrued liability
_____ Cash basis	_____ Accrued asset
_____ Accrual basis	_____ Accounting cycle
_____ Revenues	_____ Work sheet
_____ Expenses	_____ Permanent accounts
_____ Adjusting entries	_____ Temporary accounts
_____ Straight-line method	_____ Closing entries
_____ Contra account	_____ Interim statements
_____ Prepaid expense	

1. A device used at the end of the period to gather the information needed to prepare financial statements without actually recording and posting adjusting entries.

2. Inflows or other enhancements of assets or settlements of liabilities from delivering or producing goods, rendering services, or other activities.

3. Journal entries made at the end of a period by a company using the accrual basis of accounting.

4. Journal entries made at the end of the period to return the balance in all temporary accounts to zero and transfer the net income or loss and the dividends of the period to Retained Earnings.

5. A liability resulting from the receipt of cash before the recognition of revenue.

6. The name given to balance sheet accounts because they are not closed at the end of the period.

7. An asset resulting from the recognition of a revenue before the receipt of cash.

8. The amount of cash, or its equivalent, that could be received by selling an asset currently.

9. The assignment of an equal amount of depreciation to each period.

10. A series of steps performed each period and culminating with the preparation of a set of financial statements.

11. A system of accounting in which revenues are recognized when earned and expenses when incurred.

Answers on p. 197.

12. Cash has not yet been paid or received, but expense has been incurred or revenue earned.

13. Financial statements prepared monthly, quarterly, or at other intervals less than a year in duration.

14. The process of recording an item in the financial statements as an asset, liability, revenue, expense, or the like.

15. An asset resulting from the payment of cash before the incurrence of expense.

16. The name given to revenue, expense, and dividend accounts because they exist one period at time and are closed at the end of the period.

17. A system of accounting in which revenues are recognized when cash is received and expenses when cash is paid.

18. A liability resulting from the recognition of an expense before the payment of cash.

19. An account with a balance that is opposite that of a related account.

20. The amount that is paid for an asset and that is used as a basis for recognizing it on the balance sheet and carrying it on later balance sheets.

21. Outflows or other using up of assets or incurrences of liabilities resulting from delivering goods, rendering services, or carrying out other activities.

Alternate Terms

Historical cost Original cost

Permanent account Real account

Prepaid expense Deferred expense, prepaid asset

Temporary account Nominal account

Unearned revenue Deferred revenue

Warmup Exercise 4-1 *Prepaid Insurance* **LO 3**

ABC Corp. purchases a 24-month fire insurance policy on January 1, 2008, for $5,400.

Required

Prepare the necessary adjusting journal entry on January 31, 2008.

Key to the Solution Determine what proportion and therefore what dollar amount of the policy has expired after one month.

Warmup Exercise 4-2 *Depreciation* **LO 3**

DEF Corp. purchased a new car for one of its salespeople on March 1, 2008, for $25,000. The estimated useful life of the car is four years with an estimated residual value of $1,000.

Required

Prepare the necessary adjusting journal entry on March 31, 2008.

Key to the Solution Determine what dollar amount of the cost of the car should be depreciated and then how much should be depreciated each month.

Warmup Exercise 4-3 *Interest on a Note* **LO 3**

On April 1, 2008, GHI Corp. took out a 12%, 120-day, $10,000 loan at its bank.

Required

Prepare the necessary adjusting journal entry on April 30, 2008.

Key to the Solution Determine the monthly interest cost on a loan that accrues interest at the rate of 12% per year.

Solutions to Warmup Exercises

Warmup Exercise 4-1

$$\$5,400/24 \text{ months} = \$225 \text{ per month}$$

Jan. 31	Insurance Expense	225	
	Prepaid Insurance		225
	To recognize $225 of insurance expense for the month		

Assets	=	Liabilities	+	Shareholders' Equity
−225				−225

Warmup Exercise 4-2

$$\frac{\$25,000 - \$1,000}{4 \text{ years} \times 12 \text{ months}} = \$500 \text{ per month}$$

Mar. 31	Depreciation Expense	500	
	Accumulated Depreciation		500
	To recognize depreciation on car		

Assets	=	Liabilities	+	Shareholders' Equity
−500				−500

Warmup Exercise 4-3

$$\$10,000 \times 0.12 \times \tfrac{1}{12} = \$100$$

Apr. 30	Interest Expense	100	
	Interest Payable		100
	To record interest for one month on a 12%, $10,000 loan		

Assets	=	Liabilities	+	Shareholders' Equity
		+100		−100

Review Problem and Solution

The trial balance of Northern Airlines at January 31, 2008 is shown below. It was prepared after posting the recurring transactions for the month of January, but it does not reflect any month-end adjustments.

NORTHERN AIRLINES
UNADJUSTED TRIAL BALANCE
JANUARY 31, 2008

Cash	$ 75,000	
Parts Inventory	45,000	
Land	80,000	
Buildings—Hangars	250,000	
Accumulated Depreciation—Hangars		$ 24,000
Equipment—Aircraft	650,000	
Accumulated Depreciation—Aircraft		120,000
Unearned Ticket Revenue		85,000
Capital Stock		500,000
Retained Earnings		368,000
Ticket Revenue		52,000
Maintenance Expense	19,000	
Wages and Salaries Expense	30,000	
Totals	$1,149,000	$1,149,000

The following additional information is available:

a. Airplane parts needed for repairs and maintenance are purchased regularly, and the amounts paid are added to the asset account Parts Inventory. At the end of each month, the inventory is counted. At the end of January, the amount of parts on hand is $36,100. *Hint:* What adjusting entry is needed to reduce the asset account to its proper carrying value? Any expense involved should be included in Maintenance Expense.

b. The estimated useful life of the hangar is 20 years with an estimated residual value of $10,000. The original cost of the hangar was $250,000.

c. The estimated useful life of the aircraft is 10 years with an estimated residual value of $50,000. The original cost of the aircraft was $650,000.

d. As tickets are sold in advance, the amounts are added to Cash and to the liability account Unearned Ticket Revenue. A count of the redeemed tickets reveals that $47,000 worth of tickets were used during January.

e. Wages and salaries owed to employees, but unpaid, at the end of January total $7,600.

f. Northern rents excess hangar space to other companies. The amount owed to Northern but unpaid at the end of January is $2,500.

g. Assume a corporate income tax rate of 34%.

Required

1. Prepare journal entries to record all necessary month-end adjustments.
2. Set up T accounts for each of the accounts listed on the trial balance. Set up any other T accounts that will be needed to prepare adjusting entries.
3. Post the month-end adjusting entries to the T accounts.
4. Prepare a trial balance to prove the equality of debits and credits after posting the adjusting entries.

Solution to Review Problem

1.

		Debit	Credit
a.	$45,000 – $36,100 = $8,900		
	Maintenance Expense	8,900	
	Parts Inventory		8,900
b.	($250,000 – $10,000)/240 month = $1,000 per month		
	Depreciation Expense – Hangars	1,000	
	Accumulated Depreciation – Hangars		1,000
c.	($650,000 – $50,000)/120 month = $5,000 per month		
	Depreciation Expense – Aircraft	5,000	
	Accumulated Depreciation – Aircraft		5,000
d.	Unearned Ticket revenue	47,000	
	Ticket Revenue		47,000
e.	Wages and Salaries Expense	7,600	
	Wages and Salaries Payable		7,600
f.	Rent Receivable	2,500	
	Rent Revenue		2,500
g.	Income Tax Expense	10,200	
	Income Tax Payable		10,200

2. and 3.

CASH

Bal.	75,000	

LAND

Bal.	80,000	

ACCUMULATED DEPRECIATION—HANGARS

	24,000	Bal.
	1,000	**(b)**
	25,000	Bal.

RENT REVENUE

	2,500	**(f)**

INCOME TAX EXPENSE

(g)	10,200	

ACCUMULATED DEPRECIATION—AIRCRAFT

	120,000	Bal.
	5,000	**(c)**
	125,000	Bal.

CAPITAL STOCK

	500,000	Bal.

PARTS INVENTORY

Bal.	45,000	
		8,900	**(a)**
Bal.	36,100	

BUILDINGS—HANGARS

Bal.	250,000	

EQUIPMENT—AIRCRAFT

Bal.	650,000	

WAGES AND SALARIES PAYABLE

	7,600	**(e)**

INCOME TAXES PAYABLE

	10,200	**(g)**

UNEARNED TICKET REVENUE

	85,000	Bal.
(d)	47,000	
	38,000	Bal.

RETAINED EARNINGS

	368,000	Bal.

	TICKET REVENUE	
	52,000	Bal.
	47,000	(d)
	99,000	Bal.

MAINTENANCE EXPENSE		
Bal.	19,000	
(a)	8,900	
Bal.	27,900	

WAGES AND SALARIES EXPENSE		
Bal.	30,000	
(e)	7,600	
Bal.	37,600	

DEPRECIATION EXPENSE—HANGARS	
(b)	1,000

DEPRECIATION EXPENSE—AIRCRAFT	
(c)	5,000

RENT RECEIVABLE	
(f)	2,500

4.

NORTHERN AIRLINES
ADJUSTED TRIAL BALANCE
JANUARY 31, 2008

Cash	$ 75,000	
Parts Inventory	36,100	
Land	80,000	
Buildings—Hangars	250,000	
Accumulated Depreciation—Hangars		$ 25,000
Equipment—Aircraft	650,000	
Accumulated Depreciation—Aircraft		125,000
Unearned Ticket Revenue		38,000
Capital Stock		500,000
Retained Earnings		368,000
Ticket Revenue		99,000
Maintenance Expense	27,900	
Wages and Salaries Expense	37,600	
Depreciation Expense—Hangars	1,000	
Depreciation Expense—Aircraft	5,000	
Rent Receivable	2,500	
Rent Revenue		2,500
Wages and Salaries Payable		7,600
Income Tax Expense	10,200	
Income Taxes Payable		10,200
Totals	$1,175,300	$1,175,300

Appendix Review Problem and Solution

Note to the Student: The following problem is based on the information for the Northern Airlines review problem at the end of this chapter. Try to prepare the work sheet without referring to the adjusting entries you prepared in solving that problem.

Required

Refer to the unadjusted trial balance and the additional information for Northern Airlines as presented previously. Prepare a 10-column work sheet for the month of January.

NORTHERN AIRLINES
WORK SHEET
FOR THE MONTH ENDED JANUARY 31, 2008

Account Titles	Unadjusted Trial Balance Debit	Unadjusted Trial Balance Credit	Adjusting Entries Debit	Adjusting Entries Credit	Adjusted Trial Balance Debit	Adjusted Trial Balance Credit	Income Statement Debit	Income Statement Credit	Balance Sheet Debit	Balance Sheet Credit
Cash	75,000				75,000				75,000	
Parts Inventory	45,000			(a) 8,900	36,100				36,100	
Land	80,000				80,000				80,000	
Buildings—Hangars	250,000				250,000				250,000	
Accumulated Depreciation—Hangars		24,000		(b) 1,000		25,000				25,000
Equipment—Aircraft	650,000				650,000				650,000	
Accumulated Depreciation—Aircraft		120,000		(c) 5,000		125,000				125,000
Unearned Ticket Revenue		85,000	(d) 47,000			38,000				38,000
Capital Stock		500,000				500,000				500,000
Retained Earnings		368,000				368,000				368,000
Ticket Revenue		52,000		(d) 47,000		99,000		99,000		
Maintenance Expense	19,000		(a) 8,900		27,900		27,900			
Wage and Salary Expense	30,000		(e) 7,600		37,600		37,600			
	1,149,000	1,149,000								
Depreciation Expense—Hangars			(b) 1,000		1,000		1,000			
Depreciation Expense—Aircraft			(c) 5,000		5,000		5,000			
Rent Receivable			(f) 2,500		2,500				2,500	
Income Tax Expense			(g) 10,200		10,200		10,200			
Wages and Salaries Payable				(e) 7,600		7,600				7,600
Rent Revenue				(f) 2,500		2,500		2,500		
Income Taxes Payable				(g) 10,200		10,200				10,200
			82,200	82,200	1,175,300	1,175,300	81,700	101,500	1,093,600	1,073,800
Net Income							19,800			19,800
							101,500	101,500	1,093,600	1,093,600

Questions

1. What is meant by the following statement? "The items depicted in financial statements are merely *representations* of the real thing."

2. What is the meaning of the following statement? "The choice between historical cost and realizable value is a good example of the trade-off in accounting between relevance and reliability."

3. A realtor earns a 10% commission on the sale of a $150,000 home. The realtor lists the home on June 5, the sale occurs on June 12, and the seller pays the realtor the $15,000 commission on July 8. When should the realtor recognize revenue from the sale, assuming (a) the cash basis of accounting, and (b) the accrual basis of accounting?

4. What does the following statement mean? "If I want to assess the cash flow prospects for a company down the road, I look at the company's most recent statement of cash flows. An income statement prepared under the accrual basis of accounting is useless for this purpose."

5. What is the relationship between the time period assumption and accrual accounting?

6. Is it necessary for an asset to be acquired when revenue is recognized? Explain your answer.

7. When should a publisher of magazines recognize revenue?

8. What is the meaning of *depreciation* to the accountant?

9. What are the four basic types of adjusting entries? Give an example of each.

10. What are the rules of debit and credit as they apply to the contra asset account Accumulated Depreciation?

11. Which of the following steps in the accounting cycle requires the most thought and judgment by the accountant: (a) preparing a trial balance, (b) posting adjusting and closing entries, or (c) analyzing and recording transactions? Explain your answer.

12. What is the difference between a permanent account and a temporary account?

13. What two purposes are served in making closing entries?

14. Why is the Dividends account closed directly to Retained Earnings rather than to the Income Summary account?

15. Assuming the use of a work sheet, are the formal adjusting entries recorded and posted to the accounts before or after the financial statements are prepared? Explain your answer. (Appendix)

16. Some companies use an 8-column work sheet rather than the 10-column format illustrated in the chapter. Which two columns would you think are not used in the 8-column format? Why could these two columns be eliminated? (Appendix)

17. Why do the income statement columns appear before the balance sheet columns on a work sheet? (Appendix)

18. Does the Retained Earnings account that appears in the balance sheet credit column of a work sheet reflect the beginning or the ending balance in the account? Explain your answer. (Appendix)

19. One asset account will always be carried over from the unadjusted trial balance columns of a work sheet to the balance sheet columns of the work sheet without any adjustment. What account is this? (Appendix)

Exercises

Exercise 4-1 *Accruals and Deferrals* LO 3

For the following situations, indicate whether each involves a prepaid expense (PE), an unearned revenue (UR), an accrued liability (AL), or an accrued asset (AA).

Example: __PE__   Office supplies purchased in advance of their use.

_____ 1. Cash collected from subscriptions in advance of publishing a magazine

_____ 2. Income taxes owed at the end of the year

_____ 3. Interest incurred on a customer loan for which principal and interest have not yet been paid

_____ 4. One year's premium on life insurance policy paid in advance

_____ 5. Office building purchased for cash

_____ 6. Rent collected in advance from a tenant

_____ 7. Rent owed by a tenant but not yet collected

_____ 8. Wages earned by employees but not yet paid

Exercise 4-2 *Office Supplies* LO 3

Somerville Corp. purchases office supplies once a month and prepares monthly financial statements. The asset account Office Supplies on Hand has a balance of $1,450 on May 1. Purchases of supplies during May amount to $3,500. Supplies on hand at May 31 amount to $920. Prepare the necessary adjusting entry on Somerville's books on May 31. What would be the effect on net income for May if this entry is *not* recorded?

Exercise 4-3 *Prepaid Rent—Quarterly Adjustments* **LO 3**

On July 15, Northhampton Industries signed a six-month lease, effective August 1, for office space. Northhampton agreed to prepay the rent and mailed a cheque for $18,000 to the landlord on July 27. Assume that Northhampton prepares adjusting entries only four times a year, on March 31, June 30, September 30, and December 31.

Required

1. Compute the rental cost for each full month.

2. Prepare the journal entry to record the payment of rent on July 27.

3. Prepare the adjusting entry on September 30.

4. Assume that the accountant prepares the adjusting entry on September 30 but forgets to record an adjusting entry on December 31. Will net income for the year be understated or overstated? By what amount?

Exercise 4-4 *Depreciation* **LO 3**

On July 1, 2008, Red Gate Farm buys a combine for $100,000 in cash. Assume that the combine is expected to have a eight-year life and an estimated residual value of $13,600 at the end of that time.

Required

1. Prepare the journal entry to record the purchase of the combine on July 1, 2008.

2. Compute the depreciable cost of the combine.

3. Using the straight-line method, compute the monthly depreciation.

4. Prepare the adjusting entry to record depreciation at the end of July 2008.

5. Compute the combine's carrying value that will be shown on Red Gate's balance sheet prepared on December 31, 2008.

Exercise 4-5 *Prepaid Insurance—Annual Adjustments* **LO 3**

On June 1, 2008, Briggs Corp. purchases a 24-month property insurance policy for $72,000. The policy is effective immediately. Assume that Briggs prepares adjusting entries only once a year, on December 31.

Required

1. Compute the monthly cost of the insurance policy.

2. Prepare the journal entry to record the purchase of the policy on June 1, 2008.

3. Prepare the adjusting entry on December 31, 2008.

4. Assume that the accountant forgets to record an adjusting entry on December 31, 2008. Will net income for the year ended December 31, 2008, be understated or overstated? Explain your answer.

Exercise 4-6 *Subscriptions* **LO 3**

Horse Country Living publishes a monthly magazine for which a 12-month subscription costs $30. All subscriptions require payment of the full $30 in advance. On August 1, 2008, the balance in the Subscriptions Received in Advance account was $40,500. During the month of August, the company sold 950 yearly subscriptions. After the adjusting entry at the end of August, the balance in the Subscriptions Received in Advance account is $60,000.

Required

1. Prepare the journal entry to record the sale of the 950 yearly subscriptions during the month of August.

2. Prepare the adjusting journal entry on August 31.

3. Assume that the accountant made the correct entry during August to record the sale of the 950 subscriptions but forgot to make the adjusting entry on August 31. Would net income for August be overstated or understated? Explain your answer.

Exercise 4-7 *Customer Deposits* **LO 3**

Wolfe & Wolfe collected $9,000 from a customer on April 1 and agreed to provide legal services during the next six months. Wolfe & Wolfe expects to provide an equal amount of services each month.

Required

1. Prepare the journal entry for the receipt of the customer deposit on April 1.
2. Prepare the adjusting entry on April 30.
3. What would be the effect on net income for April if the entry in requirement (2) is not recorded?

Exercise 4-8 *Wages Payable* LO 3

Denton Corporation employs 50 workers in its plant. Each employee is paid $12 per hour and works seven hours per day, Monday through Friday. Employees are paid every Friday. The last payday was Friday, January 25.

Required

1. Compute the dollar amount of the weekly payroll.
2. Prepare the journal entry on Friday, January 25, for the payment of the weekly payroll.
3. Denton prepares monthly financial statements. Prepare the adjusting journal entry on Thursday, January 31, the last day of the month.
4. Prepare the journal entry on Friday, February 1, for the payment of the weekly payroll.
5. Would net income for the month of January be understated or overstated if Denton doesn't bother with an adjusting entry on January 31? Explain your answer.

Exercise 4-9 *Interest Payable* LO 3

Billings Company takes out a 6%, 90-day, $100,000 loan with First National Bank on March 1, 2008.

Required

1. Prepare the journal entry on March 1, 2008.
2. Prepare the adjusting entries for the months of March and April 2008.
3. Prepare the entry on May 30, 2008, when Billings repays the principal and interest to First National.

Exercise 4-10 *Property Taxes Payable—Annual Adjustments* LO 3

Lexington Builders owns property in Kaneland County. Lexington's 2007 property taxes amounted to $60,000. Kaneland County will send out the 2008 property tax bills to property owners during April 2009. Taxes must be paid by June 1, 2009. Assume that Lexington prepares adjusting entries only once a year, on December 31, and that property taxes for 2008 are expected to increase by 5% over those for 2007.

Required

1. Prepare the adjusting entry required to record the property taxes payable on December 31, 2008.
2. Prepare the journal entry to record the payment of the 2008 property taxes on June 1, 2009.

Exercise 4-11 *Interest Receivable* LO 3

On June 1, 2008, MicroTel Enterprises lends $60,000 to its CEO. The loan will be repaid in 60 days with interest at 8%.

Required

1. Prepare the journal entry on MicroTel's books on June 1, 2008.
2. Prepare the adjusting entry on MicroTel's books on June 30, 2008.
3. Prepare the entry on MicroTel's books on July 31, 2008, when the CEO repays the principal and interest.

Exercise 4-12 *Unbilled Accounts Receivable* LO 3

Mike and Cary repair computers for small local businesses. Heavy thunderstorms during the last week of June resulted in a record number of service calls. Eager to review the results of operations for the month of June, Mike prepared an income statement and was puzzled by the lower-than-expected amount of revenues. Cary explained that he had not yet billed the company's customers for $40,000 of work performed during the last week of the month.

(continued)

Required

1. Should revenue be recorded when services are performed or when customers are billed? Explain your answer.

2. Prepare the adjusting entry required on June 30.

Exercise 4-13 *The Effect of Ignoring Adjusting Entries on Net Income* LO 3

For each of the following independent situations, determine whether the effect of ignoring the required adjusting entry will result in an understatement (U), an overstatement (O), or no effect (NE) on net income for the period.

Situation	Effect on Net Income
Example: Taxes owed but not yet paid are ignored.	O
1. Interest due but not yet paid on a long-term note payable is ignored.	
2. Commissions earned by salespeople but not payable until the 10th of the following month are ignored.	
3. A landlord receives cash on the date a lease is signed for the rent for the first six months and credits Unearned Rent Revenue. The landlord fails to make any adjustment at the end of the first month.	
4. A company fails to record depreciation on equipment.	
5. Sales made during the last week of the period are not recorded.	
6. A company neglects to record the expired portion of a prepaid insurance policy (its cost was originally debited to an asset account).	

Exercise 4-14 *The Effect of Adjusting Entries on the Accounting Equation* LO 3

Determine whether recording each of the following adjusting entries will increase (I), decrease (D), or have no effect (NE) on each of the three elements of the accounting equation.

	Assets =	Liabilities +	Shareholders' Equity
Example: Wages earned during the period but not yet paid are accrued.	NE	I	D
1. Depreciation for the period is recorded.			
2. Revenue is recorded for the earned portion of a liability for amounts collected in advance from customers.			
3. Rent revenue is recorded for amounts owed by a tenant but not yet received.			
4. Income taxes owed but not yet paid are accrued.			
5. Prepaid insurance is reduced for the portion of the policy that has expired during the period.			
6. Interest incurred during the period but not yet paid is accrued.			

Exercise 4-15 *Reconstruction of Adjusting Entries from Unadjusted and Adjusted Trial Balances* LO 3

Following are the unadjusted and adjusted trial balances for Power Corp. on May 31, 2008:

	Unadjusted Trial Balance		Adjusted Trial Balance	
	Debit	**Credit**	**Debit**	**Credit**
Cash	$ 3,160		$ 3,160	
Accounts Receivable	7,300		9,600	
Supplies on Hand	400		150	
Prepaid Rent	2,400		2,200	
Equipment	9,000		9,000	

Accumulated Depreciation		$ 2,800		$ 3,200
Accounts Payable		2,600		2,600
Capital Stock		5,000		5,000
Retained Earnings		8,990		8,990
Service Revenue		6,170		8,470
Promotions Expense	2,050		2,050	
Wage Expense	1,250		2,250	
Wages Payable				1,000
Supplies Expense			250	
Depreciation Expense			400	
Rent Expense			200	
Totals	$25,560	$25,560	$29,260	$29,260

Required

1. Reconstruct the adjusting entries that were made on Power's books at the end of May.

2. By how much would Power's net income for May have been overstated or understated (indicate which) if these adjusting entries had not been recorded?

Exercise 4-16 *The Accounting Cycle* **LO 4**

The steps in the accounting cycle are listed below in random order. Fill in the blank next to each step to indicate its *order* in the cycle. The first step in the cycle is filled in as an example.

Order	Procedure
_____	Close the accounts.
___1___	Collect and analyze information from source documents.
_____	Prepare financial statements.
_____	Post transactions to accounts in the ledger.
_____	Record and post adjusting entries.
_____	Journalize daily transactions.

Exercise 4-17 *Trial Balance* **LO 4**

The following account titles, arranged in alphabetical order, are from the records of Hadley Realty Corporation. The balance in each account is the normal balance for that account. The balances are as of December 31, after adjusting entries have been made. Prepare an adjusted trial balance, listing the accounts in the following order: (1) assets, (2) liabilities, (3) owners' equity accounts, including dividends, (4) revenues, and (5) expenses.

Accounts Payable	$10,300
Accounts Receivable	19,230
Accumulated Depreciation—Automobiles	12,000
Accumulated Depreciation—Buildings	15,000
Automobiles	48,000
Buildings	60,000
Capital Stock	25,000
Cash	2,460
Dividends	1,500
Fees Earned	17,420
Insurance Expense	300
Interest Expense	200
Interest Payable	200
Land	40,000
Notes Payable	20,000
Office Supplies	1,680
Office Supplies Expense	5,320
Prepaid Insurance	1,200
Rent Expense	2,400
Retained Earnings	85,445
Wages and Salaries Expense	3,545
Wages and Salaries Payable	470

Exercise 4-18 *Closing Entries* **LO 4**

At the end of the year, the adjusted trial balance for Devonshire Corporation contains the following amounts for the income statement accounts (the balance in each account is the normal balance for that type of account).

Account	Balance
Advertising Fees Earned	$58,500
Interest Revenue	2,700
Wage and Salary Expense	14,300
Utilities Expense	12,500
Insurance Expense	7,300
Depreciation Expense	16,250
Interest Expense	2,600
Income Tax Expense	3,300
Dividends	2,000

Required

1. Prepare all necessary journal entries to close Devonshire Corporation's accounts at the end of the year.

2. Assume that the accountant for Devonshire forgets to record the closing entries. What will be the effect on net income for the *following* year? Explain your answer.

3. Explain why closing entries are necessary and when they should be recorded.

Exercise 4-19 *Preparation of a Statement of Retained Earnings from Closing Entries* **LO 4**

Fisher Corporation reported a Retained Earnings balance of $125,700 on January 1, 2008. Fisher Corporation made the following three closing entries on December 31, 2008 (the entry to transfer net income to Retained Earnings has been intentionally left out). Prepare a statement of retained earnings for Fisher for the year.

Dec.	31	Service Revenue	65,400	
		Interest Revenue	20,270	
		Income Summary		85,670
	31	Income Summary	62,170	
		Salary and Wage Expense		23,450
		Rent Expense		20,120
		Interest Expense		4,500
		Utilities Expense		10,900
		Insurance Expense		3,200
	31	Retained Earnings	6,400	
		Dividends		6,400

Exercise 4-20 *Reconstruction of Closing Entries* **LO 4**

The T accounts shown below summarize entries made to selected general ledger accounts of Cooper & Company. Certain entries, dated December 31, are closing entries. Prepare the closing entries that were made on December 31.

MAINTENANCE REVENUE

12/31	76,000	64,000	12/1 Bal.
		6,000	12/15
		6,000	12/30

WAGES EXPENSE

12/1 Bal.	11,000	12,000	12/31
12/15	500		
12/30	500		

SUPPLIES EXPENSE

12/1 Bal.	2,500	2,750	12/31
12/31	250		

RETAINED EARNINGS

12/31	5,000	45,600	12/1 Bal.
		75,250	12/31

DIVIDENDS

12/1 Bal.	5,000	5,000	12/31

INCOME SUMMARY

12/31	14,750	76,000	12/31
12/31	61,250		

Exercise 4-21 *The Difference between a Financial Statement and a Work Sheet (Appendix)* **LO 5**

The balance sheet columns of the work sheet for Jones Corporation show total debits and total credits of $255,000 each. Dividends for the period are $3,000. Accumulated depreciation is $12,000 at the end of the period. Compute the amount that should appear on the balance sheet (i.e., the formal financial statement) for *total assets*. How do you explain the difference between this amount and the amount that appears as the total debits and total credits on the work sheet?

Exercise 4-22 *Ten-Column Work Sheet (Appendix)* **LO 5**

Indicate whether amounts in each of the following accounts should be carried over from the adjusted trial balance columns of the work sheet to the income statement (IS) columns or to the balance sheet (BS) columns. Also indicate whether the account normally has a debit (D) balance or a credit (C) balance.

__BS-D__   **Example:** Cash

_____   **1.** Interest Receivable

_____   **2.** Interest Revenue

_____   **3.** Interest Expense

_____   **4.** Interest Payable

_____   **5.** Retained Earnings

_____   **6.** Prepaid Insurance

_____   **7.** Depreciation Expense—Trucks

_____   **8.** Office Supplies

_____   **9.** Office Supplies Expense

_____   **10.** Subscription Revenue

_____   **11.** Accumulated Depreciation—Trucks

_____   **12.** Unearned Subscription Revenue

_____   **13.** Accounts Receivable

_____   **14.** Dividends

_____   **15.** Capital Stock

Multi-Concept Exercises

Exercise 4-23 *Cash and Accrual Basis* **LO 1, 2**

Hathaway Health Club sold three-year memberships at a reduced rate during its opening promotion. It sold 1,000 three-year, nonrefundable memberships for $360 each. The club expects to sell 100 additional three-year memberships for $900 each over each of the next two years. Membership fees are paid when clients sign up. The club's bookkeeper has prepared the following income statement for the first year of business and projected income statements for Years 2 and 3.

Cash-basis income statements:

	Year 1	Year 2	Year 3
Sales	$360,000	$90,000	$90,000
Equipment*	100,000	0	0
Salaries and Wages	50,000	50,000	50,000
Advertising	5,000	5,000	5,000
Rent and Utilities	36,000	36,000	36,000
Net income (loss)	$169,000	$ (1,000)	$ (1,000)

*Equipment was purchased at the beginning of Year 1 for $100,000 and is expected to last for three years and then to be worth $1,000.

Required

1. Convert the income statements for each of the three years to the accrual basis.

2. Do you believe that the cash-basis or the accrual-basis income statements are more useful to management? to investors? Why?

Exercise 4-24 *Depreciation Expense* LO 2, 3

During 2008, Carter Company acquired three assets with the following costs, estimated useful lives, and estimated residual values:

Date	Asset	Cost	Estimated Useful Life	Estimated Residual Value
March 30	Truck	$ 20,000	5 years	$ 2,000
June 28	Computer	55,000	10 years	5,000
October 2	Building	250,000	30 years	10,000

The company uses the straight-line method to depreciate all assets and computes depreciation to the nearest month. For example, the computer system will be depreciated for six months in 2008.

Required

1. Compute the depreciation expense that Carter will record on each of the three assets for 2008.

2. Comment on the following statement: "Accountants could save time and money by simply expensing the cost of long-term assets when they are purchased. In addition, this would be more accurate because depreciation requires estimates of useful life and residual value."

Exercise 4-25 *Accrual of Interest on a Loan* LO 2, 3

On July 1, 2008, Paxson Corporation takes out a 6%, two-month, $50,000 loan at Friendly National Bank. Principal and interest are to be repaid on August 31.

Required

1. Prepare the journal entries for July 1 to record the borrowing, for July 31 to record the accrual of interest, and for August 31 to record repayment of the principal and interest.

2. Evaluate the following statement: "It would be much easier not to bother with an adjusting entry on July 31 and simply record interest expense on August 31 when the loan is repaid."

Problems

Problem 4-1 *Adjusting Entries* LO 3

Water Corporation prepares monthly financial statements and therefore adjusts its accounts at the end of every month. The following information is available for April 2008:

a. Water Corporation takes out a 90-day, 8%, $50,000 note on February 1, 2008, with interest and principal to be paid at maturity.

b. The asset account Office Supplies on Hand has a balance of $1,280 on April 1, 2008. During April, Water adds $3,750 to the account for the purchases of the period. A count of the supplies on hand at the end of April indicates a balance of $1,370.

c. The company purchased office equipment last year for $62,600. The equipment has an estimated useful life of six years and an estimated residual value of $5,000.

d. The company's plant operates five days per week with a daily payroll of $950. Wage earners are paid every Friday. The last day of the month is Wednesday, April 30.

e. The company rented an idle warehouse to a neighbouring business on February 1, 2008, at a rate of $2,000 per month. On this date, Water Corporation credited Unearned Rent Revenue for six months' rent received in advance.

f. On April 1, 2008, Water Corporation credited a liability account, Customer Deposits, for $4,800. This sum represents an amount that a customer paid in advance and that will be earned evenly by Water over a six-month period.

g. Based on its income for the month, Water Corporation estimates that federal income taxes for April amount to $3,900.

Required

For each of the preceding situations, prepare in general journal form the appropriate adjusting entry to be recorded on April 30, 2008.

Problem 4-2 *Effects of Adjusting Entries on the Accounting Equation* LO 3

Refer to the information provided for Water Corporation in Problem 4-1.

Required

1. Prepare a table to summarize the required adjusting entries as they affect the accounting equation. Use the format in Exhibit 3-1. Identify each adjustment by letter.

2. Assume that Water reports income of $23,000 before any of the adjusting entries. What net income will Water report for April?

Problem 4-3 *Adjusting Entries—Annual Adjustments* LO 3

Palmer Industries prepares annual financial statements and adjusts its accounts only at the end of the year. The following information is available for the year ended December 31, 2008:

a. Palmer purchased computer equipment two years ago for $15,000. The equipment has an estimated useful life of five years and an estimated residual value of $500.

b. The Office Supplies account had a balance of $3,600 on January 1, 2008. During 2008, Palmer added $17,600 to the account for purchases of office supplies during the year. A count of the supplies on hand at the end of December 2008 indicates a balance of $2,850.

c. On August 1, 2008, Palmer credited a liability account, Customer Deposits, for $24,000. This sum represents an amount that a customer paid in advance and that will be earned evenly by Palmer over a six-month period.

d. Palmer rented some office space on November 1, 2008, at a rate of $2,500 per month. On that date, Palmer debited Prepaid Rent for three months' rent paid in advance.

e. Palmer took out a 120-day, 9%, $200,000 note on November 1, 2008, with interest and principal to be paid at maturity.

f. Palmer operates five days per week with an average daily payroll of $500. Palmer pays its employees every Thursday. December 31, 2008, is a Sunday.

Required

1. For each of the preceding situations, prepare in general journal form the appropriate adjusting entry to be recorded on December 31, 2008.

2. Assume that Palmer's accountant forgets to record the adjusting entries on December 31, 2008. Will net income for the year be understated or overstated? By what amount? (Ignore the effect of income taxes.)

Problem 4-4 *Recurring and Adjusting Entries* LO 3

The following are Butler Realty Corporation's accounts, identified by number. The company has been in the real estate business for 10 years and prepares financial statements monthly. Following the list of accounts is a series of transactions entered into by Butler. For each transaction, enter the number(s) of the account(s) to be debited and credited.

1. Notes Payable
2. Capital Stock
3. Commissions Revenue
4. Office Supply Expense
5. Rent Expense
6. Salaries and Wages Expense
7. Depreciation Expense
8. Interest Expense
9. Income Tax Expense
10. Income Tax Payable

11. Cash
12. Accounts Receivable
13. Prepaid Rent
14. Office Supplies
15. Automobiles
16. Accumulated Depreciation
17. Land
18. Accounts Payable
19. Salaries and Wages Payable

Transaction	Debit	Credit
a. **Example:** Issued additional shares to owners.	11	2
b. Purchased automobiles for cash.	____	____
c. Purchased land; made cash down payment and signed a note for the balance.	____	____

(continued)

d. Paid cash to landlord for rent for next 12 months. _____ _____

e. Purchased office supplies on account. _____ _____

f. Collected cash for commissions from clients for the
properties sold during the month. _____ _____

g. Collected cash for commissions from clients for the
properties sold in the prior month. _____ _____

h. During the month, sold properties for which cash for
commissions will be collected from clients next month. _____ _____

i. Paid for office supplies purchased on account in an
earlier month. _____ _____

j. Recorded an adjustment to recognize salaries and wages
incurred but not yet paid. _____ _____

k. Recorded an adjustment for office supplies used during
the month. _____ _____

l. Recorded an adjusting entry for the portion of prepaid
rent that expired during the month. _____ _____

m. Made required month-end payment on note taken out
in (c); payment is part principal and part interest. _____ _____

n. Recorded adjusting entry for monthly depreciation on the autos. _____ _____

o. Recorded adjusting entry for income taxes. _____ _____

Problem 4-5 *Use of Account Balances as a Basis for Adjusting Entries—Annual Adjustments* **LO 3**

The following account balances are taken from the records of Chauncey Company at December 31, 2008. The Prepaid Insurance account represents the cost of a three-year policy purchased on August 1, 2008. The Rent Collected in Advance account represents the cash received from a tenant on June 1, 2008, for 12 months' rent, beginning on that date. The Note Payable represents a nine-month note signed on September 1, 2008. Principal and interest at an annual rate of 9% will be paid on June 1, 2009.

Prepaid Insurance	$7,200 debit	
Rent Collected in Advance		$ 6,000 credit
Note Payable		$50,000 credit

Required

1. Prepare the three necessary adjusting entries on the books of Chauncey on December 31, 2008. Assume that Chauncey prepares adjusting entries only once a year, on December 31.

2. Assume that adjusting entries are made at the end of each month rather than only at the end of the year. What would be the balance in Prepaid Insurance *before* the December adjusting entry is made? Explain your answer.

Problem 4-6 *Use of a Trial Balance as a Basis for Adjusting Entries* **LO 3**

Reynolds Realty Company records adjusting entries at the end of each month. A trial balance on April 30, 2008, *before* recording any adjusting entries, appears as follows:

REYNOLDS REALTY COMPANY
UNADJUSTED TRIAL BALANCE
APRIL 30, 2008

	Debit	Credit
Cash	$15,700	
Prepaid Insurance	900	
Office Supplies	500	
Office Equipment	50,000	
Accumulated Depreciation—Office Equipment		$ 4,500
Automobile	12,000	
Accumulated Depreciation—Automobile		3,800
Accounts Payable		6,500

Unearned Commissions		9,500
Notes Payable		10,000
Capital Stock		12,000
Retained Earnings		28,850
Dividends	2,500	
Commissions Earned		17,650
Utilities Expense	2,300	
Salaries Expense	7,400	
Advertising Expense	1,500	
Totals	$92,800	$92,800

Other Data

a. The monthly insurance cost is $100.

b. Office supplies on hand on April 30, 2008, amount to $200.

c. The office equipment was purchased on April 1, 2007. On that date, it had an estimated useful life of 10 years and a residual value of $5,000.

d. On September 1, 2006, the automobile was purchased; it had an estimated useful life of 5 years.

e. A deposit is received in advance of providing any services for first-time customers. Amounts received in advance are recorded initially in the account Unearned Commissions. Based on services provided to these first-time customers, the balance in this account at the end of April should be $4,500.

f. Repeat customers are allowed to pay for services one month after the date of the sale of their property. Services rendered during the month but not yet collected or billed to these customers amount to $1,500.

g. Interest owed on the note payable but not yet paid amounts to $50.

h. Salaries owed to employees but unpaid at the end of the month amount to $2,500.

Required

1. Prepare in general journal form the necessary adjusting entries at April 30, 2008. Label the entries (**a**) through (**h**) to correspond to the other data.

2. Note that the unadjusted trial balance reports a credit balance in Accumulated Depreciation—Office Equipment of $4,500. Explain *why* the account contains a balance of $4,500 on April 30, 2008.

Problem 4-7 *Effects of Adjusting Entries on the Accounting Equation* LO 3

Refer to the information provided for Reynolds Realty Company in Problem 4-6.

Required

1. Prepare a table to summarize the required adjusting entries as they affect the accounting equation. Use the format in Exhibit 3-1. Identify each adjustment by letter.

2. Compute the net increase or decrease in net income for the month from the recognition of the adjusting entries you prepared in requirement 1. (Ignore income taxes.)

Problem 4-8 *Reconstruction of Adjusting Entries from Account Balances* LO 3

Taggart Corp. records adjusting entries each month before preparing monthly financial statements. The following selected account balances are taken from its trial balances on June 30, 2008. The "unadjusted" columns set forth the general ledger balances before the adjusting entries were posted. The "adjusted" columns reflect the month-end adjusting entries.

	Unadjusted		Adjusted	
Account Title	**Debit**	**Credit**	**Debit**	**Credit**
Prepaid Insurance	$1,800		$1,650	
Equipment	9,600		9,600	
Accumulated Depreciation		$6,400		$6,500
Notes Payable		9,600		9,600
Interest Payable		1,360		1,440

(continued)

Required

1. The company purchased a 24-month insurance policy on June 1, 2007. Reconstruct the adjusting journal entry for insurance on June 30, 2008.

2. What was the original cost of the insurance policy? Explain your answer.

3. The equipment was purchased on February 1, 2003, for $9,600. Taggart uses straight-line depreciation and estimates that the equipment will have no residual value. Reconstruct the adjusting journal entry for depreciation on June 30, 2008.

4. What is the equipment's estimated useful life in months? Explain your answer.

5. Taggart signed a two-year note payable on January 1, 2007, for the purchase of the equipment. Interest on the note accrues on a monthly basis and will be paid at maturity along with the principal amount of $9,600. Reconstruct the adjusting journal entry for interest on June 30, 2008.

6. What is the *annual* interest rate on the loan? Explain your answer.

Problem 4-9 *Use of a Trial Balance to Record Adjusting Entries in T Accounts* LO 3

Four Star Video records adjusting entries at the end of each month. An unadjusted trial balance at May 31, 2008, follows.

FOUR STAR VIDEO
UNADJUSTED TRIAL BALANCE
MAY 31, 2008

	Debit	Credit
Cash	$ 4,000	
Prepaid Rent	6,600	
DVD Inventory	25,600	
Display Stands	8,900	
Accumulated Depreciation		$ 5,180
Accounts Payable		3,260
Unearned Subscription Revenue		4,450
Capital Stock		5,000
Retained Earnings		22,170
Rental Revenue		9,200
Wages and Salaries Expense	2,320	
Utilities Expense	1,240	
Advertising Expense	600	
Totals	$49,260	$49,260

The following additional information is available:

a. Four Star rents a store in a shopping mall and prepays the annual rent of $7,200 on April 1 of each year.

b. The asset account DVD Inventory represents the cost of DVDs purchased from suppliers. When a new title is purchased from a supplier, its cost is debited to this account. When a title has served its useful life and can no longer be rented (even at a reduced price), it is removed from the inventory in the store. Based on the monthly count, the cost of titles on hand at the end of May is $23,100.

c. The display stands have an estimated useful life of five years and an estimated residual value of $500.

d. Wages and salaries owed to employees but unpaid at the end of May amount to $1,400.

e. In addition to individual rentals, Four Star operates a popular discount subscription program. Customers pay an annual fee of $120 for an unlimited number of rentals. Based on the $10 per month earned on each of these subscriptions, the amount earned for the month of May is $400.

f. Four Star accrues income taxes using an estimated tax rate equal to 30% of the income for the month.

Required

1. Set up T accounts for each of the accounts listed in the trial balance. Based on the additional information given, set up any other T accounts that will be needed to prepare adjusting entries.

2. Post the month-end adjusting entries directly to the T accounts but do not bother to put the entries in journal format first. Use the letters (**a**) through (**f**) from the additional information to identify the entries.

3. Prepare a trial balance to prove the equality of debits and credits after posting the adjusting entries.

4. On the basis of the information you have, does Four Star appear to be a profitable business? Explain your answer.

Problem 4-10 *Effects of Adjusting Entries on the Accounting Equation* LO 3

Refer to the information provided for Four Star Video in Problem 4-9.

Required

Prepare a table to summarize the required adjusting entries as they affect the accounting equation. Use the format in Exhibit 3-1. Identify each adjustment by letter.

Multi-Concept Problems

Problem 4-11 *Accrual Accounting and Closing Entries* LO 2, 5

Two years ago, Darlene Darby opened a delivery service. Darby reports the following accounts on her income statement:

Sales	$138,000
Advertising expense	7,000
Salaries expense	78,000
Rent expense	20,000

These amounts represent two years of revenue and expenses. Darby has asked you how she can tell how much of the income is from the first year of business and how much is from the second year. She provides the following additional data:

a. Sales in the second year were double those of the first year.

b. Advertising expense is for a $1,000 opening promotion and weekly ads in the newspaper.

c. Salaries represent one employee for the first nine months and then two employees for the remainder of the time. Each is paid the same salary. No raises have been granted.

d. Rent has not changed since the business opened.

Required

1. Prepare income statements for Years 1 and 2.

2. Prepare the closing entries for each year. Prepare a short explanation for Darby about the purpose of closing temporary accounts.

Problem 4-12 *Ten-Column Work Sheet (Appendix)* LO 3, 4, 5

Ace Consulting Inc. records adjusting entries at the end of each month. The unadjusted trial balance on the next page is available for Ace Consulting Inc. on June 30, 2008.

(continued)

ACE CONSULTING INC.
UNADJUSTED TRIAL BALANCE
JUNE 30, 2008

Cash	$ 6,320	
Accounts Receivable	14,600	
Supplies on Hand	800	
Prepaid Rent	4,800	
Furniture and Fixtures	18,000	
Accumulated Depreciation		$ 5,625
Accounts Payable		5,200
Capital Stock		10,000
Retained Earnings		17,955
Consulting Revenue		12,340
Utilities Expense	4,100	
Wage and Salary Expense	2,500	
Totals	$51,120	$51,120

Required

1. Enter the unadjusted trial balance in the first two columns of a 10-column work sheet.

2. Enter the necessary adjustments in the appropriate columns of the work sheet for each of the following:

   a. Wages and salaries earned by employees at the end of June but not yet paid amount to $2,300.

   b. Supplies on hand at the end of June amount to $500.

   c. Depreciation on furniture and fixtures for June is $375.

   d. Ace prepays the rent on its office space on June 1 of each year. The rent amounts to $400 per month.

   e. Consulting services rendered and billed for which cash has not yet been received amount to $4,500.

3. Complete the remaining columns of the work sheet.

Problem 4-13 *Monthly Transactions and Financial Statements* LO 3, 4

Moonlight Bay Inn is incorporated on January 2, 2008, by its three owners, each of whom contributes $20,000 in cash in exchange for shares of the business. In addition to the sale of shares, the following transactions are entered into during the month of January:

January 2: A Victorian inn is purchased for $50,000 in cash. An appraisal performed on this date indicates that the land is worth $15,000 and the remaining balance of the purchase price is attributable to the building. The owners estimate that the building will have an estimated useful life of 25 years and an estimated residual value of $5,000.

January 3: A two-year, 12%, $30,000 note was signed at the Second Bank. Interest and principal will be repaid on the maturity date of January 3, 2010.

January 4: New furniture for the inn is purchased at a cost of $15,000 in cash. The furniture has an estimated useful life of 10 years and residual value of $3,000.

January 5: A 30-month property insurance policy is purchased for $6,000 in cash.

January 6: An advertisement for the inn is placed in the local newspaper. Moonlight Bay pays $500 cash for the ad, which will run in the paper throughout January.

January 7: Cleaning supplies are purchased on account for $900. The bill is payable within 30 days.

January 15: Wages of $4,200 for the first half of the month are paid in cash.

January 16: A guest mails the business $1,000 in cash as a deposit for a room to be rented for two weeks. The guest plans to stay at the inn during the last week of January and the first week of February.

January 31: Cash receipts from rentals of rooms for the month amount to $8,300.

January 31: Cash receipts from operation of the restaurant for the month amount to $6,600.

January 31: Each shareholder is paid $200 in cash dividends.

Required

1. Prepare journal entries to record each of the preceding transactions.
2. Post each of the journal entries to T accounts.
3. Prepare the unadjusted trial balance.
4. Prepare journal entries to record the following adjustments and post them to the ledger.

   a. Depreciation of the building
   b. Depreciation of the furniture
   c. Interest on the note
   d. Recognition of the expired portion of the insurance
   e. Recognition of the earned portion of the guest's deposit
   f. Wages earned during the second half of January amount to $5,100 and will be paid on February 3.
   g. Cleaning supplies on hand on January 31 amount to $200.
   h. A gas and electric bill that is received from the city amounts to $800 and is payable by February 5.
   i. Income taxes are to be accrued at a rate of 30% of income before taxes.

5. Prepare in good form the following financial statements:

   a. Income statement for the month ended January 31, 2008
   b. Statement of retained earnings for the month ended January 31, 2008
   c. Balance sheet at January 31, 2008

6. Prepare closing entries and post them to the ledger.
7. Assume that you are the loan officer at Second Bank (refer to the transaction on January 3). What are your reactions to Moonlight's first month of operations? Are you comfortable with the loan you made?

Alternate Problems

Problem 4-1A *Adjusting Entries* LO 3

McLeod Inc. prepares monthly financial statements and therefore adjusts its accounts at the end of every month. The following information is available for June 2008:

a. McLeod signed a $10,000, 6%, two-year note with the bank. The principal and interest are due on June 1, 2012. McLeod expects to pay the note and interest in full at that time.

b. Office supplies totaling $5,600 were purchased during the month. The asset account Supplies is debited whenever a purchase is made. A count in the storeroom on June 30, 2008, indicated that supplies on hand amount to $550. The supplies on hand at the beginning of the month total $400.

c. The company purchased machines last year for $170,000. The machines are expected to be used for four years and have an estimated residual value of $2,000.

d. On June 1, the company paid $4,500 for rent for June, July, and August. The asset Prepaid Rent was debited; it did not have a balance on June 1.

e. The company operates 5 days per week with a weekly payroll of $7,000. Wage earners are paid every Friday. The last day of the month is Monday, June 30.

f. Based on its income for the month, McLeod estimates that federal income taxes for June amount to $2,900.

Required

For each of the preceding situations, prepare in general journal form the appropriate adjusting entry to be recorded on June 30, 2008.

Problem 4-2A *Effects of Adjusting Entries on the Accounting Equation* LO 3

Refer to the information provided for McLeod Inc. in Problem 4-1A.

Required

1. Prepare a table to summarize the required adjusting entries as they affect the accounting equation. Use the format in Exhibit 3-1. Identify each adjustment by letter.
2. Assume that McLeod reports income of $35,000 before any of the adjusting entries. What net income will McLeod report for June?

Problem 4-3A *Adjusting Entries—Annual Adjustments* **LO 3**

Golden Enterprises prepares annual financial statements and adjusts its accounts only at the end of the year. The following information is available for the year ended December 31, 2008:

a. Golden purchased office furniture last year for $32,000. The furniture has an estimated useful life of eight years and an estimated residual value of $4,000.

b. The Supplies account had a balance of $1,200 on January 1, 2008. During 2008, Golden added $12,900 to the account for purchases of supplies during the year. A count of the supplies on hand at the end of December 2008 indicates a balance of $1,000.

c. On August 1, 2008, Golden credited a liability account, Customer Deposits, for $8,800. This sum represents an amount that a customer paid in advance and that will be earned evenly by Golden over an eight-month period.

d. Golden rented some warehouse space on September 1, 2008, at a rate of $4,000 per month. On that date, Golden debited Prepaid Rent for six months' rent paid in advance.

e. Golden took out a 90-day, 6%, $30,000 note on November 1, 2008, with interest and principal to be paid at maturity.

f. Golden operates five days per week with an average daily payroll of $800. Golden pays its employees every Friday. December 31, 2008, is a Tuesday.

Required

1. For each of the preceding situations, prepare in general journal form the appropriate adjusting entry to be recorded on December 31, 2008.

2. Assume that Golden's accountant forgets to record the adjusting entries on December 31, 2008. Will net income for the year be understated or overstated? By what amount? (Ignore the effect of income taxes.)

Problem 4-4A *Recurring and Adjusting Entries* **LO 5**

The following are the accounts of Fairview Inc., an interior decorator. The company has been in the decorating business for 10 years and prepares quarterly financial statements. Following the list of accounts is a series of transactions entered into by Fairview. For each transaction, enter the number(s) of the account(s) to be debited and credited.

Accounts

1. Cash	10. Interim Financing Notes Payable
2. Accounts Receivable	11. Capital Stock
3. Prepaid Rent	12. Consulting Revenue
4. Office Supplies	13. Office Supplies Expense
5. Office Equipment	14. Rent Expense
6. Accumulated Depreciation	15. Salaries and Wages Expense
7. Accounts Payable	16. Depreciation Expense
8. Salaries and Wages Payable	17. Interest Expense
9. Income Tax Payable	18. Income Tax Expense

Transaction	Debit	Credit
a. **Example:** Issued additional shares to owners.	1	11
b. Purchased office equipment for cash.	___	___
c. Purchased office supplies on account.	___	___
d. Paid office rent for the next six months.	___	___
e. Collected open accounts receivable from customer.	___	___
f. Paid salaries and wages.	___	___
g. Purchased office equipment; made a down payment in cash and signed an interim financing note.	___	___
h. Provided consulting services on account.	___	___
i. Paid interest on an interim financing note.	___	___
j. Recorded depreciation on equipment.	___	___
k. Recorded the used office supplies.	___	___
l. Recorded the used portion of prepaid rent.	___	___
m. Recorded income taxes due next month.	___	___

Problem 4-5A *Use of Account Balances as a Basis for Adjusting Entries—Annual Adjustments* **LO 3**

The following account balances are taken from the records of Island Inc. at December 31, 2008. The Supplies account represents the cost of supplies on hand at the beginning of the year plus all purchases. A physical count on December 31, 2008, shows only $1,500 of supplies on hand. The Unearned Revenue account represents the cash received from a customer on May 1, 2008, for 12 months of service, beginning on that date. The Note Payable represents a six-month promissory note signed with a supplier on September 1, 2008. Principal and interest at an annual rate of 7% will be paid on March 1, 2009.

Supplies	$5,800 debit	
Unearned Revenue		$ 1,800 credit
Note Payable		60,000 credit

Required

1. Prepare the three necessary adjusting entries on the books of Island on December 31, 2008. Assume that Island prepares adjusting entries only once a year, on December 31.

2. Assume that adjusting entries are made at the end of each month rather than only at the end of the year. What would be the balance in Unearned Revenue *before* the December adjusting entry is made? Explain your answer.

Problem 4-6A *Use of a Trial Balance as a Basis for Adjusting Entries* **LO 3**

Argyle Arts Studio records adjusting entries at the end of each month. A trial balance on June 30, 2008, *before* recording any adjusting entries, appears as follows:

ARGYLE ARTS STUDIO
UNADJUSTED TRIAL BALANCE
JUNE 30, 2008

	Debit	Credit
Cash	$ 8,000	
Prepaid Rent	18,000	
Supplies	15,210	
Office Equipment	46,120	
Accumulated Depreciation—Equipment		$ 4,000
Accounts Payable		1,800
Notes Payable		2,000
Capital Stock		50,000
Retained Earnings		25,350
Dividends	8,400	
Revenue		46,850
Utilities Expense	2,850	
Salaries Expense	19,420	
Advertising Expense	12,000	
Totals	$130,000	$130,000

Other Data

a. The monthly rent cost is $600.

b. Supplies on hand on June 30, 2008, amount to $1,200.

c. The office equipment was purchased on August 1, 2007. On that date, it had an estimated useful life of eight years and a residual value of $7,720.

d. Interest owed on the note payable but not yet paid amounts to $50.

e. Salaries of $650 are owed to employees but unpaid at the end of the month.

Required

1. Prepare in general journal form the necessary adjusting entries at June 30, 2008. Label the entries (**a**) through (**e**) to correspond to the other data.

2. Note that the unadjusted trial balance reports a credit balance in Accumulated Depreciation—Equipment of $4,000. Explain *why* the account contains a balance of $4,000 on June 30, 2008.

Problem 4-7A *Effects of Adjusting Entries on the Accounting Equation* **LO 3**

Refer to the information provided for Argyle Arts Studio in Problem 4-6A.

Required

1. Prepare a table to summarize the required adjusting entries as they affect the accounting equation. Use the format in Exhibit 3-1. Identify each adjustment by letter.

2. Compute the net increase or decrease in net income for the month from the recognition of the adjusting entries you prepared in requirement 1 (ignore income taxes).

Problem 4-8A *Reconstruction of Adjusting Entries from Account Balances* **LO 3**

Robie Corporation records adjusting entries each month before preparing monthly financial statements. The following selected account balances are taken from its trial balances on June 30, 2008. The "unadjusted" columns set forth the general ledger balances before the adjusting entries were posted. The "adjusted" columns reflect the month-end adjusting entries.

Account Title	Unadjusted Debit	Unadjusted Credit	Adjusted Debit	Adjusted Credit
Prepaid Rent	$6,000		$4,500	
Equipment	9,600		9,600	
Accumulated Depreciation		$ 1,600		$ 1,800
Notes Payable		9,600		9,600
Interest Payable		320		360

Required

1. The company paid for a six-month lease on April 1, 2008. Reconstruct the adjusting journal entry for rent on June 30, 2008.

2. What amount was prepaid on April 1, 2008? Explain your answer.

3. The equipment was purchased on September 30, 2007, for $9,600. Robie uses straight-line depreciation and estimates that the equipment will have no residual value. Reconstruct the adjusting journal entry for depreciation on June 30, 2008.

4. What is the equipment's estimated useful life in months? Explain your answer.

5. Robie signed a two-year note on September 30, 2007, for the purchase of the equipment. Interest on the note accrues on a monthly basis and will be paid at maturity along with the principal amount of $9,600. Reconstruct the adjusting journal entry for interest expense on June 30, 2008.

6. What is the *monthly* interest rate on the loan? Explain your answer.

Problem 4-9A *Use of a Trial Balance to Record Adjusting Entries in T Accounts* **LO 3**

Evan and Associates records adjusting entries at the end of each month. An unadjusted trial balance at June 30, 2008, follows:

EVAN AND ASSOCIATES
UNADJUSTED TRIAL BALANCE
JUNE 30, 2008

	Debit	Credit
Cash	$ 6,000	
Accounts Receivable	10,500	
Prepaid Rent	4,400	
Chemical Inventory	9,500	
Equipment	18,200	
Accumulated Depreciation		$ 1,200
Accounts Payable		1,100
Capital Stock		5,000
Retained Earnings		25,300
Treatment Revenue		40,600
Wages and Salaries Expense	22,500	

Utilities Expense	1,200	
Advertising Expense	900	
Totals	$73,200	$73,200

The following additional information is available:

a. Evan rents a warehouse with office space and prepays the annual rent of $4,800 on May 1 of each year.

b. The asset account Equipment represents the cost of treatment equipment, which has an estimated useful life of 10 years and an estimated residual value of $200.

c. Chemical inventory on hand equals $1,100.

d. Wages and salaries owed to employees but unpaid at the end of the month amount to $1,800.

e. Evan accrues income taxes using an estimated tax rate equal to 30% of the income for the month.

Required

1. Set up T accounts for each of the accounts listed in the trial balance. Based on the additional information given, set up any other T accounts that will be needed to prepare adjusting entries.

2. Post the month-end adjusting entries directly to the T accounts but do not bother to put the entries in journal format first. Use the letters (a) through (e) from the additional information to identify the entries.

3. Prepare a trial balance to prove the equality of debits and credits after posting the adjusting entries.

4. On the basis of the information you have, does Evan appear to be a profitable business? Explain your answer.

Problem 4-10A *Effects of Adjusting Entries on the Accounting Equation* **LO 3**
Refer to the information provided for Evan and Associates in Problem 4-9A.

Required

Prepare a table to summarize the required adjusting entries as they affect the accounting equation. Use the format in Exhibit 3-1. Identify each adjustment by letter.

Alternate Multi-Concept Problems

Problem 4-11A *Accrual Accounting and Closing Entries* **LO 2, 5**
Two years ago, Mike Lee opened an audio book rental shop. Mike Lee reports the following accounts on his income statement:

Sales	$64,000
Advertising expense	9,500
Salaries expense	10,000
Depreciation on tapes	5,000
Rent expense	18,000

These amounts represent two years of revenue and expenses. Mike has asked you how can he tell how much of the income is from the first year and how much is from the second year of business. He provides the following additional data:

a. Sales in the second year are triple those of the first year.

b. Advertising expense is for a $1,500 opening promotion and weekly ads in the newspaper.

c. Salaries represent one employee who was hired eight months ago. No raises have been granted.

d. Rent has not changed since the shop opened. All tapes were purchased at the beginning of the first year and are depreciated using the straight-line method.

Required

1. Prepare income statements for Years 1 and 2.

2. Prepare the closing entries for each year. Prepare a short explanation for Mike about the purpose of closing temporary accounts.

Problem 4-12A *Ten-Column Work Sheet and Closing Entries (Appendix)* **LO 3, 4, 5**

Green Landscaping records adjusting entries at the end of each month. The unadjusted trial balance for Green Landscaping on August 31, 2008, follows:

GREEN LANDSCAPING
UNADJUSTED TRIAL BALANCE
AUGUST 31, 2008

Cash	$ 6,460	
Accounts Receivable	23,400	
Supplies on Hand	1,260	
Prepaid Insurance	3,675	
Equipment	28,800	
Accumulated Depreciation—Equipment		$ 9,200
Buildings	72,000	
Accumulated Depreciation—Buildings		16,800
Accounts Payable		10,500
Notes Payable		10,000
Capital Stock		40,000
Retained Earnings		42,100
Service Revenue		14,200
Advertising Expense	1,200	
Gasoline and Oil Expense	1,775	
Wages and Salaries Expense	4,230	
Totals	$142,800	$142,800

Required

1. Enter the unadjusted trial balance in the first two columns of a 10-column work sheet.

2. Enter the necessary adjustments in the appropriate columns of the work sheet for each of the following:

   a. A count of the supplies on hand at the end of August reveals a balance of $730.
   b. The company paid $4,200 in cash on May 1, 2008, for a two-year insurance policy.
   c. The equipment has a four-year estimated useful life and no residual value.
   d. The buildings have an estimated useful life of 30 years and no residual value.
   e. The company leases space in its building to another company. The agreement requires the tenant to pay Green $700 on the 10th of each month for the previous month's rent.
   f. Wages and salaries earned by employees at the end of August but not yet paid amount to $3,320.
   g. The company signed a six-month note on August 1, 2008. Interest at an annual rate of 12% and the principal amount of $10,000 are due on February 1, 2009.

3. Complete the remaining columns of the work sheet.

4. Assume that Green closes its books at the end of each month before preparing financial statements. Prepare the necessary closing entries at August 31, 2008.

Problem 4-13A *Ten-Column Work Sheet and Financial Statements (Appendix)*
LO 3, 4, 5

Tenfour Trucking Company records adjusting entries at the end of each month. The following unadjusted trial balance is available for Tenfour Trucking Company on January 31, 2008:

TENFOUR TRUCKING COMPANY
UNADJUSTED TRIAL BALANCE
JANUARY 31, 2008

Cash	$ 27,340	
Accounts Receivable	41,500	
Prepaid Insurance	18,000	
Warehouse	40,000	
Accumulated Depreciation—Warehouse		$ 21,600
Truck Fleet	240,000	
Accumulated Depreciation—Truck Fleet		112,500

Land	20,000	
Accounts Payable		32,880
Notes Payable		50,000
Interest Payable		4,500
Customer Deposits		6,000
Capital Stock		100,000
Retained Earnings		40,470
Dividends	20,000	
Freight Revenue		165,670
Gas and Oil Expense	57,330	
Maintenance Expense	26,400	
Wage and Salary Expense	43,050	
Totals	$533,620	$533,620

Required

1. Enter the unadjusted trial balance in the first two columns of a 10-column work sheet.

2. Enter the necessary adjustments in the appropriate columns of the work sheet for each of the following:

   a. Prepaid insurance represents the cost of a 24-month policy purchased on January 1, 2008.

   b. The warehouse has an estimated useful life of 20 years and an estimated residual value of $4,000.

   c. The truck fleet has an estimated useful life of 6 years and an estimated residual value of $15,000.

   d. The note was signed on January 1, 2007. Interest at an annual rate of 9% and the principal of $50,000 are due on December 31, 2008.

   e. The customer deposits represent amounts paid in advance by new customers. A total of $4,500 of the balance in Customer Deposits was earned during January 2008.

   f. Wages and salaries earned by employees at the end of January but not yet paid amount to $8,200.

   g. Income taxes are accrued at a rate of 30% at the end of each month.

3. Complete the remaining columns of the work sheet.

4. Prepare in good form the following financial statements:

   a. Income statement for the month ended January 31, 2008
   b. Statement of retained earnings for the month ended January 31, 2008
   c. Balance sheet at January 31, 2008

5. Compute Tenfour's current ratio. What does this ratio tell you about the company's liquidity?

6. Describe a ratio that you believe would be a meaningful measure of profitability for a trucking company.

Cases

Reading and Interpreting Financial Statements

Case 4-1 *Comparing Two Companies in the Same Industry: CN and CP* **LO 3**
Refer to the financial information for CN and CP in Appendixes A and B at the end of the book.

CN
http://www.cn.ca
http://www.cpr.ca

Required

1. Identify the account on each company's balance sheet that is equivalent to Unearned Revenues.

2. What dollar amount does each company report in Materials and Supplies on its balance sheet at the end of 2007? When the materials and supplies are used in the future, this account will be credited. What type of account will be debited in the same entry?

3. On their balance sheets, both CN and CP report Net Amount of Property. Can you find out for each company how much the properties cost and how much of the costs had been depreciated by the end of 2007?

Making Financial Decisions

Case 4-2 *The Use of Net Income and Cash Flow to Evaluate a Company* LO 2

After you have gained five years of experience with a large CA firm, one of your clients, Oxford Inc., asks you to take over as chief financial officer for the business. Oxford advises its clients on the purchase of software products and assists them in installing the programs on their computer systems. Because the business is relatively new (it began servicing clients in January 2008), its accounting records are somewhat limited. In fact, the only statement available is an income statement for the first year:

OXFORD INC.
STATEMENT OF INCOME
FOR THE YEAR ENDED DECEMBER 31, 2008

Revenues		$1,250,000
Expenses:		
Salaries and wages	$480,000	
Supplies	65,000	
Utilities	30,000	
Rent	120,000	
Depreciation	345,000	
Interest	138,000	
Total expenses		1,178,000
Net income		$ 72,000

Based on its relatively modest profit margin of 5.76% (net income of $72,000 divided by revenues of $1,250,000), you are concerned about joining the new business. To alleviate your concerns, the president of the company is able to give you the following additional information:

a. Clients are given 90 days to pay their bills for consulting services provided by Oxford. On December 31, 2008, $230,000 of the revenue is yet to be collected in cash.

b. Employees are paid on a monthly basis. Salaries and wages of $480,000 include the December payroll of $40,000, which will be paid on January 5, 2009.

c. The company purchased $100,000 of operating supplies when it began operations in January. The balance of supplies on hand at December 31 amounts to $35,000.

d. Office space is rented in a downtown high-rise building at a monthly rental of $10,000. When the company moved into the office in January, it prepaid its rent for the next 18 months, beginning January 1, 2008.

e. On January 1, 2008, Oxford purchased its own computer system and related accessories at a cost of $1,725,000. The estimated useful life of the system is five years.

f. The computer system was purchased by signing a three-year, 8% note payable for $1,725,000 on the date of purchase. The principal amount of the note and interest for the three years are due on January 1, 2011.

Required

1. Based on the income statement and the additional information given, prepare a statement of cash flows for Oxford for 2008. (*Hint:* Simply list all of the cash inflows and outflows that relate to operations.)

2. On the basis of the income statement given and the statement of cash flows prepared in requirement 1, do you think it would be a wise decision on your part to join the company as its chief financial officer? Include in your response any additional questions that you believe are appropriate to ask before joining the company.

Case 4-3 *Depreciation* LO 2

Matrix Inc., a graphic arts studio, is considering the purchase of computer equipment and software for a total cost of $18,000. Matrix can pay for the equipment and software over three years at the rate of $6,000 per year. The equipment is expected to last 10 to 20 years, but because of changing technology, Matrix believes it may need to replace the system as soon as in three to five years. A three-year lease of similar equipment and software is available for $6,000 per year. Matrix's accountant has asked you to recommend whether the company should purchase or lease the equipment and software and to suggest the length of the period over which to depreciate the software and equipment if the company makes the purchase.

Required

Ignoring the effect of taxes, would you recommend the purchase or the lease? Why? Referring to the definition of *depreciation*, what is the appropriate useful life to use for the equipment and software?

Accounting and Ethics: What Would You Do?

Case 4-4 *Advice to a Potential Investor* LO 2

Whynot Inc. was organized 15 months ago as a management consulting firm. At that time, the owners invested a total of $50,000 cash in exchange for shares. Whynot purchased equipment for $35,000 cash and supplies to be used in the business. The equipment is expected to last seven years with no residual value. Supplies are purchased on account and paid for in the month after the purchase. Whynot normally has about $1,000 of supplies on hand. Its client base has increased so dramatically that the president and chief financial officer have approached an investor to provide additional cash for expansion. The balance sheet and income statement for the first year of business are presented below:

WHYNOT INC.
BALANCE SHEET
DECEMBER 31, 2008

Assets		Liabilities and Shareholders' Equity	
Cash	$10,100	Accounts payable	$ 2,300
Accounts receivable	1,200	Common stock	50,000
Supplies	16,500	Retained earnings	10,500
Equipment	35,000		
Total	$62,800	Total	$62,800

WHYNOT INC.
INCOME STATEMENT
FOR THE YEAR ENDED DECEMBER 31, 2008

Revenues		$82,500
Wages and salaries	$60,000	
Utilities	12,000	72,000
Net income		$10,500

Required

The investor has asked you to look at these financial statements and give an opinion about Whynot's future profitability. Are the statements prepared in accordance with generally accepted accounting principles? If not, explain why. Based on only these two statements, what would you advise? What additional information would you need in order to give an educated opinion?

Solutions to Key Terms Quiz

14	Recognition	5	Unearned revenue
20	Historical cost	12	Accrual
8	Realizable value	18	Accrued liability
17	Cash basis	7	Accrued asset
11	Accrual basis	10	Accounting cycle
2	Revenues	1	Work sheet
21	Expenses	6	Permanent accounts
3	Adjusting entries	16	Temporary accounts
9	Straight-line method	4	Closing entries
19	Contra account	13	Interim statements
15	Prepaid expense		

Integrative Problem

Completing Financial Statements, Computing Ratios, Comparing Accrual vs. Cash Income, and Evaluating the Company's Cash Needs

Norwood Home Health Inc. provides home nursing services in the Halifax region. When contacted by a client or referred by a physician, nurses visit with the patient and discuss needed services with the physician.

Norwood Home Health earns revenue from patient services. Most of the revenue comes from billing either insurance companies or the province's health care program. Amounts billed are recorded in the Billings Receivable account. Insurance companies and the province's health care program do not fully fund all procedures. For example, the province pays an average 78% of billed amounts. Norwood Home Health has already removed the uncollectible amounts from the Billings Receivable account and reports Billings Receivable and Medical Services Revenue at the net amount. Services provided but not yet recorded totaled $16,000, net of allowances for uncollectible amounts. The firm earns a minor portion of its total revenue directly from patients in the form of cash.

Employee salaries, medical supplies, depreciation, and gasoline are the major expenses. Employees are paid every Friday for work performed during the Saturday to Friday pay period. Salaries and wages amount to $800 per day. In 2008, December 31 falls on a Wednesday. Medical supplies (average use of $1,500 per week) are purchased periodically to support health care coverage. The inventory of supplies on hand on December 31 amounted to $8,653.

The firm owns five automobiles (all purchased at the same time) that average 40,000 kilometres per year and are replaced every six years. They typically have no residual value. The building has an expected life of 20 years with no residual value. Straight-line depreciation is used on all firm assets. Gasoline costs, which are a cash expenditure, average $375 per day. The firm purchases a three-year, extended warranty contract to cover maintenance costs. The contract costs $9,000 (assume equal use each year).

On December 29, 2008, Norwood Home Health declared a dividend of $10,000, payable on January 15, 2009. The firm makes annual payments of principal and interest each June 30 on the mortgage. The interest rate on the mortgage is 6%.

The following unadjusted trial balance is available for Norwood Home Health on December 31, 2008.

NORWOOD HOME HEALTH INC.
UNADJUSTED TRIAL BALANCE
DECEMBER 31, 2008

	Debit	Credit
Cash	$ 77,400	
Billings Receivable (net)	151,000	
Medical Supplies	73,000	
Prepaid Extended Warranty	6,000	
Automobiles	90,000	
Accumulated Depreciation—Automobiles		$ 60,000
Building	200,000	
Accumulated Depreciation—Building		50,000
Accounts Payable		22,000
Dividend Payable		10,000
Mortgage Payable		100,000
Capital Stock		150,000
Retained Earnings		99,900
Dividends	10,000	
Medical Services Revenue		550,000
Salary and Wages Expense	285,000	
Gasoline Expense	137,500	
Utilities Expense	12,000	
Totals	$1,041,900	$1,041,900

Required

1. Prepare journal entries to record the necessary year end adjustments.

2. Set up T accounts for each of the accounts listed on the trial balance. Based on the information provided, set up any other T accounts that will be needed to prepare adjusting entries. Post the year-end adjusting entries to the T accounts.

3. Prepare a statement of income and a statement of retained earnings for Norwood Home Health for the year ended December 31, 2008.

4. Prepare a balance sheet for Norwood Home Health as of December 31, 2008.

5. Compute the following as of December 31, 2008: **a.** Working capital   **b.** Current ratio

6. Which of the adjusting entries might cause a difference between cash- and accrual-based income?

7. Ann Rankin, controller of Norwood Home, became concerned about the company's cash flow after talking to a local bank loan officer. The firm tries to maintain a seven-week supply of cash to meet the demands of payroll, medical supply purchases, and gasoline. Determine the amount of cash Norwood Home needs to meet the seven-week supply.

COURTESY TORONTO IMAGES

PART III

Touring the Income Statement

A Word to Readers about Part III

In Part II you learned how the transactions of a company culminate in its financial statements. Part III describes in detail how revenues and expenses in the income statement are recognized and measured, how the format of an income statement enhances its usefulness, and how inventories and the costs of goods sold are recorded and valued.

CHAPTER 5

Income Measurement and the Income Statement

LEARNING OBJECTIVES

After studying this chapter, you should be able to:

LO 1 Apply the revenue recognition principle.

LO 2 Apply the matching principle to recognize expenses.

LO 3 Describe the basic format and the contents of the income statement.

LO 4 Explain additional items on the income statement.

LO 5 Discuss pro forma earnings.

LO 6 Explain the effects of sales on the statement of cash flows.

LO 7 Record sales and purchases with sales tax (Appendix).

CP PHOTO/STEVE WHITE

STUDY LINKS

A Look at the Previous Chapters

In Chapters 3 and 4 we learned accounting process, the process of recording and reporting accounting information.

A Look at This Chapter

In this Chapter, we begin a closer look at the income statement. Specifically, we focus on how incomes are recognized and reported.

A Look at the Upcoming Chapter

Chapter 6 focuses on cost of goods sold, an important expense for manufacturing and merchandising companies, and the related inventories.

Focus on Financial Results

Tim Hortons is not only an iconic symbol of Canadian living but it is also a very successful business. In the following excerpts from income statements from its 2007 annual report, we can see that Tim Hortons generated $1,896 million of sales and franchise revenues for 2007. Operating expenses totaled $1,471 million, resulting in $425 million operating income. After other expenses related to financing and investing activities and income tax expense, Tim Hortons reported $270 million net income for 2007, up almost $10 million from 2006. Chapter 5 focuses on how income is recognized and reported in the income statement. An understanding of how income is measured is important for investors, creditors, and other interested parties who use earnings information in their decision making.

TIM HORTONS INC. 2007 ANNUAL REPORT   http://www.timhortons.com

Consolidated Statements of Operations
(in thousands of Canadian dollars)

	Year ended	
	December 30, 2007	December 31, 2006
Revenues		
Sales	$1,248,574	$1,072,405
Franchise revenues		
Rents and royalties	553,441	503,375
Franchise fees	93,835	83,769
	647,276	587,144
Total revenues	1,895,850	1,659,549
Costs and expenses		
Cost of sales	1,099,248	941,947
Operating expenses	201,153	182,332
Franchise fee costs	87,077	76,658
General and administrative expenses (note 3 and note 18)	119,416	113,530
Equity (income) (note 11)	(38,460)	(35,236)
Other expense (income), net	2,307	1,102
Total costs and expenses, net	1,470,741	1,280,333
Operating income	425,109	379,216
Interest (expense)	(24,118)	(22,253)
Internet income	7,411	11,671
Affiliated interest (expense), net	—	(7,876)
Income before income taxes	408,402	360,758
Income taxes (note 6)	138,851	101,162
Net income	$ 269,551	$ 259,596

Courtesy of The TDL Group Corp.

▪ THE REVENUE RECOGNITION PRINCIPLE

LO 1 Apply the revenue recognition principle.

Revenues Increases in economic resources resulting from ordinary activities such as the sale of goods, the rendering of services, or the use by others of the entity's resources.

Revenue recognition principle Revenues are recognized in the income statement when they are earned.

In Chapter 1 we learned that the income statement reports revenues and expenses. **Revenues** are increases in economic resources—by way of either inflows or enhancements of assets, or reductions of liabilities—resulting from ordinary activities such as the sale of goods or the rendering of services. Expenses are decreases in economic resources—by way of either outflows or reductions of assets, or the incurrence of liabilities[1] that facilitate the earning of revenues. In Chapter 4 we also learned in the **revenue recognition principle** that revenues are recognized when they are earned. How do we determine exactly when revenue is earned? The *CICA Handbook* provides the following criteria as guidelines for revenue recognition:

1. The performance is achieved.
2. The amount is reasonably measurable.
3. The collection of cash is reasonably assured.[2]

The first criterion means that a company must finish doing whatever it does to earn its revenues before it can recognize them. If a company earns its revenues by selling clothing, then the clothes must be sold; if a company earns its revenues by painting houses, then the houses must already be painted. In addition, the amount of revenue earned must be known or reasonably estimable. Finally, although it is not necessary to actually collect the cash from the customers before recognizing revenue, the eventual collection of cash should be reasonably assured.

Applications of the Revenue Recognition Principle

The most common application of the revenue recognition principle is to recognize revenue at the time of sale. For instance, say a customer purchases a digital camera at an HBC store. It is fairly obvious that once the customer pays for the camera and the sales associate hands it over to the customer, all the criteria of revenue recognition have been met.

http://www.viarail.ca

However, not all sales transactions are as simple as this, and the process of generating revenue can be complex and multistaged. For instance, **VIA Rail** sells a return ticket from Halifax to Montreal on February 12 for $300, with a departure date of March 21 and a return date of March 28. The ticket is paid in full on February 12. Under the provisions of the sale, the travelling dates can be changed subject to an additional charge of $25 each way, and the ticket is refundable before departure subject to a $75 fee. However, the ticket expires one year after the date of sale if unused. When should VIA recognize the revenue from the ticket? Can any part of the ticket price be recognized as revenue before the travelling dates? The answers to these questions may not be straightforward.

In the real world, the point at which the above revenue recognition criteria are met may vary from business to business. Sometimes management will have to exercise its judgment in determining appropriate revenue recognition policies for the company. Various revenue recognition methods that are commonly used are summarized on the following pages.

Time-of-sale method The method used by merchandising and manufacturing industries to recognize revenue when goods are sold.

Manufactured Goods and Merchandise In most manufacturing and merchandising industries, revenue recognition using the **time-of-sale method** is the standard practice. When goods are sold by a manufacturer or a merchandiser, the seller usually has made sufficient effort to make the product, find the buyer, serve the buyer, reach a mutually agreed price for the product, transfer ownership of the merchandise to the buyer, and receive either the payment or the promise of payment from the buyer. As long as it is reasonable to believe that the buyer won't default on its account, all three

---

[1]AcSB section 1000, paras. 37–38.
[2]The revenue recognition criteria presented here are based on our interpretations of AcSB Section 1000, 47.

revenue recognition criteria have thus been met. Although a merchandiser does not make the products it sells, it still has to purchase the merchandise, and then complete the selling process. The following excerpt from the 2007 annual report of **Canadian Tire** is an example of recognizing revenue at the time of sale:

http://www.canadiantire.ca

> Revenue on the sale of gasoline by Canadian Tire Petroleum is recorded upon sale to the customer. Revenue for **Mark's Work Wearhouse Ltd.** is recognized at the time goods are sold by its corporate-owned stores to its customers and is net of returns.

http://www2.marks.com

⚔ Accounting for Your Decisions

You Are the Marketing Manager

The end of the year is fast approaching, and your department has not sold its quota of computers. As you understand the company's accounting policies, revenues are recorded when computers are ordered and shipped to customers. You know that if your department does not make its quota, then your job could be in jeopardy. So you get an idea. You call up some friends and tell them to order computers that they don't really need yet. In return, you'll get them a great price on the machines. Besides, if they don't want the computers, they can send them back in January and get a full refund. Meanwhile, you'll make your quota. Do you think there is anything wrong with this idea?

> **ANSWER:** Yes, there is something wrong with the idea. For one thing, it is very poor business judgment to push products on customers if you believe they will be returned. Although many customers will say no to your idea, others will go along to get a lower price, only to later regret buying something they don't need. And if the computers are indeed returned in January, then the company's auditors will be obliged to indicate that the company has not followed the generally accepted accounting principles, because the intent of the transaction was merely to boost sales in the current year. This shortcut is not only unethical but it is also in violation of the revenue recognition principle.

Long-Term Contracts   The **percentage-of-completion method** allows a contractor to recognize revenue over the life of a project rather than at its completion. For long-term contracts in which the sales price is fixed by a contract and in which the realization of revenue depends only on production, such as constructing the bridge or the dam (see the box on the following page), the method is a reasonable alternative to deferring the recognition of revenue until the project is completed. The following excerpt from the 2001 annual report of **Foster Wheeler Inc.** is an example of how revenue is recognized by most companies in the construction industry:

Percentage-of-completion method
The method used by contractors to recognize revenue before the completion of a long-term contract.

http://www.fwc.com

> The Engineering and Construction Group records profits on long-term contracts on a percentage-of-completion basis on the cost to cost method. Contracts in process are valued at cost plus accrued profits less earned revenues and progress payments on uncompleted contracts.

Franchises   Over the past 30 years, franchising has achieved enormous popularity as a way to conduct business. It has been especially prevalent in retail sales, including the restaurant (**Tim Hortons**), hotel (**Holiday Inn**), and car rental (**Hertz**) businesses. Typically, the franchisor grants the exclusive right to sell a product or service in a specific geographic area to the franchisee. A franchisor such as Tim Hortons generates franchise revenues from one or both of two sources: (1) from the sale of the franchise and related services, such as help in selecting a site and hiring employees, and (2) from continuing fees based on performance, for example, a fixed percentage of sales by the franchisee.

http://www.timhortons.com
http://www.holidayinn.com
http://www.hertz.com

Accounting For Your Decisions

You Are the Shareholder

Assume that a construction company starts two projects during the year. One is a $5 million contract for a bridge. The other is a $4 million contract for a dam. Based on actual costs incurred to date and estimates of costs yet to be incurred, the contractor estimates that at the end of the year the bridge will be 20% complete and the dam will be 50% complete. Which would be more informative to you as a shareholder of the construction company: (1) an end-of-the-year report that indicates no revenue because no contracts are finished yet or (2) an end-of-the-year report that indicates revenue of $1 million on the bridge (20% of $5 million) and $2 million on the dam (50% of $4 million), both based on the extent of completion?

ANSWER: As a shareholder, you need information on a timely basis to evaluate your various investments. The percentage-of-completion method will allow you to assess the profitability of your investment in the construction company on a regular basis rather than only at the point when projects are completed.

At what point should the revenue from the sale of a franchise be recognized? An excerpt from Tim Hortons 2007 annual report indicates how it recognizes both the initial and continuing fees:

Revenue Recognition
The Company's Tim Hortons restaurants are predominantly franchised. The Company grants franchise license or operator agreements to independent operators who in turn pay franchise fees and other payments, which may include payments for equipment, royalties and, in most cases, rent for each restaurant opened. Franchise fees and equipment sales are generally recognized as income when each restaurant commences operations and payment is received from the franchisee. Royalties, based on a percentage of monthly sales, are recognized as income on the accrual basis.
Courtesy of The TDL Group Corp.

Commodities Corn, wheat, gold, silver, and other agricultural and mining products trade on the open market at established prices. Readily convertible assets such as these are interchangeable and can be sold at a quoted price in an active market that can absorb the quantity being sold without significantly affecting the price.

Assume that a company mines gold. Revenues are realizable by the company at the time the product is mined because each ounce of gold is interchangeable with another ounce of gold and the commodities market can absorb all of the gold the company sells without having an effect on the price. This is one of the few instances in which it is considered acceptable to recognize revenue *prior* to the point of sale. The exception is justified because the important event in the revenue-generation process is the *production* of the gold, not the sale of it. The **production method** of recognizing revenue is used for precious metals, as well as for certain agricultural products and marketable securities.

Production method The method in which revenue is recognized when a commodity is produced rather than when it is sold.

Installment Sales Various real estates, such as retail land and vacation properties, are sold on an installment basis. A down payment is followed by a series of regular payments over a period of years. Default on the payments and repossession of the property by the seller are more common in these types of sales than with most other arrangements. For this reason, it is considered acceptable, in limited circumstances, to defer the recognition of revenue on an installment sale until cash is actually collected. The **installment method,** which is essentially a cash basis of accounting, is acceptable only when the seller has no reasonable basis for estimating the degree of collectibility. Note that the production and installment methods are at opposite ends of the spectrum. Under the production method, revenue is recognized *before* a sale takes place; with the installment method, revenue is recognized *after* the sale.

Installment method The method in which revenue is recognized at the time cash is collected.

Rent and Interest In some cases, revenue is earned *continuously* over time. In these cases, a product or service is not delivered at a specific point in time; instead, the earnings process takes place with the passage of time. Rent and interest are two examples. Interest is the cost associated with the use of someone else's money. When should a bank recognize the interest earned from granting a 90-day loan? Even though the interest may not be received until the loan itself is repaid, interest is earned every day the loan is outstanding. Later in the chapter, we will look at the process for recognizing interest earned but not yet received. The same procedure is used to recognize revenue from rent that is earned but uncollected.

Long-term contracts, franchises, commodities, installment sales, rent, and interest are not the only situations in which the revenue recognition principle must be interpreted. The intent in examining these particular examples was to help you think about the variety of ways in which businesses generate revenue and about the need to apply judgment in deciding when to recognize revenue. These examples should help you to realize the subjective nature of the work of an accountant and to understand that the discipline is not as precise as it may sometimes seem.

Exhibit 5-1 illustrates the various applications of the revenue recognition principle discussed previously along a time line.

Exhibit 5-1   Summary of Revenue Recognition Methods

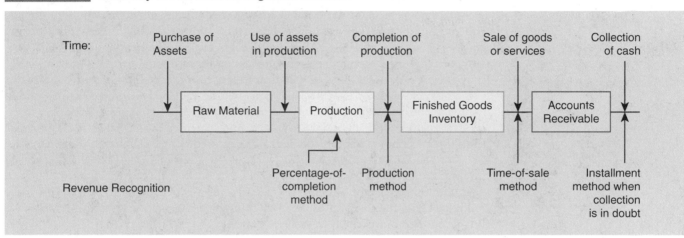

THE MATCHING PRINCIPLE AND EXPENSE RECOGNITION

There are usually many costs associated with the earning of revenues. Costs incurred to earn revenues are called expenses. The relationship between revenues and expenses means that only when revenues and the associated expenses are matched properly on the income statement can net income be a meaningful measure of profitability. Thus, in accounting the recognition of expenses is guided by the **matching principle**. Under this principle, the accountant attempts to associate the revenues for a period with the costs of generating those revenues. But how exactly expenses are matched against revenues depends on the nature of the costs that gave rise to the expenses.

> **LO 2** Apply the matching principle to recognize expenses.

Matching principle The revenues for the period are associated with the costs of generating those revenues.

Costs and Expenses

Companies incur a variety of costs: a new office building is constructed; merchandise is purchased; employees perform services; the electric meter is read. In each of these situations, the company incurs a cost, regardless of when it pays cash.

The incurrence of some costs gives rise to assets. For instance, the purchase of merchandise gives rise to merchandise inventory, which is an asset. According to the definition in Chapter 1, an asset represents a future economic benefit. Merchandise can be sold to earn revenues. Once the merchandise is sold and revenues are earned, there is no longer any future benefit to that merchandise and its costs become expenses. An asset ceases being an asset when its economic benefits expire and it becomes an expense. Assets are unexpired costs; expenses are expired costs.

Other costs, however, do not give rise to assets because no future benefits from these costs are discernible. For example, the cost of heating and lighting a building provides benefits when the heat and light are used, but it does not provide a future benefit. Such costs are treated in accounting as expiring simultaneously with their acquisition.

Direct and Indirect Matching

Certain costs directly generate revenues. Thus, these expenses can be matched directly with revenues. Other expenses are incurred to support the earning of revenues indirectly. The classic example of direct matching is cost of goods sold expense with sales revenue. Cost of goods sold is the cost of the inventory associated with a particular sale. A cost is incurred and an asset is recorded when the inventory is purchased or manufactured. The cost of inventory becomes an expense when the inventory is sold. Another example of a cost that can be matched directly with revenue is commissions. A commission is paid to a salesperson when a specific sale is completed; thus, the commission can be matched directly with the sale.

An indirect form of matching is used to recognize the benefits associated with certain types of costs, most noticeably long-term assets such as buildings and equipment. These costs benefit many periods, but usually it is not possible to match them directly with the specific sale of a product. Instead, they are matched with the periods during which they will provide benefits. For example, an office building may be useful to a company for 30 years. Depreciation is the process of allocating the cost of a tangible long-term asset over its useful life. Depreciation Expense is the account used to recognize this type of expense. Other expenses that can only be matched with a particular period include insurance, utilities, and income taxes.

The relationships among costs, assets, and expenses are depicted in Exhibit 5-2 using three examples. First, costs incurred for purchases of merchandise or manufacturing of goods result in an asset, Inventory, and are eventually matched with revenue at the time the product is sold. Second, costs incurred for office space result in an asset, Office Building, which is recognized as Depreciation Expense over the useful life of the building. Third, the cost of heating and lighting benefits only the current period and is thus recognized immediately as Utilities Expense.

Exhibit 5-2

Relationships among Costs, Assets, and Expenses

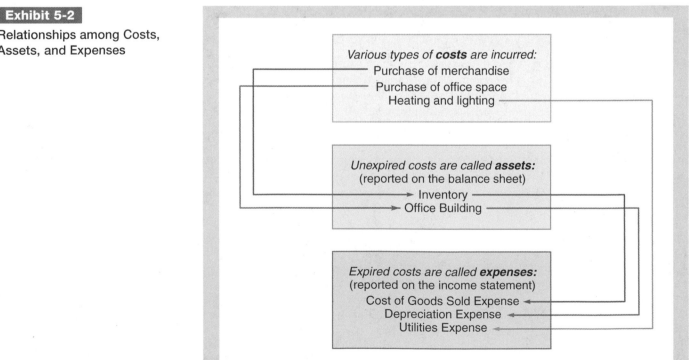

THE FORMAT AND CONTENT OF THE INCOME STATEMENT

As discussed in Chapter 1, the income statement summarizes the revenues and expenses of a particular period. Although GAAP provides some guidelines relating to the content of income statements, companies have plenty of discretion regarding how detailed their income statements must be and what format to use.

LO 3 Describe the basic format and the contents of the income statement.

Single-Step versus Multiple-Step Format for the Income Statement

The income statement of Dixon Sporting Goods Inc. in Exhibit 2-5, reproduced in Exhibit 5-3, is in single-step format. In a **single-step income statement**, all expenses and losses are added together and then subtracted from all the revenues and gains to arrive at net income in a single step. The primary advantage of the single-step form is its simplicity. No attempt is made to classify either revenues or expenses or to associate any of the expenses with any of the revenues.

The single-step income statement is acceptable. However, according to a survey of 200 companies by the CICA,[3] most Canadian companies use the multiple-step format—or at least some elements of it—for their income statements.[4]

Single-step income statement
An income statement in which all expenses are added together and subtracted from all revenues.

Exhibit 5-3 Income Statement (Single-Step Format) for Dixon Sporting Goods Inc.

DIXON SPORTING GOODS INC.
INCOME STATEMENT (SINGLE-STEP FORMAT)
FOR THE YEAR ENDED DECEMBER 31, 2008

Revenues		
Sales	$357,500	
Interest	1,500	
Total revenues		$359,000
Expenses		
Cost of goods sold	218,300	
Depreciation on store furniture and fixtures	4,200	
Advertising	13,750	
Salaries and wages for sales staff	22,000	
Depreciation on buildings and amortization of trademark	6,000	
Salaries and wages for office staff	15,000	
Insurance	3,600	
Supplies	1,050	
Interest	16,900	
Income taxes	17,200	
Total expenses		318,000
Net income		$ 41,000

In a **single-step** income statement, expenses are deducted from revenues in one step.

[3]Clarence Byrd, Ida Chen, and Joshua Smith, *Financial Reporting in Canada* (Toronto: CICA, 2005).
[4]Neither AcSB and IASB specifies the format of income statement. Instead, they typically provide a minimum list of line items that should be presented separately.

Multiple-step income statement
An income statement that shows classifications of revenues and expenses as well as important subtotals.

The purpose of the **multiple-step income statement** is to subdivide the income statement into specific sections and provide the reader with important subtotals. This format is illustrated for Dixon Sporting Goods in Exhibit 5-4.

Exhibit 5-4 Income Statement (Multiple-Step Format) for Dixon Sporting Goods

In a **multiple-step** income statement:

Sales and the costs of sales are compared. **1**

Expenses of the business are detailed.

Isolating expenses and revenues by type is useful in analyzing a business.

Operating income is highlighted. **2**

"Nonoperating" revenues and expenses are included here. **3**

4

DIXON SPORTING GOODS INC.
INCOME STATEMENT (MULTIPLE-STEP FORMAT)
FOR THE YEAR ENDED DECEMBER 31, 2008

Net sales		$357,500
Cost of goods sold		218,300
Gross profit		**$139,200**
Operating expenses		
Selling expenses		
Depreciation on store		
furniture and fixtures	$ 4,200	
Advertising	13,750	
Salaries and wages	22,000	
Total selling expenses		39,950
General and administrative expenses		
Depreciation on buildings and		
amortization of trademark	6,000	
Salaries and wages	15,000	
Insurance	3,600	
Supplies	1,050	
Total general and administrative expenses		25,650
Total operating expenses		65,600
Income from operations		73,600
Other revenues and expenses		
Interest revenue	1,500	
Interest expense	16,900	
Excess of other expenses over other revenue		15,400
Income before income taxes		58,200
Income tax expense		17,200
Net income		**$ 41,000**

Gross profit Sales less cost of goods sold, also termed gross margin.

The multiple-step income statement for Dixon indicates three important subtotals. First, **1** cost of goods sold is deducted from net sales to arrive at **gross profit**.

Second, **2** *income from operations* of $73,600 is found by subtracting *total operating expenses* of $65,600 from the gross profit of $139,200.

Third, **3** *income before income taxes* of $58,200 is shown. Interest revenue and interest expense, neither of which is an operating item, are included in *other revenues and expenses*. The excess of interest expense of $16,900 over interest revenue of $1,500, which equals $15,400, is subtracted from income from operations to arrive at income before income taxes. Finally, **4** *income tax expense* of $17,200 is deducted to arrive at *net income* of $41,000. Now we turn to a detailed discussion of the multiple-step income statement.

Net Sales

Like most companies, Dixon Sporting Goods begins its income statement with net sales. As shown in Exhibit 5-3, net sales (also called net sales revenue) typically differs from total sales (also called total sales revenue) due to two deductions: sales returns and allowances, and sales discounts. These are deducted from sales revenue to arrive at **net sales.** Sales revenue, or simply sales, is a *representation of the inflow of assets,* either cash or accounts receivable, from the sale of goods during the period:

Net sales Sales revenue less sales returns and allowances and sales discounts.

Exhibit 5-5

Net Sales Section of the Income Statement

DIXON SPORTING GOODS INC. PARTIAL INCOME STATEMENT FOR THE YEAR ENDED DECEMBER 31, 2008		
Total sales revenue	$368,000	
Less: Sales returns and allowances	6,000	
Sales discounts	4,500	
Net sales		$357,500

- *Cash sales,* most commonly seen in a retail business, are recorded daily in the journal and are based on the total amount shown on the cash register tape. For example, suppose that the cash register tape in the apparel department of Dixon shows sales on March 31, 2008, of $350. The transaction is recorded in the journal as follows:

Mar. 31   Cash   350
                  Sales Revenuc   350
              To record daily cash receipts in apparel department

Assets   =   Liabilities   +   Shareholders' Equity
+350   +350

- *Sales on credit* do not result in the immediate inflow of cash but rather in an increase in accounts receivable, that is, a promise by the customer to pay cash at a later date. The entry to record a May 4 sale of equipment on credit for $1,250 is recorded as follows:

May 4   Accounts Receivable   1,250
                  Sales Revenue   1,250
              To record sale on credit in equipment department

Assets   =   Liabilities   +   Shareholders' Equity
+1,250   +1,250

Sales Returns and Allowances

The cornerstone of marketing is to satisfy the customer. Most companies have standard policies that allow the customer to *return* merchandise within a stipulated period of time. A company's policy might be that a customer who is not completely satisfied can return the goods anytime within 30 days of purchase for a full refund. Alternatively, the customer may be given an *allowance* for spoiled or damaged goods—that is, the customer keeps the goods but receives a credit for a certain amount in the account balance. Typically, a single account, **Sales Returns and Allowances,** is used to account both for returns and for allowances. If the customer has already paid for the merchandise, either a cash refund is given or the credit amount is applied to future purchases.

The accounting for a return or allowance depends on whether the customer is given a cash refund or credit on an account. Assume that Dixon's apparel department gives a $25 cash refund on a stained T-shirt returned by a customer. The entry follows:

Sales Returns and Allowances Contra-revenue account used to record both refunds to customers and reductions of their accounts.

Apr. 25   Sales Returns and Allowances   25
                  Cash   25
              To record return of stained T-shirt by customer for a
              cash refund

Assets   =   Liabilities   +   Shareholders' Equity
−25   −25

Sales Returns and Allowances is a *contra-revenue* account. A contra account has a balance opposite to its related account and is deducted from that account on the statement. Thus, the effect of the debit to this account is the same as if Sales Revenue had been reduced (debited) directly.

The purpose of this entry is to reduce the amount of previously recorded sales. So why didn't we simply reduce Sales Revenue for $25? The reason is that management needs to be able to *monitor* the amount of returns and allowances. If Sales Revenue is reduced for returns and at some point we need to determine the total dollars of returns for the period, we would need to add up all of the individual decreases to this account. A much more efficient method is to split the sales revenue into two accounts, one that includes only sales and another that includes only returns. Thus, the total amount of returns is readily available, and decision making is more efficient and effective.

The previous entry illustrates the accounting for a return of goods. The same account is normally used when a credit is given and the customer keeps the goods. Assume that on May 7 the customer who made the $1,250 purchase from Dixon on May 4 notifies the company that the exercise equipment is rusted in certain parts. Dixon agrees to reduce the customer's unpaid account by $100 because of the rust. The entry to record the allowance follows:

May 7	Sales Returns and Allowances	100	
	Accounts Receivable		100
	To record allowance given for rusted equipment		

$$\textbf{Assets} \quad = \quad \textbf{Liabilities} \quad + \quad \textbf{Shareholders' Equity}$$
$$-100 \qquad\qquad\qquad\qquad\qquad\qquad\quad -100$$

The Sales Returns and Allowances account gives management and shareholders an important piece of data: that goods are being returned or are not completely acceptable. It does not answer the following questions, however. Why are the goods being returned? Why are customers getting partial refunds? Are the goods shoddy? Are salespeople too aggressive? Should the company's liberal policy regarding returns be changed? Answers to these questions require management to look beyond the accounting data.

Trade Discounts and Quantity Discounts

Trade discount Selling price reduction offered to a special class of customers.

Quantity discount Reduction in selling price for buying a large number of units of a product.

Various types of discounts to the list price are given to customers. A **trade discount** is a selling price reduction offered to a special class of customers. For example, Dixon's apparel department might offer a special price to sports clubs. The difference between normal selling price and this special price is called a *trade discount*. A **quantity discount** is sometimes offered to customers who are willing to buy in large quantities.

Trade discounts and quantity discounts are *not* recorded in the accounts. Although a company might track the amount of these discounts for control purposes, the reason for ignoring the quantity and trade discounts in the accounting records is that the list price is not the actual selling price. The *net* amount is a more accurate reflection of the amount of a sale. For example, assume that Dixon gives a 30% discount from the normal selling price to the local soccer clubs on soccer jerseys. The list price for each unit is $20. The selling price and the related journal entry for a club's purchase of 40 jerseys on July 2 are as follows:

List price	$ 20
Less: 30% quantity discount	6
Selling price	14
× Number of jerseys sold	× 40
Sales revenue	$560

July 2	Accounts Receivable	560	
	Sales Revenue		560
	To record sale of 40 jerseys at list price less		
	30% quantity discount		

$$\text{Assets} \quad = \quad \text{Liabilities} \quad + \quad \text{Shareholders' Equity}$$
$$+560 \qquad\qquad\qquad\qquad\qquad +560$$

Credit Terms and Sales Discounts

Most companies have a standard credit policy. Special notation is normally used to indicate a particular firm's policy for granting credit. For example, credit terms of *n/30* mean that the *net* amount of the selling price, that is, the amount determined after deducting any returns or allowances, is due within 30 days of the date of the invoice. *Net, 10 EOM* means that the net amount is due anytime within 10 days after the end of the month in which the sale took place.

Another common element of the credit terms offered to customers is sales discounts, a reduction from the selling price given for early payment. For example, assume that Dixon offers a soccer club credit terms of *1/10, n/30*. This means that the customer may deduct 1% from the selling price if the bill is paid within 10 days of the date of the invoice. Normally the discount period begins with the day *after* the invoice date. If the customer does not pay within the first 10 days, the full invoice amount is due within 30 days. Finally, note that the use of *n* for *net* in this notation is really a misnomer. Although the amount due is net of any returns and allowances, it is the *gross* amount that is due within 30 days. That is, no discount is given if the customer does not pay early.

How valuable to the customer is a 1% discount for payment within the first 10 days? Assume that a $1,000 sale is made. If the customer pays at the end of 10 days, the cash paid will be $990, rather than $1,000, a net savings of $10. The customer has saved $10 by paying 20 days earlier than required by the 30-day term. If we assume 360 days in a year, there are 360/20 or 18 periods of 20 days each in a year. Thus, a savings of $10 for 20 days is equivalent to a savings of $10 times 18, or $180 for the year. An annual return of $180/$990, or 18.2%, would be difficult to match with any other type of investment. In fact, a customer might want to consider borrowing the money to pay off the account early.

Some companies record sales *net* of any discounts for early payment; others record the *gross* amount of sales and then track sales discounts separately. Because the effect on the accounting equation does not differ between the two methods, we will concern ourselves only with the *gross method,* which assumes that customers will not necessarily take advantage of the discount offered for early payment. Sales discounts are rarely material, and companies do not normally disclose the method used on their financial statements.

Assume a sale on June 10 of $1,000 with credit terms of 2/10, net 30. The entry at the time of the sale is as follows:

June 10	Accounts Receivable	1,000	
	Sales Revenue		1,000
	To record sale on account, terms 2/10, net 30		

$$\text{Assets} \quad = \quad \text{Liabilities} \quad + \quad \text{Shareholders' Equity}$$
$$+1,000 \qquad\qquad\qquad\qquad\qquad +1,000$$

If the customer pays after the discount period, the accountant simply makes an entry to record the receipt of $1,000 cash and the reduction of accounts receivable. However, assume the customer pays its account on June 20, within the discount period. The following entry would be made:

June 20	Cash	980	
	Sales Discounts	20	
	Accounts Receivable		1,000
	To record collection on account		

$$\text{Assets} \quad = \quad \text{Liabilities} \quad + \quad \text{Shareholders' Equity}$$
$$+\ 980 \qquad\qquad\qquad\qquad\qquad\ \ -20$$
$$-1,000$$

Sales Discounts Contra-revenue account used to record discounts given customers for early payment of their accounts.

The **Sales Discounts** account is a *contra-revenue* account and thus reduces shareholders' equity, as shown in the previous accounting equation. Also note in Exhibit 5-5 that sales discounts are deducted from sales on the income statement.

The Cost of Goods Sold and Gross Profit

The recognition of cost of goods sold as an expense is an excellent example of the *matching principle.* Sales revenue represents the *inflow* of assets, in the form of cash and accounts receivable, from the sale of products during the period. Likewise, cost of goods sold represents the *outflow* of an asset, inventory, from the sale of those same products. The company needs to match the revenue of the period with one of the most important costs necessary to generate the revenue, the *cost* of the goods sold.

The Cost of Goods Sold Model

It may be helpful in understanding cost of goods sold to realize what it is *not. Cost of goods sold is not necessarily equal to the cost of purchases of merchandise or cost of goods manufactured during the period.* Except in the case of a new business, a business starts the year with a certain stock of inventory on hand, called *beginning inventory.* During the year, the business purchases goods. When the cost of goods purchased is added to beginning inventory, the result is **cost of goods available for sale.** Just as the company starts the period with an inventory on hand, a certain amount of *ending inventory* is usually on hand at the end of the year.

Cost of goods available for sale Beginning inventory plus cost of goods purchased.

As shown in Exhibit 5-6, think of cost of goods available for sale as a "pool" of costs to be distributed between what we sold and what we did not sell. If we subtract from the pool the cost of what we did *not* sell, the *ending inventory,* we will have the amount we

Exhibit 5-6

The Cost of Goods Sold Model

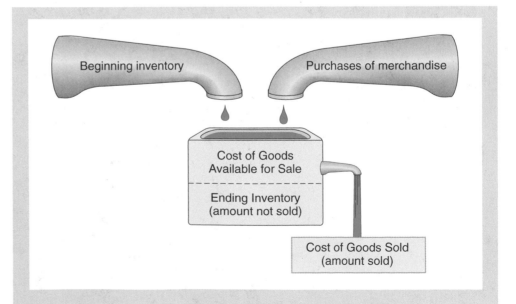

did sell, the **cost of goods sold.** Cost of goods sold is simply the difference between the cost of goods available for sale and the ending inventory:

Cost of goods sold Cost of goods available for sale minus ending inventory.

Beginning inventory — What is on hand to start the period
+ Purchases — What was acquired during the period
= Cost of goods available for sale — The "pool" of costs to be distributed
− Ending inventory — What was not sold during the period and therefore is on hand to start the next period

= Cost of goods sold — What was sold during the period

The cost of goods sold model for a merchandiser is illustrated in Exhibit 5-7. The amounts used for the illustration represent the additional inventory and cost of goods sold information of Dixon's Sporting Goods. Notice that ending inventory exceeds beginning inventory by $12,000. That means that the cost of goods purchased exceeds cost of goods sold by that same amount. Indeed, a key point for shareholders, bankers, and other users is whether inventory is building up, that is, whether a company is not selling as much inventory during the period as it is buying. A buildup may indicate that the company's products are becoming less desirable or that prices are becoming uncompetitive.

Exhibit 5-7 The Cost of Goods Sold Model: Example for a Merchandiser

Description	Item	Amount
Merchandise on hand to start the period	Beginning inventory	$ 60,000
Acquisitions of merchandise during the period	+ Cost of goods purchased	230,300
The pool of merchandise available for sale during the period	= Cost of goods available for sale	290,300
Merchandise on hand at end of period	− Ending inventory	(72,000)
The expense recognized on the income statement	= Cost of goods sold	$218,300

A $12,000 excess of ending inventory over beginning inventory means the company bought $12,000 more than it sold ($230,300 bought versus $218,000 sold).

The cost of goods sold section of the income statement for Dixon is shown in Exhibit 5-8.

Exhibit 5-8
Cost of Goods Sold Section of the Income Statement

DIXON SPORTING GOODS INC.
PARTIAL INCOME STATEMENT
FOR THE YEAR ENDED DECEMBER 31, 2008

Cost of goods sold:		
Inventory, January 1, 2008	$ 60,000	
Purchases	230,300	
Cost of goods available for sale	290,300	
Less: Inventory, December 31, 2008	72,000	
Cost of goods sold		$218,300

In the multiple-step income statement for Dixon in Exhibit 5-2, gross profit is determined by subtracting cost of goods sold from net sales. It is logical to associate cost of goods sold with the sales revenue for the year because the latter represents the selling price of the inventory sold during the period. Gross profit is an important measure of profitability for both manufacturing and merchandising businesses. The ratio of gross profit as a percentage of net sales (gross profit margin) indicates the amount of each net sales dollar left after cost of goods sold. Gross profit is the amount that can be used to cover operating expenses and other expenses.

$$\text{Gross Profit Margin} = \frac{\text{Gross Profit}}{\text{Net Sales}}$$

Inventory systems, the methods used to determine the quantity of inventory sold and left on hand, and inventory costing (i.e., methods for determining the cost of inventory sold and left on hand) are discussed in Chapter 6.

CN
http://www.cn.ca

Not all businesses have cost of goods sold and thus gross profit. For example, service companies sell services rather than goods. **CN** provides rail and other transportation services, so its income statements do not include cost of goods sold and gross profit. Instead, CN subtracts operating expenses directly from sales revenue to arrive at operating income, as shown in Exhibit 5-9 (in condensed form).

Exhibit 5-9 CN Operating and Net Income

In millions, except per share data	Year ended December 31,	2007
Total revenues		$7,897
Total operating expenses		5,021
Operating income		2,876
Interest expense		(336)
Other income (Note 14)		166
Income before income taxes and cumulative effect of change in accounting policy		2,706
Income tax expense (Note 15)		(548)
Net income		$2,158

This excerpt from CN's 2007 Annual Report appears courtesy of CN. This section of the CN Annual Report appears in the Appendix of this textbook.

Although cost of goods sold and gross profit are useful information, the separate disclosure of cost of goods sold was not mandatory in Canada until January 2008.[5] Since cost of goods sold is generally considered proprietary information, many companies were reluctant to provide it. In fact, less than half the companies surveyed by the CICA[6] report cost of goods sold separately; instead, they combine it with other operating expenses prior to AcSB section 1520.03.

Operating Expenses and Income from Operations

The second section of the multiple-step income statement reflects operating expenses and income from operations. Operating expenses are the expenses incurred pursuant to the operating activities of a company (i.e., the sales of goods or services). Operating expenses can be further subdivided into selling expenses and general and administrative expenses. Selling expenses are directly related to the selling of goods or services to customers. In Dixon's multiple-step income statement in Exhibit 5-4, selling expenses include

---

[5]AcSB section 1520.03.
[6]Clarence Byrd, Ida Chen, and Joshua Smith, *Financial Reporting in Canada* (Toronto: CICA, 2005).

depreciation on store furniture and fixtures, advertising, and salaries and wages. Depreciation on store furniture and fixtures is classified as a selling expense because the store is where sales take place. Obviously, advertising is for promoting sales. Salaries and wages are presumably for the sales associates and store managers. General and administrative expenses are incurred to support the general operations of a company. In Dixon's multiple-step income statement, general and administrative expenses include depreciation on buildings and amortization of trademark, salaries and wages, insurance, and supplies. We will assume that the buildings are offices for the administrative staff; thus, depreciation on the buildings is classified as a general and administrative expense. The trademark is related to the image of the business. Salaries and wages are for the executives and administrative staff. Insurance and supplies are both for the general operations of the company.

The income from operations is the difference between gross profit and total operating expenses. Because operating activities represent the objective of a company—in other words, what the company is in business for—income from operations is an extremely important measure of the company's financial performance. It indicates whether the company's principal business is profitable. The implication is that, since the company will presumably continue its operations, the income from operations represents the sustainable source of income. A healthy income from operations can be interpreted as indicating healthy performance in the future, a lack of income from operations as indicating future poor financial performance.

Other Revenues and Expenses and Income before Income Taxes

Revenues and expenses can also arise from *non*-operating activities. In the multiple-step income statement, revenues and expenses related to investing and financing activities—called other revenues or gains and other expenses or losses—are separated from the section for income from operations. In Dixon's income statement in Exhibit 5-4 we see two items relating to non-operating activities: interest revenue, which arises from investing activities (investments in debt securities); and interest expenses, which arise from financing activities (borrowing of debt). The net amount of other revenues and expenses is added to or subtracted from income from operations to arrive at income before income taxes.

Companies engage in investing and financing activities primarily for the purpose of supporting their operations; nevertheless, revenues and expenses arising from non-operating activities affect the financial performance of the company. Other revenues and expenses usually have different implications for the company's future financial performance from operating income. By reporting other revenues and expenses separately, a multiple-step income statement enables users to assess the different implications of the company's operating results and results from its investing and financing activities.

Income Tax Expenses and Net Income

Most businesses in Canada are required to compute income taxes based on before-tax income. The calculation of income tax expense is based on the amount of income available to pay taxes. Income tax expense is an important consideration in the decisions of shareholders, creditors, and other interested parties. After all, it is net income, not income before income taxes, that a company earns. In Exhibit 5-2, Dixon has reported $17,200 of income tax expense; this is approximately 30% of its income before income taxes.[7]

It is important to note that the single-step and multiple-step formats for income statements as discussed in this section have been standardized. The real world is rarely so black and white. In fact, quite often companies do not adhere strictly to either format for their income statements. Many companies customize their income statements to suit their unique circumstances by combining various elements from both formats.

---

[7]The income tax expense listed on the income statement may not be the actual taxes that are payable in the current period. The rules for calculating taxes are laid out in the Income Tax Act and differ in some respects from GAAP. The amount of tax that must be paid in the current period is shown as *current income taxes*; the difference between the amount of tax expense and current income tax is shown as *future income taxes*.

The ratio of net income to net sales (profit margin) indicates the amount of each net sales dollar left as profit after all expenses are covered. To improve profitability, it is necessary to keep overall expenses low.

$$\text{Profit Margin} = \frac{\text{Net Income}}{\text{Net Sales}}$$

ADDITIONAL ITEMS IN THE INCOME STATEMENT

LO 4 Explain additional items on the income statement.

Not all companies' income statements are as straightforward and easy to understand as Dixon's. Additional items may appear, albeit less frequently, in an income statement. In this section we discuss three such items: discontinued operations, extraordinary items, and unusual or infrequent items.

Discontinued Operations

Discontinued operations A line item on the income statement to reflect any gains or losses from the disposal of a segment of the business as well as any net income or loss from operating that segment.

When a company decides to either sell or otherwise dispose of one of its operations, it must separately report on that division or segment of the business on its income statement. **Discontinued operations** include any gain or loss from the disposal of the business as well as any net income or loss from operating the business until the date of disposal. Because the discontinued segment of the business will not be part of the company's operations in the future, discontinued operations are separately disclosed on the income statement. Analysts and other users would normally only consider income from continuing operations in making their decisions.

Extraordinary Items

Extraordinary item A line item on the income statement to reflect any gains or losses that arise from an event that is unusual in nature and infrequent in occurrence and, independent of management decisions.

According to accounting standards, certain events that give rise to gains or losses are deemed to be extraordinary and are thus separately disclosed on the income statement. Under current accounting standards, an **extraordinary item** is relatively rare, such as when a natural catastrophe like a tornado destroys a plant in an area not known for tornadoes. As is the case for discontinued operations, analysts and others often ignore the amount of such gains and losses in reaching their decisions since they are aware that these items are not likely to reoccur in the future.

For an item to be classified as extraordinary, it must meet all of these three conditions: it must be unusual, infrequent, and independent of management decisions.[8]

Discontinued operations and extraordinary items are distinctly different, but they also share some characteristics. First, they are all reported near the end of the income statement, after income from continuing operations. Second, they are reported separately on the income statement to call the reader's attention to their unique nature and to the fact that any additions to, or deductions from, income that they give rise to may not necessarily occur again in future periods. Finally, both items are shown net of their income tax effects; this means that any additional taxes owing because of them, or any income tax benefits arising from them, are deducted from the items themselves.

---

[8]Note under the requirement of IAS1, no items of income or expanse should be presented as extraordinary items.

Unusual or Infrequent Items

Occasionally, companies encounter revenues or expenses arising from transactions that have some characteristics of an extraordinary item but don't meet all of the three criteria of an extraordinary item. For instance, a company that is reorganizing may incur significant costs for severance pay in laying off plant employees. Or a company may write down the value of its equipment owing to obsolescence as a result of new technology. Layoffs of employees and the writing down of equipment, although unusual and infrequent, are the result of the management's decisions, thus, they can't be classified as extraordinary items. On the other hand, they are not regular business activities either and the implications of these items are different from those of other operating expenses. They are classified as unusual or infrequent items and are separated from other items. It is important for shareholders, creditors, and other interested parties to understand the nature of these unusual and infrequent items in an income statement in order to make informed decisions.

GAAP does not specify where the **unusual or infrequent items** should be reported on an income statement. It can be included in operating expenses, in other revenue and expenses, or it can be reported by itself in a separate category.

Exhibit 5-10 shows the income statement for Home & House Hardware Inc. Home & House is reporting $8,540,000 in restructuring charges. Given the nature of this item, it is not very likely to arise again next year. Analysts may very well exclude it when using the current income statement to forecast the company's future earnings.

Unusual or infrequent items
Revenues and expenses arising from transactions that are not expected to occur frequently over several years or that are not typical of the company's activities.

Exhibit 5-10 Income Statement for Home & House

HOME & HOUSE HARDWARE INC.
INCOME STATEMENT
FOR THE YEAR ENDED JANUARY 31, 2008
(IN THOUSANDS OF DOLLARS)

Net sales		$75,632
Cost of sales		42,585
Gross profit		$33,047
Operating expenses		
Selling and administrative expense	10,025	
Restructuring charges	8,540	
Total operating expenses		18,565
Income from operations		14,482
Other revenues and expenses		
Gain from sales of capital assets	2,500	
Interest expenses	6,200	
Excess of other expenses over other revenues		3,700
Income before income taxes		10,782
Income tax expense		4,310
Income from continuing operations		6,472
Discontinued operations, net of income taxes		
Loss from operation of discontinued division, net of income taxes		8,000
Gain on disposal of discontinued division, net of income taxes		5,000
Income before extraordinary items		3,472
Extraordinary loss, net of income taxes		1,000
Net income		$ 2,472

Labels at left:
- Unusual or infrequent items reported separately → (Selling and administrative expense / Restructuring charges)
- Results from ongoing operations → Income from continuing operations
- Special items that are unlikely to reoccur in the future → Discontinued operations / Extraordinary loss
- The bottom line → Net income

Estimating the Effect of Income Taxes

The unusual or infrequent items previously discussed are reported before taxes and above the line. If an analyst wants to see how much Home & House Hardware Inc. has earned in 2008 from its continuing operations excluding the restructuring charges, he or she will have to remove not only the restructuring charge, but also the tax effect of the charge.

Estimating the effect of income tax of a particular item requires the information of the applicable tax rate. While the exact tax rate of each item may not be available, it can be approximated by using the effective income tax rate. The effective tax rate can be determined by dividing the reported income tax expense by income before tax.

In Home & House Hardware's example, the effective tax rate can be estimated as the following:

$$\text{Estimated effective tax rate} = \frac{\text{Income tax expense}}{\text{Income before income taxes}} = \frac{\$4,310}{\$10,782} = 40\%$$

Restructuring charges	$ 8,540
Tax on restructuring charges	3,416
Restructuring charges (after tax)	$ 5,124
Income from continuing operations	$ 6,472
Restructuring charges (after tax)	5,124
Income from continuing operations excluding the effect of restructuring charges	$11,596

Comprehensive Income

The revenues and expenses, gains and losses are reported in the income statement. However, not all such gains and losses are included in net income. Canadian GAAP, as well as U.S. and international GAAP, now requires companies to report the gains and losses that are excluded from net income as part of the comprehensive income. Comprehensive income can either be reported following net income or in a separate statement that begins with net income. For instance, Ace Aviation, the parent company of Air Canada, reported a consolidated statement of change in comprehensive income in its 2007 annual report, shown in Exhibit 5-11 below.

Exhibit 5-11 Ace Aviation Consolidated Statement of Comprehensive Income

ACE AVIATION CONSOLIDATED STATEMENT OF COMPREHENSIVE INCOME

For the year ended December 31
(Canadian dollars in millions)

Comprehensive income	
Net income for the year	$1,398
Other comprehensive income, net of taxes	
Net change in unrealized loss on US Airways securities	(13)
Reclassification of realized gains on US Airways securities to income	(6)
Net change in unrealized gains on fuel derivatives under hedge accounting (net of taxes of $29)	88
Reclassification of net realized (gains) losses on fuel derivatives to income (net of tax of $1)	(6)
Unrealized loss on translation of self-sustaining operation (net of nil tax)	(9)
Proportional reclassification of adjustment from foreign currency translation to income related to the disposal of ACTS (net of nil tax)	7
	61
Total comprehensive income	$1,459

Courtesy of ACE Aviation. ACE Aviation Annual Report 2007.

In 2007, Ace Aviation's total comprehensive income is $1,459 million. Its net income is $1,398 million and other comprehensive income $61 million. The other comprehensive income includes certain unrealized gains or losses related to U.S. Airways securities, fuel derivatives used for hedging, cost changes, and translation of foreign operations and currencies.

▎ PRO FORMA EARNINGS

In the preceding discussion of the multiple-step income statement, we saw that there can be considerable variation in the nature and frequency of the various items reported on it. In their communications with shareholders, creditors, and other interested parties, companies often use alternative earnings measures that are not calculated according to GAAP. To differentiate net earnings reported on the income statement from net earnings arrived at through alternative measures, the former are often called GAAP earnings and the latter **pro forma earnings**, non-GAAP earnings, or Street (as in Wall Street or Bay Street) earnings.

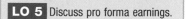

LO 5 Discuss pro forma earnings.

Why do companies use pro forma earnings? Sometimes it is because they perceive for legitimate reasons that GAAP earnings may not be the best measure for such purposes as forecasting future earnings or evaluating operating performance. In fact, various alternative earnings measures have been widely used by analysts as well as management. Popular non-GAAP earnings measures are earnings before interest and taxes (EBIT) and earnings before interest, taxes, depreciation, and amortization (EBITDA). The advantage of EBIT and EBITDA is that they remove terms such as interest and taxes from the profit benchmark, thus making comparisons across companies more transparent. For instances in its MD&A, Rogers Communications Inc. included revenue, operating profit (EBITDA) and adjusting operating profit, and net income to highlight its operating results. (See Exhibit 5-12).

Pro forma earnings Alternative earning measures that are not calculated according to GAAP.

(In millions of dollars)	2007	2006
Revenue	$10,123	$8,838
Operating profit (EBITDA)	3,099	2,878
Adjusted operating profit	3,703	2,942
Net income	637	622

Exhibit 5-12

Operating Results (Excerpt from Rogers' MD&A)

Courtesy of Rogers Communication. Connecting Matters. Rogers Communications Inc. 2007 Annual Report.

In the MD&A section of its 2007 annual report, Rogers provides the following explanation for its choice of pro forma earnings:

> We define operating profit as net income before depreciation and amortization, interest expense, income taxes and non-operating items, which include foreign exchange gains (losses), loss on repayment of long-term debt, change in fair value of derivative instruments, and other income. Operating profit is a standard measure used in the communications industry to assist in understanding and comparing operating results and is often referred to by our peers and competitors as EBITDA (earnings before interest, taxes, depreciation and amortization) or OIBDA (operating income before depreciation and amortization). We believe this is an important measure as it allows us to assess our ongoing businesses without the impact of depreciation or amortization expenses as well as non-operating factors. It is intended to indicate our ability to incur or service debt, invest in PP&E and allows us to compare our Company to our peers and competitors who may have different capital or organizational structures. This measure is not a defined term under Canadian GAAP or U.S. GAAP.

Because there is a lack of standardization in the calculation of pro forma earnings and because such earnings are usually not audited, users should be cautious when using pro forma earnings for investment and other decisions. Companies have been known to choose those pro forma earnings that are relatively more positive than GAAP earnings in order to divert investors' attention from their relatively poor GAAP earnings.

HOW SALES AFFECT THE CASH FLOW STATEMENT

LO 6 Explain the effects of sales on the statement of cash flows.

The appropriate reporting on a statement of cash flows for sales transactions depends on whether the direct or indirect method is used. If the direct method is used to prepare the Operating Activities category of the statement, the amount of cash collected from customers is shown as positive cash flow in this section of the statement.

If the indirect method is used, it is necessary to make adjustments to net income for the changes in accounts receivable, as shown in Exhibit 5-13. An increase in accounts receivable is deducted because it indicates that the company is tying up its cash in these accounts. A decrease in accounts receivable is added to net income because the company actually reduced the amount owed by customers and collected cash.

Exhibit 5-13

Sales and the Statement of Cash Flows

Item	Cash Flow Statement
	Operating Activities
	Net income **XXX**
Increase in accounts receivable ·········	➤ −
Decrease in accounts receivable ·········	➤ +
	Investing Activities
	Financing Activities

Answers to the Two-Minute Reviews

Two-Minute Review on page 209

1. The percentage-of-completion method, the production method, and the installment method are all alternatives to recognizing revenue at the point of sale. Also, franchisors normally recognize revenue when they have made substantial performance of their obligations.

2. For certain costs, such as cost of goods sold, it is possible to directly match the expense with revenue generated. For other costs, such as depreciation, an indirect form of matching is necessary in which expenses are allocated to the periods benefited, rather than matched with specific revenues. Finally, the benefits associated with the incurrence of certain costs, such as utilities, expire immediately and therefore expense is recognized as soon as the cost is incurred.

Two-Minute Review on page 214

Apr. 13	Accounts Receivable	1,000	
	Sales Revenue		1,000
	To record sale on credit		

Assets	=	Liabilities	+	Shareholders' Equity
+1,000				+1,000

Apr. 19	Sales Returns and Allowances	150	
	Accounts Receivable		150
	To record return of defective merchandise for a		
	credit on account		

	Assets	**=**	**Liabilities**	**+**	**Shareholders' Equity**
	−150				−150

Apr. 23	Cash	833	
	Sales Discounts	17	
	Accounts Receivable		850
	To record collection on account		

	Assets	**=**	**Liabilities**	**+**	**Shareholders' Equity**
	+833				−17
	−850				

Two-Minute Review on Page 218

1. Gross profit, income from operations, and income before income taxes are examples of the items that would only appear on a multiple-step income statement.

2. Advertising—selling expense;
   Depreciation on office building—general and administrative expense;
   Salespersons' commissions—selling expense; and
   Office salaries—general and administrative expense.

Appendix: Sales Taxes

The sales transactions illustrated in this textbook have been simplified. In the real world, sales taxes are often imposed by various governments when goods and services are sold and purchased in Canada. The specific forms and rates of sales tax vary from province to province; some provinces have both a provincial sales tax (PST) and the federal goods and services tax (GST); others combine PST and GST into one harmonized sales tax (HST). The accounting for businesses to record the sales tax in its various forms is similar. We use a 13% HST in this section to illustrate how sales and purchases are recorded when sales taxes are taken into account.

> **LO 7** Record sales and purchases with sales tax.

Consider the following example: A customer purchases a pair of hockey skates at one of the stores of Sports Goods Inc., paying cash. The selling price of the skates is $100. Assume that the store is in a province that has a 13% HST. The customer will have to pay $100 + ($100 × 13%), or $113. Of the $113 that Sports Goods collects, $100 is the sales revenue and $13 is the HST to be remitted to the government later on. This $13 is thus a liability. The journal entry to record the transaction is as follows:

Cash	113	
Sales Revenue		100
HST Payable		13
To record sale of a pair of skates for $100.00 and 13% HST		
collected on the sale		

	Assets	**=**	**Liabilities**	**+**	**Shareholders' Equity**
	+113		+13		+100

Businesses must pay HST on their own purchases and expenses. The HST a business pays can be deducted from the HST it collects to determine the balance to be remitted.[9]

---

[9]Similarly, in provinces where both PST and GST are used, businesses can deduct GST paid from GST collected. However, PST paid may not be deducted from PST collected in determining PST due. GST and HST are largely end-consumer taxes; by contrast PST is imposed on both businesses and end consumers.

For instance, if Sports Goods Inc. paid $100.00 plus 13% HST to purchase the skates it sold, the journal entry to record the purchase would have been as follows:

Inventory	60.00	
HST Payable	7.80	
Cash		67.80

To record purchase of a pair of skates for $60.00 and 13% HST paid on the purchase

$$\text{Assets} = \text{Liabilities} + \text{Shareholders' Equity}$$
$$-67.80 \qquad -7.80$$
$$+60.00$$

The balance of the HST Payable account after the two previous transactions follows:

HST PAYABLE

HST paid	7.80	13.00	HST collected
		5.20	Bal.

The HST that needs to be remitted is the $5.20 balance. The journal entry to record the remission is as follows:

HST Payable	5.20	
Cash		5.20

To record remission of $6 excess of HST collected and HST paid

$$\text{Assets} = \text{Liabilities} + \text{Shareholders' Equity}$$
$$-5.20 \qquad -5.20$$

For simplicity, the sales tax is ignored in the other parts of this textbook.

Chapter Highlights

1. **LO 1 Apply the revenue recognition principle (p. 204)**

   - According to the revenue recognition principle, revenues are recognized when they are earned. On a practical basis, revenue is normally recognized at the time a product or service is delivered to the customer. Certain types of sales arrangements may require different methods, such as the following:

     o Percentage-of-completion method

     o Production method

     o Installment method

2. **LO 2 Apply the matching principle to recognize expenses (p. 207)**

   - The matching principal attempts to associate with the revenue of the period all costs necessary to generate revenue.

     o A direct form of matching is possible for certain types of costs, such as cost of goods sold and sales commissions.

     o Costs such as depreciation are recognized as expense on an indirect basis.

3. **LO 3 Describe the basic format and the contents of the income statement (p. 209)**

   - The multiple-step income statement provides the reader with classifications of revenues and expenses as well as with important subtotals.

     o Net sales revenue is the total sales minus sales returns and allowance and sales returns.

   o Cost of goods sold is subtracted from the sales revenue, with the result reported as gross profit.

   o Expenses arising from operating activities are subtracted from gross profit to arrive at income from operations.

   o Revenues and expense arising from investing and financing activities are classified as other revenue or gains and other expenses or losses.

4. **LO 4 Explain additional items on the income statement (p. 218)**

   - Certain items must be reported separately, net of tax, at the bottom of the income statement. These include the following:

     o Discontinued operations

     o Extraordinary gains and losses

   - Items that have some but not all the characteristics of an extraordinary item are called Unusual or Infrequent Items.

5. **LO 5 Discuss pro forma earnings (p. 221)**

   - Instead of net income as defined by GAAP, companies sometimes use alternative earnings measures, referred to as non-GAAP earnings or pro forma earnings. These often show more positive figures than GAAP earnings. Readers should exercise caution when using non-GAAP earnings figures to make their decisions.

6. **LO 6** **Explain the effect of sales on the statement of cash flows (p. 222)**

- The cash collected from customers represents a cash inflow from operating activities on the statement of cash flows. If a company uses the indirect method, however, an adjustment is made to net income for the change in Accounts Receivable account.

7. **LO 7** **Record sales and purchases with sales tax (Appendix) (p. 223)**

- Most sales and purchases are subject to sales tax. Such taxes vary in both rate and form from province to province in Canada.

Ratio Review

$$\text{Gross Profit Margin} = \frac{\text{Gross Profit}}{\text{Net Sales}}$$

$$\text{Profit Margin} = \frac{\text{Net Income}}{\text{Net Sales}}$$

Accounts Highlighted

Account Titles	Where it Appears	In What Section	Page Number
Sales revenue	Income Statement	Revenue	211
Sales returns and allowances	Income Statement	Revenue (contra)	211
Sales discount	Income Statement	Revenue (contra)	213
HST payable	Balance Sheet	Liability	228

Key Terms Quiz

Read each of the following definitions and then write the number of that definition in the blank beside the appropriate term it defines. The quiz solutions appear at the end of the chapter.

_____ Revenue recognition principle
_____ Percentage-of-completion method
_____ Production method
_____ Installment method
_____ Matching principle
_____ Multiple-step income statement
_____ Gross profit
_____ Net sales
_____ Sales returns and allowances

_____ Trade discount
_____ Quantity discount
_____ Sales discounts
_____ Cost of goods available for sale
_____ Cost of goods sold
_____ Operating income
_____ Unusual or infrequent items
_____ Discontinued operations
_____ Extraordinary item
_____ Pro forma earnings

1. Revenues are recognized in the income statement when they are earned.

2. The association of revenue of a period with all of the costs necessary to generate that revenue.

3. Income statement with classifications of revenues and expenses as well as with important subtotals.

4. Items that are unusual, infrequent, and independent of management decisions.

5. Alternative earnings measures that differ from the earnings defined by GAAP.

6. Items that have some but not all of the characteristics of extraordinary items.

7. A line item on the income statement to reflect any gains or losses from the disposal of a segment of the business as well as any net income or loss from operating that segment.

8. Gross profit less total operating expenses.

9. The difference between net sales and cost of goods sold.

10. The method in which revenue is recognized at the time cash is collected; used for various types of consumer items, such as automobiles and appliances.

11. A reduction in selling price for buying a large number of units of a product.

12. The contra-revenue account used to record both refunds to customers and reductions of their accounts.

(continued)

13. A selling price reduction offered to a special class of customers.

14. The contra-revenue account used to record discounts given customers for early payment of their accounts.

15. Beginning inventory plus cost of goods purchased.

16. Sales revenue less sales returns and allowances and sales discounts.

17. Cost of goods available for sale minus ending inventory.

18. The method in which revenue is recognized when a commodity is produced rather than when it is sold.

19. The method used by contractors to recognize revenue before the completion of a long-term contract.

Answers on p. 241.

Alternate Terms

Cost of goods sold Cost of sales

Gross profit Gross margin

Gross profit margin Gross profit percentage

Non-GAAP earnings Pro forma earnings

Operating income Income from operations

Sales revenue Sales

Warmup Exercises and Solutions

Warmup Exercise 5-1 *Cost and Expense* **LO 2**

Explain whether each of the following costs results in an asset and, if it does, when the cost expires and becomes an expense:

1. Purchase of cleaning supplies

2. Subscription to a two-year insurance policy

3. Receipt of a telephone bill

Key to the Solution Determine whether there will be future benefit and when the future benefit expires.

Warmup Exercise 5-2 *Net Sales* **LO 3**

Victor Merchandising reported sales revenue, sales returns and allowances, and sales discounts of $57,000, $1,500, and $900, respectively, in 2008.

Required

Prepare the net sales section of Victor's 2008 income statement.

Key to the Solution Refer to Exhibit 5-3.

Warmup Exercise 5-3 *Income Statement Format* **LO 3**

Explain whether each of the following expenses is an operating expense or other expense (loss):

1. Depreciation on office equipment

2. Fire insurance premium on the company headquarters

3. Interest expense

4. Loss on sales of used equipment

5. Sales commission

Key to the Solution Determine whether expenses are related to operating, investing, or financing activities.

Solutions to Warmup Exercises

Warmup Exercise 5-1

1. Asset: supplies inventory. Expense as supplies are used.

2. Asset: prepaid insurance. Expense as time elapses.

3. Not an asset. Service already used. No future benefit.

Warmup Exercise 5-2

VICTOR MERCHANDISING
PARTIAL INCOME STATEMENT
FOR THE YEAR ENDED DECEMBER 31, 2008

Sales revenue	$57,000	
Less: Sales returns and allowances	1,500	
Sales discounts	900	
Net sales		$54,600

Warmup Exercise 5-3

1. Operating expense: general and administrative

2. Operating expense: general and administrative

3. Other expense: related financing activities

4. Other expenses: related investing activities, that is, sales of used equipment

5. Operating expense: selling

Review Problem and Solutions

The following were taken from the adjusted trial balance of Marine Equipment Inc. for the year ended December 31, 2008. The accounts are arranged in alphabetical order. Prepare a multiple-step income statement for the year, following the format described in the chapter. All amounts are in thousands of dollars.

Accounts Receivable	$36,800
Accumulated Depreciation	48,000
Advertising Expense	720
Capital Stock	50,000
Cash	78,200
Cost of Goods Sold	96,000
Depreciation and Amortization Expense	9,200
Income Tax Expense	12,000
Insurance Expense	4,000
Interest Expense	1,200
Inventory	32,000
Loss from Discontinued Operations, net of taxes	860
Loss from Sales of Equipment	870
Net Sales	160,000
Notes Payable	100,000
Patent	12,000
Property, Plant, and Equipment	80,000
Retained Earnings	22,150
Salaries and Wages Expense	12,300
Sales Commissions Expense	1,500
Write-Off on Equipment	2,500

Solution to Review Problem

MARINE EQUIPMENT INC.
INCOME STATEMENT (MULTIPLE-STEP FORMAT)
FOR THE YEAR ENDED DECEMBER 31, 2008

Net sales		$160,000	
Cost of goods sold		96,000	
Gross profit			$64,000
Operating expenses			
Selling expenses			
Sales commissions expense	1,500		
Advertising expense	720		
Total selling expense		2,220	

(continued)

General and administrative expenses			
Salaries and wages expense	12,300		
Insurance expense	4,000		
Depreciation and amortization expense	9,200		
Write-off on equipment	2,500		
Total general and administrative expenses		28,000	
Total operating expenses			30,220
Operating income			33,780
Other expenses and losses			
Interest expense		1,200	
Loss from sales of equipment		870	
Total other expenses and losses			2,070
Income before income taxes			31,710
Income tax expenses			12,000
Income from continuing operations			19,710
Loss from discontinued operations, net of taxes			860
Net income			$18,850

Questions

1. What is the justification for recognizing revenue on a long-term contract by the percentage-of-completion method?

2. What is the justification for recognizing revenue in certain industries at the time the product is *produced* rather than when it is *sold*?

3. A friend says to you: "I just don't get it. Assets cost money. Expenses reduce income. There must be some relationship among *assets*, *costs*, and *expenses*—I'm just not sure what it is!" What is the relationship? Can you give an example of it?

4. When a company gives a cash refund on returned merchandise, why doesn't it just reduce Sales revenue instead of using a contra-revenue account?

5. Why are trade discounts and quantity discounts not accorded accounting recognition? (The sale is simply recorded net of either of these types of discounts.)

6. What do credit terms of *3/20, n/60* mean? How valuable to the customer is the discount offered in these terms?

7. What is the major advantage of the multiple-step income statement over the single-step income statement?

8. Why might a company's gross profit ratio increase from one year to the next even while its profit margin ratio decreases?

9. Why are operating expenses separated from other revenues and expenses in the multiple-step income statement?

10. Why are some salary and wage expenses selling expenses even though other depreciation expenses are general and administrative expenses?

11. Why are discontinued operations and extraordinary items reported separately on the income statement?

12. How are extraordinary items and unusual or infrequent items reported differently on the income statement?

13. Why should investors be careful when using pro forma earnings in making their decisions?

14. How does a company record the sales tax it collects? (Appendix)

Exercises

Exercise 5-1 *Revenue Recognition* **LO 1**

The highway department contracted with a private company to collect tolls and maintain facilities on a highway. Users of the highway can pay cash as they approach the toll booth, or they can purchase a pass. The pass is equipped with an electronic sensor that subtracts the toll fee from the pass balance as the motorist slowly approaches a special toll booth. The passes are issued in $10 increments. Refunds are available to motorists who do not use the pass balance, but these are issued very infrequently. Last year $3,000,000 was collected at the traditional toll booths, $2,000,000 of passes were issued, and $1,700,000 of passes were used at the special toll booth. How much should the company recognize as revenue for the year? Explain how the revenue recognition principle should be applied in this case.

Exercise 5-2 *The Matching Principle* **LO 2**

This chapter has described two different kinds of costs: costs that result in assets first and become expenses when they expire, and costs that expire and become expenses immediately. Also, costs can be matched either directly or indirectly. For each of the following costs, indicate whether it results in an asset first, and whether it will be matched with revenue directly or indirectly.

1. New office copier
2. Monthly bill from the utility company for electricity

3. Office supplies

4. Biweekly payroll for office employees

5. Commissions earned by salespeople

6. Interest incurred on a six-month loan from the bank

7. Cost of inventory sold during the current period

8. Taxes owed on income earned during the current period

9. Cost of three-year insurance policy

Exercise 5-3 *Selling Expenses and General and Administrative Expenses* **LO 3**

Operating expenses are subdivided between selling expenses and general and administrative expenses when a multiple-step income statement is prepared. From the following list, identify each item as a selling expense (S) or general and administrative expense (G&A):

_____ 1. Advertising expense

_____ 2. Depreciation expense—store furniture and fixtures

_____ 3. Office rent expense

_____ 4. Office salaries expense

_____ 5. Store rent expense

_____ 6. Store salaries expense

_____ 7. Insurance expense

_____ 8. Supplies expense

_____ 9. Utilities expense

Exercise 5-4 *Missing Income Statement Amounts* **LO 3**

For each of the following independent cases, fill in the blank with the appropriate dollar amount:

	Tony's Gift Shop	Noah's Pet Shop	Sam's Flower Shop
Net sales	$35,000	$_____	$78,000
Cost of goods sold	_____	45,000	_____
Gross profit	7,000	18,000	_____
Selling expenses	3,000	_____	9,000
General and administrative expenses	1,500	2,800	_____
Total operating expenses	_____	8,800	13,600
Net income	$ 2,500	$ 9,200	$25,400

Exercise 5-5 *Income Statement Ratios* **LO 3**

The 2008 income statement of Holly's Enterprises shows net income of $45,000, comprising net sales of $134,800, cost of goods sold of $53,920, selling expenses of $18,310, general and administrative expenses of $16,990, and interest expense of $580.

Required

Compute Holly's (1) gross profit margin and (2) profit margin. What other information would you need to be able to comment on whether these ratios are favourable?

Exercise 5-6 *Journal Entries to Record Sales* **LO 3**

Prepare the journal entries to record the following transactions on the books of Amber Corp. for March 3, 2008:

a. Sold merchandise on credit for $500 with terms of 2/10, net 30. Amber records all sales at the gross amount.

b. Recorded cash sales for the day of $1,250 from the cash register tape.

c. Granted a cash refund of $135 to a customer for spoiled merchandise returned.

d. Granted a customer a credit of $190 on its outstanding bill and allowed the customer to keep a defective product.

e. Debited cash of $2,940, received through the mail, to customers' accounts. All amounts received qualify for the discount for early payment.

Exercise 5-7 *Credit Terms* LO 3

Song Company sold merchandise on credit for $2,000 on September 10, 2008, to Letson Inc. For each of the following terms, indicate the last day Letson could take the discount, the amount Letson would pay if it took the discount, and the date full payment is due.

a. 2/10, n/30

b. 3/15, n/45

c. 1/7, n/21

d. 5/15, n/30

Exercise 5-8 *Journal Entries for Sales Discounts* LO 3

Prepare the journal entries on the books of Ford Inc. for the following transactions, using the gross method to record sales discounts (all sales on credit are made with terms of 2/10, net 30).

June 2:   Sold merchandise on credit to Woodchuck Inc. for $1,500.

June 4:   Sold merchandise on credit to Hawkeye Inc. for $2,400.

June 13:   Collected cash from Hawkeye Inc.

June 30:   Collected cash from Woodchuck Inc.

Exercise 5-9 *Sales Tax* LO 7 (Appendix)

Blue Inc. operates in a province that has a 13% HST. The current month sales of Blue Inc. totaled $125,600. The merchandise purchased during the month totaled $82,500. Other expenses that were subjected to HST totaled $12,000.

Required

1. Prepare journal entries to record the sales, the purchases, and the expenses of the current month along with the applicable HST. Assume that all transactions are cash transactions.

2. What is the amount of HST payable as the result of the current month's operation?

Multi-Concept Exercise

Exercise 5-10 *Income Statement* LO 3, 4, 5

Maple Inc. has the following account balances as of December 31, 2008:

Cost of goods sold	$45,000
General and administrative expenses	3,150
Income tax expense	90
Interest expense	500
Loss from discontinued operations, net of taxes	1,860
Net sales	60,000
Selling expense	8,050
Write-off on equipment	3,100

Required

1. Prepare a multiple-step income statement for Maple Inc. for 2008.

2. Maple's manager is not too concerned about its poor performance in 2008. The manager argues that 2008 is not a typical year because of some unforeseen incidents. To convince the investors that Maple Inc. is in good shape, he or she wants the earnings to be calculated with the items that are unlikely to reoccur in the future removed. What amount of earnings should there be if the items that are unlikely to reoccur in the future are removed?

3. Why should investors be careful about non-GAAP earnings?

Problems

Problem 5-1 *The Revenue Recognition Principle* LO 1

Each of the following paragraphs describes a situation involving revenue recognition.

a. Exit Realty receives a 6% commission for every house it sells. It lists a house for a client on April 3 at a selling price of $450,000. ABC receives an offer from a buyer on April 28 to purchase the house at the asking price. The realtor's client accepts the offer on May 1. Exit Realty will receive its 6% commission at a closing scheduled for May 16.

b. Burger Club is a fast-food franchisor on the West Coast. It charges all franchisees $10,000 to open an outlet in a designated city. In return for this fee, the franchisee receives the exclusive right to operate in the area, as well as assistance from Burger Club in selecting a site. On January 5, Burger Club signs an agreement with a franchisee and receives a down payment of $4,000, with the balance of $6,000 due in three months. On March 13, Burger Club meets with the new franchisee, and the two parties agree on a suitable site for the business. On April 5, the franchisee pays Burger Club the remaining $6,000.

c. Refer to part **b**. In addition to the initial fee, Burger Club charges a continuing fee equal to 2% of the franchisee's sales each month. Each month's fee is payable by the 10th of the following month. The franchisee opens for business on June 1. On July 3, Burger Club receives a report from the franchisee indicating its sales for the month of June amount to $60,000. On July 8, Burger Club receives its 2% fee for June sales.

d. Goldstar Corp. mines and sells gold on the open market. During August, the company mines 5,000 ounces of gold. The market price throughout August is $300 per ounce. The 5,000 ounces are eventually sold on the open market on September 5 for $310 per ounce.

e. Whatadeal Inc. sells used cars. Because of the uncertainties involved in collecting from customers, Whatadeal uses the installment basis of accounting. On December 2, Whatadeal sells a car for $8,000 with a 25% down payment and six equal annual payments starting June 2, 2009. The company's accounting year ends on December 31. Whatadeal receives the first installment on June 2, 2009.

Required

For each situation, indicate when revenue should be recognized, as well as the dollar amount. Give a brief explanation for each answer.

Problem 5-2 *Costs, Assets, and Expenses* LO 2

The following costs are incurred by a restaurant:

1. New dining room furniture
2. Newspaper advertising
3. Utilities for the kitchen and the dining room
4. Wages of the waitstaff
5. Beverages to be sold to customers
6. Premiums for a two-year insurance policy
7. Manager's salary
8. Containers for takeout orders
9. New computer software for inventory management
10. Cleaning supplies

Required

1. For each of these costs, indicate whether its incurrence results in (a) an asset that will have future benefit or (b) no asset (i.e., it expires immediately).
2. Indicate whether each of these costs can be matched directly with the revenue when it expires or indirectly with a particular period when it expires.

Problem 5-3 *Multiple-Step Income Statement* LO 3

The following income statement items, arranged in alphabetical order, are taken from the records of Oxford Inc. for the year ended December 31, 2008:

Advertising expense	$ 1,500
Commissions expense	2,415
Cost of goods sold	29,200
Depreciation expense—office building	2,900
Income tax expense	1,540
Insurance expense—salesperson's auto	2,250
Interest expense	1,400
Interest revenue	1,340
Rent revenue	6,700
Salaries and wages expense—office	12,560
Sales revenue	48,300
Supplies expense—office	890

(continued)

Required

1. Prepare a multiple-step income statement for the year ended December 31, 2008.
2. Compute Oxford's gross profit margin.
3. What does this ratio tell you about Oxford's markup on its products?

Problem 5-4 *Gross Profit Margin and Profit Margin* LO 3

Corner Store is a convenience store chain. The following items appeared in the company's 2008 annual report (all amounts are in millions):

	2008	2007	2006
Sales	$3,600	$3,500	$3,800
Cost of goods sold	2,550	2,500	2,500
Net income	320	330	340

Required

1. Compute Corner Store's gross profit margin and profit margin for each of the three years.
2. Comment on the *change* in the gross profit margin and profit margin over the three-year period. What possible explanations are there for the change?

Problem 5-5 *Trade Discounts* LO 3

Essex Inc. offers the following discounts to customers who purchase large quantities:

> 10% discount: 10–25 units
> 20% discount: >25 units

Mr. Essex, the president, would like to record all sales at the list price and record the discount as an expense.

Required

1. Explain to Mr. Essex why trade discounts do not enter into the accounting records.
2. Even though trade discounts do not enter into the accounting records, is it still important to have some record of these? Explain your answer.

Problem 5-6 *Recording Sales, Sales Discounts, Sales Returns and Allowances* LO 3

The following transactions were entered into by Coast Tires Inc. during the month of June:

June 2: Sold 100 tires to Speedy at $100 per item. Terms are 2/10, net 30.

June 4: Sold 700 tires to Roadrunner garage chain at $90 per item. Terms are 2/10, net 30.

June 8: Due to defects, Roadrunner returned 12 of the tires purchased. Coast Tires issued a credit memo, indicating that the amount due had been reduced.

June 14: Roadrunner paid for the balance of the tires purchased on June 4.

June 16: Coast Tires agreed to reduce the selling price of the tires sold to Speedy by $3 per item due to late delivery. A credit memo was issued, indicating that the amount due had been reduced.

June 30: Speedy paid the balance on its June 2 purchase.

Required

1. Prepare all journal entries required to record these transactions for Coast Tires. Coast Tires uses the gross method of recording sales discounts.
2. Calculate the net sales to be included on Coast Tires' income statement for the month.

Problem 5-7 *Comparability and Consistency in Income Statements* LO 3

The following income statements were provided by Gleeson Company, a retailer:

2008 Income Statement		2007 Income Statement	
Sales	$1,700,000	Sales	$1,500,000
Cost of sales	520,000	Cost of sales	435,000
Gross profit	1,180,000	Sales salaries	398,000
Selling expense	702,000	Advertising	175,000
Administrative expense	95,000	Office supplies	54,000

Total selling and administrative expense	797,000	Depreciation—building	40,000
		Delivery expense	35,000
		Total expenses	1,137,000
Net income	$ 383,000	Net income	$ 363,000

Required

1. Identify each income statement as either single-step or multiple-step format.

2. Convert the 2007 income statement to the same format as the 2008 income statement.

3. Compute gross profit margin and profit margin for both 2008 and 2007 and comment on how Gleeson's performance has changed from 2007 to 2008.

Problem 5-8 *Financial Statements* LO 3

A list of accounts for Wellington Inc. at December 31, 2008, follows:

Accounts Receivable	$ 2,359
Advertising Expense	4,510
Buildings and Equipment, Net	55,550
Capital Stock	50,000
Cash	590
Depreciation Expense	2,300
Dividends	6,000
Income Tax Expense	3,200
Income Tax Payable	3,200
Inventory:	
January 1, 2008	6,400
December 31, 2008	7,500
Land	20,000
Prepaid Expense	100
Purchases	39,775
Retained Earnings, January 1, 2008	32,550
Salaries Expense	25,600
Salaries Payable	650
Sales	84,364
Sales Returns	780
Utilities Expense	3,600

Required

1. Determine cost of goods sold for 2008.

2. Determine net income for 2008.

3. Prepare a balance sheet dated December 31, 2008.

Problem 5-9 *Unusual or Infrequent Items on the Income Statement* LO 4, 5

The following information is summarized from the consolidated statements of operations of Banock Corp. for 2006 through 2008:

In millions of dollars	2008	2007	2006
Sales	$3,244	$2,799	$2,224
Less: Freight	239	235	215
Transportation and distribution	104	99	81
Cost of goods sold	2,220	2,085	1,621
Gross margin	681	380	307
Selling and administrative	131	96	92
Provincial mining and other taxes	93	57	68
Restructuring charges	4	264	–
Foreign exchange loss	20	52	6
Other income	(79)	(33)	(25)
Operating expenses	169	436	141
Operating income (loss)	512	(56)	167

(continued)

Interest expense	82	91	83
Income before income taxes	430	(147)	84
Income taxes	(132)	91	(30)
Net income (loss)	$ 298	$ (56)	$ 54

Required

1. Comment on the change in Banock Corp. net income (loss) over the three-year period.

2. Can you identify an item in Banock Corp. statements of earnings that is unusual or infrequent in nature?

3. Compute non-GAAP earnings for Banock Corp. by excluding any unusual or infrequent items you identified in requirement 2. Comment on the change in Banock's non-GAAP earnings over the three-year period. (The income tax rate can be estimated by dividing income taxes by earnings before income taxes.)

Problem 5-10 *Multiple-step Income Statement and Unusual or Infrequent Items on the Income Statement, Pro Forma Earnings* **LO 3, 4, 5**

Camco Inc., a medium-sized steel manufacturer, reported the income statements for the recent three years below. The chair of the board is concerned by the shrinking net income: "After implementing our plan for restructuring and refocusing, why hasn't our performance improved? It has worsened!"

	2008	2007	2006
Revenues:			
Sales	$ 72,650	$ 68,540	$ 64,520
Dividend income from investment	870	820	920
	73,520	69,360	65,440
Expenses:			
Cost of sales	34,200	32,530	36,050
Selling and administrative expense	13,250	14,250	12,630
Depreciation and amortization	9,500	9,400	4,250
Interest expense	4,300	5,200	6,500
Loss on refinancing a loan	1,600	—	—
Restructuring charges	8,000		—
Income tax expense	801	2,394	1,803
	71,651	63,774	61,233
Income from continuing operations	1,869	5,586	4,207
Earnings (loss) from discontinued operations	—	(1,000)	5,600
Net income	$ 1,869	$ 4,586	$ 9,807

Required:

1. Prepare multiple-step income statements for three years for Camco Inc.

2. Compute the gross profit margin for the three years and discuss how it has changed.

3. Compute adjusted earnings from continuing operations by excluding the restructuring charges (use an estimated effective tax rate to determine the tax effect of the item).

4. Compute adjusted profit margin, replacing net income with the adjusted earnings from continuing operations.

5. Do you agree with the chair about worsening performance?

Alternate Problems

Problem 5-1A *The Revenue Recognition Principle* **LO 1**

Each of the following paragraphs describes a situation involving revenue recognition.

a. Deangelo Inc. paints and decorates office buildings. On September 30, 2008, it received $5,750 for work to be completed over the next six months.

b. Caribbean Sun is a tanning salon franchisor in the Maritimes. It charges all franchisees a fee of $2,500 to open a salon and an ongoing fee equal to 5% of all revenue during the first five years. The $2,500 is for training and accounting systems to be used in each salon.

During January 2008, Caribbean Sun signed an agreement with five individuals to open salons over the next three months.

c. On June 1, 2008, Bridge Construction Inc. entered into a contract with the municipality to renovate an old covered bridge. The municipality gave Bridge an advance of $500,000 and agreed to pay Bridge $75,000 each month for 20 months, at which time the project should be completed.

d. Frank Cropper, a wheat grower, harvested the current year's crop and delivered it to the elevator for storage on October 1, 2008, until it is sold to one of several foreign countries. The expected sales value of the wheat is $450,000.

e. Corner Shop, a convenience store chain, constructed a strip shopping centre next to one of its stores. The spaces are being sold to individuals who will open auto parts and repair facilities. One person is planning to open a brake-repair shop, another will set up a transmission-repair shop, a third will do 10-minute oil changes, and so on. The store spaces sell for $25,000 each. There are six spaces, four of which are sold in May of 2008.

Required

For each of the preceding situations, indicate when in 2008 revenue should be recognized, as well as the dollar amount. Give a brief explanation for each answer.

Problem 5-2A *Costs, Assets, and Expenses* LO 2

The following costs are incurred by a drugstore:

1. Fees paid to courier
2. New cash register
3. Newspaper advertising
4. Utilities for the store
5. Salaries for the pharmacists
6. Bottles for dispensing medicine
7. New lighting system
8. Merchandise to be resold to customers
9. Premium of a two-year fire insurance policy
10. New paving for the parking lot

Required

1. For each of these costs, indicate whether its incurrence results in (a) an asset that will have future benefits, or (b) no asset (i.e., it expires immediately).

2. Indicate whether each of these costs will be matched directly with the revenue when it expires or indirectly with a particular period when it expires.

Problem 5-3A *Multiple-Step Income Statement* LO 3

The following income statement items, arranged in alphabetical order, are taken from the records of Lighthouse Inc., a software sales firm, for the year ended December 31, 2008:

Advertising expense	$ 18,000
Cost of goods sold	300,000
Depreciation expense—computer	9,000
Dividend revenue	5,400
Income tax expense	61,400
Interest expense	3,800
Rent expense—office	52,800
Rent expense—salesperson's car	36,000
Sales revenue	700,000
Supplies expense—office	2,600
Utilities expense	13,500
Wages expense—office	91,200

Required

1. Prepare a multiple-step income statement for the year ended December 31, 2008.
2. Compute Lighthouse's gross profit margin.
3. What does this ratio tell you about Lighthouse's markup on its products?

Problem 5-4A *Gross Profit Margin and Profit Margin* **LO 3**

Growing Concept is a furniture manufacturer that specializes in children's furniture that can be adapted to the different stages of a child's life. The following items appeared in the company's 2008 annual report (all amounts are in millions):

	2008	2007	2006
Sales	$460	$405	$346
Cost of goods sold	226	203	159
Net income	132	127	123

Required

1. Compute Growing Concept's gross profit margin and profit margin for each of the three years.

2. Comment on the *change* in the gross profit margin and profit margin over the three-year period. What possible explanations are there for the change?

Problem 5-5A *Discounts* **LO 3**

Whitefish Inc., a recording distributor, would like to offer discounts to customers who purchase large quantities. Whitefish is unsure about the terms to use and how to account for discounts extended to customers. The company also wants to consider a cash discount for early payment by customers. Whitefish expects sales of about $3 million this year. All sales are on account to about 100 different outlets located within 500 kilometres of the warehouse. Deliveries are made by Whitefish's own trucks and cost about $25 per 100 kilometres driven. A full truck will hold 1,000 units.

Required

1. Explain the difference between a quantity discount and a discount for early payment. How is each accounted for in the accounting records? What are the reasons to extend the different discounts to customers?

2. Set up a quantity discount plan and a sales discount plan for Whitefish to extend to customers. Be able to explain why you chose your bases for the discounts and the amount of discounts.

Problem 5-6A *Recording Sales, Sales Discounts, Sales Returns, and Allowances* **LO 3**

The following transactions were entered into by South Shore Shoes Inc. during the month of July:

July 1:   Sold 60 pairs of shoes to Fancy Feet at $50 per pair, the regular wholesale price. Terms are 2/10, net 30.

July 3:   Sold 500 pairs of shoes to Shoe Warehouse chain at 10% below the regular wholesale price. Terms are 1/10, net 30.

July 12:   Due to defects, Fancy Feet returned 5 pairs of the shoes purchased. South Shore Shoes issued a credit memo indicating that the amount due had been reduced.

July 13:   Shoe Warehouse paid for the balance of the shoes purchased on July 3.

July 30:   Fancy Feet paid the balance on its July 1 purchase.

Required

1. Prepare all journal entries required to record these transactions for South Shore Shoes. South Shore uses the gross method of recording sales discounts.

2. Calculate the net sales to be included in South Shore Shoes' income statement of the month.

Problem 5-7A *Comparability and Consistency in Income Statements* **LO 3**

The following income statements were provided by Clayton Inc., a retailer:

2008 Income Statement		2007 Income Statement	
Sales	$85,000	Sales	$84,000
Cost of sales	55,250	Cost of sales	57,120
Gross profit	29,750	Executive salaries	6,000
Selling expense	13,600	Sales commissions	6,300
Administrative expense	8,500	Office expense	4,120
Total selling and		Depreciation—building	3,320
administrative expense	22,100	Delivery expense	2,100
		Total expenses	78,960
Net income	$ 7,650	Net income	$ 5,040

Required

1. Identify each income statement as either single-step or multiple-step format.

2. Convert the 2007 income statement to the same format as the 2008 income statement.

3. Compute gross profit margin and profit margin for both 2008 and 2007 and comment on how Clayton's performance has changed from 2007 to 2008.

Problem 5-8A *Financial Statements* LO 3

A list of accounts for Kempt Inc. at December 31, 2008, follows:

Accounts Receivable	$ 56,359
Advertising Expense	12,900
Capital Stock	50,000
Cash	22,340
Dividends	6,000
Income Tax Expense	1,450
Income Tax Payable	1,450
Inventory	
January 1, 2008	6,400
December 31, 2008	5,900
Purchases	61,983
Retained Earnings, January 1, 2008	28,252
Salaries Payable	650
Sales	112,768
Sales Returns	1,008
Utilities Expense	1,800
Wages and Salaries Expense	23,000
Wages Payable	120

Required

1. Determine cost of goods sold for 2008.

2. Prepare a multiple-step income statement for the year ended December 31, 2008.

Alternative Multiple-Concept Problems

Problem 5-9A *Unusual or Infrequent Items* LO 4, 5

The following income statement is found in the 2005 annual report of **Reitmans** Ltd.   **http://www.reitmans.com**

FOR THE YEARS ENDED JANUARY 29, 2005, AND JANUARY 31, 2004
(IN THOUSANDS EXCEPT PER SHARE AMOUNTS)

	2005	2004
Sales	$ 912,473	$ 851,634
Cost of goods sold and selling, general and administrative expenses	788,876	766,567
	123,597	85,067
Depreciation and amortization	35,083	31,869
Lease cancellation and related costs	–	2,300
Operating earnings before the undernoted	88,514	50,898
Investment income	9,639	9,584
Interest on long-term debt	1,919	4,792
Earnings before income taxes	96,234	55,690
Income taxes	29,327	15,655
Net earnings	$ 66,907	$ 40,035

Required

1. Are there any items in the above statement that you consider unusual or infrequent? Explain.

2. Recalculate the net income for Reitmans by excluding any unusual or infrequent items. (The appropriate income tax rate can be estimated by dividing income taxes by earnings before income taxes).

Problem 5-10A *Multiple-step Income Statement and Unusual or Infrequent Items on the Income Statement, Pro Forma Earnings* **LO 3, 4, 5**

The following income statements of Master Inc. were available.

	2008	2007	2006
Sales revenue	$123,000	$122,000	$120,000
Expenses:			
Cost of goods sold	78,000	66,500	65,400
Executive salaries	15,200	13,900	12,000
Depreciation expense – building	1,200	1,200	1,200
Advertising	8,120	11,100	8,100
Sales commission	3,690	3,660	3,600
Restructuring charges	0	0	4,200
Interest expense	680	720	715
Loss (Gain) from sales of equipment	(5,000)	(73)	15
	101,890	97,007	95,230
Income before tax	21,110	24,993	24,770
Income taxes	8,444	9,997	9,908
Earnings from continuing operations	12,666	14,996	14,862
Income from discontinued operations	3,420	—	—
Net income	$ 16,086	$ 14,996	$ 14,862

Required

1. Convert the income statements to the multiple-step format.

2. Compute the gross profit margin for the three years and discuss how it has changed.

3. Compute adjusted earnings from continuing operations by excluding the restructuring charges and the gain or loss from sale of equipment (use an estimated effective tax rate to determine the tax effect of the item).

4. Compute adjusted profit margin, replacing net income with the adjusted earnings from continuing operations.

5. Discuss how Master's performance has changed over the three-year period.

Cases

Case 5-1 *Comparing Two Companies in the Same Industry: True Gold Corp. and First Mining Ltd.* **LO 3, 4, 5**

Both True Gold and First Mining are in the metal mining industry. The income statements for the two companies for the year ended December 31, 2008 and 2007, are shown below and on the next page.

TRUE GOLD CORPORATION
CONSOLIDATED STATEMENTS OF OPERATIONS
FOR THE YEARS ENDED DECEMBER 31
(IN THOUSANDS OF DOLLARS)

	2008	2007
Gold revenue	$ 92,133	$ 86,817
Expenses		
Operating costs	85,365	69,110
Depreciation and depletion	20,231	17,909
Re-start of operations	6,354	682
Warehouse fire loss	2,321	–
Other	4,528	2,041
	118,799	89,742
Mine operating (loss) earnings	(26,666)	(2,925)

Other expenses (income)

General and administrative	8,901	7,125
Interest and financing costs	7,251	6,662
General exploration	1,593	340
Stock-based compensation	4,980	3,147
Foreign exchange (gains) losses	3,311	(1,747)
Other	(690)	(133)
	25,346	15,394

Loss before taxes and other items	52,012	18,319
Realized derivative gains,	(16,895)	(2,362)
Unrealized derivative losses, net	6,087	7,481
Equity in losses of associated companies	272	94
Investment (gains) losses	(1,706)	45
Write-off of goodwill	27,344	–
Write-down of mineral properties	12,484	720
Loss before income taxes	79,598	24,297
Current income tax (recovery)	(678)	5,025
Future income tax	695	1,255
Loss for the year	$ 79,615	$ 30,576

FIRST MINING LTD.
CONSOLIDATED STATEMENTS OF EARNINGS AND DEFICIT
FOR THE YEARS ENDED DECEMBER 31
(EXPRESSED IN THOUSANDS OF DOLLARS)

	2008	2007
Revenues		
Copper	$ 103,352	$ 49,419
Acid	10,171	11,035
	113,523	60,454
Cost and expenses		
Cost of sales	53,770	41,299
Depletion and amortization	10,873	7,761
Exploration	3,063	620
Foreign exchange loss	260	969
General and administrative	6,171	2,852
Interest and financing fees on long-term debt	3,040	1,759
Other income	(985)	(419)
	76,192	54,841
Earnings before income taxes and equity earnings	37,331	5,613
Income taxes	11,006	1,397
Equity earnings	1,685	366
Net earnings for the year	$ 28,010	$ 4,582

Required

1. For each company, indicate whether the statement is in single-step format or multiple-step format, or a combination of both. Explain.

2. Compute the gross profit margins for First Mining for 2008 and 2007. Comment on the change in the ratio over the two years.

3. Can you compute gross profit margin for True Gold? Why or why not?

4. Compute the profit margin for both True Gold and First Mining. Compare the ratios of the two companies, and comment on the change in the ratio for each company over the two years.

5. Are there any items in each company's income statement that seem unusual or infrequent? Explain.

Accounting and Ethics: What Would You Do?

Case 5-2 *Revenue Recognition and the Matching Principle* LO 1, 2

Listum & Sellum Inc. is a medium-size Quebec real estate company. It was founded five years ago by its two principal shareholders, Willie Listum and Dewey Sellum. Willie is president of the company, and Dewey is vice-president of sales. Listum & Sellum has enjoyed tremendous growth since its inception by aggressively seeking out listings for residential real estate and paying a very generous commission to the selling agent.

The company receives a 6% commission for selling a client's property and gives two-thirds of this, or 4% of the selling price, to the selling agent. For example, if a house sells for $100,000, Listum & Sellum receives $6,000 and pays $4,000 of this to the selling agent. At the time of the sale, the company records a debit of $6,000 to Accounts Receivable and a credit of $6,000 to Sales Revenue. Also at the time of sale, the company debits $4,000 to Commissions Expense and credits Commissions Payable for the same amount. The accounts receivable are normally collected within 30 days. Sales agents are paid by the 15th of the month following the month of the sale. In addition to the commissions expense, Listum & Sellum's other two major expenses are advertising of listings in local newspapers and depreciation of the company fleet of Cadillacs (Dewey has always believed that all of the sales agents should drive Cadillacs). The newspaper ads are taken for one month, and the company has until the 10th of the following month to pay that month's bill. The automobiles are depreciated over four years (Dewey doesn't believe that any salesperson should drive a car that is more than four years old).

Due to a downturn in the economy in Quebec, sales have been sluggish for the first 11 months of the current year, which ends on June 30. Willie is very disturbed by the slow sales this particular year because a large note payable to the local bank is due in July and the company plans to ask the bank to renew the note for another three years. Dewey seems less concerned by the unfortunate timing of the recession and has some suggestions as to how they can "paint the rosiest possible picture for the banker" when they go for the loan extension in July. In fact, he has some very specific recommendations for you as to how to account for transactions during June, the last month in the fiscal year.

You are the controller for Listum & Sellum and have been treated very well by Willie and Dewey since joining the company two years ago. In fact, Dewey insists that you personally drive the top-of-the-line Cadillac. Following are his suggestions:

> First, for any sales made in June, we can record the 6% commission revenue immediately but delay recording the 4% commission expense until July, when the sales agent is paid. We record the sales at the same time we always have, the sales agents get paid when they always have, the bank sees how profitable we have been, we get our loan, and everybody is happy!
>
> Second, since we won't be paying our advertising bills for the month of June until July 10, we can just wait until then to record the expense. The timing seems perfect, given that we are to meet with the bank for the loan extension on July 8.
>
> Third, since we will be depreciating the fleet of Caddys for the year ending June 30, how about just changing the estimated useful life on them to eight years instead of four years? We won't say anything to the sales agents; no need to rile them up about having to drive their cars for eight years. Anyhow, the change to eight years would just be for accounting purposes. In fact, we could even switch back to four years for accounting purposes next year. Likewise, the changes in recognizing commission expense and advertising expense don't need to be permanent either; these are just slight bookkeeping changes to help us get over the hump!

Required

1. Explain why each of the three proposed changes in accounting will result in an increase in net income for the year ending June 30.

2. Identify any concerns you have with each of the three proposed changes in accounting from the perspective of generally accepted accounting principles.

3. Identify any concerns you have with each of the three proposed changes in accounting from an ethical perspective.

4. What would you do? Draft your response to Willie and Dewey in the form of a business memo.

Case 5-3 *Sales Returns and Allowances* **LO 3**

You are the controller for a large chain of discount merchandise stores. You receive a memo-randum from the sales manager for the western region. He or she raises an issue regarding the proper treatment of sales returns. The manager urges you to discontinue the "silly practice" of recording sales returns and allowances each time a customer returns a product. In the manager's mind, this is a waste of time and unduly complicates the financial statements. The manager rec-ommends, "Things could be kept a lot simpler by just reducing Sales Revenue when a product is returned."

Required

1. What do you think the sales manager's *motivation* might be for writing you the memo? Is it that he or she believes the present practice is a waste of time and unduly complicates the financial statements?

2. Do you agree with the sales manager's recommendation? Explain why you agree or disagree.

3. Write a brief memo to the sales manager outlining your position on this matter.

—————— Internet Research Case ——————

Case 5-4 Tim Hortons Inc.

Tim Hortons Inc. has dominated the Canadian market and is aggressively expanding in the United States. Go to the Tim Hortons' website and explore the site for company-related information.

INTERNET

http://www.timhortons.com

Required:

1. For the most recent year available, what are Tim Hortons' revenues? What percentage of its revenues is from sales and what percentage is from franchises?

2. Compute the gross profit of its sales. How does it compare to the previous year?

3. Find out from a source such as SEDAR.com what companies are in Tim Hortons' industry segment. Conduct an online search for news articles that compare how well the companies are performing. Then compare the sales revenues and operating income for Tim Hortons' and one of its competitors.

   a. What are each company's revenues?
   b. Over two years, how quickly is each company growing in term of revenues?
   c. Compare each company's operating income as a percentage of revenues.

—————— Solutions to Key Terms Quiz ——————

1	Revenue recognition principle	13	Trade discount
19	Percentage-of-completion method	11	Quantity discount
		14	Sales discounts
18	Production method	15	Cost of goods available for sale
10	Installment method	17	Cost of goods sold
2	Matching principle	8	Operating income
3	Multiple-step income statement	6	Unusual or infrequent items
9	Gross profit	7	Discontinued operations
16	Net sales	4	Extraordinary item
12	Sales returns and allowances	5	Pro forma earnings

CHAPTER 6

Inventories and Cost of Goods Sold

After studying this chapter, you should be able to:

LO1 Explain the differences between periodic and perpetual inventory systems.

LO2 Apply the inventory costing methods with a periodic system.

LO3 Analyze the effects of the different costing methods.

LO4 Discuss additional topics on inventory.

LO5 Explain the effects that inventory transactions have on the statement of cash flows.

LO6 Apply the inventory costing methods using a perpetual system. (Appendix)

COURTESY ALIMENTATION COUCHE-TARD INC.

STUDY LINKS

A Look at the Previous Chapters

In Chapter 5, we discussed how income is recognized and reported in the income statement.

A Look at This Chapter

In this Chapter, we focus on cost of goods sold, an often significant expense in the income statement, and the related inventories.

A Look at the Upcoming Chapters

Chapters 7 through 11 are devoted to the topics related to the reporting of various items in the balance sheet.

Focus on Financial Results

Alimentation Couche-Tard, Inc., is the leading convenience store operator in Canada and the fourth largest in North America, with a network of 4,845 convenience stores selling food, beverages, motor fuel, and other products and services. In the following statements of consolidated earnings and consolidated balance sheets, we find that the cost of sales average about 80% of revenues, and inventories make up about 50% of this company's total current assets. Given that inventory and cost of sales are significant components of the statement of earnings and the balance sheet, inventory management is of paramount importance. A small difference in how inventory is evaluated will have a significant impact on its operating results. The prices of many of the items that Alimentation Couche-Tard sells, such as motor fuel, change frequently. Also, the retail values of perishables and time-sensitive items decline quickly. How does the company keep track of its inventories sold and still on hand? How does it determine the costs of inventory sold and inventory on hand? How does the valuation of inventory affect its earnings? Chapter 6 focuses on issues related to inventories and cost of goods sold.

Consolidated Balance Sheets (Excerpt)
as at April 30, 2007, and April 30, 2006
(in millions US dollars (Note 2))

	2007	2006
Assets		
Current Assets		
Cash and cash equivalents	$ 141.7	$ 331.5
Temporary investments	–	21.4
Accounts receivable (Note 10)	199.0	153.0
Income taxes receivable (Note 7)	–	0.7
Inventories (Note 11)	382.1	322.3
Prepaid expenses	13.5	15.2
Future income taxes (Note 7)	22.7	18.9
	759.0	863.0

Consolidated Statements of Earnings (Excerpt)
For the years ended April 29, 2007; and April 30, 2006
(in millions of US dollars)

	2007 (52 weeks)	2006 (53 weeks)
Revenues	$12,087.4	$10,157.3
Cost of sales	10,082.9	8,365.8
Gross profit	2,004.5	1,791.5

Courtesy Alimentation Couche-Tard Inc.

■ INVENTORY SYSTEMS

LO 1 Explain the differences between periodic and perpetual inventory systems.

The Nature of Inventories

Inventory is an asset. Different businesses have different types of inventories. Merchandising companies such as wholesalers and retailers buy merchandise in finished form and offer it for resale without transforming the product in any way. Thus, merchandising companies report a single inventory account, often titled Merchandise Inventory, on the balance sheet. The price they pay to purchase merchandise is the only inventory cost these companies incur.

By contrast, manufacturers produce the products they sell from various raw materials. On the balance sheet, manufacturers show three inventories, which reflect the three stages in developing inventory: raw materials, work in process, and finished goods. Finished goods are the equivalent of merchandise inventory for a retailer or wholesaler, in that both represent the inventory of goods held for sale. In addition to the cost of purchasing raw materials, called the direct material cost, manufacturers incur direct labour costs, which are the amounts paid to workers to manufacture the product, as well as manufacturing overheads, which include all other costs that are related to the manufacturing process but that cannot be directly matched to specific units of output. Typical manufacturing overheads include depreciation of a factory building and the salary paid to a supervisor.

A detailed discussion of the various forms of manufacturer's inventory and of the various costs related to such inventories is a topic in managerial accounting and is beyond the scope of an introductory financial accounting textbook. For the sake of simplicity, we shall limit our discussion to merchandise inventory.

Before we discuss the various inventory systems, we need to clarify one more concept. As stated earlier, inventory is an asset; how, then, does an inventory differ from a capital asset? The owner's intentions are what distinguish inventory from a capital asset. For instance, the smart cars produced by **Daimler Chrysler** are inventories because they are intended to be sold. A smart car owned by a pizzeria, however, is a capital asset because it is to be used for delivering pizzas; the pizzeria does not intend to sell it.

http://www.daimler.com

Periodic versus Perpetual System

How do companies keep track of the units of inventory they sell? There are two different inventory systems a company may use: *periodic* and *perpetual*. All businesses use one or the other when accounting for inventory. With the **periodic system**, the Inventory account is updated only at the end of a period; with the **perpetual system**, the Inventory account is updated after each sale or purchase.

Periodic system System in which the Inventory account is updated only at the end of the period.

Perpetual system System in which the Inventory account is increased at the time of each purchase and decreased at the time of each sale.

Periodic System   In a periodic inventory system, every time goods are purchased, a temporary account called Purchases is increased, with a corresponding increase in Accounts Payable for a credit purchase, or a decrease in the Cash account for a cash purchase. Every time goods are sold, Accounts Receivable or Cash is increased and the Sales Revenue account is increased as well. Note that the Inventory account is not increased when goods are purchased, nor is it reduced when goods are sold. The Cost of Goods Sold account is not updated either.

At the end of the accounting period, the Purchases account shows all inventory purchases, the Inventory account still shows the balance at the beginning of the period, and nothing has been recorded in the Cost of Goods Sold account. To determine the inventory sold, a physical count of the inventory still on hand is necessary. The results of the inventory count multiplied by the appropriate unit costs of inventoried items generate the ending balance in the Inventory account. Cost of goods sold can then be determined through the Cost of Goods Sold model introduced in Chapter 5:

Cost of goods sold = Beginning inventory + Purchases − Ending inventory

Perpetual System   In a perpetual system, every time goods are purchased, the Inventory account is increased, with a corresponding increase in Accounts Payable for a credit purchase or a decrease in the Cash account for a cash purchase. In addition to recognizing the increases in Accounts Receivable or Cash and in Sales Revenue when goods are sold, the accountant also records an entry to recognize the *cost* of the goods sold and the decrease in the cost of inventory on hand. Thus, at any point during the period, the inventory account is up to date. It has been increased for the cost of purchases during the period and reduced for the cost of the sales.

Journal Entries of the Two Systems

To highlight the differences between the two systems, consider the following example. Assume that the inventory on hand at the beginning of a period was 200 units at $8 each and that three transactions took place during the period:

1. Sold for cash 100 units at $10 each.
2. Purchased on account 500 units at $8 each.
3. Sold on account 450 units at $10 each.

An inventory count at the end of the period indicated that 150 units were on hand. Exhibit 6-1 shows the journal entries for the three transactions and the inventory related ledger accounts under each of the two inventory systems. On the left side under the periodic system, the only entry made at the time of a sale records the revenue earned. Neither the reduction of inventory nor cost of goods sold is recorded. The purchase of 500 units of inventory is accumulated in the temporary account Purchases.

The amount to be shown on the balance sheet as inventory at the end of the period is determined by inventory count, that is 150 units at $8 each, or $1,200. The cost of goods sold is in fact a calculated figure, determined by the inventory model:

Beginning Inventory + Purchases
− Ending Inventory = Cost of goods sold
or
$1,600 + $4,000 - $1,200 = $4,400

As you see in the right-hand side of Exhibit 6-1, in a perpetual system, purchases of merchandise increase the Inventory account directly, and any returns of merchandise reduce it. Unlike the periodic system, the perpetual system requires that *two* entries be made at the time of sale. The first entry is the same as the entry made under the periodic system: to record the sales revenue. The Inventory account is kept *perpetually* up to date, however. Finally, because the Inventory account has been updated for each purchase and sale, an inventory count is not the basis for valuing the inventory at the end of the period in a perpetual system. The balance of the Inventory account, $1,200, is the ending inventory. The balance of the cost of goods sold account, $4,400, is the cost of goods sold.

For control purposes, however, most businesses that use a perpetual system count the inventory once a year. Any differences between the amount on hand per the count and the amount appearing in the Inventory account require an adjusting entry in the records and should be investigated. For example, if the Inventory account shows a balance of $1,200 at the end of the year but only $1,000 of merchandise is counted, management is able to investigate the discrepancy. No such control feature exists in a periodic system.

In addition to the loss of control, the use of a periodic system presents a dilemma when a company wants to prepare *interim* financial statements. Because most companies that use a periodic system find it cost-prohibitive to count the entire inventory more than once a year, they use estimation techniques to determine inventory for monthly or quarterly statements. (These techniques are discussed later in this chapter.)

Why don't all companies use the perpetual system? Depending on the volume of inventory transactions—that is, purchases and sales of merchandise—a perpetual system can be extremely costly to maintain. Historically, businesses that have a relatively small volume of sales at a high unit price have used perpetual systems. For example, dealers in automobiles, furniture, appliances, and jewellery normally use a perpetual system. Each purchase of a unit of merchandise, such as an automobile, can be easily identified and an increase recorded in the Inventory account. When the vehicle is sold, the dealer can easily determine the cost of the particular car sold by looking at a perpetual inventory record.

Exhibit 6-1 Comparison of the Periodic and Perpetual Inventory Systems

PERIODIC SYSTEM			PERPETUAL SYSTEM		

1. Cash   1,000
     Sales Revenue   1,000
To record sale of 100 units at $10 each

A	=	L	+	SE
+1,000				**+1,000**

1. Cash   1,000
     Sales Revenue   1,000
To record sale of 100 units at $10 each

A	=	L	+	SE
+1,000				**+1,000**

Cost of Goods Sold   800
     Inventory   800
To record 100 units sold at a cost of $8 each

A	=	L	+	SE
−800				**−800**

2. Purchases   4,000
     Accounts Payable   4,000
To record purchase of 500 units

A	=	L	+	SE
		+4,000		**−4,000**

2. Inventory   4,000
     Accounts Payable   4,000
To record purchase of 500 units

A	=	L	+	SE
+4,000		**+4,000**		

3. Accounts Receivable   4,500
     Sales Revenue   4,500
To record sale of 450 units at $10 each

A	=	L	+	SE
+4,500				**+4,500**

3. Accounts Receivable   4,500
     Sales Revenue   4,500
To record sale of 450 units at $10 each

A	=	L	+	SE
+4,500				**+4,500**

Cost of Goods Sold   3,600
     Inventory   3,600
To record 450 units sold at a cost of $8 each

A	=	L	+	SE
−3,600				**−3,600**

INVENTORY (Periodic)

Beg. Bal.	1,600	

PURCHASES

2.	4,000	

INVENTORY (Perpetual)

Beg. Bal.	1,600	800	1.
2.	4,000	3,600	3.
	5,600	4,400	
End Bal.	1,200		

COST OF GOODS SOLD

1.	800	
3.	3,600	
Bal.	4,400	

Can you imagine, however, a similar system for a supermarket or a hardware store? Consider a checkout stand in a grocery store. Through the use of a cash register tape, the sales revenue for that particular stand is recorded at the end of the day. Because of the volume of sales of various items of inventory, from cans of vegetables to boxes of soap, it may not be feasible to record the cost of goods sold every time a sale takes place. This illustrates a key point in financial information: the cost of the information should never exceed its benefit. If a store manager had to stop and update the records each time a can of soup was sold, the retailer's business would obviously be disrupted.

To a certain extent, the ability of mass merchandisers to maintain perpetual inventory records has improved with the advent of point-of-sale terminals. When a cashier

Accounting for Your Decisions

You Are the Entrepreneur

A year ago, you and your brother launched a running shoe company in your garage. You buy shoes from four of the major manufacturers and sell them over the phone. Your accountant suggests that you use a perpetual inventory system. Should you?

ANSWER: The periodic inventory system has the following advantages: The Inventory account is updated only once per year, not after every purchase; the inventory is physically counted on the last day of each period to determine ending inventory; and its cost is low. By operating out of your garage, you are focusing on keeping administrative costs down. A perpetual inventory system would be more costly and would not provide enough extra benefits at low volume. Your decision may change as your business grows, particularly if you begin taking orders over the Internet.

runs a can of corn over the sensing glass at the checkout stand and the bar code is read, the company's computer receives a message that a can of corn has been sold. In some companies, however, updating the inventory record is in units only and is used as a means to determine when a product needs to be reordered. The company still relies on a periodic system to maintain the *dollar* amount of inventory. In the remainder of this chapter, we limit our discussion to the periodic system. We discuss the perpetual system in detail in the appendix to this chapter.

Cost of Goods Purchased

To determine cost of goods purchased, purchase returns and allowances and purchase discounts should be subtracted from (and costs of transporting the goods purchased added to) the invoice price of the purchase. The cost of transporting the goods purchased that is paid by the buyer is referred to as **transportation-in**, or *freight-in*. Exhibit 6-2 shows the cost of goods purchased section of Alpha Company's income statement.

Transportation-in Adjunct account used to record freight costs paid by the buyer.

Exhibit 6-2

Cost of Goods Purchased

ALPHA COMPANY PARTIAL INCOME STATEMENT FOR THE YEAR ENDED DECEMBER 31, 2008		
Purchases	$65,000	
Less: Purchase returns and allowances	1,800	
Purchase discounts	3,700	
Net purchases	59,500	
Add: Transportation-in	3,500	
Cost of goods purchased		$63,000

Purchases Assume that Alpha buys merchandise on account from one of its wholesalers at a cost of $4,000. **Purchases** is the temporary account used in a periodic inventory system to record acquisitions of merchandise. The journal entry to record the purchase follows:

Purchases Account used in a periodic inventory system to record acquisitions of merchandise.

Feb. 8	Purchases	4,000	
	Accounts Payable		4,000
	To record the purchase of merchandise on account		

$$\text{Assets} \quad = \quad \text{Liabilities} \quad + \quad \text{Shareholders' Equity}$$
$$+4{,}000 \qquad\qquad\qquad\qquad -4{,}000$$

It is important to understand that Purchases is *not* an asset account. It is included in the income statement as an integral part of the calculation of cost of goods sold and is therefore shown as a reduction of Shareholders' equity in the accounting equation. Because Purchases is a temporary account, it is closed at the end of the period.

Purchase Returns and Allowances   We discussed returns and allowances in Chapter 5 from the seller's point of view. From the standpoint of the buyer, purchase returns and allowances are reductions in the cost to purchase merchandise. Rather than recording these reductions directly in the Purchases account, the accountant uses a separate account. This account, **Purchase Returns and Allowances,** is a *contra account* to Purchases. Because Purchases has a normal debit balance, the normal balance in Purchase Returns and Allowances is a credit balance. The use of a contra account allows management to monitor the amount of returns and allowances. For example, a large number of returns during the period relative to the amount purchased may signal that the purchasing department is not buying from reputable sources.

Suppose that Alpha returns $850 of merchandise to a wholesaler for credit on its account. The return decreases both liabilities and purchases. Note that because a return reduces purchases, it actually *increases* net income and thus also increases Shareholders' equity. The journal entry follows:

Sept. 6	Accounts Payable	850	
	Purchase Returns and Allowances		850
	To record the return of merchandise for credit to account		

Assets	=	Liabilities	+	Shareholders' Equity
		−850		+850

The entry to record an allowance for merchandise retained rather than returned is the same as the entry for a return.

Purchase Discounts   Discounts were discussed in Chapter 5, from the seller's viewpoint. Merchandising companies often purchase inventory on terms that allow for a cash discount for early payment, such as 2/10, net 30. To the buyer, a cash discount is called a *purchase discount* and results in a reduction of the cost to purchase merchandise. The same two methods that are used to account for sales discounts are used to account for purchase discounts. Regardless of the method used, management must monitor the amount of purchase discounts taken as well as those opportunities missed by not taking advantage of the discounts for early payment. Because the effect on the accounting equation does not differ between the gross and the net methods, we will limit our discussion to the use of the *gross method.*

Assume a purchase of merchandise on March 13 for $500, with credit terms of 1/10, net 30. The entry at the time of the purchase is as follows:

Mar. 13	Purchases	500	
	Accounts Payable		500
	To record purchase on account, terms 1/10, net 30		

Assets	=	Liabilities	+	Shareholders' Equity
+500		+500		−500

If the company does not pay within the discount period, the accountant simply makes an entry to record the payment of $500 cash and the reduction of accounts

Accounting for Your Decisions

You Are the President

You are the president of a mail-order computer business. Your company buys computers and related parts directly from manufacturers and sells them to consumers via direct mail. Recently, you have noticed an increase in the amount of purchase returns and allowances relative to the amount of purchases. What are some possible explanations for this increase?

ANSWER: Any number of explanations are possible. It is possible that the products are being damaged while in transit. Or it may be that the company has changed suppliers and the merchandise is not of the quality expected. Or the employees are becoming more demanding in what they accept than they used to be.

payable. However, assume the company does pay its account on March 23, within the discount period. The following entry would be made:

Mar. 23 Accounts Payable   500
      Cash   495
      Purchase Discounts   5
    To record payment on account

$$\text{Assets} \quad = \quad \text{Liabilities} \quad + \quad \text{Shareholders' Equity}$$
$$-495 \qquad\qquad -500 \qquad\qquad\qquad +5$$

The **Purchase Discounts** account is contra to the Purchases account and thus increases Shareholders' equity, as shown in the accounting equation above. Also note in Exhibit 6-2 that purchase discounts are deducted from purchases on the income statement. Finally, note that the effect on the income statement is the same as illustrated earlier for a purchase return: because purchases are reduced, net income is increased.

Shipping Terms and Transportation Costs

The *cost principle* governs the recording of all assets. All costs necessary to prepare an asset for its intended use should be included in its cost. The cost of an item to a merchandising company is not necessarily limited to its invoice price. For example, any duty paid should be included in computing total cost. Any transportation costs incurred by the buyer should likewise be included in the cost of the merchandise.

The buyer does not always pay to ship the merchandise. This depends on the terms of shipment. Goods are normally shipped either **CIF destination point** or **FOB shipping point**; *CIF* stands for "cost, insurance, and freight" and *FOB* stands for "free on board." When merchandise is shipped CIF destination point, the seller pays the costs and freight necessary to bring the products to the buyer's location. The seller is also responsible for insuring against the risk of loss or damage to the products during the transportation. Alternatively, the agreement between the buyer and the seller may provide for the goods to be shipped FOB shipping point. In this case, the products are the responsibility of the buyer as soon as they leave the seller's location. When the terms of shipment are FOB shipping point, the buyer incurs transportation costs and bears the risks of loss of or damage to the products during the transportation.[1]

Refer to Exhibit 6-2. Transportation-in represents the freight costs Alpha paid for in-bound merchandise. These costs are added to net purchases, as shown in the exhibit, and increase the cost of goods purchased. Assume that on delivery of a shipment of goods, Alpha pays an invoice for $300 from the Rocky Mountain Railway. The terms of shipment are FOB shipping point. The entry on the books of Alpha follows:

May 10 Transportation-in   300
      Cash   300
    To record the payment of freight costs

$$\text{Assets} \quad = \quad \text{Liabilities} \quad + \quad \text{Shareholders' Equity}$$
$$-300 \qquad\qquad\qquad\qquad\qquad\qquad -300$$

The total of net purchases and transportation-in is called the *cost of goods purchased*. Transportation-in will be closed at the end of the period. In summary, cost of goods purchased consists of the following:

> Purchases
> Less: Purchase returns and allowances
>   Purchase discounts
> Equals: Net purchases
> Add: Transportation-in
> Equals: Cost of goods purchased

Purchase Discounts Contra-purchases account used to record reductions in purchase price for early payment to a supplier.

CIF destination point Terms that require the seller to pay for the cost of shipping the merchandise to the buyer.

FOB shipping point Terms that require the buyer to pay for the shipping costs.

---

[1] *CIF destination point* and *FOB shipping point* are official Terms of Sale documented in the International Chamber of Commerce Terms of Trade. Variations on these terms may be found in various textbooks. For instance, many textbooks use *FOB destination*, which is an older version of *CIF destination point*, to indicate the shipping term that requires the seller to be responsible for the transportation costs and to insure against loss or damage during transportation.

How should the *seller* account for the freight costs it pays when the goods are shipped CIF destination point? This cost, sometimes called *transportation-out,* is not an addition to the cost of purchases of the seller but is instead one of the costs necessary to *sell* the merchandise. Transportation-out is classified as a *selling expense* on the income statement.

Shipping Terms and Transfer of Title to Inventory   Terms of shipment take on additional significance at the end of an accounting period. It is essential that a company establish a proper cutoff at year-end. For example, what if Alpha purchases merchandise that is in transit at the end of the year? To whom does the inventory belong, Alpha or the seller? The answer depends on the terms of shipment. If goods are shipped CIF destination point, they remain the legal property of the seller until they reach their destination. Alternatively, legal title to goods shipped FOB shipping point passes to the buyer as soon as the seller turns the goods over to the carrier.

The example in Exhibit 6-3 is intended to summarize our discussion about shipping terms and ownership of merchandise. The example involves a shipment of merchandise in transit at the end of the year. Horton Wholesale, the seller of the goods, pays the transportation charges only if the terms are CIF destination point. Horton records a sale for goods in transit at year-end, however, only if the terms of shipment are FOB shipping point. If Horton does not record a sale, because the goods are shipped CIF destination point, the inventory appears on its December 31 balance sheet. Alpha, the buyer, pays freight costs only if the goods are shipped FOB shipping point. Only in this situation does Alpha record a purchase of the merchandise and include it as an asset on its December 31 balance sheet.

It is often very difficult, however, to allocate many of these incidental costs among the various items of inventory purchased. For example, consider a $500 freight bill that a supermarket paid on a merchandise shipment that includes 100 different items of inventory. To address the practical difficulty in assigning this type of cost to the different products, many companies have a policy by which transportation costs are charged to expense of the period if they are immaterial in amount. Thus, shipments of merchandise are simply recorded at the net invoice price, that is, after taking any cash discounts for early payment. It is a practical solution to a difficult allocation problem. Once again, the company must apply the cost/benefit test to accounting information.

Exhibit 6-3

Shipping Terms and Transfer of Title to Inventory

FACTS On December 28, 2008, Giant Wholesale ships merchandise to Alpha Company. The trucking company delivers the merchandise to Alpha on January 2, 2009. Both Giant and Alpha fiscal year-end is December 31.			
		If Merchandise Is Shipped	
COMPANY		CIF DESTINATION POINT	FOB SHIPPING POINT
Giant (seller)	Pay freight costs?	Yes	No
	Record sale in 2008?	No	Yes
	Include inventory on balance sheet at December 31, 2008?	Yes	No
Alpha (buyer)	Pay freight costs?	No	Yes
	Record purchase in 2008?	No	Yes
	Include inventory on balance sheet at December 31, 2008?	No	Yes

Accounting for Your Decisions

You Are the Manager

You manage the student bookstore. To get ready for the spring term, in December you order a large shipment of books from a publisher, with terms of FOB shipping point. On December 31, the books have not yet arrived. Should this shipment be included in the year-end inventory count even though it is not on hand to count? Assume a periodic inventory system.

ANSWER: Because the books were shipped FOB shipping point, they should be included in the year-end count even though they are not on hand to count. You should review the purchase invoice to determine the number of books ordered and the unit costs.

■ INVENTORY COSTING METHODS WITH A PERIODIC SYSTEM

Valuation is the major problem in accounting for inventories. As stated earlier, because of the additional complexities involved in valuing the inventory of a manufacturer, we will concentrate on the valuation of *merchandise inventory.*

LO 2 Apply the inventory costing methods with a periodic system.

One of the fundamental concepts in accounting is the relationship between *asset valuation* and the *measurement of income.* Recall a point made in Chapter 5: assets are unexpired costs, and expenses are expired costs. Thus, the value assigned to an asset on the balance sheet determines the amount eventually recognized as an expense on the income statement. For example, the amount recorded as the cost of an item of plant and equipment will dictate the amount of depreciation expense recognized on the income statement over the life of the asset. Similarly, the amount recorded as the cost of inventory determines the amount recognized as cost of goods sold on the income statement when the asset is sold. An error in assigning the proper amount to inventory on the balance sheet will affect the amount recognized as cost of goods sold on the income statement. The relationship between inventory as an asset and cost of goods sold can be understood by recalling the cost of goods sold section of the income statement. Assume the following example:

Beginning inventory	$ 500
Add: Purchases	1,200
Cost of goods available for sale	1,700
Less: Ending inventory	(600)
Cost of goods sold	$1,100

The amount assigned to ending inventory is deducted from cost of goods available for sale to determine cost of goods sold. If the ending inventory amount is incorrect, cost of goods sold will be wrong, and thus the net income of the period will be in error as well. (We will look at inventory errors later in the chapter.)

To this point, we have assumed that the cost to purchase an item of inventory is constant. For most merchandisers, however, the unit cost of inventory changes frequently. Consider a simple example. Everett Company purchases merchandise twice during the first year of business. The dates, the number of units purchased, and the costs are as follows:

February 4	200 units purchased at $1.00 per unit	= $200
October 13	200 units purchased at $1.50 per unit	= $300

Everett sells 200 units during the first year. Individual sales of the units take place relatively evenly throughout the year. The question is: *which* 200 units did the company sell, the $1.00 units or the $1.50 units or some combination of both? Recall the earlier discussion of the relationship between asset valuation and income measurement. The question is important because the answer determines not only the value assigned to the 200 units of ending inventory *but also* the amount allocated to cost of goods sold for the 200 units sold.

One possible method of assigning amounts to ending inventory and cost of goods sold is to *specifically identify* which 200 units were sold and which 200 units are on hand. This method is feasible for a few types of businesses in which units can be identified by serial numbers or bar code, but it may be impractical in most situations. As an alternative to specific identification, we could make an *assumption* as to which units were sold and which are on hand. Three different answers are possible:

1.   200 units sold at $1.00 each   = $200 cost of goods sold
      and 200 units on hand at $1.50 each   = $300 ending inventory
      or

2.   200 units sold at $1.50 each   = $300 cost of goods sold
      and 200 units on hand at $1.00 each   = $200 ending inventory
      or

3.   200 units sold at $1.25 each   = $250 cost of goods sold
      and 200 units on hand at $1.25 each   = $250 ending inventory

The third alternative assumes an *average cost* for the 200 units on hand and the 200 units sold. The average cost is the cost of the two purchases of $200 and $300, or $500, divided by the 400 units available to sell, or $1.25 per unit.

If we are concerned with the actual *physical flow* of the units of inventory, all of the three methods illustrated may be incorrect. The only approach that will yield a "correct" answer in terms of the actual flow of *units* of inventory is the specific identification method. In the absence of a specific identification approach, it is impossible to say which particular units were *actually* sold. In fact, there may have been sales from both of the two purchases, that is, some of the $1.00 units may have been sold and some of the $1.50 units may have been sold. To solve the problem of assigning costs to identical units, accountants have developed inventory costing assumptions or methods. Each of these methods makes a specific *assumption* about the *flow of costs* rather than the physical flow of units. The only approach that uses the actual flow of the units in assigning costs is the specific identification method.

To take a closer look at specific identification as well as three alternative approaches to valuing inventory, we will use the following example:

	UNITS	UNIT COST	TOTAL COST
Beginning inventory			
January 1	500	$10	$ 5,000*
Purchases			
January 20	300	11	3,300
April 8	400	12	4,800
September 5	200	13	2,600
December 12	100	14	1,400
Total purchases	1,000		12,100
Available for sale	1,500		$17,100
Units sold	900		?
Units in ending inventory	600 units		?

*Beginning inventory of $5,000 is carried over as the ending inventory from the prior period. It is highly unlikely that the different inventory costing methods we will illustrate would result in the same dollar amount of inventory at any point in time. However, we assume the same amount of beginning inventory for the sake of simplicity.

The question marks indicate the dilemma. What portion of the cost of goods available for sale of $17,100 should be assigned to the 900 units sold? What portion should be assigned to the 600 units remaining in ending inventory? The purpose of an inventory costing method is to provide a reasonable answer to these two questions.

Specific Identification Method

It is not always necessary to make an assumption about the flow of costs. In certain situations, it may be possible to specifically identify which units are sold and which units are on hand. A serial number on an automobile allows a dealer to identify a car on hand and thus its unit cost. An appliance dealer with 15 refrigerators on hand at the end of the year can identify the unit cost of each by matching a tag number with the purchase records. To illustrate the use of the **specific identification method** for our example, assume that the merchandiser is able to identify the specific units in the inventory at the end of the year and their costs as follows:

Specific identification method An inventory costing method that relies on matching unit costs with the actual units sold.

Units on Hand

DATE PURCHASED	UNITS	COST	TOTAL COST
January 20	100	$11	$1,100
April 8	300	12	3,600
September 5	200	13	2,600
Ending inventory	600		$7,300

One of two techniques can be used to find cost of goods sold. We can deduct ending inventory from the cost of goods available for sale:

Cost of goods available for sale		$17,100
Less:	Ending inventory	7,300
Equals:	Cost of goods sold	$ 9,800

Or we can calculate cost of goods sold independently by matching the units sold with their respective unit costs. By eliminating the units in ending inventory from the original acquisition schedule, the units sold and their costs are as follows:

Units Sold

DATE PURCHASED	UNITS	COST	TOTAL COST
Beginning Inventory	500	$10	$5,000
January 20	200	11	2,200
April 8	100	12	1,200
December 12	100	14	1,400
Goods sold	900		$9,800

The practical difficulty in keeping track of individual items of inventory sold is not the only problem with the use of this method. The method also allows management to *manipulate income.* For example, assume that a company is not having a particularly good year. Management may be tempted to do whatever it can to boost net income. One way it can do this is by *selectively selling units with the lowest-possible unit cost.* By doing so, the company can keep cost of goods sold down and net income up. Because of the potential for manipulation with the specific identification method, coupled with the practical difficulty of applying it in most situations, it is not widely used.

Weighted Average Cost Method

Weighted average cost method An inventory costing method that assigns the same unit cost to all units available for sale during the period.

The **weighted average cost method** is a relatively easy approach to costing inventory. It assigns the same unit cost to all units available for sale during the period. The weighted average cost is calculated as follows for our example:

$$\frac{\text{Cost of Goods Available for Sale}}{\text{Units Available for Sale}} = \text{Weighted Average Cost}$$

$$\frac{\$17,100}{1,500} = \underline{\$11.40}$$

Ending inventory is found by multiplying the weighted average unit cost by the number of units on hand:

$$\begin{array}{ccccc}
\text{Weighted Average Cost} & \times & \text{Number of Units in Ending Inventory} & = & \text{Ending Inventory} \\
\$11.40 & \times & 600 & = & \underline{\$6,840}
\end{array}$$

Cost of goods sold can be calculated in one of two ways:

	Cost of goods available for sale	$17,100
Less:	Ending inventory	6,840
Equals:	Cost of goods sold	$10,260

or

$$\begin{array}{ccccc}
\text{Weighted Average Cost} & \times & \text{Number of Units Sold} & = & \text{Cost of Goods Sold} \\
\$11.40 & \times & 900 & = & \underline{\$10,260}
\end{array}$$

Note that the computation of the weighted average cost is based on the cost of *all* units available for sale during the period, not just the beginning inventory or purchases. Also note that the method is called the *weighted* average cost method. As the name indicates, each of the individual unit costs is multiplied by the number of units acquired at each price. The simple arithmetic average of the unit costs for the beginning inventory and the four purchases is ($10 + $11 + $12 + $13 + $14)/5 = $12. The weighted average cost is slightly less than $12 ($11.40), however, because more units were acquired at the lower prices than at the higher prices.

First-In, First-Out Method (FIFO)

FIFO method An inventory costing method that assigns the most recent costs to ending inventory.

The **FIFO method** assumes that the first units in, or purchased, are the first units out, or sold. The first units sold during the period are assumed to come from the beginning inventory. After the beginning inventory is sold, the next units sold are assumed to come from the first purchase during the period and so forth. Thus, ending inventory consists of the most recent purchases of the period. In many businesses, this cost flow assumption is a fairly accurate reflection of the *physical* flow of products. For example, to maintain a fresh stock of products, the physical flow in a grocery store is first-in, first-out.

To calculate *ending inventory*, we start with the *most recent* inventory acquired and work *backward*:

Units on Hand

DATE PURCHASED	UNITS	COST	TOTAL COST
December 12	100	$14	$1,400
September 5	200	13	2,600
April 8	300	12	3,600
Ending inventory	600		$7,600

Cost of goods sold can then be found:

Cost of goods available for sale		$17,100
Less:	Ending inventory	7,600
Equals:	Cost of goods sold	$9,500

Or, because the FIFO method assumes that the first units in are the first ones sold, cost of goods sold can be calculated by starting with the *beginning inventory* and working *forward*:

Units Sold

DATE PURCHASED	UNITS	COST	TOTAL COST
Beginning Inventory	500	$10	$5,000
January 20	300	11	3,300
April 8	100	12	1,200
Units sold	900	Cost of goods sold	$9,500

Courtesy Imperial Oil Ltd.

Last-In, First-Out Method (LIFO)

The **LIFO method** assumes that the last units in, or purchased, are the first units out, or sold. The first units sold during the period are assumed to come from the latest purchase made during the period and so forth. Can you think of any businesses where the *physical* flow of products is last-in, first-out? Although this situation is not nearly so common as a first-in, first-out physical flow, a stockpiling operation, such as in a rock quarry, operates on this basis.

Under the LIFO method, the units of inventory sold are assigned more recent costs, therefore, LIFO results in more up-to-date cost of goods sold figures compared to weighted average cost and FIFO methods. For instance, in its 2007 annual report **Imperial Oil Ltd.** provided the following justification for its decision to use the LIFO method:

> The cost of crude oil and products is determined primarily using the last-in, first-out (LIFO) method. LIFO was selected over the alternative first-in, first-out and average cost methods because it provides a better matching of current costs with the revenues generated in the period.

The LIFO method is widely used in the United States because its tax saving advantage. However, it is seldomly used in Canada because it is not permitted for tax purposes in Canada. In practice, most Canadian companies use either FIFO or the weighted average method. Starting January 2008, Canadian GAAP had changed to be consistent with the International Accounting Standards (IAS), which generally disallows the use of the LIFO method for financial reporting purposes.

LIFO method An inventory method that assigns the most recent costs to cost of goods sold.

http://www.imperialoil.com

Study Tip

There may be cases, such as this illustration of FIFO, in which it is easier to determine ending inventory and then deduct it from cost of goods available for sale to find cost of goods sold. This approach is easier in this example because there are fewer layers in ending inventory than in cost of goods sold. In other cases, it may be quicker to determine cost of goods sold first and then plug in ending inventory.

❌ Accounting for Your Decisions

You Are the Controller

Your company, McGill Systems, is a manufacturer of components for personal computers. The company uses the FIFO method to account for its inventory. The CEO, a stickler for accuracy, asks you why you can't identify each unit of inventory and place a cost on it, instead of making an assumption that the first unit of inventory is the first sold when that is not necessarily the case.

ANSWER: The CEO is suggesting the specific identification method, which works best when there are a few pieces of unique inventory, not thousands of units of identical pieces. Because the company makes thousands of identical components each year, it would be impractical to assign specific costs to each unit of inventory. The FIFO method, on the other hand, assumes that the first units in are the first units sold, an appropriate assumption under these circumstances.

In concluding this section, it is worth repeating that the inventory costing methods are based on assumptions of cost flows, not on physical flows. For instance, to apply the FIFO method, it is not necessary to actually sell first the units purchased first. FIFO simply means that the units sold first should carry the costs of earlier purchases.

▪ THE EFFECTS OF INVENTORY COSTING METHODS

LO 3 Analyze the effects of the different costing methods.

The mechanics of each of the inventory costing methods are straightforward. But how does a company decide on the best method to use to value its inventory? According to the accounting profession, *the primary determinant in selecting an inventory costing method should be the ability of the method to accurately reflect the net income of the period.* But how and why does a particular costing method affect the net income of the period?

Costing Methods, Gross Profit, Income Tax Expense, and Net Income

Comparative income statements for our example are presented in Exhibit 6-4. Given that LIFO is rarely used by Canadian companies, our comparison will focus on the weighted average method and the FIFO method.

The original data for our example involved a situation in which prices were *rising* throughout the period: beginning inventory cost $10 per unit, and the last purchase during the year was at $14. With the weighted average method, the average cost is assigned to cost of goods sold; with FIFO, the older costs are assigned to expense. Thus, in a period of rising prices, the assignment of the *higher relative* prices to cost of goods sold under the weighted average method results in a *lower gross margin* under *weighted average* than under FIFO ($7,740 for weighted average and $8,500 for FIFO). Because operating expenses are not affected by the choice of inventory method, the lower gross margin under weighted average results in lower income, which leads to lower taxes.

To summarize, *during a period of rising prices,* the two methods result in the following:

ITEM	WEIGHTED AVERAGE	RELATIVE TO	FIFO
Cost of goods sold	Higher		Lower
Gross profit	Lower		Higher
Income before taxes	Lower		Higher
Taxes	Lower		Higher
Net Income	Lower		Higher

Exhibit 6-4 Income Statements for the Inventory Costing Methods

	WEIGHTED AVERAGE	FIFO
Sales revenue—$20 each	$18,000	$18,000
Beginning inventory	5,000	5,000
Purchases	12,100	12,100
Cost of goods available for sale	17,100	17,100
Ending inventory	**6,840**	**7,600**
Cost of goods sold	**10,260**	**9,500**
Gross margin	**7,740**	**8,500**
Operating expenses	2,000	2,000
Net income before tax	**5,740**	**6,500**
Income tax expense (40%)	**2,296**	**2,600**
Net income	**$ 3,444**	**$ 3,900**

NOTE: Figures that differ between the two methods are in bold.

Accounting for Your Decisions

You Are a Student

The owner/manager of a dairy farm knows that you are an accounting student and has asked your advice about which inventory method to use to measure the cost of both the inventory and the cost of goods sold. Since the inventory of milk and milk byproducts spoils easily, does he have to use the FIFO inventory valuation method? Why or why not?

> **ANSWER:** No, he does not have to use the FIFO method just because his products are subject to spoilage. There is a difference between the actual physical flow of the product and the cost flow of that product. From a practical perspective, he would want to sell the milk and milk byproducts on a FIFO basis to minimize spoilage. However, he can keep track of the cost flows for inventory valuation and cost of goods sold purposes using the LIFO method or weighted average cost method.

Changing Inventory Methods

The purpose of each of the inventory costing methods is to *match costs with revenues*. If a company believes that a different method will result in a better matching than that being provided by the method currently being used, it should change methods. A company must be able to justify a change in methods, however. Taking advantage of price increases by using FIFO to boost reported earnings is *not* a valid justification for a change in methods.

It is very important for a company to *disclose* any change in accounting principle, including a change in the method of costing inventory. Thus, if a company changes from weighted average to FIFO, it should justify the change using, for instance, the matching principle, and disclose the effect of the change on the financial statements.

Inventory Valuation in Other Countries

Acceptable methods for valuing inventory differ considerably around the world. Countries besides Canada in which LIFO is rarely used because it is prohibited for tax purposes and/or for financial reporting include the United Kingdom, New Zealand, Sweden, Denmark, and Brazil. Some countries, such as Germany, France, Australia, and Japan, allow LIFO for inventory valuation of foreign investments but not for domestic reports. On the other hand, LIFO is widely used in the United States because of the availability of LIFO tax savings.

The use of LIFO can create additional complications. Since LIFO keeps the costs of the oldest units in inventory, when prices are rising the costs of these units will be lower than the costs of more recent purchases. The excess value of a company's inventory stated at FIFO over the value stated at LIFO is called the *LIFO reserve*. Now assume that the company sells more units than it buys during a period. Some of the units assumed to be sold will come from the older layers, with their relatively low unit costs. This situation, called *LIFO liquidation*, can distort the reported earnings. In the United States,

LIFO liquidation can also affect a company's tax bill. For these reasons, companies choosing to use LIFO for their inventories are required to provide information about the changes in their LIFO reserves—usually in the note to inventory—so that users of the financial statements can estimate LIFO's effects on income and on taxes.

In Chapter 1 we mentioned the attempts by the International Accounting Standards Board (IASB) to develop worldwide accounting standards, International Accounting Standards (IAS). IAS permits the use of either FIFO or weighted average when specific identification is not feasible. IAS generally disallows the use of LIFO.

■ ADDITIONAL TOPICS ON INVENTORY: ERRORS, LOWER OF COST OR MARKET, AND ESTIMATION

LO 4 Discuss additional topics on inventory.

In this section we discuss several additional topics relating to inventories: the effects of inventory errors, valuing inventory at lower-of-cost or market, and methods for estimating inventory value.

Inventory Errors

Earlier in the chapter we considered the inherent tie between the valuation of assets, such as inventory, and the measurement of income, such as cost of goods sold. The importance of inventory valuation to the measurement of income can be illustrated by considering inventory errors. Many different types of inventory errors exist. Some errors are mathematical; for example, a bookkeeper may incorrectly add a column total. Other errors relate specifically to the physical count of inventory at year-end. For example, the count might inadvertently omit one section of a warehouse. Other errors arise from cutoff problems at year-end.

For example, assume that merchandise in transit at the end of the year is shipped FOB (free on board) shipping point. Under these shipment terms, the inventory belongs to the buyer at the time it is shipped. Because the shipment has not arrived at the end of the year, however, it cannot be included in the physical count. Unless some type of control is in place, the amount in transit may be erroneously omitted from the valuation of inventory at year-end.

To demonstrate the effect of an inventory error on the income statement, consider the following example. Through a scheduling error, two different inventory teams were assigned to count the inventory in the same warehouse on December 31, 2008. The correct amount of ending inventory is $250,000, but because two different teams counted the same inventory in one warehouse, the amount recorded is $300,000. The effect of this error on net income is analyzed in the left half of Exhibit 6-5.

The *overstatement* of *ending inventory* in 2008 leads to an *understatement* of the 2008 cost of goods sold *expense*. Because cost of goods sold is understated, *gross profit* for the year is *overstated*. Operating expenses are unaffected by an inventory error. Thus, *net income* is *overstated* by the same amount as the overstatement of gross profit.[2] The most important conclusion from the exhibit is that an overstatement of ending inventory leads to a corresponding overstatement of net income.

Unfortunately, the effect of a misstatement of the year-end inventory is not limited to the net income for that year. As indicated in the right-hand portion of Exhibit 6-5, the error also affects the income statement for the following year. This happens simply because *the ending inventory of one period is the beginning inventory of the following period.* The *overstatement* of the 2009 *beginning inventory* leads to an *overstatement* of *cost of goods available for sale.* Because cost of goods available for sale is overstated, *cost of goods sold* is also *overstated.* The *overstatement* of cost of goods sold *expense* results in an *understatement* of *gross profit* and thus an *understatement* of *net income.*

Exhibit 6-5 illustrates the nature of a *counterbalancing error.* The effect of the overstatement of net income in the first year, 2008, is offset or counterbalanced by the understatement of net income by the same dollar amount in the following year. If the net incomes of two successive years are misstated in the opposite direction by the same

Exhibit 6-5 Effects of Inventory Error on the Income Statement

	2008			2009		
	REPORTED	CORRECTED	EFFECT OF ERROR	REPORTED	CORRECTED	EFFECT OF ERROR
Sales	$1,000*	$1,000		$1,500	$1,500	
Cost of goods sold:						
Beginning inventory	200	200		**300**	**250**	$50 OS
Add: Purchases	700	700		1,100	1,100	
Cost of goods available for sale	900	900		**1,400**	**1,350**	50 OS
Less: Ending inventory	**300**	**250**	$50 OS†	350	350	
Cost of goods sold	**600**	**650**	50 US‡	**1,050**	**1,000**	50 OS
Gross margin	**400**	**350**	50 OS	**450**	**500**	50 US
Operating expenses	100	100		120	120	
Net income	**$ 300**	**$ 250**	50 OS	**$ 330**	**$ 380**	50 US

NOTE: Figures that differ as a result of the error are in bold.
*All amounts are in thousands of dollars.

†OS = Overstatement
‡US = Understatement

amount, what is the effect on retained earnings? Assume that retained earnings at the beginning of 2008 is correctly stated at $300,000. The counterbalancing nature of the error is seen by analyzing retained earnings. For 2008 the analysis would indicate the following (OS = overstated and US = understated):

	2008 REPORTED	2008 CORRECTED	EFFECT OF ERROR
Beginning retained earnings	$300,000	$300,000	Correct
Add: Net income	300,000	250,000	$50,000 OS
Ending retained earnings	$600,000	$550,000	$50,000 OS

An analysis for 2009 would show the following:

	2009 REPORTED	2009 CORRECTED	EFFECT OF ERROR
Beginning retained earnings	$600,000	$550,000	$50,000 OS
Add: Net income	330,000	380,000	$50,000 US
Ending retained earnings	$930,000	$930,000	Correct

Thus, even though retained earnings is overstated at the end of the first year, it is correctly stated at the end of the second year. This is the nature of a counterbalancing error.

The effect of the error on the balance sheet is shown in Exhibit 6-6. The only accounts affected by the error are Inventory and Retained Earnings. The overstatement of the 2008 ending inventory results in an overstatement of total assets at the end of the first year. Similarly, as our earlier analysis indicates, the overstatement of 2008 net income leads to an overstatement of retained earnings by the same amount. Because the error is counterbalancing, the 2009 year-end balance sheet is correct; that is, ending inventory is not affected by the error, and thus the amount for total assets at the end of 2009 is also correct. The effect of the error on retained earnings is limited to the first year because of the counterbalancing nature of the error.

The effects of inventory errors on various financial statement items are summarized in Exhibit 6-7. Our analysis focused on the effects of an overstatement of inventory. The effects of an understatement are just the opposite and are summarized in the bottom portion of the exhibit.

---

[2]An overstatement of gross profit also results in an overstatement of income tax expense. Thus, because tax expense is overstated, the overstatement of net income is not as large as the overstatement of gross profit. For now we will ignore the effect of taxes, however.

Exhibit 6-6

Effects of Inventory Error on
the Balance Sheet

	2008		2009	
	REPORTED	CORRECTED	REPORTED	CORRECTED
Inventory	$ 300*	$ 250	$ 350	$ 350
All other assets	1,700	1,700	2,080	2,080
Total assets	$2,000	$1,950	$2,430	$2,430
Total liabilities	$ 400	$ 400	$ 500	$ 500
Capital stock	1,000	1,000	1,000	1,000
Retained earnings	600	550	930	930
Total liabilities and shareholders' equity	$2,000	$1,950	$2,430	$2,430

NOTE: Figures that differ as a result of the error are in bold.
*All amounts are in thousands of dollars.

Exhibit 6-7

Summary of the Effects of
Inventory Errors

Study Tip

Note the logic behind the notion
that an overstatement of ending
inventory leads to overstate-
ments of both total assets and
retained earnings at the end of
the year. This is logical because
a balance sheet must balance;
that is, the left side must equal
the right side. If the left side
(inventory) is overstated, then
the right side (retained earnings)
will also be overstated.

	Effect of Overstatement of Ending Inventory on	
	CURRENT YEAR	FOLLOWING YEAR
Cost of goods sold	Understated	Overstated
Gross margin	Overstated	Understated
Net income	Overstated	Understated
Retained earnings, end of year	Overstated	Correctly stated
Total assets, end of year	Overstated	Correctly stated

	Effect of Understatement of Ending Inventory on	
	CURRENT YEAR	FOLLOWING YEAR
Cost of goods sold	Overstated	Understated
Gross margin	Understated	Overstated
Net income	Understated	Overstated
Retained earnings, end of year	Understated	Correctly stated
Total assets, end of year	Understated	Correctly stated

Two-Minute Review

Skipper Corp. omits one section of its warehouse in the year-end inventory count.

1. Will the omission understate or overstate cost of goods sold on the income statement in the year the error is made?

2. Will the omission understate or overstate retained earnings on the balance sheet at the end of the year the error is made?

3. Will the omission affect retained earnings on the balance sheet at the end of the following year after the error is made? Explain your answer.

Answers on page 269.

Not all errors are counterbalancing. For example, if a section of a warehouse *continues* to be double counted every year, both the beginning and the ending inventory will be incorrect each year and the error will not counterbalance.

Part of the auditor's job is to perform the necessary tests to obtain reasonable assurance that inventory has not been overstated or understated. If there is an error and inventory is wrong, however, the balance sheet and the income statement will both be distorted. For example, if ending inventory is overstated, inflating total assets, then cost of goods sold will be understated, boosting profits. Thus, such an error overstates the financial health of the organization in two ways. A lender or an investor must make a decision based on the current year's statement and cannot wait until the next accounting cycle, when this error is reversed. This is one reason that investors and creditors insist on audited financial statements.

Valuing Inventory at Lower of Cost or Market

One of the components sold by an electronics firm has become economically obsolete. A particular style of suit sold by a retailer is outdated and can no longer be sold at the regular price. In each of these instances, it is likely that the retailer will have to sell the merchandise for less than the normal selling price. In these situations, a departure from the cost basis of accounting may be necessary because the *market value* of the inventory may be less than its *cost* to the company. The departure is called the **lower-of-cost-or-market (LCM) rule.**

At the end of each accounting period, the original cost, as determined using one of the costing methods such as FIFO, is compared with the market price of the inventory. If market is less than cost, the inventory is written down to the lower amount.

For example, if cost is $100,000 and market value is $85,000, the accountant would make the following entry:

Lower-of-cost-or-market (LCM) rule A conservative inventory valuation approach that is an attempt to anticipate declines in the value of inventory before its actual sale.

Dec. 31	Loss on Decline in Value of Inventory	15,000	
	Inventory		15,000
	To record decline in value of inventory		

Assets	=	Liabilities	+	Shareholders' Equity
−15,000				−15,000

Note that the entry reduces both assets, in the form of inventory, and shareholders' equity. The reduction in shareholders' equity is the result of reporting the Loss on Decline in Value of Inventory on the income statement as Cost of Goods Sold or an item of Other Expense.

Why Lower of Cost or Market Is Used

To understand why lower of cost or market (LCM) is used as a basis for comparison with original cost, consider the following example. Here the net realizable value will be used to determine the market value of inventory. Assume that a clothier pays $150 for a man's double-breasted suit and normally sells it for $200. Now assume that double-breasted suits fall out of favour with fashionistas. The retailer realizes that because of the style change, the suits will have to be offered at a reduced price. The selling price has dropped to $120. A loss of $30 ($120 - $150) will be realized on the sale of each suit. Under the LCM rule, this loss is accounted for immediately by writing down inventory to $120, rather than when the items are sold.

To compare the results with and without the use of the LCM rule, assume that the facts are the same as before and that the retailer has 10 double-breasted suits in inventory on December 31, 2008. In addition, assume that all 10 suits are sold at a clearance sale in January 2009 at the reduced price of $120 each. If the lower-of-cost-or-market rule is not used, the results for the two years will be as follows:

LCM RULE NOT USED	2008	2009	TOTAL
Sales revenue ($120 per unit)	$ 0	$ 1,200	$ 1,200
Cost of goods sold			
(original cost of $150 per unit)	0	(1,500)	(1,500)
Gross profit	$ 0	$ (300)	$ (300)

If the LCM rule is not applied, the gross profit will be distorted. A negative gross profit or gross loss will be reported in 2009 when the 10 suits are sold. If the LCM rule is applied, however, the results for the two years will be as follows:

LCM RULE USED	2008	2009	TOTAL
Sales revenue ($120 per unit)	$ 0	$1,200	$1,200
Cost of goods sold (net realizable value less normal profit margin of $120 per unit)	0	(1,200)	(1,200)
Loss on decline in value of inventory: 10 units × ($150 − $120)	300	0	(300)
Gross profit	$(300)	$ 0	$(300)

The use of the LCM rule here has served two important functions: (1) to report the loss in value of the inventory, $30 per suit or $300 in total, in the year the loss occurs and (2) to avoid reporting the loss in the year the suits are actually sold.

The term "market" is ambiguous. The AcSB recommends that "market" not be used when describing the basis of valuation. It prefers that companies use terms that are more descriptive of the method for determining market. The acceptable methods for determining market include "replacement cost," "net realizable value," and "net realizable value less normal profit margin." IAS uses Lower of Cost or Net Realizable Value, clearly indicates its preference of "market" value.

The LCM rule for inventory reflects policy setters' concern for relevance over reliability. Historical costs, although more reliable, are less useful in cases where inventory market value has significantly declined. Also, the LCM rule offers additional discretion to management in terms of, for instance, when to apply the LCM rule, what market value to use, and so on. It is management's ethical responsibility to use the LCM rule to *enhance* the informativeness of accounting information, and not to manipulate accounting numbers for their own self-interest.

Conservatism Is the Basis for the Lower-of-Cost-or-Market Rule

The departure from the cost basis is commonly justified on the basis of *conservatism*. According to the accounting profession, conservatism is a prudent reaction to uncertainties to try to ensure that uncertainties and risks inherent in business situations are adequately considered. In our example, the future selling price of a suit is uncertain because of style changes. The use of the LCM rule serves two purposes. First, the inventory of suits is written down from $150 to $120 each. Second, the decline in value of the inventory is recognized at the time it is first observed rather than waiting until the suits are sold. An investor in a company with deteriorating inventory has good reason to be alarmed. Merchandisers who do not make the proper adjustments to their product lines go out of business as they compete with the lower prices of warehouse clubs and the lower overheads of e-business and home shopping networks.

You should realize that the write-down of the suits violates the historical cost principle, which says that assets should be carried on the balance sheet at their original cost. But the LCM rule is considered a valid exception to the principle because it is a prudent reaction to the uncertainty involved and, thus, an application of conservatism in accounting.

Accounting for Your Decisions

It's October, and the accountants at Taz Industries are beginning to prepare the annual financial statements for the fiscal year that ended September 30. One of the staff members, Hudson Clark, is responsible for determining the inventory valuation.

In the current economic downturn, the depressed economy has greatly reduced the company's realizable value for its ending inventory. While he understands that inventory should be valued at the lower of cost or market, Hudson is quite concerned about writing down ending inventory because that will reduce the income reported to creditors and investors. It also will mean total assets will be much lower in value on the September 30 balance sheet.

Should Taz Industries report its September 30 inventory at cost or at the lower market value? Explain your reasoning.

ANSWER: Taz Industries should report its September 30 inventory at the lower market value. Since the net realizable value of the inventory has declined, accounting conservatism requires such decline in value be recognized at the time it is first observed. The lower market value in this case will allow the investors and creditors to adequately assess the risk and uncertainty faced by the company.

Methods for Estimating Inventory Value

Situations arise in which it may not be practicable or even possible to measure inventory at cost. At times it may be necessary to *estimate* the amount of inventory. Two similar methods are used for very different purposes to estimate the amount of inventory: the gross profit method and the retail inventory method.

Gross Profit Method   A company that uses a periodic inventory system may experience a problem if inventory is stolen or destroyed by fire, flooding, or some other type of damage. Without a perpetual inventory record, what is the cost of the inventory stolen or destroyed? The **gross profit method** is a useful technique to estimate the cost of inventory lost in these situations. The method relies *entirely* on the ability to reliably estimate the *ratio of gross profit to sales.*

Exhibit 6-8 illustrates how the normal income statement model that we use to find cost of goods sold can be rearranged to estimate inventory. The model on the left shows the components of cost of goods sold as they appear on the income statement. Assuming a periodic system, the inventory on hand at the end of the period is counted and is subtracted from cost of goods available for sale to determine cost of goods sold. The model is rearranged on the right as a basis for estimating inventory under the gross profit method. The only difference in the two models is in the reversal of the last two components: ending inventory and cost of goods sold. Rather than attempting to estimate *ending* inventory, we are trying to estimate the amount of inventory that should be on hand at a specific date, such as the date of a fire or flood. The estimate of cost of goods sold is found by estimating gross profit and deducting this estimate from sales revenue.

Gross profit method A technique used to establish an estimate of the cost of inventory stolen, destroyed, or otherwise damaged or of the amount of inventory on hand at an interim date.

INCOME STATEMENT MODEL	GROSS PROFIT METHOD MODEL
Beginning Inventory	Beginning Inventory
+ Purchases	+ Purchases
= Cost of Goods Available for Sale	= Cost of Goods Available for Sale
− Ending Inventory (per count)	− Estimated Cost of Goods Sold
= Cost of Goods Sold	= Estimated Inventory

Exhibit 6-8

The Gross Profit Method for Estimating Inventory

To understand this method, assume that on March 12, 2008, a portion of Hardluck Company's inventory is destroyed in a fire. The company determines, by a physical count, that the cost of the merchandise not destroyed is $200. Hardluck needs to estimate the cost of the inventory lost for purposes of insurance reimbursement. If the insurance company pays Hardluck an amount equivalent to the cost of the inventory destroyed, no loss will be recognized. If the cost of the inventory destroyed exceeds the amount reimbursed by the insurance company, a loss will be recorded for the excess amount.

Assume that the insurance company agrees to pay Hardluck $250 as full settlement for the inventory lost in the fire. From its records, Hardluck is able to determine the following amounts for the period from January 1 to the date of the fire, March 12:

Net sales from January 1 to March 12	$6,000
Beginning inventory—January 1	1,200
Purchases from January 1 to March 12	3,500

Assume that based on recent years' experience, Hardluck estimates its gross profit margin as 30% of net sales. The steps it will take to estimate the lost inventory follow:

1. Determine gross profit:

   Net Sales × Gross Profit Ratio = Gross Profit
   $6,000   ×   30%   = $1,800

2. Determine cost of goods sold:

   Net Sales − Gross Profit = Cost of Goods Sold
   $6,000   − $1,800   = $4,200

3. Determine cost of goods available for sale at time of fire:

   Beginning Inventory + Purchases = Cost of Goods Available for Sale
   $1,200   + $3,500   = $4,700

4. Determine inventory at time of the fire:

   Cost of Goods Available for Sale − Cost of Goods Sold = Inventory
   $4,700   − $4,200   = $500

5. Determine amount of inventory destroyed:

   Inventory at Time of Fire − Inventory Not Destroyed = Inventory Destroyed
   $500   − $200   = $300

Hardluck would record the following journal entry to recognize a loss for the excess of the cost of the lost inventory over the amount of reimbursement from the insurance company:

Mar. 12	Loss on Insurance Settlement	50	
	Cash (from insurance company)	250	
	Inventory		300
	To record the insurance settlement from fire		

Assets	=	Liabilities	+	Shareholders' Equity
+250				−50
−300				

Another situation in which the gross profit method is used is for *interim financial statements*. Most companies prepare financial statements at least once every three months. In fact, the securities commissions require quarterly reports from corporations whose shares are publicly traded. Companies using the periodic inventory system, however, find it cost-prohibitive to count the inventory every three months. The gross profit method is used to estimate the cost of the inventory at these interim dates. A company is allowed to use the method only in interim reports. Inventory reported in the annual report must be based on actual, not estimated, cost.

Retail Inventory Method   The counting of inventory in most retail businesses is a significant undertaking. Imagine the time involved to count all of the various items stocked in a hardware store. Because of the time and cost involved in counting inventory, most retail businesses take an inventory count only once a year. The **retail inventory method** is used to estimate inventory for interim statements, typically prepared monthly.

Retail inventory method A technique used by retailers to convert the retail value of inventory to a cost basis.

The retail inventory method has another important use. Consider the year-end inventory count in a large supermarket. One employee counts the number of tubes of toothpaste on the shelf and relays the relevant information either to another employee or to a scanner: "16 tubes of 130 mL ABC brand toothpaste at $1.69." The key is that the price recorded is the *selling price* or *retail price* of the product, not its cost. It is much quicker to count the inventory at retail than it would be to trace the cost of each item to purchase invoices. The retail method can then be used to convert the inventory from retail to cost. The approach taken with the retail inventory method, whether for interim statements or at year-end, is similar to the approach used with the gross profit method and is covered in detail in intermediate accounting textbooks.

Analyzing the Management of Inventory Turnover   Inventory is the lifeblood of a company that sells product. **Alimentation Couche-Tard** must strike a balance between maintaining a sufficient variety of items to meet customers' needs and incurring the high cost of carrying inventory. The cost of storage and the lost income from the money tied up in inventory make it very expensive to keep on hand. Thus, the more quickly a company can sell—that is, turn over—its inventory the better. **The inventory turnover ratio** is calculated as follows:

http://www.couche-tard.com

Inventory turnover ratio A measure of the number of times inventory is sold during a period.

$$\text{Inventory Turnover Ratio} = \text{Cost of Goods Sold / Average Inventory}$$

It is a measure of the number of times inventory sold during the period.

Use the following Ratio Decision Process to analyze the inventory of Alimentation Couche-Tard or any other public company.

1.   Formulate the Question

Managers, investors, and creditors are all interested in how well a company manages its inventory. The quicker inventory can be sold, the sooner the money will be available to invest in more inventory or to use for other purposes. Those interested must be able to answer the following question:

How many times a year does a company turn over its inventory?

2.   Gather the Information financial statements

Cost of goods sold is reported on the income statement, representing a flow for a period of time. On the other hand, inventory is an asset, respresenting a balance at a period in time. Thus, a comparison of the two requires the cost of goods sold for the year and an average of the balance in inventory:

- Cost of goods sold: From the income statement for the year
- Average inventory: From the balance sheets at the end of the two most recent years

3. Calculate the Ratio

$$\text{Inventory Turnover Ratio} = \frac{\text{Cost of Goods Sold}^3}{\text{Average Inventory}}$$

Alimentation Couche-Tard
Partial Consolidated Statement of Earnings
(in millions)

	April 29, 2007
Net sales	12,078.4
Cost of Sales	10,082.9

Alimentation Couche-Tard
Partial Consolidated Balance Sheets
(in thousands)

	April 29, 2007	April 30, 2006
Assets		
Current Assets:		
Inventories	$382.1	$322.3

Average inventories =
($382.1 + $322.3)/2 = $352.2

$$\text{Inventory Turnover} = \frac{\$\,10,082.9}{352.2} = 28.6 \text{ times}$$

4. Compare the Ratio with Others

Management compares the current year's turnover rate with prior years to see if the company is experiencing slower or faster turns of its inventory. It is also important to compare the rate with other companies in the same industry:

Inventory Turnover Comparison

ALIMENTATION COUCHE-TARD 2007	ALIMENTATION COUCHE-TARD 2008	LOBLAW
28.6 times	27.1 times	13.6 times

5. Interpret the Results

This ratio in Exhibit 6-9 tells us that in fiscal year 2007, Alimentation Couche-Tard turned over its inventory an average of 28.6 times. This is slightly faster than in the prior year, and significantly faster than its competitor, Loblaw. An alternative way to look at a

---

[3]Before January 2008 many Canadian companies did not report cost of goods sold separately, so it was impossible to compute their inventory turnover ratios using this formula. As an alternative, inventory turnover can be computed using a summary expense—such as cost of goods sold plus operating expenses—as the numerator. Alternative numerators may introduce inaccuracies in the inventory turnover ratio; however, as long as various expenses do not change drastically, such inaccuracies can be mitigated.

company's efficiency in managing its inventory is to calculate the number of days, on average, that inventory is on hand before it is sold. This measure is called the number of days' sales in inventory and is calculated as follows for the Alimentation Couche-Tard in 2007 (we will assume 360 days in a year):

$$\text{Number of Days' Sales in Inventory} = \frac{\text{Number of Days in the Period}}{\text{Inventory Turnover Ratio}}$$

$$= \frac{360}{28.6} = 13 \text{ days}$$

This measure tells us that it took Alimentation Couche-Tard 13 days, or less than two weeks, on average to sell its inventory.

■ HOW INVENTORIES AFFECT THE STATEMENT OF CASH FLOWS

The effects on the income statement and the statement of cash flows from inventory-related transactions differ significantly. We have focused our attention in the last two chapters on how the purchase and the sale of inventory are reported on the income statement. We have found that the cost of the inventory sold during the period is deducted on the income statement as cost of goods sold.

> **LO 5** Explain the effects that inventory transactions have on the statement of cash flows.

The appropriate reporting on a statement of cash flows for inventory transactions depends on whether the direct or indirect method is used. If the direct method is used to prepare the Operating Activities category of the statement, the amount of cash paid to suppliers of inventory is shown as a deduction in this section of the statement.

If the more popular indirect method is used, it is necessary to make adjustments to net income for the changes in two accounts: Inventory and Accounts Payable. These adjustments are summarized in Exhibit 6-10. An increase in Inventory is deducted because it indicates that the company is building up its inventory and thus expending cash. A decrease in Inventory is added to net income. An increase in Accounts Payable is added because it indicates that during the period, the company has increased the amount it owes suppliers and has therefore conserved its cash. A decrease in Accounts Payable is deducted because the company actually reduced the amount owed to suppliers during the period.

The Operating Activities section of consolidated cash flows and Note 9 for Alimentation Couche-Tard are presented in Exhibit 6-11. Note that the company presents only a summary of the changes in non-cash working capital in the cash flow statement and provides the details of these changes in Note 9. Accounts payable and accrued liabilities are grouped together in Note 9.

Item	Cash Flow Statement
	Operating Activities
	Net income **xxx**
Increase in Inventory	➤ −
Decrease in Inventory	➤ +
Increase in Accounts Payable	➤ +
Decrease in Accounts Payable	➤ −
	Investing Activities
	Financing Activities

Exhibit 6-10

Inventories and the Statement of Cash Flows

Consolidated Statement of Cash Flows (Excerpt)
Year ended April 29, 2007
(in millions of US dollars)

	2007
Operating activities	
Net earnings	$196.4
Adjustments to reconcile net earnings to cash flows from operating activities	
Depreciation and amortization of fixed and other assets, net of amortization of deferred credits	114.4
(Gain) on disposal of fixed and other assets	(3.8)
Future income taxes	21.7
Deferred credits	30.5
Other	13.1
Changes in non-cash working capital items (Note 9)	30.7
Cash flows from operating activities	403.0

9 – INFORMATION INCLUDED IN THE CONSOLIDATED STATEMENT OF CASH FLOWS

The changes in non-cash working capital items are detailed as follows:

	2007 $
Accounts receivable	(41.6)
Inventories	(24.4)
Prepaid expenses	1.8
Accounts payable and accrued liabilities	59.3
Income taxes	(35.6)
	30.7

Increase in inventories expands cash and thus subtracted.

Increase here conserves cash and thus added.

Courtesy Alimentation Couche-Tard Inc.

The increases in inventories in 2007 are subtracted because the purchase of these assets reduces the company's cash. Conversely, a buildup of accounts payable and accrued liabilities conserves Alimentation Couche-Tard's cash. Thus, the increase in these items in 2007 is added to net earnings.

Appendix: Inventory Costing Methods with a Perpetual System

The illustrations of the inventory costing methods in the chapter assumed the use of a periodic inventory system. In this appendix, we will see how the methods are applied when a company maintains a perpetual inventory system. Before doing so, however, it is useful to look more closely at the differences between the two systems.

LO 6 Apply the inventory costing methods using a perpetual system (Appendix).

It is important to understand the difference between inventory *costing systems* and inventory *methods*. The two inventory systems differ in terms of how often the Inventory account is updated: periodically or perpetually. However, when a company sells identical units of product and the cost to purchase each unit is subject to change, it also must choose an inventory costing method, such as FIFO, LIFO, or weighted average.

Earlier in the chapter, we illustrated the various costing methods with a periodic system. We now use the same data to illustrate how the methods differ when a perpetual system is used. Keep in mind that if a company uses specific identification, the results will be the same regardless of whether it uses the periodic or the perpetual system. To compare the periodic and perpetual systems for the other methods, we must add one important piece of information: the date of each of the sales. The original data as well as the numbers of units sold on the various dates are summarized below:

DATE	PURCHASES	SALES	BALANCE
Beginning inventory			500 units @ $10
January 20	300 units @ $11		800 units
February 18		450 units	350 units
April 8	400 units @ $12		750 units
June 19		300 units	450 units
September 5	200 units @ $13		650 units
October 20		150 units	500 units
December 12	100 units @ $14		600 units

FIFO Costing with a Perpetual System

Exhibit 6-12 illustrates the FIFO method on a perpetual basis. The basic premise of FIFO applies whether a periodic or a perpetual system is used: the first units purchased are assumed to be the first units sold. With a perpetual system, however, this concept is applied *at the time of each sale.* For example, note in the exhibit which 450 units are assumed to be sold on February 18. The 450 units sold are taken from the beginning inventory of 500 units with a unit cost of $10. Thus, the inventory or balance after this sale as shown in the last three columns is 50 units at $10 and 300 units at $11, for a total of $3,800. The purchase on April 8 of 400 units at $12 is added to the running balance. On a FIFO basis, the sale of 300 units on June 19 comes from the remainder of the beginning inventory of 50 units and another 250 units from the first purchase at $11 on January 20. The balance after this sale is 50 units at $11 and 400 units at $12. You should follow through the last three transactions in the exhibit to make sure that you understand the application of FIFO on a perpetual basis. An important point to note about the ending inventory of $7,600 is that it is the same amount that we calculated for FIFO periodic earlier in the chapter:

| FIFO periodic (Exhibit 6-4) | $7,600 |
| FIFO perpetual (Exhibit 6-12) | $7,600 |

Exhibit 6-12 Perpetual System: FIFO Cost-Flow Assumption

	Purchases			Sales			Balance		
DATE	UNITS	UNIT COST	TOTAL COST	UNITS	UNIT COST	TOTAL COST	UNITS	UNIT COST	BALANCE
1/1							500	$10	$5,000
1/20	300	$11	$3,300				500	10	
							300	11	8,300
2/18				450	$10	$4,500	50	10	
							300	11	3,800
4/8	400	12	4,800				50	10	
							300	11	
							400	12	8,600
6/19				50	10	500	50	11	
				250	11	2,750	400	12	5,350
9/5	200	13	2,600				50	11	
							400	12	
							200	13	7,950
10/20				50	11	550	300	12	
				100	12	1,200	200	13	6,200
12/12	100	14	1,400				300	12	
							200	13	
							100	14	7,600

Whether the method is applied each time a sale is made or only at the end of the period, the earliest units in are the first units out, and the two systems will yield the same ending inventory under FIFO.

Moving Average with a Perpetual System

Moving average The name given to an average cost method when it is used with a perpetual inventory system.

When a weighted average cost assumption is applied with a perpetual system, it is sometimes called a **moving average.** As indicated in Exhibit 6-13, each time a purchase is made, a new weighted average cost must be computed, thus the name *moving average.* For example, the goods available for sale after the January 20 purchase consist of 500 units at $10 and 300 units at $11, which results in an average cost of $10.38. This is the unit cost applied to the 450 units sold on February 18. The 400 units purchased on April 8 require the computation of a new unit cost, as indicated in the second footnote to the exhibit. As you might have suspected, the ending inventory with an average cost flow differs, depending on whether a periodic or a perpetual system is used:

Weighted average periodic (Exhibit 6-4)	$6,840
Moving average perpetual (Exhibit 6-13)	$7,290

Exhibit 6-13 Perpetual System: Moving Average Cost-Flow Assumption

	Purchases			Sales			Balance		
DATE	UNITS	UNIT COST	TOTAL COST	UNITS	UNIT COST	TOTAL COST	UNITS	UNIT COST	BALANCE
1/1							500	$10.00	$5,000
1/20	300	$11	$3,300				800	10.38*	8,304
2/18				450	$10.38	$4,671	350	10.38	3,633
4/8	400	12	4,800				750	11.24†	8,430
6/19				300	11.24	3,372	450	11.24	5,058
9/5	200	13	2,600				650	11.78‡	7,657
10/20				150	11.78	1,767	500	11.78	5,890
12/12	100	14	1,400				600	12.15§	7,290

The moving average prices per unit are calculated as follows:

*($5,000 + $3,300) / 800 units = $10.38 (rounded to nearest cent)

†($3,633 + $4,800) / 750 units = $11.24

‡($5,058 + $2,600) / 650 units = $11.78

§($5,890 + $1,400) / 600 units = $12.15

Chapter Highlights

1. **LO 1** **Explain the differences between periodic and perpetual inventory systems (p. 244).**
   - Inventory is a current asset held for resale in the normal course of business.
   - Companies use periodic and perpetual systems to track the units of inventory sold.
   - Under a periodic inventory system:
     - Inventory account is updated only at the end of a period.
     - Purchases of inventory are recorded in the temporary account Purchases.
     - A physical inventory at period-end is relied on to allocate costs between ending inventory and cost of goods sold in the period.
   - Under a perpetual inventory system:
     - Inventory account is updated at the time of each purchase and sale.
     - The Cost of Goods Sold account is updated at the time of each sale.

2. **LO 2** **Apply the inventory costing method with a periodic system (p. 251).**
   - The purchase of identical units of a product at varying prices necessitates the use of a costing method to assign a dollar amount to ending inventory and cost of goods sold.

   As alternatives to the use of a specific identification method, which is impractical in many instances, as well as being subject to manipulation, accountants have devised cost flow assumptions.
   - The weighted average method assigns the same average unit cost to all units available for sale during the period. It is widely used because of its simplicity.
   - The FIFO method assigns the most recent costs to ending inventory. The older costs are assigned to cost of goods sold. A FIFO approach does tend to parallel the physical flow of products in many businesses, although the actual flow is not our primary concern in choosing a costing method.
   - LIFO assigns the most recent costs to cost of goods sold, and the older costs remain in inventory. The LIFO method is used in very limited circumstances. It is permitted in Canada for neither financial reporting nor tax purposes.

3. **LO 3** **Analyze the effects of the different costing methods (p. 256).**
   - In a period of rising prices, the FIFO method results in a lower cost of goods sold, higher income before tax, higher income taxes, and higher net income than the weighted average method.

4. **LO 4** **Discuss additional topics on inventory (p. 258).**
- An understatement of ending inventory will result in an overstatement of cost of goods sold and an understatement of net income of the current period; an overstatement of ending inventory will result in an understatement of cost of goods sold and an overstatement of net income. Errors in valuing inventory affect the cost of goods sold, and thus reported net income of both the current period and the following period.

- As used in the lower-of-cost-or-market rule, market can be replacement cost, net realizable value, or net realizable value less a normal profit margin. The purpose of valuing inventory at original cost or market, whichever is lower, is to recognize a loss due to obsolescence, spoilage, or other cause in the period the loss occurs, rather than in the period the units are sold. The rule can be applied to each item, to a group of items, or to the entire inventory.

- The gross profit method is used to estimate the cost of inventory lost through theft, fire, flooding, and other types of damage. The method is also useful to estimate the amount of inventory on hand for interim reports, such as quarterly financial statements. It relies on a trustworthy estimate of gross profit margin.

- Retailers use the retail inventory method to estimate the cost of inventory for interim financial statements and to convert the year-end inventory, through a physical count, from retail to cost.

5. **LO 5** **Explain the effects that inventory transactions have on the statement of cash flows (p. 267).**
- The payment of cash to suppliers of inventory represents a cash outflow from operating activities on the statement of cash flows. If a company uses the indirect method, however, adjustments are made to net income through the changes in the Inventory and Accounts Payable accounts.

6. **LO 6** **Apply the inventory costing method with a perpetual system (Appendix) (p. 269).**
- Ending inventory cost under FIFO will be the same whether the periodic system or the perpetual system is used. This is not the case when the weighted average approach is applied. The weighted average method with a perpetual system is really a moving average approach.

Ratio Review

How well a company manages its inventory is of great interest. The quicker inventory can be sold, the more efficient the inventory is managed. The Inventory Turnover ratio and Number of Days' Sales in Inventory are commonly used ratios to indicate how quickly a company can sell its inventory.

$$\text{Inventory Turnover Ratio} = \frac{\text{Cost of Goods Sold}}{\text{Average Inventory}}$$

$$\text{Number of Days' Sales in Inventory} = \frac{\text{Number of days in the Period}}{\text{Inventory Turnover Ratio}}$$

Accounts Highlighted

Account Title	Where it Appears	In What Section	Page
Purchase	Income Statement	Expense	246
Purchase returns and allowances	Income Statement	Contra Purchase	248
Purchase discounts	Income Statement	Contra Purchase	249
Transportation-in	Income Statement	Adjunct Purchase	249
Loss on decline in value of inventory	Income Statement	Expense	261

Key Terms Quiz

Read each of the following definitions and then write the number of the definition in the blank beside the appropriate term it defines. The quiz solutions appear at the end of the chapter.

_____ Merchandise Inventory
_____ Perpetual system
_____ Periodic system
_____ Transportation-in
_____ Purchases
_____ Purchase Returns and Allowances
_____ Purchase Discounts
_____ CIF destination point
_____ FOB shipping point
_____ Specific identification method

_____ Weighted average cost method
_____ FIFO method
_____ LIFO method
_____ Net realizable value
_____ Lower-of-cost-or-market (LCM) rule
_____ Gross profit method
_____ Retail inventory method
_____ Inventory turnover ratio
_____ Number of days' sales in inventory
_____ Moving average (Appendix)

1. An inventory costing method that relies on matching unit costs with the actual units sold.

2. The account used in a periodic inventory system to record acquisitions of merchandise.

3. A measure of the number of times inventory is sold during a period.

4. The selling price of a unit of inventory less any direct selling cost.

5. The adjunct account used to record freight costs paid by the buyer.

6. The system in which the Inventory account is increased at the time of each purchase of merchandise and decreased at the time of each sale.

7. The contra-purchases account used in a periodic inventory system when a refund is received from a supplier or a reduction is given in the balance owed to the supplier.

8. Terms that require the seller to pay for the cost of shipping the merchandise to the buyer.

9. Terms that require the buyer to pay the shipping costs.

10. The system in which the Inventory account is updated only at the end of the period.

Answers on p. 291.

11. The name given to an average cost method when it is used with a perpetual inventory system.

12. An inventory costing method that assigns the same unit cost to all units available for sale during the period.

13. The account that wholesalers and retailers use to report inventory held for sale.

14. A conservative inventory valuation approach that is an attempt to anticipate declines in the value of inventory before its actual sale.

15. An inventory costing method that assigns the most recent costs to ending inventory.

16. The contra-purchases account used to record deductions in purchase price for early payment to the supplier.

17. An inventory costing method that assigns the most recent costs to cost of goods sold.

18. A measure of how long it takes to sell inventory.

19. A technique used to establish an estimate of the cost of inventory stolen, destroyed, or otherwise damaged or of the amount of inventory on hand at an interim date.

20. A technique used by retailers to convert the retail value of inventory to a cost basis.

Alternate Terms

gross profit gross margin

gross profit margin gross profit percentage

Interim statements Quarterly or monthly statements

Market (value for inventory) Net realizable value

Retail price Selling price

Transportation-in Freight-in

Warmup Exercises and Solutions

Warmup Exercise 6-1 *Inventory Valuation* LO 2

Busby Corp. began the year with 75 units of inventory that it paid $2 each to acquire. During the year, it purchased an additional 100 units for $3 each. Busby sold 150 units during the year.

Required

1. Compute cost of goods sold and ending inventory, assuming Busby uses FIFO.
2. Compute cost of goods sold and ending inventory, assuming Busby uses weighted average costing method.

Key to the Solution Review the mechanics of the methods, beginning on page 253.

Warmup Exercise 6-2 *Lower of Cost or Market* LO 6

Glendive reports its inventory on a FIFO basis and has inventory with a cost of $78,000 on December 31. The net realizable value of the inventory on this date would be only $71,000.

Required

Prepare the necessary journal entry on Glendive's books on December 31.

Key to the Solution Recall the need to write down inventory when market is less than cost.

Warmup Exercise 6-3 *Inventory Turnover* LO 7

Sidney began the year with $130,000 in merchandise inventory and ended the year with $190,000. Sales and cost of goods sold for the year were $900,000 and $640,000, respectively.

Required

1. Compute Sidney's inventory turnover ratio.
2. Compute the number of days' sales in inventory.

Key to the Solution Review how these two statistics are computed on page 268.

Solutions to Warmup Exercises

Warmup Exercise 6-1

1. Cost of goods sold: $(75 \times \$2) + (75 \times \$3) = \$375$

   Ending inventory: $25 \times \$3 = \$75$

2. Weighted average unit cost = $(100 \times \$3 + 75 \times \$2) / (100 + 75) = \$2.57$

   Cost of goods sold: $150 \times \$2.57 = \$386$

   Ending inventory: $25 \times \$2.57 = \$64$

Warmup Exercise 6-2

Dec. 31 Loss on Decline in Value of Inventory	7,000	
Inventory		7,000
To record decline in value of inventory		

$$\textbf{Assets} \quad = \quad \textbf{Liabilities} \quad + \quad \textbf{Sharehoders' Equity}$$
$$\textbf{-7,000} \qquad\qquad\qquad\qquad\qquad \textbf{-7,000}$$

Warmup Exercise 6-3

1. $$\text{Inventory Turnover Ratio} = \frac{\text{Cost of Goods Sold}}{\text{Average Inventory}}$$

   $$= \frac{\$640,000}{(\$130,000 + \$190,000)/2}$$

   $$= \frac{\$640,000}{\$160,000} = 4 \text{ times}$$

2. $$\frac{\text{Number of Days'}}{\text{Sales in Inventory}} = \frac{\text{Number of Days in the Period}}{\text{Inventory Turnover Ratio}}$$

   $$= \frac{360}{4} = 90 \text{ days}$$

Review Problem and Solution

Stewart Distributing Company sells a single product for $2 per unit and uses a periodic inventory system. The following data are available for the year:

Date	Transaction	Number of Units	Unit Cost	Total
1/1	Beginning inventory	500	$1.00	$500.00
2/5	Purchase	350	1.10	385.00
4/12	Sale	(550)		
7/17	Sale	(200)		
9/23	Purchase	400	1.30	520.00
11/5	Sale	(300)		

Required

1. Compute cost of goods sold, assuming the use of the weighted average costing method.
2. Compute the dollar amount of cost of goods sold, assuming the FIFO costing method.
3. Compute gross profit under both weighted average and FIFO methods.

Solution to Review Problem

1. Cost of goods sold, weighted average cost method:
   Cost of goods available for sale

$500 + $385 + $520 =	$1,405	
Divided by:		
Units available for sale:		
500 + 350 + 400 =	÷ 1,250	units
Weighted average cost	$1.124	per unit
× Number of units sold:		
550 + 200 + 300 =	× 1,050	units
Cost of goods sold	$1,180	

2. Ending inventory, FIFO cost method:

Units available for sale	1,250
− Units sold	− 1,050
= Units in ending inventory	200
× Most recent purchase price of	× $ 1.30
= Ending inventory	$ 260
Cost of goods available for sale (see Requirement 1)	$1,405
Ending inventory	260
Cost of goods sold	$1,145

3.

	Weighted Average	FIFO
Sales revenue: 1,050 units × $2 each	$2,100	$2,100
Cost of goods sold	1,180	1,145
Gross Profit	$ 920	$ 955

Questions

1. What is the difference between a periodic inventory system and a perpetual inventory system?

2. What is the relationship between the valuation of inventory as an asset on the balance sheet and the measurement of income?

3. What is the justification for including freight costs incurred in acquiring incoming goods in the cost of the inventory rather than simply treating the cost as an expense of the period? What is the significance of this decision for accounting purposes?

4. What are the inventory characteristics that would allow a company to use the specific identification method? Give at least two examples of inventory for which the method is appropriate.

5. How can the specific identification method allow management to manipulate income?

6. What is the significance of the adjective *weighted* in the weighted average cost method? Use an example to illustrate your answer.

7. Which inventory method, FIFO or LIFO, more nearly approximates the physical flow of products in most businesses? Explain your answer.

8. York Inc. manufactures notebook computers and has experienced noticeable declines in the purchase price of many of the components it uses, including computer chips. Which inventory costing method should York use if it wants to maximize net income? Explain your answer.

9. The president of Ace Retail is commenting on the company's new controller: "The woman is brilliant! She has shown us how we can maximize our income and at the same time minimize the amount of taxes we have to pay the government. Because the cost to purchase our inventory constantly goes up, we will use FIFO to calculate cost of goods sold on the income statement to minimize the amount charged to cost of goods sold and thus maximize net income. For tax purposes, however, we will use LIFO because this will minimize taxable income and thus minimize the amount we have to pay in taxes." Should the president be enthralled with the new controller? Explain your answer.

10. In a periodic inventory system, what kind of account is Purchases? Is it an asset or an expense or neither?

11. Why are shipping terms, such as FOB shipping point or CIF destination point, important in deciding ownership of inventory at the end of the year?

12. Is it acceptable for a company to disclose, in its annual report, that it is switching from some other inventory costing method to FIFO *to increase earnings?*

13. Delevan Corp. uses a periodic inventory system and is counting its year-end inventory. Due to a lack of communication, two different teams count the same section of the warehouse. What effect will this error have on net income?

14. What is the rationale for valuing inventory at the lower of cost or market?

15. Patterson's controller makes the following suggestion: "I have a brilliant way to save us money. Because we are already using the gross profit method for our quarterly statements, we start using it to estimate the year-end inventory for the annual report and save the money normally spent to have the inventory counted on December 31." What do you think of his suggestion?

16. Why does a company save time and money by using the retail inventory method at the end of the year?

17. Ralston Corp.'s cost of sales has remained steady over the past two years. During this same time period, however, its inventory has increased considerably. What does this information tell you about the company's inventory turnover? Explain your answer.

18. In simple terms, how do the inventory costing methods, such as FIFO and LIFO, and the inventory systems, such as periodic and perpetual, differ? (Appendix)

19. Why is the weighted average cost method called a *moving average* when a company uses a perpetual inventory system? (Appendix)

Exercises

Exercise 6-1 *Perpetual and Periodic Inventory Systems* LO 1

Following is a partial list of account balances for two different merchandising companies. The amounts in the accounts represent the balances at the end of the year *before* any adjusting or closing entries are made.

Company A		Company B	
Sales revenue	$50,000	Sales revenue	$85,000
Sales discounts	3,000	Sales discounts	2,000
Merchandise inventory	12,000	Merchandise inventory	9,000
Cost of goods sold	38,000	Purchases	41,000
		Purchase discounts	4,000
		Purchase returns and	
		allowances	1,000

Required

1. Identify which inventory system, perpetual or periodic, each of the two companies uses. Explain how you know which system each uses by looking at the types of accounts on their books.

2. How much inventory does Company A have on hand at the end of the year? What is its cost of goods sold for the year?

3. Explain why you cannot determine Company B's cost of goods sold for the year from the information available.

Exercise 6-2 *Perpetual and Periodic Inventory Systems* LO 1

From the following list, identify whether the merchandisers described would most likely use a perpetual or periodic inventory system.

_____ Appliance store

_____ Car dealership

_____ Drugstore

_____ Furniture store

_____ Grocery store

_____ Hardware store

_____ Jewellery store

How might changes in technology affect the ability of merchandisers to use perpetual inventory systems?

Exercise 6-3 *Inventoriable Costs* **LO 2**

During the first month of operations, Basinview Inc. incurred the following costs in ordering and receiving merchandise for resale. No inventory has been sold.

> List price, $100, 200 units purchased
> Volume discount, 10% off list price
> Paid freight costs, $56
> Insurance cost while goods were in transit, $32
> Long-distance phone charge to place orders, $4.35
> Purchasing department salary, $1,000
> Supplies used to label goods at retail price, $9.75
> Interest paid to supplier, $46

Required

What amount do you recommend the company record as merchandise inventory on its balance sheet? Explain your answer. For any items not to be included in inventory, indicate their appropriate treatment in the financial statements.

Exercise 6-4 *Inventory and Income Manipulation* **LO 2**

The president of Salter Inc. is concerned that the net income at year-end will not reach the expected figure. When the sales manager receives a large order on the last day of the fiscal year, the president tells the accountant to record the sale but to ignore any inventory adjustment because the physical inventory has already been taken. How will this affect the current year's net income? next year's income? What would you do if you were the accountant? Assume that Salter uses a periodic inventory system.

Exercise 6-5 *Inventory Costing Methods* **LO 2**

York Inc. reported the following information for the month of February:

Inventory, February 1	65 units @ $20
Purchases:	
February 7	50 units @ $22
February 18	60 units @ $23
February 27	45 units @ $24

During February, York sold 140 units. The company uses a periodic inventory system.

Required

What is the value of ending inventory and cost of goods sold for February under the following assumptions?

1. Of the 140 units sold, 55 cost $20, 35 cost $22, 45 cost $23, and 5 cost $24.
2. FIFO
3. Weighted average

Exercise 6-6 *Evaluation of Inventory Costing Methods* **LO 3**

Write the letter of the method that is most applicable to each statement.

a. Specific identification
b. Average cost
c. First-in, first-out (FIFO)
d. Last-in, first-out (LIFO)

_____ 1. Results in highest income taxes during periods of inflation.
_____ 2. Is not permitted for financial reporting and tax purposes in Canada.
_____ 3. Results in highest income during periods of inflation.
_____ 4. Results in highest ending inventory during periods of inflation.
_____ 5. Smooths out costs during periods of inflation.
_____ 6. Is not practical for most businesses.
_____ 7. Puts more weight on the cost of the larger number of units purchased.
_____ 8. Is an assumption that most closely reflects the physical flow of goods for most businesses.

Exercise 6-7 *Inventory Errors* LO 4

For each of the following independent situations, fill in the blanks to indicate the effect of the error on each of the various financial statement items. Indicate an understatement (U), an overstatement (O), or no effect (NE). Assume that each of the companies uses a periodic inventory system.

	Balance Sheet		Income Statement	
Error	Inventory	Retained Earnings	Cost of Goods Sold	Net Income
1. Goods in transit at year-end are not included in the physical count: they were shipped FOB shipping point.	————	————	————	————
2. One section of a warehouse is counted twice during the year-end count of inventory.	————	————	————	————
3. During the count at year-end, the inventory sheets for one of the stores of a discount retailer are lost.	————	————	————	————

Exercise 6-8 *Transfer of Title to Inventory* LO 2

For each of the following transactions, indicate which company should include the inventory on its December 31, 2008, balance sheet:

1. AD Supplies Inc. shipped merchandise to BC Sales on December 28, 2008, terms CIF destination. The merchandise arrives at BC's on January 4, 2009.

2. Melrose Inc. shipped merchandise to Fairview on December 25, 2008, CIF destination. Fairview received the merchandise on December 31, 2008.

3. St. John Inc. shipped merchandise to Stone Company on December 27, 2008, FOB shipping point. Stone Company received the merchandise on January 3, 2009.

4. Fred Company shipped merchandise to Barney Inc. on December 24, 2008, FOB shipping point. The merchandise arrived at Barney's on December 29, 2008.

Exercise 6-9 *Gross Profit Method* LO 4

On February 12, a flood destroys the entire inventory of Pentco Corp. An estimate of the amount of inventory lost is needed for insurance purposes. The following information is available:

Inventory on January 1	$ 30,800
Net sales from January 1 to February 12	210,600
Purchases from January 1 to February 12	168,500

Pentco Corp. estimates its gross profit ratio as 25% of net sales. The insurance company has agreed to pay Pentco Corp. $20,000 as a settlement for the inventory destroyed.

Required

Prepare the journal entry on Pentco Corp.'s books to recognize the inventory lost and the insurance reimbursement.

Exercise 6-10 *Impact of Transactions Involving Inventories on Statement of Cash Flows* LO 5

From the following list, identify whether the change in the account balance during the year would be added to (A) or deducted from (D) net income when the indirect method is used to determine cash flows from operating activities.

_____ Increase in Accounts Payable

_____ Decrease in Accounts Payable

_____ Increase in Inventories

_____ Decrease in Inventories

Exercise 6-11 *Effects of Transactions Involving Inventories on the Statement of Cash Flows—Direct Method* **LO 5**

Bedford Inc.'s comparative balance sheets included inventory of $180,400 at December 31, 2007, and $241,200 at December 31, 2008. Bedford's comparative balance sheets also included accounts payable of $85,400 at December 31, 2007, and $78,000 at December 31, 2008. Bedford's accounts payable balances are composed solely of amounts due to suppliers for purchases of inventory on account. Cost of goods sold, as reported by Bedford on its 2008 income statement, amounted to $1,200,000.

Required

What is the amount of cash payments for inventory that Bedford will report in the Operating Activities category of its 2008 statement of cash flows, assuming that the direct method is used?

Exercise 6-12 *Effects of Transactions Involving Inventories on the Statement of Cash Flows—Indirect Method* **LO 5**

Refer to all of the facts in Exercise 6-11.

Required

Assume instead that Bedford uses the indirect method to prepare its statement of cash flows. Indicate how each item will be reflected as an adjustment to net income in the Operating Activities category of the statement of cash flows.

Exercise 6-13 *Periodic and Perpetual Journal Entries* **LO 1**

Record the journal entries to reflect the following transactions, assuming (a) a periodic system and (b) a perpetual system. Arrange your entries in parallel columns for comparison purposes.

October   1:   Purchased 100 units on account for $7 each.
October   3:   Returned 5 defective units for full credit.
October   8:   Paid $16 freight charges on the October 1 shipment.
October 20:   Sold 75 units on account for $10 each.

Multi-Concept Exercises

Exercise 6-14 *Inventory Costing Methods—Periodic System* **LO 2, 3**

The following information is available concerning the inventory of Ford Inc.:

	Units	Unit Cost
Beginning inventory	400	$10
Purchases:		
March 5	600	11
June 12	800	12
August 23	500	13
October 2	300	15

During the year, Ford sold 2,000 units. It uses a periodic inventory system.

Required

1. Calculate ending inventory and cost of goods sold for each of the following two methods:
   a. Weighted average
   b. FIFO
2. Assume an estimated tax rate of 30%. How much more or less (indicate which) will Ford pay in taxes by using FIFO instead of weighted average? Explain your answer.

Exercise 6-15 *Lower-of-Cost-or-Market Rule* **LO 2, 4**

Medals Etc. carries an inventory of trophies and medals for local sports teams and school sports clubs. The selling price of trophies have dropped in the past year. The company has on hand considerable

(continued)

inventory that was purchased at the higher prices. The president is not pleased with the prospect that the company won't be able to recover the cost of these trophies. "Not much can be done now, but at least I don't have to worry about the loss until they are sold," he grumbled to the new staff accountant. "Not really," replied the accountant. "We have to write down the inventory to the net realizable value this year, and then next year we won't have to report any loss when the trophies are sold."

Required

Explain why the inventory can be carried at an amount less than its cost. Which accounts will be affected by the write-down? What will be the effect on income in the current year and future years?

Exercise 6-16 *Inventory Costing Methods—Perpetual System (Appendix)* LO 2, 6

The following information is available concerning Waterloo Inc.:

	Units	Unit Cost
Beginning inventory	400	$10
Purchases:		
March 5	600	11
June 12	800	12
August 23	500	13
October 2	300	15

Waterloo, which uses a perpetual system, sold 2,000 units for $22 each during the year. Sales occurred on the following dates:

	Units
February 12	300
April 30	400
July 7	400
September 6	600
December 3	300

Required

1. Calculate ending inventory and cost of goods sold for each of the following two methods:

   a. Moving average

   b. FIFO

2. For each of the two methods, compare the results with those for Ford in Exercise 6-14. Which of the methods gives a different answer depending on whether a company uses a periodic or a perpetual inventory system?

Problems

Problem 6-1 *Recording Purchases and Sales* LO 1

Leisure Time Furniture Store entered into the following transactions in the month of April:

April 3: Purchased 50 lounge chairs at $150 each with terms 2/10, net 45. The chairs were shipped CIF destination.

April 7: Sold 6 chairs for $320 each, terms 2/10, net 30.

April 8: Purchased 20 patio umbrella tables for $120 each, FOB shipping point, terms 1/10, net 30.

April 9: Due to defects, returned 5 lounge chairs purchased on April 3. Received a credit memorandum, indicating that amount due has been reduced.

April 10: Paid the trucking firm $360 for delivery of the tables purchased on April 8.

April 13: Paid for the chairs purchased on April 3.

April 17: Received payment for the chairs sold on April 7.

April 20: Paid for the tables purchased on April 8.

Required

1. Prepare all journal entries needed to record these transactions for the furniture company. Leisure Time uses the gross method of recording purchase and sales discounts. The company uses a periodic inventory system.

2. Do you think Leisure Time should change to a perpetual inventory system, given the nature of its business? Why or why not? What advantages would a company have using the perpetual system instead of the periodic system?

Problem 6-2 *Inventory System*

Memory of Banff, a souvenir shop, had $76,250 of merchandise on hand on January 1, 2008. During January, Memory of Banff purchased $22,500 of merchandise on credit. Memory of Banff recorded $31,500 of revenue, all cash, for January. A month-end inventory count revealed that merchandise on hand on January 31, 2008 totaled $68,900.

Required

1. Assume Memory of Banff uses a periodic inventory system.

   a. Prepare summary journal entries to record the purchases and sales.

   b. Determine Memory of Banff's inventory balance on January 31 and cost of goods sold for January.

   c. Prepare necessary month-end adjusting entries for January.

2. Assume Memory of Banff uses a perpetual inventory system and the cost of goods sold in January amounted to $27,210.

   a. Prepare summary journal entries to record the purchase and sales. Determine Memory of Banff's inventory balance on January 31 and cost of goods sold for January.

   b. Prepare necessary month-end adjusting entries for January.

3. Which inventory system would you recommend for Memory of Banff and why?

Problem 6-3 *Inventory Error* **LO 4**

The following highly condensed income statements and balance sheets are available for Enterprise Stores for a two-year period (all amounts are stated in thousands):

Income Statements	2008	2007
Revenues	$20,000	$15,000
Cost of goods sold	13,000	10,000
Gross profit	7,000	5,000
Operating expenses	3,000	2,000
Income before tax	$ 4,000	$ 3,000

Balance Sheets	December 31, 2008	December 31, 2007
Cash	$ 1,700	$ 1,500
Inventory	4,200	3,500
Other current assets	2,500	2,000
Long-term assets	15,000	14,000
Total assets	$23,400	$21,000
Liabilities	$ 8,500	$ 7,000
Capital stock	5,000	5,000
Retained earnings	9,900	9,000
Total liabilities and shareholders' equity	$23,400	$21,000

Before releasing the 2008 annual report, Enterprise's controller learns that the inventory of one of the stores (amounting to $500,000) was inadvertently omitted from the count on December 31, 2007. The inventory of the store was counted correctly on December 31, 2008.

(continued)

Required

1. Prepare revised income statements and balance sheets for Enterprise Stores for each of the two years. Ignore the effect of income taxes.

2. If Enterprise did not prepare revised statements before releasing the 2008 annual report, what would be the amount of overstatement or understatement of income before tax for the two-year period? What would be the overstatement or understatement of retained earnings at December 31, 2008, if revised statements were not prepared?

3. Given your answers in requirement 2, does it matter if Enterprise bothers to restate the financial statements of the two years to rectify the error? Explain your answer.

Problem 6-4 *Gross Profit Method of Estimating Inventory Losses* LO 4

On August 1, an office supply store was destroyed by an explosion in its basement. A small amount of inventory valued at $9,600 was saved. An estimate of the amount of inventory lost is needed for insurance purposes. The following information is available:

Inventory, January 1	$ 3,200
Purchases, January–July	164,000
Sales, January–July	113,500

The normal gross profit ratio is 40%. The insurance company will pay the store $65,000.

Required

1. Using the gross profit method, estimate the amount of inventory lost in the explosion.

2. Prepare the journal entry to record the inventory loss and the insurance reimbursement.

Problem 6-5 *Inventory Turnover of Two Companies in Same Industry* LO4

The following information is from the financial statements of Ingo Inc.:

	(in thousands)
Cost of goods sold for the year ended December 31:	
2008	$4,128
2007	5,817
Inventory, December 31:	
2008	1,110
2007	1,330
Net sales for the year ended December 31:	
2008	5,363
2007	7,983

The following information is from the financial statements of Airo Inc.:

	(in thousands)
Cost of goods sold for the year ended December 31:	
2008	$5,241
2007	7,541
Inventory, December 31:	
2008	965
2007	915
Net sales for the year ended December 31:	
2008	6,079
2007	9,600

Required

1. Calculate the gross margin (gross profit) ratios for Ingo and Airo for 2008 and 2007.

2. Calculate the inventory turnover ratios for both companies for 2008.

3. Which company appears to be performing better? What other information should you consider to determine how these companies are performing in this regard?

Problem 6-6 *Effects of Changes in Inventory and Accounts Payable Balances on Statement of Cash Flows* LO 5

Tudor Antiques reported a net loss of $66,400 for the year ended December 31, 2008. The following items were included on Tudor's balance sheets at December 31, 2008 and 2007:

	12/31/08	12/31/07
Cash	$130,600	$ 92,200
Trade accounts payable	247,800	187,400
Inventories	385,200	429,600

Tudor uses the indirect method to prepare its statement of cash flows. Tudor does not have any other current assets or current liabilities and did not enter into any investing or financing activities during 2008.

Required

1. Prepare Tudor's 2008 statement of cash flows.

2. Draft a brief memo to the president to explain why cash increased during such an unprofitable year.

Multi-Concept Problems

Problem 6-7 *Comparison of Inventory Costing Methods—Periodic System* **LO 2, 3**

Victoria Company's inventory records show 600 units on hand on October 1 with a unit cost of $5 each. The following transactions occurred during the month of October:

Date		Unit Purchases	Unit Sales
October	4		500 @ $10.00
	8	800 @ $5.40	
	9		700 @ $10.00
	18	700 @ $5.76	
	20		800 @ $11.00
	29	800 @ $5.90	

All expenses other than cost of goods sold amount to $3,000 for the month. The company uses an estimated tax rate of 30% to accrue monthly income tax.

Required

1. Prepare a chart comparing cost of goods sold and ending inventory using the periodic system and the following costing methods:

	Cost of Goods Sold	Ending Inventory	Total
Weighted average			
FIFO			

2. What does the Total column represent?
3. Prepare income statements for each of the two methods.

Problem 6-8 *Comparison of Inventory Costing Methods—Perpetual System (Appendix)* **LO 3, 6**

Repeat Problem 6-7 using the perpetual system.

Problem 6-9 *Inventory Costing Methods—Periodic System* **LO 2, 3**

Oxford Inc.'s inventory records for the month of November reveal the following:

Inventory, November 1	100 units @ $18.00
November 4, purchase	250 units @ $18.50
November 7, sale	300 units @ $42.00
November 13, purchase	220 units @ $18.90
November 18, purchase	150 units @ $19.00
November 22, sale	380 units @ $42.50
November 24, purchase	200 units @ $19.20
November 28, sale	110 units @ $43.00

Selling and administrative expenses for the month were $10,800. Depreciation expense was $4,000. Oxford uses an estimated tax rate of 40% to accrue monthly income tax.

(continued)

Required

1. Calculate the cost of goods sold and ending inventory under each of the following three methods (assume a periodic inventory system): (a) FIFO and (b) weighted average.

2. Calculate the gross margin and net income under each costing assumption.

Problem 6-10 *Inventory Costing Methods—Periodic System* LO 2, 3

Following is an inventory acquisition schedule for Beaver Corp. for 2008:

	Units	Unit Cost
Beginning inventory	2,000	$10
Purchases:		
February 4	3,000	9
April 12	4,000	8
September 10	2,000	7
December 5	1,000	6

During the year, Beaver sold 10,500 units at $12 each. All expenses except cost of goods sold amounted to $20,000. Beaver Corp. uses an estimated tax rate of 40% to accrue annual income tax.

Required

1. Compute cost of goods sold and ending inventory under each of the following two methods (assume a periodic inventory system): (a) weighted average, and (b) FIFO.

2. Prepare income statements under each of the two methods.

3. Which method do you recommend so that Beaver has the highest reported earnings? Explain your answer.

4. Beaver anticipates that unit costs for inventory will increase throughout 2009. Will it be able to switch from the method you recommend it use in 2008 to another method to mitigate the decline in reported earnings? Explain your answer.

Problem 6-11 *Interpreting Alimentation Couche-Tard's Inventory Accounting Policy* LO 1, 2, 3

http://www.couche-tard.com

The 2007 annual report of **Alimentation Couche-Tard** includes the following in the note that summarizes its accounting policies:

> **Inventories** Inventories are valued at the lesser of cost and the net realizable value. The cost of merchandise–distribution centres is determined according to the first-in first-out method, the cost of merchandise–retail is valued based on the retail price less a normal margin, and the cost of motor fuel inventory is determined according to the average cost method.

Required

1. What *types* of inventory cost does Alimentation Couche-Tard carry?

2. Why would the company choose three different methods to value its inventory?

3. Alimentation Couche-Tard uses first-in, first-out for its merchandise-distribution centres. Does this mean that Alimentation Couche-Tard sells its oldest merchandise first? Explain your answer.

4. Does Alimentation Couche-Tard report merchandise retail inventories on its balance sheet at their retail value? Explain your answer.

Alternate Problems

Problem 6-1A *Recording Purchases and Sales* LO 1

Baby Room entered into the following transactions in the month of April:

April 3: Purchased 50 change tables at $120 each with terms 2/10, net 45. The change tables were shipped CIF destination.

April 7: Sold 6 change tables for $256 each, terms 2/10, net 30.

April 8: Purchased 20 rocking chairs for $96 each, FOB shipping point, terms 1/10, net 30.

April 9: Due to defects, returned 5 change tables purchased on April 3. Received a credit memorandum.

April 10: Paid the trucking firm $288 for delivery of the rocking chairs purchased on April 8.

April 13: Paid for the change tables purchased on April 3.

April 17: Received payment for the change tables sold on April 7.

April 20: Paid for the rocking chairs purchased on April 8.

Required

1. Prepare all journal entries needed to record these transactions for the children's furniture store. Baby Room uses the gross method of recording purchase and sales discounts. The company uses a periodic inventory system.

2. Do you think Baby Room should change to a perpetual inventory system, given the nature of its business? Why or why not? What advantages would a company have using the perpetual system instead of the periodic system?

Problem 6-2A *Inventory System* LO 2

Reading Books, a bookstore specializing in audio books, had $126,250 of books on hand on January 1, 2008. During January, Reading Books purchased $55,000 of books on credit. Reading Books recorded $98,150 of revenue, all cash, for January. A month-end inventory count revealed that books on hand on January 31, 2008 totalled $119,990.

Required

1. Assume Reading Books uses a periodic inventory system.

   a. Prepare summary journal entries to record the purchase and sales.

   b. Determine Reading Books' inventory balance on January 31 and cost of goods sold in January.

   c. Prepare necessary month-end adjusting entries for January.

2. Assume Reading Books uses a perpetual inventory system and the cost of goods sold of January amounted to $59,970.

   a. Prepare summary journal entries to record the purchase and sales.

   b. Determine Reading Books' inventory balance on January 31 and cost of goods sold for January.

   c. Prepare necessary month-end adjusting entries for January.

3. Which inventory system would you recommend for Reading Books and why?

Problem 6-3A *Inventory Error* LO 4

The following condensed income statements and balance sheets are available for Prairie Inc. for a two-year period (all amounts are stated in thousands of dollars):

Income Statements	2008	2007
Revenues	$35,982	$26,890
Cost of goods sold	12,594	9,912
Gross profit	23,388	16,978
Operating expenses	13,488	10,578
Income before tax	$ 9,900	$ 6,400

Balance Sheets	December 31, 2008	December 31, 2007
Cash	$ 9,400	$ 4,100
Inventory	4,500	5,400
Other current assets	1,600	1,250
Long-term assets, net	24,500	24,600
Total assets	$40,000	$35,350
Current liabilities	$ 9,380	$10,600
Capital stock	18,000	18,000
Retained earnings	12,620	6,750
Total liabilities and shareholders' equity	$40,000	$35,350

Before releasing the 2008 annual report, Prairie's controller learns that the inventory of one of the stores (amounting to $750,000) was counted twice in the December 31, 2007, inventory. The inventory was counted correctly on December 31, 2008.

(continued)

Required

1. Prepare revised income statements and balance sheets for Prairie for each of the two years. Ignore income taxes.

2. Compute the current ratio at December 31, 2007, before the statements are revised, and then compute the current ratio at the same date after the statements are revised. If Prairie applied for a loan in early 2008 and the lender required a current ratio of at least 1-to-1, would the error have affected the loan? Explain your answer.

3. If Prairie did not prepare revised statements before releasing the 2008 annual report, what would be the amount of overstatement or understatement of net income for the two-year period? What would be the overstatement or understatement of retained earnings at December 31, 2008, if revised statements were not prepared?

4. Given your answers to requirements 2 and 3, does it matter if Prairie bothers to restate the financial statements of the two years to correct the error? Explain your answer.

Problem 6-4A *Gross Profit Method of Estimating Inventory Losses* LO 4

On July 1, a fire destroyed a lumber company. A small amount of inventory valued at $4,500 was saved. An estimate of the amount of inventory lost is needed for insurance purposes. The following information is available:

Inventory, January 1	$ 28,400
Purchases, January–June	154,000
Sales, January–June	187,000

The normal gross profit ratio is 70%. The insurance company will pay the supply company $100,000.

Required

1. Using the gross profit method, estimate the amount of inventory lost in the fire.

2. Prepare the journal entry to record the inventory loss and the insurance reimbursement.

Problem 6-5A *Inventory Turnover of Two Companies in Same Industry* LO 4

The following information is from the financial statements of East Coast Department Store:

	(in thousands)
Cost of goods sold for the year ended December 31:	
2008	$340,000
2007	309,000
Inventory, December 31:	
2008	45,000
2007	43,000

The following information is from the financial statements of West Coast Department Store:

	(in thousands)
Cost of goods sold for the year ended December 31:	
2008	$59,000
2007	60,000
Inventory, December 31:	
2008	11,000
2007	13,000

Required

1. Calculate the inventory turnover ratios for East Coast Department Store and West Coast Department Store for the year ended December 31, 2008.

2. Which company appears to be performing better? What other information should you consider to determine how these companies are performing in this regard?

Problem 6-6A *Effects of Changes in Inventory and Accounts Payable Balances on Statement of Cash Flows* **LO 5**

Carpet City reported net income of $39,250 for the year ended December 31, 2008. The following items were included on Carpet City's balance sheet at December 31, 2008 and 2007:

	12/31/08	12/31/07
Cash	$ 7,000	$13,150
Trade accounts payable	11,950	46,850
Inventories	52,750	42,450

Carpet City uses the indirect method to prepare its statement of cash flows. Carpet City does not have any other current assets or current liabilities and did not enter into any investing or financing activities during 2008.

Required

1. Prepare Carpet City's statement of cash flows.
2. Draft a brief memo to the president to explain why cash decreased during a profitable year.

Alternate Multi-Concept Problems

Problem 6-7A *Comparison of Inventory Costing Methods—Periodic System* **LO 2, 3**

Star Inc.'s inventory records show 600 units on hand on November 1 with a unit cost of $4 each. The following transactions occurred during the month of November:

Date		Unit Purchases	Unit Sales
November	4		400 @ $9.00
	8	1,000 @ $4.50	
	9		1,000 @ $9.00
	18	1,400 @ $4.75	
	20		800 @ $9.50
	29	1,200 @ $5.00	

All expenses other than cost of goods sold amount to $4,000 for the month. Star Inc. uses a 40% tax rate to accrue its monthy income tax expense.

Required

1. Prepare a chart comparing cost of goods sold and ending inventory using the periodic system and the following costing methods:

	Cost of Goods Sold	Ending Inventory	Total
Weighted average			
FIFO			

2. What does the Total column represent?
3. Prepare income statements for each of the two methods.

Problem 6-8A *Comparison of Inventory Costing Methods—Perpetual System* **LO 3, 6**

Repeat Problem 6-7A, using the perpetual system.

Problem 6-9A *Inventory Costing Methods—Periodic System* **LO 2, 3**

Story Company's inventory records for the month of November reveal the following:

Inventory, November 1	300 units @ $27.00
November 4, purchase	375 units @ $26.50
November 7, sale	450 units @ $63.00
November 13, purchase	330 units @ $26.00
November 18, purchase	225 units @ $25.40
November 22, sale	570 units @ $63.75
November 24, purchase	300 units @ $25.00
November 28, sale	165 units @ $64.50

Selling and administrative expenses for the month were $16,200. Depreciation expense was $6,000.

Required

1. Calculate the cost of goods sold and ending inventory under each of the following two methods (assume a periodic inventory system): (a) FIFO and (b) weighted average.

2. Calculate the gross margin and net income under each costing assumption. Story Company uses a 30% tax rate to record its monthly tax expense.

Problem 6-10A *Inventory Costing Methods—Periodic System* **LO 2, 3**

Following is an inventory acquisition schedule for First Inc. for 2008:

	Units	Unit Cost
Beginning inventory	4,000	$20
Purchases:		
February 4	2,000	18
April 12	3,000	16
September 10	1,000	14
December 5	2,500	12

During the year, First Inc. sold 11,000 units at $30 each. All expenses except cost of goods sold amounted to $60,000.

Required

1. Compute cost of goods sold and ending inventory under each of the following two methods (assume a periodic inventory system): (a) weighted average and (b) FIFO.

2. Prepare income statements under each of the two methods (assume a 30% tax rate).

3. Which method do you recommend so that First Inc. will have the higher reported earnings? Explain your answer.

4. First Inc. anticipates that unit costs for inventory will increase throughout 2009. Will it be able to switch from the method you recommend it use in 2008 to another method to mitigate the decline in reported earnings? Explain your answer.

Problem 6-11A *Interpreting Shermag Inc.'s Financial Statements* **LO 2, 3**

http://www.shermag.com

The annual report of **Shermag Inc.** includes the following note:

> **Inventory valuation** Finished goods and goods in process are valued at the lower of cost and net realizable value. Cost is determined by the average cost method.
>   Raw materials and supplies are valued at the lower of cost and replacement cost. Cost is determined by the first-in, first-out method.

Shermag. Shermag Annual Report 2007. Pg. 15. Found at: www.shermag.com.

Required

1. What *types* of inventory costs does Shermag have?

2. Why did the company choose two different methods to value its inventory?

3. Shermag uses the first-in, first-out method for raw materials. Does this mean that it always uses its oldest raw materials first?

Cases

Reading and Interpreting Financial Statements

Case 6-1 *Pricing Decision* **LO 1**

Caroline's Candy Corner sells gourmet chocolates. The company buys chocolates, in bulk, for $10.00 per kilogram plus 5% customs duty. Credit terms are 2/10, net 25, and the company always pays promptly in order to take advantage of the discount. The chocolates are shipped to Caroline FOB shipping point. Shipping costs are $0.10 per kilogram. When the chocolates arrive at the shop, Caroline's Candy repackages them into one-kilogram boxes labelled with the store name. Boxes cost $1.40 each. The company pays its employees an hourly wage of $10.50 plus a commission of $0.20 per kilogram.

Required

1. What is the cost per one-kilogram box of chocolates?

2. What price must Caroline's Candy charge in order to have a 40% gross margin?

3. Do you believe this is a sufficient margin for this kind of business? What other costs might the company still incur?

Making Financial Decisions

Case 6-2 *Inventory Costing Methods* LO 2, 3

You are the controller for Kanata Company. The following information has been accumulated during the first year of operations:

Purchases	
January	1,000 units @ $8
March	1,200 units @ 8
October	1,500 units @ 9

During the year, Kanata sold 3,000 units at $15 each. The president doesn't understand how to report inventory in the financial statements because no record of the cost of the units sold was kept as each sale was made.

Required

1. What inventory *system* must Kanata use?

2. Determine the number of units on hand at the end of the year.

3. Explain cost flow assumptions to the president and the method you recommend. Prepare income statements to justify your position, comparing your recommended method with at least one other method.

Case 6-3 *Inventory Errors* LO 4

You are the controller of a rapidly growing mass merchandiser. The company uses a periodic inventory system. As the company has grown and accounting systems have developed, errors have occurred in both the physical count of inventory and the valuation of inventory on the balance sheet. You have been able to identify the following errors as of December 2008:

■ In 2006, one section of the warehouse was counted twice. The error resulted in inventory being overstated on the December 31, 2006, balance sheet by approximately $45,600.

■ In 2007, the replacement cost of some inventory was less than the FIFO value used on the balance sheet. The inventory would have been $6,000 less on the balance sheet dated December 31, 2007.

■ In 2008, the company used the gross profit method to estimate inventory for its quarterly financial statements. At the end of the second quarter, the controller made a math error and understated the inventory by $20,000 on the quarterly report. The error was not discovered until the end of the year.

Required

What, if anything, should you do to correct each of these errors? Explain your answers.

Accounting and Ethics: What Would You Do?

Case 6-4 *Write-Down of Obsolete Inventory* LO 4

As a newly hired staff accountant, you are assigned the responsibility of physically counting inventory at the end of the year. The inventory count proceeds in a timely fashion. The inventory is outdated, however. You suggest that the inventory could not be sold for the cost at which it is carried and that the inventory should be written down to a much lower level. The controller replies that experience has taught her how the market changes and she knows that the units in the warehouse will be more marketable again. The company plans to keep the goods until they are back in style.

(continued)

Required

1. What effect will writing off the inventory have on the current year's income?
2. What effect does not writing off the inventory have on the year-end balance sheet?
3. What factors should you consider in deciding whether to persist in your argument that the inventory should be written down?

Case 6-5 *Selection of an Inventory Method* **LO 3**

As controller of a widely held public company, you are concerned with making the best decisions for the shareholders. At the end of its first year of operations, you are faced with the choice of method to value inventory. Specific identification is out of the question because the company sells a large quantity of diversified products. You are trying to decide among FIFO, LIFO, and weighted average. Inventory costs have fallen 33% over the year. The chief executive officer has instructed you to do whatever it takes in all areas to report the highest income possible.

Required

1. Which method will satisfy the CEO?
2. Which method do you believe is in the best interest of the shareholders? Explain your answer.
3. Write a brief memo to the CEO to convince him that reporting the highest income is not always the best approach for the shareholders.

Internet Research Case

INTERNET

http://www.couche-tard.com

Case 6-6 *Alimentation Couche-Tard*

Alimentation Couche-Tard Inc. is the leading convenience store operator in Canada. Read the chapter opening text, research the company, and review the financial information available on its website. Then answer the following questions:

1. What is the inventory amount shown for the most current year?
2. What is the inventory turnover for its motor fuel segment? For the entire company as a whole? Is this information significant for evaluating the segment against competition? Is it significant for evaluating the company as a whole? Why or why not?
3. What inventory system would you expect Alimentation Couche-Tard to use, perpetual or periodic? What makes you think so?
4. How could Alimentation Couche-Tard reduce its costs for carrying inventory?

13	Merchandise Inventory	12	Weighted average cost method
6	Perpetual system	15	FIFO method
10	Periodic system	17	LIFO method
5	Transportation-in	4	Net realizable value
2	Purchases	14	Lower-of-cost-or-market (LCM) rule
7	Purchase Returns and Allowances	19	Gross profit method
16	Purchase Discounts	20	Retail inventory method
8	CIF destination point	3	Inventory turnover ratio
9	FOB shipping point	18	Number of days' sales in inventory
1	Specific identification method	11	Moving average (Appendix)

Touring the Balance Sheet

A Word to Readers about Part IV

In Part III you learned how revenues and expenses in an income statement are recognized and measured and how the format of an income statement enhances its usefulness. Part IV explains how to measure and report assets, liabilities, and equity—the items provided by a balance sheet. The statement of retained earnings is also included in this part, through a discussion of shareholders' equity.

CHAPTER 7

Liquid Assets and Internal Control

LEARNING OBJECTIVES

After studying this chapter, you should be able to:

LO 1 Identify the various forms of cash reported on a balance sheet, and describe the various techniques that companies use to control cash.

LO 2 Explain how to account for accounts receivable, including bad debts.

LO 3 Explain various techniques that companies use to accelerate the inflow of cash from sales.

LO 4 Explain the effects of transactions involving liquid assets on the statement of cash flows.

LO 5 Explain the principles of internal control.

LO 6 Explain the accounting for various types of investments that companies make. (Appendix)

© OLEKSIY MAKSYMENKO/ALAMY

STUDY LINKS

A Look at Previous Chapters

Chapters 5 and 6 focused on the content and the format of the income statement, i.e., how revenues and expenses are measured and presented in the income statement.

A Look at This Chapter

In this chapter we will discuss accounting for liquid assets (assets that can be converted into cash, sold, or used in the near future), and internal control (the policies and procedures that ensure an organization is running effectively and efficiently).

A Look at Upcoming Chapters

Chapter 8 will present capital assets. The remaining chapters of this part, Chapters 9 through 11, will discuss liabilities and shareholders' equity in the balance sheet.

Focus on Financial Results

Sears Canada is one of Canada's leading department stores. It strives to offer quality services and products to its customers across Canada. Like most businesses, Sears Canada incurs various obligations during its operations. To cover current liabilities, businesses usually rely on cash and other assets that can be converted into cash quickly. On the balance sheet of Sears Canada for the year ended February 2, 2008, are $1,220 million of current liabilities; obligations require payments within a year or during the normal operating cycle if it is longer. At the same time, Sears Canada had the following liquid assets: $872 million in cash and short-term investments, $5 million in restricted cash, and $118 million in accounts receivable. What is included in the various cash accounts? How are changes in investments accounted for? How are accounts receivable valued? Chapter 7 focuses on liquid assets and on the internal control systems that businesses use to manage their resources.

SEARS CANADA INC. 2007 ANNUAL REPORT

http://www.sears.ca

Consolidated Statements of Financial Position (Excerpt)
($ in million)

	As at February 2, 2008	As at December 30, 2006
ASSETS		
Current Assets		
Cash and short-term investments	$ 871.6	$ 722.9
Restricted cash (Note 11)	5.2	10.1
Accounts receivable	118.4	135.9
Income taxes recoverable	0.4	0.6
Inventories	855.4	804.5
Prepaid expenses and other assets	115.4	120.0
Current portion of future income tax assets (Note 2)	30.6	121.2
	1,997.0	1,915.2
Capital assets (Note 3)	742.0	874.3
Deferred charges (Note 4)	205.0	220.2
Future income tax assets (Note 2)	24.9	15.2
Other long-term assets	34.2	35.4
Total Assets	$ 3,003.1	$ 3,060.3

Liquid assets are 33% of total assets.

Used with permission of Sears Canada Inc.

In Chapter 2 we looked at the distinction between current and noncurrent assets. Current assets are cash and other assets that a business expects to realize in cash, sell, or consume during its normal operating cycle or within one year if the cycle is shorter than one year. We begin our discussion of liquid assets by considering a typical business operating cycle.

Operating Cycle

A typical business operating cycle begins with the purchase of inventory from suppliers and services from employees. Inventory and services are then sold to customers. The operating cycle finishes when the cash payments are received. The length of time between when cash is paid to suppliers and employees and when cash is collected from customers varies from business to business.

http://www.sears.ca

Consider **Sears Canada**'s typical operating cycle. Assume that on August 1 it buys a camping tent from its supplier for $50.00 cash. At this point, Sears Canada has merely substituted one asset, cash, for another, inventory. Assume that on August 25, twenty-five days after it buys the tent, it sells it to Jane Jet for $100. If Jane pays cash for the tent, Sears Canada will have completed its cash-to-cash operating cycle in a total of 25 days, as shown in Exhibit 7-1.

Exhibit 7-1

Operating Cycle: Cash Sale

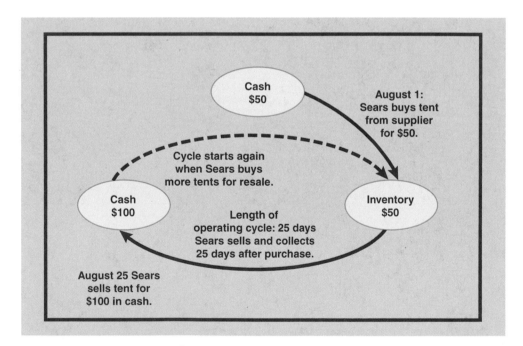

Although it is common in retail to make most sales for cash, sales between businesses are typically made on credit. Consider Sears Canada's operating cycle if it sells the tent to a Boy Scout Club on August 25 and allows it to pay in 30 days. Instead of an operating cycle of 25 days, 55 days have passed between the use of cash to buy tent from its supplier and the collection of cash from the customer, as shown in Exhibit 7-2. Obviously, a company such as Sears Canada is constantly buying more items to restock its stores and is making sales at those stores daily. We turn now to the accounting for the liquid asset accounts that arise from the operating cycle: cash and cash control; accounts receivable and cash collection; and cash investments.

Exhibit 7-2

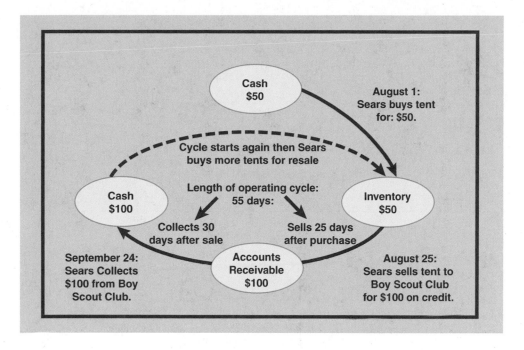

CASH AND CASH MANAGEMENT

Cash takes many different forms. Coin and currency on hand and cash on deposit in the form of chequing, savings, and money market accounts are the most obvious forms of cash. Also included in cash are various forms of cheques, including undeposited cheques from customers, cashier's cheques, and certified cheques. The proliferation of different types of financial instruments on the market today makes it very difficult to decide on the appropriate classification of these various items. The key to the classification of an amount as cash is that it be *readily available to pay debts*. Technically, a bank has the legal right to demand that a customer notify it before making withdrawals from savings accounts. Because this right is rarely exercised, however, savings accounts are normally classified as cash. In contrast, a guaranteed investment certificate has a specific maturity date and carries a penalty for early withdrawal and is therefore not included in cash.

LO 1 Identify the various forms of cash reported on a balance sheet, and describe the various techniques that companies use to control cash.

Cash Equivalents and the Statement of Cash Flows

Sometimes companies combine cash with certain other items, generally termed cash equivalents, and report it under the title 'Cash and cash equivalents.' Examples of items normally classified as cash equivalents are commercial paper issued by corporations, and money market funds offered by financial institutions. According to current accounting standards, classification as a **cash equivalent** is limited to those investments that are readily convertible to known amounts of cash and that have an original maturity to the investor of three months or less. Note that according to this definition, a 90-day guaranteed investment certificate (GIC) would be classified as a cash equivalent but a six-month GIC would not be.

The statement of cash flows that accompanies Sears' balance sheet is shown in Exhibit 7-3. Note the direct tie between this statement and the balance sheet (refer to the Current Assets section of Sears' balance sheet as shown in the chapter opener). Sears reported $722.9 million Cash and Cash Equivalents (titled "Cash and short-term investments") in its balance sheet of December 31, 2006. The net cash flows during 2007 totalled $148.7 million: $225.3 million from operating activities, $56.2 from investing activities, minus $132.8 million used for financing activities. The cash and cash equivalents balance became $871.6 million by December 31, 2007.

Cash equivalent An investment that is readily convertible to a known amount of cash and has an original maturity to the investor of three months or less.

Beginning balance in cash and cash equivalents	$ 722.9	→ 12/30/06 Balance Sheet
Add: Cash provided by operating activities	$ 225.3	
Add: Cash provided by investing activities	56.2	Statement of Cash Flows
Subtract: Cash used for financing activities	(132.8)	
Net increase in cash and cash equivalents	148.7	
Ending balance in cash and cash equivalents	$ 871.6	2/2/07 Balance Sheet

Exhibit 7-3 CONSOLIDATED STATEMENT OF CASH FLOWS OF SEARS CANADA INC.

For the 57-week period ended February 2, 2008 and the 52-week period ended December 30, 2006

(in $ millions)	2007	2006
Cash flow generated from (used for) operating activities		
Net earnings	$308.5	$152.6
Non-cash items included in net earnings, primary depreciation, pensions expense, future income taxes, the gain on sale of real estate joint ventures and capital assets	168.9	269.7
Changes in non-cash working capital balances related to operations (Note 10)	(234.9)	(106.0)
Other, principally pension contributions and changes to long-term assets and liabilities	(17.2)	(59.9)
	225.3	256.4
Cash flow generated from (used for) investing activities		
Purchases of capital assets	(54.6)	(58.4)
Proceeds from sale of capital assets	104.4	5.4
Proceeds on sale of real estate joint ventures, net of cash sold (Note 9)	5.2	—
Investments (Note 15)	(3.0)	—
Charges in restricted cash (Note 11)	4.9	(6.7)
Deferred charges	(0.7)	(0.5)
	56.2	(60.2)
Cash flow generated from (used for) investing activities		
Repayment of long-term obligations (Note 6)	(132.8)	(507.0)
Insurance of long-term obligations (Note 6)	—	300.0
Deferred charges	—	(2.6)
Dividends paid	—	(12.9)
	(132.8)	(222.5)
Increase (decrease) in cash and short-term investments	148.7	(26.3)
Cash and short-term investments at beginning of period	722.9	749.2
Cash and short-term investments at end of period	$871.6	$722.9
Cash at end of period	$ 64.7	$ 95.0
Short-term investments of end period	806.9	627.9
Total cash and short-term investments at end of period	$871.6	$722.9

Used with permission of Sears Canada Inc.

Cash Management

In addition to the need to guard against theft and other abuses related to the physical custody of cash, management of this asset is also important. Cash management is necessary to ensure that at any point in time, a company has neither too little nor too much cash on hand. The need to have enough cash on hand is obvious: suppliers, employees, taxing agencies, banks, and all other creditors must be paid on time if an entity is to remain in business. It is equally important that a company not maintain cash on hand and on deposit in chequing accounts beyond a minimal amount that is necessary to support ongoing operations, since cash is essentially a non-earning asset. Granted, some chequing accounts pay a very meagre rate of interest. However, the superior return that could be earned by investing idle cash in various forms of marketable securities dictates that companies carefully monitor the amount of cash on hand at all times.

An important tool in the management of cash, the cash flow statement, is discussed in detail in Chapter 12. Cash budgets, which are also vital to the management of cash, are discussed in management accounting and business finance texts. In this chapter, we introduce two commonly used cash management practices: bank reconciliations and petty cash funds. Before we turn to these control devices, we need to review the basic features of a bank statement.

The Bank Reconciliation

There are two fundamental principles of cash control: all cash receipts should be deposited daily intact, meaning that no disbursements should be made from this cash, and all cash payments should be made by cheque. Chequing accounts at banks are critical in this regard. These accounts allow a company to carefully monitor and control cash receipts and cash payments. Control is aided further by the monthly **bank statement.** Most banks mail their customers a monthly bank statement for each account. The statement provides a detailed list of all activities for a particular account during the month. An example of a typical bank statement is shown in Exhibit 7-4.

Bank statement A detailed list, provided by the bank, of all the activity for a particular account during the month.

Exhibit 7-4 Weber's Monthly Bank Statement—June, 2008

Date	Description	Subtractions	Additions	Balance
6-01	Previous balance			1,942.91
6-01	Cheque 498	417.25		1,525.66
6-02	Cheque 495		125.60	1,400.06
6-07	Deposit		1,023.16	2,423.22
6-13	NSF cheque	266.22		2,157.00
6-18	Cheque 499	855.40		1,301.60
6-20	Service charge	20.00		1,281.60
6-22	Deposit		2,650.10	3,931.70
6-24	Cheque 503	188.56		3,743.14
6-27	Cheque 500	450.00		3,293.14
6-30	Interest earned		15.45	3,308.59
6-30	Statement Totals	2,323.03	3,688.71	

The following items appear on Weber's bank statement:

Cancelled cheques—Weber's cheques that cleared at the bank during the month of June are listed with the corresponding cheque number and the date paid. Keep in mind that some of these cheques may have been written by Weber in a previous month but were not presented for payment to the bank until June. You also should realize that during June, Weber may have written some cheques that do not yet appear on the bank statement because they have not been presented for payment. A cheque written by a company but not yet present to the bank for payment is called **outstanding cheque**.

Outstanding cheque A cheque written by a company but not yet presented to the bank for payment.

Deposits—In keeping with the cash control principle calling for the deposit of all cash receipts intact, most companies deposit all cheques, coin, and currency on a daily basis. For the sake of brevity, we have limited to two the number of deposits that Weber made during the month. Keep in mind that Weber also may have made a deposit on the last day or two of the month and that this deposit may not yet be reflected on the bank statement. This type of deposit is called a **deposit in transit**.

Deposit in transit A deposit recorded on the books but not yet reflected on the bank statement.

NSF cheque—NSF is an abbreviation for not sufficient funds. The NSF cheque listed on the bank statement on June 13 is a customer's cheque that Weber recorded on its books, deposited, and thus included in its cash account. However, the customer did not have sufficient funds in its account when the cheque was presented for payment. Upon learning this, Coastal Bank deducted the amount from Weber's account. Weber needs to contact its customer to collect the amount due, ideally, the customer will issue a new cheque and ensure there is sufficient funds in its account.

Service charge—Banks charge for various services they provide. Among the most common bank service charges are monthly activity fees, fees for new cheques, and fees for the rental of a safety deposit box.

Interest earned—Some chequing accounts pay interest on the average daily balance in the account. Rates paid on chequing accounts are usually significantly less than could be earned on most other forms of investment.

Bank reconciliation A form used by the accountant to reconcile or resolve any differences between the balance shown on the bank statement for a particular account with the balance shown in the accounting records.

A **bank reconciliation** should be prepared for each individual bank account as soon as the bank statement is received. As the name implies, the purpose of a bank reconciliation is to *reconcile* or resolve any differences between the balance that the bank shows for an account with the balance that appears on the company's books. Differences between the two amounts are investigated, and if necessary, adjustments are made. The following are the steps in preparing a bank reconciliation:

1. Trace deposit listed on the bank statement to the books. Any deposits recorded on the books but not yet shown on the bank statement are deposit in transit. **Prepare a list of the deposits in transit.**

2. Arrange the cancelled cheques in numerical order and trace each of them to the books. Any cheques recorded on the books but not yet listed on the bank statement are outstanding cheques. **Prepare a list of the outstanding cheques**.

3. List all items, other than deposits, shown as additions on the bank statement, such as interested paid by the bank for the month. When the bank pays interest it increases or *credits* its liability to the company on its own books. For this reason, such items are called **credit memoranda**.

4. List all amounts, other than cancelled cheques, shown as subtractions on the bank statement, such as non-sufficient fund (NSF) cheques and various service changes. When the bank reduces the amount in the account, it *debits* the liability on its own books. For this reason, these items are called **debit memoranda**.

5. Identify any errors made by the bank or by the company in recording the various cash transactions.

6. Use the information collected in steps 1 through 5 to prepare a bank reconciliation.

Companies use a number of different *formats* in preparing bank reconciliations. The approach we illustrate here involves reconciling the bank balance and the book balance to an adjusted balance, rather than one to the other. As you will see, the advantage of this approach is that it yields the correct balance and makes it easy for the company to make any necessary adjustments to its books. A typical bank reconciliation for Weber Products is shown in Exhibit 7-5.

The following are explanations for the various items on the reconciliation:

1. The balance per bank statement of $3,308.59 is taken from the June statement shown in Exhibit 7-4.

2. Weber's records showed a deposit for $642.30 made on June 30 that is not reflected on the bank statement. The deposit in transit is listed as an addition to the bank statement balance.

3. The accounting records indicate three cheques written but not yet cleared on the bank statement. The three outstanding cheques are as follows:

496   $ 79.89
501   $213.20
502   $424.75

Exhibit 7-5

Bank Reconciliation

WEBER PRODUCTS
BANK RECONCILIATION
JUNE 30, 2008

Balance per bank statement, June 30		$3,308.59
Add: Deposit in transit		642.30
Deduct: Outstanding cheques:		
No. 496	$ 79.89	
No. 501	213.20	
No. 502	424.75	(717.84)
Adjusted balance, June 30		$3,233.05
Balance per books, June 30		$3,445.82
Add:		
Interest earned during June	15.45	
Error in recording cheque 498	54.00	69.45
Deduct: NSF cheque	262.22	
Service charge	20.00	(282.22)
Adjusted balance, June 30		$3,233.05

Outstanding cheques are the opposite of deposits in transit and therefore are deducted from the bank statement balance.

4. The adjusted balance of $3,233.05 is found by adding the deposit in transit and deducting the outstanding cheques from the bank statement balance.

5. The $3,445.82 book balance on June 30 is taken from the company's records as of that date.

6. An entry on June 30 on the bank statement shows an increase of $15.45 for interest earned on the bank account during June. This amount is added to the book balance.

7. A review of the cancelled cheques returned with the bank statement detected an error made by Weber. The company records indicated that cheque 498 was recorded incorrectly as $471.25; the cheque was actually written for $417.25 and reflected as such on the bank statement. This error, referred to as a *transposition error,* resulted from transposing the 7 and the 1 in recording the cheque in the books. The error is the difference between the amount of $471.25 recorded and the amount of $417.25 that should have been recorded, or $54.00. Because Weber recorded the cash payment at too large an amount, $54.00 must be added back to the book balance.

8. In addition to cancelled cheques, two other deductions appear on the bank statement. Each of these must be deducted from the book balance:

   a.   A customer's NSF cheque for $266.22

   b.   A service fee of $20.00 charged by the bank.

9. The additions of $69.45 and deductions of $282.22 resulted in an adjusted cash balance of $3,233.05. Note that this adjusted balance agrees with the adjusted bank statement balance on the bank reconciliation (see item **4**). Thus, all differences between the two balances have been explained.

The Bank Reconciliation and the Need for Adjustments to the Records

After it completes the bank reconciliation, Weber must prepare a number of adjustments to its records. In fact, all of the information for these adjustments will be from one section of the bank reconciliation. Do you think that the additions and deductions made to the bank balance or the ones made to the book balance are the basis for the adjustments? It is logical that the additions and deductions to the Cash account *on the books* should be the basis for the adjustments because these are items that Weber was unaware of before receiving the bank statement. Conversely, the additions and deductions to the bank's balance, that is, the deposits in transit and the outstanding cheques, are items that Weber has already recorded on its books.

The first entry is needed to record interest earned and paid by the bank on the average daily balance maintained in the chequing account during June:

June 30	Cash	15.45	
	Interest Revenue		15.45
	To record interest earned on chequing account		

Assets	=	Liabilities	+	Shareholders' Equity
+15.45				+15.45

Recall the error in recording cheque 498: it was actually written for $417.25, the amount paid by the bank. Weber recorded the cash disbursement on its books as $471.25, however. If we assume that the purpose of the cash payment was to buy supplies, the Cash account is understated and the Supplies account is overstated by the amount of the error. The entry needed to correct both accounts is as follows:

June 30	Cash	54.00	
	Supplies		54.00
	To correct for error in recording purchase of supplies		

Assets	=	Liabilities	+	Shareholders' Equity
+54				
−54				

The customer's NSF cheque is handled by reducing the Cash account and reinstating the account receivable:

June 30	Accounts Receivable	262.22	
	Cash		262.22
	To record customer's NSF cheque		

Assets	=	Liabilities	+	Shareholders' Equity
+262.22				
−262.22				

Finally, an entry needed to recognize the expenses incurred in connection with the fees charged by the bank for renting the safety deposit box:

June 30	Bank Service Fee	20.00	
	Cash		20.00
	To record rental charge on safety deposit box		

Assets	=	Liabilities	+	Shareholders' Equity
−20				−20

Note that we made a separate entry to record each of the increases and decreases in the Cash account. Some companies combine all of the increases in Cash in a single journal entry and all of the decreases in a second entry.

Petty Cash Fund

Recall one of the fundamental rules in controlling cash: all disbursements should be made by cheque. Most businesses make an exception to this rule in the case of minor expenditures, for which they use a **petty cash fund.** This fund consists of coin and currency kept on hand to make minor disbursements. The necessary steps in setting up and maintaining a petty cash fund follow:

Petty cash fund Money kept on hand for making minor disbursements in coin and currency rather than by writing cheques.

1. A cheque is written for a lump-sum amount, such as $100 or $500. The cheque is cashed, and the coin and currency are entrusted to a petty cash custodian.
2. A journal entry is made to record the establishment of the fund.

3. Upon presentation of the necessary documentation, employees receive minor disbursements from the fund. In essence, cash is traded from the fund in exchange for a receipt.

4. Periodically, the fund is replenished by writing and cashing a cheque in the amount necessary to bring the fund back to its original balance.

5. At the time the fund is replenished, an adjustment is made both to record its replenishment and to recognize the various expenses incurred.

The use of this fund is normally warranted on the basis of cost versus benefits. That is, the benefits in time saved in making minor disbursements from cash are thought to outweigh the cost associated with the risk of loss from decreased control over cash disbursements. The fund also serves a practical purpose for certain expenditures such as taxi fares and messengers that often must be paid in cash.

An Example of Petty Cash Fund

Assume that on August 1, the treasurer of Mickey's Marathon Sports cashed a cheque for $200 and remits the cash to the newly appointed petty cash custodian. On this date, the following journal entry is made:

Aug. 1	Petty Cash Fund	200.00	
	Cash		200.00

To record establishment of petty cash fund.

Assets	=	Liabilities	+	Shareholders' Equity
+200				
−200				

During August the custodian disburses coin and currency to various individuals who present receipts to the custodian for the following:

Canada Post	$55.00
Overnight Delivery Service	69.50
Office Supply Express	45.30
Total expenditures	$169.80

At the end of August, the custodian counts the coin and currency on hand and determines the balance to be $26.50. This means that $173.50 ($200.00–$26.50) is needed to return the balance in the account to $200.00. The discrepancy of $3.70 between the $169.80, the total expenditures for the month, and the $173.50 needed to restore the fund balance to $200.00 could be due to any number of factors, such as an error in making change. The Cash Over and Short account is necessary to record this. Next, the treasurer writes and cashes a cheque in the amount of 173.50 and remits the cash to the custodian. The following entry is made:

Aug. 31	Postage Expense	55.00	
	Delivery Expense	69.50	
	Office Expense	45.30	
	Cash Over and Short	3.70	
	Cash		173.50

To record replenishment of petty cash fund.

Assets	=	Liabilities	+	Shareholders' Equity
−173.50				−55.00
				−69.50
				−45.30
				−3.70

Any large discrepancies would be investigated, particularly if they recur. Assuming that the descrepancy is immaterial, a debit balance in the Cash Over and Short account is normally closed to Miscellaneous Expense. A credit balance in the account is closed to Other Income.

ACCOUNTS RECEIVABLE

LO 2 Explain how to account for accounts receivable, including bad debts.

Nowadays, credit sales are a significant part of sales for many businesses. Consider Canadian Tire Corporation. On its 2007 statement of earnings in its 2007 annual report, it reported total operating revenues of $8,621 million. Note 2 to those financial statements shows that the average credit card balance during the year was $3,719 million. This means that Canadian Tire's average outstanding credit card balance during the year is more than 40% of its annual sales. Given the option, companies like Canadian Tire might rather not sell on credit and would prefer to make all sales for cash. Selling on credit causes two problems: it slows down the inflow of cash to the company, and it raises the possibility that the customer may not pay its bill on time or possibly ever. To remain competitive, however, Canadian Tire and most other businesses must sell their products and services on credit. Large retailers such as Canadian Tire often extend credit by offering their own credit cards.

The types of receivables reported on a corporate balance sheet depend to some extent on a company's business. The "credit card receivables" on the balance sheet of Canadian Tire represent the interest-bearing accounts it carries with its retail customers. On the other hand, the "accounts receivable" are a result of sales of merchandise on credit by Canadian Tire to independent, owner-operated Canadian Tire stores. Accounts receivable, also called *trade receivables*, are often made on open credit to customers who promise to pay within a specified period of time. This type of account does not bear interest and often gives the customer a discount for early payment. For example, the terms of sale might be 2/10, net 30, which means the customer can deduct 2% from the amount due if the bill is paid within 10 days of the date of sale; otherwise, payment in full is required within 30 days.

The Use of a Subsidiary Ledger

As mentioned earlier, Canadian Tire provides merchandise to its owner-operated stores. Assume that it sells $25,000 of merchandise to a store on an open account. The journal entry to record the sale would be as follows:

Accounts Receivable	25,000	
Sales Revenue		25,000
To record sale on open account		

Assets	=	Liabilities	+	Shareholders' Equity
+25,000				+25,000

It is important for control purposes that Canadian Tire keeps a record of *to whom* the sale was made and includes this sale amount on a periodic statement or *bill* sent to the customer. What if a company has a hundred or a thousand different customers? Some mechanism is needed to track the balance owed by each of these customers. The mechanism companies use is called a **subsidiary ledger.**

A subsidiary ledger contains the necessary detail on each of a number of items that collectively make up a single general ledger account, called the **control account.** In theory, any one of the accounts in the general ledger could be supported by a subsidiary ledger. In addition to Accounts Receivable, two other common accounts supported by subsidiary ledgers are Plant and Equipment and Accounts Payable. An accounts payable subsidiary ledger contains a separate account for each of the suppliers or vendors from which a company purchases inventory. A plant and equipment subsidiary ledger consists of individual accounts, along with their balances, for each of the various long-term tangible assets the company owns.

It is important to understand that a subsidiary ledger does *not* take the place of the control account in the general ledger. Instead, at any point in time, the balances of the accounts that make up the subsidiary ledger should total to the single balance in the related control account. In the remainder of this chapter we will illustrate the use of only the control account. Whenever a specific customer's account is increased or decreased we will, however, note the name of the customer next to the control account in the journal entry.

Subsidiary ledger The detail for a number of individual items that collectively make up a single general ledger account.

Control account The general ledger account that is supported by a subsidiary ledger.

The Valuation of Accounts Receivable

The following presentation of receivables is taken from **Molson Coors'** 2007 annual report:

http://www.molsoncoors.com

	2007	2006
Trade receivables, less allowance for doubtful accounts ($8,827 and $10,363, respectively)	$758,526	$679,507

As you read this excerpt from the balance sheets, keep two points in mind. First, all amounts are stated in thousands of dollars. Second, these are the balances at the *end* of each of the two years.

Molson Coors does not sell its products to distributors under the assumption that any particular customer will *not* pay its bill. In fact, the credit department of a business is responsible for performing a credit check on all potential customers before they are granted credit. Management of Molson Coors is not naive enough, however, to believe that all customers will be able to pay their accounts when due. This would be the case only if (1) all customers are completely trustworthy and (2) customers never experience unforeseen financial difficulties that make it impossible to pay on time.

The reduction in Molson Coors' trade receivables for an allowance reflects the way in which most companies deal with bad debts in their accounting records. Bad debts are unpaid customer accounts that a company gives up trying to collect. Some companies such as Molson Coors describe the allowance more fully as the allowance for doubtful accounts, and others call it the allowance for uncollectible accounts. Using the end of 2007 as an example, Molson Coors believes that the *net recoverable amount* of its receivables is $758,526 thousand, even though the *gross* amount of receivables is $8,827 thousand higher than this amount. The company has reduced the gross receivables for an amount that it believes is necessary to reflect the asset on the books at the *net recoverable amount* or *net realizable value*. We now take a closer look at how a company accounts for bad debts.

Accounting for Your Decisions

You Are the Credit Manager

You are the credit manager of Department Store, which offers its customers store credit cards. An existing customer, Jane Doe, has requested a credit line increase. In processing her request, you must determine the current balance of her account. How would you use the accounting system to find her current balance? What other factors might you consider in granting Jane's request?

> **ANSWER:** You would find Jane's current balance by looking for her account in the accounts receivable subsidiary ledger. The subsidiary ledger should have a current balance because daily postings are made to each customer's account. Other factors to consider in processing Jane's request can include researching her payment history to see if she paid on time not only for this credit card but for all debts, checking to see if her income is sufficient to cover her existing debt and the new credit line increase, and verifying employment to ensure income stability.

Two Methods to Account for Bad Debts

Assume that Roberts Corp. makes a $500 sale to Dexter Inc. on November 10, 2008, with credit terms of 2/10, net 60. Roberts makes the following entry on its books on this date:

```
2008
Nov. 10   Accounts Receivable—Dexter                    500
               Sales Revenue                                      500
          To record sale on credit, terms of 2/10, net 60
```

	Assets	=	Liabilities	+	Shareholders' Equity
	+500				+500

Assume further that Dexter not only misses taking advantage of the discount for early payment but also is unable to pay within 60 days. After pursuing the account for four months into 2009, the credit department of Roberts informs the accounting department that it has given up on collecting the $500 from Dexter and advises that the account should be written off. To do so, the accounting department makes the following entry:

```
2009
May 1    Bad Debts Expense                               500
             Accounts Receivable—Dexter                          500
         To write off Dexter account
```

	Assets	=	Liabilities	+	Shareholders' Equity
	−500				−500

Direct write-off method The recognition of bad debts expense at the point an account is written off as uncollectible.

This approach to accounting for bad debts is called the **direct write-off method.** Do you see any problems with its use? What about Roberts' balance sheet at the end of 2008? By ignoring the possibility that not all of its outstanding accounts receivable will be collected, Roberts is overstating the value of this asset at December 31, 2008. Also, what about the income statement for 2008? By ignoring the possibility of bad debts on sales made during 2008, Roberts has violated the *matching principle*. This principle requires that all costs associated with making sales in a period should be matched with the sales of that period. Roberts has overstated net income for 2008 by ignoring bad debts as an expense. The problem is one of *timing*: even though any one particular account may not prove to be uncollectible until a later period (e.g., the Dexter account), the cost associated with making sales on credit (bad debts) should be recognized in the period of sale.

Accountants use the **allowance method** to overcome the deficiencies of the direct write-off method. They *estimate* the amount of bad debts before these debts actually occur. For example, assume that Roberts' total sales during 2008 amount to $600,000 and that at the end of the year the outstanding accounts receivable total $250,000. Also assume that Roberts estimates that on the basis of past experience, 1% of the sales of the period, or $6,000, eventually will prove to be uncollectible. Under the allowance method, Roberts makes the following adjusting entry at the end of 2008:

Allowance method A method of estimating bad debts on the basis of either the net credit sales of the period or the accounts receivable at the end of the period.

```
2008
Dec. 31   Bad Debts Expense                              6,000
              Allowance for Doubtful Accounts                    6,000
          To record estimated bad debts for the year
```

Assets	=	Liabilities	+	Shareholders' Equity
−6,000				−6,000

The debit recognizes the cost associated with the reduction in value of the asset Accounts Receivable. The cost is charged to the income statement, in the form of Bad Debts Expense. A contra-asset account is used to reduce the accounts receivable to its net realizable value. This is accomplished by crediting an allowance account, Allowance for Doubtful Accounts. Roberts presents accounts receivable as follows on its December 31, 2008, balance sheet:

Accounts receivable	$250,000
Less: Allowance for doubtful accounts	(6,000)
Net accounts receivable	$244,000

Study Tip

Note the similarities between the Allowance for Doubtful Accounts contra account and another contra account, Accumulated Depreciation. Both are used to reduce an asset account to a lower carrying or book value.

Write-Offs of Uncollectible Accounts with the Allowance Method

Like the direct write-off method, the allowance method reduces Accounts Receivable to write off a specific customer's account. If the account receivable no longer exists, there is no need for the related allowance account and thus this account is reduced as well. For example, assume, as we did earlier, that Dexter's $500 account is written off on May 1, 2009. Under the allowance method, the following entry is recorded:

```
2009
May 1   Allowance for Doubtful Accounts                  500
            Accounts Receivable—Dexter                          500
        To record the write-off of Dexter account
```

Assets	=	Liabilities	+	Shareholders' Equity
+500				
−500				

To summarize, whether the direct write-off method or the allowance method is used, the entry to write off a specific customer's account reduces Accounts Receivable. It is the debit that differs between the two methods: under the direct write-off method, an *expense* is increased; under the allowance method, the *allowance* account is reduced.

Recovery of Previously Written-Off Accounts

Assume by December 15, 2009, Dexter managed to raise some funds and would like to restore its credit with Roberts and paid the $500. Two journal entries are needed to record the recovery of a previously written-off account. First, the original write-off is reversed:

```
2009
December 15     Accounts Receivable—Dexter              500
                    Allowance for Doubtful Accounts              500
                To reverse the write-off of Dexter Account
```

Assets	=	Liabilities	+	Shareholders' Equity
+500				
−500				

Then the collection from Dexter is recorded.

```
2009
December 15     Cash                                    500
                    Accounts Receivable—Dexter                   500
                To record the collection from Dexter
```

Assets	=	Liabilities	+	Shareholders' Equity
+500				
−500				

Two Approaches to the Allowance Method for Bad Debts

Because the allowance method results in a better *matching*, accounting standards require the use of this method rather than the direct write-off method unless bad debts are immaterial in amount. Accountants use one of two different variations of the allowance method to estimate bad debts. One approach emphasizes matching bad debts expense with revenue on the income statement and bases bad debts on a percentage of the sales of the period. This was the method we illustrated earlier for Roberts Corp. The other approach emphasizes the net realizable amount (value) of accounts receivable on the balance sheet and bases bad debts on a percentage of the accounts receivable balance at the end of the period.

Percentage of Net Credit Sales Approach   If a company has been in business for enough years, it may be able to use the past relationship between bad debts and *net* credit sales to predict bad debt amounts. *Net* means that credit sales have been adjusted for sales discounts and returns and allowances. Assume that the accounting records for Bosco Corp. reveal the following:

YEAR	NET CREDIT SALES	BAD DEBTS
2003	$1,250,000	$ 26,400
2004	1,340,000	29,350
2005	1,200,000	23,100
2006	1,650,000	32,150
2007	2,120,000	42,700
	$7,560,000	$153,700

Although the exact percentage varied slightly over the five-year period, the average percentage of bad debts to net credit sales is very close to 2% ($153,700/$7,560,000 = 0.02033). Bosco needs to determine whether this estimate is realistic for the current period. For example, are current economic conditions considerably different from those in the prior years? Has the company made sales to any new customers with significantly different credit terms? If the answers to these types of questions are yes, Bosco should consider adjusting the 2% experience rate to estimate future bad debts. Otherwise, it should proceed with this estimate. Assuming that it uses the 2% rate and that its net credit sales during 2008 are $2,340,000, Bosco makes the following entry:

2008
Dec. 31   Bad Debts Expense   46,800
              Allowance for Doubtful Accounts   46,800
              To record estimated bad debts: 0.02 × $2,340,000

Assets	=	Liabilities	+	Shareholders' Equity
−46,800				−46,800

Thus, Bosco matches bad debt expense of $46,800 with sales revenue of $2,340,000.

The percentage-of-net-sales approach is also called the income statement method because this method estimates bad debt expense—an income statement number using Net sales—another income statement number.

Percentage of Accounts Receivable Approach
Some companies believe they can more accurately estimate bad debts by relating them to the balance in the Accounts Receivable account at the end of the period rather than to the sales of the period. The objective with both approaches is the same, however: to use past experience with bad debts to predict future amounts. Assume that the records for Cougar Corp. reveal the following:

YEAR	BALANCE IN ACCOUNTS RECEIVABLE DECEMBER 31	BAD DEBTS
2003	$ 650,000	$ 5,250
2004	785,000	6,230
2005	854,000	6,950
2006	824,000	6,450
2007	925,000	7,450
	$4,038,000	$32,330

The ratio of bad debts to the ending balance in Accounts Receivable over the past five years is $32,330/$4,038,000, or approximately 0.008 (0.8%). Assuming balances in Accounts Receivable and the Allowance for Doubtful Accounts on December 31, 2008, of $865,000 (debit) and $2,100 (credit), respectively, Cougar records the following entry:

2008
Dec. 31   Bad Debts Expense   4,820
              Allowance for Doubtful Accounts   4,820
              To record estimated bad debts:
              Credit balance required in allowance
                 account after adjustment
                 ($865,000 × 0.8%) $6,920
              Less: Credit balance in allowance
                 account before adjustment   2,100
              Amount for bad debt expense entry $4,820

Assets	=	Liabilities	+	Shareholders' Equity
−4,820				−4,820

Note the one major difference between this approach and the percentage of sales approach: *under the percentage of net credit sales approach, the balance in the allowance account is ignored, and the bad debts expense is simply a percentage of the sales of the period; under the percentage of accounts receivable approach, however, the balance in the*

Accounting for Your Decisions

You Are the Owner

Assume you own a retail business that offers credit sales. To estimate bad debts, your business uses the percentage of net credit sales approach. For the new fiscal year, how would you decide what percentage to use to estimate your bad debts?

ANSWER: To determine the bad debt percentage for the new fiscal year, you can (1) review historical records to see what the actual percentages of bad debts were, (2) check to see if credit policies have substantially changed, (3) consider current and future economic conditions, and (4) consult with your managers and salespeople to see if they are aware of any changes in customers' paying habits.

allowance account must be considered. A T account for Allowance for Doubtful Accounts with the balance before and after adjustment appears as follows:

ALLOWANCE FOR DOUBTFUL ACCOUNTS

	2,100	Bal. before adjustment
	4,820	Adjusting entry
	6,920	Bal. after adjustment

In other words, making an adjustment for $4,820 results in a balance in the account of $6,920, which is 0.8% of the Accounts Receivable balance of $865,000. The net realizable value of Accounts Receivable is determined as follows:

Accounts receivable	$865,000
Less: Allowance for doubtful accounts	(6,920)
Net realizable value	$858,080

The percentage-of-accounts-receivable approach is also called the balance sheet method because this method estimates the balance of allowance for doubtful accounts—a balance sheet number, using accounts receivable—another balance sheet number.

Aging of Accounts Receivable The most commonly used method for estimating bad debt is a variation of the percentage of accounts receivable approach called the *aging method*. This variation is actually a refinement of the approach because it considers the length of time that the receivables have been outstanding. It stands to reason that the older an account receivable is, the less likely it is to be collected. An **aging schedule** categorizes the various accounts by length of time outstanding. An example of an aging schedule is shown in Exhibit 7-6.

Aging schedule A form used to categorize the various individual accounts receivable according to the length of time each has been outstanding.

Exhibit 7-6

Use of an Aging Schedule to Estimate Bad Debts

CATEGORY	AMOUNT	ESTIMATED PERCENT UNCOLLECTIBLE	ESTIMATED AMOUNT UNCOLLECTIBLE
Current	$ 85,600	1%	$ 856
Past due:			
1–30 days	31,200	4%	1,248
31–60 days	24,500	10%	2,450
61–90 days	18,000	30%	5,400
Over 90 days	9,200	50%	4,600
Totals	$168,500		$14,554

Note that the estimated percentage of uncollectibles increases as the period of time the accounts have been outstanding lengthens. If we assume that the Allowance for Doubtful Accounts has a credit balance of $1,230 before adjustment, the adjusting entry is as follows:

2008

Dec. 31	Bad Debts Expense	13,324	
	Allowance for Doubtful Accounts		13,324
	To record estimated bad debts		

Balance required in allowance account after adjustment	$14,554
Less: Credit balance in allowance account before adjustment	1,230
Amount for bad debt expense entry	$13,324

Assets	=	Liabilities	+	Shareholders' Equity
−13,324				−13,324

The net realizable value of accounts receivable would be determined as follows:

Accounts receivable	$168,500
Less: Allowance for doubtful accounts	14,554
Net realizable value	$153,946

Two-Minute Review

1. What is the theoretical justification for recognizing bad debts under the allowance method?

2. What account titles are debited and credited at the end of the period to recognize bad debts?

3. Two approaches are available to recognize bad debts under the allowance method. What are they? Which one of the two takes into account any existing balance in the Allowance for Doubtful Accounts account when the entry is made to recognize bad debts for the period?

Answers on page 319

ACCELERATING THE INFLOW OF CASH FROM SALES

Earlier in the chapter we pointed out why cash sales are preferable to credit sales: credit sales slow down the inflow of cash to the company and create the potential for bad debts. To remain competitive, most businesses find it necessary to grant credit to customers. That is, if one company won't grant credit to a customer, the customer may find another company willing to do so. Companies have found it possible, however, to circumvent the problems inherent in credit sales. In Chapter 5 we discussed the use of sales discounts to motivate timely payment of accounts receivable. We now consider other approaches that companies use to speed up the flow of cash from sales.

LO 3 Explain various techniques that companies use to accelerate the inflow of cash from sales.

Credit Card Sales

Most retail establishments, as well as many service businesses, accept one or more major credit cards. Among the most common cards are **MasterCard**®, **VISA**®, **American Express**®, and **Discover Card**®. In return for a fee, the merchant passes the responsibility for collection on to the credit card company. Thus, the credit card issuer assumes the risk of non-payment. Assume that Joe Smith entertains clients at Club Cafe and charges $100 in meals to his American Express card. When Joe is presented with his bill at the end

http://www.mastercard.com/ca

http://www.visa.ca

https://home.americanexpress.com/home/ca

http://www.discovercard.com

Credit card draft A multiple-copy document used by a company that accepts a credit card for a sale.

of the evening, he is asked to sign a multiple-copy **credit card draft** or invoice. Joe keeps one copy of the draft and leaves the other two copies at Club Cafe. The restaurant keeps one copy as the basis for recording its sales for the day and sends the other copy to American Express for payment. American Express uses the copy of the draft it gets for two purposes: to reimburse Club Cafe $95 (keeping $5 or 5% of the original sale as a collection fee) and to include Joe Smith's $100 purchase on the monthly bill it mails him.

Generally, there is little uncertainty in payments to merchants from the major credit card companies. Some credit cards, such as MasterCard and VISA, allow a merchant to present a credit card draft directly for deposit in a bank account, in much the same way the merchant deposits cheques, coins, and currency. Many companies record sales on major credit cards as cash sales. The only difference between a cash sale and a major credit card sale is the credit card service fee charged by the major credit card companies. Assume that on July 9, Club Café's total credit card sales amount to $2,000 and that the average credit card service fee is 4%. The entry on its books on the date of deposit is as follows:

July 9	Cash	1,920	
	Credit Card Service Fee Expense	80	
	Sales Revenue		2,000
	To record credit card sales		

Assets	=	Liabilities	+	Shareholders' Equity
+1,920				−80
				+2,000

Sales of Receivables

In the normal course of operations, receivables are collected and removed from the balance sheet when due. To accelerate cash collections, it has become increasingly common for companies to sell, sometimes termed *factor*, their receivables to another company for cash before the accounts become due. Note 2 to the financial statements of Canadian Tire in the 2007 annual report indicates that $2,272 million of its $3,719 million total net managed credit card portfolio was sold at the end of 2007.

Factoring involves selling receivables to a finance company or a bank. The finance company or bank buys receivables from businesses for a fee and then collects the payments directly from the customers. Sales of receivables can be arranged under various terms. For instance, accounts can be sold either with or without recourse. When a company sells some of its accounts receivable with recourse, that company is still responsible if the customers default on their accounts; thus, the company should continue to maintain a proper allowance for doubtful accounts to cover the potential credit loss.

Notes Receivable and Discounting Notes Receivable

Some companies use promissory notes to formalize the receivables arising from credit sales. A promissory note is a written promise to repay a definite sum of money on demand or at a fixed or determinable date in the future. Promissory notes normally require the payment of interest from the borrowers. Promissory notes are negotiable, which means that they can be endorsed and given to someone else for collection. In other words, a company can sign the back of a note, just as it would a cheque, sell it to a bank, and receive cash before the note's maturity date. This process is called discounting and is another way for companies to speed the collection of cash from credit sales. A note can be sold immediately to a bank on the date it is issued, or it can be sold after it has been outstanding but before the due date.

In recent years, however, the use of credit cards and securitization of accounts receivables have largely replaced the use of promissory notes and notes discounting as means of accelerating collections from credit sales.

HOW LIQUID ASSETS AFFECT THE STATEMENT OF CASH FLOWS

As we discussed earlier in the chapter, cash equivalents are combined with cash on the balance sheet. These items are very near maturity and do not present any significant risk of collectibility. Because of this, any purchases or redemptions of cash equivalents are not considered significant activities to be reported on a statement of cash flows.

The purchase and the sale of investments are considered significant activities and are therefore reported on the statement of cash flows. Cash flows from purchases, sales, and maturities of short-term investments are classified as *investing* activities. Under the indirect method for cash from operating activities, the gain or loss from sales of investments, since they are included in net income, must be removed from the operating activities section.

The collection of accounts receivable generates cash for a business and affects the Operating Activities section of the statement of cash flows. Most companies use the indirect method of reporting cash flows and begin the statement of cash flows with the net income of the period. Net income includes the sales revenue of the period. Therefore, a decrease in accounts receivable during the period indicates that the company collected more cash than it recorded in sales revenue. Thus, *a decrease in accounts receivable must be added back to net income because more cash was collected than is reflected in the sales revenue number.* Alternatively, an increase in accounts receivable indicates that the company recorded more sales revenue than cash collected during the period. Therefore, *an increase in accounts or notes receivable requires a deduction from the net income of the period to arrive at cash flow from operating activities.* These adjustments, as well as the cash flows from buying and selling investments, are summarized in Exhibit 7-7.

LO 4 Explain the effects of transactions involving liquid assets on the statement of cash flows.

Exhibit 7-7
How Investments and Accounts Receivable Affect the Statement of Cash Flows

AN INTRODUCTION TO INTERNAL CONTROL

An employee of a large auto parts warehouse routinely takes spare parts home for personal use. A payroll clerk writes and signs two cheques for an employee and then splits the amount of the second cheque with the worker. Through human error, an invoice is paid for merchandise never received from the supplier. These cases sound quite different from one another, but they share one important characteristic. They all point to a deficiency in a company's internal control system. An **internal control system** consists of the policies and procedures necessary to ensure the safeguarding of an entity's assets, the reliability of its accounting records, and the accomplishment of its overall objectives.

LO 5 Explain the principles of internal control.

Internal control system Policies and procedures necessary to ensure the safeguarding of an entity's assets, the reliability of its accounting records, and the accomplishment of overall company objectives.

Three assets are especially critical to the operation of a merchandising company: cash, accounts receivable, and inventory. Activities related to these three assets compose the operating cycle of a business. Cash is used to buy inventory, the inventory is eventually sold, and assuming a sale on credit, the account receivable from the customer is collected. We turn now to the ways in which a company attempts to *control* the assets at its disposal.

Responsibility for Control and The Sarbanes-Oxley Act of 2002

http://www.brexcorp.com
http://www.enron.com
http://www.worldcomgroup.com

In the first few years of the new millennium, numerous corporate scandals involving questionable accounting practices by companies such as **Bre-X** and **Livent** in Canada, and **Enron** and **WorldCom** in U.S. surfaced. In an attempt to restore the public's confidence in the financial reporting system, both Canada and U.S. regulators are placing greater responsibility on management to establish and maintain effective internal control.

Most annual reports now include a management's statement of responsibility. A typical management's statement, in this case for Sears Canada, is shown in Exhibit 7-8.

The first paragraph clearly spells out management's responsibility for the fair presentation and integrity of the financial information presented in the annual report. The second paragraph states that in fulfilling its responsibilities, it is necessary for management to:

Internal audit staff Department responsible for monitoring and evaluating the internal control system.

1. Develop and maintain an extensive system of internal controls.
2. Review and evaluate the effectiveness of its internal control system through **internal audit staff**.

Exhibit 7-8 Management's Statement of Responsibility of Sears Canada (excerpt)

The preparation, presentation and integrity of the Company's consolidated financial statements, the overall accuracy of the Company's financial reporting and all information contained elsewhere in the Annual Report are the responsibility of management. The consolidated financial statements have been prepared in accordance with Canadian generally accepted accounting principles and include certain amounts that are based on management's best estimates and judgments. Financial information contained elsewhere in this Annual report is consistent with the information set out in the consolidated financial statements.

In fulfilling its responsibilities, management has developed and maintains an extensive system of internal controls designed to provide reasonable assurance that assets are safeguarded, transactions are properly recorded and reported, and financial records are reliable for the preparation of the financial statements. The Company's internal auditors, who are employees of the Company, also review and evaluate internal controls on behalf of management.

The Board of Directors monitors management's fulfillment of its responsibilities for financial reporting and internal controls principally through the Audit Committee. The Audit Committee, which is comprised solely of independent directors, meets regularly with management, the internal audit department and the Company's external auditors to review and discuss audit activity and results, internal accounting controls and financial reporting matters. The external auditors and the internal audit department have unrestricted access to the Audit Committee, management and the Company's records. The Audit Committee is also responsible for recommending to the Board of Directors the proposed nomination of the external auditors for appointment by the shareholders. Based upon the review and recommendation of the Audit Committee, the consolidated financial statements and Management's Discussion and Analysis have been approved by the Board of Directors.

First Paragraph
Management's responsibility for the financial information

Second Paragraph
System of internal control

Third Paragraph
Role of the Board of Directors and the Audit Committee

Used with permission of Sears Canada Inc.

Most large corporations today have a full-time staff of internal auditors who have the responsibility for evaluating the entity's internal control system. The primary concern of the independent public accountants, or external auditors, is whether the financial statements have been presented fairly. It is cost-prohibitive for the auditors to verify the millions of transactions recorded in a single year. Instead, the auditors rely to a certain degree on the system of internal control as assurance that transactions are properly recorded and reported. The degree of reliance that they are able to place on the company's internal controls is a significant factor in determining the extent of their testing. The stronger the system of internal control, the less testing is necessary. A weak system of internal control requires that the auditors extend their tests of the records.

The **board of directors** of a corporation usually consists of key officers of the corporation as well as a number of directors whom it does not directly employ. The outsiders often include presidents and key executive officers of other corporations and sometimes business school faculty. The board of directors is elected by the shareholders.

As referred to in the third paragraph of Exhibit 7-8, the **audit committee** is a subset of the board of directors that provides direct contact between the shareholders and the independent accounting firm. Audit committees have become much more involved in the oversight of the financial reporting system in recent years as a result of growing public concerns over reliability of corporate financial reporting.

The Sarbanes-Oxley Act (SOX) of U.S. goes even further in its effort to ensure the effectiveness of public companies' internal control system. Under SOX, a company's external auditors must also issue a report on their assessment of the company's internal control. The external auditors of a public company must issue their opinion whether the management's assessment that the company maintains effective internal control over financial reporting is fairly stated and whether the company maintains effective internal control over financial reporting.

Board of directors Group composed of key officers of a corporation and outside members responsible for general oversight of the affairs of the entity.

Audit committee Board of directors subset that acts as a direct contact between shareholders and the independent accounting firm.

The Control Environment

The success of an internal control system begins with the competence of the people in charge of it. Management's operating style will have a determinable impact on the effectiveness of various policies. An autocratic style in which a few key officers tightly control operations will result in an environment different from that of a decentralized organization in which departments have more freedom to make decisions. Personnel policies and practices form another factor in the internal control of a business. An appropriate system for hiring competent employees and firing incompetent ones is crucial to an efficient operation. After all, no internal control system will work very well if employees who are dishonest or poorly trained are on the payroll. On the other hand, too few people doing too many tasks defeats the purpose of an internal control system. Finally, the effectiveness of internal control in a business is influenced by the board of directors, particularly its audit committee.

The Accounting System

An **accounting system** consists of all the methods and records used to accurately report an entity's transactions and to maintain accountability for its assets and liabilities. Regardless of the degree of computer automation, the use of a journal to record transactions is an integral part of all accounting systems. Refinements are sometimes made to the basic components of the system, depending on the company's needs. For example, most companies use specialized journals to record recurring transactions, such as sales of merchandise on credit.

An accounting system can be completely manual, fully computerized, or as is often the case, a mixture of the two. Internal controls are important to all businesses, regardless of the degree of automation of the accounting system. The system must be capable of handling both the volume and the complexity of transactions entered into

Accounting system Methods and records used to accurately report an entity's transactions and to maintain accountability for its assets and liabilities.

© KEN REID/GETTY IMAGES

This woman is using the paper source document in her hand as a reference for entering data into the accounting system. From the standpoint of internal control, should she be the one who is ordering inventory, receiving it, and entering the information into the system? Is she authorized to make journal entries? If so, does her laptop have safeguards that prevent access by unauthorized personnel? These and other internal control procedures are part of the control environment within every company.

Administrative controls Procedures concerned with efficient operation of the business and adherence to managerial policies.

Accounting controls Procedures concerned with safeguarding the assets or the reliability of the financial statements.

by a business. Most businesses use computers because of the sheer volume of transactions. The computer is ideally suited to the task of processing large numbers of repetitive transactions efficiently and quickly.

The cost of computing has dropped so substantially that virtually every business can now afford a system. Today some computer software programs that are designed for home-based businesses cost under $100 and are meant to run on machines that cost less than $1,000. Inexpensive software programs that categorize expenses and print cheques, produce financial statements, and analyze financial ratios are available.

Internal Control Procedures

Management establishes policies and procedures on a number of different levels to ensure that corporate objectives will be met. Some procedures are formalized in writing. Others may not be written but are just as important. Certain **administrative controls** within a company are more concerned with the efficient operation of the business and adherence to managerial policies than with the accurate reporting of financial information. For example, a company policy that requires all prospective employees to be interviewed by the personnel department is an administrative control. Other **accounting controls** primarily concern safeguarding assets and ensuring the reliability of the financial statements. We now turn to a discussion of some of the most important internal control procedures:

> Proper authorizations
> Segregation of duties
> Independent verification
> Safeguarding assets and records
> Independent review and appraisal
> The design and use of business documents

Proper Authorizations Management grants specific departments the authority to perform various activities. Along with the *authority* goes *responsibility*. Most large organizations give the authority to hire new employees to the personnel department. Management authorizes the purchasing department to order goods and services for the company and the credit department to establish specific policies for granting credit to customers. By specifically authorizing certain individuals to carry out specific tasks for the business, management is able to hold these same people responsible for the outcome of their actions.

The authorizations for some transactions are general in nature; others are specific. For example, a cashier authorizes the sale of a book in a bookstore by ringing up the transaction (a general authorization). It is likely, however, that the bookstore manager's approval is required before a book can be returned (a specific authorization).

Segregation of Duties What might happen if one employee is given the authority both to prepare cheques and to sign them? What could happen if a single employee is allowed to order inventory and receive it from the shipper? Or what if the cashier at a checkout stand also records the daily receipts in the journal? If the employee in each of these situations is honest and never makes mistakes, nothing bad will happen. However, if the employee is dishonest or makes human errors, the company can experience losses. For instance, if the same employee is allowed to prepare and sign cheques, he or she may make cheques out to someone the company should not have to pay. If the same employee is allowed to both order and receive inventory, he or she may make up phantom orders and send the shipping slips for payment for inventories the company does not get. If the cashier also records the daily receipts, he or she may leave some of the cash received out of the record and pocket it. These situations all point to the need for the segregation of duties, which is one of the most fundamental of all internal control procedures. Without segregation of duties, an employee is able not only to perpetrate a fraud but also to conceal it. A good system of internal control requires that the *physical custody* of assets be separated from the *accounting* for those same assets.

Like most internal control principles, the concept of segregation of duties is an ideal that is not always completely attainable. For example, many smaller businesses simply do not have adequate personnel to achieve complete segregation of key functions. In certain instances, these businesses need to rely on the direct involvement of the owners in the business and on independent verification.

Accounting for Your Decisions

You Are the Chief Financial Officer

You have been hired by the owner of Mt. Robson Broom Company to come in and replace the out-of-date accounting systems with a system that uses modern technology. The first thing you notice is that the company's bookkeeper, Mavis, is in charge of collecting receivables, recording payments, ordering and receiving inventory, and preparing and signing cheques. When you suggest to her that she has too many duties, she gets angry and appeals to the owner. The owner backs up Mavis and tells you to focus entirely on new accounting technology. What should you do?

ANSWER: Ever so politely, you should inform the owner and Mavis in a three-way meeting that your suggestion that Mavis not do all the accounting functions is not meant as an insult but is simply good internal control. Even if Mavis is as honest as they come, there is a good chance that she will make errors, which could result in losses to the company. By having at least two people involved in a transaction, the chances are excellent that an error will be caught by one or the other.

Independent Verification Related to the principle of segregation of duties is the idea of independent verification. The work of one department should act as a check on the work of another. For example, the physical count of the inventory in a perpetual inventory system provides such a check. The accounting department maintains the general ledger account for inventory and updates it as sales and purchases are made. The physical count of the inventory by an independent department acts as a check on the work of the accounting department. As another example, consider a bank reconciliation as a control device. The reconciliation of a company's bank account with the bank statement by someone not responsible for either the physical custody of cash or the cash records acts as an independent check on the work of these parties.

Safeguarding Assets and Records Adequate safeguards must be in place to protect assets and the accounting records from losses of various kinds. Cash registers, safes, and safety deposit boxes are important safeguards for cash. Secured storage areas with limited access are essential for the safekeeping of inventory. Protection of the accounting records against misuse is equally important. For example, access to a computerized accounting record should be limited to those employees authorized to prepare journal entries. This can be done with the use of a personal identification number and a password to access the system.

Independent Review and Appraisal A well-designed system of internal control provides for periodic review and appraisal of the accounting system as well as the people operating it. The group primarily responsible for review and appraisal of the system is the internal audit staff. Internal auditors provide management with periodic reports on the effectiveness of the control system and the efficiency of operations.

The Design and Use of Business Documents *Business documents* are the crucial link between economic transactions entered into by an entity and the accounting record of these events. They are often called *source documents*. Many of these are generated by the computer, but a few may be completed manually. The source document for the recognition of the expense of an employee's wages is the time card. The source documents for a sale include the sales order, the sales invoice, and the related shipping document. Business documents must be designed so that they capture all relevant information about an economic event. They are also designed to ensure that related transactions are properly classified.

Business documents themselves must be properly controlled. For example, a key feature for documents is a *sequential numbering system* just like you have for your personal cheques. This system results in a complete accounting for all documents in the series and negates the opportunity for an employee to misdirect one. Another key feature of well-designed business documents is the use of *multiple copies*. The various departments involved in a particular activity, such as sales or purchasing, are kept informed of the status of outstanding orders through the use of copies of documents.

Two-Minute Review

1. Explain why an internal control system is important to the operation of a company that sells a product.
2. Explain the difference between administrative controls and accounting controls.
3. Explain how the concept of segregation of duties involves an evaluation of costs versus benefits.

Answers on page 319

Limitations on Internal Control

Internal control is a relative term. No system of internal control is totally foolproof. An entity's size affects the degree of control that it can obtain. In general, large organizations are able to devote a substantial amount of resources to safeguarding assets and records because these companies have the assets to justify the cost. Because the installation and maintenance of controls can be costly, an internal audit staff is a luxury that many small businesses cannot afford. The mere segregation of duties can result in added costs if two employees must be involved in a task previously performed by only one.

Segregation of duties can be effective in preventing collusion, but no system of internal control can ensure that it will not happen. It does no good to have one employee count the cash at the end of the day and to have another record it if the two act in concert to steal from the company. Rotation of duties can help to lessen the likelihood for problems of this sort. An employee is less likely to collude with someone to steal if the assignment is a temporary one. Another control feature, a system of authorizations, is meaningless if management continually overrides it. Management must believe in a system of internal control enough to support it.

Intentional acts to misappropriate company assets are not the only problem. All sorts of human errors can weaken a system of internal control. Misunderstood instructions, carelessness, fatigue, and distraction can all lead to errors. A well-designed system of internal control should result in the best-possible people being hired to perform the various tasks, but no one is perfect.

Answers to the Two-Minute Reviews

Two-Minute Review on page 304

1. The most common additions to the balance per the bank statement are deposits-in-transit and the most common deductions are outstanding cheques.
2. The most common additions to the balance per the books are collections on customers' notes and interest earned on the bank account. The most common deductions are for NSF cheques and various fees charged by the bank.

---

3. When the petty cash fund is replenished, a debit is made to various expenses incurred with a credit to cash. Any difference between the two is either debited or credited to Cash Over and Short.

Two-Minute Review on page 311

1. Use of the allowance method is an attempt by accountants to *match* bad debts as an expense with the revenue of the period in which a sale on credit took place.

2. Bad Debts expense is debited, and Allowance for Doubtful Accounts is credited.

3. The two approaches are the percentage of net credit sales approach and the percentage of accounts receivable approach. Only the latter takes into account the balance in the Allowance for Doubtful Accounts account.

Two-Minute Review on page 318

1. An effective system of internal control is critical to protecting a company's investment in three of its major assets: cash, accounts receivable, and inventory. Without an effective system, these assets are subject to misuse.

2. Administrative controls are concerned with the efficient operation of a business and adherence to managerial policies. Alternatively, accounting controls deal with safeguarding assets and ensuring the reliability of the financial statements.

3. Involving more than one employee in a specific function reduces the likelihood of theft or other misuse of company assets. However, all businesses must decide whether the benefit of segregation of duties outweighs the additional cost of involving more than one employee in a specific function such as the preparation and distribution of the payroll.

Appendix: Accounting for Short-Term Investments

The investments that companies make take a variety of forms and are made for various reasons. Corporations can invest in highly liquid financial instruments such as GICs and money market funds, in the shares and bonds of other corporations, and in bonds issued by government agencies.

Corporations invest for a number of reasons. The seasonality of certain businesses may result in excess cash being available during certain times of the year. Some businesses may need to accumulate cash in order to finance expansion projects. Because cash in its purest form does not earn a return, most companies invest their otherwise idle cash in various financial instruments as a means for earning a return. Such investments are often made in anticipation of a need for cash in the near or distant future.

Corporations frequently invest in the securities of other businesses. These investments take two forms: debt securities and equity securities.

No Significant Influence Corporations have varying motivations for investing in the stocks and bonds of other companies. We will refer to the company that invests as the *investor* and the company whose stocks and bonds are purchased as the *investee*. In addition to buying certificates of deposit and other financial instruments, companies invest excess funds in stocks and bonds over the short run. For example, **Apple** invests primarily in bonds of other companies. The seasonality of certain businesses may result in otherwise idle cash being available during certain times of the year. In other cases, stocks and bonds are purchased as a way to invest cash over the long run. Often these types of

LO 6 Explain the accounting for various types of investments that companies make.

http://www.apple.com/ca

investments are made in anticipation of a need for cash at some distant point in the future. For example, a company may invest today in a combination of stocks and bonds because it will need cash 10 years from now to build a new plant. The investor may be primarily interested in periodic income in the form of interest and dividends, in appreciation in the value of the securities, or in some combination of the two.

Significant Influence Sometimes shares in another company are bought with a different purpose in mind. If a company buys a relatively large percentage of the common stock of the investee, it may be able to secure significant influence over the policies of this company. For example, a company might buy 30% of the common stock of a supplier of its raw materials to ensure a steady source of inventory. When an investor is able to secure influence over the investee, the equity method of accounting is used. According to current accounting standards, this method is appropriate when an investor owns at least 20% of the common stock of the investee.

Control Finally, a corporation may buy stock in another company with the purpose of obtaining control over that other entity. Normally, this requires an investment in excess of 50% of the common stock of the investee. When an investor with an interest of more than 50% in another company is called the parent, and the investee in these situations is called the subsidiary.

The following chart summarizes the accounting by an investor for investments in the common stock of another company:

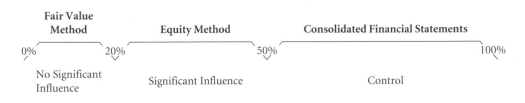

We will limit our discussion in Chapter 7 to how companies account for investments that are short-term or temporary in nature and that are classified as current assets on the balance sheet. Regardless of the type and the term of the investment, its classification as a current or non-current asset depends on whether the investor plans to sell it within the next year or next operating cycle, whichever is longer. In general, companies that engage in short-term investments do not seek significant influence or control over the other company. The equity method (accounting for investments with significant influence) and consolidation (accounting for investments with control) are covered in advanced accounting textbooks.

Companies face a number of major issues in deciding how to account for and report on investments:

1. What should be the basis for the recognition of periodic income from an investment? That is, what event causes income to be recognized?

2. How should an investment be valued and thus reported at the end of an accounting period? At original cost? At fair value?

Investments in financial instruments that are short-term in nature can generally be classified into one of three categories:

> **Held-to-maturity investments** are investments in the bonds of other companies when the investor has the positive intent and the ability to hold the securities to maturity. *Note that only bonds can qualify as held-to-maturity securities because shares do not have a maturity date.*
>
> **Trading investments** are shares and bonds that are bought and held for the purpose of selling them in the near term. These securities are usually held for only a short period of time with the objective of generating profits on short-term

Held-to-maturity investments Investments in bonds of other companies in which the investor has the positive intent and the ability to hold the securities to maturity.

Trading investments Shares and bonds of other companies bought and held for the purpose of selling them in the near term to generate profits on appreciation in their price.

appreciation in the market price of the shares and bonds. Trading investments are termed financial assets at fair value through profit or loss in International Accounting Standards.[1]

Available-for-sale investments are shares and bonds that are not classified as either held-to-maturity or trading investments.

Available-for-sale investments
Shares and bonds that are not classified as either held-to-maturity or trading investments.

Held-to-Maturity Investments

By their nature, only bonds, not shares, can qualify as held-to-maturity investments. A bond is categorized as a held-to-maturity investment if the investor plans to hold it until it matures. Note that held-to-maturity investments can be either short- or long-term investments, depending on the time remaining to maturity. Long-term held-to-maturity investments are reclassified as short-term if they mature within one year of the balance sheet date. The following accounting for held-to-maturity investments applies to both short-term and long-term held-to-maturity investments.

Consider the following example. On January 1, 1999, Simpson issues $10,000,000 of bonds that will mature in ten years. On January 1, 2008, Homer buys $100,000 in face value of these bonds on the open market at face value, which is the amount that will be repaid to the investor when the bonds mature. In many instances, bonds are purchased at an amount more or less than face value. We will limit our discussion, however, to the simpler case in which bonds are purchased for face value. The bonds pay 10% interest semiannually on June 30 and December 31. This means that Homer will receive 5% of $100,000, or $5,000, on each of these dates. The entry on Homer's books to record the purchase is as follows:

2008			
Jan. 1	Investment in Bonds	100,000	
	Cash		100,000
	To record purchase of Simpson bonds		

Assets	=	**Liabilities**	+	**Shareholders' Equity**
+100,000				
−100,000				

On June 30, Homer must record the receipt of semiannual interest. The entry on this date is as follows:

2008			
June 30	Cash	5,000	
	Interest Income		5,000
	To record interest income on Simpson bonds		

Assets	=	**Liabilities**	+	**Shareholders' Equity**
+5,000				+5,000

Note that income was recognized when interest was received. If interest is not received at the end of an accounting period, a company should accrue interest earned but not yet received. Any held-to-maturity bonds that are one year or less from maturity, however, are classified in the Current Assets section of a balance sheet.

Assume that before the maturity date, Homer needs cash and decides to sell the bonds. Keep in mind that this is a definite change in Homer's plans, since the bonds were initially categorized as held-to-maturity securities. Any difference between the proceeds received from the sale of the bonds and the amount paid for the bonds is recognized as either a gain or a loss.

---

[1] IAS 39.

Assume that on July 1, 2008, Homer sells all its Simpson bonds at 99. This means that the amount of cash received is 0.99 × $100,000, or $99,000. The entry on July 1, 2008, is as follows:

```
2008
July 1   Cash                                      99,000
         Loss on Sale of Bonds                      1,000
             Investment in Bonds                                100,000
         To record sale of Simpson bonds
```

Assets	=	Liabilities	+	Shareholders' Equity
+99,000				−1,000
−100,000				

The $1,000 loss on the sale of the bonds is the excess of the amount paid for the purchase of the bonds of $100,000 over the cash proceeds from the sale of $99,000. The loss is reported in the Other Income and Expenses section on the 2008 income statement.

Trading Investments

A company invests in trading securities as a way to profit from increases in the market prices of these securities over the short term. Because the intent is to hold them for the short term, trading investments are classified as current assets. All trading securities are recorded initially at cost, including any brokerage fees, commissions, or other fees paid to acquire the shares. Assume that Dexter Corp. invests in the following securities on November 30, 2008:

SECURITY	COST
Stuart common shares	$50,000
Menlo preferred shares	25,000
Total cost	$75,000

The entry on Dexter's books on the date of purchase is as follows:

```
2008
Nov. 30   Investment in Stuart Common Shares        50,000
          Investment in Menlo Preferred Shares      25,000
              Cash                                              75,000
          To record purchase of trading securities for cash
```

Assets	=	Liabilities	+	Shareholders' Equity
+50,000				
+25,000				
−75,000				

Many companies attempt to pay dividends every year as a signal of overall financial strength and profitability. Assume that on December 10, 2008, Dexter received dividends of $1,000 from Stuart and $600 from Menlo. The dividends received from trading securities are recognized as income, as shown in the following entry on Dexter's books:

```
2008
Dec. 10   Cash                                      1,600
              Dividend Income                                  1,600
          To record receipt of dividends on trading securities
```

Assets	=	Liabilities	+	Shareholders' Equity
+1,600				+1,600

Unlike interest on a bond or a note, dividends do not accrue over time. In fact, a company does not have a legal obligation to pay dividends until its board of directors declares them. Up to that point, the investor has no guarantee that dividends will ever be paid.

As noted earlier, trading securities are purchased with the intention of holding them for a short period of time. Assume that Dexter sells the Stuart shares on December 15, 2008, for $53,000. In this case, Dexter recognizes a gain for the excess of the cash proceeds, $53,000, over the amount recorded on the books, $50,000:

2008

Dec. 15   Cash   53,000
        Investment in Stuart Common Shares   50,000
        Gain on Sale of Shares   3,000
    To record sale of Stuart common shares

Assets	=	Liabilities	+	Shareholders' Equity
+53,000				+3,000
−50,000				

The gain is considered realized and is classified on the income statement as other income.

Assume that on December 22, 2008, Dexter replaces the Stuart shares in its portfolio by purchasing Canby common shares for $40,000. The entry on this date follows:

2008

Dec. 22   Investment in Canby Common Shares   40,000
        Cash   40,000
    To record purchase of trading securities for cash

Assets	=	Liabilities	+	Shareholders' Equity
+40,000				
−40,000				

Now assume that Dexter ends its accounting period on December 31. Should it adjust the carrying value of its investments to reflect their fair values on this date? According to GAAP, fair values should be used to report investments in trading securities on a balance sheet. The fair values are thought to be relevant information to the various users of financial statements. Assume the following information for Dexter on December 31, 2008:

SECURITY	TOTAL COST	TOTAL FAIR VALUE ON DECEMBER 31, 2008	GAIN (LOSS)
Menlo preferred shares	$25,000	$27,500	$2,500
Canby common shares	40,000	39,000	(1,000)
Totals	$65,000	$66,500	$1,500

The entry on Dexter's books on this date follows:

2008

Dec. 31   Investment in Menlo Preferred Shares   2,500
        Investment in Canby Common Shares   1,000
        Unrealized Gain—Trading Securities   1,500
          (Income Statement)
    To adjust trading securities to fair value

Assets	=	Liabilities	+	Shareholders' Equity
+2,500				+1,500
−1,000				

Note that this entry results in each security being written up or down so that it will appear on the December 31 balance sheet at its market or fair value. This type of fair value accounting for trading securities is often referred to as a *mark-to-market* approach because at the end of each period, the value of each security is adjusted or marked to its current market value. Also, it is important to realize that for trading securities, the changes in value are recognized on the income statement. The difference of $1,500 between the original cost of the two securities, $65,000, and their fair value, $66,500, is recorded in the account Unrealized Gain—Trading Securities to call attention to the fact that the securities have not been sold. Even though the gain or loss is *unrealized,* it is recognized on the income statement as a form of other income or loss.

Assume one final transaction in our Dexter example. On January 20, 2009, Dexter sells the Menlo shares for $27,000. The entry on Dexter's books on this date follows:

2009				
Jan. 20	Loss on Sale of Shares (Income Statement)		500	
	Cash		27,000	
	Investment in Menlo Preferred Shares			27,500
	To record sale of Menlo preferred shares			

Assets	=	Liabilities	+	Shareholders' Equity
+27,000				−500
−27,500				

The important point to note about this entry is that the $500 loss represents the difference between the cash proceeds of $27,000 and the *fair value of the shares at the most recent reporting date,* $27,500. Because the Menlo shares were adjusted to a fair value of $27,500 on December 31, the excess of this amount over the cash proceeds of $27,000 results in a loss of $500. Keep in mind that a gain of $2,500 was recognized last year when the shares were adjusted to their fair value at the end of the year.

Available-for-Sale Investments

Shares and bonds that do not qualify as trading securities and bonds that are not intended to be held to maturity are categorized as available-for-sale investments. The accounting for these securities is similar to the accounting for trading securities, with one major exception: *even though fair value accounting is used to report available-for-sale securities at the end of an accounting period, any gains or losses resulting from marking to market are not reported on the income statement but instead are accumulated in a shareholders' equity account.* This inconsistency is justified by the accounting profession on the grounds that the inclusion in income of fluctuations in the value of securities that are available for sale but that are not necessarily being actively traded could lead to volatility in reported earnings. Regardless, reporting gains and losses on the income statement for one class of securities but not for others is a subject of considerable debate. Investments in available-for-sale securities may be classified as either current or noncurrent assets.

To understand the use of fair value accounting for available-for-sale securities, assume that Lenox Corp. purchases two different shares late in 2008. The costs and fair values at the end of 2008 are as follows:

SECURITY	TOTAL COST	FAIR VALUE ON DECEMBER 31, 2008	GAIN (LOSS)
Adair preferred shares	$15,000	$16,000	$ 1,000
Casey common shares	35,000	32,500	(2,500)
Totals	$50,000	$48,500	$(1,500)

The entry on Lenox's books on this date is as follows:

2008			
Dec. 31	Other Comprehensive Income—Available-for-Sale		
	Securities	1,500	
	Investment in Adair Preferred Shares	1,000	

| Investment in Casey Common Shares | | 2,500 |

To adjust available-for-sale securities to fair value

Assets	**=**	**Liabilities**	**+**	**Shareholders' Equity**
+1,000				−1,500
−2,500				

Note the similarity between this entry and the one we made at the end of the period in the example for trading securities. In both instances, the individual investments are adjusted to their fair values for purposes of presenting them on the year-end balance sheet. The unrealized loss of $1,500 does not, however, affect income in this case. Instead, the loss is part of the other comprehensive income.

Now assume that Lenox sells its Casey shares for $34,500 on June 30, 2009. The entry on this date is as follows:

2009

June 30	Cash	34,500	
	Loss on Sale of Shares (Income Statement)	500	
	Investment in Casey Common Shares		32,500
	Other Comprehensive Income		
	—Available-for-Sale Securities		2,500
	To record sale of Casey common shares		

Assets	**=**	**Liabilities**	**+**	**Shareholders' Equity**
+34,500				− 500
−32,500				+2,500

Lenox recognizes a loss on the income statement of $500, which represents the excess of the cost of the shares of $35,000 over the cash proceeds of $34,500. Note, however, that the Investment in Casey Common Shares account is removed from the books at $32,500, the fair value at the end of the prior period. Thus, it is also necessary to adjust the Other Comprehensive Income account for $2,500, the difference between the original cost of $35,000 and the fair value at the end of 2008 of $32,500.

Finally, assume that Lenox does not buy any additional securities during the remainder of 2009 and that the fair value of the one investment it holds, the Adair preferred stock, is $19,000 on December 31, 2009.

The entry to adjust the Adair's shares to fair value on this date is as follows:

2009

Dec 31	Investment in Adair Preferred Shares	3,000	
	Other Comprehensive Income—Available-for-Sale		
	Securities		3,000
	To adjust available-for-sale securities to fair value.		

Assets	**=**	**Liabilities**	**+**	**Shareholders' Equity**
+3,000				+3,000

The increase in Investment in Adair Preferred Shares results in a balance of $19,000 in this account, the fair value of the shares. The account now has a *credit* balance of $4,000, as reflected in the following T account:

OTHER COMPREHENSIVE INCOME—AVAILABLE-FOR-SALE SECURITIES

12/31/08 bal.	1,500		
		2,500	6/30/09 entry
		1,000	6/30/09 bal.
		3,000	12/31/09 entry
		4,000	12/31/09 bal.

The balance of $4,000 in this account represents the excess of the $19,000 fair value of the one security now held over its original cost of $15,000.

Summary of Accounting and Reporting Requirements

A summary of the accounting and reporting requirements for each of the three categories of investments is shown in Exhibit 7-9. Periodic income from each of these types of investments is recognized in the form of interest and dividends. Held-to-maturity bonds are reported on the balance sheet at cost. (Note that we limit our discussion to the bonds purchased at face value. If bonds are purchased at an amount more or less than face value, the amortized cost will be used.) Both trading securities and available-for-sale securities are reported on the balance sheet at fair value. Unrealized gains and losses from holding trading securities are recognized on the income statement, whereas these same gains and losses for available-for-sale securities are accumulated in a shareholders' equity account.

Exhibit 7-9 Accounting for Investments without Significant Influence

CATEGORIES	TYPES	RECOGNIZE AS INCOME	REPORT ON BALANCE SHEET AT	REPORT CHANGES IN FAIR VALUE ON
Held-to-maturity	Bonds	Interest	Cost	Not applicable
Trading	Bonds, shares	Interest, dividends	Fair value	Income statement
Available-for-sale	Bonds, shares	Interest, dividends	Fair value	Balance sheet (Other comprehensive income)

Chapter Highlights

1. **LO 1** Identify the various forms of cash reported on a balance sheet and describe the various techniques that companies use to control cash (p. 297).

   - Cash can take many forms; however, the key attribute is that the asset is readily available to pay debts.
     - Cash equivalents are those investments that are readily convertible to a known amount of cash. "Readily" has been interpreted to be three months or less.
   - The liquidity of cash makes controls over it very important to have in place.
     - Cash management—managing the need to have on hand enough cash to ensure cash flow needs, but not so much that excess funds earn little return and may be more vulnerable to misappropriation.
     - Bank reconciliations use third-party documents (bank statement) to reconcile differences between the amount in the bank and on the books. Done by an independent party, bank reconciliations are effective control procedures.
     - Petty cash funds are an effective way to minimize access to large cash accounts in order to pay for relatively small expenditures.

2. **LO 2** Explain how to account for accounts receivable, including bad debts (p. 304).

   - Accounts receivable arise from sales on credit. Companies with many customers may keep detailed records of accounts receivable in a separate subsidiary ledger.
   - Because all customers pay their accounts receivable, an estimate of the accounts receivable less any doubtful accounts must be presented on the balance sheet.
   - Bad debts are estimated under the allowance method by one of two approaches:
     - Percentage of net credit sales
     - Percentage of net receivables
   - Information about net credit sales and the average accounts receivable balance may be combined to calculate the accounts receivables turnover to see how well a company is managing its collections on accounts.

3. **LO 3** Explain various techniques that companies use to accelerate the inflow of cash from sales (p. 311).

   - To be competitive, companies must make sales on credit to customers.
   - One way to avoid bad debts associated with extending credit directly to the customer, and to accelerate cash collections from sales, is by accepting credit cards for payment of goods and services.

4. **LO 4** Explain the effects of transactions involving liquid assets on the statement of cash flows (p. 313).

   - Changes in cash equivalents are not shown on the statement.
   - Cash flows related to the purchase and sale of investment are classified as Investing Activities in the statement of cash flows.
   - Under the indirect method, increases in accounts and notes receivable are deducted and decreases in these accounts are added back in the Operating Activities section of the statement.

5. **LO 5** Explain the principles of internal control (p. 313).

   - The purpose of internal control is to provide assurance that overall company objectives are met.
   - Control procedures are actions taken by company personnel to make sure policies set forth by management are followed.
   - Important accounting controls are concerned with safeguarding assets and producing accurate and timely financial statements. They include:
     - Proper authorizations—only certain personnel may authorize transactions.
     - Segregation of duties—physical custody of assets must not be combined with the ability to account for those assets.
     - Independent verification—for example, an inventory count.
     - Safeguarding assets and records—both must be adequately protected.
     - Independent review and appraisal—primarily done by internal audit.
     - Design and use of business documents—source document control.

6. **LO 6** Explain the accounting for various types of investments that companies make (Appendix) (p. 319).

   - Typically, excess cash expected to last for short periods of time is invested in highly liquid financial instruments, such as GICs.
   - Sometimes cash is also invested in securities of other corporations.
     - Equity securities—securities issued by corporations as a form of ownership in the business.
     - Debt securities—securities issued by corporations as a form of borrowing.
   - At times, a company may wish to purchase a relatively large portion of another firm's stock to acquire influence over that firm.
   - Held-to-Maturity Securities
     - These are bonds that the investor plans to hold until they mature. Interest is earned on the bonds while they are held.
   - Trading Securities
     - These are held for the short term.
     - Interest or dividends are recognized as income.
     - They are adjusted to fair value at the end of an accounting period.
     - Any increase or decrease in value if recognized on the income statement.
   - Available-for-Sale Securities
     - Those securities not classified as either held-to-maturity or trading.
     - Rules are similar to those for trading securities.
     - Primary difference is that changes in fair values are not recognized on the income statement: instead, they are reported as a separate component of shareholders' equity.

Ratio Review

$$\text{Accounts Receivable Turnover} = \frac{\text{Net Credit Sales (Income Statement)}}{\text{Average Accounts Receivable (Balance Sheet)}}$$

Accounts Highlighted

Account Titles	Where it Appears	In What Section	Page Number
Cash and Cash Equivalents	Balance Sheet	Current Assets	297
Petty Cash Fund	Balance Sheet	Current Assets	302
Cash over and under	Income Statement	Other Income/Expense	303
Accounts receivable	Balance Sheet	Current Assets	304
Bad debt expense	Income Statement	Operating Expenses	306
Allowance for doubtful accounts	Balance Sheet	Current Assets	307
Short-term Investments	Balance Sheet	Current Assets	320
Long-term Investments	Balance Sheet	Noncurrent Assets	320
Interest income	Income Statement	Other Income	320
Unrealized gain/loss—available-for-sale securities	Statement of Comprehensive Income	Other Comprehensive Income	322
Gain/loss on sale of investments	Income Statement	Other Income	322
Dividend income	Income Statement	Other Income	322
Unrealized gain/loss—trading securities	Income Statement	Other Income	329

Key Terms Quiz

Because of the large number of terms introduced in this chapter, it has two key terms quizzes. Read each of the following definitions and then write the number of the definition in the blank beside the appropriate term it defines. The quiz solutions appear at the end of the chapter.

Quiz 1: Cash and Accounts Receivable

_____ Cash equivalent	_____ Petty cash fund
_____ Bank statement	_____ Subsidiary ledger
_____ Outstanding cheque	_____ Control account
_____ Deposit in transit	_____ Direct write-off method
_____ Bank reconciliation	_____ Allowance method
_____ Credit memoranda	_____ Aging schedule
_____ Debit memoranda	_____ Credit card draft

1. Additions on a bank statement for such items as interest paid on the account and accounts collected by the bank for the customer.

2. An investment that is readily convertible to a known amount of cash and has an original maturity to the investor of three months or less.

3. Deductions on a bank statement for such items as NSF cheques and various service charges.

4. A deposit recorded on the books but not yet reflected on the bank statement.

5. A method of estimating bad debts on the basis of either the net credit sales of the period or the amount of accounts receivable at the end of the period.

6. A cheque written by a company but not yet presented to the bank for payment.

7. A multiple-copy document used by a company that accepts a credit card for a sale.

8. A detailed list, provided by the bank, of all the activity for a particular account during the month.

9. A form used by the accountant to reconcile the balance shown on the bank statement for a particular account with the balance shown in the accounting records.

10. Money kept on hand for making minor disbursements in coin and currency rather than by writing cheques.

11. A form used to categorize the various individual accounts receivable according to the length of time each has been outstanding.

12. The detail for a number of individual items that collectively make up a single general ledger account.

13. The recognition of bad debts expense at the point an account is written off as uncollectible.

14. The general ledger account that is supported by a subsidiary ledger.

Quiz 2: Internal Control and Investments

_____ Internal control system
_____ Board of directors
_____ Audit committee
_____ Accounting system
_____ Administrative controls
_____ Accounting controls
_____ Management's statement of responsibility

_____ Equity securities
_____ Debt securities
_____ Held-to-maturity-investments
_____ Trading investments
_____ Available-for-sale-investments

1. Securities issued by corporations as a form of ownership in the business.

2. The group composed of key officers of a corporation and outside members responsible for the general oversight of the affairs of the entity.

3. The methods and records used to accurately report an entity's transactions and to maintain accountability for its assets and liabilities.

4. Bonds issued by corporations and governmental bodies as a form of borrowing.

5. The board of directors subset that acts as a direct contact between the shareholders and the independent accounting firm.

6. Procedures concerned with safeguarding the assets or the reliability of the financial statements.

7. Shares and bonds of other companies bought and held for the purpose of selling them in the near term to generate profits on appreciation in their price.

8. Shares and bonds that are not classified as either held-to-maturity or trading securities.

9. Procedures concerned with efficient operation of the business and adherence to managerial policies.

10. Investments in bonds of other companies in which the investor has the positive intent and the ability to hold the securities to maturity.

11. Policies and procedures necessary to ensure the safeguarding of an entity's assets, the reliability of its accounting records, and the accomplishment of overall company objectives.

12. A written statement in the annual report indicating the responsibility of management for the financial statements.

Alternate Terms

Allowance for doubtful accounts Allowance for uncollectible accounts

Available-for-sale investments Available for sale securities

Balance sheet approach

Credit card draft Invoice

Debt securities Bonds

Equity securities Shares

Held-to-maturity investments Held-to-maturity securities

Income statement approach

Net realizable value Net recoverable amount

Percentage of accounts receivable approach

Percentage of net credit sales approach

Short-term-investments Marketable securities

Trading investments Financial assets at fair value through profit or loss

Warmup Exercises and Solutions

Warmup Exercise 7-1 *Composition of Cash* LO 1
For the following items, indicate whether each should be included (I) or excluded (E) from the line item titled Cash and Cash Equivalents on the balance sheet.

_____ 1. 60 days guaranteed investment certificate

_____ 2. Chequing account

_____ 3. Six months guaranteed investment certificate maturing in four months

_____ 4. Savings account

_____ 5. Shares of Bank of Nova Scotia

(continued)

_____ 6. Petty cash

_____ 7. Corporate bonds maturing in 30 days

_____ 8. Certified cheque

Key to the Solution Recall the key to classification as part of cash: the amount must be readily available to pay debts and cash equivalents must have an original maturity to the investor of three months or less.

Warmup Exercise 7-2 *Accounting for Bad Debts* LO 2

Brown Corp. ended the year with balances in Accounts Receivable of $60,000 and in Allowance for Doubtful Accounts of $800 (credit balance before adjustment). Net sales for the year amounted to $200,000. Prepare the necessary entry on its books at the end of the year, assuming the following:

1. Estimated percentage of net sales uncollectible is 1%.

2. Estimated percentage of year-end accounts receivable uncollectible is 4%.

Key to the Solution Recall that the percentage of net sales approach does not take into account any existing balance in the allowance account but the percentage of receivables approach does.

Warmup Exercise 7-3 *Investments* LO 6 (Appendix)

Indicate whether each of the following events will result in an increase (I), decrease (D), or no effect (NE) on net income for the period.

_____ 1. Trading securities are sold for more than their carrying value.

_____ 2. An interest cheque is received for held-to-maturity securities.

_____ 3. Available-for-sale securities increase in value during the period.

_____ 4. Available-for-sale securities are sold for less than their carrying value.

_____ 5. Trading securities decrease in value during the period.

_____ 6. Held-to-maturity securities are redeemed on their maturity date at face value.

Key to the Solution Recall from earlier in the chapter the differences in accounting for the various types of investments.

Solutions to Warmup Exercises

Warmup Exercise 7-1

1. I   2. I   3. E   4. I   5. E   6. I   7. E   8. I

Warmup Exercise 7-2

1. Bad Debts Expense   2,000
       Allowance for Doubtful Accounts   2,000
     To record estimated bad debts

Assets	=	Liabilities	+	Shareholders' Equity
−2,000				−2,000

2. Bad Debts Expense   1,600
       Allowance for Doubtful Accounts   1,600
     To record estimated bad debts

Assets	=	Liabilities	+	Shareholders' Equity
−1,600				−1,600

Warmup Exercise 7-3

1. I   2. I   3. NE   4. D   5. D   6. NE

Review Problem and Solution

The following items pertain to the Current Assets section of the balance sheet for Jackson Corp. at the end of its accounting year, December 31, 2008. Each item must be considered, and any necessary accounting entry on December 31 must be recorded. Additionally, the accountant for Jackson wants to develop the Current Assets section of the balance sheet as of the end of 2008.

a. Cash in a savings account at the First National Bank amounts to $13,200.

b. Cash on hand in the petty cash fund amounts to $400.

c. A 9%, 120-day guaranteed investment certificate was purchased on December 1, 2008, for $10,000.

d. The balance on the books for a chequing account at the First National Bank is $4,230. The bank statement indicates that one of Jackson's customers paid $1,500 owed, directly to the bank. The bank deducted a $25 collection fee from the amount it credited to Jackson's account. The statement also indicated that the bank had charged Jackson's account $50 to print new cheques.

e. Gross accounts receivable at December 31, 2008, amount to $44,000. Before adjustment, the balance in the Allowance for Doubtful Accounts is $340 (credit). Based on past experience, the accountant estimates that 3% of the gross accounts receivable outstanding at December 31, 2008, will prove to be uncollectible.

Required

1. Record the accounting entries required in items **a–e**.

2. Prepare the Current Assets section of Jackson's balance sheet as of December 31, 2008. In addition to items **a–e**, the balances in Inventory and Prepaid Insurance on this date are $65,000 and $4,800, respectively.

Solution to Review Problem

1. The following entries are recorded at December 31, 2008:

   a. & b. No entries required.

   c. Jackson needs an adjusting entry to record interest earned on the guaranteed investment certificate at the First National Bank. The GIC has been outstanding for 30 days during 2008, and therefore the amount of interest earned is calculated as follows:

   $$\$10,000 \times 0.09 \times 30/360 = \$75$$

   The adjusting entry follows:

2008			
Dec. 31	Interest Receivable	75	
	Interest Revenue		75
	To record interest earned during 2008.		

Assets	=	Liabilities	+	Shareholders' Equity
+75				+75

   d. Entries are needed to record the bank's collection of the account, the collection charge on the note, and the charge for the new cheques:

2008			
Dec. 31	Cash	1,500	
	Accounts Receivable		1,500
	To record collection of note and interest		

Assets	=	Liabilities	+	Shareholders' Equity
+1,500				
−1,500				

(continued)

2008
Dec. 31   Collection Fee Expense   25
              Cash   25
              To record deduction from account for collection fee

Assets	=	Liabilities	+	Shareholders' Equity
−25				−25

2008
Dec. 31   Miscellaneous Expense   50
              Cash   50
              To record deduction from account for new cheques

Assets	=	Liabilities	+	Shareholders' Equity
−50				−50

e. Based on gross accounts receivable of $44,000 at year-end and an estimate that 3% of this amount will be uncollectible, the balance in the Allowance for Doubtful Accounts should be $1,320 ($44,000 × 3%). Given a current balance of $340, an adjusting entry for $980 ($1,320 − $340) is needed to bring the balance to the desired amount of $1,320:

2008
Dec. 31   Bad Debts Expense   980
              Allowance for Doubtful Accounts   980
              To record estimated bad debts for the year

Assets	=	Liabilities	+	Shareholders' Equity
−980				−980

2. The Current Assets section of Jackson's balance sheet appears as follows:

JACKSON CORP.
PARTIAL BALANCE SHEET
DECEMBER 31, 2008

Current Assets

Cash		$ 19,255*
Guaranteed investment certificate		10,000
Accounts receivable	$44,000	
Less: Allowance for doubtful accounts	1,320	42,680
Interest receivable		75
Inventory		65,000
Prepaid insurance		4,800
Total current assets		$141,810

*Savings account	$13,200
Petty cash fund	400
Chequing account ($4,230 + $1,500 − $25 − $50)	5,655
Total	$19,255

Questions

1. What is a cash equivalent? Why is it included with cash on the balance sheet?

2. Why does the purchase of an item classified as a cash equivalent *not* appear on the statement of cash flows as an investing activity?

3. A friend says to you: "I understand why it is important to deposit all receipts intact and not keep coin and currency sitting around the business. Beyond this control feature, however, I believe that a company should strive to keep the maximum amount possible in chequing accounts to always be able to pay bills on time." How would you evaluate your friend's statement?

4. A friends says to you: "I'm confused. I have a memo included with my bank statement indicating a $20 service charge for printing new cheques. If the bank is deducting this amount from my account, why do they call it a 'debit memorandum'? I thought a decrease in a cash account would be a credit, not a debit." How can you explain this?

5. Different formats for bank reconciliations are possible. What is the format for a bank reconciliation in which a service charge for a safety deposit box is *added* to the balance per the bank statement? Explain your answer.

6. What is the theoretical justification for the allowance method of accounting for bad debts?

7. In estimating bad debts, why is the balance in Allowance for Doubtful Accounts considered when the percentage of accounts receivable approach is used but not when the percentage of net credit sales approach is used?

8. When estimating bad debts on the basis of a percentage of accounts receivable, what is the advantage to using an aging schedule?

9. How do the duties of an internal audit staff differ from those of the external auditors?

10. What is the typical composition of a board of directors of a publicly held corporation?

11. An order clerk fills out a purchase requisition for an expensive item of inventory and the receiving report when the merchandise arrives. The clerk takes the inventory home and then sends the invoice to the accounting department so that the supplier will be paid. What basic internal control procedure could have prevented this misuse of company assets?

12. What are some of the limitations on a company's effective system of internal control?

13. Stanzel Corp. purchased 1,000 IBM common shares. What will determine whether the shares are classified as trading securities or available-for-sale securities? (Appendix)

14. On December 31, Stockton Inc. invests idle cash in two different guaranteed investment certificates. The first is an 8%, 90-day GIC, and the second has an interest rate of 9% and matures in 120 days. How is each of these GICs classified on the December 31 balance sheet? (Appendix)

15. What is the primary difference in the accounting requirements for trading securities and those for available-for-sale securities? How is the primary difference justified? (Appendix)

16. Why are changes in the fair value of trading securities reported in the account Unrealized Gains/Losses—Trading Securities even though the gains and losses are reported on the income statement? (Appendix)

Exercises

Exercise 7-1 *Composition of Cash* **LO 1**

Using a Y for yes or an N for no, indicate whether each of the following items should be included in cash and cash equivalents on the balance sheet. If an item should not be included in cash and cash equivalents, indicate where it should appear on the balance sheet.

_____ 1. Chequing account at Third Bank

_____ 2. Petty cash fund

_____ 3. Coin and currency

_____ 4. Postage stamps

_____ 5. An IOU from an employee

_____ 6. Savings account at the Worth Bank

_____ 7. A six-month GIC

_____ 8. Undeposited customer cheques

_____ 9. A customer's cheque returned by the bank and marked NSF

_____ 10. A cashier's cheque

Exercise 7-2 *Items on a Bank Reconciliation* LO 1

Assume that a company is preparing a bank reconciliation for the month of June. It reconciles the bank balance and the book balance to the correct balance. For each of the following items, indicate whether the item is an addition to the bank balance (A-Bank), an addition to the book balance (A-Book), a deduction from the bank balance (D-Bank), a deduction from the book balance (D-Book), or would not appear on the June reconciliation (NA).

_____ 1. Cheque written in June but not yet returned to the bank for payment

_____ 2. Customer's NSF cheque

_____ 3. Customer's cheque written in the amount of $54 but recorded on the books in the amount of $45*

_____ 4. Service charge for new cheques

_____ 5. Interest on the chequing account for the month of June

_____ 6. Customer's cheque deposited on June 30 but not reflected on the bank statement

_____ 7. Cheque written on the company's account, paid by the bank, and returned with the bank statement

_____ 8. Cheque written on the company's account for $123 but recorded on the books as $132*

---

*Answer in terms of the adjustment needed to correct for the error.

Exercise 7-3 *Guaranteed Investment Certificate (Appendix)* LO 6

On May 31, 2008, Elmer Corp. purchased a 120-day, 9% guaranteed investment certificate for $50,000. The GIC was redeemed on September 28, 2008. Prepare the journal entries on Elmer's books to account for the GIC, including any entry on June 30, the end of the company's fiscal year. Assume 360 days in a year.

Exercise 7-4 *Petty Cash Fund* LO 1

On January 2, 2008, Cleaver Video Stores decided to set up a petty cash fund. The treasurer established the fund by writing and cashing a $300 cheque and placing the coin and currency in a locked petty cash drawer. Edward Haskell was designated as the custodian for the fund. During January, the following receipts were given to Haskell in exchange for cash from the fund:

Canada Post (stamps)	$76.00
Speedy Delivery Service	45.40
Cake N Cookies (party for retiring employee)	65.40
Office Supply Superstore (paper, pencils)	36.00

A count of the cash in the drawer on January 31 revealed a balance of $74.10. The treasure wrote and cashed a cheque on the same day to restore the fund to its original balance of $300. Prepare the necessary journal entries, with explanations, for January. Assume that all stamps and office supplies were used during the month.

Exercise 7-5 *Comparison of the Direct Write-Off and Allowance Methods of Accounting for Bad Debts* LO 2

In its first year of business, Rideaway Bikes has net income of $145,000, exclusive of any adjustment for bad debt expense. The president of the company has asked you to calculate net income under each of two alternatives of accounting for bad debts: the direct write-off method and the allowance method. The president would like to use the method that will result in the higher net income. So far, no entries have been made to write off uncollectible accounts or to estimate bad debts. The relevant data are as follows:

Write-offs of uncollectible accounts during the year	$ 10,500
Net credit sales	$650,000
Estimated percentage of net credit sales that will be uncollectible	2%

Required

Compute net income under each of the two alternatives. Does Rideaway have a choice as to which method to use? Should it base its choice on which method will result in the higher net income? (Ignore income taxes.)

Exercise 7-6 *Allowance Method of Accounting for Bad Debts—Comparison of the Two Approaches* LO 2

Kandel Company had the following data available for 2008 (before making any adjustments):

Accounts receivable, 12/31/08	$320,100 (dr)
Allowance for doubtful accounts	2,600 (cr)
Net credit sales, 2008	834,000 (cr)

Required

1. Prepare the journal entry to recognize bad debts under the following assumptions: (a) bad debt expense is expected to be 2% of net credit sales for the year and (b) Kandel expects it will not be able to collect 6% of the balance in accounts receivable at year end.

2. Assume instead that the balance in the allowance account is a $2,600 debit. How will this affect your answers to requirement 1?

Exercise 7-7 *Accounts Receivable Turnover* LO 3

The 2008 annual report of General Products reported the following amounts (in millions of dollars).

Sales, for the year ended December 31, 2008	$7,077.7
Receivables, less allowance for doubtful accounts of $5.7, December 31, 2008	664.0
Receivables, less allowance for doubtful accounts of $5.8, December 31, 2007	500.6

Required

1. Compute General Products' accounts receivable turnover ratio for 2008. (Assume that all sales are on credit.)

2. What is the average collection period, in days, for an account receivable? Explain your answer.

3. Do you think the average collection period for sales is reasonable? What other information do you need to fully answer this question?

Exercise 7-8 *Credit Card Sales* LO 3

Darlene's Diner accepts VISA cards from its customers. Darlene's deposits cash and credit card drafts daily but records the weekly sales on Sundays. For the week ending on Sunday, June 12, cash sales totalled $2,430 and credit card sales amounted to $3,500. VISA Company charges a 4% credit card service fee.

Required

1. Prepare journal entries to record Darlene's sales for the week ending Sunday, June 12.

2. If $100 of the $3,500 credit card sales was defaulted eventually, how will that affect Darlene's?

Exercise 7-9 *Impact of Transactions Involving Receivables on Statement of Cash Flows* LO 4

From the following list, identify whether the change in the account balance during the year would be added to or deducted from net income when the indirect method is used to determine cash flows from operating activities.

_____ Increase in accounts receivable

_____ Decrease in accounts receivable

Exercise 7-10 *Internal Control* LO 5

The university drama club is planning a raffle. The president overheard you talking about internal control to another accounting student, so she has asked you to set up some guidelines to "be sure" that all money collected for the raffle is accounted for by the club.

Required

1. Describe guidelines that the club should follow to achieve an acceptable level of internal control.

2. Comment on the president's request that she "be sure" all money is collected and recorded.

Exercise 7-11 *Segregation of Duties* LO 5

The tasks listed in the table on the next page are performed by three employees, each of whom is capable of performing all of them. Do not concern yourself with the time required to perform the tasks but with the need to provide for segregation of duties. Assign the duties by using a check mark to indicate which employee should perform each task. Remember that you may assign any one of the tasks to any of the employees.

(continued)

Task	Employee		
	Mary	**Sue**	**John**
Prepare invoices			
Mail invoices			
Pick up mail from post office			
Open mail, separate cheques			
List cheques on deposit slip in triplicate			
Post payment to customer's account			
Deposit cheques			
Prepare monthly schedule of accounts receivable			
Reconcile bank statements			

Exercise 7-12 *Classification of Investments (Appendix)* **LO 6**

Fill in the blanks below to indicate whether each of the following investments should be classified as a held-to-maturity security (HM), a trading security (T), or an available-for-sale security (AS):

_____ 1. Common shares of Nortel Network to be held indefinitely.

_____ 2. CT bonds due in 10 years. The intent is to hold them until they mature.

_____ 3. Shares of RIM. Plans are to hold the shares until the price goes up by 10% and then sell them.

_____ 4. CN bonds due in 15 years. The bonds are part of a portfolio that turns over an average of every 60 days.

_____ 5. CP bonds due in 10 years. Plans are to hold them indefinitely.

Exercise 7-13 *Investment in Bonds (Appendix)* **LO 6**

Starship Enterprises enters into the following transactions during 2008 and 2009

2008
Jan. 1: Purchased $100,000 face value of Northern Lights Inc. bonds at face value. The newly issued bonds have an interest rate of 8% paid semiannually on June 30 and December 31. The bonds mature in five years.

June 30: Received interest on the Northern Lights bonds.

Dec. 31 Received interest on the Northern Lights bonds.

2009
Jan. 1: Sold the Northern Lights Inc. bonds for $102,000.

Assume Starship classifies all bonds as held to maturity.

Required

1. Prepare all necessary journal entries on Starship's records to account for its investment on the Northern Lights bonds.

2. Why was Starship able to sell its Northern Lights bonds for $102.000.

Exercise 7-14 *Investment in Shares (Appendix)* **LO 6**

On December 1, 2008, Alpha Corp. purchases 1,000 of the preferred shares of Beta Corp. for $40 per share. Alpha expects the price of the shares to increase over the next few months and plans to sell them for a profit. On December 20, 2008, Beta declares a dividend of $1 per share to be paid on January 15, 2009. On December 31, 2008 Alpha's accounting year-end, the Beta's shares are trading on the market for $42 per share. Alpha sells the shares on February 12, 2009, at a price of $45 per share.

Required

1. Should Alpha classify its investments as held-to-maturity, trading, or available-for-sale securities? Explain your answer.

2. Prepare all necessary journal entries on Alpha's books in connection with its investment, beginning with the purchase of the preferred shares on December 1, 2008; the dividend declared on December 20, 2008; the change in market value at December 31, 2008; and the sale on February 12, 2009.

3. In what category of the balance sheet should Alpha classify its investment on its December 31, 2008, balance sheet?

Multi-Concept Exercise

Exercise 7-15 *Classification of Cash Equivalents and Investments on a Balance Sheet (Appendix)* **LO 1, 6**

Classify each of the following items as either a cash equivalent (CE), a short-term investment (STI), or a long-term investment (LTI).

_____ 1. A 120-day guaranteed investment certificate.

_____ 2. Three hundred Nortel common shares. The company plans on selling the shares in six months.

_____ 3. A 60-day GIC.

_____ 4. Ace Motor Co. bonds maturing in 15 years. The company intends to hold the bonds until maturity.

_____ 5. Commercial paper issued by ABC Corp., maturing in four months.

_____ 6. Five hundred common shares of **TD Bank**. The company plans to sell the shares in 60 days.

http://www.tdcanadatrust.com

_____ 7. Two hundred shares of ACE Aviation Holdings preferred. The company intends to hold the shares for 10 years and at that point sell them to help finance construction of a new factory.

_____ 8. 30% of Star Resources Inc.'s common shares. Star Resources Inc. is an important supplier. 30% of ownership will allow the investing company to have influence on Star Resources Inc.

Problems

Problem 7-1 *Bank Reconciliation and Journal Entries* **LO 1**

The following information is available to assist you in preparing a bank reconciliation for Packton Co. on May 31, 2008:

a. The balance on the May 31, 2008, bank statement is $8,432.11.

b. Not included on the bank statement is a $1,373.45 deposit made by Packton Co. late on May 31.

c. A comparison between the cancelled cheques returned with the bank statement and the company records indicated that the following cheques are outstanding at May 31:

No. 123	$ 23.40
No. 127	145.00
No. 128	210.80
No. 130	67.32

d. The Cash account on the company's books shows a balance of $10,430.34.

e. Interest earned on the chequing account and added to Packton Co.'s account during May was $54.60. Miscellaneous bank service charges amounted to $50.00.

f. A customer's NSF cheque in the amount of $166.00 was returned with the May bank statement.

g. The comparison of deposits per the bank statement with those per the books revealed that another customer's cheque in the amount of $101.10 was correctly added to the company's account. In recording the cheque on the company's books, however, the accountant erroneously increased the Cash account $1,011.00.

Required

1. Prepare a bank reconciliation in good form.

2. Prepare the necessary journal entries on the books of Packton Co.

3. A friend says to you: "I don't know why companies bother to prepare bank reconciliations—it seems a waste of time. Why don't they just do like I do and adjust the Cash account for any difference between what the bank shows as a balance and what shows up in the books?" Explain to your friend *why* a bank reconciliation should be prepared as soon as a bank statement is received.

Problem 7-2 *Accounts Receivable and Bad Debt Expense*

Sports Unlimited is a fast-growing retailer of athletic training equipment and accessories. At the beginning of August, Sports Unlimited has the following account balances:

Accounts receivable	$ 36,000 (Dr)
Allowance for doubtful accounts	500 (Cr)

The sales-related transactions of August are summarized below:

Cash sales	$100,000
Credit sales	250,000
Collection from customers	236,000
Write-off of uncollectible accounts	9,000
Recovery of previously written-off accounts	2,100

The company calculates its bad debt expense as 1% of the credit sales and automatically writes off all accounts that are 90 days past due.

Required

1. Prepare a summary journal entry to record the cash sales, credit sales, collection from customers, write-offs, recovery of previously written-off accounts, and the recognition of bad debt expense.
2. How should accounts receivable be reported in the balance sheet?
3. Do you think estimating bad debt expense as 1% of credit sales is adequate for Sports Unlimited? Why or why not?
4. There are two different methods of estimating bad debt expense: the percentage of credit sales, or income statement method, and the percentage of accounts receivable, or balance sheet method. Why is the percentage of credit sales called the income statement method and the percentage of accounts receivable called the balance sheet method?
5. Assume Sports Unlimited decided to switch to the percentage of accounts receivable method for bad debts and uses a 5% rate. What would be its bad debt expense for August?

Problem 7-3 *Accounts Receivable* LO 2

Linus Corp. sold merchandise for $5,000 to C. Brown on May 15, 2008, with credit terms of net 30. Subsequent to this, Brown experienced cash flow problems and was unable to pay its debt. On August 10, 2008, Linus stopped trying to collect the outstanding receivable from Brown and wrote the account off as uncollectible. On December 1, 2008, Brown sent Linus a cheque for $5,000. Linus ends its accounting year on December 31 each year, and uses the allowance method to account for bad debts.

Required

1. Prepare all of the necessary journal entries on the books of Linus Corp. from May 15, 2008, to December 31, 2008.
2. Why would Brown bother to send Linus a cheque for $5,000 on December 1, given that such a long period of time had passed since the original purchase?

Problem 7-4 *Allowance Method for Accounting for Bad Debts* LO 2

At the beginning of 2008, EZ Tech Company's Accounts Receivable balance was $140,000, and the balance in the Allowance for Doubtful Accounts was $2,350 (cr). EZ Tech's sales in 2008 were $1,050,000, 80% of which were on credit. Collections on account during the year were $670,000. The company wrote off $4,000 of uncollectible accounts during the year.

Required

1. Prepare summary journal entries related to the sale, collections, and write-offs of accounts receivable during 2008.
2. Prepare journal entries to recognize bad debts assuming (a) bad debt expense is 3% of credit sales and (b) amounts expected to be uncollectible are 6% of the year-end accounts receivable.
3. What is the net realizable value of accounts receivable on December 31, 2008, under each assumption (**a** and **b**) in requirement 2?
4. What effect does the recognition of bad debt expense have on the net realizable value? What effect does the write-off of accounts receivable have on the net realizable value?

Problem 7-5 *Aging Schedule to Account for Bad Debts* LO 2

Sparkle Jewels distributes fine stones. It sells on credit to retail jewellery stores and extends terms of 2/10, net 60.

On December 31, 2008, the credit balance in Allowance for Doubtful Accounts is $12,300. The amounts of gross receivables, by age, on this date and the estimated percentages of uncollectible accounts of each age group are as follows:

Age (days)	Amount	Estimated % of Uncollectible
≤ 30	$200,000	5%
31–60	45,000	20%
61–90	25,000	40%
90+	10,000	60%

Required

1. Prepare a schedule to estimate the amount of uncollectible accounts at December 31, 2008.

2. On the basis of the schedule in requirement 1, prepare the journal entry on December 31, 2008, to estimate bad debts.

3. Show how accounts receivable would be presented on the December 31, 2008, balance sheet.

Problem 7-6 *Credit Card Sales* LO 3

Canadian Tire rewards its customers with Canadian Tire money. These coupons can be used as payment for future purchases at Canadian Tire stores provided that customers are paying cash.

Required

1. Why does Canadian Tire offer Canadian Tire money only when a customer pays cash?

2. Assume that credit card companies charge 2.5% of the sales price when customers use credit cards. How much Canadian Tire money could Canadian Tire offer to a customer buying a set of snow tires priced at $500 with cash and still earn the same amount as if the customer paid with a credit card?

Problem 7-7 *Internal Control Procedures* LO 5

You are opening a summer business, a chain of three drive-through snow-cone stands. You have hired other students to work and have purchased a cash register with locked-in tapes. You retain one key, and the other is available to the lead person on each shift.

Required

1. Write a list of the procedures for all employees to follow when ringing up sales and giving change.

2. Write a list of the procedures for the lead person to follow in closing out at the end of the day. Be as specific as you can so that employees will have few if any questions.

3. What is your main concern in the design of internal control for the snow-cone stands? How did you address that concern? Be specific.

Problem 7-8 *Internal Control* LO 5

At Morris Mart Inc. all sales are on account. Mary Morris-Manning is responsible for mailing invoices to customers, recording the amount billed, opening mail, and recording the payment. Mary is very devoted to the family business and never takes off more than one or two days for a long weekend. The customers know Mary and sometimes send personal notes with their payments. Another clerk handles all aspects of accounts payable. Mary's brother, who is president of Morris Mart, has hired an accountant to help with expansion.

Required

1. List some problems with the current accounts receivable system.

2. What suggestions would you make to improve internal control?

3. How would you explain to Mary that she personally is not the problem?

Problem 7-9 *Investments in Bonds and Shares (Appendix)* **LO 6**

Swartz Inc. enters into the following transactions during 2008:

July 1   Paid $10,000 to acquire on the open market $10,000 face value of Gallatin bonds. The bonds have a stated annual interest rate of 6% with interest paid semiannually on June 30 and December 31. The bonds mature in one year.

Oct. 23   Purchased 600 of Eagle Rock common shares at $20 per share.

Nov. 21   Purchased 200 of Montana preferred shares at $30 per share.

Dec. 10   Received dividends of $1.50 per share on the Eagle Rock shares and $2.00 per share on the Montana shares.

Dec. 28   Sold 400 of Eagle Rock common shares at $25 per share.

Dec. 31   Received interest from the Gallatin bonds.

Dec. 31   Noted market price of $29 per share for the Eagle Rock common and $26 per share for the Montana preferred.

Required

1. Prepare all necessary journal entries on Swartz's records to account for its investments during 2008. Swartz classifies the bonds as held-to-maturity securities and all share investments as trading securities.

2. Prepare a partial balance sheet as of December 31, 2008, to indicate the proper presentation of the investments.

3. Indicate the items, and the amount of each, that will appear on the 2008 income statement relative to the investments.

Problem 7-10 *Investments in Shares (Appendix)* **LO 6**

Atlas Superstores occasionally finds itself with excess cash to invest and consequently entered into the following transactions during 2006:

Jan. 15   Purchased 200 common shares of Sears at $50 per share, plus $500 in commissions.

May 23   Received dividends of $2 per share on the Sears shares.

June 1   Purchased 100 shares of Bombardier at $74 per share, plus $300 in commissions.

Oct. 20   Sold all the Sears shares at $42 per share, less commissions of $400.

Dec. 15   Received notification from Bombardier that a $1.50 per share dividend had been declared. The cheques will be mailed to shareholders on January 10, 2009.

Dec. 31   Noted that the Bombardier shares were quoted on the stock exchange at $85 per share.

Required

1. Prepare journal entries on the books of Atlas Superstores during 2008 to record these transactions, including any necessary entry on December 15, when the dividend was declared, and at the end of the year. Assume that Atlas categorizes all investments as available-for-sale securities.

2. What is the total amount that Atlas should report on its income statement from its investments during 2008?

3. Assume all the same facts except that Atlas categorizes all investments as trading securities. How would your answer to requirement 2 change? Explain why your answer would change.

Multi-Concept Problem

Problem 7-11 *Bank Reconciliation, Accounts Receivable, and Internal Control* **LO 1, 2, 3**

General Contractor Inc. is a small but fast-growing construction company. For the last five years, the company's office manager has been responsible for preparing and mailing invoices based on project managers' purchase receipts and time sheets, collecting and opening mail, depositing cheques, writing cheques to pay bills and purchases, and recording cheques received and payments made. Due to unexpected medical reasons the office manager was out for a week. The wife of the owner-manager of the company, Mr. Mason, was asked to take over for the time being. Mrs. Mason used to help her husband until five years ago when their first child was born.

The bank statement arrived the first day Mrs. Mason was back. She was alarmed at the discrepancy between the balance shown on the statement and the cash balance in the books. She decided to prepare a bank reconciliation just to put her mind at ease. However, she could not get it to balance even after several attempts. She was always short by $1,000. The following is the related information:

    a. The balance according to the back statement was $8,642.
    b. The balance according to the ledger account was $15,173.
    c. Bank service charge was $50.
    d. Interest earned was $36.
    e. Deposit in transit amounted to $6,751.
    f. Outstanding cheques totalled $1,234.

Required

1. Prepare a bank reconciliation and see if you have the same results as Mrs. Mason's.

2. Mrs. Mason looked up the previous months' bank reconciliations and discovered that the cash balances were not reconciled either. The office manager simply debited the difference to cash over/short account and reduced the cash account accordingly. Do you think it is appropriate to treat the difference as cash over/short? Why or why not?

3. Mrs. Mason reviewed the document further and made more unsettling discoveries:

    a. The bad debt expense was a lot higher now than five years ago when she was running the office. She noticed one of the accounts written off belonged to a very good client whom she remembered as being always prompt in paying its accounts.

    b. Some of the deposits were made more than a month ago according to the cash account but they still did not show up in the bank statement.

    c. Some cheques were debited in the bank statement but there was no record in the books about these cheques.

    d. Some cheques were written to pay invoices with no packing slips to indicate anything was received.

For each scenario above, suggest an explanation of what might have happened and recommend a procedure to prevent it being undetected in the future.

Alternate Problems

Problem 7-1A *Bank Reconciliation* LO 1

The following information is available to assist you in preparing a bank reconciliation for Karen's Catering on March 31, 2008:

a. The balance on the March 31, 2008, bank statement is $6,506.10.

b. Not included on the bank statement is a deposit made by Karen's late on March 31 in the amount of $423.00.

c. A comparison between the cancelled cheques listed on the bank statement and the company records indicated that the following cheques are outstanding at March 31:

No. 112	$ 42.92
No. 117	307.00
No. 120	10.58
No. 122	75.67

d. Interest earned on the chequing account and credited to Karen's account during March was $4.30. Miscellaneous bank service charges amounted to $26.50.

e. The comparison of cheques cleared per the bank statement with those per the books revealed that the wrong amount was charged to the company's account for a cheque. The amount of the cheque was $990.00. The proof machine encoded the cheque in the amount of $909.00, the amount charged against the company's account.

(continued)

Required

1. Determine the balance on the books before any adjustments as well as the corrected balance to be reported on the balance sheet.

2. What would you recommend Karen do as a result of the bank error in item **e** on the previous page? Why?

Problem 7-2A *Accounts Receivable and Bad Debt Expense*

Fantastic Sites is a fast-growing website design firm. At the beginning of August, Fantastic Sites has the following account balances:

Accounts receivable	$ 63,000
Allowance for doubtful accounts	1,500

The sales-related transactions of August are summarized below:

Cash sales	$200,000
Credit sales	520,000
Collection from customers	486,000
Write-off of uncollectible accounts	19,000
Recovery of previously written-off accounts	3,000

The company calculates its bad debt expense as 1% of the credit sales and automatically writes off all accounts that are 90 days past due.

Required

1. Prepare a summary journal entry to record the cash sales, credit sales, collection from customers, write-offs, recovery of previously written-off accounts, and the recognition of bad debt expense.

2. How should accounts receivable be reported in the balance sheet?

3. Do you think estimating bad debt expense as 1% of credit sales is adequate for Fantastic Sites? Why or why not?

4. There are two different methods of estimating bad debt expense: the percentage of credit sales, or income statement method, and the percentage of accounts receivable, or balance sheet method. Why is the percentage of credit sales called the income statement method and the percentage of accounts receivable called the balance sheet method?

5. Assume Fantastic Sites decided to switch to the percentage of accounts receivable method for bad debts and uses a 4% rate. What would be its bad debt expense for August?

Problem 7-3A *Accounts Receivable* LO 2

Tweedy Inc. sold merchandise for $6,000 to P.D. Cat on July 31, 2008, with credit terms of net 30. Subsequent to this, Cat experienced cash flow problems and was unable to pay its debt. On December 24, 2008, Tweedy stopped trying to collect the outstanding receivable from Cat and wrote the account off as uncollectible. On January 15, 2009, Cat sent Tweedy a cheque for $6,000. Tweedy ends its accounting year on December 31 each year.

Required

1. Prepare all of the necessary journal entries on the books of Tweedy Inc. from July 31, 2008, to January 15, 2009.

2. Why would Cat bother to send Tweedy a cheque for $6,000 on January 15, given that such a long period of time had passed since the original purchase?

Problem 7-4A *Allowance Method for Accounting for Bad Debts* LO 2

At the beginning of 2008, Miyazaki Company's Accounts Receivable balance was $105,000 and the balance in the Allowance for Doubtful Accounts was $1,950 (cr). Miyazaki's sales in 2008 were $787,500, 80% of which were on credit. Collections on account during the year were $502,500. The company wrote off $3,000 of uncollectible accounts during the year.

Required

1. Prepare summary journal entries related to the sales, collections, and write-offs of accounts receivable during 2008.

2. Prepare journal entries to recognize bad debts assuming (a) bad debt expense is 3% of credit sales or (b) amounts expected to be uncollectible are 6% of the year-end accounts receivable.

3. What is the net realizable value of accounts receivable on December 31, 2008, under each assumption (**a** and **b**) in requirement 2?

4. What effect does the recognition of bad debt expense have on the net realizable value? What effect does the write-off of accounts receivable have on the net realizable value?

Problem 7-5A *Aging Schedule to Account for Bad Debts* LO 2

Rough Stuff is a distributor of large rocks. It sells on credit to commercial landscaping companies and extends terms of 2/10, net 60.

On December 31, 2008, the credit balance in Allowance for Doubtful Accounts is $34,590. The amounts of gross receivables, by age, on this date and the estimated percentage of uncollectible accounts of each age group are as follows:

Category	Amount	Estimated % of Uncollectible
≤ 60	$135,000	10%
61–90	60,300	25%
91–120	35,000	35%
120+	45,000	75%

Required

1. Prepare a schedule to estimate the amount of uncollectible accounts at December 31, 2008.

2. Rough knows that $40,000 of the $45,000 amount that is more than two months overdue is due from one customer that is in severe financial trouble. It is rumoured that the customer will be filing for bankruptcy in the near future. As controller for Rough Stuff, how would you handle this situation?

3. Show how accounts receivable would be presented on the December 31, 2008, balance sheet.

Problem 7-6A *Credit Card Sales* LO 3

A local fast-food restaurant is considering the use of major credit cards in its outlets. Current annual sales are $800,000 per outlet. The company can purchase the equipment needed to handle credit cards and have an additional phone line installed in each outlet for approximately $800 per outlet. The equipment will be an expense in the year it is installed. The employee training time is minimal. The credit card company will charge a fee equal to 1.5% of sales for the use of credit cards. The company is unable to determine by how much, if any, sales will increase and whether cash customers will use a credit card rather than cash. No other fast-food restaurants in the local area accept credit cards for payment.

Required

1. Assuming only 5% of existing cash customers will use a credit card, how much earnings should the new sales generate in order to pay for the credit card equipment in the first year?

2. What other factors might the company consider in addition to an increase in sales dollars?

Problem 7-7A *Internal Control Procedures* LO 5

The loan department in a bank is subject to regulation. Internal auditors work for the bank to ensure that the loan department complies with requirements. The internal auditors must verify that each car loan file has a note signed by the maker, verification of insurance, and a title issued by the province that names the bank as co-owner.

Required

1. Explain why the bank and the regulatory agency are concerned with these documents.

2. Describe the internal control procedures that should be in place to ensure that these documents are obtained and safeguarded.

Problem 7-8A *Internal Control* LO 5

Abbott Inc. is expanding and needs to hire more personnel in the accounting office. Barbara Barker, the chief accounting clerk, knew that her cousin Cheryl was looking for a job. Barbara and Cheryl are also roommates. Barbara offered Cheryl a job as her assistant. Barbara will be responsible for Cheryl's performance reviews and training.

Required

1. List some problems with the proposed personnel situations in the accounting department.

2. Explain why accountants are concerned with the hiring of personnel. What suggestions would you make to improve internal control at Abbott?

3. How would you explain to Barbara and Cheryl that they personally are not the problem?

Problem 7-9A *Investments in Bonds and Shares (Appendix)* **LO 6**

Nova Corp. enters into the following transactions during 2008:

July 1   Paid $10,000 to acquire on the open market $10,000 face value of Inglis bonds. The bonds have a stated annual interest rate of 8% with interest paid semiannually on June 30 and December 31. The remaining life of the bonds on the date of purchase is one year.

Oct. 23   Purchased 1,000 Robie common shares at $15 per share.

Nov. 21   Purchased 600 Tower preferred shares at $8 per share.

Dec. 10   Received dividends of $0.50 per share on the Robie shares and $1.00 per share on the Tower shares.

Dec. 28   Sold 700 Robie common shares at $19 per share.

Dec. 31   Received interest from the Inglis bonds.

Dec. 31   The Robie shares and the Tower shares have market prices of $20 per share and $11 per share, respectively.

Required

1. Prepare all necessary journal entries on Nova's records to account for its investments during 2008. Nova classifies the bonds as held-to-maturity securities and all share investments as trading securities.

2. Prepare a partial balance sheet as of December 31, 2008, to indicate the proper presentation of the investments.

3. Indicate the items, and the amount of each, that will appear on the 2008 income statement relative to the investments.

Problem 7-10A *Investments in Shares (Appendix)* **LO 6**

Trendy Supercentre occasionally finds itself with excess cash to invest and consequently entered into the following transactions during 2008:

Jan. 15   Purchased 100 RIM common shares at $130 per share, plus $250 in commissions.

May 23   Received dividends of $1 per share on the RIM shares.

June 1   Purchased 200 shares of HBC at $60 per share, plus $300 in commissions.

Oct. 20   Sold all of the RIM shares at $140 per share, less commissions of $400.

Dec. 15   Received notification from HBC that a $0.75 per share dividend had been declared. The cheques will be mailed to shareholders on January 10, 2009.

Dec. 31   Noted that the HBC shares were quoted on the stock exchange at $45 per share.

Required

1. Prepare journal entries on the books of Trendy Supercentre during 2008 to record these transactions, including any necessary entry on December 15 when the dividend was declared and at the end of the year. Assume that Trendy categorizes all investments as available-for-sale securities.

2. What is the total amount of income that Trendy should recognize from its investments during 2008?

3. Assume all of the same facts except that Trendy categorizes all investments as trading securities. How would your answer to requirement 2 change? Explain why your answer would change.

Problem 7-11A *Bank Reconciliation, Accounts Receivable, and Internal Control* **LO 1, 2, 3**

Organized Inc. is a small but fast-growing event organizer. Its staff includes Mr. Blitz, the owner and manager, six event planners, and an office manager. The office manager is responsible for preparing and mailing invoices based on project managers' purchase receipts and time sheets, collecting and opening mail, depositing cheques, writing cheques to pay bills and purchases, and recording cheques received and payments made. Last week the office manager quit abruptly without an explanation. Mr. Blitz tried to fill in for her work while looking for a replacement.

The bank statement arrived the first day after the office manager quit. Mr. Blitz was alarmed at the discrepancy between the balance shown on the statement and the cash balance in the books. He decided to prepare a bank reconciliation just to put his mind at ease. However, he couldn't get it to balance even after several attempts. He was always short by $2,150. The following is the related information:

a. The balance in the statement was $17,151.

b. The cash balance on the books was $30,245.

c. Bank service charge was $10.

d. Interest earned was $75.

e. Deposit in transit amounted to $13,264.

f. Outstanding cheques totalled $2,345.

g. A cheque of $870 issued by Organized Inc. was recorded as $780 in the books.

Required

1. Prepare a bank reconciliation and see if you have the same results as Mr. Blitz's.

2. Mr. Blitz looked up the previous months' bank reconciliations and discovered that the cash balances were not reconciled last month either. The office manager simply debited the difference to cash over/short account and reduced the cash account accordingly. Do you think it is appropriate to treat the difference as cash over/short? Why or why not?

3. Mr. Blitz spent the whole day reviewing various documents and had the following unsettling discoveries:

   a. He noticed some accounts were way past due dates. He called one of these past due clients but was told that the account had already been paid and received a cancelled cheque as proof.

   b. Some of the deposits were made more than a month ago according to the cash account but they were still deposits in transit.

   c. Some cheques from the chequebook were missing and there was no record of what happened to them.

   d. Some paycheques were made to names other than the company's employees.

4. For each scenario above, suggest an explanation of what happened and recommend a procedure to prevent it being undetected in the future.

Cases

Reading and Interpreting Financial Statements

Case 7-1 *Reading and Interpreting CN's Financial Statements* LO 2

Refer to the financial statements for 2007 included in CN's annual report. Answer each of the following questions by reference to the account titled "Accounts Receivable" and Note 4.

Required

1. What is the balance in the Allowance for Doubtful Accounts at the end of each of the two years presented? What is the net realizable value at the end of each year?

2. Calculate the ratio of the Allowance for Doubtful Accounts to Gross Accounts Receivable at the end of each of the two years.

3. Why do you think the Allowance for Doubtful Accounts percentage was decreased at the end of 2007? Does this mean that the company expects a smaller percentage of bad debts?

Making Financial Decisions

Case 7-2 *Liquidity* LO 1, 2, 6

R. Montague and J. Capulet both distribute films to movie theatres. The following are the current assets for each at the end of the year (all amounts are in millions of dollars):

	R. Montague	J. Capulet
Cash	$10	$ 5
Six-month GICs	9	0
Short-term investments in shares	0	6
Accounts receivable	15	23
Allowance for doubtful accounts	(1)	(1)
Total current assets	$33	$33

(continued)

Required

As a loan officer for the National Bank of Verona Heights, assume that both companies have come to you asking for a $10 million, six-month loan. If you could lend money to only one of the two, which one would it be? Justify your answer by writing a brief memo to the president of the bank.

Accounting and Ethics: What Would You Do?

Case 7-3 *Fair Market Values for Investments (Appendix)* LO 6

Kennedy Corp. operates a chain of discount stores. The company regularly holds shares of various companies in a trading securities portfolio. One of these investments is 10,000 shares of Clean Air Inc. purchased for $100 per share during December 2008.

Clean Air manufactures highly specialized equipment used to test automobile emissions. Unfortunately, the market price of Clean Air's stock dropped during December 2008 and closed the year trading at $75 per share. Kennedy expects the Clean Air shares to experience a turnaround, however, as provinces pass legislation to require an emissions test on all automobiles.

As controller for Kennedy, you have followed the fortunes of Clean Air with particular interest. You and the company's treasurer are both concerned by the negative impact that a write-down of the shares to fair value would have on Kennedy's earnings for 2008. You have calculated net income for 2008 to be $400,000, exclusive of the recognition of any loss on the shares.

The treasurer comes to you on January 31, 2009, with the following idea:

> Since you haven't closed the books yet for 2008, and we haven't yet released the 2008 financials, let's think carefully about how Clean Air should be classified. I realize that we normally treat these types of investments as trading securities, but if we categorize the Clean Air shares investment on the balance sheet as available-for-sale rather than a trading security, we won't need to report the adjustment to fair value on the income statement. I don't see anything wrong with this since we would still report the shares at their fair value on the balance sheet.

Required

1. Compute Kennedy's net income for 2008, under two different assumptions: (a) the shares are classified as a trading security, and (b) the shares are classified as an available-for-sale security.

2. Which classification do you believe is appropriate, according to accounting standards? Explain your answer.

3. Would you have any ethical concerns in following the treasurer's advice? Explain your answer.

Internet Research Case

INTERNET

http://www.sears.ca

Case 7-4 *Sears Canada*

Sears Canada, one of Canada's leading department stores, strives to offer quality services and products to its customers across Canada.

To answer the following questions, examine the chapter opening text and the financial statements provided there, and visit the company website.

1. What are the cash and cash equivalents for Sears for the latest year available?

2. What reason does the company give for the change in cash and equivalents for the most recent year available?

3. What are the short-term investments for the latest year available?

4. What reasons does the company give for the change in short-term investments for the latest year available?

5. What are accounts receivable for the latest year available? Can you tell from the notes how much was for accounts receivable and how much for notes receivable?

6. Comparing the latest annual report with the financial information from 2007 in the textbook, what are the three most significant changes to the financial statements? What is the most significant change to Sears as a company?

Quiz 1: Cash and Accounts Receivable

2	Cash equivalent		10	Petty cash fund
8	Bank statement		12	Subsidiary ledger
6	Outstanding cheque		14	Control account
4	Deposit in transit		13	Direct write-off method
9	Bank reconciliation		5	Allowance method
1	Credit memoranda		11	Aging schedule
3	Debit memoranda		7	Credit card draft

Quiz 2: Internal Control and Investments

11	Internal control system		1	Equity securities
2	Board of directors		4	Debt securities
5	Audit committee		10	Held-to-maturity investments
3	Accounting system		7	Trading investments
9	Administrative controls		8	Available-for-sale investments
6	Accounting controls			
12	Management's statement of responsibility			

CHAPTER 8

Capital Assets: Property, Plant, and Equipment, Natural Resources, and Intangibles

COURTESY CN RAIL

STUDY LINKS

A Look at the Previous Chapter

Chapter 7 presented the accounting for a company's current assets of accounts receivable, and investments. These assets are important aspects of short-term liquidity.

A Look at This Chapter

In this chapter we will examine a company's capital assets of property, plant, and equipment as well as natural

resources and intangibles. These assets are an important indicator of a company's ability to produce revenue in the long term.

A Look at Upcoming Chapters

Later chapters discuss the financing of long-term assets. Chapter 10 presents long-term liabilities as a source of financing. Chapter 11 describes the use of shares as a source of funds for financing long-term assets.

Focus on Financial Results

The balance sheet for CN at December 31, 2007, shows the two largest assets to be properties ($20,413 million) and intangibles and other assets ($1,999 million). These two categories of assets represent 95.5% of the total assets of CN and as such are important to the readers of these statements. Details of these amounts can be found in footnotes to the financial statements.

This chapter will help you understand many of the details in these footnotes so that you can assess the replacement practices for these assets and how CN charges its operations for the costs of these assets.

CN 2007 ANNUAL REPORT (EXCERPT)

Consolidated Balance Sheets (Excerpt)

In millions December 31,	2007	2006
Assets		
Current Assets:		
Cash and cash equivalents	$ 310	$ 179
Accounts receivable (*Note 4*)	370	692
Material and supplies	162	189
Deferred income taxes (*Note 15*)	68	84
Other	138	192
	1,048	1,336
Properties (*Note 5*)	20,413	21,053
Intangible and other assets (*Note 6*)	1,999	1,615
Total assets	$ 23,460	$ 24,004

This excerpt from CN's 2007 Annual Report appears courtesy of CN. This section of the CN Annual Report appears in the Appendix of this textbook.

CAPITAL ASSETS: PROPERTY, PLANT, AND EQUIPMENT

LO 1 Describe the balance sheet disclosures for capital assets.

Balance Sheet Presentation

Capital assets constitute the major productive assets of many companies. Current assets are important to a company's short-term liquidity; capital assets are absolutely essential to its long-term future. These assets are used to produce the goods or services the company sells to customers. The dollar amount invested in capital assets may be very large, as is the case with most manufacturing companies. On the other hand, capital assets on the balance sheet may be insignificant to a company's value, as is the case with a computer software firm or many Internet firms. Users of financial statements must assess the capital assets to make important decisions. For example, lenders are interested in the value of the capital assets as collateral when making lending decisions. Investors must evaluate whether the capital assets indicate long-term potential and can provide a return to the shareholders.

The terms used to describe the capital assets and the balance sheet presentation of those assets vary somewhat by company. Some firms refer to this category of assets as *fixed* or *plant assets*. Other firms prefer to present capital assets in two categories: **tangible** *assets* and **intangible** *assets*. The balance sheet of **CN** uses another way to classify capital assets. The company presents one line item for *property, plant, and equipment* and presents the details in the footnotes. Because the term *property* can encompass a variety of items, CN uses the more descriptive term *intangible assets* for the second category. We begin by examining the accounting issues concerned with the first category: property, plant, and equipment.

The December 31, 2007 footnotes of CN present the acquisition costs of track, roadway, rolling stock, buildings, information technology, and other, and the amount of accumulated depreciation is deducted to determine the net amount. The accumulated depreciation for track and roadway does not relate to land since land is not a depreciable item.

Tangible Having physical substance (e.g., a machine is tangible).

Intangible Lacking physical substance (e.g., a copyright is intangible).

CN
http://www.cn.ca

ACQUISITION OF PROPERTY, PLANT, AND EQUIPMENT

LO 2 Determine the acquisition cost of a capital asset.

Assets classified as property, plant, and equipment are initially recorded at acquisition cost (also referred to as *historical cost*). As indicated in CN's notes, Exhibit 8-1, these assets are normally presented on the balance sheet at original acquisition cost minus accumulated depreciation.

Exhibit 8-1

CN Properties

In millions		December 31, 2007	
	Cost	Accumulated depreciation	Net
Track and roadway [1]	$22,020	$6,433	$15,587
Rolling stock	4,702	1,606	3,096
Buildings	1,105	498	607
Information technology	667	131	536
Other	829	242	587
	$29,323	$8,910	$20,413

This excerpt from CN's 2007 Annual Report appears courtesy of CN. This section of the CN Annual Report appears in the Appendix of this textbook.

Acquisition cost The amount that includes all of the costs normally necessary to acquire an asset and prepare it for its intended use (original cost).

It is important, however, to define the term *acquisition cost* (also known as *original cost*) in a more exact manner. What items should be included as part of the original acquisition? **Acquisition cost** should include all of the costs that are normal and necessary to acquire the asset and prepare it for its intended use. Items included in acquisition cost would generally be the following:

    Purchase price
    Taxes paid at time of purchase (for example, sales tax)
    Transportation charges
    Installation costs

An accountant must exercise careful judgment to determine which costs are "normal" and "necessary" and thus should be included in the calculation of the acquisition cost of capital assets. Acquisition cost should not include expenditures unrelated to the acquisition (for example, repair costs if an asset is damaged during installation) or costs incurred after the asset was installed and use begun.

 ## Accounting for Your Decisions

You Are a Lawyer

You are a newly licensed lawyer who just opened a legal firm. As part of your office operations, you have purchased some slightly used computers. Should the cost of repairing the computers be considered as part of the acquistion cost?

ANSWER: If you were aware that the computers needed to be repaired when purchased, the repair costs are part of the cost of acquisition. If the computers were damaged after they were purchased, the costs should be treated as an expense on the income statement.

Group Purchase   Quite often a firm purchases several assets as a group and pays a lump-sum amount. This is most common when a company purchases land and a building situated on it and pays a lump-sum amount for both. It is important to measure separately the acquisition cost of the land and of the building. Land is not a depreciable asset, but the amount allocated to the building is subject to depreciation. In cases such as this, the purchase price should be allocated between land and building on the basis of the proportion of the *fair market values* of each.

For example, assume that on January 1, Payton Company purchased a building and the land that it is situated on for $100,000. The accountant was able to establish that the estimated (fair) market values of the two assets on January 1 were as follows:

Land	$ 30,000
Building	90,000
Total	$120,000

On the basis of the estimated market values, the purchase price should be allocated as follows:

To land	$100,000 × $30,000/$120,000 = $25,000
To building	$100,000 × $90,000/$120,000 = $75,000

The journal entry to record the purchase would be as follows:

Jan. 1	Land	25,000	
	Building	75,000	
	Cash		100,000
	To record the purchase of land and building		
	for a lump-sum amount		

Assets	=	Liabilities	+	Shareholders' Equity
+25,000				
+75,000				
−100,000				

Market value is best established by an independent appraisal of the property. If such appraisal is not possible, the accountant must rely on the market value of other similar assets, on the value of the assets in tax records, or on other available evidence.

These efforts to allocate dollars between land and buildings will permit the appropriate allocation for depreciation. But when an investor or lender views the balance sheet, he or she is often more interested in the current market value. The best things that can be said about historical cost are that it is a verifiable number and that it is conservative. But it is still up to the lender or the investor to determine the appropriate value for these assets.

A challenging example of this idea of fair value allocation is the situation that arose in December 2007, when CN bought the rail assets of **Athabasca Northern Railway** (ANY) for $25 million. This cost had to be allocated among the elements of ANY's assets to reflect the amounts to be included with CN's balance sheet amounts. Footnote 3 of CN's annual report describes the acquisitions by CN in 2007.

A less complex but nevertheless important example of an allocation often occurs with condominium developments that are limited non-business companies. Here, purchasers own their units individually, but the condo corporation owns the common areas such as hallways, entrances, and walkways. If the revenue of the condo corporation exceeds $500,000 per year, it must depreciate the allocated cost of the common areas (an example of the cost–benefit differential reporting described in Chapter 2).

Capitalization of Interest

We have seen that acquisition cost may include several items. But should the acquisition cost of an asset include the interest cost necessary to finance the asset? That is, should interest be treated as an asset, or should it be treated as an expense of the period?

Generally, the interest on borrowed money should be treated as an expense of the period. If a company buys an asset and borrows money to finance the purchase, the interest on the borrowed money is not considered part of the asset's cost. Financial statements generally treat investing and financing as separate decisions. Purchase of an asset, an investing activity, is treated as a business decision that is separate from the decision concerning the financing of the asset. Therefore, interest is treated as a period cost and should appear on the income statement as interest expense in the period incurred.

There is one exception to this general guideline, however. If a company constructs an asset over a period of time and borrows money to finance the construction, the amount of interest incurred during the construction period may not be treated as interest expense. Instead, the interest may be included as part of the acquisition cost of the asset. This is referred to as **capitalization of interest**. The amount of interest that is capitalized (treated as an asset) is based on the *average accumulated expenditures*. The logic of using the average accumulated expenditure is that this number represents an average amount of money tied up in the project over a year. If it takes $400,000 to construct a building, the interest should not be figured on the full $400,000 because there were times during the year when less than the full amount was being used.

When it costs $400,000 to build an asset and the amount of interest to be capitalized is $10,000, the acquisition cost of the asset is $410,000. The asset should appear on the balance sheet at that amount. Depreciation of the asset should be based on $410,000, less any residual value.

In Canada, a company has the option of capitalizing interest during the construction period. CN does not appear to use this option, but such an option can make an important difference in the cost of assets and subsequent expenses for real estate developers.

Land Improvements

It is important to distinguish between land and other costs associated with it. The acquisition cost of land should be kept in a separate account because land has an unlimited life and is not subject to depreciation. Other costs associated with land should be recorded in an account such as Land Improvements. For example, the costs of paving a parking lot or landscaping costs are properly treated as **land improvements**, which have a limited life. Therefore, the acquisition costs of land improvements should be depreciated over their useful lives.

Capitalization of interest Interest on constructed assets is added to the asset account.

Land improvements Costs that are related to land but that have a limited life.

USE AND DEPRECIATION OF PROPERTY, PLANT, AND EQUIPMENT

All items of property, plant, and equipment, except land, have a limited life and decline in usefulness over time. The accrual accounting process requires a proper *matching* of expenses and revenue to accurately measure income. Therefore, the accountant must estimate the decline in usefulness of capital assets and allocate the acquisition cost in a manner consistent with the decline in usefulness. This allocation is the process generally referred to as **depreciation.**

Unfortunately, proper matching for capital assets is not easy because of the many factors involved. An asset's decline in usefulness is related to *physical deterioration* factors such as wear and tear. In some cases, the physical deterioration results from heavy use of the asset in the production process, but it may also result from the passage of time or exposure to the elements. One refinement of depreciation can be obtained by separating larger component parts of capital assets that depreciate at different rates. For example, a roof can be separated from the walls and foundation of a building.

The decline in an asset's usefulness is also related to *obsolescence* factors. Some capital assets, such as computers, decline in usefulness simply because they have been surpassed by a newer model or newer technology. Finally, the decline in an asset's usefulness is related to a company's *repair and maintenance* policy. A company with an aggressive and extensive repair and maintenance program will not experience a decline in usefulness of capital assets as rapidly as one without such a policy.

Because the decline in an asset's usefulness is related to a variety of factors, several depreciation methods have been developed. In theory, a company should use a depreciation method that allocates the original cost of the asset to the periods benefited and that allows the company to accurately match the expense to the revenue generated by the asset. We will present three methods of depreciation: *straight-line, units-of-production,* and *accelerated methods.*

All depreciation methods are based on the asset's original acquisition cost. In addition, all methods require an estimate of two additional factors: the asset's *life* and its *residual value.* The residual value (also referred to as *salvage value*) should represent the amount that could be obtained from selling or disposing of the asset at the end of its economically useful life. Often, this may be a small amount or even zero. (Although the two terms are slightly different in their meaning, *residual* value is a more appropriate term than *salvage* value because the former relates to the end of physical life.)

Straight-Line Method The **straight-line method** of depreciation allocates the cost of the asset evenly over time. This method calculates the annual depreciation as follows:

$$\text{Depreciation} = (\text{Acquisition Cost} - \text{Residual Value})/\text{Life}$$

For example, assume that on January 1, 2008, Kemp Company purchased a machine for $20,000. The company estimated that the machine's life would be five years and that its residual value at the end of 2012 would be $2,000. The annual depreciation should be calculated as follows:

$$\text{Depreciation} = (\text{Acquisition Cost} - \text{Residual Value})/\text{Life}$$
$$\text{Depreciation} = (\$20,000 - \$2,000)/5$$
$$= \$3,600$$

An asset's **book value** is defined as its acquisition cost minus its total amount of accumulated depreciation. Thus, the book value of the machine in this example is $16,400 at the end of 2008:

$$\text{Book Value} = \text{Acquisition Cost} - \text{Accumulated Depreciation}$$
$$\text{Book Value} = \$20,000 - \$3,600$$
$$= \$16,400$$

LO 3 Compare depreciation methods, and understand the factors affecting the choice of method.

Depreciation The allocation of the original cost less residual value of a capital asset to the periods benefited by its use.

Straight-line method A method by which the same dollar amount of depreciation is recorded in each year of asset use.

Book value The original cost of an asset minus the amount of accumulated depreciation.

The book value at the end of 2009 is $12,800:

$$\text{Book Value} = \text{Acquisition Cost} - \text{Accumulated Depreciation}$$
$$\text{Book Value} = \$20,000 - (2 \times \$3,600)$$
$$= \$12,800$$

The most attractive features of the straight-line method are its ease and its simplicity. It is the most popular method for presenting depreciation in the annual report to shareholders.

Units-of-Production Method   In some cases, the decline in an asset's usefulness is directly related to wear and tear as a result of the number of units it produces. In those cases, depreciation should be calculated by the **units-of-production method.** With this method, the asset's life is expressed in terms of the number of units that the asset can produce. The depreciation *per unit* can be calculated as follows:

Units-of-production method
Depreciation is determined as a function of the number of units the asset produces.

$$\text{Depreciation per Unit} = (\text{Acquisition Cost} - \text{Residual Value})/$$
$$\text{Total Number of Units in Asset's Life}$$

The annual depreciation for a given year can be calculated based on the number of units produced during that year, as follows:

$$\text{Annual Depreciation} = \text{Depreciation per Unit} \times \text{Units Produced in Current Year}$$

For example, assume that Kemp Company in the previous example wanted to use the units-of-production method for 2008. Also assume that Kemp has been able to estimate that the total number of units that will be produced during the asset's five-year life is 18,000. During 2008 Kemp produced 4,000 units. The depreciation per unit for Kemp's machine can be calculated as follows:

$$\text{Depreciation per Unit} = (\text{Acquisition Cost} - \text{Residual Value})/\text{Life in Units}$$
$$\text{Depreciation per Unit} = (\$20,000 - \$2,000)/18,000$$
$$= \$1 \text{ per Unit}$$

The amount of depreciation that should be recorded as an expense for 2008 is $4,000:

$$\text{Annual Depreciation} = \text{Depreciation per Unit} \times \text{Units Produced in 2008}$$
$$\text{Annual Depreciation} = \$1 \text{ per Unit} \times 4,000 \text{ Units}$$
$$= \$4,000$$

Depreciation will be recorded until the asset produces 18,000 units. The machine cannot be depreciated below its residual value of $2,000.

The units-of-production method is most appropriate when the accountant is able to estimate the total number of units that will be produced over the asset's life. For example, if a factory machine is used to produce a particular item, the life of the asset may be expressed in terms of the number of units produced. Further, the units produced must be related to particular time periods so that depreciation expense can be matched accurately with the related revenue.

Accelerated Depreciation Methods   In some cases, more cost should be allocated to the early years of an asset's use and less to the later years. For those assets, an accelerated method of depreciation is appropriate. The term **accelerated depreciation** refers to several depreciation methods by which a higher amount of depreciation is recorded in the early years than in later ones.

Accelerated depreciation   A higher amount of depreciation is recorded in the early years and a lower amount in the later years.

Double-declining-balance method   Depreciation is recorded at twice the straight-line rate, but the balance is reduced each period.

One form of accelerated depreciation is the **double-declining-balance method.** Under this method, depreciation is calculated at double the straight-line rate but on a declining amount. The first step is to calculate the straight-line rate as a percentage. The straight-line rate for the Kemp asset with a five-year life is

$$100\%/5 \text{ Years} = 20\%$$

The second step is to double the straight-line rate:

$$2 \times 20\% = 40\%$$

This rate will be applied in all years to the asset's book value at the beginning of each year. As depreciation is recorded, the book value declines. Thus, a constant rate is applied to a declining amount. This constant rate is applied to the full cost or initial book value, not to cost minus residual value as in the other methods. However, the machine cannot be depreciated below its residual value.

The amount of depreciation for 2008 would be calculated as follows:

$$\text{Depreciation} = \text{Beginning Book Value} \times \text{Rate}$$

$$\text{Depreciation} = \$20{,}000 \times 40\%$$

$$= \$8{,}000$$

The amount of depreciation for 2009 would be calculated as follows:

$$\text{Depreciation} = \text{Beginning Book Value} \times \text{Rate}$$

$$\text{Depreciation} = (\$20{,}000 - \$8{,}000) \times 40\%$$

$$= \$4{,}800$$

Study Tip

Residual value is deducted for all depreciation methods except for the declining-balance methods

The complete depreciation schedule for Kemp Company for all five years of the machine's life would be as follows:

YEAR	RATE	BOOK VALUE AT BEGINNING OF YEAR	DEPRECIATION	BOOK VALUE AT END OF YEAR
2008	40%	$20,000	$ 8,000	$12,000
2009	40	12,000	4,800	7,200
2010	40	7,200	2,880	4,320
2011	40	4,320	1,728	2,592
2012	40	2,592	592	2,000
Total			$18,000	

In the Kemp Company example, the depreciation for 2012 cannot be calculated as $2,592 × 40% because this would result in an accumulated depreciation amount of more than $18,000. The total amount of depreciation recorded in Years 1 through 4 is $17,408. The accountant should record only $592 depreciation ($18,000 − $17,408) in 2012 so that the remaining value of the machine is $2,000 at the end of 2012.

The reason for stopping at a book value of $2,000 at the end of 2012 by reducing the depreciation to $592 is to prevent the book value from going below the residual value of $2,000 and thus charging operations with too much depreciation. Although the residual value is not used to calculate the depreciation when using the accelerated depreciation methods for normal periods (here, periods 2008–2011), the method stops or adjusts the depreciation in the last period to prevent an overcharge to operations and a reduction of the book value below the residual value.

The double-declining-balance method of depreciation results in an accelerated depreciation pattern. It is most appropriate for assets subject to a rapid decline in usefulness as a result of technical or obsolescence factors. Double-declining-balance depreciation is not widely used for financial statement purposes but may be appropriate for certain assets. As discussed earlier, most companies use straight-line depreciation for financial statement purposes because it generally produces the highest net income, especially in growing companies that have a stable or expanding base of assets.

Comparison of Depreciation Methods   In this section, you have learned about several methods of depreciating operating assets. Exhibit 8-2 presents a comparison of the depreciation and book values of the Kemp Company asset for 2008–2012 using the straight-line and double-declining-balance methods (we have excluded the units-of-production method). Note that both methods result in a depreciation total of $18,000 over the five-year time period. The amount of depreciation per year depends, however, on the method of depreciation chosen.

Non-accountants often misunderstand the accountant's concept of depreciation. Accountants do not consider depreciation to be a process of *valuing* the asset. That is, depreciation does not describe the increase or decrease in the market value of the asset.

Accountants consider depreciation to be a process of *cost allocation.* The purpose is to allocate the original acquisition cost to the periods benefited by the asset. The depreciation method chosen should be based on the decline in the asset's usefulness. A company can choose a different depreciation method for each individual fixed asset or for each class or category of fixed assets.

Exhibit 8-2

Comparison of Depreciation and Book Values of Straight-Line and Double-Declining-Balance Methods

YEAR	Straight-Line		Double-Declining-Balance	
	DEPRECIATION	BOOK VALUE	DEPRECIATION	BOOK VALUE
2008	$ 3,600	$16,400	$ 8,000	$12,000
2009	3,600	12,800	4,800	7,200
2010	3,600	9,200	2,880	4,320
2011	3,600	5,600	1,728	2,592
2012	3,600	2,000	592	2,000
Totals	$18,000		$18,000	

The choice of depreciation method can have a significant impact on the bottom line. If two companies are essentially identical in every other respect, a different depreciation method for fixed assets can make one company look more profitable than another. Or a company that uses accelerated depreciation for one year can find that its otherwise declining earnings are no longer declining if it switches to straight-line depreciation. Investors should pay some attention to depreciation methods when comparing companies. Statement users must be aware of the different depreciation methods to understand the calculation of income and to compare companies that may not use the same methods. For example, when ACE Aviation Holdings acquired Air Canada, it extended the lives of certain of its capital assets in September 2004. The new Air Canada reports that its buildings have a life of up to 50 years—a change from 30 years. WestJet, on the other hand, reports that its buildings have a life of up to 40 years. The reader must ask why this difference exists between the two companies and why Air Canada has changed the lives of some of its capital assets.

Some investors ignore depreciation altogether when evaluating a company, not because they do not know that assets depreciate but because they want to focus on cash flow instead of earnings. Depreciation is a "non-cash" charge that reduces net income.

Exhibit 8-3 presents the depreciation policies of CN. As footnote number 1H for CN at December 31, 2007, indicates, CN uses straight-line depreciation and groups its capital assets

Exhibit 8-3

CN's Depreciation Policies

1 H. Depreciation

The cost of properties, including those under capital leases, net of asset impairment write-downs, is depreciated on a straight-line basis over their estimated useful lives as follows:

Asset class	Annual rate
Track and roadway	2%
Rolling stock	3%
Buildings	3%
Information technology	11%
Other	8%

The Company follows the group method of depreciation for railroad properties and, as such, conducts comprehensive depreciation studies on a periodic basis to assess the reasonableness of the lives of properties based upon current information and historical activities. Changes in estimated useful lives are accounted for prospectively. In 2007, the Company completed a depreciation study for all of its U.S. assets, for which there was no significant impact on depreciation expense. The Company is also conducting a depreciation study of its Canadian properties, plant and equipment, and expects to finalize this study by the first quarter of 2008.

This excerpt from CN's 2007 Annual Report appears courtesy of CN. This section of the CN Annual Report appears in the Appendix of this textbook.

into logical categories, on which the rates are then applied. Periodic studies are conducted to help CN assure itself as to the accuracy of the lives implicit in the percentages.

Depreciation and Income Taxes Financial accounting involves the presentation of financial statements to external users of accounting information, users such as investors and creditors. When depreciating an asset for financial accounting purposes, the accountant should choose a depreciation method that is consistent with the asset's decline in usefulness and that properly allocates its cost to the periods that benefit from its use.

Depreciation (termed capital cost allowance) is also deducted for income tax purposes. Sometimes such depreciation is referred to as a *tax shield* because it reduces (as do other expenses) the amount of income tax that would otherwise have to be paid. When depreciating an asset for tax purposes, a company should generally choose a depreciation method that reduces the present value of its tax burden to the lowest possible amount over the life of the asset. Normally, this is best accomplished with an accelerated depreciation method, which allows a company to save more income tax in the early years of the asset's life. This happens because the higher depreciation charges reduce taxable income more than the straight-line method does. As a form of accelerated depreciation, it results in a larger amount of depreciation in the early years of asset life and a smaller amount in later years.

Capital cost allowance (CCA) applies the group approach (as exemplified in CN's note 1H), in which the groups are defined by the Canada Revenue Agency. CCA is sometimes used by smaller companies so that income tax depreciation is the same as accounting depreciation; however, larger companies typically use CCA for their income tax calculation and the previously noted methods (such as straight-line) for their income statements.

CCA operates in a manner similar to the accelerated method described above. The Canada Revenue Agency specifies maximum rates, which vary from 4% to 100%, with common rates of 4% for buildings, 20% for general equipment, and 30% for passenger vehicles. Rates, however, do change as illustrated by the 2007 budget, which changed new purchases of certain buildings and computer equipment.

For example, the $20,000 machine of Kemp Company would likely be grouped in class 8, which has a 20% maximum CCA. Exhibit 8-4 shows the CCA calculations for 2008–2012. Note the pattern of the calculations and in particular the ½ used in the first year. This declining balance pattern is typical of CCA calculations regardless of the maximum CCA rate.

Exhibit 8-4 shows a balance of $7,373 book value (termed *undepreciated capital cost* [UCC] for income tax purposes) of the $20,000 asset at the end of 2012. The treatment of this $7,373 UCC in 2013 and beyond depends on what Kemp Company does with the asset and this asset class in 2013. If the asset is scrapped for $0.00 and nothing is purchased to replace the asset that belongs to this CCA class, then Kemp Company will be able to deduct $7,373 in 2013 for CCA in calculating its 2013 income taxes. Such a deduction is referred to as a *terminal loss*. Any proceeds received up to the amount of $7,373 will be used to reduce the terminal loss deduction in 2013.

If Kemp Company purchases a new asset that is class 20%, then the CCA for 2013 will be calculated on the $7,373 less any proceeds of disposal in a manner reflected in the pattern followed up to 2012. The "half-year" rule shown in 2008 will be applied to the cost of the new addition purchased in 2013. Thus the balance of UCC on the original $20,000 asset will continue to be depreciated for income tax purposes even though the asset is no longer held by Kemp. For future discussions of the two alternatives in this text, we will distinguish the specific situation by indicating that the class will continue beyond the end of the life of the specific asset or be terminated. Later in the chapter, the termination of depreciation under GAAP will be presented, so it is important to note that the treatment illustrated for the asset presented in Exhibit 8-4 is for income tax purposes only.

Exhibit 8-4

Calculation of CCA

Year	CCA 20% Amount	CCA Book Value End of Year
2008	(0.20 × ½ × 20,000 =) 2,000	$18,000
2009	(0.20 × 18,000 =) 3,600	14,400
2010	(0.20 × 14,400 =) 2,880	11,520
2011	(0.20 × 11,520 =) 2,304	9,216
2012	(0.20 × 9,216 =) 1,843	7,373

Note: ½ is used in the year of acquisition regardless of the date of acquisition within the first year. CCA will continue on the book value as long as the asset is held.

Choice of Depreciation Method As we have stated, in theory a company should choose the depreciation method that best allocates the original cost of the asset to the periods benefited by the use of the asset. Theory aside, it is important to examine the other factors that affect a company's decision in choosing a depreciation method or methods. Exhibit 8-5 presents the factors that affect this decision and the likely choice that arises from each factor. Usually, the factors that are the most important are whether depreciation is calculated for presentation on the financial statements to shareholders or is calculated for income tax purposes.

When depreciation is calculated for financial statement purposes, a company generally wants to present the most favourable impression (the highest income) possible. Therefore, most companies choose the straight-line method of depreciation. In fact, more than 90% of large companies use the straight-line method for financial statement purposes.

If the objective of the company's management is to minimize its income tax liability, then the company will generally choose the maximum permitted for tax purposes. As discussed in the preceding section, maximum capital cost allowance allows the company to save more on income taxes because capital cost allowance is a tax shield.

Exhibit 8-5

Management's Choice of Depreciation Method

Factor	Likely Choice
Simplicity	The straight-line method is easiest to compute and record.
Reporting to shareholders	Usually firms wish to maximize net income in reporting to shareholders and will use the straight-line method.
Comparability	Usually firms use the same depreciation method as other firms in the same industry or line of business.
Management bonus plans	If management is paid a bonus based on net income, they are likely to use the straight-line method.
Technological competitiveness	If technology is changing rapidly, a firm should consider an accelerated method of depreciation.
Reporting to the Canada Revenue Agency	Firms will usually claim maximum capital cost allowance to minimize taxable income in reporting to the CRA.

Therefore, it is not unusual for a company to use *two* depreciation methods for the same asset, one for financial reporting purposes and another for tax purposes. This may seem somewhat confusing, but it is the direct result of the differing goals of financial and tax accounting. See Chapter 10 for more about this issue.

Accounting for Your Decisions

You Are the Sole Owner

Your accountant has presented you with three sets of financial statements—each with a different depreciation method—and asks you which depreciation method you prefer. Your answer is that other than for tax purposes, you don't really care. Should you not care?

ANSWER: For tax purposes you would prefer to use the maximum capital cost allowance permitted, which minimizes your taxable (net) income so that you can pay the minimum allowable taxes. For financial statement purposes you may use a different method. As a sole owner, you may believe that the depreciation method chosen does not matter because you are more concerned with the cash flow of the firm and depreciation is a non-cash item. However, the depreciation method is important if you are going to show your statements to external parties—for example, if you must present your statements to a banker in order to get a loan.

■ CHANGE IN DEPRECIATION ESTIMATE

An asset's acquisition cost is known at the time it is purchased, but its life and its residual value must be estimated. These estimates are then used as the basis for depreciating the asset. Occasionally, an estimate of the asset's life or residual value must be altered after the depreciation process has begun. This is an example of an accounting change that is referred to as a **change in estimate.**

LO 4 Analyze the impact of a change in the estimate of the capital asset life or residual value.

Change in estimate A change in the life of the asset or in its residual value.

Assume the same facts as in the Kemp Company example. The company purchased a machine on January 1, 2006, for $20,000. Kemp estimated that the machine's life would be five years and its residual value at the end of five years would be $2,000. Assume that Kemp has depreciated the machine using the straight-line method for two years. At the beginning of 2008, Kemp believes that the total machine life will be seven years, or another five years beyond the two years the machine has been used. Thus, depreciation must be adjusted to reflect the new estimate of the asset's life.

A change in estimate should be recorded *prospectively,* meaning that the depreciation recorded in prior years is not corrected or restated. Instead, the new estimate should affect the current year and future years. Kemp Company should depreciate the remaining depreciable amount during 2008 through 2012. The amount to be depreciated over that time period should be calculated as follows:

Acquisition Cost, January 1, 2006	$20,000
Less: Accumulated Depreciation	
(2 years at $3,600 per year)	7,200
Book Value, January 1, 2008	12,800
Less: Residual Value	2,000
Remaining Depreciable Amount	$10,800

The remaining depreciable amount should be recorded as depreciation over the remaining life of the machine. In the Kemp Company case, the depreciation amount for 2008 and the following four years would be $2,160:

Depreciation = Remaining Depreciable Amount/Remaining Life

Depreciation = $10,800/5 Years

= $2,160

The journal entry to record depreciation for the year 2008 is as follows:

```
2008
Dec. 31   Depreciation Expense                          2,160
              Accumulated Depreciation                              2,160
          To record depreciation for 2008
```

Assets	=	Liabilities	+	Shareholders' Equity
−2,160				−2,160

If the change in estimate is a material amount, the company should disclose in the footnotes to the 2008 financial statements that depreciation has changed as a result of a change in estimate. The company's auditors have to be very careful that management's decision to change its estimate of the depreciable life of the asset is not simply an attempt to manipulate earnings. Particularly in capital-intensive manufacturing concerns, lengthening the useful life of equipment can have a material impact on earnings.

A change in estimate of an asset's residual value is treated in a manner similar to a change in an asset's life. There should be no attempt to correct or restate the income statements of past periods that were based on the original estimate. Instead, the accountant should use the new estimate of residual value to calculate depreciation for the current and future years.

A change in estimate is not treated the same way as a *change in principle.* If a company changes its *method* of depreciation, for example, from accelerated depreciation to the straight-line method, this constitutes a change in accounting principle and must be disclosed separately on the financial statements.

Two-Minute Review

1. What items should be included when calculating the acquisition cost of an asset?

2. Which will be higher in the early years of an asset's life—straight-line depreciation or accelerated depreciation? Which will be higher in the later years? Which will be higher in total over the entire life of the asset?

Answers on page 376

Impairment Capital assets must be subjected to periodic review (typically yearly) to determine whether their book value exceeds the amount of benefit they are expected to generate over the remainder of their useful life. If the expected benefit from the asset or a logical group of assets is estimated to be less than their book value (cost less accumulated depreciation or amortization), then a loss must be recorded to reflect the loss of the benefit reflected in the asset on the balance sheet. A variety of factors are suggestive of potential **impairment**: a change in use, a change in law, excess costs incurred at acquisition, a history of losses, or an expected early disposal. Such factors suggest a decline in the future benefits from the capital asset from the amount reflected in its book value before an impairment is recorded.[1]

Impairment Write-down required when the expected benefit of a capital asset falls below its book value.

Say, for example, that Kemp Company purchases its asset on January 1, 2006, for $20,000 and records two years of straight-line depreciation of $3,600 per year for years 2006 and 2007 ([$20,000 − $2,000]/5 years). The book value will be $12,800 on January 1, 2008. At the end of 2008 the book value based on the original estimates will be $12,800 − $3,600 or $9,200. For the balance sheet at December 31, 2008, an assessment of future benefits of the assets suggests that $8,800 can be recovered from the use of the asset. The capital asset will be impaired and a write-down and loss will be required. At this point a special calculation may be required (the nature of which will only become clear in Chapter 9). Let it be said now, however, that the term *fair*

---

[1] AcSB, Section 3063.

value is used to describe the amount that will be reflected. Assume for now that fair value is less than $8,800 (usually the case) say $8,500, and that it reflects what the asset could be sold for at December 31, 2008. Kemp will record the following if the amounts are significant enough (termed *material*):

2008			
Dec. 31	Loss or Impairment of Capital Asset	700	
	Accumulated Depreciation		700
	$9,200 − $8,500 = $700		

Assets = Liabilities + Shareholders' Equity
−700   **−700**

The disclosure of the loss could be made as other expenses on the income statement. The new book value on December 31, 2008, would be the cost ($20,000) less the accumulated depreciation ($11,500), that is, $8,500. Depreciation for 2009 and subsequent years would be based on $8,500 − $2,000 = $6,500. Then, $6,500 ÷ 2 = $3,250 depreciation per year for 2009 and 2010, assuming that the residual value of $2,000 remained the same as originally estimated. Other potential disclosures on the income statement are possible, depending on the nature of the impairment; for example, unusual changes or part of a restructuring.

An impairment loss is a loss in the year of assessment and is assigned to income as a charge. It is not treated as a change in estimate.

■ CAPITAL VERSUS REVENUE EXPENDITURES

Accountants must often decide whether certain expenditures related to capital assets should be treated as an addition to the cost of the asset or as an expense. One of the most common examples involving this decision concerns repairs to an asset. Should the repairs constitute capital expenditures or revenue expenditures? A **capital expenditure** is a cost that is added to the acquisition cost of the capital asset. A **revenue expenditure** is not treated as part of the cost of the capital asset but as an expense on the income statement. Thus, the company must decide whether to treat an item as an asset (balance sheet) and depreciate its cost over its life or to treat it as an expense (income statement) of a single period.

The distinction between capital and revenue expenditures is a matter of judgment. Generally, the guideline that should be followed is that if an expenditure increases the life of the asset or its productivity, it should be treated as a capital expenditure and added to the asset account. If an expenditure simply maintains an asset in its normal operating condition, however, it should be treated as an expense. The *materiality* of the expenditure must also be considered. Most companies establish a policy of treating an expenditure smaller than a specified amount as a revenue expenditure (an expense on the income statement).

It is very important that a company not improperly capitalize a material expenditure that should have been written off right away. The capitalization policies of companies are closely watched by analysts who are trying to assess the value of these companies. When a company is capitalizing rather than expensing certain items to artificially boost earnings, that revelation can be very damaging to the share price.

Expenditures related to operating assets may be classified in several categories. For each type of expenditure, its treatment as capital or revenue should be as follows:

LO 5 Determine which expenditures should be capitalized as capital asset costs and which should be treated as expenses.

Capital expenditure A cost that improves the capital asset and is added to the capital asset account.

Revenue expenditure A cost that keeps an asset in its normal operating condition and is treated as an expense.

CATEGORY	EXAMPLE	ASSET OR EXPENSE
Normal maintenance	Repainting	Expense
Minor repair	Replace spark plugs	Expense
Major repair	Replace a vehicle's engine	Asset, if life or productivity is enhanced
Addition	Add a wing to a building	Asset

When an item is treated as a capital expenditure, this affects the amount of depreciation that should be recorded over the asset's remaining life. We return to the Kemp Company example to illustrate. Assume again that Kemp purchased a machine on January 1, 2006, for $20,000. Kemp estimated that its residual value at the end of five years would be $2,000 and has depreciated the machine using the straight-line method for 2006 and 2007. At the beginning of 2008, Kemp made a $3,000 overhaul to the machine, extending its life by three years. Because the expenditure qualifies as a capital expenditure, the cost of overhauling the machine should be added to the asset account. The journal entry to record the overhaul is as follows:

2008			
Jan. 1	Machine	3,000	
	Cash		3,000
	To record the overhaul of a capital asset		

Assets	=	**Liabilities**	+	**Shareholders' Equity**
+3,000				
−3,000				

For the years 2006 and 2007, Kemp recorded depreciation of $3,600 per year:

$$\text{Depreciation} = (\text{Acquisition Cost} - \text{Residual Value})/\text{Life}$$

$$\text{Depreciation} = (\$20,000 - \$2,000)/5$$

$$= \$3,600$$

 ## Accounting for Your Decisions

You Are the Owner

You are a realtor whose company car has just had its transmission rebuilt for $400. Would you classify this "repair" as a capital expenditure or a revenue expenditure? Why is it important to properly classify the $400?

> **ANSWER:** If the company car's life is not extended, then the repair should be treated as a revenue expenditure, in which the cost is expensed on the income statement. In this case, it is likely the $400 extends the life so it should be added to the asset. It is important to properly classify capital and revenue expenditures because capitalizing rather than expensing costs can artificially boost earnings. The opposite effect would occur if costs were expensed and not capitalized.

Beginning in 2008, Kemp should record depreciation of $2,300 per year, computed as follows:

Original Cost, January 1, 2006	$20,000
Less: Accumulated Depreciation (2 years × $3,600)	7,200
Book Value, January 1, 2008	12,800
Plus: Major Overhaul	3,000
Less: Residual Value	(2,000)
Remaining Depreciable Amount	$13,800

$$\text{Depreciation} = \text{Remaining Depreciable Amount}/\text{Remaining Life}$$

$$\text{Depreciation per Year} = \$13,800/6 \text{ Years}$$

$$= \$2,300$$

The entry to record depreciation for the year 2008 follows:

2008
Dec. 31   Depreciation Expense   2,300
          Accumulated Depreciation—Asset   2,300
          To record annual depreciation on operating asset

Assets	=	Liabilities	+	Shareholders' Equity
−2,300				−2,300

Note that Exhibit 8-6 describes CN's accounting policies for its properties.

1 G. Properties

Railroad properties are carried at cost less accumulated depreciation including asset impairment write-downs. Labor, materials and other costs associated with the installation of rail, ties, ballast and other track improvements are capitalized to the extent they meet the Company's minimum threshold for capitalization. Major overhauls and large refurbishments are also capitalized when they result in an extension to the useful life or increase the functionality of the asset. Included in property additions are the costs of developing computer software for internal use. Maintenance costs are expensed as incurred.

    The cost of railroad properties, less net salvage value, retired or disposed of in the normal course of business is charged to accumulated depreciation, in accordance with the group method of depreciation. The Company reviews the carrying amounts of properties held and used whenever events or changes in circumstances indicate that such carrying amounts may not be recoverable based on future undiscounted cash flows. Assets that are deemed impaired as a result of such review are recorded at the lower of carrying amount or fair value.

    Assets held for sale are measured at the lower of their carrying amount or fair value, less cost to sell. Losses resulting from significant line sales are recognized in income when the asset meets the criteria for classification as held for sale whereas losses resulting from significant line abandonments are recognized in the statement of income when the asset ceases to be used. Gains are recognized in income when they are realized.

Author's note: This method for treating disposals is not the same as illustrated later for the gain or loss on disposals. In CN's income statement, the treatment of the gain or loss on a disposal occurs because of the group method used by CN.

This excerpt from CN's 2007 Annual Report appears courtesy of CN. This section of the CN Annual Report appears in the Appendix of this textbook.

Environmental Aspects of Capital Assets

As the number of the government's environmental regulations has increased, businesses have been required to expend more money complying with them. A common example involves costs to comply with legal requirements to clean up contaminated soil surrounding plant facilities. In some cases, the costs are very large and may exceed the value of the property. Should such costs be considered an expense and recorded entirely in one accounting period, or should they be treated as a capital expenditure and added to the cost of the asset? If there is a legal obligation to clean up the property or to restore the property to its original condition, companies are required to record the cost of asset retirement obligations as part of the cost of the asset. For example, if a company owns a factory and has made a promise to restore the property that is used by the factory to its original condition, then the costs of restoring the property must be added to the asset account. Of course, it is sometimes difficult to determine whether a legal obligation exists. It is important, however, for companies at least to conduct a thorough investigation to determine the potential

Should the costs of cleaning up a contaminated factory be considered an expense of one period or a capital expenditure added to the cost of the plant asset? To make the best decision, management should gather all the facts about the extent of the cleanup and its environmental impact.

PHILIP SPEARS/PHOTODISC/GETTY IMAGES

environmental considerations that may affect the value of capital assets and to ponder carefully the accounting implications of new environmental regulations.

Canadian GAAP provides very detailed examples of how the fair (current) value of retirement obligations for capital assets can be calculated if such estimates are possible.[2] For example, in footnote 9, CN shows $83 million recorded at the end of 2007 as a long-term obligation. This amount is very small because, as described in footnote 18, section D, CN may have obligations and costs it cannot yet estimate (termed *contingencies*). CN states that of the $131 million in retirement obligations both current and long-term at the beginning of 2007, it paid $19 million in 2007 and reduced its accrual by $1 million. Thus it would appear that CN believes it was too difficult to determine some of these retirement contingencies because of the prospect of technologies or laws that will influence estimates of retirement obligations for its capital assets. Accountants cannot record what cannot be measured—something that CN and CN's auditors illustrate in the area of retirement obligations.

■ DISPOSAL OF PROPERTY, PLANT, AND EQUIPMENT

LO 6 Analyze the effect of the disposal of a capital asset at a gain or loss.

An asset may be disposed of in any of several different ways. One common method is to sell the asset for cash. Sale of an asset involves two important considerations. First, depreciation must be recorded up to the date of sale. If the sale does not occur at the fiscal year-end, usually December 31, depreciation must be recorded for a partial period from the beginning of the year to the date of sale. Second, the company selling the asset must calculate and record the gain or loss on its sale.

Refer again to the Kemp Company example. Assume that Kemp purchased a machine on January 1, 2006, for $20,000, estimating its life to be five years and the residual value to be $2,000. Kemp used the straight-line method of depreciation. Assume that Kemp sold the machine on July 1, 2008, for $12,400. Depreciation for the six-month time period from January 1 to July 1, 2008, is $1,800 ($3,600 per year $\times$ 1/2 year = $1,800) and should be recorded as follows:

2008

July 1	Depreciation Expense	1,800	
	Accumulated Depreciation—Machine		1,800
	To record depreciation for a six-month time period		

Assets	**=**	**Liabilities**	**+**	**Shareholders' Equity**
−1,800				**−1,800**

After the July 1 entry, the balance of the Accumulated Depreciation—Machine account is $9,000, which reflects depreciation for the 2½ years from the date of purchase to the date of sale. The entry to record the sale follows:

2008

July 1	Accumulated Depreciation—Machine	9,000	
	Cash	12,400	
	Machine		20,000
	Gain on Sale of Asset		1,400
	To record the sale of the machine		

Assets	**=**	**Liabilities**	**+**	**Shareholders' Equity**
+9,000				**+1,400**
+12,400				
−20,000				

---

[2] AcSB, Section 3110.

When an asset is sold, all accounts related to it must be removed. In the preceding entry, the Machine account is reduced (credited) to eliminate the account, and the Accumulated Depreciation—Machine account is reduced (debited) to eliminate it. The **Gain on Sale of Asset** indicates the amount by which the sale price of the machine *exceeds* the book value. Thus, the gain can be calculated as follows:

Asset cost	$20,000
Less: Accumulated depreciation	9,000
Book value	11,000
Sale price	12,400
Gain on sale of asset	$ 1,400

The account, Gain on Sale of Asset, is an income statement account and should appear in the Other Income/Expense category of the statement. The Gain on Sale of Asset account is not treated as revenue because it does not constitute the company's ongoing or central activity. Instead, it appears as income but in a separate category to denote its incidental nature.

The calculation of a loss on the sale of an asset is similar to that of a gain. Assume in the example on the previous page that Kemp had sold the machine on July 1, 2008, for $10,000 cash. As in the previous example, depreciation must be recorded to the date of sale, July 1. The following is the entry to record the sale of the asset:

2008			
July 1	Accumulated Depreciation—Machine	9,000	
	Cash	10,000	
	Loss on Sale of Asset	1,000	
	Machine		20,000
	To record the sale of the machine		

Assets	**=**	**Liabilities**	**+**	**Shareholders' Equity**
+9,000				−1,000
+10,000				
−20,000				

The **Loss on Sale of Asset** indicates the amount by which the asset's sales price *is less than* its book value. Thus, the loss could be calculated as follows:

Asset cost	$20,000
Less: Accumulated depreciation	9,000
Book value	11,000
Sale price	10,000
Loss on sale of asset	$ 1,000

The Loss on Sale of Asset account is an income statement account and should appear in the Other Income/Expense category of the income statement.

Capital Assets Acquired or Disposed of During Year

So far, our explanations of depreciation for capital assets acquired and capital assets disposed of have assumed that such happenings occur at the beginning of the company's fiscal year or halfway through the fiscal year. But we have also noted that CCA provides a special procedure for the first year—the ½-year rule—which is applied regardless of when the asset was acquired during the fiscal year.

Companies need to set a policy for acquisitions and disposals during a fiscal year. For example, if a capital asset such as equipment is acquired and placed in service on the 20th of a given month, should depreciation start on the first of that month or on the first of the next month? Rounding rules could be used so that from the 15th onward the depreciation would start the month following acquisition. Obviously, this is a good example of the application of materiality.

The specific procedure for using whole months for capital asset acquisitions or disposals during the year is somewhat more material. For purposes of explanation, the number of months an asset is used during the year will govern our calculations, except in the matter of capital cost allowance, which follows the ½-year rule.

For example, if Kemp Company acquired the machine described on page 355 on March 31, 2008, the straight-line depreciation for year 2008 would be:

$$([\$20,000 - \$2,000]/5) \times 9/12 = \$3,600 \times 9/12 = \$2,700$$

The units-of-production method of depreciation automatically adjusts for the time the capital asset is used, so that no correction for year 2008 is necessary.

The accelerated depreciation methods described on page 356 provide some options. If we assume that the acquisition occurred on March 31, 2008, then year 2008 could be calculated as follows:

2008:   ($20,000 × 0.40) × 9/12 = $6,000
        Book value start of 2009: ($20,000 − $6,000) = $14,000
2009: $14,000 × 0.40 = $5,600

Note that other similar options exist such as splitting each year's depreciation into monthly portions belonging to 2008 (9/12), 2009 (3/12, 9/12) or using monthly instead of yearly steps. A test for material differences should be made to justify the cost of more detailed calculations.

Methods similar to the acquisition approaches also can be used for the year of disposal of a capital asset to calculate the depreciation up to the date of disposal to reflect the use of the asset.

CAPITAL ASSETS: NATURAL RESOURCES

Balance Sheet Presentation

LO 7 Explain the balance sheet presentation of natural resources.

Natural resources Assets that are consumed during their use.

Important capital assets for some companies consist of **natural resources** such as coalfields, oil wells, other mineral deposits, and timberlands. Natural resources share one characteristic: the resource is consumed as it is used. For example, the coal a utility company uses to make electricity is consumed in the process. Most natural resources cannot be replenished in the foreseeable future. Coal and oil, for example, can be replenished only by nature over millions of years. Timberlands may be replenished in a shorter time period, but even trees must grow for many years to be usable for lumber.

Natural resources should be carried in the Property, Plant, and Equipment category of the balance sheet as a capital asset. Like other assets in the category, natural resources should initially be recorded at *acquisition cost*. Acquisition cost should include the cost of acquiring the natural resource and the costs necessary to prepare the asset for use. The preparation costs for natural resources may often be very large; for example, a company may spend large sums to remove layers of dirt before the coal can be mined. These preparation costs should be added to the cost of the asset.

Depletion of Natural Resources

When a natural resource is used or consumed, it should be treated as an expense. The process of recording the expense is similar to the depreciation or amortization process but is usually referred to as *depletion*. The amount of depletion expense each period should reflect the portion of the natural resource that was used up during the current year.

Assume, for example, that Local Coal Company purchased a coalfield on January 1, 2008, for $1 million. The company employed a team of engineering experts who estimated the total coal in the field to be 200,000 tonnes and who determined that the field's residual value after removal of the coal would be zero. Local Coal should calculate the depletion per tonne as follows:

Depletion per Tonne = (Acquisition Cost − Residual Value)/
Total Number of Tonnes in Asset's Life

= ($1,000,000 − $0)/200,000 tonnes

= $5 per tonne

Depletion expense for each year should be calculated as follows:

Depletion Expense = Depletion per Tonne × Tonnes Mined during Year

Assume that Local Coal Company mined 10,000 tonnes of coal during 2008. The depletion expense for 2008 for Local Coal follows:

$5 × 10,000 tonnes = $50,000

Local Coal should record the depletion in an Accumulated Depletion—Coalfield account, which would appear as a contra-asset on the balance sheet. The company should record the following journal entry:

2008
Dec. 31   Depletion Expense   50,000
                Accumulated Depletion—Coalfield   50,000
            To record depletion for 2008

Assets	**=**	**Liabilities**	**+**	**Shareholders' Equity**
−50,000				−50,000

Rather than using an accumulated depletion account, some companies may decrease (credit) the asset account directly.

There is an interesting parallel between depletion of natural resources and depreciation of plant and equipment. That is, depletion is very similar to depreciation using the units-of-production method. Both require an estimate of the useful life of the asset in terms of the total amount that can be produced (for the units-of-production method) or consumed (for depletion) over the asset's life.

Natural resources may be important assets for some companies. For example, Exhibit 8-7 highlights the asset portion of the 2006 balance sheet and the accompanying note of **Suncor Energy Inc.** Suncor had oil sands and natural gas properties, net of depreciation or depletion, of ($14,388 − $2,207) = $12,181 and ($2,251 − $918) = $1,333 respectively (figures in millions) as of December 31, 2006. The note indicates that the company records the cost of annual operations in relation to the total recoverable amounts.

http://www.suncor.com

Exhibit 8-7 Suncor Assets, 2006 Annual Report

2. PROPERTY, PLANT AND EQUIPMENT

($ millions)	2006 Cost	2006 Accumulated Provision	2005 Cost	2005 Accumulated Provision
Oil Sands				
Plant	7,514	1,608	6,042	1,388
Mine and mobile equipment	1,191	320	939	280
In-situ properties	1,946	147	1,608	79
Pipeline	149	34	139	30
Capital leases	38	4	30	6
Major projects in progress	2,887	–	2,484	–
Asset retirement cost	663	94	408	81
	14,388	2,207	11,650	1,864
Natural Gas				
Proved properties	1,931	867	1,632	769
Unproved properties	186	21	172	23
Other support facilities and equipment	90	23	53	13
Asset retirement cost	44	7	14	6
	2,251	918	1,871	811

Courtesy Suncor Energy

■ CAPITAL ASSETS: INTANGIBLE ASSETS

LO 8 Explain the balance sheet presentation of intangible assets.

Intangible assets Assets with no physical properties.

Intangible assets are long-term assets with no physical properties. Because one cannot see or touch most intangible assets, it is easy to overlook their importance. Intangibles are recorded as assets, however, because they provide future economic benefits to the company. In fact, an intangible asset may be the most important asset a company owns or controls. For example, a pharmaceutical company may own some property, plant, and equipment, but its most important asset may be its patent for a particular drug or process. Likewise, the company that publishes this textbook may consider the copyrights to textbooks to be among its most important revenue-producing assets.

The balance sheet includes the intangible assets that meet the accounting definition of assets. Patents, copyrights, and brand names are included because they are owned by the company and will produce a future benefit that can be identified and measured. The balance sheet, however, would indicate only the acquisition cost of those assets, not the value of the assets to the company or the sales value of the assets.

Of course, the balance sheet does not include all of the items that may produce future benefit to the company. A company's employees, its management team, its location, or the intellectual capital of a few key researchers may well provide important future benefits and value. They are not recorded on the balance sheet, however, because they do not meet the accountant's definition of *assets* and cannot be easily identified or measured.

Balance Sheet Presentation

Intangible assets are long-term capital assets and should be shown separately from property, plant, and equipment. Exhibit 8-8 provides a list of common intangible assets. Various disclosure practices are used for these assets, but as shown in the exhibit, most show general intangibles separately from goodwill because of the different treatment of each class of intangibles. Most general intangibles have a limited life—for example, in Exhibit 8-9, the licence

Exhibit 8-8

Most Common Intangible
Assets

INTANGIBLE ASSET	DESCRIPTION
Patent	Right to use, manufacture, or sell a product; granted by the federal Patent Office. Patents have a legal life of 20 years.
Copyright	Right to reproduce or sell a published work. Copyrights are granted for 50 years plus the life of the creator.
Franchise	A contractual right, granted by one party to another, that permits the franchisee to sell a product or service in a defined area.
Trademark	A symbol or name that allows a product or service to be identified; provides legal protection for 15 years (plus 5 years' probation) plus an indefinite number of renewal periods.
Goodwill	The excess of the purchase price to acquire a business over the fair value of the individual net assets acquired.

purchased by Research in Motion Limited, is similar to that for a franchise and thus is amortized. However, the modern treatment for goodwill is to not amortize it because of its indefinite life.

The nature of many intangibles is fairly evident, but goodwill is not so easily understood. **Goodwill** represents the amount of the purchase price paid in excess of the fair value of the individual net assets when a business is purchased. Goodwill is recorded only when a business is purchased. It is not recorded when a company engages in activities that do not involve the purchase of another business entity. For example, customer loyalty or a good management team may represent "goodwill," but neither meets the accountants' criteria to be recorded as an asset on a firm's financial statements.

Goodwill The excess of the purchase price of a business over the total fair value of the identifiable assets.

Acquisition Cost of Intangible Assets

As was the case with property, plant, and equipment, the acquisition cost of an intangible asset includes all of the costs to acquire the asset and prepare it for its intended use. This should include all necessary costs such as legal costs incurred at the time of acquisition. Acquisition cost also should include those costs that are incurred after acquisition and that are necessary to the existence of the asset. For example, if a firm must pay legal fees to protect a patent from infringement, the costs should be considered part of the acquisition cost and should be included in the Patent account.

Research and development costs are expenditures incurred in the discovery of new knowledge and the translation of research into a design or plan for a new product or service or into a significant improvement to an existing product or service. Firms that engage in research and development do so because they believe such activities provide future benefit to the company. In fact, many firms have become leaders in an industry by engaging in research and development and the discovery of new products or technology. It is often very difficult, however, to identify the amount of future benefits of research and development and to associate those benefits with specific time periods. Because of the difficulty in predicting future benefits, U.S. GAAP states that firms are not allowed to treat research and development costs as assets; all such expenditures must be treated as expenses in the period incurred. Many firms, especially high-technology ones, argue that this accounting rule results in seriously understated balance sheets. In their view, an important "asset" is not portrayed on their balance sheet. They also argue that they are at a competitive disadvantage when compared with foreign companies that are allowed to treat at least a portion of research and development as an asset. Users of financial statements somehow need to be aware of those "hidden assets" when analyzing the balance sheets of companies that must expense research and development costs.

Research and development costs Costs incurred in the discovery of new knowledge and the translation of research into a design or plan for a new product or service or into a significant improvement.

Canadian GAAP have permitted the recognition of research and development costs if they are acquired from other companies and if internally developed activities in this area can be reliably measured.[3]

---
[3] AcSB, Section 3450.

(United States Dollars, in thouands)

	As at	
	March 3, 2007	March 4, 2006
		(Restated - note 4)
Assets		
Current		
Total current assets	1,919,265	1,258,772
Investments (Note 5)	425,652	614,309
Capital assets (Note 7)	487,579	326,313
Intangible assets (Note 8)	138,182	85,929
Goodwill (Note 9)	109,932	29,026
Deferred income tax asset (Note 10)	8,339	–
	$3,088,949	$2,314,349

(k) Capital assets Capital assets are stated at cost less accumulated amortization. No amortization provided for construction in progress until the assets are ready for use. Amortization is provided using the following rates and methods:

Buildings, leaseholds and other	Straight-line over terms between 5 and 40 years
BlackBerry operations and other information technology	Straight-line over terms between 3 and 5 years
Manufacturing equipment, research and development equipment, and tooling	Straight-line over terms between 2 and 8 years
Furniture and fixtures	20% per annum declining balance

(l) Intangible assets Intangible assets are stated at cost less accumulated amortization and are comprised of licenses, patents and acquired technology. Licenses include licenses or agreements that the Company has negotiated with third parties upon use of third parties' technology. Patents include all costs necessary to acquire intellectual property such as patents and trademarks, as well as legal defense costs arising out of the assertion of any Company-owned patents. Acquired technology consists of purchased developed technology arising from the Company's corporate acquisitions.

Intangible assets are amortized as follows:

Acquired technology	Straight-line over 2 to 5 years
Licenses	Lesser of 5 years or on a per unit basis based upon the anticipated number of units sold during the terms of the license agreements
Patents	Straight-line over 17 years

(m) Impairment of long-lived assets The Company reviews long-lived assets such as property, plant and equipment and intangible assets with finite useful lives for impairment whenever events or changes in circumstances indicate that the carrying amount may not be recoverable. If the total of the expected undiscounted future cash flows is less than the carrying amount of the asset, a loss is recognized for the excess of the carrying amount over the fair value of the asset.

(n) Goodwill Goodwill represents the excess of the purchase price of business acquisitions over the fair value of identifiable net assets acquired in such acquisitions. Goodwill is allocated as at the date of the business combination. Goodwill is not amortized, but is tested for impairment annually, or more frequently if events or changes in circumstances indicate the asset might be impaired.

The impairment test is carried out in two steps. In the first step, the carrying amount of the reporting unit including goodwill is compared with its fair value. When the fair value of a reporting unit exceeds its carrying amount, goodwill of the reporting unit is considered not to be impaired, and the second step is unnecessary.

In the event that the fair value of the reporting unit, including goodwill, is less than the carrying value, the implied fair value of the reporting unit's goodwill is compared with its carrying amount to measure the amount of the impairment loss, if any. The implied fair value of goodwill is determined in the same manner as the value of goodwill is determined in a business combination using the fair value of the reporting unit as if it were the purchase price. When the carrying amount of the reporting unit goodwill exceeds the implied fair value of the goodwill, an impairment loss is recognized in an amount equal to the excess and is presented as a separate line item in the consolidated statements of operations.

The Company has one reporting unit which is the consolidated Company.

(continued)

8. INTANGIBLE ASSETS

Intangible assets are comprised of the following:

| | March 3, 2007 | | |
	Cost	Accumulated amortization	Net book value
Acquired technology	$ 58,639	$ 19,183	$ 39,456
Licenses	90,811	68,177	22,634
Patents	87,630	11,538	76,092
	$ 237,080	$ 98,898	$ 138,182

| | March 4, 2006 | | |
	Cost	Accumulated amortization	Net book value
Acquired technology	$ 18,373	$ 9,465	$ 8,908
Licenses	82,806	48,576	34,230
Patents	50,790	7,999	42,791
	$ 151,969	$ 66,040	$ 85,929

For the year ended March 3, 2007, amortization expense related to intangible assets was $32,858 (March 4, 2006 - $23,195; February 26, 2005 - $19,730). Total additions to intangible assets in 2007 were $85,111 (2006 - $45,384).

Based on the carrying value of the identified intangible assets as at March 3, 2007, and assuming no subsequent impairment of the underlying assets, the annual amortization expense for the next five years is expected to be as follows: 2008 - 33 million; 2009 - $17 million; 2010 - $15 million; 2011 - $13 million; and 2012 - $7 million.

The acquisitions were accounted for using the purchase method whereby identifiable assets acquired and liabilities assumed were recorded at their estimated fair value as of the date of acquisition. The excess of the purchase price over such fair value was recorded as goodwill. Acquired technology includes current and core technology, and is amortized over periods ranging from two to five years.

Courtesy Research in Motion. RIM Annual Report 2007.

It is important to distinguish between patent costs and research and development costs. Patent costs include legal and filing fees necessary to acquire a patent. Such costs are capitalized as an intangible asset, Patent. However, the Patent account should not include the costs of research and development of a new product. Those costs are not capitalized but are treated as an expense, Research and Development.

✖ Accounting for Your Decisions

You Are the Student Intern

Your colleagues at the investment house where you are doing a summer internship insist that the intangible assets on RIM's and CN's balance sheets are worthless and should be removed before any analysis can be completed on the two companies. Would you agree or disagree with their position?

ANSWER: Intangible assets are not worthless. Just because an asset is "intangible" and difficult to quantify doesn't mean it should be removed. Intangible assets such as goodwill and trademarks are frequently listed on balance sheets. They represent assets from an accounting viewpoint and may indeed be some of the most important assets of the company. The contracts acquired by RIM are assets because they will provide future benefits in the form of sales of products. In the case of CN, intangibles are so small in size that their removal would not hinder your analysis.

Amortization of Intangibles

There has been considerable discussion over the past few years about whether intangible assets should be amortized and, if so, over what period of time. The term *amortization* is very similar to depreciation of property, plant, and equipment. Amortization involves allocating the acquisition cost of an intangible asset to the periods benefited by the use of the asset. If an intangible asset is amortized, most companies use the straight-line method of amortization, and we will use that method for illustration purposes. Occasionally, however, you may see instances of an accelerated form of amortization if the decline in usefulness of the intangible asset does not occur evenly over time.

If an intangible asset has a finite life, amortization must be recognized. A finite life exists when an intangible asset is legally valid only for a certain length of time. For example, a patent is granted for a time period of 20 years and gives the patent holder the legal right to exclusive use of the patented design or invention. A copyright is likewise granted for a specified legal life. A finite life also exists when there is no legal life but the management of the company knows for certain that they will only be able to use the intangible asset for a specified period of time. For example, a company may have purchased the right to use a list of names and addresses of customers for a two-year time period. In that case, the intangible asset can only be used for two years and has a finite life.

When an intangible asset with a finite life is amortized, the time period over which amortization should be recorded must be considered carefully. The general guideline that should be followed is that *amortization should be recorded over the legal life or the useful life, whichever is shorter.* For example, patents may have a legal life of 20 years, but many are not useful for that long because new products and technology make the patent obsolete. The patent should be amortized over the number of years in which the firm receives benefits, which may be a period shorter than the legal life.

Assume that ML Company developed a patent for a new product on January 1, 2008. The costs involved with patent approval were $10,000, and the company wants to record amortization on the straight-line basis over a five-year life with no residual value. The accounting entry to record the amortization for 2008 is as follows:

2008

Dec. 31	Patent Amortization Expense	2,000	
	Accumulated Amortization—Patent		2,000
	To record amortization of patent for one year		

Assets	=	Liabilities	+	Shareholders' Equity
−2,000				−2,000

Rather than use an accumulated amortization account, some companies decrease (credit) the intangible asset account directly. In that case, the preceding transaction is recorded as follows:

2008

Dec. 31	Patent Amortization Expense	2,000	
	Patent		2,000
	To record amortization of patent for one year		

Assets	=	Liabilities	+	Shareholders' Equity
−2,000				−2,000

No matter which of the two preceding entries is used, the asset should be reported on the balance sheet at acquisition cost ($10,000) less accumulated amortization ($2,000), or $8,000, as of December 31, 2008.

While intangibles such as patents and copyrights have a finite life, many others do not. *If an intangible asset has an indefinite life, amortization should not be recognized.* For example, a television or radio station may have paid to acquire a broadcast licence. A broadcast licence is usually for a certain time period but can be renewed at the end of that time period. In that case, the life of the asset is indefinite, and amortization of the intangible asset representing the broadcast rights should not be recognized. A second example would be a trademark. For many companies, such as Honda, a trademark is a very valuable asset that provides name recognition and enhances sales. But a trademark is not subject to a legal life, and the life may be quite indefinite. The value of some trademarks may continue for a long time. Because the life of an intangible asset represented by trademarks is indefinite, amortization should not be recorded.

Goodwill is an important intangible asset on the balance sheet of many companies. Until 2002, accounting rules had required companies to record amortization of goodwill over a time period not to exceed 40 years. However, in 2002, the AcSB ruled that goodwill should be treated as an intangible asset with an *indefinite* life and companies should no longer record amortization expense related to goodwill. Companies have generally favoured the new accounting stance. Hopefully, it will allow companies to more accurately inform statement users of their true value.

While companies should not record amortization of intangible assets with an indefinite life, they are required each year to determine whether the asset has been *impaired.* Impairment means a loss should be recorded when the value of the asset has declined. For example, some trademarks, such as **Xerox** and **Polaroid**, that were quite powerful in the past have declined in value over time. By recognizing an impairment of the asset, the loss is recorded in the time period that the value declines rather than when the asset is sold. It requires a great deal of judgment to determine when intangible assets have been impaired because the true value of an intangible asset is often difficult to determine. A rather drastic example of impairment occurs when a company realizes that an intangible asset has become completely worthless and should be written off.

http://www.xerox.com
http://www.polaroid.com/ca

Assume in the ML example that ML learns on January 1, 2009, when accumulated amortization is $2,000 (or the book value of the patent is $8,000), that a competing company has developed a new product that renders ML's patent worthless. ML has a loss of $8,000 and should record an entry to write off the asset as follows:

2009			
Jan. 1	Loss on Patent	8,000	
	Accumulated Amortization—Patent	2,000	
	Patent		10,000
	To record the write-off of patent		

Assets	=	Liabilities	+	Shareholders' Equity
+2,000				−8,000
−10,000				

Capital Assets: Intangible Assets **373**

ANALYZING LONG-TERM ASSETS FOR AVERAGE LIFE AND ASSET TURNOVER

Because long-term assets constitute the major productive assets of most companies, it is important to analyze the age and composition of these assets. We will analyze the assets of CN in the following section. Analysis of the age of the assets can be accomplished fairly easily for those companies that use the straight-line method of depreciation. A rough measure of the *average life* of the assets can be calculated as follows:

Average Life = Property, Plant, and Equipment/Depreciation Expense

The *average age* of the assets can be calculated as follows:

Average Age = Accumulated Depreciation/Depreciation Expense

On December 31, 2007, CN had property and equipment of $29,323,000,000 and accumulated depreciation of $8,910,000,000. A careful reading of the statement of cash flows also indicates depreciation expense of $678,000,000 for the year ended December 31, 2007. Therefore, the average life of CN's assets is calculated as follows:

Average Life = Property, Plant, and Equipment/Depreciation Expense

Average Life = $29,323/$678

= 43.2 years

This is a rough estimate because it assumes that the company has purchased assets fairly evenly over time. Because it is an average, it indicates that some assets have a life longer than 43.2 years and others shorter lives.

The average age of CN's capital assets is calculated as follows:

Average Age = Accumulated Depreciation/Depreciation Expense

Average Age = $8,910/$678

= 13.1 years

This result indicates that CN's property assets are on average 30% (13.1/43.2) used. Thus a major investment in new properties is unlikely in the near future, although other investments will be required for specific items on an ongoing basis.

The asset category of the balance sheet is also important in analyzing the company's *profitability*. The asset turnover ratio is a measure of the productivity of the assets and is measured as follows:

Asset Turnover = Net Sales/Average Total Assets

Thus asset turnover for CN = $7,897/(($23,460 + $24,004]/2) = 0.33 per year. This ratio is a measure of how many dollars of assets are necessary for every dollar of sales. If a company is using its assets efficiently, each dollar of assets will create a high amount of sales.

HOW LONG-TERM ASSETS AFFECT THE STATEMENT OF CASH FLOWS

Determining the impact that acquisition, depreciation, and sale of long-term assets has on the statement of cash flows is important. Each of these business activities influences the statement of cash flows. Exhibit 8-10 illustrates the items discussed in this chapter and their effect on the statement of cash flows.

The acquisition of a long-term asset is an investing activity and should be reflected in the Investing Activities category of the statement of cash flows. The acquisition should appear as a deduction or negative item in that section because it requires the use of cash to purchase the asset. This applies whether the long-term asset is property, plant, and equipment or an intangible asset.

The depreciation or amortization of a long-term asset is not a cash expense. It was referred to earlier as a non-cash charge to earnings. Nevertheless, it must be presented on the statement of cash flows (if the indirect method is used for the statement). The reason is that it was deducted from earnings in calculating the net income figure. Therefore, it must be eliminated or "added back" if the net income amount is used to indicate the amount of cash generated from operations. Thus, depreciation and amortization should be presented in the Operating Activities category of the statement of cash flows as an addition to net income.

> **LO 9** Explain the impact that capital assets have on the statement of cash flows.

Item	Cash Flow Statement	
	Operating Activities	
	Net income	**xxx**
Depreciation and amortization	·······························>	+
Gain on sale of asset	·······························>	−
Loss on sale of asset	·······························>	+
	Investing Activities	
Purchase of asset	·······························>	−
Sale of asset	·······························>	+
	Financing Activities	

Exhibit 8-10

Long-Term Assets and the Statement of Cash Flows

The sale or disposition of long-term assets is an investing activity. When an asset is sold, the amount of cash received should be reflected as an addition or plus amount in the Investing Activities category of the statement of cash flows. If the asset was sold at a gain or loss, however, one additional aspect should be reflected. Because the gain or loss was reflected on the income statement, it should be eliminated from the net income amount presented in the Operating Activities category (if the indirect method is used). A sale of an asset is not an activity related to normal, ongoing operations, and all amounts involved with the sale should be removed from the Operating Activities category. Exhibit 8-11 indicates the Operating and Investing categories of the 2007 statement of cash flows of CN. The company had a net income during 2007 of $2,158 million, the first line of the Operations category of the cash flow statement. CN's performance is an excellent example of the difference between the net income on the income statement and actual cash flow. Note that the company generated a positive cash flow from operations of $2,417 million. One of the primary reasons was that depreciation and amortization of $678 million affected the income statement but do not involve a cash outflow and are therefore added on the cash flow statement. Also note that the Investing Activities category indicates major outlays of cash for new properties, and $1,387 million additions to property, plant, and equipment.

The cash flow from operations displayed in Exhibit 8-11 shows "Other $119" as a cash outflow adjustment to net income. Like most categories termed "Other," the exact contents are difficult if not impossible to discern.

An examination of the footnote for Other Income ($166 in footnote 14) shows only a small amount for the gain on disposal of properties, $14. Other components of other income, representing a gain on the disposal of a major property and a gain on the sale of an investment, are shown as separate adjustments for the removal of non-cash operating gains. Thus we cannot easily account for the $119 removed from cash flow from operations.

Note that the direct cash flow presentation for operating activities does not show depreciation and amortization. This is because only the cash elements of the income statement are presented. The indirect approach requires the presentation of adjustments to the accrual net income for items included therein that are not cash, or inclusion of cash items that are not in the net income accrued amount. In a later chapter we describe the use of each of the forms of presentation.

Answers to the Two-Minute Reviews

Two-Minute Review on page 360

1. The general rule for calculating the acquisition cost of an asset is to include all of the costs that were necessary to acquire the asset and prepare it for use. Normally, that would include the purchase price but would also include costs such as freight costs, taxes, and installation costs if they were necessary to prepare the asset for use.

2. Accelerated depreciation will be higher in the early years of the asset, and straight-line will be higher in the later years. Over the life of the asset, the total amount of depreciation will be the same under all of the methods, assuming that the same amount of salvage value is estimated for each of the methods.

Two-Minute Review on page 374

1. Intangibles are assets that have no physical properties. Examples are copyrights, trademarks, patents, franchises, and goodwill.

2. Intangibles with a finite life should be amortized over the legal life of the asset or the useful life, whichever is shorter. Most companies use the straight-line method of amortization. Accelerated methods of amortization are allowed but are not often used.

Exhibit 8-11 CN's Consolidated Statement of Cash Flows

In millions Year ended December 31,	2007	2006	2005
Operating activities			
Net income	$ 2,158	$ 2,087	$ 1,556
Adjustments to reconcile net income to net cash provided			
from operating activities:			
Depreciation and amortization	678	653	630
Deferred income taxes *(Note 15)*	(82)	3	547
Gain on sale of Central Station Complex *(Note 5)*	(92)	–	–
Gain on sale of investment in English Welsh and Scottish Railway *(Note 6)*	(61)	–	–
Other changes in:			
Accounts receivable *(Note 4)*	229	(17)	142
Material and supplies	18	(36)	(25)
Accounts payable and accrued charges	(351)	197	(156)
Other net current assets and liabilities	39	58	8
Other	(119)	6	6
Cash provided from operating activities	2,417	2,951	2,708
Investing activities			
Property additions	(1,387)	(1,298)	(1,180)
Acquisitions, net of cash acquired *(Note 3)*	(25)	(84)	
Sale of Central Station Complex *(Note 5)*	351	–	–
Sale of investment in English Welsh and Scottish Railway *(Note 6)*	114	–	–
Other, net	52	33	105
Cash used by investing activities	(895)	(1,349)	(1,075)
Financing activities			
Issuance of long-term debt	4,171	3,308	2,728
Reduction of long-term debt	(3,589)	(3,089)	(2,865)
Issuance of common shares due to exercise of stock options and			
related excess tax benefits realized *(Note 12)*	77	120	115
Repurchase of common shares *(Note 11)*	(1,584)	(1,483)	(1,418)
Dividends paid	(418)	(340)	(275)
Cash used by financing activities	(1,343)	(1,484)	(1,715)
Effect of foreign exchange fluctuations on U.S. dollar-denominated cash			
and cash equivalents	(48)	(1)	(3)
Net increase (decrease) in cash and cash equivalents	131	117	(85)
Cash and cash equivalents, beginning of year	179	62	147
Cash and cash equivalents, end of year	$ 310	$ 179	$ 62
Supplemental cash flow information			
Net cash receipts from customers and other	$ 8,139	$ 7,946	$ 7,581
Net cash payments for:			
Employee services, suppliers and other expenses	(4,323)	(4,130)	(4,075)
Interest	(340)	(294)	(306)
Workforce reductions *(Note 9)*	(31)	(45)	(87)
Personal injury and other claims *(Note 18)*	(86)	(107)	(92)
Pensions *(Note 13)*	(75)	(112)	(127)
Income taxes *(Note 15)*	(867)	(307)	(186)
Cash provided from operating activities	$ 2,417	$ 2,951	$ 2,708

This excerpt from CN's 2007 Annual Report appears courtesy of CN. This section of the CN Annual Report appears in the Appendix of this textbook.

Chapter Highlights

1. **LO 1** Describe the balance sheet disclosures for capital assets (p. 350).

   - Capital assets are normally presented on the balance sheet in one category for property, plant, and equipment and a second category for intangibles.
   - Capital assets should be presented at original acquisition cost less accumulated depreciation or amortization.

2. **LO 2** Determine the acquisition cost of a capital asset (p. 350).

   - Acquisition cost should include all costs necessary to acquire the asset and prepare it for its intended use.
   - When assets are purchased for a lump sum, acquisition cost should be determined as the proportion of the market values of the assets purchased.
   - Interest on assets constructed over time can be capitalized. The amount of interest capitalized can be the average accumulated expenditures times an interest rate.

3. **LO 3** Compare depreciation methods, and understand the factors affecting the choice of method (p. 353).

   - Several depreciation methods are available to describe the decline in usefulness of capital assets. The straight-line method is the most commonly used and assigns the same amount of depreciation to each time period over the asset's life.
   - Accelerated depreciation allocates a greater expense to the earlier years of an asset's life and less to later years. The double-declining-balance method is one form of accelerated depreciation.

4. **LO 4** Analyze the impact of a change in estimate of the capital asset life or residual value (p. 359).

   - Depreciation is based on an estimate of the life of the asset and the residual value. When it is necessary to change the estimate, the amount of depreciation expense is adjusted for the current year and future years. Past depreciation amounts are not restated.

5. **LO 5** Determine which expenditures should be capitalized as capital asset costs and which should be treated as expenses (p. 361).

   - Capital expenditures are costs that increase an asset's life or its productivity. Capital expenditures should be added to the cost of the asset. Revenue expenditures should be treated as an expense in the period in which they are incurred because they benefit only the current period.

6. **LO 6** Analyze the effect of the disposal of a capital asset at a gain or loss (p. 364).

   - The gain or loss on the disposal of an asset is the difference between the asset's book value and its selling price.

7. **LO 7** Explain the balance sheet presentation of natural resources (p. 366).

   - Depletion is used to reflect the cost of consuming natural resources.

8. **LO 8** Explain the balance sheet presentation of intangible assets (p. 368).

   - Intangible assets should be presented on the balance sheet at acquisition cost less accumulated amortization, if any. Acquisition cost should include all costs necessary to acquire the asset.
   - Research and development costs are not always treated as an intangible asset. Instead, they may be treated as an expense in the year they are incurred.
   - Intangibles with a finite life should be amortized over the shorter of their legal or useful life.

9. **LO 9** Explain the impact that capital assets have on the statement of cash flows (p. 375).

   - The acquisition of long-term assets should be reflected in the Investing Activities category of the statement of cash flows.

Ratio Review

Long-term assets are used to produce the products and services that allow a company to operate profitably. Therefore, it is important for investors and creditors to analyze whether the long-term assets are sufficient to support the company's activities. Investors and creditors should analyze the average life of the assets, the average age of the assets, and the asset turnover. The asset turnover is a measure of how many dollars of assets are necessary to generate a dollar of sales. The following ratios can be used to calculate the life, age, and turnover of the long-term assets (assuming the company is using the straight-line method of depreciation):

$$\text{Average life} = \frac{\text{Property, plant, and equipment}}{\text{Depreciation expense}}$$

$$\text{Average age} = \frac{\text{Accumulated depreciation}}{\text{Depreciation expense}}$$

$$\text{Asset turnover} = \frac{\text{Net sales}}{\text{Average total assets}}$$

The results of these ratios can be compared to previous years of the same company or to the results of other companies to yield important conclusions for the analyst.

Accounts Highlighted

Account Titles	Where it Appears	In What Section	Page Number
Land	Balance Sheet	Capital Assets	351
Buildings	Balance Sheet	Capital Assets	351
Machinery	Balance Sheet	Capital Assets	350
Accumulated depreciation (a contra account)	Balance Sheet	Capital Assets	353
Depreciation expense	Income Statement	Operating Expenses	353
Gain on sale of asset	Income Statement	Other Income	364
Loss on sale of asset	Income Statement	Other Expense	365
Depletion expense	Income Statement	Operating Expenses	367
Copyright	Balance Sheet	Intangible Capital Assets	369
Trademark	Balance Sheet	Intangible Capital Assets	369
Goodwill	Balance Sheet	Intangible Capital Assets	369
Amortization expense	Income Statements	Operating Expenses	372
Accumulated amortization (a contra account)	Balance Sheet	Intangible Capital Assets	372

Key Terms Quiz

Read each definition below and then write the number of the definition in the blank beside the appropriate term it defines. The quiz solutions appear at the end of the chapter.

_____ Acquisition cost

_____ Capitalization of interest

_____ Land improvements

_____ Depreciation

_____ Straight-line method

_____ Book value

_____ Units-of-production method

_____ Accelerated depreciation

_____ Double-declining-balance method

_____ Change in estimate

_____ Capital expenditure

_____ Revenue expenditure

_____ Gain on Sale of Capital Asset

_____ Loss on Sale of Capital Asset

_____ Natural resources

_____ Intangible capital assets

_____ Goodwill

_____ Research and development costs

1. This amount includes all of the costs normally necessary to acquire a capital asset and prepare it for its intended use.

2. Additions made to a piece of property such as paving or landscaping a parking lot. The costs are treated separately from land for purposes of recording depreciation.

3. A method by which the same dollar amount of depreciation is recorded in each year of capital asset use.

4. A method by which depreciation is determined as a function of the number of units the capital asset produces.

5. The process of treating the cost of interest on constructed capital assets as a part of the capital assets' cost rather than as an expense.

6. A change in the life of a capital asset or in its expected residual value.

7. The allocation of the original acquisition cost of a capital asset to the periods benefited by its use.

8. A cost that improves a capital asset and is added to the asset account.

9. The original acquisition cost of a capital asset minus the amount of accumulated depreciation.

10. A cost that keeps a capital asset in its normal operating condition and is treated as an expense of the period.

11. An account with an amount that indicates the selling price received on a capital asset's disposal exceeds its book value.

12. An account with an amount that indicates the book value of a capital asset exceeds the selling price received on its disposal.

13. A term that refers to several methods by which a higher amount of depreciation is recorded in the early years of a capital asset's life and a lower amount is recorded in the later years.

14. Capital assets that have no physical properties; for example, patents, copyrights, and goodwill.

15. A method by which depreciation is recorded at twice the straight-line rate but the depreciable balance is reduced in each period.

16. The amount indicating that the purchase price of a business exceeded the total fair value of the identifiable net capital assets at the time the business was acquired.

17. Expenditures incurred in the discovery of new knowledge and the translation of research into a design or plan for a new product.

18. Assets that are consumed during their use; for example, coal or oil.

Answers on p. 397.

Alternate Terms

Accumulated depreciation Allowance for depreciation

Acquisition cost Historical cost

Capitalize Treat as asset

Construction in progress Construction in process

Goodwill Purchase price in excess of the fair value of assets

Hidden assets Unrecorded or off–balance-sheet assets

Property, Plant, and Equipment Fixed assets

Prospective Current and future years

Residual value Salvage value

Revenue expenditure An expense of the period

Warmup Exercises and Solutions

Warmup Exercise 8-1 *Depreciation Methods* LO 3

Assume that a company purchases a depreciable asset on January 1 for $10,000. The asset has a four-year life and will have zero residual value at the end of the fourth year.

Required

Calculate depreciation expense for each of the four years using the straight-line method and the double-declining-balance method.

Warmup Exercise 8-2 *Depreciation and Cash Flow* LO 3

Use the information from Warmup Exercise 8-1. Assume that capital cost allowance of 20% is used for tax purposes. Also assume that the tax rate is 40%.

Required

How much will the tax savings be in the first two years as a result of using the capital cost allowance method?

Solutions to Warmup Exercises

Warmup Exercise 8-1

	Straight-Line	Double-Declining-Balance	
Year 1	$2,500*	$10,000 × 0.50**	= $5,000
2	2,500	($10,000 − $5,000) × 0.50	= 2,500
3	2,500	($10,000 − $7,500) × 0.50	= 1,250
4	2,500	($10,000 − $8,750) × 0.50	= 625

*$10,000/4 years
**Straight-line rate as a percentage is 1 year/4 years, or 25%. Double the rate is 25% × 2, or 50%.

Warmup Exercise 8-2

CCA year 1: 20% × $10,000 × ½ = $1,000
Tax savings: 40% × $1,000 = $400

CCA year 2: 20% × ($10,000 − $1,000) = $1,800
Tax savings: 40% × $1,800 = $720

Note: CCA is less than the straight-line depreciation, but CCA provides the maximum permitted for the tax returns for years 1 and 2.

Review Problem and Solution

The accountant for Becker Company wants to develop a balance sheet as of December 31, 2008. A review of the asset records has revealed the following information:

a. Asset A was purchased on July 1, 2006, for $40,000 and has been depreciated on the straight-line basis using an estimated life of six years and a residual value of $4,000.

b. Asset B was purchased on January 1, 2007, for $66,000. The straight-line method has been used for depreciation purposes. Originally, the estimated life of the asset was projected to be six years with a residual value of $6,000; however, at the beginning of 2008, the accountant learned that the remaining life of the asset was only three years with a residual value of $2,000.

c. Asset C was purchased on January 1, 2007, for $50,000. The double-declining-balance method has been used for depreciation purposes, with a four-year life and a residual value estimate of $5,000.

Required

1. Assume that these assets represent pieces of equipment. Calculate the acquisition cost, accumulated depreciation, and book value of each asset as of December 31, 2008.

2. How would the assets appear on the balance sheet on December 31, 2008?

3. Assume that Becker Company sold Asset B on January 2, 2009, for $25,000. Calculate the amount of the resulting gain or loss, and prepare the journal entry for the sale. Where would the gain or loss appear on the income statement?

Solution to Review Problem

1.

Asset A

2006	Depreciation	($40,000 − $4,000)/6 × 1/2 Year	=	$ 3,000
2007		($40,000 − $4,000)/6	=	6,000
2008		($40,000 − $4,000)/6	=	6,000
	Accumulated Depreciation			$15,000

Asset B

2007	Depreciation	($66,000 − $6,000)/6	=	$10,000
2008		($66,000 − $10,000 − $2,000)/3	=	18,000
	Accumulated Depreciation			$28,000

Note the impact of the change in estimate on 2008 depreciation.

Asset C

2007	Depreciation	$50,000 × 25% × 2	=	$25,000
2008		($50,000 − $25,000) × (25% × 2)	=	12,500
	Accumulated Depreciation			$37,500

BECKER COMPANY
SUMMARY OF ASSET COST AND ACCUMULATED DEPRECIATION
AS OF DECEMBER 31, 2008

Asset	Acquisition Cost	Accumulated Depreciation	Book Value
A	$ 40,000	$15,000	$25,000
B	66,000	28,000	38,000
C	50,000	37,500	12,500
Totals	$156,000	$80,500	$75,500

2. The assets would appear in the Long-Term Assets category of the balance sheet as follows:

Equipment	$156,000	
Less: Accumulated depreciation	80,500	
Equipment (net)		$75,500

3.

Asset B book value	$ 38,000
Selling price	25,000
Loss on sale of asset	$ 13,000

The journal entry to record the sale is as follows:

2009			
Jan. 2	Cash	25,000	
	Accumulated Depreciation	28,000	
	Loss on Sale of Asset	13,000	
	Asset B		66,000

(continued)

To record the sale of Asset B

Assets	=	Liabilities	+	Shareholders' Equity
+25,000				−13,000
+28,000				
−66,000				

The Loss on Sale of Asset account should appear in the Other Income/Other Expense category of the income statement. It is similar to an expense but is not the company's major activity.

Questions

1. What are several examples of capital assets? Why are capital assets essential to a company's long-term future?

2. What is the meaning of the term *acquisition cost of capital assets*? Give some examples of costs that should be included in the acquisition cost.

3. When assets are purchased as a group, how should the acquisition cost of the individual assets be determined?

4. Why is it important to account separately for the cost of land and building, even when the two assets are purchased together?

5. Under what circumstances should interest be capitalized as part of the cost of an asset?

6. What factors may contribute to the decline in usefulness of capital assets? Should the choice of depreciation method be related to these factors? Must a company choose just one method of depreciation for all assets?

7. Why do you think that most companies use the straight-line method of depreciation?

8. How should the residual value of a capital asset be treated when using the straight-line method? How should it be treated when using the double-declining-balance method?

9. Why do many companies use one method to calculate depreciation for the income statement developed for shareholders and another method for income tax purposes?

10. What should a company do if it finds that the original estimate of the life of an asset or the residual value of the asset must be changed?

11. What are the meanings of the terms *capital expenditures* and *revenue expenditures*? What determines whether an item is a capital or revenue expenditure?

12. How is the gain or loss on the sale of a capital asset calculated? Where would the Gain on Sale of Asset account appear on the financial statements?

13. What are several examples of items that constitute intangible assets? In what category of the balance sheet should intangible assets appear?

14. What is the meaning of the term *goodwill*? Give an example of a transaction that would result in the recording of goodwill on the balance sheet.

15. Do you agree with the U.S. GAAP ruling that all research and development costs should be treated as an expense on the income statement? Why or why not?

16. Do you agree with some accountants who argue that intangible assets have an indefinite life and therefore should not be subject to amortization?

17. When an intangible asset is amortized, should the asset's amortization occur over its legal life or over its useful life? Give an example in which the legal life exceeds the useful life.

18. Suppose that an intangible asset is being amortized over a 10-year time period but a competitor has just introduced a new product that will have a serious negative impact on the asset's value. Should the company continue to amortize the intangible asset over the 10-year life?

Exercises

Exercise 8-1 *Acquisition Cost* LO 2

Able Company purchased a piece of equipment with a list price of $30,000 on January 1, 2008. The following amounts were related to the equipment purchase:

- Terms of the purchase were 2/10, net 30. Able paid for the purchase on January 8.
- Freight costs of $500 were incurred.
- A federal agency required that a pollution-control device be installed on the equipment at a cost of $1,250.
- During installation, the equipment was damaged and repair costs of $2,000 were incurred.
- Architect's fees of $3,000 were paid to redesign the work space to accommodate the new equipment.

- Able purchased liability insurance to cover possible damage to the asset. The three-year policy cost $4,000.
- Able financed the purchase with a bank loan. Interest of $1,500 was paid on the loan during 2008.

Required

Determine the acquisition cost of the equipment.

Exercise 8-2 *Lump-Sum Purchase* LO 2

To add to his growing chain of clothing stores, on January 1, 2008, Lucas Loops bought a store from a small competitor for $260,000. An appraiser, hired to assess the value of the assets acquired, determined that the land had a market value of $100,000, the building a market value of $75,000, and the equipment a market value of $125,000.

Required

1. What is the acquisition cost of each asset? Prepare a journal entry to record the acquisition.
2. Lucas plans to depreciate the capital assets on a straight-line basis for 20 years. Determine the amount of depreciation expense for 2008 on these newly acquired assets.
3. How would the assets appear on the balance sheet as of December 31, 2008?

Exercise 8-3 *Straight-Line and Units-of-Production Methods* LO 3

Assume that Sackville Company purchased factory equipment on January 1, 2008, for $120,000. The equipment has an estimated life of five years and an estimated residual value of $12,000. Sackville's accountant is considering whether to use the straight-line or the units-of-production method to depreciate the asset. Because the company is beginning a new production process, the equipment will be used to produce 20,000 units in 2008, but production subsequent to 2008 will increase by 20,000 units each year.

Required

Calculate the depreciation expense, the accumulated depreciation, and the book value of the equipment under both methods for each of the five years of the asset's life. Do you think that the units-of-production method yields reasonable results in this situation?

Exercise 8-4 *Accelerated Depreciation* LO 3

Speedy Shipping purchased a forklift on January 1, 2008, for $12,000. It is expected to last for five years and have a residual value of $1,200. Speedy uses the double-declining-balance method for depreciation.

Required

1. Calculate the depreciation expense, the accumulated depreciation, and the book value for each year of the forklift's life.
2. Prepare the journal entry to record depreciation expense for 2009.
3. Refer to Exhibit 8-5. What factors may have influenced Speedy to use the double-declining-balance method?

Exercise 8-5 *Change in Estimate* LO 4

Assume that Cole Company purchased a new machine on January 1, 2008, for $40,000. The machine has an estimated useful life of nine years and a residual value of $4,000. Cole has chosen to use the straight-line method of depreciation. On January 1, 2010, Cole discovered that the machine would not be useful beyond December 31, 2013, and estimated its value at that time to be $1,000.

Required

1. Calculate the depreciation expense, the accumulated depreciation, and the book value of the asset for each year, 2008 to 2013.
2. Was the depreciation recorded in 2008 and 2009 wrong? If so, why was it not corrected?

Exercise 8-6 *Asset Disposal* LO 6

Assume that Lawrencetown Company purchased an asset on January 1, 2006, for $30,000. The asset had an estimated life of six years and an estimated residual value of $3,000. The company used the straight-line method to depreciate the asset. On July 1, 2008, the asset was sold for $20,000 cash.

(continued)

Required

1. Make the journal entry to record depreciation for 2008. Also record all transactions necessary for the sale of the asset.

2. How should the gain or loss on the sale of the asset be presented on the income statement?

Exercise 8-7 *Asset Disposal* **LO 6**

Refer to Exercise 8-6. Assume that Lawrencetown Company sold the asset on July 1, 2008, and received $7,500 cash and a note for an additional $7,500.

Required

1. Make the journal entry to record depreciation for 2008. Also record all transactions necessary for the sale of the asset.

2. How should the gain or loss on the sale of the asset be presented on the income statement?

Exercise 8-8 *Amortization of Intangibles* **LO 8**

For each of the following intangible assets, indicate the amount of amortization expense that should be recorded for the year 2008 and the amount of accumulated amortization on the balance sheet as of December 31, 2008.

	Copyright	Trademark	Patent
Cost	$40,000	$20,000	$25,000
Date of purchase	1/1/06	1/1/02	1/1/03
Useful life	20 years	indefinite	10 years
Legal life	50 years	undefined	20 years
Method	straight-line	straight-line	straight-line

Exercise 8-9 *Impact of Transactions Involving Capital Assets on Statement of Cash Flows* **LO 9**

From the following list, identify each item as operating (O), investing (I), financing (F), or not separately reported on the statement of cash flows (N).

_____ Purchase of land

_____ Proceeds from sale of land

_____ Gain on sale of land

_____ Purchase of equipment

_____ Depreciation expense

_____ Proceeds from sale of equipment

_____ Loss on sale of equipment

Exercise 8-10 *Impact of Transactions Involving Intangible Assets on Statement of Cash Flows* **LO 9**

From the following list, identify each item as operating (O), investing (I), financing (F), or not separately reported on the statement of cash flows (N).

_____ Cost incurred to acquire copyright

_____ Proceeds from sale of patent

_____ Gain on sale of patent

_____ Research and development costs

_____ Amortization of patent

Multi-Concept Exercises

Exercise 8-11 *Capital versus Revenue Expenditures* **LO 1, 5**

On January 1, 2006, Kentville Corporation purchased a building for $400,000 and a delivery truck for $40,000. The following expenditures have been incurred during 2008, related to the building and the truck:

■ The building was painted at a cost of $10,000.

■ To prevent leaking, new windows were installed in the building at a cost of $20,000.

- To allow an improved flow of production, a new conveyor system was installed at a cost of $80,000.
- The delivery truck was repainted with a new company logo at a cost of $2,000.
- To allow better handling of large loads, a lift system was installed on the truck at a cost of $10,000.
- The truck's engine was overhauled at a cost of $8,000.

Required

1. Determine which of these costs should be capitalized. Also record the journal entry for the capitalized costs. Assume that all costs were incurred on January 1, 2008.

2. Determine the amount of depreciation for the year 2008. The company uses the straight-line method and depreciates the building over 25 years and the truck over 6 years. Assume zero residual value for all assets.

3. How would the assets appear on the balance sheet of December 31, 2008?

Exercise 8-12 *Capitalization of Interest and Depreciation* LO 2, 3

During 2008, Kingston Company borrowed $160,000 from a local bank and, in addition, used $240,000 of cash to construct a new corporate office building. Based on average accumulated expenditures, the amount of interest capitalized during 2008 was $16,000. Construction was completed and the building was occupied on January 1, 2009.

Required

1. Determine the acquisition cost of the new building.

2. The building has an estimated useful life of 20 years and a $10,000 salvage value. Assuming that Kingston uses the straight-line basis to depreciate its operating assets, determine the amount of depreciation expense for 2008 and 2009.

Exercise 8-13 *Research and Development and Patents* LO 8

Bonita Company incurred the following costs during 2008.

a. Research and development costs of $40,000 were incurred. The research was conducted to discover a new product to sell to customers in future years. A product was successfully developed, and a patent for the new product was granted during 2008. Bonita is unsure of the period benefited by the research but believes the product will result in increased sales over the next five years.

b. Legal costs and application fees of $20,000 for the patent on the new product were incurred on January 1, 2008. The patent was granted for a life of 20 years.

c. A patent infringement suit was successfully defended at a cost of $16,000. Assume that all costs were incurred on January 1, 2009.

Required

Determine how the costs in parts **a** and **b** should be presented on Bonita's financial statements as of December 31, 2008. Also determine the amount of amortization of intangible assets that Bonita should record in 2008 and 2009.

Problems

Problem 8-1 *Balance Sheet and Note Disclosures for Cape Britain Air Ltd.* LO 1

The June 30, 2008, balance sheet of Cape Britain Air Ltd. revealed the following information in the property and equipment category:

	2008	2007
Flight equipment	$6,789	$5,826
Less: Accumulated depreciation	2,160	1,887
	$4,629	$3,939
Ground property and equipment	$1,806	$1,656
Less: Accumulated depreciation	963	909
	$ 843	$ 747

(continued)

The notes that accompany the financial statements revealed the following:

> Depreciation and Amortization—Owned flight equipment is depreciated on a straight-line basis to residual values over its estimated life. Ground property and equipment are depreciated on a straight-line basis over their estimated service lives, which range from 3 years to 30 years.

Required

1. Assume that Cape Britain Air Ltd. did not dispose of any ground property and equipment during the fiscal year 2008. Calculate the amount of depreciation expense for the year.

2. What was the average life of the flight equipment as of 2008?

3. What was the average age of the ground property and equipment as of 2008?

Problem 8-2 *Lump-Sum Purchase of Assets and Subsequent Events* LO 2

Minas Developments purchased, for cash, a large tract of land that was immediately plotted and deeded into smaller sections:

> Section 1, retail development with road frontage
>
> Section 2, apartment development
>
> Section 3, single-family homes in the largest section

Based on recent sales of similar property, the fair market values of the three sections are as follows:

> Section 1, $1,260,000
>
> Section 2, $756,000
>
> Section 3, $504,000

Required

1. What value is assigned to each section of land if the tract was purchased for (a) $2,520,000, (b) $3,120,000, or (c) $2,000,000?

2. How does the purchase of the tract affect the balance sheet?

3. Why would Minas be concerned with the value assigned to each section? Would Minas be more concerned with the values assigned if instead of purchasing three sections of land, it purchased land with buildings? Why or why not?

Problem 8-3 *Capital Cost Allowance as a Tax Shield* LO 3

The term *tax shield* refers to the amount of income tax saved by deducting CCA for income tax purposes. Assume that Irving Company is considering the purchase of an asset as of January 1, 2008. The cost of the asset is $200,000 and it is considered to be class 8, 20%, for income tax purposes. The company expects to use the asset for the next five years and to dispose of it for its tax book value at the end of that time.

Irving's income for tax purposes before recording capital cost allowance on the asset will be $100,000 per year for the next five years. The company is currently taxed at 25% on its taxable income.

Required

Calculate the amount of income tax Irving must pay each year for years 2008 to 2012 if the asset is not purchased. Calculate the amount of income tax Irving must pay each year for years 2008 to 2012 if the asset is purchased. What is the amount of the CCA tax shield?

Problem 8-4 *Book Depreciation Versus Capital Cost Allowance* LO 3

Supreme Courier Service purchased a delivery truck for $67,200. The truck has an estimated useful life of six years with no salvage value. For income tax purposes, Supreme follows the practice of claiming maximum CCA for class 10, 30%, with an assumption of a replacement truck being purchased in year 7.

Required

1. What is the difference between straight-line depreciation and CCA tax expense for years 1 to 6?

2. Supreme's president has asked why you have used one method for the books and another for calculating taxes. "Can you do this? Is it legal? Don't we take the same total depreciation either way?" she asked. Write a brief memo answering her question and explaining the reasons for the two methods.

Problem 8-5 *Depreciation and Cash Flow* **LO 9**

Able Company's only asset as of January 1, 2008, was an automobile. During 2008, only three transactions occurred:

- Provided services of $200,000 on account.
- Collected all accounts receivable.
- Depreciation on the automobile was $30,000.

Required

1. Develop an income statement for Able for 2008.
2. Determine the amount of the net cash inflow for Able for 2008.
3. Explain in one or more sentences why the amount of the net income on Able's income statement does not equal the amount of the net cash inflow.
4. If Able developed a cash flow statement for 2008 using the indirect method, what amount would appear in the category titled Cash Flow from Operating Activities?

Problem 8-6 *Reconstruct Net Book Values Using Statement of Cash Flows* **LO 9**

Capital Stores Ltd. had property, plant, and equipment, net of accumulated depreciation of $3,377,000; and intangible assets, net of accumulated amortization, of $2,019,000 at December 31, 2008. The company's 2008 statement of cash flows, prepared using the indirect method, included the following items.

The Cash Flows from Operating Activities section included three additions to net income: (1) depreciation expense in the amount of $2,016,000, (2) amortization expense in the amount of $99,000, and (3) the loss on the sale of equipment in the amount of $105,000. The Cash Flows from Operating Activities section also included a subtraction from net income for the gain on the sale of a copyright of $165,000. The Cash Flows from Investing Activities section included outflows for the purchase of a building in the amount of $876,000 and $45,000 for the payment of legal fees to protect a patent from infringement. The Cash Flows from Investing Activities section also included inflows from the sale of equipment in the amount of $945,000 and the sale of a copyright in the amount of $225,000.

Required

1. Determine the book values of the assets that were sold during 2008.
2. Reconstruct the amount of property, plant, and equipment, net of accumulated depreciation, that was reported on the company's balance sheet at December 31, 2007.
3. Reconstruct the amount of intangibles, net of accumulated amortization, that was reported on the company's balance sheet at December 31, 2007.

Multi-Concept Problems

Problem 8-7 *Cost of Assets, Subsequent Book Values, and Balance Sheet Presentation* **LO 1, 2, 3, 5, 6**

The following events took place at Ken's Construction Company during 2008:

a. On January 1, Ken bought a used truck for $28,000. He added a tool chest and side racks for ladders for $9,600. The truck is expected to last four years and then be sold for $1,600. Ken uses straight-line depreciation.

b. On January 1, he purchased several items at an auction for $4,800. These items had fair market values as follows:

10 cases of paint trays and roller covers	$ 400
Storage cabinets	1,200
Ladders and scaffolding	4,800

Ken will use all the paint trays and roller covers this year. The storage cabinets are expected to last nine years, and the ladders and scaffolding for four years.

c. On February 1, Ken paid the city $3,000 for a three-year licence to operate the business.

d. On September 1, Ken sold an old truck for $9,600. The truck had cost $24,000 when it was purchased on September 1, 2003. It had been expected to last eight years and have a salvage value of $1,600.

(continued)

Required

1. For each situation, explain the value assigned to the asset when it was purchased (or for part **d,** the book value when sold).

2. Determine the amount of depreciation or other expense to be recorded for each asset for 2008.

3. How would these assets appear on the balance sheet as of December 31, 2008?

Problem 8-8 *Cost of Assets and the Effect on Depreciation* LO 2, 3

Early in its first year of business, Heart Company, a fitness centre, purchased new workout equipment. The acquisition included the following costs:

Purchase price	$75,000
Tax	7,500
Transportation	2,000
Setup*	12,500
Painting*	1,500

*The equipment was adjusted to Heart's specific needs
and painted to match the other equipment in the gym.*

The bookkeeper recorded an asset, Equipment, $82,500 (purchase price and tax). The remaining costs were expensed for the year. Heart used straight-line depreciation. The equipment was expected to last 10 years with zero salvage value.

Required

1. How much depreciation did Heart report on its income statement related to this equipment in year 1? What do you believe is the correct amount of depreciation to report in year 1 related to this equipment?

2. Income is $50,000, before costs related to the equipment are reported. How much income will Heart report in year 1? What amount of income should it report? You may ignore income tax.

3. Using the equipment as an example, explain the difference between a cost and an expense.

Problem 8-9 *Capital Expenditures, Depreciation, and Disposal* LO 3, 5, 6

Burnside Company purchased a factory building at a cost of $1,092,000 on January 1, 2007. Burnside estimated that the building's life would be 25 years and the residual value at the end of 25 years would be $42,000.

On January 1, 2008, the company made several expenditures related to the building. The entire building was painted and floors were refinished at a cost of $63,000. A federal agency required Burnside to install additional pollution-control devices in the building at a cost of $126,000. With the new devices, Burnside believed it was possible to extend the life of the building by an additional six years.

In 2009 Burnside altered its corporate strategy dramatically. The company sold the factory building on April 1, 2009, for $1,176,000 in cash and relocated all operations in another province.

Required

1. Determine the amount of depreciation that should be reflected on the income statement for 2007 and 2008.

2. Explain why the cost of the pollution-control equipment was not expensed in 2008. What conditions would have allowed Burnside to expense the equipment? If Burnside has a choice, would it prefer to expense or capitalize the equipment?

3. What amount of gain or loss did Burnside record when it sold the building? What amount of gain or loss would have been reported if the pollution-control equipment had been expensed in 2008?

Problem 8-10 *Amortization of Intangible, Revision of Rate* LO 4, 8

During 2003, Rockingham Ltd.'s R&D department developed a new manufacturing process. R&D costs were $170,000. The process was patented on October 1, 2003. Legal costs to acquire the patent were $23,800. Rockingham decided to expense the patent over a 20-year time period. Rockingham's fiscal year ends on September 30.

On October 1, 2008, Rockingham's competition announced that it had obtained a patent on a new process that would make Rockingham's patent completely worthless.

Required

1. How should Rockingham record the $170,000 and $23,800 costs?

2. How much amortization expense should Rockingham report in each year through the year ended September 30, 2008?

3. What amount of loss should Rockingham report in the year ended September 30, 2009?

Problem 8-11 *Purchase and Disposal of Capital Asset and Effects on Statement of Cash Flows* **LO 6, 9**

On January 1, 2008, Castlehill Company purchased some machinery for its production line for $208,000. Using an estimated useful life of eight years and a residual value of $16,000, the annual straight-line depreciation of the machinery was calculated to be $24,000. Castlehill used the machinery during 2008 and 2009 but then decided to automate its production process. On December 31, 2009, Castlehill sold the machinery at a loss of $10,000 and purchased new, fully automated machinery for $410,000.

Required

1. How would the transactions described above be presented on Castlehill's statements of cash flows for the years ended December 31, 2008 and 2009?

2. Why would Castlehill sell at a loss machinery that had a remaining useful life of six years and purchase new machinery with a cost almost twice that of the old?

Problem 8-12 *Amortization of Intangibles and Effects on Statement of Cash Flows* **LO 8, 9**

Larsen Ltd. purchased a patent a number of years ago. The patent is being amortized on a straight-line basis over its estimated useful life. The company's comparative balance sheets as of December 31, 2008 and 2007, included the following line item:

	12/31/08	**12/31/07**
Patent, less accumulated amortization of $238,000 (2008) and $204,000 (2007)	$340,000	$374,000

Required

1. How much amortization expense was recorded during 2008?

2. What was the patent's acquisition cost? When was it acquired? What is its estimated useful life? How was the acquisition of the patent reported on that year's statement of cash flows?

3. Assume that Larsen uses the indirect method to prepare its statement of cash flows. How is the amortization of the patent reported annually on the statement of cash flows?

4. How would the sale of the patent on January 1, 2009, for $400,000 be reported on the 2009 statement of cash flows?

Problem 8-13 *Depletion and Impairment* **LO 7, 9**

Suncor Energy Inc. is a large Canadian oil and gas company engaged in numerous oil and gas projects, and the development of the oil sands of the West. It reports $14,388 million in oil sands developments at December 31, 2006, $2,251 million in natural gas properties, $2,466 million in energy marketing and refining assets in Canada, and $904 million of refining and marketing assets in the United States.

http://www.suncor.com

Three major factors—depreciation, depletion, and impairment—are involved in accounting for the expenses of the four types of property, plant, equipment, and intangibles.

Required

1. Explain how Suncor might determine the allocated costs of PP&E for oil sands and gas plant facilities.

2. Explain the possible allocation of the cost of proved properties for natural gas. How can oil and gas costs be allocated for the same properties when they are not of the same nature?

3. How would you expect Suncor to handle potential impairments? Given the behaviour of oil and gas prices, would you expect impairments?

Alternate Problems

Problem 8-1A *Disclosures of Capital Assets* **LO 1**

The notes to the December 31, 2008, financial statements of East/West included the following disclosures for the Property, Plant, and Equipment account:

Property, Plant, and Equipment (in millions)	2008	2007
Land and Buildings	$1,926	$1,924
Cable Television Equipment	2,070	1,882
Furniture, Fixtures, and Other Equipment	2,800	2,674
	6,796	6,480
Less: Accumulated Depreciation	(2,814)	(2,302)
Totals	$3,982	$4,178

Required

Assume that East/West disposed of Property, Plant, and Equipment during 2008 with accumulated depreciation of $1,200 million.

1. Based on the note disclosures, what was the amount of depreciation expense for fiscal year 2008 for Property, Plant, and Equipment?
2. What was the average life of the assets in the Property, Plant, and Equipment categories?
3. What was the average age of the assets in the Property, Plant, and Equipment categories?

Problem 8-2A *Lump-Sum Purchase of Assets and Subsequent Events* **LO 2**

Regina Processing purchased, for cash, three large pieces of equipment. Based on recent sales of similar equipment, the fair market values are as follows:

Piece 1	$100,000
Piece 2	$100,000
Piece 3	$220,000

Required

1. What value is assigned to each piece of equipment if the equipment was purchased for (a) $480,000, (b) $340,000, or (c) $400,000?
2. How does the purchase of the equipment affect total assets?

Problem 8-3A *Depreciation as a Tax Shield* **LO 3**

The term *tax shield* refers to the amount of income tax saved by deducting CCA for income tax purposes. Assume that Hector Company is considering the purchase of an asset as of January 1, 2008. The cost of the asset with a five-year life and zero residual value is $120,000.

Hector's income for tax purposes before recording depreciation on the asset will be $124,000 per year for the next five years. The corporation is currently in the 30% tax bracket and determines that the asset is in the 30% CCA class.

Required

Calculate the amount of income tax that Hector must pay each year if the asset is not purchased and then the amount of income tax that Hector must pay each year for years 2008 to 2012 if the asset is purchased. What is the amount of tax shield over the life of the asset?

Problem 8-4A *Book Depreciation versus Capital Cost Allowance* **LO 3**

Prompt Courier Service purchased a delivery truck for $56,400. The truck will have a useful life of six years and a zero salvage value for financial statement purposes. Prompt will use straight-line depreciation for its financial statements. Prompt will use class 10, 30% for CCA.

Required

1. What would be the difference between straight-line depreciation and the maximum CCA for each of the six years?
2. Prompt's president has asked why you have used one method for financial statement purposes and CCA for income tax purposes. Write a memo to the president explaining the situation and the reasons for the two methods.

Problem 8-5A *Amortization and Cash Flow* **LO 9**

Thompson Company's only asset as of January 1, 2008, was a copyright. During 2008, only three transactions occurred:

- Royalties earned from copyright use, $250,000 in cash
- Cash paid for advertising and salaries, $31,250
- Depreciation, $25,000

Required

1. What amount of income will Thompson report in 2008?

2. What is the amount of cash on hand at December 31, 2008?

3. Explain how the cash balance increased from zero at the beginning of the year to its end-of-year balance. Why does the increase in cash not equal the income?

Problem 8-6A *Reconstruct Net Book Values Using Statement of Cash Flows* **LO 9**

Wilsons Canners Ltd. had property, plant, and equipment, net of accumulated depreciation, of $3,110,000; and intangible assets, net of accumulated amortization, of $68,000 at December 31, 2008. The company's 2008 statement of cash flows, prepared using the indirect method, included the following items.

The Cash Flows from Operating Activities section included three additions to net income: (1) depreciation expense in the amount of $410,000, (2) amortization expense in the amount of $6,000, and (3) the loss on the sale of land in the amount of $34,000. The Cash Flows from Operating Activities section also included a subtraction from net income for the gain on the sale of a trademark of $14,000. The Cash Flows from Investing Activities section included outflows for the purchase of equipment in the amount of $554,000 and $12,000 for the payment of legal fees to protect a copyright from infringement. The Cash Flows from Investing Activities section also included inflows from the sale of land in the amount of $374,000 and the sale of a trademark in the amount of $242,000.

Required

1. Determine the book values of the assets that were sold during 2008.

2. Reconstruct the amount of property, plant, and equipment, net of accumulated depreciation, that was reported on the company's balance sheet at December 31, 2007.

3. Reconstruct the amount of intangibles, net of accumulated amortization, that was reported on the company's balance sheet at December 31, 2007.

Alternate Multi-Concept Problems

Problem 8-7A *Cost of Assets, Subsequent Book Values, and Balance Sheet Presentation* **LO 1, 3, 6, 8**

The following events took place at Happy Eats Ltd., a pizza shop that specializes in home delivery, during 2008:

a. January 1, purchased a truck for $32,000 and added a cap and oven at a cost of $21,800. The truck is expected to last five years and be sold for $600 at the end of that time. The company uses straight-line depreciation for its trucks.

b. January 1, purchased equipment for $5,400 from a competitor who was retiring. The equipment is expected to last three years with zero salvage value. The company uses the double-declining-balance method to depreciate its equipment.

c. April 1, sold a truck for $3,000. The truck had been purchased for $16,000 exactly five years earlier, had an expected salvage value of $2,000, and was depreciated over an eight-year life using the straight-line method.

d. July 1, purchased a $28,000 patent for a unique baking process to produce a new product. The patent is valid for 15 more years; however, the company expects to produce and market the product for only four years. The patent's value at the end of the four years will be zero.

Required

For each situation, explain the amount of depreciation or amortization recorded for each asset in the current year and the book value of each asset at the end of the year. For part **c**, indicate the accumulated depreciation and book value at the time of sale.

Problem 8-8A *Cost of Assets and the Effect on Depreciation* **LO 2, 3**

Early in its first year of business, AID Inc., a security consultant, purchased new equipment. The acquisition included the following costs:

Purchase price	$84,000
Tax	8,250
Transportation	2,200
Setup*	550
Operating cost for first year	13,200

The equipment was adjusted to AID's specific needs.

The bookkeeper recorded the asset, Equipment, at $108,200. AID used straight-line depreciation. The equipment was expected to last 10 years with zero residual value.

Required

1. Was $108,200 the proper amount to record for the acquisition cost? If not, explain how each expenditure should be recorded.

2. How much depreciation did AID report on its income statement related to this equipment in year 1? How much should have been reported?

3. If AID's income before the costs associated with the equipment is $27,500, what amount of income did AID report? What amount should it have reported? You may ignore income tax.

4. Explain how AID should determine the amount to capitalize when recording an asset. What is the effect on the income statement and balance sheet of AID's error?

Problem 8-9A *Capital Expenditures, Depreciation, and Disposal* **LO 3, 5, 6**

Wedgewood Company purchased a retail shopping centre at a cost of $1,224,000 on January 1, 2007. Wagner estimated that the life of the building would be 25 years and the residual value at the end of 25 years would be $24,000.

On January 1, 2008, the company made several expenditures related to the building. The entire building was painted and floors were refinished at a cost of $230,400. A local zoning agency required Wedgewood to install additional fire-protection equipment, including sprinklers and built-in alarms, at a cost of $175,200. With the new protection, Wedgewood believed it was possible to increase the residual value of the building to $60,000.

In 2009, Wedgewood altered its corporate strategy dramatically. The company sold the retail shopping centre on January 1, 2009, for $720,000 of cash.

Required

1. Determine the amount of depreciation that should be reflected on the income statement for 2007 and 2008.

2. Explain why the cost of the fire-protection equipment was not expensed in 2008. What conditions would have allowed Wedgewood to expense it? If Wedgewood has a choice, would it prefer to expense or capitalize the improvement?

3. What amount of gain or loss did Wedgewood record when it sold the building? What amount of gain or loss would have been reported if the fire-protection equipment had been expensed in 2008?

Problem 8-10A *Amortization of Intangible, Revision of Rate* **LO 4, 8**

During 2003, Discovery Ltd.'s R&D department developed a new manufacturing process. R&D costs were $700,000. The process was patented on October 1, 2003. Legal costs to acquire the patent were $47,600. Discovery decided to expense the patent over a 20-year time period using the straight-line method. Discovery's fiscal year ends on September 30.

On October 1, 2008, Discovery's competition announced that it had obtained a patent on a new process that would make Discovery's patent completely worthless.

Required

1. How should Discovery record the $700,000 and $47,600 costs?

2. How much amortization expense should Discovery report in each year through the year ended September 30, 2008?

3. What amount of loss should Discovery report in the year ended September 30, 2009?

Problem 8-11A *Purchase and Disposal of Capital Asset and Effects on Statement of Cash Flows* **LO 6, 9**

On January 1, 2008, Maitland Inc. purchased a medium-sized delivery truck for $45,000. Using an estimated useful life of five years and a residual value of $5,000, the annual straight-line depreciation of the truck was calculated to be $8,000. Maitland used the truck during 2008 and 2009 but then decided to purchase a much larger delivery truck. On December 31, 2009, Maitland sold the medium-sized delivery truck at a loss of $12,000 and purchased a new, larger delivery truck for $80,000.

Required

1. How would the transactions described above be presented on Mansfield's statements of cash flows for the years ended December 31, 2008 and 2009?

2. Why would Maitland sell a truck that had a remaining useful life of three years at a loss and purchase a new truck with a cost almost twice that of the old?

Problem 8-12A *Amortization of Intangibles and Effects on Statement of Cash Flows* **LO 8, 9**

Liquidity Inc. acquired a patent a number of years ago. The patent is being amortized on a straight-line basis over its estimated useful life. The company's comparative balance sheets as of December 31, 2008 and 2007, included the following line item:

	12/31/08	12/31/07
Patent, less accumulated amortization of $830,500 (2008) and $755,000 (2007)	$678,500	$754,000

Required

1. How much amortization expense was recorded during 2008?

2. What was the patent's acquisition cost? When was it acquired? What is its estimated useful life? How was the acquisition of the patent reported on that year's statement of cash flows?

3. Assume that Liquidity uses the indirect method to prepare its statement of cash flows. How is the amortization of the patent reported annually on the statement of cash flows?

4. How would the sale of the patent on January 1, 2009, for $850,000 be reported on the 2009 statement of cash flows?

Problem 8-13A *Impairment* **LO 8, 9**

In 2006, Loblaw Companies Limited reported an $800 million charge for the impairment of goodwill acquired when it purchased Provigo Inc. in 1998. After the impairment charge, operating income for the year ended December 30, 2006, was $289 million. Goodwill of $794 million remained after the 2006 impairment write-down.

Required:

1. How would Loblaw Companies Limited assess the potential of impairment?

2. How would Loblaw calculate the impairment?

3. How would Loblaw disclose the impairment? Why would such a disclosure be necessary?

Cases

Reading and Interpreting Financial Statements

CN
http://www.cn.ca

Case 8-1 *CN* LO 1, 8

Refer to the financial statements and notes included in the 2007 annual report of **CN**.

Required

1. What items does CN list in the Property and Equipment category?
2. What method is used to depreciate the capital assets?
3. What is the estimated useful life of the capital assets?
4. What are the accumulated depreciation and book values of property for the most recent fiscal year?
5. Were any capital assets purchased or sold during the most recent fiscal year?

Case 8-2 *CN's Statement of Cash Flows* LO 9

Refer to the statement of cash flows in CN's 2007 annual report and answer the following questions:

1. What amount of cash was used to purchase property and equipment during 2007?
2. Did CN sell any property and equipment during 2007?
3. What amount was reported for depreciation and amortization during 2007? Does the fact that depreciation and amortization is listed in the Cash Flow from Operating Activities section mean that CN created cash by reporting depreciation?

Case 8-3 *Comparing Two Companies in the Same Industry: CN and CP* LO 1, 8

http://www.cpr.ca

The following information was taken from the 2007 annual report of CP, one of CN's competitors in the transportation industry.

Property note:

Property consists of the following:

	December 31 2007	December 31 2006
	(in millions)	
Track and roadway	$ 8,828.0	$ 8,615.1
Buildings	342.4	344.8
Rolling stock	3,593.7	3,548.3
Other	1,632.9	1,625.6
	14,397.0	14,133.8
Less: Accumulated depreciation	5,103.9	5,010.9
Totals	$ 9,293.1	$ 9,122.9

Accounting policy note excerpt:

Depreciation is calculated on the straight-line basis at rates based on the estimated service life, taking into consideration the projected annual usage of depreciable property, except for rail and other track in the United States, which is based directly on usage. Usage is based on volumes of traffic.

Estimated service life used for principal categories of properties is as follows:

Assets	Years
Diesel locomotives	28 to 35
Freight cars	21 to 46
Ties	35 to 41
Rails – in first position	27 to 29
– in other than first position	55
Computer system development costs	5 to 15

Source: CP footnote, pages 67 and 79 of 2007 Annual Report in Appendix B. Courtesy CP Rail.

Refer to the annual reports in Appendices A and B at the end of the text for any additional information you might need about CP or CN.

Required

1. Compare the list of property, plant, and equipment represented in the CP note to the list on the CN balance sheet. How are these lists similar? Note the differences between these lists and provide a logical reason for the differences.

2. What method is used by each company to depreciate the assets? Why do you think each company has chosen the method it uses?

3. What are the accumulated depreciation and book values of the property and equipment for each company? What does this information tell you about these competitors?

4. What is the estimated life of the CP assets? How does this compare to the estimated life of the CN assets?

5. Refer to the investing activities portion of the cash flow statements of the two companies. Were any assets purchased or sold by either company during the year? This section of the statements does not tell if there was a gain or loss on the sale of long-term assets. Where would you find that information?

Making Financial Decisions

Case 8-4 *Comparing Companies* LO 1, 3

Assume that you are a financial analyst attempting to compare the financial results of two companies. The 2008 income statement of Simple Company is as follows:

Sales		$1,440,000
Cost of goods sold		720,000
Gross profit		720,000
Administrative costs	$ 192,000	
Depreciation expense	240,000	432,000
Income before tax		288,000
Tax expense (40%)		115,200
Net income		$172,800

Simple Company depreciates all capital assets using the straight-line method for the annual report provided to shareholders. All capital assets were purchased on the same date, and all assets had an estimated life of five years when purchased. Simple Company's balance sheet reveals that on December 31, 2008, the balance of the Accumulated Depreciation account was $480,000.

You want to compare the annual report of Simple Company to that of Speedy Company. Both companies are in the same industry, and both have exactly the same assets, sales, and expenses.

Required

Develop Speedy Company's 2008 income statement. As a financial analyst interested in investing in one of the companies, do you find Simple or Speedy more attractive? Because depreciation is a "non-cash" expense, should you be indifferent between the two companies? Explain your answer.

Case 8-5 *Depreciation Alternatives* LO 3

Ho Supply Ltd. produces supplies used in hospitals and nursing homes. Its sales, production, and costs to produce are expected to remain constant over the next five years. The corporate income tax rate is expected to increase over the next three years. The current rate, 15%, is expected to increase to 20% next year and then to 25% and continue at that rate indefinitely.

Ho Supply is considering the purchase of new equipment that is expected to last for five years and to cost $300,000 with zero salvage value. As the controller, you are aware that the company can use one method of depreciation for accounting purposes and another method for tax purposes. CCA for these assets is 30%.

Required

Recommend which method to use for accounting purposes and which to use for tax purposes. Be able to justify your answer on both a numerical and a theoretical basis. How does a non-cash adjustment to income, such as depreciation, affect cash flow?

Accounting and Ethics: What Would You Do?

Case 8-6 *Valuing Assets* LO 2

Berwick Company recently hired Tom Traves as an accountant. He was given responsibility for all accounting functions related to fixed asset accounting. Heather Pace, Tom's boss, asked him to review all transactions involving the current year's acquisition of fixed assets and to take necessary action to ensure that acquired assets were recorded at proper values. Tom is satisfied that all transactions are proper except for an April 15 purchase of an office building and the land on which it is situated. The purchase price of the acquisition was $400,000. Berwick Company has not separately reported the land and building, however.

Tom hired an appraiser to determine the market values of the land and the building. The appraiser reported that his best estimates of the values were $300,000 for the building and $140,000 for the land. When Tom proposed that these values be used to determine the acquisition cost of the assets, Heather disagreed. She told Tom to request another appraisal of the property and asked him to stress to the appraiser that the land component of the acquisition could not be depreciated for tax purposes. The second appraiser estimated that the values were $360,000 for the building and $80,000 for the land. Tom and Heather agreed that the second appraisal should be used to determine the acquisition cost of the assets.

Required

Did Tom and Heather act ethically in this situation? Explain your answer.

Case 8-7 *Depreciation Estimates* LO 3

Morse Production is planning for a new project. Usually Morse depreciates long-term equipment for 10 years. The equipment for this project is specialized and will have no further use at the end of the project in three years. The manager of the project wants to depreciate the equipment over the usual 10 years and plans on writing off the remaining book value at the end of year 3 as a loss. You believe that the equipment should be depreciated over the three-year life.

Required

Which method do you think is conceptually better? What should you do if the manager insists on depreciating the equipment over 10 years?

Internet Research Cases

INTERNET

http://www.rim.com

Case 8-8 RIM

RIM (Research in Motion Limited) is the maker of the famous BlackBerry. Its annual report for March 3, 2007, describes some of its operations. Its balance sheet using Canadian GAAP shows capital assets of $487,579,000, intangibles of $138,182,000, and goodwill of $109,932,000, all in U.S. dollars. Footnotes 1, 7, 8, and 9 describe details of the capital assets and intangibles, their accounting, and activities relevant to these two balance sheet accounts.

Required

Access the company's annual report and answer the following questions:

1. What depreciation and amortization policy does RIM use?
2. How did RIM increase its goodwill during 2006/07?
3. How did RIM deal with impairments? Comment on the reasonableness of the impairment practices used.

Case 8-9 Prospective Developments in Accounting for Capital Assets

Numerous developments are happening in accounting standards that may influence accounting for capital assets. Review the accounting standards for the IASB available on the CICA web site or that of the IASB and answer the following requirements.

Required

1. What alternative value is possible to historical cost for recording capital assets?
2. What refinements are stated to determine the depreciation calculations for the group approach used by CN and the aggregate cost approach commonly inferred from Canadian GAAP? Why is it useful to refine Canadian GAAP in this regard?

3. Impairment is part of IASB standards but IASB standards carry impairment a step further than Canadian standards stated in the text chapter 8. What is the added feature in the IASB standards that would significantly alter the current Canadian standards for impairment?

Solutions to Key Terms Quiz

1	Acquisition cost	6	Change in estimate
5	Capitalization of interest	8	Capital expenditure
2	Land improvements	10	Revenue expenditure
7	Depreciation	11	Gain on Sale of Capital Asset
3	Straight-line method	12	Loss on Sale of Capital Asset
9	Book value	18	Natural resources
4	Units-of-production method	14	Intangible capital assets
13	Accelerated depreciation	16	Goodwill
15	Double-declining-balance method	17	Research and development costs

Part IV

Integrative Problem

Correct an income statement and statement of cash flows. Assess the effect of a bad-debt recognition.

The following income statement, statement of cash flows, and additional information are available for Pictou Company:

PICTOU COMPANY
INCOME STATEMENT (IN 000's)
FOR THE YEAR ENDING DECEMBER 31, 2008

Sales revenue		$625,000
Cost of goods sold		318,250
Gross profit		306,750
Depreciation on plant equipment	29,200	
Depreciation on buildings	6,000	
Interest expense	16,900	
Other expenses	41,900	94,000
Income before taxes		212,950
Income tax expense (30% rate)		63,825
Net income		$148,925

PICTOU COMPANY
STATEMENT OF CASH FLOW (IN 000's)
FOR THE YEAR ENDING DECEMBER 31, 2008

Cash flows from operating activities	
Net income	$148,925
Depreciation expense	35,200
Net cash provided by operating activities	184,125
Cash flows from financing activities	
Dividends	17,500
Net increase in cash	$166,625

Additional information:

a. Beginning inventory and purchases for the one product the company sells are as follows:

	Units	Unit Cost
Beginning inventory	$25,000	$2.00
Purchases:		
February 10	12,500	2.10
March 15	15,000	2.20
April 20	20,000	2.50
June 8	37,500	3.00
September 12	30,000	3.10
October 8	20,000	3.25

b. During the year, the company sold 125,000 unit at $5 each.

c. Pictou uses the periodic FIFO method to value its inventory and the straight-line method to depreciate all of its long-term assets.

d. During the year-end audit, it was discovered that a January 2, 2008, transaction for the lump-sum purchase of a machine and a heater was not recorded. The fair market value of the machine and the heater were $100,000 and $50,000, respectively. The machine had an estimated useful life of 10 years with no residual value expected while the heater had a useful life of 7 years. The purchase of the assets was financed by issuing a $135,000 five-year note directly to the seller. Interest of 4% is paid annually on December 31.

In addition, it was unclear if the cost of goods sold was determined correctly.

Required

1. Prepare a revised income statement and a revised statement of cash flows to take into account the omission of the entry to record the purchase of the two assets. (Hint: You will need to take into account any change in income taxes as a result of changes in any income statement items. Assume that income taxes are paid on December 31 of each year. Also look for a potential error in the statement of cash flows.)

2. Assume the same fact as above, except that the company is considering the use of an accelerated method rather than the straight-line method for the assets purchased on January 2, 2008. All other assets would continue to be depreciated on a straight-line basis. Prepare a revised income statement and a revised statement of cash flows, assuming the company decides to use the accelerated method for these two assets rather than the straight-line method.

Treat the answer in requirement 3 as independent of the other parts

3. Assume Pictou failed to record an estimate of bad debts for 2008 (bad debt expense is normally included in "other expenses"). Before any adjustment, the balance in Allowance for Doubtful Accounts is $4,100. The credit manager estimates that 3% of the $400,000 of sales on account will prove to be uncollectible. Based on this informantion, compute the effect (amount of increase or decrease) of recognition of the bad-debt estimate on other expenses, income tax expense, and net income.

CHAPTER 9

Current Liabilities, Contingencies, and the Time Value of Money

After studying this chapter, you should be able to:

LO 1 Identify the components of the current liability category of the balance sheet.

LO 2 Demonstrate the treatment of deductions and expenses for payroll.

LO 3 Determine when contingent liabilities should be presented on the balance sheet or disclosed in notes, and how to calculate their amounts.

LO 4 Demonstrate how changes in current liabilities affect the statement of cash flows.

LO 5 Calculate interest using various concepts. (Appendix)

COURTESY CN RAIL

A Look at Previous Chapters

Chapters 7 and 8 presented accounting for assets: Chapter 7 focuses on current assets and Chapter 8 on long-term capital assets.

A Look at This Chapter

In this chapter we will begin to discuss liabilities. The current chapter focuses on

current liabilities and contingencies. It also covers the time value of money. The concept will be applied in the valuation of long-term liabilities.

A Look at the Upcoming Chapter

Chapter 10 will examine the reporting of long-term liabilities.

Focus on Financial Results

Over the next three chapters we analyze the three main categories in the liabilities and shareholders' equity portion of the balance sheet. Chapter 9 discusses current liabilities and provides the tools required to interpret the current portion of long-term debt. Chapter 10 examines long-term debt, deferred income taxes, and deferred credits. Chapter 11 analyzes the components of shareholders' equity.

Accounts payable and accrued charges, which arise from the purchase of supplies and services by CN, represent the ongoing debts to suppliers. Accrued charges were encountered in Chapter 4, when liabilities were needed to reflect internal adjustments for incomplete external transactions such as interest payable and salaries, wages, and deductions payable.

A question that statement users should assess is whether CN is able to generate sufficient cash to pay its current liabilities in the near term.

Consolidated Balance Sheet (Excerpt)

(in millions) December 31,	2007	2006
Liabilities and shareholders' equity		
Current liabilities		
Accounts payable and accrued charges *(Note 8)*	$ 1,282	$ 1,823
Current portion of long-term debt *(Note 10)*	254	218
Other	54	73
	1,590	2,114
Deferred income taxes *(Note 15)*	4,908	5,215
Other liabilities and deferred credits *(Note 9)*	1,422	1,465
Long-term debt *(Note 10)*	5,363	5,386
Shareholders' equity		
Common shares *(Note 11)*	4,283	4,459
Accumulated other comprehensive loss *(Note 20)*	(31)	(44)
Retained earnings	5,925	5,409
	10,177	9,824
Total liabilities and shareholders' equity	$ 23,460	$ 24,004

This excerpt from CN's 2007 Annual Report appears courtesy of CN. This section of the CN Annual Report appears in the Appendix of this textbook.

▌ CURRENT LIABILITIES

LO 1 Identify the components of the current liability category of the balance sheet.

CN
http://www.cn.ca

Current liability An obligation that will be satisfied within the next operating cycle or within one year if the cycle is shorter than one year.

A classified balance sheet presents financial statement items by category in order to provide more information to financial statement users. The balance sheet generally presents two categories of liabilities, current and long-term.

Current liabilities finance the working capital of the company. At any given time during the year, current liabilities may fluctuate substantially. It is important that the company generates sufficient cash flow to retire these debts as they come due. As long as the company's ratio of current assets to current liabilities stays fairly constant from quarter to quarter or year to year, financial statement users are not going to be too concerned.

Footnote 8 of the 2007 balance sheet of CN, highlighted in Exhibit 9-1, presents specifics about accounts payable and accrued charges. Some companies list the accounts in the current liability category in the order of payment due date. That is, the account that requires payment first is listed first, the account that requires payment next is listed second, and so forth. This allows users of the statement to assess the cash flow implications of each account. CN lists its trade payables, commonly termed *accounts payable*, first.

Current liabilities were first introduced to you in Chapter 2 of this text. In general, a **current liability** is an obligation that will be satisfied within one year. Although current liabilities are not due immediately, they are still recorded at face value; that is, the time until payment is not taken into account. If it were, current liabilities would be recorded at a slight discount to reflect interest that would be charged between now and the due date. The face value amount is generally used for all current liabilities because the time period involved is short enough that it is not necessary to record or calculate an interest factor. In addition, when interest rates are low, one need not worry about the interest that could be earned in this short period of time. In Chapter 10 we will find that many long-term liabilities must be stated at their present value (interest taken into account) on the balance sheet.

The current liability classification is important because it is closely tied to the concept of *liquidity*. Management of the firm must be prepared to pay current liabilities within a very short time period. Therefore, management must have access to liquid assets, cash, or other assets that can be converted to cash in amounts sufficient to pay the current liabilities. Firms that do not have sufficient resources to pay their current liabilities are often said to have a liquidity problem.

Exhibit 9-1 CN, 2004 Consolidated Balance Sheet, Footnote 8

8 Accounts payable and accrued charges

In millions December 31,	2007	2006
Trade payables	$ 457	$ 529
Payroll-related accruals	234	232
Accrued charges	146	184
Income and other taxes	123	566
Accrued interest	118	124
Personal injury and other claims provision	102	115
Workforce reduction provisions	19	23
Other	83	50
	$ 1,282	$ 1,823

This excerpt from CN's 2007 Annual Report appears courtesy of CN. This section of the CN Annual Report appears in the Appendix of this textbook.

A handy ratio to help creditors or potential creditors determine a company's liquidity is the current ratio. A current ratio of current assets to current liabilities of 2:1 is usually a very comfortable margin. If the firm has a large amount of inventory, it is sometimes useful to exclude inventory (prepayments are also excluded) when computing the ratio. That provides the "quick" ratio. Usually, one would want a quick ratio of at least 1.5:1 to feel secure that the company could pay its bills on time. Of course, the guidelines given for the current ratio, 2:1, and the quick ratio, 1.5:1, are only general guides. The actual current and quick ratios of companies vary widely and depend on the company, the management policies, and the type of industry. Exhibit 9-2 presents the current and quick ratios for companies in various industries. They reflect wide variations and the importance of industry effects.

COMPANY	INDUSTRY	CURRENT RATIO	QUICK RATIO*
CN	Transport	0.66	0.43
CP	Transport	0.87	0.68
Loblaw	General Merchandise	1.13	0.51
RIM	Technology	3.51	2.93

*Typical Definitions: (Current Assets − Inventory − Prepaids) / Current Liabilities or (Cash + Accounts Receivable + Short-term Investments) / Current Liabilities

Exhibit 9-2

Current and Quick Ratios of Selected Companies for 2007

Accounting for current liabilities is an area in which Canadian accounting standards are very similar to those of most other countries. Nearly all countries encourage firms to provide a breakdown of liabilities into current and long-term to allow users to evaluate liquidity.

Accounting for Your Decisions

You Are a Student

What types of current liabilities could you, as a student, have? What makes them liabilities? What makes them current?

ANSWER: Your current liabilities might include the current payments due from (1) student loans, (2) car loans, (3) loans from family members, (4) rent or mortgage payments, (5) credit card charges, (6) cafeteria charges, and similar charges. These items are current liabilities because they are obligations that will be satisfied within a year.

Accounts Payable

Accounts payable represent amounts owed for the purchase of inventory, goods, or services acquired in the normal course of business. Often, Accounts Payable is the first account listed in the current liability category because it requires the payment of cash before other current liabilities.

Normally, a firm has an established relationship with suppliers, and formal contractual arrangements with those suppliers are unnecessary. Accounts payable usually do not require the payment of interest, but terms may be given to encourage early payment. For example, terms may be stated as 2/10, n/30, which means that a 2% discount is available if payment occurs within the first 10 days and that if payment is not made within 10 days, the full amount must be paid within 30 days.

Timely payment of accounts payable is an important aspect of the management of cash flow. Generally, it is to the company's benefit to take advantage of discounts when they are available. After all, if your supplier is going to give you a 2% discount for paying on Day 10 instead of Day 30, that means you are earning 2% on your money over 20/360 of a year. If you took the 2% discount throughout the year, you would be getting a 36% annual return on your money, since there are 18 periods of 20 days each in a year. It is essential, therefore, that the accounts payable system be established in a manner that alerts management to take advantage of offered discounts.

Accounts payable Amounts owed for inventory, goods, or services acquired in the normal course of business.

Notes Payable

Note payable Amounts owed that are represented by a formal contract.

How is a note payable different from an account payable? The most important difference is that an account payable is not composed of individual formal contractual arrangements, whereas a **note payable** is represented by a formal agreement or note signed by the parties to the transaction. Notes payable may arise from dealing with a supplier or from acquiring a cash loan from a bank or creditor, but in each case a specific contract is signed for each transaction. Those notes that are expected to be paid within one year of the balance sheet date should be classified as current liabilities.

The accounting for notes payable depends on whether the interest is paid on the note's due date or is deducted before the borrower receives the loan proceeds. With the first type of note, the terms stipulate that the borrower receives a short-term loan and agrees to repay the principal and interest at the note's due date. For example, assume that Lamanski Company receives a one-year loan from First Bank on January 1. The face amount of the note of $1,000 must be repaid on December 31 along with interest at the rate of 12%. Lamanski would make the following entries to record the loan and its repayment:

Jan. 1	Cash	1,000	
	Notes Payable		1,000
	To record a loan of $1,000		

Assets	**=**	**Liabilities**	**+**	**Shareholders' Equity**
+1,000		+1,000		

Dec. 31	Notes Payable	1,000	
	Interest Expense	120	
	Cash		1,120
	To record the repayment of loan with interest		

Assets	**=**	**Liabilities**	**+**	**Shareholders' Equity**
−1,120		−1,000		−120

If a note is issued in one accounting period and matures in another, any interest incurred but unpaid at an accounting period-end must be accrued, i.e., interest expense and interest payable must be recorded. Assume that Lamanski's fiscal year ends on December 31 and another one-year, 12%, $2,000 note was issued on April 1, 2008, with both the interest and the principal to be paid at maturity:

2008			
Apr. 1	Cash	2,000	
	Notes Payable		2,000
	To record a loan of $2,000		

Assets	**=**	**Liabilities**	**+**	**Shareholders' Equity**
+2,000		+2,000		

On December 31, 2008, Lamanski's fiscal year-end, it must make an adjusting entry to record the interest accrued on the note as the result of the passage of time since its signing. From April 1 to December 31, 2008, nine months have passed. At a 12% annual rate, the nine-month interest on a $2,000 note is $180, or $2,000 × 12% × 9/12.

2008			
Dec. 31	Interest expense	180	
	Interest Payable		180
	To record interest accrued		

Assets	**=**	**Liabilities**	**+**	**Shareholders' Equity**
		+180		−180

The interest recognized here is an example of accrued liabilities. In previous chapters, particularly Chapter 4, we covered many examples of accrued liabilities. Accrued liabilities include any amount that has been incurred due to the passage of time but which has not been paid as of the balance sheet date.

On March 31, 2009, the note's maturity date, Lamanski repaid the note, plus all the interest on the note. Since the 2008's portion of interest was recognized already on December 31, 2008, only 2009's portion needed to be recognized. The three months' interest from January 1 to March 31, 2009 is $60, or $2,000 × 12% × 3/12.

```
2009
Mar. 31   Notes Payable                              2,000
          Interest Payable                             180
          Interest Expense                              60
              Cash                                               2,240
          To record the repayment of note and interest
```

Assets = Liabilities + Shareholders' Equity
−2,240   −2,000
**   −180   −60**

Banks also use another form of note, one in which the interest is deducted in advance. Suppose that on January 1, 2008, First Bank granted to Lamanski a $1,000 loan, due on December 31, 2008, but deducted the interest in advance and gave Lamanski the remaining amount of $880 ($1,000 face amount of the note less interest of $120). This is sometimes referred to as *discounting a note* because a Discount on Notes Payable account is established when the loan is recorded. On January 1, Lamanski must make the following entry:

```
Jan. 1    Cash                                        880
          Discount on Notes Payable                   120
              Notes Payable                                      1,000
          To record a loan of $1,000 less interest deducted in advance
```

Assets = Liabilities + Shareholders' Equity
+880   −120
**   +1,000**

The **Discount on Notes Payable** account should be treated as a reduction of Notes Payable (and should have a debit balance). If a balance sheet was developed immediately after the January 1 loan, the note would appear in the current liability category as follows:

Notes Payable	$1,000
Less: Discount on Notes Payable	120
Net Liability	$ 880

Discount on notes payable A contra-liability that represents interest deducted from a loan in advance.

The original balance in the Discount on Notes Payable account represents interest that must be transferred to interest expense over the life of the note. Before Lamanski presents its year-end financial statements, it must make an adjustment to transfer the discount to interest expense. The effect of the adjustment on December 31 is as follows:

```
Dec. 31   Interest Expense                            120
              Discount on Notes Payable                          120
          To record interest on note payable
```

Assets = Liabilities + Shareholders' Equity
**   +120   −120**

Thus, the balance of the Discount on Notes Payable account is zero, and $120 has been transferred to Interest Expense. When the note is repaid on December 31, Lamanski must repay the full amount of the note as follows:

```
Dec. 31   Notes Payable                             1,000
              Cash                                             1,000
          To record payment of the note on its due date
```

Assets = Liabilities + Shareholders' Equity
−1,000   −1,000

It is important to compare the two types of notes payable. In the previous two examples, the stated interest rate on each note was 12%. The dollar amount of interest incurred in each case was $120. However, the interest *rate* on a discounted note, the second example, is always higher than it appears. Lamanski received the use of only $880, yet it was required to repay $1,000. Therefore, the interest rate incurred on the note was actually $120/$880, or approximately 13.6%.

Current Portion of Long-Term Debt

Current portion of long-term debt
The portion of a long-term liability that will be paid within one year.

Another account that appears in the current liability category of CN's balance sheet is **Current Portion of Long-Term Debt.** On other companies' balance sheets, this item may be termed Long-Term Debt, Current Portion. This account should appear when a firm has a liability and must make periodic payments. For example, assume that on January 1, 2008, your firm obtained a $10,000 loan from the bank. The terms of the loan require you to make payments in the amount of $1,000 per year for 10 years, payable each January 1, beginning January 1, 2009. On December 31, 2008, an entry should be made to classify a portion of the balance as a current liability as follows:

2008			
Dec. 31	Long-Term Liability	1,000	
	Current Portion of Liability		1,000
	To record the current portion of bank loan		

Assets	**=**	**Liabilities**	**+**	**Shareholders' Equity**
		−1,000		
		+1,000		

The December 31, 2008, balance sheet should indicate that the liability for the note payable is classified into two portions: a $1,000 current liability that must be repaid within one year and a $9,000 long-term liability.

On January 1, 2009, the company must pay $1,000, and the entry should be recorded as follows:

2009			
Jan. 1	Current Portion of Liability	1,000	
	Cash		1,000
	To record payment of $1,000 on bank loan		

Assets	**=**	**Liabilities**	**+**	**Shareholders' Equity**
−1,000		−1,000		

On December 31, 2009, the company should again record the current portion of the liability. Therefore, the 2009 year-end balance sheet should indicate that the liability is classified into two portions: a $1,000 current liability and an $8,000 long-term liability. The process should be repeated each year until the bank loan has been fully paid. When an investor or creditor reads a balance sheet, he or she wants to distinguish between debt that is long-term and debt that is short-term. Therefore, it is important to segregate that portion of the debt that becomes due within one year.

The balance sheet account labeled Current Portion of Long-Term Debt should include only the amount of principal to be paid. The amount of interest that has been incurred but is unpaid should be listed separately in an account such as Interest Payable.

Income Taxes Payable

Corporations pay a variety of taxes, including federal and provincial income taxes, property taxes, and other taxes. Usually, the largest dollar amount is incurred for federal and provincial income taxes. Taxes are an expense of the business and should be accrued in the same manner as any other business expense. A company that ends its accounting year on December 31 is not required to calculate the amount of tax owed to the government until the following February 28 or March 31, depending on the nature of the business.

Therefore, the business must make an accounting entry, usually as one of the year-end adjusting entries, to record the amount of income tax that has been incurred but is unpaid.

For example, assume Rockingham Inc., a small business, reported $135,000 income before income taxes during 2008. Rockingham calculated its income tax expense for the year using a 32% rate. The income taxes were paid on February 28, 2009.

2008
Dec. 31

Income Tax Expense	43,200	
Income Tax Payable		43,200
To record 2008 income tax expense		

Assets	**=**	**Liabilities**	**+**	**Shareholders' Equity**
		+43,200		−43,200

2009
Feb. 28

Income Tax Payable	43,200	
Cash		43,200
To record the payment of 2008 income taxes		

Assets	**=**	**Liabilities**	**+**	**Shareholders' Equity**
−43,200		−43,200		

The calculation of the amount of tax a business owes is very complex. The determination of income taxes is governed by the Canadian *Income Tax Act* and the Canada Revenue Agency's rules and regulations. The income tax expense a company records may not be the same as the income tax it has to pay each year for that period.

For now, the important point is that taxes are an expense when incurred (not when they are paid) and must be recorded as a liability as incurred.

CN shows $123 million in income tax and other taxes owing at December 31, 2007. It is important to note here that CN would have paid twelve monthly installments on its income taxes for 2007 beginning January 31, 2007.

Some analysts prefer to measure a company's profits before tax expense for several reasons. For one thing, tax rates change from year to year. A small change in the tax rate may drastically change a firm's profitability. Also, investors should realize that taxes occur in every year but that tax changes are not a recurring element of a business. Additionally, taxes are somewhat beyond the control of a company's management. For these reasons, it is important to consider a firm's operations *before* taxes to better evaluate management's ability to control operations.

Sales Taxes Payable

The rates, the terms, and calculation of sales taxes vary from province to province. Typically, sales taxes include a federal Goods and Service Tax (GST) and a Provincial Sales Tax (PST). The GST is 5% currently and PSTs range from 0% to 10%. PST can be applied either on the before-tax selling price alone or on the selling price plus the GST. Nova Scotia, New Brunswick, and Newfoundland and Labrador combine the GST and the PST into one Harmonized Sales Tax (HST). Exhibit 9-3 summarizes the sales taxes of different provinces and territories in Canada.

Companies collect the sales taxes from customers when sales are made, and periodically remit the taxes collected to the designated federal and provincial government agencies. Companies do not incur sales tax expense, however, because sales taxes are end-consumer taxes. Companies merely act as collecting agents for the government. In the case of GST and HST, taxes paid by a company for its purchases of goods or services can be deducted from the taxes collected, with only the difference remitted. In the event that a company paid more than it collected, the government will issue a refund.

Exhibit 9-3

Summary of Sales Taxes in
Canada

Province	GST	PST	HST
Alberta	5%	–	–
British Colombia	5%	7%	–
Manitoba	5%	7%	–
New Brunswick	–	–	13%
Newfoundland and Labrador	–	–	13%
Northwest Territories	5%	–	–
Nova Scotia	–	–	13%
Nunavut	5%	–	–
Ontario	5%	8%	–
Prince Edward Island*	5%	10%*	–
Quebec*	5%	7.5%*	–
Saskatchewan	5%	5%	–
Yukon	5%	–	–

* Provincial sales tax is calculated on GST as well.

For example, On-The-Run, a retail store in Ontario, sold a pair of running shoes priced at $100 before taxes. The following journal entry will be made.

Cash	113	
Revenue		100
PST Payable		8
GST Payable		5
To record the revenue earned on the sale		

Assets	=	**Liabilities**	+	**Shareholders' Equity**
+113		+8		+100
		+7		

If On-The-Run sold a total 200 pairs of running shoes in the first quarter of 2008, it would have collected $1,000 of GST ($100 × 200 × 5%) and $1,600 of PST ($100 × 200 × 8%). Assume that it also paid $300 GST in same period for purchases of supplies and services, then the amount of GST to be remitted is $700 ($1,000 – $300).

Unearned Revenue

Companies sometimes require their customers to make down payments or deposits before receiving goods or services. According to the revenue recognition principle, the seller should not recognize such advance collections as revenue because the criteria of revenue recognition have not been met at this point, i.e., the goods or services have not been delivered. The seller must record advance collections as liabilities, known as unearned revenue. Unearned revenues are realized when the goods or services are delivered.

For example, assume VIA Rail sold a round-trip ticket from Toronto to Montreal on December 1, 2008, for $160. The passenger traveled to Montreal from Toronto on December 22, 2008, and returned to Toronto on January 5, 2009.

2008			
Dec. 1	Cash	160	
	Unearned Revenue		160
	To record the advance sale of ticket		

Assets	=	**Liabilities**	+	**Shareholders' Equity**
+160		+160		

Dec. 22	Unearned Revenue	80	
	Revenue		80

To record the revenue earned on the ticket used.

Assets	=	Liabilities	+	Shareholders' Equity
		−80		+80

The value of return portion of the ticket, $80, will be a current liability of VIA Rail on December 31, 2008, its fiscal year-end.

2009

Jan. 5	Unearned Revenue	80	
	Revenue		80

To record the revenue earned on the ticket used.

Assets	=	Liabilities	+	Shareholders' Equity
		−80		+80

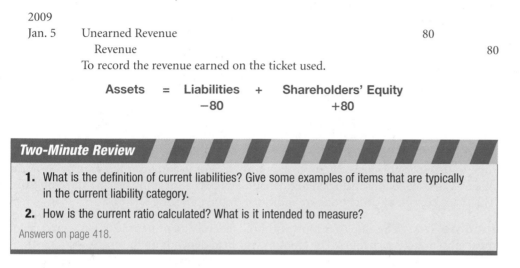

Two-Minute Review

1. What is the definition of current liabilities? Give some examples of items that are typically in the current liability category.
2. How is the current ratio calculated? What is it intended to measure?

Answers on page 418.

▪ PAYROLL ACCOUNTING

Salaries payable was one of the current liabilities discussed in Chapter 2. At the end of each accounting period, the accountant must accrue salaries that have been earned by the employees but have not yet been paid. To this point, we have not considered the accounting that must be done for payroll deductions and other payroll expenses.

> **LO 2** Demonstrate the treatment of deductions and expenses for payroll.

Payroll deductions and expenses occur not only at year-end but every time, throughout the year, that employees are paid. The amount of cash paid for salaries and wages is the largest cash outflow for many firms. For example, CN's largest expense is $1,701 million for labour and fringe benefits. It is imperative that sufficient cash be available not only to meet the weekly or monthly payroll but also to remit the payroll taxes to the appropriate government agencies when required. Tracking and remitting payroll deductions and payroll taxes is important both legally and ethically. Government agencies may levy fines for inaccurate deductions. Potentially serious personal liabilities can be attached to directors of companies and even to directors of charitable organizations for deductions that are not remitted if the organization cannot pay. The directors can be held personally responsible for those deductions. The purpose of this section is to introduce the calculations and the accounting entries that are necessary when payroll is recorded.

The issue of payroll expenses is of great concern to businesses, particularly small entrepreneurial ones. One of the large issues facing companies is how to meet the increasing cost of hiring people. Salary is just one component. How are they going to pay salaries plus benefits such as health insurance, life insurance, disability, unemployment benefits, workers' compensation, and so on? More and more companies are trying to keep their payrolls as small as possible in order to avoid these costs. Unfortunately, this has been a contributing factor in the trends of using more part-time employees and of outsourcing some business functions. Outsourcing, or hiring independent contractors, allows the company to reduce salary expense and the expenses related to fringe benefits. However, it does not necessarily improve the company's profitability. The expenses that are increased as a result of hiring outside contractors must also be considered. A manager must carefully consider all of the costs that are affected before deciding whether to hire more employees or go with an independent contractor.

Calculation of Gross Wages

Gross wages The amount of wages before deductions.

We will cover the payroll process by indicating the basic steps that must be performed. The first step is to calculate the **gross wages** of all employees. The gross wage represents the wage amount before deductions. Companies often have two general classes of employees, hourly and salaried. The gross wage of each hourly employee is calculated by multiplying the number of hours worked by his or her hourly wage rate. Salaried employees are not paid on a per-hour basis but at a flat rate per week, month, or year. For both hourly and salaried employees, the payroll accountant must also consider any overtime, bonus, or other salary supplement that may affect gross wages.

Calculation of Net Pay

Net pay The amount of wages after deductions.

The second step in the payroll process is to calculate the deductions from each employee's paycheque to determine **net pay**. Deductions from the employees' cheques represent a current liability to the employer because the employer must remit the amounts at a future time to the proper agencies or government offices, for example, to the Canada Revenue Agency. The deductions that are made depend on the type of company and the employee. The most important deductions are indicated in the following sections.

Income Tax   The employer must withhold federal and provincial income taxes from most employees' paycheques. The amount withheld depends on the employee's earnings and the number of *exemptions* claimed by that employee. An exemption reflects the number of dependants a taxpayer can claim. The more exemptions, the lower is the withholding amount required by the government. Tables or computer formulas are available from the Canada Revenue Agency[1] to calculate the proper amount that should be withheld. This amount must be remitted to the Canada Revenue Agency periodically; the frequency depends on the company's payroll period. Income tax withheld represents a liability to the employer and is normally classified as a current liability.

All provinces also have an income tax. The employer must often withhold additional amounts for this tax. (Quebec, however, requires their portion be remitted directly to the Ministère du Revenu du Québec.)

CPP and EI—Employees' Share   EI stands for Employment Insurance, a national program where the employee must pay 1.73% of earnings up to $41,100 per year. CPP stands for Canada Pension Plan, the national program for all provinces except Quebec. For CPP, the employee pays 4.95% of earnings up to $44,900 (in 2008). Both EI and CPP rates change and have specific rules, so the Canada Revenue Agency provides ongoing specifics for each type of deduction.

CPP and EI withheld from employees' cheques represent a liability to the employer until remitted. It is important to remember that the employees' portion of CPP and EI does not represent an expense to the employer.

Voluntary Deductions   If you have ever received a paycheque, you probably noticed that a variety of items are deducted from the amount earned. Many of these are voluntary deductions chosen by the employee. They may include health insurance, pension or retirement contributions, savings plans, contributions to charities, and union dues. Each of these items is deducted from the employees' cheques, is held by the employer, and is remitted at a future time. Therefore, each represents a current liability to the employer until remitted.

Employer Payroll Taxes

The payroll deductions discussed thus far do not represent expenses to the employer because they are assessed on the employees and deducted from their paycheques. However, there are taxes that the employer must pay. The two most important are CPP and EI.

---

[1]http://www.cra.gc.ca/payroll

CPP—Employer's Share CPP is assessed on both the employee and the employer. The employee amount is withheld from the employees' paycheques and represents a liability but is not an expense to the employer. Normally, an equal amount is assessed on the employer. Therefore, the employer must pay an additional 4.95% of employee wages to the government. The employer's portion represents an expense to the employer and should be reflected in a Payroll Benefit Expense account or similar type of account. This portion is a liability to the employer until it is remitted.

EI Most employers must also pay EI. The employer's EI rate is 3.42% of earnings up to a $711 contribution per employee (in 2008). This charge for the employer's portion of EI is an expense in the period when the employee earns the salary or wage.

An Example

Assume that Kori Company has calculated the gross salaries and wages of all employees for the month of July to be $100,000. Also assume that the following amounts have been withheld from the employees' paycheques:

Income Tax	$20,000
CPP	4,950
EI	1,950
United Way Contributions	5,000
Union Dues	3,000

In addition, assume that Kori's employees have not reached the limit, and that Kori's portion of CPP matches the employees' share. Kori must make the following entries to record the payroll, to pay the employees, and to record the employer's payroll expenses.

July 31	Salaries and Wages Expense	100,000	
	Salaries and Wages Payable		65,100
	Income Tax Deduction Payable		20,000
	CPP Payable		4,950
	EI Payable		1,950
	United Way Payable		5,000
	Union Dues Payable		3,000
	To record July salaries and wages and deductions		

Assets	=	Liabilities	+	Shareholders' Equity
		+65,100		−100,000
		+20,000		
		+4,950		
		+1,950		
		+5,000		
		+3,000		

July 31	Salaries and Wages Payable	65,100	
	Cash		65,100
	To record payment of employee salaries and wages		

Assets	=	Liabilities	+	Shareholders' Equity
−65,100		−65,100		

July 31	Payroll Benefits Expense	7,680	
	CPP Payable		4,950
	EI Payable		2,730
	To record employer's payroll taxes		

Assets	=	Liabilities	+	Shareholders' Equity
		+4,950		−7,680
		+2,730		

Periodically, Kori must remit amounts to the appropriate government body or agency. The accounting entry to record remittance, assuming remittance is the middle of August, is as follows:

August 15 Income Tax Deduction Payable	20,000	
CPP Payable	9,900	
United Way Payable	5,000	
Union Dues Payable	3,000	
EI Payable	4,680	
Cash		42,580
To record remittance of withheld amounts		

Assets	=	Liabilities	+	Shareholders' Equity
−42,580		−20,000		
		−9,900		
		−5,000		
		−3,000		
		−4,680		

Compensated Absences

Most employers allow or are required to permit employees to accumulate a certain number of sick days and to take a certain number of paid vacation days each year. This causes an accounting question when recording payroll amounts. When should the sick days and vacation days be treated as an expense—in the period they are earned or in the period they are taken by the employee?

Compensated absences Employee absences for which the employee will be paid.

Compensated absences is the term coined for these benefits. These are absences from employment, such as vacation, illness, and holidays, for which it is expected that employees will be paid. The AcSB has ruled that an expense should be accrued if certain conditions are met: the services have been rendered, the rights (days) accumulate, and payment is probable and can be reasonably estimated, typically a legal requirement. The result of the AcSB ruling is that most employers are required to record a liability and expense for vacation days when earned; however, sick days are not recorded until employees are actually absent.

Compensated absence is another example of the matching principle at work, and so it is consistent with good accounting theory. Unfortunately, it has also resulted in some complex calculations and additional work for payroll accountants. Part of the complexity is due to unresolved legal issues about compensatedabsences.

Accounting standards on this issue are much more detailed and extensive than the standards of many foreign countries. As a result, companies may believe that they are subject to higher record-keeping costs than their foreign competitors.

CONTINGENT LIABILITIES

LO 3 Determine when contingent liabilities should be presented on the balance sheet or disclosed in notes, and how to calculate their amounts.

Contingent liability An existing condition for which the outcome is not known but depends on some future event.

We have seen that accountants must exercise a great deal of expertise and judgment in deciding what to record and in determining the amount to record. This is certainly true regarding contingent liabilities. A **contingent liability** is an obligation that involves an existing condition for which the outcome is not known with certainty and depends on some event that will occur in the future. The actual amount of the liability must be estimated because we cannot clearly predict the future. The important accounting issues are whether contingent liabilities should be recorded and, if so, in what amounts.

This is a judgment call that is usually resolved through discussions among the company's management and its outside auditors. Management usually would rather not disclose contingent liabilities until they come due. The reason is that investors' and creditors' judgment of management is based on the company's earnings, and the recording of a contingent liability must be accompanied by a charge to (reduction in) earnings.

Auditors, on the other hand, want management to disclose as much as possible because the auditors are essentially representing the interests of investors and creditors, who want to have as much information as possible.

Contingent Liabilities That Are Recorded

A contingent liability should be accrued and presented on the balance sheet if it is probable and if the amount can be reasonably estimated. But when is an event *probable*, and what does *reasonably estimated* mean? The terms must be defined based on the facts of each situation. A financial statement user would want the company to err on the side of full disclosure. On the other hand, the company should not be required to disclose every remote possibility.

A common contingent liability that must be presented as a liability by firms involves product warranties or guarantees. Many firms sell products for which they provide the customer a warranty against defects that may develop in the products. If a product becomes defective within the warranty period, the selling firm ensures that it will repair or replace the item. This is an example of a contingent liability because the expense of fixing a product depends on some of the products becoming defective—an uncertain, although likely, event.

At the end of each period, the selling firm must estimate how many of the products sold in the current year will become defective in the future and the cost of repair or replacement. This type of contingent liability is often referred to as an **estimated liability** to emphasize that the costs are not known at year-end and must be estimated.

As an example, assume that Quickkey Computer sells a computer product for $5,000. When the customer buys the product, Quickkey provides a one-year warranty in case it must be repaired. Assume that in 2008 Quickkey sold 100 computers for a total sales revenue of $500,000. At the end of 2008, Quickkey must record an estimate of the warranty costs that will occur on 2008 sales. Using an analysis of past warranty records, Quickkey estimates that repairs will average 2% of total sales. Therefore, Quickkey should record the following transaction at the end of 2008:

Dec. 31	Warranty Expense	10,000	
	Estimated Warranty Liability		10,000
	To record estimated liability at 2% of sales		

Assets	=	Liabilities	+	Shareholders' Equity
		+10,000		−10,000

The amount of warranty costs that a company presents as an expense is of interest to investors and potential creditors. If the expense as a percentage of sales begins to rise, one might conclude that the product is becoming less reliable.

Warranties are an excellent example of the matching principle. In our Quickkey example, the warranty costs related to 2008 sales were estimated and recorded in 2008. This was done to match the 2008 sales with the expenses related to those sales. If actual repairs of the computers occurred in 2009, they do not result in an expense. The repair costs incurred in 2009 should be treated as a reduction in the liability that had previously been estimated.

For example, if in February 2009 Able Company returned to Quickkey for repair one of the computers it purchased in November 2008, Quickkey might well incur a cost for the warranty repair. Suppose that Quickkey incurred $175 for parts and $150 for labour to repair the computer. Quickkey would charge the $325 to the estimated liability it set up in 2008 when the sale was made. Quickkey would record the transaction as follows in February 2009:

Estimated Warranty Liability	325	
Parts Inventory		175
Accrued Salaries and Wages		150
To record the parts cost and labour cost to repair Able's computer		

Assets	=	Liabilities	+	Shareholders' Equity
− 175		− 325		
		+ 150		

> **Study Tip**
>
> Contingent liabilities are recorded only if they are probable and if the amount can be reasonably estimated.

Estimated liability A contingent liability that is accrued and reflected on the balance sheet.

Because items such as warranties involve estimation, you may wonder what happens if the amount estimated is not accurate. The company must analyze past warranty records carefully and incorporate any changes in customer buying habits, usage, technological changes, and other changes. Still, even with careful analysis, the actual amount of the expense is not likely to equal the estimated amount. Generally, firms do not change the amount of the expense recorded in past periods for such differences. They may adjust the amount recorded in future periods, however.

Warranties provide an example of a contingent liability that must be estimated and recorded. Another example is premium or coupon offers that accompany many products. Cereal boxes are an everyday example of premium offers. The boxes often allow customers to purchase a toy or game at a reduced price if the purchase is accompanied by cereal box tops or proof of purchase. The offer given to cereal customers represents a contingent liability. At the end of each year, the cereal company must estimate the number of premium offers that will be redeemed and the cost involved and must report a contingent liability for that amount.

Legal claims that have been filed against a firm are also examples of contingent liabilities. In today's business environment, lawsuits and legal claims are a fact of life. They represent a contingent liability because an event has occurred but the outcome of that event, the resolution of the lawsuit, is not known. The defendant in the lawsuit must make a judgment about the outcome of the lawsuit in order to decide whether the item should be recorded on the balance sheet or should be disclosed in the notes. If an unfavourable outcome to the legal claim is deemed to be probable, then an amount should be recorded as a contingent liability on the balance sheet. Exhibit 9-4 provides portions of a note disclosure that accompanied the 2007 financial statements of CN. The note concerned litigation over personal injury that was alleged to have occurred as a result of the company's activities. In this case, CN believed that an unfavourable outcome had become probable and, as a result, recorded a contingent liability of $197 million as an estimate of the amount that would be owed at the eventual outcome of this claim at the end of 2007.

As you might imagine, firms are not usually eager to record contingent lawsuits as liabilities because the amount of loss is often difficult to estimate. Also, some may view the accountant's decision as an admission of guilt if a lawsuit is recorded as a liability

Exhibit 9-4

Note Disclosure for Contingent Liability from CN's Financial Statements

18 Major commitments and contingencies

C. Contingencies

Employee injuries are governed by the workers' compensation legislation in each province whereby employees may be awarded either a lump sum or future stream of payments depending on the nature and severity of the injury. Accordingly, the Company accounts for costs related to employee work-related injuries based on actuarially developed estimates of the ultimate cost associated with such injuries, including compensation, health care and third-party administration costs. For all other legal actions, the Company maintains, and regularly updates on a case-by-case basis, provisions for such items when the expected loss is both probable and can be reasonably estimated based on currently available information.

At December 31, 2007, 2006 and 2005, the Company's provision for personal injury and other claims in Canada was as follows:

In millions	2007	2006	2005
Balance January 1	$ 195	$ 205	$ 204
Accruals and other	41	60	46
Payments	(40)	(70)	(45)
Balance December 31	$ 196	$ 195	$ 205

This excerpt from CN's 2007 Annual Report appears courtesy of CN. This section of the CN Annual Report appears in the Appendix of this textbook.

before the courts have finalized a decision. Accountants must often consult with lawyers or other legal experts to determine the probability of the loss of a lawsuit. In cases involving contingencies, it is especially important that the accountant make an independent judgment based on the facts and not be swayed by the desires of other parties.

Contingent Liabilities That Are Disclosed

Any contingent liability that both is probable and can be reasonably estimated must be reported as a liability. We now must consider contingent liabilities that do not meet the probable criterion or cannot be reasonably estimated. In either case, a contingent liability must be disclosed in the financial statement notes but not reported on the balance sheet if the contingent liability is at least reasonably possible.

Although information in the notes to the financial statements contains very important data on which investors base decisions, some accountants believe that note disclosure does not have the same impact as does recording a contingent liability on the balance sheet. For one thing, note disclosure does not affect the important financial ratios that investors use to make decisions.

In the previous section, we presented a legal claim involving CN as an example of a contingent liability that was probable and therefore was recorded on the balance sheet as a liability. Most lawsuits, however, are not recorded as liabilities either because the risk of loss is not considered probable or because the amount of the loss cannot be reasonably estimated. If a company does not record a lawsuit as a liability, it must still consider whether the lawsuit should be disclosed in the notes to the financial statements. If the risk of loss is at least *reasonably possible,* then the company should provide note disclosure. This is the course of action taken for most contingent liabilities involving lawsuits.

Exhibit 9-5 contains excerpts from the notes to the 2007 financial statements of CN (from Footnote 18). A portion of Exhibit 9-5 indicates that CN is subject to a variety of actions, which arise from environmental claims and other matters. CN describes in the note why it has difficulty estimating the full amount of its liabilities for environmental matters. At the conclusion of the note it describes the amount that it actually has recorded, net of recoveries.

You should note that the excerpts in Exhibit 9-5 are examples of contingent liabilities that have been disclosed in the notes to the financial statements *but have not been recorded as liabilities on the balance sheet.* Readers of the financial statements, and analysts, must carefully read the notes to determine the impact of such contingent liabilities.

Exhibit 9-5 Note Disclosure for Contingencies from CN's 2007 Annual Report

18. Major commitments and contingencies

D. Environmental Matters*

While the Company believes that it has identified the costs likely to be incurred in the next several years, based on known information, for environmental matters, the Company's ongoing efforts to identify potential environmental concerns that may be associated with its properties may lead to future environmental investigations, which may result in the identification of additional environmental costs and liabilities. The magnitude of such additional liabilities and the costs of complying with environmental laws and containing or remediating contamination cannot be reasonably estimated due to:

(*i*) the lack of specific technical information available with respect to many sites;

(*ii*) the absence of any government authority, third-party orders, or claims with respect to particular sites;

(*iii*) the potential for new or changed laws and regulations and for development of new remediation technologies and uncertainty regarding the timing of the work with respect to particular sites;

(*iv*) the ability to recover costs from any third parties with respect to particular sites; and

therefore, the likelihood of any such costs being incurred or whether such costs would be material to the Company cannot be determined at this time.

---

* Authors' note: Footnote 18D of Appendix A contains a further discussion of the environmental matters. This excerpt from CN's 2007 Annual Report appears courtesy of CN. This section of the CN Annual Report appears in the Appendix of this textbook.

The amount and the timing of the cash outlays associated with contingent liabilities are especially difficult to determine. Lawsuits, for example, may extend several years into the future, and the dollar amount of possible loss may be subject to great uncertainty.

 ## Accounting for Your Decisions

You Are the CEO

You run a high-technology company that grows fast some quarters and disappoints investors in other quarters. As a result, your company's share price fluctuates widely, and you have attracted the unwanted attention of a law firm that filed a lawsuit on behalf of disgruntled shareholders. How do you reflect this lawsuit on your financial statements?

ANSWER: Your legal counsel should be consulted to determine whether the plaintiff's case has merit. If a loss is probable and the amount can be estimated, the lawsuit should be recorded as a liability. Unfortunately, lawsuits have become very common for many companies. In some cases, the lawsuits are totally without merit and are frivolous. If your lawyers agree that this case will not result in a loss, then no disclosure would be required.

Contingent Liabilities versus Contingent Assets

Contingent assets An existing condition for which the outcome is not known but by which the company stands to gain.

Contingent liabilities that are probable and can be reasonably estimated must be presented on the balance sheet before the outcome of the future events is known. This accounting rule applies only to contingent losses or liabilities. It does not apply to contingencies by which the firm may gain. Generally, contingent gains or **contingent assets** are not reported until the gain actually occurs. That is, contingent liabilities may be accrued, but contingent assets are not accrued. Remember, however, that accounting is a discipline based on a conservative set of principles. It is prudent and conservative to delay the recording of a gain until an asset is actually received but to record contingent liabilities in advance.

Of course, even though the contingent assets are not reported, the information may still be important to investors. Analysts make their living trying to place a value on contingent assets that they believe will result in future benefits. By buying shares of a company that has unrecorded assets, or advising their clients to do so, investment analysts hope to make money when those assets become a reality.

Two-Minute Review

1. Under what circumstances should contingent liabilities be reported in the financial statements?
2. Under what circumstances should contingent liabilities be disclosed in the notes and not recorded in the financial statements?
3. Are contingent assets treated the same as contingent liabilities?

Answers on page 419.

READING THE STATEMENT OF CASH FLOWS FOR CHANGES IN CURRENT LIABILITIES

It is important to understand the impact that current liabilities have on a company's cash flows. Exhibit 9-6 illustrates the placement of current liabilities on the statement of cash flows (using the indirect method) and their effect. Most current liabilities are directly related to a firm's ongoing operations. Therefore, the change in the balance of each current liability account should be reflected in the Operating Activities category of the statement of cash flows. A decrease in a current liability account indicates that cash has been used to pay the liability and should appear as a deduction on the cash flow statement. An increase in a current liability account indicates a recognized expense that has not yet been paid. Look for it as an increase in the Operating Activities category of the cash flow statement.

The cash flow statement of CN is presented in Exhibit 9-6. Note that one of the items in the 2007 Operating Activities category is listed as accounts payable and accrued charges, $351 million. This means that the balance of those current liabilities decreased by $351 million, resulting in an decrease of cash.

Almost all current liabilities appear in the Operating Activities category of the statement of cash flows, but there are exceptions. If a current liability is not directly related to operating activities, it should not appear in that category. Therefore, note borrowings and repayments are reflected in the Financing Activities rather than the Operating Activities category (see Exhibit 9-7).

An interesting observation can be made between the Current Portion of Long-Term Debt at the end of 2006 as stated in the balance sheet on page 401, amount $218 million, and the reduction of long-term debt in the Financing section of the statement of cash flows, Exhibit 9-7, amount $3,589 million. One would expect the reduction of long-term debt for 2007 to be equal to the current portion of long-term debt shown on the December 31, 2006, balance sheet. However, such is not the case here. What appears to have occurred is that CN paid $218 million but redeemed and reissued $3,371 ($3,589–$218) million in long-term debt.

LO 4 Demonstrate how changes in current liabilities affect the statement of cash flows.

Item	Cash Flow Statement		
	Operating Activities		
	Net income		**xxx**
Increase in current liability			**+**
Decrease in current liability			**–**
	Investing Activities		
	Financing Activities		
Increase in notes payable			**+**
Decrease in notes payable			**–**

Exhibit 9-6

Current Liabilities on the Statement of Cash Flows

Exhibit 9-7 CN's 2007 Consolidated Statement of Cash Flows

In millions	*Year ended December 31,*	**2007**
Operating activities		
Net income		$ 2,158
Adjustments to reconcile net income to net cash provided from operating activities:		
Depreciation and amortization		678
Deferred income taxes *(Note 15)*		(82)
Gain on sale of Central Station Complex *(Note 5)*		(92)
Gain on sale of investment in English Welsh and Scottish Railway *(Note 6)*		(61)
Other changes in:		
Accounts receivable *(Note 4)*		229
Material and supplies		18
Accounts payable and accrued charges		(351)
Other net current assets and liabilities		39
Other		(119)
Cash provided from operating activities		2,417
Investing activities		
Property additions		(1,387)
Acquisitions, net of cash acquired *(Note 3)*		(25)
Sale of Central Station Complex *(Note 5)*		351
Sale of investment in English Welsh and Scottish Railway *(Note 6)*		114
Other, net		52
Cash used by investing activities		(895)
Financing activities		
Issuance of long-term debt		4,171
Reduction of long-term debt		(3,589)
Issuance of common shares due to exercise of stock options and related excess tax benefits realized *(Note 12)*		77
Repurchase of common shares *(Note 11)*		(1,584)
Dividends paid		(418)
Cash used by financing activities		(1,343)
Effect of foreign exchange fluctuations on U.S. dollar-denominated cash and cash equivalents		(48)
Net increase in cash and cash equivalents		131
Cash and cash equivalents, beginning of year		179
Cash and cash equivalents, end of year		$ 310

This excerpt from CN's 2007 Annual Report appears courtesy of CN. This section of the CN Annual Report appears in the Appendix of this textbook.

Answers to the Two-Minute Reviews

Two-Minute Review on page 409

1. Current liabilities are defined as items that will be paid within one year of the balance sheet date. Examples of current liabilities include accounts payable, notes payable if due within one year, taxes payable, and other accrued liabilities. Also, if a portion of a long-term debt will be paid within one year, that portion should be reported as a current liability.

2. The current ratio is calculated as total current assets divided by total current liabilities. It is a measure of the liquidity of the company, or the ability of the company to pay its short-term obligations.

Appendix: Time Value of Money Concepts

In this section we will study the impact that interest has on decision making because of the time value of money. The **time value of money** concept means that people prefer a payment at the present time rather than in the future because of the interest factor. If an amount is received at the present time, it can be invested, and the resulting accumulation will be larger than if the same amount were received in the future. Thus, there is a *time value* to cash receipts and payments. This time value concept is important to every student for two reasons: it affects your personal financial decisions, and it affects accounting valuation decisions.

Exhibit 9-8 indicates some of the personal and accounting decisions affected by the time value of money concept. In your personal life, you make decisions based on the time value of money concept nearly every day. When you invest money, you are interested in how much will be accumulated, and you must determine the *future value* based on the amount of interest that will be compounded. When you borrow money, you

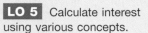
LO 5 Calculate interest using various concepts.

Time value of money An immediate amount should be preferred over an amount in the future.

Personal Financial Decision	Action
■ How much money will accumulate if you invest in a money market account? →	Calculate the future value based on compound interest.
■ If you take out a car loan, what will be the monthly loan payments? →	Calculate the payments based on the present value of the loan.
■ If you invest in the bond market, what should you pay for a bond? →	Calculate the present value of the bond based on compound interest.
■ If you win the lottery, should you take an immediate payment or payment over time? →	Calculate the present value of the alternatives based on compound interest.

Valuation Decisions on the Financial Statements	Valuation
■ Long-term assets ⟶	Historical cost, but not higher than present value of the cash flows
■ Notes receivable ⟶	Present value of the cash flows
■ Loan payments ⟶	Based on the present value of the loan
■ Bond issue price ⟶	Present value of the cash flows
■ Leases ⟶	Present value of the cash flows

Exhibit 9-8

Importance of the Time Value of Money

must determine the amount of the payments on the loan. You may not always realize it, but the amount of the loan payment is based on the *present value* of the loan, another time value of money concept.

Time value of money is also important because of its implications for accounting valuations. We will discover in Chapter 10 that the issue price of a bond is based on the present value of the cash flows that the bond will produce. The valuation of the bond and the recording of the bond on the balance sheet are based on this concept. Further, the amount that is considered interest expense on the financial statements is also based on time value of money concepts. The bottom portion of Exhibit 9-8 indicates that the valuations of many other accounts, including Notes Receivable and Leases, are based on compound interest calculations.

The time value of money concept is used in virtually every advanced business course. Investment courses, marketing courses, and many other business courses will use the time value of money concept. *In fact, it is probably the most important decision-making tool to master in preparation for the business world.* This section of the text begins with an explanation of how simple interest and compound interest differ and then proceeds to the concepts of present values and future values.

Simple Interest

Simple interest Interest is calculated on the principal amount only.

Simple interest is interest earned on the principal amount. If the amount of principal is unchanged from year to year, the interest per year will remain the same. Interest can be calculated by the following formula:

$$I = P \times R \times T$$

where

I = Dollar amount of interest per year

P = Principal

R = Interest rate as a percentage

T = Time in years

For example, assume that our firm has signed a two-year note payable for $3,000. Interest and principal are to be paid at the due date with simple interest at the rate of 10% per year. The amount of interest on the note would be $600, calculated as $3,000 $\times$ 0.10 $\times$ 2. We would be required to pay $3,600 on the due date: $3,000 principal and $600 interest.

Compound Interest

Compound interest Interest calculated on the principal plus previous amounts of interest.

Compound interest means that interest is calculated on the principal plus previous amounts of accumulated interest. Thus, interest is compounded, or we can say that there is interest on interest. For example, assume a $3,000 note payable for which interest and principal are due in two years with interest compounded annually at 10% per year. Interest would be calculated as follows:

YEAR	PRINCIPAL AMOUNT AT BEGINNING OF YEAR	INTEREST AT 10%	ACCUMULATED AT YEAR-END
1	$3,000	$300	$3,300
2	3,300	330	3,630

We would be required to pay $3,630 at the end of two years, $3,000 principal and $630 interest. A comparison of the note payable with 10% simple interest in the first example with the note payable with 10% compound interest in the second example clearly indicates that the amount accumulated with compound interest is always a higher amount because of the interest-on-interest feature.

Interest Compounding

For most accounting problems, we will assume that interest is compounded annually. In actual business practice, compounding usually occurs over much shorter intervals. This can be confusing because the interest rate is often stated as an annual rate even though it is compounded over a shorter period. If compounding is not done annually, you must adjust the interest rate by dividing the annual rate by the number of compounding periods per year.

For example, assume that the note payable from the previous example carried a 10% interest rate compounded semiannually for two years. The 10% annual rate should be converted to 5% per period for four semiannual periods. The amount of interest would be compounded, as in the previous example, but for four periods instead of two. The compounding process is as follows:

PERIOD	PRINCIPAL AMOUNT AT BEGINNING OF PERIOD	INTEREST AT 5% PER PERIOD	ACCUMULATED AT END OF PERIOD
1	$3,000	$150	$3,150
2	3,150	158	3,308
3	3,308	165	3,473
4	3,473	174	3,647

The example illustrates that compounding more frequently results in a larger amount accumulated. In fact, many banks and financial institutions now compound interest on savings accounts on a daily basis.

In the remainder of this section, we will assume that compound interest is applicable. Four compound interest calculations must be understood:

1. Future value of a single amount
2. Present value of a single amount
3. Future value of an annuity
4. Present value of an annuity

Accounting for Your Decisions

You Invest Some Unexpected Cash

You want to invest some extra money you received from a long-lost uncle. You have narrowed your options down to two: (1) invest in a bond that offers 10% interest compounded semiannually, or (2) invest in a certificate of deposit that offers 10% interest compounded quarterly. Both options cover a one-year time period. Using the time value of money concepts you have learned in this accounting course, would you choose Option 1 or 2? Why?

ANSWER: You should choose Option 2, offering the same interest rate as the first option but compounding on a quarterly basis instead of a semiannual basis. More frequent compounding results in more interest, thus making Option 2's quarterly compounding more appealing than Option 1's semiannual compounding.

Future Value of a Single Amount

We are often interested in the amount of interest plus principal that will be accumulated at a future time. This is called a *future amount* or *future value*. The future amount is always larger than the principal amount (payment) because of the interest that accumulates. The formula to calculate the **future value of a single amount** is as follows:

$$FV = p(1 + i)^n$$

Future value of a single amount Amount accumulated at a future time from a single payment or investment.

where

$$FV = \text{Future value to be calculated}$$
$$p = \text{Present value or principal amount}$$
$$i = \text{Interest rate per compounding period}$$
$$n = \text{Number of periods of compounding}$$

Example 1: Your three-year-old son, Robert, just inherited $50,000 in cash and securities from his grandmother. If the funds were left in the bank and in the stock market and received an annual return of 10%, how much would be there in 15 years when Robert starts university?

Solution:
$$FV = \$50,000(1 + 0.10)^{15}$$
$$= \$50,000(4.177)$$
$$= \$208,850$$

In some cases, we will use time diagrams to illustrate the relationships. A time diagram to illustrate a future value would be of the following form:

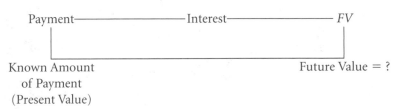

Payment————————————Interest————————————FV

Known Amount   Future Value = ?
of Payment
(Present Value)

Assume you won the lottery and this cheque is yours. Which payment option would you take—a lump sum or an equal amount every year for 10 years? Only by understanding time value of money concepts could you make an intelligent choice.

Example 2: Consider a $2,000 note payable that carries interest at the rate of 10% compounded annually. The note is due in two years, and the principal and interest must be paid at that time. The amount that must be paid in two years is the future value. The future value can be calculated in the manner we have used in the previous examples:

YEAR	PRINCIPAL AMOUNT AT BEGINNING OF YEAR	INTEREST AT 10%	ACCUMULATED AT YEAR-END
1	$2,000	$200	$2,200
2	2,200	220	2,420

The future value can also be calculated by using the following formula:

$$FV = \$2,000(1 + 0.10)^2$$
$$= \$2,000(1.21)$$
$$= \$2,420$$

Rather than using a formula, there are other methods to calculate future value. Tables can be constructed to assist in the calculations. Table 9-1 on page 436 indicates the future value of $1 at various interest rates and for various time periods. To find the future value of a two-year note at 10% compounded annually, you read across the line for two periods and down the 10% column and see an interest rate factor of 1.210. Because the table has been constructed for future values of $1, we would determine the future value of $2,000 as follows:

$$FV = \$2,000 \times 1.210$$
$$= \$2,420$$

Many financial calculators are also available to perform future value calculations. We will illustrate the calculations with a widely used calculator, **Texas Instruments'** **Advanced Business Analyst®** (BA II). All financial calculators perform the calculations in the same manner, but you should be aware that the methods to enter the data, the keystrokes, might vary somewhat from one calculator to another.[2]

http://www.ti.com

To calculate the future value in our example, you should perform the following steps:

ENTER	DISPLAY
2 N	N = 2
10 I/Y	I/Y = 10
0 PMT	PMT = 0
2000 PV	PV = 2,000
CPT FV	FV = 2,420

A third method used to perform the calculations is to use the built-in functions of a computerized spreadsheet. We will illustrate how to use a common spreadsheet program, Microsoft® Excel, to perform the same calculations.

---

[2] Some preliminary steps are necessary before using the calculator for the calculations we will illustrate. First, we will assume that your calculator is set to accommodate annual payments, rather than monthly payments. See your calculator instruction manual to set it to annual payments if necessary. Second, when we calculate the present value or future value of an annuity of payments, we will assume that the payments constitute an ordinary annuity, also called an annuity in arrears. That is, we will assume the payments occur at the end of each period. Your calculator should be set to end-of-period payments. Again, refer to your instruction manual to make sure it is set correctly.

To view the Excel functions, click on the Insert function of the Excel toolbar and choose the Financial option. Several different calculations are available. We will illustrate two of them: FV and PV. The problem involving the calculation of the future value can be done using the FV function of Excel as follows:

```
┌─FV──────────────────────────────────────────────────────┐
│                                                          │
│         Rate  10%                          ▦  = 0.1      │
│                                                          │
│         Nper  2                            ▦  = 2        │
│                                                          │
│          Pmt  0                            ▦  = 0        │
│                                                          │
│           Pv  2000                         ▦  = 2000     │
│                                                          │
│         Type                               ▦  = number   │
│                                                          │
│                                               = -2420    │
│   Returns the future value of an investment based on     │
│   periodic, constant payments and a constant interest    │
│   rate.                                                   │
│                                                          │
│          Pv is the present value, or the lump-sum amount │
│          that a series of future payments is worth now.  │
│          If omitted, Pv = 0.                             │
│  ──────────────────────────────────────────────────     │
│   Formula result =        -2420                          │
│                                                          │
│   Help on this function              [  OK  ] [ Cancel ] │
└──────────────────────────────────────────────────────────┘
```

The future value of is $2,420. We mentioned that compounding does not always occur annually. How does this affect the calculation of future value amounts?

Example 3: Suppose we want to find the future value of a $2,000 note payable due in two years. The note payable requires interest to be compounded quarterly at the rate of 12% per year. To calculate the future value, we must adjust the interest rate to a quarterly basis by dividing the 12% rate by the number of compounding periods per year, which in the case of quarterly compounding is four:

$$12\%/4 \text{ quarters} = 3\% \text{ per quarter}$$

Also, the number of compounding periods is eight—four per year times two years.

The future value of the note can be found in two ways. First, we can insert the proper values into the future value formula:

$$FV = \$2,000(1 + 0.03)^8$$
$$= \$2,000(1.267)$$
$$= \$2,534$$

We can arrive at the same future value amount with the use of Table 9-1. Refer to the interest factor in the table indicated for 8 periods and 3%. The future value would be calculated as follows:

$$FV = \$2,000(\text{interest factor})$$
$$= \$2,000(1.267)$$
$$= \$2,534$$

The steps using the calculator are as follows:

ENTER	DISPLAY
8 N	N = 8
3 I/Y	I/Y = 3
0 PMT	PMT = 0
2000 PV	PV = 2,000
CPT FV	FV = 2,534

This problem can also be calculated using the FV function of Excel as follows:

The future value is $2,534 (rounded to the nearest dollar).

Present Value of a Single Amount

In many situations, we do not want to calculate how much will be accumulated at a future time. Rather, we want to determine the present amount that is equivalent to an amount at a future time. This is the present value concept. The **present value of a single amount** represents the value today of a single amount to be received or paid at a future time. This can be portrayed in a time diagram as follows:

Present value of a single amount Amount at a present time that is equivalent to a payment or investment at a future time.

PV ——————————————Discount————————————Payment

PV = ?

Known Amount
of Payment
(Future Value)

The time diagram portrays discount, rather than interest, because we often speak of "discounting" the future payment back to the present time.

Example 4: Suppose you know that you will receive $2,000 in two years. You also know that if you had the money now, it could be invested at 10% compounded annually. What is the present value of the $2,000? Another way to ask the same question is, What amount must be invested today at 10% compounded annually in order to have $2,000 accumulated in two years?

The formula used to calculate present value is as follows:

$$PV = \text{Future value} \times 1/(1 + i)^n = \text{Future value} \times (1 + i)^{-n}$$

where

$$PV = \text{Present value amount in dollars}$$

$$\text{Future value} = \text{Amount to be received in the future}$$

$$i = \text{Interest rate or discount rate per compounding period}$$

$$n = \text{Number of periods}$$

We can use the present value formula to solve for the present value of the $2,000 note as follows:

$$PV = \$2,000 \times (1 + 0.10)^{-2}$$
$$= \$2,000 \times (0.826)$$
$$= \$1,652$$

Tables have also been developed to determine the present value of $1 at various interest rates and number of periods. Table 9-2 on page 439 presents the present value or discount factors for an amount of $1 to be received at a future time. To use the table for our two-year note (Example 4), you must read across the line for two periods and down the 10% column to the discount factor of 0.826. The present value of $2,000 would be calculated as follows:

$$PV = \$2,000(\text{discount factor})$$
$$= \$2,000(0.826)$$
$$= \$1,652$$

The steps using the calculator are as follows:

ENTER	DISPLAY
2 N	N = 2
10 I/Y	I/Y = 10
0 PMT	PMT= 0
2000 FV	FV = 2,000
CPT PV	PV = 1,653

The problem involving the calculation of the present can be done using the PV function of Excel as follows:

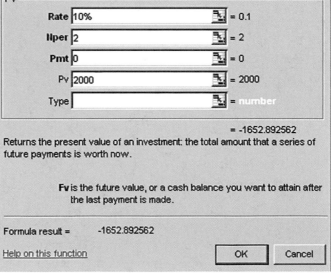

The present value is $1,653 (rounded to the nearest dollar). *Note that the numbers produced by each method may differ by a few dollars because of rounding differences. You should ignore those small differences and concentrate on the methods used to perform the interest rate calculations.*

Two other points are important. First, the example illustrates that the present value amount is always less than the future payment. This happens because of the discount factor. In other words, if we had a smaller amount at the present (the present value), we could invest it and earn interest that would accumulate to an amount equal to the larger amount (the future payment). Second, study of the present value and future value formulas indicates that each is the reciprocal of the other. When we want to calculate a present value amount, we normally use Table 9-2 and multiply a discount factor times the payment. However, we could also use Table 9-1 and divide by the interest factor. Thus, the present value of the $2,000 to be received in the future could also be calculated as follows:

$$PV = \$2,000/1.210$$
$$= \$1,652$$

Example 5: A recent magazine article projects that it will cost $120,000 to attend a four-year university program 10 years from now. If that is true, how much money would you have to put into an account today to fund that education, assuming a 5% rate of return?

$$PV = \$120,000(1 + 0.05)^{-10}$$
$$= \$120,000(0.614)$$
$$= \$73,680$$

Study Tip

When interest rates *increase*, present values *decrease*. This is called an *inverse relationship*.

Using Table 9-2 on page 437 the discount factor for 10 periods at 5% is 0.614. The present value of $120,000 would be calculated as follows:

$$PV = \$120,000(\text{discount factor})$$
$$= \$120,000(0.614)$$
$$= \$73,680$$

The steps using the calculator are as follows:

ENTER	DISPLAY
10 N	N = 10
5 I/Y	I/Y = 5
0 PMT	PMT = 0
120000 FV	FV = 120,000
CPT PV	PV = 73,670

The present value can also be calculated using the PV function of Excel as follows:

FV

Rate	5%	= 0.05
Nper	10	= 10
Pmt	0	= 0
Pv	120000	= 120000
Type		= number

= -73699.59042

Returns the future value of an investment based on periodic, constant payments and a constant interest rate.

Pv is the present value, or the lump-sum amount that a series of future payments is worth now. If omitted, Pv = 0.

Formula result =   -73699.59042

Help on this function   OK   Cancel

The present value is $73,670 (rounded to the nearest dollar).

Future Value of an Annuity

Annuity A series of payments of equal amounts. Note that each payment must be at the same time and the interest rate must remain constant.

The present value and future value amounts are useful when a single amount is involved. Many accounting situations involve an annuity, however. **Annuity** means a series of payments of equal amounts. We will now consider the calculation of the future value when a series of payments is involved.

Example 6: Suppose that you are to receive $3,000 per year at the end of each of the next four years. Also assume that each payment could be invested at an interest rate of 10% compounded annually. How much would be accumulated in principal and interest by the end of the fourth year? This is an example of an annuity of payments of equal amounts. A time diagram would portray the payments as follows:

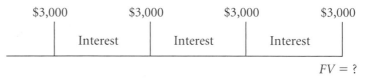

Because we are interested in calculating the future value, we could use the future value of $1 concept and calculate the future value of each $3,000 payment using Table 9-1 as follows:

$3,000 × 1.331 Interest for 3 Periods	$ 3,993
3,000 × 1.210 Interest for 2 Periods	3,630
3,000 × 1.100 Interest for 1 Period	3,300
3,000 × 1.000 Interest for 0 Periods	3,000
Total Future Value	$13,923

It should be noted that four payments would be received but that only three of them would draw interest because the payments are received at the end of each period.

Future value of an annuity Amount accumulated in the future when a series of payments is invested and accrues interest.

Fortunately, there is an easier method to calculate the **future value of an annuity**. Table 9-3 on page 440 has been constructed to indicate the future value of a series of payments of $1 per period at various interest rates and number of periods. The table can be used for Example 6 by reading across the four-period line and down the 10% column to a table factor of 4.641. The future value of an annuity of $3,000 per year can be calculated as follows:

$$FV = \$3,000(\text{table factor})$$
$$= \$3,000(4.641)$$
$$= \$13,923$$

The steps using the calculator are as follows:

ENTER	DISPLAY
4 N	N = 4
10 I/Y	I/Y = 10
3000 PMT	PMT = 3,000
0 PV	PV = 0
CPT FV	FV = 13,923

This problem can be done using the FV function of Excel as follows:

```
┌─FV─────────────────────────────────────────────────────────────┐
│        Rate │10%              │  ▤ = 0.1                        │
│        Nper │4                │  ▤ = 4                          │
│        Pmt  │3000             │  ▤ = 3000                       │
│        Pv   │0                │  ▤ = 0                          │
│        Type │                 │  ▤ = number                     │
│                                                                 │
│                                          = -13923               │
│  Returns the future value of an investment based on periodic,   │
│  constant payments and a constant interest rate.                │
│                                                                 │
│        Pv is the present value, or the lump-sum amount that a   │
│        series of future payments is worth now. If omitted,      │
│        Pv = 0.                                                  │
│                                                                 │
│  Formula result =      -13923                                   │
│  Help on this function                    [  OK  ]  [ Cancel ]  │
└─────────────────────────────────────────────────────────────────┘
```

The future value of the series of payments is $13,923. Note that the payments are simply entered as the Pmt variable in the spreadsheet.

Example 7: Your cousin just had a baby girl two weeks ago and is already thinking about sending her to university. When the girl is 15, how much money will be in her university account if your cousin deposits $2,000 into it on each of her 15 birthdays? The interest rate is 10%.

$$FV = \$2,000(\text{table factor})$$
$$= \$2,000(31.772)$$
$$= \$63,544$$

The steps using the calculator are as follows:

ENTER	DISPLAY
15 N	N = 15
10 I/Y	I/Y = 10
2000 PMT	PMT= 2,000
0 PV	PV = 0
CPT FV	FV = 63,545

You could use the Excel FV function as follows:

```
┌─FV─────────────────────────────────────────────────────────────┐
│        Rate │10%              │  ▤ = 0.1                        │
│        Nper │15               │  ▤ = 15                         │
│        Pmt  │2000             │  ▤ = 2000                       │
│        Pv   │0                │  ▤ = 0                          │
│        Type │                 │  ▤ = number                     │
│                                                                 │
│                                          = -63544.96339         │
│  Returns the future value of an investment based on periodic,   │
│  constant payments and a constant interest rate.                │
│                                                                 │
│        Pv is the present value, or the lump-sum amount that a   │
│        series of future payments is worth now. If omitted,      │
│        Pv = 0.                                                  │
│                                                                 │
│  Formula result =      -63544.96339                             │
│  Help on this function                    [  OK  ]  [ Cancel ]  │
└─────────────────────────────────────────────────────────────────┘
```

The future value amount is $63,545 (rounded to the nearest dollar).

When compounding occurs more frequently than annually, adjustments must be made to the interest rate and number of periods, adjustments similar to those discussed previously for single amounts.

Example 8: How would the future value be calculated if the previous example was modified so that we deposited $1,000 semiannually and the interest rate was 10% compounded semiannually (or 5% per period) for 15 years? Table 9-3 could be used by reading across the line for 30 periods and down the column for 5% to obtain a table factor of 66.439. The future value would be calculated as follows:

$$FV = \$1,000(\text{table factor})$$
$$= \$1,000(66.439)$$
$$= \$66,439$$

The steps using the calculator are as follows:

ENTER	DISPLAY
30 N	N = 30
5 I/Y	I/Y = 5
1000 PMT	PMT= 1,000
0 PV	PV = 0
CPT FV	FV = 66,439

Because the compounding is semiannual, you should use the FV function of Excel as follows:

FV

Rate	5%	= 0.05
Nper	30	= 30
Pmt	1000	= 1000
Pv	0	= 0
Type		= number

= -66438.8475

Returns the future value of an investment based on periodic, constant payments and a constant interest rate.

Pv is the present value, or the lump-sum amount that a series of future payments is worth now. If omitted, Pv = 0.

Formula result =   -66438.8475

Help on this function   OK   Cancel

The future value is $66,439 (rounded to the nearest dollar).

Comparing Examples 7 and 8 illustrates once again that more frequent compounding results in larger accumulated amounts.

Present Value of an Annuity

Many accounting applications of the time value of money concept concern situations for which we want to know the present value of a series of payments that will occur in the future. This involves calculating the present value of an annuity. An annuity is a series of payments of equal amounts.

Example 9: Suppose that you will receive an annuity of $4,000 per year for four years, with the first payment received one year from today. The amounts received can be invested at a rate of 10% compounded annually. What amount would you need at the present time to have an amount equivalent to the series of payments and interest in the future? To answer this question, you must calculate the **present value of an annuity.** A time diagram of the series of payments would appear as follows:

Present value of an annuity The amount at the present time that is equivalent to a series of payments and interest in the future.

	$4,000	$4,000	$4,000	$4,000
	Discount	Discount	Discount	Discount

$PV = ?$

Because you are interested in calculating the present value, you could refer to the present value of $1 concept and discount each of the $4,000 payments individually using table factors from Table 9-2 as follows:

$4,000 × 0.683 Factor for Four Periods	$ 2,732
4,000 × 0.751 Factor for Three Periods	3,004
4,000 × 0.826 Factor for Two Periods	3,304
4,000 × 0.909 Factor for One Period	3,636
Total Present Value	$12,676

For a problem of any size, it is very cumbersome to calculate the present value of each payment individually. Therefore, tables have been constructed to ease the computational burden. Table 9-4 on page 441 provides table factors to calculate the present value of an annuity of $1 per year at various interest rates and number of periods. Example 9 can be solved by reading across the four-year line and down the 10% column to obtain a table factor of 3.170. The present value would then be calculated as follows:

$$PV = \$4,000(\text{table factor})$$
$$= \$4,000(3.170)$$
$$= \$12,680$$

You should note that there is a $4 difference in the present values calculated by the first and second methods. This difference is caused by a small amount of rounding in the table factors that were used.

The steps using the calculator are as follows:

ENTER	DISPLAY
4 N	N = 4
10 I/Y	I/Y = 10
4000 PMT	PMT = 4,000
0 FV	FV = 0
CPT PV	PV = 12,680

This problem can also be calculated using the PV function of Excel as follows:

The present value of $12,679 (rounded to the nearest dollar) differs slightly from that derived when using the tables because of rounding in the table factors.

Example 10: You just won the lottery. You can take your $1 million in a lump sum today, or you can receive $100,000 per year over the next 12 years. Assuming a 5% interest rate, which would you prefer?

Solution:
$$PV = \$100,000(\text{table factor})$$
$$= \$100,000(8.863)$$
$$= \$886,300$$

The steps using the calculator are as follows:

ENTER	DISPLAY
12 N	N = 12
5 I/Y	I/Y = 5
100,000 PMT	PMT = 100,000
0 FV	FV = 0
CPT PV	PV = 886,325

You could use the PV function of Excel as follows:

Because the present value of the payments over 12 years is $886,325 (rounded to the nearest dollar) and is less than the $1 million that can be received immediately, you should choose the immediate payment.

On each of the tables for the interest factors, an Excel formula is provided that will enable the calculation of an interest factor for any i and any n. These formulas inserted in Excel will permit the calculation of interest factors for any of the four tables when the tables do not contain the interest rate or time needed for a specific problem. When employing these formulas it is important to note the specific parentheses so that the formula will be calculated correctly.

Solving for Unknowns

In some cases, the present value or future value amounts will be known but the interest rate or the number of payments must be calculated. The formulas that have been presented thus far can be used for such calculations, but you must be careful to analyze each problem to be sure that you have chosen the correct relationship. We will use two examples to illustrate the power of the time value of money concepts.

Assume that you have just purchased a new automobile for $14,420 and must decide how to pay for it. Your local bank has graciously granted you a five-year loan. Because you are a good credit risk, the bank will allow you to make annual payments on the loan at the end of each year. The amount of the loan payments, which include principal and interest, is $4,000 per year. You are concerned that your total payments will be $20,000 ($4,000 per year for five years) and want to calculate the interest rate that is being charged on the loan.

Because the market or present value of the car, as well as the loan, is $14,420, a time diagram of our example would appear as follows:

$4,000	$4,000	$4,000	$4,000	$4,000
Discount	Discount	Discount	Discount	Discount

$PV = 14,420$

Appendix: Time Value of Money Concepts **433**

The interest rate that we must solve for represents the discount rate that was applied to the $4,000 payments to result in a present value of $14,420. Therefore, the applicable formula is the following:

$$PV = \$4,000(\text{table factor})$$

In this case, PV is known, so the formula can be rearranged as follows:

$$\text{Table factor} = PV/\$4,000$$
$$= \$14,420/\$4,000$$
$$= 3.605$$

The value of 3.605 represents a table factor in Table 9-4. We must read across the five-year line until we find a table factor of 3.605. In this case, that table factor is found in the 12% column. Therefore, the rate of interest being paid on the auto loan is 12%. The steps using the calculator are as follows:

ENTER	DISPLAY
5 N	N = 5
14420 PV	PV = 14,420
4000 PMT +/−	PMT = −4,000
0 FV	FV = 0
CPT I/Y	I/Y = 11.99

[**Note:** On many calculators, including Texas Instruments' BA II, the payment amount (PMT) must be entered as a negative value in order to calculate I/Y.]

[**Note:** Where I is known and N is not, the steps to solve for N follow a similar pattern to those shown when solving for I.]

Chapter Highlights

1. **LO 1** **Identify the components of the current liability category of the balance sheet (p. 402).**
   - Current liabilities are obligations of a company that generally must be satisfied within one year. Some companies list them in the balance sheet in order of the account that requires payment first.
   - Current liability accounts include:
     - Accounts payable
     - Notes payable
     - Current portion of L/T debt
     - Income tax payable
     - Sales tax payable
     - Unearned revenue
     - Interest payable
     - Salaries payable
     - Estimated warranty obligation

2. **LO 2** **Demonstrate the deductions and expenses for payroll (p. 409).**
   - Payroll-related expenses must often be accrued at the end of the period, and the accounting involves some specialized accounts.
     - Net pay is the cash disbursed to employees. It is the gross pay less income tax withheld for the employee, CPP, EI, and any voluntary deductions specified by the employee.
     - The employer has expenses for salaries and wages beyond those amounts themselves. Two of the most important are CPP (same amount as employee) and EI (1.4 times per employee's contribution).
     - Most employers allow employees to take paid vacation and to accumulate a certain number of sick days per year. These represent compensated absences. Normally the expense and related liability for vacation days is recorded when earned, but sick days are not recorded until actually taken.

3. **LO 3** Determine when contingent liabilities should be presented on the balance sheet or disclosed in notes, and how to calculate their amounts. (p. 412).

- Contingent liabilities should be accrued and disclosed only when the event that they depend upon is probable and the amount can reasonably be estimated.
- The amount of a contingent liability is often an estimate made by experts both inside the firm (managers for amounts of warranty expenses) and outside the firm (e.g., attorneys for amounts in a lawsuit).

4. **LO 4** Demonstrate how changes in current liabilities affect the statement of cash flows. (p. 417).

- Most current liabilities are directly related to the ongoing operations of a company.
  o Decreases in current liabilities indicate that cash has been used to satisfy obligations and are cash outflows not represented by some expenses in the income statement.
  o Increases in current liabilities indicate that some expenses in the income statement have not been paid in cash and are not cash outflows represented by some expenses on the income statement.

5. **LO 5** Calculate interest using various concepts. (Appendix) (p. 419).

- Simple interest is earned only on the principal amount, whereas compound interest is earned on the principal plus previous amounts of accumulated interest.
- Present and future value calculations are made for four different scenarios:
  o Future value of a single amount
  o Present value of a single amount
  o Future value of an annuity
  o Present value of an annuity
- Often all of the variables necessary to calculate amounts related to present and future value concepts will be available except for one unknown amount that can be solved for.
- Financial calculators allow for these situations and easily solve for unknown values such as present or future value, payments, and interest rate.

——— *Ratio Review* ———

Working Capital* = Current Assets – Current Liabilities

Current Ratio = Current Assets/Current Liabilities

Quick Ratio = Quick Assets**/Current Liabilities

---

*Working capital is defined and discussed in Chapter 2.
**Quick assets are those assets that can be converted into cash quickly. It may be measured differently by different companies but generally it is measured as Total Current Assets – Inventory – Prepaid Expenses.

——— *Accounts Highlighted* ———

Account Titles	Where it Appears	In What Section	Page Number
Notes Payable	Balance Sheet	Current Liabilities	404
Discount on Payable	Balance Sheet	Contra Current Liabilities	405
Current Portion of L/T Debt	Balance Sheet	Current Liabilities	406
Income Tax Payable	Balance Sheet	Current Liabilities	407
Sales Tax Payable	Balance Sheet	Current Liabilities	407
Unearned Revenue	Balance Sheet	Current Liabilities	408
Salaries and Wages Payable	Balance Sheet	Current Liabilities	411
Income Tax Deduction Payable	Balance Sheet	Current Liabilities	411
CPP Payable	Balance Sheet	Current Liabilities	411
EI Payable	Balance Sheet	Current Liabilities	411
Estimated Warranty Liability	Balance Sheet	Current or Long-term Liabilities (depending upon when it will be paid)	413

TABLE 9-1 Future Value of $1 Formula $(1 + i)^n$

(n) PERIODS	2	3	4	5	6	7	8	9	10	11	12	15
					Rate of Interest in %							
1	1.020	1.030	1.040	1.050	1.060	1.070	1.080	1.090	1.100	1.110	1.120	1.150
2	1.040	1.061	1.082	1.103	1.124	1.145	1.166	1.188	1.210	1.232	1.254	1.323
3	1.061	1.093	1.125	1.158	1.191	1.225	1.260	1.295	1.331	1.368	1.405	1.521
4	1.082	1.126	1.170	1.216	1.262	1.311	1.360	1.412	1.464	1.518	1.574	1.749
5	1.104	1.159	1.217	1.276	1.338	1.403	1.469	1.539	1.611	1.685	1.762	2.011
6	1.126	1.194	1.265	1.340	1.419	1.501	1.587	1.677	1.772	1.870	1.974	2.313
7	1.149	1.230	1.316	1.407	1.504	1.606	1.714	1.828	1.949	2.076	2.211	2.660
8	1.172	1.267	1.369	1.477	1.594	1.718	1.851	1.993	2.144	2.305	2.476	3.059
9	1.195	1.305	1.423	1.551	1.689	1.838	1.999	2.172	2.358	2.558	2.773	3.518
10	1.219	1.344	1.480	1.629	1.791	1.967	2.159	2.367	2.594	2.839	3.106	4.046
11	1.243	1.384	1.539	1.710	1.898	2.105	2.332	2.580	2.853	3.152	3.479	4.652
12	1.268	1.426	1.601	1.796	2.012	2.252	2.518	2.813	3.138	3.498	3.896	5.350
13	1.294	1.469	1.665	1.886	2.133	2.410	2.720	3.066	3.452	3.883	4.363	6.153
14	1.319	1.513	1.732	1.980	2.261	2.579	2.937	3.342	3.797	4.310	4.887	7.076
15	1.346	1.558	1.801	2.079	2.397	2.759	3.172	3.642	4.177	4.785	5.474	8.137
16	1.373	1.605	1.873	2.183	2.540	2.952	3.426	3.970	4.595	5.311	6.130	9.358
17	1.400	1.653	1.948	2.292	2.693	3.159	3.700	4.328	5.054	5.895	6.866	10.761
18	1.428	1.702	2.026	2.407	2.854	3.380	3.996	4.717	5.560	6.544	7.690	12.375
19	1.457	1.754	2.107	2.527	3.026	3.617	4.316	5.142	6.116	7.263	8.613	14.232
20	1.486	1.806	2.191	2.653	3.207	3.870	4.661	5.604	6.727	8.062	9.646	16.367
21	1.516	1.860	2.279	2.786	3.400	4.141	5.034	6.109	7.400	8.949	10.804	18.822
22	1.546	1.916	2.370	2.925	3.604	4.430	5.437	6.659	8.140	9.934	12.100	21.645
23	1.577	1.974	2.465	3.072	3.820	4.741	5.871	7.258	8.954	11.026	13.552	24.891
24	1.608	2.033	2.563	3.225	4.049	5.072	6.341	7.911	9.850	12.239	15.179	28.625
25	1.641	2.094	2.666	3.386	4.292	5.427	6.848	8.623	10.835	13.585	17.000	32.919
26	1.673	2.157	2.772	3.556	4.549	5.807	7.396	9.399	11.918	15.080	19.040	37.857
27	1.707	2.221	2.883	3.733	4.822	6.214	7.988	10.245	13.110	16.739	21.325	43.535
28	1.741	2.288	2.999	3.920	5.112	6.649	8.627	11.167	14.421	18.580	23.884	50.066
29	1.776	2.357	3.119	4.116	5.418	7.114	9.317	12.172	15.863	20.624	26.750	57.575
30	1.811	2.427	3.243	4.322	5.743	7.612	10.063	13.268	17.449	22.892	29.960	66.212

Excel formula for the future value of $1 is $(1+i)^\wedge n$ where i is any interest rate (eg: 0.055) and n is the number of compounding (interest) periods.

TABLE 9-2 Present Value of $1 Formula $(1 + i)^{-n}$

(n) PERIODS	Rate of Interest in %											
	2	3	4	5	6	7	8	9	10	11	12	15
1	0.980	0.971	0.962	0.952	0.943	0.935	0.926	0.917	0.909	0.901	0.893	0.870
2	0.961	0.943	0.925	0.907	0.890	0.873	0.857	0.842	0.826	0.812	0.797	0.756
3	0.942	0.915	0.889	0.864	0.840	0.816	0.794	0.772	0.751	0.731	0.712	0.658
4	0.924	0.888	0.855	0.823	0.792	0.763	0.735	0.708	0.683	0.659	0.636	0.572
5	0.906	0.863	0.822	0.784	0.747	0.713	0.681	0.650	0.621	0.593	0.567	0.497
6	0.888	0.837	0.790	0.746	0.705	0.666	0.630	0.596	0.564	0.535	0.507	0.432
7	0.871	0.813	0.760	0.711	0.665	0.623	0.583	0.547	0.513	0.482	0.452	0.376
8	0.853	0.789	0.731	0.677	0.627	0.582	0.540	0.502	0.467	0.434	0.404	0.327
9	0.837	0.766	0.703	0.645	0.592	0.544	0.500	0.460	0.424	0.391	0.361	0.284
10	0.820	0.744	0.676	0.614	0.558	0.508	0.463	0.422	0.386	0.352	0.322	0.247
11	0.804	0.722	0.650	0.585	0.527	0.475	0.429	0.388	0.350	0.317	0.287	0.215
12	0.788	0.701	0.625	0.557	0.497	0.444	0.397	0.356	0.319	0.286	0.257	0.187
13	0.773	0.681	0.601	0.530	0.469	0.415	0.368	0.326	0.290	0.258	0.229	0.163
14	0.758	0.661	0.577	0.505	0.442	0.388	0.340	0.299	0.263	0.232	0.205	0.141
15	0.743	0.642	0.555	0.481	0.417	0.362	0.315	0.275	0.239	0.209	0.183	0.123
16	0.728	0.623	0.534	0.458	0.394	0.339	0.292	0.252	0.218	0.188	0.163	0.107
17	0.714	0.605	0.513	0.436	0.371	0.317	0.270	0.231	0.198	0.170	0.146	0.093
18	0.700	0.587	0.494	0.416	0.350	0.296	0.250	0.212	0.180	0.153	0.130	0.081
19	0.686	0.570	0.475	0.396	0.331	0.277	0.232	0.194	0.164	0.138	0.116	0.070
20	0.673	0.554	0.456	0.377	0.312	0.258	0.215	0.178	0.149	0.124	0.104	0.061
21	0.660	0.538	0.439	0.359	0.294	0.242	0.199	0.164	0.135	0.112	0.093	0.053
22	0.647	0.522	0.422	0.342	0.278	0.226	0.184	0.150	0.123	0.101	0.083	0.046
23	0.634	0.507	0.406	0.326	0.262	0.211	0.170	0.138	0.112	0.091	0.074	0.040
24	0.622	0.492	0.390	0.310	0.247	0.197	0.158	0.126	0.102	0.082	0.066	0.035
25	0.610	0.478	0.375	0.295	0.233	0.184	0.146	0.116	0.092	0.074	0.059	0.030
26	0.598	0.464	0.361	0.281	0.220	0.172	0.135	0.106	0.084	0.066	0.053	0.026
27	0.586	0.450	0.347	0.268	0.207	0.161	0.125	0.098	0.076	0.060	0.047	0.023
28	0.574	0.437	0.333	0.255	0.196	0.150	0.116	0.090	0.069	0.054	0.042	0.020
29	0.563	0.424	0.321	0.243	0.185	0.141	0.107	0.082	0.063	0.048	0.037	0.017
30	0.552	0.412	0.308	0.231	0.174	0.131	0.099	0.075	0.057	0.044	0.033	0.015

Excel formula for the present value of $1 is $(1+i)^{\wedge}n$ where i is any interest rate (eg: 0.055) and n is the number of compounding (interest) periods.

TABLE 9-3 Future Value of Annuity of $1   Formula $((1 + i)^n - 1)/i$

(n) PERIODS	2	3	4	5	6	7	8	9	10	11	12	15
						Rate of Interest in %						
1	1.000	1.000	1.000	1.000	1.000	1.000	1.000	1.000	1.000	1.000	1.000	1.000
2	2.020	2.030	2.040	2.050	2.060	2.070	2.080	2.090	2.100	2.110	2.120	2.150
3	3.060	3.091	3.122	3.153	3.184	3.215	3.246	3.278	3.310	3.342	3.374	3.473
4	4.122	4.184	4.246	4.310	4.375	4.440	4.506	4.573	4.641	4.710	4.779	4.993
5	5.204	5.309	5.416	5.526	5.637	5.751	5.867	5.985	6.105	6.228	6.353	6.742
6	6.308	6.468	6.633	6.802	6.975	7.153	7.336	7.523	7.716	7.913	8.115	8.754
7	7.434	7.662	7.898	8.142	8.394	8.654	8.923	9.200	9.487	9.783	10.089	11.067
8	8.583	8.892	9.214	9.549	9.897	10.260	10.637	11.028	11.436	11.859	12.300	13.727
9	9.755	10.159	10.583	11.027	11.491	11.978	12.488	13.021	13.579	14.164	14.776	16.786
10	10.950	11.464	12.006	12.578	13.181	13.816	14.487	15.193	15.937	16.722	17.549	20.304
11	12.169	12.808	13.486	14.207	14.972	15.784	16.645	17.560	18.531	19.561	20.655	24.349
12	13.412	14.192	15.026	15.917	16.870	17.888	18.977	20.141	21.384	22.713	24.133	29.002
13	14.680	15.618	16.627	17.713	18.882	20.141	21.495	22.953	24.523	26.212	28.029	34.352
14	15.974	17.086	18.292	19.599	21.015	22.550	24.215	26.019	27.975	30.095	32.393	40.505
15	17.293	18.599	20.024	21.579	23.276	25.129	27.152	29.361	31.772	34.405	37.280	47.580
16	18.639	20.157	21.825	23.657	25.673	27.888	30.324	33.003	35.950	39.190	42.753	55.717
17	20.012	21.762	23.698	25.840	28.213	30.840	33.750	36.974	40.545	44.501	48.884	65.075
18	21.412	23.414	25.645	28.132	30.906	33.999	37.450	41.301	45.599	50.396	55.750	75.836
19	22.841	25.117	27.671	30.539	33.760	37.379	41.446	46.018	51.159	56.939	63.440	88.212
20	24.297	26.870	29.778	33.066	36.786	40.995	45.762	51.160	57.275	64.203	72.052	102.444
21	25.783	28.676	31.969	35.719	39.993	44.865	50.423	56.765	64.002	72.265	81.699	118.810
22	27.299	30.537	34.248	38.505	43.392	49.006	55.457	62.873	71.403	81.214	92.503	137.632
23	28.845	32.453	36.618	41.430	46.996	53.436	60.893	69.532	79.543	91.148	104.603	159.276
24	30.422	34.426	39.083	44.502	50.816	58.177	66.765	76.790	88.497	102.174	118.155	184.168
25	32.030	36.459	41.646	47.727	54.865	63.249	73.106	84.701	98.347	114.413	133.334	212.793
26	33.671	38.553	44.312	51.113	59.156	68.676	79.954	93.324	109.182	127.999	150.334	245.712
27	35.344	40.710	47.084	54.669	63.706	74.484	87.351	102.723	121.100	143.079	169.374	283.569
28	37.051	42.931	49.968	58.403	68.528	80.698	95.339	112.968	134.210	159.817	190.699	327.104
29	38.792	45.219	52.966	62.323	73.640	87.347	103.966	124.135	148.631	178.397	214.583	377.170
30	40.568	47.575	56.085	66.439	79.058	94.461	113.283	136.308	164.494	199.021	241.333	434.745

Excel formula for the future value of $1 deposits is $(((1 + i)^\wedge n) - 1)/i$ where i is any interest rate (eg: 0.055) and n is the number of compounding periods.

TABLE 9-4 Present Value of Annuity of $1   Formula $(1-(1+i)^{-n})/i$

(n) PERIODS	Rate of Interest in %											
	2	3	4	5	6	7	8	9	10	11	12	15
1	0.980	0.971	0.962	0.952	0.943	0.935	0.926	0.917	0.909	0.901	0.893	0.870
2	1.942	1.913	1.886	1.859	1.833	1.808	1.783	1.759	1.736	1.713	1.690	1.626
3	2.884	2.829	2.775	2.723	2.673	2.624	2.577	2.531	2.487	2.444	2.402	2.283
4	3.808	3.717	3.630	3.546	3.465	3.387	3.312	3.240	3.170	3.102	3.037	2.855
5	4.713	4.580	4.452	4.329	4.212	4.100	3.993	3.890	3.791	3.696	3.605	3.352
6	5.601	5.417	5.242	5.076	4.917	4.767	4.623	4.486	4.355	4.231	4.111	3.784
7	6.472	6.230	6.002	5.786	5.582	5.389	5.206	5.033	4.868	4.712	4.564	4.160
8	7.325	7.020	6.733	6.463	6.210	5.971	5.747	5.535	5.335	5.146	4.968	4.487
9	8.162	7.786	7.435	7.108	6.802	6.515	6.247	5.995	5.759	5.537	5.328	4.772
10	8.983	8.530	8.111	7.722	7.360	7.024	6.710	6.418	6.145	5.889	5.650	5.019
11	9.787	9.253	8.760	8.306	7.887	7.499	7.139	6.805	6.495	6.207	5.938	5.234
12	10.575	9.954	9.385	8.863	8.384	7.943	7.536	7.161	6.814	6.492	6.194	5.421
13	11.348	10.635	9.986	9.394	8.853	8.358	7.904	7.487	7.103	6.750	6.424	5.583
14	12.106	11.296	10.563	9.899	9.295	8.745	8.244	7.786	7.367	6.982	6.628	5.724
15	12.849	11.938	11.118	10.380	9.712	9.108	8.559	8.061	7.606	7.191	6.811	5.847
16	13.578	12.561	11.652	10.838	10.106	9.447	8.851	8.313	7.824	7.379	6.974	5.954
17	14.292	13.166	12.166	11.274	10.477	9.763	9.122	8.544	8.022	7.549	7.120	6.047
18	14.992	13.754	12.659	11.690	10.828	10.059	9.372	8.756	8.201	7.702	7.250	6.128
19	15.678	14.324	13.134	12.085	11.158	10.336	9.604	8.950	8.365	7.839	7.366	6.198
20	16.351	14.877	13.590	12.462	11.470	10.594	9.818	9.129	8.514	7.963	7.469	6.259
21	17.011	15.415	14.029	12.821	11.764	10.836	10.017	9.292	8.649	8.075	7.562	6.312
22	17.658	15.937	14.451	13.163	12.042	11.061	10.201	9.442	8.772	8.176	7.645	6.359
23	18.292	16.444	14.857	13.489	12.303	11.272	10.371	9.580	8.883	8.266	7.718	6.399
24	18.914	16.936	15.247	13.799	12.550	11.469	10.529	9.707	8.985	8.348	7.784	6.434
25	19.523	17.413	15.622	14.094	12.783	11.654	10.675	9.823	9.077	8.422	7.843	6.464
26	20.121	17.877	15.983	14.375	13.003	11.826	10.810	9.929	9.161	8.488	7.896	6.491
27	20.707	18.327	16.330	14.643	13.211	11.987	10.935	10.027	9.237	8.548	7.943	6.514
28	21.281	18.764	16.663	14.898	13.406	12.137	11.051	10.116	9.307	8.602	7.984	6.534
29	21.844	19.188	16.984	15.141	13.591	12.278	11.158	10.198	9.370	8.650	8.022	6.551
30	22.396	19.600	17.292	15.372	13.765	12.409	11.258	10.274	9.427	8.694	8.055	6.566

Excel formula for the present value of deposits of $1 is $(1-(1/((1+i)^n)))/i$ where i is any interest rate (eg: 0.055) and n is the number of compounding periods.

Key Terms Quiz

Read each definition below, and then write the number of the definition in the blank beside the appropriate term it defines. The quiz solutions appear at the end of the chapter.

_____ Current liability
_____ Accounts payable
_____ Notes payable
_____ Discount on Notes Payable
_____ Current Portion of Long-Term Debt
_____ Accrued liability
_____ Contingent liability
_____ Estimated liability
_____ Contingent asset
_____ Time value of money
_____ Simple interest (Appendix)
_____ Compound interest (Appendix)

_____ Future value of a single amount (Appendix)
_____ Present value of a single amount (Appendix)
_____ Annuity (Appendix)
_____ Future value of an annuity (Appendix)
_____ Present value of an annuity (Appendix)
_____ Gross wages
_____ Net pay
_____ Compensated absences

1. Accounts that will be satisfied within one year or the next operating cycle.

2. The amount needed at the present time to be equivalent to a series of payments and interest in the future.

3. Amounts owed for the purchase of inventory, goods, or services acquired in the normal course of business.

4. A contra-liability account that represents interest deducted from a loan or note in advance.

5. A series of payments of equal amount.

6. The portion of a long-term liability that will be paid within one year of the balance sheet date.

7. A liability that has been incurred but has not been paid as of the balance sheet date.

8. Amounts owed that are represented by a formal contractual agreement. These amounts usually require the payment of interest.

9. A liability that involves an existing condition for which the outcome is not known with certainty and depends on some future event.

10. Interest that is earned or paid on the principal amount only.

11. A contingent liability that is accrued and is reflected on the balance sheet. Common examples are warranties, guarantees, and premium offers.

12. An amount that involves an existing condition dependent on some future event by which the company stands to gain. These amounts are not normally reported until realized.

13. Interest calculated on the principal plus previous amounts of interest accumulated.

14. The concept that indicates that people should prefer to receive an immediate amount at the present time over an equal amount in the future.

15. The amount that will be accumulated in the future when one amount is invested at the present time and accrues interest until the future time.

16. The amount that will be accumulated in the future when a series of payments is invested and accrues interest until the future time.

17. The present amount that is equivalent to an amount at a future time.

18. The amount of an employee's wages before deductions.

19. Employment absences, such as sick days and vacation days, for which it is expected that employees will be paid.

20. The amount of an employee's paycheque after deductions.

Answers on p. 459.

Alternate Terms

Accrued interest Interest payable

Compensated absences Accrued vacation or sick pay

Compound interest Interest on interest

Contingent asset Contingent gain

Contingent liability Contingent loss

Current liability Short-term liability

Current portion of long-term debt Long-term debt, current portion

CPP Government pension

Discounting a note Interest in advance

EI Employment Insurance

Future value of an annuity Amount of an annuity

Gross wages Gross pay

Income tax liability Income tax payable

Warranties Guarantees

Warmup Exercises and Solutions

Warmup Exercise 9-1 LO 1

A company has the following current assets: Cash, $10,000; Accounts Receivable, $70,000; and Inventory, $20,000. The company also has current liabilities of $40,000. Calculate the company's current ratio and quick ratio.

Warmup Exercise 9-2 LO 4

A company has the following current liabilities at the beginning of the period: Accounts Payable, $30,000; Taxes Payable $10,000. At the end of the period the balances of the accounts are as follows: Accounts Payable, $20,000; Taxes Payable, $15,000. What amounts will appear in the cash flow statement, and in what category of the statement will they appear?

Solutions to Warmup Exercises

Warmup Exercise 9-1

Current Ratio: Current Assets/Current Liabilities

Cash ($10,000) + Accounts Receivable ($70,000) + Inventory ($20,000) = $100,000

$100,000/$40,000 = 2.5 Current Ratio

Quick Ratio: Quick Assets/Current Liabilities

Cash ($10,000) + Accounts Receivable ($70,000) = $80,000

$80,000/$40,000 = 2.0 Quick Ratio

Warmup Exercise 9-2

The amounts appearing in the cash flow statement should be in the Operating Activities category of the statement. The amounts shown should be the *changes* in the balances of the accounts.

■ Accounts Payable decreased by $10,000 and should appear as a decrease in the cash flow statement.

■ Taxes Payable increased by $5,000 and should appear as an increase in the cash flow statement.

Review Problem and Solution

The accountant for Lunn Express wants to develop a balance sheet as of December 31, 2008. The following items pertain to the liability category and must be considered in order to determine the items that should be reported in the Current Liabilities section of the balance sheet. You may assume that Lunn began business on January 1, 2008, and therefore the beginning balance of all accounts was zero.

a. During 2008 Lunn purchased $100,000 of inventory on account from suppliers. By year-end, $40,000 of the balance has been eliminated as a result of payments. All items were purchased on terms of 2/10, n/30. Lunn uses the gross method of recording payables.

b. On April 1, 2008, Lunn borrowed $10,000 on a one-year note payable from Philips Bank. Terms of the loan indicate that Lunn must repay the principal and 12% interest at the due date of the note.

c. On October 1, 2008, Lunn also borrowed $8,000 from Dove Bank on a one-year note payable. Dove Bank deducted 10% interest in advance and gave Lunn the net amount. At the due date, Lunn must repay the principal of $8,000.

d. On January 1, 2008, Lunn borrowed $20,000 from Owens Bank by signing a 10-year note payable. Terms of the note indicate that Lunn must make annual payments of principal each January 1 beginning in 2009 and also must pay interest each January 1 in the amount of 8% of the outstanding balance of the loan.

(continued)

e. The accountant for Lunn has completed an income statement for 2008 that indicates that income before taxes was $10,000. Lunn must pay tax at the rate of 40% and must remit the tax to the Canada Revenue Agency by April 15, 2009.

f. As of December 31, 2008, Lunn owes to employees salaries of $3,000 for work performed in 2008. The employees will be paid on the first payday of 2009.

g. During 2008 two lawsuits were filed against Lunn. In the first lawsuit, a customer sued for damages because of an injury that occurred on Lunn's premises. Lunn's legal counsel advised that it is probable that the lawsuit will be settled in 2009 at an amount of $7,000. The second lawsuit involves a patent infringement suit of $14,000 filed against Lunn by a competitor. The legal counsel has advised that there is some possibility that Lunn may be at fault but that a loss does not appear probable at this time.

Required

Develop the Current Liabilities section of Lunn's balance sheet as of December 31, 2008. To make investment decisions about this company, what additional data would you need? You may ignore the need for notes that accompany the balance sheet. (Note: You may wish to consult the first few pages of the appendix to this chapter to assist with the interest calculations.)

Solution to Review Problem

The accountant's decisions for items **a** through **g** should be as follows:

a. The balance of the Accounts Payable account should be $60,000. The payables should be reported at the gross amount, and discounts would not be reported until the time of payment.

b. The note payable to Philips Bank of $10,000 should be included as a current liability. Also, interest payable of $900 ($10,000 × 12% × 9/12) should be considered a current liability.

c. The note payable to Dove Bank should be considered a current liability and listed at $8,000 minus the contra account Discount on Note Payable of $600 ($8,000 × 10% × 9/12 remaining).

d. The debt to Owens Bank should be split between current liability and long-term liability with the current portion shown as $2,000. Also, interest payable of $1,600 ($20,000 × 8% × 1 year) should be considered a current liability.

e. Income taxes payable of $4,000 ($10,000 × 40%) is a current liability.

f. Salaries payable of $3,000 represent a current liability.

g. The lawsuit involving the customer must be reported as a current liability of $7,000 because the possibility of loss is probable. The second lawsuit should not be reported but should be disclosed as a note to the balance sheet.

LUNN EXPRESS
PARTIAL BALANCE SHEET
AS AT DECEMBER 31, 2008

Current Liabilities

Accounts payable		$60,000
Interest payable ($900 + $1,600)		2,500
Salaries payable		3,000
Taxes payable		4,000
Note payable to Philips Bank		10,000
Note payable to Dove Bank	$8,000	
Less: Discount on note payable	(600)	7,400
Current maturity of long-term debt		2,000
Contingent liability for pending lawsuit		7,000
Total Current Liabilities		$95,900

Other data necessary to make an investment decision might include current assets, total assets, and current liabilities as of December 31, 2007 and 2008. If current assets are significantly larger than current liabilities, you can be comfortable that the company is capable of paying its short-term debt. The dollar amount of current assets and liabilities must be evaluated with regard to the size of the company. The larger the company, the less significant $95,900 in current liabilities would be. Knowing last year's current liabilities would give you an idea about the trend in current liabilities. If they are rising, you would want to know why.

Review Problem (Appendix)

a. What amount will be accumulated by January 1, 2012, if $5,000 is invested on January 1, 2008, at 10% interest compounded semiannually?

b. Assume that we are to receive $5,000 on January 1, 2012. What amount at January 1, 2008, is equivalent to the $5,000 that is to be received in 2012? Assume that interest is compounded annually at 10%.

c. What amount will be accumulated by January 1, 2012, if $5,000 is invested each semiannual period for eight periods beginning with June 30, 2008, and ending December 31, 2011? Interest will accumulate at 10% (annual rate) compounded semiannually.

d. Assume that we are to receive $5,000 each semiannual period for eight periods beginning on June 30, 2008. What amount at January 1, 2008, is equivalent to the future series of payments? Assume that interest will accrue at 10% (annual rate) compounded semiannually.

e. Assume that a new bank has begun a promotional campaign to attract savings accounts. The bank advertisement indicates that customers who invest $1,000 will double their money in 10 years. Assuming annual compounding of interest, what rate of interest is the bank offering?

Required

1. Answer the five questions.

Solution to Review Problem

a.

$$FV = \$5,000(\text{table factor})$$
$$= \$5,000(1.477)$$
$$= \$7,385$$

using Table 9-1
where $i = 5\%$, $n = 8$

a.

ENTER	DISPLAY
8 N	N = 8
5 I/Y	I/Y = 5
0 PMT	PMT= 0
5000 PV	PV = 5,000
CPT FV	FV = 7,387

b.

$$PV = \$5,000(\text{table factor})$$
$$= \$5,000(0.683)$$
$$= \$3,415$$

using Table 9-2
where $i = 10\%$, $n = 4$

b.

ENTER	DISPLAY
4 N	N = 4
10 I/Y	I/Y = 10
0 PMT	PMT= 0
5000 FV	FV = 5,000
CPT PV	PV = 3,415

c. FV annuity

$$= \$5,000(\text{table factor})$$
$$= \$5,000(9.549)$$
$$= \$47,745$$

using Table 9-3
where $i = 5\%$, $n = 8$

c.

ENTER	DISPLAY
8 N	N = 8
5 I/Y	I/Y = 5
5000 PMT	PMT= 5,000
0 PV	PV = 0
CPT FV	FV = 47,746

(continued)

d. PV annuity = $5,000(table factor)   using Table 9-4

         = $5,000(6.463)   where $i = 5\%, n = 8$

         = $32,315

d.

ENTER	DISPLAY
8 N	N = 8
5 I/Y	I/Y = 5
5000 PMT	PMT = 5,000
0 FV	FV = 0
CPT PV	PV = 32,316

e. FV = $1,000(table factor)   using Table 9-1

Because the future value is known to be $2,000, the formula can be written as

         $2,000 = $1,000(table factor)

and rearranged as

Table factor = $2,000/$1,000 = 2.0.

In Table 9-1, the table factor of 2.0 and 10 years corresponds with an interest rate of between 7% and 8%.

e.

ENTER	DISPLAY
10 N	N = 10
0 PMT	PMT = 0
1000 PV +/−	PV = −1,000
2000 FV	FV = 2,000
CPT I/Y	I/Y = 7.177

(**Note:** In this case, the present value must be entered as a negative amount.)

Questions

1. What is the definition of *current liabilities?* Why is it important to distinguish between current and long-term liabilities?

2. Most firms attempt to pay their accounts payable within the discount period to take advantage of the discount. Why is that normally a sound financial move?

3. Assume that your local bank gives you a $1,000 loan at 10% per year but deducts the interest in advance. Is 10% the "real" rate of interest that you will pay? How could the true interest rate be calculated?

4. Is the account Discount on Notes Payable an income statement or a balance sheet account? Does it have a debit or a credit balance?

5. A firm's year ends on December 31. Its tax is computed and submitted to the Canada Revenue Agency on February 28 of the following year. When should the taxes be reported as a liability?

6. What is a contingent liability? Why are contingent liabilities accounted for differently than contingent assets?

7. Many firms believe that it is very difficult to estimate the amount of a possible future contingency. Should a contingent liability be reported even if the dollar amount of the loss is not known? Should it be disclosed in the notes to the financial statements?

8. Assume that a lawsuit has been filed against your firm. Your legal counsel has assured you that the likelihood of loss is not probable. How should the lawsuit be disclosed on the financial statements?

9. What is the difference between simple interest and compound interest? Would the amount of interest be higher or lower if the interest is simple rather than compound? (Appendix)

10. What is the effect if interest is compounded quarterly versus annually? (Appendix)

11. What is the meaning of the terms *present value* and *future value?* How can you determine whether to calculate the present value of an amount versus the future value? (Appendix)

12. What is the meaning of the word *annuity?* Could the present value of an annuity be calculated as a series of single amounts? If so, how? (Appendix)

13. Assume that you know the total dollar amount of a loan and the amount of the monthly interest payments on the loan. How could you determine the interest rate of the loan? (Appendix)

14. The present value and future value concepts are applied to measure the amount of several accounts commonly encountered in accounting. What are some accounts that are valued in this manner? (Appendix)

15. Your employer withholds federal income tax from your paycheque and remits it to the Canada Revenue Agency. How is the federal tax treated on the employer's financial statements?

16. EI tax is a tax on the employer. How should EI tax be treated on the employer's financial statements?

17. What is the meaning of the term *compensated absences?* Give some examples.

18. Do you agree or disagree with the following statement: "Vacation pay should be reported as an expense when the employee takes the vacation"?

Exercises

Exercise 9-1 *Current Liabilities* LO 1

The items listed below are accounts on Highland Inc.'s balance sheet of December 31, 2008.

Taxes Payable
Accounts Receivable
Notes Payable, 9%, due in 90 days
Investment in RBC shares.
Capital Stock
Accounts Payable
Estimated Warranty Payable in 2009
Retained Earnings
Trademark
Mortgage Payable ($10,000 due every year until 2023)

Required

Identify which of the above accounts should be classified as a current liability on Highland's balance sheet. For each item that is not a current liability, indicate the category of the balance sheet in which it would be classified.

Exercise 9-2 *Current Liabilities* LO 1

The following items all represent liabilities on a firm's balance sheet of December 31, 2008.

a. An amount of money owed to a supplier based on the terms 2/20, net 40

b. An amount of money owed to a creditor on a note due April 30, 2009

c. An amount of money owed to a creditor on a note due August 15, 2010

d. An amount of money owed to employees for work performed during the last week in December, 2008

e. An amount of money owed to a bank for the use of borrowed funds due on March 1, 2009

f. An amount of money owed to a creditor as an annual installment payment on a 10-year note

g. An amount of money owed to the federal government, based on the company's annual income

Required

1. For each lettered item, state whether it should be classified as a current liability on the December 31, 2008, balance sheet. Assume that the operating cycle is shorter than one year. If the item should not be classified as a current liability, indicate where on the balance sheet it should be presented.

2. For each item identified as a current liability in requirement 1, state the account title that is normally used to report the item on the balance sheet.

3. Why would an investor or creditor be interested in whether an item is a current or a long-term liability?

Exercise 9-3 *Current Liabilities Section* LO 1

Kennedy Company had the following accounts and balances on December 31, 2008:

Income Taxes Payable	$61,250
Allowance for Doubtful Accounts	17,800
Accounts Payable	24,400
Interest Receivable	5,000
Unearned Revenue	4,320
Wages Payable	6,000
Notes Payable, 10%, due June 2, 2009	1,000
Accounts Receivable	67,500
Discount on Notes Payable	150
Current Portion of Long-Term Debt	6,900
Interest Payable	3,010

Required

Prepare the Current Liabilities section of Kennedy Company's balance sheet as of December 31, 2008.

Exercise 9-4 *Transaction Analysis* **LO 1**

Polly's Cards & Gifts Shop had the following transactions during the year:

a. Polly's purchased inventory on account from a supplier for $8,000. Assume that Polly's uses a periodic inventory system.

b. On May 1, land was purchased for $44,500. A 20% down payment was made, and an 18-month, 8% note was signed for the remainder.

c. Polly's returned $450 worth of inventory purchased in item **a**, which was found to be broken when the inventory was received.

d. Polly's paid the balance due on the purchase of inventory.

e. On June 1, Polly signed a one-year, $15,000 note to First Bank and received $13,800.

f. Polly's sold 200 gift certificates for $25 each for cash. Sales of gift certificates are recorded as a liability. At year-end, 35% of the gift certificates had been redeemed.

g. Sales for the year were $120,000, of which 90% were for cash. HST of 13% applied to all sales and must be remitted to the Canada Revenue Agency by January 31 of next year.

Required

1. Record all necessary journal entries relating to these transactions.

2. Assume that Polly's accounting year ends on December 31. Prepare any necessary adjusting journal entries.

3. What is the total of the current liabilities at the end of the year?

Exercise 9-5 *Current Liabilities and Ratios* **LO 1**

Listed below are several accounts that appeared on Kruse's 2008 balance sheet.

Accounts Payable	$ 55,000
Temporary Investments	40,000
Accounts Receivable	180,000
Notes Payable, 12%, due in 60 days	20,000
Capital Stock	1,150,000
Salaries Payable	10,000
Cash	15,000
Equipment	950,000
Taxes Payable	15,000
Retained Earnings	250,000
Inventory	85,000
Allowance for Doubtful Accounts	20,000
Land	600,000

Required

1. Prepare the Current Liabilities section of Kruse's 2008 balance sheet.

2. Compute Kruse's working capital.

3. Compute Kruse's current ratio. What does this ratio indicate about Kruse's condition?

Exercise 9-6 *Discounts* **LO 1**

Each of the following situations involves the use of discounts.

1. How much discount may Seals Inc. take in each of the following transactions? What was the annualized interest rate?

   a. Seals purchases inventory costing $450, 2/10, n/40.

   b. Seals purchases new office furniture costing $1,500, terms 1/10, n/30.

2. Calculate the discount rate Croft Co. received in each of these transactions.

   a. Croft purchased office supplies costing $200 and paid within the discount period with a cheque for $196.

   b. Croft purchased merchandise for $2,800. It paid within the discount period with a cheque for $2,674.

Exercise 9-7 *Notes Payable and Interest* **LO 1**

On July 1, 2008, Jo's Flower Shop borrowed $25,000 from the bank. Jo signed a 10-month, 8% promissory note for the entire amount. Jo's uses a calendar year-end.

Required

1. Prepare the journal entry on July 1 to record the issuance of the promissory note.
2. Prepare any adjusting entries needed at year-end.
3. Prepare the journal entry on May 1 to record the payment of principal and interest.

Exercise 9-8 *Non-Interest-Bearing Notes Payable* **LO 1**

On October 1, 2008, Ratkowski Inc. signed a 12-month, $18,000 non-interest bearing note with National Bank. The bank discounted the note at 9%.

Required

1. Prepare the journal entry needed to record the issuance of the note.
2. Prepare the journal entry needed at December 31, 2008, to accrue interest.
3. Prepare the journal entry to record the payment of the note on October 1, 2009.
4. What effective rate of interest did Ratkowski pay?

Exercise 9-9 *Payroll Entries* **LO 2**

During the month of January, VanderSalm Company's employees earned $385,000. The following rates apply to VanderSalm's gross payroll:

Income Tax Rate	28%
CPP Rate	4.95%
EI	2.42%

In addition, employee deductions were $7,000 for health insurance and $980 for union dues.

Required

1. Prepare the journal entry the company made to record the January payroll.
2. Prepare the journal entry the company made to record the employer's portion of payroll taxes for January.
3. If the company paid fringe benefits, such as employees' health insurance coverage, how would these contributions affect the payroll entries?

Exercise 9-10 *Payroll, Employer's Portion* **LO 2**

Tasty Bakery Shop has six employees on its payroll. Payroll records include the following information on employee earnings for each employee:

Name	Earnings from 1/1 to 6/30/2008	Earnings for 3rd Quarter, 2008
Dell	$ 23,490	$11,710
Fin	4,240	2,660
Hook	34,100	15,660
Patty	63,300	26,200
Tuss	30,050	19,350
Woo	6,300	3,900
Totals	$161,480	$79,480

CPP is levied at 4.95% on the first $41,000 of each employee's current year's earnings. The unemployment insurance rates are 3.4% of salaries up to $40,000 for both the employee and the employer.

Required

1. Calculate the employer's portion of payroll taxes incurred by Tasty Bakery for each employee for the third quarter of 2008. Round your answers to the nearest dollar.
2. Prepare the journal entry that Tasty's should make to record the employer's portion of payroll taxes for the third quarter.

Exercise 9-11 *Compensated Absences* **LO 2**

Wonder Inc. has a monthly payroll of $72,000 for its 24 employees. In addition to their salary, employees earn one day of vacation and one sick day for each month that they work. There are 20 workdays in a month.

Required

1. Prepare the end-of-the-month journal entry, if necessary, to record (a) vacation benefits and (b) sick days.

2. From the owner's perspective, should the company offer the employees vacation and sick pay that accumulates year to year?

Exercise 9-12 *Warranties* **LO 3**

Clean Corporation manufactures and sells dishwashers. Clean provides all customers with a two-year warranty guaranteeing to repair, free of charge, any defects reported during this time period. During the year, it sold 100,000 dishwashers, for $325 each. Analysis of past warranty records indicates that 12% of all sales will be returned for repair within the warranty period. Clean expects to incur expenditures of $14 to repair each dishwasher. The account Estimated Liability for Warranties had a balance of $120,000 on January 1. Clean incurred $150,000 in actual expenditures during the year.

Required

Prepare all journal entries necessary to record the events related to the warranty transactions during the year. Determine the adjusted ending balance in the Estimated Liability for Warranties account.

Exercise 9-13 *Impact of Transaction Involving Current Liabilities of Statement of Cash Flows* **LO 4**

From the following list, identify whether the change in the account balance during the year would be reported as an operating (O), investing (I), or financing (F) activity, or not separately reported on the statement of cash flows (N). Assume that indirect method is used to determine the cash flows from operating activities.

_____ Accounts payable
_____ Current portion of long-term debt
_____ Notes payable
_____ Other accrued liabilities
_____ Salaries and wages payable
_____ Taxes payable

Exercise 9-14 *Compare Alternatives (Appendix)* **LO 5**

Jane Bauer has won the lottery and has four options for receiving her winnings:

1. Receive $100,000 at the beginning of the current year
2. Receive $108,000 at the end of the year
3. Receive $20,000 at the end of each year for 8 years
4. Receive $10,000 at the end of each year for 30 years

Jane can invest her winnings at an interest rate of 8% compounded annually at a major bank. Which of the payment options should Jane choose?

Exercise 9-15 *Two Situations (Appendix)* **LO 5**

The following situations involve the application of the time value of money concepts.

1. Sampson Company just purchased a piece of equipment with a value of $53,300. Sampson financed this purchase with a loan from the bank and must make annual loan payments of $13,000 at the end of each year for the next five years. Interest is compounded annually on the loan. What is the interest rate on the bank loan?

2. Simon Company needs to accumulate $200,000 to repay bonds due in six years. Simon estimates it can save $12,000 at the end of each semiannual period at a local bank offering an annual interest rate of 8% compounded semiannually. Will Simon have enough money saved at the end of six years to repay the bonds?

Exercise 9-16 *Comprehensive Time Value of Money (Appendix)* LO 5

Mary Everest is 30 and plans to retire at age 55. She is analyzing alternative plans regarding saving, investment, and pension. She expects to live to 80 years of age.

1. If she invests $500 a month in an account that yields 6%, how much will she have upon her retirement at 55?

2. Instead of investing monthly, if she invests $6,000 at the end of each year in an account that yields 6%, how much will she have upon her retirement at 55?

3. If she invests $500 a month in an account that yields 12%, how much will she have upon her retirement at 55?

4. If she invests $500 a month in an account that yields 6% until she retires at 55, how much pension can she draw from the account each month after her retirement so that she will just use up all her savings at the age of 80?

5. If she wishes to draw $3,000 a month in her retirement until she is 80, how much must she invest each month during her employment years, assuming a 6% yield rate?

(Note: Assume all deposits and withdrawals are made at end of the period.)

Problems

Problem 9-1 *Notes and Interest* LO 1

Glencoe Inc. operates with a June 30 year-end. During 2008, the following transactions occurred:

a. January 1: Signed a one-year, 10% loan for $25,000. Interest and principal are to be paid at maturity.

b. January 10: Signed a line of credit with the Local Bank to establish a $400,000 line of credit. Interest of 9% will be charged on all borrowed funds.

c. February 1: Issued a $20,000 non-interest-bearing, six-month note to pay for a new machine. Interest on the note, at 12%, was deducted in advance.

d. March 1: Borrowed $150,000 on the line of credit.

e. June 1: Repaid $100,000 on the line of credit, plus accrued interest.

f. June 30: Made all necessary adjusting entries.

g. August 1: Repaid the non-interest-bearing note.

h. September 1: Borrowed $200,000 on the line of credit.

i. November 1: Issued a three-month, 8%, $12,000 note in payment of an overdue open account.

j. December 31: Repaid the one-year loan (from item **a**) plus accrued interest.

Required

1. Record all journal entries necessary to report these transactions.

2. As of December 31, which notes are outstanding, and how much interest is due on each?

Problem 9-2 *Payroll Entries* LO 2

Vivian Company has calculated the gross wages of all employees for the month of August to be $210,000. The following amounts have been withheld from the employees' paycheques:

Income Tax	$42,500
CPP	16,000
EI	5,600
Heart Fund Contributions	5,800
Union Dues	3,150

Vivian's EI rate is 3%, and its portion of CPP matches the employees' share.

Required

1. Prepare the journal entry to record the payroll as an amount payable to employees.

2. Prepare the journal entry that would be recorded to pay the employees.

3. Prepare the journal entry to record the employer's payroll costs.

4. Prepare the journal entry to remit the withholdings.

Problem 9-3 *Compensated Absences* LO 2

Hetzel Inc. pays its employees every Friday. For every four weeks that employees work, they earn one vacation day. For every six weeks that they work without calling in sick, they earn one sick day. If employees quit or retire, they can receive a lump-sum payment for their unused vacation days and unused sick days.

Required

Write a short memo to the bookkeeper to explain how and when he should report vacation and sick days. Explain how the matching principle applies and why you believe that the timing you recommend is appropriate.

Problem 9-4 *Warranties* LO 3

Clearview Company manufactures and sells high-quality television sets. The most popular line sells for $1,000 each and is accompanied by a three-year warranty to repair, free of charge, any defective unit. Average costs to repair each defective unit will be $90 for replacement parts and $60 for labour. Clearview estimates that warranty costs of $12,600 will be incurred during 2008. The company actually sold 600 television sets and incurred replacement part costs of $3,600 and labour costs of $5,400 during the year. The adjusted 2008 ending balance in the Estimated Liability for Warranties account is $10,200.

Required

1. How many defective units from this year's sales does Clearview Company estimate will be returned for repair?

2. What percentage of sales does Clearview Company estimate will be returned for repair?

3. What steps should Clearview take if actual warranty costs incurred during 2009 are significantly higher than the estimated liability recorded at the end of 2008?

Problem 9-5 *Warranties* LO 3

Bombeck Company sells a product for $1,500. When the customer buys it, Bombeck provides a one-year warranty. Bombeck sold 120 products during 2008. Based on analysis of past warranty records, Bombeck estimates that repairs will average 3% of total sales.

Required

1. Prepare the journal entry to record the estimated liability.

2. Assume that products under warranty must be repaired during 2008 using repair parts from inventory costing $4,950. Prepare the journal entry to record the repair of products.

Problem 9-6 *Contingent Liabilities* LO 3

Listed below are several items for which the outcome of events is unknown at year-end.

a. A company offers a two-year warranty on sales of new computers. It believes that 4% of the computers will require repairs.

b. The company is involved in a trademark infringement suit. The company's legal experts believe an award of $500,000 in the company's favour will be made.

c. A company is involved in an environmental clean-up lawsuit. The company's legal counsel believes it is possible the outcome will be unfavourable but has not been able to estimate the costs of the possible loss.

d. A soap manufacturer has included a coupon offer in the Sunday newspaper supplements. The manufacturer estimates that 25% of the 50-cent coupons will be redeemed.

e. A company has been sued by the federal government for price fixing. The company's legal counsel believes there will be an unfavourable verdict and has made an estimate of the probable loss.

Required

1. Identify which of the items **a** through **e** should be recorded at year-end.

2. Identify which of the items **a** through **e** should not be recorded but should be disclosed in the year-end financial statements.

Problem 9-7 *Effects of Current Liabilities on a Statement of Cash Flows* LO 4

The following items are classified as current liabilities on Lee Corporation's consolidated balance sheet at June 30, 2008, and July 1, 2007 (in millions):

	2008	2007
Notes payable	$ 101	$2,054
Accounts payable	1,505	1,762
Accrued liabilities:		
Payroll and employee benefits	812	928
Advertising and promotions	343	421
Taxes other than payroll and income	84	104
Income taxes	423	55
Other	1,210	1,054
Current maturities of long-term debt	480	381

Required

1. Lee uses the indirect method to prepare its statement of cash flows. Prepare the Operating Activities section of the cash flow statement, which indicates how each item will be reflected as an adjustment to net income. If you did not include any of the items set forth above, explain why not.

2. How would you decide whether Lee has the ability to pay these liabilities as they become due?

Problem 9-8 *Effects of Changes in Current Assets and Liabilities on a Statement of Cash Flows* LO 4

The following items, listed in alphabetical order, are included in the Current Assets and Current Liabilities categories on the consolidated balance sheet of Tommy Corporation at March 31, 2008 and 2007:

	2008	2007
Accounts payable	$ 4,828	$ 3,911
Accounts receivable	29,677	27,639
Accrued expenses and other liabilities	21,455	29,179
Short-term borrowings	–0–	65
Inventories	25,681	27,349
Other current assets	11,294	12,963

Required

1. Tommy uses the indirect method to prepare its statement of cash flows. Prepare the Operating Activities section of the cash flow statement, which indicates how each item will be reflected as an adjustment to net income.

2. If you did not include any of the items set forth above in your answer to requirement 1, explain how these items would be reported on the statement of cash flows.

Problem 9-9 *Evaluation of Purchase Options (Appendix)* LO 5

Stanley Inc. is evaluating its options in financing the acquisition of a new presser. Stanley's interest rate is 6%. The dealer offers the following three alternatives:

a. Cash purchase price of $50,000.

b. $30,000 down payment and five annual payments of $5,000 each, to be made at the end of each of the next five years.

c. Delayed payment of $70,000 to be made at the end of the fifth year.

Required

1. Which option would you recommend Stanley take and why?
2. If Stanley's interest rate is 8%, would your answer to Requirement 1 change? How and why?

Multi-Concept Problems

Problem 9-10 *Current and Contingent Liabilities* LO 1, 3

Sun Source Inc. is a new company specializing in solar energy-powered lighting systems. The company offers two types of products: standard systems and custom-made systems. Sun Source's fiscal year ends December 31. It began selling its products in 2008 and had the following liability-related transactions:

a. Sun Source signed a 1-year, $20,000, 6% promissory note on April 1, 2008. The interest is due on the note's maturity date.

b. It purchased $50,000 of materials on credit. The transaction is subjected to 13% HST.

c. It sold standard systems for $80,000 cash. The 13% HST is applicable to the sales.

d. It received a $10,000 deposit from a customer to manufacture custom-made lighting systems for the 50 condominiums the customer is building. Lighting systems for 20 condominiums have been delivered by the end of the year. The price of each custom-made system is $450 and the 13% HST is applicable.

e. Sun Source offers a one-year limited warranty for manufacturing defects in its products. It estimated that the warranty cost should be about 2% of its sales revenue. Sales in Items **c** and **d** are the only sales of 2008.

f. Sun Source processed 150 returns and replacements in 2008 under its limited one-year warranty policy. The total cost of these replacements is $750.

g. Sun Source reported $22,250 income before tax and uses a 40% effective income tax rate to accrue its tax expense at the end of each year.

Required

1. Prepare journal entries to record the above transactions and any adjustments necessary at the end of 2008.
2. Indicate how the liabilities resulting from the above transaction should be reported in the balance sheet for Sun Source as of December 31, 2008.
3. Prepare journal entries to record the following follow-up transactions:
   a. The HST was remitted January 15, 2009.
   b. The remaining custom-made systems were delivered at the end of February 2009.
   c. The promissory note matured, and the interest and the principal were paid on March 31, 2009.
   d. 2008 income taxes were paid on March 31, 2009.

Alternate Problems

Problem 9-1A *Notes and Interest* LO 1

McLaughlin Inc. operates with a June 30 year-end. During 2008, the following transactions occurred:

a. January 1: Signed a one-year, 10% loan for $35,000. Interest and principal are to be paid at maturity.

b. January 10: Signed a line of credit with the Local Bank to establish a $560,000 line of credit. Interest of 9% will be charged on all borrowed funds.

c. February 1: Issued a $28,000 non-interest-bearing, six-month note to pay for a new machine. Discount on the note, at 12%, was deducted in advance.

d. March 1: Borrowed $210,000 on the line of credit.

e. June 1: Repaid $140,000 on the line of credit, plus accrued interest.

f. June 30: Made all necessary adjusting entries.

g. August 1: Repaid the non-interest-bearing note.

h. September 1: Borrowed $280,000 on the line of credit.

i. November 1: Issued a three-month, 8%, $16,800 note in payment of an overdue open account.

j. December 31: Repaid the one-year loan (from Item **a**) plus accrued interest.

Required

1. Record all journal entries necessary to report these transactions.
2. As of December 31, what are the accrued interests on the outstanding notes and on the balance on the line of credit?

Problem 9-2A *Payroll Entries* LO 2

Calvin Company has calculated the gross wages of all employees for the month of August to be $336,000. The following amounts have been withheld from the employees' paycheques:

Income Tax	$68,000
CPP	25,600
EI	8,736
Heart Fund Contributions	9,280
Union Dues	5,040

Calvin's EI tax rate is 3%, and its portion of CPP matches the employees' share.

Required

1. Prepare the journal entry to record the payroll as an amount payable to employees.
2. Prepare the journal entry that would be recorded to pay the employees.
3. Prepare the journal entry to record the employer's payroll costs.
4. Prepare the journal entry to remit the withholdings, including CPP and EI.

Problem 9-3A *Compensated Absences* LO 2

Assume that you are the accountant for a large company with several divisions. The manager of Division B has contacted you with a concern. During 2008, several employees retired from Division B. The company's policy is that employees can be paid for days of sick leave accrued at the time they retire. Payment occurs in the year following retirement. The manager has been told by corporate headquarters that she cannot replace the employees in 2009 because the payment of the accrued sick pay will be deducted from Division B's budget in that year.

Required

In a memo to the manager of Division B, explain the proper accounting for accrued sick pay. Do you think that the policies of corporate headquarters should be revised?

Problem 9-4A *Warranties* LO 3

Sound Company manufactures and sells high-quality stereo sets. The most popular line sells for $2,000 each and is accompanied by a three-year warranty to repair, free of charge, any defective unit. Average costs to repair each defective unit will be $180 for replacement parts and $120 for labour. Sound estimates that warranty costs of $25,200 will be incurred during 2008. The company actually sold 600 sets and incurred replacement part costs of $7,200 and labour costs of $10,800 during the year. The adjusted 2008 ending balance in the Estimated Liability for Warranties account is $20,400.

Required

1. How many defective units from this year's sales does Sound Company estimate will be returned for repair?
2. What percent of sales does Sound Company estimate will be returned for repair?

Problem 9-5A *Warranties* LO 3

Beck Company sells a product for $3,200. When the customer buys it, Beck provides a one-year warranty. Beck sold 120 products during 2008. Based on analysis of past warranty records, Beck estimates that repairs will average 4% of total sales.

Required

1. Prepare the journal entry to record the estimated liability.
2. Assume that during 2008, products under warranty must be repaired using repair parts from inventory costing $10,200. Prepare the journal entry to record the repair of products.
3. Assume that the balance of the Estimated Liability for Warranties account as of the beginning of 2008 was $1,100. Calculate the balance of the account as of the end of 2008.

Problem 9-6A *Contingent Liabilities* LO 3

Listed below and on the following page are several events for which the outcome is unknown at year-end.

a. A company has been sued by the federal government for price fixing. The company's legal counsel believes there will be an unfavorable verdict and has made an estimate of the probable loss.

(continued)

b. A company is involved in an environmental clean-up lawsuit. The company's legal counsel believes it is possible the outcome will be unfavourable but has not been able to estimate the cost of the possible loss.

c. A company is involved in a trademark infringement suit. A company's legal experts believe an award of $750,000 in the company's favour will be made.

d. A company offers a three-year warranty on sales of new computers. It believes that 6% of the computers will require repairs.

e. A snack food manufacturer has included a coupon offer in the Sunday newspaper supplements. The manufacturer estimates that 30% of the 40-cent coupons will be redeemed.

Required

1. Identify which of the items **a** through **e** should be recorded at year-end.

2. Identify which of the items **a** through **e** should not be recorded but should be disclosed on the year-end financial statements.

Problem 9-7A *Effects of Current Liabilities on A Statement of Cash Flows* **LO 4**

The following items are classified as current liabilities on Beeline Company's consolidated statements of financial condition (or balance sheet) at December 31 (in millions):

	2008	2007
Accounts payable and other liabilities	$6,936	$6,156
Advances from customers in excess of related costs	2,153	1,758
Income taxes payable	454	933
Short-term debt and current portion of long-term debt	699	616

Required

1. Beeline uses the indirect method to prepare its statement of cash flows. Prepare the Operating Activities section of the cash flow statement, which indicates how each item will be reflected as an adjustment to net income. If you did not include any of the items set forth above, explain why not.

2. How would you decide whether Beeline has the ability to pay these liabilities as they become due?

Problem 9-8A *Effects of Changes in Current Assets and Liabilities on A Statement of Cash Flows* **LO 4**

The following items, listed in alphabetical order, are included in the Current Assets and Current Liabilities categories on the consolidated balance sheet of Nice Inc. at May 31, 2008 and 2007:

	2008	2007
Accounts payable	$ 144	$ 181
Accounts receivable	540	523
Accrued liabilities	157	207
Current portion of long-term debt	2	17
Income taxes payable	7	–0–
Inventories	475	482
Notes payable	285	308
Prepaid expenses	54	72
Deferred income tax	38	37

Required

1. Nice uses the indirect method to prepare its statement of cash flows. Prepare the Operating Activities section of the cash flow statement, which indicates how each item will be reflected as an adjustment to net income.

2. If you did not include any of the items set forth above in your answer to requirement **1**, explain how these items would be reported on the statement of cash flows.

Problem 9-9A *Evaluation of Purchase Options (Appendix)* **LO 5**

Morgan Inc. is evaluating its options in financing the acquisition of a new delivery truck. Morgan's interest rate is 6%. The dealer offers the following three alternatives:

a. Cash purchase price of $25,000.
b. $10,000 down payment and 10 annual payments of $2,000 each, to be made at the end of each of the next 10 years.
c. No down payment, five annual payments of $6,000, to be made at the end of each of the next five years.

Required

1. Which option would you recommend Morgan take and why?
2. If Morgan's interest rate is 5%, would your answer to Requirement 1 change? How and why?

Alternate Multi-Concept Problem

Problem 9-10A *Current and Contingent Liabilities* **LO 1, 3**

Peddler's Pal Inc. is a new company specializing in manufacturing bicycle trailers. The company offers two types of products: standard and custom-made. Peddler's Pal's fiscal year ends December 31. It began selling its products in 2008 and had the following liability-related transactions:

a. Peddler's Pal signed a 1-year, $30,000, 9% note on April 1, 2008. The interest is due on the note's maturity date.
b. It purchased $60,000 of materials on credit. The transaction is subjected to 13% HST.
c. It sold standard products for $125,000 cash. The 13% HST is applicable to the sales.
d. It received a $6,000 deposit from a customer, a cycling club, to manufacture 30 custom-made trailers for the club's cross-country expedition. Ten trailers have been delivered by the end of the year. The price of each custom-made trailer is $500, and the 13% HST is applicable.
e. Peddler's Pal offers a one-year limited warranty for manufacturing defects in its products. It estimated that the warranty cost should be about 2% of its sales revenue.
f. Peddler's Pal spent $250 in parts and $1,000 in labour serving warranty claims in 2008 under its limited one-year warranty policy.
g. Peddler's Pal reported $32,500 income before tax and uses a 30% effective income tax rate to accrue its income tax expense at the end of each year.

Required

1. Prepare journal entries to record the above transactions and any adjustments necessary at the end of 2008.
2. Prepare the partial liability section of the balance sheet for Peddler's Pal as of December 31, 2008.
3. Prepare journal entries to record the follow-up transactions:
   a. The HST was remitted January 15, 2009.
   b. The remaining custom-made trailers were delivered at the end of February 2009.
   c. The note matured, and the interest and the principal were paid on March 31, 2009.
   d. 2008 income taxes were paid on March 31, 2009.

Cases

Reading and Interpreting Financial Statements

Case 9-1 *CN's Current Liabilities* **LO 1**

Refer to **CN**'s 2007 annual report. Using the company balance sheet and accompanying notes, write a response to the following questions.

http://www.cn.ca

Required

1. Determine the company's current ratio for fiscal years 2007 and 2006. What do the ratios indicate about the liquidity of the company?

(continued)

2. Explain why personal injury claims are current liabilities in the amount of $102 million when Footnote 18 indicates that the total expected claims in Canada and the United States are $446 million.

3. Explain why current liabilities show a workforce reduction provision of $19 million when the footnote states that $72 million is the liability.

Case 9-2 *RIM's Contingent Liability* LO 3

Footnote 13 of RIM's balance sheet describes the details of its product warranty from 2005 to 2008. Footnote 17(c) provides information about how RIM discloses these warranties on its balance sheet and cash flow statement.

Required

1. Describe the practice used by RIM to determine its treatment of product warranty.

2. Determine the amount of warranty expense, liability, and warranty cash flow for the fiscal year 2008.

3. What is the adjustment for a change in estimate in the amount of $4,219 million (US) noted in Footnote 13 for 2006? Where would RIM present this amount in its financial statements?

Case 9-3 *CN's Cash Flow Statement* LO 4

Refer to CN's statement of cash flows in its 2007 annual report to answer the following questions.

Required

1. The net cash provided by operating activities decreased significantly in fiscal year 2007. What were the primary reasons for the decrease?

2. In fiscal year 2007, accounts receivable appears as a positive amount on the cash flow statement while accounts payable and accrued charges are negative. Explain whether these accounts actually increased or decreased. What do the changes in these accounts indicate about the company's liquidity and its future performance?

Case 9-4 *Comparing Two Companies in the Same Industry: CN and CP* LO 4

http://www.cpr.ca Refer to the 2007 cash flow statements of **CP** and of CN in Appendixes A and B at the end of the text.

Required

1. CP's net cash provided by operating activities increased significantly in fiscal year 2007. What were the primary reasons for the increase?

2. Compare the Operating Activities categories of both companies' cash flow statements. Which company was able to generate more cash from its operating activities in 2007 than 2006? What appears to be the top three reasons for the difference?

3. For each company, look at the following line items listed in the operating activities section of its 2007 cash flow statement:
   - CP: accounts receivable, materials and supplies, and accounts payable
   - CN: accounts receivable, material and supplies, and accounts payable and accrued charges.

   Did cash flow increase or decrease for each of these line items? What do the changes in these accounts indicate about each company's liquidity and its future performance?

Making Financial Decisions

Case 9-5 *Current Ratio Loan Provision* LO 1

Assume that you are the controller of a small, growing sporting goods company. The prospects for your firm in the future are quite good, but like most other firms, it has been experiencing some cash flow difficulties because all available funds have been used to purchase inventory and finance start-up costs associated with a new business. At the beginning of the current year, your local bank advanced a loan to your company. Included in the loan is the following provision:

> The company is obligated to make interest payments each month for the next five years. Principal is due and must be paid at the end of Year 5. The company is further obligated to maintain a current assets to current liabilities ratio of 2 to 1 as indicated on quarterly statements to be submitted to the bank. If the company fails to meet any loan provisions, all amounts of interest and principal are due immediately upon notification by the bank.

You, as controller, have just gathered the following information as of the end of the first month of the current quarter:

Current liabilities:	
Accounts payable	$400,000
Taxes payable	100,000
Accrued expenses	50,000
Total current liabilities	$550,000

You are concerned about the loan provision that requires a 2:1 ratio of current assets to current liabilities.

Required

1. Indicate what actions could be taken during the next two months to meet the loan provision. Which of the available actions should be recommended?

2. What is the meaning of the term *window-dressing* financial statements? What are the long-run implications of actions taken to window-dress financial statements?

Case 9-6 *Alternative Payment Options (Appendix)* LO 5

Kathy Clark owns a small company that makes ice machines for restaurants and food-service facilities. Kathy knows a lot about producing ice machines but is less familiar with the best terms to extend to her customers. One customer is opening a new business and has asked Kathy to consider any of the following options to pay for his new $20,000 ice machine.

■ Option 1: 10% down, the remainder paid at the end of the year plus 8% simple interest.

■ Option 2: 10% down, the remainder paid at the end of the year plus 8% interest, compounded quarterly.

■ Option 3: $0 down, but $21,600 due at the end of the year.

Required

Make a recommendation to Kathy. She believes that 8% is a fair return on her money at this time. Should she accept Option 1, 2, or 3, or take the $20,000 cash at the time of the sale? Justify your recommendation with calculations. What factors, other than the actual amount of cash received from the sale, should be considered?

Accounting and Ethics: What Would You Do?

Case 9-7 *Warranty Cost Estimate* LO 3

John Walton is an accountant for ABC Auto Dealers, a large auto dealership in a metropolitan area. ABC sells both new and used cars. New cars are sold with a five-year warranty, the cost of which is carried by the manufacturer. For several years, however, ABC has offered a two-year warranty on used cars. The cost of the warranty is an expense to ABC, and John has been asked by his boss, Mr. Sawyer, to review warranty costs and recommend the amount to accrue on the year-end financial statements.

For the past several years, ABC has recorded as warranty expense 5% of used car sales. John has analyzed past repair records and found that repairs, although fluctuating somewhat from year to year, have averaged near the 5% level. John is convinced, however, that 5% is inadequate for the coming year. He bases his judgment on industry reports of increased repair costs and on the fact that several cars that were recently sold on warranty have experienced very high repair costs. John believes that the current-year repair accrual will be at least 10%. He discussed the higher expense amount with Mr. Sawyer, who is the controller of ABC.

Mr. Sawyer was not happy with John's decision concerning warranty expense. He reminded John of the need to control expenses during the recent sales downturn. He also reminded John that ABC is seeking a large loan from the bank and that the bank loan officers may not be happy with recent operating results, especially if ABC begins to accrue larger amounts for future estimated amounts such as warranties. Finally, Mr. Sawyer reminded John that most of the employees of ABC, including Mr. Sawyer, were members of the company's profit-sharing plan and would not be happy with the reduced share of profits. Mr. Sawyer thanked John for his judgment concerning warranty costs but told him that the accrual for the current year would remain at 5%.

(continued)

John left the meeting with Mr. Sawyer somewhat frustrated. He was convinced that his judgment concerning the warranty costs was correct. He knew that the owner of ABC would be visiting the office the next week and wondered whether he should discuss the matter with him personally at that time. John also had met one of the loan officers from the bank several times and considered calling her to discuss his concern about the warranty expense amount on the year-end statements.

Required

Discuss the courses of action available to John. What should John do concerning his judgment of warranty costs?

Case 9-8 *Retainer Fees As Sales* LO 3

Bunch o' Balloons markets balloon arrangements to companies who want to thank clients and employees. Bunch o' Balloons has a unique style that has put it in high demand. Consequently, Bunch o' Balloons has asked clients to establish an account. Clients are asked to pay a retainer fee equal to about three months of client purchases. The fee will be used to cover the cost of arrangements delivered and will be reevaluated at the end of each month. At the end of the current month Bunch o' Balloons has $43,900 of retainer fees in its possession. The controller is eager to show this amount as sales because "it represents certain sales for the company."

Required

Do you agree with the controller? When should the sales be reported? Why would the controller be eager to report the cash receipts as sales?

Internet Research Case

INTERNET

http://www.rim.com

Case 9-9 *RIM Reporting Contingencies* LO 3

In footnotes 12(b) and (c) to its annual report for the year ended March 1, 2008. **Research in Motion** (RIM) disclosed several legal actions against it in the United Kingdom, Europe, and the United States. In footnote 12(c) it disclosed the investigations by Ontario Securities Commission and the office of the United States Attorney of the Southern District of New York into the company's stock option-granting practices, triggered by the 2006 restatement of stock-option based compensation expenses.

Required

1. Describe how the lawsuit filed by Visto Corporation against RIM for alleging infringement of four patents is reported in 2008.

2. What developments occurred since March 1, 2008, regarding the Visto–RIM case?

3. How is the investigation by the Ontario Securities Commission and the United States Attorney Office reported in 2008?

Solutions to Key Terms Quiz

1	Current liability	**15**	Future value of a single amount (Appendix)
3	Accounts payable		
8	Notes payable	**17**	Present value of a single amount (Appendix)
4	Discount on Notes Payable		
6	Current Portion of Long-Term Debt	**5**	Annuity (Appendix)
7	Accrued liability	**16**	Future value of an annuity (Appendix)
9	Contingent liability		
11	Estimated liability	**2**	Present value of an annuity (Appendix)
12	Contingent asset		
14	Time value of money	**18**	Gross wages
10	Simple interest (Appendix)	**20**	Net pay
13	Compound interest (Appendix)	**19**	Compensated absences

CHAPTER 10

Long-Term Liabilities

PHOTOS.COM

STUDY LINKS

A Look at the Previous Chapter

Chapter 9 was concerned with current liabilities and short term liquidity. We also introduced the concept of the time value of money.

A Look at This Chapter

In this chapter we examine the use of long-term liabilities as an important source of financing a company's needs. We will

utilize the time value of money concept because it is the basis for the value of all long-term liabilities.

A Look at the Upcoming Chapter

Chapter 11 will examine the presentation of shareholders' equity, the other major category on the right-hand side of the balance sheet.

Focus on Financial Results

CN's balance sheet shows a substantial amount of debt, termed *liabilities*. Current liabilities are $1,590 million and are due within the upcoming year. The much larger portion—$4,908 million, $1,422 million, and $5,363 million—is not due within the coming year; these amounts are considered long-term liabilities. Notes 9, 10, and 15 provide some details of the deferred income taxes, other liabilities and deferred credits, and long-term debt. The nature and impact of these three items on the finances and reports of CN are of concern to investors as well as to CN's managers.

Of particular interest are those liabilities that are not reflected in the three long-term amounts shown on the balance sheet—termed *current portion of long-term debt*—because these represent debts that must be paid within the next year. Other items of concern are obligations that fall outside the GAAP rules for long-term debt—termed off-balance-sheet financing—which may be relevant to the ratios and analyses of statement users. This chapter discusses such issues in the context of bonds, leases and mortgages, deferred taxes, and pension liabilities.

CN 2007 ANNUAL REPORT			http://www.cn.ca

Consolidated Balance Sheet (Excerpt)

In millions December 31,	**2007**	2006
Liabilities and shareholders' equity		
Current Liabilities		
Accounts payable and accrued charges *(Note 8)*	$ 1,282	$ 1,823
Current portion of long-term debt *(Note 10)*	254	218
Other	54	73
	1,590	2,114
Deferred income taxes *(Note 15)*	4,908	5,215
Other liabilities and deferred credits *(Note 9)*	1,422	1,465
Long-term debt *(Note 10)*	5,363	5,386
Shareholders' equity		
Common shares *(Note 11)*	4,283	4,459
Accumulated other comprehensive loss *(Note 20)*	(31)	(44)
Retained earnings	5,925	5,409
	10,177	9,824
Total Liabilities and shareholders' equity	$ 23,460	$ 24,004

This excerpt from CN's 2007 Annual Report appears courtesy of CN. This section of the CN Annual Report appears in the Appendix of this textbook.

BALANCE SHEET PRESENTATION

LO 1 Identify the components of the long-term liability category of the balance sheet.

Long-term liability An obligation that will not be satisfied within one year or the current operating cycle.

CN

http://www.cn.ca

In general, **long-term liabilities** are obligations that will not be satisfied within one year. Essentially, all liabilities that are not classified as current liabilities are classified as long-term. We will concentrate on the long-term liabilities of bonds or notes, mortgages, leases, deferred taxes, and pension obligations. On the balance sheet, the items are listed after current liabilities. For example, the long-term debt for **CN**'s balance sheet is highlighted on the previous page and shown in detail in Exhibit 10-1. CN has acquired financing through a combination of long-term debt, share issuance, and internal growth or retained earnings. The balance sheet exhibit indicates that long-term debt is one portion of the long-term liability category of the balance sheet. But the balance sheet also reveals two other items that must be considered part of the long-term liability category: deferred (future) income taxes, and other liabilities and deferred credits. We begin by looking at a particular type of long-term debt: bonds payable. Exhibit 10-1 provides the specifics of the bonds, notes, and debentures of CN.

BONDS PAYABLE

LO 2 Determine the important impacts of bonds payable.

Characteristics of Bonds (Notes, Debentures)

A bond is a security or financial instrument that allows firms to borrow money and repay the loan over a long period of time. The bonds are sold, or *issued,* to investors who have amounts to invest and want a return on their investment. The *borrower* (issuing firm) promises to pay interest on specified dates, usually annually or semiannually. The borrower also promises to repay the principal on a specified date, the *due date* or maturity date.

Face value The principal amount of the bond as stated on the bond certificate.

A bond certificate, illustrated in Exhibit 10-2, is issued at the time of purchase and indicates the *terms* of the bond. Generally, bonds are issued in denominations of $1,000. The denomination of the bond is usually referred to as the **face value** or par value. This is the amount that the firm must pay at the maturity date of the bond.

In Exhibit 10-1, CN describes some of its long-term debt as notes or debentures. Notes and debentures are similar to bonds in that they represent combined payments of principal and interest at specified dates. Because bonds and notes are legal contracts between CN and its creditors, various titles are used to reflect the nature of the contract. Some of these titles, such as Puttable Reset Securities and income debentures, are rather unusual. So we will focus our discussion on notes and debentures, which are much more common, and which we will term *bonds* for the sake of ease of discussion.

Firms issue bonds in very large amounts, often in millions in a single issue. After bonds are issued, they may be traded on a bond exchange in the same way that shares are sold on the stock exchanges. Therefore, bonds are not always held until maturity by the initial investor but may change hands several times before their eventual due date. Because bond maturities are as long as 30 years, the "secondary" market in bonds—the market for bonds already issued—is a critical factor in a company's ability to raise money. Investors in bonds may want to sell them if interest rates paid by competing investments become more attractive or if the issuer becomes less creditworthy. Buyers of these bonds may be betting that interest rates will reverse course or that the company will get back on its feet. Trading in the secondary market does not affect the financial statements of the issuing company.

We have described the general nature of bonds, but it should not be assumed that all bonds have the same terms and features. Following are some important features that often appear in the bond certificate.

Debenture bonds Bonds that are not backed by specific collateral.

Collateral The bond certificate should indicate the *collateral* of the loan. Collateral represents the assets that back the bonds in case the issuer cannot make the interest and principal payments and must default on the loan. **Debenture bonds** are not backed by specific collateral of the issuing company. Rather, the investor must examine the general creditworthiness of the issuer. If a bond is a *secured bond,* the certificate indicates specific assets that serve as collateral in case of default.

Exhibit 10-1 Footnote 10, CN's Balance Sheet

10. Long-term debt

In millions	Maturity	U.S dollar-denominated amount	December 31,	2007	2006
Debentures and notes (A)					
Canadian National series:					
4.25% 5-year notes *(B)*	Aug. 1, 2009	$300		$ 297	$ 350
6.38% 10-year notes *(B)*	Oct. 15, 2011	400		397	466
4.40% 10-year notes *(B)*	Mar. 15, 2013	400		397	466
5.80% 10-year notes *(B)*	June 1, 2016	250		248	291
5.85% 10-year notes *(B)*	Nov. 15, 2017	250		248	–
6.80% 20-year notes *(B)*	July 15, 2018	200		198	233
7.63% 30-year debentures	May 15, 2023	150		149	175
6.90% 30-year notes *(B)*	July 15, 2028	475		471	554
7.38% 30-year debentures *(B)*	Oct. 15, 2031	200		198	233
6.25% 30-year notes *(B)*	Aug. 1, 2034	500		496	583
6.20% 30-year notes *(B)*	June 1, 2036	450		446	524
6.71% Puttable Reset Securities PURS^{SM} *(B)(C)*	July 15, 2036	250		248	291
6.38% 30-year debentures *(B)*	Nov. 15, 2037	300		297	–
Illinois Central series:					
6.98% 12-year notes	July 12, 2007	50		–	58
6.63% 10-year notes	June 9, 2008	20		20	23
5.00% 99-year income debentures	Dec. 1, 2056	7		7	9
7.70% 100-year debentures	Sept. 15, 2096	125		124	146
Wisconsin Central series:					
6.63% 10-year notes	April 15, 2008	150		149	175
				4,390	4,577
BC Rail series:					
Non-interest bearing 90-year subordinated notes *(D)*	July 14, 2094	–		842	842
Total debentures and notes				5,232	5,419
Other:					
Commercial paper *(E) (Note 7)*				122	–
Capital lease obligations and other *(F)*				1,114	1,038
Total Other				1,236	1,038
				6,468	6,457
Less:					
Current portion of long-term debt				254	218
Net unamorized discount				851	853
				1,105	1,071
				$ 5,363	$ 5,386

(continued)

Exhibit 10-1 Footnote 10, CN's Balance Sheet *(continued)*

G. Long-term debt maturities, including repurchase arrangements and capital lease repayments on debt outstanding as at December 31, 2007, for the next five years and thereafter, are as follows:

In millions

2008	$ 254
2009	409
2010	48
2011	628
2012	27
2013 and thereafter	4,251

H. The aggregate amount of debt payable in U.S. currency as at December 31, 2007 was U.S.$5,280 million (Cdn$5,234 million) and U.S.$4,636 million (Cdn$5,403 million) as at December 31, 2006.

I. The Company has U.S.$2.5 billion available under its currently effective shelf prospectus and registration statement, expiring in January 2010, providing for the issuance of debt securities in one or more offerings.

This excerpt from CN's 2007 Annual Report appears courtesy of CN. This section of the CN Annual Report appears in the Appendix of this textbook.

The term "collateral" implies that if the debt agreement is violated—in particular, if interest or principal is not paid—the collateral assets will be claimed by the bond holders as a means of payment.

Due Date The bond certificate specifies the date that the bond principal must be repaid. Normally, bonds are *term bonds,* meaning that the entire principal amount is due on a single date. Alternatively, bonds may be issued as **serial bonds,** meaning that not all of the principal is due on the same date. For example, a firm may issue serial bonds that have a portion of the principal due each year for the next 10 years. Issuing firms may prefer serial bonds because a firm does not need to accumulate the entire amount for principal repayment at one time.

Serial bonds Bonds that do not all have the same due date; a portion of the bonds comes due each time period.

Other Features Some bonds are issued as convertible or callable bonds. *Convertible bonds* can be converted into common shares at a future time. This feature allows the investor to buy a security that pays a fixed interest rate but that can be converted at a future date into an equity security (shares) if the issuing firm is growing and profitable. The conversion feature is also advantageous to the issuing firm because convertible bonds normally carry a lower rate of interest.

Callable bonds may be retired before their specified due date. *Callable* generally refers to the issuer's right to retire the bonds. If the buyer or investor has the right to retire the bonds, they are referred to as *redeemable bonds.* Usually, callable bonds stipulate the price to be paid at redemption; this price is referred to as the *redemption*

Callable bonds Bonds that may be redeemed or retired before their specified due date.

Exhibit 10-2 The Structure of Notes and Bonds

In today's environment, notes and bonds can take many forms but all will have a general legal structure similar to what follows:

On January 1, 2014, Canadian Railway Company promises to pay $5,000 to the Canadian Bank plus interest at the rate of 6% per annum, every six months beginning July 1, 2008.

Signed: Canadian Railway Company
Dated: January 15, 2008

Note the specifics of the legal agreement can be altered to suit the circumstances of the specific loan from a lender such as Canadian Bank.

price or the *reacquisition price.* The callable feature is like an insurance policy for the company. Say a bond pays 10%, but interest rates plummet to 6%. Rather than continuing to pay 10%, the company is willing to offer a slight premium over face value for the right to retire those 10% bonds so that it can borrow at 6%. Of course, the investor is invariably disappointed when the company invokes its call privilege.

As you can see, various terms and features are associated with bonds. Each firm seeks to structure the bond agreement in the manner that best meets its financial needs and will attract investors at the most favourable rates.

Bonds are a popular source of financing because of the tax advantages to the issuer when compared with the issuance of shares. Interest paid on bonds is deductible for tax purposes, but dividends paid on shares are not. This may explain why the amount of debt on many firms' balance sheets has increased in recent years. Debt became popular in the 1980s to finance *mergers,* the term applied to the purchase of one business by another, and again in recent years when interest rates reached 20-year lows. Still, investors and creditors tend to downgrade a company when the amount of debt it has on the balance sheet is deemed to be excessive.

http://www2.standardand
poors.com
http://www.dbrs.com

http://www.cpr.ca

http://www.dmerail.com

Bond rating agencies, such as **Standard & Poor's** and Canada's **Dominion Bond Rating Service** (DBRS), provide investors with ratings for various bonds and notes. For example, **CP**'s unsecured bonds, debentures, and notes were rated BBB during the fourth quarter of 2007, a drop from a BBB high, by DBRS. CN does not report its bond ratings. CP's decline is a matter of strategic importance to CP's management because it wishes to obtain an improved rating after its acquisition of the **Dakota, Minnesota, & Eastern Railroad Corporation** in October 2007 for $1,493 million (Footnote 11). BBB is viewed as adequate; however, companies with this rating are reported to be fairly susceptible to adverse changes in economic conditions. DBRS's rating system requires careful study, as do those of all such rating services. DBRS ranges its ratings from AAA, the highest quality, to D, the lowest. D indicates that the firm has missed or will miss a scheduled payment. C represents speculative debt that has a danger of default.

Issuance of Bonds

When bonds are issued, the issuing firm must recognize the incurrence of a liability in exchange for cash. If bonds are issued at their face amount, the accounting entry is straightforward. For example, assume that on April 1, a firm issues bonds with a face amount of $10,000 and receives $10,000. In this case, the asset Cash and the liability Bonds Payable are both increased by $10,000. The accounting entry is as follows:

Apr. 1	Cash	10,000	
	Bonds Payable		10,000
	To record the issuance of bonds at face value		

Assets	=	**Liabilities**	+	**Shareholders' Equity**
+10,000		+10,000		

Factors Affecting Bond Price

With bonds payable, two interest rates are always involved. The **face rate of interest** (also called the *stated rate, nominal rate, contract rate,* or *coupon rate*) is the rate specified on the bond certificate. It is the amount of interest that will be paid each interest period. For example, if $10,000 worth of bonds is issued with an 8% annual face rate of interest, then interest of $800 ($10,000 $\times$ 8% $\times$ 1 year) would be paid at the end of each annual period. Alternatively, bonds often require the payment of

Face rate of interest The rate of interest on the bond certificate.

interest semiannually. If the bonds in our example required the 8% annual face rate to be paid semiannually (at 4%), then interest of $400 ($10,000 × 8% × ½ year) would be paid each semiannual period.

The second important interest rate is the **market rate of interest** (also called the *effective rate* or *bond yield*). The market rate of interest is the rate that bondholders could obtain by investing in other bonds that are similar to the issuing firm's bonds. The issuing firm does not set the market rate of interest. That rate is determined by the bond market on the basis of many transactions for similar bonds. The market rate incorporates all of the "market's" knowledge about economic conditions and all its expectations about future conditions. Normally, issuing firms try to set a face rate that is equal to the market rate. However, because the market rate changes daily, there are almost always small differences between the face rate and the market rate at the time bonds are issued.

In addition to the number of interest payments and the maturity length of the bond, the face rate and the market rate of interest must both be known in order to calculate the issue price of a bond. The **bond issue price** equals the *present value* of the cash flows that the bond will produce. Bonds produce two types of cash flows for the investor: interest receipts and repayment of principal (face value). The interest receipts constitute an annuity of payments each interest period over the life of the bonds. The repayment of principal (face value) is a one-time receipt that occurs at the end of the term of the bonds. We must calculate the present value of the interest receipts (using Table 9-4) and the present value of the principal amount (using Table 9-2). The total of the two present-value calculations represents the issue price of the bond.

An Example   Suppose that on January 1, 2008, Discount Firm wants to issue bonds with a face value of $10,000. The face or coupon rate of interest has been set at 8%. The bonds will pay interest annually, and the principal amount is due in four years. Also suppose that the market rate of interest for other similar bonds is currently 10%. Because the market rate of interest exceeds the coupon rate, investors will not be willing to pay $10,000 but something less. We want to calculate the amount that will be obtained from the issuance of Discount Firm's bonds.

Discount's bond will produce two sets of cash flows for the investor: an annual interest payment of $800 ($10,000 × 8%) per year for four years and repayment of the principal of $10,000 at the end of the fourth year. To calculate the issue price, we must calculate the present value of the two sets of cash flows. A time diagram portrays the cash flows as follows:

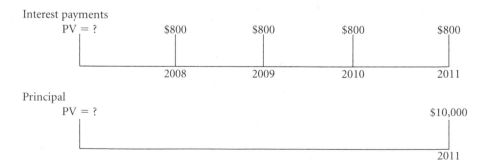

We can calculate the issue price by using the compound-interest tables found in Chapter 9, as follows:

$800 × 3.170 (factor from Table 9-4 for 4 periods, 10%)	$2,536
$10,000 × 0.683 (factor from Table 9-2 for 4 periods, 10%)	6,830
Issue price	$9,366

Study Tip

Calculating the issue price of a bond always involves a calculation of the present value of the cash flows.

Bond issue price The present value of the annuity of interest payments plus the present value of the principal.

Accounting for Your Decisions

You Rate the Bonds

One of the factors that determine the rate of interest on a bond is a rating by a rating agency such as Dominion Bond Rating Service, Standard & Poor's, or **Moody's Investors Service**. Bonds with a higher rating are considered less risky and can be issued for a lower rate of interest. You have been given an assignment to rate the bonds issued by CN. What factors would you consider in your rating?

http://www.moodys.com

> **ANSWER:** There are many factors that affect your evaluation of the riskiness of the company's bonds. One factor would be the amount of debt on CN's books, which can be found by examining the liability section of the balance sheet. It is important to relate the amount of debt to the total equity of the company; this is often done by computing the debt-to-equity ratio. Another important factor is the company's competitive position within its industry. If CN can operate profitably, it will generate cash that can be used to pay the interest and principal on the bonds.

The factors used to calculate the present value represent four periods and 10% interest. This is a key point. The issue price of a bond is always calculated using the market rate of interest. The face rate of interest determines the amount of the interest payments, but the market rate determines the present value of the payments and the present value of the principal (and therefore the issue price).

Our example of Discount Firm reveals that the bonds with a $10,000 face value amount would be issued for $9,366. The bond markets and the financial press often state the issue price as a percentage of the face amount. The percentage for Discount's bonds can be calculated as ($9,366/$10,000) × 100, or 93.66%.

Exhibit 10-3 illustrates how bonds are actually listed in the reporting of bond markets. The exhibit lists three bonds that had a price on a particular day. The information following the company name indicates (for example) that the face rate of interest is 6.50%, that the due date of the bonds is January 19, 2011, and that a bond investor who purchased the bonds on that day for 102.362 will receive a yield of 5.565%. These bonds are trading at a premium because the face rate (6.50%) is greater than the market rate of 5.565%. Each of the other bonds was trading at a premium as well.

Exhibit 10-3

Listing of Bonds on the Bond Market

COMPANY	COUPON %	MATURITY DATE	BID PRICE	YIELD %
Loblaw Companies	6.5	1/19/2011	102.362	5.565
Royal Bank of Canada	6.3	4/12/2011	104.243	4.768
Suncor Energy Inc.	6.7	8/22/2011	108.693	3.918

Source: National Bank Financial April 2008.

Premium or Discount on Bonds

Premium or **discount** represents the difference between the face value and the issue price of a bond. We may state the relationship as follows:

Premium = Issue Price − Face Value
Discount = Face Value − Issue Price

In other words, when issue price exceeds face value, the bonds have sold at a premium, and when the face value exceeds the issue price, the bonds have sold at a discount.

Premium The excess of the issue price over the face value of the bonds.

Discount The excess of the face value of bonds over the issue price.

We will continue with the Discount Firm example to illustrate the accounting for bonds sold at a discount. Discount Firm's bonds sold at a discount calculated as follows:

$$Discount = \$10,000 - \$9,366$$
$$= \$634$$

Discount Firm would record both the discount and the issuance of the bonds in the following journal entry:

Jan. 1	Cash	9,366	
	Discount on Bonds Payable	634	
	Bonds Payable		10,000
	To record the issuance of bonds payable		

Assets	=	Liabilities	+	Shareholders' Equity
+9,366		−634		
		+10,000		

The Discount on Bonds Payable account is shown as a contra liability on the balance sheet in conjunction with the Bonds Payable account and is a deduction from that account. If Discount Firm prepared a balance sheet immediately after the bond issuance, the following would appear in the Long-Term Liabilities category of the balance sheet:

Long-term liabilities:	
Bonds payable	$10,000
Less: Discount on bonds payable	634
	$9,366

The Discount Firm example has illustrated a situation in which the market rate of a bond issue is higher than the face rate. Now we will examine the opposite situation, when the face rate exceeds the market rate. Again, we are interested in calculating the issue price of the bonds.

Issuing at a Premium   Suppose that on January 1, 2008, Premium Firm wants to issue the same bonds as in the previous example: $10,000 face value bonds, with an 8% face rate of interest and with interest paid annually each year for four years. Assume, however, that the market rate of interest is 6% for similar bonds. The issue price is calculated as the present value of the annuity of interest payments plus the present value of the principal at the market rate of interest. The calculations are as follows:

$800 × 3.465 (factor from Table 9-4 for 4 periods, 6%)	$ 2,772
$10,000 × 0.792 (factor from Table 9-2 for 4 periods, 6%)	7,920
Issue price	$ 10,692

We have calculated that the bonds would be issued for $10,692. Because the bonds would be issued at an amount that is higher than the face value amount, they would be issued at a premium. The amount of the premium is calculated as follows:

$$Premium = \$10,692 - \$10,000$$
$$= \$692$$

The premium is recorded at the time of bond issuance in the following entry:

Jan. 1	Cash	10,692	
	Bonds Payable		10,000
	Premium on Bonds Payable		692
	To record the issuance of bonds payable		

Assets	=	Liabilities	+	Shareholders' Equity
+10,692		+10,000		
		+692		

The account Premium on Bonds Payable is an addition to the Bonds Payable account. If Premium Firm presented a balance sheet immediately after the bond issuance, the Long-Term Liabilities category of the balance sheet would appear as follows:

Long-term liabilities:	
Bonds payable	$10,000
Plus: Premium on bonds payable	692
	$10,692

> **Study Tip**
>
> When interest rates increase, present value decreases. This is called an *inverse relationship*.

You should learn two important points from the Discount Firm and Premium Firm examples. First, you should be able to determine whether a bond will sell at a premium or discount by the relationship that exists between the face rate and the market rate of interest. *Premium* and *discount* do not mean "good" and "bad." Premium or discount arises solely because of the difference that exists between the face rate and the market rate of interest for a bond issue. The same relationship always exists, so that the following statements hold true:

If Market Rate = Face Rate, then bonds are issued at face value amount.
If Market Rate > Face Rate, then bonds are issued at a discount.
If Market Rate < Face Rate, then bonds are issued at a premium.

The examples also illustrate a second important point. The relationship between interest rates and bond prices is always inverse. To understand the term *inverse relationship,* refer to the Discount Firm and Premium Firm examples. The bonds of the two firms are identical in all respects except for the market rate of interest. When the market rate was 10%, the bond issue price was $9,366 (the Discount Firm example). When the market rate was 6%, the bond issue price increased to $10,692 (the Premium Firm example). The examples illustrate that as interest rates decrease, prices on the bond markets increase and that as interest rates increase, bond prices decrease.

Many investors in the stock market perceive that they are taking a great deal of risk with their capital. In truth, bond investors are taking substantial risks too. The most obvious risk is that the company will fail and not be able to pay its debts. But another risk is that interest rates on comparable investments will rise. Interest rate risk can have a devastating impact on the current market value of bonds. One way to minimize interest rate risk is to hold the bond to maturity, at which point the company must pay the face amount.

A review of the financial press does not reveal market quotes for CN's long-term debt. This implies that there is little if any trading in CN's debt at the date reviewed. This situation can occur if the debt has been placed with institutional investors, such as banks or pension plans, that are not interested in trading the debt. Footnote 19 of CN's annual report states that the fair value of the company's long-term debt plus its current portion is $5,850 million. The carrying value is $5,617 million, which suggests that the market rate of interest demanded for debt such as CN's has declined, the result being an increase in current market value above the amortized historical amount shown on the balance sheet.

Bond Amortization

Purpose of Amortization The amount of interest expense that should be reflected on a firm's income statement for bonds payable is the true, or effective, interest. The effective interest should reflect the face rate of interest as well as interest that results from issuing the bond at a premium or discount. To reflect that interest component, the amount initially recorded in the Premium on Bonds Payable or the Discount on Bonds Payable account must be amortized or spread over the life of the bond.

Amortization refers to the process of transferring an amount from the discount or premium account to interest expense each time period to adjust interest expense. One commonly used method of amortization is the effective interest method. We will illustrate how to amortize a discount amount and then how to amortize a premium amount.

To illustrate amortization of a discount, we need to return to our Discount Firm example introduced earlier. We have seen that the issue price of the bond could be calculated as $9,366, resulting in a contra-liability (debit) balance of $634 in the Discount on Bonds Payable account (see the entry on page 468). But what does the initial balance of the Discount account really represent? The discount should be thought of as additional interest that Discount Firm must pay over and above the 8% face rate. Remember that Discount received only $9,366 but must repay the full principal of $10,000 at the bond due date. For that reason, the $634 discount is an additional interest cost that must be reflected as interest expense. It is reflected as interest expense by the process of amortization. In other words, interest expense is made up of two components: cash interest and amortization. We will now consider how to amortize premium or discount.

Effective interest method of amortization The process of transferring a portion of the premium or discount to interest expense; this method results in a constant effective interest rate.

Carrying value The face value of a bond plus the amount of unamortized premium or minus the amount of unamortized discount.

Effective Interest Method: Impact on Expense The **effective interest method of amortization** amortizes discount or premium in a manner that produces a constant effective interest rate from period to period. The *dollar amount* of interest expense will vary from period to period, but the rate of interest will be constant. This interest rate is referred to as the *effective interest rate* and is equal to the market rate of interest at the time the bonds are issued.

To illustrate this point, we introduce two new terms. The **carrying value** of bonds is represented by the following:

Carrying Value = Face Value − Unamortized Discount

For example, the carrying value of the bonds for our Discount Firm example, as of the date of issuance of January 1, 2008, could be calculated as follows:

$$\$10,000 - \$634 = \$9,366$$

In those situations in which there is a premium instead of a discount, carrying value is represented by the following:

Carrying Value = Face Value + Unamortized Premium

For example, the carrying value of the bonds for our Premium Firm example, as of the date of issuance of January 1, 2008, could be calculated as follows:

$$\$10,000 + \$692 = \$10,692$$

The second term has been suggested earlier. The *effective rate of interest* is represented by the following:

Effective Rate = Annual Interest Expense/Carrying Value

Effective Interest Method: An Example The amortization table in Exhibit 10-4 illustrates effective interest amortization of the bond discount for our Discount Firm example.

As illustrated in Exhibit 10-4, the effective interest method of amortization is based on several important concepts. The relationships can be stated in equation form as follows:

Cash Interest (in Column 1)	= Bond Face Value × Face Rate
Interest Expense (in Column 2)	= Carrying Value × Effective Rate
Discount Amortized (in Column 3)	= Interest Expense − Cash Interest

Exhibit 10-4

Discount Amortization: Effective Interest Method of Amortization

DATE	COLUMN 1 CASH INTEREST	COLUMN 2 INTEREST EXPENSE	COLUMN 3 DISCOUNT AMORTIZED	COLUMN 4 CARRYING VALUE
	8%	10%	Col. 2 − Col. 1	
1/1/2008	—	—	—	$ 9,366
12/31/2008	$800	$937	$137	9,503
12/31/2009	800	950	150	9,653
12/31/2010	800	965	165	9,818
12/31/2011	800	982	182	10,000

The first column of the exhibit indicates that the cash interest to be paid is $800 ($10,000 × 8%). The second column indicates the annual interest expense at the effective rate of interest (market rate at the time of issuance). This is a constant rate of interest (10% in our example) and is calculated by multiplying the carrying value *as of the beginning of the period* by the market rate of interest. In 2008, the interest expense is $937 ($9,366 × 10%). Note that the amount of interest expense changes each year because the carrying value changes as discount is amortized. The amount of discount amortized each year in Column 3 is the difference between the cash interest in Column 1 and the interest expense in Column 2. Again, note that the amount of discount amortized changes in each of the four years. Finally, the carrying value in Column 4 is the previous year's carrying value plus the discount amortized in Column 3. When bonds are issued at a discount, the carrying value starts at an amount less than face value and increases each period until it reaches the face value amount.

The amortization table in Exhibit 10-4 is the basis for the accounting entries that must be recorded. Discount Firm may record two entries for each period. The first entry at the end of 2008 is recorded to reflect the cash interest payment:

Dec. 31	Interest Expense	800	
	Cash		800
	To record annual interest payment on bonds payable		

Assets	**=**	**Liabilities**	**+**	**Shareholders' Equity**
−800				−800

The second entry is recorded to amortize a portion of the discount and to reflect that amount as an adjustment of interest expense:

Dec. 31	Interest Expense	137	
	Discount on Bonds Payable		137
	To amortize annual portion of discount on bonds payable		

Assets	**=**	**Liabilities**	**+**	**Shareholders' Equity**
		+137		−137

Instead of making two entries, firms often make one entry that combines the two. Thus, the entry for 2008 could also be recorded in the following manner:

Dec. 31	Interest Expense	937	
	Cash		800
	Discount on Bonds Payable		137
	To record annual interest payment and to amortize annual portion of discount on bonds payable		

Assets	**=**	**Liabilities**	**+**	**Shareholders' Equity**
−800		+137		−937

The T accounts of the issuing firm as of December 31, 2008, would appear as follows:

BONDS PAYABLE		
	10,000	1/1/08

DISCOUNT ON BONDS PAYABLE			
1/1/08	634		
		137	12/31/08
Bal.	497		

INTEREST EXPENSE		
12/31/08	800	
12/31/08	137	
Bal.	937	

The balance of the Discount on Bonds Payable account as of December 31, 2008, would be calculated as follows:

Beginning balance, January 1, 2008	$634
Less: Amount amortized	137
Ending balance, December 31, 2008	$497

The December 31, 2008, balance represents the amount *unamortized,* or the amount that will be amortized in future time periods. On the balance sheet presented as of December 31, 2008, the unamortized portion of the discount appears as the balance of the Discount on Bonds Payable account as follows:

Long-term liabilities	
Bonds payable	$10,000
Less: Discount on bonds payable	497
	$ 9,503

The process of amortization would continue for four years, until the balance of the Discount on Bonds Payable account has been reduced to zero. By the end of 2011, all of the balance of the Discount on Bonds Payable account will have been transferred to the Interest Expense account and represents an increase in interest expense each period.

The amortization of a premium has an impact opposite that of the amortization of a discount. We will use our Premium Firm example to illustrate. Recall that on January 1, 2008, Premium Firm issued $10,000 face value bonds with a face rate of interest of 8%. At the time the bonds were issued, the market rate was 6%, resulting in an issue price of $10,692 and a credit balance in the Premium on Bonds Payable account of $692.

The amortization table in Exhibit 10-5 illustrates effective interest amortization of the bond premium for Premium Firm. As the exhibit illustrates, effective interest amortization of a premium is based on the same concepts as amortization of a discount. The following relationships still hold true:

Cash Interest (in Column 1) = Bond Face Value × Face Rate
Interest Expense (in Column 2) = Carrying Value × Effective Rate

DATE	COLUMN 1 CASH INTEREST	COLUMN 2 INTEREST EXPENSE	COLUMN 3 PREMIUM AMORTIZED	COLUMN 4 CARRYING VALUE
	8%	6%	Col. 1 − Col. 2	
1/1/2008	—	—	—	$10,692
12/31/2008	$800	$642	$158	10,534
12/31/2009	800	632	168	10,366
12/31/2010	800	622	178	10,188
12/31/2011	800	612	188	10,000

The first column of the exhibit indicates that the cash interest to be paid is $800 ($10,000 × 8%). The second column indicates the annual interest expense at the effective rate. In 2008 the interest expense is $642 ($10,692 × 6%). Note, however, two differences between Exhibit 10-4 and Exhibit 10-5. In the amortization of a premium, the cash interest in Column 1 exceeds the interest expense in Column 2. Therefore, the premium amortized is defined as follows:

Premium Amortized (in Column 3) = Cash Interest − Interest Expense

Also note that the carrying value in Column 4 starts at an amount higher than the face value of $10,000 ($10,692) and is amortized downward until it reaches face value. Therefore, the carrying value at the end of each year is the carrying value at the beginning of the period minus the premium amortized for that year. For example, the carrying value in Exhibit 10-5 at the end of 2008 ($10,534) was calculated by subtracting the premium amortized for 2008 ($158 in Column 3) from the carrying value at the beginning of 2008 ($10,692).

The amortization table in Exhibit 10-5 again serves as the basis for the accounting entries that must be recorded. Premium Firm may record two entries for each period. The first entry at the end of 2008 is recorded to reflect the cash interest payment:

Dec. 31	Interest Expense	800	
	Cash		800
	To record annual interest payment on bonds payable		

Assets = Liabilities + Shareholders' Equity
−800 −800

The second entry is recorded to amortize a portion of the premium and to reflect that amount as an adjustment of interest expense:

Dec. 31	Premium on Bonds Payable	158	
	Interest Expense		158
	To amortize annual portion of premium on bonds payable		

Assets = Liabilities + Shareholders' Equity
−158 +158

Of course, Premium Firm could combine the preceding two entries into one entry as follows:

Dec. 31	Interest Expense	642	
	Premium on Bonds Payable	158	
	Cash		800
	To record annual interest payment and to amortize annual portion of premium on bonds payable		

Assets = Liabilities + Shareholders' Equity
−800 −158 −642

The balance of the Premium on Bonds payable account as of December 31, 2008, would be calculated as follows:

Beginning balance, January 1, 2008	$692
Less: Amount amortized	158
Ending balance, December 31, 2008	$534

The December 31, 2008, balance represents the amount *unamortized*, or the amount that will be amortized in future time periods. On the balance sheet presented as of December 31, 2008, the unamortized portion of the premium appears as the balance of the Premium on Bonds Payable account as follows:

Long-term liabilities:	
Bonds payable	$10,000
Plus: Premium on bonds payable	534
	$10,534

The process of amortization would continue for four years, until the balance of the Premium on Bonds Payable account has been reduced to zero. By the end of 2011, all of the balance of the Premium on Bonds Payable account will have been transferred to the Interest Expense account and represents a reduction of interest expense each period.

Two-Minute Review

1. How do you calculate the issue price of a bond?

2. What effect does amortizing a premium have on the amount of interest expense for the bond? What effect does amortizing a discount have?

Answers on page 486

Redemption of Bonds

Redemption at Maturity The term *redemption* refers to retirement of bonds by repayment of the principal. If bonds are retired on their due date, the accounting entry is not difficult. Refer again to the Discount Firm example. If Discount Firm retires its bonds on the due date of December 31, 2011, it must repay the principal of $10,000, and Cash is reduced by $10,000. The following entry is recorded:

Dec. 31	Bonds Payable	10,000	
	Cash		10,000
	To record the retirement of bonds payable		

Assets	=	Liabilities	+	Shareholders' Equity
−10,000		−10,000		

This assumes that the interest payment that was paid on December 31, 2011, and the discount amortization on that date has already been recorded. The balance of the Discount on Bonds Payable account is zero, since it has been fully amortized.

Notice that no gain or loss is incurred because the carrying value of the bond at that point is $10,000.

Retired Early at a Gain A firm may want to retire bonds before their due date for several reasons. A firm may simply have excess cash and may determine that the best use of those funds is to repay outstanding bond obligations. Bonds may also be retired early because of changing interest rate conditions. If interest rates in the economy decline, firms may find it advantageous to retire bonds that have been issued at higher rates. Of course, what is advantageous to the issuer is not necessarily so for the investor. Early retirement of callable bonds is always a possibility that must be anticipated. Large institutional investors expect such a development and merely reinvest the money elsewhere. Many individual investors are more seriously inconvenienced when a bond issue is called.

Bond terms generally specify that if bonds are retired before their due date, they are not retired at the face value amount but at a call price or redemption price indicated on the bond certificate. Also, the amount of unamortized premium or discount on the bonds must be considered when bonds are retired early. The retirement results in a **gain or loss on redemption** that must be calculated as follows:

> **Gain = Carrying Value − Redemption Price**
> **Loss = Redemption Price − Carrying Value**

Gain or loss on redemption The difference between the carrying value and the redemption price at the time bonds are redeemed.

In other words, the issuing firm must calculate the carrying value of the bonds at the time of redemption and compare it with the total redemption price. If the carrying value is higher than the redemption price, the issuing firm must record a gain. If the carrying value is lower than the redemption price, the issuing firm must record a loss.

We will use the Premium Firm example to illustrate the calculation of gain or loss. Assume that on December 31, 2008, Premium Firm wants to retire its bonds due in 2011. Assume, as in the previous section, that the bonds were issued at a premium of $692 at the beginning of 2008. Premium Firm has used the effective interest method of amortization and has recorded the interest and amortization entries for the year (see page 472). This has resulted in a balance of $534 in the Premium on Bonds Payable account as of December 31, 2008. Assume also that Premium Firm's bond certificates indicate that the bonds may be retired early at a call price of 102 (meaning 102% of face value). Thus, the redemption price is 102% of $10,000, or $10,200.

Premium Firm's retirement of bonds would result in a gain. The gain can be calculated using two steps. First, we must calculate the carrying value of the bonds as of the date they are retired. The carrying value of Premium Firm's bonds at that date is calculated as follows:

> **Carrying Value = Face Value + Unamortized Premium**
> = $10,000 + $534
> = $10,534

Note that the carrying value we have calculated is the same amount indicated for December 31, 2008, in Column 4 of the effective interest amortization table of Exhibit 10-5.

The second step is to calculate the gain:

$$\text{Gain} = \text{Carrying Value} - \text{Redemption Price}$$
$$= \$10,534 - (\$10,000 \times 1.02)$$
$$= \$10,534 - \$10,200$$
$$= \$334$$

It is important to remember that when bonds are retired, the balance of the Bonds Payable account and the remaining balance of the Premium on Bonds Payable account must be eliminated from the balance sheet.

Retired Early at a Loss

To illustrate retirement of bonds at a loss, assume that Premium Firm retires bonds at December 31, 2008, as in the previous section. However, assume that the call price for the bonds is 107 (or 107% of face value).

We can again perform the calculations in two steps. The first step is to calculate the carrying value:

$$\text{Carrying Value} = \text{Face Value} + \text{Unamortized Premium}$$
$$= \$10,000 + \$534$$
$$= \$10,534$$

The second step is to compare the carrying value with the redemption price to calculate the amount of the loss:

$$\text{Loss} = \text{Redemption Price} - \text{Carrying Value}$$
$$= (\$10,000 \times 1.07) - \$10,534$$
$$= \$10,700 - \$10,534$$
$$= \$166$$

In this case, a loss of $166 has resulted from the retirement of Premium Firm bonds. A loss means that the company paid more to retire the bonds than the amount at which the bonds were recorded on the balance sheet.

Financial Statement Presentation of Gain or Loss

The accounts Gain on Bond Redemption and Loss on Bond Redemption are income statement accounts. A gain on bond redemption increases Premium Firm's income; a loss decreases its income. In most cases, a gain or loss should not be considered "unusual" or "infrequent" and therefore should not be placed in the section of the income statement where extraordinary items are presented. While gains and losses should be treated as part of the company's operating income, some statement users may consider them as "one-time" events and wish to exclude them when predicting a company's future income. For that reason, it would be very helpful if companies would present their gains and losses separately on the income statement so that readers could determine whether such amounts will affect future periods.

Recent changes in the presentation of bonds and other financial instruments require the presentation of the fair value of these instruments at the balance sheet date. While some flexibility in the specifics of the fair value presentation is permitted, CP provides detailed amounts in its footnote 15 of its annual report for 2007. The section of footnote 15 shown in Exhibit 10-6 displays the carrying value (the balance sheet amounts) of each of its financial liabilities together with the corresponding fair value. As indicated, the terms of similar debt with a market price or a present value calculation based on current interest rates are used to determine the fair value. The nature of the swaps and forward contracts mentioned are beyond the scope of this chapter of the textbook but will be described in later courses.

Why these fair value amounts are not reflected in the financial statements is a difficult question to answer. As CP indicates in the footnote presented in Exhibit 10-6, significant judgments are needed to obtain these fair values. Also, companies and standard setters are concerned that market fluctuations in the fair value could cause significant variations in net income that in turn could affect investors. Thus, footnote disclosures are the compromise approach selected at present.

15. FINANCIAL INSTRUMENTS

Interest Rate Exposure and Fair Values

The Company's exposure to interest rate risk along with the total carrying amounts and fair values of its financial instruments are summarized in the following tables:

2007 (In millions of Canadian dollars)	At floating interest rates	2008	Fixed interest rate maturing in 2009 to 2012	2013 and after	Total carrying value	Fair value
Financial assests						
Cash and short term investments	$ 378.1	$ –	$ –	$ –	$ 378.1	$ 378.1
Crude oil swaps, unrealized gain	–	–	–	–	21.4	21.4
Financial liabilities						
Short-term borrowings	229.7	–	–	–	229.7	229.7
6.250 % Notes	–	–	396.5		396.5	413.8
7.125 % Debentures	–	–	–	347.0	347.0	374.0
9.450 % Debentures	–	–	–	247.8	247.8	300.5
5.750 % Debentures	–	–	–	247.8	247.8	226.2
5.950 % 30-year notes	–	–	–	446.1	446.1	403.8
4.90 % Medium Term Notes	–	–	350.0	–	350.0	351.9
5.41 % Senior Secured Notes	–	2.8	13.7	95.6	112.1	123.6
6.91 % Secured Equipment Notes	–	7.0	33.3	176.3	216.6	244.6
7.49 % Equipemnt Trust Certificates	–	4.4	42.6	98.2	145.2	124.4
Secured Equipment Loan	133.1	–	–	–	133.1	145.2
4 % Consolidated Debenture Stock	–	–	–	38.1	38.1	33.8
Obligations under captial·leases	–	8.3	46.7	222.0	277.0	296.8
Bridge financing	1,259.0	–	–	–	1,259.0	1,259.0
Bank loan payable on demand	–	5.1	–	–	5.1	5.0
Transaction costs	–	–	–	–	(44.2)	–
Total long-term debt	1,392.1	27.6	882.8	1,918.9	4,177.2	4,302.6

The Company has determined the estimated fair values of its financial instruments based on appropriate valuation methodologies. However, considerable judgment is necessary to develop these estimates. Accordingly, the estimates presented herein are not necessarily indicative of what the Company could realize in a current market exchange. The use of different assumption or methodologies may have a material effect on the estimated fair value amounts.

The following methods and assumptions were used to estimate the fair value of each class of financial instrument:

• Short-term financial assets and liabilities are valued at their carrying amounts as presented on the Consolidation Balance Sheet, which are reasonable estimates of fair value due to the relatively short period to maturity of these instruments.

• The fair value of publicly traded long-term debt is determined based on market prices at December 31, 2007 and 2006. The fair value of other long-term debt is estimated based on rates currently available to the Company for long-term borrowings, with terms and conditions similar to those borrowings in place at the applicable Consolidated Balance Sheet date.

This excerpt from CP's 2007 Annual Report appears courtesy of CP. This section of CP's Annual Report is presented in Appendix B of this textbook.

▌ LIABILITY FOR LEASES

Long-term bonds and notes payable are important sources of financing for many large corporations and are quite prominent in the Long-Term Liabilities category of the balance sheet for many firms. But other important elements of that category of the balance sheet also represent long-term obligations. We introduce leases because they are a major source of financing for many companies.

LO 3 Determine whether a lease agreement must be reported as a liability on the balance sheet and compare it to a mortgage agreement.

Leases

A *lease*, a contractual arrangement between two parties, allows one party, the *lessee*, the right to use an asset in exchange for making payments to its owner, the *lessor*. A common example of a lease arrangement is the rental of an apartment. The tenant is the lessee and the landlord is the lessor.

Lease agreements are a form of financing. In some cases, it is more advantageous to lease an asset than to borrow money to purchase it. The lessee can conserve cash because a lease does not require a large initial cash outlay. A wide variety of lease arrangements exists, ranging from simple agreements to complex ones that span a long time period. Lease arrangements are popular because of their flexibility. The terms of a lease can be structured in many ways to meet the needs of the lessee and lessor. This results in difficult accounting questions:

1. Should the right to use property be reported as an asset by the lessee?
2. Should the obligation to make payments be reported as a liability by the lessee?
3. Should all leases be accounted for in the same manner regardless of the terms of the lease agreement?

The answers are that some leases should be reported as an asset and a liability by the lessee and some should not. The accountant must examine the terms of the lease agreement and compare those terms with an established set of criteria.

Lease A contractual arrangement between two parties that permits one party, the lessee, the right to use an asset in exchange for payments to its owner, the lessor.

✖ Accounting for Your Decisions

Should You Lease or Buy?

You want to acquire a new car and are considering leasing instead of buying. What factors should you consider to determine whether leasing is the better alternative?

ANSWER: To make this decision, answer the following questions: Do you have the cash to buy the car? If not, what is the cost of borrowing? How long will the car be used? Will another car be needed in the near future? What is the purpose of the car? How will the lease payments compare with the purchase payments? Will you own the car at the end of the lease?

Operating lease A lease that does not meet any of the four criteria and is not recorded as an asset by the lessee.

Capital lease A lease that is recorded as an asset by the lessee.

Lease Criteria   From the viewpoint of the lessee, there are two types of lease agreements: operating and capital leases. In an **operating lease,** the lessee acquires the right to use an asset for a limited period of time. The lessee is *not* required to record the right to use the property as an asset or to record the obligation for payments as a liability. Therefore, the lessee is able to attain a form of *off-balance-sheet financing.* That is, the lessee has obtained the right to use property but has not recorded that right, or the accompanying obligation, on the balance sheet. By escaping the balance sheet, the lease does not add to debt or impair the debt-to-equity ratio that investors usually calculate. Management has a responsibility to make sure that such off-balance-sheet financing is not in fact a long-term obligation. The company's auditors are supposed to analyze the terms of the lease carefully to make sure that management has exercised its responsibility.

The second type of lease agreement is a **capital lease.** In this type of lease, the lessee has acquired sufficient rights of ownership and control of the property to be considered its owner. The lease is called a *capital lease* because it is capitalized (recorded) on the balance sheet by the lessee.

A lease should be considered a capital lease by the lessee if one or more of the following criteria are met:[1]

1.   The lease transfers ownership of the property to the lessee at the end of the lease term.
2.   The lease contains a bargain-purchase option to purchase the asset at an amount lower than its fair market value at the end of the lease.
3.   The lease term is 75% or more of the property's economic life.
4.   The present value of the minimum lease payments is 90% or more of the fair market value of the property at the inception of the lease.

If none of the criteria are met, the lease agreement is accounted for as an operating lease. This is an area in which it is important for the accountant to exercise professional judgment. In some cases, firms may take elaborate measures to evade or manipulate the criteria that would require lease capitalization. The accountant should determine what is full and fair disclosure based on an unbiased evaluation of the substance of the transaction.

Operating Leases   You have already accounted for operating leases in previous chapters when recording rent expense and prepaid rent. A rental agreement for a limited time period is also a lease agreement.

Suppose, for example, that Lessee Firm wants to lease a car for a new salesperson. A lease agreement is signed with Lessor Dealer on January 1, 2008, to lease a car for the year for $4,000, payable on December 31, 2008. Typically, a car lease does not transfer title at the end of the term, does not include a bargain-purchase price, and does not last for more than 75% of the car's life. In addition, the present value of the lease payments is not 90% of the car's value. Because the lease does not meet any of the specified criteria, it should be presented as an operating lease. Lessee Firm would simply record lease expense, or rent expense, of $4,000 for the year.

Although operating leases are not recorded on the balance sheet by the lessee, they are mentioned in financial statement notes. The AcSB requires note disclosure of the amount of future lease obligations for leases that are considered operating leases. Exhibit 10-7 provides a portion of the note from CN's 2007 annual report. The note reveals that CN has used operating leases as an important source of financing and has significant off-balance-sheet commitments in future periods as a result. An investor might want to add this off-balance-sheet item to the debt on the balance sheet to get a conservative view of the company's obligations.

---

[1]*AcSB, Section 3065, Leases.*

Exhibit 10-7

CN's 2007 Note Disclosure of Leases (Footnote 18).

18. MAJOR COMMITMENTS AND CONTINGENCIES

A. Leases

The Company has operating and capital leases, mainly for locomotives, freight cars and intermodal equipment. Of the capital leases, many provide the option to purchase the leased items at fixed values during or at the end of the lease term. As at December 31, 2007, the Company's commitments under these operating and capital leases were $879 million and $1,620 million, respectively. Minimum rental payments for operating leases having initial non-cancelable lease terms of one year or more and minimum lease payments for capital leases in each of the next five years and thereafter are as follows:

In millions	Operating	Capital
2008	$152	$ 145
2009	125	165
2010	106	100
2011	84	164
2012	68	75
2013 and thereafter	344	971
	$879	$ 1,620
Less: imputed interest on capital leases at rates ranging from approximately 3.0% to 7.9%		515
Present value of minimum lease payments included in debt		$ 1,105

The Company also has operating lease agreements for its automotive fleet with minimum one-year non-cancelable terms for which its practice is to renew monthly thereafter. The estimated annual rental payments for such leases are approximately $30 million and generally extend over a few years.

Rent expense for all operating leases was $207 million, $202 million and $233 million for the years ended December 31, 2007, 2006, and 2005, respectively. Contingent rentals and sublease rentals were not significant.

This excerpt from CN's 2007 Annual Report appears courtesy of CN. This section of the CN Annual Report appears in the Appendix of this textbook.

Capital Leases   Capital leases are presented as assets and liabilities by the lessee because they meet one or more of the capital lease criteria. Suppose that Lessee Firm in the previous example wanted to lease a car for a longer period of time. Assume that on January 1, 2008, Lessee signs a lease agreement with Lessor Dealer to lease a car. The terms of the agreement specify that Lessee will make annual lease payments of $4,000 per year for five years, payable each December 31. Assume also that the lease specifies that at the end of the lease agreement, the title to the car is transferred to Lessee Firm. Lessee must decide how to account for the lease agreement.

The contractual arrangement between Lessee Firm and Lessor Dealer is called a lease agreement, but clearly the agreement is much different from a year-to-year lease arrangement. Essentially, Lessee Firm has acquired the right to use the asset for its entire life and does not need to return it to Lessor Dealer. You may call this agreement a lease, but it actually represents a purchase of the asset by Lessee with payments made over time.

The lease should be treated as a capital lease by Lessee because it meets at least one of the four criteria (it meets the first criterion concerning transfer of title). A capital lease must be recorded at its present value by Lessee as an asset and as an obligation. As of January 1, 2008, we must calculate the present value of the annual payments. If we assume an interest rate of 8%, the present value of the payments is $15,972 ($4,000 × an annuity factor of 3.993 from Table 9-4).

Study Tip

It is called a *capital lease* because the lease is capitalized, or put on the books of the lessee as an asset and a corresponding liability.

The first entry is made on the basis of the present value as follows:

Jan. 1   Leased Asset   15,972
               Lease Obligation   15,972
           To record a capital lease agreement

Assets   =   Liabilities   +   Shareholders' Equity
+15,972   +15,972

The Leased Asset account is a long-term asset similar to plant and equipment and represents the fact that Lessee has acquired the right to use and retain the asset. Because the leased asset represents depreciable property, depreciation must be reported for each of the five years of asset use. On December 31, 2008, Lessee records depreciation of $3,194 ($15,972/5 years) as follows, assuming that the straight-line method is adopted:

Dec. 31   Depreciation Expense   3,194
               Accumulated Depreciation—Leased Assets   3,194
           To record depreciation of leased assets

Assets   =   Liabilities   +   Shareholders' Equity
−3,194   −3,194

Depreciation of leased assets is referred to as *amortization* by some firms.

On December 31, Lessee Firm also must make a payment of $4,000 to Lessor Dealer. A portion of each payment represents interest on the obligation (loan), and the remainder represents a reduction of the principal amount. Each payment, termed a *blended payment*, must be separated into its principal and interest components. Generally, the effective interest method is used for that purpose. An effective interest table can be established using the same concepts as were used to amortize a premium or discount on bonds payable.

Exhibit 10-8 illustrates the effective interest method applied to the Lessee Firm example. Note that the table begins with an obligation amount equal to the present value of the payments of $15,972. Each payment is separated into principal and interest amounts so that the amount of the loan obligation at the end of the lease agreement equals zero. The amortization table is the basis for the amounts that are reflected on the financial statement. Exhibit 10-8 indicates that the $4,000 payment in 2008 should be considered as interest of $1,278 (8% of $15,972) and reduction of principal of $2,722. On December 31, 2008, Lessee Firm records the following entry for the annual payment:

Dec. 31   Interest Expense   1,278
           Lease Obligation   2,722
               Cash   4,000
           To record annual lease payment

Assets   =   Liabilities   +   Shareholders' Equity
−4,000   −2,722   −1,278

Exhibit 10-8

Lease Amortization: Effective Interest Method of Amortization

DATE	COLUMN 1 LEASE PAYMENT	COLUMN 2 INTEREST EXPENSE	COLUMN 3 REDUCTION OF OBLIGATION	COLUMN 4 LEASE OBLIGATION
		8%	Col. 1 − Col. 2	
1/1/2008	—	—	—	$15,972
12/31/2008	$4,000	$1,278	$2,722	13,250
12/31/2009	4,000	1,060	2,940	10,310
12/31/2010	4,000	825	3,175	7,135
12/31/2011	4,000	571	3,429	3,706
12/31/2012	4,000	294	3,706	−0−

Therefore, for a capital lease, Lessee Firm must record both an asset and a liability. The asset is reduced by the process of depreciation. The liability is reduced by reductions of principal using the effective interest method. According to Exhibit 10-8, the total lease obligation as of December 31, 2008, is $13,250. This amount must be separated into current and long-term categories. The portion of the liability that will be paid within one year of the balance sheet should be considered a current liability. Reference to Exhibit 10-8 indicates that the liability will be reduced by $2,940 in 2009, and that amount should be considered a current liability. The remaining amount of the liability, $10,310 ($13,250 − $2,940), should be considered long-term. On the balance sheet as of December 31, 2008, Lessee Firm reports the following balances related to the lease obligation:

Assets:		
Leased assets	$15,972	
Less: Accumulated depreciation	3,194	$12,778
Current liabilities:		
Lease obligation (Next year's liability payment)		$ 2,940
Long-term liabilities:		
Lease obligation (Long-term liability payments)		$10,310

Notice that the depreciated asset does not equal the present value of the lease obligation. This is not unusual. For example, an automobile often may be completely depreciated but still have payments due on it. Notice as well that the interest portion of each lease payment is not part of the liability for the lease on the balance sheet. The reason for this is a peculiarity of interest. Interest is an obligation and an expense of using the debt. Thus it is recorded only after time passes, which represents the use of the debt. The obligation portion for the lease liability is the reduction of the obligation represented by the present value (interest removed) of the lease payment.

The criteria used to determine whether a lease is an operating or a capital lease have provided a standard accounting treatment for all leases. The accounting for leases in foreign countries generally follows guidelines similar to those used in Canada. The criteria used in foreign countries to determine whether a lease is a capital lease are usually less detailed and less specific, however. As a result, capitalization of leases occurs less frequently in foreign countries than in Canada because of the increased judgment necessary in applying the accounting rules. Leases for a vehicle or an apartment have lease payments required at the beginning of each period. This annuity due requires a relatively simple adaptation of the annuity formula or tables shown in Chapter 9 that future courses will explore.

Two-Minute Review

1. When a lease is considered a capital lease to the lessee, what entry is made to initially record the lease agreement?

2. When the lessee makes a lease payment on a capital lease, how is the payment recorded?

Answers on page 486

Mortgages

Smaller companies and individuals may use mortgages as a method of obtaining debt financing from banks and other financial institutions. Mortgages provide security to the creditor by transferring legal title to the property (usually land and buildings) to the creditor if the debt is not paid. Thus the land and buildings serve as collateral for the mortgage debt. Financial statements should provide the details of the assets under mortgages and should also make it clear that the debt is a mortgage loan.

Accounting for mortgages parallels the demonstrations provided for capital leases. Each mortgage payment is a blend of principal and interest, the same as the lessee firm's treatment illustrated in Exhibit 10-8.

To illustrate, assume Lessee firm borrows $15,972 from the Local Bank to finance the purchase of a storage building.

Lessee would record the cash receipt as follows:

Jan. 1	Cash	15,972	
	Mortgage Payable		15,972
	To record the receipt of cash from Local Bank		

Assets	=	Liabilities	+	Shareholders' Equity
+15,972		+15,972		

Lessee would use the cash to buy the building and record the transaction as follows:

Jan. 1	Building	15,972	
	Cash		15,972
	To record the purchase of the building		

Assets	=	Liabilities	+	Shareholders' Equity
+15,972				
−15,972				

If we assume only a single payment in year 1 in order to reduce the size of the illustration, the December year-end entries would be:

Dec. 31	Depreciation Expense	3,194	
	Accumulated Depreciation		3,194
	To record the depreciation expense of the mortgaged building		

Calculation: $15,972/5 = $3,194

Assets	=	Liabilities	+	Shareholders' Equity
−3,194				−3,194

To record the payment of the mortgage in year 1, the following entry is made by the Lessee:

Dec. 31	Interest Expense	1,278	
	Mortgage Payable	2,722	
	Cash		4,000
	To record the year 1 mortgage payment		

Assets	=	Liabilities	+	Shareholders' Equity
−4,000		−2,722		−1,278

A comparison of the capital lease entries with the mortgage entries shows the parallel of the two financing situations. Treatment of capital leases attempts to achieve this parallel.

Mortgages and leases are financial contracts and thus are designed to satisfy the market conditions and the peculiarities of the companies involved. For example, mortgages often involve monthly payments with interest compounding every six months. Variable rate mortgages involve an interest rate that can change every month with monthly compounding of interest. As mentioned earlier, leases may have lease payments required at the start of each month as well as various terms applied to the end of the lease. These variations require the analyst to know how interest calculations are made and to perform a careful reading of the contract terms of the mortgage or lease.

Analyzing Debt to Assess a Firm's Ability to Pay Its Liabilities

Long-term liabilities are a component of the "capital structure" of the company and are included in the calculation of the debt-to-equity ratio:

$$\text{Debt-to-Equity Ratio} = \frac{\text{Total Liabilities}}{\text{Total Shareholders' Equity}}$$

For example, refer to the Liabilities category of CN's balance sheet, provided at the beginning of the chapter. CN's total liabilities are $13,283 million (current liabilities of $1,590, long-term debt of $5,363, other liabilities of $1,422, and deferred income taxes of $4,908). Its total shareholders' equity is $10,177 million. Therefore, the debt-to-equity ratio is $13,283 / $10,177, or 1.31, which means that CN has 1.3 times as much debt as equity—a situation that is not uncommon for companies in the transportation industry.

Most investors would prefer to see equity rather than debt on the balance sheet. Debt and its interest charges make up a fixed obligation that must be repaid in a finite period of time. In contrast, equity never has to be repaid, and the dividends that are declared on it are optional. Share investors view debt as a claim against the company that must be satisfied before they get a return on their money.

Other ratios used to measure the degree of debt obligation include the times interest earned ratio and the debt service coverage ratio:

$$\text{Times Interest Earned Ratio} = \frac{\text{Income Before Interest and Tax}}{\text{Interest Expense}}$$

$$\text{Debt Service Coverage Ratio} = \frac{\text{Cash Flow from Operations Before Interest and Tax}}{\text{Interest and Principal Payments}}$$

Lenders want to be sure that borrowers can pay the interest and repay the principal on a loan. Both of the preceding ratios, which will be explored in more detail in Chapter 13, reflect the degree to which a company can make its debt payments out of current cash flow.

HOW LONG-TERM LIABILITIES AFFECT THE STATEMENT OF CASH FLOWS

LO 4 Explain the effects that transactions involving long-term liabilities have on the statement of cash flows.

Exhibit 10-9 indicates the impact that long-term liabilities have on a company's cash flow and their placement on the cash flow statement.

Most long-term liabilities are related to a firm's financing activities. Therefore, the change in the balance of each long-term liability account should be reflected in the Financing Activities category of the statement of cash flows. The decrease in a long-term liability account indicates that cash has been used to pay the liability. Therefore, in the cash flow statement, a decrease in a long-term liability account should appear as a subtraction or reduction. The increase in a long-term liability account indicates that the firm has obtained additional cash via a long-term obligation. Therefore, an increase in a long-term liability account should appear in the cash flow statement as an addition.

Exhibit 10-9

Long-Term Liabilities on the Statement of Cash Flows

Item	Statement of Cash Flows
	Operating Activities
	Net income xxx
Increase in current liability	➤ +
Decrease in current liability	➤ −
	Investing Activities
	Financing Activities
Increase in long-term liability	➤ +
Decrease in long-term liability	➤ −

The cash flow statement of CN is presented in Exhibit 10-10. Note that the Financing Activities category contains two items related to long-term liabilities. In 2007, long-term debt was issued for $4,171 million and is an addition to cash. This indicates that CN increased its cash position by borrowing. Second, the payment of debt is listed as a deduction of $3,589 million. This indicates that CN paid long-term liabilities resulting in a reduction of cash.

Although most long-term liabilities are reflected in the Financing Activities category of the statement of cash flows, there are exceptions. The most notable exception involves the Deferred Tax account (discussed in the Appendix at the end of this chapter). The change in this account is reflected in the Operating Activities category of the statement of cash flows. This presentation is necessary because the Deferred Tax account is related to an operating item, income tax expense. For example, in Exhibit 10-10, CN listed $82 million in the Operating Activities category of the 2007 statement of cash flows. This indicates that $82 million more was recorded as expense than was paid out in cash. Therefore, the amount is a positive amount in, or an addition to, the Operating Activities category.

In the case of CN, the issue and reduction of long-term debt does not easily relate to the balance sheet changes in long-term debt. One would expect the $218 current portion shown at the end of 2006 on the balance sheet at the start of the chapter to be the repayment of long-term debt during 2007 shown on the cash flow statement. However, this is not the case, because the cash flow statement shows $3,589 repaid on long-term debt. In addition, the balance sheet shows a decrease in long-term debt of $23($5,363 − $5,386) plus the portion shown in the current section of $254—a total of $277 reduction. The cash flow statement shows new long-term debt issued of $4,171. No footnote explaining the composition of the long-term debt cash flow is provided, so it is difficult to understand these differences. Some differences result from changes in foreign currency, because of the movement of the U.S.-dollar debt relative to the Canadian dollar shown on the balance sheet. Some differences may have resulted from the revolving credit creating cash outflow and inflow that cannot be observed from the ending balances. For the sake of expediency, we will give up the analysis.

Exhibit 10-10 CN's 2007 Consolidated Statement of Cash Flows

See accompanying notes to consolidated financial statements

In millions Year ended December 31,	2007	2006	2005
Operating activities			
Net income	2,158	2,087	1,556
Adjustments to reconcile net income to net cash provided from operating activities:			
Depreciation and amortization	678	653	630
Deferred income taxes *(Note 15)*	(82)	3	547
Gain on sale of Central Station Complex *(Note 5)*	(92)	–	–
Gain on sale of investment in English Welsh and Scottish Railway *(Note 6)*	(61)	–	–
Other changes in:			
Accounts receivable *(Note 4)*	229	(17)	142
Material and supplics	18	(36)	(25)
Accounts payable and accrued charges	(351)	197	(156)
Other net current assets and liabilities	39	58	8
Other	(119)	6	6
Cash provided from operating activities	2,417	2,951	2708
Investing activities			
Property additions	(1,387)	(1,298)	(1,180)
Acquisitions, net of cash acquired *(Note 3)*	(25)	(84)	–
Sale of Central Station Complex *(Note 5)*	351	–	–
Sale of investment in English Welsh and Scottish Railway *(Note 6)*	114	–	–
Other, net	52	33	105
Cash used by investing activities	(895)	(1,349)	(1,075)
Financing activities			
Issuance of long-term debt	4,171	3308	2,728
Reduction of long-term debt	(3,589)	(3,089)	(2,865)
Issuance of common shares due to exercise of stock options and			
related excess tax benefits realized *(Note 12)*	77	120	115
Repurchase of common shares *(Note 11)*	(1,584)	(1,483)	(1,418)
Dividends paid	(418)	(340)	(275)
Cash used by financing activities	(1,343)	(1,484)	(1,715)
Effect of foreign exchange fluctuations on U.S. dollar-denominated cash and cash equivalents	(48)	(1)	(3)
Net increase (decrease) in cash and cash equivalents	131	117	(85)
Cash and cash equivalents, beginning of year	179	62	147
Cash and cash equivalents, end of year	310	179	62
Supplemental cash flow information			
Net cash recipts from customers and other	8,139	7,946	7,581
Net cash payments for:			
Employee services, suppliers and other expenses	(4,323)	(4,130)	(4,075)
Interest	(340)	(294)	(306)
Workforce reductions *(Note 9)*	(31)	(45)	(87)
Personal injury and other claims *(Note 18)*	(86)	(107)	(92)
Pensions *(Note 13)*	(75)	(112)	(127)
Income taxes *(Note 15)*	(867)	(307)	(186)
Cash provided from operating expenses	2,417	2,951	2,708

This excerpt from CN's 2007 Annual Report appears courtesy of CN. This section of the CN Annual Report aapears in the Appendix of this textbook.

Appendix A: Accounting Tools: Deferred (Future) Tax

LO 5 Explain deferred (future) taxes and calculate the deferred (future) tax liability.

In these Appendices we will discuss two additional items that are found in the Long-Term Liabilities category of many companies: deferred taxes and pensions. Both items are complex financial arrangements, and our primary purpose is to make you aware of their existence when reading financial statements.

The financial statements of most major firms include an item titled Deferred Income Taxes or Future Tax. In most cases, the account appears in the Long-Term Liabilities section of the balance sheet, and the dollar amount may be large enough to catch the user's attention. For another example, Exhibit 10-11 (page 491) illustrates the presentation of deferred tax in the 2007 comparative balance sheets of CN. The Deferred (Future) Income Taxes account is listed immediately after current liabilities and for CN should be considered a long-term liability. At the end of 2007, the firm had more than $4,908 million of deferred tax. The size of that account relative to the other liabilities should raise questions concerning its exact meaning. In fact, deferred income taxes represent one of the most misunderstood aspects of financial statements. In this section, we will attempt to address some of the questions concerning deferred taxes.

The terms *future tax* and *deferred tax* are used interchangeably to refer to a specific feature of tax accounting that reflects the difference between the income taxes imposed by provincial and federal acts and the income tax determined according to GAAP. *Deferred tax* is the older term and is still used by some companies (such as CN) and is the term used in the United States. *Future tax* is a more recent term and is reflected in current GAAP (and used by CP). To be consistent with modern terminology, we will use *future tax* to reflect the ideas described in the following section.

Future tax is an amount that reconciles the difference between the amount recorded as income tax expense for purposes of financial reporting to shareholders ("book" purposes) and the accounting done for income tax calculation purposes. It may surprise you that firms are allowed to use accounting methods for financial reporting that differ from those used for tax calculations. The reason is that the Canada Revenue Agency defines income and expense differently than does the AcSB. As a result, companies tend to use accounting methods that minimize income for tax purposes but maximize income in the

Future tax The account used to reconcile the difference between the amount recorded as income tax expense and the amount that is payable as income tax.

annual report to shareholders. This is not true in some foreign countries where financial accounting and tax accounting are more closely aligned. Firms in those countries do not report deferred tax, because the difference between methods is not significant.

When differences between financial and tax reporting do occur, we can classify them into two types: permanent and temporary. **Permanent differences** occur when an item is included in the tax calculation and is never included for book purposes—or vice versa, when an item is included for book purposes but not for tax purposes.

For example, the tax laws allow taxpayers to exclude dividends on certain investments from their income. These are generally called *dividends from taxable Canadian corporations*. If a corporation buys share investments, it does not have to declare the dividends as income for tax purposes. When the corporation develops its income statement for shareholders (book purposes), however, the dividends are included and appear in the Investment Income account. Therefore, tax-exempt dividends represent a permanent difference between tax and book calculations.

Other common permanent differences relate to fines and legal penalties, which are treated as expenses for accounting purposes but not for income tax purposes. Certain entertainment expenses and club dues are excluded from tax expenses, while a percentage (typically 50%) of certain defined gains, termed *capital gains*, are not taken into taxable income but are accounting income.

Temporary differences occur when an item affects both the book and the tax calculations but not in the same time period. A difference caused by depreciation methods is the most common type of temporary difference. In previous chapters you have learned that depreciation may be calculated using a straight-line method or an accelerated method such as the double-declining-balance method. Most firms do not use the same depreciation method for book and tax purposes, however.

Generally, straight-line or other depreciation methods are used for book purposes while capital cost allowance (CCA) is used for income tax purposes. (See Chapter 8 for a detailed example of CCA.) Over the life of the asset, depreciation may be greater or less than CCA in any particular year, but the amounts will approximate each other over the life of the asset. This situation creates a temporary difference between the tax expense (CCA) and the accounting depreciation expense.

Other common temporary differences relate to bad debts, warranty expenses, pension expense, certain contingent expenses such as lawsuits, and revenues received in advance from subscriptions and rentals. Typically, the income tax calculation requires a cash basis focus for its recognition while GAAP uses an accrual approach. In this way a temporary difference is created.

The Future Tax account is used to reconcile the differences between the accounting for book purposes and for tax purposes. It is important to distinguish between permanent and temporary differences because the AcSB has ruled that not all differences should affect the Future Tax account. The Future Tax account should reflect temporary differences but not items that are permanent differences between book accounting and tax reporting.[2]

Example of Future Tax   Assume that Startup Company begins business on January 1, 2008. During 2008 the firm has sales of $6,000 and has no expenses other than depreciation and income tax at the rate of 40%. Startup has depreciation on only one asset. That asset was purchased on July 1, 2008, for $10,000 and has a four-year life. Startup has decided to use the straight-line depreciation method for financial reporting purposes. Startup uses the maximum CCA for tax purposes, which for illustration here is 30% on a declining balance basis.

Permanent difference A difference that affects the tax records but not the accounting records, or vice versa.

Temporary difference A difference that affects both book and tax records but not in the same time period.

---

[2]AcSB, Section 3465.

The depreciation amounts for each of the five years for Startup's asset are as follows:

Year	CCA	Book Depreciation	Difference
2008	$1,500	$ 1,250	$ 250
2009	2,550	2,500	50
2010	1,785	2,500	−715
2011	1,250	2,500	−1,250
2012	875	1,250	−375
	$7,960	$10,000	$−2,040

For a single asset, it is possible that CCA will be less than accounting depreciation in any given year. This difference will create a future tax asset initially and later a future tax liability when the difference is sufficient to reverse the former and generate an opposite difference where the CCA exceeds the depreciation expense. To illustrate only the key point here, we keep the relationship between CCA and accounting depreciation simplified. Chapter 8 provides opportunities to witness more complex patterns of temporary differences between CCA and depreciation.

Startup's tax calculation for 2008 is based on the CCA of $1,500, as follows:

Sales	$6,000
CCA	1,500
Taxable Income	4,500
× Tax Rate	40%
Tax Payable	$1,800

For the year 2008, Startup owes $1,800 of tax to the governments. This amount is ordinarily recorded as tax payable until the time it is remitted.

Startup wants also to develop an income statement to send to the shareholders. What amount should be shown as tax expense on the income statement? You may guess that the Tax Expense account on the income statement should reflect $1,800 because that is the amount to be paid to the governments. That is not true in this case, however. Remember that the tax payable amount was calculated using the CCA method. The income statement must be calculated using the straight-line method, which Startup uses for book purposes. Therefore, Startup's income statement for 2008 appears as follows:

Sales	$6,000
Depreciation Expense	1,250
Income before Tax	4,750
Tax Expense (40%)	1,900
Net Income	$2,850

Startup must make the following accounting entry to record the amount of tax expense and tax payable for 2008:

Dec. 31	Tax Expense	1,900	
	Tax Payable		1,800
	Future Tax Liability		100
	To record income tax for the year 2008.		

Assets	=	Liabilities	+	Shareholders' Equity
		+1,800		−1,900
		+100		

The Future Tax account is a balance sheet account. A balance in it reflects the fact that Startup has received a tax benefit by recording accelerated depreciation, in effect delaying the ultimate obligation to Canadian governments. To be sure, the amount of future tax still represents a liability of Startup. The Future Tax account balance of $100 represents the amount of the 2008 temporary difference of $250 times the tax rate of 40% ($250 × 40% = $100).

What can we learn from the Startup example? First, when you see a firm's income statement, the amount listed as tax expense does not represent the amount of cash paid to governments for taxes. Accrual accounting procedures require that the tax expense amount be calculated using the accounting methods chosen for book purposes.

Second, when you see a firm's balance sheet, the amount in the Future Tax account reflects all of the temporary differences between the accounting methods chosen for tax and book purposes. The accounting and financial communities are severely divided on whether the Future Tax account represents a "true" liability. For one thing, many investment analysts do not view it as a real liability because they have noticed that it continues to grow year after year. Others look at it as a bookkeeping item that is simply there to balance the books. The AcSB has taken the stance that future tax is an amount that results in a future obligation and meets the definition of a liability. The controversy concerning future taxes is likely to continue for many years.

Before we examine a more detailed situation as illustrated in the published financial statements of CN, it is worth noting a potential confusion in the tax numbers that is important when statement analysis is conducted.

Note that the income tax rate set by Canadian governments as assumed in our illustration of Startup Company was 40%. This is termed the statutory rate. When we divide the tax expense of $1,900 by the income before tax of $4,750, the effective tax rate is also 40%. The statutory and the effective tax rates are the same here because the only differences between the accounting income before tax ($4,750) and the taxable income of $4,500 is the temporary difference of $250 resulting from the difference between the accounting depreciation and the CCA for 2008. This relationship between the statutory tax rate and the effective rate would continue as long as permanent income differences do not appear.

To illustrate the effect of permanent differences, consider Startup to have revenue from dividends of $1,000 from a Canadian investment and sales of $5,000. The income results would be as follows:

	Tax	Accounting
Sales	$5,000	$5,000
Dividend Revenue	–	1,000
	5,000	6,000
CCA/ Depreciation	1,500	1,250
Tax Income/ Income before tax	3,500	4,750
Tax Expense 40%	1,400	1,500*
Net income	$2,100	$3,250

*($5,000-$1,250) × .40 = $1,500

The statutory tax rate is 40% of the tax income. The effective tax rate based on the accounting income before tax is $1,500/$4,750 or 31.6%. For doing statement analysis, the effective tax rate of 31.6% would typically be used to determine after-tax amounts. The nature of why this difference appears is presented in the footnote disclosure of published financial statements, as illustrated in Exhibit 10-11.

Footnote 15 from CN's 2007 annual report reflects a complex array of information, some of which is beyond the scope of the explanation possible here. However, some interpretation is possible. The footnote presented in Exhibit 10-11 begins by showing the difference between the tax expense using only the federal statutory tax rate (amounting to $598) and the actual tax expense ($548). This major difference arises, in part, because provincial taxes are $318. CN also shows a reduction of its deferred taxes of $317 resulting from tax rate reductions. Note that the cash paid is $867—substantially more than the expense of $548. The cash payment amount would be the amount presented in the cash flow statement as part of the operating section.

The next section shows a breakdown of tax expense between the income amount, which does not include temporary differences ($630), and the future tax recovery of $82, which is the tax impact of temporary differences.

The final section shows the future tax asset of $277, which is made up of temporary differences from workforce reduction accruals, personal injury claims, post-retirement benefits (similar to pensions), and loss carry-forwards. Loss carry-forward is a special treatment of operating losses that CN can use to offset future income tax. These items create future tax assets, which are then netted against the future tax liabilities created by prepaid pension benefits and accelerated CCA ($5,117). CN then shows the net long-term future tax liability of $4,840 and a short-term future tax asset of $68, which it expects to use to offset future tax payments within the next year.

Thus reading the income tax footnote permits a detailed analysis of both permanent differences and temporary differences. Unfortunately, a full understanding of each individual item requires a solid knowledge of income tax rules—and perhaps insider information for the smaller items that have been aggregated into "other" categories.

An alternative presentation for income tax expense is illustrated in Exhibit 10-11 by CN. It is possible to separate the income tax expense into the portion that is future (termed "deferred" by CN) and the portion that belongs to the ordinary tax expense. The ordinary tax expense is typically the tax expense associated with what is the current period charge without temporary differences. CN shows $630 for current tax purposes and $82 for deferred tax recovery of expense.

To illustrate how this separation would occur, we use the 2008 entry for Startup Company:

December 31

Current Expense	1,800	
Future Tax Expense	100	
Taxes Payable		1,800
Future Tax Liability		100

Assets	=	Liabilities	+	Shareholders' Equity
		+ 1,800		− 1,800
		+ 100		− 100

As the entry suggests, the logic of the future tax procedure and disclosure is not changed; however, the separation of the expense into two categories does provide somewhat more information to the statement reader.

To continue the Startup Company's operations to 2009, the CCA will be $2,550 while the straight-line depreciation will become $2,500. The temporary difference in 2009 is $2,550 − $2,500, or $50 extra tax depreciation. If the tax rate is still 40%, this temporary difference translates to 0.40 × $50 or $20. If the rate is kept the same, one can observe that the future tax liability set up in 2008 will be reversed as follows:

Tax Expense [(6,000 − 2,500) × 0.40]	1,400	
Future Tax Liability [50 × 0.40]		20
Taxes Payable [(6,000 − 2,550) × 0.40]		1,380

Assets	=	Liabilities	+	Shareholders' Equity
		+1,380		−1,400
		+ 20		

To continue to 2010:

Tax Expense [(6,000 − 2,500) × 0.40]	1,400	
Future Tax Asset (1,785 − 2,500) × 0.40 − 120]	166	
Future Tax Liability (100 + 20)	120	
Taxes Payable [(6,000 − 1,785) × 0.40]		1,686

Assets	=	Liabilities	+	Shareholders' Equity
+166		+1,686		− 1,400
		− 120		

Exhibit 10-11 CN's Future (Deferred) Taxes

15. Income taxes

The Company's consolidated effective income tax rate differs from the Canadian statutory Federal tax rate. The reconciliation of income tax expense is as follows:

In millions	Year ended December 31,	**2007**	2006	2005
Federal tax rate		**22.1%**	22.1%	22.1%
Income tax expense at the statutory				
Federal tax rate		**$ (598)**	$ (603)	$ (516)
Income tax (expense) recovery resulting from:				
Provincial and other taxes		**(318)**	(354)	(331)
Deferred income tax adjustments due to rate enactments		**317**	228	(14)
Other[1]		**51**	87	80
Income tax expense		**$ (548)**	$ (642)	$ (781)
Cash payments for income taxes		**$ 867**	$ 307	$ 186

(1) Includes adjustments relating to the resolution of matters pertaining to prior years' income taxes and other items.

The following table provides tax information for Canada and the United States

In millions	Year ended December 31,	**2007**	2006	2005
Income before income taxes				
Canada		**$1,983**	$2,009	$1,769
U.S.		**723**	720	568
		$2,706	$2,729	$2,337
Current income tax expense				
Canada		**$ (418)**	$ (440)	$ (95)
U.S.		**(212)**	(199)	(139)
		$ (630)	$ (639)	$ (234)
Deferred income tax recovery (expense)				
Canada		**$ 141**	$ 102	$ (488)
U.S.		**(59)**	(105)	(59)
		$ 82	$ (3)	$ (547)

Significant components of deferred income tax assets and liabilities are as follows:

In millions	December 31,	**2007**	2006
Deferred income tax assets			
Workforce reduction provisions		**$ 22**	$ 32
Personal injury claims and other reserves		**146**	215
Other postretirement benefits liability		**85**	99
Losses and tax credit carryforwards		**24**	14
		277	360
Deferred income tax liabilities			
Net pension asset		**429**	330
Properties and other		**4,688**	5,161
		5,117	5,491
Total net deferred income tax liability		**$ 4,840**	$ 5,131
Total net deferred income tax liability			
Canada		**$ 2,191**	$ 2,050
U.S.		**2,649**	3,081
		$ 4,840	$ 5,131
Total net deferred income tax liability		**$ 4,840**	$ 5,131
Net current deferred income tax asset		**68**	84
Long-term deferred income tax liability		**$ 4,908**	$ 5,215

This excerpt from CN's 2007 Annual Report appears courtesy of CN. This section of the CN Annual Report appears in the Appendix of this textbook.

The future tax asset will continue to build up if Startup has only a single asset. If it invests in other CCA permitted assets, then the overall situation may shift the future tax asset to a future tax liability.

If Startup ceases operations in 2012 and disposes of its 30% CCA asset for $0.00, then it can claim for tax purposes all the unused CCA in 2012, $2,040. Such a claim is called a terminal loss and only occurs if no further assets are purchased for this 30% class in 2012. Otherwise, Startup would claim a further 30% CCA after 2012 to add to what it would claim on the new asset placed in the 30% CCA class. Thus we can see that the CCA may continue beyond the straight-line life of the asset as long as the claim is continued by the purchase of a new asset for the class. If the class does not continue, CCA will end in the year the class is closed, and a deduction or a recapture (gain for tax purposes) will occur in this year.

The disclosure of Future Tax as an asset or a liability, current or long term, depends on the timing of the reversal of the temporary differences. Thus when Future Taxes are noted on the balance sheet, no special concern exists because of the classification of the Future Tax balance.

The overall long-term CCA tax effect for various classes can be calculated using what is termed a *tax shield formula*. Exploring this formula is beyond the scope of the discussion of future taxes but will be explained in future accounting or finance courses.

Appendix B: Accounting Tools: Pensions

Pension An obligation to pay employees for service rendered while employed.

Many large firms establish pension plans to provide income to employees after their retirement. These pension plans often cover a large number of employees and involve millions of dollars. The large amounts in pension funds have become a major force in our economy, representing billions of dollars in shares and bonds. In fact, pension funds are among the major "institutional investors" and have an enormous economic impact on our stock and bond exchanges.

Pensions are complex financial arrangements that involve difficult estimates and projections developed by specialists, termed *actuaries*. Pension plans also involve very difficult accounting issues requiring a wide range of estimates and assumptions about future cash flows.

We will concern ourselves with two accounting questions related to pensions. First, the employer must report the cost of the pension plan as an expense for the time period of the income statement. How should that expense be reported? Second, the employer's financial statements should reflect a measure of the liability associated with a pension plan. What is the liability for future pension amounts from existing or previous efforts by employees, and how should it be recorded or disclosed? Our discussion will begin with the recording of pension expense.

Pensions on the Income Statement Most pension plans are of the following form:

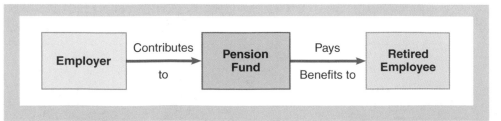

Funding payment A payment made by the employer to the pension fund or its trustee.

Normally, the employer must make payments to the pension fund at least annually, perhaps more frequently. This is often referred to as *funding the pension* or as the **funding payment.** *Funding* simply means that the employer has contributed cash to the pension fund. The pension fund is usually administered by a trustee, often a bank or other financial institution. The trustee must invest the employer's funds so that they earn interest and dividends sufficient to pay the amounts owed to retired employees. As the term trustee implies, the pension fund assets are not assets of the employer but rather are held for the benefit of the employees.

Our first accounting question concerns the amount that should be shown by the employer as pension expense. This is another example of the difference between cash-basis accounting and accrual accounting. The cash paid as the funding payment is not the same as the expense. When using the accrual basis of accounting, we must consider the amount of pension cost incurred, not the amount paid. Pension expense should be accrued in the period that the employee earns the benefits, regardless of the amount paid to the pension trustee. The amount expensed and the amount paid involve two separate decisions.

The AcSB has specified the methods that should be used to calculate the amount of annual pension expense to record on the employer's income statement.[3] The accountant must determine the costs of the separate components of the pension and total them to arrive at the amount of pension expense. The components include the employee's service during the current year, the interest cost, the earnings on pension investments, and other factors. The details of those calculations are beyond our discussion.

To illustrate, suppose that Employer Firm has calculated its annual pension expense to be $80,000 for 2008. Also suppose that Employer has determined that it will make a funding payment of $60,000 to the pension fund. On the basis of those decisions, Employer should make the following accounting entry for the year:

Dec. 31	Pension Expense	80,000	
	Cash		60,000
	Accrued Pension Cost		20,000
	To record annual pension expense and funding payment		

Assets	**=**	**Liabilities**	**+**	**Shareholders' Equity**
−60,000		+20,000		−80,000

The Pension Expense account is an income statement account and is reflected on Employer's 2008 income statement.

Pensions on the Balance Sheet

The **Accrued Pension Cost** account in the preceding example is a balance sheet account. The account could represent an asset or a liability, depending on whether the amount expensed is more or less than the amount of the funding payment. If the amount expensed is less than the amount paid, it is reported by Employer Firm as an asset and labelled as Prepaid Pension Cost. Normally, the amount expensed is greater than the amount paid, as in the example here. In that case, the Accrued Pension Cost is reported by Employer Firm as a long term liability.

But what is the meaning of the Accrued Pension Cost account? Is it really a liability? It certainly is not a measure of the amount that is owed to employees at the time of retirement. In fact, the only true meaning that can be given to the account is to say that it is the difference between the amount expensed and the amount funded.[4] In that regard, the Accrued Pension Cost account is inadequate in determining a firm's liability to its employees for future retirement benefits. The AcSB requires a great deal of note information for pension plans. This note section can be used to develop a clearer picture of the status of a firm's pension obligation.

Pension Note Information

Readers of financial statements are often interested in the *funding status* of pension plans. This indicates whether sufficient assets are available in the pension fund to cover the amounts to be paid to employees as retirement benefits. We will use the note disclosures of an actual firm to illustrate the use of pension information.

Exhibit 10-12 presents portions of the 2007 pension footnote for CN. CN is a large company with thousands of employees who are covered by the company's pension plans. Analysts who follow the industry must assess whether CN's pension is adequate for its employees. The amounts on the balance sheet give some indication about the status of the

Accrued Pension Cost The difference between the amount of pension recorded as an expense and the amount of the funding payment.

---

[3] *AcSB, Section 3461.*
[4] Some pension plans that are underfunded may be required to report an additional amount as a liability. This is referred to as the *minimum liability provision.*

Exhibit 10-12

CN's Pension Note for 2007
(Footnote 13)

	Pension (in millions)	
	2007	2006
Fair value of plan assets	$16,000	$15,625
Obligation at end of year- salary increases not included - ABO	13,801	13,774
Funding status (1)	$ 2,199	$ 1,851
Obligation at end of year- salary increases included - PBO	$14,419	$14,545
Funding status (2)	$ 1,581	$ 1,080
Balance Sheet		
Prepaid cost (asset)	$ 1,768	$ 1,275
Accrued benefit cost (liability)	(187)	(195)
Net amount recognized by accrual accounting	$ 1,581	$ 1,080
Pension Expense	$ 29	$ 66

This excerpt from CN's 2007 Annual Report appears courtesy of CN. This section of the CN Annual Report aapears in the Appendix of this textbook.

plan, but a more complete picture is provided in the company's notes. Fortunately, the notes can assist us as we determine whether the pension plans could be considered underfunded or overfunded. Several items in the note need to be defined. First, CN has disclosed the amount of plan assets at fair value. This is a measure of the total amount of assets that has been accumulated in the pension fund. The footnote indicates that as of year-end 2007, CN had assets of $16,000 million. Second, CN disclosed a $13,801 million (1) obligation to retirees at the end of 2007. When the obligation is larger than the amount of assets available in the pension fund, the fund is referred to as underfunded. At December 31, 2007, CN's pension funds were overfunded. CN also disclosed a second obligation, namely $14,419 million, for 2007. The second amount (2) reflects the obligation ($16,000 − $14,419 = $1,581) to pensioners if future expected salary increases are included. The disclosure of the two amounts for pension obligations indicates some of the differences between Canadian and U.S. GAAP. The U.S. introduced changes effective December 15, 2006 to show the PBO as the obligation and to make accrual accounting agree with the funding status of the plan as evident in Exhibit 10-12. The overfunded status of $1,581 million equals the accrual balance sheet amount of $1,581 million. The ABO which has the projected salary increases removed from the obligation is the original amount required by Canadian GAAP and currently reflects the Canadian position. Currently Canada and the IASB are attempting to resolve the differences from U.S. GAAP to create some harmony in the area of pensions.

"Fair value of plan assets" represents the estimated market value of the invested contributions by the employer together with the contributions made by employees held by the trustee at the balance sheet date. These investments and the cash held in trust are used or will be used to pay pension benefits to employees upon retirement, or upon leaving the firm if legal title has passed to the employee (termed "vesting").

"Obligations at end of year" represent what the estimated obligation is to employees for services rendered up to the end of the current period as determined by the actuarial specialist. Actuaries estimate the future benefits from the plan and refunds for employees who leave together with what the rate of return will be on resources deposited in the plan. The assumptions, which are based on "defined benefits," involve numerous estimates, which must be constantly revisited as the life of the plan progresses. Details on the assumptions and revisions made are sometimes provided in the footnotes to the pension balance sheet accounts, as prepaid costs or accrued benefit costs. Usually, however, the pension expense is contained within the salaries, wages, and benefits expense and thus may be invisible unless indicated (as CN did in its footnote).

In footnote 13, (an excerpt is shown in Exhibit 10-12), CN disclosed that the funding status and the balance sheet accrual accounting agree if the PBO is used as the pension obligation. CP in its footnote 20 presented in Appendix B to this book, uses the ABO as its pension obligation, the current Canadian position. Also CP showed the variety of factors that typically reflect the differences between the funding status and the accrual accounting results. Differences result from actual gains (losses) in the plan assets compared to the expected gains (losses). Also they result from changes in assumptions, termed actuarial revaluations, as dictated by changes in circumstances or as past service benefits awarded to employees. Traditionally these differences were only taken into balance sheet accruals over a future amortization period such as average working lives much like depreciation. The recent U.S. GAAP changes eliminate these unrecognized differences between the economic and accrual accounting results.

CN's pension plans are overfunded. Not all firms are as fortunate. There have been many press reports of firms whose pension plans are seriously underfunded and for which it is quite questionable whether sufficient assets are available to pay impending retirement benefits. Such underfunded plans must be considered an off-balance-sheet liability by investors or creditors in assessing the company's health.

Users of the financial statements of Canadian and American firms are somewhat fortunate because the disclosure of pensions on the balance sheet and in the notes is quite extensive. The accounting for pensions by firms outside Canada and the United States varies considerably. Many countries do not require firms to accrue pension costs, and the expense is reported only when paid to retirees. Furthermore, within the statements and notes, there is much less disclosure, making an assessment of the funding status of pensions much more difficult. The IASB is attempting to rectify these issues with its updated standards.

A second class of pension plans, defined contribution plans, are seen for some companies. The footnote and balance sheet disclosures for a defined contribution plan are very similar to what was shown on the previous page. The difference relates to the difference in the financial risk between defined contributions and defined benefits—a risk that is significant because with a defined contribution plan, the employer agrees to make stipulated contributions to the plan. The employee's future benefits, however, depend on the accumulated assets that are attributable to the employee. With a defined benefits plan, the future benefits are stipulated or a formula is provided (e.g., 70% of the best three years' earnings by the employee); thus the employer bears the risk because supplemental contributions may be necessary by the employer if the fund cannot keep up in terms of providing the defined benefits.

Post-Retirement Benefits

Pensions represent a benefit paid to employees after their retirement. In addition to pensions, other benefits may be paid to employees after their retirement. For example, many firms promise to pay a portion of retirees' health care costs. The accounting question is whether post-retirement benefits should be considered an expense when paid or during the period that the employee worked for the firm.

A few years ago, most firms treated post-retirement benefits as an expense when they were paid to the retiree. It was widely believed that costs such as those for health care after retirement were too uncertain to be accrued as an expense and that such costs did not meet the definition of a liability and thus did not merit recording. The result of this expense-as-you-pay accounting was that firms had an obligation that was not recorded as a liability. As health care costs began to escalate, this unrecorded—and often undisclosed—cost became a concern for many firms as well as for shareholders, analysts, and employees.

The AcSB has modified the accounting for post-employment benefits to be consistent with pension costs. Under the matching principle, post-retirement costs must now be accrued as an expense during the period that the employee helps the firm generate revenues and thus *earns* the benefits. The accountant must determine the costs of the separate components of post-retirement benefits and total them to calculate the amount of the expense. The amount of the expense is reflected on the income statement in the Post-Retirement Expense account. The balance sheet should normally reflect the Accrued Post-Retirement Cost account. That account should be classified as a liability in the long-term liability category; it indicates the employer's obligation to present and future retirees.

The dollar amount of the liability represented by post-retirement obligations is very large for many companies. For example, in 2007, CN's Footnote 9 to the financial statements reveals the obligation to its employees for these retirement costs was $248 million long-term and $18 million short-term, with an expense in the current period of $14 million (in addition to its pension plan amounts, disclosed in Exhibit 10-12).

There is still much controversy concerning the accounting for post-retirement costs. Many firms object to the accounting requirements because of the uncertainty involved in measuring an obligation that extends far into the future. They also object because the requirements result in reduced profits on the income statement and huge liabilities on the balance sheet. Interestingly, this accounting rule had little impact on the stock market because the investment community already knew the magnitude of the post-retirement obligations.

Chapter Highlights

1. **LO 1 Identify the components of the long-term liability category of the balance sheet (p. 462).**

   - Balance sheets generally have two categories of liabilities: current liabilities and long-term liabilities. Long-term liabilities are obligations that will not be satisfied within one year.

2. **LO 2 Determine the important impacts of bonds payable (p. 462).**

   - The terms of a bond payable are given in the bond certificate. The denomination of a bond is its face value. The interest rate stated in the bond certificate is referred to as the *face rate* or *stated rate of interest*. Term bonds all have the same due date. Serial bonds are not all due on the same date. Convertible bonds can be converted into common shares by the bondholders. Callable bonds may be redeemed or retired before their due date.

   - The issue price of a bond is the present value of the cash flows that the bond will provide to the investor. To determine the price, you must calculate the present values of the annuity of interest payments and of the principal amount. The present values must be calculated at the market rate of interest.

   - A bond sells at a discount or premium, depending on the relationship of the face rate to the market rate of interest. If the face rate exceeds the market rate, a bond is issued at a premium. If the face rate is less than the market rate, it will be issued at a discount.

   - Premiums or discounts must be amortized by transferring a portion of the premium or the discount each period to interest expense. The effective interest method of amortization reduces the balance of the premium or discount such that the effective interest rate on the bond is constant over its life.

   - The carrying value of the bond equals the face value plus unamortized premium or minus unamortized discount.

   - When bonds are redeemed before their due date, a gain or loss on redemption results. The gain or loss is the difference between the bonds' carrying value at the date of redemption and the redemption price.

3. **LO 3 Determine whether a lease agreement must be reported as a liability on the balance sheet and compare it to a mortgage agreement (p. 477).**

   - A lease, a contractual arrangement between two parties, allows the lessee the right to use property in exchange for making payments to the lessor.

   - There are two major categories of lease agreements: operating and capital. The lessee does not report an operating lease as an asset and does not present the obligation to make payments as a liability. Capital leases are reported as assets and liabilities by the lessee. Leases are reported as capital leases if they meet one or more of four criteria.

   - Capital lease assets must be depreciated by the lessee over the life of the lease agreement. Capital lease payments must be separated into interest expense and reduction of principal using the effective interest method. Mortgages used to fund certain businesses are treated in a manner similar to capital leases.

4. **LO 4 Explain the effects that transactions involving long-term liabilities have on the statement of cash flows (p. 484).**

   - Long-term liabilities represent methods of financing. Therefore, changes in the balances of long-term liability accounts should be reflected in the Financing Activities category of the statement of cash flows.

5. **LO 5 Explain deferred (future) taxes and calculate the deferred (future) tax liability (Appendix) (p. 486).**

   - There are many differences between the accounting for tax purposes and the accounting for financial reporting purposes. Permanent differences occur when an item affects one calculation but never affects the other. Temporary differences affect both book and tax calculations but not in the same time period. (Appendix)

   - The amount of tax payable is calculated using the accounting method chosen for tax purposes. The amount of tax expense is calculated using the accounting method chosen for financial reporting purposes. The Future Tax account reconciles the differences between tax expense and tax payable. It reflects all of the temporary differences times the tax rate. Future taxes account a controversial item on the balance sheet, raising questions as to whether they are a true liability. (Appendix)

6. **LO 6 Demonstrate an understanding of the meaning of a pension obligation and the effect of pensions on the long-term liability category of the balance sheet (Appendix) (p. 492).**

   - Pensions represent an obligation to compensate retired employees for service performed while employed. (Appendix)

- Pension expense is presented on the income statement and is calculated on the basis of several complex components that have been specified by the AcSB. (Appendix)
- Pension expense does not represent the amount of cash paid by the employer to the pension fund. The cash payment is referred to as the *funding payment*. The Accrued Pension account is recorded as the difference between the amount of pension expense and the amount of the funding. (Appendix)
- The required note information on pensions can be used to evaluate the funding status of a firm's pension plan. If the amount of assets in the pension fund exceeds the pension obligation, the fund is considered to be overfunded, generally indicating that it is healthy and well managed. An overfunded plan is an example of an "off-balance-sheet" asset that an investor can count toward the value of the company's shares. (Appendix)

Ratio Review

Reporting and analyzing financial statement information related to a company's long-term debt:
The impact of debt in investment and credit decisions can be significant. Because the company must meet its debt obligations in order to remain in business, investors and creditors carefully review its financial information. The following ratios are key to determining whether the company is likely to have resources to pay its liabilities: (a) the proportion of current income, before interest and tax expenses (EBIT), to the current interest expense and (b) the amount of net cash, before interest and taxes have been paid, currently created by company operations when compared to the amount of interest and principal payments that have been paid in the current period. In addition, the ratio of total debt to total equity indicates how heavily the company is burdened by its liabilities.

In this chapter, you learned about three new ratios used for decision making. These ratios are presented below:

$$\text{Times Interest Earned Ratio} = \frac{\text{Income Before Interest and Tax (EBIT)}}{\text{Interest Expense}}$$

$$\text{Debt Service Coverage Ratio} = \frac{\text{Cash Flow from Operations (with Interest and Tax payments added back)}}{\text{Interest and Principal Payments}^*}$$

$$\text{Debt-to-Equity Ratio} = \frac{\text{Total Liabilities}}{\text{Total Shareholders' Equity}}$$

*When the statement of cash flows is prepared under the indirect method, the interest payment amount is disclosed in the notes to the financial statements. Under the direct method, explained in detail in Chapter 12, the interest amount appears on the statement of cash flows in the Operating Activities section.

Accounts Highlighted

Account Titles	Where it Appears	In What Section	Page Number
Bonds Payable	Balance Sheet	Long-Term Liabilities	465
Premium on Bonds Payable	Balance Sheet	Long-Term Liabilities	467
Discount on Bonds Payable	Balance Sheet	Long-Term Liabilities as a contra account	467
Gain on Bond Redemption	Income Statement	Other Income/Expenses	474
Loss on Bond Redemption	Income Statement	Other Income/Expenses	474
Leased Asset	Balance Sheet	Property, Plant and Equipment	477
Lease Obligation	Balance Sheet	Long-Term Liabilities	477
Deferred Income Tax	Balance Sheet	Maybe Asset or Liability	486

Key Terms Quiz

Read each definition below and then write the number of that definition in the blank beside the appropriate term it defines. The quiz solutions appear at the end of the chapter.

_____ Long-term liability	_____ Carrying value
_____ Face value	_____ Gain or loss on redemption
_____ Debenture bonds	_____ Operating lease
_____ Serial bonds	_____ Capital lease
_____ Callable bonds	_____ Future tax (Appendix)
_____ Face rate of interest	_____ Permanent difference (Appendix)
_____ Market rate of interest	_____ Temporary difference (Appendix)
_____ Bond issue price	_____ Pension (Appendix)
_____ Premium	_____ Funding payment (Appendix)
_____ Discount	_____ Accrued pension cost (Appendix)
_____ Effective interest method of amortization	_____ Benefit obligation (Appendix)

1. The principal amount of the bond as stated on the bond certificate.

2. Bonds that do not all have the same due date. A portion of the bonds comes due each time period.

3. The interest rate stated on the bond certificate. It is also called the _nominal or coupon rate._

4. The total of the present value of the cash flows produced by a bond. It is calculated as the present value of the annuity of interest payments plus the present value of the principal.

5. An obligation that will not be satisfied within one year.

6. The excess of the issue price over the face value of bonds. It occurs when the face rate on the bonds exceeds the market rate.

7. Bonds that are backed by the general creditworthiness of the issuer and are not backed by specific collateral.

8. The excess of the face value of bonds over the issue price. It occurs when the market rate on the bonds exceeds the face rate.

9. Bonds that may be redeemed or retired before their specified due date.

10. The process of transferring a portion of premium or discount to interest expense. This method transfers an amount resulting in a constant effective interest rate.

11. The face value of a bond plus the amount of unamortized premium or minus the amount of unamortized discount.

12. The interest rate that bondholders could obtain by investing in other bonds that are similar to the issuing firm's bonds.

Answers on p. 515

13. The difference between the carrying value and the redemption price at the time bonds are redeemed. This amount is presented as an income statement account.

14. A lease that does not meet any of four criteria and is not recorded by the lessee as an asset and liability.

15. A payment made by the employer to the pension fund or its trustee.

16. A lease that meets one or more of four criteria and is recorded as an asset by the lessee.

17. A difference between the accounting for tax purposes and the accounting for financial reporting purposes. This type of difference affects both book and tax calculations but not in the same time period.

18. The account used to reconcile the difference between the amount recorded as income tax expense and the amount that is payable as income tax.

19. A difference between the accounting for tax purposes and the accounting for financial reporting purposes. This type of difference occurs when an item affects one set of calculations but never affects the other set.

20. An obligation to pay retired employees as compensation for service performed while employed.

21. An account that represents the difference between the amount of pension recorded as an expense and the amount of the funding payment made to the pension fund.

22. A measure of the amount owed to employees for pensions if the employees retire at their existing salary levels.

Alternate Terms

Bond face value Bond par value

Bonds payable Notes payable

Bond retirement Extinguishment of bonds

Carrying value of bond Book value of bond

Effective interest amortization Interest method of amortization

Face rate of interest Stated rate or nominal rate or coupon rate of interest

Long-term liabilities Non-current liabilities

Market rate of interest Yield or effective rate of interest

Postretirement costs Other post-employment benefits

Benefit obligation Projected Benefits Obligation (PBO)/ Accumulated Benefits Obligation (ABO)

Redemption price Reacquisition price

Temporary difference Timing difference

Warmup Exercise 10-1

A bond due in 10 years, with face value of $1,000 and face rate of interest of 8%, is issued when the market rate of interest is 6%.

Required

1. What is the issue price of the bond?

2. What is the amount of premium or discount on the bond at the time of issuance?

3. What amount of interest expense will be shown on the income statement for the first year of the bond?

4. What amount of the premium or discount will be amortized during the first year of the bond?

Warmup Exercise 10-2

You have signed an agreement to lease a car for four years and will make annual payments of $4,000 at the end of each year. (Assume that the lease meets the criteria for a capital lease.)

Required

1. Calculate the present value of the lease payments, assuming an 8% interest rate.

2. What is the journal entry to record the leased asset?

3. When the first lease payment is made, what portion of the payment will be considered interest?

Solutions to Warmup Exercises

Warmup Exercise 10-1

1. The issue price of the bond would be calculated at the present value:

$80(7.360)$	$= \$\ 588.80$	using Table 9-4, where $i = 6\%$ and $n = 10$
$\$1,000(0.558)$	$= \underline{\quad 558.00}$	using Table 9-2, where $i = 6\%$ and $n = 10$
Issue price	$\$1,146.80$	

2. The amount of the premium is the difference between the issue price and the face value:

    $$\text{Premium} = \$1,146.80 - \$1,000$$
    $$= \$146.80$$

3. The amount of interest expense can be calculated as follows:

    $$\text{Interest Expense} = \$1,146.80 \times 0.06$$
    $$= \$68.81$$

4. The amount that will be amortized can be calculated as follows:

    $$\text{Amortized} = \text{Cash Interest} - \text{Interest Expense}$$
    $$= (\$1,000 \times 0.08) - (\$1,146.80 \times 0.06)$$
    $$= \$80.00 - \$68.81$$
    $$= \$11.19$$

Warmup Exercise 10-2

1. The present value of the lease payments can be calculated as follows:

    $$\text{Present Value} = \$4,000(3.312) \text{ using Table 9-4, where } i = 8\%, n = 4$$
    $$= \$13,248$$

2. The journal entry to record the lease agreement:

Leased Asset	13,248	
Lease Obligation		13,248

3. The amount of interest can be calculated as follows:

    $$\text{Interest} = \$13,248 \times 0.08$$
    $$= \$1,059.84$$

The following items pertain to the liabilities of Brent Foods. You may assume that Brent Foods began business on January 1, 2008, and therefore the beginning balance of all accounts was zero.

a. On January 1, 2008, Brent Foods issued bonds with a face value of $50,000. The bonds are due in five years and have a face interest rate of 10%. The market rate on January 1 for similar bonds was 12%. The bonds pay interest annually each December 31. Brent has chosen to use the effective interest method of amortization for any premium or discount on the bonds.

b. On December 31, Brent Foods signed a lease agreement with Cordova Leasing. The agreement requires Brent to make annual lease payments of $3,000 per year for four years, with the first payment due on December 31, 2009. The agreement stipulates that ownership of the property is transferred to Brent at the end of the four-year lease. Assume that an 8% interest rate is used for the leasing transaction.

c. On January 1, 2009, Brent redeems its bonds payable at the specified redemption price of 101. Because this item occurs in 2009, it does not affect the balance sheet prepared for year-end 2008.

Required

1. Make the accounting entries necessary on December 31, 2008, to record the interest adjustment in item **a** and the signing of the lease in item **b**.

2. Develop the Long-Term Liabilities section of Brent Foods' balance sheet as of December 31, 2008, based on items **a** and **b**. You do not need to consider the notes that accompany the balance sheet.

3. Would the company prefer to treat the lease in item **b** as an operating lease? Why or why not?

4. Calculate the gain or loss on the bond redemption for item **c**.

Solution to Review Problem

1. **a.** The issue price of the bonds on January 1, must be calculated at the present value of the interest payments and the present value of the principal, as follows:

$5,000 × 3.605	$18,025
$50,000 × 0.567	28,350
Issue price	$46,375

The amount of the discount is calculated as follows:

$$\$50,000 - \$46,375 = \$3,625$$

The following is the entry on December 31, 2008, to record interest and to amortize discount:

Dec. 31	Interest Expense	5,565	
	Cash		5,000
	Discount on Bonds Payable		565
	To record interest and amortize discount		

Assets	=	**Liabilities**	+	**Shareholders' Equity**
−5,000		+565		−5,565

The interest expense is calculated using the effective interest method by multiplying the carrying value of the bonds times the market rate of interest ($46,375 × 12%).

Brent must show two accounts in the Long-Term Liabilities section of the balance sheet: Bonds Payable of $50,000 and Discount on Bonds Payable of $3,060 ($3,625 less $565 amortized).

b. The lease meets the criteria to be a capital lease. Brent must report the lease as an asset and report the obligation for lease payments as a liability. The transaction should be reported at the present value of the lease payments, $9,936 (computed by multiplying $3,000 by the annuity factor of 3.312). The accounting entry should be as follows:

Dec. 31	Leased Asset	9,936	
	Lease Obligation		9,936
	To record lease as a capital lease		

Assets = Liabilities + Shareholders' Equity
+9,936   +9,936

Because the lease agreement was signed on December 31, 2008, it is not necessary to amortize the Lease Obligation account in 2008. The account should be stated in the Long-Term Liabilities section of Brent's balance sheet at $9,936.

2. The Long-Term Liabilities section of Brent's balance sheet for December 31, 2008, on the basis of items **a** and **b** is as follows:

BRENT FOODS
PARTIAL BALANCE SHEET
AS OF DECEMBER 31, 2008

Long-term liabilities:		
Bonds payable	$50,000	
Less: Unamortized discount on bonds payable	3,060	$46,940
Lease obligation		9,936
Total long-term liabilities		$56,876

3. The company would prefer that the lease be an operating lease because it would not have to report the asset or liability on the balance sheet. This off–balance-sheet financing may give a more favourable impression of the company.

4. Brent must calculate the loss on the bond redemption as the difference between the carrying value of the bonds ($46,940) and the redemption price ($50,000 × 1.01). The amount of the loss is calculated as follows:

$50,500 – $46,940 = $3,560 loss on redemption

Questions

1. Which interest rate, the face rate or the market rate, should be used when calculating the issue price of a bond? Why?

2. What is the tax advantage that companies experience when bonds are issued instead of shares?

3. Does the issuance of bonds at a premium indicate that the face rate is higher or lower than the market rate of interest?

4. How does the effective interest method of amortization result in a constant rate of interest?

5. What is the meaning of the following sentence: "Amortization affects the amount of interest expense"? How does amortization of a premium affect the amount of interest expense? How does amortization of a discount affect the amount of interest expense?

6. Does amortization of a premium increase or decrease the bond carrying value? Does amortization of a discount increase or decrease the bond carrying value?

7. Is there always a gain or loss when bonds are redeemed? How is the gain or loss calculated?

8. What are the reasons that not all leases are accounted for in the same manner? Do you think it would be possible to develop a new accounting rule that would treat all leases in the same manner?

9. What is the meaning of the term *off-balance-sheet financing?* Why do some firms want to engage in off-balance-sheet transactions?

10. What are the effects on the financial statements if a lease is considered an operating rather than a capital lease?

11. Should depreciation be reported on leased assets? If so, over what period of time should depreciation occur?

12. Why do firms have a Future Tax account? Where should that account be shown on the financial statements? (Appendix)

13. How can you determine whether an item should reflect a permanent or a temporary difference when calculating the future tax amount? (Appendix)

14. Does the amount of income tax expense presented on the income statement represent the amount of tax actually paid? Why or why not? (Appendix)

15. When an employer has a pension plan for employees, what information is shown on the financial statements concerning the pension plan? (Appendix)

16. How can you determine whether a pension plan is overfunded or underfunded? (Appendix)

17. Do you agree with this statement: "All liabilities could be legally enforced in a court of law"? (Appendix)

Exercise 10-1 *Relationships* **LO 2**

The following components are computed annually when a bond is issued for other than its face value:

■ Cash interest payment

■ Interest expense

■ Amortization of discount/premium

■ Carrying value of bond

Required

State whether each component will increase (I), decrease (D), or remain constant (C) as the bond approaches maturity, given the following situations:

1. Issued at a discount.

2. Issued at a premium.

Exercise 10-2 *Issue Price* **LO 2**

Bedford Ltd. plans to issue $250,000 face value bonds with a stated interest rate of 4%. They will mature in 10 years. Interest will be paid semiannually. At the date of issuance, assume the market rate is (a) 4%, (b) 3%, and (c) 6%.

Required

For each market interest rate, answer the following questions:

1. What is the amount due at maturity?

2. How much cash interest will be paid every six months?

3. At what price will the bond be issued?

Exercise 10-3 *Issue Price* **LO 2**

The following terms relate to independent bond issues:

a. 500 bonds; $1,000 face value; 6% stated rate; 5 years; annual interest payments

b. 500 bonds; $1,000 face value; 6% stated rate; 5 years; semiannual interest payments

c. 800 bonds; $1,000 face value; 6% stated rate; 10 years; semiannual interest payments

d. 2,000 bonds; $500 face value; 8% stated rate; 15 years; semiannual interest payments

Required

Assuming the market rate of interest is 8%, calculate the selling price for each bond issue.

Exercise 10-4 *Impact of Two Bond Alternatives* **LO 2**

Ping Company wants to issue 100 bonds, $1,000 face value, in January. The bonds will have a 10-year life and pay interest annually. The market rate of interest on January 1, will be 8%. Ping is considering two alternative bond issues: (a) bonds with a face rate of 6% and (b) bonds with a face rate of 9%.

Required

1. Could the company save money by issuing bonds with a 6% face rate? If it chooses alternative (a), what would be the interest cost as a percentage?

2. Could the company benefit by issuing bonds with a 9% face rate? If it chooses alternative (b), what would be the interest cost as a percentage?

Exercise 10-5 *Redemption of Bonds* **LO 2**

Rhyno Corporation issued $150,000 face value bonds at a discount of $5,000. The bonds contain a call price of 103. Rhyno decides to redeem the bonds early when the unamortized discount is $3,500.

Required

1. Calculate Rhyno Corporation's gain or loss on the early redemption of the bonds.

2. Describe how the gain or loss would be reported on the income statement and in the notes to the financial statements.

Exercise 10-6 *Redemption of a Bond at Maturity* LO 2

On May 31, 2008, Bayside Ltd. issued $500,000 face value bonds at a discount of $14,000. The bonds were retired at their maturity date, May 31, 2018.

Required

Assuming the last interest payment and the amortization of discount have already been recorded, calculate the gain or loss on the redemption of the bonds on May 31, 2018. Prepare the journal entry to record the redemption of the bonds.

Exercise 10-7 *Leased Asset* LO 3

Lam Corporation signed a 10-year capital lease on January 1, 2008. The lease requires annual payments of $16,000 every December 31.

Required

1. Assuming an interest rate of 9%, calculate the present value of the minimum lease payments.

2. Explain why the value of the leased asset and the accompanying lease obligation are not initially reported on the balance sheet at $160,000.

Exercise 10-8 *Financial Statement Impact of a Lease* LO 3

Burnside Storage signed a six-year capital lease on January 1, 2008, with payments due every December 31. Interest is calculated annually at 5%, and the present value of the minimum lease payments is $26,130.

Required

1. Calculate the amount of the annual payment that Burnside must make every December 31.

2. Calculate the amount of the lease obligation that would be presented on the December 31, 2009, balance sheet (after two lease payments have been made).

Exercise 10-9 *Leased Assets* LO 3

Able Ltd. signed a four-year lease for a trucklift on January 1, 2008. Annual lease payments of $3,020, based on an interest rate of 4%, are to be made every December 31, beginning with December 31, 2008.

Required

1. Assume the lease is treated as an operating lease.

   a. Will the value of the trucklift appear on Able's balance sheet?

   b. What account will indicate lease payments have been made?

2. Assume the lease is treated as a capital lease.

   a. Prepare any journal entries needed when the lease is signed. Explain why the value of the leased asset is not recorded at $12,080 ($3,020 × 4).

   b. Prepare the journal entry to record the first lease payment on December 31, 2008.

   c. Prepare the adjusting entry to record depreciation expense on December 31, 2008.

   d. At what amount would the lease obligation be presented on the balance sheet as of December 31, 2008?

Exercise 10-10 *Impact of Transactions Involving Bonds on Statement of Cash Flows* LO 4

From the following list, identify each item as operating (O), investing (I), financing (F), or not separately reported on the statement of cash flows (N).

Proceeds from issuance of bonds payable

Interest expense

Redemption of bonds payable at maturity

Exercise 10-11 *Impact of Transactions Involving Capital Leases on Statement of Cash Flows* **LO 4**

Assume that Lois Company signs a lease agreement with Marion Ltd. to lease a piece of equipment and determines that the lease should be treated as a capital lease. Lois records a leased asset in the amount of $106,800 and a lease obligation in the same amount on its balance sheet.

Required

1. Indicate how this transaction would be reported on Lois's statement of cash flows.

2. From the following list of transactions relating to this lease, identify each item as operating (O), investing (I), financing (F), or not separately reported on the statement of cash flows (N).

   Reduction of lease obligation (principal portion of lease payment)

   Interest expense

   Depreciation expense—leased assets

Exercise 10-12 *Impact of Transactions Involving Tax Liabilities on Statement of Cash Flows (Appendix)* **LO 5**

From the following list, identify each item as operating (O), investing (I), financing (F), or not separately reported on the statement of cash flows (N). For items identified as operating, indicate whether the related amount would be added to or deducted from net income in determining the cash flows from operating activities.

   Decrease in taxes payable

   Increase in future taxes

Exercise 10-13 *Temporary and Permanent Differences (Appendix)* **LO 5**

Leo Ltd. wants to determine the amount of future tax that should be reported on its 2008 financial statements. It has compiled a list of differences between the accounting conducted for tax purposes and the accounting used for financial reporting (book) purposes.

Required

For each of the following items, indicate whether the difference should be classified as a permanent or a temporary difference.

1. During 2008, Leo received dividends on shares of another Canadian company purchased as an investment.

2. During 2008, Leo paid for a life insurance premium on two key executives. Leo's accountant has indicated that the amount of the premium cannot be deducted for income tax purposes.

3. During December 2008, Leo received money for renting a building to a tenant. Leo must report the rent as income on its 2008 tax return. For book purposes, however, the rent will be considered income on the 2009 income statement.

4. Leo owns several pieces of equipment that it depreciates using the straight-line method for book purposes. CCA is used for tax purposes, however.

5. Leo offers a warranty on the product it sells. The corporation records the expense of the warranty repair costs in the year the product is sold (the accrual method) for book purposes. For tax purposes, however, Leo is not allowed to deduct the expense until the period when the product is repaired.

6. During 2008, Leo was assessed a large fine by the federal government for polluting the environment. Leo's accountant has indicated that the fine cannot be deducted as an expense for income tax purposes.

Exercise 10-14 *Future Tax (Appendix)* **LO 5**

On July 1, 2008, Alan Corporation purchased an asset for $64,000. Assume this is the only asset owned by the company. Alan has decided to use the straight-line method to depreciate it over five years. For tax purposes, it will be in the 30% CCA class. Assume that Alan Corporation is subject to a 40% tax rate and that the CCA class will be closed for income tax purposes in 2013.

Required

Calculate the balance that should be reflected in the Future Tax account for Alan Corporation for each year 2008 through 2013.

Exercise 10-15 *Pension Analysis (Appendix)* **LO 6**

The following information was extracted from a note found in the 2008 annual report of a company.

Plan Assets	$5.2 billion
Benefit Obligation	$4.2 billion

Required

1. Determine whether the pension plan is overfunded or underfunded.

2. Explain what your response to requirement 1 implies about the ability of the plan to provide benefits to future retirees.

Exercise 10-16 *Issuance of a Bond at Face Value* **LO 2**

On January 1, 2008, Spencer Ltd. issued 600, $1,000 face value bonds. The bonds have a five-year life and pay interest at the rate of 8%. Interest is paid semiannually on July 1 and January 1. The market rate of interest on January 1 was 8%.

Required

1. Calculate the issue price of the bonds and record the issuance of the bonds on January 1, 2008.

2. Explain how the issue price would have been affected if the market rate of interest had been higher than 8%.

3. Prepare the journal entry to record the payment of interest on July 1, 2008.

4. Prepare the journal entry to record the accrual of interest on December 31, 2008.

Multi-Concept Exercises

Exercise 10-17 *Impact of a Discount* **LO 1, 2**

Kingston Ltd. sold 20-year bonds on January 1, 2008. The face value of the bonds was $200,000, and they carry a 4.5% stated rate of interest, which is paid on December 31 of every year. Kingston received $187,558 in return for the issuance of the bonds when the market rate was 5%. Any premium or discount is amortized using the effective interest method.

Required

1. Prepare the journal entry to record the sale of the bonds on January 1, 2008, and the proper balance sheet presentation on this date.

2. Prepare the journal entry to record interest expense on December 31, 2008, and the proper balance sheet presentation on this date.

3. Explain why it was necessary for Kingston to issue the bonds for only $187,558 rather than $200,000.

Exercise 10-18 *Impact of a Premium* **LO 1, 2**

Assume the same set of facts for Kingston Ltd. as in Exercise 10-17 except that it received $213,510 in return for the issuance of the bonds when the market rate was 4%.

Required

1. Prepare the journal entry to record the sale of the bonds on January 1, 2008, and the proper balance sheet presentation on this date.

2. Prepare the journal entry to record interest expense on December 31, 2008, and the proper balance sheet presentation on this date.

3. Explain why the company was able to issue the bonds for $213,510 rather than for the face amount.

Problems

Problem 10-1 *Factors That Affect the Bond Issue Price* LO 2

Fisher Company is considering the issue of $200,000 face value, 10-year term bonds. The bonds will pay 6% interest each December 31. The current market rate is 6%; therefore, the bonds will be issued at face value.

Required

1. For each of the following independent situations, indicate whether you believe that the company will receive a premium on the bonds or will issue them at a discount or at face value. Without using numbers, explain your position.

   a. Interest is paid semiannually instead of annually.

   b. Assume instead that the market rate of interest is 7%; the nominal rate is still 6% payable annually.

2. For each situation in requirement 1, prove your statement by determining the issue price of the bonds given the changes in parts **a** and **b** of requirement 1.

Problem 10-2 *Amortization of Discount* LO 2

Shearwater issued five-year, 5% bonds with face value of $20,000 on January 1, 2008. Interest is paid annually on December 31. The market rate of interest on this date is 6%, and Shearwater receives proceeds of $19,152 on the bond issuance.

Required

1. Prepare a five-year table (similar to Exhibit 10-4) to amortize the discount using the effective interest method.

2. What is the total interest expense over the life of the bonds? cash interest payment? discount amortization?

3. Prepare the journal entry for the payment of interest and the amortization of discount on December 31, 2010 (the third year), and determine the balance sheet presentation of the bonds on that date.

Problem 10-3 *Amortization of Premium* LO 2

Assume the same set of facts for Shearwater as in Problem 10-2 except that the market rate of interest on January 1, 2008, is 4% and the proceeds from the bond issuance equal $20,892.

Required

1. Prepare a five-year table (similar to Exhibit 10-5) to amortize the premium using the effective interest method.

2. What is the total interest expense over the life of the bonds? cash interest payments? premium amortization?

3. Prepare the journal entry for the payment of interest and the amortization of premium on December 31, 2010 (the third year), and determine the balance sheet presentation of the bonds on that date.

Problem 10-4 *Redemption of Bonds* LO 2

MacDonald Company issued $400,000 face value bonds at a premium of $9,000. The bonds contain a call provision of 101. MacDonald decides to redeem the bonds, due to a significant decline in interest rates. On that date, MacDonald had amortized only $2,000 of the premium.

Required

1. Calculate the gain or loss on the early redemption of the bonds.

2. Calculate the gain or loss on the redemption, assuming that the call provision is 103 instead of 101.

3. Indicate where the gain or loss should be presented on the financial statements.

4. Why do you suppose the call price is normally higher than 100?

Problem 10-5 *Financial Statement Impact of a Lease* LO 3

On January 1, 2008, Amour Trucking Company leased a semi-tractor and trailer for five years. Annual payments of $56,600 are to be made every December 31, beginning December 31, 2008. Interest expense is based on a rate of 8%. The present value of the minimum lease payments is $226,000 and has been determined to be greater than 90% of the fair market value of the asset on January 1, 2008. Amour uses straight-line depreciation on all assets.

Required

1. Prepare a table similar to Exhibit 10-8 to show the five-year amortization of the lease obligation.
2. Prepare the journal entry for the lease transaction on January 1, 2008.
3. Prepare all necessary journal entries on December 31, 2009 (the second year of the lease).
4. Prepare the balance sheet presentation as of December 31, 2009, for the leased asset and the lease obligation.
5. Repeat the above journal entries (2, 3) assuming Armour borrowed the required funds with a mortgage.

Problem 10-6 *Future Tax (Appendix)* LO 5

Arin Ltd. has compiled its 2008 financial statements. Included in the Long-Term Liabilities category of the balance sheet are the following amounts:

	2008	2007
Future tax	$180	$100

Included in the income statement are the following amounts related to income taxes:

	2008	2007
Income before tax	$500	$400
Tax expense	200	160
Net income	$300	$240

In the notes that accompany the 2008 statement are the following amounts:

	2008
Current tax expense	$120
Future tax expense	80

Required

1. Prepare the journal entry in 2008 for income tax expense, future tax, and income tax payable.
2. Assume that a shareholder has inquired about the meaning of the numbers recorded and disclosed about future tax. Explain why the Future Tax liability account exists. Also, what do the terms current tax expense and future tax expense mean? Why is the future amount in the note $80 when the future amount on the 2008 balance sheet is $180?

Problem 10-7 *Future Tax Calculations (Appendix)* LO 5

Cole Ltd. reported income from operations, before taxes and depreciation, for 2006–2008 as follows:

2006	$420,000
2007	480,000
2008	560,000

When calculating income, Cole deducted depreciation on plant equipment. The equipment was purchased July 1, 2006, at a cost of $176,000. The equipment is expected to last three years and have $16,000 residual value. Cole uses straight-line depreciation for book purposes. For tax purposes, CCA on the equipment is 45% beginning in 2006. Assume the class will continue beyond 2008. Cole's tax rate is 35%.

Required

1. How much did Cole pay in income tax each year?
2. How much income tax expense did Cole record each year?
3. What is the balance in the Future Income Tax account at the end of 2006, 2007, and 2008?

Problem 10-8 *Financial Statement Impact of a Pension (Appendix)* **LO 6**

Cable Ltd. prepared the following schedule relating to its pension expense and pension-funding payment for the years 2006 through 2008.

Year	Expense	Payment
2006	$200,000	$180,000
2007	170,000	210,000
2008	224,000	200,000

At the beginning of 2006, the Prepaid/Accrued Pension Cost account was reported on the balance sheet as an asset with a balance of $8,000.

Required

1. Prepare the journal entries to record Cable Ltd.'s pension expense for 2006, 2007, and 2008.

2. Calculate the balance in the Prepaid/Accrued Pension Cost account at the end of 2008. Does this represent an asset or a liability?

3. Explain the effects that pension expense, the funding payment, and the balance in the Prepaid/Accrued Pension Cost account have on the 2008 income statement and balance sheet.

Multi-Concept Problems

Problem 10-9 *Bond Transactions* **LO 2, 4**

Bond Company issued $500,000 face value, eight-year, 6% bonds on April 1, 2008, when the market rate of interest was 6%. Interest payments are due every October 1 and April 1. Bond uses a calendar year-end.

Required

1. Prepare the journal entry to record the issuance of the bonds on April 1, 2008.

2. Prepare the journal entry to record the interest payment on October 1, 2008.

3. Explain why additional interest must be recorded on December 31, 2008. What impact does this have on the amounts paid on April 1, 2009?

4. Determine the total cash inflows and outflows that occurred on the bonds over the eight-year life.

Problem 10-10 *Partial Classified Balance Sheet for Wylie* **LO 1, 5, 6**

The following items, listed alphabetically, appear on Wylie's consolidated balance sheet at August 31, 2008.

Accrued expenses and other liabilities	$1,407
Future income tax (long-term)	204
Income taxes payable	129
Other non-current liabilities	717
Short-term borrowings	660
Trade accounts payable	2,319

Required

1. Prepare the Current Liabilities and Long-Term Liabilities sections of Wylie's classified balance sheet at August 31, 2008.

2. Wylie's had total liabilities of $4,305 and total shareholders' equity of $6,351 at August 31, 2007. Total shareholders' equity at August 31, 2008, amounted to $7,812. Compute the company's debt-to-equity ratio at August 31, 2008 and 2007, respectively. As an investor, how would you react to the changes in this ratio?

3. What other related ratios would the company's lenders use to assess the company? What do these ratios measure?

Problem 10-1A *Factors that Affect the Bond Issue Price* LO 2

Riverside Ltd. is considering the issuance of $1,000,000 face value, 10-year term bonds. The bonds will pay 5% interest each December 31. The current market rate is 5%; therefore, the bonds will be issued at face value.

Required

1. For each of the following independent situations, indicate whether you believe that the company will receive a premium on the bonds or will issue them at a discount or at face value. Without using numbers, explain your position.

   a. Interest is paid semiannually instead of annually.

   b. Assume instead that the market rate of interest is 4%; the nominal rate is still 5% annually.

2. For each situation in requirement 1, prove your statement by determining the issue price of the bonds given the changes in parts **a** and **b** of requirement 1.

Problem 10-2A *Amortization of Discount* LO 2

Ottawa Corporation issued five-year, 5% bonds with face value of $100,000 on January 1, 2008. Interest is paid annually on December 31. The market rate of interest on this date is 8%, and Ottawa Corporation receives proceeds of $88,065 on the bond issuance.

Required

1. Prepare a five-year table (similar to Exhibit 10-4) to amortize the discount using the effective interest method.

2. What is the total interest expense over the life of the bonds? cash interest payment? discount amortization?

3. Prepare the journal entry to record interest expense on December 31, 2010 (the third year), and the balance sheet presentation of the bonds on that date.

Problem 10-3A *Amortization of Premium* LO 2

Assume the same set of facts for Ottawa Corporation as in Problem 10-2A except that the market rate of interest of January 1, 2008, is 4% and the proceeds from the bond issuance equal $104,460.

Required

1. Prepare a five-year table (similar to Exhibit 10-5) to amortize the premium using the effective interest method.

2. What is the total interest expense over the life of the bonds? cash interest payments? premium amortization?

3. Prepare the journal entry to record interest expense on December 31, 2010 (the third year), and the balance sheet presentation of the bonds on that date.

Problem 10-4A *Redemption of Bonds* LO 2

Albert Company issued $200,000 face value bonds at a premium of $11,000. The bonds contain a call provision of 101. Albert decides to redeem the bonds, due to a significant decline in interest rates. On that date, Albert has amortized only $4,000 of the premium.

Required

1. Calculate the gain or loss on the early redemption of the bonds.

2. Calculate the gain or loss on the redemption, assuming that the call provision is 104 instead of 101.

3. Indicate how the gain or loss would be reported on the income statement and in the notes to the financial statements.

4. Why do you suppose that the call price of the bonds is normally an amount higher than 100?

Problem 10-5A *Financial Statement Impact of a Lease* **LO 3**

On January 1, 2008, Kentville Processing Ltd. leased a factory machine for six years. Annual payments of $43,960 are to be made every December 31, beginning December 31, 2008. Interest expense is based on a rate of 9%. The present value of the minimum lease payments is $197,200 and has been determined to be greater than 90% of the fair market value of the machine on January 1, 2008. Kentville uses straight-line depreciation on all assets.

Required

1. Prepare a table similar to Exhibit 10-8 to show the six-year amortization of the lease obligation.
2. Prepare the journal entry to record the signing of the lease on January 1, 2008.
3. Prepare all journal entries necessary on December 31, 2009 (the second year of the lease).
4. Prepare the balance sheet presentation as of December 31, 2009, for the leased asset and the lease obligation.
5. Repeat the requirements for parts 2 and 3 assuming Kentville purchased the machine using the funds for a mortgage.

Problem 10-6A *Future Tax (Appendix)* **LO 5**

John Ltd. has compiled its 2008 financial statements. Included in the Long-Term Liabilities category of the balance sheet are the following amounts:

	2008	2007
Future tax	$180	$200

Included in the income statement are the following amounts related to income taxes:

	2008	2007
Income before tax	$500	$400
Tax expense	100	150
Net income	$400	$250

Required

1. Prepare the journal entry recorded in 2008 for income tax expense, future tax, and income tax payable.
2. Assume that a shareholder has inquired about the meaning of the numbers recorded. Explain why the Future Tax liability account exists.

Problem 10-7A *Future Tax Calculations (Appendix)* **LO 5**

Yarmouth Ltd. has reported income for book purposes as follows for the past three years:

(in Thousands)	Year 1	Year 2	Year 3
Income before taxes and depreciation	$240	$240	$240

Yarmouth has identified two items that are treated differently in the financial records and in the tax records. The first one is dividend income on investments in shares of another Canadian corporation, which is recognized on the financial reports to the extent of $10,000 each year but does not show up as a revenue item on the company's tax return. The other item is equipment that is depreciated using the straight-line method, at the rate of $40,000 each year, for financial accounting but is a 30% CCA class. Note the original cost was $200,000 five years prior to the most recent year. Assume that the CCA class continues beyond Year 3.

Required

1. Determine the amount of cash paid for income taxes each year by Yarmouth. Assume that a 40% tax rate applies to all three years.
2. Calculate the balance in the Future Tax account at the end of Years 1, 2, and 3. How does this account appear on the balance sheet?

Problem 10-8A *Financial Statement Impact of a Pension (Appendix)* **LO 6**

Benefit Company prepared the following schedule relating to its pension expense and pension-funding payment for the years 2006 through 2008:

Year	Expense	Payment
2006	$200,000	$220,000
2007	170,000	160,000
2008	224,000	200,000

At the beginning of 2006, the Prepaid/Accrued Pension Cost account was reported on the balance sheet as an asset with a balance of $10,000.

Required

1. Prepare the journal entries to record Benefit Company's pension expense for 2006, 2007, and 2008.

2. Calculate the balance in the Prepaid/Accrued Pension Cost account at the end of 2008.

3. Explain the effects that pension expense, the funding payment, and the balance in the Prepaid/Accrued Pension Cost account have on the 2008 income statement and balance sheet.

Problem 10-9A *Financial Statement Impact of a Bond* **LO 2**

Vancouver Company issued $2,000,000 face value, six-year, 6% bonds on July 1, 2008, when the market rate of interest was 8%. Interest payments are due every July 1 and January 1. Vancouver uses a calendar year-end.

Required

1. Prepare the journal entry to record the issuance of the bonds on July 1, 2008.

2. Prepare the adjusting journal entry on December 31, 2008, to accrue interest expense.

3. Prepare the journal entry to record the interest payment on January 1, 2009.

4. Prepare the journal entry to record the retirement of the bonds on the maturity date.

Alternate Multi-Concept Problems

Problem 10-10A *Partial Classified Balance Sheet* **LO 1, 5, 6**

The following items appear on the consolidated balance sheet of LED Ltd. at December 31, 2008. The information in parentheses was added to aid in your understanding.

Accounts payable and other liabilities	$9,248
Accrued retiree healthcare	3,578
Advances from customers in excess of related costs	834
Short-term debt and current portion of long-term debt	932
Income tax payable	606
Long-term debt	7,244
Future income taxes (long-term)	118
Unearned lease income (long-term)	414

Required

1. Prepare the Current Liabilities and Long-Term Liabilities sections of LED's classified balance sheet at December 31, 2008.

2. LED had total liabilities of $24,598 and total shareholders' equity of $7,346 at December 31, 2007. Total shareholders' equity amounted to $7,216 at December 31, 2008. Compute LED's debt-to-equity ratio at December 31, 2008 and 2007. As an investor, how would you react to the change in this ratio?

3. What other related ratios would the company's lenders use to assess the company? What do these ratios measure?

Cases

Reading and Interpreting Financial Statements

CN

http://www.cn.ca

http://www.cpr.ca

Case 10-1 *Comparing Two Companies in the Same Industry: CN and CP.* **LO 1, 2, 3**

The Current Liabilities and Long-Term Liabilities sections of CN's and CP's balance sheet as of December 31, 2007, and December 31, 2006, are presented in Appendixes A and B of this text.

Required

1. Calculate the debt-to-equity ratio on December 31, 2007, for CP and CN. How do the two ratios compare? What does that tell you about the two companies?

2. Comment on the reasons for the change in CP's total liabilities from December 31, 2006, to December 31, 2007. What are the most important changes? What impact do these changes have on the company's cash flow?

3. Note 14 of CP's annual report for 2007 describes various elements of the long-term debt.
   a. Speculate on the meaning of the 6.91% Secured Equipment Notes. Are these notes secured? How?
   b. Explain the nature of the 2008–2015 secured equipment loan amounting to $144.2 million. How is the interest calculated?

4. What is the amount of the payment on the cash flow statement for long-term debt expected based on Footnote 14 in 2007? What was paid on the long-term debt? How does it appear CP paid its debt in 2007?

Case 10-2 *CP's Taxes and Pensions* **LO 5, 6**

CP's annual report in Appendix B of this book describes income taxes in Footnote 6, and pensions and other benefits in Footnote 20.

Required

1. Determine the amount of off–balance-sheet debt CP has that resulted from its pension and benefit obligations to its employees, as of December 31, 2007.

2. Ascertain the amount of tax expense shown by CP for 2007. How much did CP owe the government at the end of 2007? Explain the possible reasons why the current tax expense for 2007 does not equal the taxes payable at the end of 2007.

3. Explain the nature of the difference between the current income tax expense and the total income tax expense.

Case 10-3 *CN's Cash Flows* **LO 4, 5, 6**

Refer to the annual report of CN, presented in Appendix A of this book.

Required

1. Determine how CN paid $218 million for the current portion of long-term debt shown at the end of 2006. Could CN have paid the debt with its cash flow from operations for 2007?

2. Explain the specific effect of deferred income tax on cash flow from operations for 2007.

3. Determine how much of the benefits to employees must be paid in 2008 (refer to Footnote 13). What was the benefits expense for 2007? What amount is shown on the balance sheet at the end of 2007? How much did the pension plan actually pay to CN's employees for 2007?

Making Financial Decisions

Case 10-4 *Making a Loan Decision* **LO 1, 4**

Assume that you are a loan officer in charge of reviewing loan applications from potential new clients at a major bank. You are considering an application from Mosher Ltd., which is a fairly new company with a limited credit history. It has provided a balance sheet for its most recent fiscal year as follows:

MOSHER LTD.
BALANCE SHEET
DECEMBER 31, 2008

Assets		Liabilities	
Cash	$ 20,000	Accounts payable	$ 200,000
Receivables	100,000	Notes payable	400,000
Inventory	200,000		
Equipment	1,000,000	**Shareholders' Equity**	
		Common stock	160,000
		Retained earnings	560,000
		Total liabilities and	
Total assets	$1,320,000	shareholders' equity	$1,320,000

Your bank has established certain guidelines that must be met before making a favourable loan recommendation. These include minimum levels for several financial ratios. You are particularly concerned about the bank's policy that loan applicants must have a total-assets-to-debt ratio of at least 2-to-1 to be acceptable. Your initial analysis of Mosher's balance sheet has indicated that the firm has met the minimum total-assets-to-debt ratio requirement. On reading the notes that accompany the financial statements, however, you discover the following statement:

> Mosher has engaged in a variety of innovative financial techniques resulting in the acquisition of $400,000 of assets at very favourable rates. The company is obligated to make a series of payments over the next five years to fulfill its commitments in conjunction with these financial instruments. Current generally accepted accounting principles do not require the assets acquired or the related obligations to be reflected on the financial statements.

Required

1. How should this note affect your evaluation of Mosher's loan application? Calculate a revised total-assets-to-debt ratio for Mosher.

2. Do you believe that the bank's policy concerning a minimum total-assets-to-debt ratio can be modified to consider financing techniques that are not reflected on the financial statements? Write a statement that expresses your position on this issue.

Case 10-5 *Bond Redemption Decision* LO 2, 5

Hughes Ltd., a truck training school, issued $200,000 of 20-year bonds at face value when the coupon rate was 8%. The bonds have been outstanding for 10 years. The company pays annual interest on January 1. The current rate for similar bonds is 6%. On January 1, the controller would like to purchase the bonds on the open market, retire the bonds, then issue $200,000 of 10-year bonds to pay 6% annual interest.

Required

Draft a memo to the controller advising him to retire the outstanding bonds and issue new debt. Ignore taxes. (*Hint:* Find the selling price of bonds that pay 8% when the market rate is 6%.)

Accounting and Ethics: What Would You Do?

Case 10-6 *Determination of Asset Life* LO 1, 3

Jane Smith is an accountant for Hector's Manufacturing Company. Hector's has entered into an agreement to lease a piece of equipment from Home Leasing. Jane must decide how to report the lease agreement on Hector's financial statements.

(continued)

Jane has reviewed the lease contract carefully. She has also reviewed the four lease criteria specified in the accounting rules. She has been able to determine that the lease does not meet three of the criteria. However, she is concerned about the criterion that indicates that if the term of the lease is 75% or more of the life of the property, the lease should be classified as a capital lease. Jane is fully aware that Hector's does not want to record the lease agreement as a capital lease but prefers to show it as a type of off-balance-sheet financing.

Jane's reading of the lease contract indicates that the asset has been leased for seven years. She is unsure of the life of such assets, however, and has consulted two sources to determine it. One of them states that equipment similar to that owned by Hector's is depreciated over nine years. The other, a trade publication of the equipment industry, indicates that equipment of this type will usually last for 12 years.

Required

1. How should Jane report the lease agreement in the financial statements?

2. If Jane decides to present the lease as an off-balance-sheet arrangement, has she acted ethically?

Case 10-7 *Overfunded Pension Plan (Appendix)* LO 1, 6

Concern Company has sponsored a pension plan for employees for several years. Each year Concern has paid cash to the pension fund, and the pension trustee has used that cash to invest in stocks and bonds. Because the trustee has invested wisely, the amount of the pension assets exceeds the accumulated benefit obligation as of December 31, 2008.

The president of Concern Company wants to pay a dividend to the shareholders at the end of 2008. The president believes that it is important to maintain a stable dividend pattern. Unfortunately, the company, though profitable, does not have enough cash on hand to pay a dividend and must find a way to raise the necessary cash if the dividend is declared. Several executives of the company have recommended that assets be withdrawn from the pension fund. They have pointed out that the fund is currently "overfunded." Further, they have stated that a withdrawal of assets will not have an impact on the financial statements because the overfunding is an "off-balance-sheet item."

Required

Comment on the proposal to withdraw assets from the pension fund to pay a dividend to shareholders. Do you believe it is unethical?

Internet Research Case

INTERNET

http://www.ypg.com

Case 10-8 Yellow Pages Income Fund LO 2, 4, 5, 6

Yellow Pages Income Fund is a special type of business entity termed a *trust*. Its overall operations are focused on the yellow pages available on the Web and in telephone books in Canada. Access to its annual report for December 31, 2007, can be obtained from its website or from *www.sedar.com*.

Required

1. Using its balance sheet, determine the debt-to-equity (unit holders' equity) ratio for 2007. Did it increase or decrease from 2006?

2. How can Yellow Pages pay its long-term debt? Examine its cash flow statement.

3. What is the Future Tax balance shown on the balance sheet at the end of 2007?

4. What is the employee benefits obligation at the end of 2007?

Solutions to Key Terms Quiz

__5__	Long-term liability	__11__	Carrying value
__1__	Face value	__13__	Gain or loss on redemption
__7__	Debenture bonds	__14__	Operating lease
__2__	Serial bonds	__16__	Capital lease
__9__	Callable bonds	__18__	Future tax (Appendix)
__3__	Face rate of interest	__19__	Permanent difference (Appendix)
__12__	Market rate of interest	__17__	Temporary difference (Appendix)
__4__	Bond issue price	__20__	Pension (Appendix)
__6__	Premium	__15__	Funding payment (Appendix)
__8__	Discount	__21__	Accrued pension cost (Appendix)
__10__	Effective interest method of amortization	__22__	Benefit obligation (Appendix)

Shareholders' Equity

After studying this chapter, you should be able to:

LO 1   Identify the components of the Shareholders' Equity category of the balance sheet and the accounts found in each component.

LO 2   Describe the characteristics of different classes of shares.

LO 3   Determine the financial statement impact when shares are issued for cash or for other consideration.

LO 4   Explain the difference between cash and stock dividends, and stock dividends and stock splits.

LO 5   Interpret the statement of shareholders' equity.

LO 6   Describe how investors use ratios to evaluate shareholders' equity.

LO 7   Explain the effects that transactions involving shareholders' equity have on the statement of cash flows.

LO 8   Describe the important differences between the sole proprietorship and partnership forms of organization versus the corporate form. (Appendix)

JOHN JAMES WOOD / INDEX STOCK IMAGERY

STUDY LINKS

A Look at the Previous Chapter

The previous chapter indicated how companies use long-term debt as a means of financing the company.

A Look at This Chapter

In this chapter we will concentrate on the issues concerned with the shareholders' equity of the balance sheet. The use of

equity is an important source of financing for all corporations. This chapter also considers the various types of dividends paid to shareholders.

A Look at the Upcoming Chapter

In Chapter 12 we turn our attention to an expanded discussion of the preparation and use of the statement of cash flows.

Focus on Financial Results

CN's shares have traded recently on the Toronto Stock Exchange for $51.10 per share. Footnote 11 to the balance sheet suggests that the company had 485.2 million shares outstanding on December 31, 2007. These two numbers indicate a shareholders' market value of $24,794 million, or about 2.4 times the balance sheet amount of $10,177. To properly interpret the financial results of a company like CN, an investor or analyst needs to understand the nature of shareholders' equity and the reasons for such a difference in the two shareholders' equity amounts.

CN 2007 ANNUAL REPORT (EXCERPT)   http://www.cn.ca

Liabilities and shareholders' equity		
Current liabilities		
Accounts payable and accrued charges *(Note 8)*	$ 1,282	$ 1,823
Current portion of long-term debt *(Note 10)*	254	218
Other	54	73
	1,590	2,114
Deferred income taxes *(Note 15)*	4,908	5,215
Other liabilities and deferred credits *(Note 9)*	1,422	1,465
Long-term debt *(Note 10)*	5,363	5,386
Shareholders' equity		
Common shares *(Note 11)*	4,283	4,459
Accumulated other comprehensive loss *(Note 20)*	(31)	(44)
Retained earnings	5,925	5,409
	10,177	9,824
Total liabilities and shareholders' equity	**$23,460**	$24,004

This excerpt from CN's 2007 Annual Report appears courtesy of CN. This section of the CN Annual Report appears in the Appendix of this textbook.

Equity as a Source of Financing

Whenever a company needs to raise money, it must choose from the alternative financing sources that are available. Financing can be divided into two general categories: debt (borrowing from banks or other creditors) and equity (issuing shares). The company's management must consider the advantages and disadvantages of each alternative. Exhibit 11-1 indicates a few of the factors that must be considered.

Issuing shares is a very popular method of financing because of its flexibility. It provides advantages for the issuing company and the investors (shareholders). Investors are primarily concerned with the return on their investment. With shares, the return may be in the form of dividends paid to the investors but may also be the price appreciation of the shares. Shares are popular because they generally provide a higher rate of return (but also a higher degree of risk) than can be obtained by creditors who receive interest from lending money. Shares are popular with issuing companies because dividends on them can be adjusted according to the company's profitability; higher dividends can be paid when the firm is profitable and lower dividends when it is not. Interest on debt financing, on the other hand, is generally fixed and is a legal liability that cannot be adjusted when a company experiences lower profitability.

There are several disadvantages in issuing shares. Shares usually have voting rights, and issuing shares allows new investors to vote. Existing investors may not want to share the control of the company with new shareholders. From the issuing company's viewpoint, there is also a serious tax disadvantage to shares versus debt. As indicated in Chapter 10, interest on debt is tax deductible and results in lower taxes. Dividends on shares, on the other hand, are not tax deductible and do not result in tax savings to the issuing company. Finally, the following sections of this chapter indicate the impact that issuing shares has on the company's financial statements. Issuing shares decreases several important financial ratios, such as earnings per share. Issuing debt does not have a similar effect on the earnings per share ratio.

Management should consider many other factors in deciding between debt and equity financing. The company's goal should be financing the company in a manner that results in the lowest overall cost of capital to the firm. Usually, companies attain that goal by having a reasonable balance of both debt and equity financing.

Accounting for Your Decisions

You Are the Investor

You have the opportunity to buy a company's bonds that pay 6% interest or the same company's shares. The shares have paid a 6% dividend rate for the past few years. The company is a large, reputable firm and has been profitable during recent times. Should you be indifferent between the two alternatives?

ANSWER: Interest on bonds is a fixed obligation. Unless the company goes out of business, you can count on receiving the 6% interest if you invest in the bonds. Dividends on shares are not fixed. There is no guarantee that the company will continue to pay 6% as the dividend on your investment. If the company is not profitable, it may decrease the size of the dividend. On the other hand, if the company becomes more profitable, it may pay a larger dividend.

Shareholders' Equity on the Balance Sheet

The basic accounting equation is often stated as follows:

Assets = Liabilities + Shareholders' Equity

Shareholders' equity is viewed as a residual amount. That is, the owners of a corporation have a claim to all assets after the claims represented by liabilities to creditors have been satisfied.

Advantages of Financing with Shares   ADVANTAGES   DISADVANTAGES

1. Flexibility ⟶ Dividends on shares can be increased in profitable years, reduced when the company is less profitable. Debt interest is fixed. (An advantage for issuing company)

2. Exchanges facilitate trading ⟶ Large companies have ready markets for shares through the stock exchanges. (An advantage for issuing company and investors) Sometimes debt is not as widely traded.

3. Return on investment ⟶ Shares generally provide a higher return in dividends and in growth than interest on debt. (An advantage for investors)

ADVANTAGES   DISADVANTAGES

Disadvantages of Financing with Shares

1. Control ⟶ Issuing shares involves giving voting rights to new investors, less control of the company for existing shareholders. (A disadvantage for issuing company)

2. Tax consequences ⟶ Interest on debt is tax deductible for the issuing company, dividends on shares are not. (A disadvantage for issuing company)

3. Impact on ratios ⟶ Issuing shares decreases several important financial ratios, including earnings per share. (A disadvantage for issuing company)

In this chapter, we concentrate on the corporate form of organization and refer to the owners' equity as *shareholders' equity*. Therefore, the basic accounting equation for a corporation can be restated as follows:

Assets = Liabilities + Shareholders' Equity

The shareholders are the owners of a corporation. They have a residual interest in its assets after the claims of all creditors have been satisfied.

The shareholders' equity category of all corporations has two major components or subcategories:

Total Shareholders' Equity = Contributed Capital
+
Retained Earnings

Contributed capital represents the amount the corporation has received from the sale of shares to shareholders. Retained earnings is the amount of net income that the corporation has earned but not paid as dividends. Instead, the corporation retains and reinvests the income.

Although all corporations maintain the two primary categories of contributed capital and retained earnings, within these categories they use a variety of accounts that have several alternative titles. The next section examines two important items: income and dividends, and their impact on the Retained Earnings account.

How Income and Dividends Affect Retained Earnings

The Retained Earnings account plays an important role because it serves as a link between the income statement and the balance sheet. The term *articulated statements* refers to the fact that the information on the income statement is related to the information on the balance sheet. The bridge (or link) between the two statements is the Retained Earnings account. Exhibit 11-2 presents this relationship graphically. As the exhibit indicates, the income statement is used to calculate a company's net income for a given period of time. The amount of the net income is transferred to the statement of retained earnings and is added to the beginning balance of retained earnings (with dividends deducted) to calculate the ending balance of retained earnings. The ending balance of retained earnings is the amount that is portrayed on the balance sheet in the shareholders' equity category. That is why you must always prepare the income statement before you prepare the balance sheet, as you have discovered when developing financial statements in previous chapters of the text.

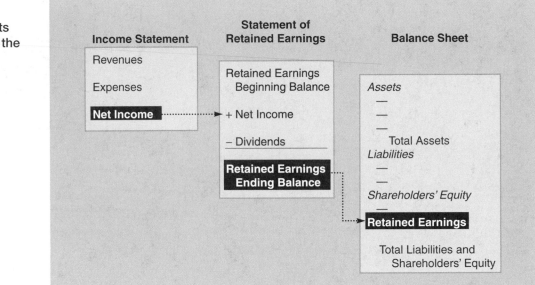

IDENTIFYING THE COMPONENTS OF THE SHAREHOLDERS' EQUITY SECTION OF THE BALANCE SHEET

LO 1 Identify the components of the Shareholders' Equity category of the balance sheet and the accounts found in each component.

CN
http://www.cn.ca

Authorized shares The maximum number of shares a corporation may issue as indicated in the corporate charter.

Issued shares The number of shares sold or distributed to shareholders.

Outstanding shares The number of shares issued less the number of shares held as treasury stock if any.

The Liabilities and Shareholders' Equity portion of the balance sheet of **CN** is provided at the beginning of the chapter and in Exhibit 11-3. We will focus on the Shareholders' Equity category of the balance sheet. All corporations, including CN, begin the Shareholders' Equity category with a list of the firm's contributed capital. In some cases, there are two categories of shares: common shares and preferred shares (class A and class B). Common shares normally carry voting rights. The common shareholders elect the officers of the corporation and establish its by-laws and governing rules. It is not unusual for corporations to have more than one type of common shares, each with different rights or terms. *Preferred shares* is the traditional term for the class of shares that has preference rights to dividends or liquidation over common shares. Currently the terms *class A* and *class B* are replacing *preferred* and *common* shares because they better reflect companies laws in Canada. Up until 2002, CN had preferred shares.

Number of Shares   It is important to determine the number of shares for each share account. Corporate balance sheets report the number of shares in three categories: **authorized**, **issued**, and **outstanding shares**.

To become incorporated, a business must develop articles of incorporation and apply to the proper government authorities for a certificate of incorporation. The corporation must specify the maximum number of shares that it will be allowed to issue. This maximum number of shares is called the *authorized capital stock*. A corporation applies for authorization to issue many more shares than it will issue immediately, to allow for future growth and other events that may occur over its long life. For example, Footnote 11, parts A and B, of CN's balance sheet describes the authorized capital stock as an unlimited number of no par common shares, and an unlimited number of class A preferred and class B preferred shares, both no par. Issued and outstanding shares are common shares because all of the preferred shares were converted to common in July 2002. CN issued and had outstanding 485.2 million no par common at the end of 2007.

The number of shares *issued* indicates the number of shares that have been sold or transferred to shareholders. The number of shares issued does not necessarily mean, however, that those shares are currently outstanding. The term *outstanding* indicates shares actually in the hands of the shareholders. Shares that have been issued by the corporation and then repurchased are counted as shares issued but not as shares outstanding. Quite often corporations repurchase their own shares as treasury stock (explained in more detail later in this chapter). Treasury stock reduces the number of shares outstanding. Typically, however, Canadian companies will not have treasury stock but rather will immediately reduce their issued shares when they buy back outstanding shares. CN notes it has approval to repurchase 33.0 million shares over the period July 26, 2007 and July 25, 2008. Up to December 31, 2008, it had repurchased 17.7 million shares for $897 million. CN also repurchased 12.5 million shares for $687 million from a previous year's program for a total repurchased of $1,584 million in 2007.

Exhibit 11-3 **CN Partial Footnote on Contributed Capital**

11. Capital stock

A. Authorized capital stock
The authorized capital stock of the Company is as follows:
- Unlimited number of Common Shares, without par value
- Unlimited number of Class A Preferred Shares, without par value, issuable in series
- Unlimited number of Class B Preferred Shares, without par value, issuable in series

B. Issued and outstanding common shares
During 2007, the Company issued 3.0 million shares (5.1 million shares in 2006 and 6.6 million shares in 2005) related to stock options exercised. The total number of common shares issued and outstanding was 485.2 million as at December 31, 2007.

C. Shares repurchase programs
In July 2007, the Board of Directors of the Company approved a new share repurchase program which allows for the repurchase of up to 33.0 million common shares between July 26, 2007 and July 25, 2008 pursuant to a normal course issuer bid, at prevailing market prices or such other price as may be permitted by the Toronto Stock Exchange.

As at December 31, 2007, under this current share repurchase program, the Company repurchased 17.7 million common shares for $897 million, at a weight-average price of $50.70 per share.

In June 2007, the Company completed its 28.0 million share repurchase program, which began on July 25, 2006, for a total of $1,453 million, at a weighted-average price of $51.88 per share. Of this amount, 12.5 million common shares were repurchased in 2007 for $687 million, at a weighted-average price of $54.93 per share.

This excerpt from CN's 2007 Annual Report appears courtesy of CN. This section of the CN Annual Report appears in the Appendix of this textbook.

Par Value Shares

The Shareholders' Equity category for capital stock illustrated to this point has used the term *no par shares*. The issue of no par or par is determined by the rules governing legal capital as specified by the laws of the incorporating jurisdiction. In Canada the laws use no par. In other countries, particularly the United States, companies can still employ par shares. **Par value** is an arbitrary amount stated on the face of the share certificate and represents the legal capital of the corporation. Most corporations that still use par value

Par value An arbitrary amount stated on the face of the share certificate representing the legal capital of the corporation.

set the par amount very low because there are legal difficulties if the shares are sold at less than par. Therefore, par value does not indicate the share value or the amount that is obtained when it is sold on the stock exchange; it is simply an arbitrary amount that exists to fulfill legal requirements. A company's legal requirement depends on the laws of the jurisdiction of incorporation.

Par value was used historically to prevent companies from depleting their legal capital except by a special resolution of their shareholders. Some jurisdictions still use this legal idea, but in Canada the depletion of legal capital is restricted by specific rules stating how much depletion can occur. These rules negate the need for par values; thus in Canada rarely will companies use par value. CN, for example, issues only no par shares, where all of the amount paid by the shareholders is recorded in the capital stock account.

For par value jurisdictions, the amount of the par value is the amount presented in the capital stock account; thus, the dollar amount in a firm's account can be calculated as its par value per share times the number of shares issued. For example, the dollar amount appearing in the Common Stock account can be calculated as follows:

$1 Par Value per Share $\times$ 182,278,766 Shares Issued =
$182 million (rounded) balance in the Common Stock account

Additional Paid-in Capital   The dollar amounts of capital stock accounts in the Shareholders' Equity category do not indicate the amount received when the shares were sold, as they did in the case of no par shares. When shares are issued for an amount greater than the par value of the shares, the excess is reported as **additional paid-in capital**. Alternative terms that may be used are *paid-in capital in excess of par*, or *premium on shares*, or *capital surplus*. Regardless of the title, the account represents the amount received in excess of the par when the shares were issued.

Retained Earnings: The Amount *Not* Paid as Dividends   **Retained earnings** represents net income that the firm has earned but has *not* paid as dividends plus or minus miscellaneous specified items. Remember that retained earnings is an amount that is accumulated over the entire life of the corporation and does not represent the income or dividends for a specific year. For example, the balance of the Retained Earnings account on CN's balance sheet at December 31, 2007, is $5,925 million. That does not mean that CN had a net income of this amount in 2007; it simply means that over the life of the corporation, CN has retained $5,925 million more net income than it has paid out as dividends to shareholders.

Additional paid-in capital An amount received that is greater than the par value of the shares when shares were issued.

Retained earnings Net income that has been made by the corporation but not paid out as dividends plus or minus miscellaneous specified items.

A prospective shareholder may purchase shares and receive certificates, like this one, either directly from the company or through a stockbroker. Usually, a broker purchases shares in its own name for the investor's account—and the investor never sees a certificate.

Courtesy CN Rail

It is also important to remember that the balance of the Retained Earnings account does not mean that liquid assets of that amount are available to the shareholders. Corporations decide to retain income because they have needs other than paying dividends to shareholders. The needs may include the purchase of assets, the retirement of debt, or other financial needs. Money spent for those needs usually benefits the shareholders in the long run, but liquid assets equal to the balance of the Retained Earnings account are not necessarily available to shareholders. In theory, income should be retained whenever the company can reinvest the money and get a better return within the business than the shareholders can get on their own. In summary, Retained Earnings is a shareholders' equity account. Although the company's assets have increased, retained earnings does not represent a pool of liquid assets.

▪ WHAT ARE PREFERRED SHARES?

Many companies have a class of shares called *preferred shares*. One of the advantages of preferred shares is the flexibility they provide because their terms and provisions can be tailored to meet the firm's needs. These terms and provisions are detailed in the share certificate. Generally, preferred shares offer holders a preference to dividends declared by the corporation. That is, if dividends are declared, the preferred sharcholders must receive dividends first, before the holders of common shares.

LO 2 Describe the characteristics of different classes of shares.

The dividend rate on preferred shares may be stated in two ways. First, it may be stated as a percentage of the share's par value. For example, if a share is presented on the balance sheet as $100 par, 7% preferred stock, its dividend rate is $7 per share ($100 times 7%). Second, the dividend may be stated as a per-share amount, necessary for the more common no par shares. For example, a share may appear on the balance sheet as $7, no par preferred stock, meaning that the dividend rate is $7 per share. Investors in common shares should note the dividend requirements of the preferred shareholder. The greater the obligation to the preferred shareholder, the less desirable the common shares become.

Several important provisions of preferred shares relate to the payment of dividends. Some preferred share issues have a **cumulative feature**, which means that if a dividend is not declared to the preferred shareholders in one year, dividends are considered to be *in arrears*. Before a dividend can be declared to common shareholders in a subsequent period, the preferred shareholders must be paid all dividends in arrears as well as the current year's dividend. The cumulative feature ensures that the preferred shareholders will receive a dividend before one is paid to common shareholders. It does not guarantee a dividend to preferred shareholders, however. There is no legal requirement mandating that a corporation declare a dividend, and preferred shareholders have a legal right to receive a dividend only when it has been declared.

Cumulative feature The right to dividends in arrears before the current-year dividend is distributed.

Preferred shares may also be convertible or callable. The **convertible feature** allows the preferred shareholders to convert their shareholdings to common shares. Convertible preferred shares offer shareholders the advantages of the low risk generally associated with preferred shares and the possibility of the higher return that is associated with common shares. The **callable feature** allows the issuing firm to retire the shares after they have been issued. Normally, the call price is specified as a fixed dollar amount. Firms may exercise the call option to eliminate a certain class of preferred shares so that control of the corporation is maintained in the hands of fewer shareholders. The call option also may be exercised when the dividend rate on the preferred shares is too high and other, more cost-effective financing alternatives are available.

Convertible feature Allows preferred shares to be exchanged for common shares.

Callable feature Allows the firm to eliminate a class of shares by paying the shareholders a specified amount.

Preferred shares are attractive to many investors because they offer a return in the form of a dividend at a level of risk that is lower than that of most common shares. Usually, the dividend available on preferred shares is more stable from year to year, and as a result, the market price of the shares is also more stable. In fact, if preferred shares carry certain provisions, the shares are very similar to bonds or notes payable. Management must evaluate whether such securities really represent debt and should be presented in the Liabilities category of the balance sheet or whether they represent equity and should be presented in the Equity category. Such a decision involves the concept of *substance over form*. That is, a company must look not only at the legal form but also at the economic substance of the security to decide whether it is debt or equity. In 2006, 36 companies of 200 surveyed had preferred shares in the broad sense of the preference class of shares.[1]

◾ ISSUANCE OF SHARES

<table>
<tr><td>**LO 3** Determine the financial statement impact when shares are issued for cash or for other consideration.</td></tr>
</table>

Shares Issued for Cash

Shares may be issued in several different ways. They may be issued for cash or for non-cash assets. When shares are issued for cash, the amount of cash received should be reported in the share account. For example, assume that on July 1 a firm issued 1,000 shares of no par common stock for $15 per share. The transaction is recorded as follows:

July 1	Cash	15,000	
	Common Stock		15,000
	To record the issuance of 1,000 shares of no par common at $15 per share		

	Assets	=	Liabilities	+	Shareholders' Equity
	+15,000				+15,000

The amount, $15,000, is the contributed capital component of the corporation.

Shares Issued for Non-cash Consideration

Occasionally, shares are issued in return for something other than cash. For example, a corporation may issue shares to obtain land or buildings. When such a transaction occurs, the company faces the difficult task of deciding what value to place on the transaction. This is especially difficult when the market values of the elements of the transaction are not known with complete certainty. According to the general guideline, the transaction should be reported at fair market value. Market value may be indicated by the value of the consideration given (shares) or the value of the consideration received (property), whichever can be most readily determined.

Assume that on July 1 a firm issues 500 shares of no par preferred stock to acquire a building. The shares are not widely traded, and the current market value of the shares is not evident. The building has recently been appraised by an independent firm as having a market value of $12,000. In this case, the issuance of the shares should be recorded as follows:

July 1	Building	12,000	
	Preferred Stock		12,000
	To record the issuance of preferred shares for building		

	Assets	=	Liabilities	+	Shareholders' Equity
	+12,000				+12,000

In other situations, the market value of the shares may be more readily determined and should be used as the best measure of the value of the transaction. Market value may be represented by the current stock market quotation or by a recent cash sale of the shares. The company should attempt to develop the best estimate of the market value of the non-cash transaction and should neither intentionally overstate nor intentionally understate the assets received by the issuance of shares.

---

[1] Nadi Chlala, Diane Paul, Louise Martel, and Andrée Lavigne, *Financial Reporting in Canada* (Toronto: CICA, 2007).

REPURCHASE OF COMPANY CAPITAL STOCK

What Is Treasury Stock?

The Shareholders' Equity category of a balance sheet may include **treasury stock**. The Treasury Stock account is created when a corporation buys its own shares sometime after issuing them. For an amount to be treated as treasury stock, (1) it must be the corporation's own shares, (2) it must have been issued to the shareholders at some point, (3) it must have been repurchased from the shareholders, and (4) it must not be retired but must be held for some purpose. Treasury shares are not considered outstanding shares and do not have voting rights.

> **Treasury stock** Shares issued by the firm and then repurchased but not retired.

Only 8 of 200 companies surveyed in 2006 in Canada showed treasury shares.[2] Canadian disclosures used by a number of balance sheets for treasury stock are illustrated in the Shareholders' Equity section of Rezin's balance sheet on February 1, 2008:

Common stock, no par value	
1,000 shares issued, 900 outstanding	$22,000
Total contributed capital	22,000
Less: Treasury stock, 1,000 shares at cost	2,500
	19,500
Retained earnings	15,000
Total shareholders' equity	$34,500

Note that *income statement accounts are never involved* in treasury stock transactions. Regardless of whether treasury stock is reissued for more or less than its cost, the effect is reflected in the shareholders' equity accounts. It is simply not possible for a firm to engage in transactions involving its own shares and have the result affect the performance of the firm as reflected on the income statement.

Two-Minute Review

1. Where does the Treasury Stock account appear on the balance sheet?
2. What is the effect on shareholders' equity when shares are purchased as treasury stock?
3. How does treasury stock affect the number of shares issued and outstanding?

Answers on page 537.

Retirement of Shares

Retirement of shares occurs when a corporation buys back shares after they have been issued to investors and does not intend to reissue the shares. Retirement often occurs because the corporation wants to eliminate a particular class of shares or a particular group of shareholders. When shares are repurchased and retired, the balance of the share account that was created when the shares were issued must be eliminated. When the original issue price is higher than the repurchase price of the shares, the difference is reflected in the Contributed Surplus account. When the repurchase price of the shares is more than the original issue price, the difference reduces the Retained Earnings account. The general principle for retirement of shares is the same as for treasury stock transactions. No income statement accounts are affected by the retirement. The effect is reflected in the Cash account and the shareholders' equity accounts.

> **Retirement of shares** When the shares are repurchased with no intention to reissue at a later date.

For example, CN describes in Note 11 the repurchase of common stock in 2007. CN repurchased 30.2 million common shares for $1,584 million ($52.45 per share). Of this, $265 million was removed from the Common Stock account representing $8.77 per share, the original issue amount. The remaining balance of $1,319 million reduced Retained Earnings. Thus the income statement did not reflect any of the differences between the price paid, $52.45, and the original book value of $8.77.

---

[2]Ibid.

DIVIDENDS: DISTRIBUTION OF INCOME TO SHAREHOLDERS

LO 4 Explain the difference between cash and stock dividends, and stock dividends and stock splits.

Cash Dividends

Corporations may declare and issue several different types of dividends, the most common of which is a cash dividend to shareholders. Cash dividends may be declared quarterly, annually, or at other intervals. Normally, cash dividends are declared on one date, referred to as the *date of declaration*, and are paid out on a later date, referred to as the *payment date*. The dividend is paid to the shareholders that own the shares as of a particular date, the *date of record*.

Generally, two requirements must be met before the board of directors can declare a cash dividend. First, sufficient cash must be available by the payment date to pay to the shareholders. Second, the Retained Earnings account must have a sufficient positive balance. Specifically, Section 42 of the Canada Business Corporations Act describes the modern requirements that must be satisfied to permit the payment of dividends: "A corporation shall not declare, or pay a dividend if there are reasonable grounds for believing that (a) the corporation is, or would after payment, be unable to pay its liabilities as they become due; or (b) the realizable value of the corporation's assets would thereby be less than the aggregate of its liabilities and stated capital of all classes."[3] Most firms have an established policy concerning the portion of income that will be declared as dividends. The **dividend payout ratio** is calculated as the annual dividend amount divided by the annual net income. The dividend payout ratios in various industries are given in Exhibit 11-4. Typically, utilities pay a high proportion of their earnings. In contrast, fast-growing companies in technology often pay nothing to shareholders. Some investors want and need the current income of a high dividend payout, but others would rather not receive dividend income and prefer to gamble that the share price will appreciate.

Dividend payout ratio The annual dividend amount divided by the annual net income.

Exhibit 11-4

2007 Dividend Payout Ratios to Common Shareholders of selected firms.

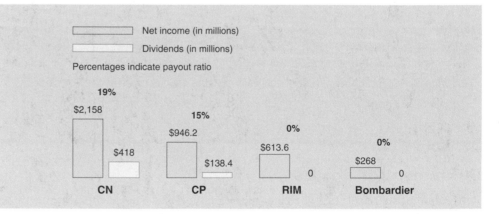

Study Tip

A dividend is not an expense on the income statement. It is a reduction of retained earnings and appears on the retained earnings statement. If it is a cash dividend, it also reduces the cash balance when paid.

Cash dividends become a liability on the date they are declared. An accounting entry should be recorded on that date to acknowledge the liability and reduce the balance of the Retained Earnings account. For example, assume that on July 1 the board of directors of Grant Company declared a cash dividend of $7,000 to be paid on September 1. Grant reflects the declaration as a reduction of Retained Earnings and an increase in Cash Dividend Payable as follows:

July 1	Retained Earnings	7,000	
	Cash Dividend Payable		7,000
	To record the declaration of a cash dividend		

Assets	=	Liabilities	+	Shareholders' Equity
		+7,000		−7,000

The Cash Dividend Payable account is a liability and is normally shown in the Current Liabilities section of the balance sheet.

---

[3]Consolidated Canada Business Corporations Act and Regulations, 25th edition (Toronto: Thomson/Carswell, 2005).

Grant records the following accounting transaction on September 1 when the cash dividend is paid:

Sept. 1	Cash Dividend Payable	7,000	
	Cash		7,000
	To record the payment of a cash dividend		

Assets	=	**Liabilities**	+	**Shareholders' Equity**
−7,000		−7,000		

The important point to remember is that dividends reduce the amount of retained earnings *when declared*. When dividends are paid, the company reduces the liability to shareholders reflected in the Cash Dividend Payable account.

Stock Dividends

Cash dividends are the most popular and widely used form of a dividend, but corporations may at times use stock dividends instead of, or in addition to, cash dividends. A **stock dividend** occurs when a corporation declares and issues its own additional shares to its existing shareholders. Firms use stock dividends for several reasons. First, a corporation may simply not have sufficient cash available to declare a cash dividend. Stock dividends do not require the use of the corporation's resources and allow cash to be retained for other purposes. Second, stock dividends result in additional shares outstanding and may decrease the market price per share if the dividend is large (small stock dividends tend to have little effect on market price). The lower price may make the shares more attractive to a wider range of investors and allow enhanced financing opportunities.

Stock dividend The issuance of additional shares to existing shareholders.

Similar to cash dividends, stock dividends are normally declared by the board of directors on a specific date, and the shares are distributed to the shareholders at a later date. The corporation recognizes the stock dividend on the date of declaration. Assume that Sable Company's Shareholders' Equity category of the balance sheet appears as follows as of January 1, 2008:

Common stock, 5,000 no par shares issued and outstanding	$ 80,000
Retained earnings	70,000
Total shareholders' equity	$150,000

Assume that on January 2, 2008, Sable declares a 10% stock dividend to common shareholders to be distributed on April 1, 2008. Small stock dividends (usually those of 20% to 25% or less) normally are recorded at the *market value* of the shares as of the date of declaration. Assume that Sable's common stock is selling at $40 per share on that date. Therefore, the total market value of the stock dividend is $20,000 (10% of 5,000 shares outstanding, or 500 shares, times $40 per share). Sable records the transaction on the date of declaration as follows:

Jan. 2	Retained Earnings	20,000	
	Common Stock Dividend Distributable		20,000
	To record the declaration of a stock dividend		

Assets	=	**Liabilities**	+	**Shareholders' Equity**
				−20,000
				+20,000

The Common Stock Dividend Distributable account represents shares to be issued; it is not a liability account because no cash or assets are to be distributed to the shareholders. Thus, it should be treated as an account in the Shareholders' Equity section of the balance sheet and is a part of the contributed capital component of equity.

Note that the declaration of a stock dividend does not affect the total shareholders' equity of the corporation, although the retained earnings are reduced. That is, the

Shareholders' Equity section of Sable's balance sheet on January 2, 2008, is as follows after the declaration of the dividend:

Common stock, 5,000 no par	
shares issued and outstanding	$ 80,000
Common stock dividend distributable, 500 shares	20,000
Retained earnings	50,000
Total shareholders' equity	$150,000

The account balances are different, but total shareholders' equity is $150,000 both before and after the declaration of the stock dividend. In effect, retained earnings has been capitalized (transferred permanently to the contributed capital accounts). When a corporation actually issues a stock dividend, it is necessary to transfer an amount from the Stock Dividend Distributable account to the appropriate stock account.

Our stock dividend example has illustrated the general rule that stock dividends should be reported at fair market value. That is, in the transaction to reflect the stock dividend, retained earnings is decreased in the amount of the fair market value per share times the number of shares to be distributed. When a large stock dividend is declared, however, accountants do not follow the general rule we have illustrated. A large stock dividend is a stock dividend of more than 20% to 25% of the number of shares outstanding. In that case, the stock dividend is reported at *book value* rather than at fair market value. That is, Retained Earnings is decreased in the amount of the book value per share times the number of shares to be distributed. The *Canada Business Corporations Act* provides some flexibility by requiring only that the stated capital be increased by the declared amount of the stock dividend.[4]

Refer again to the Sable Company example. Assume that instead of a 10% dividend, on January 2, 2008, Sable declares a 60% stock dividend to be distributed on April 1, 2008. The stock dividend results in 3,000 additional shares being issued and certainly meets the definition of a large stock dividend. Sable records the following transaction on January 2, the date of declaration:

Jan. 2	Retained Earnings	48,000	
	Common Stock Dividend Distributable		48,000
	To record the declaration of a large stock dividend, where		
	($16 × 3,000 =) $48,000 is the original book value per share		

Assets	=	**Liabilities**	+	**Shareholders' Equity**
				−48,000
				+48,000

The accounting transaction to be recorded when the shares are actually distributed is as follows:

Apr. 1	Common Stock Dividend Distributable	48,000	
	Common Stock		48,000
	To record the distribution of a stock dividend		

Assets	=	**Liabilities**	+	**Shareholders' Equity**
				−48,000
				+48,000

The Shareholders' Equity category of Sable's balance sheet as of April 1 after the stock dividend is as follows:

Common stock, 8,000 no par	
shares issued and outstanding	$128,000
Retained earnings	22,000
Total shareholders' equity	$150,000

---

[4]Ibid. section 43 (2).

Again, you should note that the stock dividend has not affected total shareholders' equity. Sable has $150,000 of shareholders' equity both before and after the stock dividend. The difference between large and small stock dividends is the amount transferred from retained earnings to the contributed capital portion of equity.

Stock Splits

A **stock split** is similar to a stock dividend in that it results in additional shares outstanding. In fact, firms may use a stock split for nearly the same reasons as a stock dividend: to increase the number of shares, reduce the market price per share, and make the shares more accessible to a wider range of investors. There is an important legal difference, however. Stock splits reduce the book value per share. There also is an important accounting difference. An accounting transaction is *not recorded* when a corporation declares and executes a stock split. None of the shareholders' equity accounts are affected by the split. Rather, the note information accompanying the balance sheet must disclose the additional shares and the reduction of the book value per share.

Stock split The creation of additional shares with a reduction of the book value of the shares.

Return to the Sable Company example. Assume that on January 2, 2008, Sable issued a 2-for-1 stock split instead of a stock dividend. The split results in an additional 5,000 shares outstanding but should not be recorded in a formal accounting transaction. Therefore, the Shareholders' Equity section of Sable Company immediately after the stock split on January 2, 2008, is as follows:

Common stock, 10,000 no par shares issued and outstanding	$ 80,000
Retained earnings	70,000
Total shareholders' equity	$150,000

You should note that the book value per share has been reduced from $16 to $8 per share as a result of the split. Like a stock dividend, the split does not affect total shareholders' equity because no assets have been transferred. Therefore, the split simply results in more shares with claims to the same net assets of the firm.

Exhibit 11-5 CN Stock Split

Footnote 11 E. Common stock split
On January 27, 2004, the Board of Directors of the Company approved a three-for-two common stock split which was effected in the form of a stock dividend of one-half additional common share of CN payable for each share held. The stock dividend was paid on February 27, 2004, to shareholders of record on February 23, 2004. All equity-based benefit plans were adjusted to reflect the issuance of additional shares or options due to the declaration of the stock split. All share and per share data has been adjusted to reflect the stock split.

This excerpt from CN's 2007 Annual Report appears courtesy of CN. This section of the CN Annual Report appears in the Appendix of this textbook.

▪ STATEMENT OF SHAREHOLDERS' EQUITY

In addition to a balance sheet, an income statement, and a cash flow statement, many annual reports contain a **statement of shareholders' equity**. The purpose of this statement is to explain all the reasons for the difference between the beginning and the ending balances of each of the accounts in the Shareholders' Equity category of the balance sheet. Of course, if the only changes are the result of income and dividends, a statement of retained earnings is sufficient. When other changes have occurred in shareholders' equity accounts, this more complete statement is necessary.

LO 5 Interpret the statement of shareholders' equity.

Statement of shareholders' equity Reflects the differences between beginning and ending balances for all accounts in the Shareholders' Equity category of the balance sheet.

The statement of shareholders' equity of CN is presented in Exhibit 11-6 for the year 2007. The statement starts with the beginning balances of each of the accounts as of January 2007. CN's shareholders' equity is presented in three categories.

The statement of shareholders' equity indicates the items or events that affected shareholders' equity during 2007. The items or events were as follows:

ITEM OR EVENT	EFFECT ON SHAREHOLDERS' EQUITY
Net earnings ⟶	Increased retained earnings by $2,158 million
Dividends ⟶	Decreased retained earnings by $418 million
Shares repurchased ⟶	Decreased common stock by $265 million and retained earnings by $1,319 million

Exhibit 11-6 CN's Statement of Changes in Shareholders' Equity, 2007

Consolidated Statement of Changes in Shareholders' Equity, 2007

In millions	Issued and outstanding common shares	Common shares	Accumulated other comprehensive loss	Retained earnings	Total shareholders' equity
Balances December 31, 2006	512.4	$4,459	$(44)	$5,409	$ 9,824
Adoption of accounting pronouncements (Note 2)	-	-	-	95	95
Restated balance, beginning of year	512.4	4,459	(44)	5,504	9,919
Net income	-	-	-	2,158	2,158
Stock options exercised and others (Notes 11, 12)	3.0	89	-	-	89
Share repurchase program (Note 11)	(30.2)	(265)	-	(1,319)	(1,584)
Other comprehensive income (Note 20)	-	-	13	-	13
Dividends ($0.84 per share)	-	-	-	(418)	(418)
Balances December 31, 2007	485.2	$4,283	$(31)	$5,925	$10,177

This excerpt from CN's 2007 Annual Report appears courtesy of CN. This section of the CN Annual Report appears in the Appendix of this textbook.

The last line of the statement of shareholders' equity indicates the ending balances of the shareholders' equity accounts as of the balance sheet date, December 31, 2007. The statement of shareholders' equity is useful in explaining the reasons for the changes that occurred.

What Is Comprehensive Income?

There has always been some question about which items or transactions should be shown on the income statement and should be included in the calculation of net income. Generally, the accounting rule-making bodies have held that the income statement should reflect an *all-inclusive* approach. That is, all events and transactions that affect income should be shown on the income statement. This approach prevents the manipulation of the income figure by those who would like to show "good news" on the income statement and "bad news" directly on the retained earnings statement or the statement of shareholders' equity. The result of the all-inclusive approach is that the income statement includes items that are not necessarily under management's control, such as losses from natural disasters, and thus the income statement may not be a true reflection of a company's future potential.

The AcSB has accepted certain exceptions to the all-inclusive approach and has allowed items to be recorded directly to the shareholders' equity category. This text has discussed one such item: unrealized gains and losses on investment securities. Exhibit 11-7 presents several additional items that are beyond the scope of this text. Items such as these have been excluded from the income statement for various reasons. Quite often, the justification is a concern for the volatility of the net income number. The items we have cited are often large dollar amounts; if included in the income statement, they would cause income to fluctuate widely from period to period. Therefore, the income statement is deemed to be more useful if the items are excluded.

A new term has been coined to incorporate the "income-type" items that escape the income statement. **Comprehensive income** is the net asset increase resulting from all transactions during a time period (except for investments by owners and distributions to owners). Exhibit 11-7 presents the statement of comprehensive income and its relationship to the traditional income statement. It illustrates that comprehensive income encompasses all the revenues and expenses that are presented on the income statement to calculate net income and also includes items that are not presented on the income statement but affect total shareholders' equity. The comprehensive income measure is truly all-inclusive because it includes such transactions as unrealized gains and prior period adjustments that affect shareholders' equity. Firms are required to disclose comprehensive income because it provides a more complete measure of performance.

Comprehensive income The total change in net assets from all sources except investments by or distributions to the owners.

Exhibit 11-7 The Relationship of the Income Statement and Statement of Comprehensive Income

**Income Statement
For Year Ended December 31, 20XX**

Revenues	XXX
Expenses	XXX
Other gains and losses	XXX
Income before tax	XXX
Income tax expense	XXX
Net income	XXX

All-Inclusive Earnings
These items, excluded from the income statement, are included on a statement of comprehensive income.

**Statement of Comprehensive Income
for Year Ended December 31, 20XX**

Net income	XXX
Foreign currency translation adjustment	XXX
Unrealized holding gains/losses	XXX
Minimum pension liability adjustment	XXX
Other comprehensive income	XXX
Comprehensive income	XXX

In Exhibit 11-6 CN showed a $13 positive amount for 2007 for Other Comprehensive Income. This amount began in 2007 with a $44 negative amount, which was decreased by $13, resulting in the ending $31 negative amount.

Beginning in October 2006, Section 1530 of the AcSB pronouncements required the use in Canada of a statement of comprehensive income comparable to what the FASB requires in the United States. For the general structure of this statement, examine Exhibit 11-8, which presents the statement prepared by CN under U.S. GAAP.

Exhibit 11-8   Other Comprehensive Income for CN (U.S. GAAP)

Canadian National Railway Company   U.S. GAAP

December 31,	2007	2006
Shareholders' equity:		
Common shares *(Note 11)*	$ 4,283	$ 4,459
Accumulated other comprehensive loss *(Note 20)**	(31)	(44)
Retained earnings	5,925	5,409
	10,177	9,824
Total liabilities and shareholders' equity	$23,460	$24,004

The components of Accumulated other comprehensive loss
are as follows:

Footnote 20

In millions December 31,	2007	2006
Unrealized foreign exchange loss	$ (762)	$ (455)
Pension and other postretment benefit plans	723	403
Derivative instruments	8	8
Accumulated other comprehensive loss	$ (31)	$ (44)

The components of other comprehensive income (loss) and the
related tax effects are as follows:

In millions Year ended December 31,	2007	2006	2005
Accumulated other comprehensive loss – Balance at January 1	$ (44)	$ (222)	$ (148)
Other comprehensive income (loss):			
Unrealized foreign exchange loss (net of income tax (expense) recovery of $(91), $(231), and $27, for 2007, 2006 and 2005, respectively)[1]	(307)	(232)	(54)
Pension and other postretirement benefit plans (net of income tax expense of $(129), nil, and $(1), for 2007, 2006 and 2005, respectively) *(Note 9, 13)*	320	1	3
Derivative Instruments (net of income tax recovery of $1, $18, and $12, for 2007, 2006 and 2005, respectively) *(Note 19)*	–	(39)	(23)
Deferred income tax rate enactment	–	34	–
Other comprehensive income (loss)	13	(236)	(74)
Adjustment to reflect the funded status of benefit plans *(Note 2)*			
Net actuarial gain (net of income tax expense of $(200) for 2006)			
Prior service cost (net of income tax recovery of $14 for 2006)	–	434	–
Reversal of minimum pension liability adjustment (net of income tax	–	(31)	–
expense of $(6) for 2006)	–	11	–
Accumulated other comprehensive loss – Balance at December 31	$ (31)	$ (44)	$ (222)

(1) In 2006 the Company adjusted its deferred income tax liability for changes in income tax rates applied to certain temporary differences and also for the income tax effect on the currency translation amount resulting from the different between the accounting and tax basis of its net investment in foreign subsidiaries. As a result, the Company recorded a $180 million net charge for deferred income taxes in Other comprehensive income (loss).

*The net income portion of the comprehensive income of $2,158 for 2007 is included in the retained earnings as shown in Exhibit 11-6.

WHAT ANALYZING SHAREHOLDERS' EQUITY REVEALS ABOUT A FIRM'S VALUE

Book Value per Share

LO 6 Describe how investors use ratios to evaluate shareholders' equity.

Earlier, the term *book value per share* was used when shares were repurchased and cancelled. In that case the book value per share was for the Capital Stock account only, namely, the balance of the Capital Stock account divided by the number of shares represented by that account. On December 31, 2007, CN had $4,283 in its Common Shares account, representing 485.2 shares, or a book value per share in the account of $8.83 (see Exhibit 11-6).

The term book value per share is also used to signify a larger amount with a broader interpretation. This broader book value will be explained in the following section.

Users of financial statements are often interested in computing the value of a corporation's shares. This is a difficult task because value is not a well-defined term and means different things to different users. One measure of value is the book value of the shares. **Book value per share** of common represents the rights that each share of common stock has to the net assets of the corporation. The term *net assets* refers to the total assets of the firm minus total liabilities. In other words, net assets equal the total shareholders' equity of the corporation. Therefore, when only common stock is present, book value per share is measured as follows:

Book value per share Total shareholders' equity divided by the number of common shares outstanding.

$$\text{Book Value per Share} = \frac{\text{Total Shareholders' Equity}}{\text{Number of Common Shares Outstanding}}$$

Refer again to the statement of shareholders' equity of CN that appears in Exhibit 11-6. As of December 31, 2007, total shareholders' equity is $10,177 million and the number of outstanding common shares is 485.2 million. Therefore, the book value per share for CN is $20.97, calculated as follows:

$$\$10,177/485.2 = \$20.97$$

This means that the company's common shareholders have the right to $20.97 per share of net assets in the corporation.

The book value per share indicates the recorded minimum value per share. In a sense, it indicates the rights of the common shareholders in the event that the company is liquidated. It does not indicate the market value of the common shares. That is, book value per share does not indicate the price that should be paid by those who want to buy or sell the shares on the stock exchange. Book value is also an incomplete measure of value because the corporation's net assets are normally measured on the balance sheet at the original historical cost, not at the current value of the assets. Thus, book value per share does not provide a very accurate measure of the price that a shareholder would be willing to pay for a share. The book value of a share is often thought to be the "floor" of a share price. An investor's decision to pay less than book value for a share suggests that he or she thinks that the company is going to continue to lose money, thus shrinking book value.

Two-Minute Review

1. What effect does a stock dividend have on a firm's shareholders' equity?
2. What effect does a stock split have on a firm's shareholders' equity?
3. How is book value per share calculated?

Answers on page 537.

Calculating Book Value When Preferred Stock Is Present

The focus of the computation of book value per share is always on the book value per share of the *common* stock. Therefore, the computation must be adjusted for corporations that have both preferred and common stock. The numerator of the fraction, total shareholders' equity, should be reduced by the rights that preferred shareholders have to the corporation's net assets. Normally, this can be accomplished by deducting the redemption value or liquidation value of the preferred shares along with any dividends in arrears on cumulative preferred stock. The denominator should not include the number of preferred shares.

To illustrate the computation of book value per share when both common and preferred stock are present, we will refer to the shareholders' equity category of Hope Air. When calculating book value per share, we want to consider only the *common* shareholders' equity. Hope Air's total shareholders' equity in 2008 was $3,769 million, but preferred shareholders had a right to $452 million in the event of liquidation. Therefore, $452 million must be deducted to calculate the rights of the common shareholders:

$$\$3,769 - \$452 = \$3,317 \text{ common shareholders' equity}$$

The number of common shares *outstanding* is 123.2. Therefore, the computation of book value per share is as follows:

$$\$3,317/123.2 = \$26.92 \text{ Book Value per Share}$$

This indicates that if the company were liquidated and the assets sold at their recorded values, the common shareholders would receive $26.92 per share. Of course, if the company went bankrupt and had to liquidate assets at distressed values, shareholders would receive something less than book value.

Market Value per Share

Market value per share The selling price of the shares as indicated by the most recent transactions.

http://www.cpr.ca

The market value of the shares is a more meaningful measure of the value of the shares to those financial statement users interested in buying or selling shares. The **market value per share** is the price at which shares are currently selling. When shares are sold on a stock exchange, the price can be determined by their most recent selling price. For example, the listing for **CP** shares for a 2007 indicates the following:

52-Week	
HIGH	LOW
91.00	57.30

The market value of the shares depends on many factors. Shareholders must evaluate a corporation's earnings and liquidity as indicated in the financial statements. They must also consider a variety of economic factors and project all of the factors into the future to determine the proper market value per share. Many investors use sophisticated investment techniques, including large databases, to identify factors that affect a company's share price.

Shares or Derivative Share Compensation

Companies such as CN may compensate employees and managers for services using company shares or derivatives of company shares (commonly termed *stock options*). Up until 2004 in Canada, some question existed as to the whether the benefit conveyed to employees was an expense. The reason for the question was the fact that expenses typically involve the payment of an asset such as cash, or the incurrence of a liability that is later settled by the consumption of an asset. Share plans settle the employee benefit obligation using company shares, which are equity, not assets. Thus the question: Is the share or share derivative value an expense of the company?

CN indicates that it began to recognize expenses for the share plans on January 1, 2003, when it backdated such expenses to January 1, 2002, to provide comparative results for 2003.

CN uses four stock-based compensation plans and describes them in Footnote 12 of the financial statements (see Appendix A of this text). The footnote discloses expenses of $62 million before tax.

A popular plan for many companies, termed a *stock option plan*, is described in the partial Footnote 12 for CN presented in Exhibit 11-9. A stock option plan is a legal contract given to managers to provide them with the option to purchase company shares at a specified price during a specified period—10 years in this case. A total of 0.9 million options were granted in 2007 to senior management employees. The 14.7 million options outstanding at the end of 2007 represent an accumulation of options from earlier times. Two valuations described in the CN footnote—intrinsic value and Black-Scholes—are approaches to calculating the fair value of these options. These valuation methods will be described in later studies.

Exhibit 11-9 CN's Stock Plans, Footnote 12 (Excerpt)

(ii). Stock options awards

The Company has stock option plans for eligible employees to acquire common shares of the Company upon vesting at a price equal to the market value of the common shares at the date of granting. The options are exercisable during a period not exceeding 10 years. The right to exercise options generally accrues over a period of four years of continuous employment. Options are not generally exercisable during the first 12 months after the date of grant. At December 31, 2007, an additional 14.4 million common shares remained authorized for future issuances under these plans.

Options issued by the Company include conventional options, which vest over a period of time; performance options, which vest upon the attainment of Company targets relating to the operating ratio and unlevered return on investment; and performance-accelerated options, which vest on the sixth anniversary of the grant or prior if certain Company targets relating to return on investment and revenues are attained.

Changes in the Company's stock options are as follows:

	Options outstanding	
	Number of options	Weighted-average exercise price
	In millions	
Outstanding at December 31, 2006[1]	16.9	$23.29
Granted	0.9	$52.73
Forfeited	(0.1)	$37.35
Exercised	(3.0)	$20.09
Vested	N/A	N/A
Outstanding at December 31, 2007[1]	14.7	$24.55
Exercisable at December 31, 2007[1]	12.4	$21.17

(1) Stock options with a U.S. dollar exercise price have been translated to Canadian dollars using the foreign exchange rate in effect at the balance sheet date.

This excerpt from CN's 2007 Annual Report appears courtesy of CN. This section of the CN Annual Report appears in the Appendix of this textbook.

HOW CHANGES IN SHAREHOLDERS' EQUITY AFFECT THE STATEMENT OF CASH FLOWS

LO 7 Explain the effects that transactions involving shareholders' equity have on the statement of cash flows.

It is important to determine the effects that the issuance of shares, the repurchase of shares, and the payment of dividends have on the statement of cash flows. Each of these business activities' impact on cash must be reflected on the statement. Exhibit 11-10 indicates how these shareholders' equity transactions affect cash flow and where the items should be placed on the statement of cash flows.

Exhibit 11-10

The Effect of Shareholders' Equity Items on the Statement of Cash Flows

Item	Statement of Cash Flows
	Operating Activities
	Net income xxx
	Investing Activities
	Financing Activities
Issuance of shares	............................➤ +
Retirement or repurchase of shares	............................➤ −
Payment of dividends	............................➤ −

The issuance of shares is a method to finance business. Therefore, the cash *inflow* from the sale of shares to shareholders should be reflected as an inflow in the Financing Activities section of the statement of cash flows. One amount is listed to indicate the total inflow of cash.

The repurchase or retirement of shares also represents a financing activity. Therefore, the cash *outflow* should be reflected as a reduction of cash in the Financing Activities section of the statement of cash flows. One amount is generally listed to indicate the total cash outflow to retire shares.

Dividends paid to shareholders represent a cost of financing the business with shares. Therefore, dividends paid should be reflected as a cash *outflow* in the Financing Activities section of the statement of cash flows. It is important to distinguish between the declaration of dividends and the payment of dividends. The cash outflow occurs at the time the dividend is paid and should be reflected on the statement of cash flows in that period.

The 2007 statement of cash flows for CN is given in Exhibit 11-11. Note in particular three lines in the Financing Activities category of the cash flow statement. First, the cash dividends line indicates cash payments of $418 million for the payment of dividends. Also, a line for the issuance of shares indicates the company had cash inflows during 2007 of $77 million from such transactions. Finally, CN during the year made cash payments of $1,584 million to repurchase shares.

Study Tip

Transactions affecting the Shareholders' Equity category of the balance sheet will appear in the Financing Activities category of the cash flow statement. Dividends are included in the cash flow statement when actually paid rather than when they are declared.

Exhibit 11-11 CN 2007 Statement of Cash Flows (Excerpt)

Consolidated Statement of Cash Flows

In millions	*Year ended December 31,*	2007	2006	2005
Cash provided from operating activities		2,417	2,951	2,708
Cash used by investing activities		(895)	(1,349)	(1,075)
Financing activities				
Issuance of long-term debt		4,171	3,308	2,728
Reduction of long-term debt		(3,589)	(3,089)	(2,865)
Issuance of common shares due to exercise of stock options and related excess tax benefits realized *(Note 12)*		77	120	115
Repurchase of common shares *(Note 11)*		(1,584)	(1,483)	(1,418)
Dividends paid		(418)	(340)	(275)
Cash used by financing activities		(1,343)	(1,484)	(1,715)
Effect of foreign exchange fluctuations on U.S. dollar-denominated cash and cash equivalents		(48)	(1)	(3)
Net increase (decrease) in cash and cash equivalents		131	117	(85)
Cash and cash equivalents, beginning of year		179	62	147
Cash and cash equivalents, end of year		$ 310	$ 179	$ 62

This excerpt from CN's 2007 Annual Report appears courtesy of CN. This section of the CN Annual Report appears in the Appendix of this textbook.

Answers to the Two-Minute Reviews

Two-Minute Review on page 525

1. Treasury stock is a contra-equity account, and the balance should appear as a reduction in the Shareholders' Equity category of the balance sheet.

2. When treasury stock is purchased, it reduces total shareholders' equity.

3. Treasury stock represents shares that have been issued and so does not affect the number of shares issued. But they are shares that are held by the company, rather than the shareholders, and the purchase of treasury stock reduces the number of shares outstanding.

Two-Minute Review on page 533

1. A stock dividend does not change a firm's total shareholders' equity but does affect the balances of accounts within that category of the balance sheet. Generally, a stock dividend will reduce the retained earnings account and will increase the capital stock account.

2. A stock split does not affect total shareholders' equity or the accounts within shareholders' equity. No accounting entry is made for a stock split.

3. Book value per share is determined by dividing total shareholders' equity (less an amount representing the rights of preferred shareholders) by the number of common shares outstanding.

Appendix: Accounting Tools: Unincorporated Businesses

LO 8 Describe the important differences between the sole proprietorship and partnership forms of organization versus the corporate form. (Appendix)

The focus of Chapter 11 has been on the corporate form of organization. Most large, influential companies are organized as corporations. They have a legal and economic existence that is separate from that of the owners of the business, the shareholders. Yet many other organizations in the economy have been formed as sole proprietorships or partnerships. The purpose of this appendix is to show briefly how the characteristics of such organizations affect the accounting, particularly the accounting for the Owners' Equity category of the balance sheet.

Sole Proprietorships

Sole proprietorship A business with a single owner.

A **sole proprietorship** is a business owned by one person. Most sole proprietorships are small in size, with the owner serving as the operator or manager of the company. The primary advantage of the sole proprietorship form of organization is its simplicity. The Owner's Equity category of the balance sheet consists of one account, the owner's capital account. The owner answers to no one but himself or herself. A disadvantage of the sole proprietorship is that all the responsibility for the success or failure of the venture attaches to the owner, who often has limited resources.

There are three important points to remember about this form of organization. First, a sole proprietorship is not a separate entity for legal purposes. This means that the law does not distinguish between the assets of the business and those of its owner. If an owner loses a lawsuit, for example, the law does not limit an owner's liability to the amount of assets of the business but extends liability to the owner's personal assets. Thus, the owner is said to have *unlimited liability*.

Second, accountants adhere to the *entity principle* and maintain a distinction between the owner's personal assets and the assets of the sole proprietorship. The balance sheet of a sole proprietorship should reflect only the "business" assets and liabilities, with the difference reflected as owner's capital.

Third, a sole proprietorship is not treated as a separate entity for income tax purposes. That is, the sole proprietorship does not pay tax on its income. Rather, the business income must be declared as income on the owner's personal tax return, and income tax is assessed at the personal tax rate rather than the rate that applies to companies organized as corporations. This may or may not be advantageous, depending on the amount of income involved and the owner's tax situation.

Typical Transactions When the owners of a corporation, the shareholders, invest in the corporation, they normally do so by purchasing shares. When investing in a sole proprietorship, the owner simply contributes cash, or other assets, into the business. For example, assume that on January 1, 2008, Peter Tom began a new business by investing $10,000 cash. Peter Tom Company records the transaction as follows:

Jan. 1	Cash	10,000	
	Peter Tom, Capital		10,000
	To record the investment of cash in the business		

Assets	=	Liabilities	+	Owner's Equity
+10,000				+10,000

The Peter Tom, Capital account is an owner's equity account and reflects the rights of the owner to the business assets.

An owner's withdrawal of assets from the business is recorded as a reduction of owner's equity. Assume that on July 1, 2008, Peter Tom took an auto valued at $6,000 from the business to use as his personal auto. The transaction is recorded as follows:

July 1	Peter Tom, Drawing	6,000	
	Equipment		6,000
	To record the withdrawal of an auto from the business		

Assets	=	Liabilities	+	Owner's Equity
−6,000				−6,000

The Peter Tom, Drawing account is a contra-equity account. Sometimes a drawing account is referred to as a *withdrawals account,* as in Peter Tom, Withdrawals. An increase (debit) in the account reduces the owner's equity. At the end of the fiscal year, the drawing account should be closed to the capital account as follows:

Dec. 31	Peter Tom, Capital	6,000	
	Peter Tom, Drawing		6,000
	To close the drawing account to capital		

Assets	=	Liabilities	+	Owner's Equity
				−6,000
				+6,000

The amount of the net income of the business should also be reflected in the capital account. Assume that all revenue and expense accounts of Peter Tom Company have been closed to the Income Summary account, resulting in a credit balance of $4,000, the net income for the year. The Income Summary account is closed to capital as follows:

Dec. 31	Income Summary	4,000	
	Peter Tom, Capital		4,000
	To close Income Summary to the capital account		

Assets	=	Liabilities	+	Owner's Equity
				−4,000
				+4,000

The Owner's Equity section of the balance sheet for Peter Tom Company consists of one account, the capital account, calculated as follows:

Beginning balance, Jan. 1, 2008	$ 0
Plus: Investments	10,000
Net income	4,000
Less: Withdrawals	(6,000)
Ending balance, Dec. 31, 2008	$ 8,000

Partnerships

A **partnership** is an organization owned by two or more persons. Like sole proprietorships, most partnerships are fairly small businesses formed when individuals combine their capital and managerial talents for a common business purpose. Other partnerships are large, national organizations.

Partnerships have characteristics similar to those of sole proprietorships. The following are the most common important characteristics of partnerships:

1. *Unlimited liability.* Legally, the assets of the business are not separate from the partners' personal assets. Each partner is personally liable for the debts of the partnership. Creditors have a legal claim first to the assets of the partnership and then to the assets of the individual partners.

Partnership A business owned by two or more individuals and with the characteristic of unlimited liability.

2. *Limited life.* Corporations have a separate legal existence and an unlimited life; partnerships do not. The life of a partnership is limited; it exists as long as the contract between the partners is valid. The partnership ends when a partner withdraws or a new partner is added. A new partnership must be created for the business to continue.

3. *Not taxed as a separate entity.* Partnerships are subject to the same tax features as sole proprietorships. The partnership itself does not pay income tax. Rather, the income of the partnership is treated as personal income on each of the partners' individual tax returns and is taxed as personal income. All partnership income is subject to income tax on the individual partners' returns even if it is not distributed to the partners. A variety of other factors affect the tax consequences of partnerships versus the corporate form of organization. These aspects are quite complex and beyond the scope of this text.

Partnership agreement Specifies how much the owners will invest, their salaries, and how income will be shared.

A partnership is based on a **partnership agreement.** It is very important that the partners agree, in writing, about all aspects of the partnership. The agreement should detail items such as how much capital each partner is to invest, the time each is expected to devote to the business, the salary of each, and how income and losses of the partnership are to be divided. If a partnership agreement is not present, the courts may be forced to settle disputes among partners. Therefore, the partners should develop a partnership agreement when the firm is first established and should review the agreement periodically to determine whether changes are necessary.

Investments and Withdrawals
In a partnership, it is important to account separately for the capital of each of the partners. A capital account should be established in the Owners' Equity section of the balance sheet for each partner of the partnership. Investments into the partnership should be credited to the partner making the investment. For example, assume that on January 1, 2008, Page Thoms and Amy Rebec begin a partnership named AP Company. Page contributes $10,000 cash, and Amy contributes equipment valued at $5,000. The accounting transaction recorded by AP Company follows:

Jan. 1	Cash	10,000	
	Equipment	5,000	
	Page Thoms, Capital		10,000
	Amy Rebec, Capital		5,000
	To record the contribution of assets to the business		

Assets	=	Liabilities	+	Owners' Equity
+10,000				+10,000
+5,000				+5,000

A drawing account also should be established for each owner of the partnership to account for withdrawals of assets. Assume that on April 1, 2008, each owner withdraws $2,000 of cash from AP Company. The accounting entry is recorded:

Apr. 1	Page Thoms, Drawing	2,000	
	Amy Rebec, Drawing	2,000	
	Cash		4,000
	To record the withdrawal of assets from the business		

Assets	=	Liabilities	+	Owners' Equity
−4,000				−2,000
				−2,000

Distribution of Income
The partnership agreement governs the manner in which income should be allocated to partners. The distribution may recognize the partners' relative investment in the business, their time and effort, their expertise and talents, or other factors. We will illustrate three methods of income allocation, but you should be aware that partnerships use many other allocation methods. Although these allocation methods are straightforward, partnerships dissolve often because one or more of the partners believes that the allocation is unfair. It is very difficult to devise a method that will make all partners happy.

One way to allocate income is to divide it evenly between or among the partners. In fact, when a partnership agreement is not present, the courts specify that an equal allocation must be applied, regardless of the relative contributions or efforts of the partners. For example, assume that AP Company has $30,000 of net income for the period and has established an agreement that income should be allocated evenly between the two partners, Page and Amy. The accounting entry that AP Company records during the closing entry process is as follows:

Dec. 31	Income Summary	30,000	
	Page Thoms, Capital		15,000
	Amy Rebec, Capital		15,000
	To record the allocation of income between partners		

Assets = Liabilities + Owners' Equity
−30,000
+15,000
+15,000

An equal distribution of income to all partners is easy to apply but is not fair to those partners who have contributed more in money or time to the partnership.

Another way to allocate income is to specify in the partnership agreement that income be allocated according to a *stated ratio*. For example, Page and Amy may specify that all income of AP Company should be allocated on a 2-to-1 ratio, with Page receiving the larger portion. If that allocation method is applied to the preceding example, AP Company records the following transaction at year-end:

Dec. 31	Income Summary	30,000	
	Page Thoms, Capital		20,000
	Amy Rebec, Capital		10,000
	To record the allocation of income between partners		

Assets = Liabilities + Owners' Equity
−30,000
+20,000
+10,000

Finally, we illustrate an allocation method that more accurately reflects the partners' input. It is based on salaries, interest on invested capital, and a stated ratio. Assume that the partnership agreement of AP Company specifies that Page and Amy be allowed a salary of $6,000 and $4,000 respectively, that each partner receive 10% on her capital balance, and that any remaining income be allocated equally. Assume that AP Company has been in operation for several years and the capital balances of the owners at the end of 2008, before the income distribution, are as follows:

Page Thoms, Capital	$40,000
Amy Rebec, Capital	50,000

If AP Company calculated that its 2008 net income (before partner salaries) was $30,000, income would be allocated between the partners as follows:

	PAGE	AMY
Distributed for salaries:	$ 6,000	$ 4,000
Distributed for interest:		
Page: ($40,000 × 10%)	4,000	
Amy: ($50,000 × 10%)		5,000
Remainder = $30,000 − $10,000 − $9,000 = $11,000		
Remainder distributed equally:		
Page: ($11,000/2)	5,500	
Amy: ($11,000/2)		5,500
Total distributed	$15,500	$14,500

The accounting transaction to transfer the income to the capital accounts is as follows:

Dec. 31	Income Summary	30,000	
	Page Thoms, Capital		15,500
	Amy Rebec, Capital		14,500
	To record the allocation of income to partners		

Assets	=	Liabilities	+	Owners' Equity
				−30,000
				+15,500
				+14,500

This indicates that the amounts of $15,500 and $14,500 were allocated to Page and Amy respectively. It does not indicate the amount actually paid to (or withdrawn by) the partners. However, for tax purposes, the income of the partnership is treated as personal income on the partners' individual tax returns regardless of whether the income is actually paid in cash to the partners. This aspect often encourages partners to withdraw income from the business and makes it difficult to retain sufficient capital for the business to operate profitably.

The auditors' report for CN indicates that the auditor is KPMG LLP. KPMG stands for the names of the original partners who formed the firm many decades ago, in 1840. Currently, Swiss-based KPMG has 123,000 professionals worldwide and according to its website, www.KPMG.ca, it operates in 145 countries. In 1996 KPMG became the international standardized name for the firm. One of the recent characteristics of this very large partnership and other such partnerships is signified by *LLP (limited liability partnership)*. *LLP* signifies that the partners of KPMG have their liability for the firm's debts limited by their partnership agreement. No longer are the many partners responsible for all of the firm's liabilities resulting from Canadian or worldwide activities. Thus, many of the limited liability characteristics of corporations are present with these LLP partnerships.

A second form of partnership that has become popular in recent years, particularly to take advantage of the specifics in income tax law, operates through what is termed an *income trust*. The income trust is a special legal entity that has "units" that it can sell on the stock market. Two possibilities are used by these trusts to make the tax advantages beneficial to the unit holders. The simplest is for the trust to buy an operating company with mostly debt so that what is distributed to the trust has little income tax taken out. Thus the income of the trust can be the interest paid by the operating company and this income flows directly to the unit holders of the trust.

The other form is where the trust buys limited partnership rights in the partnership that operates the business. The income from the business flows to the limited partners and in turn to the trust. The trust then distributes the profits to its unit holders. The federal government announced in the November 2006 budget that the original tax-exempt status of income trusts would be removed in stages over future years.[5]

The nature of LLPs and income trusts demonstrates a few of the complexities of modern business arrangements. Regardless, the principles described to date do provide a foundation for understanding such complex arrangements.

Chapter Highlights

1. **LO 1** Identify the components of the Shareholders' Equity category of the balance sheet and the accounts found in each component (p. 520).

- The Shareholders' Equity category is composed of two parts. Contributed capital is the amount derived from shareholders and other external parties. Retained earnings is the amount of net income not paid as dividends.

- The Shareholders' Equity category reveals the number of shares authorized, issued, and outstanding. Treasury stock is shares that the firm has issued and repurchased but not retired.

2. **LO 2** Describe the characteristics of different classes of shares (p. 523).

- *Preferred stock* refers to shares that have preference to dividends declared. If a dividend is declared, the preferred shareholders must receive a dividend before the common shareholders.

3. **LO 3** Determine the financial statement impact when shares are issued for cash or for other consideration (p. 524).

- When shares are issued for cash, the amount received should be reported in the capital stock account.

---

[5]Simon Ramano, "Income Trusts: How They Work," *Shareowner*, September–October 2005, at Canadian Shareowner Magazine Inc., http://proquest.umi.com.

- When shares are issued for a non-cash asset, the transaction should reflect the value of the shares given or the value of the property received, whichever is more evident.

- When shares are repurchased, the book value of the original shares is removed from the Common Stock account and the excess is added to the contributed surplus if the amount paid is below the book value. The difference, where the amount paid exceeds the book value, is charged against retained earnings.

- The amount of cash dividends to be paid to common and preferred shareholders depends on the terms of the preferred stock. If the shares are cumulative, preferred shareholders have the right to dividends in arrears before current-year dividends are paid.

4. **LO 4** Explain the difference between cash and stock dividends, and stock dividends and stock splits (p. 526).

- Stock dividends involve the issuance of additional shares. The dividend should normally reflect the fair market value of the additional shares.

- Stock splits are similar to stock dividends except that splits reduce the book value per share. No accounting transaction is necessary for splits.

5. **LO 5** Interpret the statement of shareholders' equity (p. 529).

- The statement of shareholders' equity reflects the changes in the balances of all shareholders' equity accounts.

6. **LO 6** Describe how investors use ratios to evaluate shareholders' equity (p. 533).

- Book value per share is calculated as net assets divided by the number of common shares outstanding. It indicates the rights that shareholders have, based on recorded values, to the net assets in the event of liquidation and is therefore not a measure of the market value of the shares.

- When a corporation has both common and preferred shares, the net assets attributed to the rights of the preferred shareholders must be deducted from the amount of net assets to determine the book value per share of the common stock.

7. **LO 7** Explain the effects that transactions involving shareholders' equity have on the statement of cash flows (p. 536).

- Transactions involving shareholders' equity accounts should be reflected in the Financing Activities category of the statement of cash flows.

8. **LO 8** Describe the important differences between the sole proprietorship and partnership forms of organization versus the corporate form (Appendix) (p. 538).

- A sole proprietorship is a business owned by one person. It is not a separate entity for legal purposes and does not pay taxes on its income. However, a balance sheet should present the assets and liabilities of the business separate from those of the owner. (Appendix)

- A partnership is a business owned by two or more persons. Like sole proprietorships, partnerships are not a separate legal or tax entity. The balance sheet of the partnership should present the assets and liabilities of the business separate from those of the owners. (Appendix)

Ratio Review

Reporting and analyzing financial statement information related to a company's shareholders' equity:

The book value per share represents the *right* each share has to the net assets of the company. This is an estimate since, should the company be sold, the amount received by shareholders for each share owned may be more or less than the book value per share.

$$\text{Book Value per Share} = \frac{\text{Total Shareholders' Equity*}}{\text{Number of outstanding common shares}}$$

*When there is preferred stock outstanding, the redemption value or liquidation value (disclosed on the preferred stock line or in the notes) of the preferred stock must be subtracted from total shareholders' equity.

Accounts Highlighted

Account Titles	Where it Appears	In What Section	Page Number
Common Stock	Balance Sheet	Contributed Capital	520
Preferred Stock	Balance Sheet	Contributed Capital	523
Retained Earnings	Balance Sheet	Retained Earnings	522
Treasury Stock	Balance Sheet	(bottom portion of shareholders' Equity as a contra account)	525
Cash Dividend Payable	Balance Sheet	Current Liabilities	527
Stock Dividend Distributable	Balance Sheet	Contributed Capital	527

Key Terms Quiz

Read each definition below and then write the number of the definition in the blank beside the appropriate term it defines. The quiz solutions appear at the end of the chapter.

——	Authorized shares	——	Dividend payout ratio
——	Issued shares	——	Stock dividend
——	Outstanding shares	——	Stock split
——	Par value	——	Statement of shareholders' equity
——	Contributed surplus	——	Comprehensive income
——	Retained earnings	——	Book value per share
——	Cumulative feature	——	Market value per share
——	Convertible feature	——	Sole proprietorship (Appendix)
——	Callable feature	——	Partnership (Appendix)
——	Treasury stock	——	Partnership agreement (Appendix)
——	Retirement of shares		

1. The number of shares sold or distributed to shareholders.

2. An arbitrary amount that is stated on the face of the share certificate and that represents the legal capital of the firm.

3. Net income that has been made by the corporation but not paid out as dividends.

4. The right to dividends in arrears before the current-year dividend is distributed.

5. Allows preferred shares to be returned to the corporation in exchange for common stock.

6. Shares issued by the firm and then repurchased but not retired.

7. The annual dividend amount divided by the annual net income.

8. A statement that reflects the differences between beginning and ending balances for all accounts in the Shareholders' Equity category.

9. Creation of additional shares and reduction of the book value of the shares in the Common Stock account.

10. Total shareholders' equity divided by the number of common shares outstanding.

11. The total change in net assets from all sources except investments by or distributions to the owners.

12. The selling price of the shares as indicated by the most recent share transactions on, for example, the stock exchange.

13. The maximum number of shares a corporation may issue as indicated in the corporate charter.

14. The number of shares issued less the number of shares held as treasury stock.

15. The amount paid for the purchase of shares that is less than the book value of the shares in the Common Stock account.

16. Allows the issuing firm to eliminate a class of shares by paying the shareholders a fixed amount.

17. When the shares of a corporation are repurchased with no intention to reissue at a later date.

18. A corporation's declaration and issuance of additional shares of its own stock to existing shareholders.

19. A business owned by two or more individuals and with the characteristic of unlimited liability.

20. A document that specifies how much each owner should invest, the salary of each owner, and how profits are to be shared.

21. A business with a single owner.

Answers on p. 564

Alternate Terms

Additional paid-in capital Contributed surplus

Callable Redeemable

Capital account Owners' equity account

Retained earnings Retained income

Shareholders' equity Owners' equity

Warmup Exercises and Solutions

Warmup Exercise 11-1

A company has a retained earnings account with a January 1 balance of $500,000. The accountant has reviewed the following information for the current year:

Increase in cash balance	$50,000
Net income	80,000
Dividends declared	30,000
Dividends paid	20,000
Decrease in accounts receivable balance	10,000

Required

Calculate the ending balance of the Retained Earnings account.

Key to the Solution   Cash and accounts receivable do not affect retained earnings. Also note that dividends are deducted from retained earnings at the time they are declared rather than when they are paid.

Warmup Exercise 11-2

A company begins business on January 1 and issues 100,000 shares of common stock. On July 1, the company declares and issues a 2-for-1 stock split. On October 15, the company purchases 20,000 shares and issues 5,000 shares by the end of the month.

Required

Calculate the number of shares issued and the number of shares outstanding as of the end of the first year of operations.

Warmup Exercise 11-3

A. Company A has total shareholders' equity at year-end of $500,000 and has 10,000 shares.

B. Company B has total shareholders' equity at year-end of $500,000 and has 10,000 shares. The company also has 50,000 shares of preferred stock, which have a liquidation value of $3 per share.

Required

Calculate the book value per share for Company A and Company B.

Key to the Solution   Book value per share is calculated for the common shareholder. If preferred stock is present, an amount must be deducted that represents the amount the preferred shareholder would receive at liquidation.

Solution to Review Problem

Warmup Exercise 11-1

The ending balance of the Retained Earnings account should be calculated as follows:

Beginning balance	$500,000
Plus: Net income	80,000
Less: Dividends declared	(30,000)
Ending balance	$550,000

Warmup Exercise 11-2

The number of shares issued is 200,000, or 100,000 times 2 because of the stock split. The number of shares outstanding is 185,000, calculated as follows:

Number of shares after split	100,000 × 2 = 200,000
Less purchase of shares	(20,000)
Plus shares issued	5,000
Total outstanding	185,000 shares

Warmup Exercise 11-3

A. Book value per share is $50, or $500,000/10,000.

B. Book value per share is $35, or ($500,000 − $150,000)/10,000.

——————— *Review Problem and Solution* ———————

Andrew Company was incorporated on January 1, 2008, under a corporate charter that authorized the issuance of 50,000 shares of no par common stock and 20,000 shares of $8 no par preferred stock. The following events occurred during 2008. Andrew wants to record the events and develop financial statements on December 31, 2008.

a. Issued for cash 10,000 common shares at $25 per share and 1,000 preferred shares at $110 per share on January 15, 2008.

(continued)

b. Acquired a patent on April 1 in exchange for 2,000 common shares. At the time of the exchange, the common shares were selling on the local stock exchange for $30 per share.

c. Repurchased 500 shares of common stock on May 1 at $20 per share. The corporation cancelled the shares.

d. Declared a cash dividend of $1 per share to common shareholders and an $8 dividend to preferred shareholders on July 1. The dividend will be distributed on August 1.

e. Distributed the cash dividend on August 1.

f. Declared and distributed to preferred shareholders a 10% stock dividend on September 1. At the time of the dividend declaration, preferred shares were valued at $130 per share.

g. On December 31, calculated the net income for the year to be $200,000.

Required

1. Record the accounting entries for items **a** through **g**.

2. Develop the Shareholders' Equity section of Andrew Company's balance sheet at December 31, 2008. You do not need to consider the notes that accompany the balance sheet.

3. Determine the book value per share of the common stock. Assume that the preferred shares can be redeemed at $100 per share.

Solution to Review Problem

1. The following entries should be recorded:

   a. The entry to record the issuance of shares:

Jan. 15	Cash	360,000	
	Common Stock		250,000
	Preferred Stock		110,000
	To record the issuance of shares for cash		

Assets	=	Liabilities	+	Shareholders' Equity
+360,000				+250,000
				+110,000

   b. The patent received for shares should be recorded at the value of the shares:

Apr. 1	Patent	60,000	
	Common Stock		60,000
	To record the issuance of shares for patent		

Assets	=	Liabilities	+	Shareholders' Equity
+60,000				+60,000

   c. Shares reacquired should be recorded as follows:

May 1	Common Stock (500 × 25)	12,500	
	Cash		10,000
	Contributed Surplus		2,500
	To record the purchase of shares		

Assets	=	Liabilities	+	Shareholders' Equity
−10,000				−12,500
				+ 2,500

   d. A cash dividend should be declared on the number of shares outstanding as of July 1. The dividend is recorded as follows:

July 1	Retained Earnings	19,500	
	Dividends Payable—Common		11,500
	Dividends Payable—Preferred		8,000
	To record the declaration of a cash dividend		

Assets	=	Liabilities	+	Shareholders' Equity
		+11,500		−19,500
		+8,000		

The number of shares of common stock outstanding should be calculated as the number of shares issued (11,500). The preferred dividend should be calculated as 1,000 shares times $8 per share.

e. The entry to record the distribution of a cash dividend is as follows:

Aug. 1	Dividends Payable—Common	11,500	
	Dividends Payable—Preferred	8,000	
	Cash		19,500
	To record the payment of cash dividend		

Assets	**=**	**Liabilities**	**+**	**Shareholders' Equity**
−19,500		**−11,500**		
		−8,000		

f. A stock dividend should be based on the number of shares outstanding and should be declared and recorded at the market value of the shares as follows:

Sept. 1	Retained Earnings	13,000	
	Preferred Stock		13,000
	To record the declaration of a stock dividend		

Assets	**=**	**Liabilities**	**+**	**Shareholders' Equity**
				−13,000
				+13,000

The amount of the debit to Retained Earnings should be calculated as the number of shares outstanding (1,000) times 10% times $130 per share.

g. The entry to close the Income Summary account to shareholders' equity should be recorded as follows:

Dec. 31	Income Summary	200,000	
	Retained Earnings		200,000
	To record the annual net income		

Assets	**=**	**Liabilities**	**+**	**Shareholders' Equity**
				−200,000
				+200,000

2. The Shareholders' Equity for Andrew Company after completing these transactions appears as follows:

Preferred stock, $8 no par	
20,000 shares authorized, 1,100 issued	$123,000
Common stock,	
50,000 no par shares authorized, 11,500 issued	297,500
Contributed Surplus	2,500
Retained earnings	167,500*
Total shareholders' equity	$590,500

*$200,000 − $19,500 − $13,000 = $167,500

3. The book value per common share is calculated as follows:

($590,500 − $123,000)/11,500 shares = $40.65

Questions

1. What are the two major components of shareholders' equity? Which accounts generally appear in each component?

2. Corporations disclose the number of shares authorized, issued, and outstanding. What is the meaning of these terms? What causes a difference between the number of shares issued and the number outstanding?

3. If a firm has a net income for the year, will the balance in the Retained Earnings account equal the net income? What is the meaning of the balance of the account?

4. What is the meaning of the statement that preferred shares have a preference to dividends declared by the corporation? Do preferred shareholders have the right to dividends in arrears on preferred shares?

5. Why might some shareholders be inclined to buy preferred rather than common shares? What are the advantages of investing in preferred shares?

6. Why are common shareholders sometimes called *residual owners* when a company has both common and preferred shares outstanding?

7. When shares are issued in exchange for an asset, at what amount should the asset be reported? How could the fair market value be determined?

8. What is treasury stock? Why do firms use it? Where does it appear on a corporation's financial statements?

9. When shares are bought and sold by the company, the transactions do not result in gains or losses reported on the income statement. What account or accounts are used instead? Why are no income statement amounts recorded?

10. Many firms operate at a dividend payout ratio of less than 50%. Why do firms not pay a larger percentage of income as dividends?

11. What is a *stock dividend?* How should it be recorded?

12. Would you rather receive a cash dividend or a stock dividend from a company? Explain.

13. What is the difference between stock dividends and stock splits? How should stock splits be recorded?

14. How is the book value per share calculated? Does the amount calculated as book value per share mean that shareholders will receive a dividend equal to the book value?

15. Can the market value per share be determined by the information on the income statement?

16. What is the difference between a statement of shareholders' equity and a retained earnings statement?

17. What is an advantage of organizing a company as a corporation rather than a partnership? Why don't all companies incorporate? (Appendix)

18. What are some ways that partnerships could share income among the partners? (Appendix)

Exercises

Exercise 11-1 *Shareholders' Equity Accounts* **LO 1**

MJ Company has identified the following items. Indicate whether each item is included in an account in the Shareholders' Equity category of the balance sheet and identify the account title. Also indicate whether the item would increase or decrease shareholders' equity.

1. Preferred shares issued by MJ
2. Dividends in arrears on MJ preferred shares
3. Cash dividend declared but unpaid on MJ shares
4. Stock dividend declared but unissued by MJ
5. Treasury stock
6. Amount paid in excess of the share account book value when shares are repurchased by MJ
7. Retained earnings

Exercise 11-2 *Solve for Unknowns* **LO 1**

The Shareholders' Equity category of SMU Company's balance sheet appears below.

Common stock, 18,400 no par shares issued, and	
outstanding	$??
Total contributed capital	700,000
Retained earnings	200,000
Total shareholders' equity	$900,000

Required

Determine the missing value that is indicated by question marks and the book value per common share for contributed capital.

Exercise 11-3 *Share Issuance* **LO 3**

Harold Company had the following transactions during 2008, its first year of business.

a. Issued 5,000 no par common shares for cash at $30 per share.

b. Issued 7,000 common shares on May 1 to acquire a factory building from Bonita Company. Bonita had acquired the building in 2004 at a price of $300,000. Harold estimated that the building was worth $350,000 on May 1, 2008.

c. Issued 2,000 shares on June 1 to acquire a patent. The accountant has been unable to estimate the value of the patent but has determined that Harold's common shares were selling at $50 per share on June 1.

Required

1. Record an entry for each of the transactions.

2. Determine the balance sheet amount for common shares.

Exercise 11-4 *Share Issuances* LO 3

The following transactions are for Weaver Company in 2008:

a. On March 1, the corporation was organized and received authorization to issue 10,000 shares of $4 no par value preferred stock and 4,000,000 shares of no par value common stock.

b. On March 10, Weaver issued 10,000 common shares at $17.50 per share.

c. On March 18, Weaver issued 200 preferred shares at $60 per share.

d. On April 12, Weaver issued another 20,000 common shares at $22.50 per share.

Required

1. Determine the effect on the accounting equation of each of the events. Prepare journal entries when they are appropriate.

2. Prepare the Shareholders' Equity section of the balance sheet as of December 31, 2008.

3. Does the balance sheet indicate the market value of the shares at year-end? Explain.

Exercise 11-5 *Repurchase of Shares* LO 3

The Shareholders' Equity category of Baillie Company's balance sheet on January 1, 2008, appeared as follows:

Common stock, 20,000 no par shares issued	
and outstanding	$300,000
Retained earnings	160,000
Total shareholders' equity	$460,000

The following transactions occurred during 2008:

a. Reacquired 4,000 common shares at $20 per share on July 1.

b. Reacquired 800 common shares at $18 per share on August 1.

Required

1. Record the entries in journal form.

2. Assume the company sold the shares at $28 per share on October 1. Did the company benefit from the repurchase transaction? If so, where is the "gain" presented on the balance sheet?

Exercise 11-6 *Repurchase of Shares* LO 3

The shareholders' equity category of Lakeside's balance sheet on January 1, 2008, appeared as follows:

Common stock, 80,000 no par shares issued	
and outstanding	$580,000
Retained earnings	200,000
Total shareholders' equity	$780,000

The following transactions occurred during 2008:

a. Reacquired 10,000 common shares at $20 per share on March 1.

b. Reacquired 2,400 common shares at $13 per share on May 1.

Required

1. Record the entries in journal form.

2. Assume that the shares were reissued on October 1 at $12 per share. Did the company benefit from the share reissuance? Where is the "gain" or "loss" presented on the financial statements?

3. What effect did the two transactions to purchase the shares and the later reissuance of those shares have on the Shareholders' Equity section of the balance sheet?

Exercise 11-7 *Cash Dividends* LO 3

Gerry Company has 2,000 $9 no par preferred shares and 20,000 shares of no par value common shares outstanding. The preferred shares are cumulative. Dividends were paid in 2004. Since 2004, Gerry has declared and paid dividends as follows:

2005	$ 0
2006	20,000
2007	40,000
2008	50,000

(continued)

Required

1. Determine the amount of the dividends to be allocated to preferred and common shareholders for each year, 2006 to 2008.

2. If the preferred shares had been non-cumulative, how much would have been allocated to the preferred and common shareholders each year?

Exercise 11-8 *Cash Dividends* **LO 3**

The Shareholders' Equity category of Jerry Company's balance sheet as of January 1, 2008, appeared as follows:

Preferred stock, $8 no par,	
4,000 shares issued and outstanding	$ 400,000
Common stock,	
10,000 no par shares issued and outstanding	700,000
Total contributed capital	1,100,000
Retained earnings	800,000
Total shareholders' equity	$1,900,000

The notes that accompany the financial statements indicate that Jerry has not paid dividends for the two years prior to 2008. On July 1, 2008, Jerry declares a dividend of $200,000 to be paid to preferred and common shareholders on August 1.

Required

1. Determine the amounts of the dividend to be allocated to preferred and common shareholders, assuming that the preferred stock is non-cumulative.

2. Record the appropriate journal entries on July 1 and August 1, 2008.

3. Determine the amounts of the dividend to be allocated to preferred and common shareholders, assuming instead that the preferred shares are cumulative.

Exercise 11-9 *Stock Dividends* **LO 4**

The Shareholders' Equity category of Wendy Company's balance sheet as of January 1, 2008, appeared as follows:

Common stock,	
80,000 no par shares issued and outstanding	$1,000,000
Retained earnings	800,000
Total shareholders' equity	$1,800,000

The following transactions occurred during 2008:

a. Declared a 10% stock dividend to common shareholders on February 15. At the time of the dividend, the common shares were selling for $30 per share. The stock dividend was to be issued to shareholders on March 3, 2008.

b. Distributed the stock dividend to the shareholders on March 3, 2008.

Required

1. Record the 2008 transactions in journal form.

2. Develop the Shareholders' Equity category of Wendy Company's balance sheet as of March 31, 2008, after the stock dividend was issued. What effect did these transactions have on total shareholders' equity?

Exercise 11-10 *Stock Dividends versus Stock Splits* **LO 4**

Wally Company wants to increase the number of shares of its common stock outstanding and is considering a stock dividend versus a stock split. The Shareholders' Equity of the firm on its most recent balance sheet appeared as follows:

Common stock,	
100,000 no par shares issued and outstanding	$1,000,000
Retained earnings	3,260,000
Total shareholders' equity	$4,260,000

If a stock dividend is chosen, the firm wants to declare a 100% stock dividend. Because the stock dividend qualifies as a "large stock dividend," it is recorded to be at book value. If a stock split is chosen, Wally will declare a 2-for-1 split.

Required

1. Compare the effects of the stock dividends and stock splits on the accounting equation.
2. Develop the Shareholders' Equity category of Wally's balance sheet (a) after the stock dividend and (b) after the stock split.

Exercise 11-11 *Stock Dividends and Stock Splits* LO 4

Milton Company's Shareholders' Equity section of the balance sheet on December 31, 2007, was as follows:

Common stock,	
30,000 no par shares issued and outstanding	$ 540,000
Retained earnings	620,000
Total shareholders' equity	$1,160,000

On May 1, 2008, Milton declared and issued a 15% stock dividend, when the shares were selling for $20 per share. Then on November 1, it declared and issued a 2-for-1 stock split.

Required

1. How many shares are outstanding at year-end?
2. What is the book value per share of these shares in the Common Stock account at December 31, 2008?
3. Develop the Shareholders' Equity category of Milton's balance sheet as of December 31, 2008.

Exercise 11-12 *Reporting Changes in Shareholders' Equity Items* LO 5

On July 1, 2007, Ryder Ltd. had common share capital of $821,500 and retained earnings of $1,506,500. Ryder did not purchase or sell any common shares during the year. The company reported net income of $278,000 and declared dividends in the amount of $39,000 during the year ended June 30, 2008.

Required

Prepare a financial statement that explains all the reasons for the differences between the beginning and ending balances for the accounts in the Shareholders' Equity category of the balance sheet.

Exercise 11-13 *Comprehensive Income* LO 5

Assume that you are the accountant for Ellen Company, which has issued its 2008 annual report. You have received an inquiry from a shareholder who has questions about several items in the annual report, including why Ellen has not shown certain transactions on the income statement. In particular, Ellen's 2008 balance sheet revealed two accounts in Shareholders' Equity (Unrealized Gain/Loss—Available-for-Sale Securities and Loss on Foreign Currency Translation Adjustments) for which the dollar amounts involved were not reported on the income statement.

Required

Draft a written response to the shareholder's inquiry that explains the nature of the two accounts and the reason that the amounts involved were not recorded on the 2008 income statement. Do you think the concept of comprehensive income would be useful to explain the impact of all events for Ellen Corporation?

Exercise 11-14 *Dividend Payout Ratio and Book Value per Share* LO 6

David Company has developed a statement of shareholders' equity for the year 2008 as follows:

	Preferred Stock	Common Stock	Retained Earnings
Balance Jan. 1	$300,000	$220,000	$100,000
Stock issued		55,000	
Net income			40,000
Cash dividend			− 22,500
Stock dividend	30,000		− 7,500
Balance Dec. 31	$330,000	$275,000	$110,000

(continued)

David's preferred shares are $8 no par. If the 2,200 preferred shares outstanding are liquidated or redeemed, shareholders are entitled to $120 per share. There are no dividends in arrears on the shares. There are 40,000 no par common shares outstanding.

Required

1. Determine the dividend payout ratio for the common shares.
2. Determine the book value per share of David's common shares.

Exercise 11-15 *Impact of Transactions Involving Issuance of Shares on Statement of Cash Flows* LO 7

Identify each of the following items as operating (O), investing (I), financing (F), or not separately reported on the statement of cash flows (N).

———— Issuance of common shares for cash

———— Issuance of preferred shares for cash

———— Issuance of common shares for equipment

———— Issuance of preferred shares for land and building

———— Conversion of preferred shares into common shares

Exercise 11-16 *Impact of Transactions Involving Repurchase of Shares on Statement of Cash Flows* LO 7

Identify each of the following items as operating (O), investing (I), financing (F), or not separately reported on the statement of cash flows (N).

———— Repurchase of common shares

———— Issuance of common shares

Exercise 11-17 *Impact of Transactions Involving Dividends on Statement of Cash Flows* LO 7

Identify each of the following items as operating (O), investing (I), financing (F), or not separately reported on the statement of cash flows (N).

———— Payment of cash dividend on common shares

———— Payment of cash dividend on preferred shares

———— Distribution of stock dividend

———— Declaration of stock split

Exercise 11-18 *Determining Dividends Paid on Statement of Cash Flows* LO 7

Clark Company's comparative balance sheet included dividends payable of $40,000 at December 31, 2007, and $50,000 at December 31, 2008. Dividends declared by Clark during 2008 amounted to $200,000.

Required

1. Calculate the amount of dividends actually paid to shareholders during 2008.
2. How will Clark report the dividend payments on its 2008 statement of cash flows?

Exercise 11-19 *Sole Proprietorship (Appendix)* LO 8

Velma King opened Sub Par Golf as a sole proprietor by investing $100,000 cash on January 1, 2008. Because the business was new, it operated at a net loss of $20,000 for 2008. During the year, Velma withdrew $40,000 from the business for living expenses. Velma also had $8,000 of interest income from sources unrelated to the business.

Required

1. Record all the necessary entries for 2008 on the books of Sub Par Golf.
2. Present the Owner's Equity category of Sub Par Golf's balance sheet as of December 31, 2008.

Exercise 11-20 *Partnerships (Appendix)* LO 8

Sports Central is a sporting goods store owned by Lill, Jason, and Jill in partnership. On January 1, 2008, their capital balances were as follows:

Lill, Capital	$30,000
Jason, Capital	60,000
Jill, Capital	40,000

During 2008, Lill withdrew $10,000; Jason, $24,000; and Jill, $18,000. Income for the partnership for 2008 was $60,000.

Required

If the partners agreed to allocate income equally, what was the ending balance in each of their capital accounts on December 31, 2008?

Problems

Problem 11-1 *Shareholders' Equity Category* LO 1

Wang Company was incorporated as a new business on January 1, 2008. The corporate articles approved on that date authorized the issuance of 2,000 shares of $7 no par cumulative, preferred stock and 20,000 shares of no par common stock. On January 15, Wang issued for cash 1,000 preferred shares at $120 per share and 8,000 common shares at $80 per share. On January 30, it issued 2,000 common shares to acquire a building site, at a time when the shares were selling for $70 per share.

During 2008, Wang established an employee benefit plan and acquired 1,000 common shares at $60 per share for that purpose. Later in 2008, it resold 200 shares at $65 per share.

On December 31, 2008, Wang determined its net income for the year to be $80,000. The firm declared the annual cash dividend to preferred shareholders and a cash dividend of $5 per share to the common shareholders. The dividends will be paid in 2009.

Required

Develop the Shareholders' Equity category of Wang's balance sheet as of December 31, 2008. Indicate on the statement the number of shares authorized, issued, and outstanding, both preferred and common.

Problem 11-2 *Evaluating Alternative Investments* LO 2

James Ho received a windfall from one of his investments. He would like to invest $200,000 of the money in Leewood Ltd., which is offering common shares, preferred shares, and bonds on the open market. The common shares have paid $8 per share in dividends for the past three years and the company expects to be able to perform as well in the current year. The current market price of the common shares is $100 per share. The preferred shares have an $8 dividend rate, cumulative and selling for $100 each. The bonds are selling at par with an 8% stated rate.

1. What are the advantages and disadvantages of each type of investment?

2. Recommend one type of investment over the others to James, and justify your reason.

Problem 11-3 *Dividends for Preferred and Common Stock* LO 3

The Shareholders' Equity category of Parkland Company's balance sheet as of December 31, 2006, appeared as follows:

Preferred stock, $8 no par,	
2,000 shares issued and outstanding	$ 200,000
Common stock,	
40,000 no par shares issued and outstanding	900,000
Total contributed capital	1,100,000
Retained earnings	900,000
Total shareholders' equity	$2,000,000

(continued)

The notes to the financial statements indicate that dividends were not declared or paid for 2006 or 2007. Parkland wants to declare a dividend of $118,000 for 2008.

Required

Determine the total and the per-share amounts that should be declared to the preferred and common shareholders under the following assumptions:

1. The preferred shares are non-cumulative.
2. The preferred shares are cumulative.

Problem 11-4 *Effect of Stock Dividend* LO 4

Amos Company has a history of paying cash dividends on its common shares. The firm did not have a particularly profitable year, however, in 2008. At the end of the year, Amos found itself without the necessary cash for a dividend and therefore declared a stock dividend to its common shareholders. A 50% stock dividend was declared to shareholders on December 31, 2008. The board of directors is unclear about a stock dividend's effect on Amos's balance sheet and has requested your assistance.

Required

1. Write a statement to indicate the effect that the stock dividend has on the financial statements of Amos Company.
2. A group of common shareholders has contacted the firm to express its concern about the effect of the stock dividend and to question the effect the stock dividend may have on the market price of the shares. Write a statement to address the shareholders' concerns.

Problem 11-5 *Dividends and Stock Splits* LO 4

On January 1, 2008, Moncton Ltd.'s Shareholders' Equity category appeared as follows:

Preferred stock, $5.60 no par,	
9,000 shares issued and outstanding	$ 900,000
Common stock,	
45,000 no par shares issued and outstanding	1,125,000
Total contributed capital	2,025,000
Retained earnings	6,300,000
Total shareholders' equity	$8,325,000

The preferred shares are non-cumulative. During 2008, the following transactions occurred:

a. On May 1, declared a cash dividend of $50,400 on preferred shares. Paid the dividend on June 1.
b. On August 1, declared a 5% stock dividend on common shares. The current market price of the common shares was $18. The shares were issued on September 1.
c. On October 1, declared a cash dividend of $0.50 per share on the common shares; paid the dividend on November 1.
d. On December 15, issued a 2-for-1 stock split of common shares, when the shares were selling for $50 per share.

Required

1. Explain each transaction's effect on the shareholders' equity accounts and the total shareholders' equity.
2. Develop the Shareholders' Equity category of the December 31, 2008, balance sheet. Assume the net income for the year was $1,950,000.
3. Write a paragraph that explains the difference between a stock dividend and a stock split.

Problem 11-6 *Statement of Shareholders' Equity* LO 5

Refer to all the facts in Problem 11-1.

Required

Develop a statement of shareholders' equity for Wang Company for 2008. The statement should start with the beginning balance of each shareholders' equity account and explain the changes that occurred in each account to arrive at the 2008 ending balances.

Problem 11-7 *Wilco Comprehensive Income* **LO 5**

The consolidated statement of shareholders' equity of Wilco Stores, Inc. for the year ended December 31, 2008, appears below:

Consolidated Statement of Shareholders' Equity

	Number of Shares	Common Stock	Contributed Surplus	Retained Earnings	Accumulated Comprehensive Income	Total
Balance, January 31, 2007	4,470	$446	$1,412	$30,168	$ (684)	$31,342
Comprehensive Income						
Net income				3,336		3,336
Other accumulated comprehensive income						
Foreign currency translation adjustment					(472)	(472)
Hedge accounting adjustment					(112)	(112)
Total Comprehensive Income						2,752
Cash dividends ($0.28 per share)				(624)		(624)
Purchase of Company shares	(24)	(2)	(31)	(575)		(608)
Stock options exercised and other	6		67			67
Balance, January 31, 2008	4,452	$444	$1,448	$32,305	$(1,268)	$32,929

Required

1. Which items were included in comprehensive income? If these items had been included on the income statement as part of net income, what would have been the effect?

2. Do you think that the concept of comprehensive income would be useful to explain the impact of all the events that took place during 2008 to the shareholders of Wilco?

Problem 11-8 *Effects of Shareholders' Equity Transactions on Statement of Cash Flows* **LO 7**

Refer to all the facts in Problem 11-1.

Required

Indicate how each of the transactions affects the cash flows of Wang Company, by preparing the Financing Activities section of the 2008 statement of cash flows. Provide an explanation for the exclusion of any of these transactions from the Financing Activities section of the statement.

Problem 11-9 *Income Distribution of a Partnership (Appendix)* **LO 8**

Chunmei Ho and Philip King are partners in an entertainment business. The partnership agreement specifies the manner in which income of the business is to be distributed. Chunmei is to receive a salary of $40,000 for managing the club, and Philip is to receive interest at the rate of 10% on his capital balance of $600,000. Remaining income is to be distributed on a 2-to-1 ratio.

Required

Determine the amount that should be distributed to each partner, assuming the following business net incomes:

1. $30,000
2. $100,000
3. $160,000

Problem 11-10 *Sole Proprietorships (Appendix)* **LO 8**

On March 1, Hosie Keep deposited $60,000 of his own savings in a separate bank account to start a copying business. He purchased printing machines for $21,000. Expenses for the year, including depreciation on the printing machines, were $42,000. Sales for the year, all in cash, were $54,000. Keep withdrew $6,000 during the year.

Required

1. Prepare the journal entries for the following transactions: the March 1 initial investment, Hosie's withdrawal of cash, and the December 31 closing entries. Hosie closes revenues and expenses to an Income Summary account.

(continued)

2. What is the balance in Hosie's capital account at the end of the year?

3. Explain why the balance in Hosie's capital account is different from the amount of cash on hand.

Problem 11-11 *Partnerships (Appendix)* LO 8

Pat Cameron and Hilda MacDonald agreed to form a partnership to operate a sandwich shop. Pat contributed $50,000 cash and will manage the store. Hilda contributed computer equipment worth $16,000 and $184,000 cash. Hilda will keep the financial records. During the year, sales were $180,000 and expenses were $152,000. Pat withdrew $1,000 per month. Hilda withdrew $8,000 (total). Their partnership agreement specified that Pat would receive a salary of $14,400 for the year. Hilda would receive 6% interest on her initial capital investment. All remaining income or loss would be equally divided.

Required

Calculate the ending balance in the equity account of each of the partners.

Multi-Concept Problems

Problem 11-12 *Analysis of Shareholders' Equity* LO 1, 3, 6

The Shareholders' Equity section of the December 31, 2008, balance sheet of May Company appeared as follows:

Preferred stock,	
2,450 no par shares authorized, and issued	$ 61,400
Common stock,	
5,000 no par shares authorized, 3,500 shares issued	315,000
Contributed surplus	500
Total contributed capital	376,900
Retained earnings	20,000
Total shareholders' equity	$??

Required

Determine the following items, based on May's balance sheet:

1. The number of preferred shares issued
2. The number of preferred shares outstanding
3. The average per-share sales price of the preferred shares when issued
4. The average per-share sales price of the common shares when issued
5. The total shareholders' equity
6. The per-share book value of the common shares, assuming that there are no dividends in arrears and that the preferred shares can be redeemed at their book value

Problem 11-13 *Effects of Shareholders' Equity Transactions on the Balance Sheet* LO 3, 4

The following transactions occurred at Grand Ltd. during its first year of operation:

a. Issued 50,000 common shares at $5 each; 500,000 no par shares are authorized.
b. Issued 5,000 common shares for a building and land. The building was appraised for $10,000, but the value of the land is undeterminable. The shares are selling for $10 on the open market.
c. Purchased 500 of its own common shares on the open market for $16 per share.
d. Declared a dividend of $0.10 per share on outstanding common stock. The dividend is to be paid after the end of the first year of operations. Market value of the shares is $26.
e. Declared a 2-for-1 stock split. The market value of the stock was $37 before the stock split.
f. Reported $90,000 of income for the year.

Required

1. Indicate each transaction's effect on the assets, liabilities, and shareholders' equity of Grand Ltd.
2. Prepare the Shareholders' Equity section of the balance sheet.
3. Write a paragraph that explains the number of shares issued and outstanding at the end of the year.

Problem 11-14 *Shareholders' Equity Section of the Balance Sheet* LO 1, 3

The newly hired accountant at Robert Ltd. prepared the following balance sheet:

Assets	
Cash	$ 7,000
Accounts receivable	10,000
Repurchased 800 common shares	1,000
Plant, property, and equipment	216,000
Retained earnings	2,000
Total assets	$236,000
Liabilities	
Accounts payable	$ 11,000
Dividends payable	3,000
Shareholders' Equity	
Common stock,	
200,000 no par shares issued	222,000
Total liabilities and shareholders' equity	$236,000

Required

1. Prepare a corrected balance sheet. Write a short explanation for each correction.
2. Why does the Retained Earnings account have a negative balance?

—————— Alternate Problems ——————

Problem 11-1A *Shareholders' Equity Category* LO 1

Kennie Company was incorporated as a new business on January 1, 2008. The corporate articles approved on that date authorized the issuance of 4,000 shares of $7 no par cumulative, preferred stock and 40,000 shares of no par common stock. On March 10, Kennie issued for cash 2,000 preferred shares at $120 per share and 16,000 common shares at $80 per share. On March 20, it issued 4,000 common shares to acquire a building site, at a time when the shares were selling for $70 per share.

During 2008 Kennie established an employee benefit plan and acquired 2,000 common shares at $60 per share for that purpose. Later in 2008, it sold 200 shares at $65 per share.

On December 31, 2008, Kennie determined its net income for the year to be $160,000. The firm declared the annual cash dividend to preferred shareholders and a cash dividend of $5 per share to the common shareholders. The dividend will be paid in 2009.

Required

Develop the Shareholders' Equity category of Kennie's balance sheet as of December 31, 2008. Indicate on the statement the number of shares authorized, issued, and outstanding, both preferred and common.

Problem 11-2A *Evaluating Alternative Investments* LO 2

Betty Kerr would like to invest $200,000 in Travanti Ltd., which is offering common shares, preferred shares, and bonds on the open market. The common shares have paid $1 per share in dividends for the past three years, and the company expects to be able to double the dividend in the current year. The current market price of the common shares is $10 per share. The preferred shares have an $8 dividend rate. The bonds are selling at par with a 5% stated rate.

(continued)

Required

1. Explain Tarvanti's obligation to pay dividends or interest on each instrument.

2. Recommend one type of investment over the others to Betty, and justify your reason.

Problem 11-3A *Dividends for Preferred and Common Stock* **LO 3**

The Shareholders' Equity category of Irving Company's balance sheet as of December 31, 2008, appeared as follows:

Preferred stock,	
6,000 $8 no par shares issued and outstanding	$ 600,000
Common stock,	
120,000 no par shares issued and outstanding	2,700,000
Total contributed capital	3,300,000
Retained earnings	2,700,000
Total shareholders' equity	$6,000,000

The notes to the financial statements indicate that dividends were not declared or paid for 2006 or 2007. Irving wants to declare a dividend of $354,000 for 2008.

Required

Determine the total and the per-share amounts that should be declared to the preferred and common shareholders under the following assumptions:

1. The preferred shares are non-cumulative.

2. The preferred shares are cumulative.

Problem 11-4A *Effect of Stock Dividend* **LO 4**

Traves Company has a history of paying cash dividends on its common shares. Although the firm has been profitable this year, the board of directors has been planning construction of a second manufacturing plant. To reduce the amount that they must borrow to finance the expansion, the directors are contemplating replacing their usual cash dividend with a 40% stock dividend. The board is unsure what the effect of a stock dividend will be on the company's balance sheet and has requested your assistance.

Required

1. Write a statement to indicate the effect that the stock dividend has on the financial statements of Traves Company.

2. A group of common shareholders has contacted the firm to express its concern about the effect of the stock dividend and to question the effect that the stock dividend may have on the market price of the shares. Write a statement to address the shareholders' concerns.

Problem 11-5A *Dividends and Stock Splits* **LO 4**

On January 1, 2008, Mayflower Ltd.'s Shareholders' Equity category appeared as follows:

Preferred stock, $6.40 no par,	
2,000 shares issued and outstanding	$ 280,000
Common stock,	
20,000 no par shares issued and outstanding	650,000
Total contributed capital	930,000
Retained earnings	3,960,000
Total shareholders' equity	$4,890,000

The preferred shares are non-cumulative. During 2008, the following transactions occurred:

a. On May 1, declared a cash dividend of $12,800 on preferred shares. Paid the dividend on June 1.

b. On August 1, declared an 8% stock dividend on common shares. The current market price of the common shares was $26. The shares were issued on September 1.

c. On October 1, declared a cash dividend of $0.70 per share on the common shares; paid the dividend on November 1.

d. On December 1, issued a 3-for-1 stock split of common shares, when the shares were selling for $30 per share.

Required

1. Explain each transaction's effect on the shareholders' equity accounts and the total shareholders' equity.

2. Develop the Shareholders' Equity category of the balance sheet. Assume the net income for the year was $1,440,000.

3. Write a paragraph that explains the difference between a stock dividend and a stock split.

Problem 11-6A *Statement of Shareholders' Equity* **LO 5**

Refer to all the facts in Problem 11-1A.

Required

Develop a statement of shareholders' equity for Kennie Company for 2008. The statement should start with the beginning balance of each shareholders' equity account and explain the changes that occurred in each account to arrive at the 2008 ending balance.

Problem 11-7A *MIA's Comprehensive Income* **LO 5**

The consolidated statement of shareholders' equity of MIA Corporation for the year ended December 31, 2008, appears below.

MIA CORPORATION
CONSOLIDATED STATEMENT OF SHAREHOLDERS' EQUITY
(MILLIONS OF DOLLARS)

	Common Stock	Contributed Surplus	Treasury Stock	Accumulated Other Comprehensive Loss	Retained Earnings	Total
Balance at December 31, 2007	$182	$1,640	$(1,240)	$ (1)	$2,975	$3,556
Net loss	—	—	—	—	(1,081)	(1,081)
Adjustment for minimum pension liability, net of tax of $60	—	—	—	(100)	—	(100)
Changes in fair value of derivative financial instruments, net of tax of $28	—	—	—	(46)	—	(46)
Unrealized gain on investments, net of tax of $2	—	—	—	4	—	4
Total comprehensive loss*						(1,223)
Issuance of 221,000 shares from treasury pursuant to stock option, deferred stock, and restricted stock incentive plans, net of tax of $58	—	(45)	80	—	—	35
Balance at December 31, 2008	$182	$1,595	$(1,160)	$(143)	$1,894	$2,368

*$1081 + $100 + $46 – $4 = $1,223

Required

1. Explain the items that caused MIA's net income to be different from its comprehensive income. What does the term *unrealized gain* mean? What does a positive amount of $4 for unrealized gain on investments mean?

2. Do you think that MIA's shareholders would find the concept of comprehensive income useful to evaluate the performance of the company?

Problem 11-8A *Effects of Shareholders' Equity Transactions on the Statement of Cash Flows* **LO 7**

Refer to all the facts in Problem 11-1A.

Required

Indicate how each of the transactions affects the cash flows of Kennie Company, by preparing the Financing Activities section of the 2008 statement of cash flows. Provide an explanation for the exclusion of any of these transactions from the Financing Activities section of the statement.

Problem 11-9A *Income Distribution of a Partnership (Appendix)* **LO 8**

Allison Chat and Christy Hoe are partners in a cleaning business. The partnership agreement specifies the manner in which income of the business is to be distributed. Allison is to receive a salary of $50,000 for managing the business. Christy is to receive interest at the rate of 8% on her capital balance of $600,000. Remaining income is to be distributed on a 2-to-1 ratio.

Required

Determine the amount that should be distributed to each partner, assuming the following business net incomes:

1. $50,000
2. $125,000
3. $180,000

Problem 11-10A *Sole Proprietorships (Appendix)* **LO 8**

On March 1, Will Richey deposited $300,000 of his own savings in a business bank account to start a business. He purchased machines for $105,000. Expenses for the year, including depreciation on the machines, were $210,000. Sales for the year, all in cash, were $270,000. Will withdrew $30,000 during the year.

Required

1. Prepare the journal entries for the following transactions: the March 1 initial investment, Will's withdrawal of cash, and the December 31 closing entries. Will closes revenues and expenses to an Income Summary account.
2. What is the balance in Will's capital account at the end of the year?
3. Explain why the balance in Will's capital account is different from the amount of cash on hand.

Problem 11-11A *Partnerships (Appendix)* **LO 8**

May Song and Karen Young agreed to form a partnership to operate a restaurant. May contributed $70,000 cash and will manage the restaurant. Karen contributed computer equipment worth $22,400 and $257,600 cash. Karen will keep the financial records. During the year, sales were $252,000 and expenses were $212,800. May withdrew $1,400 per month. Karen withdrew $11,200 (total). Their partnership agreement specified that May would receive a salary of $21,600 for the year. Karen would receive 6% interest on her initial capital investment. All remaining income or loss would be equally divided.

Required

Calculate the ending balance in the equity account of each of the partners.

Alternate Multi-Concept Problems

Problem 11-12A *Analysis of Shareholders' Equity* **LO 1, 3, 6**

The Shareholders' Equity section of the December 31, 2008, balance sheet of Sackville Company appeared as follows:

Preferred stock,	
20,000 no par shares authorized, 16,000 shares issued	$ 824,000
Common stock,	
40,000 no par shares authorized, 28,000 shares issued,	2,520,000
Contributed surplus—shares repurchased	4,000
Total contributed capital	3,348,000
Retained earnings	160,000
Less: Treasury stock, preferred, 400 shares	(25,600)
Total shareholders' equity	$??

Determine the following items, based on Sackville's balance sheet.

1. The number of preferred shares outstanding
2. The average per-share sales price of the preferred shares when issued
3. The book value of the common shares in the Common Stock account

4. The average per-share sales price of the common shares when issued

5. The cost of the treasury stock per share

6. The total shareholders' equity

7. The per-share book value of the common shares, assuming that there are no dividends in arrears and that the preferred shares can be redeemed at book value

Problem 11-13A *Effects of Shareholders' Equity Transactions on Balance Sheet* **LO 3, 4**

The following transactions occurred at Hanna Inc. during its first year of operation:

a. Issued 20,000 common shares at $10 each; 200,000 shares are authorized at no par value.

b. Issued 20,000 common shares for a patent, which is expected to be effective for the next 15 years. The value of the patent is undeterminable. The shares are selling for $10 on the open market.

c. Purchased 2,000 of its own common shares on the open market for $10 per share.

d. Declared a dividend of $0.50 per share of outstanding common stock. The dividend is to be paid after the end of the first year of operations. Market value of the shares is $10.

e. Income for the year is reported as $680,000.

Required

1. Indicate each transaction's effect on the assets, liabilities, and shareholders' equity of Hanna Inc.

2. Hanna's president has asked you to explain the difference between contributed capital and retained earnings. Discuss these terms as they relate to Hanna.

3. Determine the book value per share at the end of the year.

Problem 11-14A *Shareholders' Equity Section of the Balance Sheet* **LO 1, 3**

The newly hired accountant at Larsen Inc. is considering the following list of accounts as he prepares the balance sheet. All of the accounts have positive balances. The company is authorized to issue 2,000,000 common shares and 20,000 preferred shares.

Retained earnings	$109,800
Dividends payable	3,000
Common stock, 200,000 no par	306,800
Preferred stock, $0.50 no par, 10,000 issued	100,000

Required

1. Prepare the Shareholders' Equity section of the balance sheet for Larsen.

2. Explain why some of the listed accounts are not shown in the Shareholders' Equity section.

Cases

Reading and Interpreting Financial Statements

Case 11-1 *CN's Shareholders' Equity Category* **LO 1, 5, 6**

Refer to CN's 2007 annual report.

CN

http://www.cn.ca

Required

1. What are the numbers of common shares authorized, issued, and outstanding as of the balance sheet date?

2. Calculate the book value per common share.

3. The balance of the Reinvested Earnings account increased during the year. What are the possible factors that affect its balance?

4. The total shareholders' equity as of December 31, 2007, is $10,177 million. Does that mean that shareholders will receive that amount if the company is liquidated?

Case 11-2 *Comparing Two Companies in the Same Industry: CN and CP* **LO 1, 5, 6**

Refer to the Shareholders' Equity section of the balance sheets of CP, and CN as of December 31, 2007, as provided in Appendixes A and B at the end of the text.

http://www.cpr.ca

(continued)

Required

1. For each company, what are the numbers of common shares authorized, issued, and outstanding as of the balance sheet date?

2. Calculate the book value per share for each company on its balance sheet date. What does this information tell you?

3. Did the balance of the Retained Earnings account of each company increase or decrease during the year? What are the possible factors that affect the Retained Earnings balance?

4. How does the total shareholders' equity of each company compare to the other company? Does the difference mean that one company's shares are more valuable than the other? Explain your answer.

Case 11-3 *Reading CN's Statement of Cash Flows* LO 7

A portion of the cash flow statement of CN for the year ended December 31, 2007, is as follows:

	Year Ended December 31,		
(In thousands)	**2007**	**2006**	**2005**
Cash flows from financing activities			
Payments for purchase of common shares	$(1,584)	$(1,483)	$(1,418)
Payments of cash dividends	(418)	(340)	(275)
Proceeds from issuance of common shares	77	120	115
Net cash used by financing activities and capital transactions	$(1,925)	$(1,703)	$(1,578)

Required

1. Explain how each of the items in the Financing Activities category affected the amount of the company's cash.

2. CN generated cash by selling shares during the year. What are possible reasons for selling shares? Why would a company repurchase common shares?

3. The cash flow statement indicates a use of cash for dividends paid. How do dividends affect the Shareholders' Equity category of the balance sheet?

Making Financial Decisions

Case 11-4 *Debt versus Preferred Shares* LO 1, 2, 6

Assume that you are an analyst attempting to compare the financial structures of two companies. In particular, you must analyze the debt and equity categories of the two firms and calculate a debt-to-equity ratio for each firm. The liability and equity categories of First Company at year-end appeared as follows:

Liabilities	
Accounts payable	$ 250,000
Loan payable	400,000
Shareholders' Equity	
Common stock	150,000
Retained earnings	300,000
Total liabilities and equity	$1,100,000

First Company's loan payable bears interest at 4%, which is paid annually. The principal is due in five years.

The liability and equity categories of Second Company at year-end appeared as follows:

Liabilities	
Accounts payable	$ 250,000
Shareholders' Equity	
Common stock	150,000
Preferred stock	400,000
Retained earnings	300,000
Total liabilities and equity	$1,100,000

Second Company's preferred shares are $4, cumulative and were issued at $100 per share. A provision of the share agreement specifies that the shares must be redeemed at face value in five years.

Required

1. It appears that the loan payable of First Company and the preferred shares of Second Company are very similar. What are the differences between the two securities?

2. When calculating the debt-to-equity ratio, do you believe that the Second Company preferred shares should be treated as debt or as shareholders' equity? Write a statement expressing your position on this issue.

Case 11-5 *Preferred versus Common Stock* LO 2

Rhondda Inc. needs to raise $1,000,000. It is considering two options:

a. Issue preferred shares, $8 no par, cumulative, callable at $110. The shares could be issued at $100 per share.

b. Issue common shares, no par, market $10. Currently, the company has 800,000 shares outstanding equally in the hands of five owners. The company has never paid a dividend.

Required

Rhondda has asked you to consider both options and make a recommendation. It is equally concerned with cash flow and company control. Write your recommendations.

Accounting and Ethics: What Would You Do?

Case 11-6 *Inside Information* LO 6

Hilda Space was an accountant with Hali Ltd., a large corporation with shares that were publicly traded on the Toronto Stock Exchange. One of Hilda's duties was to manage the corporate reporting department, which was responsible for developing and issuing Hali's annual report. At the end of 2008, Hali closed its accounting records, and initial calculations indicated a very profitable year. In fact, the net income exceeded the amount that had been projected during the year by the financial analysts who followed Hali's shares.

Hilda was very pleased with the company's financial performance. In January 2009, she suggested that her mother buy Hali's shares because she was sure the price would increase when the company announced its 2008 results. Hilda's mother followed the advice and bought a block of shares at $25 per share.

On March 15, 2009, Hali announced its 2008 results and issued the annual report. The company received favourable press coverage about its performance, and the share price on the stock exchange increased to $32 per share.

Required

What was Hilda's professional responsibility to Hali Ltd. concerning the issuance of the 2008 annual report? Did Hilda act ethically in this situation?

Case 11-7 *Dividend Policy* LO 4

Schooner Ltd. is owned by nearly 50 shareholders. Jim Stretch owns 48% of the shares. He needs cash to fulfill his commitment to donate the funds to construct a new church. Some of his friends have agreed to vote for Schooner to pay a larger-than-normal dividend to shareholders. Jim has asked you to vote for the large dividend because he knows that you also support the church. When informed that the dividend may create a working capital hardship on Schooner, Jim responded: "There is plenty of money in Retained Earnings. The dividend will not affect the cash of the company." Respond to his comment. What ethical questions do you and Jim face? How would you vote?

—————— *Internet Research Cases*——————————————

Case 11-8 *WestJet* LO 1, 5, 6

WestJet operates in the highly volatile airline industry. It must respond to competition and to innovative technology, and it must do so in ways that continue to build shareholder value. Search the Web to obtain WestJet's most recent annual report, or use library resources to obtain company information to answer the following:

1. Based on the latest information available, what is WestJet's (a) authorized number of common shares, (b) issued number of shares, (c) outstanding number of shares, and (d) average issue price for those shares?

INTERNET

http://www.westjet.com

(continued)

2. For the most recent year available, what dividend per common share did WestJet pay its shareholders?

3. Locate the past 52-week high and low and the most current market price for WestJet common shares. What financial factors may have affected the company's share price over the past three to six months? Would you buy WestJet's shares at this time? Explain your response.

Optional Research. Use an online reservation system to investigate how the prices of WestJet tickets compare with those of the other airlines. Are they higher or lower? Are there some routes where WestJet has a competitive advantage?

Case 11-9 *Yellow Pages* LO 1, 5, 8

The Yellow Pages found in most telephone books and on the Web is an income trust. On the Yellow Pages website (www.ypg.com) or at www.sedar.com, locate the Annual Information Form and the annual report issued in the second month after the December 31 year-end.

Required

1. Describe the structure of the Yellow Pages Income Fund.
2. Describe the distribution policy of the fund and the other parts of the organization.
3. Determine the consolidated net earnings of the fund, using its annual report.
4. Determine whether the distributions to unit holders were more or less than the earnings for the year.

Solutions to Key Terms Quiz

13	Authorized shares		7	Dividend payout ratio
1	Issued shares		18	Stock dividend
14	Outstanding shares		9	Stock split
2	Par value		8	Statement of shareholders' equity
15	Contributed surplus		11	Comprehensive income
3	Retained earnings		10	Book value per share
4	Cumulative feature		12	Market value per share
5	Convertible feature		21	Sole proprietorship (Appendix)
16	Callable feature		19	Partnership (Appendix)
6	Treasury stock		20	Partnership agreement (Appendix)
17	Retirement of shares			

Integrative Problem–Financing

Evaluating financing options for asset acquisition and their impact on financial statements

Following are the financial statements for Granville Ltd. for the year 2008.

**GRANVILLE LTD.
BALANCE SHEET
DECEMBER 31, 2008
(IN THOUSANDS)**

Assets		Liabilities	
Cash	$ 32	Current portion of lease	
Other current assets	128	obligation	$ 100
Leased assets (net of		Other current liabilities	60
accumulated depreciation)	700	Lease obligation—long-term	600
Other long-term assets	900	Other long-term liabilities	120
		Total liabilities	880
		Shareholders' Equity	
		Preferred stock	60
		Common stock	400
		Retained earnings	420
		Total shareholders' equity	880
		Total liabilities and	
Total assets	$1,760	shareholders' equity	$1,760

(continued)

GRANVILLE LTD.
INCOME STATEMENT
FOR THE YEAR ENDED DECEMBER 31, 2008
(IN THOUSANDS EXCEPT FOR PER SHARE AMOUNTS)

Revenues		$1,000
Expenses:		
Depreciation of leased asset	$100	
Depreciation—Other assets	64	
Interest on leased asset	50	
Other expenses	548	
Income tax (30% rate)	71	
Total expenses		(833)
Income before extraordinary loss		167
Extraordinary loss (net of		
$18 taxes)		(42)
Net income		$ 125
EPS before extraordinary loss		$3.925
EPS extraordinary loss		(1.05)
EPS—Net income		$2.875

Additional Information:

Granville Inc. has authorized 50,000 shares of $1 no par value cumulative preferred stock. There were 10,000 shares issued and outstanding at all times during 2008. The firm has also authorized 500,000 shares of no par common stock, with 40,000 shares issued and outstanding.

On January 1, 2008, Granville Ltd. acquired an asset, a piece of specialized equipment, for $800,000 with a capital lease. The lease contract indicates that the term of the lease is eight years. Payments of $150,000 are to be made each December 31. The first lease payment was made December 31, 2008, and consisted of $100,000 principal and $50,000 of interest expense. The capital lease is depreciated using the straight-line method over eight years with zero salvage value.

Required

1. Assuming the equipment was acquired using a capital lease, provide the entries for the acquisition, depreciation, and the lease payment.

2. The management of Granville Ltd. is considering the financial statement impact of methods of financing, other than the capital lease, that could have been used to acquire the equipment. For each following alternative **a**, **b**, and **c**, provide all necessary entries, each entry's impact on the accounting equation, and revised 2008 financial statements and calculate, as revised, the following amounts or ratios:

> Current ratio
> Debt-to-equity ratio
> Net income
> EPS—Net income

Assume that the following alternative actions would have taken place on January 1, 2008.

a. Instead of acquiring the equipment with a capital lease, the company negotiated an operating lease to use the asset. The lease requires annual year-end payments of $150,000 and results in "off-balance-sheet" financing. (*Hint:* The $150,000 should be treated as rental expense.)

b. Instead of acquiring the equipment with a capital lease, Granville Ltd. issued bonds for $800,000 and purchased the equipment with the proceeds of the bond issue. Assume the bond interest of $50,000 was accrued and paid on December 31, 2008. A portion of the principal also is paid each year for eight years. On December 31, 2008, the company paid $100,000 of principal and anticipated another $100,000 of principal to be paid in 2009. Assume the equipment would have an eight-year life and would be depreciated on a straight-line basis with zero salvage value.

c. Instead of acquiring the equipment with a capital lease, Granville Ltd. issued 20,000 additional shares of $1 preferred stock to raise $800,000 and purchased the equipment for $800,000 with the proceeds from the share issue. Dividends on the shares are declared and paid annually. Assume that a dividend payment was made on December 31, 2008. Assume the equipment would have an eight-year life and would be depreciated on a straight-line basis with zero salvage value.

COURTESY CN RAIL

Touring the Cash Flow Statement

A Word to Readers About Part V

Part V discusses the statement of cash flows which complements the other financial statements by focusing on the sources and uses of cash—a vital resource for any organization if it is to operate successfully.

CHAPTER 12

The Statement of Cash Flows

LEARNING OBJECTIVES

After studying this chapter, you should be able to:

LO 1 Explain the purpose of a statement of cash flows.

LO 2 Describe operating, investing, and financing activities, and give examples of each.

LO 3 Describe the difference between the direct and indirect methods of computing cash flow from operating activities.

LO 4 Use a work sheet to prepare a statement of cash flows.

LO 5 Interpret the statement of cash flows.

SUSAN QUINLAND-STRINGER/SHUTTERSTOCK

STUDY LINKS

A Look at the Previous Chapter

In Chapters 7 through 11, we discussed the items reported on the balance sheet in detail.

A Look at This Chapter

This chapter will focus on the statement of cash flows.

A Look at the Upcoming Chapter

Chapter 13 will focus on how financial information is used in decision making.

Focus on Financial Results

For managers, shareholders, creditors, analysts, and other users of financial statements, net income (along with its companion, earnings per share) is the single most important indicator of a company's overall performance. In recent years, however, experts have grown wary of relying too heavily on any one number. As you know by now from your study of accounting, you can't pay bills with net income; you need cash! The cash flow statement provides important information about how a company generates and uses its cash—information that often is not obvious in the other financial statements. For instance, CN reported $2,158 million of net income for 2007 but produced only $131 million of cash flow during the same period. How is this possible? Chapter 12 discusses the format and contents of the cash flow statement, how the cash flow statement is assembled, and how to interpret the cash flow statement.

CN 2007 ANNUAL REPORT

Consolidated Statement of Cash Flows

In millions Year ended December 31,	2007	2006	2005
Operating activities			
Net income	$2,158	$2,087	$1,556
Adjustments to reconcile net income to net cash provided from operating activities:			
Depreciation and amortization	678	653	630
Deferred income taxes (Note 15)	(82)	3	547
Gain on sale of Central Station Complex (Note 5)	(92)	-	-
Gain on sale of investment in English Welsh and Scottish Railway (Note 6)	(61)	-	-
Other changes in:			
Accounts receivable (Note 4)	229	(17)	142
Material and supplies	18	(36)	(25)
Accounts payable and accrued charges	(351)	197	(156)
Other net current assets and liabilities	39	58	8
Other	(119)	6	6
Cash provided from operating activities	2,417	2,951	2,708
Investing activities			
Property activities	(1,387)	(1,298)	(1,180)
Acquisitions, net of cash acquired (Note 3)	(25)	(84)	-
Sale of Central Station Complex (Note 5)	531	-	-
Sale of investment in English Welsh and Scottish Railway (Note 6)	114	-	-
Other, net	52	33	105
Cash used by investing activities	(895)	(1,349)	(1,075)
Financing activities			
Issuance of long-term debt	4,171	3,308	2,728
Reduction of long-term debt	(3,589)	(3,089)	(2,865)
Issuance of common shares due to exercise of stock options and related excess tax benefits realized (Note 12)	77	120	115
Repurchase of common shares (Note 11)	(1,584)	(1,483)	(1,418)
Dividends paid	(418)	(340)	(275)
Cash used by financing activities	1,343	(1,484)	(1,715)
Effect of foreign exchange fluctuations on U.S. dollar-denominated cash equivalents	(48)	(1)	(3)
Net increase (decrease) in cash and cash equivalents	131	117	(85)
Cash and cash equivalents, beginning of year	179	62	147
Cash and cash equivalents, end of year	$ 310	$ 179	$ 62
Supplemental cash flow information			
Net cash receipts from customers and other	$8,139	$7,946	$7,581
Net cash payments for:			
Employee services, suppliers, and other expenses	(4,323)	(4,130)	(4,075)
Interest	(340)	(294)	(306)
Workforce reductions (Note 9)	(31)	(45)	(87)
Personal injury and other claims (Note 18)	(86)	(107)	(92)
Pensions (Note 13)	(75)	(112)	(127)
Income taxes (Note 15)	(867)	(307)	(186)
Cash provided from operating activities	$2,417	$2,951	$2,708

This excerpt from CN's 2007 Annual Report appears courtesy of CN. This section of the CN Annual Report appears in the Appendix of this textbook.

▪ PURPOSE OF THE STATEMENT OF CASH FLOWS

LO 1 Explain the purpose of a statement of cash flows.

Statement of cash flows The financial statement that summarizes an entity's cash receipts and cash payments during the period from operating, investing, and financing activities.

The **statement of cash flows** is an important complement to the other major financial statements. It summarizes the operating, investing, and financing activities of a business over a period of time. The balance sheet summarizes the cash on hand and the balances in the other asset, liability, and owners' equity accounts, providing a snapshot at a specific point in time. The statement of cash flows reports the changes in cash over a period of time and, most important, *explains these changes.*

The income statement summarizes performance on an accrual basis. As you have learned in your study of accrual accounting, income on this basis is considered a better indicator of *future* cash inflows and outflows than is a statement limited to current cash flows. The statement of cash flows complements the accrual-based income statement by allowing users to assess a company's performance on a cash basis. As we will see in the following simple example, however, it also goes beyond presenting data related to operating performance and looks at other activities that affect a company's cash position.

An Example

Consider the following discussion between the owner of Fox River Realty and the company accountant. After a successful first year in business in 2007, in which it earned a profit of $100,000, the owner reviews the income statement for the second year, as presented in Exhibit 12-1.

Exhibit 12-1

Income Statement for Fox River Realty

FOX RIVER REALTY INCOME STATEMENT FOR THE YEAR ENDED DECEMBER 31, 2008	
Revenues	$400,000
Depreciation expense	50,000
All other expenses	100,000
Total expenses	150,000
Net income	$250,000

The owner is pleased with the results and asks to see the balance sheet. Comparative balance sheets for the first two years are presented in Exhibit 12-2.

Exhibit 12-2

Comparative Balance Sheets for Fox River Realty

FOX RIVER REALTY COMPARATIVE BALANCE SHEETS DECEMBER 31		
	2008	**2007**
Cash	$ 50,000	$150,000
Buildings	600,000	350,000
Accumulated depreciation	(150,000)	(100,000)
Total assets	$500,000	$400,000
Notes payable	$100,000	$150,000
Common shares	250,000	200,000
Retained earnings	150,000	50,000
Total liabilities and shareholders' equity	$500,000	$400,000

Where Did the Cash Go?   At first glance, the owner is surprised to see the significant decline in the Cash account. She immediately presses the accountant for answers. With such a profitable year, where has the cash gone? Specifically, why has cash decreased from $150,000 to $50,000, even though income rose from $100,000 in the first year to $250,000 in the second year?

The accountant begins his explanation to the owner by pointing out that income on a cash basis is even *higher* than the reported $250,000. Because depreciation expense is an expense that does not use cash (cash is used when the buildings are purchased, not when they are depreciated), cash provided from operating activities is calculated as follows:

Net income	$250,000
Add back: Depreciation expense	50,000
Cash provided by operating activities	$300,000

Further, the accountant reminds the owner of the additional $50,000 that she invested in the business during the year. Now the owner is even more bewildered: with cash from operations of $300,000 and her own infusion of $50,000, why did cash *decrease* by $100,000? The accountant refreshes the owner's memory on three major outflows of cash during the year. First, even though the business earned $250,000, she withdrew $150,000 in dividends during the year. Second, the comparative balance sheets indicate that notes payable with the bank were reduced from $150,000 to $100,000, requiring the use of $50,000 in cash. Finally, the comparative balance sheets show an increase in buildings for the year from $350,000 to $600,000—a sizable investment of $250,000 in new long-term assets.

Statement of Cash Flows   To summarize what happened to the cash, the accountant prepares a statement of cash flows as shown in Exhibit 12-3. Although the owner is not particularly happy with the decrease in cash for the year, she is at least satisfied with the statement as an explanation of where the cash came from and how it was used. The statement summarizes the important cash activities for the year and fills a void created with the presentation of just an income statement and a balance sheet.

FOX RIVER REALTY
STATEMENT OF CASH FLOWS
FOR THE YEAR ENDED DECEMBER 31, 2008

Cash provided (used) by operating activities:	
Net income	$ 250,000
Add back: Depreciation expense	50,000
Net cash provided (used) by operating activities	300,000
Cash provided (used) by investing activities:	
Purchase of buildings	(250,000)
Cash provided (used) by financing activities:	
Additional investment by owner	50,000
Cash dividends paid to owner	(150,000)
Repayment of notes payable to bank	(50,000)
Net cash provided (used) by financing activities	(150,000)
Net increase (decrease) in cash	(100,000)
Cash balance at beginning of year	150,000
Cash balance at end of year	$ 50,000

Exhibit 12-3

Statement of Cash Flows for Fox River Realty

The purpose of the statement of cash flows is to provide information about a company's cash inflows and outflows. As discussed early in Chapter 7, certain items are recognized as being equivalent to cash and are combined with cash on the balance sheet. A cash equivalent is an investment that is readily convertible to a known amount of cash and with a maturity to the investor of three months or less. For the same reason that cash equivalents are combined with cash on the balance sheet, they are also combined with cash in the statement of cash flows.

CLASSIFICATION OF CASH FLOWS

LO 2 Describe operating, investing, and financing activities, and give examples of each.

For the statement of cash flows, companies are required to classify activities into three categories: operating, investing, or financing. These categories represent the major functions of an entity, and classifying activities in this way allows users to look at important relationships. For example, one important financing activity for many businesses is borrowing money. Grouping the cash inflows from borrowing money during the period with the cash outflows from repayments of loans during the period makes it easier for analysts and other users of the statements to evaluate the company.

Each of the three types of activities can result in both cash inflows and cash outflows to the company. Thus, the general format for the statement is as shown in Exhibit 12-4. Note the direct tie between the bottom portion of this statement and the balance sheet. The beginning and ending balances in cash and cash equivalents, shown as the last two lines on the statement of cash flows, are taken directly from the comparative balance sheets. Some companies end their statement of cash flows with the figure for the net increase or decrease

Exhibit 12-4

Format for the Statement of Cash Flows

THE SMITH CORPORATION STATEMENT OF CASH FLOWS FOR THE YEAR ENDED DECEMBER 31, 2008		
Cash flows from operating activities:		
Inflows	$ xxx	
Outflows	(xxx)	
Net cash provided (used) by operating activities		$xxx
Cash flows from investing activities:		
Inflows	xxx	
Outflows	(xxx)	
Net cash provided (used) by investing activities		xxx
Cash flows from financing activities:		
Inflows	xxx	
Outflows	(xxx)	
Net cash provided (used) by financing activities		xxx
Net increase (decrease) in cash and cash equivalents		xxx
Cash and cash equivalents at beginning of year		xxx
Cash and cash equivalents at end of year		$xxx

in cash and cash equivalents and do not report the beginning and ending balances in cash and cash equivalents directly on the statement of cash flows. Instead, the reader must turn to the balance sheet for these amounts. We now take a closer look at the types of activities that appear in each of the three categories on the statement of cash flows.

Operating activities Activities concerned with the acquisition and sale of products and services.

Operating Activities   **Operating activities** involve acquiring and selling products and services. The specific activities of a business depend on its type. For example, for a retailer, the purchase of inventory from a distributor constitutes an operating activity. For a realty company, the payment of a commission to a salesperson is an operating activity. Both types of businesses sell either products or services, and their sales are important operating activities.

A statement of cash flows reflects the cash effects, either inflows or outflows, associated with each of these activities. For example, the retailer's payment for purchases of inventories results in a cash outflow. The receipt of cash from collecting an account receivable results in a cash inflow. The income statement reports operating activities on an accrual basis. The statement of cash flows reflects a company's operating activities on a cash basis.

The notion that the income statement and the operating section of the statement of cash flows report the results of the same activities also helps us to understand why certain items, such as interest paid, are considered operating cash flows. Interest paid is related to a financing activity—borrowing on debts, thus, it is natural to think interest paid should be a financing cash flow. AcSB specifies that since interest paid and interest and dividends received are reported on the income statement, they are also reported in the operating section in the statement of cash flows. Dividends paid, on the other hand, are reported in the statement of retained earnings and are thus not included in the operating section, but in the financing section in a statement of cash flows.

Investing Activities **Investing activities** involve acquiring and disposing of long-term assets. Replacing worn-out plant and equipment and expanding the existing base of long-term assets are essential to all businesses. In fact, cash paid for these acquisitions, often called *capital expenditures*, is usually the largest single item in the Investing Activities section of the statement. The following example of the Investing Activities section of a statement of cash flows indicates that the company spent $5,660 million for **1** plant, rental machines, and other property during the year (all amounts are in millions of dollars):

Investing activities Activities concerned with the acquisition and disposal of long-term assets.

Cash flow from investing activities:

1	Payments for plant, rental machines, and other property	$(5,660)
2	Proceeds from disposition of plant, rental machines, and other property	1,165
3	Acquisitions	(916)
4	Purchases of marketable securities and other investments	(778)
5	Proceeds from marketable securities and other investments	738
	Net cash used in investing activities	(5,451)

Sales of long-term assets, such as plant and equipment, are not generally a significant source of cash. These assets are acquired to be used in producing goods and services, or to support this function, rather than to be resold, as is true for inventory. Occasionally, however, plant and equipment may wear out or no longer be needed and are offered for sale. In fact, the above example indicates that it generated $1,165 million of cash during the year from **2** disposals of plant, rental machines, and other property.

In Chapter 7, we explained why companies sometimes invest in the shares and bonds of other companies. The acquisition of one company by another, whether in the form of a merger or of a share acquisition, is an important *investing* activity to bring to the attention of statement readers. The above company spent $916 million to **3** acquire other companies during the year. Note also that during the year it **4** spent $778 million to buy marketable securities and other investments and **5** generated $738 million from selling these investments.

Financing Activities All businesses rely on internal financing, external financing, or a combination of the two in meeting their needs for cash. Initially, a new business must have a certain amount of investment by the owners to begin operations. After this, many companies use notes, bonds, and other forms of debt to provide financing. Issuing shares and various forms of debt results in cash inflows that appear as **financing activities** on the statement of cash flows. On the other side, the repurchase of a company's own shares and the repayment of borrowings are important cash outflows to be reported in the Financing Activities section of the statement. Another important activity listed in the Financing Activities section of the statement is the payment of

Financing activities Activities concerned with the raising and repayment of funds in the form of debt and equity.

dividends to shareholders. The following example lists most of the common cash inflows and outflows from financing activities (amounts in millions of dollars):

Cash flow from financing activities:

1	Proceeds from new debt	4,535
	Short-term borrowings less than 90 days—net	2,926
2	Payments to settle debt	(7,898)
	Preferred share repurchase	(254)
	Common share repurchase	(3,652)
	Cash dividends paid	(966)
	Net cash used in financing activities	(5,309)

During the year, the company **1** received $4,535 million from issuing new debt and **2** paid $7,898 million to retire old debt. In analyzing the company, you would probably next read the long-term debt note to see whether the company essentially refinanced the old debt with new debt at a lower interest rate and, if it did, what the interest saving is, because this will continue to be a benefit for many years.

Summary of the Three Types of Activities   To summarize the categorization of the activities of a business as operating, investing, and financing, refer to Exhibit 12-5. The exhibit lists examples of each of the three activities along with the related accounts on the balance sheet and the account classifications on the balance sheet.

In the exhibit, operating activities centre on the acquisition and sale of products and services and related costs, such as wages and taxes. Two important observations can be made about the cash flow effects from the operating activities of a business. *First, the cash flows from these activities are the cash effects of transactions that enter into the determination of net income.* For example, the sale of a product enters into the calculation of net income. The cash effect of this transaction—that is, the collection of the account receivable—results in a cash inflow from operating activities. *Second, cash flows from operating activities usually relate to an increase or decrease in either a current asset or a current liability.* For example, the payment of taxes to the government results in a decrease in taxes payable, which is a current liability on the balance sheet.

Exhibit 12-5   Classification of Items on the Statement of Cash Flows

ACTIVITY	EXAMPLES	EFFECT ON CASH	RELATED BALANCE SHEET ACCOUNT	CLASSIFICATION ON BALANCE SHEET
Operating	Collection of customer accounts	Inflow	Accounts receivable	Current asset
	Payment to suppliers for inventory	Outflow	Accounts payable Inventory	Current liability Current asset
	Payment of wages	Outflow	Wages payable	Current liability
	Payment of taxes	Outflow	Taxes payable	Current liability
Investing	Capital expenditures	Outflow	Plant and equipment	Long-term asset
	Purchase of another company	Outflow	Long-term investment	Long-term asset
	Sale of plant and equipment	Inflow	Plant and equipment	Long-term asset
	Sale of another company	Inflow	Long-term investment	Long-term asset
Financing	Issuance of capital stock	Inflow	Capital stock	Shareholders' equity
	Issuance of bonds	Inflow	Bonds payable	Long-term liability
	Issuance of bank note	Inflow	Notes payable	Long-term liability
	Repurchase of shares	Outflow	Capital stock and retained earnings	Shareholders' equity
	Retirement of bonds	Outflow	Bonds payable	Long-term liability
	Repayment of notes	Outflow	Notes payable	Long-term liability
	Payment of dividends	Outflow	Retained earnings	Shareholders' equity

Note that investing activities normally relate to long-term assets on the balance sheet. For example, the purchase of new plant and equipment increases long-term assets, and the sale of these same assets reduces long-term assets on the balance sheet.

Finally, *note that financing activities usually relate to either long-term liabilities or shareholders' equity accounts.* There are exceptions to these observations about the type of balance sheet account involved with each of the three types of activities, but these rules of thumb are useful as we begin to analyze transactions and attempt to determine their classification on the statement of cash flows.

TWO METHODS OF REPORTING CASH FLOW FROM OPERATING ACTIVITIES

Companies use one of two different methods to report the amount of cash flow from operating activities. The first approach, called the **direct method,** involves reporting major classes of gross cash receipts and cash payments. For example, cash collected from customers is reported separately from any interest and dividends received. Each of the major types of cash payments related to the company's operations follows, such as cash paid for inventory, for salaries and wages, for interest, and for taxes. An acceptable alternative to this approach is the **indirect method.** Under the indirect method, net cash flow from operating activities is computed by adjusting net income to remove the effect of all deferrals of past operating cash receipts and payments and all accruals of future operating cash receipts and payments.

Although the direct method is preferred by the AcSB, it is used much less frequently than the indirect method in practice.

To compare and contrast the two methods, assume that Canmore Company begins operations as a corporation on January 1, 2008, with the owners' investment of $10,000 in cash. An income statement for 2008 and a balance sheet as of December 31, 2008, are presented in Exhibits 12-6 and 12-7, respectively.

Direct Method   To report cash flow from operating activities under the direct method, we look at each of the items on the income statement and determine how much cash each of these activities either generated or used.

LO 3 Describe the difference between the direct and indirect methods of computing cash flow from operating activities.

Direct method For preparing the Operating Activities section of the statement of cash flows, the approach in which cash receipts and cash payments are reported.

Indirect method For preparing the Operating Activities section of the statement of cash flows, the approach in which net income is reconciled to net cash flow from operations.

Exhibit 12-6

Canmore Company Income Statement

CANMORE COMPANY INCOME STATEMENT FOR THE YEAR ENDED DECEMBER 31, 2008	
Revenues	$80,000
Operating expenses	(64,000)
Income before tax	16,000
Income tax expense	(4,000)
Net income	$12,000

Exhibit 12-7

Canmore Company Balance Sheet

CANMORE COMPANY BALANCE SHEET AS OF DECEMBER 31, 2008			
Assets		**Liabilities and Shareholders' Equity**	
Cash	$15,000	Accounts payable	$ 6,000
Accounts receivable	13,000	Capital stock	10,000
		Retained earnings	12,000
Total	$28,000	Total	$28,000

A T account of the related balance sheet items can be used to determine cash collections and payments. A T account for Accounts Receivable with the beginning and ending balances and the sales of the period is provided below:

ACCOUNTS RECEIVABLE

Bal. Jan. 1	0		
Sales	80,000	?	Cash collection
Bal. Dec. 31	13,000		

Since Beginning Accounts Receivable	$ -0-	
+ Sales Revenue	80,000	
− Collections	(X)	
= Ending Accounts Receivable	$ 13,000	

Solving for X, we can find the cash collection:

$$\$0 + \$80,000 - X = \$13,000$$
$$X = \$67,000$$

Revenues for the period were $80,000. Since the balance sheet at the end of the period shows a balance in Accounts Receivable of $13,000, however, Canmore collected only $80,000 − $13,000, or $67,000, from its sales of the period. Thus, the first line on the statement of cash flows in Exhibit 12-8 reports $67,000 in cash collected from customers. Remember that the *net increase* in Accounts Receivable must be deducted from sales to find cash collected. For a new company, this is the same as the ending balance because the company starts the year without a balance in Accounts Receivable.

The same logic can be applied to determine the amount of cash expended for operating purposes.

A T account for Accounts Payable with the beginning and ending balances and the Operating Expenses of the period is shown below:

ACCOUNTS PAYABLE

		0	Bal. Jan. 1
Cash payment	?	64,000	Operating expenses
		6,000	Bal. Dec. 31

Exhibit 12-8

Statement of Cash Flows
Using the Direct Method

CANMORE COMPANY STATEMENT OF CASH FLOWS FOR THE YEAR ENDED DECEMBER 31, 2008	
Cash flows from operating activities	
Cash collected from customers	$ 67,000
Cash payments for operating purposes	(58,000)
Cash payments for taxes	(4,000)
Net cash inflow from operating activities	5,000
Cash flows from financing activities	
Issuance of capital stock	10,000
Net increase in cash	15,000
Cash balance, beginning of period	–0–
Cash balance, end of period	$ 15,000

	Since	Beginning Accounts Payable	$ 0
		+ Operating Expenses	64,000
		− Cash payment	(X)
		= Ending Accounts Payable	$ 6,000

Solving for X, we can find the cash payment:

$$\$0 + \$64,000 - X = \$6,000$$

$$X = \$58,000$$

Operating expenses on the income statement are reported at $64,000. According to the balance sheet, however, $6,000 of the expense is unpaid at the end of the period as evidenced by the balance in Accounts Payable. Thus, the amount of cash expended for operating purposes as reported on the statement of cash flows in Exhibit 12-8 is $64,000 − $6,000, or $58,000. The other cash payment in the Operating Activities section of the statement is $4,000 for income taxes. Because no liability for income taxes is reported on the balance sheet, we know that $4,000 represents both the income tax expense of the period and the amount paid to the government. The only other item on the statement of cash flows in Exhibit 12-8 is the cash inflow from financing activities for the amount of cash invested by the owner in return for capital stock.

Indirect Method   When the indirect method is used, the first line in the Operating Activities section of the statement of cash flows as shown in Exhibit 12-9 is the net income of the period. Net income is then *adjusted* to reconcile it to the amount of cash provided by operating activities. As reported on the income statement, this net income figure includes the sales of $80,000 for the period. As we know, however, the amount of cash collected was $13,000 less than this because not all customers paid Canmore the amount due. *The increase in Accounts Receivable for the period is deducted from net income on the statement because the increase indicates that the company sold more during the period than it collected in cash.*

Exhibit 12-9

Statement of Cash Flows Using the Indirect Method

CANMORE COMPANY STATEMENT OF CASH FLOWS FOR THE YEAR ENDED DECEMBER 31, 2008	
Cash flows from operating activities	
Net income	$ 12,000
Adjustments to reconcile net income to net cash from operating activities:	
Increase in accounts receivable	(13,000)
Increase in accounts payable	6,000
Net cash inflow from operating activities	5,000
Cash flows from financing activities	
Issuance of capital stock	10,000
Net increase in cash	15,000
Cash balance, beginning of period	–0–
Cash balance, end of period	$ 15,000

The logic for the addition of the increase in Accounts Payable is similar, although the effect is the opposite. The amount of operating expenses deducted on the income statement was $64,000. We know, however, that the amount of cash paid was $6,000 less than this, as the balance in Accounts Payable indicates. *The increase in Accounts Payable for the period is added back to net income on the statement because the increase indicates that the company paid less during the period than it recognized in expense on the income statement.* One observation can be noted about this example. Because this is the first year of operations for Canmore, we wouldn't be too concerned that accounts receivable are increasing faster than accounts payable. If this becomes a trend, however, we would try to improve the accounts receivable collections process.

Two important observations should be made in comparing the two methods illustrated in Exhibits 12-8 and 12-9. First, the amount of cash provided by operating activities is the same under the two methods: $5,000; the two methods are simply different computational approaches to arrive at the cash generated from operations. Second, the remainder of the statement of cash flows is the same, regardless of which method is used. The only difference between the two methods is in the Operating Activities section of the statement.

Both the direct and the indirect methods are acceptable for financial reporting purposes. AcSB recommends the direct method as the preferred method but also requires a reconciliation of net income and cash from operating activities. In practice, most companies use the indirect method for cash from operating activities.

Non-cash Investing and Financing Activities

Occasionally, companies engage in important investing and financing activities that do not affect cash. For example, assume that Canmore issues shares to an inventor in return for the exclusive rights to a patent. Although the patent has no ready market value, the shares could have been sold on the open market for $25,000. Thus, the following entry is made on Canmore's books:

Patent	25,000	
Capital Stock		25,000
To record issuance of shares in exchange for patent		

Assets	=	Liabilities	+	Shareholders' Equity
+25,000				+25,000

This transaction does not involve cash and is therefore not reported on the statement of cash flows. However, what if we changed the scenario slightly? Assume that Canmore wants the patent but the inventor is not willing to accept shares in return for it. So instead Canmore sells shares on the open market for $25,000 and then pays this amount in cash to the inventor for the rights to the patent. Now Canmore records two journal entries. The first is as follows:

Cash	25,000	
Capital Stock		25,000
To record issuance of capital stock for cash		

Assets	=	Liabilities	+	Shareholders' Equity
+25,000				+25,000

It next records this entry:

Patent	25,000	
Cash		25,000
To record acquisition of patent for cash		

Assets	=	Liabilities	+	Shareholders' Equity
+25,000				
−25,000				

How would each of these two transactions be reported on a statement of cash flows? The first transaction appears as a cash inflow in the Financing Activities section of the statement; the second is reported as a cash outflow in the Investing Activities section. The point is that even though the *form* of this arrangement (with shares sold for cash and then the cash paid to the inventor) differs from the form of the first arrangement (with shares exchanged directly for the patent), the *substance* of the two arrangements is the same. That is, both involve a significant financing activity, the issuance of shares, and an important investing activity, the acquisition of a patent. Because the substance is what matters, accounting standards require that any significant non-cash transactions be reported in a note to the financial statements. For our transaction in which shares were issued directly to the inventor, presentation in a note is as follows:

Shares were issued to acquire patent valued at $25,000

To this point, we have concentrated on the purpose of a statement of cash flows and the major reporting requirements related to it. We turn our attention next to a methodology to use in actually preparing the statement.

Two-Minute Review

1. What are cash equivalents, and why are any increases or decreases in them not reported on a statement of cash flows?

2. What are the three types of activities reported on a statement of cash flows?

3. What are the two methods of reporting cash flow from operating activities, and how do they differ?

Answers on page 598.

HOW THE STATEMENT OF CASH FLOWS IS PUT TOGETHER

Two interesting observations can be made about the statement of cash flows. First, the "answer" to a statement of cash flows is known before we start to prepare it. That is, the change in cash for the period is known by comparing two successive balance sheets. Thus, it is not the change in cash itself that is emphasized on the statement of cash flows but the *explanations* for the change in cash. That is, each item on a statement of cash flows helps to explain why cash changed by the amount it did during the period. The second important observation about the statement of cash flows relates even more specifically to how we prepare it. Both an income statement and a balance sheet are prepared simply by taking the balances in each of the various accounts in the general ledger and putting them in the right place on the right statement. This is not true for the statement of cash flows, however. Instead, it is necessary to analyze the transactions during the period and attempt to (1) determine which of these affected cash and (2) classify each of the cash effects into one of the three categories.

In the simple examples presented so far in the chapter, we prepared the statement of cash flows without the use of any special tools. In more complex situations, however, some type of methodology is needed. We first will review the basic accounting equation and then illustrate a work sheet approach for preparing the statement.

LO 4 Use a work sheet to prepare a statement of cash flows.

The Accounting Equation and the Statement of Cash Flows

The basic accounting equation is as follows:

Next, consider this refinement of the equation:

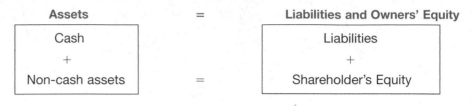

The equation can be rearranged so only cash is on the left side and all other items are on the right side:

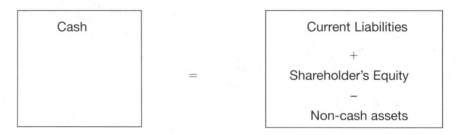

Therefore, any changes in cash on the left side must be accompanied by a corresponding change in the right side of the equation. For example, an increase or inflow of cash could result from an *increase* in liabilities in the form of borrowing from the bank by signing a note. Or an increase in cash could come from a *decrease* in assets in the form of sales of capital assets. Remember, no matter how the accounts change, the basic accounting equation remains balanced. This provides us with the basis to determine how the changes in the rest of the accounts affect cash. The following are some examples of how cash is affected by the changes in other balance sheet accounts:

Example 1: $500 decrease in accounts receivable – Collection of $500 for the outstanding accounts results in a decrease in accounts receivable and an increase in cash.

	Assets	=	Liabilities	+	Shareholders' Equity
– 500 (Accounts Receivable)					
+500 (Cash)					

Example 2: $1,200 increase in prepaid insurance – Paying insurance premium causes prepaid insurance to increase and cash to decrease.

	Assets	=	Liabilities	+	Shareholders' Equity
+1,200 (Prepaid Insurance)					
– 1,200 (Cash)					

Example 3: $1,500 decrease in notes payable – repaying bank loan results in a decrease in liabilities and a decrease in cash.

Assets	=	Liabilities	+	Shareholders' Equity
–1,500 (Cash)		–1,500 (Notes Payable)		

Example 4: $2,000 increase in retained earnings – selling goods or services for cash will increase cash as well as retained earnings through an increase in sales revenue.

Assets	=	Liabilities	+	Shareholders' Equity
+2,000 (Cash)				+2,000 (Retained Earnings)

By considering these examples we see that inflows and outflows of cash relate to increases and decreases in the various balance sheet accounts. We now turn to analyzing these accounts as a way to assemble a statement of cash flows.

A Work Sheet Approach to Preparing the Statement of Cash Flows

The following steps can be used to prepare a statement of cash flows:

1. *List all operating, investing, and financing activities in three separate sections.*

   The income statement provides the details of the operating activities. Additional information is often required to determine the investing and financing activities.

2. *List the accrual amount of each activity on the income statement.*

   Note that investing and financing activities usually are not reported on the income statement; thus, only the operating activities should be entered. There are exceptions to this rule—for instance, the gain from the disposal of a capital asset and the loss from the retirement of a long-term debt are included on the income statement. The cash flows associated with these activities—that is, the proceeds from disposal of a capital asset and the payment to retire a long-term debt—are considered cash from investing and financing activities, respectively. The non-operating items on the income statement should be moved out of the Operating Activities section and placed in the Investing Activities and Financing Activities sections, as appropriate.

3. *Adjust for the difference between the accrual amount and the cash amount for each item to derive the cash flow.*

   The changes in the balance sheet account during the period provide the information needed for the adjustments. In the Operating Activities section, decreases in non-cash current assets and increases in current liabilities are added, and increases in non-cash current assets and decreases in current liabilities are subtracted.

   In the Investing Activities section, decreases in non-current assets are added, and increases in non-current assets are subtracted. In the Financing Activities section, increases in non-current liabilities and shareholders' equity are added and decreases in non-current liabilities and shareholders' equity are subtracted. The adjustments are entered in **Column B** and cash flows in **Column C**. The amount in Column C should be the sum of Columns A and B.

4. *Prepare the statement of cash flows.*

   Statement of cash flows can be prepared using the information in the worksheet prepared following steps 1–3.

To illustrate this approach, we will refer to the income statement in Exhibit 12-10 and to the comparative balance sheets and the additional information provided for Julian Corp. in Exhibit 12-11.

Exhibit 12-10

Julian Corp. Income Statement

JULIAN CORP.
INCOME STATEMENT
FOR THE YEAR ENDED DECEMBER 31, 2008

Revenues and gains:		
Sales revenue	$685,000	
Gain on sale of equipment	5,000	
Total revenues and gains		$690,000
Expenses and losses:		
Cost of goods sold	390,000	
Salaries and wages	60,000	
Depreciation	40,000	
Insurance	12,000	
Interest	15,000	
Income taxes	53,000	
Total expenses and losses		570,000
Net income		$120,000

Exhibit 12-11

Julian Corp. Comparative
Balance Sheets

JULIAN CORP.
COMPARATIVE BALANCE SHEETS

	December 31	
	2008	**2007**
Cash	$ 35,000	$ 46,000
Accounts receivable	63,000	57,000
Inventory	84,000	92,000
Prepaid insurance	12,000	18,000
Total current assets	194,000	213,000
Land	150,000	100,000
Property and equipment	440,000	370,000
Accumulated depreciation	(100,000)	(75,000)
Total long-term assets	490,000	395,000
Total assets	$684,000	$608,000
Accounts payable	$ 38,000	$ 31,000
Salaries and wages payable	7,000	9,000
Income taxes payable	8,000	5,000
Total current liabilities	53,000	45,000
Notes payable	285,000	235,000
Total liabilities	338,000	280,000
Capital stock	100,000	75,000
Retained earnings	246,000	253,000
Total shareholders' equity	346,000	328,000
Total liabilities and shareholders' equity	$684,000	$608,000

Additional Information

1. Land was purchased by issuing a $50,000 note payable.

2. Equipment was purchased for $105,000.

3. Equipment with an original cost of $35,000 and a book value of $20,000 was sold for $25,000.

4. Capital stock was issued in exchange for $25,000 in cash.

5. Cash dividends of $127,000 were declared and paid.

First, we list in a table all the activities engaged in by Julian Corp. during 2008; see Exhibit 12-12. The income statement (Exhibit 12-10) contains the operating activities. We can use the additional information at the bottom of Exhibit 12-11 to determine the investing and financing activities. The amounts in Column A are taken from the income statement in Exhibit 12-10. Next we adjust each item in Column A according to the changes in the related balance sheet accounts in Column B to determine the cash flow of each item. The cash flow of each item is shown in Column C.

Exhibit 12-12 Cash Flow Statement Work Sheet of Julian Corp. (Highlighted for Direct Method for CFO)

(In thousands of dollars) Activities	(A) Income Statement	(B) Adjusting for the Difference Between Accrual and Cash Amounts	(C) = A + B Cash Received (Paid)
Operating Activities			
1 Sales	685	−6 Increase in accounts receivable	679
2 Sale of equipment	5	−5 An investing activity, moved to #11	
3 Cost of goods sold	−390	8 Decrease in inventory 7 Increase in accounts payable	−375
4 Salaries and wages	−60	−2 Decrease in salaries and wages payable	−62
5 Depreciation	−40	40 Increase in accumulated depreciation	
6 Insurance	−12	6 Decrease in prepaid insurance	−6
7 Interest incurred	−15	No interest payable	−15
8 Income taxes	−53	3 Increase in income tax payable	−50
Net income	<u>120</u>		
Investing Activities			
9 Purchase of land		−50 Increase in land 50 Increase in notes payable	
10 Purchase of equipment		−105 Increase in property and equipment	−105
11 Sale of equipment	5	35 Decrease in property and equipment −15 Decrease in accumulated depreciation	25
Financing Activities			
12 Issuance of shares		25 Increase in capital stock	25
13 Dividends payment		−127 Decrease in retained earnings	−127

How the Statement of Cash Flows Is Put Together

#1 Sales Revenue. Sales as reported on the income statement in Exhibit 12-10 amounted to $685,000. Accounts receivable increased by $6,000 for the period. This indicates that Julian had $6,000 more sales to its customers than it collected in cash from them (assuming that all sales are on credit). Thus the $6,000 increase in Accounts Receivable should be subtracted to determine the cash collections. The cash collection in Column C is $685,000 – $6,000, or $679,000. The following summary journal entry explains the sales, the cash collected from customers, and the change in Accounts Receivable:

		DEBIT	CREDIT
#1	Cash	679,000	
	Accounts Receivable	6,000	
	Sales		685,000

Note that the above journal entry is not part of the bookkeeping. Rather, it is used here to explain the total effects of sales and collections on the Cash, Accounts Receivable, and Sales accounts.

#2 Sale of Equipment. A gain on the sale of the equipment of $5,000 is reported as the next line on the income statement. Any cash received from the sale of a long-term asset is reported in the Investing Activities section of the cash flow statement. We move it out of the Operating Activities section by deducting $5,000 from Column B and adding that amount to #11. Thus, there is no cash flow from this item in the Operating Activities section in Column C.

#3 Cost of Goods Sold. Cost of goods sold, as reported on the income statement, amounted to $390,000. The $390,000 is not the amount of cash paid to suppliers of inventory. This is because first, cost of goods sold represents the cost of the inventory sold during the period, not the amount purchased. Since the Inventory account decreased by $8,000, the amount of inventory purchased must be $8,000 less than the goods sold. Second, the amount of purchases is not the same as the cash paid to suppliers, because purchases are normally on account. Since Accounts Payable increased by $7,000 during the year, the amount of cash paid to suppliers must be $7,000 less than the purchases. The $8,000 increase in Inventory and the $7,000 decrease in Accounts Payable are entered in Column B as negative adjustments to Cost of Goods Sold. The cash flow in Column C is –$390,000 + $8,000 + $7,000, or –$375,000. The journal entry to explain Cost of Goods Sold, change in Inventory, and change in Accounts Payable is as follows:

		DEBIT	CREDIT
#3	Cost of Goods Sold	390,000	
	Inventory		8,000
	Accounts Payable		7,000
	Cash		375,000

#4 Salaries and Wages. Salaries and Wages reported on the income statement are $60,000; and Salaries and Wages Payable decreased by $2,000 during the year. Thus, the salaries and wages paid during the year must be $2,000 more than salaries and wages recognized. The $2,000 decrease in Salaries and Wages Payable negatively affects the cash flow and thus is subtracted in Column B. The cash flow associated with salaries and wages in Column C is –$60,000 – $2,000, or –$62,000. The journal entry to explain Salaries and Wages Expenses, change in Salaries and Wages Payable, and salaries and wages paid is as follows:

		DEBIT	CREDIT
#4	Salaries and Wages Expenses	60,000	
	Salaries and Wages Payable	2,000	
	Cash		62,000

#5 Depreciation.
The depreciation of capital assets is different from most other expenses in that it has no effect on cash flow. The only related cash flows are from the purchase and sale of these capital assets, which are reported in the Investing Activities section of the cash flow statement. The Accumulated Depreciation account will be increased by the amount depreciated during the year. The increase in Accumulated Depreciation, a contra-asset, is added in Column B. Thus, no cash flow associated with depreciation is shown in Column C. The journal entry to explain Depreciation Expense and Accumulated Depreciation is as follows:

		DEBIT	CREDIT
#5	Depreciation Expense	40,000	
	Accumulated Depreciation		40,000

#6 Insurance.
According to the income statement in Exhibit 12-10, Julian recorded Insurance Expense of $12,000 during 2008. This amount cannot reflect cash payments for insurance, however, because Julian's Prepaid Insurance decreased by $6,000 during the period. The decrease in Prepaid Insurance, a current asset, is added in Column B. The cash flow associated with insurance expense in Column C is –$12,000 + $6,000, or –$6,000:

		DEBIT	CREDIT
#6	Insurance Expense	12,000	
	Prepaid Insurance		6,000
	Cash		6,000

#7 Interest Incurred.
The amount of interest expense reported on the income statement is $15,000. Because the balance sheet does not report an accrual of interest owed but not paid (an Interest Payable account), we know that $15,000 is also the amount of cash paid. The journal entry to explain the Interest Expense and interest payment is as follows:

		DEBIT	CREDIT
#7	Interest Expense	15,000	
	Cash		15,000

#8 Income Tax Expense.   Income tax expense as reported on the income statement is $53,000. There is also a $3,000 increase in Income Tax Payable. Thus, the income tax paid is $3,000 less than the income tax expense recognized. The $3,000 increase in current liabilities is added in Column B as a positive adjustment. The income tax paid in Column C is –$53,000 + $3,000, or –$50,000:

		DEBIT	CREDIT
#8	Income Tax Expense	53,000	
	Income Tax Payable		3,000
	Cash		50,000

#9 Land.   Item 1 in the additional information indicates that Julian purchased land by issuing a $50,000 note payable. This entry obviously does not involve cash. In Column B, the increase in Land is subtracted; simultaneously, the increase in Notes Payable is added. Thus, no cash flow should show in Column C. The journal entry to explain the purchase of land and the issuance of a note follows:

		DEBIT	CREDIT
#9	Land	50,000	
	Notes Payable		50,000

This transaction has important investing and financing components. The issuance of the note is a financing activity, and the acquisition of land is an investing activity. Because no cash was involved, the transaction is reported as follows in a note, instead of directly on the cash flow statement:

A note of $50,000 was issued in exchange of land.

#10 The Purchase of Equipment.   Property and Equipment increased by $70,000 during the year. However, Julian both acquired equipment and sold equipment (items 1 and 2 in the additional information). The acquisition of the equipment resulted in a cash payment of $105,000. The journal entry to explain the purchase of property and equipment with a cash payment follows:

		DEBIT	CREDIT
#10	Property and Equipment	105,000	
	Cash		105,000

#11 Sale of Equipment.   Item 3 in the additional information in Exhibit 12-11 reports the sale of a machine with an original cost of $35,000 and a book value of $20,000 for $25,000. This means that the accumulated depreciation on the sold machine was $15,000. In Column B, the $35,000 decrease in Property and Equipment is added, and the $15,000 decrease in Accumulated Depreciation is subtracted. Thus, the cash flow from the sale of the machine is $5,000 + $35,000 – $15,000, or $25,000. The journal entry to explain the sale of the machine at a gain is as follows:

		DEBIT	CREDIT
#11	Cash	25,000	
	Accumulated Depreciation	15,000	
	Property and Equipment		35,000
	Gain on sale of machine		5,000

#12 Issuance of Shares. Item 4 in the additional information in Exhibit 12-11 indicates that shares were issued for $25,000 in cash. The $25,000 increase in the Capital Stock account confirms this. The increase in the Capital Stock account is added in Column B, and the cash flow from the issuance of shares in Column C is $25,000. The journal entry to explain the issuance of shares for cash is as follows:

	DEBIT	CREDIT
#12 Cash	25,000	
Capital Stock		25,000

#13 Dividends. Item 5 in the additional information in Exhibit 12-11 indicates that dividends for the year were $127,000. The fact that Retained Earnings decreased by $7,000 during the year while earnings were $120,000 confirms this. The $127,000 decrease in Retained Earnings represents the dividends declared during the year. However, since there was no Dividends Payable account at the beginning of the year, Julian must have paid the same amount of dividends that it declared during the year. The $127,000 decrease in Retained Earnings is subtracted in Column B. The journal entry to explain the cash dividend is as follows:

	DEBIT	CREDIT
#13 Retained Earnings	127,000	
Cash		127,000

Statement of Cash Flows: Direct Method

We have now recorded all the changes in the balance sheet accounts. Note that the changes in the Retained Earnings account caused by net income are recorded through revenues and expenses in the income statement. The changes in the Cash account are listed in Column C of Exhibit 12-12's cash inflows and cash outflows for various purposes. A cash flow statement that uses the direct method for cash from operating activities is presented in Exhibit 12-13.

Exhibit 12-13

Completed Statement of Cash Flows for Julian Corp.

JULIAN CORP. STATEMENT OF CASH FLOWS (DIRECT METHOD) FOR THE YEAR ENDED DECEMBER 31, 2008	
Cash flows from operating activities	
Cash receipts from:	
Sales on account	$ 679,000
Cash payments for:	
Inventory purchases	(375,000)
Salaries and wages	(62,000)
Insurance	(6,000)
Interest	(15,000)
Taxes	(50,000)
Total cash payments	(508,000)
Net cash provided by operating activities	171,000
Cash flows for investing activities	
Purchase of property and equipment	(105,000)
Sale of equipment	25,000
Net cash used by investing activities	(80,000)
Cash flows for financing activities	
Issuance of shares	25,000
Payment of cash dividends	(127,000)
Net cash used by financing activities	(102,000)

(continued)

How the Statement of Cash Flows Is Put Together

Exhibit 12-13

Completed Statement of
Cash Flows for Julian Corp.
(continued)

Net decrease in cash	(11,000)
Cash balance, December 31, 2007	46,000
Cash balance, December 31, 2008	$ 35,000
Note on investing and financing activities	
Acquisition of land in exchange for note payable	$ 50,000

What does Julian's statement of cash flows tell us? Cash flow from operations totalled $171,000. Cash used to acquire investments and equipment amounted to $80,000, after $25,000 was received from the sale of equipment. A net amount of $102,000 was used for financing activities. Thus, Julian used $11,000 more cash than it generated, and that's why the cash balance declined from $46,000 to $35,000. That's okay for a year or two, but if this continues, the company won't be able to pay its bills.

Accounting for Your Decisions

You Decide for Your Investment Club

You are a member of an investment club and have been given the assignment of analyzing the statements of cash flows for the Yarmouth Corp. for the last three years. The company has neither issued nor retired any shares during this time period. You notice that the company's cash balance has increased steadily during this period but that a majority of the increase is due to a large net inflow of cash from financing activities in each of the three years. Should you be concerned?

ANSWER: The net inflow of cash from financing activities indicates that the company is borrowing more than it is repaying. Certainly borrowing can be an attractive means of financing the purchase of new plant and equipment. At some point, however, the debt, along with interest, will need to be repaid. The company must be able to generate sufficient cash from its operations to make these payments.

Statement of Cash Flows: Indirect Method

The purpose of the Operating Activities section of the statement changes when we use the indirect method. Instead of reporting cash receipts and cash payments, *the objective is to reconcile net income to net cash flow from operating activities.*

The information for preparing a cash flow statement using the indirect method is also available from the work sheet in Exhibit 12-12. We have reproduced the work sheet in Exhibit 12-14, highlighting the items reported on the cash flow statement using the indirect method. Note that the net income is the summary of the income statement; thus the net income adjusted for the items as the Operating Activities section of Column B provides the same information to the Operating Activities section of Column C. The statement of cash flows of Julian with the Operating Activities section prepared using the indirect method is shown in Exhibit 12-15.

Note in Exhibit 12-15 the Investing Activities and Financing Activities sections are unchanged. The choice of the indirect or the direct method for presenting cash flow from operating activities does not affect these two sections.

(In thousands of dollars) Activities	(A) Income Statement		(B) Adjusting for the Difference Between Accrual and Cash Amounts	(C) = A + B Cash Received (Paid)
Operating Activities				
1 Sales	685	−6	Increase in accounts receivable	679
2 Sale of equipment	5	−5	An investing activity, moved to #11	
3 Cost of goods sold	−390	8	Decrease in inventory	−375
		7	Increase in accounts payable	
4 Salaries and wages	−60	−2	Decrease in salaries and wages payable	−62
5 Depreciation	−40	40	Increase in accumulated depreciation	
6 Insurance	−12	6	Decrease in prepaid insurance	−6
7 Interest incurred	−15		No interest payable	−15
8 Income taxes	−53	3	Increase in income tax payable	−50
Net income	**120**			
Investing Activities				
9 Purchase of land		50	Increase in land	
		−50	Increase in notes payable	
10 Purchase of equipment		−105	Increase in property and equipment	−105
11 Sale of equipment	5	35	Decrease in property and equipment	25
		−15	Decrease in accumulated depreciation	
Financing Activities				
12 Issuance of shares		25	Increase in capital stock	25
13 Dividends payment		−127	Decrease in retained earnings	−127

JULIAN CORP.
PARTIAL STATEMENT OF CASH FLOWS
FOR THE YEAR ENDED DECEMBER 31, 2008

Net cash flows from operating activities	
Net income	$120,000
Adjustments to reconcile net income to net cash provided by operating activities:	
Increase in accounts receivable	(6,000)
Gain on sale of equipment	(5,000)
Decrease in inventory	8,000
Increase in accounts payable	7,000
Decrease in salaries and wages payable	(2,000)
Depreciation expense	40,000
Decrease in prepaid insurance	6,000
Increase in income taxes payable	3,000
Net cash provided by operating activities	$171,000

Exhibit 12-15

Indirect Method for Reporting Cash Flows from Operating Activities

(continued)

Cash flows for investing activities	
Purchase of property and equipment	(105,000)
Sale of equipment	25,000
Net cash used by investing activities	(80,000)
Cash flows for financing activities	
Issuance of shares	25,000
Payment of cash dividends	(127,000)
Net cash used by financing activities	(102,000)
Net decrease in cash	(11,000)
Cash balance, December 31, 2007	46,000
Cash balance, December 31, 2008	$ 35,000
Note on investing and financing activities	
Acquisition of land in exchange for note payable	$ 50,000

Note that the work sheet demonstrates clearly how operating activities reported on the income statement can be adjusted for the changes in the related non-cash working capital accounts to determine the cash flow for these activities. The work sheet is also a useful tool for preparing a cash flow statement for the operating activities section using both the direct and the indirect methods. However, a work sheet is not always necessary to prepare a cash flow statement, especially when the indirect method is used. The Cash from Operating Activities section of a cash flow statement can be prepared by making necessary adjustments to the net income based on the change in non-cash working capital accounts.

Summary of Adjustments to Net Income under the Indirect Method

The following is a list of the most common adjustments to net income when the indirect method is used to prepare the Operating Activities section of the statement of cash flows:

ADDITIONS TO NET INCOME	DEDUCTIONS FROM NET INCOME
Decrease in accounts receivable	Increase in accounts receivable
Decrease in inventory	Increase in inventory
Decrease in prepayments	Increase in prepayments
Increase in accounts payable	Decrease in accounts payable
Increase in accrued liabilities	Decrease in accrued liabilities
Losses on sales of long-term assets	Gains on sales of long-term assets
Losses on retirements of bonds	Gains on retirements of bonds
Depreciation, amortization, and depletion	

Comparison of the Indirect and Direct Methods

Earlier in the chapter we pointed out that the amount of cash provided by operating activities is the same under the direct and the indirect methods. The relative merits of the two methods, however, have stirred considerable debate in the accounting profession. The AcSB has expressed a strong preference for the direct method but allows companies to use the indirect method.

Advocates of the direct method believe that the information provided with this approach is valuable in evaluating a company's operating efficiency. For example, the use of the direct method allows the analyst to follow any trends in cash receipts from customers and compare them with cash payments to suppliers. The information presented in the Operating Activities section of the statement under the direct method is certainly user-friendly. Someone without a technical background in accounting can easily tell where cash came from and where it went during the period.

You Are an Entrepreneur

You operate a coffee cart in the lobby of an office building. You started the business this year by investing $5,000 of your own money to buy the coffee cart. Even though you think the cart will last for five years, a friend has advised you to recognize the entire cost of the cart as an expense the first year. He reasons that "the first year is very crucial to any business and since depreciation is added back in the Operating Activities section of the statement of cash flows, why not add back the maximum amount so that you will maximize the cash flow from operations?" Is your friend's reasoning sound?

ANSWER: Your friend is correct in stating that depreciation is added back in the Operating Activities section, assuming use of the indirect method. The only reason that depreciation is added back, however, is because it was deducted as an expense on the income statement but does not use any cash. Depreciation is not a cash flow, and any manipulation of the amount of depreciation expensed in any one year will not affect the amount of cash generated from operations.

Advocates of the indirect method argue two major points. Many companies believe that the use of the direct method reveals too much about their business by telling readers exactly the amount of cash receipts and cash payments from operations. Whether the use of the direct method tells the competition too much about a company is subject to debate. The other argument made for the indirect method is that it focuses attention on the differences between income on an accrual basis and a cash basis. In fact, this reconciliation of net income and cash provided by operating activities is considered to be important enough that *if a company uses the direct method, it must present a separate schedule to reconcile net income to net cash from operating activities.* This schedule, in effect, is the same as the Operating Activities section for the indirect method.

INTERPRETING THE CASH FLOW STATEMENT

The cash flow statement provides important information for current and potential shareholders, creditors, and other interested parties to help them predict future cash flows as part of their decision-making processes. However, like all financial statements, the cash flow statement reports historical cash flows. The interpretation of a cash flow statement is rarely straightforward and should be based on a solid understanding of the business. Sometimes the cash flow statement does not provide definitive answers; rather it flags issues to be further investigated. Following are some general observations.

LO 5 Interpret the statement of cash flows.

DAVID COOPER/CP PHOTO

Managers, investors, and brokers gauge the relative strengths of retailers by observing which stores are the most popular. But they also study the financial statements, particularly the statement of cash flows and its indicators of cash flow adequacy, as the most fundamental way to measure a firm's strength.

Cash from Operating Activities (CFO)

No business can succeed without generating significant positive cash from operating activities in the long term. Operating activities represent the normal business activities of a company, so they are the only sustainable source of cash. CFO is a key indicator as to whether the company's normal operations have generated sufficient cash flows to repay loans, maintain operating capability, make new investments, and provide distributions to the owners without having to rely on external sources of financing. For example, Exhibit 12-16 shows that Loblaw generated $1,180 million from its operating activities in 2006—insufficient to finance its $1,308 investing needs, it had to raise additional $120 million through issuing debt or equity to make up for the difference.

Negative CFO means that the operating activities are not producing enough cash to cover the payments required by the process. Generally speaking, negative CFO should

Exhibit 12-16
Cash Flow Patterns of
Selected Companies

(IN MILLIONS OF DOLLARS)	2006
Loblaw Companies Limited	
Cash from Operating Activities	$ 1,180
Cash used for Investing Activities	(1,308)
Cash used for Financing Activities	(120)
Rogers Communications Inc.	
Cash from Operating Activities	$ 2,449
Cash used for Investing Activities	(1,633)
Cash used for Financing Activities	(731)
Biomira	
Cash used for Operating Activities	$ (15.6)
Cash used for Investing Activities	(9.9)
Cash from Financing Activities	31.8

be a cause of concern. However, there are a variety of situations where CFO can be negative, so we need to resist oversimplifying our interpretation. For instance, the negative CFO of a mature company, if caused by its inability to compete and to control its spending, is bad news. However, the negative CFO of a startup company that is developing some great ideas can actually attract investors. It can take time for a new or growing company to realize the full benefit of its investment, and in the meantime, many expenses may still arise. So it is likely that the negative CFO of a new or growing company is only temporary.

A company with a negative CFO is not necessarily unprofitable. How well a company manages its accounts receivable, inventory, and prepaid expenses, and how well it utilizes its suppliers' credit and various accrued liabilities, can have a significant effect on CFO. The CFO section of a cash flow statement that uses the indirect method is especially helpful in assessing the effects that changes in accruals and deferrals have on the difference between accrual income and CFO. In fact, since net income is an accrual measure and its quality can be compromised by the use of accruals and deferrals, some analysts believe that a comparison between net income and CFO allows them to gauge the quality of accrual earnings.

A company with a negative CFO will have to raise the cash it needs from investing and financing activities. Next we discuss how to interpret CFI and CFF.

Cash from Investing Activities (CFI)

Cash paid to acquire capital assets and cash received from the disposal of capital assets are classified as CFI in the cash flow statement. It is important to recognize that a company must spend regularly on capital assets in order to maintain its capacity. Even a company that is not growing needs to replace or upgrade equipment, buildings, and other capital assets as they become worn out. When interpreting CFI, one must consider the cash required for the company to maintain the capacity of its existing capital assets. Note that depreciation is the cost of capital assets expensed during the period; thus, it provides a rough measure of the cash required to maintain the capacity of capital assets. However, unlike depreciation (which tends to spread more evenly over the years), capital investments can vary significantly from year to year. Therefore, to gain better insight into a company's investing activities, we should look not just at the current-period CFI but also at the CFI of several periods.

A company that is not generating enough cash from its operating activities can raise cash by selling capital assets and investments. Companies in financial difficulty often use this strategy to raise much-needed cash. However, a company's ability to generate cash from investing activities is limited. A company that sells significant amounts of its capital assets is drastically affecting its ability to continue in business. Thus again, being able to generate sufficient CFO is crucial for a company to succeed.

Cash from Financing Activities (CFF)

Issuing debt and equity is an important way for a company to raise significant amounts of cash, especially at startup and during major growth and expansion. However, creditors and shareholders will not provide an endless supply of cash. As a company's debt increases, so do its interest costs and, it follows, the risks it faces. This increased risk level will make future borrowing more costly. When shareholders invest in a company, they expect to earn a return. A company that cannot generate the expected returns will reduce its ability to raise cash by issuing additional equity. This reinforces how important it is for a company to raise cash through operating activities.

Cash Flow Patterns

When interpreting a company's cash flow statement, it is important to understand how the business life cycle affects such statements. There are many possible combinations of cash from operating, investing, and financing activities, and each combination tells a different story. Exhibit 12-16 presents the cash flow patterns of some companies.

Loblaw is a mature food retailer and distributor. Recently it made a strategic decision to expand into general household merchandise. Its cash from operating activities provided $1,180 million, which was insufficient for its expansion needs of $1,308 million. $120 million was also used for financing activities, consequently, the cash balance must have decreased. Rogers is a successful company in the fast-growing telecommunications industry. It produced positive cash flows from its operating activities of $2,449 million, which was sufficient to finance its investment needs of $1,633 million. The surplus cash then was used to either reduce the debt or pay dividends, as evidenced by the $731 million outflow in financing activities. Biomira is a pharmaceutical company at an early stage of its business cycle. Its primary product, a cancer treatment medicine, is still undergoing clinical testing. It is not ready to market the product, yet expenses still must be paid. During 2006, **Biomira** relied primarily on financing activities to raise cash ($31.8 million) to cover cash outflows from operating activities, which totalled $17.6 million, and for investments.

http://www.biomira.com

✕ Accounting for Your Decisions

You Are the Banker

You and your old university roommate are having an argument. You say that cash flow is all that matters when looking at a company's prospects. Your roommate says that the most important number is earnings per share. Who's right?

> **ANSWER:** You're both wrong. True, bankers are interested in cash flow to make sure that a company can pay back its loans. But earnings per share is important also because it is less easily manipulated. After all, companies can decide when they want to finance expansion, pay down debt, or invest in new businesses. A company with strong earnings can appear weak from a cash flow perspective if it invests too much in new operating assets or other businesses. On the other hand, a company that wants to appear cash-rich can avoid making all of the investments that it ought to be making. Although companies can manipulate earnings to some extent, the matching principle ensures that revenues and expenses relating to those revenues take place during the same period.

The Use of Cash Flow Information

The statement of cash flows is a critical disclosure to a company's investors and creditors. Many investors focus on cash flow from operations, rather than net income, as their key statistic. Similarly, many bankers are as concerned with cash flow from operations as they are with net income because they care about a company's ability to pay its bills. There is the concern that accrual accounting can mask cash flow problems. For example, a company with smooth earnings could be building up accounts receivable and inventory. This may not become evident until the company is in deep trouble.

The statement of cash flows provides investors, analysts, bankers, and other users with a valuable starting point as they attempt to evaluate a company's financial health. From this point, these groups must decide *how* to use the information presented on the statement. They pay particular attention to the *relationships* among various items on the statement, as well as to other financial statement items. In fact, many large banks have their own cash flow models, which typically involve a rearrangement of the items on the statement of cash flows to suit their needs. We now turn our attention to two examples of how various groups use cash flow information.

Quality-of-earnings The portion of earnings realized in cash.

Quality-of-Earnings Ratio

The **quality-of-earnings** ratio measures the portion of earnings realized in cash. Quality-of-earnings ratio can be computed as follows:

$$\text{Quality-of-Earnings} = \frac{\textbf{Cash Flow from Operating Activities}}{\textbf{Net Income}}$$

A higher quality-of-earnings ratio also indicates that the company is more likely to be conservative in recognizing its revenues. Note that the quality-of-earnings ratio should be used based on an understanding of the business's operations. Like many other financial ratios and data, the quality-of-earnings ratio does not always provide definitive answers. Many factors, such as the business life cycle, business seasonality, revenue and expense recognition methods, and the approach to managing working capital assets and liabilities can affect the quality-of-earnings ratio. For instance, a low ratio could be caused by a seasonal decline in sales or by the adoption of a more aggressive revenue recognition method.

As an example of the calculation of this ratio, consider the following amounts from CN's statements of cash flows from 2005 through 2007:

CN
http://www.cn.ca

	2007	2006	2005
Net income	$2,158	$2,087	$1,556
Cash flow from operating activities	2,417	2,951	2,708
Quality-of-earnings ratio	1.12	1.41	1.74

It appears that even though CN's quality-of-earnings ratio is still high, it has been on a slight decline. What do you think will happen if CN's quality-of-earnings ratio keeps changing in this direction?

Free cash flow Cash available for expansion, debt reduction, and paying dividends.

Free Cash Flow

As mentioned earlier, CFO is of great significance because of its sustainability. **Free cash flow**—a term gaining increasing popularity among analysts— is a measure of the amount of cash available to finance planned expansion of operating capacity, to reduce debt, to pay dividends, and/or to repurchase shares outstanding. Free cash flow is commonly defined as the company's operating cash flows less cash outlays to replace existing operating capacity such as buildings, equipment, and furnishings, which are approximated by depreciation and amortization expenses.

Free Cash Flow can be computed as follows:

Free Cash Flow = Cash Flow from Operating Activities – Depreciation and Amortization

As an example, CN's free cash flows from 2005 through 2007 can be computed as follows:

	2007	2006	2005
Cash flow provided from operating activities	$2,417	$2,951	$2,708
Depreciation and amortization	677	650	627
Free cash flow	$1,740	$2,301	$2,081

It appears that CN's free cash flow has been substantial for all three years, although it somewhat declined in 2007. This means that significant cash was generated each year for dividends, debt reduction, and future expansion.

Cash flow adequacy   Banks and other creditors are especially concerned with a company's ability to meet its principle and interest obligations. Cash flow adequacy is a measure intended to help in this regard. It gauges the cash available to meet future debt obligations after paying taxes and interest costs and making capital expenditures. Because capital expenditures on new plant and equipment are a necessity for most companies, analysts are concerned with the cash available to repay debt *after* the company has replaced and updated its existing base of long-term assets.

Cash flow adequacy can be computed as follows:

Cash Flow adequacy = Cash Flow from Operating Activities - Capital Expenditures
Average Amount of debt Maturing over Next Five Years

How could you use the information in an annual report to measure a company's cash flow adequacy? First, whether a company uses the direct or indirect method to report cash flow from operating activities, this number represents cash flow after paying interest and taxes. The numerator of the ratio is determined by deducting capital expenditures, as they appear in the Investing Activities section of the statement, from cash flow from operating activities. A disclosure required by the AcSB Handbook provides the information needed to calculate the denominator of the ratio. This regulatory body requires companies to report the annual amount of long-term debt maturing over each of the next five years.

As an example of the calculation of this ratio, consider the following amounts from CN's statement of cash flows for 2007 (amounts in millions of dollars):

Total cash provided by operating activities from continuing operations	$2,417
Additions to property and equipment	$ 895

Note 10 in CN's 2007 annual report provides the following information on maturities of long-term debt, including repurchase arrangements and capitalized leases:

FISCAL YEAR		
2008	$ 254	
2009	409	Average amount of debt maturing in next five years =
2010	48	$\dfrac{1{,}366}{5} = \$273$
2011	628	
2012	27	
	$1,366	

$$\text{Cash Flow adequacy} = \frac{\$2{,}417 - \$898}{\$273} = 5.6$$

CN's cash flow adequacy may be compared to prior years

	CN 2007	CN 2006
Cash Flow Adequacy	5.6	5.2

CN ratio of 5.6 is a slight improvement over the prior year and indicates that its 2007 cash flow was more than sufficient to repay its average annual debt over the next five years.

Cash flow adequacy Gauges the cash available to meet future debt obligations.

Chapter Highlights

1. **LO 1 Explain the purpose of a statement of cash flows.** (p. 572)

   - The statement of cash flows helps investors to understand cash inflows and outflows of an entity based on its operating, investing, and financing activities. It provides compl mentary information to the accrual-based income statements.

2. **LO 2 Describe operating, investing, and financing activities, and give examples of each.** (p. 574)

   - Operating activities are generally the effects of items that enter into the determination of net income, such as the effects of buying and selling products and services. Other operating activities include payments of compensation to employees, taxes to the government, and interest to creditors. Preparation of operating activities section of the statement cash flows requires an analysis of the changes in current assets and current liabilities.

   - Investing activities are critical to the success of a business because they involve the replacement of existing productive assets and the addition of new ones. Capital expenditures are normally the single largest cash outflow for most businesses. Occasionally, companies generate cash from the sales of existing plant and equipment. The information needed to prepare the investing activities section of the statement of cash flows is found by analyzing the changes in long-term asset accounts.

   - All businesses rely on financing in one form or another. At least initially, all corporations sell shares to raise funds. Many turn to external sources as well, generating cash from the issuance of notes and bonds. The repayment of debt and reacquisition of capital stock are important uses of cash for some companies. Given the nature of financings activities, long-term liability and shareholders' equity accounts must be examined in preparing that section of the statement of cash flows.

3. **LO 3 Describe the difference between the direct and indirect method of computing cash flow from operating activities.** (p. 577)

   - Two different methods are acceptable to report cash flow from operating activities: the direct method and the indirect method.

     ○ Under the direct method, cash receipts and cash payments related to operations are reported.

     ○ Under the indirect method, net income is reconciled to net cash flow from operating activities.

     ○ Regardless of which method is used, the amount of cash generated from operations is the same.

4. **LO 4 Use a work sheet to prepare a statement of cash flows.** (p. 581)

   - A work sheet is used as a tool to aid in the preparation of a statement of cash flows. In the work sheet, the accrual measures of a company's activities are converted to cash measures through the adjustment of changes in the related balance sheet accounts.

   - Preparation of the operating activities section under the direct method requires the conversion of income statement items from an accrual basis to a cash basis. Certain items, such as depreciation, do not have a cash effect and are not included on the statement of cash flows. Gains and losses typically related to either investing or financial activities are not included in the operating activities section of the statement.

- When the indirect method is used, the reconciliation of net income to net cash flow from operating activities appears on the face of the statement. Adjustments are made for the changes in each of the operating-related current asset and current liability account, as well as adjustments for non-cash items such as deprecation. The effects of gains and losses on net income must also be removed to convert to a cash basis.

5. **LO 5** **Interpret the statement of cash flows. (p. 593)**
   - Cash from operating activities is crucial for the success of a company, because such cash flows are sustainable.
   - Growing companies often require net cash outflows for investing activities. It is important even for mature companies to invest in capital assets to maintain operating capacity.
   - Financing activities are important sources of cash. It is important to understand that debt and equity issuances can increase financial risk and cost of capital.

Ratio Review

$$\text{Quality-of-Earnings} = \frac{\text{Cash Flow from Operating Activities}}{\text{Net Income}}$$

$$\text{Free Cash Flow} = \text{Cash Flow from Operating Activities} - \text{Depreciation and Amortization}$$

$$\text{Cash Flow Adequacy} = \frac{\text{Cash Flow from Operating Activities} - \text{Capital Expenditures (Statement of Cash Flows)}}{\text{Average Amount of Debt Maturing over Next Five Years (Notes to the Financial Statements)}}$$

Key Terms Quiz

Read each definition below and then write the number of that definition in the blank beside the appropriate term it defines. The quiz solutions appear at the end of the chapter.

_____ Statement of cash flows   _____ Financing activities

_____ Cash equivalent   _____ Direct method

_____ Operating activities   _____ Indirect method

_____ Investing activities

1. Activities concerned with the acquisition and sale of products and services.

2. For preparing the Operating Activities section of the statement of cash flows, the approach in which net income is reconciled to net cash flow from operations.

3. The financial statement that summarizes an entity's cash receipts and cash payments during the period from operating, investing, and financing activities.

4. An item readily convertible to a known amount of cash and with a maturity to the investor of three months or less.

5. Activities concerned with the acquisition and disposal of long-term assets.

6. For preparing the Operating Activities section of the statement of cash flows, the approach in which cash receipts and cash payments are reported.

7. Activities concerned with the raising and repayment of funds in the form of debt and equity.

Answers on p. 625.

Alternate Terms

Bottom line Net income

Cash flow from operating activities Cash flow from operations

Statement of cash flows Cash flows statement

Warmup Exercises and Solutions

Warmup Exercise 12-1 *Purpose of the Statement of Cash Flows* LO 1

Most companies begin the statement of cash flows by indicating the amount of net income and end it with the beginning and ending cash balances. Why is the statement necessary if net income already appears on the income statement and the cash balances can be found on the balance sheet?

Key to the Solution   Recall the *purpose* of the statement of cash flows as described in the beginning of the chapter.

Warmup Exercise 12-2 *Classification of Activities* LO 2

For each of the following activities, indicate whether it should appear on the statement of cash flows as an operating (O), investing (I), or financing (F) activity. Assume the company uses the direct method of reporting in the Operating Activities section.

—————— 1. New equipment is acquired for cash.

—————— 2. Thirty-year bonds are issued.

—————— 3. Cash receipts from the cash register are recorded.

—————— 4. The biweekly payroll is paid.

—————— 5. Common shares are issued for cash.

—————— 6. Land that was being held for future expansion is sold at book value.

Key to the Solution   Recall the general rules for each of the categories: operating activities involve acquiring and selling products and services; investing activities deal with acquiring and disposing of long-term assets; and financing activities are concerned with the raising and repayment of funds in the form of debt and equity.

Warmup Exercise 12-3 *Adjustments to Net Income with the Indirect Method* LO 3

Assume that a company uses the indirect method to prepare the Operating Activities section of the statement of cash flows. For each of the following items, indicate whether it would be added to net income (A), deducted from net income (D), or not reported in this section of the statement under the indirect method (NR).

—————— 1. Decrease in accounts payable

—————— 2. Increase in accounts receivable

—————— 3. Decrease in prepaid insurance

—————— 4. Purchase of new factory equipment

—————— 5. Depreciation expense

—————— 6. Gain on retirement of bonds

Key to the Solution   Refer to the summary of adjustments to net income under the indirect method on page 592.

Solutions to Warmup Exercises

Warmup Exercise 12-1

The statement of cash flows is a complement to the other statements in that it summarizes the operating, investing, and financing activities over a period of time. Even though the net income and cash balances are available on other statements, the statement of cash flows explains to the reader *why* net income is different than cash flow from operations and *why* cash changed by the amount it did during the period.

Warmup Exercise 12-2

1. I   2. F   3. O   4. O   5. F   6. I

Warmup Exercise 12-3

1. D   2. D   3. A   4. NR   5. A   6. D

An income statement and comparative balance sheets for Dexter Company are shown below:

DEXTER COMPANY
INCOME STATEMENT
FOR THE YEAR ENDED DECEMBER 31, 2008

Sales revenue	$89,000
Cost of goods sold	57,000
Gross margin	32,000
Depreciation expense	6,500
Advertising expense	3,200
Salaries expense	12,000
Total operating expenses	21,700
Operating income	10,300
Loss on sale of land	2,500
Income before tax	7,800
Income tax expense	2,600
Net income	$ 5,200

DEXTER COMPANY
COMPARATIVE BALANCE SHEETS

	December 31	
	2008	**2007**
Cash	$ 12,000	$ 9,500
Accounts receivable	22,000	18,400
Inventory	25,400	20,500
Prepaid advertising	10,000	8,600
Total current assets	69,400	57,000
Land	120,000	80,000
Equipment	190,000	130,000
Accumulated depreciation	(70,000)	(63,500)
Total long-term assets	240,000	146,500
Total assets	$309,400	$203,500
Accounts payable	$ 15,300	$ 12,100
Salaries payable	14,000	16,400
Income taxes payable	1,200	700
Total current liabilities	30,500	29,200
Capital stock	200,000	100,000
Retained earnings	78,900	74,300
Total shareholders' equity	278,900	174,300
Total liabilities and shareholders' equity	$309,400	$203,500

Additional Information
1. Land was acquired during the year for $70,000.

2. An unimproved parcel of land was sold during the year for $27,500. Its original cost to Dexter was $30,000.

3. A specialized piece of equipment was acquired in exchange for capital stock in the company. The value of the capital stock was $60,000.

4. In addition to the capital stock issued in item **3**, shares were sold for $40,000.

5. Dividends of $600 were paid.

Required
1. Prepare a statement of cash flows for 2008 using the direct method for the operating activities section.

2. Prepare the Operating Activities section of the 2008 statement of cash flows using the indirect method.

3. Prepare a note to disclose any non-cash financing and investing activities.

Solution to Review Problem

Activities	(A) Income Statement		Adjusting for the Difference Between (B) Accrual and Cash Amounts	(C) = A + B Cash Received (Paid)
Operating Activities				
1 Sales	89,000	−3,600	Increase in accounts receivable	85,400
2 Cost of goods sold	−57,000	−4,900	Increase in inventory	−58,700
		3,200	Increase in accounts payable	
3 Depreciation	−6,500	6,500	Increase in accumulated depreciation	–
4 Advertising	−3,200	−1,400	Increase in prepaid advertising	−4,600
5 Salaries expense	−12,000	−2,400	Decrease in salaries payable	−14,400
6 Sale of land	−2,500	2,500	Investing activity, moved to #9	–
7 Income taxes	−2,600	500	Increase in income taxes payable	−2,100
Net income	**5,200**			
Investing Activities				
8 Purchase of land		−70,000	from additional information 1	−70,000
9 Sale of land	−2,500	30,000	from additional information 2 (#8 and #9 explain increase in land)	27,500
10 Purchase of equipment		−60,000	from additional information 3	–
		60,000	from additional information 3	
Financing Activities				
11 Issuance of shares		40,000	from additional information 4 (also increase in capital stock)	40,000
12 Dividend payment		−600	from additional information 5 (net income and #12 explain increase in retained earnings)	−600

1.

DEXTER COMPANY
STATEMENT OF CASH FLOWS (DIRECT METHOD)
FOR THE YEAR ENDED DECEMBER 31, 2008

Cash flows from operating activities

Cash collections from customers	$ 85,400
Cash payments:	
To suppliers	(58,700)
For advertising	(4,600)
To employees	(14,400)
For income taxes	(2,100)
Total cash payments	(79,800)
Net cash provided by operating activities	5,600

Cash flows from investing activities

Purchase of land	(70,000)
Sale of land	27,500
Net cash used by investing activities	(42,500)

Cash flows from financing activities

Issuance of capital stock	40,000
Payment of cash dividends	(600)

(continued)

Net cash provided by financing activities		39,400
Net increase in cash		2,500
Cash balance, December 31, 2007		9,500
Cash balance, December 31, 2008		$ 12,000

2.

DEXTER COMPANY
STATEMENT OF CASH FLOWS (INDIRECT METHOD)
FOR THE YEAR ENDED DECEMBER 31, 2008

Cash flows from operating activities

Net income		$ 5,200
Adjustments to reconcile net income to net		
cash provided by operating activities:		
Increase in accounts receivable	(3,600)	
Increase in inventory	(4,900)	
Increase in prepaid advertising	(1,400)	
Increase in accounts payable	3,200	
Decrease in salaries payable	(2,400)	
Increase in income taxes payable	500	
Depreciation expense	6,500	
Loss on sale of land	2,500	
Net cash provided by operating activities		$ 5,600

3. **Note on non-cash investing and financing activities**
Shares were issued in exchange of special equipment valued at $60,000.

Questions
---

1. What is the purpose of the statement of cash flow? As a flow statement, explain how it differs from the income statement.

2. Companies are required to classify cash flows as operating, investing, or financing. Which of these three categories do you think will most likely have a net cash *outflow* over a number of years? Explain your answer.

3. A fellow student says to you: "The statement of cash flows is the easiest of the basic financial statements to prepare because you know the answer before you start. You compare the beginning and ending balances in cash on the balance sheet and compute the net inflow or outflow of cash. What could be easier?" Do you agree? Explain your answer.

4. What is your evaluation of the following statement? "Depreciation is responsible for providing some of the highest amounts of cash for capital-intensive businesses. This is obvious from examining the Operating Activities section of the statement of cash flows. Other than the net income of the period, depreciation is often the largest amount reported in this section of the statement."

5. Which method for preparing the Operating Activities section of the statement of cash flows, the direct or the indirect method, do you believe provides more information to users of the statement? Explain your answer.

6. Assume that a company uses the indirect method to prepare the Operating Activities section of the statement of cash flows. Why would a decrease in accounts receivable during the period be added back to net income?

7. Why is it necessary to analyze both inventory and accounts payable in trying to determine cash payments to suppliers when the direct method is used?

8. A company has a very profitable year. What explanations might there be for a decrease in cash?

9. A company reports a net loss for the year. Is it possible that cash could increase during the year? Explain your answer.

10. What effect does a decrease in income taxes payable for the period have on cash generated from operating activities? Does it matter whether the direct or the indirect method is used?

11. Is it logical that interest paid is classified as a cash outflow in the *Operating* Activities section of the statement of cash flows but that dividends paid are included in the *Financing* Activities section? Explain your answer.

12. Jackson Company prepays the rent on various office facilities. The beginning balance in Prepaid Rent was $9,600, and the ending balance was $7,300. The income statement reports Rent Expense of $45,900. Under the direct method, what amount would appear for cash paid in rent in the Operating Activities section of the statement of cash flows?

13. Baxter Inc. buys 2,000 of its own common shares at $20 per share. How is this transaction reported on the statement of cash flows?

14. Duke Corp. sold a delivery truck for $9,000. Its original cost was $25,000, and the book value at the time of the sale was $11,000. How does the transaction to record the sale appear on a statement of cash flows prepared under the indirect method?

(continued)

15. Billings Company has a patent on its books with a balance at the beginning of the year of $24,000. The ending balance for the asset was $20,000. The company neither bought nor sold any patents during the year, nor does it use an Accumulated Amortization account. Assuming that the company uses the indirect method in preparing a statement of cash flows, how is the decrease in the Patents account reported on the statement?

16. Ace Inc. declared and distributed a 10% stock dividend during the year. Explain how, if at all, you think this transaction should be reported on a statement of cash flows.

Exercises

Exercise 12-1 *Statement of Cash Flows* LO 1

Indicate the likely corresponding cash flow items of the following items:

1. Sales revenue
2. Cost of goods sold
3. Depreciation expense
4. Income tax expense

Exercise 12-2 *Classification of Activities* LO 2

For each of the following transactions reported on a statement of cash flows, fill in the blank to indicate if it would appear in the Operating Activities section (O), in the Investing Activities section (I), or in the Financing Activities section (F). Put an (S) in the blank if the transaction does not affect cash but is reported in a supplemental schedule of non-cash activities. Assume the company uses the direct method in the Operating Activities section.

_____ 1. A company purchases its own common shares in the open market and immediately retires them.

_____ 2. A company issues preferred shares in exchange for land.

_____ 3. A six-month bank loan is obtained.

_____ 4. Twenty-year bonds are issued.

_____ 5. A customer's accounts receivable are collected.

_____ 6. Income taxes are paid.

_____ 7. Cash sales for the day are recorded.

_____ 8. Cash dividends are declared and paid.

_____ 9. A creditor is given common shares of the company in return for cancellation of a long-term loan.

_____ 10. A new piece of machinery is acquired for cash.

_____ 11. Shares of another company are acquired as an investment.

_____ 12. Interest is paid on a bank loan.

_____ 13. Factory workers are paid.

Exercise 12-3 *Retirement of Bonds Payable on the Statement of Cash Flows—Indirect Method* LO 3

Redstone Inc. has the following debt outstanding on December 31, 2008:

10% bonds payable, due 12/31/12	$500,000	
Discount on bonds payable	(40,000)	$460,000

On this date, Redstone retired the entire bond issue by paying cash of $510,000.

Required

1. Prepare the journal entry to record the bond retirement.
2. Describe how the bond retirement would be reported on the statement of cash flows, assuming that Redstone uses the indirect method.

Exercise 12-4 *Cash Collections—Direct Method* LO 4

Stanley Company's comparative balance sheets included accounts receivable of $80,800 at December 31, 2007, and $101,100 at December 31, 2008. Sales reported by Stanley on its 2008 income statement amounted to $1,450,000. What is the amount of cash collections that Stanley will report in the Operating Activities section of its 2008 statement of cash flows, assuming that the direct method is used?

Exercise 12-5 *Cash Payments—Direct Method* **LO 4**

Lester Enterprises' comparative balance sheets included inventory of $90,000 at December 31, 2007, and $70,600 at December 31, 2008. Lester's comparative balance sheets also included accounts payable of $57,700 at December 31, 2007, and $39,200 at December 31, 2008. Lester's accounts payable balances are composed solely of amounts due to suppliers for purchases of inventory on account. Cost of goods sold, as reported by Lester on its 2008 income statement, amounted to $770,900. What is the amount of cash payments for inventory that Lester will report in the Operating Activities section of its 2008 statement of cash flows, assuming that the direct method is used?

Exercise 12-6 *Operating Activities Section—Direct Method* **LO 4**

The following account balances for the non-cash current assets and current liabilities of Windsor Company are available:

	December 31	
	2008	**2007**
Accounts receivable	$ 4,000	$ 6,000
Inventory	32,000	27,500
Office supplies	7,000	7,500
Accounts payable	7,500	4,500
Salaries and wages payable	1,500	2,500
Interest payable	500	1,000
Income taxes payable	4,500	3,000

In addition, the income statement for 2008 is as follows:

	2008
Sales revenue	$100,000
Cost of goods sold	75,000
Gross profit	25,000
Office supply expense	1,000
Salaries and wages	7,000
Depreciation expense	3,000
Total operating expenses	11,000
Income before interest and taxes	14,000
Interest expense	3,000
Income before tax	11,000
Income tax expense	5,000
Net income	$ 6,000

Required

1. Prepare the Operating Activities section of the statement of cash flows using the direct method.

2. What does the use of the direct method reveal about a company that the indirect method does not?

Exercise 12-7 *Determination of Missing Amounts—Cash Flow from Operating Activities* **LO 4**

The computation of cash provided by operating activities requires analysis of the non-cash current asset and current liability accounts. Determine the missing amounts for each of the following independent cases:

Case 1

Accounts receivable, net, beginning of year	$300,000
Accounts receivable, net, end of year	130,000
Credit sales for the year	350,000
Cash sales for the year	120,000
Total cash collections for the year (from cash sales and collections on account)	?

Case 2

Inventory, beginning of year	$160,000
Inventory, end of year	110,000

(continued)

Accounts payable, beginning of year	50,000
Accounts payable, end of year	30,000
Cost of goods sold	350,000
Cash payments for inventory (assume all purchases of inventory are on account)	?

Case 3

Prepaid insurance, beginning of year	$ 34,000
Prepaid insurance, end of year	40,000
Insurance expense	30,000
Cash paid for new insurance policies	?

Case 4

Income taxes payable, beginning of year	$190,000
Income taxes payable, end of year	230,000
Income tax expense	600,000
Cash payments for taxes	?

Exercise 12-8 *Dividends on the Statement of Cash Flows* LO 4

The following selected account balances are available from the records of Newtown Company:

	December 31	
	2008	**2007**
Dividends payable	$ 30,000	$ 20,000
Retained earnings	375,000	250,000

Other information available for 2008 follows:

a. Newtown reported $320,000 net income for the year.

b. It declared and distributed a stock dividend of $50,000 during the year.

c. It declared cash dividends at the end of each quarter and paid them within the next 30 days of the following quarter.

Required

1. Determine the amount of cash dividends *paid* during the year for presentation in the Financing Activities section of the statement of cash flows.

2. Should the stock dividend described in part **b** appear on a statement of cash flows? Explain your answer.

Exercise 12-9 *Adjustments to Net Income with the Indirect Method* LO 4

Assume that a company uses the indirect method to prepare the Operating Activities section of the statement of cash flows. For each of the following items, fill in the blank to indicate whether it would be added to net income (A), deducted from net income (D), or not reported in this section of the statement under the indirect method (NR).

_____ 1. Depreciation expense

_____ 2. Gain on sale of used delivery truck

_____ 3. Bad debts expense

_____ 4. Increase in accounts payable

_____ 5. Purchase of new delivery truck

_____ 6. Loss on retirement of bonds

_____ 7. Increase in prepaid rent

_____ 8. Decrease in inventory

_____ 9. Increase in short-term investments

_____ 10. Amortization of patents

Exercise 12-10 *Operating Activities Section—Indirect Method* **LO 4**

The following account balances for the non-cash current assets and current liabilities of Sheffield Company are available:

	December 31	
	2008	**2007**
Accounts receivable	$45,000	$35,000
Inventory	30,000	40,000
Prepaid rent	17,000	15,000
Totals	$90,000	$90,000
Accounts payable	$26,000	$19,000
Income taxes payable	6,000	10,000
Interest payable	15,000	12,000
Totals	$47,000	$41,000

Net income for 2008 is $40,000. Depreciation expense is $20,000. Assume that all sales and all purchases are on account.

Required

1. Prepare the Operating Activities section of the statement of cash flows using the indirect method.
2. Provide a brief explanation as to why cash flow from operating activities is more or less than the net income of the period.

Multi-Concept Exercises

Exercise 12-11 *Classification of Activities* **LO 1, 2**

Use the following legend to indicate how each of the following transactions would be reported on the statement of cash flows:

II = Inflow from investing activities
OI = Outflow from investing activities
IF = Inflow from financing activities
OF= Outflow from financing activities
CE= Classified as a cash equivalent and included with cash for purposes of preparing the statement of cash flows

_____   1. Purchased a six-month GIC.

_____   2. Purchased a 60-day GIC.

_____   3. Issued 1,000 common shares.

_____   4. Purchased 1,000 shares of another company.

_____   5. Purchased 1,000 of its own shares.

_____   6. Invested $1,000 in a money market fund.

_____   7. Sold 500 shares of another company.

_____   8. Purchased 20-year bonds of another company.

_____   9. Issued 30-year bonds.

_____   10. Repaid a six-month bank loan.

Exercise 12-12 *Classification of Activities* **LO 2, 3**

Use the following legend to indicate how each of the following transactions would be reported on the statement of cash flows (assume that the company uses the direct method in the Operating Activities section):

IO =Inflow from operating activities
OO=Outflow from operating activities

(continued)

II = Inflow from investing activities
OI = Outflow from investing activities
IF = Inflow from financing activities
OF = Outflow from financing activities
NR = Not reported in the body of the statement of cash flows but included in a supplemental schedule

_____ 1. Collected $10,000 in cash from customers' accounts receivable for the period.

_____ 2. Paid one of the company's inventory suppliers $500 in settlement of an account payable.

_____ 3. Purchased a new copier for $6,000; signed a 90-day note payable.

_____ 4. Issued bonds at face value of $100,000.

_____ 5. Made $23,200 in cash sales for the week.

_____ 6. Purchased an empty lot adjacent to the factory for $50,000. The seller of the land agrees to accept a five-year promissory note as consideration.

_____ 7. Renewed the property insurance policy for another six months. Cash of $1,000 is paid for the renewal.

_____ 8. Purchased a machine for $10,000.

_____ 9. Paid cash dividends of $2,500.

_____ 10. Reclassified as short-term a long-term note payable of $5,000 that is due within the next year.

_____ 11. Purchased 500 of the company's own shares on the open market for $4,000.

www.nike.com   _____ 12. Sold 500 shares of **Nike** for book value of $10,000.

Exercise 12-13 *Long-Term Assets on the Statement of Cash Flows—Indirect Method* LO 2, 4

The following account balances are taken from the records of McCain Corp. for the past two years (credit balances are in parentheses):

	December 31	
	2008	**2007**
Plant and equipment	$ 750,000	$ 500,000
Accumulated depreciation	(160,000)	(200,000)
Patents	92,000	80,000
Retained earnings	(825,000)	(675,000)

Other information available for 2008 follows:

a. Net income for the year was $200,000.

b. Depreciation expense on plant and equipment was $50,000.

c. Plant and equipment with an original cost of $150,000 were sold for $64,000 (you will need to determine the book value of the assets sold).

d. Amortization expense on patents was $8,000.

e. Both new plant and equipment and patents were purchased for cash during the year.

Required

Indicate, with amounts, how all items related to these long-term assets would be reported in the 2008 statement of cash flows, including any adjustments in the Operating Activities section of the statement. Assume that McCain uses the indirect method.

Exercise 12-14 *Income Statement, Statement of Cash Flows (Direct Method), and Balance Sheet* LO 1, 4

The following events occurred at Cutting Edge Grooming Company during its first year of business:

a. To establish the company, the two owners contributed a total of $50,000 in exchange for common shares.

b. Grooming service revenue for the first year amounted to $130,000, of which $40,000 was on account.

c. Customers owe $10,000 at the end of the year from the services provided on account.

d. At the beginning of the year a storage building was rented. The company was required to sign a three-year lease for $12,000 per year and make a $2,000 refundable security deposit. The first year's lease payment and the security deposit were paid at the beginning of the year.

e. At the beginning of the year the company purchased a patent at a cost of $100,000 for a revolutionary system to be used for dog grooming. The patent is expected to be useful for 10 years. The company paid 20% down in cash and signed a four-year note at the bank for the remainder.

f. Operating expenses, including amortization of the patent and rent on the storage building, totalled $80,000 for the first year. No expenses were accrued or unpaid at the end of the year.

g. The company declared and paid a $20,000 cash dividend at the end of the first year.

Required

1. Prepare an income statement for the first year.

2. Prepare a statement of cash flows for the first year, using the direct method in the Operating Activities section.

3. Did the company generate more or less cash flow from operations than it earned in net income? Explain why there is a difference.

4. Prepare a balance sheet as of the end of the first year.

Problems

Problem 12-1 *Statement of Cash Flows—Indirect Method* LO 4

The following balances are available for Cohen Company:

	December 31	
	2008	**2007**
Cash	$ 8,000	$ 15,000
Accounts receivable	20,000	15,000
Inventory	15,000	25,000
Prepaid rent	9,000	6,000
Land	75,000	75,000
Plant and equipment	400,000	300,000
Accumulated depreciation	(65,000)	(30,000)
Totals	$462,000	$406,000
Accounts payable	$ 12,000	$ 10,000
Income taxes payable	3,000	5,000
Short-term notes payable	35,000	25,000
Bonds payable	75,000	105,000
Common shares	200,000	150,000
Retained earnings	137,000	111,000
Totals	$462,000	$406,000

Bonds were retired during 2008 at face value, plant and equipment were acquired for cash, and common stock was issued for cash. Depreciation expense for the year was $35,000. Net income was reported at $26,000.

Required

Prepare a statement of cash flows for 2008, using the indirect method in the Operating Activities section.

Problem 12-2 *Statement of Cash Flows—Indirect Method* **LO 4**

Pedra Corp. has just completed another very successful year, as indicated by the following income statement:

	For the Year Ended December 31, 2008
Sales revenue	$1,250,000
Cost of goods sold	700,000
Gross profit	550,000
Depreciation	50,000
Salaries and wages	88,000
Insurance expense	12,000
Income before interest and taxes	400,000
Interest expense	25,000
Income before taxes	375,000
Income tax expense	150,000
Net income	$ 225,000

Presented below are comparative balance sheets:

	December 31	
	2008	2007
Cash	$ 52,000	$ 80,000
Accounts receivable	180,000	130,000
Inventory	230,000	200,000
Prepaid insurance	15,000	25,000
Total current assets	477,000	435,000
Land	750,000	600,000
Plant and equipment	700,000	500,000
Accumulated depreciation	(250,000)	(200,000)
Total long-term assets	1,200,000	900,000
Total assets	$1,677,000	$1,335,000
Accounts payable	$ 130,000	$ 148,000
Salaries and wages payable	68,000	63,000
Income taxes payable	90,000	100,000
Total current liabilities	288,000	311,000
Long-term bank loan payable	350,000	300,000
Common shares	550,000	400,000
Retained earnings	489,000	324,000
Total shareholders' equity	1,039,000	724,000
Total liabilities and shareholders' equity	$1,677,000	$1,335,000

Other information follows:

a. Dividends of $60,000 were declared and paid during the year.

b. Land and plant and equipment were acquired for cash, and additional shares were issued for cash. Cash was also received from additional bank loans.

Required

Prepare a statement of cash flows for 2008, using the indirect method in the Operating Activities section.

Problem 12-3 *Statement of Cash Flows Direct Method* **LO 4**

Refer to all of the facts in Problem 12-2.

Required

Prepare a statement of cash flows for 2008, using the direct method in the Operating Activities section.

Multi-Concept Problems

Problem 12-4 *Statement of Cash Flows—Indirect Method* **LO 4, 5**

The income statement for Arrow Inc. for 2008 follows:

	For the Year Ended December 31, 2008
Sales revenue	$ 500,000
Cost of goods sold	400,000
Gross profit	100,000
Depreciation	70,000
Salaries and wages	92,000
Insurance expense	18,000
Loss before interest and taxes	(80,000)
Interest expense	20,000
Net loss	$(100,000)

Presented below are comparative balance sheets:

	December 31	
	2008	2007
Cash	$ 100,000	$ 80,000
Accounts receivable	50,000	75,000
Inventory	145,000	195,000
Prepaid insurance	10,000	-
Total current assets	305,000	350,000
Land	475,000	400,000
Plant and equipment	870,000	800,000
Accumulated depreciation	(370,000)	(300,000)
Total long-term assets	975,000	900,000
Total assets	$1,280,000	$1,250,000
Accounts payable	$ 130,000	$ 100,000
Salaries and wages payable	35,000	45,000
Interest payable	15,000	10,000
Total current liabilities	180,000	155,000
Long-term bank loan payable	340,000	250,000
Common shares	450,000	400,000
Retained earnings	310,000	445,000
Total shareholders' equity	760,000	845,000
Total liabilities and shareholders' equity	$1,280,000	$1,250,000

Other information follows:

a. Dividends of $35,000 were declared and paid during the year.

b. Land and plant and equipment were acquired for cash, and additional shares were issued for cash. Cash was also received from additional bank loans.

The president has asked you some questions about the year's results. He is disturbed with the $100,000 net loss for the year. He notes, however, that the cash position at the end of the year has improved. He is confused about what appear to be conflicting signals: "How could we have possibly added to our bank accounts during such a terrible year of operations?"

Required

1. Prepare a statement of cash flows for 2008, using the indirect method in the Operating Activities section.

2. On the basis of your statement in requirement 1, draft a brief memo to the president to explain why cash increased during such an unprofitable year. Include in your memo your recommendations for improving the company's bottom line.

Problem 12-5 *Statement of Cash Flows—Direct Method* **LO 3, 4**

Refer to all of the facts in Problem 12-4.

Required

1. Prepare a statement of cash flows for 2008, using the direct method in the Operating Activities section.

2. Evaluate the following statement: "Whether a company uses the direct or the indirect method to report cash flows from operations is irrelevant because the amount of cash flow from operating activities is the same regardless of which method is used."

Problem 12-6 *Year-End Balance Sheet and Statement of Cash Flows—Indirect Method* **LO 4, 5**

The balance sheet of Bell Company at the end of 2007 is presented below, along with certain other information for 2008:

	December 31, 2007
Cash	$ 140,000
Accounts receivable	155,000
Total current assets	295,000
Land	300,000
Plant and equipment	500,000
Accumulated depreciation	(150,000)
Investments	100,000
Total long-term assets	750,000
Total assets	$1,045,000
Current liabilities	$ 205,000
Bonds payable	300,000
Common shares	400,000
Retained earnings	140,000
Total shareholders' equity	540,000
Total liabilities and shareholders' equity	$1,045,000

Other information follows:

a. Net income for 2008 was $70,000.
b. Included in operating expenses was $20,000 in depreciation.
c. Cash dividends of $25,000 were declared and paid.
d. An additional $150,000 of bonds were issued for cash.
e. Common shares of $50,000 were purchased for cash.
f. Cash purchases of plant and equipment during the year were $200,000.
g. An additional $100,000 of bonds were issued in exchange for land.
h. Sales exceeded cash collections on account during the year by $30,000. All sales are on account.
i. The amount of current liabilities remained unchanged during the year.

Required

1. Prepare a statement of cash flows for 2008, using the indirect method in the Operating Activities section. Include a note for non-cash activities.

2. Prepare a balance sheet at December 31, 2008.

3. Provide a possible explanation as to why Bell decided to issue additional bonds for cash during 2008.

Problem 12-7 *Statement of Cash Flows—Indirect Method* **LO 3, 4**

Highand Corp. is in the process of preparing its statement of cash flows for the year ended June 30, 2008. An income statement for the year and comparative balance sheets follow:

	For the Year Ended June 30, 2008
Sales revenue	$550,000
Cost of goods sold	350,000
Gross profit	200,000
Rent expense	15,000
Salaries and wages	40,000
Depreciation expense	75,000
Loss on sale of plant assets	5,000
Total expenses and losses	135,000
Income before interest and taxes	65,000
Interest expense	15,000
Income before taxes	50,000
Income tax expense	24,000
Net income	$ 26,000

	June 30	
	2008	**2007**
Cash	$ 24,000	$ 40,000
Accounts receivable	90,000	75,000
Inventory	80,000	95,000
Prepaid rent	12,000	16,000
Total current assets	206,000	226,000
Land	250,000	170,000
Plant and equipment	750,000	600,000
Accumulated depreciation	(310,000)	(250,000)
Total long-term assets	690,000	520,000
Total assets	$896,000	$746,000
Accounts payable	$155,000	$148,000
Salaries and wages payable	32,000	26,000
Income taxes payable	8,000	10,000
Total current liabilities	195,000	184,000
Long-term bank loan payable	100,000	130,000
Common shares	350,000	200,000
Retained earnings	251,000	232,000
Total shareholders' equity	601,000	432,000
Total liabilities and shareholders' equity	$896,000	$746,000

Dividends of $7,000 were declared and paid during the year. New plant assets were purchased for $195,000 in cash during the year. Also, land was purchased for cash. Plant assets were sold during 2008 for $25,000 in cash. The original cost of the assets sold was $45,000, and their book value was $30,000. Additional shares were issued for cash, and a portion of the bank loan was repaid.

(continued)

Required

1. Prepare a statement of cash flows, using the indirect method in the Operating Activities section.

2. Explain why Highland's cash decreased during a profitable year.

3. Evaluate the following statement: "Since depreciation is added in determining cash from operating activities, depreciation must be a source of cash."

Problem 12-8 *Statement of Cash Flows—Direct Method* **LO 3, 4**

Refer to all of the facts in Problem 12-7.

Required

1. Prepare a statement of cash flows for 2008, using the direct method in the Operating Activities section.

2. What are the relative merits of the direct and the indirect methods for reporting cash flows from operating activities?

Problem 12-9 *Statement of Cash Flows—Direct Method* **LO 1, 4**

Song Company has not yet prepared a formal statement of cash flows for 2008. Comparative balance sheets (thousands omitted) as of December 31, 2008 and 2007, and a statement of income and retained earnings for the year ended December 31, 2008, follow:

SONG COMPANY
BALANCE SHEET
DECEMBER 31

	2008	2007
Current assets:		
Cash	$ 90	$ 100
GIC (six-month)	–0–	50
Accounts receivable	610	500
Inventory	720	600
Total current assets	1,420	1,250
Long-term assets:		
Land	80	70
Buildings and equipment	710	600
Accumulated depreciation	(180)	(120)
Patents (less amortization)	105	130
Total long-term assets	715	680
Total assets	$2,135	$1,930
Current liabilities:		
Accounts payable	$ 360	$ 300
Income tax payable	25	20
Notes payable	400	400
Total current liabilities	785	720
Term notes payable—due 2010	330	200
Total liabilities	1,115	920
Shareholders' equity:		
Common shares outstanding	700	700
Retained earnings	320	310
Total shareholders' equity	1,020	1,010
Total liabilities and shareholders' equity	$2,135	$1,930

SONG COMPANY
STATEMENT OF INCOME AND RETAINED EARNINGS
FOR THE YEAR ENDED DECEMBER 31, 2008

Sales		$2,408
Less expenses and interest:		
Cost of goods sold	$1,100	
Salaries and benefits	850	
Heat, light, and power	75	
Depreciation	60	
Property taxes	18	
Patent amortization	25	
Miscellaneous expense	10	
Interest	55	2,193
Net income before income taxes		215
Income taxes		105
Net income		110
Retained earnings—January 1, 2008		310
		420
Dividend declared and distributed		100
Retained earnings—December 31, 2008		$ 320

Required

1. For the purposes of a statement of cash flows, is the GIC a cash equivalent? If not, how should it be classified? Explain your answers.
2. Prepare a statement of cash flows for 2008, using the direct method in the Operating Activities section. (CMA adapted)

———— Alternate Problems ————

Problem 12-1A *Statement of Cash Flows—Indirect Method* **LO 4**

The following balances are available for Burlington Company:

	December 31	
	2008	**2007**
Cash	$ 13,000	$ 10,000
Accounts receivable	10,000	12,000
Inventory	8,000	7,000
Prepaid rent	1,200	1,000
Land	75,000	75,000
Plant and equipment	200,000	150,000
Accumulated depreciation	(75,000)	(25,000)
Totals	$232,200	$230,000
Accounts payable	$ 15,000	$ 15,000
Income taxes payable	2,500	2,000
Short-term notes payable	20,000	22,500
Bonds payable	75,000	50,000
Common stock	100,000	100,000
Retained earnings	19,700	40,500
Totals	$232,200	$230,000

Bonds were issued during 2008 at face value, and plant and equipment were acquired for cash. Depreciation expense for the year was $50,000. A net loss of $20,800 was reported.

Required

Prepare a statement of cash flows for 2008, using the indirect method in the Operating Activities section.

Problem 12-2A *Statement of Cash Flows—Indirect Method* **LO 4**

Power Corp. has just completed another very successful year, as indicated by the following income statement:

	For the Year Ended December 31, 2008
Sales revenue	$2,460,000
Cost of goods sold	1,400,000
Gross profit	1,060,000
Depreciation	25,000
Salaries and wages	375,000
Insurance expense	60,000
Income before interest and taxes	600,000
Interest expense	100,000
Income before taxes	500,000
Income tax expense	150,000
Net income	$ 350,000

The following are comparative balance sheets:

	December 31	
	2008	2007
Cash	$ 140,000	$ 200,000
Accounts receivable	60,000	145,000
Inventory	200,000	180,000
Prepaid insurance	15,000	25,000
Total current assets	415,000	550,000
Land	600,000	700,000
Plant and equipment	850,000	600,000
Accumulated depreciation	(225,000)	(200,000)
Total long-term assets	1,225,000	1,100,000
Total assets	$1,640,000	$1,650,000
Accounts payable	$ 140,000	$ 110,000
Salaries and wages payable	50,000	55,000
Income taxes payable	80,000	115,000
Total current liabilities	270,000	280,000
Long-term bank loan payable	200,000	250,000
Common shares	450,000	400,000
Retained earnings	720,000	720,000
Total shareholders' equity	1,170,000	1,120,000
Total liabilities and shareholders' equity	$1,640,000	$1,650,000

Other information follows:

a. Dividends of $350,000 were declared and paid during the year.

b. Land was sold for its book value, and new plant and equipment were acquired for cash.

c. Part of the bank loan was repaid, and additional common shares were issued for cash.

The president has asked you some questions about the year's results. She is very impressed with the profit margin of 14% (net income divided by sales revenue). She is bothered, however, by the decline in the company's cash balance during the year. One of the conditions of the existing bank loan is that the company maintain a minimum cash balance of $100,000.

Required

Prepare a statement of cash flows for 2008, using the indirect method in the Operating Activities section.

Problem 12-3A Statement of Cash Flows—Direct Method LO 4

Refer to all of the facts in Problem 12-2A.

Required

Prepare a statement of cash flows for 2008, using the direct method in the Operating Activities section.

Alternate Multi-Concept Problems

Problem 12-4A *Statement of Cash Flows—Indirect Method* LO 4, 5

The income statement for Bridget Inc. for 2008 follows:

	For the Year Ended December 31, 2008
Sales revenue	$350,000
Cost of goods sold	150,000
Gross profit	200,000
Depreciation	40,000
Salaries and wages	180,000
Insurance expense	30,000
Loss before interest	(50,000)
Interest expense	20,000
Net loss	$(70,000)

Presented below are comparative balance sheets:

	December 31	
	2008	2007
Cash	$ 15,000	$ 10,000
Accounts receivable	30,000	80,000
Inventory	100,000	100,000
Prepaid insurance	36,000	35,000
Total current assets	181,000	225,000
Land	300,000	200,000
Plant and equipment	500,000	250,000
Accumulated depreciation	(90,000)	(50,000)
Total long-term assets	710,000	400,000
Total assets	$891,000	$625,000
Accounts payable	$ 50,000	$ 10,000
Salaries and wages payable	40,000	20,000
Interest payable	22,000	12,000
Total current liabilities	112,000	42,000
Long-term bank loan payable	450,000	100,000
Common stock	300,000	300,000
Retained earnings	29,000	183,000
Total shareholders' equity	329,000	483,000
Total liabilities and shareholders' equity	$891,000	$625,000

Other information follows:

a. Dividends of $84,000 were declared and paid during the year.

b. Land and plant and equipment were acquired for cash. Cash was received from additional bank loans.

The president has asked you some questions about the year's results. He is disturbed with the net loss of $70,000 for the year. He notes, however, that the cash position at the end of the year is improved. He is confused about what appear to be conflicting signals: "How could we have possibly added to our bank accounts during such a terrible year of operations?"

Required

1. Prepare a statement of cash flows for 2008, using the indirect method in the Operating Activities section.

2. Based on the statement of cash flows in requirement 1, draft a brief memo to the president to explain why cash increased during such an unprofitable year. Include in your memo your recommendations for improving the company's bottom line.

Problem 12-5A *Statement of Cash Flows—Direct Method* **LO 3, 4**

Refer to all of the facts in Problem 12-4A.

Required

1. Prepare a statement of cash flows for 2008, using the direct method in the Operating Activities section.

2. Evaluate the following statement: "Whether a company uses the direct or indirect method to report cash flow from operations is irrelevant because the amount of cash flow from operating activities is the same regardless of which method is used."

Problem 12-6A *Year-End Balance Sheet and Statement of Cash Flows—Indirect Method* **LO 4, 5**

The balance sheet of Koko Company at the end of 2007 is presented below along with certain other information for 2008:

	December 31, 2007
Cash	$ 155,000
Accounts receivable	140,000
Total current assets	295,000
Land	100,000
Plant and equipment	700,000
Accumulated depreciation	(175,000)
Investments	125,000
Total long-term assets	750,000
Total assets	$1,045,000
Current liabilities	$ 325,000
Bonds payable	100,000
Common stock	500,000
Retained earnings	120,000
Total shareholders' equity	620,000
Total liabilities and shareholders' equity	$1,045,000

Other information follows:

a. Net income for 2008 was $60,000.

b. Included in operating expenses was $25,000 in depreciation.

c. Cash dividends of $40,000 were declared and paid.

d. An additional $50,000 of common shares were issued for cash.

e. Bonds payable of $100,000 were purchased for cash and retired at no gain or loss.

f. Cash purchases of plant and equipment during the year were $60,000.

g. An additional $200,000 of land was acquired in exchange for a long-term note payable.

h. Sales exceeded cash collections on account during the year by $15,000. All sales are on account.

i. The amount of current liabilities decreased by $20,000 during the year.

Required

1. Prepare a statement of cash flows for 2008, using the indirect method in the Operating Activities section. Include a note for non-cash activities.

2. Prepare a balance sheet at December 31, 2008.

3. What primary uses did Koko make of the cash it generated from operating activities?

Problem 12-7A *Statement of Cash Flows—Indirect Method* LO 3, 4

Bodeck Corp. is in the process of preparing its statement of cash flows for the year ended June 30, 2008. An income statement for the year and comparative balance sheets follow:

	For the Year Ended June 30, 2008
Sales revenue	$400,000
Cost of goods sold	220,000
Gross profit	180,000
Salaries and wages	20,000
Rent expense	20,000
Depreciation expense	80,000
Loss on sale of plant assets	10,000
Total expenses and losses	130,000
Income before interest and taxes	50,000
Interest expense	15,000
Income before taxes	35,000
Income tax expense	5,000
Net income	$ 30,000

	June 30	
	2008	2007
Cash	$ 15,000	$ 40,000
Accounts receivable	110,000	69,000
Inventory	75,000	50,000
Prepaid rent	2,000	18,000
Total current assets	202,000	177,000
Land	60,000	150,000
Plant and equipment	575,000	500,000
Accumulated depreciation	(310,000)	(250,000)
Total long-term assets	325,000	400,000
Total assets	$ 527,000	$ 577,000
Accounts payable	$ 145,000	$ 140,000
Salaries and wages payable	50,000	45,000
Income taxes payable	5,000	15,000
Total current liabilities	200,000	200,000
Long-term bank loan payable	75,000	150,000
Common shares	100,000	100,000
Retained earnings	157,000	127,000
Total shareholders' equity	252,000	227,000
Total liabilities and shareholders' equity	$ 527,000	$ 577,000

Dividends of $5,000 were declared and paid during the year. New plant assets were purchased for $125,000 in cash during the year. Also, land was sold for cash at its book value. Plant assets were sold during 2008 for $20,000 in cash. The original cost of the assets sold was $50,000, and their book value was $30,000. A portion of the bank loan was repaid.

Required

1. Prepare a statement of cash flows for 2008, using the indirect method in the Operating Activities section.

2. Explain why Bodeck's cash decreased during a profitable year.

3. Evaluate the following statement: "Since depreciation is added to determine the cash flows from operating activities depreciation must be a source of cash."

Problem 12-8A *Statement of Cash Flows—Direct Method* **LO 3, 4**

Refer to all of the facts in Problem 12-7A.

Required

1. Prepare a statement of cash flows for 2008, using the direct method in the Operating Activities section.

2. What are the relative merits of the direct and the indirect methods for reporting cash flows from operating activities?

Problem 12-9A *Statement of Cash Flows—Direct Method* **LO 1, 4**

Moses Company has not yet prepared a formal statement of cash flows for 2008. Comparative balance sheets as of December 31, 2008 and 2007, and a statement of income and retained earnings for the year ended December 31, 2008, follow:

MOSES COMPANY
BALANCE SHEET
DECEMBER 31
(THOUSANDS OMITTED)

Assets	2008	2007
Current assets:		
Cash	$ 50	$ 75
GIC (six-month)	45	0
Accounts receivable	125	200
Inventory	525	500
Total current assets	745	775
Long-term assets:		
Land	100	80
Buildings and equipment	510	450
Accumulated depreciation	(190)	(150)
Patents (less amortization)	90	110
Total long-term assets	510	490
Total assets	$1,255	$1,265

Liabilities and Shareholders' Equity		
Current liabilities:		
Accounts payable	$ 410	$ 330
Income Taxes payable	10	20
Notes payable	300	400
Total current liabilities	720	750
Term notes payable—due 2010	200	200
Total liabilities	920	950
Shareholders' equity:		
Common shares outstanding	200	200
Retained earnings	135	115
Total shareholders' equity	335	315
Total liabilities and owners' equity	$1,255	$1,265

MOSES COMPANY
STATEMENT OF INCOME AND RETAINED EARNINGS
YEAR ENDED DECEMBER 31, 2008
(THOUSANDS OMITTED)

Sales		$1,416
Less expenses and interest:		
Cost of goods sold	$990	
Salaries and benefits	195	
Heat, light, and power	70	

(continued)

Depreciation	40	
Property taxes	2	
Patent amortization	20	
Miscellaneous expense	2	
Interest	45	1,364
Net income before income taxes		52
Income taxes		12
Net income		40
Retained earnings—January 1, 2008		115
		155
Stock dividend distributed		20
Retained earnings—December 31, 2008		$ 135

Required

1. For the purposes of a statement of cash flows, is a GIC a cash equivalent? If not, how should it be classified? Explain your answers.

2. Prepare a statement of cash flows for 2008, using the direct method in the Operating Activities section. (CMA adapted)

Cases

Reading and Interpreting Financial Statements

Case 12-1 *Reading and Interpreting CN's Statement of Cash Flows* LO 2, 5

Refer to **CN's** statement of cash flows for 2007 and any other pertinent information in its annual report.

CN
http://www.cn.ca

Required

1. According to a note in the annual report, how does the company define cash equivalents?

2. According to the statement of cash flows, did accounts receivable increase or decrease during the most recent year? Explain your answer.

3. What are the major reasons for the difference between net income and net cash provided by operating activities?

4. What was CN's largest source of cash during the most recent year? the largest use of cash?

5. In the Financing Activities section of its statement of cash flows, CN reports an amount used for the purchase of common shares. Locate this same amount on the statement of changes in shareholders' equity and explain why this amount appears on both statements.

Case 12-2 *Comparing Two Companies in the Same Industry: CN and CP* LO 2, 5

Refer to the financial statement information of CN and **CP** in Appendixes A and B at the end of the text. Use the cash flow statements in the annual reports for 2007 to answer the following questions.

http://www.cpr.ca

Required

1. Did material and supplies increase or decrease for CP during 2007? How does that compare to the change in material and supplies for CN? What are logical reasons for these changes in inventory levels?

2. In 2007, CP expanded through an acquisition of another company. What impact did this have on the Investing Activities and Financing Activities portions of the cash flows statement? Was there similar activity reported by CN in its 2007 cash flow statement?

3. What is the primary source of cash for financing activities for each of the two companies in 2007? Why do you think the companies did not use shares more extensively in 2007 as a way to acquire cash? Do you think this was a good strategic move? Why or why not?

(continued)

Case 12-3 *Reading and Interpreting the Statement of Cash Flows* **LO 1, 5**

The consolidated statement of cash flows for **Killam Properties Inc.** is presented below.

Killam Properties. Killam Properties Annual Report 2007

	December 31, 2005
Operating Activities	
Net income	$ 4,847
Add items not affecting cash	
Depreciation and amortization	10,412,556
Non-cash debenture interest	119,804
Non-cash compensation expense	172,669
Future income taxes	212,855
Funds from operations	10,922,731
Net change in non-cash working capital items	3,992,949
Cash provided by operating activities	14,915,680
Financing Activities	
Issue of common shares for cash	14,549,924
Issuance and retirements of debt financing	153,322,991
Cash provided by financing activities	167,872,915
Investing Activities	
Purchase of capital assets	(182,071,540)
Cash used in investing activities	(182,071,540)
Net increase in cash and cash equivalent:	717,055
Cash and cash equivalent, beginning of period	4,168,071
Cash and cash equivalent, end of period	$ 4,885,126

Required

1. Why is operating cash flow different from net income? What does this tell you? Explain.

2. Operating cash flow was not sufficient to provide all necessary cash for purchase of capital assets. Does this mean that cash flow was not adequate? Explain.

3. Why are the above statements divided into three sections? What key information is provided by each section?

4. What is the relationship between investing and financing activities for this company?

5. Does this cash flow statement provide any indication as to the weaknesses of the company?

Acknowledgment *Peter Secord, Saint Mary's University*

Making Financial Decisions

Case 12-4 *Dividend Decision and the Statement of Cash Flows—Direct Method* **LO 1, 4, 5**

Bailey Corp. just completed the most profitable year in its 25-year history. Reported earnings of $1,020,000 on sales of $8,000,000 resulted in a very healthy profit margin of 12.75%. Each year before releasing the financial statements, the board of directors meets to decide on the amount of dividends to declare for the year. For each of the past nine years, the company has declared a dividend of $1 per share of common shares, which has been paid on January 15 of the following year.

Presented below and on the following page are the income statement for the year and comparative balance sheets as of the end of the last two years.

	For the Year Ended December 31, 2008
Sales revenue	$8,000,000
Cost of goods sold	4,500,000
Gross profit	3,500,000
Operating expenses	1,450,000
Income before interest and taxes	2,050,000
Interest expense	350,000
Income before taxes	1,700,000
Income tax expense 40%	680,000
Net income	$1,020,000

	December 31	
	2008	**2007**
Cash	$ 480,000	$ 450,000
Accounts receivable	250,000	200,000
Inventory	750,000	600,000
Prepayments	60,000	75,000
Total current assets	1,540,000	1,325,000
Land	3,255,000	2,200,000
Plant and equipment	4,200,000	2,500,000
Accumulated depreciation	(1,250,000)	(1,000,000)
Long-term investments	500,000	900,000
Patents	650,000	750,000
Total long-term assets	7,355,000	5,350,000
Total assets	$8,895,000	$6,675,000
Accounts payable	$ 350,000	$ 280,000
Other accrued liabilities	285,000	225,000
Income taxes payable	170,000	100,000
Dividends payable	0	200,000
Notes payable due within next year	200,000	0
Total current liabilities	1,005,000	805,000
Long-term notes payable	300,000	500,000
Bonds payable	2,200,000	1,500,000
Total long-term liabilities	2,500,000	2,000,000
Common stock	2,500,000	2,000,000
Retained earnings	2,890,000	1,870,000
Total shareholders' equity	5,390,000	3,870,000
Total liabilities and shareholders' equity	$8,895,000	$6,675,000

Additional information follows:

a. All sales are on account, as are all purchases.

b. Land was purchased through the issuance of bonds. Additional land (beyond the amount purchased through the issuance of bonds) was purchased for cash.

c. New plant and equipment were acquired during the year for cash. No plant assets were retired during the year. Depreciation expense is included in operating expenses.

d. Long-term investments were sold for cash during the year.

e. No new patents were acquired, and none were disposed of during the year. Amortization expense is included in operating expenses.

f. "Notes payable due within next year" represents the amount reclassified from long-term to short-term.

g. Two hundred thousand common shares were outstanding at beginning of the year. Fifty thousand common shares were issued during the year.

As Bailey's controller, you have been asked to recommend to the board whether to declare a dividend this year and, if so, whether the precedent of paying a $1 per share dividend can be maintained. The president is eager to keep the dividend at $1 in view of the successful year just completed. He is also concerned, however, about the effect of a dividend on the company's cash position. He is particularly concerned about the large amount of notes payable that comes due next year. He further notes the aggressive growth pattern in recent years, as evidenced this year by large increases in land and plant and equipment.

Required

1. Using the format in Exhibit 12-12, convert the income statement from an accrual basis to a cash basis.

2. Prepare a statement of cash flows, using the direct method in the Operating Activities section.

3. What do you recommend to the board of directors concerning the declaration of a cash dividend? Should the $1 per share dividend be declared? Should a smaller amount be declared? Should no dividend be declared? Support your answer with any necessary computations. Include in your response your concerns, from a cash flow perspective, about the following year.

Case 12-5 *Equipment Replacement Decision and Cash Flows from Operations*
LO 1, 4

Conrad Company has been in operation for four years. The company is pleased with the continued improvement in net income but is concerned about a lack of cash available to replace existing equipment. Land, buildings, and equipment were purchased at the beginning of Year 1. No subsequent fixed asset purchases have been made, but the president believes that equipment will need to be replaced in the near future. The following information is available (all amounts are in millions of dollars):

	Year of Operation			
	Year 1	**Year 2**	**Year 3**	**Year 4**
Net income (loss)	$(10)	$ (2)	$15	$20
Depreciation expense	30	25	15	14
Increase (decrease) in:				
Accounts receivable	32	5	12	20
Inventories	26	8	5	9
Prepayments	0	0	10	5
Accounts payable	15	3	(5)	(4)

Required

1. Compute the cash flow from operations for each of Conrad's first four years of operation.
2. Write a memo to the president explaining why the company is not generating sufficient cash from operations to pay for the replacement of equipment.

Accounting and Ethics: What Would You Do?

Case 12-6 *Loan Decision and the Statement of Cash Flows—Indirect Method* **LO 1, 4**

St. Lawrence Inc. is in the process of negotiating an extension of its existing loan agreements with a major bank. The bank is particularly concerned with St. Lawrence's ability to generate sufficient cash flow from operating activities to meet the periodic principal and interest payments. In conjunction with the negotiations, the controller prepared the following statement of cash flows to present to the bank:

ST. LAWRENCE INC.
STATEMENT OF CASH FLOWS
FOR THE YEAR ENDED DECEMBER 31, 2008
(ALL AMOUNTS IN MILLIONS OF DOLLARS)

Cash flows from operating activities		
Net income		$ 65
Adjustments to reconcile net income to net		
cash provided by operating activities:		
Depreciation and amortization		56
Increase in accounts receivable		(19)
Decrease in inventory		27
Decrease in accounts payable		(42)
Increase in other accrued liabilities		18
Net cash provided by operating activities		105
Cash flows for investing activities		
Acquisitions of other businesses		(234)
Acquisitions of plant and equipment		(125)
Sale of other businesses		300
Net cash used by investing activities		(59)
Cash flows for financing activities		
Additional borrowings		150
Repayments of borrowings		(180)
Cash dividends paid		(50)
Net cash used by financing activities		(80)
Net decrease in cash		(34)
Cash balance, January 1, 2008		42
Cash balance, December 31, 2008		$ 8

During 2008, St. Lawrence sold one of its businesses in Quebec. A gain of $200 million was included in 2008 income as the difference between the proceeds from the sale of $500 million and the book value of the business of $300 million. The entry to record the sale is as follows:

Cash	500	
Quebec Properties		300
Gain on Sale of Business		200
To record sale of a business		

Required

1. Comment on the presentation of the sale of the Quebec business on the statement of cash flows. Does the way in which the sale was reported violate generally accepted accounting principles? Regardless of whether it violates GAAP, does the way in which the transaction was reported on the statement result in a misstatement of the net decrease in cash for the period? Explain your answers.

2. Prepare a revised statement of cash flows for 2008, with the proper presentation of the sale of the Quebec business.

3. Has the controller acted in an unethical manner in the way the sale was reported on the statement of cash flows? Explain your answer.

Internet Research Case

Case 12-7 *CN*

Like most Canadian companies, **CN** reports its cash flow statement using the indirect method for cash from operations. However, in 2007 it also provided the cash flow from operations using the direct method.

INTERNET

CN
http://www.cn.ca

Required

1. Compare the latest information available with the cash flow statement in the chapter opener. Are there any significant changes in the adjustments made to net income to arrive at cash from operations? Are there any significant changes in net receipts from customers and net cash payments for the various operating activities?

2. Based on the latest financial information, what is the amount of CN's (a) cash flows from operating activities; (b) cash flows from investing activities; and (c) cash flows from financing activities? How do these compare to the corresponding numbers from 2007 in the "Focus on Financial Results" vignette at the start of the chapter? What is the trend?

3. What are three major changes in line items you see in the latest year's statement of cash flows? Using information available in the annual report, and in business news services, what changes do they represent within the company?

Solutions to Key Terms Quiz

_3_	Statement of cash flows		_7_	Financing activities
_4_	Cash equivalent		_6_	Direct method
_1_	Operating activities		_2_	Indirect method
_5_	Investing activities			

COURTESY CN RAIL

Chapter 13

Financial Statement Analysis

Final Destination

A Word to Readers About Part VI

Parts I to V present the principles of financial reporting, approaches to recording and processing accounting information, and the financial statements. We are now ready to look at how decision makers use accounting information to enhance their decisions.

CHAPTER 13

Financial Statement Analysis

LEARNING OBJECTIVES

After studying this chapter, you should be able to:

LO 1 Use comparative financial statements to analyze a company over time (horizontal analysis).

LO 2 Use common-size financial statements to compare various financial statement items (vertical analysis).

LO 3 Compute and use various ratios to assess liquidity.

LO 4 Compute and use various ratios to assess solvency.

LO 5 Compute and use various ratios to assess profitability.

LO 6 Discuss additional topics on financial statement analysis.

COURTESY JAMES LALANDE

STUDY LINKS

A Look at Previous Chapters

In Chapter 2, we introduced a few key financial ratios and saw the way that investors and creditors use them to better understand a company's financial statements. In many of the subsequent chapters we introduced ratios relevant to the particular topic being discussed.

A Look at This Chapter

Ratio analysis is one important type of analysis used to interpret financial statements. In this chapter, we expand our discussion of ratio analysis and introduce other valuable techniques used by investors, creditors, and analysts in reaching informed decisions. We will find that ratios and other forms of analysis can provide additional insight beyond that available from merely reading the financial statements.

Focus on Financial Results

Relevant and reliable information plays an important role in investment and business decisions. For example, a potential investor who is deciding whether to buy CN or CP shares will want to know what kind of return he might earn from each. A banker will want to know the likelihood that a loan will be repaid before lending money to a company. A supplier will want to know whether it will collect on time before granting an open line of credit to a company. The objective of financial reporting is to provide useful information to help various interested parties make decisions; however, financial statements do not answer directly such questions,

for two reasons: (1) financial statements are primarily historical information, whereas the information needed to answer the questions is future oriented; and (2) financial statements are general information, whereas different groups focus on different questions in their decisions. Financial statement analysis is a process of making financial statement information more relevant to decisions by relating items from various statements and different time periods. Chapter 13 focuses on techniques and issues relating to financial statement analysis.

CN AND CP 2007 ANNUAL REPORTS (EXCERPTS)

http://www.cn.ca
http://www.cpr.ca

Selected Information at December 31, 2007 or for the year Ended December 31, 2007

(in millions of dollars)	CN	CP
Revenues	$ 7,897	$ 4,707.6
Operating income	2,876	1,164.2
Net income	2,158	946.2
Total current assets	1,048	1,167.7
Total assets	23,460	13,365.0
Total current liabilities	1,590	1,344.8
Total liabilities	13,283	7,907.1
Total shareholders' equity	10,177	5,457.9
Cash from operating activities	2,417	1,314.6
Net cash flow	131	253.8

These excerpts from CN and CP's 2007 Annual Reports appear courtesy of CN and CP Rail. These sections of the Annual Reports appear in the Appendices of this textbook.

ANALYSIS OF COMPARATIVE AND COMMON-SIZE STATEMENTS

Horizontal analysis A comparison of financial statement items over a period of time.

Vertical analysis A comparison of various financial statement items within a single period with the use of common-size statements.

We will begin by looking at the comparative statements of a company for a two-year period. The analysis of the statements over a series of years is often called **horizontal analysis.** We will then see how the statements can be recast as what are referred to as *common-size statements.* The analysis of common-size statements is called **vertical analysis.** Next, we will consider the use of a variety of ratios to analyze a company. Finally, we will discuss additional issues such as benchmarking, forward-looking analysis, and the limitations of financial statement analysis.

HORIZONTAL ANALYSIS

LO 1 Use comparative financial statements to analyze a company over time (horizontal analysis).

Exhibit 13-1 shows comparative statements of income and retained earnings for Henderson for 2008 and 2007. At first glance, **1** the 20% increase in sales to $24 million appears promising, but management was not able to limit the increase in either **2** cost of goods sold or **3** selling, general, and administrative expense to 20%. The analysis indicates that cost of goods sold increased by 29% and that selling, general, and administrative expense increased by 50%. The increases in these two expenses more than offset the increase in sales and resulted in a **4** decrease in operating income of 25%.

Companies that experience sales growth often become lax about controlling expenses. Their managements sometimes forget that it is the bottom line that counts, not the top line. Perhaps the salespeople are given incentives to increase sales without considering the costs of the sales. Maybe management is spending too much on overhead, including its own salaries. The owners of the business will have to address these concerns if they want to receive a reasonable return on their investment.

Exhibit 13-1 Comparative Statements of Income and Retained Earnings—Horizontal Analysis

HENDERSON COMPANY
COMPARATIVE STATEMENTS OF INCOME AND RETAINED EARNINGS
FOR THE YEARS ENDED DECEMBER 31, 2008 AND 2007
(ALL AMOUNTS IN THOUSANDS OF DOLLARS)

	December 31 2008	December 31 2007	Increase (Decrease) Dollars	Increase (Decrease) Percent	
Net sales	$24,000	$20,000	$ 4,000	**1** 20%	
Cost of goods sold	18,000	14,000	4,000	**2** 29	These three increases in revenue and expenses resulted in an operating income *decrease* of 25%.
Gross profit	6,000	6,000	–0–	–0–	
Selling, general, and administrative expense	3,000	2,000	1,000	**3** 50	
Operating income	3,000	4,000	(1,000)	**4** (25)	
Interest expense	140	160	(20)	(13)	
Income before tax	2,860	3,840	(980)	(26)	
Income tax expense	1,140	1,540	(400)	(26)	
Net income	1,720	2,300	$ (580)	(25)%	
Preferred dividends	50	50			
Income available to common	1,670	2,250			
Common dividends	250	250			
To retained earnings	1,420	2,000			
Retained earnings, 1/1	6,000	4,000			
Retained earnings, 12/31	$ 7,420	$ 6,000			

NOTE: Referenced amounts boldfaced for convenience.

Comparative balance sheets for a hypothetical entity, Henderson Company, are presented in Exhibit 13-2. The increase or decrease in each of the major accounts on the balance sheet is shown both in absolute dollars and as a percentage. The base year for computing the percentage increase or decrease in each account is the first year, 2007, and is normally shown on the right side. By reading across from right to left (thus the term *horizontal analysis*), the analyst can quickly spot any unusual changes in accounts from the previous year. Three accounts stand out: **1** Cash decreased by 76%, **2** Inventory increased by 73%, and **3** Accounts Payable increased by 70%. (These lines are also boldfaced for convenience.) Individually, each of these large changes is a red flag. Taken together, these changes send the financial statement user the warning that the business may be deteriorating. Each of these large changes should be investigated further.

Horizontal analysis can be extended to include more than two years of results. At a minimum, publicly held companies are required to include income statements and statements of cash flows for the two most recent years and balance sheets as of the end of the two most recent years. Many annual reports include, as supplementary information, financial summaries of operations for extended periods of time. Tracking items over a series of years, a practice called *trend analysis*, can be a very powerful tool for the analyst. Advanced statistical techniques are available for analyzing trends in financial data and, most important, for projecting those trends to future periods.

Exhibit 13-2 Comparative Balance Sheets—Horizontal Analysis

Read from earlier year to later year. Usually this is from right to left.

HENDERSON COMPANY
COMPARATIVE BALANCE SHEETS
DECEMBER 31, 2008 AND 2007
(ALL AMOUNTS IN THOUSANDS OF DOLLARS)

The base year is normally on the right.

	December 31		Increase (Decrease)		
	2008	**2007**	**Dollars**	**Percent**	
Cash	$ 320	$ 1,350	$ (1,030) **1**	(76)%	Dollar change from year to year.
Accounts receivable	5,500	4,500	1,000	22	
Inventory	**4,750**	**2,750**	**2,000** **2**	**73**	
Prepaid insurance	150	200	(50)	(25)	Percentage change from one year to the next year.
Total current assets	10,720	8,800	1,920	22	
Land	2,000	2,000	–0–	–0–	
Buildings and equipment	6,000	4,500	1,500	33	In **horizontal analysis**, read right to left to compare one year's results with the next as a dollar amount of change and as a percentage of change from year to year.
Accumulated depreciation	(1,850)	(1,500)	(350)	(23)	
Total long-term assets	6,150	5,000	1,150	23	
Total assets	$16,870	$13,800	$ 3,070	22%	
Accounts payable	**$ 4,250**	**$ 2,500**	**$ 1,750** **3**	**70%**	
Taxes payable	2,300	2,100	200	10	
Notes payable	600	800	(200)	(25)	
Current portion of bonds	100	100	–0–	–0–	
Total current liabilities	7,250	5,500	1,750	32	
Bonds payable	700	800	(100)	(13)	
Total liabilities	7,950	6,300	1,650	26	
Preferred shares	500	500	–0–	–0–	
Common shares (1 million shares)	1,000	1,000	–0–	–0–	
Retained earnings	7,420	6,000	1,420	24	
Total shareholders' equity	8,920	7,500	1,420	19	
Total liabilities and shareholders' equity	$16,870	$13,800	$ 3,070	22%	

NOTE: Referenced amounts boldfaced for convenience.

Some of the techniques, such as time series analysis, have been used extensively in forecasting sales trends.

Historically, attention has focused on the balance sheet and income statement in analyzing a company's position and results of operations. Only recently have analysts and other users begun to appreciate the value in incorporating the statement of cash flows into their analyses.

Comparative statements of cash flows for Henderson appear in Exhibit 13-3. Henderson's financing activities remained constant over the two-year period, as indicated in that section of the statements. Each year the company paid $200,000 on notes, another $100,000 to retire bonds, and $300,000 to shareholders in dividends. Cash outflow from investing activities slowed down somewhat in 2008, with the purchase of $1,500,000 in new buildings, compared with $2,000,000 the year before.

The most noticeable difference between Henderson's statements of cash flows for the two years is in the Operating Activities section. Operations **1** generated almost $2 million less in cash in 2008 than in 2007 ($1.07 million in 2008 versus $2.95 million in 2007). The decrease in net income **2** was partially responsible for this reduction in cash from operations. However, the increases in **3** accounts receivable and **4** inventory in 2008 had a significant impact on the decrease in cash generated from operating activities.

Exhibit 13-3 Comparative Statements of Cash Flows—Horizontal Analysis

HENDERSON COMPANY
COMPARATIVE STATEMENTS OF CASH FLOWS
FOR THE YEARS ENDED DECEMBER 31, 2008 AND 2007
(ALL AMOUNTS IN THOUSANDS OF DOLLARS)

			Increase (Decrease)	
	2008	2007	Dollars	Percent
Net Cash Flows from Operating Activities				
2 Net income	$1,720	$2,300	$ (580)	(25)%
Adjustments:				
Depreciation expense	350	300		
Changes in:				
3 Accounts receivable	(1,000)	500		
4 Inventory	(2,000)	(300)		
Prepaid insurance	50	50		
Accounts payable	1,750	(200)		
Taxes payable	200	300		
Net cash provided by operating activities **1** Unfavourable	1,070 ⋯⋯	2,950	$(1,880)	(64)
Net Cash Flows from Investing Activities				
Purchase of buildings	(1,500)	(2,000)	$ (500)	(25)
Net Cash Flows from Financing Activities				
Repayment of notes	(200)	(200)	–0–	–0–
Retirement of bonds	(100)	(100)	–0–	–0–
Cash dividends—preferred	(50)	(50)	–0–	–0–
Cash dividends—common	(250)	(250)	–0–	–0–
Net cash used by financing activities	(600)	(600)	–0–	–0–
Net increase (decrease) in cash	(1,030)	350		
Beginning cash balance	1,350	1,000		
Ending cash balance	$ 320	$ 1,350		

NOTE: Referenced amounts boldfaced for convenience.

VERTICAL ANALYSIS

Often it is easier to examine comparative financial statements if they have been standardized. *Common-size statements* recast all items on the statement as a percentage of a selected item on the statement. This excludes size as a relevant variable in the analysis. One could use this type of analysis to compare **CN** with the smaller **CP**. It is also a convenient way to compare the same company from year to year.

Vertical analysis involves looking at the relative size and composition of various items on a particular financial statement. Common-size comparative income statements for Henderson are presented in Exhibit 13-4. The *base*, or benchmark, on which all other items in the income statement are compared is **1** net sales. Again, observations from the comparative statements alone are further confirmed by examining the common-size statements. Although the **gross profit margin**—*gross profit as a percentage of net sales*—was 30% in 2007, the same ratio for 2008 is only 25% **2**. Recall the earlier observation that although sales increased by 20% from one year to the next, **3** cost of goods sold increased by 29%.

In addition to the gross profit ratio, an important relationship from Exhibit 13-4 is the *ratio of net income to net sales,* or **profit margin.** The ratio, an overall indicator of management's ability to control expenses, reflects the amount of income for each dollar of sales. Some analysts prefer to look at income before tax, rather than final net income, because taxes are not typically an expense that can be controlled. Further, if the company does not earn a profit before tax, it will incur no tax expense. Note **4** the decrease in Henderson's profit margin: from 11.5% in 2007 to 7.2% in 2008 (or from 19.2% to 11.9% on a before-tax basis).

Common-size comparative balance sheets for Henderson Company are presented in Exhibit 13-5. Note that all asset accounts are stated as a percentage of total assets. Similarly, all liability and shareholders' equity accounts are stated as a percentage of total liabilities and shareholders' equity. The combination of the comparative balance sheets for the two years and the common-size feature allows the analyst to spot critical changes in the composition of the assets. We noted in Exhibit 13-2 that cash had decreased by 76% over the past year. The decrease of cash from 9.8% of total assets to only 1.9% **1** is highlighted in Exhibit 13-5.

> **LO 2** Use common-size financial statements to compare various financial statement items (vertical analysis).

CN
http://www.cn.ca
http://www.cpr.ca

Gross profit margin Gross profit to net sales.

Profit margin Net income to net sales.

Exhibit 13-4 Common-Size Comparative Income Statements—Vertical Analysis

HENDERSON COMPANY
COMMON-SIZE COMPARATIVE INCOME STATEMENTS
FOR THE YEARS ENDED DECEMBER 31, 2008 AND 2007
(ALL AMOUNTS IN THOUSANDS OF DOLLARS)

	2008		2007	
	Dollars	Percent	Dollars	Percent
Net sales	$24,000	**1** 100.0%	$20,000	100.0%
Cost of goods sold	**3** 18,000	75.0	14,000	70.0
Gross profit	6,000	**2** 25.0	6,000	30.0
Selling, general, and administrative expense	3,000	12.5	2,000	10.0
Operating income	3,000	12.5	4,000	20.0
Interest expense	140	0.6	160	0.8
Income before tax	2,860	11.9	3,840	19.2
Income tax expense	1,140	4.7	1,540	7.7
Net income	$ 1,720	**4** 7.2%	$ 2,300	11.5%

Gross profit as a percentage of sales is the **gross profit margin.**

The ratio of net income to net sales is the **profit margin.**

NOTE: Referenced amounts boldfaced for convenience.

One can also observe in the exhibit that **2** total current assets have continued to represent just under two-thirds (63.5%) of total assets. If cash has decreased significantly in terms of the percentage of total assets, what accounts have increased to maintain current assets at two-thirds of total assets? We can quickly determine from the data in Exhibit 13-5 that **3** although inventory represented 19.9% of total assets at the end of 2007, the percentage is up to 28.1% at the end of 2008. This change in the relative composition of current assets between cash and inventory may have important implications. The change, for instance, may signal that the company is having trouble selling inventory.

Total current liabilities **4** represent a slightly higher percentage of total liabilities and shareholders' equity at the end of 2008 than at the end of 2007. The increase is balanced by a slight decrease in the relative percentages of **5** long-term debt (the bonds) and of **6** shareholders' equity. We will return later to further analysis of the composition of both the current and the non-current accounts.

Exhibit 13-5 Common-Size Comparative Balance Sheets—Vertical Analysis

HENDERSON COMPANY
COMMON-SIZE COMPARATIVE BALANCE SHEETS
DECEMBER 31, 2008 AND 2007
(ALL AMOUNTS IN THOUSANDS OF DOLLARS)

	2008		2007	
	Dollars	Percent	Dollars	Percent
Cash	$ 320	1.9%	$ 1,350 **1**	9.8%
Accounts receivable	5,500	32.6	4,500	32.6
Inventory	4,750	28.1	2,750 **3**	19.9
Prepaid insurance	150	0.9	200	1.5
Total current assets	10,720	**2** 63.5	8,800	63.8
Land	2,000	11.9	2,000	14.5
Buildings and equipment, net	4,150	24.6	3,000	21.7
Total long-term assets	6,150	36.5	5,000	36.2
Total assets	$16,870	100.0%	$13,800	100.0%
Accounts payable	$ 4,250	25.2%	$ 2,500	18.1%
Taxes payable	2,300	13.6	2,100	15.2
Notes payable	600	3.6	800	5.8
Current portion of bonds	100	0.6	100	0.7
Total current liabilities	7,250	**4** 43.0	5,500	39.9
Bonds payable	700	**5** 4.1	800	5.8
Total liabilities	7,950	47.1	6,300	45.7
Preferred shares	500	3.0	500	3.6
Common shares	1,000	5.9	1,000	7.2
Retained earnings	7,420	44.0	6,000	43.5
Total shareholders' equity	8,920	**6** 52.9	7,500	54.3
Total liabilities and shareholders' equity	$16,870	100.0%	$13,800	100.0%

Compare percentages across years to spot year-to-year trends.

In **vertical analysis**, compare each line item as a percentage of total (100%) to highlight a company's overall condition.

NOTE: Referenced amounts boldfaced for convenience.

Summary Report—Horizontal and Vertical Analyses

Horizontal and vertical analyses provide some preliminary indicators of where investigations need to be made. For example, why did costs increase faster than sales? Can Henderson manage its cash decline resulting from its operations, its inventory, and receivable increases, and keep its creditors happy? Investing and financing activities appear to be controlled even in the face of a significant decline in cash flow from operations.

Ratios for liquidity, solvency, and profitability may confirm the horizontal and vertical analyses or provide further insights.

LIQUIDITY ANALYSIS AND THE MANAGEMENT OF WORKING CAPITAL

Two ratios were discussed in the last section: the *gross profit margin* and the *profit margin.* A ratio is simply the relationship, normally stated as a percentage, between two financial statement amounts. In this section, we consider a wide range of ratios used by management, analysts, and others for a variety of purposes. We classify the ratios in three main categories according to their use in performing: (1) liquidity analysis, (2) solvency analysis, and (3) profitability analysis.

LO 3 Compute and use various ratios to assess liquidity.

Liquidity can have slightly different meanings when used in different contexts. Liquidity of an asset is a relative measure of the nearness to cash of the assets and liabilities of a company. Nearness to cash deals with the length of time before cash is realized. **Liquidity** of a company concerns the company's ability to pay its debts as they come due. Recall the distinction between the current and long-term classifications on the balance sheet. Current assets are assets that will be either converted into cash or consumed within one year or the operating cycle, if the cycle is longer than one year. The operating cycle for a manufacturing company is the length of time between the purchase of raw materials and the eventual collection of any outstanding accounts receivable from the sale of the product. Current liabilities are a company's obligations that require the use of current assets or the creation of other current liabilities to satisfy them. Thus, a comparison of current assets and current liabilities provides some indications of the company's ability to pay its bills as they become due.

Liquidity The company's ability to pay its debts as they become due.

The nearness to cash of the current assets is indicated by their placement on the balance sheet. Current assets are listed on the balance sheet in descending order of their nearness to cash. Liquidity is, of course, a matter of degree, with cash being the most liquid of all assets. With few exceptions, such as prepaid insurance, most current assets are convertible into cash. However, accounts receivable are closer to being converted into cash than is inventory. An account receivable need only be collected to be converted to cash. An item of inventory must first be sold, and then, assuming that sales of inventory are on account, the account must be collected before cash is realized.

Working Capital

Working capital is the excess of current assets over current liabilities at a point in time:

Working Capital = Current Assets − Current Liabilities

Working capital Current assets minus current liabilities.

Reference to Henderson's comparative balance sheets in Exhibit 13-1 indicates the following:

	December 31	
	2008	**2007**
Current assets	$10,720,000	$8,800,000
Current liabilities	7,250,000	5,500,000
Working capital	$ 3,470,000	$3,300,000

The management of working capital is an extremely important task for any business. A comparison of Henderson's working capital at the end of each of the two years indicates a slight increase in the degree of protection for short-term creditors of the company. Management must always strive for the ideal balance of current assets and current liabilities. The amount of working capital is limited in its informational value, however. For example, it tells us nothing about the composition of the current accounts. Also, the dollar amount of working capital may not be useful for comparison with other companies of different sizes in the same industry. Working capital of $3,470,000 may be adequate for Henderson Company, but it might signal impending bankruptcy for a company much larger than Henderson.

Current Ratio

Current ratio The ratio of current assets to current liabilities.

The **current ratio** is one of the most widely used of all financial statement ratios and is calculated as follows:

$$\text{Current Ratio} = \frac{\text{Current Assets}}{\text{Current Liabilities}}$$

For Henderson Company, the ratio at each year-end is as follows:

	December 31	
	2008	**2007**
	$\dfrac{\$10{,}720{,}000}{\$ 7{,}250{,}000} = 1.48 \text{ to } 1$	$\dfrac{\$8{,}800{,}000}{\$5{,}500{,}000} = 1.60 \text{ to } 1$

At the end of 2008, Henderson had $1.48 of current assets for every $1 of current liabilities. Is this current ratio adequate? Or is it a sign of impending financial difficulties? There is no definitive answer to either of these questions. Some analysts use a general rule of thumb of 2:1 for the current ratio as a sign of short-term financial health. The answer depends first on the industry. Companies in certain industries have historically operated with current ratios much less than 2:1.

A second concern in interpreting the current ratio involves the composition of the current assets. Cash is usually the only acceptable means of payment for most liabilities. Therefore, it is important to consider the makeup, or *composition,* of the current assets. Refer to Exhibit 13-5 and Henderson's common-size balance sheets. Not only did the current ratio decline during 2008 but also the proportion of the total current assets made up by inventory increased whereas the proportion made up by accounts receivable remained the same. Recall that accounts receivable are only one step removed from cash, whereas inventory requires both sale and collection of the subsequent account.

Acid-Test Ratio

The **acid-test** or **quick ratio** is a stricter test of a company's ability to pay its current debts as they are due. Specifically, it is intended to deal with the composition problem because it *excludes* inventories and prepaid assets from the numerator of the fraction:

$$\text{Acid-Test or Quick Ratio} = \frac{\text{Quick Assets}}{\text{Current Liabilities}}$$

where

Quick Assets = Cash + Short-term Investments + Current Receivables

Henderson's quick assets consist of only cash and accounts receivable, and its quick ratios are as follows:

December 31

2008	2007
$\dfrac{\$320{,}000 + \$5{,}500{,}000}{\$7{,}250{,}000} = 0.80$ to 1	$\dfrac{\$1{,}350{,}000 + \$4{,}500{,}000}{\$5{,}500{,}000} = 1.06$ to 1

Does the quick ratio of less than 1:1 at the end of 2008 mean that Henderson will be unable to pay creditors on time? *For many companies, an acid-test ratio below 1 is not desirable because it may signal the need to liquidate marketable securities to pay bills, regardless of the current trading price of the securities.* Although the quick ratio is a better indication of short-term debt-paying ability than the current ratio, it is still not perfect. For example, we would want to know the normal credit terms that Henderson extends to its customers, as well as the credit terms that the company receives from its suppliers.

Assume that Henderson requires its customers to pay their accounts within 30 days and that the normal credit terms extended by Henderson's suppliers allow payment anytime within 60 days. The relatively longer credit terms extended by Henderson's suppliers give it some cushion in meeting its obligations. The due date of the $2,300,000 in taxes payable could also have a significant effect on the company's ability to remain in business.

Cash Flow from Operations to Current Liabilities

Two limitations exist with either the current ratio or the quick ratio as a measure of liquidity. First, almost all debts require the payment of cash. Thus, a ratio that focuses on cash is more useful. Second, both ratios focus on liquid assets at a *point in time*. Cash flow from operating activities, as reported on the statement of cash flows, can be used to indicate the flow of cash during the year to cover the debts due.[1] The **cash flow from operations to current liabilities ratio** is computed as follows:

$$\text{Cash Flow from Operations to Current Liabilities Ratio} = \frac{\text{Net Cash Provided by Operating Activities}}{\text{Average Current Liabilities}}$$

Note the use of *average* current liabilities in the denominator. This results in a denominator that is consistent with the numerator, which reports the cash flow over a period of time. Because we need to calculate the *average* current liabilities for both years, it is necessary to add the ending balance sheet for 2006 for use in the analysis.

Acid-test or quick ratio A stricter test of liquidity than the current ratio; excludes inventory and prepayments from the numerator.

Cash flow from operations to current liabilities ratio A measure of the ability to pay current debts from operating cash flows.

---

[1]For a detailed discussion on the use of information contained in the statement of cash flows in performing ratio analysis, see Charles A. Carslaw and John R. Mills, "Developing Ratios for Effective Cash Flow Statement Analysis," *Journal of Accountancy* (November 1991), pp. 63–70.

NEL

Liquidity Analysis and the Management of Working Capital **637**

The balance sheet for Henderson on December 31, 2006, is given in Exhibit 13-6. The ratio for Henderson for each year is as follows:

2008	2007
$\dfrac{\$1,070,000}{(\$7,250,000 + \$5,500,000)/2} = 16.8\%$	$\dfrac{\$2,950,000}{(\$5,500,000 + \$5,600,000)/2} = 53.2\%$

Exhibit 13-6

Henderson's Balance Sheet, End of 2006

HENDERSON COMPANY BALANCE SHEET DECEMBER 31, 2006 (ALL AMOUNTS IN THOUSANDS OF DOLLARS)	
Cash	$ 1,000
Accounts receivable	5,000
Inventory	2,450
Prepaid insurance	250
Total current assets	8,700
Land	2,000
Buildings and equipment, net	1,300
Total long-term assets	3,300
Total assets	$12,000
Accounts payable	$ 2,700
Taxes payable	1,800
Notes payable	1,000
Current portion of bonds	100
Total current liabilities	5,600
Bonds payable	900
Total liabilities	6,500
Preferred shares	500
Common shares	1,000
Retained earnings	4,000
Total shareholders' equity	5,500
Total liabilities and shareholders' equity	$12,000

Two factors are responsible for the large decrease in this ratio from 2007 to 2008. First, cash generated from operations during 2008 was less than half what it was during 2007 (the numerator). Second, average current liabilities were smaller in 2007 than in 2008 (the denominator). In examining the health of the company in terms of its liquidity, an analyst would concentrate on the reason for these decreases.

Accounts Receivable Analysis

The analysis of accounts receivable is an important component in the management of working capital. A company must be willing to extend credit terms that are liberal enough to attract and maintain customers, but at the same time, management must continually monitor the accounts to ensure collection on a timely basis. One measure of the efficiency of the collection process is the **accounts receivable turnover ratio:**

Accounts receivable turnover ratio
A measure of the number of times accounts receivable are collected in a period.

$$\text{Accounts Receivable Turnover Ratio} = \frac{\text{Net Credit Sales}}{\text{Average Accounts Receivable}}$$

Note an important distinction between this ratio and either the current or the quick ratio. Although both of those ratios measure liquidity at a point in time and all numbers come from the balance sheet, a turnover ratio is an *activity* ratio and consists of an activity (sales, in this case) divided by a base to which it is naturally related (accounts receivable). Because an activity such as sales is for a period of time (a year, in this case), the base should be stated as an average for that same period of time.

The accounts receivable turnover ratios for both years can now be calculated (we assume that all sales are on account):

2008	2007
$\dfrac{\$24,000,000}{(\$5,500,000 + \$4,500,000)/2} = 4.8$ times	$\dfrac{\$20,000,000}{(\$4,500,000 + \$5,000,000)/2} = 4.2$ times

Accounts turned over, on average, 4.2 times in 2007, compared with 4.8 times in 2008. This means that the average number of times accounts were collected during each year was between four and five times. What does this mean about the average length of time that an account was outstanding? Another way to measure efficiency in the collection process is to calculate the **number of days' sales in receivables:**

$$\text{Number of Days' Sales in Receivables} = \frac{\text{Number of Days in the Period}}{\text{Accounts Receivable Turnover}}$$

Number of days' sales in receivables A measure of the average age of accounts receivable.

For simplicity, we assume 360 days in a year:

2008	2007
$\dfrac{360 \text{ days}}{4.8 \text{ times}} = 75$ days	$\dfrac{360 \text{ days}}{4.2 \text{ times}} = 86$ days

The average number of days an account is outstanding, or the average collection period, is 75 days in 2008, down from 86 days in 2007. Is this acceptable? The answer depends on the company's credit policy. If Henderson's normal credit terms require payment within 60 days, further investigation is needed, even though the number of days outstanding has decreased from the previous year.

Management needs to be concerned with both the collectibility of an account as it ages and the cost of funds tied up in receivables. For example, a $1 million average receivable balance that requires an additional month to collect suggests that the company is forgoing $10,000 in lost profits if we assume that the money could be reinvested in the business to earn 1% per month, or 12% per year.

Accounting for Your Decisions

You Examine Your Business's Trends

You are a small business owner and have noticed that over the past two years, sales have increased but the accounts receivable turnover ratio has decreased. Should you be concerned?

ANSWER: You should certainly be pleased with an increase in sales, but a decrease in accounts receivable turnover should concern you. A decline in this ratio indicates that the average time to collect an open account is increasing. Regardless of the specific reason for this change (e.g., more liberal credit terms, change in creditworthiness of customers, lack of follow-up on overdue accounts), the increase in the time to collect may result in cash flow problems for you.

Inventory Analysis

A similar set of ratios can be calculated to analyze the efficiency in managing inventory. The **inventory turnover ratio** is as follows:

$$\text{Inventory Turnover Ratio} = \frac{\text{Cost of Goods Sold}}{\text{Average Inventory}}$$

Inventory turnover ratio A measure of the number of times inventory is sold during a period.

The ratio for each of the two years follows:

2008	2007
$\dfrac{\$18,000,000}{(\$4,750,000 + \$2,750,000)/2} = 4.8$ times	$\dfrac{\$14,000,000}{(\$2,750,000 + \$2,450,000)/2} = 5.4$ times

Henderson was slightly more efficient in 2007 in moving its inventory. The number of "turns" each year varies widely for different industries. For example, a wholesaler of perishable fruits and vegetables may turn over inventory at least 50 times per year. An airplane manufacturer, however, may turn over its inventory once or twice a year. What does the number of turns per year tell us about the average length of time it takes to sell an item of inventory? The **number of days' sales in inventory** is an alternative measure of the company's efficiency in managing inventory. It is the number of days between the date an item of inventory is purchased and the date it is sold:

Number of days' sales in inventory
A measure of how long it takes to sell inventory.

$$\text{Number of Days' Sales in Inventory} = \frac{\text{Number of Days in the Period}}{\text{Inventory Turnover}}$$

The number of days' sales in inventory for Henderson is as follows:

2008	2007
$\frac{360 \text{ days}}{4.8 \text{ times}} = 75 \text{ days}$	$\frac{360 \text{ days}}{5.4 \text{ times}} = 67 \text{ days}$

This measure can reveal a great deal about inventory management. For example, an unusually low turnover (and, of course, high number of days in inventory) may signal a large amount of obsolete inventory or problems in the sales department. Or, it may indicate that the company is pricing its products too high and the market is reacting by reducing demand for the company's products.

Accounts Payable Analysis

Accounts payable turnover ratio
A measure of the number of times accounts payable are paid in a period.

Another set of ratios can be calculated to analyze a company's efficiency in managing its accounts payable. The **accounts payable turnover ratio** is as follows:

$$\text{Accounts Payable Turnover Ratio} = \frac{\text{Purchases}}{\text{Average Accounts Payable}}$$

The ratios for each of the two years are as follows:

2008	2007
$\frac{\$20,000,000}{(\$4,250,000 + \$2,500,000)/2} = 5.9 \text{ times}$	$\frac{\$14,300,000}{(\$2,500,000 + \$2,700,000)/2} = 5.5 \text{ times}$

The amount for purchases is not directly available from the financial statement; however, it can be determined from the Cost of Goods Sold account adjusted for changes in the Inventory account. The cost of goods sold for 2008 was $18,000,000, and inventory changed from $2,750,000 to $4,750,000—a $2,000,000 increase. Thus the purchases for the year must be $18,000,000 + $2,000,000, or $20,000,000. Similarly, since the cost of goods sold for 2007 was $14,000,000 and the inventory changed from $2,450,000 to $2,750,000, the purchases for 2007 must be $14,300,000.

Number of days' purchases in payables A measure of the average age of accounts payable.

The accounts payable ratios indicate that Henderson was more prompt in paying its accounts in 2008 than in 2007. What does the number of turns per year tell us about the average length of time it takes to pay for a purchase? The **number of days' purchases in payables** is an alternative measure of how a company manages its payables. It tells us the average number of days between the date an item was purchased and the date the purchase was paid for:

2008	2007
$\frac{360 \text{ days}}{5.9 \text{ times}} = 61 \text{ days}$	$\frac{360 \text{ days}}{5.5 \text{ times}} = 65 \text{ days}$

This measure tells us how promptly the company pays its accounts. A low turnover (high number of days in payables) can mean that the company is able to lengthen the period in which it uses the cash it has "borrowed" from suppliers. Alternatively, it could mean that the company is behind in paying its suppliers.

Cash Operating Cycle

The **cash to cash operating cycle** is the length of time between the payment for the purchase of inventory and the eventual collection of the cash from the sale. One method to approximate the number of days in a company's operating cycle involves combining three measures:

> **Cash to Cash Operating Cycle = Number of Days' Sales in Inventory**
> **+ Number of Days' Sales in Receivables**
> **− Number of Days' Purchases in Payables**

Cash to cash operating cycle The length of time from the payment for the purchase of inventory to the collection of any receivable from the sale.

Henderson's operating cycles for 2008 and 2007 are as follows:

2008	2007
75 days + 75 days − 61 days = 89 days	67 days + 86 days − 65 days = 88 days

The average length of time between inventory having to be paid for and the collection of cash from the sale of that inventory was 89 days in 2008 and 88 days in 2007. This means that for both years, the length of time between paying for inventory and collecting cash from the sale of that inventory was nearly 88 days. Cash would have been needed to bridge this gap between the payment and the collection. Note that the length of the operating cycle did not change significantly from 2007 to 2008, but the composition did change: there was an increase in the number of days in inventory, a decrease in the number of days in receivables, and a decrease in the number of days in payables.

Summary Report—Liquidity

The specifics of each report written about liquidity depend on the findings and on the comparisons undertaken in the analysis. In the case of Henderson, the comparisons were limited to the previous year (2007). Industry comparisons or comparisons to other companies are possible along with investigations into the operational reasons for the ratio findings.

The ratios for liquidity indicated a slight decline in liquidity because of increases in inventory (75 days versus 67 days) and a slight decrease in payables (61 days versus 65 days). Also, cash flow from operations as a percentage of current liabilities declined significantly to 16.8% versus 53.2%. Overall, Henderson seems to have managed its liquidity issues by drawing down its cash and increasing its collection of receivables. Future investigations would determine if inventory and payables can be managed to bring liquidity in line with 2007 levels.

▪ SOLVENCY ANALYSIS

LO 4 Compute and use various ratios to assess solvency.

Solvency refers to a company's ability to remain in business over the long term. It is related to liquidity but differs in time. Liquidity relates to the firm's ability to pay next year's debts as they come due; solvency concerns the ability of the firm to stay financially healthy over the period of time that existing debt (short- and long-term) will be outstanding.

Solvency The ability of a company to remain in business over the long term.

Due to the perishable nature of their products, grocery chains have high inventory turnovers and short cash-to-cash operating cycles. Firms in other segments have relatively longer cycles.

RACHEL L. SELLERS/ SHUTTERSTOCK

Debt-to-Equity Ratio

Debt-to-equity ratio The ratio of total liabilities to total shareholders' equity.

Capital structure is the focal point in solvency analysis. This refers to the composition of the right side of the balance sheet and the mix between debt and shareholders' equity. The composition of debt and equity in the capital structure is an important determinant of the cost of capital to a company. We will have more to say later about the effects that the mix of debt and equity has on profitability. For now, consider the **debt-to-equity ratio:**

$$\text{Debt-to-Equity Ratio} = \frac{\text{Total Liabilities}}{\text{Total Shareholders' Equity}}$$

Henderson's debt-to-equity ratio at each year-end is as follows:

December 31			
2008		**2007**	
$\dfrac{\$7,950,000}{\$8,920,000} = 0.89 \text{ to } 1$		$\dfrac{\$6,300,000}{\$7,500,000} = 0.84 \text{ to } 1$	

The 2008 ratio indicates that for every $1 of capital that shareholders provided, creditors provided $0.89. Variations of the debt-to-equity ratio are sometimes used to assess solvency. For example, an analyst might calculate the ratio of total liabilities to the sum of total liabilities and shareholders' equity. This results in a ratio that differs from the debt-to-equity ratio, but the objective of the measure is the same—to determine the degree to which the company relies on outsiders for funds.

What is an *acceptable* ratio of debt to equity? As with all ratios, the answer depends on the company, the industry, and many other factors. You should not assume that a lower debt-to-equity ratio is better. Certainly taking on additional debt is risky. Many companies are able to benefit from borrowing money, however, by putting the cash raised to good uses in their businesses. Later in the chapter we discuss the concept of leverage: using borrowed money to benefit the company and its shareholders.

Times Interest Earned

The debt-to-equity ratio is a measure of the company's overall long-term financial health. Management must also be aware of its ability to meet current interest payments to creditors. The **times interest earned ratio** indicates the company's ability to meet current-year interest payments out of current-year earnings:

$$\text{Times Interest Earned Ratio} = \frac{\text{Net Income} + \text{Interest Expense} + \text{Income Tax Expense}}{\text{Interest Expense}}$$

Both interest expense and income tax expense are added back to net income in the numerator because interest is a deduction in arriving at the amount of income subject to tax. Stated slightly differently, if a company had just enough income to cover the payment of interest, tax expense would be zero. Note that the numerator is also called earnings before interest and taxes (EBIT). The greater the interest coverage is, the better, as far as lenders are concerned. Bankers often place more importance on the times interest earned ratio than even on earnings per share. The ratio for Henderson for each of the two years indicates a great deal of protection in this regard:

2008	2007
$\dfrac{\$1,720,000 + \$140,000 + \$1,140,000}{\$140,000}$	$\dfrac{\$2,300,000 + \$160,000 + \$1,540,000}{\$160,000}$
= 21.4 to 1	= 25 to 1

Debt Service Coverage

Two problems exist with the times interest earned ratio as a measure of the ability to pay creditors. First, the denominator of the fraction considers only *interest.* Management must also be concerned with the *principal* amount of loans maturing in the next year. The second problem deals with the difference between the cash and the accrual bases of accounting. The numerator of the times interest earned ratio is not a measure of the *cash* available to repay loans. Keep in mind the various non-cash adjustments, such as depreciation, that enter into the determination of net income. Also, recall that the denominator of the times interest earned ratio is a measure of interest expense, not interest payments. The **debt service coverage ratio** is a measure of the amount of cash that is generated from operating activities during the year and that is available to repay interest due and any maturing principal amounts (that is, the amount available to "service" the debt):

$$\text{Debt Service Coverage Ratio} = \frac{\text{Cash Flow from Operations Before Interest and Tax Payments}}{\text{Interest and Principal Payments}}$$

Some analysts use an alternative measure in the numerator of this ratio, as well as for other purposes. The alternative is referred to as EBITDA, which stands for earnings before interest, taxes, depreciation, and amortization. Whether EBITDA is a good substitute for cash flow from operations before interest and tax payments depends on whether there were significant changes in current assets and current liabilities during the period. If significant changes in these accounts occurred during the period, cash flow from operations before interest and tax payments is a better measure of a company's ability to cover interest and debt payments.

Henderson's cash flow from operations is available on the comparative statement of cash flows in Exhibit 13-3. As was the case with the times interest earned ratio, the net cash provided by operating activities is adjusted to reflect the amount available *before* paying interest and taxes.

Keep in mind that Henderson's income statement in Exhibit 13-4 reflects the *expense* for interest and taxes each year. The amounts of interest and taxes *paid* each year would be shown as supplemental information to the statement of cash flows in Exhibit 13-3 and are relevant in computing the debt service coverage ratio.

We must include any principal payments with interest paid in the denominator of the debt service coverage ratio. According to the Financing Activities section of the statements of cash flows in Exhibit 13-3, Henderson repaid $200,000 each year on the notes payable and $100,000 each year on the bonds. The debt service coverage ratios for the two years are calculated as follows:

2008

$$\frac{\$1,070,000 + \$140,000 + \$940,000}{\$140,000 + \$200,000 + \$100,000} = 4.89 \text{ times}$$

2007

$$\frac{\$2,950,000 + \$160,000 + \$1,240,000}{\$160,000 + \$200,000 + \$100,000} = 9.46 \text{ times}$$

Calculations: $1,140,000 − $200,000 = $940,000;
$1,540,000 − $300,000 = $1,240,000

Like Henderson's times interest earned ratio, its debt service coverage ratio decreased during 2008. According to the calculations, however, Henderson still generated almost $5 of cash from operations during 2008 to "cover" every $1 of required interest and principal payments.

Summary Report—Solvency

Can Henderson manage its debts in the long term? Slight problems with inventory and the expansion of sales and the issue of collections of receivables were evident from the liquidity analysis. Solvency analysis suggests a minor increase in the proportion of debt to equity, indicating some increase in debt payment risk. Times interest earned and debt service coverage portray some dangers for Henderson because of the decline in profits and cash flow from operations. The reduction in cash flow from operations significantly reduced the coverage of capital expenditures. Financing may be required in the future to continue investing. These solvency issues will require near-term attention by management if long-term solvency is to return to 2007 levels.

Cash Flow from Operations to Capital Expenditures Ratio

Cash flow from operations to capital expenditures ratio A measure of the ability of a company to finance long-term asset acquisitions with cash from operations.

One final measure is useful in assessing the solvency of a business. The **cash flow from operations to capital expenditures ratio** measures a company's ability to use operations to finance its acquisitions of productive assets. To the extent that a company is able to do this, it should rely less on external financing or additional contributions by the owners to replace and add to the existing capital base. The ratio is computed as follows:

$$\frac{\text{Cash Flow from Operations}}{\text{to Capital Expenditures Ratio}} = \frac{\text{Cash Flow from Operations – Total Dividends Paid}}{\text{Cash Paid for Acquisitions}}$$

Not that the numerator of the ratio measures the cash flow *after* meeting all dividend payments.[2] The calculation of the ratios for Henderson follows:

2008		2007	
$\frac{\$1,070,000 - \$300,000}{\$1,500,000}$	$= 51.3\%$	$\frac{\$2,950,000 - \$300,000}{\$2,000,000}$	$= 132.5\%$

---

[2] Dividends paid are reported on the statement of cash flows in the Financing Activities section. The amount *paid* should be used for this calculation rather than the amount declared, which appears on the statement of retained earnings.

Although the amount of capital expenditures was less in 2008 than in 2007, the company generated considerably less cash from operations in 2008 to cover these acquisitions. In fact, the ratio of less than 100% in 2008 indicates that Henderson was not able to finance all of its capital expenditures from operations *and* cover its dividend payments.

Two-Minute Review

1. Explain the difference between liquidity and solvency as it relates to a company's financial position.

2. Assume that you are a supplier and are considering whether to sell to a company on account. Which of the two, liquidity or solvency, are you more concerned with?

Answers on page 655.

PROFITABILITY ANALYSIS

Liquidity analysis and solvency analysis deal with management's ability to repay short- and long-term creditors. Creditors are concerned with a company's profitability because a profitable company is more likely to be able to make principal and interest payments. Of course, shareholders care about a company's profitability because it affects the market price of the shares and the ability of the company to pay dividends. Various measures of **profitability** indicate how well management is using the resources at its disposal to earn a return on the funds invested by various groups. Two frequently used profitability measures, the gross profit ratio and the profit margin ratio, were discussed earlier in the chapter. We now turn to other measures of profitability.

> **LO 5** Compute and use various ratios to assess profitability.

Profitability How well management is using company resources to earn a return on the funds invested by various groups.

Rate of Return on Assets

Before computing the rate of return, we must answer an important question: *return to whom? Every return ratio is a measure of the relationship between the income earned by the company and the investment made in the company by various groups.* The broadest rate of return ratio is the **return on assets ratio** because it considers the investment made by *all* providers of capital, from short-term creditors to bondholders to shareholders. Therefore, the denominator, or base, for the return on assets ratio is average total liabilities and shareholders' equity—which of course is the same as average total assets.

The numerator of a return ratio will be some measure of the company's income for the period. The income selected for the numerator must match the investment or base in the denominator. For example, if average total assets is the base in the denominator, it is necessary to use an income number that is applicable to all providers of capital. Therefore, the income number used in the rate of return on assets is income *after* adding back interest expense. This adjustment considers creditors as one of the groups that have provided funds to the company. In other words, we want the amount of income before either creditors or shareholders have been given any distributions (that is, interest to creditors or dividends to shareholders). Interest expense must be added back on a net-of-tax basis. Net-of-tax here means interest expense taxes on the interest expense. Because net income is on an after-tax basis, for consistency purposes interest must also be placed on a net, or after-tax, basis.

The return on assets ratio is as follows:

$$\text{Return on Assets Ratio} = \frac{\text{Net Income} + \text{Interest Expense, Net of Tax}}{\text{Average Total Assets}}$$

Return on assets ratio A measure of a company's success in earning a return for all providers of capital.

The tax rate used here should be the effective tax rate, which is the ratio of income tax expense to income before tax. If the effective tax rate for Henderson is 40%, we determine its return on assets ratios as follows:

		2008		2007
Net income		$ 1,720,000		$ 2,300,000
Add back:				
Interest expense	$140,000		$160,000	
× (1 − tax rate)	× 0.6	84,000	× 0.6	96,000
Numerator		$ 1,804,000		$ 2,396,000
Assets, beginning of year		$13,800,000		$12,000,000
Assets, end of year		16,870,000		13,800,000
Total		30,670,000		25,800,000
Denominator:				
Average total assets				
(total above divided by 2)		$15,335,000		$12,900,000
		$ 1,804,000		$ 2,396,000
		$15,335,000		$12,900,000
Return on assets ratio		= 11.76%		= 18.57%

Components of Return on Assets

What caused Henderson's return on assets to decrease so dramatically from the previous year? The answer can be found by considering the two individual components that make up the return on assets ratio. The first of these components is the **return on sales ratio** and is calculated as follows:

Return on sales ratio A variation of the profit margin ratio; measures earnings before payments to creditors.

$$\text{Return on Sales Ratio} = \frac{\text{Net Income} + \text{Interest Expense, Net of Tax}}{\text{Net Sales}}$$

The return on sales ratios for Henderson for the two years follow:

2008	2007
$\dfrac{\$1,720,000 + \$84,000}{\$24,000,000} = 7.52\%$	$\dfrac{\$2,300,000 + \$96,000}{\$20,000,000} = 11.98\%$

The ratio for 2008 indicates that for every $1 of sales, the company was able to earn a profit, before the payment of interest, of between 7 and 8 cents, as compared with a return of almost 12 cents on the dollar in 2007.

The other component of the rate of return on assets is the **asset turnover ratio.** The ratio is similar to both the inventory turnover and the accounts receivable turnover ratios because it is a measure of the relationship between some activity (net sales, in this case) and some investment base (average total assets):

Asset turnover ratio The relationship between net sales and average total assets.

$$\text{Asset Turnover Ratio} = \frac{\text{Net Sales}}{\text{Average Total Assets}}$$

For Henderson, the ratio for each of the two years follows:

2008	2007
$\dfrac{\$24,000,000}{\$15,335,000} = 1.57 \text{ times}$	$\dfrac{\$20,000,000}{\$12,900,000} = 1.55 \text{ times}$

It now becomes evident that the explanation for the decrease in Henderson's return on assets lies in the drop in the return on sales, since the asset turnover ratio was almost the same. To summarize, note the relationship among the three ratios:

Return on Assets = Return on Sales × Asset Turnover

For 2008, Henderson's return on assets consists of the following:

$$\frac{\$1,804,000}{\$24,000,000} \times \frac{\$24,000,000}{\$15,335,000} = 7.52\% \times 1.57 = 11.8\%$$

Finally, notice that net sales cancels out of both ratios, leaving the net income adjusted for interest divided by average assets as the return on assets ratio.

Return on Common Shareholders' Equity

Reasoning similar to that used to calculate return on assets can be used to calculate the return on capital provided by the common shareholder. Because we are interested in the return to the common shareholder, our base is no longer average total assets but average common shareholders' equity. Similarly, the appropriate income figure for the numerator is net income less preferred dividends because we are interested in the return to the common shareholder after all claims have been settled. Income taxes and interest expense have already been deducted in arriving at net income, but preferred dividends have not been because dividends are a distribution of profits, not an expense.

The **return on common shareholders' equity ratio** is computed as follows:

$$\text{Return on Common Shareholders' Equity Ratio} = \frac{\text{Net Income} - \text{Preferred Dividends}}{\text{Average Common Shareholders' Equity}}$$

Return on common shareholders' equity ratio A measure of a company's success in earning a return for the common shareholders.

The average common shareholders' equity for Henderson is calculated using information from Exhibits 13-2 and 13-6:

	Account Balances at December 31		
	2008	2007	2006
Common shares	$1,000,000	$1,000,000	$1,000,000
Retained earnings	7,420,000	6,000,000	4,000,000
Total common equity	$8,420,000	$7,000,000	$5,000,000

Average common equity:
2007: ($7,000,000 + $5,000,000)/2 = $6,000,000
2008: ($8,420,000 + $7,000,000)/2 = $7,710,000

Net income less preferred dividends—or "income available to common," as it is called—can be found by referring to net income on the income statement and to preferred dividends on the statement of retained earnings. The combined statement of income and retained earnings in Exhibit 13-1 gives the relevant amounts for the numerator. Henderson's return on equity for the two years is as follows:

2008	2007
$\frac{\$1,720,000 - \$50,000}{\$7,710,000} = 21.66\%$	$\frac{\$2,300,000 - \$50,000}{\$6,000,000} = 37.50\%$

Even though Henderson's return on shareholders' equity ratio decreased significantly from one year to the next, most shareholders would be very happy to achieve these returns on their money. Very few investments offer much more than 10% return unless substantial risk is involved.

Return on Assets, Return on Equity, and Leverage

The return on assets for 2008 was 11.8%. But the return to the common shareholders was much higher: 21.7%. How do you explain this phenomenon? Why are the shareholders receiving a higher return on their money than all of the providers of money combined are getting? A partial answer to these questions can be found by reviewing the cost to Henderson of the various sources of capital.

Exhibit 13-2 indicates that notes, bonds, and preferred shares are the primary sources of capital other than common shares (accounts payable and taxes payable are *not* included because they represent interest-free loans to the company from suppliers and the government). These sources and the average amount of each outstanding during 2008 follow:

	Account Balances at December 31		
	2008	2007	AVERAGE
Notes payable	$ 600,000	$ 800,000	$ 700,000
Current portion of bonds	100,000	100,000	100,000
Bonds payable—Long-term	700,000	800,000	750,000
Total liabilities	$1,400,000	$1,700,000	$1,550,000
Preferred shares	$ 500,000	$ 500,000	$ 500,000

What was the cost to Henderson of each of these sources? The cost of the money provided by the preferred shareholders is clearly the amount of dividends of $50,000. The cost as a percentage is $50,000/$500,000, or 10%. The average cost of the borrowed money can be approximated by dividing the 2008 interest expense of $140,000 by the average of the notes payable and bonds payable of $1,550,000. The result is an average cost of these two sources of $140,000/$1,550,000, or approximately 9%.

Leverage The use of borrowed funds and amounts contributed by preferred shareholders to earn an overall return higher than the cost of these funds.

The concept of **leverage** refers to the practice of using borrowed funds and amounts received from preferred shareholders in an attempt to earn an overall return that is higher than the cost of these funds. Recall the rate of return on assets for 2008: 11.8%. Because this return is on an after-tax basis, it is necessary, for comparative purposes, to convert the average cost of borrowed funds to an after-tax basis. Although we computed an average cost for borrowed money of 9%, the actual cost of the borrowed money is 5.4% [9% × (100% − 40%)] after taxes. Because dividends are *not* tax-deductible, the cost of the money provided by preferred shareholders is 10%, as calculated earlier.

Has Henderson successfully employed favourable leverage? That is, has it been able to earn an overall rate of return on assets that is higher than the amounts that it must pay creditors and preferred shareholders? Henderson has been successful in using outside money: neither of the sources must be paid a rate in excess of the 11.8% overall rate on assets used. Also keep in mind that Henderson has been able to borrow some amounts on an interest-free basis. As mentioned earlier, the accounts payable and taxes payable represent interest-free loans from suppliers and the government, although the loans are typically for a short period of time, such as 30 days.

In summary, the excess of the 21.7% return on equity over the 11.8% return on assets indicates that the Henderson management has been successful in employing leverage; that is, there is favourable leverage. Is it possible to be unsuccessful in this pursuit; that is, can there be unfavourable leverage? If the company must pay more for the amounts provided by creditors and preferred shareholders than it can earn overall, as indicated by the return on assets, there will, in fact, be unfavourable leverage. This may occur when interest requirements are high and net income is low. A company would likely have a high debt-to-equity ratio as well when there is unfavourable leverage.

Earnings per Share

Earnings per share A company's bottom line stated on a per-share basis.

Earnings per share is one of the most quoted statistics for publicly traded companies. Shareholders and potential investors want to know what their share of profits is, not just the total dollar amount. Presentation of profits on a per-share basis also allows the shareholder to relate earnings to what he or she paid for a share or to the current trading price of a share.

In simple situations, such as our Henderson Company example, earnings per share (EPS) is calculated as follows:

$$\text{Earnings per Share} = \frac{\textbf{Net Income} - \textbf{Preferred Dividends}}{\textbf{Weighted Average Number of Common Shares Outstanding}}$$

Because Henderson had 1,000,000 common shares outstanding throughout both 2007 and 2008 (see exhibit 13-2), its EPS for each of the two years is as follows:

2008	2007
$\dfrac{\$1,720,000 - \$50,000}{1,000,000 \text{ shares}} = \$1.67 \text{ per share}$	$\dfrac{\$2,300,000 - \$50,000}{1,000,000 \text{ shares}} = \$2.25 \text{ per share}$

A number of complications can arise in the computation of EPS, and the calculations can become exceedingly complex for a company with many different types of securities in its capital structure. These complications are beyond the scope of this book and are discussed in more advanced accounting courses.

Price/Earnings Ratio

Earnings per share is an important ratio for an investor because of its relationship to dividends and market price. Shareholders hope to earn a return by receiving periodic dividends or eventually selling the shares for more than they paid for them, or both. Although earnings are related to dividends and market price, the latter two are of primary interest to the shareholder.

We mentioned earlier the desire of investors to relate the earnings of the company to the market price of the shares. Now that we have stated Henderson's earnings on a per-share basis, we can calculate the **price/earnings (P/E) ratio.** What market price is relevant? Should we use the market price that the investor paid for a share, or should we use the current market price? Because earnings are based on the most recent evaluation of the company for accounting purposes, it seems logical to use current market price, which is based on the stock market's current assessment of the company. Therefore, the ratio is computed as follows:

Price/earnings (P/E) ratio The relationship between a company's performance according to the income statement and its performance in the stock market.

$$\text{Price/Earnings Ratio} = \frac{\textbf{Current Market Price}}{\textbf{Earnings per Share}}$$

Assume that the current market price for Henderson's common stock is $15 per share at the end of 2008 and $18 per share at the end of 2007. The price/earnings ratio for each of the two years is as follows:

2008	2007
$\dfrac{\$15 \text{ per share}}{\$1.67 \text{ per share}} = 9 \text{ to } 1$	$\dfrac{\$18 \text{ per share}}{\$2.25 \text{ per share}} = 8 \text{ to } 1$

What is normal for a P/E ratio? As is the case for all other ratios, it is difficult to generalize as to what is good or bad. The P/E ratio compares the stock market's assessment of a company's performance with its success as reflected on the income statement. A relatively high P/E ratio may indicate that the market expects higher earnings from the company in the future, perhaps because the company has high growth potential. On the other hand, if the market's expectations are overly optimistic, a high P/E ratio could indicate that the market has overpriced the shares.

The P/E ratio is also thought to indicate the "quality" or the "conservativeness" of a company's earnings. For example, assume that Companies A and B have an identical EPS ratio of $2.00. Why should investors be willing to pay $20 (10 times earnings) for each share of Company A but only $14 (or 7 times earnings) for each share of Company B? One possible reason could relate to differences in accounting practices between the two companies. Assume that Company A uses the double-declining-balance method for depreciation and that Company B uses the straight-line method. Here, Company A's EPS would be more conservative than Company B's. Had Company A used the straight-line method, it would have reported a higher EPS. The difference in the P/E ratios of the two companies reflects the market's assessment of the two companies' accounting policies.

The P/E ratio should be used in conjunction with a good understanding of both the underlying business and the nature of the industry, as well as with other financial ratios of the company. There is no straightforward answer as to whether a particular P/E ratio is good or bad. In addition to growth potential and accounting policies, many other factors—such as general economic conditions, the outlook for the particular industry, and pending lawsuits—can affect the trading price of a company's shares.

Summary Report—Profitability

Profitability analysis completes the review of the numbers contained in the financial statements. Previous reviews—vertical and horizontal, liquidity and solvency—have indicated profitability problems resulting from excessive cost increases. The analysis of profitability will permit confirmation of these conclusions and add more in-depth review of the profit picture.

Return on assets presents the profitability of assets independent of how they were financed. The return declined to 11.76% from 18.57% as a result of the return on sales. The relation of assets to sales remained nearly constant, indicating that the decline in return resulted from the expense increase at a rate faster than sales.

The return to common shareholders declined to 22% from 38% as a result of the profit decline and the increase in shareholders' equity. Notice, however, that the return to common shareholders exceeded the return on assets by approximately 10%.

This means financial leverage is positive because the after-tax cost of debt of 5.4% is below the return on assets purchased with the debt, nearly 12%. Thus the financial risk of debt has not resulted in a negative financial leverage to common shareholders.

Earnings per share declined $0.58, resulting in the decline in the return to common shareholders to 1/9 or 11% from 1/8 or 12.5%. The decline in earnings and perhaps the increased risk of business operations resulted in the decline in share price to $15 from $18.

Accounting for Your Decisions

You Are the CEO

You have just been promoted to the chief executive officer position at Orange Computer, a company that has recently fallen on hard times. Sales and earnings have been sluggish. Part of the reason that the prior CEO was dismissed by the board was the lagging share price. Although the typical computer company share price is roughly 25 times earnings, Orange Computer is languishing at just 8 times earnings. What can you do to restore the company's share price?

> **ANSWER:** The best way to boost your company's share price is to restore earnings to levels comparable to those of other companies in the industry. If investors see that you are cutting costs, boosting sales, and restoring earnings, they may see a future earnings and dividends stream from Orange Computer that matches other competing investments. Investors' optimism may well translate to an improved share price.

Summary of Selected Financial Ratios

We have now completed our review of the various ratios used to assess a company's liquidity, solvency, and profitability. For ease of reference, Exhibit 13-7 summarizes the ratios discussed. Keep in mind that this list is not all-inclusive and that certain ratios used by analysts and others may be specific to a particular industry or type of business. Some of the ratios in Exhibit 13-7 were discussed earlier in the textbook; the chapters in which they were discussed are indicated in the exhibit as well.

As noted in the chapter, ratios are not the final answer. Operational investigations and summary writeups of the ratio results provide the conclusions needed to make investment and operational decisions.

Exhibit 13-7 Summary of Selected Financial Ratios

Liquidity Analysis

Working capital	Current Assets − Current Liabilities	Chapter 2
Current ratio	$\dfrac{\text{Current Assets}}{\text{Current Liabilities}}$	Chapter 2
Acid-test ratio (quick ratio)	$\dfrac{\text{Cash + Marketable Securities + Current Receivables}}{\text{Current Liabilities}}$	Chapter 9
Cash flow from operations to current liabilities ratio	$\dfrac{\text{Net Cash Provided by Operating Activities}}{\text{Average Current Liabilities}}$	Chapter 13
Accounts receivable turnover ratio	$\dfrac{\text{Net Credit Sales}}{\text{Average Accounts Receivable}}$	Chapter 7
Number of days' sales in receivables	$\dfrac{\text{Number of Days in the Period}}{\text{Accounts Receivable Turnover}}$	Chapter 13
Inventory turnover ratio	$\dfrac{\text{Cost of Goods Sold}}{\text{Average Inventory}}$	Chapter 6
Number of days' sales in inventory	$\dfrac{\text{Number of Days in the Period}}{\text{Inventory Turnover}}$	Chapter 6
Accounts payable turnover ratio	$\dfrac{\text{Purchases}}{\text{Average Accounts Payable}}$	Chapter 13
Number of days' purchases in payables	$\dfrac{\text{Number of Days in the Period}}{\text{Accounts Payable Turnover}}$	Chapter 13
Cash to cash operating cycle	Number of Days' Sales in Inventory + Number of Days' Sales in Receivables − Number of Days' Purchases in Payables	Chapter 13

Solvency Analysis

Debt-to-equity ratio	$\dfrac{\text{Total Liabilities}}{\text{Total Shareholders' Equity}}$	Chapter 10
Times interest earned ratio	$\dfrac{\text{Net Income + Interest Expense + Income Tax Expense}}{\text{Interest Expense}}$	Chapter 10
Debt service coverage ratio	$\dfrac{\text{Cash Flow from Operations Before Interest and Tax Payments}}{\text{Interest and Principal Payments}}$	Chapter 10

(continued)

Exhibit 13-7 Summary of Selected Financial Ratios (continued)

Cash Flow from Operations to Capital Expenditures Ratio	$\dfrac{\text{(Cash Flow from Operations} - \text{Total Dividends Paid)}}{\text{Cash Paid for Acquisitions}}$	Chapter 13
Profitability Analysis		
Gross profit margin	$\dfrac{\text{Gross Profit}}{\text{Net Sales}}$	Chapter 5
Profit margin	$\dfrac{\text{Net Income}}{\text{Net Sales}}$	Chapter 2
Return on assets ratio	$\dfrac{\text{Net Income} + \text{Interest Expense, Net of Tax}}{\text{Average Total Assets}}$	Chapter 13
Return on sales ratio	$\dfrac{\text{Net Income} + \text{Interest Expense, Net of Tax}}{\text{Net Sales}}$	Chapter 13
Asset turnover ratio	$\dfrac{\text{Net Sales}}{\text{Average Total Assets}}$	Chapter 8
Return on assets	Return on Sales × Asset Turnover	Chapter 13
Return on common shareholders' equity ratio	$\dfrac{\text{Net Income} - \text{Preferred Dividends}}{\text{Average Common Shareholders' Equity}}$	Chapter 13
Earnings per share	$\dfrac{\text{Net Income} - \text{Preferred Dividends}}{\text{Weighted Average Number of Common Shares Outstanding}}$	Chapter 13
Price/earnings ratio	$\dfrac{\text{Current Market Price}}{\text{Earnings per Share}}$	Chapter 13

▪ ADDITIONAL TOPICS ON FINANCIAL STATEMENT ANALYSIS

Benchmarking[3]

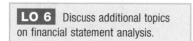
LO 6 Discuss additional topics on financial statement analysis.

What kind of return on a particular company should be considered satisfactory? What level of current ratio indicates adequate liquidity? What level of debt/equity ratio indicates a manageable risk level? As stated before in this book, there are no standard answers to these questions. For example, the number of days' sales in inventory typically runs a couple of weeks for food retailers because of the perishable nature of most of their inventory, whereas the number of days' sales in inventory for a department store is usually several months. This means that the financial ratios of a single company for a single period yield limited information.

Analysts usually compare a company's ratios against some kind of "standard" or "benchmark" when assessing its financial performance and condition. For example, a comparison of the financial ratios of the same company over several periods can reveal recent changes that might affect future profitability and financial condition. A comparison of the ratios of a given company with those of industry leaders can reveal unrealized

---

[3]The word benchmark here means a reference point used for comparison. In management science, benchmark is more specifically defined as the best practice.

potential. Various organizations publish summaries of selected ratios in specific industries. For example, *Dun & Bradstreet's Industry Norms and Key Business Ratios* is an annual review that organizes companies into major industry segments and approximately 800 specific lines of business. Exhibit 13-8 shows the selected ratios of companies in Canada's Retail Trade sector, published by Statistics Canada.

Exhibit 13-8 Selected Ratios of the Companies in the Segment of Retail Trade

	THIRD QUARTER 2006	FOURTH QUARTER 2006	FIRST QUARTER 2007	SECOND QUARTER 2007	THIRD QUARTER 2007
Selected financial ratios					
Debt to equity (ratio)	1.187	1.122	1.157	1.169	1.099
Profit margin (%)	3.4	3.4	3.7	3.7	3.8
Return on equity (%)	15.8	9.4	19.4	16.2	16.8
Return on capital employed (%)	9.8	7.4	10.7	9.8	10.2

Source: Statistics Canada. Quarterly Financial Statistics for Enterprises, Third Quarter 2007. Catalogue No. 61-008, p. 38.

Although comparisons within a given industry are useful, caution is necessary when interpreting the results of such analyses. Few companies in today's economy operate within a single industry. *Conglomerates*—companies operating in more than one industry—present a special challenge to the analysts.

Forecast Financial Information

Financial statements reported under GAAP are based on transactions that have already taken place. A key characteristic of financial statements is that predictions can be developed from them. Analysts routinely publish forecasts of key financial information, such as EPS, sales revenue, cash flow, and net book values. Exhibit 13-9 shows financial analysts'

Exhibit 13-9 I/B/E/S Forecasts of CN's Earnings per Share and Cash Flow per Share

FORECASTS PROVIDED BY IBES CANADIAN NATIONAL RAILWAY COMPANY							
Consensus Recommendation of 13 Analysts							Buy
Consensus Target Price of 12 Analysts							$58.15
Consensus Information – EPS $							
Periods	Date	# Ests.	Mean	High	Low	Up	Down
Quarter Ending:	Mar/08	10	0.68	0.82	0.60	0	1
Quarter Ending:	Jun/08	9	0.98	1.02	0.93	0	1
Quarter Ending:	Sep/08	9	1.00	1.03	0.91	0	1
Quarter Ending:	Dec/08	9	0.96	1.04	0.92	0	1
2008	Dec	12	3.63	3.70	3.54	0	1
2009	Dec	10	4.18	4.35	4.02	0	0
LTG %		1	11.00	11.00	11.00	0	0
Consensus Information – Cash Flow Per Share $							
Periods	Date	# Ests.	Mean	High	Low	Up	Down
Quarter Ending:	Mar/08	2	0.53	1.01	0.04	0	0
Quarter Ending:	Jun/08	2	0.97	1.44	0.49	0	0
Quarter Ending:	Sep/08	2	0.87	1.44	0.29	0	0
Quarter Ending:	Dec/08	2	0.88	1.36	0.39	0	0
2008	Dec	6	4.83	6.23	1.19	0	1
2009	Dec	6	5.39	6.55	1.61	1	0

Source: Institutional Brokers Estimate System.

forecasts of CN's earnings per share and cash flow per share made by the International Brokers Estimate System (I/B/E/S), a subdivision of Standard & Poor's (S&P).

Managers often used forecasted financial statements, referred to as pro forma statements, when communicating their predictions to current and potential investors and creditors. The management of a public company is required to discuss the company's future in the annual report in a Management Discussion and Analysis (MD&A) section. Public companies that intend to issue shares or bonds are required to release projected financial statements in a document called a prospectus. Entrepreneurs seeking capital or a loan to finance a business often prepare a business plan that includes a set of projected financial statements, the purpose being to communicate their vision of the business. Forecasted financial statements can be prepared based on some basic forecasts such as sales volume, sales price, costs of material and labour, and so on. Financial ratios can be used to estimate other items in order to complete the financial statements.

For example, if forecasted annual sales revenue is $200,000 for a company in the industry with an average accounts receivable turnover ratio of 8, the ending balance of Accounts Receivable can be estimated as follows:

Accounts Receivable Turnover Ratio = Sales Revenue / Accounts Receivable
Accounts Receivable = Sales Revenue / Accounts Receivable Turnover
= $200,000/8 = $25,000

Assume that the industry's average gross profit margin is 40% and that the inventory turnover ratio is 6 times:

Cost of Goods Sold = Sales Revenue × (1 − Gross Profit Margin)
= $200,000 × (1 − 40%) = $120,000

Since

Inventory Turnover Ratio = Cost of Goods Sold / Inventory

Thus,

Inventory = Cost of Goods Sold / Inventory Turnover Ratio
= $120,000/6 = $20,000

Limitations of Financial Statement Analysis

It is important to understand that there are limitations to financial statement analysis and that care should be taken when drawing conclusions based on financial statement analysis. In the next section we discuss the potential effects of alternative accounting methods and inflation.

Alternative Accounting Methods   The effects of every set of financial statements are based on various assumptions. For example, a cost-flow method must be assumed when valuing inventory and recognizing cost of goods sold. The accountant chooses FIFO, LIFO, or one of the other acceptable methods. The analyst or other user finds this type of information in the notes to the financial statements. The selection of a particular inventory valuation method has a significant effect on certain key ratios. Recognition of the acceptable alternatives is especially important when two or more companies are being compared. *Changes* in accounting methods, such as a change in the depreciation method, also make comparing results for a given company over time more difficult. Again, the reader must turn to the notes for information regarding these changes.

Besides the flexibility with GAAP, the GAAP rules are in the process of change. Two general types of changes are occurring. Public companies (some refinement of the application of GAAP beyond public companies exists in practice) such as CN and CP are the main focus of the GAAP rules presented in this book, and the major emphasis of the CICA Handbook. These accounting standards in Canada and the United States are migrating to GAAP published by the IASB. The deadline for this migration in Canada has been set for 2011. The specifics of the changes are somewhat unclear at present but the proposals do suggest the need for monitoring future developments.

Smaller companies (often termed private companies, technically termed non publicly accountable firms) are also in the process of changing their GAAP. These companies are by far the most numerous in Canada but they are typically smaller in size and do not sell their shares to the general public. Whether they will migrate to IASB GAAP for Canada is unclear at present, but credit analysts and investors in such companies will need to monitor upcoming changes so that misinterpretations do not occur.

The Possible Effects of Inflation   Inflation, or an increase in the level of prices, is another important consideration in analyzing financial statements. Statements are based on historical costs and are not adjusted for the effects of increasing prices. For example, consider the following trend in a company's sales for the past three years:

	2008	2007	2006
Net sales	$121,000	$110,000	$100,000

As measured by the actual dollars of sales, sales have increased by 10% each year. Caution is necessary in concluding that the company is better off in each succeeding year because of the increase in sales *dollars*. Assume, for example, that 2006 sales of $100,000 are the result of selling 100,000 units at $1 each. Are 2007 sales of $110,000 the result of selling 110,000 units at $1 each or of selling 100,000 units at $1.10 each? Although on the surface it may seem unimportant which accounts for the sales increase, the answer can have significant ramifications. If the company found it necessary to increase the selling price to $1.10 in the face of increasing *costs,* it may be no better off than it was in 2006 in terms of gross profit. On the other hand, if the company is able to increase sales revenue by 10% primarily based on growth in unit sales, then its performance would be considered stronger than if the increase were merely due to a price increase. The point to be made is one of caution: published financial statements are stated in historical costs and therefore have not been adjusted for the effects of inflation.

Answers to the Two-Minute Reviews

Two-Minute Review on page 635

1. Horizontal analysis is used to compare a particular financial statement item over a period of time, whereas vertical analysis allows someone to compare various financial statement items within a single period. With vertical analysis, all of the items are stated as a percentage of a specific item on that statement, such as sales on the income statement or total assets on the balance sheet.

2. Horizontal analysis could be used to examine the trend in accounts receivable over recent years.

3. Vertical analysis could be used to examine the relationship between selling and administrative expenses and sales. However, you may also want to compare this percentage with the ratio in prior years (thus, you would be performing horizontal analysis as well).

Two-Minute Review on page 645

1. Liquidity is a relative measure of the nearness to cash of the assets and liabilities of a company. Measures of liquidity are intended to determine the company's ability to pay its debts as they come due. Solvency refers to a company's ability to remain in business over the long term. Liquidity and solvency are certainly related, but the latter takes a much more long-term view of the financial health of the company.

2. Because you need to assess the ability of the company to pay its account on a timely basis, you would be more concerned with the liquidity of the company over the short term.

Chapter Highlights

1. **LO 1** Use comparative financial statements to analyze a company over time (horizontal analysis) (p. 630).

   - Horizontal analysis uses comparative financial statements to examine the increases and decreases in items from one period to the next. The analysis can look at the change in items over an extended period of time. Many companies present a summary of selected financial items for a 5- or 10-year period.

2. **LO 2** Use common-size financial statements to compare various financial statement items (vertical analysis) (p. 633).

   - Vertical analysis involves stating all items on a particular financial statement as a percentage of one item on the statement. For example, all expenses on a common-size income statement are stated as a percentage of net sales. This technique, along with horizontal analysis, can be useful in spotting problem areas within a company.

3. **LO 3** Compute and use various ratios to assess liquidity (p. 635).

   - Ratios can be categorized according to their primary purpose. Liquidity ratios indicate the company's ability to pay its bills as they are due. The focus of liquidity analysis is on a company's current assets and current liabilities.

4. **LO 4** Compute and use various ratios to assess solvency (p. 641).

   - Solvency ratios deal with a company's long-term financial health, that is, its ability to repay long-term creditors. The right side of the balance sheet is informative in this respect because it reports on the various sources of capital to the business.

5. **LO 5** Compute and use various ratios to assess profitability (p. 645).

   - Profitability ratios measure how well management has used the assets at its disposal to earn a return for the various providers of capital. Return on assets indicates the return to all providers; return on common shareholders' equity measures the return to the residual owners of the business. Certain other ratios are used to relate a company's performance according to the financial statements with its performance in the stock market.

6. **LO 6** Discuss additional topics on financial statement analysis (p. 652).

   - Financial ratios are much more revealing when compared with some kind of "standard" or "benchmark." Ratios can be used to prepare forward-looking financial statements. Knowledge of GAAP details and upcoming changes can help prevent misinterpretations.

Key Terms Quiz

Because of the number of terms introduced in this chapter, there are two key terms quizzes. For each quiz, read each of the following definitions and then write the number of that definition in the blank beside the appropriate term it defines. The quiz solutions appear at the end of the chapter.

Quiz 1:

_____ Horizontal analysis	_____ Accounts receivable turnover ratio
_____ Vertical analysis	_____ Number of days' sales in receivables
_____ Gross profit margin	_____ Inventory turnover ratio
_____ Profit margin	_____ Number of days' sales in inventory
_____ Liquidity	_____ Accounts payable turnover
_____ Working capital	_____ Number of days' purchases in payables
_____ Current ratio	
_____ Acid-test or quick ratio	_____ Cash to cash operating cycle
_____ Cash flow from operations to current liabilities ratio	

1. A stricter test of liquidity than the current ratio; excludes inventory and prepayments from the numerator.
2. Current assets minus current liabilities.
3. The ratio of current assets to current liabilities.
4. A measure of the average age of accounts receivable.
5. A measure of the ability to pay current debts from operating cash flows.
6. A measure of the number of times accounts receivable are collected in a period.
7. A measure of how long it takes to sell inventory.
8. The length of time from the payment of the purchase of inventory to the collection of any receivable from the sale.

9. A measure of the number of times inventory is sold during a period.
10. Gross profit to net sales.
11. A comparison of various financial statement items within a single period with the use of common-size statements.
12. Net income to net sales.
13. The ability to pay bills as they become due.
14. A comparison of financial statement items over a period of time.
15. A measure of the number of times accounts payable are paid in a period.
16. A measure of average age of accounts payable.

Quiz 2:

_____	Solvency	_____	Asset turnover ratio
_____	Debt-to-equity ratio	_____	Return on common shareholders' equity ratio
_____	Times interest earned ratio		
_____	Debt service coverage ratio	_____	Leverage
_____	Profitability	_____	Earnings per share
_____	Return on assets ratio	_____	Price/earnings (P/E) ratio
_____	Return on sales ratio		

1. A measure of a company's success in earning a return for the common shareholders.

2. The relationship between a company's performance according to the income statement and its performance in the stock market.

3. The ability of a company to remain in business over the long term.

4. A variation of the profit margin ratio; measures earnings before payments to creditors.

5. A company's bottom line stated on a per-share basis.

6. How well management is using company resources to earn a return on the funds invested by various groups.

7. The ratio of total liabilities to total shareholders' equity.

8. A measure of a company's success in earning a return for all providers of capital.

9. The relationship between net sales and total assets.

10. The use of borrowed funds and amounts contributed by preferred shareholders to earn an overall return higher than the cost of these funds.

11. An income statement measure of the ability of a company to meet its interest payments.

12. A statement of cash flows measure of the ability of a company to meet its interest and principal payments.

Answers on p. 687.

Alternate Terms

Acid-test ratio Quick ratio
Horizontal analysis Trend analysis

Number of days' sales in receivables Average collection period
Price/earnings ratio P/E ratio

Warmup Exercises and Solutions

Warmup Exercise 13-1 *Types of Ratios* LO 3, 4, 5

Fill in the blanks that follow to indicate whether each of the following ratios is concerned with a company's liquidity (L), its solvency (S), or its profitability (P).

_____ 1. Return on assets ratio
_____ 2. Current ratio
_____ 3. Debt-to-equity ratio
_____ 4. Earnings per share
_____ 5. Inventory turnover ratio
_____ 6. Gross profit ratio

Key to the Solution Review the summary of selected ratios in Exhibit 13-7.

Warmup Exercise 13-2 *Accounts Receivable Turnover* LO 3

Company X reported sales during the year of $500,000. Its average accounts receivable balance during the year was $125,000. Company Y reported sales during the same year of $200,000 and had an average accounts receivable balance of $20,000.

Required

1. Compute the accounts receivable turnover for both companies.

2. What is the average length of time each company takes to collect its receivables?

Key to the Solution Review the summary of selected ratios in Exhibit 13-7.

Warmup Exercise 13-3 *Earnings Per Share* LO 5

Company P reported net income during the year of $45,000 and paid dividends of $75,000 to its common shareholders and $5,000 to its preferred shareholders. During the year, 10,000 common shares were outstanding and 5,000 preferred shares were outstanding.

Required

Compute earnings per share for the year.

(continued)

Key to the Solution Recall that earnings per share only has relevance to the common shareholders and therefore it is a measure of the earnings per common share outstanding, after taking into account any claims of preferred shareholders.

Solutions to Warmup Exercises

Warmup Exercise 13-1
1. P 2. L 3. S 4. P 5. L 6. P

Warmup Exercise 13-2
1. Company X turns over its accounts receivable, on the average, 4 times during the year ($500,000/$125,000) and Company Y 10 times during the year ($200,000/$20,000).

2. Assuming 360 days in a year, Company X takes, on the average, 90 days to collect its accounts receivable, and Company Y takes, on the average, 36 days.

Warmup Exercise 13-3
Earnings per share: ($45,000 − $5,000)/10,000 shares = $4 per share.

Review Problem and Solutions

On pages 659–662 are the comparative financial statements for Chew Company, a chewing gum manufacturer.

Required

1. Compute the following ratios for the two years 2008 and 2007, either for each year or as of the end of each of the years, as appropriate. Beginning balances for 2007 are not available; that is, you do not have a balance sheet as of the end of 2006. Therefore, to be consistent, use year-end balances for both years where you would normally use average amounts for the year. To compute the return on assets ratio, you will need to find the tax rate. Use the relationship between income taxes and earnings before taxes to find the rate for each year.

   a. Current ratio
   b. Quick ratio
   c. Cash flow from operations to current liabilities ratio
   d. Number of days' sales in receivables
   e. Number of days' sales in inventory
   f. Debt-to-equity ratio
   g. Debt service coverage ratio
   h. Return on assets ratio
   i. Return on common shareholders' equity ratio

2. Comment on Chew's liquidity. Has it improved or declined over the two-year period?

3. Does Chew appear to be solvent to you? Does there appear to be anything unusual about its capital structure?

4. Comment on Chew's profitability. Would you buy shares of the company?

Solution to Review Problem

1. Ratios:

   a. 2008: $913,843/$332,324 = 2.75
      2007: $828,715/$288,210 = 2.88

   b. 2008: ($307,785 + $25,450 + $239,885)/$332,324 = 1.72
      2007: ($300,599 + $29,301 + $191,570)/$288,210 = 1.81

   c. 2008: $390,491/$332,324 = 1.18
      2007: $448,283/$288,210 = 1.56

Chew Company Consolidated Statement of Earnings

	2008	2007
EARNINGS		
Net sales	$2,429,646	$2,145,706
Cost of sales	997,054	904,266
Gross profit	1,432,592	1,241,440
Selling and general administrative expense	919,236	778,197
Operating income	513,356	463,243
Investment income	18,553	19,185
Other expense	(4,543)	(3,116)
Earnings before income taxes	527,366	479,312
Income taxes	164,380	150,370
Net earnings	$ 362,986	$ 328,942
PER SHARE AMOUNTS		
Net earnings per common share (basic and diluted)	$ 1.61	$ 1.45
Dividends paid per common share	$ 0.745	$ 0.70

d. 2008: 360 days/[($2,429,646/$239,885)] = 360/10.13 = <u>36 days</u>

   2007: 360 days/[($2,145,706/$191,570)] = 360/11.20 = <u>32 days</u>

e. 2008: 360 days/[($997,054/$278,981)] = 360/3.57 = <u>101 days</u>

   2007: 360 days/[($904,266/$253,291)] = 360/3.57 = <u>101 days</u>

f. 2008: ($332,324 + $43,206 + $113,921)/$1,276,197 = <u>0.38</u>

   2007: ($288,210 + $40,144 + $113,489)/$1,132,897 = <u>0.39</u>

g. 2008: ($390,491 + $146,858 + $1,101)/$1,101 = <u>489</u>

   2007: ($448,283 + $136,311 + $749)/$749 = <u>781</u>

h. 2008: $362,986 + [$1,101[a](1 − 0.31[b])]/$1,765,648 = <u>20.6%</u>

   2007: $328,942 + [$749[a](1 − 0.31[b])]/$1,574,740 = <u>20.9%</u>

i. 2008: $362,986/$1,276,197[c] = <u>28.4%</u>

   2007: $328,942/$1,132,897[c] = <u>29.0%</u>

---

[a]Chew does not separately disclose interest expense on its income statement; the amounts of interest paid that are reported at bottom of statement of cash flows have been used for the calculations.

[b]The effective tax rate for each of the two years:

  2008: $164,380/$527,366 = 0.31

  2007: $150,370/$479,312 = 0.31

[c]In addition to its common shares, Chew has outstanding Class B common shares. Because this is a second class of shares (similar in many respects to preferred shares), the contributed capital attributable to it should be deducted from total shareholders' equity in the denominator. Similarly, any dividends paid on the Class B common shares should be deducted from net income in the numerator to find the return to the regular common shareholders. We have ignored the difficulties involved in determining these adjustments in our calculations of return on equity.

Chew Company Consolidated Statement of Cash Flows

	2008	2007
OPERATING ACTIVITIES		
Net earnings	$362,986	$328,942
Adjustments to reconcile net earnings to net cash provided by operating activities:		
Depreciation	68,326	57,880
Loss on sales of property, plant and equipment	2,910	778
(Increase) Decrease in:		
Accounts receivable	(53,162)	(18,483)
Inventories	(29,487)	(2,812)
Other current assets	(8,079)	199
Deferred charges and other assets	(6,931)	30,408
Increase in:		
Accounts payable	20,365	12,988
Accrued expenses	16,532	18,015
Income and other taxes payable	9,565	14,670
Future income taxes	5,570	2,546
Other non-current liabilities	1,896	3,152
Net cash provided by operating activities	390,491	448,283
INVESTING ACTIVITIES		
Additions to property, plant, and equipment	(181,760)	(125,068)
Proceeds from property retirements	2,376	1,128
Purchases of short-term investments	(24,448)	(125,728)
Maturities of short-term investments	26,835	115,007
Net cash used in investing activities	(176,997)	(134,661)
FINANCING ACTIVITIES		
Dividends paid	(167,922)	(159,138)
Common shares purchased, net	(34,173)	(131,765)
Net cash used in financing activities	(202,095)	(290,903)
Effect of exchange rate changes on cash and cash equivalents	(4,213)	(10,506)
Net increase in cash and cash equivalents	7,186	12,213
Cash and cash equivalents at beginning of year	300,599	288,386
Cash and cash equivalents at end of year	$307,785	$300,599
SUPPLEMENTAL CASH FLOW INFORMATION		
Income taxes paid	$146,858	$136,311
Interest paid	$ 1,101	$ 749
Interest and dividends received	$ 18,570	$ 19,243

Chew Company Consolidated Balance Sheet

	2008	2007
ASSETS		
Current assets:		
Cash and cash equivalents	$ 307,785	$ 300,599
Short-term investments, at amortized cost	25,450	29,301
Accounts receivable		
(less allowance for doubtful accounts: 2008—$7,712; 2007—$7,065)	239,885	191,570
Inventories		
Finished goods	75,693	64,676
Raw materials and supplies	203,288	188,615
	278,981	253,291
Other current assets	46,896	39,728
Future income taxes—current	14,846	14,226
Total current assets	913,843	828,715
Marketable equity securities, at fair value	25,300	28,535
Deferred charges and other assets	115,745	83,713
Future income taxes—non-current	26,381	26,743
Property, plant, and equipment, at cost:		
Land	39,933	39,125
Buildings and building equipment	359,109	344,457
Machinery and equipment	857,054	756,050
	1,256,096	1,139,632
Less accumulated depreciation	571,717	532,598
Net property, plant, and equipment	684,379	607,034
TOTAL ASSETS	$1,765,648	$1,574,740

(continued)

2. Although both the current ratio and the quick ratio declined during 2008, neither was a very significant decrease. Cash flow from operations to current liabilities declined more significantly, although the ratio at the end of 2008 was still greater than 1 to 1 overall. Chew appears to be quite liquid and should have no problems meeting its short-term obligations.

3. Chew is extremely solvent. Its capital structure reveals that it does not rely in any significant way on long-term debt to finance its business. The amount of non-current liabilities is less than 10% of total liabilities and shareholders' equity at the end of each year. In fact, a majority of Chew's debt is in the form of interest-free current liabilities. Most revealing is the debt service coverage ratio of 489 times in 2008 and 781 times in 2007. The total interest expense each year is insignificant.

Consolidated Balance Sheet (continued)

	2008	2007
LIABILITIES AND SHAREHOLDERS' EQUITY		
Current liabilities:		
Accounts payable	$ 91,225	$ 73,129
Accrued expenses	128,436	113,779
Dividends payable	42,741	39,467
Income and other taxes payable	68,467	60,976
Future income taxes—current	1,455	859
Total current liabilities	332,324	288,210
Future income taxes—non-current	43,206	40,144
Other non-current liabilities	113,921	113,489
Shareholders' equity:		
Preferred stock		
Authorized: 20,000 shares		
Issued: None		
Common stock		
Common Stock		
Authorized: 400,000 shares		
Issued: 2008—189,800 shares; 2007—188,368 shares	12,646	12,558
Class B Common Stock—convertible		
Authorized: 80,000 shares		
Issued and outstanding:		
2008—42,641 shares; 2007—44,073 shares	2,850	2,938
Retained earnings	1,246,427	1,100,050
Unrealized holding gains on marketable equity securities	14,274	17,351
Total shareholders' equity	1,276,197	1,132,897
TOTAL LIABILITIES AND SHAREHOLDERS' EQUITY	$1,765,648	$1,574,740

4. The return on assets for 2008 is 20.6%, and the return on common shareholders' equity is 28.4%. Although these return ratios are down slightly from the prior year, they indicate a very profitable company. It should be noted that the company paid nearly half of its 2008 earnings in dividends. Chew appears to be a very sound investment, but many other factors, including information on the current market price of the shares, should be considered before making a decision.

1. Two companies are in the same industry. Company A uses the weighted average method of inventory valuation, and Company B uses FIFO. What difficulties does this present when comparing the two companies?

2. You are told to compare the company's results for the year, as measured by various ratios, with one of the published surveys that arranges information by industry classification. What are some of the difficulties you may encounter when making comparisons using industry standards?

3. What types of problems does inflation cause in analyzing financial statements?

4. Distinguish between horizontal and vertical analysis. Why is the analysis of common-size statements called *vertical* analysis? Why is horizontal analysis sometimes called *trend* analysis?

5. A company experiences a 15% increase in sales over the previous year. However, gross profit actually decreased by 5% from the previous year. What are some of the possible causes for an increase in sales but a decline in gross profit?

6. A company's total current assets have increased by 5% over the prior year. Management is concerned, however, about the composition of the current assets. Why is the composition of current assets important?

7. Ratios were categorized in the chapter according to their use in performing three different types of analysis. What are the three types of ratios?

8. Describe the operating cycle for a retail company.

9. What accounts for the order in which current assets are presented on a balance sheet?

10. A company has a current ratio of 1.25 but an acid-test or quick ratio of only 0.65. How can this difference in the two ratios be explained? What are some concerns that you would have about this company?

11. Explain the basic concept underlying all turnover ratios. Why is it advisable in computing a turnover ratio to use an average in the denominator (for example, average inventory)?

12. Sanders Company's accounts receivable turned over nine times during the year. The credit department extends terms of 2/10, net 30. Does the turnover ratio indicate any problems that management should investigate?

13. The turnover of inventory for Ace Company has slowed from 6.0 times per year to 4.5 times. What are some of the possible explanations for this decrease?

14. A higher accounts receivable turnover ratio means greater efficiency in managing accounts, and thus is more desirable. Is the same true for the accounts payable turnover ratio?

15. What is the difference between liquidity analysis and solvency analysis?

16. Why is the debt service coverage ratio a better measure of solvency than the times interest earned ratio?

17. A friend tells you that the best way to assess solvency is by comparing total debt to total assets. Another friend says that solvency is measured by comparing total debt to total shareholders' equity. Which one is right?

18. A company is in the process of negotiating with a bank for an additional loan. Why will the bank be very interested in the company's debt service coverage ratio?

19. What is the rationale for deducting dividends when computing the ratio of cash flow from operations to capital expenditures?

20. The rate of return on assets ratio is computed by dividing net income and interest expense, net of tax, by average total assets. Why is the numerator net income and interest expense, net of tax, rather than just net income?

21. A company has a return on assets of 14% and a return on common shareholders' equity of 11%. The president of the company has asked you to explain the reason for this difference. What causes the difference? How is the concept of financial leverage involved?

22. What is meant by the "quality" of a company's earnings? Explain why the price/earnings ratio for a company may indicate the quality of earnings.

23. Some ratios are more useful for management, whereas others are better suited to the needs of outsiders, such as shareholders and bankers. What is an example of a ratio that is primarily suited to management use? What is one that is more suited to use by outsiders?

24. The needs of service-oriented companies in analyzing financial statements differ from those of product-oriented companies. Why is this true? Give an example of a ratio that is meaningless to a service business.

Exercises

Exercise 13-1 *Accounts Receivable Analysis* **LO 3**

The following account balances are taken from the records of the Fresh Advertising Agency:

	December 31		
	2008	**2007**	**2006**
Accounts receivable	$300,000	$200,000	$160,000

	2008	**2007**	
Net credit sales	$1,200,000	$1,080,000	

Fresh extends credit terms requiring full payment in 60 days, with no discount for early payment.

(continued)

Required

1. Compute Fresh's accounts receivable turnover ratio for 2008 and 2007.

2. Compute the number of days' sales in receivables for 2008 and 2007. Assume 360 days in a year.

3. Comment on the efficiency of Fresh's collection efforts over the two-year period.

Exercise 13-2 *Inventory Analysis* LO 3

The following account balances are taken from the records of Jake's Ltd., a wholesaler of fresh fruits and vegetables:

	December 31		
	2008	**2007**	**2006**
Merchandise inventory	$100,000	$75,000	$60,000
	2008	**2007**	
Cost of goods sold	$3,550,000	$4,050,000	

Required

1. Compute Jake's inventory turnover ratio for 2008 and 2007.

2. Compute the number of days' sales in inventory for 2008 and 2007. Assume 360 days in a year.

3. Comment on your answers in requirements 1 and 2 relative to the company's management of inventory over the two years. What problems do you see in its inventory management?

Exercise 13-3 *Accounts Receivable and Inventory Analyses for Two Companies in the Same Industry* LO 3

The following has been extracted from the financial statements of two frozen food companies, Cold Company and Frozen Company:

(in thousands)		Cold	Frozen
Accounts receivable, net	12/31/08	$ 941	$ 1,071
	12/31/07	878	1,064
Inventories	12/31/08	528	655
	12/31/07	533	596
Accounts payable	12/31/08	310	366
	12/31/07	317	374
Net sales	2008	10,046	13,468
	2007	9,945	12,739
Cost of goods sold	2008	3,022	5,377
	2007	3,102	5,113

Required

1. Using the information provided above, compute the following for each company for 2008:

   a. Accounts receivable turnover ratio

   b. Number of days' sales in receivables

   c. Inventory turnover ratio

   d. Number of days' sales in inventory

   e. Accounts payable turnover

   f. Number of days' purchases in payables

   g. Cash to cash operating cycle

2. Comment briefly on the liquidity of each of these two companies.

Exercise 13-4 *Liquidity Analyses for Two Companies* **LO 3**

The following information was summarized from the balance sheets of two frozen food companies, Cold Company and Frozen Company:

(in thousands)	Cold	Frozen
Cash and cash equivalents	$ 933	$ 341
Short-term investments/marketable securities	34	483
Accounts receivable, net	941	1,071
Inventories	528	655
Prepaid expenses and other current assets	1,150	376
Total current assets	$3,586	$2,926
Current liabilities	$4,215	$2,499
Other liabilities	1,311	4,012
Shareholders' equity	5,683	4,337

Required

1. Using the information provided above, compute the following for each company at the end of 2008:

    a. Current ratio

    b. Quick ratio

2. Comment briefly on the liquidity of each of these two companies. Which appears to be more liquid?

3. What other ratios would help you to more fully assess the liquidity of these companies?

Exercise 13-5 *Solvency Analyses* **LO 4**

The following information was obtained from the comparative financial statements of Clothes Inc. (all amounts are in thousands of dollars):

	March 31, 2008	March 31, 2007
Total liabilities	$497	$552
Total shareholders' equity	674	639

For the Fiscal Years Ended March 31

	2008	2007
Interest expense	$ 21	$ 21
Provision for income taxes	21	28
Net income	65	86
Net cash provided by operating activities	95	116
Total dividends paid	—	—
Cash used to purchase property and equipment	37	76
Payments on long-term debt	25	20

Required

1. Using the information provided above, compute the following for 2008 and 2007:

    a. Debt-to-equity ratio (at each year-end)

    b. Times interest earned ratio

    c. Debt service coverage ratio

    d. Cash Flow from operations to capital expenditures ratio

2. Comment briefly on the company's solvency.

Exercise 13-6 *Solvency Analysis* LO 4

The following information is available from the balance sheets at the ends of the two most recent years and the income statement for the most recent year of Maggie Company:

	December 31	
	2008	**2007**
Accounts payable	$ 130,000	$ 100,000
Accrued liabilities	50,000	70,000
Taxes payable	120,000	90,000
Short-term notes payable	0	150,000
Bonds payable due within next year	400,000	400,000
Total current liabilities	700,000	810,000
Bonds payable	1,200,000	1,600,000
Common shares	2,000,000	2,000,000
Retained earnings	1,300,000	1,000,000
Total shareholders' equity	3,300,000	3,000,000
Total liabilities and shareholders' equity	$5,200,000	$5,410,000

	2008
Sales revenue	$3,200,000
Cost of goods sold	1,900,000
Gross profit	1,300,000
Selling and administrative expense	600,000
Operating income	700,000
Interest expense	178,000
Income before tax	522,000
Income tax expense	222,000
Net income	$ 300,000

Other Information

a. Short-term notes payable represents a 12-month loan that matured in November 2008. Interest of 6% was paid at maturity.

b. Two million dollars of serial bonds had been issued 10 years earlier. The first series of $400,000 matured at the end of 2008, with interest of 4% payable annually.

c. Cash flow from operations was $370,000 in 2008. The amounts of interest and taxes paid during 2008 were $178,000 and $192,000, respectively.

Required

1. Compute the following for Maggie Company:

    a. The debt-to-equity ratio at December 31, 2008, and December 31, 2007

    b. The times interest earned ratio for 2008

    c. The debt service coverage ratio for 2008

2. Comment on Maggie's solvency at the end of 2008. Do the times interest earned ratio and the debt service coverage ratio differ in their indication of Impact's ability to pay its debts?

Exercise 13-7 *Return Ratios and Leverage* LO 5

The following selected data are taken from the financial statements of Enviro Company:

Sales revenue	$1,300,000
Cost of goods sold	800,000
Gross profit	500,000
Selling and administrative expense	200,000
Operating income	300,000
Interest expense	100,000
Income before tax	200,000
Income tax expense (40%)	80,000
Net income	$ 120,000

Accounts payable	$ 90,000
Accrued liabilities	140,000
Income taxes payable	20,000
Interest payable	50,000
Short-term loans payable	300,000
Total current liabilities	600,000
Long-term bonds payable	1,000,000
Preferred stock, $10, 5,000 shares issued and outstanding	500,000
Common stock	1,200,000
Retained earnings	700,000
Total shareholders' equity	2,400,000
Total liabilities and shareholders' equity	$4,000,000

Required

1. Compute the following ratios for Enviro Company:

   a. Return on sales

   b. Asset turnover (assume that total assets at the beginning of the year were $3,200,000)

   c. Return on assets

   d. Return on common shareholders' equity (assume that the only changes in shareholders' equity during the year were from the net income for the year and dividends on the preferred shares)

2. Comment on Enviro's use of leverage. Has it successfully employed leverage? Explain.

Exercise 13-8 *Relationships Among Return on Assets, Return on Sales, and Asset Turnover* **LO 5**

A company's return on assets is a function of its ability to turn over its investment (asset turnover) and earn a profit on each dollar of sales (return on sales). For each of the *independent* cases below, determine the missing amounts. (*Note:* Assume in each case that the company has no interest expense; that is, net income is used as the definition of income in all calculations.)

Case 1

Net income	$5,000
Net sales	$40,000
Average total assets	$30,000
Return on assets	?

Case 2

Net income	$12,500
Average total assets	$125,000
Return on sales	2%
Net sales	?

Case 3

Average total assets	$40,000
Asset turnover	1.5 times
Return on sales	6%
Return on assets	?

Case 4

Return on assets	10%
Net sales	$100,000
Asset turnover	1.25 times
Net income	?

Case 5

Return on assets	15%
Net income	$40,000
Return on sales	5%
Average total assets	?

Exercise 13-9 *EPS and P/E Ratio* **LO 5**

The shareholders' equity section of the balance sheet for North Co. at the end of 2008 appears as follows:

$8, preferred shares, 200,000 shares authorized,	
25,000 shares issued and outstanding	$ 3,750,000
Common shares, 500,000 shares authorized,	
200,000 shares issued and outstanding	10,000,000
Retained earnings	18,750,000
Total shareholders' equity	$32,500,000

Net income for the year was $650,000. The closing market price for the common shares on December 31, 2008, was $12.50 per share.

Required

1. Compute the following ratios for the common shares:

   a. Earnings per share

   b. Price/earnings ratio

2. Assume that you are an investment adviser. What other information would you want to have before advising a client regarding the purchase of North Co. shares?

Exercise 13-10 *Earnings Per Share and Extraordinary Items* **LO 5**

The shareholders' equity section of the balance sheet for Lahey Construction Company at the end of 2008 follows:

$9, preferred	
500,000 shares authorized,	
100,000 shares issued and outstanding	$ 4,750,000
Common shares, 2,500,000 authorized,	
750,000 issued and outstanding	11,250,000
Retained earnings	12,750,000
Total shareholders' equity	$28,750,000

The lower portion of the 2008 income statement indicates the following:

Net income before tax		$ 4,875,000
Income tax expense (40%)		(1,950,000)
Income before extraordinary items		2,925,000
Extraordinary loss from flood	$(3,100,000)	
Less related tax effect (40%)	1,240,000	(1,860,000)
Net income		$ 1,065,000

Assume the number of shares outstanding did not change during the year.

Required

1. Compute earnings per share *before* extraordinary items.

2. Compute earnings per share *after* the extraordinary loss.

3. Which of the two EPS ratios is more useful to management? Explain your answer. Would your answer be different if the ratios were to be used by an outsider, for example, by a potential shareholder? Why?

Multi-Concept Exercises

Exercise 13-11 *Common-Size Balance Sheets and Horizontal Analysis* **LO 1, 2**

Comparative balance sheets for Harbour Company for the past two years are as follows:

	December 31	
	2008	2007
Cash	$ 8,000	$ 10,000
Accounts receivable	20,000	15,000
Inventory	15,000	25,000
Prepaid rent	9,000	6,000
Total current assets	52,000	56,000

Land	75,000	75,000
Plant and equipment	400,000	300,000
Accumulated depreciation	(65,000)	(30,000)
Total long-term assets	410,000	345,000
Total assets	$462,000	$401,000
Accounts payable	$ 12,000	$ 10,000
Income taxes payable	3,000	5,000
Short-term notes payable	35,000	25,000
Total current liabilities	50,000	40,000
Bonds payable	75,000	100,000
Common shares	200,000	150,000
Retained earnings	137,000	111,000
Total shareholders' equity	337,000	261,000
Total liabilities and shareholders' equity	$462,000	$401,000

Required

1. Using the format in Exhibit 13-5, prepare common-size comparative balance sheets for the two years for Harbour Company.

2. What observations can you make about the changes in the relative composition of Harbour's accounts from the common-size balance sheets? List at least five observations.

3. Using the format in Exhibit 13-2, prepare comparative balance sheets for Harbour Company, including columns both for the dollars and for the percentage increase or decrease in each item on the statement.

4. Identify the five items on the balance sheet that experienced the largest change from one year to the next. For each of these, explain where you would look to find additional information about the change.

Exercise 13-12 *Common-Size Income Statements and Horizontal Analysis* **LO 1, 2**

Income statements for Moose Corp. for the past two years follow:

	(Amounts in Thousands of Dollars)	
	2008	**2007**
Sales revenue	$120,000	$100,000
Cost of goods sold	84,000	60,000
Gross profit	36,000	40,000
Selling and administrative expense	18,000	10,000
Operating income	18,000	30,000
Interest expense	4,000	4,000
Income before tax	14,000	26,000
Income tax expense	4,000	8,000
Net income	$ 10,000	$ 18,000

Required

1. Using the format in Exhibit 13-4, prepare common-size comparative income statements for the two years for Moose Corp.

2. What observations can you make about the common-size statements? List at least four observations.

3. Using the format in Exhibit 13-1, prepare comparative income statements for Moose Corp., including columns both for the dollars and for the percentage increase or decrease in each item on the statement.

4. Identify the two items on the income statement that experienced the largest change from one year to the next. For each of these, explain where you would look to find additional information about the change.

Exercise 13-13 *Ratios and Projected Financial Statements* **LO 3, 4, 5, 6**

Dave Batman is planning to set up a company, to be called Uniforms Ltd., to design and print promotional sport shirts for businesses and non-business organizations. Batman estimated the following information and gathered the following industry average ratios:

Forecasts

Annual sales revenue	$240,000
Minimum cash balance to be maintained	$14,000
Annual rent	$24,000
Annual salaries	$60,000
Miscellaneous expenses	5% of sales
Cost of printing equipment (10 years)	$100,000
Cost of borrowing	5%

Industry average ratios

Gross profit margin	50%
Current ratio	1.2:1
Accounts receivable turnover	10 times
Inventory turnover	12 times
Accounts payable turnover	5 times
Debt-to-equity ratio	2:1

Required

1. Prepare a forecasted income statement and balance sheet for Uniforms for its first year of operations.
2. What kind of financing should Dave Batman be seeking?
3. Does Uniforms Ltd. appear to be a viable business?

Problems

Problem 13-1 *Effect of Transactions on Working Capital, Current Ratio, and Quick Ratio* **LO 3**

The following account balances are taken from the records of Air Liquid Inc.:

Cash	$ 140,000
Trading securities (short-term)	120,000
Accounts receivable	160,000
Inventory	200,000
Prepaid insurance	20,000
Accounts payable	150,000
Taxes payable	50,000
Salaries and wages payable	80,000
Short-term loans payable	120,000

Required

1. Use the information provided above to compute the amount of working capital and Air Liquid's current and quick ratios (round to two decimal places).
2. Determine the effect that each of the following transactions will have on Air Liquid's working capital, current ratio, and quick ratio by recalculating each and then indicating whether the measure is increased, decreased, or not affected by the transaction. (For the ratios, round to three decimal places.) Consider each transaction independently; that is, assume that it is the *only* transaction that takes place.

	Effect of Transaction on		
Transaction	**Working Capital**	**Current Ratio**	**Quick Ratio**
a. Purchased inventory on account for $40,000.			
b. Purchased inventory for cash, $30,000.			
c. Paid suppliers on account, $60,000.			
d. Received cash on account, $80,000.			
e. Paid insurance for next year, $40,000.			
f. Made sales on account, $120,000.			

g. Repaid short-term loans at bank, $50,000.

h. Borrowed $80,000 at bank for 90 days.

i. Declared and paid $90,000 cash dividend.

j. Purchased $40,000 of trading securities (classified as current assets).

k. Paid $60,000 in salaries.

l. Accrued additional $30,000 in taxes.

Problem 13-2 *Goals for Sales and Return on Assets* LO 5

The president of Budget Ltd. is reviewing with his vice-presidents the operating results of the year just completed. Sales increased by 15% from the previous year to $30,000,000. Average total assets for the year were $20,000,000. Net income, after adding back interest expense, net of tax, was $2,500,000.

The president is happy with the performance over the past year but is never satisfied with the status quo. He has set two specific goals for next year: (1) a 20% growth in sales, and (2) a return on assets of 15%.

To achieve the second goal, the president has stated his intention to increase the total asset base by 12.5% over the base for the year just completed.

Required

1. For the year just completed, compute the following ratios:

   a. Return on sales

   b. Asset turnover

   c. Return on assets

2. Compute the necessary asset turnover for next year to achieve the president's goal of a 20% increase in sales.

3. Calculate the income needed next year to achieve the goal of a 15% return on total assets. (*Note:* Assume that *income* is defined as net income plus interest, net of tax.)

4. Based on your answers to requirements **2** and **3**, comment on the reasonableness of the president's goals. What must the company focus on to attain these goals?

Problem 13-3 *Goals for Sales and Income Growth* LO 5

Sackville Ltd. is a major regional retailer. The chief executive officer (CEO) is concerned with the slow growth both of sales and of net income and the subsequent effect on the trading price of the common shares. Selected financial data for the past three years follow.

SACKVILLE LTD.
(IN MILLIONS)

	2008	2007	2006
1. Sales	$100.0	$96.3	$93.5
2. Net income	3.0	2.9	2.8
December 31 balances:			
3. Shareholders' equity	35.0	33.2	31.6
4. Debt	15.0	14.9	15.1
Selected year-end financial ratios			
Net income to sales	3.0%	3.0%	3.0%
Asset turnover	2 times	2 times	2 times
5. Return on shareholders' equity*	8.6%	8.7%	8.9%
6. Debt to total assets	30.0%	30.9%	32.4%

*Based on year-end balances in shareholders' equity.

The CEO believes that the price of the shares has been adversely affected by the downward trend of the return on equity. To improve the price of the shares, she wants to improve the return on equity. She believes that the company should be able to meet these objectives by increasing sales and net income at an annual rate of 10% a year.

The 10% annual sales increase will be accomplished through a new promotional program. The president believes that the present net income to sales ratio of 3% will be unchanged by the cost of this new program and any interest paid on new debt. She expects that the company can accomplish this sales and income growth while maintaining the current relationship of total

(continued)

assets to sales. Any capital that is needed to maintain this relationship and that is not generated internally would be acquired through long-term debt financing. The company is to maintain its dividends of $1.25 million a year unchanged. The CEO hopes that debt would not exceed 35% of total liabilities and shareholders' equity.

Required

1. Using the CEO's program, prepare a schedule that shows the appropriate data for the years 2009, 2010, and 2011 for the items numbered 1 through 6 on the preceding schedule.

2. Can the CEO meet all of her requirements if a 10% per year growth in income and sales is achieved? Explain your answer.

3. What alternative actions should the CEO consider to improve the return on equity and to support increased dividend payments?

4. Explain the reasons that the CEO might have for wanting to limit debt to 35% of total liabilities and shareholders' equity.

(CMA adapted)

Multi-Concept Problems

Problem 13-4 *Basic Financial Ratios* LO 3, 4, 5

The accounting staff of Calgary Corp. has completed the financial statements for the 2008 calendar year. The statement of income for 2008 and the comparative statements of financial position for 2008 and 2007 follow.

CALGARY CORP.
STATEMENT OF INCOME
FOR THE YEAR ENDED DECEMBER 31, 2008

Revenue:	
Net sales	$400,000
Other	30,000
Total revenue	430,000
Expenses:	
Cost of goods sold	270,000
Research and development	12,500
Selling and administrative	77,500
Interest	10,000
Total expenses	370,000
Income before income taxes	60,000
Income taxes	24,000
Net income	$ 36,000

CALGARY CORP.
COMPARATIVE STATEMENTS OF FINANCIAL POSITION
DECEMBER 31, 2008 AND 2007

	2008	2007
Assets		
Current assets:		
Cash and short-term investments	$ 13,000	$ 10,500
Receivables, less allowance for doubtful accounts		
($550 in 2008 and $700 in 2007)	24,000	25,000
Inventories, at lower of FIFO cost or market	32,500	31,000
Prepaid items and other current assets	2,500	1,500
Total current assets	72,000	68,000
Other assets:		
Investments, at cost	53,000	53,000
Deposits	5,000	4,000
Total other assets	58,000	57,000
Property, plant, and equipment:		
Land	6,000	6,000
Buildings and equipment, less		
accumulated depreciation ($63,000 in		
2008 and $61,000 in 2007)	134,000	124,000
Total property, plant, and equipment	140,000	130,000
Total assets	$270,000	$255,000

Liabilities and Shareholders' Equity

Current liabilities:		
Short-term loans	$ 11,000	$ 12,000
Accounts payable	36,000	35,500
Salaries, wages, and other	13,000	13,500
Total current liabilities	60,000	61,000
Long-term debt	80,000	85,500
Total liabilities	140,000	146,500
Shareholders' equity:		
Common stock	54,000	51,500
Retained earnings	76,000	57,000
Total shareholders' equity	130,000	108,500
Total liabilities and shareholders' equity	$270,000	$255,000

Required:

1. Calculate the following financial ratios for 2008 for Calgary Corp.:

   a. Times interest earned

   b. Return on total assets

   c. Return on common shareholders' equity

   d. Debt-equity-ratio (at December 31, 2008)

   e. Current ratio (at December 31, 2008)

   f. Quick (acid-test) ratio (at December 31, 2008)

   g. Accounts receivable turnover ratio (assume that all sales are on credit)

   h. Number of days' sales in receivables

   i. Inventory turnover ratio (assume that all purchases are on credit)

   j. Number of days' sales in inventory

   k. Accounts payable turnover

   l. Number of days' purchases in payables

   m. Number of days in cash operating cycle

2. Prepare a few brief comments on the overall financial health of Calgary Corp. For each comment, indicate any information that is not provided in the problem and that you would need to fully evaluate the company's financial health.

(CMA adapted)

Problem 13-5 *Projected Results to Meet Corporate Objectives* LO 4, 5, 6

Whistler Ltd. is a wholly owned subsidiary of Rocky Co. The philosophy of Rocky's management is to allow the subsidiaries to operate as independent units. Corporate control is exercised through the establishment of minimum objectives for each subsidiary, accompanied by substantial rewards for success and penalties for failure. The time period for performance review is long enough for competent managers to display their abilities.

Each quarter the subsidiary is required to submit financial statements. The statements are accompanied by a letter from the subsidiary president explaining the results to date, a forecast for the remainder of the year, and the actions to be taken to achieve the objectives if the forecast indicates that the objectives will not be met.

Rocky management, in conjunction with Whistler management, had set the objectives listed below for the year ending May 31, 2009. These objectives are similar to those set in previous years.

■ Sales growth of 20%

■ Return on shareholders' equity of 15%

■ A long-term debt-to-equity ratio of not more than 1.0

■ Payment of a cash dividend of 50% of net income, with a minimum payment of at least $200,000

Whistler's controller has just completed the financial statements for the six months ended November 30, 2008, and the forecast for the year ending May 31, 2009. The statements are presented on the next page.

(continued)

After a cursory glance at the financial statements, Whistler's president concluded that not all objectives would be met. At a staff meeting of the Whistler management, the president asked the controller to review the projected results and recommend possible actions that could be taken during the remainder of the year so that Whistler would be more likely to meet the objectives.

WHISTLER LTD.
INCOME STATEMENT
(THOUSANDS OMITTED)

	Year Ended May 31, 2008	Six Months Ended November 30, 2008	Forecast for Year Ending May 31, 2009
Sales	$12,500	$ 7,500	$15,000
Cost of goods sold	6,500	4,000	8,000
Selling expenses	2,500	1,750	3,500
Administrative expenses and interest	2,000	1,250	2,500
Income taxes (40%)	600	200	400
Total expenses and taxes	11,600	7,200	14,400
Net income	900	300	600
Dividends declared and paid	300	0	300
Income retained	$ 600	$ 300	$ 300

WHISTLER LTD.
STATEMENT OF FINANCIAL POSITION
(THOUSANDS OMITTED)

	May 31, 2008	November 30, 2008	Forecast for May 31, 2009
Assets			
Cash	$ 200	$ 250	$ 250
Accounts receivable (net)	2,050	3,250	3,550
Inventory	3,500	4,250	4,300
Plant and equipment (net)	3,250	3,500	3,650
Total assets	$9,000	$11,250	$11,750
Liabilities and Equities			
Accounts payable	$1,500	$ 2,000	$ 2,000
Accrued taxes	150	100	100
Long-term borrowing	3,000	4,500	5,000
Common shares	2,500	2,500	2,500
Retained earnings	1,850	2,150	2,150
Total liabilities and equities	$9,000	$11,250	$11,750

Required

1. Calculate the projected results for each of the four objectives established for Whistler Ltd. State which results will not meet the objectives by year-end.

2. From the data presented, identify the factors that seem to contribute to the failure of Whistler Ltd. to meet all of its objectives.

3. Explain the possible actions that the controller could recommend in response to the president's request.

(CMA adapted)

Problem 13-6 *Comparison with Industry Averages* LO 3, 4, 5, 6

Amherst Ltd. is a medium-sized company that has been in business for 20 years. The industry has become very competitive in the last few years, and Amherst has decided that it must grow if it is going to survive. It has approached the bank for a sizable five-year loan, and the bank has requested its most recent financial statements as part of the loan package.

The industry in which Amherst operates consists of approximately 20 companies relatively equal in size. The trade association to which all of the competitors belong publishes an annual survey of the industry, including industry averages for selected ratios for the competitors. All companies voluntarily submit their statements to the association for this purpose.

Amherst's controller is aware that the bank has access to this survey and is very concerned about how the company fared this past year compared with the rest of the industry. The ratios included in the publication, and the averages for the past year, are as follows:

Ratio	Industry Average
Current ratio	1.23
Acid-test (quick) ratio	0.75
Accounts receivable turnover	33 times
Inventory turnover	29 times
Debt-to-equity ratio	0.53
Times interest earned	8.65 times
Return on sales	6.57%
Asset turnover	1.95 times
Return on assets	12.81%
Return on common shareholders' equity	17.67%

The financial statements to be submitted to the bank in connection with the loan follow:

AMHERST LTD.
STATEMENT OF INCOME AND RETAINED EARNINGS
FOR THE YEAR ENDED DECEMBER 31, 2008
(THOUSANDS OMITTED)

Sales revenue	$271,375
Cost of goods sold	(217,825)
Gross margin	53,550
Selling, general, and administrative expenses	(32,890)
Loss on sales of securities	(110)
Income before interest and taxes	20,550
Interest expense	(4,637)
Income before taxes	15,913
Income tax expense	(6,365)
Net income	9,548
Retained earnings, January 1, 2008	29,243
	38,791
Dividends paid on common stock	(6,000)
Retained earnings, December 31, 2008	$ 32,791

AMHERST LTD.
COMPARATIVE STATEMENTS OF FINANCIAL POSITION
(THOUSANDS OMITTED)

	December 31, 2008	December 31, 2007
Assets		
Current assets:		
Cash	$ 568	$ 375
Short-term investment	625	1,125
Accounts receivable, net of allowances	7,825	6,190
Inventories	6,340	7,935
Prepaid items	192	210
Total current assets	15,550	15,835
Long-term investments	212	212
Property, plant, and equipment:		
Land	16,000	16,000
Buildings and equipment, net of accumulated depreciation	108,000	103,000
Total property, plant, and equipment	124,000	119,000
Total assets	$139,762	$135,047

(continued)

Liabilities and Shareholders' Equity

Current liabilities:		
Short-term notes	$ 4,375	$ 6,375
Accounts payable	10,045	7,190
Salaries and wages payable	987	1,215
Income taxes payable	1,565	1,025
Total current liabilities	16,972	15,805
Long-term bonds payable	40,000	40,000
Shareholders' equity:		
Common shares	50,000	50,000
Retained earnings	32,790	29,243
Total shareholders' equity	82,790	79,243
Total liabilities and shareholders' equity	$139,762	$135,048

Required

1. Prepare a columnar report for the controller of Amherst Ltd., comparing the industry averages for the ratios published by the trade association with the comparable ratios for Amherst. For Amherst, compute the ratios as of December 31, 2008, or for the year ending December 31, 2008, whichever is appropriate.

2. Briefly evaluate Amherst's ratios relative to the industry averages.

3. Do you think that the bank will approve the loan? Explain your answer.

Alternate Problems

Problem 13-1A *Effect of Transactions on Debt-to-Equity Ratio* LO 4

The following account balances are taken from the records of Montreal's Ltd.:

Current liabilities	$300,000
Long-term liabilities	750,000
Shareholders' equity	800,000

Required

1. Use the information provided above to compute Montreal's debt-to-equity ratio (round to three decimal places).

2. Determine the effect that each of the following transactions will have on Montreal's debt-to-equity ratio by recalculating the ratio and then indicating whether the ratio is increased, decreased, or not affected by the transaction. (Round to three decimal places.) Consider each transaction independently; that is, assume that it is the *only* transaction that takes place.

Transaction	Effect of Transaction on Debt-To-Equity Ratio
a. Purchased inventory on account for $40,000.	
b. Purchased inventory for cash, $30,000.	
c. Paid suppliers on account, $60,000.	
d. Received cash on account, $80,000.	
e. Paid insurance for next year, $40,000.	
f. Made sales on account, $120,000.	
g. Repaid short-term loans at bank, $50,000.	
h. Borrowed $80,000 at bank for 90 days.	
i. Declared and paid $90,000 cash dividend.	
j. Purchased $40,000 of trading securities (classified as current assets).	
k. Paid $60,000 in salaries.	
l. Accrued additional $30,000 in taxes.	

Problem 13-2A *Goals for Sales and Return on Assets* **LO 5**

The president of Thunder Bay Ltd. is reviewing with her department managers the operating results of the year just completed. Sales increased by 12% from the previous year to $1,500,000. Average total assets for the year were $800,000. Net income, after adding back interest expense, net of tax, was $120,000.

The president is happy with the performance over the past year but is never satisfied with the status quo. She has set two specific goals for next year: (1) a 15% growth in sales, and (2) a return on assets of 20%.

To achieve the second goal, the president has stated her intention to increase the total asset base by 10% over the base for the year just completed.

Required

1. For the year just completed, compute the following ratios:

   a. Return on sales

   b. Asset turnover

   c. Return on assets

2. Compute the necessary asset turnover for next year to achieve the president's goal of a 15% increase in sales.

3. Calculate the income needed next year to achieve the goal of a 20% return on total assets. (*Note:* Assume that *income* is defined as net income plus interest, net of tax.)

4. Based on your answers to requirements **2** and **3**, comment on the reasonableness of the president's goals. What must the company focus on to attain these goals?

Problem 13-3A *Goals for Sales and Income Growth* **LO 5**

Saskatoon Corp. is a major regional retailer. The chief executive officer (CEO) is concerned with the slow growth both of sales and of net income and the subsequent effect on the trading price of the common shares. Selected financial data for the past three years follow.

SASKATOON CORP.
(IN MILLIONS)

	2008	2007	2006
1. Sales	$200.0	$193.4	$186.6
2. Net income	6.0	5.8	5.6
3. Dividends declared and paid	2.4	2.4	2.4
December 31 balances:			
4. Shareholders' equity	80.0	76.4	73.0
5. Debt	20.0	20.4	20.4
Selected year-end financial ratios			
Net income to sales	3.0%	3.0%	3.0%
Asset turnover	2 times	2 times	2 times
6. Return on shareholders' equity*	7.5%	7.6%	7.7%
7. Debt to total assets	20.0%	21.1%	21.8%

*Based on year-end balances in shareholders' equity.

The CEO believes that the price of the shares has been adversely affected by the downward trend of the return on equity. To improve the price of the shares, he wants to improve the return on equity.

He believes that the company should be able to meet these objectives by increasing sales and net income at an annual rate of 10% a year.

The 10% annual sales increase will be accomplished through a product enhancement program. The president believes that the present net income to sales ratio of 3% will be unchanged by the cost of this new program and any interest paid on new debt. He expects that the company can accomplish this sales and income growth while maintaining the current relationship of total assets to sales. Any capital that is needed to maintain this relationship and that is not generated internally would be acquired through long-term debt financing. The company is to maintain its $2.4 million dividend per year unchanged. The CEO hopes that debt would not exceed 25% of total liabilities and shareholders' equity.

(continued)

Required

1. Using the CEO's program, prepare a schedule that shows the appropriate data for the years 2009, 2010, and 2011 for the items numbered 1 through 7 on the preceding schedule.

2. Can the CEO meet all of his requirements if a 10% per-year growth in income and sales is achieved? Explain your answers.

3. What alternative actions should the CEO consider to improve the return on equity and to support increased dividend payments?

(CMA adapted)

Alternate Multi-Concept Problems

Problem 13-4A *Basic Financial Ratios* LO 3, 4, 5

The accounting staff of Eassons Ltd. has completed the financial statements for the 2008 calendar year. The statement of income for the current year and the comparative statements of financial position for 2008 and 2007 follow.

EASSONS LTD.
STATEMENT OF INCOME
YEAR ENDED DECEMBER 31, 2008

Revenue:	
Net sales	$1,200,000
Other	90,000
Total revenue	1,290,000
Expenses:	
Cost of goods sold	810,000
Research and development	36,000
Selling and administrative	240,000
Interest	30,000
Total expenses	1,116,000
Income before income taxes	174,000
Income taxes	54,000
Net income	$ 120,000

EASSONS LTD.
COMPARATIVE STATEMENTS OF FINANCIAL POSITION
DECEMBER 31, 2008 AND 2007

	2008	2007
Assets		
Current assets:		
Cash and short-term investments	$ 54,000	$ 40,000
Receivables, less allowance for doubtful accounts		
($2,200 in 2008 and $2,800 in 2007)	72,000	74,000
Inventories, at lower of FIFO cost or market	70,000	84,000
Prepaid items and other current assets	4,000	2,000
Total current assets	200,000	200,000
Property, plant, and equipment:		
Land	18,000	18,000
Buildings and equipment, less accumulated depreciation ($148,000 in 2008 and $124,000 in 2007)	382,000	372,000
Total property, plant, and equipment	400,000	390,000
Total assets	$600,000	$590,000

Liabilities and Shareholders' Equity

Current liabilities:		
Short-term loans	$ 40,000	$ 30,000
Accounts payable	160,000	136,000
Salaries, wages, and other	10,000	14,000
Total current liabilities	210,000	180,000
Long-term debt	30,000	80,000
Total liabilities	240,000	260,000
Shareholders' equity:		
Common shares	150,000	150,000
Retained earnings	210,000	180,000
Total shareholders' equity	360,000	330,000
Total liabilities and shareholders' equity	$600,000	$590,000

Required

1. Calculate the following financial ratios for 2008 for Eassons Ltd.:

   a. Times interest earned

   b. Return on total assets

   c. Return on common shareholders' equity

   d. Debt-equity-ratio (at December 31, 2008)

   e. Current ratio (at December 31, 2008)

   f. Quick (acid-test) ratio (at December 31, 2008)

   g. Accounts receivable turnover ratio (assume that all sales are on credit)

   h. Number of days' sales in receivables

   i. Inventory turnover ratio (assume that all purchases are on credit)

   j. Number of days' sales in inventory

   k. Accounts payable turnover

   l. Number of days' purchases in payables

   m. Number of days in cash operating cycle

2. Prepare a few brief comments on the overall financial health of Eassons Ltd. For each comment, indicate any information that is not provided in the problem and that you would need to fully evaluate the company's financial health.

(CMA adapted)

Problem 13-5A *Projected Results to Meet Corporate Objectives* LO 4, 5, 6

Moncton Ltd. is a wholly owned subsidiary of Toronto Corp. The philosophy of Toronto's management is to allow the subsidiaries to operate as independent units. Corporate control is exercised through the establishment of minimum objectives for each subsidiary, accompanied by substantial rewards for success and penalties for failure. The time period for performance review is long enough for competent managers to display their abilities.

Each quarter the subsidiary is required to submit financial statements. The statements are accompanied by a letter from the subsidiary president explaining the results to date, a forecast for the remainder of the year, and the actions to be taken to achieve the objectives if the forecast indicates that the objectives will not be met.

Toronto's management, in conjunction with Moncton's management, had set the objectives listed below for the year ending September 30, 2009. These objectives are similar to those set in previous years.

- Sales growth of 10%
- Return on shareholders' equity of 20%
- A long-term debt-to-equity ratio of not more than 1.0
- Payment of a cash dividend of 50% of net income, with a minimum payment of at least $500,000

Moncton's controller has just completed preparing the financial statements for the six months ended March 31, 2009, and the forecast for the year ending September 30, 2009. The statements are presented on the following page.

(continued)

After a cursory glance at the financial statements, Moncton's president concluded that not all objectives would be met. At a staff meeting of the Moncton management, the president asked the controller to review the projected results and recommend possible actions that could be taken during the remainder of the year so that Moncton would be more likely to meet the objectives.

MONCTON LTD.
INCOME STATEMENT
(THOUSANDS OMITTED)

	Year Ended September 30, 2008	Six Months Ended March 31, 2009	Forecast for Year Ending September 30, 2009
Sales	$10,000	$6,000	$12,000
Cost of goods sold	6,000	4,000	8,000
Selling expenses	1,500	900	1,800
Administrative expenses and interest	1,000	600	1,200
Income taxes	500	300	600
Total expenses and taxes	9,000	5,800	11,600
Net income	1,000	200	400
Dividends declared and paid	500	0	400
Income retained	$ 500	$ 200	$ 0

MONCTON LTD.
STATEMENT OF FINANCIAL POSITION
(THOUSANDS OMITTED)

	September 30, 2008	March 31, 2009	Forecast for September 30, 2009
Assets			
Cash	$ 400	$ 500	$ 500
Accounts receivable (net)	2,100	3,400	2,600
Inventory	7,000	8,500	8,400
Plant and equipment (net)	2,800	2,500	3,200
Total assets	$12,300	$14,900	$14,700
Liabilities and Equities			
Accounts payable	$ 3,000	$ 4,000	$ 4,000
Accrued taxes	300	200	200
Long-term borrowing	4,000	5,500	5,500
Common shares	4,000	4,000	4,000
Retained earnings	1,000	1,200	1,000
Total liabilities and equities	$12,300	$14,900	$14,700

Required

1. Calculate the projected results for each of the four objectives established for Moncton Ltd. State which results will not meet the objectives by year-end.

2. From the data presented, identify the factors that seem to contribute to the failure of Moncton Ltd. to meet all of its objectives.

3. Explain the possible actions that the controller could recommend in response to the president's request.

(CMA adapted)

Problem 13-6A *A Comparison with Industry Averages* **LO 3, 4, 5, 6**
Sunbury Ltd. is a medium-sized company that has been in business for 20 years. The industry has become very competitive in the last few years, and Sunbury has decided that it must grow if it is going to survive. It has approached the bank for a sizable five-year loan, and the bank has requested its most recent financial statements as part of the loan package.

The industry in which Sunbury operates consists of approximately 20 companies relatively equal in size. The trade association to which all of the competitors belong publishes an annual survey of the industry, including industry averages for selected ratios for the competitors. All companies voluntarily submit their statements to the association for this purpose.

Sunbury's controller is aware that the bank has access to this survey and is very concerned about how the company fared this past year compared with the rest of the industry. The ratios included in the publication, and the averages for the past year, are as follows:

Ratio	Industry Average
Current ratio	1.20
Acid-test (quick) ratio	0.50
Inventory turnover	35 times
Debt-to-equity ratio	0.50
Times interest earned	25 times
Return on sales	3%
Asset turnover	3.5 times
Return on common shareholders' equity	20%

The financial statements to be submitted to the bank in connection with the loan follow:

SUNBURY LTD.
STATEMENT OF INCOME AND RETAINED EARNINGS
FOR THE YEAR ENDED DECEMBER 31, 2008
(THOUSANDS OMITTED)

Sales revenue	$841,000
Cost of goods sold	(600,000)
Gross margin	241,000
Selling, general, and administrative expenses	(170,000)
Income before interest and taxes	71,000
Interest expense	(17,200)
Income before taxes	53,800
Income tax expense	(24,000)
Net income	29,800
Retained earnings, January 1, 2008	24,800
	54,600
Dividends paid on common	(22,400)
Retained earnings, December 31, 2008	$ 32,200

SUNBURY LTD.
COMPARATIVE STATEMENTS OF FINANCIAL POSITION
(THOUSANDS OMITTED)

	December 31, 2008	December 31, 2007
Assets		
Current assets:		
Cash	$ 3,580	$ 5,200
Marketable securities	2,400	3,400
Accounts receivable, net of allowances	800	1,200
Inventories	17,400	14,800
Prepaid items	700	800
Total current assets	24,880	25,400
Long-term investments	1,120	800
Property, plant, and equipment:		
Land	24,000	24,000
Buildings and equipment, net of accumulated depreciation	174,000	165,800
Total property, plant, and equipment	198,000	189,800
Total assets	$224,000	$216,000

(continued)

Liabilities and Shareholders' Equity

Current liabilities:

Short-term notes	$ 1,600	$ 1,200
Accounts payable	12,080	13,550
Salaries and wages payable	3,000	2,400
Income taxes payable	3,120	2,050
Total current liabilities	19,800	19,200
Long-term bonds payable	72,000	72,000
Shareholders' equity:		
Common shares	100,000	100,000
Retained earnings	32,200	24,800
Total shareholders' equity	132,200	124,800
Total liabilities and shareholders' equity	$224,000	$216,000

Required

1. Prepare a columnar report for the controller of Sunbury Ltd., comparing the industry averages for the ratios published by the trade association with the comparable ratios for Sunbury. For Sunbury, compute the ratios as of December 31, 2008, or for the year ending December 31, 2008, whichever is appropriate.

2. Briefly evaluate Sunbury's ratios relative to the industry.

3. Do you think that the bank will approve the loan? Explain your answer.

Cases

Reading and Interpreting Financial Statements

CN
www.cn.ca

Case 13-1 *Horizontal Analysis for CN* LO 1

Refer to CN's comparative income statements included in its annual report.

Required

1. Prepare a work sheet with the following headings:

	Increase (Decrease) from			
	2006 to 2007		**2005 to 2006**	
Income Statement Accounts	**Dollars (millions)**	**Percent**	**Dollars (millions)**	**Percent**

2. Complete the work sheet using each of the account titles on CN's income statement. Round dollar amounts to the nearest one-tenth of $1 million and percentages to the nearest one-tenth of a percent.

3. What observations can you make from this horizontal analysis? What is your overall analysis of operations? Have the company's operations improved over the three-year period?

Case 13-2 *Vertical Analysis for CN* LO 2

Refer to CN's financial statements included in its annual report.

Required

1. Using the format in Exhibit 13-5, prepare common-size comparative income statements for 2007 and 2006. Round dollar amounts to the nearest one-tenth of $1 million and percentages to the nearest one-tenth of a percent.

2. What changes do you detect in the income statement relationships from 2006 to 2007?

3. Using the format in Exhibit 13-4, prepare common-size comparative balance sheets at the end of 2007 and 2006. Round dollar amounts to the nearest one-tenth of $1 million and percentages to the nearest one-tenth of a percent.

4. What observations can you make about the relative composition of CN's assets from the common-size statements? What observations can be made about the changes in the relative composition of liabilities and shareholders' equity accounts?

Case 13-3 *Comparing Two Companies in the Same Industry: CN and CP* LO 2

This case should be completed after responding to the requirements in Case 13-2. Refer to the financial statement information of CN and **CP** in Appendices A and B at the end of the text.

www.cpr.ca

Required:

1. Using the format in Exhibit 13-4, prepare common-size comparative income statements for 2007 and 2006 for CP. Round dollar amounts to the nearest one-tenth of $1 million and percentages to the nearest one-tenth of a percent.

2. The common-size comparative income statements indicates the relative importance of items on the statement. Compare the common-size income statements of CP and CN. What are the most important differences between the two companies' income statements?

3. Using the format in Exhibit 13-5, prepare common-size balance sheets at the end of 2007 and 2006 CP. Round the dollar amounts to the nearest one-tenth of $1 million and percentages to the nearest one-tenth of a percent.

4. The common-size comparative balance sheets indicates the relative importance of items on the statement. Compare the common-size balance sheets of CP and CN. What are the most important differences between the two companies' balance sheets?

Case 13-4 *Ratio Analysis for CN* LO 3, 4, 5

Refer to CN's financial statements included in its annual report.

Required

1. Compute the following ratios and other amounts for each of the two years, 2007 and 2006. Because only two years of data are given on the balance sheets, to be consistent you should use year-end balances for each year in lieu of average balances. Assume 360 days to a year and use the effective tax rate if necessary. State any other necessary assumptions in making the calculations. Round all ratios to the nearest one-tenth of a percent.

   a. Working capital

   b. Current ratio

   c. Acid-test ratio

   d. Cash flow from operations to current liabilities

   e. Number of days' sales in receivables

   f. Number of days' sales in inventory

   g. Number of days' purchases in payables

   h. Debt-to-equity ratio

   i. Asset turnover

   j. Return on sales

   k. Return on assets

   l. Return on common shareholders' equity

2. What is your overall analysis of the financial health of CN? What do you believe are the company's strengths and weaknesses?

Making Financial Decisions

Case 13-5 *Acquisition Decision* LO 3, 4, 5

Deno Corp. is a conglomerate and is continually in the market for new acquisitions. The company has grown rapidly over the last 10 years through buyouts of medium-sized companies. Deno does not limit itself to companies in any one industry but looks for firms with a sound financial base and the ability to stand on their own financially.

The president of Deno recently told a meeting of the company's officers: "I want to impress two points on all of you. First, we are not in the business of looking for bargains. Deno has achieved success in the past by acquiring companies with the ability to be a permanent member of the corporate family. We don't want companies that may appear to be a bargain on paper but can't survive in the long run. Second, a new member of our family must be able to come in and make it on its own—the parent is not organized to be a funding agency for struggling subsidiaries."

(continued)

Jane Hope is the vice-president of acquisitions for Deno, a position she has held for five years. She is responsible for making recommendations to the board of directors on potential acquisitions. Because you are one of her assistants, she recently brought you a set of financials for a manufacturer, Capable Ltd. Hope believes that Capable is a "can't-miss" opportunity for Deno and asks you to confirm her hunch by performing basic financial statement analysis on the company. The most recent income statement and comparative balance sheets for the company follow:

CAPABLE LTD.
STATEMENT OF INCOME AND RETAINED EARNINGS
FOR THE YEAR ENDED DECEMBER 31, 2008

Sales revenue	$1,750,500
Cost of goods sold	1,085,500
Gross margin	665,000
Selling, general, and administrative expenses	528,720
Operating income	136,280
Interest expense	90,000
Net income before taxes and extraordinary items	46,280
Income tax expense	18,500
Income before extraordinary items	27,780
Extraordinary gain, less taxes of $6,000	18,000
Net income	45,780
Retained earnings, January 1, 2008	339,640
	385,420
Dividends paid on common shares	20,000
Retained earnings, December 31, 2008	$ 365,420

CAPABLE LTD.
COMPARATIVE STATEMENTS OF FINANCIAL POSITION

	December 31, 2008	December 31, 2007
Assets		
Current assets:		
Cash	$ 97,000	$ 49,960
Temporary investments	7,500	0
Accounts receivable, net of allowances	256,840	168,240
Inventories	271,700	193,560
Prepaid items	15,200	18,600
Total current assets	648,240	430,360
Long-term investments	111,780	111,780
Property, plant, and equipment:		
Land	90,000	90,000
Buildings and equipment, less accumulated depreciation of $770,000 in 2008 and $650,000 in 2007	1,090,000	1,210,000
Total property, plant, and equipment	1,180,000	1,300,000
Total assets	$1,940,020	$1,842,140
Liabilities and Shareholders' Equity		
Current liabilities:		
Short-term notes	$ 160,000	$ 120,000
Accounts payable	130,700	97,520
Salaries and wages payable	28,720	27,680
Income taxes payable	5,180	7,300
Total current liabilities	324,600	252,500
Long-term bonds payable, due 2013	550,000	550,000
Shareholders' equity:		
Common shares	700,000	700,000
Retained earnings	365,420	339,640
Total shareholders' equity	1,065,420	1,039,640
Total liabilities and shareholders' equity	$1,940,020	$1,842,140

Required

1. How liquid is Capable Ltd.? Support your answer with any ratios that you believe are necessary to justify your conclusion. Also indicate any other information that you would want to have in making a final determination on its liquidity.

2. In light of the president's comments, should you be concerned about the solvency of Capable Ltd.? Support your answer with the necessary ratios. How does the maturity date of the outstanding debt affect your answer?

3. Has Capable demonstrated the ability to be a profitable member of the Deno family? Support your answer with the necessary ratios.

4. What will you tell your boss? Should she recommend to the board of directors that Deno put in a bid for Capable Ltd.?

Case 13-6 *Pricing Decision* LO 2

Moose Jaw's management believes that the company has been successful at increasing sales because it has not increased the selling price of the products, even though its competition has increased prices and costs have increased. Price and cost relationships in Year 1 were established because they represented industry averages. The following income statements are available for Moose Jaw's first three years of operation:

	Year 3	Year 2	Year 1
Sales	$250,000	$220,000	$200,000
Cost of goods sold	124,000	98,000	80,000
Gross profit	126,000	122,000	120,000
Operating expenses	106,000	98,000	90,000
Net income	$ 20,000	$ 24,000	$ 30,000

Required

1. Using the format in Exhibit 13-4, prepare common-size comparative income statements for the three years.

2. Explain why net income has decreased while sales have increased.

3. Prepare an income statement for Year 4. Sales volume in units is expected to increase by 10%, and costs are expected to increase by 8%.

4. Do you think Moose Jaw should raise its prices or maintain the same selling prices? Explain your answer.

Accounting and Ethics: What Would You Do?

Case 13-7 *Provisions in a Loan Agreement* LO 3, 4

As assistant controller of Quebec Company, you are reviewing the financial statements for the year just ended. During the review, you are reminded of an existing loan agreement with Commerce Bank. Quebec has agreed to the following conditions:

■ The current ratio will be maintained at a minimum level of 1.5 to 1.0 at all times.

■ The debt-to-equity ratio will not exceed 0.5 to 1.0 at any time.

You have drawn up the following preliminary, condensed balance sheet for the year just ended:

QUEBEC COMPANY
BALANCE SHEET
DECEMBER 31
(IN MILLIONS OF DOLLARS)

Current assets	$32	Current liabilities	$20
Long-term assets	128	Long-term debt	30
		Shareholders' equity	110
Total	$160	Total	$160

You want to discuss two items with the controller. First, long-term debt currently includes a $10 million note payable, to Royal Bank, that is due in six months. The plan is to go to Royal before the note is due and ask it to extend the maturity date of the note for five years. You do not believe that Quebec needs to include the $10 million in current liabilities because the plan is to roll the note over.

(continued)

Second, in December of this year, Quebec received a $4 million deposit from the province for a major road project. The contract calls for the work to be performed over the next 18 months. You recorded the $4 million as revenue this year because the contract is with the province; there shouldn't be any question about being able to collect.

Required

1. Based on the balance sheet you prepared, is Quebec in compliance with its loan agreement with Commerce? Support your answer with any necessary computations.

2. What would you do with the two items in question? Do you see anything wrong with the way you handled each of them? Explain your answer.

3. Prepare a revised balance sheet based on your answer to requirement **2.** Also, compute a revised current ratio and debt-to-equity ratio. Based on the revised ratios, is Quebec in compliance with its loan agreement?

Case 13-8 *Inventory Turnover* LO 3

Halifax Ltd. is a wholesaler of fresh fruit and vegetables. Each year it submits a set of financial ratios to a trade association. Even though the association doesn't publish the individual ratios for each company, the president of Halifax thinks it is important for public relations that his company look as good as possible. Due to the nature of the fresh fruit and vegetable business, one of the major ratios tracked by the association is inventory turnover. Halifax's inventory stated at FIFO cost was as follows:

| | Year Ended December 31 | |
	2008	2007
Fruits	$20,000	$18,000
Vegetables	60,000	66,000
Totals	$80,000	$84,000

Sales revenue for the year ended December 31, 2008, is $7,380,000. The company's gross profit ratio is normally 40%.

Based on these data, the president thinks the company should report an inventory turnover ratio of 90 times per year.

Required

1. Explain, using the necessary calculations, how the president came up with an inventory turnover ratio of 90 times.

2. Do you think the company should report a turnover ratio of 90 times? If not, explain why you disagree and explain, with calculations, what you think the ratio should be.

3. Assume you are the controller for Halifax. What will you tell the president?

Internet Research Cases

INTERNET

http://www.cpr.ca

Case 13-9 *CP* LO 3, 4, 5, 6

CP is the second largest railway company in Canada. By reading its financial statements and notes and using them to calculate selected ratios, you can develop a current picture of CP's performance that will help you interpret how CP has performed most recently.

1. Based on the financial information for the last two years available, compute the ratios required in Case 13-4 on page 683.

2. Comment on CP's liquidity. Has it improved or declined over the two-year period?

3. Comment on CP's solvency and CP's capital structure.

4. Comment on CP's profitability.

5. Examine various sources such as the financial news and CP's most recent annual report. What management plans and initiatives, such as announced increases in building of plants or increases in hiring, are likely to change your analysis of CP's performance the most in future years?

Case 13-10 *CN Results and Expectations*

CN's MD&A provides an analysis by management of the operations for 2007 and some of the prospects it has for 2008. The nature of the analysis provides insights into the financial statements of CN and insights into the management of CN. Such insights are important to financial analysts in their review of a company.

CN
http://www.cn.ca

Required:

1. Using the revenue analysis of 2007 given in the MD&A and footnote 16 of the Annual Report of CN, determine the major causes of the decline in revenues for 2007 and assess the expectations for 2008 against the actual results that are shown in the 2008 MD&A of CN, when available.

2. Using the operating expense analysis of 2007 given in the MD&A of CN, determine the reasons for the increase in operating expenses for 2007. Assess the expectations for these expenses in 2008 by comparing the stated expectations against the actual results shown in the 2008 MD&A, when available.

3. Determine from the 2007 MD&A presented in CN's Annual Report presented in Appendix A of this textbook, the reasons for the changes in Other Expenses and Other Income. Assess whether or not these changes are recurring or one-time effects. Assess your conclusions by examining the 2008 results when they are available.

4. What were the stated reasons for changes in CN's liquidity in 2007 evident in its MD&A? Using the results for 2008, assess the reasonableness of expectations presented in 2007. Compare the stated contractual obligations for 2008 as presented in 2007 against actual spending in 2008 when known.

5. Compare share repurchases expected in 2008 as stated in the 2007 MD&A against the actual repurchases made in 2008. Why would CN repurchase its shares?

6. Did the study of depreciation policies of Canadian property to begin in 2008 result in any changes for depreciation or impairment in 2008? What happened as a result of the 2007 study of U.S. properties?

7. Environmental matters, personal injury claims, labour negotiations, regulation and economic conditions are all stated as areas where events can affect the 2008 results of CN. Assess the outcomes of these matters in 2008 and determine if they will have a material effect on 2008 operations. Did the 2008 events have an effect that is greater or less than the outcomes evident in 2007?

Solutions to Key Terms Quiz

Quiz 1:

14	Horizontal analysis
11	Vertical analysis
10	Gross profit margin
12	Profit margin
13	Liquidity
2	Working capital
3	Current ratio
1	Acid-test or quick ratio
5	Cash flow from operations to current liabilities ratio
6	Accounts receivable turnover ratio
4	Number of days' sales in receivables
9	Inventory turnover ratio
7	Number of days' sales in inventory
15	Accounts payable turnover
16	Number of days' purchases in payables
8	Cash to cash operating cycle

Quiz 2:

3	Solvency
7	Debt-to-equity ratio
11	Times interest earned ratio
12	Debt service coverage ratio
6	Profitability
8	Return on assets ratio
4	Return on sales ratio
9	Asset turnover ratio
1	Return on common shareholders' equity ratio
10	Leverage
5	Earnings per share
2	Price/earnings (P/E) ratio

Part VI

Integrative Problem

Presented below and on the next page are comparative balance sheets and a statement of income and retained earnings for Victoria Ltd., which operates a national chain of sporting goods stores:

VICTORIA LTD.
COMPARATIVE BALANCE SHEETS
DECEMBER 31, 2008 AND 2007
(ALL AMOUNTS IN THOUSANDS OF DOLLARS)

	December 31	
	2008	**2007**
Cash	$ 420	$ 1,350
Accounts receivable	6,250	4,500
Inventory	4,000	2,750
Prepaid insurance	50	200
Total current assets	10,720	8,800
Land	2,000	2,000
Buildings and equipment	6,000	4,500
Accumulated depreciation	(1,850)	(1,500)
Total long-term assets	6,150	5,000
Total assets	$16,870	$13,800
Accounts payable	$ 3,650	$ 2,500
Taxes payable	2,300	2,100
Notes payable	1,200	800
Current portion of bonds	100	100
Total current liabilities	7,250	5,500
Bonds payable	700	800
Total liabilities	7,950	6,300
Preferred shares	500	500
Common shares	1,000	1,000
Retained earnings	7,420	6,000
Total shareholders' equity	8,920	7,500
Total liabilities and shareholders' equity	$16,870	$13,800

VICTORIA LTD.
STATEMENT OF INCOME AND RETAINED EARNINGS
FOR THE YEAR ENDED DECEMBER 31, 2008
(ALL AMOUNTS IN THOUSANDS OF DOLLARS)

Net sales	$24,000
Cost of goods sold	18,000
Gross profit	6,000
Selling, general, and administrative expense	3,000
Operating income	3,000
Interest expense	140
Income before tax	2,860
Income tax expense	1,140
Net income	1,720
Preferred dividends	50
Income available to common	1,670
Common dividends	250
To retained earnings	1,420
Retained earnings, 1/1	6,000
Retained earnings, 12/31	$ 7,420

Required

1. Prepare a statement of cash flows for Victoria Ltd. for the year ended December 31, 2008, using the **indirect** method in the Operating Activities section of the statement.

2. Victoria's management is concerned with both its short-term liquidity and its solvency over the long run. To help it evaluate these, compute the following ratios, rounding all answers to the nearest one-tenth of a percent:

   a. Current ratio

   b. Acid-test ratio

   c. Cash flow from operations to current liabilities ratio

   d. Accounts receivable turnover ratio

   e. Number of days' sales in receivables

   f. Inventory turnover ratio

   g. Number of days' sales in inventory

   h. Accounts payable turnover ratio

   i. Number of days' purchases in payables

   j. Debt-to-equity ratio

   k. Debt service coverage ratio

   l. Cash flow from operations to capital expenditures ratio.

3. Comment on Victoria's liquidity and its solvency. What additional information do you need to fully evaluate the company?

Appendix A: CN Rail Annual Report

Financial Section (U.S. GAAP)

Contents

Canadian National Railway Company

Notes to Consolidated Financial Statements

Selected Railroad Statistics [1]

Year ended December 31,	2007	2006	2005
Statistical operating data			
Rail freight revenues *($ millions)*	7,186	7,254	6,793
Gross ton miles (GTM) *(millions)*	347,898	352,972	342,894
Revenue ton miles (RTM) *(millions)*	184,148	185,610	179,701
Carloads *(thousands)*	4,744	4,824	4,841
Route miles *(includes Canada and the U.S.)*	20,421	20,264	19,221
Employees *(end of year)*	22,696	22,250	21,961
Employees *(average for the year)*	22,389	22,092	22,637
Productivity			
Operating ratio *(%)*	63.6	61.8	64.8
Rail freight revenue per RTM *(cents)*	3.90	3.91	3.78
Rail freight revenue per carload *($)*	1,515	1,504	1,403
Operating expenses per GTM *(cents)*	1.44	1.39	1.41
Labor and fringe benefits expense per GTM *(cents)*	0.49	0.52	0.54
GTMs per average number of employees *(thousands)*	15,539	15,977	15,148
Diesel fuel consumed *(U.S. gallons in millions)*	392	401	403
Average fuel price *($/U.S. gallon)* [2]	2.40	2.13	1.72
GTMs per U.S. gallon of fuel consumed	887	880	851
Safety indicators			
Injury frequency rate per 200,000 person hours [3]	1.9	2.1	2.4
Accident rate per million train miles [3]	2.7	2.4	1.8

(1) Includes data relating to companies acquired as of the date of acquisition.

(2) Includes the impact of the Company's fuel hedging program that expired in September 2006.

(3) Based on Federal Railroad Administration (FRA) reporting criteria. For 2006, the Injury frequency rate per 200,000 person hours and the Accident rate per million train miles, prepared on a proforma basis to include the acquisitions of Mackenzie Northern Railway and Savage Alberta Railway, Inc., as of January 1, 2006, would have been 2.1 and 2.5, respectively, for the year ended December 31, 2006.

Certain of the 2006 and 2005 comparative figures have been reclassified in order to be consistent with the 2007 presentation. Certain statistical data and related productivity measures are based on estimated data available at such time and are subject to change as more complete information becomes available.

Management's discussion and analysis (MD&A) relates to the financial condition and results of operations of Canadian National Railway Company, together with its wholly-owned subsidiaries, collectively "CN" or "the Company." Canadian National Railway Company's common shares are listed on the Toronto and New York stock exchanges. Except where otherwise indicated, all financial information reflected herein is expressed in Canadian dollars and determined on the basis of United States generally accepted accounting principles (U.S. GAAP). The Company's objective is to provide meaningful and relevant information reflecting the Company's financial condition and results of operations. In certain instances, the Company may make reference to certain non-GAAP measures that, from management's perspective, are useful measures of performance. The reader is advised to read all information provided in the MD&A in conjunction with the Company's 2007 Annual Consolidated Financial Statements and Notes thereto.

Business profile

CN is engaged in the rail and related transportation business. CN's network of approximately 20,400 route miles of track spans Canada and mid-America, connecting three coasts: the Atlantic, the Pacific and the Gulf of Mexico. CN's extensive network, in addition to co-production arrangements, routing protocols, marketing alliances, and interline agreements, provide CN customers access to all three North American Free Trade Agreement (NAFTA) nations.

CN's freight revenues are derived from seven commodity groups representing a diversified and balanced portfolio of goods transported between a wide range of origins and destinations. This product and geographic diversity better positions the Company to face economic fluctuations and enhances its potential for growth opportunities. In 2007, no individual commodity group accounted for more than 20% of revenues. From a geographic standpoint, 19% of revenues came from United States (U.S.) domestic traffic, 32% from transborder traffic, 23% from Canadian domestic traffic and 26% from overseas traffic. The Company originates approximately 87% of traffic moving along its network, which allows it both to capitalize on service advantages and build on opportunities to efficiently use assets.

Corporate organization

The Company manages its rail operations in Canada and the United States as one business segment. Financial information reported at this level, such as revenues, operating income and cash flow from operations, is used by the Company's corporate management in evaluating financial and operational performance and allocating resources across CN's network. The Company's strategic initiatives, which drive its operational direction, are developed and managed centrally by corporate management and are communicated to its regional activity centers (the Western Region, Eastern Region and Southern Region), whose role is to manage the day-to-day service requirements of their respective territories, control direct costs incurred locally, and execute the corporate strategy and operating plan established by corporate management.

See Note 16 – Segmented information, to the Company's 2007 Annual Consolidated Financial Statements for additional information on the Company's corporate organization, as well as selected financial information by geographic area.

Strategy overview

CN's focus is on running a safe and efficient railroad. While remaining at the forefront of the rail industry, CN's goal is to be internationally regarded as one of the best-performing transportation companies.

CN's commitment is to create value for both its customers and shareholders. By providing quality and cost-effective service, CN seeks to create value for its customers. By striving for sustainable financial performance through profitable growth, solid free cash flow and a high return on investment, CN seeks to deliver increased shareholder value.

CN has a unique business model, which is anchored on five key principles: providing quality service, controlling costs, focusing on asset utilization, committing to safety, and developing people. "Precision railroading" is at the core of CN's business model. It is a highly disciplined process whereby CN handles individual rail shipments according to a specific trip plan and manages all aspects of railroad operations to meet customer commitments efficiently and profitably.

Precision railroading demands discipline to execute the trip plan, the relentless measurement of results, and the use of such results to generate further execution improvements. Precision railroading increases velocity, improves reliability, lowers costs, enhances asset utilization and, ultimately, helps the Company grow the top line. It has been a key contributor to CN's earnings growth and improved return.

The Company sees further opportunities to grow the business and improve productivity. While the slowdown in the economy has affected CN in specific markets such as key forest products and construction materials, there are several opportunities that extend beyond business-cycle considerations. In Intermodal, the Prince Rupert Intermodal Terminal, opened in the fourth quarter of 2007, will allow CN to leverage the potential of the growing container trade between Asia and North America. In Bulk, the Company expects to continue to benefit from increased resource demand, particularly as it relates to recent coal mine expansion. In Merchandise, the Company sees growth potential for a number of commodities, particularly pipes, machinery and equipment, condensate and other commodities associated with oil and gas development in western Canada. While there is an increasing risk of recession in the U.S. economy, the Company's assumption is that economic growth in North America and globally will continue to slow down in 2008, but that a recession will not take place. In addition, the Company's assumption is that the risks outlined in the Business risks section of this MD&A will not result in a material impact on its financial statements.

The Company, on an ongoing basis, invests in various strategic initiatives to grow the business. Some of these recent initiatives include the proposed acquisition of the Elgin, Joliet and Eastern Railway Company (EJ&E), which is pending approval by the U.S. Surface Transportation Board (STB); the acquisition of short lines in Alberta to help oil sands operators meet growing demand for energy; the development of CN WorldWide International, the Company's international freight-forwarding subsidiary, with offices in Europe and China; and the formation of CN WorldWide North America, a new operating entity, to manage and expand the scope and scale of the Company's existing non-rail capabilities such as warehousing and distribution, customs services, truck brokerage and supply chain visibility tools across North America.

The opportunities to further improve productivity extend across all functions in the organization. In Transportation, the Company is aiming to continue to increase productivity on the track and in the yards. Yard throughput is being improved through SmartYard, an innovative use of real-time traffic information to sequence cars effectively and get them out on the line more quickly in the face of constantly changing conditions. In Engineering, the Company is working to increase the productivity of its field forces, again through better use of traffic information and, as a result, better management of its engineering forces on the track. The Company also intends to maintain a solid focus on reducing accidents and related costs, and also costs for legal claims and health care.

CN's capital programs support the Company's commitment to the five key principles and its ability to grow the business profitably. In 2008, CN plans to invest approximately $1.5 billion on capital programs, of which over $1 billion is targeted towards track infrastructure to maintain a safe railway and to improve the productivity and fluidity of the network, and includes the replacement of rail, ties, and other track materials, bridge improvements, as well as upgrades to the recently acquired rail assets of the Athabasca Northern Railway (ANY). This amount also includes funds for strategic initiatives, such as siding extensions to accommodate container traffic from the Prince Rupert Intermodal Terminal, the upgrade of the Company's freight car classification yard in Memphis, Tennessee, and additional enhancements to the track infrastructure in western Canada to take advantage of growth prospects in North American trade with Asia and in western Canada.

CN's equipment spending, targeted to reach approximately $140 million in 2008, is intended to develop growth opportunities and to improve the quality of the fleet to meet customer requirements. This amount includes the acquisition of new fuel-efficient locomotives, as well as improvements to the existing fleet. CN also expects to spend more than $300 million on facilities to grow the business, including transloads and distribution centers; on information technology to improve service and operating efficiency; and on other projects to increase productivity.

The Company's commitment to safety is reflected in the wide range of initiatives that CN is pursuing and the size of its capital programs. Comprehensive plans are in place to address safety, security, employee well-being and environmental management. CN's Integrated Safety Plan is the framework for putting safety at the center of its day-to-day operations. This proactive plan is designed to minimize risk and drive continuous improvement in the reduction of injuries and accidents, is fully supported by senior management, and engages employees at all levels of the organization.

Environmental protection is also an integral part of CN's day-to-day activities. A combination of key resource people, training, policies, monitoring and environmental assessments helps to ensure that the Company's operations comply with CN's Environmental Policy, a copy of which is available on CN's website.

CN's ability to develop the best railroaders in the industry has been a key contributor to the Company's success. CN recognizes that without the right people – no matter how good a service plan or business model a company may have – it will not be able to fully execute. The Company is focused on recruiting the right people, developing employees with the right skills, motivating them to do the right thing, and training them to be the future leaders of the Company.

The forward-looking statements provided in the above section and in other parts of this MD&A are subject to risks and uncertainties that could cause actual results or performance to differ materially from those expressed or implied in such statements and are based on certain factors and assumptions which the Company considers reasonable, about events, developments, prospects and opportunities that may not materialize or that may be offset entirely or partially by other events and developments. See the Business risks section of this MD&A for assumptions and risk factors affecting such forward-looking statements.

Financial outlook

During the year, the Company issued and updated its financial outlook. The 2007 actual results are in line with the latest financial outlook provided by the Company.

Financial and statistical highlights

$ in millions, except per share data, or unless otherwise indicated	2007	2006	2005
Financial results			
Revenues [a]	$ 7,897	$ 7,929	$ 7,446
Operating income	$ 2,876	$ 3,030	$ 2,624
Net income [b][c]	$ 2,158	$ 2,087	$ 1,556
Operating ratio [a]	63.6%	61.8%	64.8%
Basic earnings per share [b][c]	$ 4.31	$ 3.97	$ 2.82
Diluted earnings per share [b][c]	$ 4.25	$ 3.91	$ 2.77
Dividend declared per share	$ 0.84	$ 0.65	$ 0.50
Financial position			
Total assets	$23,460	$24,004	$22,188
Total long-term financial liabilities	$11,693	$12,066	$10,981
Statistical operating data and productivity measures			
Employees (average for the year)	22,389	22,092	22,637
Gross ton miles (GTM) per average number of employees (thousands)	15,539	15,977	15,148
GTMs per U.S. gallon of fuel consumed	887	880	851

(a) The 2006 and 2005 comparative figures have been reclassified in order to be consistent with the 2007 presentation (see the Revenue reclassification section of this MD&A).

(b) The 2007 figures included a deferred income tax recovery of $328 million ($0.66 per basic share or $0.64 per diluted share), resulting mainly from the enactment of corporate income tax rate changes in Canada, and the gains on sale of the Central Station Complex of $92 million, or $64 million after-tax ($0.13 per basic or diluted share) and the Company's investment in English Welsh and Scottish Railway (EWS) of $61 million, or $41 million after-tax ($0.08 per basic or diluted share).

(c) The 2006 figures included a deferred income tax recovery of $277 million ($0.53 per basic share or $0.51 per diluted share), resulting primarily from the enactment of lower corporate income tax rates in Canada and the resolution of matters pertaining to prior years' income taxes.

Financial results

2007 compared to 2006

In 2007, net income increased by $71 million, or 3%, to $2,158 million, when compared to 2006, with diluted earnings per share rising 9%, to $4.25. Included in the 2007 figures was a deferred income tax recovery of $328 million ($0.66 per basic share or $0.64 per diluted share), resulting mainly from the enactment of corporate income tax rate changes in Canada, and the gains on sale of the Central Station Complex of $64 million after-tax ($0.13 per basic or diluted share) and the Company's investment in EWS of $41 million after-tax ($0.08 per basic or diluted share). Included in the 2006 figures was a deferred income tax recovery of $277 million ($0.53 per basic share or $0.51 per diluted share), resulting primarily from the enactment of lower corporate income tax rates in Canada and the resolution of matters pertaining to prior years' income taxes.

Revenues for the year ended December 31, 2007 totaled $7,897 million compared to $7,929 million in 2006. The decrease of $32 million, relatively flat on a percentage basis, was mainly due to the translation impact of the stronger Canadian dollar on U.S. dollar-denominated revenues, weakness in specific markets, particularly forest products, and the impact of the United Transportation Union (UTU) strike and adverse weather conditions in the first half of 2007. Partly offsetting these factors was the impact of net freight rate increases, which includes lower fuel surcharge revenues as a result of applicable fuel prices, and an overall improvement in traffic mix.

Operating expenses increased by $122 million, or 2%, to $5,021 million, mainly due to increased fuel costs and equipment rents, which were partly offset by the translation impact of the stronger Canadian dollar on U.S. dollar-denominated expenses and decreased labor and fringe benefits.

The operating ratio, defined as operating expenses as a percentage of revenues, was 63.6% in 2007 compared to 61.8% in 2006, a 1.8-point increase.

In addition to the weather conditions and operational challenges in the first half of the year, the Company's results in 2007 included the impact of a first-quarter strike by 2,800 members of the UTU in Canada for which the Company estimated the negative impact on first-quarter operating income and net income to be approximately $50 million and $35 million, respectively ($0.07 per basic or diluted share).

Foreign exchange fluctuations have had an impact on the comparability of the results of operations. In 2007, the strengthening of the Canadian dollar relative to the U.S. dollar, which affected the conversion of the Company's U.S. dollar-denominated revenues and expenses, resulted in a reduction to net income of approximately $35 million.

Revenues

In millions, unless otherwise indicated Year ended December 31,	2007	2006	% Change
Rail freight revenues	$7,186	$7,254	(1%)
Other revenues	711	675	5%
Total revenues	$7,897	$7,929	–
Rail freight revenues:			
Petroleum and chemicals	$1,226	$1,171	5%
Metals and minerals	826	835	(1%)
Forest products	1,552	1,747	(11%)
Coal	385	370	4%
Grain and fertilizers	1,311	1,258	4%
Intermodal	1,382	1,394	(1%)
Automotive	504	479	5%
Total rail freight revenues	$7,186	$7,254	(1%)
Revenue ton miles (RTM) *(millions)*	184,148	185,610	(1%)
Rail freight revenue/RTM *(cents)*	3.90	3.91	–
Carloads *(thousands)*	4,744	4,824	(2%)
Rail freight revenue/carload *(dollars)*	1,515	1,504	1%

Certain of the 2006 comparative figures have been reclassified in order to be consistent with the 2007 presentation (see the Revenue reclassification section of this MD&A).

Revenues for the year ended December 31, 2007 totaled $7,897 million compared to $7,929 million in 2006. The decrease of $32 million was mainly due to the translation impact of the stronger Canadian dollar on U.S. dollar-denominated revenues of approximately $220 million; weakness in specific markets, particularly forest products; and the impact of the UTU strike and adverse weather conditions in the first half of 2007. Partly offsetting these factors was the impact of net freight rate increases of approximately $170 million, which includes lower fuel surcharge revenues as a result of applicable fuel prices, and an overall improvement in traffic mix.

In 2007, revenue ton miles (RTM), measuring the relative weight and distance of rail freight transported by the Company, declined 1% relative to 2006. Rail freight revenue per revenue ton mile, a measurement of yield defined as revenue earned on the movement of a ton of freight over one mile, was flat compared to 2006, partly due to net freight rate increases that were offset by the translation impact of the stronger Canadian dollar.

Petroleum and chemicals

Year ended December 31,	2007	2006	% Change
Revenues *(millions)*	$1,226	$1,171	5%
RTMs *(millions)*	32,761	31,868	3%
Revenue/RTM *(cents)*	3.74	3.67	2%

Petroleum and chemicals comprises a wide range of commodities, including chemicals, sulfur, plastics, petroleum products and liquefied petroleum gas products. The primary markets for these commodities are within North America, and as such, the performance of this commodity group is closely correlated with the North American economy. Most of the Company's petroleum and chemicals shipments originate in the Louisiana petrochemical corridor between New Orleans and Baton Rouge; in northern Alberta, which is a major center for natural gas feedstock and world scale petrochemicals and plastics; and in eastern Canadian regional plants. These shipments are destined for customers in Canada, the United States and overseas. For the year ended December 31, 2007, revenues for this commodity group increased by $55 million, or 5%, from 2006. The increase in this commodity group was mainly due to net freight rate increases; the continued growth of condensate movements, both from the west coast of Canada and the U.S.; and increased volumes in petroleum products, driven by higher shipments of diesel and heavy fuel oils in Canada and alternative fuels in the U.S. These gains were partly offset by the translation impact of the stronger Canadian dollar; areas of market weakness for plastic feedstocks, driven largely by a customer plant closure, and for PVC plastics and chemicals; and the impact of the UTU strike and adverse weather conditions in the first half of 2007. Revenue per revenue ton mile increased by 2% in 2007, mainly due to net freight rate increases and an improvement in traffic mix that were partly offset by the translation impact of the stronger Canadian dollar.

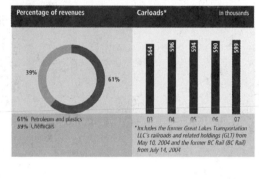

Percentage of revenues

39%   61%

61% Petroleum and plastics
39% Chemicals

Carloads*   In thousands

564   596   594   590   599

03   04   05   06   07

*Includes the former Great Lakes Transportation LLC's railroads and related holdings (GLT) from May 10, 2004 and the former BC Rail (BC Rail) from July 14, 2004

U.S. GAAP

Metals and minerals

Year ended December 31,	2007	2006	% Change
Revenues *(millions)*	$826	$835	(1%)
RTMs *(millions)*	16,719	17,467	(4%)
Revenue/RTM *(cents)*	4.94	4.78	3%

The metals and minerals commodity group consists primarily of nonferrous base metals, concentrates, iron ore, steel, construction materials, machinery and dimensional (large) loads. The Company provides unique rail access to aluminum, mining, steel and iron ore producing regions, which are among the most important in North America. This access, coupled with the Company's transload and port facilities, has made CN a leader in the transportation of copper, lead, zinc, concentrates, iron ore, refined metals and aluminum. Mining, oil and gas development and non-residential construction are the key drivers for metals and minerals. For the year ended December 31, 2007, revenues for this commodity group decreased by $9 million, or 1%, from 2006. The decrease in this commodity group was mainly due to the translation impact of the stronger Canadian dollar and softer demand for construction materials, primarily caused by fewer shipments of cement and roofing material. Partly offsetting these factors were net freight rate increases, strong shipments of steel slabs and plates, and increased volumes of machinery and dimensional loads. Revenue per revenue ton mile increased by 3% in 2007, mainly due to net freight rate increases and a reduction in the average length of haul, largely caused by the recovery of short-haul iron ore volumes. Partly offsetting these factors was the translation impact of the stronger Canadian dollar.

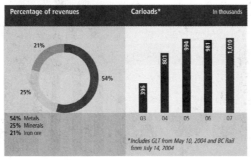

Percentage of revenues / Carloads* (In thousands)

54% Metals
25% Minerals
21% Iron ore

*Includes GLT from May 10, 2004 and BC Rail from July 14, 2004

Forest products

Year ended December 31,	2007	2006	% Change
Revenues *(millions)*	$1,552	$1,747	(11%)
RTMs *(millions)*	39,808	42,488	(6%)
Revenue/RTM *(cents)*	3.90	4.11	(5%)

The forest products commodity group includes various types of lumber, panels, paper, wood pulp and other fibers such as logs, recycled paper and wood chips. The Company has superior rail access to the western and eastern Canadian fiber-producing regions, which are among the largest fiber source areas in North America. In the United States, the Company is strategically located to serve both the Midwest and southern U.S. corridors with interline connections to other Class I railroads. The key drivers for the various commodities are: for newsprint, advertising lineage, non-print media and overall economic conditions, primarily in the United States; for fibers (mainly wood pulp), the consumption of paper in North American and offshore markets; and for lumber and panels, housing starts and renovation activities in the United States. Although demand for forest products can be cyclical, the Company's geographical advantages, unique access and product diversity tend to reduce the overall impact of market fluctuations. For the year ended December 31, 2007, revenues for this commodity group decreased by $195 million, or 11%, when compared to 2006. The decrease in 2007 was mainly due to weak market conditions, the translation impact of the stronger Canadian dollar and the impact of the UTU strike and adverse weather conditions in the first half of 2007. Partly offsetting these factors were improvements in traffic mix as a result of extended routings and net freight rate increases. Revenue per revenue ton mile decreased by 5% in 2007, mainly due to an increase in the average length of haul and the translation impact of the stronger Canadian dollar, which were partly offset by net freight rate increases.

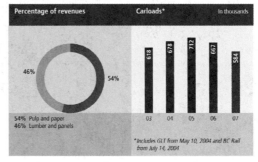

Percentage of revenues / Carloads* (In thousands)

54% Pulp and paper
46% Lumber and panels

*Includes GLT from May 10, 2004 and BC Rail from July 14, 2004

U.S. GAAP

Canadian National Railway Company **35**

Coal

Year ended December 31,	2007	2006	% Change
Revenues *(millions)*	$385	$370	4%
RTMs *(millions)*	13,776	13,727	–
Revenue/RTM *(cents)*	2.79	2.70	3%

The coal commodity group consists primarily of thermal grades of bituminous coal. Canadian thermal coal is delivered to power utilities primarily in eastern Canada; while in the United States, thermal coal is transported from mines served in southern Illinois, or from western U.S. mines via interchange with other railroads, to major utilities in the Midwest and southeast United States. The coal business also includes the transport of Canadian metallurgical coal, which is largely exported via terminals on the west coast of Canada to steel producers. For the year ended December 31, 2007, revenues for this commodity group increased by $15 million, or 4%, from 2006. The improvement in this commodity group was mainly due to increased shipments of metallurgical coal in western Canada, largely driven by a new mine start-up, positive changes in traffic mix and net freight rate increases. Partly offsetting these gains were reduced shipments of imported metallurgical coke to the U.S., the cessation by the Company of certain short-haul U.S. coal shipments and the impact of the UTU strike and adverse weather conditions in the first half of 2007. The revenue per revenue ton mile increase of 3% in 2007 was mainly due to a positive change in traffic mix and net freight rate increases, which were partly offset by the translation impact of the stronger Canadian dollar.

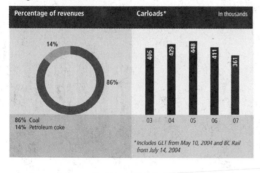

Percentage of revenues
14%
86%
86% Coal
14% Petroleum coke

Carloads* — In thousands
405 | 429 | 448 | 411 | 361
03 | 04 | 05 | 06 | 07
*Includes GLT from May 10, 2004 and BC Rail from July 14, 2004

Grain and fertilizers

Year ended December 31,	2007	2006	% Change
Revenues *(millions)*	$1,311	$1,258	4%
RTMs *(millions)*	45,359	44,096	3%
Revenue/RTM *(cents)*	2.89	2.85	1%

The grain and fertilizers commodity group depends primarily on crops grown and fertilizers processed in western Canada and the U.S. Midwest. The grain segment consists of three primary segments: food grains (mainly wheat, oats and malting barley), feed grains (including feed barley, feed wheat, and corn), and oilseeds and oilseed products (primarily canola seed, oil and meal, and soybeans). Production of grain varies considerably from year to year, affected primarily by weather conditions, seeded and harvested acreage, the mix of grains produced and crop yields. Grain exports are sensitive to the size and quality of the crop produced, international market conditions and foreign government policy. The majority of grain produced in western Canada and moved by CN is exported via the ports of Vancouver, Prince Rupert and Thunder Bay. Certain of these rail movements are subject to government regulation and to a "revenue cap," which effectively establishes a maximum revenue entitlement that railways can earn. In the U.S., grain grown in Illinois and Iowa is exported, as well as transported to domestic processing facilities and feed markets. The Company also serves major producers of potash in Canada, as well as producers of ammonium nitrate, urea and other fertilizers across Canada and the U.S. For the year ended December 31, 2007, revenues for this commodity group increased by $53 million, or 4%, from 2006. The improvement in this commodity group was mainly due to net freight rate increases and increased volumes, particularly of potash into the U.S., ethanol and Canadian grain exports. These gains were partly offset by the translation impact of the stronger Canadian dollar, lower U.S. corn shipments and the impact of the UTU strike and adverse weather conditions in the first half of 2007. Revenue per revenue ton mile increased by 1% in 2007, largely due to net freight rate increases and a positive change in traffic mix that were partly offset by the translation impact of the stronger Canadian dollar.

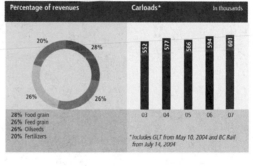

Percentage of revenues
20%
28%
26%
26%
28% Food grain
26% Feed grain
26% Oilseeds
20% Fertilizers

Carloads* — In thousands
552 | 577 | 566 | 594 | 601
03 | 04 | 05 | 06 | 07
*Includes GLT from May 10, 2004 and BC Rail from July 14, 2004

Intermodal

Year ended December 31,	2007	2006	% Change
Revenues (millions)	$1,382	$1,394	(1%)
RTMs (millions)	32,607	32,922	(1%)
Revenue/RTM (cents)	4.24	4.23	–

The intermodal commodity group is comprised of two segments: domestic and international. The domestic segment transports consumer products and manufactured goods, operating through both retail and wholesale channels, within domestic Canada, domestic U.S., Mexico and transborder, while the international segment handles import and export container traffic, directly serving the major ports of Vancouver, Prince Rupert, Montreal, Halifax and New Orleans. The domestic segment is driven by consumer markets, with growth generally tied to the economy. The international segment is driven by North American economic and trade conditions. For the year ended December 31, 2007, revenues for this commodity group decreased by $12 million, or 1%, from 2006. The decrease in this commodity group was mainly due to the translation impact of the stronger Canadian dollar, reduced overseas traffic due to lower volumes through the ports of Halifax and Montreal and the impact of the UTU strike and adverse weather conditions in the first half of 2007. Partly offsetting these factors were net freight rate increases, an increase in volume through the port of Vancouver and the opening of the Port of Prince Rupert in the fourth quarter. Revenue per revenue ton mile remained relatively flat in 2007, mainly due to net freight rate increases that were offset by the translation impact of the stronger Canadian dollar.

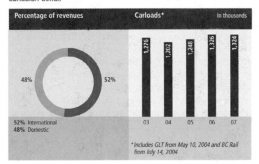

52% International
48% Domestic

*Includes GLT from May 10, 2004 and BC Rail from July 14, 2004

Automotive

Year ended December 31,	2007	2006	% Change
Revenues (millions)	$504	$479	5%
RTMs (millions)	3,118	3,042	2%
Revenue/RTM (cents)	16.16	15.75	3%

The automotive commodity group moves both finished vehicles and parts throughout North America, providing rail access to all vehicle assembly plants in Canada; eight assembly plants in Michigan; and one in Mississippi. The Company also serves more than 20 vehicle distribution facilities in Canada and the U.S., as well as parts production facilities in Michigan and Ontario. CN's broad coverage enables it to consolidate full trainloads of automotive traffic for delivery to connecting railroads at key interchange points. The Company serves shippers of import vehicles via the ports of Halifax and Vancouver, and through interchange with other railroads. The Company's automotive revenues are closely correlated to automotive production and sales in North America. For the year ended December 31, 2007, revenues for this commodity group increased by $25 million, or 5%, from 2006. The improvement in this commodity group was mainly due to increased market share of finished vehicles coming out of the U.S. into western Canada, increases in finished vehicles entering North America through CN-served ports, the benefit of new facilities in Ontario and Michigan and net freight rate increases that were partly offset by the translation impact of the stronger Canadian dollar. Revenue per revenue ton mile increased by 3% in 2007, largely due to net freight rate increases that were partly offset by the translation impact of the stronger Canadian dollar.

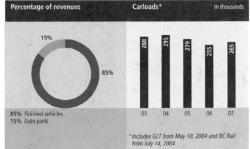

85% Finished vehicles
15% Auto parts

*Includes GLT from May 10, 2004 and BC Rail from July 14, 2004

Other revenues
Other revenues mainly includes revenues from non-rail transportation services, interswitching, and maritime operations. In 2007, Other revenues increased by $36 million, or 5%, when compared to 2006, mainly due to an increase in non-rail transportation services revenues and higher optional service revenues which were partly offset by the translation impact of the stronger Canadian dollar.

Operating expenses

Operating expenses amounted to $5,021 million in 2007 compared to $4,899 million in 2006. The increase of $122 million, or 2%, in 2007 was mainly due to increased fuel costs and equipment rents, which were partly offset by the translation impact of the stronger Canadian dollar on U.S dollar-denominated expenses of approximately $135 million and decreased labor and fringe benefits. The first-quarter 2007 UTU strike did not have a significant impact on total operating expenses as lower labor and fringe benefits expense was mostly offset by increases in purchased services and other expenses.

In millions	Year ended December 31,	2007	2006	% Change	Percentage of revenues 2007	2006
Labor and fringe benefits		$1,701	$1,823	7%	21.5%	23.0%
Purchased services and material		1,045	1,027	(2%)	13.2%	13.0%
Fuel		1,026	892	(15%)	13.0%	11.2%
Depreciation and amortization		677	650	(4%)	8.6%	8.2%
Equipment rents		247	198	(25%)	3.1%	2.5%
Casualty and other		325	309	(5%)	4.2%	3.9%
Total operating expenses		$5,021	$4,899	(2%)	63.6%	61.8%

Certain of the 2006 comparative figures have been reclassified in order to be consistent with the 2007 presentation (see the Revenue reclassification section of this MD&A).

Labor and fringe benefits: Labor and fringe benefits expense includes wages, payroll taxes, and employee benefits such as incentive compensation, stock-based compensation, health and welfare, pensions and other postretirement benefits. Certain incentive and stock-based compensation plans are based on financial and market performance targets and the related expense is recorded in relation to the attainment of such targets. Labor and fringe benefits expense decreased by $122 million, or 7%, in 2007 as compared to 2006. The decrease was mainly due to lower annual employee incentive costs, the translation impact of the stronger Canadian dollar, a reduction in net periodic benefit cost for pensions, lower stock-based compensation expense and net savings due to the first-quarter UTU strike. Partly offsetting these factors were higher workforce levels, particularly in the second half of 2007, and annual wage increases.

Purchased services and material: Purchased services and material expense primarily includes the costs of services purchased from outside contractors, materials used in the maintenance of the Company's track, facilities and equipment, transportation and lodging for train crew employees, utility costs and the net costs of operating facilities jointly used by the Company and other railroads. These expenses increased by $18 million, or 2%, in 2007 as compared to 2006. The increase was mainly due to higher costs for outsourced non-rail transportation services, higher repairs and maintenance expenses and higher costs as a result of the first-quarter UTU strike, which were partly offset by the translation impact of the stronger Canadian dollar.

Fuel: Fuel expense includes the cost of fuel consumed by locomotives, intermodal equipment and other vehicles. These expenses increased by $134 million, or 15%, in 2007 as compared to 2006. The increase was mainly due to a 13% increase in the average price per U.S. gallon of fuel when compared to the 2006 average price, which included the benefits of the fuel hedging program that expired in September 2006. Partly offsetting these factors were the translation impact of the stronger Canadian dollar, a decrease in freight volumes and improvements in fuel productivity.

Depreciation and amortization: Depreciation and amortization expense relates to the Company's rail operations. These expenses increased by $27 million, or 4%, in 2007 as compared to 2006. The increase was mainly due to the impact of net capital additions, which was partly offset by the translation impact of the stronger Canadian dollar.

Equipment rents: Equipment rents expense includes rental expense for the use of freight cars owned by other railroads or private companies and for the short- or long-term lease of freight cars, locomotives and intermodal equipment, net of rental income from other railroads for the use of the Company's cars and locomotives. These expenses increased by $49 million, or 25%, in 2007 as compared to 2006. The increase was mainly due to lower car hire income as a result of the reduction in traffic for forest products, shorter car cycles offline, increased car hire expense due to reduced velocity online related to the impact of the UTU strike and adverse weather conditions in western Canada in the first half of 2007. Partly offsetting these factors was the translation impact of the stronger Canadian dollar.

Casualty and other: Casualty and other expense includes expenses for personal injuries, environmental, freight and property damage, insurance, bad debt and operating taxes, as well as travel expenses. These expenses increased by $16 million, or 5%, in 2007 as compared to 2006. The increase was due primarily to increased accident costs as well as expenses incurred for the deployment of management employees as a result of the first-quarter UTU strike. Partly offsetting these factors was a lower expense for U.S. personal injury claims reflecting the results of the actuarial valuations in 2007.

Other

Interest expense: Interest expense increased by $24 million, or 8%, for the year ended December 31, 2007 as compared to 2006, mainly due to a higher average debt balance that was partly offset by the translation impact of the stronger Canadian dollar.

Other income: In 2007, the Company recorded Other income of $166 million compared to $11 million in 2006. The increase was mainly due to the gains on sale of the Central Station Complex of $92 million and the Company's investment in EWS of $61 million.

Income tax expense: The Company recorded income tax expense of $548 million for the year ended December 31, 2007 compared to $642 million in 2006. Included in the 2007 income tax expense was a deferred income tax recovery of $328 million, resulting mainly from the enactment of corporate income tax rate changes in Canada. Included in the 2006 income tax expense was a deferred income tax recovery of $277 million, resulting primarily from the enactment of lower corporate income tax rates in Canada and the resolution of matters pertaining to prior years' income taxes. The effective tax rate for 2007 was 20.3% compared to 23.5% in 2006. Excluding the deferred income tax recoveries, the effective tax rates for 2007 and 2006 were 32.4% and 33.7%, respectively. The decrease in the effective tax rate, excluding the deferred income tax recoveries, was mainly due to lower corporate income tax rates in Canada.

2006 compared to 2005

In 2006, net income increased by $531 million, or 34%, to $2,087 million, when compared to 2005, with diluted earnings per share rising 41%, to $3.91. Included in the 2006 figures was a deferred income tax recovery of $277 million ($0.53 per basic share or $0.51 per diluted share), resulting primarily from the enactment of lower corporate income tax rates in Canada and the resolution of matters pertaining to prior years' income taxes.

Revenues increased by $483 million, or 6%, to $7,929 million, mainly due to freight rate increases and volume growth, particularly for grain, intermodal and metals and minerals, which were partly offset by the translation impact of the stronger Canadian dollar on U.S. dollar-denominated revenues.

Operating expenses increased by $77 million, or 2%, to $4,899 million, mainly due to increased fuel costs, purchased services and material expense and depreciation. Partly offsetting these factors was the translation impact of the stronger Canadian dollar on U.S. dollar-denominated expenses and lower casualty and other expense.

The operating ratio, defined as operating expenses as a percentage of revenues, was 61.8% in 2006 compared to 64.8% in 2005, a 3.0-point betterment.

Foreign exchange fluctuations have had an impact on the comparability of the results of operations. In 2006, the continued appreciation in the Canadian dollar relative to the U.S. dollar, which has affected the conversion of the Company's U.S. dollar-denominated revenues and expenses, resulted in a reduction to net income of approximately $60 million.

Revenues

In millions, unless otherwise indicated Year ended December 31,	2006	2005	% Change
Rail freight revenues	$7,254	$6,793	7%
Other revenues	675	653	3%
Total revenues	$7,929	$7,446	6%
Rail freight revenues:			
Petroleum and chemicals	$1,171	$1,093	7%
Metals and minerals	835	777	7%
Forest products	1,747	1,742	–
Coal	370	324	14%
Grain and fertilizers	1,258	1,118	13%
Intermodal	1,394	1,252	11%
Automotive	479	487	(2%)
Total rail freight revenues	$7,254	$6,793	7%
Revenue ton miles (RTM) *(millions)*	185,610	179,701	3%
Rail freight revenue/RTM *(cents)*	3.91	3.78	3%
Carloads *(thousands)*	4,824	4,841	–
Rail freight revenue/carload *(dollars)*	1,504	1,403	7%

Certain of the 2006 and 2005 comparative figures have been reclassified in order to be consistent with the 2007 presentation (see the Revenue reclassification section of this MD&A).

Revenues for the year ended December 31, 2006 totaled $7,929 million compared to $7,446 million in 2005. The increase of $483 million, or 6%, was mainly due to freight rate increases of approximately $500 million, of which approximately 40% was due to higher fuel surcharge revenues that mainly resulted from increases in applicable fuel prices; and volume growth, particularly for grain, intermodal and metals and minerals. Partly offsetting these gains was the translation impact of the stronger Canadian dollar on U.S. dollar-denominated revenues of approximately $255 million.

In 2006, revenue ton miles increased by 3% relative to 2005. Rail freight revenue per revenue ton mile increased by 3% in 2006 when compared to 2005, largely due to freight rate increases that were partly offset by the translation impact of the stronger Canadian dollar on U.S. dollar-denominated revenues and an increase in the average length of haul.

Petroleum and chemicals

Year ended December 31,	2006	2005	% Change
Revenues *(millions)*	$1,171	$1,093	7%
RTMs *(millions)*	31,868	31,235	2%
Revenue/RTM *(cents)*	3.67	3.50	5%

Revenues for the year ended December 31, 2006 increased by $78 million, or 7%, from 2005. The improvement in this commodity group was mainly due to freight rate increases and increased shipments of condensate for oil sands-related development, and plastics and petrochemicals.

These gains were partly offset by the translation impact of the stronger Canadian dollar; lower petroleum products shipments in the second quarter of 2006 due to a temporary refinery shutdown; reduced spot shipments of heavy fuel oils in eastern Canada; lower liquefied petroleum gas shipments on account of warmer weather conditions; and a reduction in sulfur shipments in western Canada, particularly in the fourth quarter of 2006 due to inclement weather. Revenue per revenue ton mile increased by 5% in 2006, largely due to freight rate increases that were partly offset by the translation impact of the stronger Canadian dollar and an increase in the average length of haul.

Metals and minerals

Year ended December 31,	2006	2005	% Change
Revenues *(millions)*	$835	$777	7%
RTMs *(millions)*	17,467	16,848	4%
Revenue/RTM *(cents)*	4.78	4.61	4%

Revenues for the year ended December 31, 2006 increased by $58 million, or 7%, from 2005. The improvement in this commodity group was mainly due to freight rate increases; strong shipments of Canadian long steel products, primarily pipes for oil sands-related development; increased volumes of U.S. iron ore and raw materials for steel production due to higher demand, despite temporary fourth-quarter 2006 production issues at a customer plant; and strong machinery and dimensional loads traffic also for oil sands-related development. Partly offsetting these gains was the translation impact of the stronger Canadian dollar and reduced construction material shipments, particularly in the fourth quarter of 2006 due to softening demand. Revenue per revenue ton mile increased by 4% in 2006, mainly due to freight rate increases that were partly offset by the translation impact of the stronger Canadian dollar and an increase in the average length of haul.

Forest products

Year ended December 31,	2006	2005	% Change
Revenues *(millions)*	$1,747	$1,742	–
RTMs *(millions)*	42,488	42,330	–
Revenue/RTM *(cents)*	4.11	4.12	–

Revenues for the year ended December 31, 2006 increased by $5 million, remaining relatively flat when compared to 2005. The improvement in this commodity group was mainly due to freight rate increases and increased lumber shipments originating from western Canada in the first half of 2006. Largely offsetting these gains was the translation impact of the stronger Canadian dollar; a reduction in pulp and paper shipments due to continued weak market conditions and related mill closures; and lower lumber shipments originating from eastern Canada, particularly driven by mill closures in the fourth quarter of 2006. Revenue per revenue ton mile was flat in 2006 when compared to 2005, mainly due to freight rate increases that were offset by the translation impact of the stronger Canadian dollar and an increase in the average length of haul.

Coal

Year ended December 31,	2006	2005	% Change
Revenues *(millions)*	$370	$324	14%
RTMs *(millions)*	13,727	13,576	1%
Revenue/RTM *(cents)*	2.70	2.39	13%

Revenues for the year ended December 31, 2006 increased by $46 million, or 14%, from 2005. The improvement in this commodity group was mainly due to the expansion of metallurgical coal mines in western Canada and freight rate increases. Partly offsetting these gains was a decline in CN shipments originating from U.S. coal mines; the translation impact of the stronger Canadian dollar; and the loss of export shipments of petroleum coke due to adverse market conditions. The revenue per revenue ton mile increase of 13% in 2006 was mainly due to freight rate increases, which were partly offset by the translation impact of the stronger Canadian dollar and an increase in the average length of haul.

Grain and fertilizers

Year ended December 31,	2006	2005	% Change
Revenues *(millions)*	$1,258	$1,118	13%
RTMs *(millions)*	44,096	40,393	9%
Revenue/RTM *(cents)*	2.85	2.77	3%

Revenues for the year ended December 31, 2006 increased by $140 million, or 13%, from 2005. The improvement in this commodity group was mainly due to freight rate increases; higher shipments of U.S. corn mainly due to a larger harvest; stronger volumes of Canadian wheat due to a high quality crop; and increased shipments of canola. These gains were partly offset by the translation impact of the stronger Canadian dollar; decreased shipments of potash and other fertilizers due in part to soft North American market conditions; and decreased Canadian barley shipments. Revenue per revenue ton mile increased by 3% in 2006, largely due to freight rate increases that were partly offset by the translation impact of the stronger Canadian dollar and an increase in the average length of haul.

Intermodal

Year ended December 31,	2006	2005	% Change
Revenues *(millions)*	$1,394	$1,252	11%
RTMs *(millions)*	32,922	32,184	2%
Revenue/RTM *(cents)*	4.23	3.89	9%

Revenues for the year ended December 31, 2006 increased by $142 million, or 11%, from 2005. The improvement in this commodity group was mainly due to freight rate increases; growth in international container traffic, primarily from Asia; and increased domestic movements, particularly to transborder markets and western Canada. Partly offsetting these gains was the translation impact of the stronger Canadian dollar. The revenue per revenue ton mile increase of 9% in 2006 was largely due to freight rate increases and a decrease in the average length of haul, which were partly offset by the translation impact of the stronger Canadian dollar.

Automotive

Year ended December 31,	2006	2005	% Change
Revenues *(millions)*	$479	$487	(2%)
RTMs *(millions)*	3,042	3,135	(3%)
Revenue/RTM *(cents)*	15.75	15.53	1%

Revenues for the year ended December 31, 2006 decreased by $8 million, or 2%, from 2005. The translation impact of the stronger Canadian dollar and reduced shipments from domestic producers, primarily driven by production slowdowns, was partly offset by the benefit of freight rate increases and higher shipments of import vehicles via CN-served ports. Revenue per revenue ton mile increased by 1% in 2006, largely due to freight rate increases that were partly offset by the translation impact of the stronger Canadian dollar and an increase in the average length of haul.

Other revenues

In 2006, Other revenues increased by $22 million, or 3%, when compared to 2005, mainly due to increased interswitching, rental and maritime operations.

Operating expenses

Operating expenses amounted to $4,899 million in 2006 compared to $4,822 million in 2005. The increase of $77 million, or 2%, in 2006 was mainly due to increased fuel costs, purchased services and material expense and depreciation. Partly offsetting these factors was the translation impact of the stronger Canadian dollar on U.S. dollar-denominated expenses of approximately $150 million and lower casualty and other expense.

					Percentage of revenues	
In millions	*Year ended December 31,*	2006	2005	% Change	2006	2005
Labor and fringe benefits		$1,823	$1,856	2%	23.0%	24.9%
Purchased services and material		1,027	993	(3%)	13.0%	13.3%
Fuel		892	730	(22%)	11.2%	9.8%
Depreciation and amortization		650	627	(4%)	8.2%	8.5%
Equipment rents		198	192	(3%)	2.5%	2.6%
Casualty and other		309	424	27%	3.9%	5.7%
Total operating expenses		$4,899	$4,822	(2%)	61.8%	64.8%

Certain of the 2006 and 2005 comparative figures have been reclassified in order to be consistent with the 2007 presentation (see the Revenue reclassification section of this MD&A).

Labor and fringe benefits: Labor and fringe benefits expense decreased by $33 million, or 2%, in 2006 as compared to 2005. The decrease was mainly due to lower stock-based compensation expense, largely due to an acceleration of a grant payout in 2005; the translation impact of the stronger Canadian dollar; the impact of a reduced workforce and ongoing productivity improvements; and an increase in the first quarter of 2005 to the workforce reduction provision mainly for increased health care costs. Partly offsetting these factors were annual wage increases and an increase in net periodic benefit cost for pensions, mainly as a result of a decrease in the Company's discount rate used in 2006 relative to 2005.

Purchased services and material: Purchased services and material expense increased by $34 million, or 3%, in 2006 as compared to 2005. The increase was mainly due to higher expenses for various services, particularly for the Company's maritime activities, higher expenses for locomotive maintenance, lower income from joint facilities, and costs related to the upgrading of track shared with another railroad. Partly offsetting these factors was the translation impact of the stronger Canadian dollar.

Fuel: Fuel expense increased by $162 million, or 22%, in 2006 as compared to 2005. The increase was mainly due to a 24% increase in the average price per U.S. gallon of fuel, net of the benefits from CN's fuel hedging program, and higher freight volumes. Partly offsetting these factors were the translation impact of the stronger Canadian dollar and productivity improvements.

Depreciation and amortization: Depreciation and amortization expense increased by $23 million, or 4%, in 2006 as compared to 2005. The increase was mainly due to the impact of net capital additions and higher depreciation rates for the information technology asset class, which were partly offset by the translation impact of the stronger Canadian dollar.

Equipment rents: Equipment rents expense increased by $6 million, or 3%, in 2006 as compared to 2005. The increase was due to lower car hire income, mainly due to shorter routes and offline cycles, that was partly offset by lower lease and car hire expense, and the translation impact of the stronger Canadian dollar.

Casualty and other: Casualty and other expense decreased by $115 million, or 27%, in 2006 as compared to 2005. The decrease was largely due to a net reduction to the provision for U.S. personal injuries following the 2006 actuarial studies; a lower expense for occupational disease claims; and lower derailment-related expenses, mainly due to costs that were incurred for the incident at Wabamun Lake in 2005. Partly offsetting these items were higher operating taxes and increased environmental expenses for ongoing site restoration.

Other

Interest expense: Interest expense increased by $13 million, or 4%, for the year ended December 31, 2006 as compared to 2005, mainly due to interest on 2006 debt issuances and higher capital lease obligations that were partly offset by the translation impact of the stronger Canadian dollar.

Other income: In 2006, the Company recorded Other income of $11 million compared to $12 million in 2005. The decrease was mainly due to lower investment income, which was largely offset by higher foreign exchange gains and lower costs related to the securitization program.

Income tax expense: The Company recorded income tax expense of $642 million for the year ended December 31, 2006 compared to $781 million in 2005. Included in the 2006 income tax expense was a deferred income tax recovery of $277 million, resulting primarily from the enactment of lower corporate income tax rates in Canada and the resolution of matters pertaining to prior years' income taxes. Excluding this deferred income tax recovery, the effective tax rate for the year ended December 31, 2006 was 33.7% compared to 33.4% in 2005.

Summary of quarterly financial data – unaudited

In millions, except per share data

	2007 Quarters				2006 Quarters			
	Fourth	Third	Second	First	Fourth	Third	Second	First
Revenues (a)	$ 1,941	$ 2,023	$ 2,027	$ 1,906	$ 2,000	$ 2,032	$ 2,000	$ 1,897
Operating income	$ 736	$ 768	$ 811	$ 561	$ 756	$ 844	$ 805	$ 625
Net income	$ 833	$ 485	$ 516	$ 324	$ 499	$ 497	$ 729	$ 362
Basic earnings per share	$ 1.70	$ 0.97	$ 1.02	$ 0.64	$ 0.97	$ 0.95	$ 1.38	$ 0.68
Diluted earnings per share	$ 1.68	$ 0.96	$ 1.01	$ 0.63	$ 0.95	$ 0.94	$ 1.35	$ 0.66
Dividend declared per share	$0.2100	$0.2100	$0.2100	$0.2100	$0.1625	$0.1625	$0.1625	$0.1625

(a) The 2006 comparative figures have been reclassified in order to be consistent with the 2007 presentation (see the Revenue reclassification section of this MD&A).

Revenues generated by the Company during the year are influenced by seasonal weather conditions, general economic conditions, cyclical demand for rail transportation, and competitive forces in the transportation marketplace. Operating expenses reflect the impact of freight volumes, seasonal weather conditions, labor costs, fuel prices, and the Company's productivity initiatives. The continued fluctuations in the Canadian dollar relative to the U.S. dollar have also affected the conversion of the Company's U.S. dollar-denominated revenues and expenses and resulted in fluctuations in net income in the rolling eight quarters presented above.

The Company's quarterly results included items that impacted the quarter-over-quarter comparability of the results of operations as discussed herein:

In millions, except per share data

	2007 Quarters				2006 Quarters			
	Fourth	Third	Second	First	Fourth	Third	Second	First
Deferred income tax recoveries	$ 284	$ 14	$ 30	$ –	$ 27	$ –	$ 250	$ –
Gain on sale of Central Station Complex (after-tax)	64	–	–	–	–	–	–	–
Gain on sale of investment in EWS (after-tax)	41	–	–	–	–	–	–	–
UTU strike (after-tax)	–	–	–	(35)	–	–	–	–
Impact on net income	$ 389	$ 14	$ 30	$ (35)	$ 27	$ –	$ 250	$ –
Basic earnings per share	$0.79	$0.03	$0.06	$(0.07)	$0.05	$ –	$0.48	$ –
Diluted earnings per share	$0.78	$0.03	$0.06	$(0.07)	$0.05	$ –	$0.46	$ –

Revenue reclassification

Certain of the 2006 and 2005 comparative figures have been reclassified in order to be consistent with the 2007 presentation as discussed herein. As a result of the Company's expansion of its existing non-rail transportation services, in combination with its rail service, the Company has become primarily responsible for the fulfillment of the transportation of goods involving non-rail activities. In order to be consistent with the presentation of other non-rail transportation services, the Company reclassified certain operating expenses incurred for non-rail transportation services, which were previously netted with their related revenues, to reflect the gross reporting of revenues where appropriate. This change had no impact on the Company's operating income and net income, as both revenues and operating expenses were increased by $213 million for 2006 and $206 million for 2005. In addition, the Company reclassified its non-rail transportation revenues to Other revenues. Previously, various revenues for non-rail transportation services were reported in both Rail freight revenues and Other revenues.

Liquidity and capital resources

The Company's principal source of liquidity is cash generated from operations. The Company also has the ability to fund liquidity requirements through its revolving credit facility, the issuance of debt and/or equity, and the sale of a portion of its accounts receivable through a securitization program. In addition, from time to time, the Company's liquidity requirements can be supplemented by the disposal of surplus properties and the monetization of assets.

Operating activities: Cash provided from operating activities was $2,417 million for the year ended December 31, 2007 compared to $2,951 million for 2006. Net cash receipts from customers and other were $8,139 million for the year ended December 31, 2007, an increase of $193 million when compared to 2006, mainly due to an increase in the proceeds received under the Company's accounts receivable securitization program. In 2007, payments for employee services, suppliers and other expenses were $4,323 million, an increase of $193 million when compared to 2006, principally due to higher payments for labor and fringe benefits, fuel and car hire. Payments for income taxes in 2007 were $867 million, an increase of $560 million when compared to 2006, mainly due to the final payment for Canadian income taxes, in respect of the 2006 fiscal year. Also consuming cash in 2007 were payments for interest, workforce reductions and personal injury and other claims of $340 million, $31 million and $86 million, respectively, compared to $294 million, $45 million and $107 million, respectively, in 2006. In 2007 and 2006, pension contributions were $75 million and $112 million, respectively. In 2008, payments for workforce reductions, pension contributions and income taxes are expected to be $19 million, $100 million and approximately $500 million (see the Income taxes section of this MD&A), respectively. There are currently no specific or unusual requirements relating to working capital other than the items disclosed.

Investing activities: Cash used by investing activities in 2007 amounted to $895 million compared to $1,349 million in 2006. The Company's investing activities in 2007 included property additions of $1,387 million, an increase of $89 million when compared to 2006; and $25 million for the acquisition of the rail assets of ANY. Also included in investing activities are the net proceeds of $465 million from the disposition of the Central Station Complex and the Company's investment in EWS. The following table details property additions for 2007 and 2006:

In millions	Year ended December 31,	2007	2006
Track and roadway		$1,069	$1,012
Rolling stock		281	349
Buildings		172	35
Information technology		97	81
Other		69	82
Gross property additions		1,688	1,559
Less: capital leases (a)		301	261
Property additions		$1,387	$1,298

(a) During 2007, the Company recorded $213 million ($264 million in 2006) in assets it acquired through equipment leases and $90 million relating to the leaseback arrangement from the Central Station Complex transaction, for which an equivalent amount was recorded in debt.

On an ongoing basis, the Company invests in capital programs for the renewal of the basic plant, the acquisition of rolling stock and other investments to take advantage of growth opportunities and to improve the Company's productivity and the fluidity of its network. For 2008, the Company expects to invest approximately $1.5 billion for its capital programs.

Free cash flow
The Company generated $828 million of free cash flow for the year ended December 31, 2007, compared to $1,343 million in 2006. Free cash flow does not have any standardized meaning prescribed by GAAP and therefore, may not be comparable to similar measures presented by other companies. The Company believes that free cash flow is a useful measure of performance as it demonstrates the Company's ability to generate cash after the payment of capital expenditures and dividends. The Company defines free cash flow as cash provided from operating activities, excluding changes in the accounts receivable securitization program and changes in cash and cash equivalents resulting from foreign exchange fluctuations, less cash used by investing activities and the payment of dividends, calculated as follows:

In millions	Year ended December 31,	2007	2006
Cash provided from operating activities		$2,417	$ 2,951
Cash used by investing activities		(895)	(1,349)
Cash provided before financing activities		1,522	1,602
Adjustments:			
Change in accounts receivable securitization		(228)	82
Dividends paid		(418)	(340)
Effect of foreign exchange fluctuations on U.S. dollar-denominated cash and cash equivalents		(48)	(1)
Free cash flow		$ 828	$ 1,343

Financing activities: Cash used by financing activities totaled $1,343 million for the year ended December 31, 2007 compared to $1,484 million in 2006. In September 2007, the Company issued U.S.$250 million (Cdn$250 million) of 5.85% Notes due 2017 and U.S.$300 million (Cdn$300 million) of 6.375% Debentures due 2037. The Company used the net proceeds of U.S.$544 million to repay a portion of its outstanding commercial paper and to reduce its accounts receivable securitization program. In 2007 and 2006, issuances and repayments of long-term debt related principally to the Company's commercial paper program.

Cash received from options exercised during 2007 and 2006 was $61 million and $101 million, respectively, and the related tax benefit realized upon exercise was $16 million and $19 million, respectively.

In 2007, the Company repurchased 30.2 million common shares under its share repurchase programs for $1,584 million: 17.7 million common shares for $897 million (weighted-average price of $50.70 per share) under its new 33.0 million share repurchase program and 12.5 million common shares for $687 million (weighted-average price of $54.93 per share) under its previous 28.0 million share repurchase program, which was completed in the second quarter of 2007. In 2006, the Company used $1,483 million to repurchase 29.5 million common shares under its previous share repurchase programs.

During 2007, the Company paid dividends totaling $418 million to its shareholders at the quarterly rate of $0.21 per share, compared to $340 million at the quarterly rate of $0.1625 per share in 2006.

Credit measures

Management believes that adjusted debt-to-total capitalization is a useful credit measure that aims to show the true leverage of the Company. Similarly, adjusted debt-to-adjusted earnings before interest, income taxes, depreciation and amortization (EBITDA) is another useful credit measure because it reflects the Company's ability to service its debt. The Company excludes Other income in the calculation of EBITDA. However, since these measures do not have any standardized meaning prescribed by GAAP, they may not be comparable to similar measures presented by other companies and, as such, should not be considered in isolation.

Adjusted debt-to-total capitalization ratio

December 31,	2007	2006
Debt-to-total capitalization ratio [(a)]	35.6%	36.3%
Add: Present value of operating lease commitments plus securitization financing [(b)]	4.8%	4.1%
Adjusted debt-to-total capitalization ratio	40.4%	40.4%

Adjusted debt-to-adjusted EBITDA

$ in millions, unless otherwise indicated Year ended December 31,	2007	2006
Debt	$5,617	$5,604
Add: Present value of operating lease commitments plus securitization financing [(b)]	1,287	1,044
Adjusted debt	6,904	6,648
EBITDA	3,553	3,680
Add: Deemed interest on operating leases	41	38
Adjusted EBITDA	$3,594	$3,718
Adjusted debt-to-adjusted EBITDA	1.9 times	1.8 times

(a) Debt-to-total capitalization is calculated as total long-term debt plus current portion of long-term debt divided by the sum of total debt plus total shareholders' equity.

(b) The operating lease commitments have been discounted using the Company's implicit interest rate for each of the periods presented.

The Company has access to various financing arrangements:

Revolving credit facility

The Company's U.S.$1 billion revolving credit facility, expiring in October 2011, is available for general corporate purposes, including back-stopping the Company's commercial paper program, and provides for borrowings at various interest rates, including the Canadian prime rate, bankers' acceptance rates, the U.S. federal funds effective rate and the London Interbank Offer Rate, plus applicable margins. The credit facility agreement has one financial covenant, which limits debt as a percentage of total capitalization, and with which the Company is in compliance. As at December 31, 2007, the Company had letters of credit drawn on its revolving credit facility of $57 million ($308 million as at December 31, 2006).

Commercial paper

The Company has a commercial paper program, which is backed by a portion of its revolving credit facility, enabling it to issue commercial paper up to a maximum aggregate principal amount of $800 million, or the U.S. dollar equivalent. Commercial paper debt is due within one year but is classified as long-term debt, reflecting the Company's intent and contractual ability to refinance the short-term borrowings through subsequent issuances of commercial paper or drawing down on the long-term revolving credit facility. As at December 31, 2007, the Company had total borrowings of $122 million, of which $114 million was denominated in Canadian dollars and $8 million was denominated in U.S. dollars (U.S.$8 million). The weighted-average interest rate on these borrowings was 5.01%. The Company had no commercial paper outstanding as at December 31, 2006.

Shelf prospectus and registration statement

In December 2007, the Company filed a new shelf prospectus and registration statement, which expires in January 2010, providing for the issuance of up to U.S.$2.5 billion of debt securities in one or more offerings.

In September 2007, the Company had utilized the remaining U.S.$550 million borrowing capacity of its previous shelf prospectus and registration statement to issue U.S.$250 million (Cdn$250 million) of 5.85% Notes due 2017 and U.S.$300 million (Cdn$300 million) of 6.375% Debentures due 2037. The Company used the net proceeds of U.S.$544 million to repay a portion of its outstanding commercial paper and to reduce its accounts receivable securitization program.

The Company's access to current and alternate sources of financing at competitive costs is dependent on its credit rating. The Company is not currently aware of any material adverse trend, event or condition that would significantly affect the Company's credit rating.

All forward-looking information provided in this section is subject to risks and uncertainties and is based on assumptions about events and developments that may not materialize or that may be offset entirely or partially by other events and developments. See the Business risks section of this MD&A for a discussion of assumptions and risk factors affecting such forward-looking statements.

Contractual obligations

In the normal course of business, the Company incurs contractual obligations. The following table sets forth the Company's contractual obligations for the following items as at December 31, 2007:

In millions	Total	2008	2009	2010	2011	2012	2013 & thereafter
Long-term debt obligations [a]	$ 4,512	$ 170	$ 299	$ –	$ 517	$ –	$3,526
Interest on long-term debt obligations	5,428	277	267	254	252	223	4,155
Capital lease obligations [b]	1,620	145	165	100	164	75	971
Operating lease obligations [c]	879	152	125	106	84	68	344
Purchase obligations [d]	952	492	156	108	52	36	108
Other long-term liabilities reflected on the balance sheet [e]	950	73	60	51	44	41	681
Total obligations	$14,341	$1,309	$1,072	$619	$1,113	$443	$9,785

(a) Presented net of unamortized discounts, of which $836 million relates to non-interest bearing Notes due in 2094, and excludes capital lease obligations of $1,105 million which are included in "Capital lease obligations."

(b) Includes $1,105 million of minimum lease payments and $515 million of imputed interest at rates ranging from 3.0% to 7.9%.

(c) Includes minimum rental payments for operating leases having initial non-cancelable lease terms of one year or more. The Company also has operating lease agreements for its automotive fleet with minimum one-year non-cancelable terms for which its practice is to renew monthly thereafter. The estimated annual rental payments for such leases are approximately $30 million and generally extend over five years.

(d) Includes commitments for railroad ties, rail, freight cars, locomotives and other equipment and services, and outstanding information technology service contracts and licenses.

(e) Includes expected payments for workers' compensation, workforce reductions, postretirement benefits other than pensions and environmental liabilities that have been classified as contractual settlement agreements.

For 2008 and the foreseeable future, the Company expects cash flow from operations and from its various sources of financing to be sufficient to meet its debt repayments and future obligations, and to fund anticipated capital expenditures. The Company is not aware of any trends, events or conditions or expected fluctuations in liquidity that would create any deficiencies. See the Business risks section of this MD&A for a discussion of assumptions and risk factors affecting such forward-looking statement.

Agreement to acquire Elgin, Joliet and Eastern Railway Company (EJ&E)

In September 2007, the Company entered into an agreement with the U.S. Steel Corporation (U.S. Steel) for the acquisition of the key operations of EJ&E for a purchase price of approximately U.S.$300 million. Under the terms of the agreement, the Company will acquire substantially all of the railroad assets and equipment of EJ&E, except those that support the Gary Works site in Northwest Indiana and the steelmaking operations of U.S. Steel. The acquisition will be financed by debt and cash on hand.

In accordance with the terms of the agreement, the Company's obligation to consummate the acquisition is subject to the Company having obtained from the STB a final, unappealable decision that approves the acquisition or exempts it from regulation and does not impose on the parties conditions that would significantly and adversely affect the anticipated economic benefits of the acquisition to the Company.

On November 26, 2007, the STB accepted the Company's application to consider the acquisition as a minor transaction that would normally provide for a decision by mid-2008. The STB, however, is also requiring an Environmental Impact Statement (EIS) for the transaction, and it has indicated that its decision on the transaction will not be issued until the EIS process is completed. The Company believes that the STB should be able to conclude its environmental review and issue a decision that would enable the transaction to close by late 2008. If the transaction is approved by the STB, the Company will account for the acquisition using the purchase method of accounting.

Acquisition of Athabasca Northern Railway (ANY)

In December 2007, the Company acquired the rail assets of ANY for $25 million, for which it plans to invest $135 million in rail-line upgrades over the next three years.

Investment in English Welsh and Scottish Railway (EWS)

In November 2007, Germany's state-owned railway, Deutsche Bahn AG, acquired all of the shares of EWS, a company that provides most of the rail freight services in Great Britain and operates freight trains through the English Channel Tunnel, and in which the Company had a 32% ownership interest. The Company accounted for its investment in EWS using the equity method. The Company's share of the cash proceeds was $114 million (net after-tax proceeds are expected to approximate $84 million) resulting in a gain on disposition of the investment of $61 million ($41 million after-tax) which was recorded in Other income. An additional £18 million (Cdn$36 million) was placed in escrow and will be recognized when defined contingencies are resolved.

Sale of Central Station Complex

In November 2007, CN finalized an agreement with Homburg Invest Inc., to sell its Central Station Complex in Montreal for proceeds of $355 million before transaction costs. Under the agreement, CN has entered into long-term arrangements to lease back its corporate headquarters building and the Central Station railway passenger facilities. The transaction

Management's Discussion and Analysis

resulted in a gain on disposition of $222 million, including amounts related to the corporate headquarters building and the Central Station railway passenger facilities, which are being deferred and amortized over their respective lease terms. A gain of $92 million ($64 million after-tax) was recognized immediately in Other income.

Off balance sheet arrangements

Accounts receivable securitization program
The Company has a five-year agreement, expiring in May 2011, to sell an undivided co-ownership interest for maximum cash proceeds of $600 million in a revolving pool of freight receivables to an unrelated trust. Pursuant to the agreement, the Company sells an interest in its receivables and receives proceeds net of the retained interest as stipulated in the agreement.

The Company has retained the responsibility for servicing, administering and collecting the receivables sold. At December 31, 2007, the servicing asset and liability were not significant. Subject to customary indemnifications, the trust's recourse is generally limited to the receivables.

The Company accounted for the accounts receivable securitization program as a sale, because control over the transferred accounts receivable was relinquished. Due to the relatively short collection period and the high quality of the receivables sold, the fair value of the undivided interest transferred to the trust approximated the book value thereof.

The Company is subject to customary reporting requirements for which failure to perform could result in termination of the program. In addition, the trust is subject to customary credit rating requirements, which if not met, could also result in termination of the program. The Company monitors the reporting requirements and is currently not aware of any trends, events or conditions that could cause such termination.

The accounts receivable securitization program provides the Company with readily available short-term financing for general corporate use. Under the agreement, the Company may change the level of receivables sold at any time. In the event the program is terminated before its scheduled maturity, the Company expects to meet its future payment obligations through its various sources of financing, including its revolving credit facility and commercial paper program, and/or access to capital markets.

At December 31, 2007, the Company had sold receivables that resulted in proceeds of $588 million under the accounts receivable securitization program ($393 million at December 31, 2006), and recorded the retained interest of approximately 10% of this amount in Other current assets (retained interest of approximately 10% recorded at December 31, 2006).

Guarantees and indemnifications
In the normal course of business, the Company, including certain of its subsidiaries, enters into agreements that may involve providing certain guarantees or indemnifications to third parties and others, which may extend beyond the term of the agreement. These include, but are not

limited to, residual value guarantees on operating leases, standby letters of credit and surety and other bonds, and indemnifications that are customary for the type of transaction or for the railway business.

The Company is required to recognize a liability for the fair value of the obligation undertaken in issuing certain guarantees on the date the guarantee is issued or modified. In addition, where the Company expects to make a payment in respect of a guarantee, a liability will be recognized to the extent that one has not yet been recognized.

The nature of these guarantees or indemnifications, the maximum potential amount of future payments, the carrying amount of the liability, if any, and the nature of any recourse provisions are disclosed in Note 18 – Major commitments and contingencies, to the Company's Annual Consolidated Financial Statements.

Stock plans

The Company has various stock-based incentive plans for eligible employees. A description of the plans is provided in Note 12 – Stock plans, to the Company's Annual Consolidated Financial Statements. Total compensation expense for awards under all stock-based compensation plans was $62 million, $79 million and $120 million for the years ended December 31, 2007, 2006 and 2005, respectively. The total tax benefit recognized in income in relation to stock-based compensation expense for the years ended December 31, 2007, 2006 and 2005 was $23 million, $22 million and $34 million, respectively. Additional disclosures are provided in Note 12 – Stock plans, to the Company's Annual Consolidated Financial Statements.

Financial instruments

The Company has limited involvement with derivative financial instruments and does not use them for trading purposes. At December 31, 2007, the Company did not have any derivative financial instruments outstanding.

Fuel
To mitigate the effects of fuel price changes on its operating margins and overall profitability, the Company had a hedging program which called for entering into swap positions on crude and heating oil to cover a target percentage of future fuel consumption up to two years in advance. However, with an increased application of fuel surcharge on revenues, no additional swap positions were entered into since September 2004. As such, the Company terminated this program in late 2006.

Since the changes in the fair value of the swap positions were highly correlated to changes in the price of fuel, the fuel hedges were accounted for as cash flow hedges, whereby the effective portion of the cumulative change in the market value of the derivative instruments had been recorded in Accumulated other comprehensive loss.

During 2006, the Company's remaining swap positions matured and were settled. As a result, the related unrealized gains previously recorded in Accumulated other comprehensive loss were reclassified into income as realized gains (unrealized gains of $57 million, $39 million after-tax at December 31, 2005). The Company is currently not hedged through financial markets.

Total realized gains from the Company's fuel hedging activities, which are recorded as a reduction in fuel expense, were $64 million and $177 million for the years ended December 31, 2006 and 2005, respectively.

The Company did not recognize any material gains or losses in each of 2006 and 2005 due to hedge ineffectiveness as the Company's derivative instruments were highly effective in hedging the changes in cash flows associated with forecasted purchases of diesel fuel.

Interest rate

The Company is exposed to interest rate risk related to the funded status of its pension and postretirement plans and on a portion of its long-term debt and does not currently hold any financial instruments that mitigate this risk. At December 31, 2007, Accumulated other comprehensive loss included an unamortized gain of $11 million, $8 million after-tax ($12 million, $8 million after-tax at December 31, 2006) relating to treasury lock transactions settled in 2004.

Income taxes

Uncertain tax positions

On January 1, 2007, the Company adopted Financial Accounting Standards Board (FASB) Interpretation (FIN) No. 48, "Accounting for Uncertainty in Income Taxes," which prescribes the criteria for financial statement recognition and measurement of a tax position taken or expected to be taken in a tax return. This Interpretation also provides guidance on derecognition, classification, interest and penalties, disclosure, and transition. The application of FIN No. 48 on January 1, 2007 had the effect of decreasing the net deferred income tax liability and increasing Retained earnings by $98 million.

At December 31, 2007, the total amount of gross unrecognized tax benefits was $158 million, before considering tax treaties and other arrangements between taxation authorities, of which $45 million related to accrued interest and penalties. If recognized, all of the unrecognized tax benefits would affect the effective tax rate.

The Company recognizes interest accrued and penalties related to unrecognized tax benefits in Income tax expense in the Company's Consolidated Statement of Income.

In Canada, the federal income tax returns filed for the years 2003 to 2006 and the provincial income tax returns filed for the years 1998 to 2006 remain subject to examination by the taxation authorities. In the U.S., the income tax returns filed for the years 2003 to 2006 remain subject to examination by the taxation authorities.

Additional disclosures required pursuant to FIN No. 48 are provided in Note 15 – Income taxes, to the Company's Annual Consolidated Financial Statements.

Payments for income taxes

The Company is required to make scheduled installment payments as prescribed by the tax authorities. In Canada, payments in 2007 were $724 million, of which $367 million related to the final payment for the 2006 taxation year ($130 million was paid in 2006). In the U.S., payments in 2007 were $143 million ($177 million in 2006). There are no expected amounts payable in the first quarter of 2008 for income taxes in respect of the 2007 fiscal year. For the 2008 fiscal year, the Company expects to pay approximately $500 million of taxes based on forecasted 2008 taxable income.

See the Business risks section of this MD&A for a discussion of assumptions and risk factors affecting such forward-looking statements.

Deferred income tax recoveries

In 2007, the Company recorded a deferred income tax recovery of $328 million in the Consolidated Statement of Income, resulting mainly from the enactment of corporate income tax rate changes in Canada.

In 2006, the Company recorded a deferred income tax recovery of $277 million in the Consolidated Statement of Income, resulting primarily from the enactment of lower corporate income tax rates in Canada and the resolution of matters pertaining to prior years' income taxes.

Common stock

Share repurchase programs

In July 2007, the Board of Directors of the Company approved a new share repurchase program which allows for the repurchase of up to 33.0 million common shares between July 26, 2007 and July 25, 2008 pursuant to a normal course issuer bid, at prevailing market prices or such other price as may be permitted by the Toronto Stock Exchange.

As at December 31, 2007, under this current share repurchase program, 17.7 million common shares have been repurchased for $897 million, at a weighted-average price of $50.70 per share.

The Company's previous share repurchase program, initiated in 2006, allowed for the repurchase of up to 28.0 million common shares between July 25, 2006 and July 24, 2007, pursuant to a normal course issuer bid, at prevailing market prices. In June 2007, the Company completed this share repurchase program for a total of $1,453 million, at a weighted-average price of $51.88 per share. Of this amount, 12.5 million common shares were repurchased in 2007 for $687 million, at a weighted-average price of $54.93 per share and 15.5 million common shares in 2006 for $766 million, at a weighted-average price of $49.43 per share.

Outstanding share data

As at February 11, 2008, the Company had 484.2 million common shares outstanding.

Recent accounting pronouncements

In December 2007, FASB issued Statement of Financial Accounting Standards (SFAS) No. 141(R), "Business Combinations," which requires that assets acquired and liabilities assumed be measured at fair value as of the acquisition date and goodwill acquired from a bargain purchase (previously referred to as negative goodwill) be recognized in the Consolidated Statement of Income in the period the acquisition occurs. The Standard also prescribes disclosure requirements to enable users of financial statements to evaluate and understand the nature and financial effects of the business combination. The Standard is effective for business combinations with an acquisition date on or after the beginning of the first annual reporting period beginning on or after December 15, 2008. The Company will apply SFAS No. 141(R) on a prospective basis. The Standard may have a material impact on the reporting of future acquisitions in the Company's financial statements.

In February 2007, the FASB issued SFAS No. 159, "The Fair Value Option for Financial Assets and Financial Liabilities, including an amendment of FASB Statement No. 115," which permits entities to elect to measure eligible items at fair value at specified election dates. For items for which the fair value option has been elected, an entity shall report unrealized gains and losses in earnings at each subsequent reporting date. The fair value option: (i) may be applied instrument by instrument, such as investments otherwise accounted for by the equity method; (ii) is irrevocable (unless a new election date occurs); and (iii) is applied only to entire instruments and not to portions of instruments. This Standard is effective as of an entity's first fiscal year beginning after November 15, 2007. The Company does not expect this Standard to have a significant impact on its financial statements.

Critical accounting policies

The preparation of financial statements in conformity with generally accepted accounting principles requires management to make estimates and assumptions that affect the reported amounts of revenues and expenses during the period, the reported amounts of assets and liabilities, and the disclosure of contingent assets and liabilities at the date of the financial statements. On an ongoing basis, management reviews its estimates based upon currently available information. Actual results could differ from these estimates. The Company's policies for personal injury and other claims, environmental claims, depreciation, pensions and other postretirement benefits, and income taxes, require management's more significant judgments and estimates in the preparation of the Company's consolidated financial statements and, as such, are considered to be critical. The following information should be read in conjunction with the Company's Annual Consolidated Financial Statements and Notes thereto.

Management discusses the development and selection of the Company's critical accounting estimates with the Audit Committee of the Company's Board of Directors, and the Audit Committee has reviewed the Company's related disclosures.

Personal injury and other claims

In the normal course of its operations, the Company becomes involved in various legal actions, including claims relating to personal injuries, occupational disease and damage to property.

Canada

Employee injuries are governed by the workers' compensation legislation in each province whereby employees may be awarded either a lump sum or future stream of payments depending on the nature and severity of the injury. Accordingly, the Company accounts for costs related to employee work-related injuries based on actuarially developed estimates of the ultimate cost associated with such injuries, including compensation, health care and third-party administration costs. For all other legal actions, the Company maintains, and regularly updates on a case-by-case basis, provisions for such items when the expected loss is both probable and can be reasonably estimated based on currently available information.

At December 31, 2007, 2006 and 2005, the Company's provision for personal injury and other claims in Canada was as follows:

In millions	2007	2006	2005
Balance January 1	$195	$205	$204
Accruals and other	41	60	46
Payments	(40)	(70)	(45)
Balance December 31	$196	$195	$205

Assumptions used in estimating the ultimate costs for Canadian employee injury claims consider, among others, the discount rate, the rate of inflation, wage increases and health care costs. The Company periodically reviews its assumptions to reflect currently available information. Over the past three years, the Company has not significantly changed any of these assumptions. For all other legal claims in Canada, estimates are based on the specifics of the case, trends and judgment.

United States

Employee work-related injuries, including occupational disease claims, are compensated according to the provisions of the Federal Employers' Liability Act (FELA), which requires either the finding of fault through the U.S. jury system or individual settlements, and represent a major liability for the railroad industry. The Company follows an actuarial-based approach and accrues the expected cost for personal injury and property damage claims and asserted and unasserted occupational disease claims, based on actuarial estimates of their ultimate cost.

In 2007, 2006 and 2005, the Company recorded net reductions to its provision for U.S. personal injury and other claims pursuant to the results of external actuarial studies of $97 million, $62 million and $21 million, respectively. The reductions were mainly attributable to decreases in the Company's estimates of unasserted claims and costs related to asserted claims as a result of its ongoing risk mitigation strategy focused on prevention, mitigation of claims and containment of injuries, lower settlements for existing claims and reduced severity relating to non-occupational disease claims.

Due to the inherent uncertainty involved in projecting future events related to occupational diseases, which include but are not limited to, the number of expected claims, the average cost per claim and the legislative and judicial environment, the Company's future obligations may differ from current amounts recorded.

At December 31, 2007, 2006 and 2005, the Company's provision for U.S. personal injury and other claims was as follows:

In millions	2007	2006	2005
Balance January 1	$407	$452	$438
Accruals and other	(111)	(8)	61
Payments	(46)	(37)	(47)
Balance December 31	$250	$407	$452

For the U.S. personal injury and other claims liability, historical claim data is used to formulate assumptions relating to the expected number of claims and average cost per claim (severity) for each year. Changes in any one of these assumptions could materially affect Casualty and other expense as reported in the Company's results of operations. For example, a 5% change in the probability level for the number of claims or severity would have the effect of changing the provision by approximately $20 million and the annual expense by approximately $3 million.

Environmental claims

Regulatory compliance

A risk of environmental liability is inherent in railroad and related transportation operations; real estate ownership, operation or control; and other commercial activities of the Company with respect to both current and past operations. As a result, the Company incurs significant compliance and capital costs, on an ongoing basis, associated with environmental regulatory compliance and clean-up requirements in its railroad operations and relating to its past and present ownership, operation or control of real property. Environmental expenditures that relate to current operations are expensed unless they relate to an improvement to the property. Expenditures that relate to an existing condition caused by past operations and which are not expected to contribute to current or future operations are expensed.

Known existing environmental concerns

The Company is subject to environmental clean-up and enforcement actions. In particular, the Federal Comprehensive Environmental Response, Compensation and Liability Act of 1980 (CERCLA), also known as the Superfund law, as well as similar state laws generally impose joint and several liability for clean-up and enforcement costs on current and former owners and operators of a site without regard to fault or the legality of the original conduct. The Company has been notified that it is a potentially responsible party for study and clean-up costs at approximately 21 sites governed by the Superfund law (and other similar federal and state laws) for which investigation and remediation payments are or will be made or are yet to be determined and, in many instances, is one of several potentially responsible parties.

The ultimate cost of known contaminated sites cannot be definitely established, and the estimated environmental liability for any given site may vary depending on the nature and extent of the contamination, the available clean-up techniques, the Company's share of the costs and evolving regulatory standards governing environmental liability. As a result, liabilities are recorded based on the results of a four-phase assessment conducted on a site-by-site basis. Cost scenarios established by external consultants based on extent of contamination and expected costs for remedial efforts are used by the Company to estimate the costs related to a particular site. A liability is initially recorded when environmental assessments occur and/or remedial efforts are likely, and when costs, based on a specific plan of action in terms of the technology to be used and the extent of the corrective action required, can be reasonably estimated. Adjustments to initial estimates are recorded as additional information becomes available. Based on the information currently available, the Company considers its provisions to be adequate.

In 2005, the Company had recorded a liability related to a derailment at Wabamun Lake, Alberta. Over the last two years, this liability was adjusted for additional environmental and legal claims and reduced by payments made pursuant to the clean-up performed. At December 31, 2007, the Company has an amount receivable for the remaining estimated recoveries from the Company's insurance carriers who covered substantially all expenses related to the derailment above the self-insured retention of $25 million, which was recorded in operating expenses in 2005.

At December 31, 2007, most of the Company's properties not acquired through recent acquisitions have reached the final assessment stage and therefore costs related to such sites have been anticipated. The final assessment stage can span multiple years. For properties acquired through recent acquisitions, the Company obtains assessments from both external and internal consultants and a liability has been or will be accrued based on such assessments.

Unknown existing environmental concerns

The Company's ongoing efforts to identify potential environmental concerns that may be associated with its properties may lead to future environmental investigations, which may result in the identification of additional environmental costs and liabilities. The magnitude of such additional liabilities and the costs of complying with environmental laws and containing or remediating contamination cannot be reasonably estimated due to:

(i) the lack of specific technical information available with respect to many sites;

(ii) the absence of any government authority, third-party orders, or claims with respect to particular sites;

(iii) the potential for new or changed laws and regulations and for development of new remediation technologies and uncertainty regarding the timing of the work with respect to particular sites;

(iv) the ability to recover costs from any third parties with respect to particular sites;

and as such, costs related to any future remediation will be accrued in the period they become known.

U.S. GAAP *Canadian National Railway Company* **49**

Future occurrences

In railroad and related transportation operations, it is possible that derailments, explosions or other accidents may occur that could cause harm to human health or to the environment. As a result, the Company may incur costs in the future, which may be material, to address any such harm, including costs relating to the performance of clean-ups, natural resource damages and compensatory or punitive damages relating to harm to individuals or property.

At December 31, 2007, 2006 and 2005, the Company's provision for specific environmental sites and remediation, net of potential and actual insurance recoveries was as follows:

In millions	2007	2006	2005
Balance January 1	$131	$124	$113
Accruals and other	(1)	17	35
Payments	(19)	(10)	(24)
Balance December 31	$111	$131	$124

The Company also incurs expenses related to environmental regulatory compliance and clean-up requirements. Such expenses amounted to $10 million in 2007 ($10 million in 2006 and $9 million in 2005).

Depreciation

Railroad properties are carried at cost less accumulated depreciation including asset impairment write-downs. The Company follows the group method of depreciation for railroad properties and, as such, depreciates the cost of railroad properties, less net salvage value, on a straight-line basis over their estimated useful lives. In addition, under the group method of depreciation, the cost of railroad properties, less net salvage value, retired or disposed of in the normal course of business, is charged to accumulated depreciation.

Assessing the reasonableness of the estimated useful lives of properties requires judgment and is based on currently available information, including periodic depreciation studies conducted by the Company. The Company's U.S. properties are subject to comprehensive depreciation studies as required by the Surface Transportation Board (STB). Depreciation studies for Canadian properties are not required by regulation and are therefore conducted internally. Studies are performed on specific asset groups on a periodic basis. The studies consider, among others, the analysis of historical retirement data using recognized life analysis techniques, and the forecasting of asset life characteristics. Changes in circumstances, such as technological advances, changes to the Company's business strategy, changes in the Company's capital strategy or changes in regulations can result in the actual useful lives differing from the Company's estimates.

A change in the remaining useful life of a group of assets, or their estimated net salvage value, will affect the depreciation rate used to amortize the group of assets and thus affect depreciation expense as reported in the Company's results of operations. A change of one year in the composite useful life of the Company's fixed asset base would impact annual depreciation expense by approximately $15 million.

Depreciation studies are a means of ensuring that the assumptions used to estimate the useful lives of particular asset groups are still valid and where they are not, they serve as the basis to establish the new depreciation rates to be used on a prospective basis. In 2007, the Company completed a depreciation study for all of its U.S. assets, for which there was no significant impact on depreciation expense. The Company is also conducting a depreciation study of its Canadian properties, plant and equipment, and expects to finalize this study by the first quarter of 2008.

In 2007, the Company recorded total depreciation and amortization expense of $678 million ($653 million in 2006 and $630 million in 2005). At December 31, 2007, the Company had Properties of $20,413 million, net of accumulated depreciation of $8,910 million ($21,053 million in 2006, net of accumulated depreciation of $9,458 million).

Pensions and other postretirement benefits

In 2007, the Company's plans have a measurement date of December 31. The Company's pension asset, pension liability and accrual for postretirement benefits liability at December 31, 2007 were $1,768 million, $187 million and $266 million, respectively ($1,275 million, $195 million and $286 million at December 31, 2006, respectively). The descriptions in the following paragraphs pertaining to pensions relate generally to the Company's main pension plan, the CN Pension Plan (the Plan), unless otherwise specified.

Calculation of net periodic benefit cost

The Company accounts for net periodic benefit cost for pensions and other postretirement benefits as required by SFAS No. 87, "Employers' Accounting for Pensions," and SFAS No. 106, "Employers' Accounting for Postretirement Benefits Other Than Pensions," respectively. Under these standards, assumptions are made regarding the valuation of benefit obligations and performance of plan assets. In the calculation of net periodic benefit cost, these standards allow for a gradual recognition of changes in benefit obligations and fund performance over the expected average remaining service life of the employee group covered by the plans.

In accounting for pensions and other postretirement benefits, assumptions are required for, among others, the discount rate, the expected long-term rate of return on plan assets, the rate of compensation increase, health care cost trend rates, mortality rates, employee early retirements, terminations and disability. Changes in these assumptions result in actuarial gains or losses, which pursuant to SFAS No. 158, will be recognized in Other comprehensive income (loss). In accordance with SFAS No. 87 and SFAS No. 106, the Company has elected to amortize these gains or losses into net periodic benefit cost over the expected average remaining service life of the employee group covered by the plans only to the extent that the unrecognized net actuarial gains and losses are in excess of the corridor threshold, which is calculated as 10% of the greater of the beginning of year balances of the projected benefit obligation or market-related value of plan assets. The Company's net periodic benefit cost for future periods is dependent on demographic experience, economic conditions and investment performance. Recent demographic experience has revealed no material net gains or losses on termination, retirement, disability and mortality. Experience with respect to economic conditions and investment performance is further discussed herein.

The Company recorded consolidated net periodic benefit cost for pensions of $29 million, $66 million and $17 million in 2007, 2006 and 2005, respectively. Consolidated net periodic benefit cost for other postretirement benefits was $14 million, $17 million and $24 million in 2007, 2006 and 2005, respectively.

At December 31, 2007 and 2006, the pension benefit obligation, accumulated postretirement benefit obligation (APBO), and other postretirement benefits liability were as follows:

In millions	December 31,	2007	2006
Pension benefit obligation		$14,419	$14,545
Accumulated postretirement benefit obligation		266	286
Other postretirement benefits liability		266	286

Discount rate assumption

The Company's discount rate assumption, which is set annually at the end of each year, is used to determine the projected benefit obligation at the end of the year and the net periodic benefit cost for the following year. The discount rate is used to measure the single amount that, if invested at the measurement date in a portfolio of high-quality debt instruments with a rating of AA or better, would provide the necessary cash flows to pay for pension benefits as they become due. The discount rate is determined by management with the aid of third-party actuaries. The Company's methodology for determining the discount rate is based on a zero-coupon bond yield curve, which is derived from a semi-annual bond yield curve provided by a third party. The portfolio of hypothetical zero-coupon bonds is expected to generate cash flows that match the estimated future benefit payments of the plans as the bond rate for each maturity year is applied to the plans' corresponding expected benefit payments of that year. A discount rate of 5.53%, based on bond yields prevailing at December 31, 2007 (5.12% at December 31, 2006), was considered appropriate by the Company to match the approximately 12-year average duration of estimated future benefit payments. As a result, in 2008, the Company's net periodic benefit cost for all plans is expected to decrease by approximately $70 million, since the cumulative unrecognized actuarial loss has decreased to $962 million at December 31, 2007 from $1,804 million at December 31, 2006, mainly resulting from an increase in the level of interest rates and an increase in the market-related value of plan assets. The current estimate for the expected average remaining service life of the employee group covered by the plans is approximately nine years.

For the year ended December 31, 2007, a one-percentage-point decrease in the 5.12% discount rate used to determine net periodic benefit cost at January 1, 2007 would have resulted in an increase of approximately $160 million in net periodic benefit cost, whereas a one-percentage-point increase would have resulted in a decrease of approximately $50 million, given that the Company amortizes net actuarial gains and losses over the expected average remaining service life of the employee group covered by the plans, only to the extent they are in excess of the corridor threshold.

Expected long-term rate of return assumption

To develop its expected long-term rate of return assumption used in the calculation of net periodic benefit cost applicable to the market-related value of assets, the Company considers both its past experience and future estimates of long-term investment returns, the expected composition of the plans' assets as well as the expected long-term market returns in the future. The Company has elected to use a market-related value of assets, whereby realized and unrealized gains/losses and appreciation/depreciation in the value of the investments are recognized over a period of five years, while investment income is recognized immediately. If the Company had elected to use the market value of assets, which at December 31, 2007 exceeded the market-related value of Plan assets by $1,999 million, net periodic benefit cost would decrease by approximately $150 million for 2007, assuming all other assumptions remained constant. The Company follows a disciplined investment strategy, which limits concentration of investments by asset class, foreign currency, sector or company. The Investment Committee of the Board of Directors has approved an investment policy that establishes long-term asset mix targets based on a review of historical returns achieved by worldwide investment markets. Investment managers may deviate from these targets but their performance is evaluated in relation to the market performance of the target mix. The Company does not anticipate the return on plan assets to fluctuate materially from related capital market indices. The Investment Committee reviews investments regularly with specific approval required for major investments in illiquid securities. The policy also permits the use of derivative financial instruments to implement asset mix decisions or to hedge existing or anticipated exposures. The Plan does not invest in the securities of the Company or its subsidiaries. During the last 10 years ended December 31, 2007, the Plan earned an annual average rate of return of 9.6%. The actual, market-related value, and expected rates of return on plan assets for the last five years were as follows:

Rates of return	2007	2006	2005	2004	2003
Actual	8.0%	10.7%	20.5%	11.7%	9.6%
Market-related value	12.7%	11.4%	8.6%	6.3%	7.0%
Expected	8.0%	8.0%	8.0%	8.0%	8.0%

The Company's expected long-term rate of return on plan assets reflects management's view of long-term investment returns and the effect of a 1% variation in such rate of return would result in a change to the net periodic benefit cost of approximately $65 million.

Plan asset allocation

Based on the fair value of the assets held as at December 31, 2007, the Plan assets are comprised of 51% in Canadian and foreign equities, 34% in debt securities, 2% in real estate assets and 13% in other assets. The long-term asset allocation percentages are not expected to differ materially from the current composition.

Rate of compensation increase and health care cost trend rate

Another significant assumption is the rate of compensation increase, which is determined by the Company based upon its long-term plans for such increases. For 2007, a rate of compensation increase of 3.5% was used to determine the benefit obligation and the net periodic benefit cost.

For postretirement benefits other than pensions, the Company reviews external data and its own historical trends for health care costs to determine the health care cost trend rates. For measurement purposes, the projected health care cost trend rate for prescription drugs was assumed to be 13% in 2007, and it is assumed that the rate will decrease gradually to 6% in 2013 and remain at that level thereafter. For the year ended December 31, 2007, a one-percentage-point change in either the rate of compensation increase or the health care cost trend rate would not cause a material change to the Company's net periodic benefit cost for both pensions and other postretirement benefits.

Funding of pension plans

For pension funding purposes, an actuarial valuation is required at least on a triennial basis. However, the Company has conducted actuarial valuations on an annual basis to account for pensions. The latest actuarial valuation of the CN Pension Plan was conducted as at December 31, 2006 and indicated a funding excess. Total contributions for all of the Company's pension plans are expected to be approximately $100 million in each of 2008, 2009 and 2010 based on the plans' current position. The assumptions discussed above are not expected to have a significant impact on the cash funding requirements of the pension plans.

Information disclosed by major pension plan

The following table provides the Company's plan assets by category, benefit obligation at end of year, and Company and employee contributions by major pension plan:

In millions December 31, 2007	CN Pension Plan	BC Rail Ltd Pension Plan	U.S. and other plans	Total
Plan assets by category				
Equity securities	$ 7,730	$283	$110	$ 8,123
Debt securities	5,149	229	73	5,451
Real estate	247	9	1	257
Other	2,082	76	11	2,169
Total	$15,208	$597	$195	$16,000
Benefit obligation at end of year	$13,538	$513	$368	$14,419
Company contributions in 2007	$ 64	$ 2	$ 9	$ 75
Employee contributions in 2007	$ 54	$ –	$ –	$ 54

Income taxes

The Company follows the asset and liability method of accounting for income taxes. Under the asset and liability method, the change in the net deferred income tax asset or liability is included in the computation of net income. Deferred income tax assets and liabilities are measured using enacted income tax rates expected to apply to taxable income in the years in which temporary differences are expected to be recovered or settled. As a result, a projection of taxable income is required for those years, as well as an assumption of the ultimate recovery/settlement period for temporary differences. The projection of future taxable income is based on management's best estimate and may vary from actual taxable income. On an annual basis, the Company assesses its need to establish a valuation allowance for its deferred income tax assets, and if it is deemed more likely than not that its deferred income tax assets will not be realized based on its taxable income projections, a valuation allowance is recorded. As at December 31, 2007, the Company expects that the large majority of its deferred income tax assets will be recovered from future taxable income. In addition, Canadian and U.S. tax rules and regulations are subject to interpretation and require judgment by the Company that may be challenged by the taxation authorities upon audit of the filed income tax returns. In 2006, the Canadian taxation authorities completed their assessments of income tax returns filed for the years 1998 to 2001. Accordingly, the Company has made adjustments to its provision for income taxes in 2006. The Company believes that its provisions for income taxes at December 31, 2007 are adequate pertaining to any future assessments from the taxation authorities. The Company's deferred income tax assets are mainly composed of temporary differences related to accruals for workforce reductions, personal injury

and other claims, environmental and other postretirement benefits, and losses and tax credit carryforwards. The majority of these accruals will be paid out over the next five years. The Company's deferred income tax liabilities are mainly composed of temporary differences related to properties and the net pension asset. The reversal of temporary differences is expected at future-enacted income tax rates which could change due to fiscal budget changes and/or changes in income tax laws. As a result, a change in the timing and/or the income tax rate at which the components will reverse, could materially affect deferred income tax expense as recorded in the Company's results of operations. A one-percentage-point change in the Company's reported effective income tax rate would have the effect of changing the income tax expense by $27 million in 2007.

From time to time, the federal, provincial, and state governments enact new corporate income tax rates resulting in either lower or higher tax liabilities. Such enactments occurred in each of 2007, 2006 and 2005 and resulted in a deferred income tax recovery of $317 million, a deferred income tax recovery of $228 million and a deferred income tax expense of $14 million, respectively, with corresponding adjustments to the Company's net deferred income tax liability.

In 2006, for certain items reported in Accumulated other comprehensive loss, the Company adjusted its deferred income tax liability for changes in income tax rates applied to certain temporary differences and also for the income tax effect on the currency translation amount resulting from the difference between the accounting and tax basis of its net investment in foreign subsidiaries. As a result, the Company recorded a $180 million net charge for deferred income taxes in Other comprehensive income (loss).

For the year ended December 31, 2007, the Company recorded total income tax expense of $548 million ($642 million in 2006 and $781 million in 2005), of which $82 million was a deferred income tax recovery and included $328 million resulting mainly from the enactment of corporate income tax rate changes in Canada. In 2006, $3 million of the reported income tax expense was for deferred income taxes, and included $277 million resulting from the enactment of lower corporate income tax rates in Canada and the resolution of matters pertaining to prior years' income taxes ($547 million in 2005). The Company's net deferred income tax liability at December 31, 2007 was $4,840 million ($5,131 million at December 31, 2006).

Business risks

Certain information included in this report may be "forward-looking statements" within the meaning of the United States Private Securities Litigation Reform Act of 1995 and under Canadian securities laws. CN cautions that, by their nature, forward-looking statements involve risks, uncertainties and assumptions and while there is an increasing risk of recession in the U.S. economy, implicit in these statements, particularly in respect of growth opportunities, are the Company's assumptions that economic growth in North America and globally will continue to slow down in 2008, but that a recession will not take place, and that its business risks described below will not result in a material impact on its financial statements. This assumption, although considered reasonable by the Company at the time of preparation, may not materialize. Such forward-looking statements are not guarantees of future performance and involve known and unknown risks, uncertainties and other factors which may cause the actual results or performance of the Company or the rail industry to be materially different from the outlook or any future results or performance implied by such statements. Such factors include the specific risks set forth below as well as other risks detailed from time to time in reports filed by the Company with securities regulators in Canada and the United States.

Competition

The Company faces significant competition from a variety of carriers, including Canadian Pacific Railway Company (CP) which operates the other major rail system in Canada, serving most of the same industrial and population centers as the Company; long distance trucking companies; and in many markets, major U.S. railroads and other Canadian and U.S. railroads. Competition is generally based on the quality and reliability of services provided, price, and the condition and suitability of carriers' equipment. Competition is particularly intense in eastern Canada where an extensive highway network and population centers, located relatively close to one another, have encouraged significant competition from trucking companies. In addition, much of the freight carried by the Company consists of commodity goods that are available from other sources in competitive markets. Factors affecting the competitive position of suppliers of these commodities, including exchange rates, could materially adversely affect the demand for goods supplied by the sources served by the Company and, therefore, the Company's volumes, revenues and profit margins.

In addition to trucking competition, and to a greater degree than other rail carriers, the Company's subsidiary, Illinois Central Railroad Company (ICRR), is vulnerable to barge competition because its main routes are parallel to the Mississippi River system. The use of barges for some commodities, particularly coal and grain, often represents a lower cost mode of transportation. Barge competition and barge rates are affected by navigational interruptions from ice, floods and droughts, which can cause widely fluctuating barge rates. The ability of ICRR to maintain its market share of the available freight has traditionally been affected by the navigational conditions on the river.

The significant consolidation of rail systems in the United States has resulted in larger rail systems that are able to offer seamless services in larger market areas and accordingly, compete effectively with the Company in certain markets. This consolidation requires the Company to consider arrangements or other initiatives that would similarly enhance its own service. There can be no assurance that the Company will be able to compete effectively against current and future competitors in the railroad industry and that further consolidation within the railroad industry will not adversely affect the Company's competitive position. No assurance can be given that competitive pressures will not lead to reduced revenues, profit margins or both.

Environmental matters

The Company's operations are subject to numerous federal, provincial, state, municipal and local environmental laws and regulations in Canada and the United States concerning, among other things, emissions into the air; discharges into waters; the generation, handling, storage, transportation, treatment and disposal of waste, hazardous substances and other materials; decommissioning of underground and aboveground storage tanks; and soil and groundwater contamination. A risk of environmental liability is inherent in railroad and related transportation operations; real estate ownership, operation or control; and other commercial activities of the Company with respect to both current and past operations. As a result, the Company incurs significant compliance and capital costs, on an ongoing basis, associated with environmental regulatory compliance and clean-up requirements in its railroad operations and relating to its past and present ownership, operation or control of real property.

While the Company believes that it has identified the costs likely to be incurred in the next several years for environmental matters, based on known information, the Company's ongoing efforts to identify potential environmental concerns that may be associated with its properties may lead to future environmental investigations, which may result in the identification of additional environmental costs and liabilities.

In railroad and related transportation operations, it is possible that derailments, explosions or other accidents may occur that could cause harm to human health or to the environment. In addition, the Company is also exposed to liability risk, faced by the railroad industry generally, in connection with the transportation of toxic-by-inhalation hazardous materials such as chlorine and anhydrous ammonia, commodities that are essential to the public health and welfare and that, as a common carrier, the Company has a duty to transport. As a result, the Company may incur costs in the future, which may be material, to address any such harm, including costs relating to the performance of clean-ups, natural resource damages and compensatory or punitive damages relating to harm to individuals or property.

The ultimate cost of known contaminated sites cannot be definitively established, and the estimated environmental liability for any given site may vary depending on the nature and extent of the contamination, the available clean-up techniques, the Company's share of the costs and evolving regulatory standards governing environmental liability. Also, additional contaminated sites yet unknown may be discovered or future operations may result in accidental releases. For these reasons, there can be no assurance that material liabilities or costs related to environmental matters will not be incurred in the future, or will not have a material adverse effect on the Company's financial position or results of operations in a particular quarter or fiscal year, or that the Company's liquidity will not be adversely impacted by such environmental liabilities or costs.

Personal injury and other claims

In the normal course of its operations, the Company becomes involved in various legal actions, including claims relating to personal injuries, occupational disease and damage to property. The Company maintains provisions for such items, which it considers to be adequate for all of its outstanding or pending claims. The final outcome with respect to actions outstanding or pending at December 31, 2007, or with respect to future claims, cannot be predicted with certainty, and therefore there can be no assurance that their resolution will not have a material adverse effect on the Company's financial position or results of operations in a particular quarter or fiscal year.

Labor negotiations

Canadian workforce

As at December 31, 2007, CN employed a total of 16,074 employees in Canada, of which 12,602 were unionized employees.

As of January 2008, the Company had in place labor agreements covering its entire Canadian unionized workforce, including the 2,800 employees represented by the UTU, whose agreements were extended by virtue of federal back-to-work legislation.

In September 2006, the Company had begun negotiating with the UTU to renew the collective agreements covering conductors and yard crews. Following a conciliation process and the completion of required legislated processes, the union claimed it was in a legal strike position, and the Company would have been legally permitted to lockout the members of the UTU bargaining unit or promulgate work rule changes unilaterally on February 9, 2007. The UTU commenced a general strike on February 10, 2007. The Company sought to have the UTU work stoppage declared illegal by the Canada Industrial Relations Board (CIRB). On February 19, 2007, the CIRB issued an oral decision dismissing CN's application to have the strike declared illegal. On February 23, 2007, the Minister of Labour tabled a motion to expedite back-to-work legislation to end the strike at CN. However, the Company and the UTU continued to meet to try to resolve the impasse and reached a tentative settlement on February 24, 2007. On April 10, 2007, the ratification results were

announced. The tentative settlement was rejected by a majority of the UTU membership. The UTU notified the Company that it would renew strike activity on April 10, 2007.

On April 17, 2007, the Minister of Labour passed the motion to expedite back-to-work legislation to end the strike at CN, which was originally tabled on February 23, 2007. The act, titled *An Act to Provide for the Resumption and Continuation of Railway Operations*, provided for an immediate return to work as well as a final and binding arbitration (final offer selection) process to resolve outstanding collective bargaining issues between the UTU and CN. The Act was passed into law on April 18, 2007. The Company and the union presented their final offers to the appointed arbitrator on June 25, 2007. The arbitrator rendered his binding decision on July 20, 2007 and selected the Company's final offer, which effectively renews the collective agreements between the Company and the UTU for a three-year period ending July 22, 2010. Pursuant to the Act, the collective agreements are binding upon the UTU and any other trade union certified by the CIRB to represent the employees.

The Company has an agreement with the UTU for its Northern Quebec line, which expired on December 15, 2007. The agreement remains in effect until the bargaining process has been exhausted. Negotiations are ongoing to renew that collective agreement, and neither party has, as of date, requested conciliation assistance. In September 2007, CN began bargaining with two other national unions, the United Steelworkers of America (USW) and the International Brotherhood of Electrical Workers (IBEW), whose agreements expired December 31, 2007. CN reached tentative agreements with both the USW and the IBEW to renew their collective agreements in November 2007. The IBEW advised the Company on December 28, 2007 that its membership had ratified a five-year collective agreement which will expire on December 31, 2012. On January 16, 2008, the USW announced that its members have ratified the tentative agreement to renew the collective agreement.

The Company's collective agreements with the Teamsters Canada Rail Conference, who represent locomotive engineers in one bargaining unit, and rail traffic controllers, also known as train dispatchers, in a separate bargaining unit, and with the Canadian National Railways Police Association (CNRP) will expire on December 31, 2008.

The Company's collective agreement covering employees working on the Mackenzie Northern Railway expires on May 2, 2008. These employees are covered by a single collective agreement but are represented by the Teamsters Canada Rail Conference and the Canadian Auto Workers.

There can be no assurance that the Company will be able to renew and have ratified its collective agreements without any strikes or lockouts or that the resolution of these collective bargaining negotiations will not have a material adverse effect on the Company's financial position or results of operations.

U.S. workforce

As at December 31, 2007, CN employed a total of 6,622 employees in the United States, of which 5,610 were unionized employees.

As of January 2008, the Company had in place agreements with bargaining units representing the entire unionized workforce at Grand Trunk Western Railroad Incorporated (GTW); Duluth, Winnipeg and Pacific Railway Company (DWP); ICRR; companies owned by CCP Holdings, Inc. (CCP); Duluth, Missabe & Iron Range Railway Company (DMIR); Bessemer & Lake Erie Railroad Company (BLE); The Pittsburgh and Conneaut Dock Company (PCD); and the unionized workforce at companies owned by Wisconsin Central Transportation Corporation (WC). Agreements in place have various moratorium provisions, ranging from 2004 to 2011, which preserve the status quo in respect of given areas during the terms of such moratoriums. Several of these agreements are currently under renegotiation.

The general approach to labor negotiations by U.S. Class I railroads is to bargain on a collective national basis. GTW, DWP, ICRR, CCP, WC, DMIR, BLE and PCD have bargained on a local basis rather than holding national, industry-wide negotiations because they believe it results in agreements that better address both the employees' concerns and preferences, and the railways' actual operating environment. However, local negotiations may not generate federal intervention in a strike or lockout situation, since a dispute may be localized. The Company believes the potential mutual benefits of local bargaining outweigh the risks.

Negotiations are ongoing with the bargaining units with which the Company does not have agreements or settlements. Until new agreements are reached or the processes of the Railway Labor Act have been exhausted, the terms and conditions of existing agreements generally continue to apply. On July 19, 2006, one of the unions representing 250 GTW employees took a one-day strike action during the mediation process. However, a U.S. District Court subsequently determined that the strike action was improper and enjoined employees from further action. The employees returned to work and the Company continues to be in mediation with that union. The union filed an appeal concerning portions of the District Court decision which was heard by the appellate court on July 19, 2007. The appellate court ruled in favor of the Company and entered a preliminary injunction prohibiting the union from striking over the issues involved in the July 19, 2006 strike. There can be no assurance that there will not be any work action by any of the bargaining units with which the Company is currently in negotiations or that the resolution of these negotiations will not have a material adverse effect on the Company's financial position or results of operations.

Regulation

The Company's rail operations in Canada are subject to (i) regulation as to rate setting, level of service and network rationalization by the Canadian Transportation Agency (the Agency) under the Canada Transportation Act (the CTA), and (ii) safety regulation by the federal Minister of Transport under the Railway Safety Act and certain other statutes. The Company's U.S. rail operations are subject to (i) economic regulation by the STB and (ii) safety regulation by the Federal Railroad Administration (FRA). As such, various Company business transactions must gain prior regulatory approval, with attendant risks and uncertainties, and the Company is subject to government oversight with respect to rate, service and business practice issues. In particular, the STB completed a proceeding on January 26, 2007 in which it reviewed the practice of rail carriers, including the Company and the majority of other large railroads operating within the U.S., of assessing a fuel surcharge computed as a percentage of the base rate for service. Following its review, the STB

directed carriers to change that practice and adjust their fuel surcharge programs within 90 days on a basis more closely related to the amount of fuel consumed on individual movements. The Company announced a mileage-based fuel surcharge, effective April 26, 2007, to conform to the STB's decision. To make its rate dispute resolution procedures more affordable and accessible to shippers, the STB also completed a proceeding on September 5, 2007, in which it modified its rate guidelines for handling medium-size and smaller rate disputes. The Company is also subject to a variety of health, safety, security, labor, environmental and other regulations, all of which can affect its competitive position and profitability.

The Company's ownership of the former Great Lakes Transportation vessels is subject to regulation by the U.S. Coast Guard and the Department of Transportation, Maritime Administration, which regulate the ownership and operation of vessels operating on the Great Lakes and in U.S. coastal waters. While recent Congressional legislation and Coast Guard rulemakings have not adversely affected CN's ownership of these vessels, no assurance can be given that any future legislative or regulatory initiatives by the U.S. federal government will not materially adversely affect the Company's operations or its competitive and financial position.

With respect to safety, rail safety regulation in Canada is the responsibility of Transport Canada, which administers the Canadian Railway Safety Act, as well as the rail portions of other safety-related statutes. In the U.S., rail safety regulation is the responsibility of the FRA, which administers the Federal Railroad Safety Act, as well as the rail portions of other safety statutes. In addition, safety matters related to security are overseen by the Transportation Security Administration (TSA), which is part of the U.S. Department of Homeland Security and the Pipeline and Hazardous Materials Safety Administration (PHMSA), which, like the FRA, is part of the U.S. Department of Transportation.

The federal government carries out a review of Canadian transportation legislation periodically. The latest review resulted in a report to the Minister of Transport, released to the public on July 18, 2001, which contains numerous recommendations for legislative changes affecting all modes of transportation, including rail. On February 25, 2003, the Canadian Minister of Transport released the policy document *Straight Ahead – A Vision for Transportation in Canada*. On April 24, 2006, the Minister of Transport tabled Bill C-3, entitled *International Bridges and Tunnels Act*, relating to the safety and security and the construction and alteration of international bridges and tunnels. The Bill became law on February 1, 2007. On May 4, 2006, the Minister of Transport tabled Bill C-11, entitled *Transportation Amendment Act*, relating to passenger service providers, noise, mergers and other issues. The Bill became law on June 22, 2007. On December 14, 2006, the federal government announced a full review of the Railway Safety Act. Members of the panel to conduct the review were appointed in February 2007 and have submitted their report to the Minister of Transport in November 2007. On October 29, 2007, the Minister of Transport tabled Bill C-8, entitled *An Act to amend the Canada Transportation Act (railway transportation)* proposing to extend the availability of the Final Offer Arbitration recourse to groups of shippers and adding a new shipper recourse to the Agency in respect of charges for incidental services provided by a railway company other than transportation services. No assurance can be given that any current or future legislative action by the federal government or other future government initiatives will not materially adversely affect the Company's financial position or results of operations.

In the United States, the Bush Administration submitted to Congress in 2007 its legislative proposal to reauthorize the Federal Railroad Safety Act. In addition, the U.S. House of Representatives is considering its own rail safety legislation (H.R. 2095) covering a broad range of safety issues, including fatigue management, positive train control, track safety standards, and other matters. The United States Senate is also considering its own safety legislation (S. 1889), which will cover a broad range of issues. Separate legislation passed by the U.S. House (H.R. 1401) in March 2007 included language that would have undermined much of the federal preemption of state and local regulation of railroads; this provision was modified in the final bill enacted into law to address litigation issues related to rail safety incidents while retaining federal preemption of rail safety regulations.

The U.S. Congress has had under consideration for several years various pieces of legislation that would increase federal economic regulation of the railroad industry, and additional legislation has been introduced in 2007 in both Houses of Congress. In addition, the Senate Judiciary Committee approved legislation in September 2007 (S. 772) to repeal the railroad industry's limited antitrust exemptions; comparable legislation has been introduced in the U.S. House of Representatives.

The STB is authorized by statute to commence regulatory proceedings if it deems them to be appropriate. On August 14, 2007, the STB proposed to change its methodology for calculating the rail industry's cost of capital that is used to evaluate the adequacy of carrier revenues and in assessing reasonableness of challenged rates. No assurance can be given that this or any future regulatory initiatives by the U.S. federal government will not materially adversely affect the Company's operations, or its competitive and financial position.

The Company is subject to statutory and regulatory directives in the United States addressing homeland security concerns, as well as by regulation by the Canada Border Services Agency (CBSA). In the U.S., these include border security arrangements, pursuant to an agreement the Company and CP entered into with U.S. Customs and Border Protection (CBP) and the CBSA. These requirements include advance electronic transmission of cargo information for U.S.-bound traffic and cargo screening (including gamma ray and radiation screening), as well as U.S. government-imposed restrictions on the transportation into the United States of certain commodities. These also include participation in CBP's Customs-Trade Partnership Against Terrorism (C-TPAT) program and designation as a low-risk carrier under CBSA's Customs Self-Assessment (CSA) program; in the third quarter of 2007, the Company successfully completed the CBP C-TPAT validation process. In the fourth quarter of 2003, the CBP issued regulations to extend advance notification requirements to all modes of transportation and the U.S. Food and Drug Administration promulgated interim final rules requiring advance notification by all modes for certain food imports into the United States. CBSA is also working on implementation of advance notification requirements for Canadian-bound traffic. In 2006, the U.S. Department of Agriculture (USDA) issued a proposed interim rule, which would remove the current exemption from inspection for imported fruits and vegetables grown in Canada and the exemptions for all transport modes from the agricultural quarantine and inspection (AQI) user fee for traffic entering the U.S. from Canada. The rule took effect for surface modes on June 1, 2007.

The Company has also worked with the Association of American Railroads to develop and put in place an extensive industry-wide security plan to address terrorism and security-driven efforts by state and local governments seeking to restrict the routings of certain hazardous materials. If such state and local routing restrictions were to go into force, they would be likely to add to security concerns by foreclosing the Company's most optimal and secure transportation routes, leading to increased yard handling, longer hauls, and the transfer of traffic to lines less suitable for moving hazardous materials, while also infringing upon the exclusive and uniform federal oversight over railroad security matters. In addition to recommended security action items for the rail transportation of toxic inhalation hazard (TIH) materials jointly announced by the TSA and the FRA on June 23, 2006 and November 21, 2006, the TSA and the PHMSA also separately issued, on December 21, 2006, related notices of proposed rulemakings. Among other things, the TSA's regulations would require rail carriers operating within the U.S. to provide upon request, within one hour, location and shipping information on cars on their networks containing TIH materials and certain radioactive or explosive materials, and ensure the secure, attended transfer of all such cars to and from shippers, receivers and other carriers. The PHMSA's regulations would require carriers to report annually the volume and route-specific data for cars containing these commodities; conduct a safety and security risk analysis for each used route; identify a commercially practicable alternative route for each used route; and select for use the practical route posing the least safety and security risk. The final TSA and PHMSA regulations are expected to be issued in the first half of 2008.

While the Company will continue to work closely with the CBSA, CBP, and other Canadian and U.S. agencies, as described above, no assurance can be given that these and future decisions by the U.S., Canadian, provincial, state, or local governments on homeland security matters, legislation on security matters enacted by the U.S. Congress, or joint decisions by the industry in response to threats to the North American rail network, will not materially adversely affect the Company's operations, or its competitive and financial position.

Business prospects and other risks

In any given year, the Company, like other railroads, is susceptible to changes in the economic conditions of the industries and geographic areas that produce and consume the freight it transports or the supplies it requires to operate. In addition, many of the goods and commodities carried by the Company experience cyclicality in demand. Many of the bulk commodities the Company transports move offshore and are affected more by global rather than North American economic conditions. The Company's results of operations can be expected to reflect these conditions because of the significant fixed costs inherent in railroad operations.

Global as well as North American trade conditions, including trade barriers on certain commodities, may interfere with the free circulation of goods across Canada and the United States.

The Company, like other railway companies in North America, may experience demographic challenges in the employment levels of its workforce. Changes in employee demographics, training requirements and the availability of qualified personnel could negatively impact the Company's ability to meet demand for rail service. The Company is monitoring employment levels to ensure that there is an adequate supply of personnel to meet rail service requirements. However, the Company's efforts to attract and retain qualified personnel may be hindered by increased demand in the job market. No assurance can be given that the demographic challenges will not materially adversely affect the Company's operations or its financial position.

The Company, like other railroads, is susceptible to the volatility of fuel prices due to changes in the economy or supply disruptions. Rising fuel prices could materially adversely affect the Company's expenses. As such, CN has implemented a fuel surcharge program with a view of off-setting the impact of rising fuel prices. No assurance can be given that continued increases in fuel prices or supply disruptions will not materially adversely affect the Company's operations or its financial position.

Overall return in the capital markets and the level of interest rates affect the funded status of the Company's pension plans as well as the Company's results of operations. Adverse changes with respect to pension plan returns and the level of interest rates from the date of the last actuarial valuation may increase future pension contributions and could have a material adverse effect on the Company's results of operations. The funding requirements, as well as the impact on the results of operations, will be determined following the completion of future actuarial valuations.

Potential terrorist actions can have a direct or indirect impact on the transportation infrastructure, including railway infrastructure in North America, and interfere with the free flow of goods. International conflicts can also have an impact on the Company's markets.

The Company conducts its business in both Canada and the U.S. and as a result, is affected by currency fluctuations. Based on the Company's current operations, the estimated annual impact on net income of a year-over-year one-cent change in the Canadian dollar relative to the U.S. dollar is approximately $10 million. Changes in the exchange rate between the Canadian dollar and other currencies (including the U.S. dollar) make the goods transported by the Company more or less competitive in the world marketplace and thereby further affect the Company's revenues and expenses.

Should a recession occur in North America or other key markets, or should major industrial restructuring take place, the volume of rail shipments carried by the Company may be adversely affected.

In order to grow the business, the Company implements strategic initiatives to expand the scope and scale of existing rail and non-rail operations. CN WorldWide International, the Company's international freight-forwarding subsidiary, was formed to leverage existing non-rail capabilities. This subsidiary operates in a highly competitive market and no assurance can be given that the expected benefits will be realized given the nature and intensity of the competition in that market.

In addition to the inherent risks of the business cycle, the Company's operations are occasionally susceptible to severe weather conditions, which can disrupt operations and service for the railroad as well as for the Company's customers. In recent years, severe drought conditions in western Canada, for instance, significantly reduced bulk commodity revenues, principally grain.

Generally accepted accounting principles require the use of historical cost as the basis of reporting in financial statements. As a result, the cumulative effect of inflation, which has significantly increased asset replacement costs for capital-intensive companies such as CN, is not reflected in operating expenses. Depreciation charges on an inflation-adjusted basis, assuming that all operating assets are replaced at current price levels, would be substantially greater than historically reported amounts.

Controls and procedures

The Company's Chief Executive Officer and its Chief Financial Officer, after evaluating the effectiveness of the Company's "disclosure controls and procedures" (as defined in Exchange Act Rules 13a-15(e) and 15d-15(e)) as of December 31, 2007, have concluded that the Company's disclosure controls and procedures were adequate and effective to ensure that material information relating to the Company and its consolidated subsidiaries would have been made known to them.

During the fourth quarter ending December 31, 2007, there was no change in the Company's internal control over financial reporting that has materially affected, or is reasonably likely to materially affect, the Company's internal control over financial reporting.

As of December 31, 2007, management has assessed the effectiveness of the Company's internal control over financial reporting using the criteria set forth by the Committee of Sponsoring Organizations of the Treadway Commission (COSO) in Internal Control – Integrated Framework. Based on this assessment, management has determined that the Company's internal control over financial reporting was effective as of December 31, 2007, and issued Management's Report on Internal Control over Financial Reporting dated February 11, 2008 to that effect.

Additional information, including the Company's 2007 Annual Information Form (AIF) and Form 40-F, as well as the Company's Notice of Intention to Make a Normal Course Issuer Bid, may be found on SEDAR at *www.sedar.com* and on EDGAR at *www.sec.gov*. Copies of such documents may be obtained by contacting the Corporate Secretary's office.

Montreal, Canada
February 11, 2008

Management's Report on Internal Control over Financial Reporting

Management is responsible for establishing and maintaining adequate internal control over financial reporting. Internal control over financial reporting is a process designed to provide reasonable assurance regarding the reliability of financial reporting and the preparation of financial statements for external purposes in accordance with generally accepted accounting principles. Because of its inherent limitations, internal control over financial reporting may not prevent or detect misstatements.

Management has assessed the effectiveness of the Company's internal control over financial reporting as of December 31, 2007 using the criteria set forth by the Committee of Sponsoring Organizations of the Treadway Commission (COSO) in Internal Control – Integrated Framework. Based on this assessment, management has determined that the Company's internal control over financial reporting was effective as of December 31, 2007.

KPMG LLP, an independent registered public accounting firm, has issued an unqualified audit report on the effectiveness of the Company's internal control over financial reporting as of December 31, 2007 and has also expressed an unqualified opinion on the Company's 2007 consolidated financial statements as stated in their Reports of Independent Registered Public Accounting Firm dated February 11, 2008.

E. Hunter Harrison
President and Chief Executive Officer

February 11, 2008

Claude Mongeau
Executive Vice-President and Chief Financial Officer

February 11, 2008

Report of Independent Registered Public Accounting Firm

To the Board of Directors and Shareholders of the Canadian National Railway Company:

We have audited the accompanying consolidated balance sheets of the Canadian National Railway Company (the "Company") as of December 31, 2007 and 2006, and the related consolidated statements of income, comprehensive income, changes in shareholders' equity and cash flows for each of the years in the three-year period ended December 31, 2007. These consolidated financial statements are the responsibility of the Company's management. Our responsibility is to express an opinion on these consolidated financial statements based on our audits.

We conducted our audits in accordance with Canadian generally accepted auditing standards and with the standards of the Public Company Accounting Oversight Board (United States). Those standards require that we plan and perform the audit to obtain reasonable assurance about whether the financial statements are free of material misstatement. An audit includes examining, on a test basis, evidence supporting the amounts and disclosures in the financial statements. An audit also includes assessing the accounting principles used and significant estimates made by management, as well as evaluating the overall financial statement presentation. We believe that our audits provide a reasonable basis for our opinion.

In our opinion, the consolidated financial statements referred to above present fairly, in all material respects, the financial position of the Company as of December 31, 2007 and 2006, and the results of its operations and its cash flows for each of the years in the three-year period ended December 31, 2007, in conformity with generally accepted accounting principles in the United States.

We also have audited, in accordance with the standards of the Public Company Accounting Oversight Board (United States), the Company's internal control over financial reporting as of December 31, 2007, based on criteria established in Internal Control – Integrated Framework issued by the Committee of Sponsoring Organizations of the Treadway Commission (COSO), and our report dated February 11, 2008 expressed an unqualified opinion on the effectiveness of the Company's internal control over financial reporting.

KPMG LLP
Chartered Accountants

Montreal, Canada
February 11, 2008

Report of Independent Registered Public Accounting Firm

To the Board of Directors and Shareholders of the Canadian National Railway Company:

We have audited the Canadian National Railway Company's (the "Company") internal control over financial reporting as of December 31, 2007, based on the criteria established in Internal Control – Integrated Framework issued by the Committee of Sponsoring Organizations of the Treadway Commission ("COSO"). The Company's management is responsible for maintaining effective internal control over financial reporting and for its assessment of the effectiveness of internal control over financial reporting included in the accompanying Management's Report on Internal Control over Financial Reporting. Our responsibility is to express an opinion on the Company's internal control over financial reporting based on our audit.

We conducted our audit in accordance with the standards of the Public Company Accounting Oversight Board (United States). Those standards require that we plan and perform the audit to obtain reasonable assurance about whether effective internal control over financial reporting was maintained in all material respects. Our audit included obtaining an understanding of internal control over financial reporting, assessing the risk that a material weakness exists, and testing and evaluating the design and operating effectiveness of internal control based on the assessed risk. Our audit also included performing such other procedures as we considered necessary in the circumstances. We believe that our audit provides a reasonable basis for our opinion.

A company's internal control over financial reporting is a process designed to provide reasonable assurance regarding the reliability of financial reporting and the preparation of financial statements for external purposes in accordance with generally accepted accounting principles. A company's internal control over financial reporting includes those policies and procedures that (1) pertain to the maintenance of records that, in reasonable detail, accurately and fairly reflect the transactions and dispositions of the assets of the company; (2) provide reasonable assurance that transactions are recorded as necessary to permit preparation of financial statements in accordance with generally accepted accounting principles, and that receipts and expenditures of the company are being made only in accordance with authorizations of management and directors of the company; and (3) provide reasonable assurance regarding prevention or timely detection of unauthorized acquisition, use, or disposition of the company's assets that could have a material effect on the financial statements.

Because of its inherent limitations, internal control over financial reporting may not prevent or detect misstatements. Also, projections of any evaluation of effectiveness to future periods are subject to the risk that controls may become inadequate because of changes in conditions, or that the degree of compliance with the policies or procedures may deteriorate.

In our opinion, the Company maintained, in all material respects, effective internal control over financial reporting as of December 31, 2007, based on criteria established in Internal Control – Integrated Framework issued by the COSO.

We also have audited, in accordance with Canadian generally accepted auditing standards and with the standards of the Public Company Accounting Oversight Board (United States), the consolidated balance sheets of the Company as of December 31, 2007 and 2006, and the related consolidated statements of income, comprehensive income, changes in shareholders' equity and cash flows for each of the years in the three-year period ended December 31, 2007, and our report dated February 11, 2008 expressed an unqualified opinion on those consolidated financial statements.

KPMG LLP

KPMG LLP
Chartered Accountants

Montreal, Canada
February 11, 2008

Consolidated Statement of Income

In millions, except per share data	Year ended December 31,	2007	2006	2005
Revenues[(1)]		**$7,897**	$7,929	$7,446
Operating expenses[(1)]				
Labor and fringe benefits		**1,701**	1,823	1,856
Purchased services and material		**1,045**	1,027	993
Fuel		**1,026**	892	730
Depreciation and amortization		**677**	650	627
Equipment rents		**247**	198	192
Casualty and other		**325**	309	424
Total operating expenses		**5,021**	4,899	4,822
Operating income		**2,876**	3,030	2,624
Interest expense		**(336)**	(312)	(299)
Other income *(Note 14)*		**166**	11	12
Income before income taxes		**2,706**	2,729	2,337
Income tax expense *(Note 15)*		**(548)**	(642)	(781)
Net income		**$2,158**	$2,087	$1,556
Earnings per share (Note 17)				
Basic		**$ 4.31**	$ 3.97	$ 2.82
Diluted		**$ 4.25**	$ 3.91	$ 2.77

(1) Certain of the 2006 and 2005 comparative figures have been reclassified in order to be consistent with the 2007 presentation (see Note 21).

See accompanying notes to consolidated financial statements.

60 *Canadian National Railway Company*　　　　　　　U.S. GAAP

Consolidated Statement of Comprehensive Income

In millions Year ended December 31,	2007	2006	2005
Net income	$ 2,158	$2,087	$1,556
Other comprehensive income (loss) *(Note 20)*:			
Unrealized foreign exchange gain (loss) on:			
Translation of the net investment in foreign operations	(1,004)	32	(233)
Translation of U.S. dollar-denominated long-term debt designated as a hedge of the net investment in U.S. subsidiaries	788	(33)	152
Pension and other postretirement benefit plans *(Notes 9, 13)*:			
Net actuarial gain arising during the period	391	–	–
Prior service cost arising during the period	(12)	–	–
Amortization of net actuarial loss included in net periodic benefit cost	49	–	–
Amortization of prior service cost included in net periodic benefit cost	21	–	–
Minimum pension liability adjustment	–	1	4
Derivative instruments *(Note 19)*	(1)	(57)	(35)
Other comprehensive income (loss) before income taxes	232	(57)	(112)
Income tax recovery (expense) on Other comprehensive income (loss)	(219)	(179)	38
Other comprehensive income (loss)	13	(236)	(74)
Comprehensive income	$ 2,171	$1,851	$1,482

See accompanying notes to consolidated financial statements.

U.S. GAAP   *Canadian National Railway Company* **61**

Consolidated Balance Sheet

In millions	December 31,	2007	2006
Assets			
Current assets			
Cash and cash equivalents		$ 310	$ 179
Accounts receivable *(Note 4)*		370	692
Material and supplies		162	189
Deferred income taxes *(Note 15)*		68	84
Other		138	192
		1,048	1,336
Properties *(Note 5)*		20,413	21,053
Intangible and other assets *(Note 6)*		1,999	1,615
Total assets		$23,460	$24,004
Liabilities and shareholders' equity			
Current liabilities			
Accounts payable and accrued charges *(Note 8)*		$ 1,282	$ 1,823
Current portion of long-term debt *(Note 10)*		254	218
Other		54	73
		1,590	2,114
Deferred income taxes *(Note 15)*		4,908	5,215
Other liabilities and deferred credits *(Note 9)*		1,422	1,465
Long-term debt *(Note 10)*		5,363	5,386
Shareholders' equity			
Common shares *(Note 11)*		4,283	4,459
Accumulated other comprehensive loss *(Note 20)*		(31)	(44)
Retained earnings		5,925	5,409
		10,177	9,824
Total liabilities and shareholders' equity		$23,460	$24,004

On behalf of the Board:

David G.A. McLean
Director

E. Hunter Harrison
Director

See accompanying notes to consolidated financial statements.

62   *Canadian National Railway Company*   U.S. GAAP

Consolidated Statement of Changes in Shareholders' Equity

In millions	Issued and outstanding common shares	Common shares	Accumulated other comprehensive loss	Retained earnings	Total shareholders' equity
Balances December 31, 2004	566.2	$4,706	$(148)	$4,726	$ 9,284
Net income	–	–	–	1,556	1,556
Stock options exercised and other *(Notes 11, 12)*	6.6	176	–	–	176
Share repurchase programs *(Note 11)*	(36.0)	(302)	–	(1,116)	(1,418)
Other comprehensive loss *(Note 20)*	–	–	(74)	–	(74)
Dividends ($0.50 per share)	–	–	–	(275)	(275)
Balances December 31, 2005	536.8	4,580	(222)	4,891	9,249
Net income	–	–	–	2,087	2,087
Stock options exercised and other *(Notes 11, 12)*	5.1	133	–	–	133
Share repurchase programs *(Note 11)*	(29.5)	(254)	–	(1,229)	(1,483)
Other comprehensive loss *(Note 20)*	–	–	(236)	–	(236)
Adjustment to Accumulated other comprehensive loss *(Notes 2, 20)*	–	–	414	–	414
Dividends ($0.65 per share)	–	–	–	(340)	(340)
Balances December 31, 2006	512.4	4,459	(44)	5,409	9,824
Adoption of accounting pronouncements *(Note 2)*	–	–	–	95	95
Restated balance, beginning of year	512.4	4,459	(44)	5,504	9,919
Net income	–	–	–	2,158	2,158
Stock options exercised and other *(Notes 11, 12)*	3.0	89	–	–	89
Share repurchase programs *(Note 11)*	(30.2)	(265)	–	(1,319)	(1,584)
Other comprehensive income *(Note 20)*	–	–	13	–	13
Dividends ($0.84 per share)	–	–	–	(418)	(418)
Balances December 31, 2007	**485.2**	**$4,283**	**$ (31)**	**$5,925**	**$10,177**

See accompanying notes to consolidated financial statements.

U.S. GAAP

Canadian National Railway Company **63**

726 **Appendix A**

NEL

Consolidated Statement of Cash Flows

In millions Year ended December 31,	2007	2006	2005
Operating activities			
Net income	$ 2,158	$ 2,087	$ 1,556
Adjustments to reconcile net income to net cash provided from operating activities:			
Depreciation and amortization	678	653	630
Deferred income taxes *(Note 15)*	(82)	3	547
Gain on sale of Central Station Complex *(Note 5)*	(92)	–	–
Gain on sale of investment in English Welsh and Scottish Railway *(Note 6)*	(61)	–	–
Other changes in:			
Accounts receivable *(Note 4)*	229	(17)	142
Material and supplies	18	(36)	(25)
Accounts payable and accrued charges	(351)	197	(156)
Other net current assets and liabilities	39	58	8
Other	(119)	6	6
Cash provided from operating activities	2,417	2,951	2,708
Investing activities			
Property additions	(1,387)	(1,298)	(1,180)
Acquisitions, net of cash acquired *(Note 3)*	(25)	(84)	–
Sale of Central Station Complex *(Note 5)*	351	–	–
Sale of investment in English Welsh and Scottish Railway *(Note 6)*	114	–	–
Other, net	52	33	105
Cash used by investing activities	(895)	(1,349)	(1,075)
Financing activities			
Issuance of long-term debt	4,171	3,308	2,728
Reduction of long-term debt	(3,589)	(3,089)	(2,865)
Issuance of common shares due to exercise of stock options and related excess tax benefits realized *(Note 12)*	77	120	115
Repurchase of common shares *(Note 11)*	(1,584)	(1,483)	(1,418)
Dividends paid	(418)	(340)	(275)
Cash used by financing activities	(1,343)	(1,484)	(1,715)
Effect of foreign exchange fluctuations on U.S. dollar-denominated cash and cash equivalents	(48)	(1)	(3)
Net increase (decrease) in cash and cash equivalents	131	117	(85)
Cash and cash equivalents, beginning of year	179	62	147
Cash and cash equivalents, end of year	$ 310	$ 179	$ 62
Supplemental cash flow information			
Net cash receipts from customers and other	$ 8,139	$ 7,946	$ 7,581
Net cash payments for:			
Employee services, suppliers and other expenses	(4,323)	(4,130)	(4,075)
Interest	(340)	(294)	(306)
Workforce reductions *(Note 9)*	(31)	(45)	(87)
Personal injury and other claims *(Note 18)*	(86)	(107)	(92)
Pensions *(Note 13)*	(75)	(112)	(127)
Income taxes *(Note 15)*	(867)	(307)	(186)
Cash provided from operating activities	$ 2,417	$ 2,951	$ 2,708

See accompanying notes to consolidated financial statements.

Canadian National Railway Company, together with its wholly owned subsidiaries, collectively "CN" or "the Company," is engaged in the rail and related transportation business. CN spans Canada and mid-America, from the Atlantic and Pacific oceans to the Gulf of Mexico, serving the ports of Vancouver, Prince Rupert, B.C., Montreal, Halifax, New Orleans and Mobile, Alabama, and the key cities of Toronto, Buffalo, Chicago, Detroit, Duluth, Minnesota/Superior, Wisconsin, Green Bay, Wisconsin, Minneapolis/St. Paul, Memphis, St. Louis, and Jackson, Mississippi, with connections to all points in North America. CN's freight revenues are derived from the movement of a diversified and balanced portfolio of goods, including petroleum and chemicals, grain and fertilizers, coal, metals and minerals, forest products, intermodal and automotive.

1 Summary of significant accounting policies

These consolidated financial statements are expressed in Canadian dollars, except where otherwise indicated, and have been prepared in accordance with United States generally accepted accounting principles (U.S. GAAP). The preparation of financial statements in conformity with generally accepted accounting principles requires management to make estimates and assumptions that affect the reported amounts of revenues and expenses during the period, the reported amounts of assets and liabilities, and the disclosure of contingent assets and liabilities at the date of the financial statements. On an ongoing basis, management reviews its estimates, including those related to personal injury and other claims, environmental claims, depreciation, pensions and other postretirement benefits, and income taxes, based upon currently available information. Actual results could differ from these estimates.

A. Principles of consolidation

These consolidated financial statements include the accounts of all subsidiaries. The Company's investments in which it has significant influence are accounted for using the equity method and all other investments are accounted for using the cost method.

B. Revenues

Freight revenues are recognized using the percentage of completed service method based on the transit time of freight as it moves from origin to destination. Costs associated with movements are recognized as the service is performed. Revenues are presented net of taxes collected from customers and remitted to governmental authorities.

C. Foreign exchange

All of the Company's United States (U.S.) operations are self-contained foreign entities with the U.S. dollar as their functional currency. Accordingly, the U.S. operations' assets and liabilities and the Company's foreign equity investment are translated into Canadian dollars at the rate in effect at the balance sheet date and the revenues and expenses are translated at average exchange rates during the year. All adjustments resulting from the translation of the foreign operations are recorded in Other comprehensive income (loss) (see Note 20).

The Company designates the U.S. dollar-denominated long-term debt of the parent company as a foreign exchange hedge of its net investment in U.S. subsidiaries. Accordingly, unrealized foreign exchange gains and losses, from the dates of designation, on the translation of the U.S. dollar-denominated long-term debt are also included in Other comprehensive income (loss).

D. Cash and cash equivalents

Cash and cash equivalents include highly liquid investments purchased three months or less from maturity and are stated at cost, which approximates market value.

E. Accounts receivable

Accounts receivable are recorded at cost net of billing adjustments and an allowance for doubtful accounts. The allowance for doubtful accounts is based on expected collectibility and considers historical experience as well as known trends or uncertainties related to account collectibility. Any gains or losses on the sale of accounts receivable are calculated by comparing the carrying amount of the accounts receivable sold to the total of the cash proceeds on sale and the fair value of the retained interest in such receivables on the date of transfer. Costs related to the sale of accounts receivable are recognized in earnings in the period incurred.

F. Material and supplies

Material and supplies, which consist mainly of rail, ties, and other items for construction and maintenance of property and equipment, as well as diesel fuel, are valued at weighted-average cost.

G. Properties

Railroad properties are carried at cost less accumulated depreciation including asset impairment write-downs. Labor, materials and other costs associated with the installation of rail, ties, ballast and other track improvements are capitalized to the extent they meet the Company's minimum threshold for capitalization. Major overhauls and large refurbishments are also capitalized when they result in an extension to the useful life or increase the functionality of the asset. Included in property additions are the costs of developing computer software for internal use. Maintenance costs are expensed as incurred.

The cost of railroad properties, less net salvage value, retired or disposed of in the normal course of business is charged to accumulated depreciation, in accordance with the group method of depreciation. The Company reviews the carrying amounts of properties held and used whenever events or changes in circumstances indicate that such carrying amounts may not be recoverable based on future undiscounted cash flows. Assets that are deemed impaired as a result of such review are recorded at the lower of carrying amount or fair value.

Assets held for sale are measured at the lower of their carrying amount or fair value, less cost to sell. Losses resulting from significant line sales are recognized in income when the asset meets the criteria for classification as held for sale whereas losses resulting from significant line abandonments are recognized in the statement of income when the asset ceases to be used. Gains are recognized in income when they are realized.

1 Summary of significant accounting policies *(continued)*

H. Depreciation

The cost of properties, including those under capital leases, net of asset impairment write-downs, is depreciated on a straight-line basis over their estimated useful lives as follows:

Asset class	Annual rate
Track and roadway	2%
Rolling stock	3%
Buildings	3%
Information technology	11%
Other	8%

The Company follows the group method of depreciation for railroad properties and, as such, conducts comprehensive depreciation studies on a periodic basis to assess the reasonableness of the lives of properties based upon current information and historical activities. Changes in estimated useful lives are accounted for prospectively. In 2007, the Company completed a depreciation study for all of its U.S. assets, for which there was no significant impact on depreciation expense. The Company is also conducting a depreciation study of its Canadian properties, plant and equipment, and expects to finalize this study by the first quarter of 2008.

I. Intangible assets

Intangible assets relate to customer contracts and relationships assumed through past acquisitions and are being amortized on a straight-line basis over 40 to 50 years.

J. Pensions

Pension costs are determined using actuarial methods. Net periodic benefit cost is charged to income and includes:

(i) the cost of pension benefits provided in exchange for employees' services rendered during the year,

(ii) the interest cost of pension obligations,

(iii) the expected long-term return on pension fund assets,

(iv) the amortization of prior service costs and amendments over the expected average remaining service life of the employee group covered by the plans, and

(v) the amortization of cumulative net actuarial gains and losses in excess of 10% of, the greater of the beginning of year balances of the projected benefit obligation or market-related value of plan assets, over the expected average remaining service life of the employee group covered by the plans.

The pension plans are funded through contributions determined in accordance with the projected unit credit actuarial cost method.

K. Postretirement benefits other than pensions

The Company accrues the cost of postretirement benefits other than pensions using actuarial methods. These benefits, which are funded by the Company as they become due, include life insurance programs, medical benefits and free rail travel benefits.

The Company amortizes the cumulative net actuarial gains and losses in excess of 10% of the projected benefit obligation at the beginning of the year, over the expected average remaining service life of the employee group covered by the plans.

L. Personal injury and other claims

In Canada, the Company accounts for costs related to employee work-related injuries based on actuarially developed estimates of the ultimate cost associated with such injuries, including compensation, health care and third-party administration costs.

In the U.S., the Company accrues the expected cost for personal injury, property damage and occupational disease claims, based on actuarial estimates of their ultimate cost.

For all other legal actions in Canada and the U.S., the Company maintains, and regularly updates on a case-by-case basis, provisions for such items when the expected loss is both probable and can be reasonably estimated based on currently available information.

M. Environmental expenditures

Environmental expenditures that relate to current operations are expensed unless they relate to an improvement to the property. Expenditures that relate to an existing condition caused by past operations and which are not expected to contribute to current or future operations are expensed. Liabilities are recorded when environmental assessments occur and/or remedial efforts are probable, and when the costs, based on a specific plan of action in terms of the technology to be used and the extent of the corrective action required, can be reasonably estimated.

N. Income taxes

The Company follows the asset and liability method of accounting for income taxes. Under the asset and liability method, the change in the net deferred tax asset or liability is included in the computation of net income. Deferred tax assets and liabilities are measured using enacted tax rates expected to apply to taxable income in the years in which temporary differences are expected to be recovered or settled.

O. Derivative financial instruments

The Company uses derivative financial instruments from time to time in the management of its interest rate and foreign currency exposures. Derivative instruments are recorded on the balance sheet at fair value and the changes in fair value are recorded in earnings or Other comprehensive income (loss) depending on the nature and effectiveness of the hedge transaction. Income and expense related to hedged derivative financial instruments are recorded in the same category as that generated by the underlying asset or liability.

P. Stock-based compensation

The Company follows the fair value based approach for stock option awards based on the grant-date fair value using the Black-Scholes option-pricing model. The Company expenses the fair value of its stock option awards on a straight-line basis, over the period during which an employee is required to provide service (vesting period) or until retirement eligibility is attained, whichever is shorter. The Company also follows the fair value based approach for cash settled awards. Compensation cost for cash settled awards is based on the fair value of the awards at period-end and is recognized over the period during which an employee is required to provide service (vesting period) or until retirement eligibility is attained, whichever is shorter. See Note 12 – Stock plans, for the assumptions used to determine fair value and for other required disclosures.

Q. Recent accounting pronouncements

In December 2007, the Financial Accounting Standards Board (FASB) issued Statement of Financial Accounting Standards (SFAS) No. 141(R), "Business Combinations," which requires that assets acquired and liabilities assumed be measured at fair value as of the acquisition date and goodwill acquired from a bargain purchase (previously referred to as negative goodwill) be recognized in the Consolidated Statement of Income in the period the acquisition occurs. The Standard also prescribes disclosure requirements to enable users of financial statements to evaluate and understand the nature and financial effects of the business combination. The Standard is effective for business combinations with an acquisition date on or after the beginning of the first annual reporting period beginning on or after December 15, 2008. The Company will apply SFAS No. 141(R) on a prospective basis. The Standard may have a material impact on the reporting of future acquisitions in the Company's financial statements.

In February 2007, the FASB issued SFAS No. 159, "The Fair Value Option for Financial Assets and Financial Liabilities, including an amendment of FASB Statement No. 115," which permits entities to elect to measure eligible items at fair value at specified election dates. For items for which the fair value option has been elected, an entity shall report unrealized gains and losses in earnings at each subsequent reporting date. The fair value option: (i) may be applied instrument by instrument, such as investments otherwise accounted for by the equity method; (ii) is irrevocable (unless a new election date occurs); and (iii) is applied only to entire instruments and not to portions of instruments. This Standard is effective as of an entity's first fiscal year beginning after November 15, 2007. The Company does not expect this Standard to have a significant impact on its financial statements.

 Accounting changes

2007

Income taxes

On January 1, 2007, the Company adopted FASB Interpretation (FIN) No. 48, "Accounting for Uncertainty in Income Taxes," which prescribes the criteria for financial statement recognition and measurement of a tax position taken or expected to be taken in a tax return. This Interpretation also provides guidance on derecognition, classification, interest and penalties, disclosure, and transition. The application of FIN No. 48 on January 1, 2007 had the effect of decreasing the net deferred income tax liability and increasing Retained earnings by $98 million. Disclosures prescribed by FIN No. 48 are presented in Note 15 – Income taxes.

Pensions and other postretirement benefits

On January 1, 2007, pursuant to SFAS No. 158, "Employers' Accounting for Defined Benefit Pension and Other Postretirement Plans, an amendment of FASB Statements No. 87, 88, 106, and 132(R)," the Company early adopted the requirement to measure the defined benefit plan assets and the projected benefit obligation as of the date of the fiscal year-end statement of financial position for its U.S. plans. The Company elected to use the 15-month transition method, which allows for the extrapolation of net periodic benefit cost based on the September 30, 2006 measurement date to the fiscal year-end date of December 31, 2007. As a result, the Company recorded a reduction of $3 million to Retained earnings at January 1, 2007, which represented the net periodic benefit cost pursuant to the actuarial valuation attributable to the period between the early measurement date of September 30, 2006 and January 1, 2007 (the date of adoption).

2006

Stock-based compensation

On January 1, 2006, the Company adopted SFAS No. 123(R), "Share-Based Payment," which required the expensing of all options issued, modified or settled based on the grant date fair value over the period during which an employee is required to provide service (vesting period) or until retirement eligibility is attained, whichever is shorter. Compensation cost for cash settled awards is based on the fair value of the awards at period-end and is recognized over the period during which an employee is required to provide service (vesting period) or until retirement eligibility is attained, whichever is shorter.

The Company adopted SFAS No. 123(R) using the modified prospective approach, which required application of the standard to all awards granted, modified, repurchased or cancelled on or after January 1, 2006, and to all awards for which the requisite service had not been rendered as at such date. Since January 1, 2003, the Company had been following the fair value based approach prescribed by SFAS No. 123, "Accounting for Stock-Based Compensation," as amended by SFAS No. 148, "Accounting for Stock-Based Compensation – Transition and Disclosure," for stock option awards granted, modified or settled on or after such date, while cash settled awards were measured at their intrinsic value at each reporting period until December 31, 2005. As such, the application of SFAS No. 123(R) on January 1, 2006 to all awards granted prior to its adoption did not have a significant impact on the financial statements. In accordance with the modified prospective approach, prior period financial statements were not restated to reflect the impact of SFAS No. 123(R).

For the year ended December 31, 2006, the application of SFAS No. 123(R) had the effect of increasing stock-based compensation expense and decreasing net income by $16 million and $12 million, respectively, or $0.02 per basic and diluted earnings per share. Disclosures prescribed by SFAS No. 123(R) for the Company's various stock-based compensation plans are presented in Note 12 – Stock plans.

2 Accounting changes *(continued)*

Pension and other postretirement plans

On December 31, 2006, the Company adopted SFAS No. 158, "Employers' Accounting for Defined Benefit Pension and Other Postretirement Plans, an amendment of FASB Statements No. 87, 88, 106, and 132(R)," which requires the Company to recognize the funded status of its various benefit plans in its Consolidated Balance Sheet. As such, on December 31, 2006, the Company increased its pension asset by $599 million, to $1,275 million, and decreased its pension and other postretirement benefits liability by $7 million, to $481 million. Pursuant to SFAS No. 158, the Company recognizes changes in the funded status in the year in which the changes occur, through Other comprehensive income (loss). The actuarial gains/losses and prior service costs/credits that arise during the period but are not recognized as components of net periodic benefit cost will be recognized as a component of Other comprehensive income (loss). These amounts recognized in Accumulated other comprehensive loss will be adjusted as they are subsequently recognized as components of net periodic benefit cost. Prior to December 31, 2006, actuarial gains/ losses and prior service costs/credits were deferred in their recognition, and amortized into net periodic benefit cost over the expected average remaining service life of the employee group covered by the plans. The adoption of SFAS No. 158 had no impact on years prior to 2006 as retrospective application was not allowed. This Standard has no effect on the computation of net periodic benefit cost for pensions and other postretirement benefits. See Note 9 – Other liabilities and deferred credits and Note 13 – Pensions, for the prospective application of SFAS No. 158 to the Company's benefit plans.

The following table illustrates the incremental effect of applying SFAS No. 158 on individual line items in the Company's Consolidated Balance Sheet at December 31, 2006:

In millions	Assets		Liabilities				Shareholders' equity	
	Pension	Total	Other postretirement benefits	Pension[1]	Net deferred income tax	Total	Accumulated other comprehensive loss	Total
Balance at December 31, 2006 before application of SFAS No. 158	$ 676	$23,405	$313	$175	$4,939	$13,995	$(458)	$9,410
Adjustments	599	599	(27)	20	192	185	414	414
Balance at December 31, 2006 after application of SFAS No. 158	$1,275	$24,004	$286	$195	$5,131	$14,180	$ (44)	$9,824

(1) On December 31, 2006, just prior to the adoption of SFAS No. 158, the Company had a minimum pension liability recorded of $17 million, with the offsetting amount recorded in Accumulated other comprehensive loss ($11 million after-tax).

3 Acquisitions

2007

Agreement to acquire Elgin, Joliet and Eastern Railway Company (EJ&E)

In September 2007, the Company entered into an agreement with the U.S. Steel Corporation (U.S. Steel) for the acquisition of the key operations of EJ&E for a purchase price of approximately U.S.$300 million. Under the terms of the agreement, the Company will acquire substantially all of the railroad assets and equipment of EJ&E, except those that support the Gary Works site in northwest Indiana and the steelmaking operations of U.S. Steel. The acquisition will be financed by debt and cash on hand.

In accordance with the terms of the agreement, the Company's obligation to consummate the acquisition is subject to the Company having obtained from the U.S. Surface Transportation Board (STB) a final, unappealable decision that approves the acquisition or exempts it from regulation and does not impose on the parties conditions that would significantly and adversely affect the anticipated economic benefits of the acquisition to the Company.

On November 26, 2007, the STB accepted the Company's application to consider the acquisition as a minor transaction that would normally provide for a decision by mid-2008. The STB, however, is also requiring an Environmental Impact Statement (EIS) for the transaction, and it has indicated that its decision on the transaction will not be issued until the EIS process is completed. The Company believes that the STB should be able to conclude its environmental review and issue a decision that would enable the transaction to close by late 2008. If the transaction is approved by the STB, the Company will account for the acquisition using the purchase method of accounting.

Acquisition of Athabasca Northern Railway (ANY)

In December 2007, the Company acquired the rail assets of ANY for $25 million, for which it plans to invest $135 million in rail-line upgrades over the next three years.

2006

In 2006, the Company acquired the following three entities for a total acquisition cost of $84 million, paid in cash:

(i) Alberta short-line railways, composed of the 600-mile Mackenzie Northern Railway, the 118-mile Lakeland & Waterways Railway and the 21-mile Central Western Railway,

(ii) Savage Alberta Railway, Inc., a 345-mile short-line railway, and

(iii) the remaining 51% of SLX Canada Inc., a company engaged in equipment leasing in which the Company previously had a 49% interest that had been consolidated.

All acquisitions were accounted for using the purchase method of accounting. As such, the Company's consolidated financial statements include the assets, liabilities and results of operations of the acquired entities from the dates of acquisition.

4 Accounts receivable

In millions	December 31,	2007	2006
Freight		$146	$398
Non-freight		251	313
		397	711
Allowance for doubtful accounts		(27)	(19)
		$370	$692

The Company has a five-year agreement, expiring in May 2011, to sell an undivided co-ownership interest for maximum cash proceeds of $600 million in a revolving pool of freight receivables to an unrelated trust. Pursuant to the agreement, the Company sells an interest in its receivables and receives proceeds net of the retained interest as stipulated in the agreement.

The Company has retained the responsibility for servicing, administering and collecting the receivables sold. At December 31, 2007, the servicing asset and liability were not significant. Subject to customary indemnifications, the trust's recourse is generally limited to the receivables.

The Company accounted for the accounts receivable securitization program as a sale, because control over the transferred accounts receivable was relinquished. Due to the relatively short collection period and the high quality of the receivables sold, the fair value of the undivided interest transferred to the trust approximated the book value thereof.

At December 31, 2007, the Company had sold receivables that resulted in proceeds of $588 million under the accounts receivable securitization program ($393 million at December 31, 2006), and recorded the retained interest of approximately 10% of this amount in Other current assets (retained interest of approximately 10% recorded at December 31, 2006).

Other income included $24 million in 2007, $12 million in 2006 and $16 million in 2005, for costs related to the agreement, which fluctuate with changes in prevailing interest rates.

5 Properties

In millions	December 31, 2007			December 31, 2006		
	Cost	Accumulated depreciation	Net	Cost	Accumulated depreciation	Net
Track and roadway [1]	$22,020	$6,433	$15,587	$22,579	$6,445	$16,134
Rolling stock	4,702	1,606	3,096	4,833	1,676	3,157
Buildings	1,105	498	607	1,251	609	642
Information technology	667	131	536	622	101	521
Other	829	242	587	1,226	627	599
	$29,323	$8,910	$20,413	$30,511	$9,458	$21,053
Capital leases included in properties						
Track and roadway [1]	$ 457	$ 38	$ 419	$ 450	$ 25	$ 425
Rolling stock	1,591	310	1,281	1,442	275	1,167
Buildings	119	2	117	38	3	35
Information technology	14	2	12	20	6	14
Other	211	63	148	188	41	147
	$ 2,392	$ 415	$ 1,977	$ 2,138	$ 350	$ 1,788

(1) Includes the cost of land of $1,530 million and $1,746 million as at December 31, 2007 and 2006, respectively, of which $108 million was for right-of-way access and was recorded as a capital lease in both years.

Sale of Central Station Complex

In November 2007, CN finalized an agreement with Homburg Invest Inc., to sell its Central Station Complex in Montreal for proceeds of $355 million before transaction costs. Under the agreement, CN has entered into long-term arrangements to lease back its corporate headquarters building and the Central Station railway passenger facilities. The transaction resulted in a gain on disposition of $222 million, including amounts related to the corporate headquarters building and the Central Station railway passenger facilities, which are being deferred and amortized over their respective lease terms. A gain of $92 million ($64 million after-tax) was recognized immediately in Other income (see Note 14).

Notes to Consolidated Financial Statements

6 Intangible and other assets

In millions	December 31,	2007	2006
Pension asset *(Notes 2, 13)*		$1,768	$1,275
Investments *(A)*		24	142
Other receivables		106	95
Intangible assets *(B)*		54	65
Other		47	38
		$1,999	$1,615

A. Investments

As at December 31, 2007, the Company had $17 million ($134 million at December 31, 2006) of investments accounted for under the equity method and $7 million ($8 million at December 31, 2006) of investments accounted for under the cost method.

In November 2007, Germany's state-owned railway, Deutsche Bahn AG, acquired all of the shares of English Welsh and Scottish Railway (EWS), a company that provides most of the rail freight services in Great Britain and operates freight trains through the English Channel Tunnel, and in which the Company had a 32% ownership interest. The Company accounted for its investment in EWS using the equity method. The Company's share of the cash proceeds was $114 million (net after-tax proceeds are expected to approximate $84 million) resulting in a gain on disposition of the investment of $61 million ($41 million after-tax) which was recorded in Other income (see Note 14). An additional £18 million (Cdn$36 million) was placed in escrow and will be recognized when defined contingencies are resolved.

B. Intangible assets

Intangible assets relate to customer contracts and relationships assumed through past acquisitions.

7 Credit facility

The Company has a U.S.$1 billion revolving credit facility expiring in October 2011. The credit facility is available for general corporate purposes, including back-stopping the Company's commercial paper program, and provides for borrowings at various interest rates, including the Canadian prime rate, bankers' acceptance rates, the U.S. federal funds effective rate and the London Interbank Offer Rate, plus applicable margins. The credit facility agreement has one financial covenant, which limits debt as a percentage of total capitalization, and with which the Company is in compliance. As at December 31, 2007, the Company had no outstanding borrowings under its revolving credit facility (nil as at December 31, 2006) and had letters of credit drawn of $57 million ($308 million as at December 31, 2006).

The Company's commercial paper program is backed by a portion of its revolving credit facility. As at December 31, 2007, the Company had total borrowings under its commercial paper program of $122 million, of which $114 million was denominated in Canadian dollars and $8 million was denominated in U.S. dollars (U.S.$8 million). The weighted-average interest rate on these borrowings was 5.01%. The Company had no commercial paper outstanding as at December 31, 2006.

8 Accounts payable and accrued charges

In millions	December 31,	2007	2006
Trade payables		$ 457	$ 529
Payroll-related accruals		234	232
Accrued charges		146	184
Income and other taxes		123	566
Accrued interest		118	124
Personal injury and other claims provision		102	115
Workforce reduction provisions		19	23
Other		83	50
		$1,282	$1,823

9 Other liabilities and deferred credits

In millions	December 31,	2007	2006
Personal injury and other claims provision, net of current portion		$ 344	$ 487
Other postretirement benefits liability, net of current portion *(A)*		248	269
Pension liability *(Note 13)*		187	195
Environmental reserve, net of current portion		83	106
Workforce reduction provisions, net of current portion *(B)*		53	74
Deferred credits and other		507	334
		$1,422	$1,465

A. Other postretirement benefits liability

The following disclosures in relation to the Company's other postretirement benefit plans are made pursuant to SFAS No. 158 requirements.

(i) Obligations and funded status

In millions Year ended December 31,	2007	2006
Change in benefit obligation		
Benefit obligation at beginning of year	$286	$300
Amendments	12	2
Adoption of SFAS No. 158 measurement date provision *(Note 2)*	2	–
Actuarial gain	(7)	(19)
Interest cost	15	16
Service cost	5	4
Curtailment gain	(9)	–
Foreign currency changes	(21)	–
Benefits paid	(17)	(17)
Benefit obligation at end of year	$266	$286
Unfunded status	$266	$286

(ii) Amount recognized in the Consolidated Balance Sheet

In millions December 31,	2007	2006
Current liabilities	$ 18	$ 17
Noncurrent liabilities	248	269
Total amount recognized	$266	$286

(iii) Amounts recognized in Accumulated other comprehensive loss (Note 20)

In millions December 31,	2007	2006
Net actuarial gain	$27	$34
Prior service cost	(8)	(7)

(iv) Components of net periodic benefit cost

In millions Year ended December 31,	2007	2006	2005
Service cost	$ 5	$ 4	$ 5
Interest cost	15	16	19
Curtailment gain	(4)	–	–
Amortization of prior service cost	2	2	1
Recognized net actuarial gain	(4)	(5)	(1)
Net periodic benefit cost	$14	$17	$24

The estimated prior service cost and net actuarial gain for other postretirement benefits that will be amortized from Accumulated other comprehensive loss into net periodic benefit cost over the next fiscal year are $3 million and $2 million, respectively.

(v) Weighted-average assumptions

The following assumptions are used in accounting for other postretirement benefits:

December 31,	2007	2006	2005
To determine benefit obligation			
Discount rate	5.84%	5.44%	5.30%
Rate of compensation increase	3.50%	3.50%	3.75%
To determine net periodic benefit cost			
Discount rate	5.44%	5.30%	5.90%
Rate of compensation increase	3.50%	3.75%	3.75%

(vi) Health care cost trend rate

For measurement purposes, increases in the per capita cost of covered health care benefits were assumed to be 12% for 2008 and 13% for 2007. It is assumed that the rate will decrease gradually to 6% in 2013 and remain at that level thereafter.

A one-percentage-point change in the assumed health care cost trend rates would have the following effect:

In millions	One-percentage-point	
	Increase	Decrease
Effect on total service and interest costs	$ 2	$ (1)
Effect on benefit obligation	17	(14)

(vii) Estimated future benefit payments

The estimated future benefit payments for each of the next five years and the subsequent five-year period are as follows:

In millions	
2008	$ 18
2009	18
2010	19
2011	19
2012	20
Years 2013 to 2017	107

B. Workforce reduction provisions

The workforce reduction provisions, which cover employees in both Canada and the United States, are mainly comprised of payments related to severance, early retirement incentives and bridging to early retirement, the majority of which will be disbursed within the next four years. In 2007, net charges and adjustments increased the provisions by $6 million (nil for the year ended December 31, 2006). Payments have reduced the provisions by $31 million for the year ended December 31, 2007 ($45 million for the year ended December 31, 2006). As at December 31, 2007, the aggregate provisions, including the current portion, amounted to $72 million ($97 million as at December 31, 2006).

Notes to Consolidated Financial Statements

 Long-term debt

In millions	Maturity	U.S. dollar-denominated amount	December 31, 2007	December 31, 2006
Debentures and notes: (A)				
Canadian National series:				
4.25% 5-year notes *(B)*	Aug. 1, 2009	$300	$ 297	$ 350
6.38% 10-year notes *(B)*	Oct. 15, 2011	400	397	466
4.40% 10-year notes *(B)*	Mar. 15, 2013	400	397	466
5.80% 10-year notes *(B)*	June 1, 2016	250	248	291
5.85% 10-year notes *(B)*	Nov. 15, 2017	250	248	–
6.80% 20-year notes *(B)*	July 15, 2018	200	198	233
7.63% 30-year debentures	May 15, 2023	150	149	175
6.90% 30-year notes *(B)*	July 15, 2028	475	471	554
7.38% 30-year debentures *(B)*	Oct. 15, 2031	200	198	233
6.25% 30-year notes *(B)*	Aug. 1, 2034	500	496	583
6.20% 30-year notes *(B)*	June 1, 2036	450	446	524
6.71% Puttable Reset Securities PURSᴿᴹ *(B)(C)*	July 15, 2036	250	248	291
6.38% 30-year debentures *(B)*	Nov. 15, 2037	300	297	–
Illinois Central series:				
6.98% 12-year notes	July 12, 2007	50	–	58
6.63% 10-year notes	June 9, 2008	20	20	23
5.00% 99-year income debentures	Dec. 1, 2056	7	7	9
7.70% 100-year debentures	Sept. 15, 2096	125	124	146
Wisconsin Central series:				
6.63% 10-year notes	April 15, 2008	150	149	175
			4,390	4,577
BC Rail series:				
Non-interest bearing 90-year subordinated notes *(D)*	July 14, 2094	–	842	842
Total debentures and notes			5,232	5,419
Other:				
Commercial paper *(E) (Note 7)*			122	–
Capital lease obligations and other *(F)*			1,114	1,038
Total other			1,236	1,038
			6,468	6,457
Less:				
Current portion of long-term debt			254	218
Net unamortized discount			851	853
			1,105	1,071
			$5,363	$5,386

A. The Company's debentures, notes and revolving credit facility are unsecured.

B. These debt securities are redeemable, in whole or in part, at the option of the Company, at any time, at the greater of par and a formula price based on interest rates prevailing at the time of redemption.

C. On July 15, 2006, the interest rate on the Company's U.S.$250 million Puttable Reset Securities PURS^{SM} (PURS) was reset at a new rate of 6.71% for the remaining 30-year term ending July 15, 2036. The remarketing did not trigger an extinguishment of debt, as the provisions for the reset of the interest rate were set forth in the original PURS. As such, the original PURS remain outstanding but accrue interest at the new rate until July 2036. Under securities laws, the remarketing required utilization of the Company's shelf prospectus and registration statement.

D. The Company records these notes as a discounted debt of $6 million, using an imputed interest rate of 5.75%. The discount of $836 million is included in the net unamortized discount.

E. The Company has a commercial paper program, which is backed by a portion of its revolving credit facility, enabling it to issue commercial paper up to a maximum aggregate principal amount of $800 million, or the U.S. dollar equivalent. Commercial paper debt is due within one year but is classified as long-term debt, reflecting the Company's intent and contractual ability to refinance the short-term borrowings through subsequent issuances of commercial paper or drawing down on the long-term revolving credit facility.

F. During 2007, the Company recorded $213 million ($264 million in 2006) in assets it acquired through equipment leases and $90 million relating to the leaseback arrangement from the Central Station Complex transaction (see Note 5), for which an equivalent amount was recorded in debt.

Interest rates for capital lease obligations range from approximately 3.0% to 7.9% with maturity dates in the years 2008 through 2037. The imputed interest on these leases amounted to $515 million as at December 31, 2007 and $384 million as at December 31, 2006.

The capital lease obligations are secured by properties with a net carrying amount of $1,566 million as at December 31, 2007 and $1,368 million as at December 31, 2006.

G. Long-term debt maturities, including repurchase arrangements and capital lease repayments on debt outstanding as at December 31, 2007, for the next five years and thereafter, are as follows:

In millions	
2008	$ 254
2009	409
2010	48
2011	628
2012	27
2013 and thereafter	4,251

H. The aggregate amount of debt payable in U.S. currency as at December 31, 2007 was U.S.$5,280 million (Cdn$5,234 million) and U.S.$4,636 million (Cdn$5,403 million) as at December 31, 2006.

I. The Company has U.S.$2.5 billion available under its currently effective shelf prospectus and registration statement, expiring in January 2010, providing for the issuance of debt securities in one or more offerings.

11 Capital stock

A. Authorized capital stock

The authorized capital stock of the Company is as follows:
- Unlimited number of Common Shares, without par value
- Unlimited number of Class A Preferred Shares, without par value, issuable in series
- Unlimited number of Class B Preferred Shares, without par value, issuable in series

B. Issued and outstanding common shares

During 2007, the Company issued 3.0 million shares (5.1 million shares in 2006 and 6.6 million shares in 2005) related to stock options exercised. The total number of common shares issued and outstanding was 485.2 million as at December 31, 2007.

C. Share repurchase programs

In July 2007, the Board of Directors of the Company approved a new share repurchase program which allows for the repurchase of up to 33.0 million common shares between July 26, 2007 and July 25, 2008 pursuant to a normal course issuer bid, at prevailing market prices or such other price as may be permitted by the Toronto Stock Exchange.

As at December 31, 2007, under this current share repurchase program, the Company repurchased 17.7 million common shares for $897 million, at a weighted-average price of $50.70 per share.

In June 2007, the Company completed its 28.0 million share repurchase program, which began on July 25, 2006, for a total of $1,453 million, at a weighted-average price of $51.88 per share. Of this amount, 12.5 million common shares were repurchased in 2007 for $687 million, at a weighted-average price of $54.93 per share.

12 Stock plans

The Company has various stock-based incentive plans for eligible employees. A description of the Company's major plans is provided below:

A. Employee Share Investment Plan

The Company has an Employee Share Investment Plan (ESIP) giving eligible employees the opportunity to subscribe for up to 10% of their gross salaries to purchase shares of the Company's common stock on the open market and to have the Company invest, on the employees' behalf, a further 35% of the amount invested by the employees, up to 6% of their gross salaries.

12 **Stock plans** *(continued)*

The number of participants holding shares at December 31, 2007 was 14,206 (12,590 at December 31, 2006 and 11,010 at December 31, 2005). The total number of ESIP shares purchased on behalf of employees, including the Company's contributions, was 1.3 million in 2007, 1.3 million in 2006 and 1.6 million in 2005, resulting in a pre-tax charge to income of $16 million, $15 million and $12 million for the years ended December 31, 2007, 2006 and 2005, respectively.

B. Stock-based compensation plans

Compensation cost for awards under all stock-based compensation plans was $62 million, $79 million and $120 million for the years ended December 31, 2007, 2006 and 2005, respectively. The total tax benefit recognized in income in relation to stock-based compensation expense for the years ended December 31, 2007, 2006 and 2005 was $23 million, $22 million and $34 million, respectively.

(i) Cash settled awards
Restricted share units

The Company has granted restricted share units (RSUs), 0.7 million in 2007, 0.8 million in 2006, and 0.9 million in 2005, to designated management employees entitling them to receive payout in cash based on the Company's share price. The RSUs granted are generally scheduled for payout after three years ("plan period") and vest upon the attainment of targets relating to return on invested capital over the plan period and to the Company's share price during the last three months of the plan period. Given that the targets related to the 2005 grant were met at December 31, 2007, a payout of $47 million occurred in February of 2008, which was based on the Company's share price during the 20-day period ending on January 31, 2008. As at December 31, 2007, 0.1 million of RSUs remained authorized for future issuance under this plan.

Vision 2008 Share Unit Plan

In the first quarter of 2005, the Board of Directors of the Company approved a special share unit plan with a four-year term to December 31, 2008, entitling designated senior management employees to receive cash payout in January 2009. The Company granted 0.9 million share units which vest conditionally upon the attainment of targets relating to the Company's share price during the six-month period ending December 31, 2008. Payout is conditional upon the attainment of targets relating to return on invested capital over the four-year period and to the Company's share price during the 20-day period ending on December 31, 2008. The award payout will be equal to the number of share units vested on December 31, 2008 multiplied by the Company's 20-day average share price ending on such date. As at December 31, 2007, 0.1 million share units remained authorized for future issuance under this plan.

Voluntary Incentive Deferral Plan

The Company has a Voluntary Incentive Deferral Plan (VIDP), providing eligible senior management employees the opportunity to elect to receive their annual incentive bonus payment and other eligible incentive payments in deferred share units (DSUs). A DSU is equivalent to a common share of the Company and also earns dividends when normal cash dividends are paid on common shares. The number of DSUs received by each participant is established using the average closing price for the 20 trading days prior to and including the date of the incentive payment. For each participant, the Company will grant a further 25% of the amount elected in DSUs, which will vest over a period of four years. The election to receive eligible incentive payments in DSUs is no longer available to a participant when the value of the participant's vested DSUs is sufficient to meet the Company's stock ownership guidelines. The value of each participant's DSUs is payable in cash at the time of cessation of employment. The Company's liability for DSUs is marked-to-market at each period-end based on the Company's closing stock price.

The following table provides the 2007 activity for all cash settled awards:

In millions	RSUs		Vision		VIDP	
	Nonvested	Vested	Nonvested	Vested	Nonvested	Vested
Outstanding at December 31, 2006	2.0	–	0.8	–	0.3	1.9
Granted	0.7	–	0.1	–	–	–
Forfeited	–		(0.1)	–	–	–
Vested during period	(1.1)	1.1	–	–	(0.1)	0.1
Payout	–	(0.1)	–	–	–	(0.2)
Conversion into VIDP	–	(0.1)	–	–	–	0.1
Outstanding at December 31, 2007	1.6	0.9	0.8	–	0.2	1.9

The following table provides valuation and expense information for all cash settled awards:

In millions, unless otherwise indicated	RSUs [1]				Vision [1]	VIDP [2]	Total
Year of grant	2007	2006	2005	2004	2005	2003 onwards	
Stock-based compensation expense recognized over vesting period							
Year ended December 31, 2007	$ 11	$ 8	$ 14	$ 5	$ 2	$ 11	$ 51
Year ended December 31, 2006	N/A	$ 21	$ 19	$ 6	$ 8	$ 11	$ 65
Year ended December 31, 2005	N/A	N/A	$ 15	$ 74	$ –	$ 13	$ 102
Liability outstanding							
December 31, 2007	$ 11	$ 29	$ 48	$ 4	$ 8	$ 95	$ 195
December 31, 2006	N/A	$ 21	$ 34	$ 8	$ 8	$ 99	$ 170
Fair value per unit							
December 31, 2007	$28.56	$38.88	$46.65	$46.65	$17.54	$46.65	N/A
Fair value of awards vested during period							
Year ended December 31, 2007	$ –	$ 1	$ 48	$ 9	$ –	$ 5	$ 63
Year ended December 31, 2006	N/A	$ –	$ –	$ 4	$ –	$ 5	$ 9
Year ended December 31, 2005	N/A	N/A	$ –	$ 105	$ –	$ 2	$ 107
Nonvested awards at December 31, 2007							
Unrecognized compensation cost	$ 7	$ 8	$ –	$ 4	$ 3	$ 7	$ 29
Remaining recognition period *(years)*	2.0	1.0	–	1.0	1.0	3.0	N/A
Assumptions [3]							
Stock price *($)*	$46.65	$46.65	$46.65	$46.65	$46.65	$46.65	N/A
Expected stock price volatility [4]	20%	20%	N/A	N/A	20%	N/A	N/A
Expected term *(years)* [5]	2.0	1.0	N/A	N/A	1.0	N/A	N/A
Risk-free interest rate [6]	3.74%	3.90%	N/A	N/A	3.49%	N/A	N/A
Dividend rate *($)* [7]	$ 0.84	$ 0.84	N/A	N/A	$ 0.84	N/A	N/A

(1) *Beginning in 2006, compensation cost is based on the fair value of the awards at period-end using the lattice-based valuation model that uses the assumptions as presented herein, except for time-vested RSUs. In 2005, compensation cost was measured using intrinsic value.*

(2) *Compensation cost is based on intrinsic value.*

(3) *Assumptions used to determine fair value are at period-end.*

(4) *Based on the historical volatility of the Company's stock over a period commensurate with the expected term of the award.*

(5) *Represents the remaining period of time that awards are expected to be outstanding.*

(6) *Based on the implied yield available on zero-coupon government issues with an equivalent term commensurate with the expected term of the awards.*

(7) *Based on the annualized dividend rate.*

(ii) Stock option awards

The Company has stock option plans for eligible employees to acquire common shares of the Company upon vesting at a price equal to the market value of the common shares at the date of granting. The options are exercisable during a period not exceeding 10 years. The right to exercise options generally accrues over a period of four years of continuous employment. Options are not generally exercisable during the first 12 months after the date of grant. At December 31, 2007, 14.4 million common shares remained authorized for future issuances under these plans.

Options issued by the Company include conventional options, which vest over a period of time; performance options, which vest upon the attainment of Company targets relating to the operating ratio and unlevered return on investment; and performance-accelerated options, which vest on the sixth anniversary of the grant or prior if certain Company targets relating to return on investment and revenues are attained. As at December 31, 2007, the Company's performance and performance-accelerated stock options were fully vested.

For 2007, 2006 and 2005, the Company granted approximately 0.9 million, 1.1 million and 1.3 million, respectively, of conventional stock options to designated senior management employees that vest over a period of four years of continuous employment.

The total number of options outstanding at December 31, 2007, for conventional, performance and performance-accelerated options was 10.6 million, 0.6 million and 3.5 million, respectively.

U.S. GAAP *Canadian National Railway Company* **75**

Notes to Consolidated Financial Statements

12 Stock plans *(continued)*

The following table provides the activity of stock option awards during 2007, and for options outstanding and exercisable at December 31, 2007, the weighted-average exercise price.

	Options outstanding		Nonvested options	
	Number of options	Weighted-average exercise price	Number of options	Weighted-average grant date fair value
	In millions		*In millions*	
Outstanding at December 31, 2006 [1]	16.9	$23.29	2.1	$11.61
Granted	0.9	$52.73	0.9	$13.36
Forfeited	(0.1)	$37.35	(0.1)	$12.06
Exercised	(3.0)	$20.19	N/A	N/A
Vested	N/A	N/A	(0.6)	$11.20
Outstanding at December 31, 2007 [1]	14.7	$24.55	2.3	$12.34
Exercisable at December 31, 2007 [1]	12.4	$21.17	N/A	N/A

(1) Stock options with a U.S. dollar exercise price have been translated to Canadian dollars using the foreign exchange rate in effect at the balance sheet date.

The following table provides the number of stock options outstanding and exercisable as at December 31, 2007 by range of exercise price and their related intrinsic value, and for options outstanding, the weighted-average years to expiration. The table also provides the aggregate intrinsic value for in-the-money stock options, which represents the amount that would have been received by option holders had they exercised their options on December 31, 2007 at the Company's closing stock price of $46.65.

	Options outstanding				Options exercisable		
Range of exercise prices	Number of options	Weighted-average years to expiration	Weighted-average exercise price	Aggregate intrinsic value	Number of options	Weighted-average exercise price	Aggregate intrinsic value
	In millions			*In millions*	*In millions*		*In millions*
$8.90–$11.90	1.5	1.6	$ 11.29	$ 53	1.5	$ 11.29	$ 53
$13.54–$19.83	2.6	2.4	$ 16.19	79	2.6	$ 16.19	79
$20.27–$27.07	7.5	4.5	$ 23.12	176	7.5	$ 23.12	176
$28.93–$40.55	1.2	7.1	$ 31.69	18	0.5	$ 31.57	9
$41.40–$46.27	1.1	8.5	$ 44.42	2	0.2	$ 44.53	–
$46.73–$57.38	0.8	8.6	$ 52.00	–	0.1	$ 51.29	–
Balance at December 31, 2007 [1]	14.7	4.6	$24.55	$328	12.4	$21.17	$317

(1) Stock options with a U.S. dollar exercise price have been translated to Canadian dollars using the foreign exchange rate in effect at the balance sheet date. As at December 31, 2007, the total number of in-the-money stock options outstanding was 13.9 million with a weighted-average exercise price of $23.06. The weighted-average years to expiration of exercisable stock options is 3.9 years.

Notes to Consolidated Financial Statements

The following table provides valuation and expense information for all stock option awards:

In millions, unless otherwise indicated					
Year of grant	2007	2006	2005	Prior to 2005	Total
Stock-based compensation expense recognized over requisite service period [1]					
Year ended December 31, 2007	$ 6	$ 2	$ 3	$ –	$ 11
Year ended December 31, 2006	N/A	$ 8	$ 3	$ 3	$ 14
Year ended December 31, 2005	N/A	N/A	$ 2	$ 16	$ 18
Fair value per unit					
At grant date ($)	$13.36	$13.80	$ 9.19	$ 8.61	N/A
Fair value of awards vested during period					
Year ended December 31, 2007	$ –	$ 4	$ 3	$ –	$ 7
Year ended December 31, 2006	N/A	$ –	$ 3	$ 34	$ 37
Year ended December 31, 2005	N/A	N/A	$ –	$ 34	$ 34
Nonvested awards at December 31, 2007					
Unrecognized compensation cost	$ 5	$ 4	$ 3	$ –	$ 12
Remaining recognition period (years)	3.1	2.1	1.1	–	N/A
Assumptions					
Grant price ($)	$52.79	$51.51	$36.33	$23.59	N/A
Expected stock price volatility [2]	24%	25%	25%	30%	N/A
Expected term (years) [3]	5.2	5.2	5.2	6.2	N/A
Risk-free interest rate [4]	4.12%	4.04%	3.50%	5.13%	N/A
Dividend rate ($) [5]	$ 0.84	$ 0.65	$ 0.50	$ 0.30	N/A

(1) Compensation cost is based on the grant date fair value using the Black-Scholes option-pricing model that uses the assumptions at the grant date.

(2) Based on the historical volatility of the Company's stock over a period commensurate with the expected term of the award.

(3) Represents the period of time that awards are expected to be outstanding. The Company uses historical data to estimate option exercise and employee termination, and groups of employees that have similar historical exercise behavior are considered separately.

(4) Based on the implied yield available on zero-coupon government issues with an equivalent term commensurate with the expected term of the awards.

(5) Based on the annualized dividend rate.

The following table provides information related to options exercised during the years ended December 31, 2007, 2006 and 2005:

In millions	Year ended December 31,	2007	2006	2005
Total intrinsic value		$105	$156	$139
Cash received upon exercise of options		$ 61	$101	$115
Related tax benefits realized		$ 16	$ 19	$ 21

Prior to January 1, 2006, the Company followed the fair value based approach for stock option awards and had prospectively applied this method of accounting to all awards granted, modified or settled on or after January 1, 2003, and measured cash settled awards at their intrinsic value at period-end. For the year ended December 31, 2005, if compensation cost had been determined based upon fair values at the date of grant for awards under all plans, the Company's pro forma net income and earnings per share would have been as follows:

In millions, except per share data	Year ended December 31,	2005
Net income, as reported		$1,556
Add (deduct) compensation cost, net of applicable taxes, determined under:		
Fair value method for all awards granted after Jan. 1, 2003 (SFAS No. 123)		86
Fair value method for all awards (SFAS No. 123)		(110)
Pro forma net income		$1,532
Basic earnings per share, as reported		$ 2.82
Basic earnings per share, pro forma		$ 2.78
Diluted earnings per share, as reported		$ 2.77
Diluted earnings per share, pro forma		$ 2.73

U.S. GAAP   Canadian National Railway Company   77

13 Pensions

The Company has various retirement benefit plans under which substantially all of its employees are entitled to benefits at retirement age, generally based on compensation and length of service and/or contributions. The information in the tables that follow pertains to all such plans. However, the following descriptions relate solely to the Company's main pension plan, the CN Pension Plan (the Plan), unless otherwise specified.

A. Description of the Plan

The Plan is a contributory defined benefit pension plan that covers the majority of CN employees. It provides for pensions based mainly on years of service and final average pensionable earnings and is generally applicable from the first day of employment. Indexation of pensions is provided after retirement through a gain/loss sharing mechanism, subject to guaranteed minimum increases. An independent trust company is the Trustee of the Canadian National Railways Pension Trust Funds (CN Pension Trust Funds). As Trustee, the trust company performs certain duties, which include holding legal title to the assets of the CN Pension Trust Funds and ensuring that the Company, as Administrator, complies with the provisions of the Plan and the related legislation. The Company utilizes a measurement date of December 31 for the Plan.

B. Funding policy

Employee contributions to the Plan are determined by the plan rules. Company contributions are in accordance with the requirements of the Government of Canada legislation, The Pension Benefits Standards Act, 1985, and are determined by actuarial valuations conducted at least on a triennial basis. These valuations are made in accordance with legislative requirements and with the recommendations of the Canadian Institute of Actuaries for the valuation of pension plans. The latest actuarial valuation of the Plan was conducted as at December 31, 2006 and indicated a funding excess. Total contributions for all of the Company's pension plans are expected to be approximately $100 million in each of 2008, 2009 and 2010 based on the plans' current position. All of the Company's contributions are expected to be in the form of cash.

C. Description of fund assets

The assets of the Plan are accounted for separately in the CN Pension Trust Funds and consist of cash and short-term investments, bonds, mortgages, Canadian and foreign equities, real estate, and oil and gas assets. The assets of the Plan have a fair market value of $15,208 million as at

December 31, 2007 ($14,812 million at December 31, 2006). The Plan's target percentage allocation and weighted-average asset allocations as at December 31, 2007 and 2006, by asset category are as follows:

Plan assets by category	Target allocation	December 31, 2007	2006
Equity securities	53%	51%	52%
Debt securities	40%	34%	38%
Real estate	4%	2%	2%
Other	3%	13%	8%
	100%	100%	100%

The Company follows a disciplined investment strategy, which limits concentration of investments by asset class, foreign currency, sector or company. The Investment Committee of the Board of Directors has approved an investment policy that establishes long-term asset mix targets based on a review of historical returns achieved by worldwide investment markets. Investment managers may deviate from these targets but their performance is evaluated in relation to the market performance of the target mix. The Company does not anticipate the return on plan assets to fluctuate materially from related capital market indices. The Investment Committee reviews investments regularly with specific approval required for major investments in illiquid securities. The policy also permits the use of derivative financial instruments to implement asset mix decisions or to hedge existing or anticipated exposures. The Plan does not invest in the securities of the Company or its subsidiaries.

D. Weighted-average assumptions

The following assumptions are used in accounting for pension benefits:

December 31,	2007	2006	2005
To determine benefit obligation			
Discount rate	5.53%	5.12%	5.00%
Rate of compensation increase	3.50%	3.50%	3.75%
To determine net periodic benefit cost			
Discount rate	5.12%	5.00%	5.75%
Rate of compensation increase	3.50%	3.75%	3.75%
Expected return on plan assets	8.00%	8.00%	8.00%

To develop its expected long-term rate of return assumption used in the calculation of net periodic benefit cost applicable to the market-related value of assets, the Company considers both its past experience and future estimates of long-term investment returns, the expected composition of the plans' assets as well as the expected long-term market returns in the future. The Company has elected to use a market-related value of assets, whereby realized and unrealized gains/losses and appreciation/depreciation in the value of the investments are recognized over a period of five years, while investment income is recognized immediately.

E. Information about the Company's defined benefit pension plans

The following disclosures in relation to the Company's defined benefit pension plans are made pursuant to SFAS No. 158 requirements.

(i) Obligations and funded status

In millions Year ended December 31,	2007	2006
Change in benefit obligation		
Benefit obligation at beginning of year	$14,545	$14,346
Adoption of SFAS No. 158 measurement date provision *(Note 2)*	3	–
Interest cost	742	713
Actuarial (gain) loss	(195)	237
Service cost	150	146
Plan participants' contributions	54	55
Foreign currency changes	(33)	(1)
Benefit payments and transfers	(847)	(951)
Benefit obligation at end of year	$14,419	$14,545
Component representing future salary increases	(618)	(771)
Accumulated benefit obligation at end of year	$13,801	$13,774
Change in plan assets		
Fair value of plan assets at beginning of year	$15,625	$14,874
Employer contributions	75	112
Plan participants' contributions	54	55
Foreign currency changes	(26)	1
Actual return on plan assets	1,119	1,534
Benefit payments and transfers	(847)	(951)
Fair value of plan assets at end of year	$16,000	$15,625
Funded status (Excess of fair value of plan assets over benefit obligation at end of year)	$ 1,581	$ 1,080

(ii) Amounts recognized in the Consolidated Balance Sheet

In millions December 31,	2007	2006
Noncurrent assets *(Note 6)*	$1,768	$1,275
Noncurrent liability *(Note 9)*	(187)	(195)
Total amount recognized	$1,581	$1,080

(iii) Amounts recognized in Accumulated other comprehensive loss (Note 20)

In millions December 31,	2007	2006
Net actuarial gain	$1,039	$600
Prior service cost	(19)	(38)

(iv) Information for the pension plan with an accumulated benefit obligation in excess of plan assets

In millions December 31,	2007	2006
Projected benefit obligation	$266	$386
Accumulated benefit obligation	229	337
Fair value of plan assets	79	177

(v) Components of net periodic benefit cost

In millions Year ended December 31,	2007	2006	2005
Service cost	$ 150	$146	$ 138
Interest cost	742	713	742
Expected return on plan assets	(935)	(903)	(884)
Amortization of prior service cost	19	19	18
Recognized net actuarial loss	53	91	3
Net periodic benefit cost	$ 29	$ 66	$ 17

The estimated prior service cost and net actuarial loss for defined benefit pension plans that will be amortized from Accumulated other comprehensive loss into net periodic benefit cost over the next fiscal year are $19 million and nil, respectively.

(vi) Estimated future benefit payments

The estimated future benefit payments for each of the next five years and the subsequent five-year period are as follows:

In millions	
2008	$ 847
2009	879
2010	912
2011	942
2012	971
Years 2013 to 2017	5,245

14 Other income

In millions Year ended December 31,	2007	2006	2005
Gain on disposal of Central Station Complex *(Note 5)*	$ 92	$ –	$ –
Gain on disposal of investment in EWS *(Note 6)*	61	–	–
Foreign exchange	24	18	12
Gain on disposal of properties	14	16	26
Equity in earnings of EWS *(Note 6)*	5	(6)	4
Net real estate costs	(6)	(12)	(12)
Costs related to the Accounts receivable securitization program	(24)	(12)	(16)
Other	–	7	(2)
	$166	$ 11	$ 12

U.S. GAAP

Notes to Consolidated Financial Statements

 Income taxes

The Company's consolidated effective income tax rate differs from the Canadian statutory Federal tax rate. The reconciliation of income tax expense is as follows:

In millions Year ended December 31,	2007	2006	2005
Federal tax rate	22.1%	22.1%	22.1%
Income tax expense at the statutory Federal tax rate	$(598)	$(603)	$(516)
Income tax (expense) recovery resulting from:			
Provincial and other taxes	(318)	(354)	(331)
Deferred income tax adjustments due to rate enactments	317	228	(14)
Other [1]	51	87	80
Income tax expense	$(548)	$(642)	$(781)
Cash payments for income taxes	$ 867	$ 307	$ 186

(1) Includes adjustments relating to the resolution of matters pertaining to prior years' income taxes and other items.

The following table provides tax information for Canada and the United States:

In millions Year ended December 31,	2007	2006	2005
Income before income taxes			
Canada	$1,983	$2,009	$1,769
U.S.	723	720	568
	$2,706	$2,729	$2,337
Current income tax expense			
Canada	$ (418)	$ (440)	$ (95)
U.S.	(212)	(199)	(139)
	$ (630)	$ (639)	$ (234)
Deferred income tax recovery (expense)			
Canada	$ 141	$ 102	$ (488)
U.S.	(59)	(105)	(59)
	$ 82	$ (3)	$ (547)

Significant components of deferred income tax assets and liabilities are as follows:

In millions December 31,	2007	2006
Deferred income tax assets		
Workforce reduction provisions	$ 22	$ 32
Personal injury claims and other reserves	146	215
Other postretirement benefits liability	85	99
Losses and tax credit carryforwards	24	14
	277	360
Deferred income tax liabilities		
Net pension asset	429	330
Properties and other	4,688	5,161
	5,117	5,491
Total net deferred income tax liability	$4,840	$5,131
Total net deferred income tax liability		
Canada	$2,191	$2,050
U.S.	2,649	3,081
	$4,840	$5,131
Total net deferred income tax liability	$4,840	$5,131
Net current deferred income tax asset	68	84
Long-term deferred income tax liability	$4,908	$5,215

It is more likely than not that the Company will realize the majority of its deferred income tax assets from the generation of future taxable income, as the payments for provisions, reserves and accruals are made and losses and tax credit carryforwards are utilized. At December 31, 2007, the Company had no operating loss carryforwards available to reduce future taxable income. The Company has not recognized a deferred tax asset on the foreign exchange loss recorded in Accumulated other comprehensive loss on its permanent investment in U.S. rail subsidiaries, as the Company does not expect this temporary difference to reverse in the foreseeable future.

The Company recognized tax credits of $4 million in each of 2007, 2006 and 2005 for eligible research and development expenditures, which reduced the cost of properties.

The following table provides reconciliation for unrecognized tax benefits for Canada and the United States:

In millions	
Gross unrecognized tax benefits as at January 1, 2007	$140
Additions:	
Tax positions related to the current year	14
Tax positions related to prior years	11
Interest accrued on tax positions	15
Deductions:	
Tax positions related to prior years	(11)
Interest accrued on tax positions	(6)
Settlements	(5)
Gross unrecognized tax benefits as at December 31, 2007	$158
Adjustments to reflect tax treaties and other arrangements	(81)
Net unrecognized tax benefits as at December 31, 2007	$ 77

At December 31, 2007, the total amount of gross unrecognized tax benefits was $158 million, before considering tax treaties and other arrangements between taxation authorities, of which $45 million related to accrued interest and penalties. If recognized, all of the net unrecognized tax benefits would affect the effective tax rate.

The Company recognizes interest accrued and penalties related to unrecognized tax benefits in Income tax expense in the Company's Consolidated Statement of Income.

In Canada, the federal income tax returns filed for the years 2003 to 2006 and the provincial income tax returns filed for the years 1998 to 2006 remain subject to examination by the taxation authorities. In the U.S., the income tax returns filed for the years 2003 to 2006 remain subject to examination by the taxation authorities.

 Segmented information

The Company manages its operations as one business segment over a single network that spans vast geographic distances and territories, with operations in Canada and the United States. Financial information reported at this level, such as revenues, operating income, and cash flow from operations, is used by corporate management, including the Company's chief operating decision-maker, in evaluating financial and operational performance and allocating resources across CN's network.

The Company's strategic initiatives, which drive its operational direction, are developed and managed centrally by corporate management and are communicated to its regional activity centers (the Western Region, Eastern Region and Southern Region). Corporate management is responsible for, among others, CN's marketing strategy, the management of large customer accounts, overall planning and control of infrastructure and rolling stock, the allocation of resources, and other functions such as financial planning, accounting and treasury.

The role of each region is to manage the day-to-day service requirements within their respective territories and control direct costs incurred locally. Such cost control is required to ensure that pre-established efficiency standards set at the corporate level are met. The regions execute the overall corporate strategy and operating plan established by corporate management, as their management of throughput and control of direct costs does not serve as the platform for the Company's decision-making process. Approximately 90% of the Company's freight revenues are from national accounts for which freight traffic spans North America and touches various commodity groups. As a result, the Company does not manage revenues on a regional basis since a large number of the movements originate in one region and pass through and/or terminate in another region.

The regions also demonstrate common characteristics in each of the following areas:

(i) each region's sole business activity is the transportation of freight over the Company's extensive rail network;

(ii) the regions service national accounts that extend over the Company's various commodity groups and across its rail network;

(iii) the services offered by the Company stem predominantly from the transportation of freight by rail with the goal of optimizing the rail network as a whole;

(iv) the Company and its subsidiaries, not its regions, are subject to single regulatory regimes in both Canada and the U.S.

For the reasons mentioned herein, the Company reports as one operating segment.

The following tables provide information by geographic area:

In millions	Year ended December 31,	2007	2006	2005
Revenues				
Canada		$5,265	$ 5,293	$ 4,839
U.S.		2,632	2,636	2,607
		$7,897	$ 7,929	$ 7,446

In millions	Year ended December 31,	2007	2006	2005
Net income				
Canada		$1,706	$ 1,671	$ 1,186
U.S.		452	416	370
		$2,158	$ 2,087	$ 1,556

In millions	December 31,	2007	2006
Properties			
Canada		$11,777	$11,129
U.S.		8,636	9,924
		$20,413	$21,053

17 Earnings per share

Year ended December 31,	2007	2006	2005
Basic earnings per share	$4.31	$3.97	$2.82
Diluted earnings per share	$4.25	$3.91	$2.77

The following table provides a reconciliation between basic and diluted earnings per share:

In millions	Year ended December 31,	2007	2006	2005
Net income		$2,158	$2,087	$1,556
Weighted-average shares outstanding		501.2	525.9	551.7
Effect of stock options		6.8	8.4	10.5
Weighted-average diluted shares outstanding		508.0	534.3	562.2

For the years ended December 31, 2007 and 2006, the weighted-average number of stock options that were not included in the calculation of diluted earnings per share, as their inclusion would have had an anti-dilutive impact, were 0.1 million and 0.2 million, respectively. For the year ended December 31, 2005, all stock options were dilutive.

18 Major commitments and contingencies

A. Leases

The Company has operating and capital leases, mainly for locomotives, freight cars and intermodal equipment. Of the capital leases, many provide the option to purchase the leased items at fixed values during or at the end of the lease term. As at December 31, 2007, the Company's commitments under these operating and capital leases were $879 million and $1,620 million, respectively. Minimum rental payments for operating leases having initial non-cancelable lease terms of one year or more and minimum lease payments for capital leases in each of the next five years and thereafter are as follows:

In millions	Operating	Capital
2008	$152	$ 145
2009	125	165
2010	106	100
2011	84	164
2012	68	75
2013 and thereafter	344	971
	$879	1,620
Less: imputed interest on capital leases at rates ranging from approximately 3.0% to 7.9%		515
Present value of minimum lease payments included in debt		$1,105

The Company also has operating lease agreements for its automotive fleet with minimum one-year non-cancelable terms for which its practice is to renew monthly thereafter. The estimated annual rental payments for such leases are approximately $30 million and generally extend over five years.

Rent expense for all operating leases was $207 million, $202 million and $233 million for the years ended December 31, 2007, 2006 and 2005, respectively. Contingent rentals and sublease rentals were not significant.

U.S. GAAP

Canadian National Railway Company **81**

18 Major commitments and contingencies *(continued)*

B. Other commitments

As at December 31, 2007, the Company had commitments to acquire railroad ties, rail, freight cars, locomotives and other equipment and services, as well as outstanding information technology service contracts and licenses, at an aggregate cost of $952 million. The Company also had agreements with fuel suppliers to purchase approximately 84% of its anticipated 2008 volume, 59% of its anticipated 2009 volume and 28% of its anticipated 2010 volume, at market prices prevailing on the date of the purchase.

C. Contingencies

In the normal course of its operations, the Company becomes involved in various legal actions, including claims relating to personal injuries, occupational disease and damage to property.

Canada

Employee injuries are governed by the workers' compensation legislation in each province whereby employees may be awarded either a lump sum or future stream of payments depending on the nature and severity of the injury. Accordingly, the Company accounts for costs related to employee work-related injuries based on actuarially developed estimates of the ultimate cost associated with such injuries, including compensation, health care and third-party administration costs. For all other legal actions, the Company maintains, and regularly updates on a case-by-case basis, provisions for such items when the expected loss is both probable and can be reasonably estimated based on currently available information.

At December 31, 2007, 2006 and 2005, the Company's provision for personal injury and other claims in Canada was as follows:

In millions	2007	2006	2005
Balance January 1	$195	$205	$204
Accruals and other	41	60	46
Payments	(40)	(70)	(45)
Balance December 31	$196	$195	$205

United States

Employee work-related injuries, including occupational disease claims, are compensated according to the provisions of the Federal Employers' Liability Act (FELA), which requires either the finding of fault through the U.S. jury system or individual settlements, and represent a major liability for the railroad industry. The Company follows an actuarial-based approach and accrues the expected cost for personal injury and property damage claims and asserted and unasserted occupational disease claims, based on actuarial estimates of their ultimate cost.

In 2007, 2006 and 2005, the Company recorded net reductions to its provision for U.S. personal injury and other claims pursuant to the results of external actuarial studies of $97 million, $62 million and $21 million, respectively. The reductions were mainly attributable to decreases in the Company's estimates of unasserted claims and costs related to asserted claims as a result of its ongoing risk mitigation

strategy focused on prevention, mitigation of claims and containment of injuries, lower settlements for existing claims and reduced severity relating to non-occupational disease claims.

Due to the inherent uncertainty involved in projecting future events related to occupational diseases, which include but are not limited to, the number of expected claims, the average cost per claim and the legislative and judicial environment, the Company's future obligations may differ from current amounts recorded.

At December 31, 2007, 2006 and 2005, the Company's provision for U.S. personal injury and other claims was as follows:

In millions	2007	2006	2005
Balance January 1	$407	$452	$438
Accruals and other	(111)	(8)	61
Payments	(46)	(37)	(47)
Balance December 31	$250	$407	$452

Although the Company considers such provisions to be adequate for all its outstanding and pending claims, the final outcome with respect to actions outstanding or pending at December 31, 2007, or with respect to future claims, cannot be predicted with certainty, and therefore there can be no assurance that their resolution will not have a material adverse effect on the Company's financial position or results of operations in a particular quarter or fiscal year.

D. Environmental matters

The Company's operations are subject to numerous federal, provincial, state, municipal and local environmental laws and regulations in Canada and the United States concerning, among other things, emissions into the air; discharges into waters; the generation, handling, storage, transportation, treatment and disposal of waste, hazardous substances, and other materials; decommissioning of underground and aboveground storage tanks; and soil and groundwater contamination. A risk of environmental liability is inherent in railroad and related transportation operations; real estate ownership, operation or control; and other commercial activities of the Company with respect to both current and past operations. As a result, the Company incurs significant compliance and capital costs, on an ongoing basis, associated with environmental regulatory compliance and clean-up requirements in its railroad operations and relating to its past and present ownership, operation or control of real property.

The Company is subject to environmental clean-up and enforcement actions. In particular, the Federal Comprehensive Environmental Response, Compensation and Liability Act of 1980 (CERCLA), also known as the Superfund law, as well as similar state laws generally impose joint and several liability for clean-up and enforcement costs on current and former owners and operators of a site without regard to fault or the legality of the original conduct. The Company has been notified that it is a potentially responsible party for study and clean-up costs at approximately 21 sites governed by the Superfund law (and other similar federal and state laws) for which investigation and remediation payments are or will be made or are yet to be determined and, in many instances, is one of several potentially responsible parties.

While the Company believes that it has identified the costs likely to be incurred in the next several years, based on known information, for environmental matters, the Company's ongoing efforts to identify potential environmental concerns that may be associated with its properties may lead to future environmental investigations, which may result in the identification of additional environmental costs and liabilities. The magnitude of such additional liabilities and the costs of complying with environmental laws and containing or remediating contamination cannot be reasonably estimated due to:

(i) the lack of specific technical information available with respect to many sites;

(ii) the absence of any government authority, third-party orders, or claims with respect to particular sites;

(iii) the potential for new or changed laws and regulations and for development of new remediation technologies and uncertainty regarding the timing of the work with respect to particular sites;

(iv) the ability to recover costs from any third parties with respect to particular sites; and

therefore, the likelihood of any such costs being incurred or whether such costs would be material to the Company cannot be determined at this time. There can thus be no assurance that material liabilities or costs related to environmental matters will not be incurred in the future, or will not have a material adverse effect on the Company's financial position or results of operations in a particular quarter or fiscal year, or that the Company's liquidity will not be adversely impacted by such environmental liabilities or costs. Although the effect on operating results and liquidity cannot be reasonably estimated, management believes, based on current information, that environmental matters will not have a material adverse effect on the Company's financial condition or competitive position. Costs related to any future remediation will be accrued in the year in which they become known.

In 2005, the Company had recorded a liability related to a derailment at Wabamun Lake, Alberta. Over the last two years, this liability was adjusted for additional environmental and legal claims and reduced by payments made pursuant to the clean-up performed. At December 31, 2007, the Company has an amount receivable for the remaining estimated recoveries from the Company's insurance carriers who covered substantially all expenses related to the derailment above the self-insured retention of $25 million, which was recorded in operating expenses in 2005.

At December 31, 2007, 2006 and 2005, the Company's provision for specific environmental sites and remediation, net of potential and actual insurance recoveries was as follows:

In millions	2007	2006	2005
Balance January 1	$131	$124	$113
Accruals and other	(1)	17	35
Payments	(19)	(10)	(24)
Balance December 31	$111	$131	$124

The Company anticipates that the majority of the liability at December 31, 2007 will be paid out over the next five years.

The Company also incurs expenses related to environmental regulatory compliance and clean-up requirements. Such expenses amounted to $10 million in 2007 ($10 million in 2006 and $9 million in 2005). In addition, environmental capital expenditures were $14 million in 2007, $18 million in 2006 and $11 million in 2005. The Company expects to incur capital expenditures relating to environmental conditions of approximately $11 million in 2008, $12 million in 2009 and $9 million in 2010.

E. Guarantees and indemnifications

In the normal course of business, the Company, including certain of its subsidiaries, enters into agreements that may involve providing certain guarantees or indemnifications to third parties and others, which may extend beyond the term of the agreement. These include, but are not limited to, residual value guarantees on operating leases, standby letters of credit and surety and other bonds, and indemnifications that are customary for the type of transaction or for the railway business.

The Company is required to recognize a liability for the fair value of the obligation undertaken in issuing certain guarantees on the date the guarantee is issued or modified. In addition, where the Company expects to make a payment in respect of a guarantee, a liability will be recognized to the extent that one has not yet been recognized.

(i) Guarantee of residual values of operating leases
The Company has guaranteed a portion of the residual values of certain of its assets under operating leases with expiry dates between 2008 and 2017, for the benefit of the lessor. If the fair value of the assets, at the end of their respective lease term, is less than the fair value, as estimated at the inception of the lease, then the Company must, under certain conditions, compensate the lessor for the shortfall. At December 31, 2007, the maximum exposure in respect of these guarantees was $145 million. There are no recourse provisions to recover any amounts from third parties.

(ii) Other guarantees
The Company, including certain of its subsidiaries, has granted irrevocable standby letters of credit and surety and other bonds, issued by highly rated financial institutions, to third parties to indemnify them in the event the Company does not perform its contractual obligations. As at December 31, 2007, the maximum potential liability under these guarantees was $462 million, of which $384 million was for workers' compensation and other employee benefits and $78 million was for equipment under leases and other. During 2007, the Company granted guarantees for which no liability has been recorded, as they relate to the Company's future performance.

As at December 31, 2007 and 2006, the Company had not recorded any additional liability with respect to these guarantees, as the Company does not expect to make any additional payments associated with these guarantees. The majority of the guarantee instruments mature at various dates between 2008 and 2010.

18 Major commitments and contingencies *(continued)*

(iii) CN Pension Plan, CN 1935 Pension Plan and BC Rail Ltd Pension Plan

The Company has indemnified and held harmless the current trustee and the former trustee of the Canadian National Railways Pension Trust Funds, the trustee of the BC Rail Ltd Pension Trust Fund, and the respective officers, directors, employees and agents of such trustees, from any and all taxes, claims, liabilities, damages, costs and expenses arising out of the performance of their obligations under the relevant trust agreements and trust deeds, including in respect of their reliance on authorized instructions of the Company or for failing to act in the absence of authorized instructions. These indemnifications survive the termination of such agreements or trust deeds. As at December 31, 2007, the Company had not recorded a liability associated with these indemnifications, as the Company does not expect to make any payments pertaining to these indemnifications.

(iv) General indemnifications

In the normal course of business, the Company has provided indemnifications, customary for the type of transaction or for the railway business, in various agreements with third parties, including indemnification provisions where the Company would be required to indemnify third parties and others. Indemnifications are found in various types of contracts with third parties, which include, but are not limited to:

(a) contracts granting the Company the right to use or enter upon property owned by third parties such as leases, easements, trackage rights and sidetrack agreements;

(b) contracts granting rights to others to use the Company's property, such as leases, licenses and easements;

(c) contracts for the sale of assets and securitization of accounts receivable;

(d) contracts for the acquisition of services;

(e) financing agreements;

(f) trust indentures, fiscal agency agreements, underwriting agreements or similar agreements relating to debt or equity securities of the Company and engagement agreements with financial advisors;

(g) transfer agent and registrar agreements in respect of the Company's securities;

(h) trust and other agreements relating to pension plans and other plans, including those establishing trust funds to secure payment to certain officers and senior employees of special retirement compensation arrangements;

(i) pension transfer agreements;

(j) master agreements with financial institutions governing derivative transactions; and

(k) settlement agreements with insurance companies or other third parties whereby such insurer or third party has been indemnified for any present or future claims relating to insurance policies, incidents or events covered by the settlement agreements.

To the extent of any actual claims under these agreements, the Company maintains provisions for such items, which it considers to be adequate. Due to the nature of the indemnification clauses, the maximum exposure for future payments may be material. However, such exposure cannot be determined with certainty.

The Company has entered into various indemnification contracts with third parties for which the maximum exposure for future payments cannot be determined with certainty. As a result, the Company was unable to determine the fair value of these guarantees and accordingly, no liability was recorded. There are no recourse provisions to recover any amounts from third parties.

19 Financial instruments

A. Risk management

The Company has limited involvement with derivative financial instruments in the management of its foreign currency and interest rate exposures, and does not use them for trading purposes. At December 31, 2007, the Company did not have any derivative financial instruments outstanding.

(i) Credit risk

In the normal course of business, the Company monitors the financial condition of its customers and reviews the credit history of each new customer. The Company believes there are no significant concentrations of credit risk.

(ii) Fuel

To mitigate the effects of fuel price changes on its operating margins and overall profitability, the Company had a hedging program which called for entering into swap positions on crude and heating oil to cover a target percentage of future fuel consumption up to two years in advance. However, with an increased application of fuel surcharge on revenues, no additional swap positions were entered into since September 2004. As such, the Company terminated this program in late 2006.

Since the changes in the fair value of the swap positions were highly correlated to changes in the price of fuel, the hedges were accounted for as cash flow hedges, whereby the effective portion of the cumulative change in the market value of the derivative instruments had been recorded in Accumulated other comprehensive loss.

During 2006, the Company's remaining swap positions matured and were settled. As a result, the related unrealized gains previously recorded in Accumulated other comprehensive loss were reclassified into income as realized gains (unrealized gains of $57 million, $39 million after-tax at December 31, 2005).

Total realized gains from the Company's fuel hedging activities, which are recorded as a reduction in fuel expense were $64 million and $177 million for the years ended December 31, 2006 and 2005, respectively.

The Company did not recognize any material gains or losses in each of 2006 and 2005 due to hedge ineffectiveness as the Company's derivative instruments were highly effective in hedging the changes in cash flows associated with forecasted purchases of diesel fuel.

(iii) Interest rate

The Company is exposed to interest rate risk related to the funded status of its pension and postretirement plans and on a portion of its long-term debt and does not currently hold any financial instruments that mitigate this risk. At December 31, 2007, Accumulated other comprehensive loss included an unamortized gain of $11 million, $8 million after-tax ($12 million, $8 million after-tax at December 31, 2006) relating to treasury lock transactions settled in 2004.

(iv) Foreign currency

The Company conducts its business in both Canada and the U.S. and as a result, is affected by currency fluctuations. Changes in the exchange rate between the Canadian dollar and other currencies (including the U.S. dollar) make the goods transported by the Company more or less competitive in the world marketplace and thereby further affect the Company's revenues and expenses.

For the purpose of minimizing volatility of earnings resulting from the conversion of U.S. dollar-denominated long-term debt into the Canadian dollar, the Company designates the U.S. dollar-denominated long-term debt of the parent company as a foreign exchange hedge of its net investment in U.S. subsidiaries. As a result, from the dates of designation, unrealized foreign exchange gains and losses on the translation of the Company's U.S. dollar-denominated long-term debt are recorded in Accumulated other comprehensive loss.

B. Fair value of financial instruments

Generally accepted accounting principles define the fair value of a financial instrument as the amount at which the instrument could be exchanged in a current transaction between willing parties. The Company uses the following methods and assumptions to estimate the fair value of each class of financial instruments for which the carrying amounts are included in the Consolidated Balance Sheet under the following captions:

(i) Cash and cash equivalents, Accounts receivable, Other current assets, Accounts payable and accrued charges, and Other current liabilities: The carrying amounts approximate fair value because of the short maturity of these instruments.

(ii) Other assets:

Investments: The Company has various equity investments for which the carrying value approximates the fair value, with the exception of certain cost investments for which the fair value was estimated based on the Company's proportionate share of its net assets.

(iii) Long-term debt:

The fair value of the Company's long-term debt is estimated based on the quoted market prices for the same or similar debt instruments, as well as discounted cash flows using current interest rates for debt with similar terms, company rating, and remaining maturity.

The following table presents the carrying amounts and estimated fair values of the Company's financial instruments as at December 31, 2007 and 2006 for which the carrying values on the Consolidated Balance Sheet are different from their fair values:

In millions	December 31, 2007		December 31, 2006	
	Carrying amount	Fair value	Carrying amount	Fair value
Financial assets				
Investments	$ 24	$ 95	$ 142	$ 215
Financial liabilities				
Long-term debt (including current portion)	$5,617	$5,850	$5,604	$5,946

Notes to Consolidated Financial Statements

20 Accumulated other comprehensive loss

The components of Accumulated other comprehensive loss are as follows:

In millions	December 31,	2007	2006
Unrealized foreign exchange loss		$(762)	$(455)
Pension and other postretirement benefit plans		723	403
Derivative instruments		8	8
Accumulated other comprehensive loss		$ (31)	$ (44)

The components of Other comprehensive income (loss) and the related tax effects are as follows:

In millions	Year ended December 31,	2007	2006	2005
Accumulated other comprehensive loss – Balance at January 1		$ (44)	$(222)	$(148)
Other comprehensive income (loss):				
Unrealized foreign exchange loss (net of income tax (expense) recovery of $(91), $(231), and $27, for 2007, 2006 and 2005, respectively) [1]		(307)	(232)	(54)
Pension and other postretirement benefit plans (net of income tax expense of $(129), nil, and $(1), for 2007, 2006 and 2005, respectively) (Notes 9, 13)		320	1	3
Derivative instruments (net of income tax recovery of $1, $18, and $12, for 2007, 2006 and 2005, respectively) (Note 19)		–	(39)	(23)
Deferred income tax rate enactment		–	34	–
Other comprehensive income (loss)		13	(236)	(74)
Adjustment to reflect the funded status of benefit plans (Note 2):				
Net actuarial gain (net of income tax expense of $(200) for 2006)		–	434	–
Prior service cost (net of income tax recovery of $14 for 2006)		–	(31)	–
Reversal of minimum pension liability adjustment (net of income tax expense of $(6) for 2006)		–	11	–
Accumulated other comprehensive loss – Balance at December 31		$ (31)	$ (44)	$(222)

(1) In 2006, the Company adjusted its deferred income tax liability for changes in income tax rates applied to certain temporary differences and also for the income tax effect on the currency translation amount resulting from the difference between the accounting and tax basis of its net investment in foreign subsidiaries. As a result, the Company recorded a $180 million net charge for deferred income taxes in Other comprehensive income (loss).

21 Comparative figures

Certain of the 2006 and 2005 comparative figures have been reclassified in order to be consistent with the 2007 presentation as discussed herein. As a result of the Company's expansion of its existing non-rail transportation services, in combination with its rail service, the Company has become primarily responsible for the fulfillment of the transportation of goods involving non-rail activities. In order to be consistent with the presentation of other non-rail transportation services, the Company reclassified certain operating expenses incurred for non-rail transportation services, which were previously netted with their related revenues, to reflect the gross reporting of revenues where appropriate. This change had no impact on the Company's operating income and net income, as both revenues and operating expenses were increased by $213 million for 2006 and $206 million for 2005. In addition, the Company reclassified its non-rail transportation revenues to Other revenues. Previously, various revenues for non-rail transportation services were reported in both Rail freight revenues and Other revenues.

Non-GAAP Measures – unaudited

The Company makes reference to non-GAAP measures in this Annual Report that do not have any standardized meaning prescribed by U.S. GAAP and are, therefore, not necessarily comparable to similar measures presented by other companies and, as such, should not be considered in isolation. Management believes that non-GAAP measures such as adjusted net income and the resulting adjusted performance measures for such items as operating income, operating ratio and per share data are useful measures of performance that can facilitate period-to-period comparisons as they exclude items that do not arise as part of the normal day-to-day operations or that could potentially distort the analysis of trends in business performance. The exclusion of the specified items in the adjusted measures below do not, however, imply that such items are necessarily non-recurring. The Company also believes that free cash flow is a useful measure of performance as it demonstrates the Company's ability to generate cash after the payment of capital expenditures and dividends. Free cash flow does not have any standardized meaning prescribed by GAAP and therefore, may not be comparable to similar measures presented by other companies. The Company defines free cash flow as cash provided from operating activities, excluding changes in the accounts receivable securitization program and changes in cash and cash equivalents resulting from foreign exchange fluctuations, less cash used by investing activities and the payment of dividends. A reconciliation of the various non-GAAP measures presented in this Annual Report to their comparable U.S. GAAP measures is provided herein:

Reconciliation of adjusted performance measures – 2007 and 2006

In millions, except per share data, or unless otherwise indicated

Year ended December 31,	2007			2006		
	Reported	Adjustments [1]	Adjusted	Reported	Adjustments [2]	Adjusted
Revenues	$7,897	$ –	$7,897	$7,929	$ –	$7,929
Operating expenses	5,021	–	5,021	4,899	–	4,899
Operating income	2,876	–	2,876	3,030	–	3,030
Interest expense	(336)	–	(336)	(312)	–	(312)
Other income	166	(153)	13	11	–	11
Income before income taxes	2,706	(153)	2,553	2,729	–	2,729
Income tax expense	(548)	(280)	(828)	(642)	(277)	(919)
Net income	$2,158	$(433)	$1,725	$2,087	$(277)	$1,810
Operating ratio	63.6%		63.6%	61.8%		61.8%
Diluted earnings per share	$ 4.25	$(0.85)	$ 3.40	$3.91	$(0.51)	$ 3.40

(1) Adjusted to exclude the impact of a deferred income tax recovery of $328 million ($0.64 per diluted share) that resulted mainly from the enactment of corporate income tax rate changes in Canada, as well as the gains on sale of the Central Station Complex of $92 million, or $64 million after-tax ($0.13 per diluted share) and the Company's investment in English Welsh and Scottish Railway of $61 million, or $41 million after tax ($0.08 per diluted share).

(2) Adjusted to exclude the impact of a deferred income tax recovery of $277 million ($0.51 per diluted share) that resulted primarily from the enactment of lower corporate income tax rates in Canada and the resolution of matters pertaining to prior years' income taxes.

Free cash flow – 2007 and 2006

In millions

	Year ended December 31,	2007	2006
Cash provided from operating activities		$2,417	$ 2,951
Cash used by investing activities		(895)	(1,349)
Cash provided before financing activities		1,522	1,602
Adjustments:			
Change in accounts receivable securitization		(228)	82
Dividends paid		(418)	(340)
Effect of foreign exchange fluctuations on U.S. dollar-denominated cash and cash equivalents		(48)	(1)
Free cash flow		$ 828	$1,343

CN is committed to being a good corporate citizen. At CN, sound corporate citizenship touches nearly every aspect of what we do, from governance to business ethics, from safety to environmental protection. Central to this comprehensive approach is our strong belief that good corporate citizenship is simply good business.

CN has always recognized the importance of good governance. As it evolved from a Canadian institution to a North American publicly traded company, CN voluntarily followed certain corporate governance requirements that, as a company based in Canada, it was not technically compelled to follow. We continue to do so today. Since many of our peers – and shareholders – are based in the United States, we want to provide the same assurances of sound practices as our U.S. competitors.

Hence, we adopt and adhere to corporate governance practices that either meet or exceed applicable Canadian and U.S. corporate governance standards. As a Canadian reporting issuer with securities listed on the Toronto Stock Exchange (TSX) and the New York Stock Exchange (NYSE), CN complies with applicable rules adopted by the Canadian Securities Administrators and the rules of the U.S. Securities and Exchange Commission giving effect to the provisions of the U.S. *Sarbanes-Oxley Act of 2002*.

As a Canadian company, we are not required to comply with many of the NYSE corporate governance rules, and instead may comply with Canadian governance practices. However, except as summarized on our website (*www.cn.ca/cngovernance*), our governance practices comply with the NYSE corporate governance rules in all significant respects.

Consistent with the belief that ethical conduct goes beyond compliance and resides in a solid governance culture, the governance section on the CN website contains CN's Corporate Governance Manual (including the charters of our Board and of our Board committees) and CN's Code of Business Conduct. Printed versions of these documents are also available upon request to CN's Corporate Secretary.

Because it is important to CN to uphold the highest standards in corporate governance and that any potential or real wrongdoings be reported, CN has also adopted methods allowing employees and third parties to report accounting, auditing and other concerns, as more fully described on our website.

We are proud of our corporate governance practices. For more information on these practices, please refer to our website, as well as to our proxy circular – mailed to all shareholders and also available on our website.

Appendix B: CP Rail
Annual Report

These excerpts from CP's 2007 Annual Report appear Courtesy of CP Rail.

Financial Section (U.S. GAAP)

Contents

Canadian Pacific Railway Company

Notes to Consolidated Financial Statements

MANAGEMENT'S RESPONSIBILITY FOR FINANCIAL REPORTING

The information in this report is the responsibility of management. The consolidated financial statements have been prepared by management in accordance with Canadian generally accepted accounting principles and include some amounts based on management's best estimates and careful judgment. The consolidated financial statements include the accounts of Canadian Pacific Railway Limited, Canadian Pacific Railway Company and all of its subsidiaries (the "Company"). The financial information of the Company included in the Company's Annual Report is consistent with that in the consolidated financial statements. The consolidated financial statements have been approved by the Board of Directors.

Our Board of Directors is responsible for reviewing and approving the consolidated financial statements and for overseeing management's performance of its financial reporting responsibilities. The Board of Directors carries out its responsibility for the consolidated financial statements principally through its Audit, Finance and Risk Management Committee (the Audit Committee), consisting of six members, all of whom are outside directors. The Audit Committee reviews the consolidated financial statements and Management's Discussion and Analysis with management and the independent auditors prior to submission to the Board for approval. The Audit Committee meets regularly with management, internal auditors, and the independent auditors to review accounting policies, and financial reporting. The Audit Committee also reviews the recommendations of both the independent and internal auditors for improvements to internal controls, as well as the actions of management to implement such recommendations. The internal and independent auditors have full access to the Audit Committee, with or without the presence of management.

MANAGEMENT'S REPORT ON INTERNAL CONTROL OVER FINANCIAL REPORTING

Management is responsible for establishing and maintaining adequate internal control over financial reporting for the Company. Because of its inherent limitations, internal control over financial reporting may not prevent or detect misstatements. Also, projections of any evaluation of effectiveness to future periods are subject to the risk that controls may become inadequate because of changes in conditions, or that the degree of compliance with the policies or procedures may deteriorate.

Management has assessed the effectiveness of the Company's internal controls over financial reporting in accordance with the criteria set forth by the Committee of Sponsoring Organizations of the Treadway Commission in "Internal Control-Integrated Framework". Based on this assessment, management determined that the Company maintained effective internal control over financial reporting as of December 31, 2007.

The effectiveness of the Company's internal control over financial reporting as of December 31, 2007 has been audited by PricewaterhouseCoopers LLP, independent auditors, as stated in their report, which is included herein.

MICHAEL LAMBERT
Executive Vice-President
and Chief Financial Officer

February 19, 2008

FRED J. GREEN
Chief Executive Officer

INDEPENDENT AUDITORS' REPORT

TO THE SHAREHOLDERS OF CANADIAN PACIFIC RAILWAY LIMITED

We have completed integrated audits of the consolidated financial statements and internal control over financial reporting of Canadian Pacific Railway Limited as of December 31, 2007 and 2006 and an audit of its 2005 consolidated financial statements. Our opinions, based on our audits, are presented below.

CONSOLIDATED FINANCIAL STATEMENTS

We have audited the accompanying consolidated balance sheets of Canadian Pacific Railway Limited as at December 31, 2007 and December 31, 2006, and the related consolidated statements of income, comprehensive income, changes in shareholders' equity and cash flows for each of the years in the three year period ended December 31, 2007. These financial statements are the responsibility of the Company's management. Our responsibility is to express an opinion on these financial statements based on our audits.

We conducted our audits of the Company's financial statements as at December 31, 2007 and December 31, 2006 and for each of the years then ended in accordance with Canadian generally accepted auditing standards and the standards of the Public Company Accounting Oversight Board (United States). We conducted our audit of the Company's financial statements for the year ended December 31, 2005 in accordance with Canadian generally accepted auditing standards. Those standards require that we plan and perform an audit to obtain reasonable assurance about whether the financial statements are free of material misstatement. An audit of financial statements includes examining, on a test basis, evidence supporting the amounts and disclosures in the financial statements. A financial statement audit also includes assessing the accounting principles used and significant estimates made by management, and evaluating the overall financial statement presentation. We believe that our audits provide a reasonable basis for our opinion.

In our opinion, the consolidated financial statements referred to above present fairly, in all material respects, the financial position of the Company as at December 31, 2007 and December 31, 2006 and the results of its operations and its cash flows for each of the years in the three year period ended December 31, 2007 in accordance with Canadian generally accepted accounting principles.

INTERNAL CONTROL OVER FINANCIAL REPORTING

We have also audited Canadian Pacific Railway Limited's internal control over financial reporting as of December 31, 2007, based on criteria established in Internal Control – Integrated Framework issued by the Committee of Sponsoring Organizations of the Treadway Commission (COSO). The Company's management is responsible for maintaining effective internal control over financial reporting and for its assessment of the effectiveness of internal control over financial reporting, included in the accompanying Management's Assessment of Internal Control over Financial Reporting. Our responsibility is to express an opinion on the effectiveness of the Company's internal control over financial reporting based on our audit.

We conducted our audit of internal control over financial reporting in accordance with the standards of the Public Company Accounting Oversight Board (United States). Those standards require that we plan and perform the audit to obtain reasonable assurance about whether effective internal control over financial reporting was maintained in all material respects. An audit of internal control over financial reporting includes obtaining an understanding of internal control over financial reporting, assessing the risk that a material weakness exists, testing and evaluating the design and operating effectiveness of internal control based on the assessed risk, and performing such other procedures as we consider necessary in the circumstances. We believe that our audit provides a reasonable basis for our opinions.

A company's internal control over financial reporting is a process designed to provide reasonable assurance regarding the reliability of financial reporting and the preparation of financial statements for external purposes in accordance with generally accepted accounting principles. A company's internal control over financial reporting includes those policies and procedures that (i) pertain to the maintenance of records that, in reasonable detail, accurately and fairly reflect the transactions and dispositions of the assets of the company; (ii) provide reasonable assurance that transactions are recorded as necessary to permit preparation of financial statements in accordance with generally accepted accounting principles, and that receipts and expenditures of the company are being made only in accordance with authorizations of management and directors of the company; and (iii) provide reasonable assurance regarding prevention or timely detection of unauthorized acquisition,

use, or disposition of the company's assets that could have a material effect on the financial statements.

Because of its inherent limitations, internal control over financial reporting may not prevent or detect misstatements. Also, projections of any evaluation of effectiveness to future periods are subject to the risk that controls may become inadequate because of changes in conditions, or that the degree of compliance with the policies or procedures may deteriorate.

In our opinion, the Company maintained, in all material respects, effective internal control over financial reporting as of December 31, 2007 based on criteria established in Internal Control — Integrated Framework issued by the COSO.

PricewaterhouseCoopers LLP

PRICEWATERHOUSECOOPERS LLP
Chartered Accountants
Calgary, Alberta

February 19, 2008

STATEMENT OF CONSOLIDATED INCOME

Year ended December 31 (in millions of Canadian dollars, except per share data)	2007	2006	2005
Revenues			
Freight (Note 23)	$ 4,555.2	$ 4,427.3	$ 4,266.3
Other	152.4	155.9	125.3
	4,707.6	4,583.2	4,391.6
Operating expenses			
Compensation and benefits	1,284.2	1,327.6	1,322.1
Fuel	746.8	650.5	588.0
Materials	215.5	212.9	203.3
Equipment rents	207.5	181.2	210.0
Depreciation and amortization	472.0	464.1	445.1
Purchased services and other	617.4	618.3	621.6
	3,543.4	3,454.6	3,390.1
Operating income, before the following:	1,164.2	1,128.6	1,001.5
Special credit for environmental remediation (Note 18)	–	–	(33.9)
Special charge for labour restructuring (Note 18)	–	–	44.2
Operating income	1,164.2	1,128.6	991.2
Other income and charges (Note 4)	17.3	27.8	18.1
Change in fair value of Canadian third party asset-backed commercial paper (Note 11)	21.5	–	–
Foreign exchange (gain) loss on long-term debt	(169.8)	0.1	(44.7)
Net interest expense (Note 5)	204.3	194.5	204.2
Income tax expense (Note 6)	144.7	109.9	270.6
Net income	$ 946.2	$ 796.3	$ 543.0
Basic earnings per share (Note 7)	$ 6.14	$ 5.06	$ 3.43
Diluted earnings per share (Note 7)	$ 6.08	$ 5.02	$ 3.39

See Notes to Consolidated Financial Statements.

60
2007
ANNUAL
REPORT

CONSOLIDATED STATEMENT OF COMPREHENSIVE INCOME

Year ended December 31 (in millions of Canadian dollars)		2007		2006		2005
Comprehensive income						
Net income	$	946.2	$	796.3	$	543.0
Net change in foreign currency translation adjustments, net of hedging activities		(7.4)		(1.6)		(7.4)
Net change in losses on derivatives designated as cash flow hedges		(36.8)		–		–
Other comprehensive loss before income taxes		(44.2)		(1.6)		(7.4)
Income tax recovery (expense)		3.4		0.5		(2.1)
Other comprehensive loss (Note 9)		(40.8)		(1.1)		(9.5)
Comprehensive income	$	905.4	$	795.2	$	533.5

See Notes to Consolidated Financial Statements.

CONSOLIDATED BALANCE SHEET

As at December 31 (in millions of Canadian dollars)	2007	2006
Assets		
Current assets		
Cash and cash equivalents	$ 378.1	$ 124.3
Accounts receivable and other current assets (Note 8)	542.8	615.7
Materials and supplies	179.5	158.6
Future income taxes (Note 6)	67.3	106.3
	1,167.7	1,004.9
Investments (Note 11)	1,668.6	64.9
Net properties (Note 12)	9,293.1	9,122.9
Other assets and deferred charges (Note 13)	1,235.6	1,223.2
Total assets	$ 13,365.0	$ 11,415.9
Liabilities and shareholders' equity		
Current liabilities		
Short-term borrowing	$ 229.7	$ —
Accounts payable and accrued liabilities	980.8	1,002.6
Income and other taxes payable	68.8	16.0
Dividends payable	34.5	29.1
Long-term debt maturing within one year (Note 14)	31.0	191.3
	1,344.8	1,239.0
Deferred liabilities (Note 16)	714.6	725.7
Long-term debt (Note 14)	4,146.2	2,813.5
Future income taxes (Note 6)	1,701.5	1,781.2
Shareholders' equity		
Share capital (Note 19)	1,188.6	1,175.7
Contributed surplus (Note 19)	42.4	32.3
Accumulated other comprehensive income (Note 9)	39.6	66.4
Retained income	4,187.3	3,582.1
	5,457.9	4,856.5
Total liabilities and shareholders' equity	$ 13,365.0	$ 11,415.9

Commitments and contingencies (Note 22).
See Notes to Consolidated Financial Statements.

Approved on behalf of the Board:

J.E. Cleghorn, Director

R. Phillips, Director

62

2007
ANNUAL
REPORT

STATEMENT OF CONSOLIDATED CASH FLOWS

Year ended December 31 (in millions of Canadian dollars)	2007	2006	2005
Operating activities			
Net income	$ 946.2	$ 796.3	$ 543.0
Add (deduct) items not affecting cash			
Depreciation and amortization	472.0	464.1	445.1
Future income taxes (Note 6)	38.7	75.3	258.0
Change in fair value of Canadian third party asset-backed commercial paper (Note 11)	21.5	–	–
Environmental remediation charge (Note 18)	–	–	(30.9)
Restructuring and impairment charge (Note 18)	–	–	44.2
Foreign exchange (gain) loss on long-term debt	(169.8)	0.1	(44.7)
Amortization of deferred charges	12.1	16.5	19.5
Restructuring and environmental payments (Note 18)	(61.0)	(96.3)	(69.0)
Other operating activities, net	4.6	(103.4)	(91.2)
Change in non-cash working capital balances related to operations (Note 10)	50.3	(101.6)	(23.3)
Cash provided by operating activities	1,314.6	1,051.0	1,050.7
Investing activities			
Additions to properties (Note 12)	(893.2)	(793.7)	(884.4)
Reduction in investments and other assets	0.2	2.2	2.0
Net proceeds from disposal of transportation properties	14.9	97.8	13.2
Acquisition of Dakota, Minnesota & Eastern Railroad Corporation (Note 11)	(1,492.6)	–	–
Investment in Canadian third party asset-backed commercial paper (Note 11)	(143.6)	–	–
Cash used in investing activities	(2,514.3)	(693.7)	(869.2)
Financing activities			
Dividends paid	(133.1)	(112.4)	(89.5)
Issuance of CP Common Shares	30.4	66.6	31.8
Purchase of CP Common Shares (Note 19)	(231.1)	(286.4)	(80.6)
Increase in short-term borrowing	229.7	–	–
Issuance of long-term debt (Note 14)	1,745.3	2.8	–
Repayment of long-term debt	(187.7)	(25.4)	(274.4)
Cash provided by (used in) financing activities	1,453.5	(354.8)	(412.7)
Cash position			
Increase (decrease) in cash and cash equivalents	253.8	2.5	(231.2)
Cash and cash equivalents at beginning of year	124.3	121.8	353.0
Cash and cash equivalents at end of year	$ 378.1	$ 124.3	$ 121.8

See Notes to Consolidated Financial Statements.

CONSOLIDATED STATEMENT OF CHANGES IN SHAREHOLDERS' EQUITY

Year ended December 31 (in millions of Canadian dollars)	2007	2006
Share capital		
Balance, beginning of year	$ 1,175.7	$ 1,141.5
Shares issued under stock option plans (Note 19)	37.4	71.0
Shares purchased (Note 19)	(24.5)	(36.8)
Balance, end of year	1,188.6	1,175.7
Contributed surplus		
Balance, beginning of year	32.3	245.1
Movement in stock-based compensation	10.1	10.3
Shares purchased	–	(223.1)
Balance, end of year	42.4	32.3
Accumulated other comprehensive income		
Balance, beginning of year	66.4	67.5
Adjustment for change in accounting policy (Note 2)	14.0	–
Adjusted balance, beginning of year	80.4	67.5
Other comprehensive loss (Note 9)	(40.8)	(1.1)
Balance, end of year	39.6	66.4
Retained income		
Balance, beginning of year	3,582.1	2,930.0
Adjustment for change in accounting policy (Note 2)	4.0	–
Adjusted balance, beginning of year	3,586.1	2,930.0
Net income for the year	946.2	796.3
Shares purchased (Note 19)	(206.6)	(26.5)
Dividends	(138.4)	(117.7)
Balance, end of year	4,187.3	3,582.1
Total accumulated other comprehensive income and retained income	4,226.9	3,648.5
Shareholders' equity, end of year	$ 5,457.9	$ 4,856.5

See Notes to Consolidated Financial Statements.

NOTES TO CONSOLIDATED FINANCIAL STATEMENTS

December 31, 2007

1. Summary of significant accounting policies

PRINCIPLES OF CONSOLIDATION

These consolidated financial statements include the accounts of Canadian Pacific Railway Limited ("CPRL") and all of its subsidiaries, including variable-interest entities ("VIE") for which CPRL is the primary beneficiary and the proportionate share of the accounts of jointly controlled enterprises (collectively referred to as "CP" or "the Company"), and have been prepared in accordance with Canadian generally accepted accounting principles ("GAAP").

These consolidated financial statements are expressed in Canadian dollars, except where otherwise indicated. The preparation of these financial statements in conformity with Canadian GAAP requires management to make estimates and assumptions that affect the reported amounts of revenues and expenses during the period, the reported amounts of assets and liabilities, and the disclosure of contingent assets and liabilities at the date of the financial statements. Management regularly reviews its estimates, including those related to restructuring and environmental liabilities, pensions and other benefits, depreciable lives of properties, future income tax assets and liabilities, as well as legal and personal injury liabilities based upon currently available information. Actual results could differ from these estimates.

PRINCIPAL SUBSIDIARIES

The following list sets out CPRL's principal railway operating subsidiaries, including the jurisdiction of incorporation and the percentage of voting securities owned directly or indirectly by CPRL as of December 31, 2007.

Principal subsidiary	Incorporated under the laws of	Percentage of voting securities held directly or indirectly by CPRL
Canadian Pacific Railway Company	Canada	100 %
Soo Line Railroad Company ("Soo Line")	Minnesota	100 %
Delaware and Hudson Railway Company, Inc. ("D&H")	Delaware	100 %
Mount Stephen Properties Inc. ("MSP")	Canada	100 %

Dakota, Minnesota and Eastern Railroad Corporation ("DM&E") was acquired in October, 2007 and is wholly owned. The purchase is subject to review and approval by the U.S. Surface Transportation Board ("STB"), during which time the shares of DM&E have been placed in a voting trust.

REVENUE RECOGNITION

Railway freight revenues are recognized based on the percentage of completed service method. Other revenue is recognized as service is performed or contractual obligations are met. Volume rebates are accrued as a reduction of freight revenues based on estimated volumes and contract terms as freight service is provided.

CASH AND CASH EQUIVALENTS

Cash and cash equivalents includes marketable short-term investments that are readily convertible to cash with original maturities of less than 3 months. Short-term investments are stated at fair value, which approximates cost.

FOREIGN CURRENCY TRANSLATION

Assets and liabilities denominated in foreign currencies, other than those held through self-sustaining foreign subsidiaries, are translated into Canadian dollars at the year-end exchange rate for monetary items and at the historical exchange rates for non-monetary items. Foreign currency revenues and expenses are translated at the exchange rate in effect on the dates of the related transactions. Foreign currency gains and losses, other than those arising from the translation of the Company's net investment in self-sustaining foreign subsidiaries, are included in income.

The accounts of the Company's self-sustaining foreign subsidiaries are translated into Canadian dollars using the year-end exchange rate for assets and liabilities and the average exchange rates during the year for revenues and expenses. Exchange gains and losses arising from translation of these foreign subsidiaries' accounts are included in other comprehensive loss. A portion of the U.S. dollar-denominated long-term debt has been designated as a hedge of the net investment in self-sustaining foreign subsidiaries. As a result, unrealized foreign exchange gains and losses on a portion of the U.S. dollar-denominated long-term debt are offset against foreign exchange gains and losses arising from translation of self-sustaining foreign subsidiaries' accounts.

PENSIONS AND OTHER BENEFITS

Pension costs are actuarially determined using the projected-benefit method prorated over the credited service periods of employees. This method incorporates management's best estimates of expected plan investment performance, salary escalation and retirement ages of employees. The expected return on fund assets is calculated using market-related asset values developed from a five-year average of market values for the fund's public equity securities (with each prior year's market value adjusted to the current date for assumed investment income during the intervening period) plus the market value of the fund's fixed income, real estate and infrastructure securities. The discount rate used to determine the benefit obligation is based on market interest rates on high-quality corporate debt instruments with matching cash flows. Unrecognized actuarial gains and losses in excess of 10 % of the greater of the benefit obligation and the market-related value of plan assets are amortized over the expected average remaining service period of active employees expected to receive benefits under the plan (approximately 11 years). Prior service costs arising from plan amendments are amortized over the expected average remaining service period of active employees who were expected to receive benefits under the plan at the date of amendment. Transitional assets and obligations, which arose from implementing the CICA Accounting Standard Section 3461 "Employee Future Benefits" effective January 1, 2000, are being amortized over the expected average remaining service period of active employees who were expected to receive benefits under the plan at January 1, 2000 (approximately 13 years).

Benefits other than pensions, including health care, some workers' compensation and long-term disability benefits in Canada and life insurance, are actuarially determined and accrued on a basis similar to pension costs.

MATERIALS AND SUPPLIES

Materials and supplies on hand are valued at the lower of average cost and replacement value.

NET PROPERTIES

Fixed asset additions and major renewals are recorded at cost, including direct costs, directly attributable indirect costs and attributed carrying costs. The Company capitalizes development costs for major new computer systems, including the related variable indirect costs. In addition, CP capitalizes the cost of major overhauls and large refurbishments. When depreciable property is retired or otherwise disposed of in the normal course of business, the book value, less net salvage proceeds, is charged to accumulated depreciation. However, when removal costs exceed the salvage value on assets and the Company had no legal obligation to remove, the net removal cost is charged to income in the period in which the asset is removed and is not charged to accumulated depreciation. When there is a legal obligation associated with the retirement of property, plant and equipment, a liability is initially recognized at its fair value and a corresponding asset retirement cost is added to the gross book value of the related asset and amortized to expense over the estimated term to retirement. The Company reviews the carrying amounts of its properties whenever changes in circumstances indicate that such carrying amounts may not be recoverable based on future undiscounted cash flows. When such properties are determined to be impaired, recorded asset values are revised to the fair value and an impairment loss is recognized.

Depreciation is calculated on the straight-line basis at rates based on the estimated service life, taking into consideration the projected annual usage of depreciable property, except for rail and other track material in the U.S., which is based directly on usage. Usage is based on volumes of traffic.

Assets to be disposed of are included in "Other assets and deferred charges" on the Consolidated Balance Sheet. They are reported at the lower of the carrying amount and fair value, less costs to sell, and are no longer depreciated.

Equipment under capital lease is included in properties and depreciated over the period of expected use.

Estimated service life used for principal categories of properties is as follows:

Assets	Years
Diesel locomotives	28 to 35
Freight cars	21 to 46
Ties	35 to 41
Rails – in first position	27 to 29
– in other than first position	55
Computer system development costs	5 to 15

DERIVATIVE FINANCIAL AND COMMODITY INSTRUMENTS

Derivative financial and commodity instruments may be used from time to time by the Company to manage its exposure to price risks relating to foreign currency exchange rates, stock-based compensation, interest rates and fuel prices. When CP utilizes derivative instruments in hedging relationships, CP identifies, designates and documents those hedging transactions and regularly tests the transactions to demonstrate effectiveness in order to continue hedge accounting.

Commencing January 1, 2007, all derivative instruments are recorded at their fair value. Any change in the fair value of derivatives not designated as hedges is recognized in the period in which the change occurs in the Statement of Consolidated Income in the line item to which the derivative instrument is related. On the Consolidated Balance Sheet they are classified in "Other assets and deferred charges", "Deferred liabilities", "Accounts receivable and other current assets" or "Accounts payable and accrued liabilities" as applicable. Prior to 2007, only derivative instruments that did not qualify as hedges or were not designated as hedges were carried at fair value on the Consolidated Balance Sheet in "Other assets and deferred charges" or "Deferred liabilities". Gains and losses arising from derivative instruments affect the following income statement lines: "Revenues", "Compensation and benefits", "Fuel", "Other income and charges", "Foreign exchange (gains) losses on long-term debt" and "Interest expense".

For fair value hedges, the periodic change in value is recognized in income, on the same line as the changes in values of the hedged items are also recorded. For a cash flow hedge, the change in value of the effective portion is recognized in "Other comprehensive loss". Any ineffectiveness within an effective cash flow hedge is recognized in income as it arises in the same income account as the hedged item when realized. Should a cash flow hedge relationship become ineffective, previously unrealized gains and losses remain within "Accumulated other comprehensive income" ("AOCI") until the hedged item is settled and, prospectively, future changes in value of the derivative are recognized in income. The change in value of the effective portion of a cash flow hedge remains in "AOCI" until the related hedged item settles, at which time amounts recognized in "AOCI" are reclassified to the same income or balance sheet account that records the hedged item. Prior to January 1, 2007, the periodic change in the fair value of an effective hedging instrument prior to settlement was not recognized in the financial statements.

In the Statement of Consolidated Cash Flows, cash flows relating to derivative instruments designated as hedges are included in the same line as the related item.

The transitional date for the assessment of embedded derivatives was January 1, 2001.

The Company from time to time enters into foreign exchange forward contracts to hedge anticipated sales in U.S. dollars, the related accounts receivable and future capital acquisitions. Foreign exchange translation gains and losses on foreign currency-denominated derivative financial instruments used to hedge anticipated U.S. dollar-denominated sales are recognized as an adjustment of the revenues when the sale is recorded. Those used to hedge future capital acquisitions are recognized as an adjustment of the property amount when the acquisition is recorded.

The Company also occasionally enters into foreign exchange forward contracts as part of its short-term cash management strategy. These contracts are not designated as hedges due to their short-term nature and are carried on the Consolidated Balance Sheet at fair value. Changes in fair value are recognized in income in the period in which the change occurs.

The Company enters into interest rate swaps to manage the risk related to interest rate fluctuations. These swap agreements require the periodic exchange of payments without the exchange of the principal amount on which the payments are based. Interest expense on the debt is adjusted to include the payments owing or receivable under the interest rate swaps.

The Company from time to time enters into bond forwards to fix interest rates for anticipated issuances of debt. These agreements are accounted for as cash flow hedges.

The Company has a fuel-hedging program under which CP acquires future crude oil contracts for a portion of its diesel fuel purchases to reduce the risk of price volatility affecting future cash flows. In addition, foreign exchange forward contracts are used as part of the fuel-hedging program to manage the foreign exchange variability component of CP's fuel price risk. The gains or losses on the hedge contracts are applied against the corresponding fuel purchases in the period during which the hedging contracts mature.

The Company enters into derivatives called Total Return Swaps ("TRS") to mitigate fluctuations in stock appreciation rights ("SAR"), deferred share units ("DSU"), performance share units ("PSU") and restricted share units ("RSU"). These are not designated as hedges and are recorded at market value with the offsetting gain or loss reflected in "Compensation and benefits".

RESTRUCTURING ACCRUAL AND ENVIRONMENTAL REMEDIATION

Restructuring liabilities are recorded at their present value. The discount related to liabilities incurred in 2003 and subsequent years is amortized to "Compensation and benefits" and "Purchased services and other" over the payment period. The discount related to liabilities incurred prior to 2003 is amortized to "Other income and charges" over the payment period. Environmental remediation accruals cover site-specific remediation programs. Provisions for labour restructuring and environmental remediation costs are recorded in "Deferred liabilities", except for the current portion, which is recorded in "Accounts payable and accrued liabilities".

INCOME TAXES

The Company follows the liability method of accounting for income taxes. Future income tax assets and liabilities are determined based on differences between the financial reporting and tax bases of assets and liabilities using substantively enacted tax rates and laws that will be in effect when the differences are expected to reverse. The effect of a change in income tax rates on future income tax assets and liabilities is recognized in income in the period during which the change occurs.

EARNINGS PER SHARE

Basic earnings per share are calculated using the weighted average number of Common Shares outstanding during the year. Diluted earnings per share are calculated using the Treasury Stock Method for determining the dilutive effect of options.

STOCK-BASED COMPENSATION

CP follows the fair value based approach to accounting for stock-based compensation applying to options issued for years beginning in 2003. Compensation expense and an increase in contributed surplus are recognized for stock options over their vesting period based on their estimated fair values on the date of grants, as determined using the Black-Scholes option-pricing model. Forfeitures and cancellations of options are accounted for when they occur except for tandem options where forfeitures are estimated on the grant date.

Any consideration paid by employees on exercise of stock options is credited to share capital when the option is exercised and the recorded fair value of the option is removed from contributed surplus and credited to share capital. Compensation expense is also recognized for SARs, DSUs, PSUs and RSUs, using the intrinsic method, and employee share purchase plans, using the issue price, by amortizing the cost over the vesting period or over the period from the grant date to the date employees become eligible to retire when this is shorter than the vesting period, with the liability for SARs, DSUs, PSUs and RSUs marked to market until exercised. Forfeitures and cancellations of SARs, DSUs, PSUs and RSUs are accounted for when they occur. The SAR liability is settled to "Share capital" when a SAR is cancelled due to the exercise of a tandem option.

2.   New accounting policies

FINANCIAL INSTRUMENTS, HEDGING AND COMPREHENSIVE INCOME

On January 1, 2007, the Company adopted the following accounting standards issued by the Canadian Institute of Chartered Accountants ("CICA"): Section 3855 "Financial Instruments – Recognition and Measurement", Section 3861 "Financial Instruments – Disclosure and Presentation", Section 3865 "Hedges", Section 1530 "Comprehensive Income" and Section 3251 "Equity". These sections require certain financial instruments and hedge positions to be recorded at their fair value. They also introduce the concept of comprehensive income and AOCI. Adoption of these standards was on a retrospective basis without restatement of prior periods, except for the restatement of equity balances to reflect the reclassification of "Foreign currency translation adjustments" to "AOCI" and "Other Comprehensive Loss".

The impact of the adoption of these standards on January 1, 2007, was an increase in net assets of $18.0 million, a reduction in "Foreign currency translation adjustments" of $66.4 million, an increase in "Retained income" of $4.0 million, and the recognition of "AOCI" of $80.4 million.

The fair value of hedging instruments at January 1, 2007, was $31.7 million reflected in "Other assets and deferred charges" and "Accounts receivable and other current assets" and $4.8 million reflected in "Deferred liabilities" and "Accounts payable and accrued liabilities". The inclusion of transaction costs within "Long-term debt" at amortized cost reduced "Long-term debt" by $33.4 million with an associated reduction in "Other assets and deferred charges" of $26.9 million. Deferred gains and losses on previously settled hedges were reclassified to "AOCI" and "Retained income" with a resultant decrease in "Other assets and deferred charges" of $4.8 million. The recognition of certain other financial instruments at fair value or amortized cost resulted in reductions in "Long-term debt" of $2.8 million, "Investments" of $1.5 million and "Other assets and deferred charges" of $0.4 million. The adoption of these standards increased the liability for "Future income taxes" by $11.6 million. AOCI is comprised of foreign currency gains and losses on the net investment in self-sustaining foreign subsidiaries, foreign currency gains and losses related to long-term debt designated as a hedge of the net investment in self-sustaining foreign subsidiaries' effective portions of gains and losses resulting from changes in the fair value of cash flow hedging instruments, and the reclassification of cumulative foreign currency translation adjustments. The adjustment to opening retained income reflects the change in measurement basis, from original cost to fair value or amortized cost, of certain financial assets, financial liabilities, transaction costs associated with the Company's long-term debt and previously deferred gains and losses on derivative instruments that were settled in prior years and which, had they currently existed, did not meet the criteria for hedge accounting under Accounting Standard Section 3865. The amounts recorded on the adoption of these standards differed from the estimated amounts disclosed in Note 3 to the 2006 annual financial statements as a result of the refinement of certain estimates used at the year end.

ACCOUNTING CHANGES

Effective from January 1, 2007, the CICA has amended Accounting Standard Section 1506 "Accounting Changes" to prescribe the criteria for changing accounting policies and related accounting treatment and disclosures of accounting changes. Changes in accounting policies are permitted when required by a primary source of GAAP, for example when a new accounting section is first adopted, or when the change in accounting policy results in more reliable and relevant financial information being reflected in the financial statements.

The adoption of this amended accounting standard did not impact the financial statements of the Company.

3. Future accounting changes

FINANCIAL INSTRUMENT AND CAPITAL DISCLOSURES

The CICA has issued the following accounting standards effective for fiscal years beginning on or after January 1, 2008: Section 3862 "Financial Instruments – Disclosures", Section 3863 "Financial Instruments – Presentation", and Section 1535 "Capital Disclosures".

Section 3862 "Financial Instruments – Disclosures" and Section 3863 "Financial Instruments – Presentation" replace Section 3861 "Financial Instruments – Disclosure and Presentation", revising disclosures related to financial instruments, including hedging instruments, and carrying forward unchanged presentation requirements.

Section 1535 "Capital Disclosures" will require the Company to provide disclosures about the Company's capital and how it is managed.

The adoption of these new accounting standards will not impact the amounts reported in the Company's financial statements as they primarily relate to disclosure.

INVENTORIES

Effective January 1, 2008, the CICA has issued accounting standard Section 3031 "Inventories". Section 3031 "Inventories" will provide guidance on the method of determining the cost of CP's materials and supplies. The new accounting standard specifies that inventories are to be valued at the lower of cost and net realizable value. CP currently reflects materials and supplies at the lower of cost and replacement value. The standard requires the reversal of previously recorded write downs to realizable value when there is clear evidence that net realizable value has increased. Additional disclosures will also be required. It is not anticipated that the adoption of Section 3031 "Inventories" will have a material impact on CP's financial statements. Any adjustment on the adoption of Section 3031 "Inventories" will be recognized in 2008 as an adjustment to opening inventory and opening retained income.

GOODWILL AND INTANGIBLE ASSETS

In February 2008, the CICA has issued accounting standard Section 3064 "Goodwill, and intangible assets", replacing accounting standard Section 3062 "Goodwill and other intangible assets" and accounting standard Section 3450 "Research and development costs". Various changes have been made to other sections of the CICA Handbook for consistency purposes. The new Section will be applicable to financial statements relating to fiscal years beginning on or after October 1, 2008. Accordingly, the Company will adopt the new standards for its fiscal year beginning January 1, 2009. Section 3064 establishes standards for the recognition, measurement, presentation and disclosure of goodwill subsequent to its initial recognition and of intangible assets by profit-oriented enterprises. Standards concerning goodwill are unchanged from the standards included in the previous Section 3062. The Company is currently evaluating the impact of the adoption of this new Section.

4. Other income and charges

(in millions of Canadian dollars)	2007	2006	2005
Amortization of discount on accruals recorded at present value	$ 8.1	$ 10.0	$ 15.4
Other exchange losses (gains)	5.8	6.5	(2.2)
Loss on sale of accounts receivable (Note 8)	5.8	5.0	3.5
Loss (gain) on non-hedging derivative instruments	1.5	(1.2)	(6.6)
Equity income in Dakota, Minnesota & Eastern Railroad Corporation, net of tax (Note 11)	(12.3)	–	–
Other	8.4	7.5	8.0
Total other income and charges	$ 17.3	$ 27.8	$ 18.1

5. Interest expense

(in millions of Canadian dollars)	2007	2006	2005
Interest expense	$ 219.6	$ 200.5	$ 211.8
Interest income	(15.3)	(6.0)	(7.6)
Net interest expense	$ 204.3	$ 194.5	$ 204.2
Gross cash interest payments	$ 208.9	$ 192.8	$ 199.6

Interest expense includes interest on capital leases of $21.6 million for the year ended December 31, 2007 (2006 – $24.2 million; 2005 – $24.7 million).

6. Income taxes

The following is a summary of the major components of the Company's income tax expense:

(in millions of Canadian dollars)		2007		2006		2005
Canada (domestic)						
Current income tax expense	$	69.8	$	3.3	$	10.3
Future income tax expense						
Origination and reversal of temporary differences		163.8		194.7		213.9
Effect of tax rate decreases		(162.9)		(176.0)		–
Recognition of previously unrecorded tax losses		–		–		(17.2)
Effect of hedge of net investment in self-sustaining foreign subsidiaries		(9.7)		0.6		(2.1)
Other		(6.9)		(2.3)		(1.0)
Total future income tax expense		(15.7)		17.0		193.6
Total income taxes (domestic)	$	54.1	$	20.3	$	203.9
Other (foreign)						
Current income tax expense	$	36.2	$	31.3	$	2.3
Future income tax expense						
Origination and reversal of temporary differences		64.7		62.5		64.4
Other		(10.3)		(4.2)		–
Total future income tax expense		54.4		58.3		64.4
Total income taxes (foreign)	$	90.6	$	89.6	$	66.7
Total						
Current income tax expense	$	106.0	$	34.6	$	12.6
Future income tax expense		38.7		75.3		258.0
Total income taxes (domestic and foreign)	$	144.7	$	109.9	$	270.6

The provision for future income taxes arises from temporary differences in the carrying values of assets and liabilities for financial statement and income tax purposes and the effect of loss carry forwards. The items comprising the future income tax assets and liabilities are as follows:

(in millions of Canadian dollars)	2007	2006
Future income tax assets		
Restructuring liability	$ 39.7	$ 64.5
Amount related to tax losses carried forward	53.9	83.6
Liabilities carrying value in excess of tax basis	35.6	84.1
Future environmental remediation costs	35.1	42.7
Other	28.7	21.4
Total future income tax assets	193.0	296.3
Future income tax liabilities		
Capital assets carrying value in excess of tax basis	1,495.5	1,567.3
Other long-term assets carrying value in excess of tax basis	300.0	338.0
Other	33.7	65.9
Total future income tax liabilities	1,827.2	1,971.2
Total net future income tax liabilities	1,634.2	1,674.9
Current future income tax assets	67.3	106.3
Long-term future income tax liabilities	$ 1,701.5	$ 1,781.2

The Company's consolidated effective income tax rate differs from the expected statutory tax rates. Expected income tax expense at statutory rates is reconciled to income tax expense as follows:

(in millions of Canadian dollars)	2007	2006	2005
Expected income tax expense at Canadian enacted statutory tax rates	$ 333.6	$ 298.6	$ 291.8
Increase (decrease) in taxes resulting from:			
Large corporations tax	–	(5.6)	8.3
Gains and equity income not subject to tax	(62.5)	(22.0)	(22.0)
Foreign tax rate differentials	33.8	6.6	2.7
Effect of tax rate decreases	(162.9)	(176.0)	–
Recognition of previously unrecorded tax losses	–	–	(17.2)
Other	2.7	8.3	7.0
Income tax expense	$ 144.7	$ 109.9	$ 270.6

The Company has no unbenefited capital losses at December 31, 2007 and 2006.

In 2007, legislation was enacted to reduce Canadian federal corporate income tax rates over a period of several years. As a result of these changes, the Company recorded a $162.9 million benefit in future tax liability and income tax expense related to the revaluation of its future income tax balances as at December 31, 2006.

In 2006, federal and provincial legislation was substantively enacted to reduce Canadian corporate income tax rates over a period of several years. As a result of these changes, the Company recorded a $176.0 million reduction in future tax liability and income tax expense related to the revaluation of its future income tax balances as at December 31, 2005.

Cash taxes paid in the year ended December 31, 2007, was $6.7 million (2006 – $50.9 million; 2005 – $7.6 million).

7. Earnings per share

At December 31, 2007, the number of shares outstanding was 153.3 million (2006 – 155.5 million).

Basic earnings per share have been calculated using net income for the year divided by the weighted average number of CPRL shares outstanding during the year.

Diluted earnings per share have been calculated using the Treasury Stock Method, which gives effect to the dilutive value of outstanding options. After the spin-off of CP from Canadian Pacific Limited ("CPL") in October 2001, CPL stock options held by CPL employees were exchanged for CP replacement options. At December 31, 2007, there were 0.2 million replacement options outstanding (2006 – 0.2 million; 2005 – 0.4 million). Since the spin-off, CPRL has issued new stock options to CP employees. At December 31, 2007, there were 4.3 million new options outstanding (2006 – 4.3 million; 2005 – 5.5 million). These new option totals at December 31, 2007 exclude 2.4 million options (2006 – 2.3 million; 2005 – 2.0 million) for which there are tandem SARs outstanding (see Note 21), as these are not included in the dilution calculation.

The number of shares used in the earnings per share calculations is reconciled as follows:

(in millions)	2007	2006	2005
Weighted average shares outstanding	154.0	157.3	158.4
Dilutive effect of stock options	1.6	1.5	1.7
Weighted average diluted shares outstanding	155.6	158.8	160.1

(in dollars)	2007	2006	2005
Basic earnings per share	$ 6.14	$ 5.06	$ 3.43
Diluted earnings per share	$ 6.08	$ 5.02	$ 3.39

In 2007, 3,183 options (2006 – 379,908; 2005 – 1,000) were excluded from the computation of diluted earnings per share because their effects were not dilutive.

8. Accounts receivable

The Company maintains an adequate allowance for doubtful accounts based on expected collectibility of accounts receivable. Credit losses are based on specific identification of uncollectible accounts and the application of historical percentages by aging category. At December 31, 2007, allowances of $18.4 million (2006 – $19.2 million) were recorded in "Accounts receivable". During 2007, provisions of $2.7 million of accounts receivable (2006 – $6.5 million) were recorded within "Purchased services and other".

The Company renewed its accounts receivable securitization program for a term of five years to September 2009. Under the terms of the renewal, the Company sold an undivided co-ownership interest in $120.0 million of eligible freight receivables to an unrelated trust. The trust is a multi-seller trust and CP is not the primary beneficiary. The Company may increase the sale amount up to a program limit of $200.0 million. At December 31, 2007, the outstanding undivided co-ownership interest held by the trust under the accounts receivable securitization program was $120.0 million (2006 – $120.0 million).

The undivided co-ownership interest is sold on a fully serviced basis and the Company receives no fee for ongoing servicing responsibilities. The average servicing period is approximately one month. A servicing asset of $0.1 million and a liability of $0.1 million have been recorded, as the benefit the Company derives from servicing the receivables approximates the value of the activity.

Receivables funded under the securitization program may not include delinquent, defaulted or written-off receivables, nor receivables that do not meet certain obligor-specific criteria, including concentrations in excess of prescribed limits.

The Company provides a credit enhancement amount to absorb credit losses. The trust has no recourse to the co-ownership interest in receivables retained by the Company, other than in respect of the credit enhancement amount. This amount is recognized by the Company as a retained interest and included in accounts receivable. At December 31, 2007, the fair value of the retained interest was 18.7 % of the receivables sold or $22.5 million (2006 – 19.1 % or $22.9 million). The fair value approximated carrying value as a result of the short collection cycle and negligible credit losses. The Company cannot enter into an agreement with a third party with respect to its retained interest.

The securitization program is subject to standard reporting and credit-rating requirements for CP. The reporting includes provision of a monthly portfolio report that the pool of eligible receivables satisfies pre-established criteria that are reviewed and approved by Dominion Bond Rating Service and are standard for agreements of this nature. Failure to comply with these provisions would trigger termination of the program.

In 2007, the Company recognized a loss of $5.8 million (2006 – $5.0 million; 2005 – $3.5 million) on the securitization program. The loss is included in "Other income and charges" on the Statement of Consolidated Income.

The table below summarizes certain cash flows related to the transfer of receivables:

(in millions of Canadian dollars)	2007	2006	2005
Proceeds from collections reinvested	$ 1,478.9	$ 1,475.7	$ 1,480.6

9. Other comprehensive loss and accumulated other comprehensive income

Components of other comprehensive loss and the related tax effects are as follows:

(in millions of Canadian dollars)	Before tax amount	Income tax (expense) recovery	Net of tax amount
For the year ended December 31, 2007			
Unrealized foreign exchange gain on translation of U.S. dollar-denominated long-term debt designated as a hedge of the net investment in U.S. subsidiaries	$ 71.0	$ (9.7)	$ 61.3
Unrealized foreign exchange loss on translation of the net investment in U.S. subsidiaries	(78.4)	–	(78.4)
Realized gain on cash flow hedges settled in the period	(12.8)	4.8	(8.0)
Increase in unrealized holding losses on cash flow hedges	(26.2)	9.1	(17.1)
Realized loss on cash flow hedges settled in prior periods	2.2	(0.8)	1.4
Other comprehensive loss	$ (44.2)	$ 3.4	$ (40.8)
For the year ended December 31, 2006			
Unrealized foreign exchange loss on translation of U.S. dollar-denominated long-term debt designated as a hedge of the net investment in U.S. subsidiaries	$ (3.7)	$ 0.5	$ (3.2)
Unrealized foreign exchange gain on translation of the net investment in U.S. subsidiaries	2.1	–	2.1
Other comprehensive loss	$ (1.6)	$ 0.5	$ (1.1)
For the year ended December 31, 2005			
Unrealized foreign exchange gain on translation of U.S. dollar-denominated long-term debt designated as a hedge of the net investment in U.S. subsidiaries	$ 11.7	$ (2.1)	$ 9.6
Unrealized foreign exchange loss on translation of the net investment in U.S. subsidiaries	(19.1)	–	(19.1)
Other comprehensive loss	$ (7.4)	$ (2.1)	$ (9.5)

Changes in the balances of each classification within AOCI are as follows:

(in millions of Canadian dollars)	Opening balance Jan. 1		Adjustment for change in accounting policy (Note 2)		Adjusted opening balance Jan. 1 (Note 2)		Period change		Closing balance Dec. 31
Year ended December 31, 2007									
Foreign exchange on U.S. dollar debt designated as a hedge of the net investment in U.S. subsidiaries	$	234.9	$	0.4	$	235.3	$	61.3	$ 296.6
Foreign exchange on net investment in U.S. subsidiaries		(168.5)		–		(168.5)		(78.4)	(246.9)
Increase (decrease) in unrealized effective gains (losses) on cash flow hedges		–		18.9		18.9		(25.1)	(6.2)
Deferred loss on settled hedge instruments		–		(5.3)		(5.3)		1.4	(3.9)
Accumulated other comprehensive income	$	66.4	$	14.0	$	80.4	$	(40.8)	$ 39.6
Year ended December 31, 2006									
Foreign exchange on U.S. dollar debt designated as a hedge of the net investment in U.S. subsidiaries	$	238.1					$	(3.2)	$ 234.9
Foreign exchange on net investment in U.S. subsidiaries		(170.6)						2.1	(168.5)
Accumulated other comprehensive income	$	67.5					$	(1.1)	$ 66.4

During the next twelve months, the Company expects $10.9 million of unrealized holding gains on derivative instruments to be realized and recognized in the Statement of Consolidated Income. Derivative instruments designated as cash flow hedges will mature during the period ending December 2009.

10. Change in non-cash working capital balances related to operations

(in millions of Canadian dollars)	2007		2006		2005
(Use) source of cash:					
Accounts receivable and other current assets	$ 70.6	$	(101.0)	$	(61.8)
Materials and supplies	(28.7)		(15.8)		(14.6)
Accounts payable and accrued liabilities	(45.5)		(0.4)		39.1
Income and other taxes payable	53.9		15.6		14.0
Change in non-cash working capital	$ 50.3	$	(101.6)	$	(23.3)

11. Investments

For the year ended December 31 (in millions of Canadian dollars)	2007	2006
Rail investments accounted for on an equity basis	$ 1,528.6	$ 37.9
Other investments	140.0	27.0
Total investments	$ 1,668.6	$ 64.9

DAKOTA, MINNESOTA & EASTERN RAILROAD CORPORATION ("DM&E")

Effective October 4, 2007, the Company acquired all of the issued and outstanding shares of Dakota, Minnesota & Eastern Railroad Corporation and its subsidiaries (DM&E), a Class II railroad with approximately 2,500 miles of track in the U.S. Midwest, for a purchase price of approximately US$1.5 billion, including acquisition costs.

The transaction is subject to review and approval by the United States Surface Transportation Board (STB), pending which the shares of DM&E have been placed into an independent voting trust. The voting trust is required by U.S. law so the Company does not exercise control over DM&E prior to approval of the transaction by the STB. The Company is currently accounting for the purchase by the equity method until such time as the acquisition has been approved by the STB; upon final approval the acquisition will be accounted for using the purchase method of accounting. This final approval is not expected to be received until late 2008. As such the accompanying consolidated financial statements include the equity investment and equity earnings of DM&E for the period October 4 to December 31, 2007. The equity income from the Company's investment in DM&E, which is recorded net of tax, was $12.3 million in 2007, and is recorded in "Other income and charges" on the Statement of Consolidated Income.

The purchase price included a $1.473 billion cash payment at the closing and future contingent payments of up to approximately US$1.05 billion, which may become payable upon achievement of certain milestones and transaction costs of $20 million incurred to December 31, 2007. The Company drew down US$1.27 billion from an eighteen-month credit agreement entered into in October 2007 specifically to fund the acquisition of DM&E. Future contingent payments of US$350 million would become due when construction starts of the Powder River Basin expansion project prior to December 31, 2025. Further future contingent payments of up to approximately US$700 million would become due upon the movement of specified volumes over the Powder River Basin extension prior to December 31, 2025. The contingent payments would be accounted for as an increase in the purchase price. Intangible assets acquired are subject to amortization. Neither the amortization of intangible assets nor goodwill are deductible for tax purposes.

The following table reflects the purchase price allocation, based on the fair value of DM&E's assets, owned and leased, and liabilities acquired at acquisition, which is subject to final valuations, the impact of which is not expected to have a material effect on the result of operations.

October 4, 2007 (in millions of Canadian dollars)	2007
Current assets	$ 91
Railroad properties	1,935
Intangible assets	50
Goodwill	163
Other assets	2
Total assets acquired	2,241
Current liabilities	104
Future income taxes	576
Debt and other liabilities	68
Total liabilities assumed	748
Investment in net assets of DM&E	$ 1,493

ASSET-BACKED COMMERCIAL PAPER ("ABCP")

At December 31, 2007, the Company held Canadian third party asset-backed commercial paper ("ABCP") issued by a number of trusts with an original cost of $143.6 million. At the dates the Company acquired these investments they were rated R1 (High) by Dominion Bond Rating Service ("DBRS"), the highest credit rating issued for commercial paper, and backed by R1 (High) rated assets and liquidity agreements. These investments matured during the third quarter of 2007 but, as a result of liquidity issues in the ABCP market, did not settle on maturity. As a result, the Company has classified its ABCP as long-term assets within Investments after initially classifying them as Cash and cash equivalents.

On August 16, 2007, an announcement was made by a group representing banks, asset providers and major investors that they had agreed in principle to a long-term proposal and interim agreement to convert the ABCP into long-term floating rate notes maturing no earlier than the scheduled maturity of the underlying assets. On September 6, 2007, a pan-Canadian restructuring committee consisting of major investors was formed. The committee was created to propose a solution to the liquidity problem affecting the ABCP market and has retained legal and financial advisors to oversee the proposed restructuring process.

The ABCP in which the Company has invested has not traded in an active market since mid-August 2007 and there are currently no market quotations available. The ABCP in which the Company has invested continues to be rated R1 (High, Under Review with Developing Implications) by DBRS.

A Standstill Agreement is in place that commits investors not to take any action that would precipitate an event of default. It is expected that the restructuring of the ABCP will occur in April 2008 if approval by investors is obtained to do so. This approval will be requested on a trust by trust basis most likely during April 2008.

On December 23, 2007, the pan-Canadian restructuring committee provided certain details about the expected restructuring. Based on this and other public information it is estimated that, of the $143.6 million of ABCP in which the Company has invested:

◻ $12.5 million is represented by traditional securitized assets and the Company will, on restructuring, receive replacement long-term floating rate notes that are expected to receive a AAA credit rating;

◻ $119.0 million is represented by a combination of leveraged collaterized debt, synthetic assets and traditional securitized assets and the Company will, on restructuring, receive replacement senior and subordinated long-term floating rate notes. The senior notes are expected to obtain a AAA rating while the subordinated notes are likely to be unrated; and

◻ $12.1 million is represented by assets that have an exposure to U.S. sub-prime mortgages. On restructuring, the Company is likely to receive long-term floating rate notes that may be rated, although at this time the pan-Canadian restructuring committee has provided no indication of the likely rating these notes may receive.

The valuation technique used by the Company to estimate the fair value of its investment in ABCP at December 31, 2007, incorporates probability weighted discounted cash flows considering the best available public information regarding market conditions and other factors that a market participant would consider for such investments. The assumptions used in determining the estimated fair value reflect the public statements made by the pan-Canadian restructuring committee that it expects the ABCP will be converted into various long-term floating rate notes, as discussed above, with maturities matching the maturities of the underlying assets and bearing market interest rates commensurate with the nature of the underlying assets and their associated cash flows and the credit rating and risk associated with the long-term floating rate notes.

The interest rates and maturities of the various long-term floating rate notes, discount rates and credit losses modelled are:

Probability weighted average interest rate	4.6 %
Weighted average discount rate	5.3 %
Maturity of long-term floating rate notes	five to seven years
Credit losses	nil to 25 % on a going concern basis 5 % to 50 % on a liquidation basis

Interest rates and credit losses vary by each of the different replacement long-term floating rate notes that are expected to be issued as each has different credit ratings and risks. Interest rates and credit losses also vary by the different probable cash flow scenarios that have been modelled.

Discount rates vary dependent upon the credit rating of the replacement long-term floating rate notes.

Maturities vary by different replacement long-term floating rate notes as a result of the expected maturity of the underlying assets.

One of the probable cash flow scenarios modelled is a liquidation scenario whereby, if the restructuring is not successfully completed, recovery of the Company's investment is through the liquidation of the underlying assets of the ABCP trusts.

In addition, assumptions have also been made as to the amount of restructuring costs that the Company will bear.

Based on additional information that became publicly available during the fourth quarter of 2007, the probability weighted cash flows resulted in an estimated fair value of the Company's investment in ABCP of $122.1 million at December 31, 2007. This was unchanged from the estimated fair value at September 30, 2007. The reduction in the fair value of $21.5 million compared to the original cost of the ABCP was recorded as a charge to income in the third quarter of 2007 with no further charges required in the fourth quarter of 2007.

In view of the continuing uncertainties regarding the value of the assets which underlie the ABCP, the amount and timing of cash flows and the outcome of the restructuring process could give rise to a further material change in the value of the Company's investment in ABCP and could impact the Company's near term earnings.

OTHER INVESTMENTS

Effective January 1, 2005 , CP's 50 % investment in the Detroit River Tunnel Partnership ("DRTP") has been accounted for on a proportionate consolidation basis. Summarized financial information for the Company's interest in the DRTP is as follows:

(in millions of Canadian dollars)	2007	2006
Current assets	$ 0.8	$ 0.9
Long-term assets	51.0	48.0
Current liabilities	2.5	2.1
Long-term liabilities	0.5	0.5
Revenues	12.9	12.8
Expenses	2.4	1.7
Net income	10.5	11.1
Cash provided by operating activities	9.4	8.9
Cash used in investing activities	1.9	1.4
Cash used in financing activities	7.7	7.3

Income before tax from CP's investment in the DRTP was $10.5 million in 2007 (2006 – $11.1 million; 2005 – $8.2 million). The equity income (loss) from the Company's investment in the CNCP Niagara-Windsor Partnership was $0.2 million in 2007 (2006 – ($0.6) million; 2005 – ($0.6) million). CP's investment in the Indiana Harbor Belt Railroad Company generated equity income of $4.1 million in 2007 (2006 – $3.6 million; 2005 – $3.0 million). Equity income (loss) is recorded in "Other" revenues on the Statement of Consolidated Income.

12. Net properties

(in millions of Canadian dollars)	Cost	Accumulated depreciation	Net book value
2007			
Track and roadway	$ 8,828.0	$ 2,852.1	$ 5,975.9
Buildings	342.4	136.0	206.4
Rolling stock	3,593.7	1,485.4	2,108.3
Other	1,632.9	630.4	1,002.5
Total net properties	$ 14,397.0	$ 5,103.9	$ 9,293.1
2006			
Track and roadway	$ 8,615.1	$ 2,770.5	$ 5,844.6
Buildings	344.8	154.1	190.7
Rolling stock	3,548.3	1,450.9	2,097.4
Other	1,625.6	635.4	990.2
Total net properties	$ 14,133.8	$ 5,010.9	$ 9,122.9

At December 31, 2007, software development costs of $612.5 million (2006 – $609.8 million) and accumulated depreciation of $239.1 million (2006 – $239.8 million) were included in the category "Other". Additions during 2007 were $48.8 million (2006 – $37.6 million; 2005 – $39.6 million) and depreciation expense was $50.5 million (2006 – $53.2 million; 2005 – $52.3 million).

At December 31, 2007, net properties included $503.4 million (2006 – $522.5 million) of assets held under capital lease at cost and related accumulated depreciation of $127.5 million (2006 – $112.4 million).

During 2007, capital assets were acquired under the Company's capital program at an aggregate cost of $908.5 million (2006 – $818.6 million; 2005 – $906.0 million), $12.1 million of which were acquired by means of capital leases (2006 – $21.6 million; 2005 – $0.6 million), and $4.6 million of which were acquired by means of a non-monetary transaction. Cash payments related to capital purchases were $893.2 million in 2007 (2006 – $793.7 million; 2005 – $884.4 million). At December 31, 2007, $2.1 million (2006 – $3.5 million; 2005 – $9.4 million) remained in accounts payable related to the above purchases.

13. Other assets and deferred charges

(in millions of Canadian dollars)	2007	2006
Prepaid pension costs	$ 1,104.1	$ 1,081.2
Other [1]	131.5	142.0
Total other assets and deferred charges	$ 1,235.6	$ 1,223.2

[1] At December 31, 2007, the category "Other" included assets held for sale that had a carrying value of $17.0 million (2006 – $1.0 million) that were reclassified from "Net properties".

14. Long-term debt

(in millions of Canadian dollars)	Currency in which payable	2007	2006
6.250 % Notes due 2011	US$	$ 398.8	$ 466.2
7.125 % Debentures due 2031	US$	341.4	407.9
9.450 % Debentures due 2021	US$	244.4	291.4
5.750 % Debentures due 2033	US$	235.5	291.4
4.90 % Medium Term Notes due 2010	CDN$	349.8	350.0
5.95 % 30 – year Notes	US$	432.1	–
5.41 % Senior Secured Notes due 2024	US$	130.4	160.3
6.91 % Secured Equipment Notes due 2008 – 2024	CDN$	212.9	223.2
7.49 % Equipment Trust Certificates due 2008 – 2021	US$	111.2	134.9
Secured Equipment Loan due 2007	US$	–	141.6
Secured Equipment Loan due 2008 – 2015	CDN$	144.2	149.6
Obligations under capital leases due 2008 – 2022 (5.20 % – 6.99 %)	US$	263.5	317.0
Obligations under capital leases due 2008 – 2031 (5.64 % – 5.65 %)	CDN$	13.5	21.9
Bridge financing due 2009	US$	1,256.3	–
Bank loan payable on demand due 2010 (5.883 %)	CDN$	5.1	4.7
		4,139.1	2,960.1
Perpetual 4 % Consolidated Debenture Stock	US$	30.3	35.7
Perpetual 4 % Consolidated Debenture Stock	GB£	7.8	9.0
		4,177.2	3,004.8
Less: Long-term debt maturing within one year		31.0	191.3
		$ 4,146.2	$ 2,813.5

At December 31, 2007, the gross amount of long-term debt denominated in U.S. dollars was US$3,513.8 million (2006 – US$1,927.5 million).

Interest on each of the following instruments is paid semi-annually: 6.250 % Notes and 7.125 % Debentures on April 15 and October 15; 9.450 % Debentures on February 1 and August 1; 5.750 % Debentures on March 15 and September 15; and 4.90 % Medium Term Notes on June 15 and December 15 of each year. All of these Notes and Debentures are unsecured but carry a negative pledge.

The 5.41 % Senior Secured Notes due 2024 are secured by specific locomotive units with a carrying value at December 31, 2007, of $185.2 million. Equal blended semi-annual payments of principal and interest are made on March 3 and September 3 of each year, up to and including September 3, 2023. Final payment of the remaining interest and principal will be made on March 3, 2024.

The 6.91 % Secured Equipment Notes are full recourse obligations of the Company secured by a first charge on specific locomotive units with a carrying value at December 31, 2007 of $187.3 million. The Company made semi-annual payments of interest in the amount of $8.1 million on April 1 and October 1 of each year, up to and including October 1, 2004. Commencing April 1, 2005, and continuing on April 1 and October 1 of each year, the Company pays equal blended semi-annual payments of principal and interest of $10.9 million. Final payment of principal and interest is due October 1, 2024.

The 7.49 % Equipment Trust Certificates are secured by specific locomotive units with a carrying value at December 31, 2007, of $120.8 million. Semi-annual interest payments of US$4.4 million were made on January 15 and July 15 of each year, up to and including January 15, 2005. Beginning on July 15, 2005, and continuing on January 15 and July 15 of each year, the Company makes semi-annual payments that vary in amount and are interest-only payments or blended principal and interest payments. Final payment of the principal is due January 15, 2021.

The Secured Equipment Loan due 2008-2015 is secured by specific locomotive units with a carrying value of $154.2 million at December 31, 2007. The floating interest rate is calculated based on a six-month average Canadian Dollar Offered Rate (calculated based on an average of Bankers'

Acceptance rates) plus 53 basis points (2007 – 4.91 %; 2006 – 3.89 %). The Company makes blended payments of principal and interest semi-annually on February 1 and August 1 of each year.

The bank loan payable on demand matures in 2010 and carries an interest rate of 5.883 %. The amount of the loan at December 31, 2007, was $195.4 million (2006 – $184.2 million). The Company has offset against this loan a financial asset of $190.3 million (2006 – $179.5 million) with the same financial institution.

The Consolidated Debenture Stock, created by an Act of Parliament of 1889, constitutes a first charge upon and over the whole of the undertaking, railways, works, rolling stock, plant, property and effects of the Company, with certain exceptions.

During 2007, the Company issued US$450 million of 5.95 % 30 – year notes for net proceeds of CDN$485.1 million. The notes are unsecured, but carry a negative pledge. Interest is paid semi-annually in arrears on May 15 and November 15 of each year.

In October 2007, the Company obtained bridge financing in the amount of US$1.27 billion for net proceeds of CDN$1.26 billion. The bridge financing is repayable in 2009 and is unsecured. The interest rate is floating and is calculated based on London Interbank Offered Rate ("LIBOR") plus a spread (2007 – 5.53 %).

The Secured Equipment Loan due 2007 was secured by specific units of rolling stock. The interest rate was floating and was calculated based on a blend of one-month and three-month average LIBOR plus a spread (2007 – 7.43 %; 2006 – 5.57 %). The Company made blended payments of principal and interest quarterly on February 20, May 20, August 20 and November 20 of each year. The final interest and principal payment occurred on February 20, 2007.

Annual maturities and sinking fund requirements, excluding those pertaining to capital leases, for each of the five years following 2007 are (in millions): 2008 – $252.4; 2009 – $1,277.5; 2010 – $373.3; 2011 – $424.6; 2012 – $35.2.

At December 31, 2007, capital lease obligations included in long-term debt were as follows:

(in millions of Canadian dollars)	Year	Capital leases
	2008	$ 27.8
	2009	28.9
	2010	41.5
	2011	22.2
	2012	24.5
	Thereafter	302.4
Total minimum lease payments		447.3
Less: Imputed interest		(170.3)
Present value of minimum lease payments		277.0
Less: Current portion		(8.3)
Long-term portion of capital lease obligations		$ 268.7

The carrying value of the assets securing the capital lease obligations was $375.8 million at December 31, 2007.

15. Financial instruments

FOREIGN EXCHANGE FORWARD CONTRACTS

During 2007, the company entered into a currency forward to fix the exchange rate on US$400 million 6.250 % Notes due 2011. At December 31, 2007, the unrealized loss on this currency forward was $15.7 million which has been recorded to "Foreign exchange on long-term debt".

COMMODITY CONTRACTS

Exposure to fluctuations in fuel prices has been partially managed by selling or purchasing crude oil swaps. At December 31, 2007, the Company had entered into futures contracts, which are accounted for as cash flow hedges, to purchase approximately 396,000 barrels (2006 – 1,116,000 barrels) over the 2008-2009 period at average annual prices ranging from US$30.59 to US$38.19 per barrel (2006 – US$32.24 to US$41.59 over the 2007-2009 period). At December 31, 2007, the unrealized gain on crude oil futures was CDN$21.4 million (2006 – CDN$31.7 million). The Company from time to time uses foreign exchange forward contracts to manage the risk caused by foreign exchange variability on fuel purchases and commodity hedges. The Company enters into purchase contracts of U.S. dollars because the Canadian dollar cost of fuel increases if the U.S. dollar appreciates relative to the Canadian dollar. Gains and losses on the crude oil swaps, coupled with foreign exchange forward contracts, offset increases and decreases in the cash cost of fuel. At December 31, 2007, the Company had entered into foreign exchange forward contracts totaling US$14.2 million over the 2008-2009 period at exchange rates ranging from 1.2276 to 1.3008 (2006 – US$45.8 million over the 2007-2009 period at exchange rates ranging from 1.1759 to 1.3008), which are accounted for as cash flow hedges. At December 31, 2007, the unrealized loss on these forward contracts was CDN$3.5 million (2006 – CDN$3.1 million).

INTEREST RATE CONTRACTS

At December 31, 2007, the Company had outstanding interest rate swap agreements, classified as a fair value hedge, for a nominal amount of US$200 million (2006 – US$200.0 million). The swap agreements converted a portion of the Company's fixed-interest-rate liability into a variable-rate liability for the 6.250 % Notes. At December 31, 2007, the unrealized gains on these interest rate swap agreements was CDN$5.5 million (2006 – CDN$2.8 million).

The following table discloses the terms of the swap agreements at December 31, 2007:

	October 15, 2011
Expiration	
Notional amount of principal (in CDN$ millions)	$ 198.3
Fixed receiving rate	6.250%
Variable paying rate	6.655%

Based on U.S. three-month LIBOR.

During 2007, the Company entered into agreements that established the benchmark rate on CDN$350.0 million of long-term debt, which is expected to be issued in 2008. The fair value of this instrument, which is accounted for as a cash flow hedge, was a loss of CDN$30.6 million at December 31, 2007. During the year, losses of CDN$2.3 million were recognised and recorded in "Net income" and unrealized losses of CDN$28.3 million were recorded in "Other comprehensive loss".

In 2004 , the Company entered into agreements that established the borrowing rate on US$200.0 million of long-term debt, which was expected to be issued in the first half of 2005. Unrealized gains on this arrangement, which was accounted for as a cash flow hedge, were CDN$1.8 million at December 31, 2004. In the first quarter of 2005, the hedge was terminated as the Company decided not to issue the debt and the $5.8-million gain on settlement was recorded in "Other income and charges".

CREDIT RISK MANAGEMENT

Counterparties to financial instruments expose the Company to credit losses in the event of non-performance. However, the Company does not anticipate non-performance that would materially impact the Company's financial statements because dealings have been with counterparties of high credit quality and adequate provisions have been made. In addition, the Company believes there are no significant concentrations of credit risk [1].

INTEREST RATE EXPOSURE AND FAIR VALUES

The Company's exposure to interest rate risk along with the total carrying amounts and fair values of its financial instruments are summarized in the following tables [1]:

2007 (in millions of Canadian dollars)	At floating interest rates	Fixed interest rate maturing in			Total carrying value	Fair value
		2008	2009 to 2012	2013 and after		
Financial assets [1]						
Cash and short-term investments	$ 378.1	$ –	$ –	$ –	$ 378.1	$ 378.1
Crude oil swaps, unrealized gain	–	–	–	–	21.4	21.4
Financial liabilities						
Short-term borrowings	229.7	–	–	–	229.7	229.7
6.250 % Notes	–	–	396.5	–	396.5	413.8
7.125 % Debentures	–	–	–	347.0	347.0	374.0
9.450 % Debentures	–	–	–	247.8	247.8	300.5
5.750 % Debentures	–	–	–	247.8	247.8	226.2
5.950 % 30-year notes	–	–	–	446.1	446.1	403.8
4.90 % Medium Term Notes	–	–	350.0	–	350.0	351.9
5.41 % Senior Secured Notes	–	2.8	13.7	95.6	112.1	123.6
6.91 % Secured Equipment Notes	–	7.0	33.3	176.3	216.6	244.6
7.49 % Equipment Trust Certificates	–	4.4	42.6	98.2	145.2	124.4
Secured Equipment Loan	133.1	–	–	–	133.1	145.2
4 % Consolidated Debenture Stock	–	–	–	38.1	38.1	33.8
Obligations under capital leases	–	8.3	46.7	222.0	277.0	296.8
Bridge financing	1,259.0	–	–	–	1,259.0	1,259.0
Bank loan payable on demand	–	5.1	–	–	5.1	5.0
Transaction costs	–	–	–	–	(44.2)	–
Total long-term debt	1,392.1	27.6	882.8	1,918.9	4,177.2	4,302.6

		Notional amounts				Fair value
Foreign exchange forward contracts on fuel, unrealized loss	–	–	–	–	3.5	3.5
Interest rate swaps, unrealized loss	198.3	–	(198.3)	–	5.5	5.5
Total return swap, unrealized loss	–	–	–	–	3.8	3.8
Interest rate forward, unrealized loss	–	–	–	–	30.6	30.6
Currency forward, unrealized loss	–	–	–	–	15.7	15.7

[1] The discussion provided relating to credit risk management and interest rate exposure and fair values and the information in the table above does not consider risks related to the Company's investment in ABCP which is discussed in more detail in Note 11.

2006 (in millions of Canadian dollars)	At floating interest rates	Fixed interest rate maturing in 2007	Fixed interest rate maturing in 2008 to 2011	Fixed interest rate maturing in 2012 and after	Total carrying value	Fair value
Financial assets						
Cash and short-term investments	$ 124.3	$ –	$ –	$ –	$ 124.3	$ 124.3
Crude oil swaps, unrealized gain	–	–	–	–	–	31.7
Financial liabilities						
6.250 % Notes	–	–	466.2	–	466.2	487.0
7.125 % Debentures	–	–	–	407.9	407.9	484.3
9.450 % Debentures	–	–	–	291.4	291.4	381.7
5.750 % Debentures	–	–	–	291.4	291.4	300.6
4.90 % Medium Term Notes	–	–	350.0	–	350.0	355.3
5.41 % Senior Secured Notes	–	3.8	17.5	139.0	160.3	157.8
6.91 % Secured Equipment Notes	–	6.6	31.1	185.5	223.2	259.0
7.49 % Equipment Trust Certificates	–	3.1	14.8	117.0	134.9	155.7
Secured Equipment Loan	141.6	–	–	–	141.6	141.6
Secured Equipment Loan	149.6	–	–	–	149.6	149.6
4 % Consolidated Debenture Stock	–	–	–	44.7	44.7	37.4
Obligations under capital leases	–	27.0	50.4	261.5	338.9	358.2
Bank loan payable on demand	–	4.7	–	–	4.7	4.7
Total long-term debt	291.2	45.2	930.0	1,738.4	3,004.8	3,272.9

		Notional amounts				Fair value
Foreign exchange forward contracts on fuel, unrealized loss	–	–	–	–	–	3.1
Interest rate swaps, unrealized loss	233.1	–	(233.1)	–	–	2.8
Total return swap	–	–	–	–	1.2	1.2

The Company has determined the estimated fair values of its financial instruments based on appropriate valuation methodologies. However, considerable judgment is necessary to develop these estimates. Accordingly, the estimates presented herein are not necessarily indicative of what the Company could realize in a current market exchange. The use of different assumptions or methodologies may have a material effect on the estimated fair value amounts.

The following methods and assumptions were used to estimate the fair value of each class of financial instrument:

□ Short-term financial assets and liabilities are valued at their carrying amounts as presented on the Consolidated Balance Sheet, which are reasonable estimates of fair value due to the relatively short period to maturity of these instruments.

□ The fair value of publicly traded long-term debt is determined based on market prices at December 31, 2007 and 2006. The fair value of other long-term debt is estimated based on rates currently available to the Company for long-term borrowings, with terms and conditions similar to those borrowings in place at the applicable Consolidated Balance Sheet date.

□ The fair value of derivative instruments is calculated based on market prices or rates at December 31, 2007 and 2006, which generally reflects the estimated amount the Company would receive or pay to terminate the contracts at the applicable Consolidated Balance Sheet date.

STOCK-BASED COMPENSATION EXPENSE MANAGEMENT

The Company entered into a TRS, effective in May 2006, in order to reduce the volatility and total cost to the Company over time of four types of stock-based compensation: SARs, DSUs, RSUs and PSUs. The value of the TRS derivative is linked to the market value of our stock and is intended to mitigate the impact on expenses of share value movements on SARs, DSUs, RSUs and PSUs. "Compensation and benefits" expense increased by $2.6 million (2006 – $1.2 million) for the year ended December 31, 2007 due to unrealized losses for these swaps. These losses substantially offset the benefits recognized in these stock-based compensation programs due to fluctuations in share price during the period the TRS was in place.

FAIR VALUE OF FINANCIAL INSTRUMENTS

The fair value of a financial instrument is the amount of consideration that would be agreed upon in an arm's length transaction between willing parties. The Company uses the following methods and assumptions to estimate fair value of each class of financial instruments for which carrying amounts are included in the Consolidated Balance Sheet as follows:

Loans and Receivables

Accounts receivable and other current assets The carrying amounts included in the Consolidated Balance Sheet approximate fair value because of the short maturity of these instruments.

Investments Long-term receivable balances are carried at amortized cost based on an initial fair value determined using discounted cash flow analysis using observable market based inputs.

Financial Liabilities

Accounts payable and accrued liabilities and short-term borrowings The carrying amounts included in the Consolidated Balance Sheet approximate fair value because of the short maturity of these instruments.

Long-term debt The carrying amount of long-term debt is at amortized cost based on an initial fair value determined using the quoted market prices for the same or similar debt instruments.

Available for Sale

Investments The Company's equity investments recorded on a cost basis have a carrying value that equals cost as fair value cannot be reliably established as there are no quoted prices in an active market for these investments. The Company's equity investments recorded on an equity basis have a carrying value equal to cost plus the Company's share of the investees net income, less any dividends received. These investments are not traded on a liquid market.

Held for Trading

Other assets and deferred charges and deferred liabilities Derivative instruments that are designated as hedging instruments are measured at fair value determined using the quoted market prices for the same or similar instruments. Derivative instruments that are not designated in hedging relationships are classified as held for trading and measured at fair value determined by using quoted market prices for the same or similar instruments and changes in the fair values of such derivative instruments are recognized in net income as they arise.

Cash and cash equivalents The carrying amounts included in the Consolidated Balance Sheet approximate fair value because of the short maturity of these instruments.

Investments ABCP is carried at fair value, which has been determined using valuation techniques that incorporate probability weighted discounted future cash flows reflecting market conditions and other factors that a market participant would consider (see Note 11).

Carrying Value and Fair Value of Financial Instruments

The carrying values of financial instruments equal or approximate their fair values with the exception of long-term debt which has a carrying value of approximately $4,177.2 million and a fair value of approximately $4,302.6 million at December 31, 2007.

16. Deferred liabilities

(in millions of Canadian dollars)		2007		2006
Provision for restructuring and environmental remediation (Note 18)	$	234.0	$	309.0
Deferred workers' compensation and personal injury accruals		161.4		162.5
Accrued employee benefits		222.0		208.4
Asset retirement obligations (Note 17)		29.1		30.9
Deferred revenue on rights-of-way license agreements		48.0		45.8
Deferred income credits		32.0		27.3
Stock-based compensation liabilities		75.0		76.6
Financial instruments		13.7		–
Other		92.1		54.1
		907.3		914.6
Less: Amount payable/realizable within one year		192.7		188.9
Total deferred liabilities	$	714.6	$	725.7

Deferred revenue on rights-of-way license agreements is being amortized to income on a straight-line basis over the related lease terms.

17. Asset retirement obligations

The Company has two liabilities related to asset retirement obligations ("ARO") recorded in "Deferred liabilities". These liabilities are discounted at 6.25 %. The accretion expense related to these AROs in 2007 was $1.9 million (2006 – $2.0 million; 2005 – $2.1 million), offset by payments made of $0.7 million and a reduction of $0.8 million due to a sale of a related asset (2006 – payments of $0.7 million and a reduction of $3.4 million due to a sale of a related asset; 2005 – payments of $0.6 million and a reduction of $1.0 million due to the sale of the related asset), and revisions to the estimated cash flows of $2.2 million thereby decreasing the ARO liability to $29.1 million at December 31, 2007 (2006 – $30.9 million; 2005 – $32.9 million). Accretion expense is included in "Depreciation and amortization" on the Statement of Consolidated Income.

Upon the ultimate retirement of grain-dependent branch lines, the Company has to pay a fee, levied under the Canada Transportation Act, of $30,000 per mile of abandoned track. The undiscounted amount of the liability was $50.4 million at December 31, 2007 (2006 – $51.9 million), which, when present valued, was $27.7 million at December 31, 2007 (2006 – $29.6 million). The payments are expected to be made in the 2008-2044 period.

The Company also has a liability on a joint facility that will have to be settled upon retirement based on a proportion of use during the life of the asset. The estimate of the obligation at December 31, 2007, was $16.0 million (2006 – $15.3 million), which, when present valued, was $1.4 million at December 31, 2007 (2006 – $1.3 million). For purposes of estimating this liability, the payment related to the retirement of the joint facility is anticipated to be in 37 years.

18. Restructuring accrual and environmental remediation

At December 31, 2007, the provision for restructuring and environmental remediation was $234.0 million (2006 – $309.0 million). The restructuring provision was primarily for labour liabilities for restructuring plans. Payments are expected to continue in diminishing amounts until 2025. The environmental remediation liability includes the cost of a multi-year soil remediation program for various sites, as well as a special charge taken in 2004 related to a specific property.

Set out below is a reconciliation of CP's liabilities associated with its restructuring and environmental remediation programs:

(in millions of Canadian dollars)	Opening balance Jan. 1		Accrued (reduced)		Payments		Amortization of discount[1]		Foreign exchange impact		Closing balance Dec. 31
Year ended December 31, 2007											
Labour liability for terminations and severances	$	187.4	$	(12.8)	$	(46.8)	$	6.1	$	(4.7)	$	129.2
Other non-labour liabilities for exit plans		1.4		(0.2)		(0.2)		–		(0.2)		0.8
Total restructuring liability		188.8		(13.0)		(47.0)		6.1		(4.9)		130.0
Environmental remediation program		120.2		7.5		(14.0)		–		(9.7)		104.0
Total restructuring and environmental remediation liability	$	309.0	$	(5.5)	$	(61.0)	$	6.1	$	(14.6)	$	234.0
Year ended December 31, 2006											
Labour liability for terminations and severances	$	263.6	$	(14.1)	$	(71.8)	$	9.8	$	(0.1)	$	187.4
Other non-labour liabilities for exit plans		5.8		0.7		(5.0)		0.1		(0.2)		1.4
Total restructuring liability		269.4		(13.4)		(76.8)		9.9		(0.3)		188.8
Environmental remediation program		129.4		10.5		(19.5)		–		(0.2)		120.2
Total restructuring and environmental remediation liability	$	398.8	$	(2.9)	$	(96.3)	$	9.9	$	(0.5)	$	309.0
Year ended December 31, 2005											
Labour liability for terminations and severances	$	269.7	$	33.6	$	(50.5)	$	12.0	$	(1.2)	$	263.6
Other non-labour liabilities for exit plans		6.1		(0.1)		(0.1)		0.1		(0.2)		5.8
Total restructuring liability		275.8		33.5		(50.6)		12.1		(1.4)		269.4
Environmental remediation program		172.9		(22.4)		(18.4)		–		(2.7)		129.4
Total restructuring and environmental remediation liability	$	448.7	$	11.1	$	(69.0)	$	12.1	$	(4.1)	$	398.8

[1] Amortization of discount is charged to income as "Compensation and benefits" (2007 – $3.3 million; 2006 – $5.1 million; 2005 – $0.7 million), "Purchased services and other" (2007 – nil; 2006 – nil; 2005 – $2.3 million) and "Other income and charges" (2007 – $2.8 million; 2006 – $4.8 million; 2005 – $9.2 million), as applicable.

New accruals and adjustments to previous accruals were a net reduction of $5.5 million in 2007, compared with net reduction of $2.9 million in 2006 and a net increase of $11.1 million in 2005.

In 2007, CP recorded a net reduction in the restructuring liability included in "Deferred liabilities", of $13.0 million, mainly due to experience gains on termination costs for previously accrued labour initiatives. This reduction was partially offset by an increase in the environmental remediation liability, also included in "Deferred liabilities", of $7.5 million. This net reduction was recorded in "Compensation and benefits" and "Purchased services and other".

In 2006, CP recorded a net reduction in the restructuring liability included in "Deferred liabilities", of $13.4 million, mainly due to experience gains on termination costs for previously accrued labour initiatives. This reduction was partially offset by an increase in the environmental remediation liability, also included in "Deferred liabilities", of $10.5 million. This net reduction was recorded in "Compensation and benefits" and "Purchased services and other".

In 2005, CP established new restructuring initiatives to reduce labour costs, primarily in management and administrative areas, which were completed in 2006. These initiatives required recording a special charge of $44.2 million for labour restructuring, which included $43.1 million for labour restructuring liabilities and $1.1 million for accelerated recognition of stock-based compensation (included elsewhere in "Deferred liabilities" and in "Contributed surplus"). This charge was partially offset by a net reduction of $9.6 million (included in "Compensation and benefits" and "Purchased services and other"), largely due to experience gains on previously accrued amounts and minor new initiatives. The adjustment to the environmental remediation program was largely due to a binding settlement reached during the third quarter of 2005 with a potentially responsible party, resulting in a reduction of $33.9 million to the special charge recorded in 2004, including a $30.3-million reduction in the environmental liability. The $30.3-million reduction was partially offset by $7.9 million of other adjustments, due largely to monitoring and technical support costs related to multi-year sites.

In the fourth quarter of 2004, CP recorded a special charge of $90.9 million for investigation, characterization, remediation and other applicable actions related to environmental contamination at a CP-owned property in the U.S., which includes areas previously leased to third parties. CP is participating in the State of Minnesota's voluntary investigation and clean-up program at the east side of the property. The property is the subject of ongoing fieldwork being undertaken in conjunction with the appropriate state authorities to determine the extent and magnitude of the contamination and the appropriate remediation plan. In 2005, CP filed with the State of Minnesota a response action plan for the east side of the property.

In the third quarter of 2005, a binding settlement was reached relating to a lawsuit with a potentially responsible party in relation to portions of past environmental contamination at the above-mentioned CP-owned property. As a result, the lawsuit against this party was dismissed. CP reduced accrued liabilities related to this property and recognized in 2005 a total reduction of $33.9 million to the special charge for environmental remediation recorded in 2004.

In the fourth quarter of 2005, CP recorded a special charge of $44.2 million for a labour restructuring initiative. The job reductions, mostly in management and administrative positions, were completed in 2006.

19. Shareholders' equity

AUTHORIZED AND ISSUED SHARE CAPITAL

The Company's Articles of Incorporation authorize for issuance an unlimited number of Common Shares and an unlimited number of First Preferred Shares and Second Preferred Shares. At December 31, 2007, no Preferred Shares had been issued.

An analysis of Common Share balances is as follows:

(in millions)	2007 Number	2006 Number
Share capital, January 1	155.5	158.2
Shares issued under stock option plans	1.0	2.3
Shares repurchased	(3.2)	(5.0)
Share capital, December 31	153.3	155.5

The change in the Share capital balance includes $5.1 million (2006 – $3.3 million) related to the cancellation of the SARs liability on exercise of tandem stock options, and $0.7 million (2006 – $1.1 million) of stock-based compensation transferred from "Contributed surplus".

The balance remaining in contributed surplus of $42.4 million relates to stock-based compensation recognized to date on unexercised options and will be attributed to share capital as options are exercised.

In May 2005, the Company completed the necessary filings for a normal course issuer bid to purchase, for cancellation, up to 2.5 million of its outstanding Common Shares, representing 1.6 % of the approximately 159.0 million Common Shares outstanding just prior to the filing date. In March 2006, the normal course issuer bid was amended to increase the number of Common Shares eligible to be purchased to 3.3 million. Share repurchases were made during the 12-month period beginning June 6, 2005, and ending June 5, 2006. In June 2006, the Company completed the acquisition of Common Shares under the previous normal course issuer bid and filed a new normal course issuer bid to purchase, for cancellation, up to 3.9 million of its outstanding Common Shares. Under this filing, share purchases could have been made during the 12-month period beginning June 6, 2006, and ending June 5, 2007. Of the 3.9 million shares authorized for purchase under this filing, 3.4 million were purchased in 2006 at an average price per share of $56.66 and 0.2 million shares were purchased during the three months ended March 31, 2007 at an average price per share of $64.11.

In March 2007, the Company completed the filing for a new normal course issuer bid ("2007 NCIB") to cover the period of March 28, 2007 to March 27, 2008 to purchase, for cancellation, up to 5.0 million of its outstanding Common Shares. Effective April 30, 2007, the 2007 NCIB was amended to purchase, for cancellation, up to 15.3 million of its outstanding Common Shares. Of the 15.3 million shares authorized under the 2007 NCIB, 2.7 million shares were purchased at an average price per share of $73.64.

In addition, pursuant to a notice of intention to make an exempt issuer bid filed on March 23, 2007, the Company purchased, for cancellation, 0.3 million shares through a private agreement with an arm's length third party on March 29, 2007 at an average price of $63.12.

The purchases are made at the market price on the day of purchase, with consideration allocated to share capital up to the average carrying amount of the shares, and any excess allocated to contributed surplus and retained income. When shares are purchased, it takes three days before the transaction is settled and the shares are cancelled. The cost of shares purchased in a given month and settled in the following month is accrued in the month of purchase.

The table below summarizes the allocation of the cost of shares repurchased between share capital, contributed surplus and retained income.

(in millions of Canadian dollars)		2007		2006
Share capital	$	24.5	$	36.8
Contributed surplus		–		223.1
Retained income		206.6		26.5
CP Common Shares repurchased	$	231.1	$	286.4

20. Pensions and other benefits

The Company has both defined benefit ("DB") and defined contribution ("DC") pension plans.

The DB plans provide for pensions based principally on years of service and compensation rates near retirement. Pensions for Canadian pensioners are partially indexed to inflation. Annual employer contributions to the DB plans, which are actuarially determined, are made on the basis of being not less than the minimum amounts required by federal pension supervisory authorities.

Other benefits include post-retirement health and life insurance for pensioners, and post-employment long-term disability and workers' compensation benefits, which are based on Company-specific claims.

At December 31, the elements of defined benefit cost for DB pension plans and other benefits recognized in the year included the following components:

(in millions of Canadian dollars)	Pensions			Other benefits		
	2007	2006	2005	2007	2006	2005
Current service cost (benefits earned by employees in the year)	$ 97.6	$ 101.9	$ 75.7	$ 16.8	$ 15.1	$ 13.8
Interest cost on benefit obligation	420.0	400.0	405.0	26.7	26.6	27.3
Actual return on fund assets	(275.9)	(927.4)	(849.8)	(1.2)	(0.6)	(0.7)
Actuarial (gain) loss	(1.4)	35.2	693.7 [1]	(1.1)	(2.9)	29.8
Plan amendments	22.5	1.3	56.5	–	(1.2)	(6.7)
Settlement gain	–	–	–	(10.7) [2]	–	–
Elements of employee future benefit cost, before adjustments to recognize the long-term nature of employee future benefit costs	262.8	(389.0)	381.1	30.5	37.0	63.5
Adjustments to recognize the long-term nature of employee future benefit costs:						
Amortization of transitional (asset) obligation	(16.2)	(16.2)	(16.2)	12.4	12.4	12.7
Difference between expected return and actual return on fund assets	(278.3)	401.2	351.2	0.6	–	–
Difference between actuarial loss (gain) recognized and actual actuarial loss (gain) on benefit obligation	99.9	64.9	(638.1)	6.8	9.1	(25.6)
Difference between amortization of prior service costs and actual plan amendments	(5.8)	14.5	(41.3)	(0.2)	1.0	6.7
Net benefit cost	$ 62.4	$ 75.4	$ 36.7	$ 50.1	$ 59.5	$ 57.3

[1] Actuarial loss for 2005 was largely a result of a decrease in the discount rate.

[2] Settlement gain from certain post-retirement benefit obligations being assumed by a U.S. national multi-employer benefit plan.

Information about the Company's DB pension plans and other benefits, in aggregate, is as follows:

(in millions of Canadian dollars)	Pensions		Other benefits	
	2007	2006	2007	2006
Change in benefit obligation:				
Benefit obligation at January 1	$ 7,892.7	$ 7,732.2	$ 509.5	$ 498.9
Current service cost	97.6	101.9	16.8	15.1
Interest cost	420.0	400.0	26.7	26.6
Employee contributions	53.4	53.9	0.2	0.2
Benefits paid	(436.9)	(432.1)	(35.7)	(33.2)
Foreign currency changes	(22.1)	0.3	(9.3)	0.3
Actuarial loss (gain)	(1.4)	35.2	(1.1)	(2.9)
Plan amendments and other	22.5	1.3	–	4.5
Release due to settlement	–	–	(15.4)	–
Benefit obligation at December 31	$ 8,025.8	$ 7,892.7	$ 491.7	$ 509.5
Change in fund assets:				
Fair value of fund assets at January 1	$ 7,649.2	$ 6,890.1	$ 11.9	$ 11.9
Actual return on fund assets	275.9	927.4	1.2	0.6
Employer contributions	86.4	209.5	34.9	32.4
Employee contributions	53.4	53.9	0.2	0.2
Benefits paid	(436.9)	(432.1)	(35.7)	(33.2)
Foreign currency changes	(17.5)	0.4	–	–
Fair value of fund assets at December 31	$ 7,610.5	$ 7,649.2	$ 12.5	$ 11.9
Funded status – plan deficit	$ (415.3)	$ (243.5)	$ (479.2)	$ (497.6)
Unamortized prior service cost	132.6	126.9	(0.7)	(1.0)
Unamortized net transitional (asset) obligation	(80.3)	(96.5)	61.7	74.1
Unamortized experience losses:				
Deferred investment losses due to use of market-related value to determine net benefit cost	(181.2)	(568.9)	–	–
Unamortized net actuarial loss	1,647.3 [1]	1,861.7 [1]	101.9	118.9
Accrued benefit asset (liability) on the Consolidated Balance Sheet	$ 1,103.1	$ 1,079.7	$ (316.3)	$ (305.6)

[1] The amount by which these losses exceed the 10 % corridor (representing 10 % of the benefit obligation) was equal to $844.7 million at December 31, 2007 (2006 – $1,072.4 million). Any such excess is amortized, commencing in the following year, over the expected average remaining service period of active employees expected to receive benefits under the plan (December 31, 2007 – 11 years; December 31, 2006 – 11 years). In 2007, $98.5 million was amortized and included in the net benefit cost (2006 – $100.1 million).

The accrued benefit asset (liability) is included on the Company's Consolidated Balance Sheet as follows:

	Pensions		Other benefits	
(in millions of Canadian dollars)	2007	2006	2007	2006
Other assets and deferred charges	$ 1,104.1	$ 1,081.2	$ –	$ –
Accounts payable and accrued liabilities	(0.2)	(0.3)	(38.3)	(21.5)
Other long-term liabilities	(0.8)	(1.2)	(278.0)	(284.1)
Accrued benefit asset (liability) on the Consolidated Balance Sheet	$ 1,103.1	$ 1,079.7	$ (316.3)	$ (305.6)

The measurement date used to determine the plan assets and the accrued benefit obligation is December 31 (November 30 for U.S. pension plans). The most recent actuarial valuations for pension funding purposes were performed as at January 1, 2007. The next actuarial valuations for pension funding purposes will be performed as at January 1, 2008.

Included in the benefit obligation and fair value of fund assets at year end were the following amounts in respect of plans where the benefit obligation exceeded the fund assets:

	Pensions		Other benefits	
(in millions of Canadian dollars)	2007	2006	2007	2006
Benefit obligation	$ (8,025.8)	$ (7,892.7)	$ (491.7)	$ (509.5)
Fair value of fund assets	7,610.5	7,649.2	12.5	11.9
	$ (415.3)	$ (243.5)	$ (479.2)	$ (497.6)

Actuarial assumptions used were approximately:

(percentages)	2007	2006	2005
Benefit obligation at December 31:			
Discount rate	5.60	5.40	5.25
Projected future salary increases	3.00	3.00	3.00
Health care cost trend rate	9.50 [1]	10.00 [1]	10.00 [1]
Benefit cost for year ended December 31:			
Discount rate	5.40	5.25	6.00
Expected rate of return on fund assets	8.00	8.00	8.00
Projected future salary increases	3.00	3.00	3.00
Health care cost trend rate	10.00 [1]	10.00 [1]	8.50 [2]

[1] The health care cost trend rate is projected to decrease by 0.5 % per year from a 10.0 % rate in 2006 and 2007 to approximately 5.0 % per year in 2017.

[2] For this prior period, the health care cost trend rate was projected to decrease by 0.5 % per year to approximately 4.5 % per year in 2012.

Assumed health care cost trend rates have a significant effect on the amounts reported for the health care plans. A one-percentage-point change in the assumed health care cost trend rate would have the following effects:

Favourable (unfavourable) (in millions of Canadian dollars)	One percentage point increase	One percentage point decrease
Effect on the total of service and interest costs	$ (1.2)	$ 1.1
Effect on post-retirement benefit obligation	$ (14.8)	$ 14.0

PLAN ASSETS

The Company's pension plan asset allocation, and the current weighted average permissible range for each major asset class, were as follows:

		Percentage of plan assets at December 31	
Asset allocation (percentage)	Current permissible range	2007	2006
Equity securities	47 – 53	49.4	56.3
Debt securities	37 – 43	41.6	38.1
Real estate and infrastructure	8 – 12	9.0	5.6
Total		100.0	100.0

The Company's investment strategy is to achieve a long-term (five- to ten-year period) real rate of return of 5.5 %, net of all fees and expenses. The Company's best estimate of long-term inflation of 2.5 % yields a long-term nominal target of 8.0 %, net of all fees and expenses. In identifying the asset allocation ranges, consideration was given to the long-term nature of the underlying plan liabilities, the solvency and going-concern financial position of the plan, long-term return expectations and the risks associated with key asset classes as well as the relationships of their returns with each other, inflation and interest rates. When advantageous and with due consideration, derivative instruments may be utilized, provided the total value of the underlying asset represented by financial derivatives, excluding currency forwards, is limited to 20 % of the market value of the fund.

At December 31, 2007, fund assets consisted primarily of listed stocks and bonds, including 54,440 of the Company's Common Shares (2006 – 132,600) at a market value of $3.5 million (2006 – $8.1 million) and 6.91 % Secured Equipment Notes issued by the Company at a par value of $3.9 million (2006 – $4.1 million) and at a market value of $4.3 million (2006 – $4.7 million).

CASH FLOWS

In 2007, the Company contributed $82.9 million to its registered pension plans (2006 – $202.0 million), including $3.2 million to the defined contribution plan (2006 – $3.1 million). In addition, the Company made payments directly to employees, their beneficiaries or estates or to third-party benefit administrators of $40.7 million (2006 – $42.0 million) with respect to supplemental pension plan benefits and other benefits.

DEFINED CONTRIBUTION PLAN

Canadian non-unionized employees have the option to participate in the DC plan. The DC plan provides a pension based on total employee and employer contributions plus investment income earned on those contributions. Employee contributions are based on a percentage of salary. The Company matches employee contributions to a maximum percentage each year. In 2007, the net cost of this plan, which generally equals the employer's required contribution, was $3.2 million (2006 – $3.0 million; 2005 – $3.1 million).

POST-EMPLOYMENT RESTRUCTURING BENEFITS

The Company accrues post-employment labour liabilities as part of its restructuring accruals (see Note 18) that are discounted at rates of 5.25 % and 6.75 %. The labour portion of the Company's accrued restructuring liability was as follows:

(in millions of Canadian dollars)	2007	2006
Change in liability:		
Restructuring labour liability at January 1	$ 160.8	$ 224.8
Plan adjustment	(12.8)	(14.1)
Interest cost	8.9	12.0
Benefits paid	(36.8)	(61.8)
Foreign currency changes	(4.7)	(0.1)
Restructuring labour liability at December 31	115.4	160.8
Unfunded restructuring labour amount	(115.4)	(160.8)
Unamortized net transitional amount	(13.8)	(26.6)
Accrued restructuring labour liability on the Consolidated Balance Sheet	$ (129.2)	$ (187.4)

21. Stock-based compensation

At December 31, 2007, the Company had several stock-based compensation plans, including a stock option plan, tandem SARs, a DSU plan, a RSU plan, a PSU plan and an employee stock savings plan. These plans resulted in a compensation cost in 2007 of $33.7 million (2006 – $52.1 million; 2005 – $38.7 million).

REPLACEMENT OPTIONS AND SARS

Due to the reorganization of Canadian Pacific Limited ("CPL") and the spin-off of its subsidiary companies in October 2001, all CPL employees who held CPL options at the date of the spin-off received in exchange for their CPL options fully-vested replacement options and SARs in the spun-off companies, according to the reorganization ratio used for Common Shares. The exercise price of the CPL options and SARs was allocated among the replacement options and SARs of each of the spun-off companies, based on a formula using the weighted average trading price of the spun-off companies for their first 10 days of trading.

By agreement between CP and its former affiliates, the difference between the strike price and the exercise price of SARs of the former affiliates held by CP employees is recognized as an expense by CP. The difference between the strike price and the exercise price of CP SARs held by employees of the former affiliates is recovered from the former affiliates.

SARs are attached to 50 % of the options and there is a one-to-one cancellation ratio between those options and SARs.

STOCK OPTION PLANS AND SARS

Under the Company's stock option plans, options are granted to eligible employees to purchase Common Shares of the Company at a price equal to the market value of the shares at the grant date. CP follows the fair value-based approach to accounting for stock-based compensation for options issued for years beginning in 2003. Compensation expense is recognized for stock options over the shorter of the vesting period or employee service period based on their estimated fair values on the dates of grant, as determined by the Black-Scholes option-pricing model. Options granted between January 1 and December 31, 2002, are not recorded at fair value and, as such, no compensation expense has been recorded for these options.

Pursuant to the employee plan, options may be exercised upon vesting, which is between 24 and 36 months after the grant date, and will expire after 10 years ("regular options").

Some options vest after 48 months, unless certain performance targets are achieved, in which case vesting is accelerated and will expire five years after the grant date ("performance-accelerated options"). Some options will only vest when certain performance targets are achieved and will expire, if the performance targets are not achieved within a specific time frame, and will expire five years and three months after the grant date ("performance-contingent options").

At December 31, 2007, there were 3,602,761 (2006 – 669,864; 2005 – 1,836,254) Common Shares available for the granting of future options under the stock option plans, out of the 15,578,642 (2006 –11,500,000; 2005 – 11,500,000) Common Shares currently authorized.

With the granting of regular options, employees are simultaneously granted SARs equivalent to one-half the number of regular options granted. A SAR entitles the holder to receive payment of an amount equal to the excess of the market value of a Common Share at the exercise date of the SAR over the related option exercise price. On an ongoing basis, a liability for SARs is accrued on the incremental change in the market value of the underlying stock and amortized to income over the vesting period. SARs may be exercised no earlier than two years and no later than 10 years after the grant date.

Where an option granted is a tandem award, the holder can choose to exercise an option or a SAR of equal intrinsic value.

In 2007, the expense for stock options was $10.7 million (2006 – $11.1 million; 2005 – $9.8 million) and for SARs was $8.7 million (2006 – $26.1 million; 2005 – $16.8 million).

The following is a summary of the Company's fixed stock option plan as of December 31:

	2007		2006	
	Number of options	Weighted average exercise price	Number of options	Weighted average exercise price
Outstanding, January 1	6,807,644	$ 38.50	7,971,917	$ 32.07
New options granted	1,304,500	62.60	1,467,900	57.80
Exercised	(972,281)	31.99	(2,330,664)	28.59
Forfeited/cancelled	(158,755)	35.76	(301,509)	39.07
Outstanding, December 31	6,981,108	$ 43.97	6,807,644	$ 38.50
Options exercisable at December 31	4,035,008	$ 34.12	2,918,294	$ 29.64

At December 31, 2007, the details of the stock options outstanding were as follows:

	Options outstanding			Options exercisable	
Range of exercise prices	Number of options	Weighted average years to expiration	Weighted average exercise price	Number of options	Weighted average exercise price
$14.07 – $18.96	184,225	2	$ 14.49	184,225	$ 14.49
$27.62 – $36.64	2,812,483	4	31.31	2,812,483	31.31
$42.05 – $74.89	3,984,400	7	54.21	1,038,300	45.21
Total	6,981,108	6	$ 43.97	4,035,008	$ 34.12

DEFERRED SHARE UNIT PLAN AND OTHER

The Company established the DSU plan as a means to compensate and assist in attaining share ownership targets set for certain key employees and Directors. A DSU entitles the holder to receive, upon redemption, a cash payment equivalent to the market value of a Common Share at the redemption date. DSUs vest over various periods of up to 36 months and are only redeemable for a specified period after employment is terminated.

Key employees may choose to receive DSUs in lieu of cash payments for certain incentive programs. In addition, when acquiring Common Shares to meet share ownership targets, key employees may be granted a matching number of DSUs up to 33 % of the shares and DSUs acquired during the first six months after becoming eligible under the plan and, thereafter, up to 25 %. Key employees have five years to meet their ownership targets.

An expense to income for DSUs is recognized over the vesting period for both the initial subscription price and the change in value between reporting periods. At December 31, 2007, there were 284,968 (2006 – 335,177; 2005 – 295,224) DSUs outstanding. In 2007, 46,050 (2006 – 65,781; 2005 – 47,891) DSUs were granted. In 2007, 96,259 (2006 – 26,137; 2005 – 44,167) DSUs were redeemed. In 2007, the expense for DSUs was $4.1 million (2006 – $6.8 million; 2005 – $4.1 million).

The Company issued 16,921 RSUs in 2007. The RSUs are subject to time vesting. They will vest on May 31, 2010, and will be cashed out based on the average closing price for the 10 days prior to May 31, 2010. An expense to income for RSUs is recognized over the vesting period. The Company issued 30,000 RSUs in 2005. These RSUs were forfeited in 2006 prior to vesting. An expense to income for RSUs was being recognized over the vesting period and was recovered upon cancellation. In 2007, the expense was $0.2 million (2006 – expense recovery of $0.6 million; 2005 – $0.6 million).

The Company issued 23,855 PSUs in 2007. The PSUs are contingent upon achieving certain performance targets, and would not become payable until 2010. The actual value of the PSUs will be based on the average closing price for the 10 days prior to the entitlement date. An expense to income for PSUs is recognized over the vesting period. In 2007, the expense was $0.7 million (2006 – nil; 2005 – nil).

Under the fair value method, the fair value of options at the grant date was $11.3 million for options issued in 2007 (2006 – $12.4 million; 2005 – $10.1 million). The weighted average fair value assumptions were approximately:

	2007	2006	2005
Expected option life (years)	4.00	4.50	4.50
Risk-free interest rate	3.90%	4.07%	3.49%
Expected stock price volatility	22%	22%	24%
Expected annual dividends per share	$ 0.90	$ 0.75	$ 0.53
Weighted average fair value of options granted during the year	$ 12.97	$ 12.99	$ 9.66

EMPLOYEE SHARE PURCHASE PLAN

The Company has an employee share purchase plan whereby both employee and Company contributions are used to purchase shares on the open market for employees. The Company's contributions are expensed over the one-year vesting period. Under the plan, the Company matches $1 for every $3 contributed by employees up to a maximum employee contribution of 6 % of annual salary.

At December 31, 2007, there were 12,181 participants (2006 – 11,682; 2005 – 8,989) in the plan. The total number of shares purchased in 2007 on behalf of participants, including the Company contribution, was 745,374 (2006 – 657,530; 2005 – 795,728). In 2007, the Company's contributions totalled $10.4 million (2006 – $10.0 million; 2005 – $8.8 million) and the related expense was $8.9 million (2006 – $8.6 million; 2005 – $7.4 million).

22. Commitments and contingencies

In the normal course of its operations, the Company becomes involved in various legal actions, including claims relating to injuries and damage to property. The Company maintains provisions it considers to be adequate for such actions. While the final outcome with respect to actions outstanding or pending at December 31, 2007, cannot be predicted with certainty, it is the opinion of management that their resolution will not have a material adverse effect on the Company's financial position or results of operations.

At December 31, 2007, the Company had committed to total future capital expenditures amounting to $504.2 million for the years 2008-2016.

At December 31, 2007, the Company had a committed unused line of credit of $408.0 million available for short-term financing, effective until December 2012. The interest rate for this credit facility varies based on bank prime, Bankers' Acceptances or LIBOR. At December 31, 2007, the Company also had a committed unused credit facility of US$530.0 million available for short-term financing requirements related to the acquisition of DM&E and related capital programs. The interest rate for this facility varies based on LIBOR.

Minimum payments under operating leases were estimated at $614.9 million in aggregate, with annual payments in each of the five years following 2007 of (in millions): 2008 – $120.3; 2009 – $86.8; 2010 – $68.9; 2011 – $60.9; 2012 – $58.0.

GUARANTEES

In the normal course of operating the railway, the Company enters into contractual arrangements that involve providing certain guarantees, which extend over the term of the contracts. These guarantees include, but are not limited to:

□ residual value guarantees on operating lease commitments of $321.7 million at December 31, 2007;

□ guarantees to pay other parties in the event of the occurrence of specified events, including damage to equipment, in relation to assets used in the operation of the railway through operating leases, rental agreements, easements, trackage and interline agreements;

□ indemnifications of certain tax-related payments incurred by lessors and lenders; and

□ certain amounts related to the Company's investment in the DM&E. These include minimum lease payments of $46.2 million, residual value guarantees of $11.0 million, and a line of credit of US$10 million (see Note 11).

The maximum amount that could be payable under these guarantees, excluding residual value guarantees, cannot be reasonably estimated due to the nature of certain of these guarantees. All or a portion of amounts paid under guarantees to other parties in the event of the occurrence of specified events could be recoverable from other parties or through insurance. The Company has accrued for all guarantees that it expects to pay. At December 31, 2007, these accruals amounted to $7.0 million (2006 – $6.2 million).

INDEMNIFICATIONS

Pursuant to a trust and custodial services agreement with the trustee of the Canadian Pacific Railway Company Pension Trust Fund, we have undertaken to indemnify and save harmless the trustee, to the extent not paid by the fund, from any and all taxes, claims, liabilities, damages, costs and expenses arising out of the performance of the trustee's obligations under the agreement, except as a result of misconduct by the trustee. The indemnity includes liabilities, costs or expenses relating to any legal reporting or notification obligations of the trustee with respect to the defined contribution option of the pension plans or otherwise with respect to the assets of the pension plans that are not part of the fund. The indemnity survives the termination or expiry of the agreement with respect to claims and liabilities arising prior to the termination or expiry. At December 31, 2007, we had not recorded a liability associated with this indemnification, as we do not expect to make any payments pertaining to it.

Pursuant to our by-laws, we indemnify all our current and former directors and officers. In addition to the indemnity provided for in our by-laws, we also indemnify our directors and officers pursuant to indemnity agreements. We carry a liability insurance policy for directors and officers, subject to a maximum coverage limit and certain deductibles in cases where a director or officer is reimbursed for any loss covered by the policy.

23. Segmented information

OPERATING SEGMENT

The Company operates in only one operating segment: rail transportation. Operating results by geographic areas, railway corridors or other lower level components or units of operation are not reviewed by the Company's chief operating decision maker to make decisions about the allocation of resources to, or the assessment of performance of, such geographic areas, corridors, components or units of operation.

At December 31, 2007, one customer comprised 11.5 % (2006 – 11.5 %, 2005 – 14.5 %) of CP's total revenues. At December 31, 2007, accounts receivable from this customer represented 6.2 % (2006 – 5.6 %) of CP's "Accounts receivable and other current assets".

During 2005, the Company prospectively recorded a $23.4-million adjustment to increase revenues in 2005 related to services provided in 2004. The adjustment reflected a change in estimate primarily as a result of a contract settlement with a customer.

GEOGRAPHIC INFORMATION

(in millions of Canadian dollars)	Canada	United States	Total
2007			
Revenues	$ 3,716.4	$ 991.2	$ 4,707.6
Net properties	$ 7,745.1	$ 1,548.0	$ 9,293.1
2006			
Revenues	$ 3,575.1	$ 1,008.1	$ 4,583.2
Net properties	$ 7,539.3	$ 1,583.6	$ 9,122.9
2005			
Revenues	$ 3,404.1	$ 987.5	$ 4,391.6

The Company's accounts have been adjusted to reflect an accounting basis that is more comparable with that employed by other Class 1 railways in North America. CP's principal subsidiaries present unconsolidated financial statements in accordance with generally accepted accounting practices for railways as prescribed in the regulations of the Canadian Transportation Agency and the Surface Transportation Board in the United States.

The condensed income statement and balance sheet information, which follows, includes the Canadian operations prepared in accordance with the Uniform Classification of Accounts issued by the Canadian Transportation Agency. The changes required to consolidate the Company's operations are identified as consolidating entries.

CONSOLIDATING INFORMATION – 2007

(in millions of Canadian dollars)	Canada	United States	Other countries	Consolidating entries	Total
Revenues	$ 3,715.9	$ 991.2	$ –	$ 0.5	$ 4,707.6
Operating expenses	2,949.9	688.6	0.1	(95.2)	3,543.4
Operating income (loss)	766.0	302.6	(0.1)	95.7	1,164.2
Interest and other income and charges	230.7	43.8	(30.9)	(0.5)	243.1
Foreign exchange (gain) loss on long-term debt	(255.6)	–	84.4	1.4	(169.8)
Income taxes	99.8	89.5	0.7	(45.3)	144.7
Net income (loss)	$ 691.1	$ 169.3	$ (54.3)	$ 140.1	$ 946.2
Current assets	$ 1,014.1	$ 358.0	$ (89.8)	$ (114.6)	$ 1,167.7
Net properties	5,925.7	1,487.5	–	1,879.9	9,293.1
Other long-term assets	2,766.7	1,559.8	515.1	(1,937.4)	2,904.2
Total assets	$ 9,706.5	$ 3,405.3	$ 425.3	$ (172.1)	$ 13,365.0
Current liabilities	$ 1,158.7	$ 232.1	$ 0.3	$ (46.3)	$ 1,344.8
Long-term liabilities	5,648.9	1,809.0	–	(895.6)	6,562.3
Shareholders' equity	2,898.9	1,364.2	425.0	769.8	5,457.9
Total liabilities and shareholders' equity	$ 9,706.5	$ 3,405.3	$ 425.3	$ (172.1)	$ 13,365.0

CONSOLIDATING INFORMATION – 2006

(in millions of Canadian dollars)	Canada	United States	Other countries	Consolidating entries	Total
Revenues	$ 3,571.2	$ 1,008.1	$ –	$ 3.9	$ 4,583.2
Operating expenses	2,833.9	736.5	–	(115.8)	3,454.6
Operating income	737.3	271.6	–	119.7	1,128.6
Interest and other income and charges	196.5	42.0	(25.2)	9.0	222.3
Foreign exchange (gain) loss on long-term debt	1.2	–	(1.3)	0.2	0.1
Income taxes	69.6	86.7	0.5	(46.9)	109.9
Net income	$ 470.0	$ 142.9	$ 26.0	$ 157.4	$ 796.3
Current assets	$ 813.5	$ 293.2	$ 18.1	$ (119.9)	$ 1,004.9
Net properties	5,673.0	1,569.3	–	1,880.6	9,122.9
Other long-term assets	1,241.7	67.9	414.4	(435.9)	1,288.1
Total assets	$ 7,728.2	$ 1,930.4	$ 432.5	$ 1,324.8	$ 11,415.9
Current liabilities	$ 924.3	$ 227.7	$ 0.2	$ 86.8	$ 1,239.0
Long-term liabilities	4,299.0	1,076.2	–	(54.8)	5,320.4
Shareholders' equity	2,504.9	626.5	432.3	1,292.8	4,856.5
Total liabilities and shareholders' equity	$ 7,728.2	$ 1,930.4	$ 432.5	$ 1,324.8	$ 11,415.9

CONSOLIDATING INFORMATION – 2005

(in millions of Canadian dollars)	Canada	United States	Other countries	Consolidating entries	Total
Revenues	$ 3,397.9	$ 987.5	$ –	$ 6.2	$ 4,391.6
Operating expenses	2,731.1	779.0	–	(109.7)	3,400.4
Operating income	666.8	208.5	–	115.9	991.2
Interest and other income and charges	194.9	42.6	(22.1)	6.9	222.3
Foreign exchange (gain) loss on long-term debt	(53.8)	–	13.7	(4.6)	(44.7)
Income taxes	165.8	65.0	0.7	39.1	270.6
Net income	$ 359.9	$ 100.9	$ 7.7	$ 74.5	$ 543.0

24. Reconciliation of Canadian and United States generally accepted accounting principles

The consolidated financial statements of the Company have been prepared in accordance with GAAP in Canada. The material differences between Canadian and U.S. GAAP relating to measurement and recognition are explained below, along with their effect on the Company's Statement of Consolidated Income and Consolidated Balance Sheet. Certain additional disclosures required under U.S. GAAP have not been provided, as permitted by the United States Securities and Exchange Commission.

ACCOUNTING FOR DERIVATIVE INSTRUMENTS AND HEDGING

Effective January 1, 2007, the Company adopted the following CICA accounting standards Section 3855 "Financial Instruments, Recognition and Measurement", Section 3861 "Financial Instruments, Presentation and Disclosure", Section 3865 "Hedging", Section 1530 "Comprehensive Income" and Section 3251 "Equity" on a retrospective basis without restatement of prior periods, with the exception that "Foreign currency translation adjustments" was reclassified to "AOCI" and "Other comprehensive income", which largely harmonized the measurement and recognition rules for derivative instruments and hedging with U.S. GAAP. Transaction costs have been added to the fair value of the "Long-term debt" under Canadian GAAP whereas under U.S. GAAP such costs are recorded separately with "Other assets and deferred charges".

Prior to January 1, 2007, the Company followed the CICA Accounting Guideline No. 13 "Hedging Relationships" ("AcG 13"), which harmonized the documentation standards for financial instruments and hedging with U.S. GAAP, as required by Financial Accounting Standards Board ("FASB") Statement No. 133 "Accounting for Derivative Instruments and Hedging Activities" ("FASB 133"). Under both Canadian and U.S. GAAP, gains or losses were included in the income statement when the hedged transaction occurs. However, under U.S. GAAP, the ineffective portion of a hedging derivative was immediately recognized in income and the effective portion of changes in the fair value of derivatives that was designated and qualified as cash flow hedges were recorded as a component of AOCI. Changes in the fair value of derivatives that were designated and qualified as fair value hedges were recorded in income along with adjustments to the hedged item. Under Canadian GAAP, derivative instruments that qualified as hedges were not recorded on the balance sheet. Under U.S. GAAP, all derivative instruments were recognized on the balance sheet at fair value. Canadian GAAP required that gains and losses on derivatives meeting hedge accounting requirements be deferred and recognized when the hedged transaction occurs.

PENSIONS AND POST-RETIREMENT BENEFITS

The CICA Section 3461 "Employee Future Benefits" permits amortization of net actuarial gains and losses only if the unamortized portion of these gains and losses exceeds 10 % of the greater of the benefit obligation and the market-related value of the plan assets the ("corridor"). This harmonized the Canadian GAAP treatment with FASB Statement No. 87 "Employers' Accounting for Pensions" ("FASB 87") and FASB Statement No. 106 "Employers' Accounting for Post-retirement Benefits Other Than Pensions" ("FASB 106").

Prior to January 1, 2000, all actuarial gains and losses were amortized under Canadian GAAP. Upon transition to the CICA Section 3461 effective January 1, 2000, all unamortized gains and losses, including prior service costs, were accumulated into a net transitional asset, which is being amortized to income over approximately 13 years. This created a difference with U.S. GAAP in 2007, 2006 and 2005, under which prior service costs continued to be amortized over the expected average remaining service period and all other net gains accumulated prior to January 1, 2000, fell within the corridor. In 2007, 2006 and 2005, the difference was reduced due to amortization of losses outside the corridor for Canadian GAAP (see Note 20).

FASB Statement No. 158 "Employers' Accounting for Defined Benefit Pension and Other Postretirement Plans, an amendment of FASB Statements No. 87, 88, 106 and 123R" ("FASB 158") requires that the over or under funded status of defined benefit pension and other post-retirement plans be recognized on the balance sheet. FASB 158 became effective for years ending after December 15, 2006. The over or under funded status is measured as the difference between the fair value of the plan assets and the benefit obligation, being the projected benefit obligation for pension plans and the accumulated benefit obligation for other post-retirement plans. In addition, any previously unrecognized actuarial gains and losses and prior service costs and credits that arise during the period will be recognized as a component of other comprehensive loss, net of tax. Under Canadian GAAP, the over or under funded status of defined benefit plans are not recognized on the balance sheet, nor does Canadian GAAP currently require the recognition of other comprehensive loss related to defined benefit pension and other post-retirement plans.

Adoption of FASB 158 on a prospective basis at December 31, 2006 resulted in a reduction in "Other assets and deferred charges" of $881.9 million, an increase in "Deferred liabilities" of $345.3 million, a reduction in "AOCI" of $838.8 million and an increase in deferred income tax assets of $388.4 million. The adoption of FASB 158 was reflected as an adjustment to closing "AOCI" at December 31, 2006. In addition, the "Minimum pension liability" of $43.6 million and an intangible asset of $3.9 million at December 31, 2006, with an associated $25.7 million (after tax) balance in "AOCI", was reclassified to "Unfunded status of defined benefit pension and post-retirement plans". Prior periods have not been restated.

Prior to the adoption of FASB 158 in 2006, and in accordance with FASB 87, an additional minimum pension liability was required for unfunded plans. The additional minimum pension liability represented the excess of the unfunded accumulated benefit obligation over previously recorded pension cost liabilities and was also charged directly to shareholders' equity, net of related deferred income taxes.

Under Canadian GAAP, there is no requirement to set up an unfunded pension liability based on an annual funded position test.

POST-EMPLOYMENT BENEFITS

Post-employment benefits are covered by the CICA recommendations for accounting for employee future benefits. Consistent with accounting for post-retirement benefits, the policy permits amortization of actuarial gains and losses only if they fall outside of the corridor. Under FASB Statement No. 112 "Employers' Accounting for Post-employment Benefits" ("FASB 112"), such gains and losses on post employment benefits that do not vest or accumulate are included immediately in income.

TERMINATION AND SEVERANCE BENEFITS

Termination and severance benefits are covered by the CICA Section 3461 and the CICA Emerging Issues Committee Abstract 134 "Accounting for Severance and Termination Benefits" ("EIC 134"). Upon transition to the CICA Section 3461 effective January 1, 2000, a net transitional asset was created and is being amortized to income over approximately 13 years. Under U.S. GAAP, the expected benefits were not accrued and are expensed when paid.

STOCK-BASED COMPENSATION

FASB issued a revision to Statement No. 123 "Share-based Payment" ("FASB 123R") which was effective for CP from January 1, 2006. FASB 123R requires the use of an option-pricing model to fair value, at the grant date, share-based awards issued to employees, including stock options, SARs and DSUs. SARs and DSUs are subsequently re-measured at fair value at each reporting period. Under Canadian GAAP, liability awards, such as SARs and DSUs, are accounted for using the intrinsic method. FASB 123R also requires that CP account for forfeitures on an estimated basis. Under Canadian GAAP, CP has elected to account for forfeitures on an actual basis as they occur. CP adopted FASB 123R on January 1, 2006 without restatement of prior periods using the modified prospective approach. In addition, on adoption of FASB 123R, CP has recognized compensation cost attributable to stock-based awards over the period from the grant date to the date the employee becomes eligible to retire when this is shorter than the vesting period (the "non-substantive vesting period approach").

Previously CP recognized the compensation cost over the vesting period (the "nominal vesting period approach"). Canadian GAAP has similar provisions for the recognition of the compensation cost attributable to stock-based awards over the shorter of the period from grant date to vesting or eligibility for retirement. However, Canadian GAAP introduced these provisions with effect for the year ended December 31, 2006 and the Company adopted them with retroactive restatement of prior periods.

As a result of the adoption of FASB 123R, CP recorded a charge against income in 2006 of $3.0 million ($2.0 million net of tax) as a cumulative effect of the change in accounting principle and 2006 "Compensation and benefit" expense was decreased by $1.5 million ($0.9 million net of tax). There was no impact to cash flow amounts as a result of the adoption of FASB 123R.

Under FASB Interpretation No. 44 "Accounting for Certain Transactions Involving Stock Compensation" ("FIN 44"), compensation expense must be recorded if the intrinsic value of stock options is not exactly the same immediately before and after an equity restructuring. As a result of the CPL corporate reorganization in 2001, CPL underwent an equity restructuring, which resulted in replacement options in CPRL stock having a different intrinsic value after the restructuring than prior to it. Canadian GAAP did not require the revaluation of these options. The Company adopted on a prospective basis effective January 2003 the CICA Section 3870 "Stock-based Compensation and Other Stock-based Payments", which requires companies to account for stock options at their fair value. Concurrently, the Company elected to adopt the fair value option under FASB Statement No. 123 "Accounting for Stock-based Compensation" ("FASB 123").

INTERNAL USE SOFTWARE

Under the American Institute of Certified Public Accountants Statement of Position No. 98-1 "Accounting for the Costs of Computer Software Developed or Obtained for Internal Use" ("SOP 98-1"), certain costs, including preliminary project phase costs, are to be expensed as incurred. These costs are capitalized under Canadian GAAP.

CAPITALIZATION OF INTEREST

The Company expenses interest related to capital projects undertaken during the year unless specific debt is attributed to a capital program. FASB Statement No. 34 "Capitalization of Interest Cost" ("FASB 34") requires interest costs to be capitalized for all capital programs. Differences in GAAP result in additional capitalization of interest under U.S. GAAP and subsequent related depreciation.

COMPREHENSIVE INCOME

Under U.S. GAAP, all derivative instruments are recognized on the balance sheet as either an asset or a liability measured at fair value. Changes in the fair value of derivatives are either recognized in earnings or in other comprehensive loss depending on whether specific hedge criteria are met. On January 1, 2007, the Company adopted the equivalent Canadian standard for comprehensive income on a prospective basis, which is largely harmonized with FASB Statement No. 130 "Reporting Comprehensive Income" ("FASB 130").

FASB 130 requires disclosure of the change in equity from transactions and other events related to non-owner sources during the period. In 2007 and the comparative periods presented, other comprehensive loss arose from foreign currency translation on the net investment in self-sustaining foreign subsidiaries, foreign currency translation related to long-term debt designated as a hedge of the net investment in self-sustaining foreign subsidiaries, unfunded pension liability (minimum pension liability in 2005) and changes in the fair value of derivative instruments. In 2006, the Company made an adjustment to reduce deferred income tax liability and reduce deferred income tax expense included in "Other comprehensive loss" by $54.6 million for amounts accumulated in "Other comprehensive loss" prior to 2003.

JOINT VENTURE

The CICA Section 3055 "Interest in Joint Ventures" requires the proportionate consolidation method to be applied to the recognition of interests in joint ventures in consolidated financial statements. The Company has a joint-venture interest in the DRTP. FASB Accounting Principles Board Opinion No. 18 "The Equity Method of Accounting for Investments in Common Stock" ("APB 18") requires the equity method of accounting to be applied to interests in joint ventures. This has no effect on net income as it represents a classification difference within the income statement and balance sheet. Equity income from DRTP in 2007 was $10.5 million (2006 – $11.2 million, 2005 – $8.2 million).

OFFSETTING CONTRACTS

FASB Financial Interpretation No. 39 "Offsetting of Amounts Relating to Certain Contracts" ("FIN 39") does not allow netting of assets and liabilities among three parties. In 2003, the Company and one of its subsidiaries entered into a contract with a financial institution. Under Canadian GAAP, offsetting amounts with the same party and with a legal right to offset are netted against each other.

START-UP COSTS

Under EIC 27 "Revenues and Expenditures during the Pre-operating Period", costs incurred for projects under development may be deferred until the projects are substantially complete. Upon completion, these costs are amortized based on the expected period and pattern of benefit of the expenditures. Under U.S. GAAP, these costs are to be expensed as incurred.

UNCERTAINTY IN TAX POSITIONS

In July 2006, FASB issued FASB Interpretation No. 48 "Accounting for Uncertainty in Income Tax Positions" ("FIN 48") introducing recognition and measurement criteria for income tax positions. An income tax position is a position taken in a filed tax return or a position that will be taken in a future tax return which has been reflected in the recognition and measurement of income or deferred tax assets or liabilities. Under the provisions of FIN 48 a tax position must be evaluated using a more likely than not recognition threshold based on the technical merits of the position and can only be recognized if it is more likely than not that this position will be sustainable on audit. If the position does not meet this threshold, no amount may be accrued. Additionally, the recognized tax position will be measured at the largest amount that is greater than 50 % likely to be realized on settlement. FIN 48 is effective for the Company commencing on January 1, 2007. The adoption of FIN 48 had no impact on the financial statements of the Company.

CAPITAL LEASES

Under FASB Statement No. 13 "Accounting for Leases" ("FASB 13"), which prescribes certain recognition criteria for a capital lease, certain leases, which the Company has recorded as capital leases under Canadian GAAP, do not meet the criteria for capital leases and are recorded as operating leases.

STATEMENT OF CASH FLOWS

There are no material differences in the Statement of Consolidated Cash Flows under U.S. GAAP.

FUTURE ACCOUNTING CHANGES

Measurement date of defined benefit pension

FASB 158 also requires, effective in 2008, that pension and other post-retirement benefit plans be measured as of the balance sheet date. The Company's Canadian plans are already measured as of the balance sheet date, however, the U.S. pension plans currently have a November 30 measurement date. FASB 158 provides two approaches to transition to a fiscal year-end measurement date, both of which are applied prospectively. Under the first approach, the plan assets are measured on November 30, 2007, and then re-measured on January 1, 2008. Under the alternative approach, the plan assets are measured on November 30, 2007 and the next re-measurement is not until December 31, 2008. CP plans has elected to adopt this change in measurement date using the latter approach. The impact of adopting a plan measurement date at the balance sheet date for the Company's U.S. plans is not anticipated to be material in 2008.

Fair value measurement

In September 2006, FASB issued FASB No. 157 "Fair Value Measurement" ("FASB 157"). This Statement provides guidance for using fair values to measure assets and liabilities. Under the standard, the definition of fair value focuses on the price that would be received to sell the asset or paid to transfer the liability (an exit price), not the price that would be paid to acquire the asset or received to assume the liability (an entry price). FASB 157 clarifies that fair value is a market-based measurement, not an entity-specific measurement, and sets out a fair value hierarchy with the highest priority being quoted prices in active markets and the lowest priority being company specific unobservable data. FASB 157 is effective January 1, 2008. The potential impact of adoption on the Company's financial statements is not anticipated to be material.

Fair value option for financial assets and financial liabilities

In February 2007, FASB issued FASB No. 159 "The Fair Value Option for Financial Assets and Financial Liabilities" ("FASB 159"). This standard permits an entity to irrevocably elect fair value on a contract by contract basis as the initial and subsequent measurement attribute for many financial instruments and certain other items. An entity electing the fair value option would be required to recognize changes in fair value in earnings. FASB 159 is effective January 1, 2008. At this time the Company has not elected to account for any instruments at fair value under the fair value option of FASB 159.

Business combinations

In December 2007, FASB issued FASB Statement No. 141 (revised 2007) "Business Combinations" ("FASB 141(revised)") which replaces FASB Statement No. 141 "Business Combinations". The new standard requires the acquiring entity in a business combination to recognize all the assets acquired and liabilities assumed in the transaction; and recognize and measure the goodwill acquired in the business combination or a gain from a bargain purchase. FASB 141 (revised) will be applied prospectively to business combinations for which the acquisition date is on or after January 1, 2009. The adoption of this accounting standard will not impact the current financial statements of the Company.

Non-controlling interests in consolidated financial statements

In December 2007, FASB issued FASB Statement No. 160 "Non-controlling Interests in Consolidated Financial Statements" ("FASB 160") which requires the Company to report non-controlling interests in subsidiaries as equity in the consolidated financial statements; and all transactions between an entity and non-controlling interests as equity transactions. FASB 160 is effective for the Company commencing on January 1, 2009 and its adoption is unlikely to impact the financial statements of the Company at that time.

COMPARATIVE INCOME STATEMENT

Consolidated net income and Other comprehensive loss is reconciled from Canadian to U.S. GAAP in the following manner:

(in millions of Canadian dollars, except per share data)	2007	2006	2005
Net income – Canadian GAAP	$ **946.2**	$ 796.3	$ 543.0
Increased (decreased) by:			
Pension costs	**5.8**	5.1	7.7
Post-retirement benefits costs	**9.4**	9.1	9.2
Post-employment benefits costs	**7.2**	6.7	(4.0)
Termination and severance benefits	**(8.8)**	(8.2)	(9.4)
Internal use software – additions	**(12.0)**	(9.2)	(9.8)
Internal use software – depreciation	**8.0**	7.1	6.1
Stock-based compensation	**(1.7)**	(3.0)	(3.4)
Loss on ineffective portion of hedges	**(0.4)**	(0.9)	(6.6)
Capitalized interest – additions	**14.0**	4.1	4.4
Capitalized interest – depreciation	**(4.5)**	(3.9)	(3.9)
Start-up costs	**(0.8)**	(10.8)	–
Fair value of financial instruments	**–**	(2.3)	–
Future/deferred income tax expense related to net income	**(40.7)**	(19.0)	1.7
Income before cumulative catch-up adjustment	**921.7**	771.1	535.0
Cumulative catch-up adjustment on adoption of FASB 123R, net of tax	**–**	(2.0)	–
Net income – U.S. GAAP	$ **921.7**	$ 769.1	$ 535.0
Other comprehensive loss – Canadian GAAP	**(40.8)**	(1.1)	(9.5)
Increased (decreased) by:			
Unrealized foreign exchange gain on designated net investment hedge	**0.4**	0.6	4.8
Unfunded pension and post-retirement liability adjustment	**(186.6)**	–	–
Minimum pension liability adjustment	**–**	783.3	(254.3)
Change in fair value of derivative instruments	**–**	16.6	86.5
Gain on derivative instruments realized in net income	**–**	(42.5)	(55.9)
Future (deferred) income tax recovery (expense) related to other comprehensive loss	**35.7**	(210.7)	76.6
Other comprehensive (loss) income – U.S. GAAP	$ **(191.3)**	$ 546.2	$ (151.8)
Earnings per share – U.S. GAAP			
Basic earnings per share before cumulative catch-up adjustment on adoption of FASB 123R, net of tax	$ **5.98**	$ 4.90	$ 3.38
Basic earnings per share after cumulative catch-up adjustment on adoption of FASB 123R, net of tax	$ **5.98**	$ 4.89	$ 3.38
Diluted earnings per share before cumulative catch-up adjustment on adoption of FASB 123R, net of tax	$ **5.92**	$ 4.86	$ 3.34
Diluted earnings per share after cumulative catch-up adjustment on adoption of FASB 123R, net of tax	$ **5.92**	$ 4.84	$ 3.34

A summary of comprehensive income resulting from Canadian and U.S. GAAP differences is as follows:

(in millions of Canadian dollars)		2007		2006		2005
Comprehensive income						
Canadian GAAP	$	905.4	$	795.2	$	533.5
U.S. GAAP	$	730.4	$	1,315.3	$	383.2

A summary of operating income resulting from Canadian and U.S. GAAP differences is as follows:

(in millions of Canadian dollars)		2007		2006		2005
Operating income						
Canadian GAAP	$	1,164.2	$	1,128.6	$	991.2
U.S. GAAP	$	1,166.5	$	1,122.3	$	981.5

The differences between U.S. and Canadian GAAP operating income are itemized in the comparative net income reconciliation, excluding the effect of future income taxes.

2007
ANNUAL
REPORT

105

802   Appendix B

NEL

CONSOLIDATED BALANCE SHEET

Had the Consolidated Balance Sheet been prepared under U.S. GAAP, the differences would have been as follows (higher/(lower)):

(in millions of Canadian dollars)	2007	2006
Assets		
Current assets		
Cash		
Investment in joint ventures	$ (0.2)	$ (0.4)
Accounts receivable and other current assets		
Investment in joint ventures	1.4	1.9
Long-term assets		
Investments		
Investment in joint ventures	48.9	87.8
Capital commitments and mortgages	–	(2.3)
Start-up costs	(11.6)	(10.8)
Properties		
Capitalized interest	160.0	150.4
Internal use software	(55.2)	(51.2)
Investment in joint ventures	(36.1)	(71.5)
Capital leases	(10.4)	–
Other assets and deferred charges		
Pension	(1,103.1)	(1,079.7)
Long-term receivable (FIN 39)	190.3	179.5
Derivative instruments	–	31.7
Transaction costs on long-term debt	36.0	–
Investment in joint ventures	(14.8)	(22.2)
Total assets	$ (794.8)	$ (786.8)

106
2007
ANNUAL
REPORT

NEL

Canadian Pacific Railway 2007 Annual Report   **803**

CONSOLIDATED BALANCE SHEET (CONTINUED)

(in millions of Canadian dollars)	2007	2006
Liabilities and shareholders' equity		
Current liabilities		
Accounts payable and accrued liabilities		
Investment in joint ventures	$ (0.4)	$ (1.3)
Income and other taxes payable		
Investment in joint ventures	(0.1)	(0.2)
Long-term debt maturing within one year		
Capital leases	(0.7)	–
Long-term liabilities		
Deferred liabilities		
Termination and severance benefits	(10.2)	(19.0)
Post-employment benefit liability	5.2	16.4
Under funded status of defined benefit pension and other post-retirement plans	573.0	421.0
Derivative instruments	–	4.8
Investment in joint ventures	(0.5)	(2.7)
Stock-based compensation	0.2	(0.6)
Long-term debt		
Marked-to-market hedged portion of debt	–	(2.8)
Bank loan (FIN 39)	190.3	179.5
Capital leases	(9.7)	–
Transaction costs on long-term debt	36.0	–
Future/deferred income tax liability	(441.2)	(437.2)
Total liabilities	341.9	157.9
Shareholders' equity		
Share capital		
Stock-based compensation	20.9	16.9
Contributed surplus		
Stock-based compensation	5.2	8.3
Retained income	(156.8)	(128.4)
Accumulated other comprehensive income		
Foreign currency translation adjustments	–	(2.1)
Funding status of defined benefit pension and other post-retirement plans	(1,010.2)	(858.8)
Derivative instruments (FASB 133)	4.2	19.4
Total liabilities and shareholders' equity	$ (794.8)	$ (786.8)

FIVE-YEAR SUMMARY

(in millions)	2007		2006		2005 [1]		2004 [1]		2003 [1] [2]
Income Statement									
Revenues									
Freight									
Grain	$	938.9	$	904.6	$	754.5	$	668.2	$	644.4
Coal		573.6		592.0		728.8		530.3		444.0
Sulphur and fertilizers		502.0		439.3		447.1		460.0		417.4
Forest products		275.8		316.4		333.9		322.0		328.8
Industrial and consumer products [3]		627.9		603.8		542.9		481.4		459.9
Intermodal [3]		1,318.0		1,256.8		1,161.1		1,034.7		926.4
Automotive		319.0		314.4		298.0		288.5		304.2
		4,555.2		4,427.3		4,266.3		3,785.1		3,525.1
Other [3] [4] [6]		152.4		155.9		125.3		117.8		135.6
Total revenues [4] [6]		4,707.6		4,583.2		4,391.6		3,902.9		3,660.7
Operating expenses									
Compensation and benefits		1,284.2		1,327.6		1,322.1		1,261.5		1,166.4
Fuel		746.8		650.5		588.0		440.0		393.6
Materials		215.5		212.9		203.3		178.5		179.2
Equipment rents		207.5		181.2		210.0		218.5		238.5
Depreciation		472.0		464.1		445.1		407.1		372.3
Purchased services and other		617.4		618.3		621.6		610.7		583.6
Total operating expenses, before other specified items [4] [6]		3,543.4		3,454.6		3,390.1		3,116.3		2,933.6
Operating income, before other specified items [4] [6]		1,164.2		1,128.6		1,001.5		786.6		727.1
Other income and charges, before foreign exchange gains and losses on long-term debt and other specified items [4] [5] [6]		17.3		27.8		18.1		36.1		33.5
Interest expense		204.3		194.5		204.2		218.6		218.7
Income tax expense, before foreign exchange gains and losses on long-term debt and income tax on other specified items [4] [5] [6]		269.8		278.8		250.8		172.4		147.0
Income, before foreign exchange gains and losses on long-term debt and other specified items [4] [5] [6]		672.8		627.5		528.4		359.5		327.9
Foreign exchange gain (loss) on long-term debt (net of income tax) [5]		125.5		(7.2)		22.3		94.4		224.4
Other specified items (net of income tax) [4]		147.9		176.0		(7.7)		(42.8)		(153.2)
Net income	$	946.2	$	796.3	$	543.0	$	411.1	$	399.1

108
2007
ANNUAL
REPORT

NEL

Canadian Pacific Railway 2007 Annual Report   805

(1) Certain comparative period figures have been restated for retroactive application of a new accounting pronouncement on stock-based compensation for employees eligible to retire before vesting date.

(2) Restated. Effective January 1, 2004, CP adopted retroactively with restatement the Canadian Institute of Chartered Accountants' new accounting standard for asset retirement obligations.

(3) In 2005, CP reclassified from "Other" revenue certain intermodal-related revenue items consisting of container storage revenue and terminal service fees as part of the intermodal line of business. Also, items relating to food and consumer products have been reclassed from the intermodal group to the renamed Industrial and Consumer Products group.

(4) Before other specified items as follows: For 2007, a $162.9 million income tax benefit was recorded due to Federal income tax rate reductions which was offset by a $21.5 million change in estimated fair value of Canadian third party asset-backed commercial paper ($15.0 million after tax); for 2006, a $176.0-million income tax benefit was recorded due to Federal and Provincial income tax rate reductions; for 2005, a $33.9-million ($20.6 million after tax) reduction to environmental remediation and a $44.2-million ($28.3 million after tax) special charge for labour restructuring; for 2004, a $19.0-million ($12.4 million after tax) reduction of a labour restructuring liability and a $90.9-million ($55.2 million after tax) special charge for environmental remediation; for 2003, a $215.1-million ($141.4 million after tax) special charge for labour restructuring and asset impairment, a $28.9-million ($18.4 million after tax) for a loss on transfer of assets to an outsourcing firm, a $59.3-million favourable adjustment related to the revaluation of future income taxes, and an unfavourable impact of $52.7 million for an increase in future income taxes resulting from the repeal of previously legislated income tax reductions.

(5) Before foreign exchange gain (loss) on long-term debt as follows: For 2007, a $169.8 million ($125.5 million after tax) foreign exchange gain on long-term debt; for 2006, a $0.1-million ($7.2 million after tax) foreign exchange loss on long-term debt; for 2005, a $44.7-million ($22.3 million after tax) foreign exchange gain on long-term debt; for 2004, a $94.4-million ($94.4 million after tax) foreign exchange gain on long-term debt; for 2003, a $209.5-million ($224.4 million after tax) foreign exchange gain on long-term debt.

(6) These are earnings measures that are not in accordance with GAAP and may not be comparable to similar measures of other companies. CP's results, before foreign exchange gains and losses and other specified items as defined in this summary, are presented to provide the reader with information that is readily comparable to prior years' results. By excluding foreign exchange gains and losses on long-term debt, the impact of volatile short-term exchange rate fluctuations, which can only be realized when long-term debt matures or is settled, is largely eliminated. By also excluding other specified items, the results better reflect ongoing operations at CP.

2007
ANNUAL
REPORT

109

806   **Appendix B**

NEL

SHAREHOLDER INFORMATION

COMMON SHARE MARKET PRICES

	2007		2006	
Toronto Stock Exchange (Canadian dollars)	**High**	**Low**	High	Low
First Quarter	66.33	60.06	60.85	45.55
Second Quarter	78.48	63.75	65.17	52.55
Third Quarter	91.00	67.37	57.97	51.05
Fourth Quarter	73.00	59.48	65.29	54.95
Year	91.00	59.48	65.29	45.55
New York Stock Exchange (U.S. dollars)	**High**	**Low**	High	Low
First Quarter	56.61	51.23	53.00	39.10
Second Quarter	73.95	55.36	57.73	47.10
Third Quarter	87.23	62.66	52.17	44.85
Fourth Quarter	74.38	60.31	57.32	48.75
Year	87.23	51.23	57.73	39.10

Number of registered shareholders at year end	18,152
Market prices at year end	
Toronto Stock Exchange	CDN$ 64.22
New York Stock Exchange	US$ 64.64

SHAREHOLDER ADMINISTRATION

Common Shares

Computershare Investor Services Inc., with transfer facilities in Montreal, Toronto, Calgary and Vancouver, serves as transfer agent and registrar for the Common Shares in Canada. Computershare Trust Company NA, Denver, Colorado, serves as co-transfer agent and co-registrar for the Common Shares in the United States.

For information concerning dividends, lost share certificates, estate transfers or for change in share registration or address, please contact the transfer agent and registrar by telephone at 1-877-427-7245 toll free North America or International (514) 982-7555, visit their website at www.computershare.com; or write to:

Computershare Investor Services Inc.
100 University Avenue, 9th Floor
Toronto, Ontario Canada M5J 2Y1

Glossary

Accelerated depreciation A higher amount of depreciation is recorded in the early years and a lower amount in the later years. (p. 354)

Account Record used to accumulate amounts for each individual asset, liability, revenue, expense, and component of owners' equity. (p. 102)

Accounting The process of identifying, measuring, and communicating economic information to various users. (p. 11)

Accounting controls Procedures concerned with safeguarding the assets or the reliability of the financial statements. (p. 316)

Accounting cycle A series of steps performed each period and culminating with the preparation of a set of financial statements. (p. 161)

Accounting system Methods and records used to accurately report an entity's transactions and to maintain accountability for its assets and liabilities. (p. 315)

Accounts payable Amounts owed for inventory, goods, or services acquired in the normal course of business. (p. 403)

Accounts payable turnover ratio A measure of the number of times accounts payable are paid in a period. (p. 640)

Accounts receivable turnover ratio A measure of the number of times accounts receivable are collected in a period. (p. 638)

Accrual basis A system of accounting in which revenues are recognized when earned and expenses when incurred. (p. 147)

Accrued asset An asset resulting from the recognition of a revenue before the receipt of cash. (p. 156)

Accrued liability A liability resulting from the recognition of an expense before the payment of cash. (p. 156)

Accrued pension cost The difference between the amount of pension recorded as an expense and the amount of the funding payment. (p. 493)

Acid-test or quick ratio A stricter test of liquidity than the current ratio; it excludes inventory and prepayments from the numerator. (p. 637)

Acquisition cost The amount that includes all of the costs normally necessary to acquire an asset and prepare it for its intended use. (p. 350)

Additional paid-in capital An amount received that is greater than the par value of the shares when the shares were issued. (p. 522)

Adjusting entries Journal entries made at the end of a period by a company using the accrual basis of accounting. (p. 149)

Administrative controls Procedures concerned with efficient operation of the business and adherence to managerial policies. (p. 316)

Aging schedule A form used to categorize the various individual accounts receivable according to the length of time each has been outstanding. (p. 310)

Allowance method A method of estimating bad debts on the basis of either the net credit sales of the period or the accounts receivable at the end of the period. (p. 307)

Annuity A series of payments of equal amounts. (p. 428)

Asset A future economic benefit. (p. 10)

Asset turnover ratio The relationship between net sales and average total assets. (p. 646)

Audit committee Board of directors subset that acts as a direct contact between shareholders and the independent accounting firm. (p. 315)

Auditing The process of examining the financial statements and the underlying records of a company in order to render an opinion as to whether the statements are fairly represented. (p. 22)

Auditors' report The opinion rendered by a public accounting firm concerning the fairness of the presentation of the financial statements. (p. 23)

Authorized shares The maximum number of shares a corporation may issue as indicated in the corporate charter. (p. 520)

Available-for-sale investments Shares and bonds that are not classified as either held-to-maturity or for trading investments. (p. 321)

Balance sheet The financial statement that summarizes the assets, liabilities, and owners' equity at a specific point in time. (p. 14)

Bank reconciliation A form used by the accountant to reconcile the balance shown on the bank statement for a particular account with the balance shown in the accounting records. (p. 300)

Bank statement A detailed list, provided by the bank, of all the activity for a particular account during the month. (p. 299)

Board of directors Group composed of key officers of a corporation and outside members responsible for general oversight of the affairs of the entity. (p. 315)

Bond A certificate that represents a corporation's promise to repay a certain amount of money and interest in the future. (p. 7)

Bond issue price The present value of the annuity of interest payments plus the present value of the principal. (p. 466)

Book value The original cost of an asset minus the amount of accumulated depreciation. (p. 353)

Book value per share Total shareholders' equity divided by the number of common shares outstanding. (p. 533)

Callable bonds Bonds that may be redeemed or retired before their specified due date. (p. 464)

Callable feature Allows the firm to eliminate a class of shares by paying the shareholders a specified amount. (p. 523)

Canadian Academic Accounting Association The professional organization for accounting educators. (p. 23)

Capital expenditure A cost that improves the capital asset and is added to the capital asset account. (p. 361)

Capitalization of interest Interest on constructed capital assets is added to the capital asset account. (p. 352)

Capital lease A lease that is recorded as an asset by the lessee. (p. 478)

Capital stock Indicates the owners' contributions to a corporation. (p. 8)

Carrying value The face value of a bond plus the amount of unamortized premium or minus the amount of unamortized discount. (p. 470)

Cash basis A system of accounting in which revenues are recognized when cash is received and expenses when cash is paid. (p. 147)

Cash equivalent An investment that is readily convertible to a known amount of cash and with a maturity to the investor of three months or less. (p. 297)

Cash Flow Adequacy Gauges the cash available to meet future debt obligations. (p. 597)

Cash flow from operations to capital expenditures ratio A measure of the ability of a company to finance long-term asset aquisition with cash from operations. (p. 644)

Cash flow from operations to current liabilities ratio A measure of the ability to pay current debts from operating cash flows. (p. 637)

Cash to cash operating cycle The length of time from the purchase of inventory to the collection of any receivable from the sale. (p. 641)

Change in estimate A change in the life of the asset or in its residual value. (p. 359)

Chart of accounts A numerical list of all the accounts used by a company. (p. 102)

CIF destination point Terms that require the seller to pay for the cost of shipping the merchandise to the buyer. (p. 249)

Closing entries Journal entries made at the end of the period to return the balance in all temporary accounts to zero and transfer the net income or loss and the dividends to Retained Earnings. (p. 162)

Comparability For accounting information, the quality that allows a user to analyze two or more companies and look for similarities and differences. (p. 55)

Compensated absences Employee absences for which the employee will be paid. (p. 412)

Compound interest Interest calculated on the principal plus previous amounts of interest. (p. 420)

Comprehensive income The total change in net assets from all sources except investments by or distributions to the owners. (p. 531)

Consistency For accounting information, the quality that allows a user to compare two or more accounting periods for a single company. (p. 56)

Contingent asset An existing condition for which the outcome is not known but by which the company stands to gain. (p. 416)

Contingent liability An existing condition for which the outcome is not known but depends on some future event. (p. 412)

Contra account An account with a balance that is opposite that of a related account. (p. 151)

Control account The general ledger account that is supported by a subsidiary ledger. (p. 305)

Controller The chief accounting officer for a company. (p. 21)

Convertible feature Allows preferred shares to be exchanged for common shares. (p. 523)

Corporation A form of entity organized under the laws of a particular province or the federal government; ownership is evidenced by shares. (p. 7)

Cost of goods available for sale Beginning inventory plus cost of goods purchased. (p. 214)

Cost of goods sold Cost of goods available for sale minus ending inventory. (p. 215)

Cost principle Assets recorded at the cost to acquire them. (p. 19)

Credit An entry on the right side of an account. (p. 104)

Credit card draft A multiple-copy document used by a company that accepts a credit card for a sale. (p. 312)

Creditor Someone to whom a company or person has a debt. (p. 10)

Cumulative feature The right to dividends in arrears before the current-year dividend is distributed. (p. 523)

Current asset An asset that is expected to be realized in cash or sold or consumed during the operating cycle or within one year if the cycle is shorter than one year. (p. 59)

Current liability An obligation that will be satisfied within the next operating cycle or within one year if the cycle is shorter than one year. (pp. 62, 402)

Current portion of long-term debt The portion of a long-term liability that will be paid within one year. (p. 406)

Current ratio Current assets divided by current liabilities. (pp. 63, 636)

Debenture bonds Bonds that are not backed by specific collateral. (p. 462)

Debit An entry on the left side of an account. (p. 104)

Debt service coverage ratio A statement of cash flows measure of the ability of a company to meet its interest and principal payments. (p. 643)

Debt-to-equity ratio The ratio of total liabilities to total shareholders' equity. (p. 642)

Deposit in transit A deposit recorded on the books but not yet reflected on the bank statement. (p. 299)

Depreciation The process of allocating the cost of a long-term tangible asset over its useful life. (pp. 55, 151, 353)

Direct method For preparing the Operating Activities section of the statement of cash flows, the approach in which cash receipts and cash payments are reported. (p. 577)

Direct write-off method The recognition of bad debts expense at the point an account is written off as uncollectible. (p. 306)

Discontinued operations A line item on the income statement to reflect any gains or losses from the disposal of a segment of the business as well as any net income or loss from operating that segment. (p. 218)

Discount The excess of the face value of bonds over the issue price. (p. 467)

Discount on notes payable A contra-liability that represents interest deducted from a loan in advance. (p. 405)

Dividend payout ratio The annual dividend amount divided by the annual net income. (p. 526)

Dividends A distribution of the net income of a business to its owners. (p. 14)

Double declining-balance method Depreciation is recorded at twice the straight-line rate, but the balance is reduced each period. (p. 354)

Double-entry system A system of accounting in which every transaction is recorded with equal debits and credits and the accounting equation is kept in balance. (p. 107)

Earnings per share A company's bottom line stated on a per-share basis. (p. 648)

Economic entity concept The assumption that a single, identifiable unit must be accounted for in all situations. (p. 6)

Effective interest method of amortization The process of transferring a portion of the premium or discount to interest expense; this method results in a constant effective interest rate. (p. 470)

Estimated liability A contingent liability that is accrued and reflected on the balance sheet. (p. 413)

Event A happening of consequence to an entity. (p. 94)

Expense Outflows of assets resulting from the sale of goods and services. (p. 10)

External event An event involving interaction between an entity and its environment. (p. 94)

Extraordinary item A line item on the income statement to reflect any gains or losses that arise from an event that is both unusual in nature and infrequent in occurrence, and independent of management decisions (p. 218)

Face rate of interest The rate of interest on the bond certificate. (p. 465)

Face value The principal amount of the bond as stated on the bond certificate. (p. 462)

FIFO method An inventory costing method that assigns the most recent costs to ending inventory. (p. 254)

Financial accounting The branch of accounting concerned with the preparation of financial statements for outsider use. (p. 12)

Financial Accounting Standards Board (FASB) The group in the private sector with authority to set accounting standards. (p. 21)

Financing activities Activities concerned with the raising and repayment of funds in the form of debt and equity. (p. 575)

FOB shipping point Terms that require the buyer to pay for the shipping costs. (p. 249)

Free cash flow Cash available for expansion, debt reduction, and paying dividends. (p. 596)

Funding payment A payment made by the employer to the pension fund or its trustee. (p. 492)

Future Tax The account used to reconcile the difference between the amount recorded as income tax expense and the amount that is payable as income tax. (p. 486)

Future value of an annuity Amount accumulated in the future when a series of payments is invested and accrues interest. (p. 428)

Future value of a single amount Amount accumulated at a future time from a single payment or investment. (p. 421)

Gain on sale of asset The excess of the selling price over the asset's book value. (p. 365)

Gain or loss on redemption The difference between the carrying value and the redemption price at the time bonds are redeemed. (p. 474)

General journal The journal used in place of a specialized journal. (p. 107)

Generally accepted accounting principles (GAAP) The various methods, rules, practices, and other procedures that have evolved over time in response to the need to regulate the preparation of financial statements. (p. 20)

Going concern The assumption that an entity is not in the process of liquidation and that it will continue indefinitely. (p. 19)

Goodwill The excess of the purchase price of a business over the total market value of identifiable assets. (p. 369)

Gross profit Sales less cost of goods sold. (p. 210)

Gross profit method A technique used to establish an estimate of the cost of inventory stolen, destroyed, or otherwise damaged, or of the amount of inventory on hand at an interim date. (p. 263)

Gross profit margin Gross profit to net sales. (p. 633)

Gross wages The amount of wages before deductions. (p. 410)

Held-to-maturity investments Investments in bonds of other companies in which the investor has the positive intent and the ability to hold the securities to maturity. (p. 320)

Historical cost The amount paid for an asset and used as a basis for recognizing it on the balance sheet and carrying it on later balance sheets. (p. 144)

Horizontal analysis A comparison of financial statement items over a period of time. (p. 630)

Impairment Writedown required when the expected benefit of a capital asset falls below its book value. (p. 360)

Income statement A statement that summarizes revenues and expenses. (p. 14)

Indirect method For preparing the Operating Activities section of the statement of cash flows, the approach in which net income is reconciled to net cash flow from operations. (p. 577)

Installment method The method in which revenue is recognized at the time cash is collected. (p. 206)

Intangible Lacking physical substance (e.g., a copyright is intangible). (p. 350)

Intangible assets Assets with no physical properties. (p. 368)

Interim statements Financial statements prepared monthly, quarterly, or at other intervals less than a year in duration. (p. 164)

Internal auditing The department responsible in a company for the review and appraisal of its accounting and administrative controls. (p. 21)

Internal audit staff Department responsible for monitoring and evaluating the internal control system. (p. 314)

Internal control system Policies and procedures necessary to ensure the safeguarding of an entity's assets, the reliability of its accounting records, and the accomplishment of overall company objectives. (p. 313)

Internal event An event occurring entirely within an entity. (p. 94)

International Accounting Standards Board (IASB) The organization formed to develop worldwide accounting standards. (p. 21)

Inventory turnover ratio A measure of the number of times inventory is sold during a period. (pp. 265, 639)

Investing activities Activities concerned with the acquisition and disposal of long-term assets. (p. 575)

Issued shares The number of shares sold or distributed to shareholders. (p. 520)

Journal A chronological record of transactions, also known as the book of original entry. (p. 107)

Land improvements Costs that are related to land but that have a limited life. (p. 352)

Lease A contractual arrangement between two parties that permits one party, the lessee, the right to use an asset in exchange for payments to its owner, the lessor. (p. 477)

Ledger A book, file, hard drive, or other device containing all the accounts. (p. 111)

Leverage The use of borrowed funds and amounts contributed by preferred shareholders to earn an overall return higher than the cost of these funds. (p. 648)

Liability An obligation of a business. (p. 8)

LIFO method An inventory method that assigns the most recent costs to cost of goods sold. (p. 255)

Liquidity The ability of a company to pay its debts as they come due. (pp. 62, 635)

Long-term liability An obligation that will not be satisfied within one year or the current operating cycle. (p. 462)

Loss on sale of asset The amount by which selling price is less than book value. (p. 365)

Lower-of-cost-or-market (LCM) rule A conservative inventory valuation approach that is an attempt to anticipate declines in the value of inventory before its actual sale. (p. 261)

Management accounting The branch of accounting concerned with providing management with information to facilitate planning and control. (p. 12)

Market rate of interest The rate that investors could obtain by investing in other bonds that are similar to the issuing firm's bonds. (p. 466)

Market value per share The selling price of the shares as indicated by the most recent transactions. (p. 534)

Matching principle The revenues for the period are associated with the costs of generating those revenues. (p. 207)

Materiality The magnitude of an accounting information omission or misstatement that will affect the judgment of someone relying on the information. (p. 56)

Monetary unit The yardstick used to measure amounts in financial statements, the dollar. (p. 19)

Moving average The name given to an average cost method when it is used with a perpetual inventory system. (p. 270)

Multiple-step income statement An income statement that shows classifications of revenues and expenses as well as important subtotals. (p. 210)

Natural resources Assets that are consumed during their use. (p. 366)

Net pay The amount of wages after deductions. (p. 410)

Net sales Sales revenue less sales returns and allowances and sales discounts. (p. 211)

Non-business entity Organization operated for some purpose other than to earn a profit. (p. 7)

Note payable A liability resulting from the signing of a promissory note. (p. 404)

Number of days' purchases in payables A measure of the average age of accounts payable. (p. 640)

Number of days' sales in inventory A measure of how long it takes to sell inventory. (p. 640)

Number of days' sales in receivables A measure of the average age of accounts receivable. (p. 639)

Operating activities Activities concerned with the acquisition and sale of products and services. (p. 574)

Operating cycle The period of time between the purchase of inventory and the collection of any receivable from the sale of the inventory. (p. 58)

Operating lease A lease that does not meet any of the four criteria and is not recorded as an asset by the lessee. (p. 478)

Organization A collection of individuals pursuing the same goal or objective. (p. 6)

Outstanding cheque A cheque written by a company but not yet presented to the bank for payment. (p. 299)

Outstanding shares The number of shares issued less the number of shares held as treasury stock if any. (p. 520)

Owners' equity The owners' claim on the assets of an entity. (p. 13)

Partnership A business owned by two or more individuals and with the characteristic of unlimited liability. (pp. 7, 539)

Partnership agreement Specifies how much the owners will invest, their salaries, and how income will be shared. (p. 540)

Par value An arbitrary amount stated on the face of the share certificate representing the legal capital of the corporation. (p. 521)

Pension An obligation to pay employees for service rendered while employed. (p. 492)

Percentage-of-completion method The method used by contractors to recognize revenue before the completion of a long-term contract. (p. 205)

Periodic system System in which the Inventory account is updated only at the end of the period. (p. 244)

Permanent accounts The name given to balance sheet accounts because they are permanent and are not closed at the end of the period. (p. 162)

Permanent difference A difference that affects the tax records but not the accounting records, or vice versa. (p. 487)

Perpetual system System in which the inventory account is increased at the time of each purchase and decreased at the time of each sale. (p. 244)

Petty cash fund Money kept on hand for making minor disbursements in coin and currency rather than by writing cheques. (p. 302)

Posting The process of transferring amounts from a journal to the ledger accounts. (p. 111)

Premium The excess of the issue price over the face value of the bonds. (p. 467)

Prepaid expense An asset resulting from the payment of cash before the incurrence of expense. (p. 156)

Present value of an annuity The amount at a present time that is equivalent to a series of payments and interest in the future. (p. 431)

Present value of a single amount Amount at the present time that is equivalent to a payment or investment at a future time. (p. 425)

Price/earnings (P/E) ratio The relationship between a company's performance according to the income statement and its performance in the stock market. (p. 649)

Pro forma earnings Alternative earning measures that are not calculated according to GAAP. (p. 221)

Production method The method in which revenue is recognized when a commodity is produced rather than when it is sold. (p. 206)

Profit margin Net income divided by sales. (pp. 64, 633)

Profitability How well management is using company resources to earn a return on the funds invested by various groups. (p. 645)

Purchase Discounts Contra-purchases account used to record reductions in purchase price for early payment to a supplier. (p. 249)

Purchase Returns and Allowances Contra-purchases account used in a periodic inventory system when a refund is received from a supplier or a reduction given in the balance owed to a supplier. (p. 248)

Purchases Account used in a periodic inventory system to record acquisitions of merchandise. (p. 247)

Quality of earning The portion of earnings realized in cash. (p. 596)

Quantity discount Reduction in selling price for buying a large number of units of a product. (p. 212)

Realizable value The amount of cash, or its equivalent, that could be received by selling an asset currently. (p. 145)

Recognition The process of including an item in the financial statements. (p. 144)

Relevance The capacity of information to make a difference in a decision. (p. 54)

Reliability The quality that makes accounting information dependable in representing the events that it purports to represent. (p. 55)

Research and development costs Costs incurred in the discovery of new knowledge and the translation of research into a design or plan for a new product or service or into a significant improvement. (p. 369)

Retail inventory method A technique used by retailers to convert the retail value of inventory to a cost basis. (p. 265)

Retained earnings The part of owners' equity that represents the income earned less dividends paid over the life of an entity. (pp. 14, 522)

Retirement of shares When the shares are repurchased with no intention to reissue at a later date. (p. 525)

Return on assets ratio A measure of a company's success in earning a return for all providers of capital. (p. 645)

Return on common shareholders' equity ratio A measure of a company's success in earning a return for the common shareholders. (p. 647)

Return on sales ratio A variation of the profit margin ratio; measures earnings before payments to creditors. (p. 646)

Revenue Inflows of assets resulting from the sale of products and services. (p. 10)

Revenue expenditure A cost that keeps an asset in its normal operating condition and is treated as an expense. (p. 361)

Revenue recognition principle Revenues are recognized in the income statement when they are earned. (p. 204)

Revenues Increases is economic resources resulting from ordinary activities such as the sale of goods, the rendering of services, or the use by others of the entity's resources. (p. 204)

Sales Discounts Contra-revenue account used to record discounts given customers for early payment of their accounts. (p. 214)

Sales Returns and Allowances Contra-revenue account used to record both refunds to customers and reductions of their accounts. (p. 211)

Securities and Exchange Commission (SEC) The U.S. federal agency with ultimate authority to determine the rules in preparing statements for companies whose sold to the public. (p. 20)

Serial bonds Bonds that do not all have the same due date; a portion of the bonds comes due each time period. (p. 464)

Share A certificate that acts as ownership in a corporation. (p. 7)

Shareholder Someone who buys shares in a company. (p. 8)

Shareholders' equity The owners' equity in a corporation. (p. 13)

Simple interest Interest is calculated on the principal amount only. (p. 420)

Single-step income statement An income statement in which all expenses are added together and subtracted from all revenues. (pp. 64, 209)

Sole proprietorship A business with a single owner. (pp. 6, 538)

Solvency The ability of a company to remain in business over the long term. (p. 641)

Source document A piece of paper that is used as evidence to record a transaction. (p. 94)

Specific identification method An inventory costing method that relies on matching unit costs with the actual units sold. (p. 253)

Statement of cash flows The financial statement that summarizes an entity's cash receipts and cash payments during the period from operating, investing, and financing activities. (p. 572)

Statement of retained earnings The statement that summarizes the income earned and dividends paid over the life of a business. (p. 16)

Statement of shareholders' equity Reflects the differences between beginning and ending balances for all accounts in the Shareholders' Equity category of the balance sheet. (p. 529)

Stock dividend The issuance of additional shares to existing shareholders. (p. 527)

Stock split The creation of additional shares with a reduction of the book value of the shares. (p. 529)

Straight-line method A method by which the same dollar amount of depreciation is recorded in each year of asset use. (pp. 151, 353)

Subsidiary ledger The detail for a number of individual items that collectively make up a single general ledger account. (p. 305)

Tangible Having physical substance (e.g., a machine is tangible). (p. 350)

Temporary accounts The name given to revenue, expense, and dividend accounts because they are temporary and are closed at the end of the period. (p. 162)

Temporary difference A difference that affects both book and tax records but not in the same time period. (p. 487)

Time-of-sale method The method used by merchandising and manufacturing industries to recognize revenue when goods are sold. (p. 204)

Time period Artificial segment on the calendar, used as the basis for preparing financial statements. (p. 20)

Times interest earned ratio An income statement measure of the ability of a company to meet its interest payments. (p. 643)

Time value of money An immediate amount should be preferred over an amount in the future. (p. 419)

Trade discount Selling price reduction offered to a special class of customers. (p. 212)

Trading investments Shares and bonds of other companies bought and held for the purpose of selling them in the near term to generate profits on appreciation in their price. (p. 320)

Transaction Any event that is recognized in a set of financial statements. (p. 94)

Transportation-in Adjunct account used to record freight costs paid by the buyer. (p. 247)

Treasurer The officer responsible in an organization for the safeguarding and efficient use of a company's liquid assets. (p. 21)

Treasury stock Shares issued by the firm and then repurchased but not retired. (p. 525)

Trial balance A list of each account and its balance; it is used to prove equality of debits and credits. (p. 114)

Understandability The quality of accounting information that makes it comprehensible to those willing to spend the necessary time. (p. 54)

Unearned revenue A liability resulting from the receipt of cash before the recognition of revenue. (p. 156)

Units-of-production method Depreciation is determined as a function of the number of units the asset produces. (p. 354)

Unusual or infrequent items Revenues and expenses arising from transactions that are not expected to occur frequently over several years or that are not typical of the company's activities. (p. 219)

Vertical analysis A comparison of various financial statement items within a single period with the use of common-size statements. (p. 630)

Weighted average cost method An inventory costing method that assigns the same unit cost to all units available for sale during the period. (p. 254)

Work sheet A device used at the end of the period to gather the information needed to prepare financial statements without actually recording and posting adjusting entries. (p. 165)

Working capital Current assets minus current liabilities. (pp. 63, 635)

Company Index

Subject Index